THE HARVEST
OF MYSTICISM IN
MEDIEVAL GERMANY

A six-volume series

**THE PRESENCE OF GOD:
A HISTORY OF WESTERN CHRISTIAN MYSTICISM**

THE HARVEST OF MYSTICISM IN MEDIEVAL GERMANY (1300–1500)

Vol. IV of
The Presence of God:
A History of Western Christian Mysticism

by
Bernard McGinn

A Herder & Herder Book
The Crossroad Publishing Company
New York

The Crossroad Publishing Company
16 Penn Plaza – 481 Eighth Avenue, Suite 1550
New York, NY 10001

This book is set in 10.5/13 Baskerville BE.

Printed in the United States of America

Library of Congress Cataloging-in-Publication data is available.

ISBN 0-8245-2345-8

1 2 3 4 5 6 7 8 9 10   09 08 07 06 05

To Dan, Gina, and Maeve
with love

Contents

Preface

THIS VOLUME of *The Presence of God: A History of Western Christian Mysticism* has been long in gestation. Over the course of five years its scope and arrangement have evolved in ways that I had not foreseen, yet that became increasingly clear and even necessary as the research and writing progressed.

The original plan for a volume entitled *The Harvest of Mysticism* envisaged a study of all the major mystical literature between ca. 1300 and ca. 1500. The greater number of these texts are in the developing vernacular languages of Western Europe, especially German, Dutch, English, and Italian; but there is also a significant body of learned Latin texts of a mystical character. (Some of the most popular vernacular texts were translated into Latin to give them an international audience.) While the fourteenth century has been rightly called "the Golden Age of English mysticism," and while Italian mysticism boasts the towering figure of Catherine of Siena, and Dutch mysticism that of John Ruusbroec (let alone the other important writers in both languages), I think it fair to say it was in German-speaking lands in the fourteenth and fifteenth centuries that the greatest production of mystical literature, a true harvest, is to be found. These two centuries saw the emergence of so many significant mystics and so extensive a proliferation of mystical texts that it eventually proved impossible to include it all in a single book—at least one of the character that I have intended for the volumes in this ongoing account of Western mysticism.

The writing of the volume began in early 2000, during the year when I was fortunate enough to enjoy the hospitality and scholarly fellowship of the National Humanities Center in North Carolina. I began work on what I hoped would be the chapter (or chapters) devoted to

Meister Eckhart, the central figure of late medieval Germany and one of the premier mystics of the Christian tradition. Although I had read, taught, and translated Eckhart for decades, and written several shorter studies of his mystical thought, it was a revelation for me to reread the whole of his corpus and the recent extensive literature on the Dominican, much of it corrective of previous studies. The upshot was a book, rather than a long chapter or series of chapters. The volume was published by Crossroad-Herder in 2001 under the title _The Mystical Thought of Meister Eckhart: The Man from Whom God Hid Nothing_. In the course of writing that book I identified a key mystical theme, that of the _grunt_, or ground, the "explosive metaphor" (_Sprengmetapher_) expressing the fused identity of God and human that for me stood at the heart of Eckhart's mystical teaching. Created by Eckhart, utilized and transformed by his successors, the mysticism of the ground is a way of identifying much of what is new about late medieval German mysticism. A considerably shorter, and in some particulars revised, version of that volume on Eckhart appears as the longest chapter in this book. It is introduced by a short chapter on the nature of the mysticism of the ground.

By 2002 I was at work on two major mystics, Henry Suso and John Tauler, who were students of Eckhart, at least in the broad sense. Suso was probably the most read mystic of the late Middle Ages, with many hundreds of manuscripts surviving. Tauler, on the other hand, especially owing to his influence on Luther and acceptance in the Protestant tradition has the distinction of being the most continuously read of medieval German mystics, by both Catholics and Protestants. These two Dominicans developed Eckhart's mysticism in their own ways, despite the papal condemnation of some of the master's views in 1329. It would be a mistake to reduce these significant mystics to the status of mere followers of Eckhart, but it would be difficult to provide an adequate account of their thought without attention to how they used Eckhart's mysticism of the ground within their own attempts to deal with the intimate encounter between God and human that is the core of mysticism.

In order to understand the theological background for the mysticism of the ground presented by these three towering Germans, one needs to look at their Dominican predecessors, particularly the way the preachers read the fountainhead of all mystical theology in the Middle Ages, the pseudo-apostolic Dionysius. Hence, there was need for an introductory chapter investigating the mystical theology of Thomas Aquinas, the official doctor of the Dominican order, as well as that of his teacher, the German master

Albert the Great, who was the founding father of a distinctive German Dominican philosophical and theological school.

Eckhart's condemnation was both a symptom and a cause: symptom, in the sense of reflecting growing suspicions of dangerous mysticism in the late Middle Ages; cause, because of the impact it continued to have on debates on mysticism over the next two centuries and more. Hence, a chapter on the relation of mysticism and heresy in the late Middle Ages soon emerged as a second prolegomenon for understanding the German mystics, and indeed all later Western mysticism.

These six chapters already constituted a decent-sized book. By late 2003 I reluctantly realized that to do justice to the wealth of other mystical literature (and art) in late medieval Germany it would be impossible to include the major mystical traditions of England, the Low Countries, and Italy in this volume. I had already decided that a chapter would have to be devoted to the mystical elements in the thought of that prodigious thinker Nicholas of Cusa. The Renaissance cardinal's contributions were many, and in many fields, not least in mystical theology. But the resources for the story of mysticism in late medieval Germany were by no means to be exhausted by consideration of the giants from Eckhart to Cusa. One of the most striking things about mysticism in German-speaking lands between 1300 and 1500 is the way in which mystical teaching was disseminated on a broad level to a much wider audience than ever before. Although the fourteenth century was the era of the most impressive creativity, the manuscript and early printed evidence shows that the fifteenth century was the age of greater spread of mystical literature. This phenomenon could not be neglected.

As I sought to bring the remaining materials into some coherent shape during 2004, I was privileged to be the recipient of an Emeritus Faculty Research Grant from the Andrew W. Mellon Foundation. I am indebted to the Mellon Foundation for its generosity, which has done much to expedite the completion of this long volume. During this final year of its gestation, the now entitled *Harvest of Mysticism in Medieval Germany* achieved final shape in the ten chapters presented here. Along with the chapter on Nicholas of Cusa, chapters 7 to 9 were written during this time to provide a structure for beginning to appreciate the variety and the originality of the wealth that survives from this rich harvest.

No brief preface can repay the debt of gratitude I owe to the many friends and colleagues who have contributed to making this volume possible. Along with the National Humanities Center and the Andrew W. Mellon

Foundation, my heartfelt thanks go to the Divinity School of the University of Chicago, my intellectual home and support for over three decades, especially in the person of its present Dean, Richard Rosengarten, who was always ready with a generous response when I appealed to him. Former volumes in this history have been dedicated to my students and colleagues at the Divinity School. This volume too could have easily carried such a dedication. Given the German theme of this volume, I am grateful for the encouragement and assistance I have received from colleagues in Europe, especially in Germany and Switzerland, who have been my teachers in so much that relates to *die deutsche Mystik.* Their generosity has expressed itself in many ways, especially through the books and articles they forwarded to me over the decades that have not only helped keep me abreast of new literature, but also deepened my understanding of mysticism in Germany. I especially would like to mention Werner Beierwaltes, Alois M. Haas, William J. Hoye, Hildegard Keller, Freimuth Löser, Georg Steer, Loris Sturlese, Marie-Anne Vannier, and Werner Williams-Krapp.

Not being a native German speaker, let alone a student of Middle High German, is a barrier to someone attemping to penetrate the world of mystical theology in late medieval Germany. Like poems, and unlike technical or scientific manuals, mystical texts maintain a surplus of meaning in their original form that resists translation and that often remains partly hidden to outsiders. The effect of this barrier may be mitigated by the fact that my own approach, as in the previous volumes in this history, has been primarily theological rather than linguistic, but it would be a mistake to exaggerate the differences between the two. The union of solid philology and original philosophical and theological insight has been evident in many of the books and studies that my colleagues in Europe have shared with me over the years—a true marriage of Mercury and Philology. I hope to do all I can to further this happy union.

Along with European colleagues, I have an equally weighty indebtedness to friends in the English and American academic world of Germanic Studies and the history of medieval thought, especially to Oliver Davies, Donald Duclow, Jeffrey Hamburger, Niklaus Largier, and Kenneth Northcott. My deepest thanks go to my old friend Frank Tobin, who read many of these chapters and offered many helpful suggestions and corrections. As ever, I feel fortunate to have been able to work with the staff at the Crossroad Publishing Company, who have been understanding of the delay in bringing this volume to its conclusion and ever helpful in the editing and production process. Special thanks to Gwendolin Herder, the publisher, and to my editor, John Jones.

Over the past year, as *The Harvest of Mysticism in Medieval Germany* assumed its final form, my research assistant, David C. Albertson, has contributed much to the last stages. I am grateful for his keen eye as a proofreader and for his many suggestions for making the book clearer and more cogent in its argument. As ever, the last word goes to my wife, Patricia. She too has lived with this book over its long and sometimes difficult gestation. She too has read and even reread it—correcting, emending, suggesting, and quietly encouraging countless improvements along the way.

The volume is dedicated to our son, Daniel McGinn, to his wife, Gina Maria McGinn, and to their daughter, Maeve, who joined our family as this book was coming to be.

CHICAGO
FEBRUARY 2005

Abbreviations

AASS   *Acta Sanctorum.* Paris: Palmé, 1863–. 3rd edition.

CC   *Corpus Christianorum. Series Latina.* Turnhout: Brepols, 1954-.

CCCM   *Corpus Christianorum. Continuatio Mediaevalis.* Turnhout: Brepols, 1970-.

CSEL   *Corpus scriptorum ecclesiasticorum latinorum.* Vienna: Hoelder-Pichler-Tempsky, 1866–.

The Dionysian Corpus. The writings ascribed to Dionysius the Areopagite are available in the critical edition of Beate Regina Suchla, Gunther Heil, and Adolf Martin Ritter, *Corpus Dionysiacum,* 2 vols. (Berlin: Walter de Gruyter, 1990–91). This edition continues to use the standard column numbers found in the old edition in PG 3, which will also be employed here with the following abbreviations:

    CH   *De caelesti hierarchia (The Celestial Hierarchy)*
    DN   *De divinis nominibus (The Divine Names)*
    EH   *De ecclesiastica hierarchia (The Ecclesiastical Hierarchy)*
    Ep   *Epistulae (Letters)*
    MT   *De mystica theologia (The Mystical Theology)*

DS   *Dictionnaire de spiritualité ascétique et mystique doctrine et histoire.* 17 volumes. Paris: Beauchesne, 1937–97.

Eckhart. The critical edition of the writings of Meister Eckhart is: *Meister Eckhart: Die deutschen und lateinischen Werke herausgegeben im Auftrag der deutschen Forschungsgemeinschaft* (Stuttgart/Berlin: Kohlhammer, 1936–). The two sections of this edition are *Die lateinischen Werke* (LW) and *Die deutschen Werke* (DW). Eckhart's writings will be cited by volume, page, and

line number where necessary. In addition, the Latin writings have
numbered subsections (n. and nn.). The following abbreviations
will be employed for the individual writings:

Latin Works:

Acta	*Acta Echardiana* (LW 5:149–520)
In Eccli.	*Sermones et Lectiones super Ecclesiastici c. 24:23-31* (LW 2:29-300)
In Ex.	*Expositio Libri Exodi* (LW 2:1–227)
In Gen.I	*Expositio Libri Genesis* (LW 1:185–444)
In Gen.II	*Liber Parabolorum Genesis* (LW 1:447–702)
In Ioh.	*Expositio sancti Evangelii secundum Iohannem* (LW 3)
In Sap.	*Expositio Libri Sapientiae* (LW 2:301–643)
Proc.Col.I	*Processus Coloniensis I* (=Acta nn. 46 and 48 in LW 5:197–226, and 275–317)
Proc.Col.II	*Processus Coloniensis II* (=Acta nn. 47 and 48 in LW 5:227–47, and 318–54)
Prol.gen.	*Prologus generalis in Opus tripartitum* (LW 1:148–65)
Prol.op.expos.	*Prologus in Opus expositionum* (LW 1:183–84)
Prol.op.prop.	*Prologus in Opus propositionum* (LW 1:166–82)
Qu.Par.	*Quaestiones Parisienses* (LW 1:27–83)
S. and SS.	*Sermones* (LW 4)

German Works:

BgT	*Daz buoch der goetlîchen troestunge* (DW 5:1–105)
Pr. and Prr.	*Predigt/Predigten* (DW 1–4)
RdU	*Die rede der underscheidunge* (DW 5:137–376)
Vab	*Von dem edeln menschen* (DW 5:106–36)

GCS   *Die griechischen christlichen Schriftsteller der ersten drei Jahrhunderte.* Berlin: Akademie-Verlag, 1897–.

Geschichte Kurt Ruh, *Die Geschichte der abendländische Mystik.* 4 volumes. Munich: Beck, 1990–99.

MGH   *Monumenta Germaniae Historica inde ab a.C. 500 usque ad a. 1500.* Hannover and Berlin, 1826–. Various publishers and sections.

MHG   Middle High German

ms./mss. manuscript/s

PG   *Patrologia cursus completus. Series graeca.* 161 volumes. Paris: J. P. Migne, 1857–66.

PL   *Patrologia cursus completus. Series latina.* 221 volumes. Paris: J. P.
        Migne, 1844–64.
SC   *Sources chrétiennes.* Paris: Éditions du Cerf, 1940–.
STh   Thomas Aquinas, *Summa theologiae*
Vg   Latin Vulgate version of the Bible. See *Biblia sacra iuxta Vulgatam
        Versionem.* Stuttgart: Deutsche Bibelgemeinschaft, 1983.
VL   *Die deutsche Literatur des Mittelalters Verfasserlexikon.* 2nd edition.
        Edited by Kurt Ruh et al. Berlin: Walter de Gruyter, 1978–.

Illustrations

See the photo insert between pp. 484 and 485.

Introduction

I
T WAS PERHAPS INEVITABLE that a book devoted to mysticism between 1300 and 1500 should be entitled *The Harvest of Mysticism*. The harvest metaphor has fascinated historians of the late Middle Ages since Johan Huizinga published his brilliant and enigmatic book *Herfsttij der Middeleeuwen* in 1919—a title rendered in different languages variously as "Harvest," "Autumn," "Waning," "Decline," or "Evening of the Middle Ages." (The Dutch term means "tide of autumn.")[1] Although Huizinga himself gave his book several titles during its gestation, and by now the title has been generally regularized to "Autumn," the agricultural metaphor "harvest" with its autumnal connotations has proven to have a rare evocative power. As Margaret Aston pointed out in a discussion of Huizinga's masterpiece, "harvest" suggests a fullness lacking in the more negative term "waning."[2]

History lives on metaphor, though not on metaphor alone. The peculiar attraction of the metaphor of the harvest lies in its double-sidedness, signifying on the one hand completion, richness, surplus, and on the other finality, and even decay and death. John Keats's "To Autumn" hymns a "Season of mists and mellow fruitfulness," and portrays how the season conspires with the sun to "fill all fruit with ripeness to the core," until the bees "think warm days will never cease." But warm days do cease, and extreme ripeness is the last stage of the growing season that inevitably results in death and new forms of life.

Late medieval mysticism in Germany fits both sides of the metaphorical ambiguity of the autumn harvest. The dates that appear in my title are themselves somewhat metaphorical (more on this below), but

1

the period ca. 1300–ca. 1500 witnessed a production of mystical literature in Germany that was as remarkable for its originality as it was for its proliferation. Few if any periods in the history of Christianity have shown greater fascination with mysticism. While mysticism flourished across Western Europe in the late Middle Ages, German-speaking lands stand out both for the quantity of the texts produced and for the creativeness of the great mystics of the time, as the names of Eckhart, Suso, Tauler, and Nicholas of Cusa show. It was truly a time of the harvest of many plantings, both early and late, in the history of Christian mysticism.

There were, however, also signs, if not of finality and death, at least of the emergence of problems that were to trouble the later history of Western Christian mysticism. Foremost among these was the growth of fears about dangerous forms of union with God and the institutional reaction these provoked beginning in the early years of the fourteenth century. This volume contains a chapter explicitly devoted to what is usually called the heresy of the Free Spirit, but the other chapters show that most mystical writers after 1300 were concerned with the need to distinguish good from bad forms of mysticism. Furthermore, it is evident that the fourteenth century was the time of greatest creativity, while the fifteenth century, with the exception of Nicholas of Cusa, was the age more of the physical dissemination of texts and treatises than of new departures.[3] In this limited sense at least, mysticism in Germany had gathered in its harvest and was to wait for many years until new religious developments, especially the variety of reformations of the sixteenth century, helped provide the impetus for new configurations of mystical traditions.

The harvest metaphor gained further attraction for intellectual historians and historical theologians by the fact that another great Dutch scholar, Heiko A. Oberman, entitled his ground-breaking 1963 study of late medieval nominalist thought *The Harvest of Late Medieval Theology*.[4] Oberman and his students have been at the forefront of those who insisted that the last centuries of the Middle Ages were more than a time of confusion and decline (the older Catholic view), or alternatively of preparation for the Reformation (often put forth by Protestant scholars); rather, they formed a period that deserved to be studied in its own right, not only in literature and art but also, and perhaps more surprisingly to some, in science, in philosophy, and in theology. This at one time revisionist viewpoint has been increasingly accepted, though viewed in different ways by different authors.[5] It has also meant that the year 1500, once the dividing line between the Middle Ages and the early modern period, has diminished in significance, though perhaps not to the point of becoming a "mythological year" of importance only to collectors of incunabula.[6] The late-nineteenth-century dispute between Wilhelm Dilthey (d. 1911), who saw the Renaissance and the early Reformation as a new eruption in the history of the West, and Ernst Troeltsch (d. 1923), who viewed Luther and the early reformers as the concluding stage in the long debates over reform that had percolated through Christendom from the thirteenth century, took on new life in the past forty years with a decided tilt in favor of Troeltsch's view. Though periodization is always the artifice of historians, there is considerable agreement at present that the more useful artifice is one that takes the late Middle Ages and the sixteenth century together, whether the parameters of this time of transition are viewed more broadly (ca. 1250–1550), or more narrowly (ca. 1400–1600).[7]

A similar sense of period is true with regard to mysticism. The year 1500 does not mark any decisive shift in the development of what I have called the new mysticism that emerged in Europe ca. 1200.[8] The layered interaction of different forms of mysticism that I argue helps provide a structure for understanding this long and varied religious tradition, beginning with the monastic mysticism of the early church, followed by the overlay of the twelfth-century ordering of love, and then the eruption of the new mysticism and its excessive and vernacular forms, and finally the appearance of the mysticism of the ground associated with Eckhart and his followers to be studied in this volume, did not see important new developments around the year 1500. In that sense, the date of 1500 that appears in my title is a round number, somewhat artificial, pointing to the fact that by the end of the fifteenth century the productive era of medieval German mysticism had played itself out. (Indeed, nothing important happened after ca. 1465, when Cusa was already dead and the energies of those who had engaged with him in debating the relation of love and knowledge in mystical theology were exhausted.) The date 1300 is more accurate, if still not chronologically exact. It was during the years 1295–1305 that Eckhart first began his mystical preaching. In this same decade the startling message of his contemporary the beguine Marguerite Porete started to attract the attention of suspicious bishops and inquisitors. Although understanding Eckhart's mysticism requires a look backward half a century to the teaching of Albert the Great and Thomas Aquinas (see chapter 1), in Germany at least, 1300 does mark a new day.

Both Huizinga and Oberman recognized the importance of mysticism for their respective understandings of what constituted the harvest, or the autumn, of the fourteenth and fifteenth centuries. Huizinga, quoting Eckhart, Suso, and Tauler, along with Ruusbroec, Gerson, and Denis the

Carthusian, has some evocative comments on the paradox of the way in which what he calls "the lonely heights of an individual, solitary, formless, and imageless mysticism," also helped engender a movement "dignifying the practical element"—a form of "sober mysticism," as he calls it.[9] In his *Harvest* Oberman argued for a neglected relation between nominalism and mysticism in such figures as Jean Gerson and Gabriel Biel,[10] and he later expanded his interest in late medieval mysticism in several essays, especially a classic account of Luther's relation to mysticism.[11] What the reader will find in this volume, however, is different from what either Huizinga or Oberman had in mind, though I hope that on a deeper level it testifies to how these two major thinkers have reshaped the way we think about the late Middle Ages.

The Late Medieval Context of Mysticism

The figures investigated in this volume were active mostly during the century and a half between 1300 and 1450.[12] This period is customarily seen as a time of tribulation for Western society and the church, not least in Germany. There can be no question that the fourteenth century witnessed a series of calamities, both natural and human-made, that crippled society, induced widespread discouragement and even despair, and provoked anguished reactions. But not all was black, even in the fourteenth century. This period saw the foundation of the first universities in imperial Germany, beginning with Prague in 1348. Despite the difficult economic conditions, the towns continued to grow, and with them the urban middle class, who encouraged new forms of piety and who made up much of the audience for spiritual and mystical literature.[13] The fifteenth century in imperial Germany saw even more new initiatives, economic, social, and cultural.[14]

The fourteenth century abounded in natural disasters. Agricultural societies such as medieval Christendom were always prone to famine and other trials of nature. Late medieval agriculture was not helped by the fact that the fourteenth century saw the beginning of a major climatic change, a general cooling that produced a "little ice age" of several centuries duration. Several devastating earthquakes visited Germany during the century. The greatest disaster, of course, was the Great Plague, or Black Death. Bubonic plague had been absent from the West since 787, but it returned in full force between 1347 and 1350 to kill more than 50 percent of the population in many areas.[15] The demographic, economic, and social impact of the slaughter is difficult to calculate but was obviously devastating.[16] The plague returned at roughly ten- or twenty-year intervals down to 1503.

Perhaps more troubling to the spiritually sensitive were the political crises and struggles of the time, and especially the troubles that afflicted the church. The endemic violence of much of medieval history seems to have grown in the fourteenth century. The long tragedy of the Hundred Years' War between France and England (1337–1453) did not directly affect Germany and the imperial lands, but still testified to how dynastic struggles ravaged late medieval society. In the welter of princely domains and cities that made up the German Empire, there were always tensions, and often open conflicts. The most serious political trial of the fourteenth century, at least from the religious perspective, was the conflict between Pope John XXII and the emperor-elect Lewis of Bavaria that divided Germany between 1324 and 1347. The pope refused to recognize the emperor's election; the emperor in turn denounced the pope as a heretic. The pope excommunicated Lewis and put those areas in Germany that adhered to him under interdict (a ban on public celebration of mass and distribution of the sacraments). It was a foolish dispute, even in the eyes of contemporaries, but one that tried the patience of all believers.

Later German rulers avoided such confrontations, if only because the fourteenth-century papacy, the central institution of the medieval church, came close to self-destruction as the century progressed. Much has been written about the tribulations and triumphs of the late medieval papacy in the two centuries of 1300–1500. Some of the issues debated then, such as the role of a general council in relation to papal authority, are still alive today. Late medieval mystics lived in the midst of severe crises in the life of the church. Some mystics seem to have remained relatively oblivious to the trying times; others felt compelled to become deeply involved on one side or the other of the disputes on the nature of the church and the best way to proceed in its reform.[17]

One thing that was the subject of well-nigh universal agreement, at least among sincere Christians, was the need for the reform of the church "in head and members," that is, from top to bottom. The cry for reform, the cleansing of the church from manifest abuses both institutional and personal, was the leitmotif of the late Middle Ages.[18] Mystics have often been conceived of as eschewing interest in external reform in favor of stressing the need for interior change of heart, but in Christianity it is hard to conceive of the one without the other. Some medieval mystics and mystical writers, such as Catherine of Siena, Jean Gerson, and Nicholas of Cusa, owing to accidents of location or vocation, were actively involved in efforts for reform on the highest levels. Others concentrated their energies more narrowly, but without denying the need for reform and conversion for all in Christendom.

The drama of the late medieval papacy played out in four acts during the time under consideration in this volume. The first act was the period when the popes fled Rome to take up residence at Avignon (1305–78), often described as the "Babylonian Captivity" of the papacy. The papal flight was in large part a reaction to the disturbed condition in Italy following the defeat of Boniface VIII in his conflict with Philip the Fair of France. Modern scholarship has modified the dark picture of the Avignon popes inherited from their medieval opponents, but that has not altered the fundamental fact that the seven popes who resided at Avignon were seen as too subservient to the French monarchy, too interested in enriching themselves and their relatives at the expense of the church, and too ineffective, whatever their good intentions, in implementing serious church reform. The return of Gregory XI to Rome in 1378 (at least partly due to the efforts of Catherine of Siena) seemed to presage a new day, but instead a far more serious crisis ensued. Gregory died and a deeply split College of Cardinals, under pressure from many sides, elected two popes in quick succession: Urban VI (1378–89), who took up residence in Rome, and Clement VII (1378–94), who returned to Avignon. The Great Western Schism with its two papal lines of Rome and Avignon had begun.

The schism (1378–1417) was possibly the most severe trial of all for devout believers. Who was the real pope? Whose ordinations, appointments, and sacraments were valid? How could God have left his church in such a position? Europe split into two camps; kings and other rulers played the field between the claimants for their own advantage; clerics and theologians strove to work out ways to overcome the split; pious believers, even canonized saints, supported one side or the other. No wonder that we are told that a popular belief emerged after some years that no one had entered heaven since the schism had begun.[19] Something needed to be done because, as one contemporary religious leader, Jean Gerson, once put it, "Papal power was given for the construction of the church, not for its destruction."[20]

The scandal of the divided papacy moved canonists and theologians to give new thought to the role of general councils in relation to the papal office. Conciliarism, as Brian Tierney showed fifty years ago, was not a new movement, but was rooted deep in medieval ecclesiology.[21] The conciliar option for solving the schism led first to a failed council held at Pisa in 1409, which succeeded only in making things worse by electing a third claimant to the papacy. The support of the German ruler Sigismund (1410–37) helped ensure the modified success of the council held at Constance between 1414 and 1418. Constance produced a consensus pope, Martin V (1417–31). It did not really get to work on reform issues, but did issue two decrees that might have helped further this work. The first, called "Haec sancta" (April 6, 1415), affirmed that a general council has "its powers directly from Christ and that all persons of whatever rank or dignity, even a pope, are bound to obey it in matters relating to faith, the end of the schism, and the general reformation of the church of God in head and members."[22] The second decree ("Frequens" of October 9, 1417) established a schedule of regular councils to pursue needed reform of the church.

These decrees introduced the third act in this drama, that of the conflict between the papalist and conciliar views of reform that strove for supremacy between 1417 and 1460. Martin V and his successor Eugene IV (1431–47) put their efforts into reestablishing a strong papacy based once again in Rome.[23] They had no intention of implementing the plan of regular councils, beset as they were with factions and special interests. (We must not think of the medieval councils as "democratic" institutions, though they did represent a wider range of interests than the papal curia.) A major confrontation erupted in the 1430s when Eugene refused to recognize the council gathered at Basel. After years of conflict, a complete break eventuated in 1439, when Eugene dissolved the council and called for his own council to meet in Italy. Many of the Basel representatives had already gone over to the papal side; those who remained followed the time-worn medieval precedent of electing an antipope. But conciliarism was doomed. In 1451 the few council representatives left at Basel recognized Eugene's successor, Nicholas V, as true pope. In 1460 Pope Pius II, himself once a conciliarist adherent at Basel, issued the bull "Execrabilis," condemning conciliarism as a "horrible abuse, unheard of in earlier times," and contrary to canon law.

The papal resurgence after a century and a half of turmoil was won at a price. A certain narrowing of political claims and horizons was in evidence in the papacy from the time of the return of the popes to Rome after Constance. The final decades of the fifteenth century saw the emergence of a new kind of papacy, the fourth and final act in the drama. Western European rulers had used the time of papal weakness, especially during the schism, to increase control over the church in their own lands in return for the political support they offered to one or another papal claimant. Such rights, especially when put in writing, were hard to win back. Although the popes of the late fifteenth century did not abandon the rhetoric of universal papal claims, they were increasingly willing to make arrangements (concordats) with territorial rulers for immediate political gain. The succession of Renaissance princely pontiffs that began with the humanists Nicholas V (1447–55) and Pius II (1458–64) included great patrons of the arts and wily politicians. A few even paid lip-service to the cries for reform. Even by the standards of the much-maligned popes of Avignon, they could not be called spiritual men. The age of the Renaissance popes was to last down to 1555 and the election of Paul IV, the first of the Counter-Reformation popes.

What effect this succession of crises had on late medieval mysticism is difficult to evaluate. It is all too easy to read the emphasis on interiorization that was central to so much late medieval mysticism as a reaction to the sad state of the external institutional church. To some historians, the broad diffusion of mysticism, especially in Germany, is a sign that late medieval believers were increasingly driven to a search for an interior contact with God that bypassed or questioned the structures of the corrupt institutional church. The appearance of radical mystical heretics, the Free Spirits as they were called, seems to confirm this. But the situation was actually far more complex. Meister Eckhart and John Tauler, for all their insistence on finding God within in the ground of the soul, also taught that living out of the divine ground enabled a person to break through the old separation between the active and contemplative lives and to combine both Mary (the contemplative dimension) and Martha (the active). As Eckhart once put it: "One is to seek God in all creatures through all kinds of activity and with flaming love" (Pr. 86). The mystics to be considered here were not revolutionaries, or even subversive of the established order of sacraments, laws, and moral regulations. They may have condemned evil-living clerics, but they did not attack the clerical status itself, however much they thought that simple believers were often closer to God. These mystics continued to live within the structures of late medieval Christianity and to view the *ecclesia romana* as God's necessary instrument of salvation. What the mystics of medieval Germany did insist on, however, was that instruments are always only instruments. They should not be confused with the goal, which is finding God within and living out of that stupendous discovery.

PART I

Background

Contemplata aliis tradere: *Mystic Knowing in Albert the Great and Thomas Aquinas*

T HE DOMINICANS WERE NEVER AS LARGE a group as the Franciscans, either in their established or semi-established forms, but the role of the *ordo praedicatorum* in late medieval spirituality and mysticism was no less significant. The Franciscans often seem to have been obsessed with the need to affirm conformity with a foundational form of spirituality, especially one in harmony with the archetypal figure of Francis. The Dominicans were inclined to be suspicious of attempts to define a single or unique Dominican spirituality or mysticism.[1] These different approaches reflect the wider problematic of unity and diversity in Christian spirituality in general. Theologically speaking, Christians believe that the one Gospel message is communicated by the Holy Spirit in multiple forms through the ages, but always as modalities of a spiritual conformity to Christ.[2] This affirmation, however, does not obviate the work of the historian to study the almost bewildering variety of spiritualities over the centuries.

The role the Dominican order played in the "harvest of mysticism" in the fourteenth and fifteenth centuries was large and varied. Different aspects of the Dominican impact on late medieval mysticism will appear in most of the chapters in this volume. Without attempting to analyze the characteristic features of the Dominican way of life,[3] there is one essential feature of the life of the preachers that casts particular light on their role in late medieval mysticism. In a famous passage in his *Summa Theologiae*, Thomas Aquinas said that "it is a greater thing to hand on to others what has been contemplated than merely to contemplate" (*ita maius est contemplata aliis tradere quam solum contemplari* [STh

IIaIIae, q. 188, a. 6c]). Handing on the fruits of contemplation, both doctrinal and mystical, was essential to the Dominican way of life.

The lives of the two greatest Dominican teachers of the thirteenth century, Albert the Great (ca. 1200–1280) and Thomas Aquinas (1225–1274), are good illustrations of *contemplata aliis tradere*. Neither of these teachers speaks of his own life of prayer or inner states; nor did they write mystical treatises or engage in mystical preaching in the manner of some later Dominicans. We need not consider Albert and Thomas as mystics in the usual sense, though some have so treated them,[4] in order to vindicate their significance in the history of mysticism. Their teaching was foundational for the powerful current of the mysticism that arose at the turn of the fourteenth century in Germany in the preaching and writing of Meister Eckhart. Later Dominican mystics, even those like Catherine of Siena who did not receive formal theological training, were influenced to a greater or lesser degree by the synthesis of Thomas, which, as Jean-Pierre Torrell has shown, "is as deeply spiritual as it is doctrinal."[5] Without some consideration of key aspects of the thought of Albert and of Thomas, a good deal of late medieval mysticism will be difficult to understand. Needless to say, what follows is not to be taken as an attempt to present a synthesis of the thought of either of these teachers. My intention is merely to touch upon some features of their teaching that are significant for comprehending late medieval mysticism.

Albert the Great and Intellective Dionysianism

The year 1248 was a crucial date in the history of mysticism. In the summer of that year the learned German Dominican Albert of Lauingen, master of theology, left Paris at his order's command to set up a *studium generale*, or theological faculty, at Cologne.[6] Among the student friars who accompanied him was a young Italian, Thomas of Aquino. The internationally famous theological center that Albert created in the Rhineland city, though not technically a university, was in reality the first German university and the only one for a century. In the following decades a number of brilliant students studied and taught there, theologians and mystics who shaped a distinctive German Dominican philosophy, theology, and mysticism. "This is why," as Loris Sturlese says, "the year 1248 has epochal significance for German intellectual history."[7]

Albert's sojourn as head of the Cologne *studium* was relatively brief (1248–54 and 1258–60), but filled with intellectual activity. It was during this time that he began the commentaries on Aristotle (thirty-six in all were eventually written) that were to be so influential in bringing the full range of the philosopher's works to theologians despite the condemnations of Aristotle in 1210 and 1215.[8] Deeply informed by Greco-Arabian philosophy, especially the thought of Avicenna and Averroes, Albert initiated a critical correlation between philosophy and theology that was to be carried on, though in a somewhat different way, by his greatest student, Thomas Aquinas. Though diverse views of the nature and coherence of Albert's intellectual project continue,[9] there is a growing consensus that the *doctor universalis* was not merely an eclectic compiler of material but an original thinker of wide-ranging influence. The fifteenth-century chronicler Johannes Meyer praised him in the following terms: "They say of this holy, great, highly learned Albert, who wrote so many large books in the divine and natural sciences, 'Wer er nit gewessen, Deutschelant wer ein eysel blyben'" (Had he not lived, Germany would have remained an ass).[10]

Albert was a scientist and philosopher, but also a theologian—and a mystical theologian to boot.[11] Albert's mystical theology, as found especially in his commentaries on the Dionysian writings,[12] goes back to his time at Cologne.[13] Albert was not the first systematic commentator on the Dionysian corpus. Between about 1224 and 1244, Thomas Gallus, a Paris-educated Victorine canon at Vercelli, composed first an *Extract* (i.e., a paraphrase) and then a long *Explanation* of the Dionysian corpus.[14] Gallus's original attempt to see the Dionysian writings as the theoretical or speculative side of the practical theology of mystical joining with God described in the Song of Songs resulted in what is usually called affective Dionysianism, that is, a reading of the corpus in which the "unknowing knowing" that is the goal of Dionysius's mystical ascent to union is reinterpreted in terms of the superiority of an experience of affective love beyond all cognition.[15]

The glossed version of the *corpus dionysiacum* that Albert knew as a student and master at Paris during the years 1240–48 included Gallus's *Extract*, but Albert would have none of his reading. For the learned Dominican, Dionysius tells us "how it is necessary to be united to God through intellect and to praise him by word."[16] If Gallus's Dionysianism can be characterized as affective, Albert's equally impressive and influential reading is resolutely intellective.[17]

Albert's reading of the Dionysian texts is central to his impact on medieval mystical theology, though it does not exhaust the full scope of his thinking about mysticism.[18] The great historian of medieval thought Martin Grabmann long ago noted the importance of Albert for late medieval German mysticism—a judgment that has become more clear in recent decades.[19] Albert's mystical thought is so deeply intertwined with his whole program that it is difficult to characterize in any simple way. In what follows I will briefly touch on two intertwined areas of import: Albert's metaphysics of flow (*fluxus*) as a significant basis for later German mysticism; and the Dominican's intellective Dionysian understanding of mystical theology.

The Metaphysics of Flow

Albert's innovative metaphysics is important for understanding the mysticism of his Dominican students and successors,[20] but exactly how best to characterize the main lines of Albert's metaphysics remains under discussion. The *doctor universalis* was deeply influenced by the Peripatetic tradition, that is, Aristotle, his Greek commentators, and the Arab philosophers who used them. Some have seen a triumph of philosophical rationalism in Albert's emphasis on the role of reason,[21] but the Dominican teacher also attacked philosophical views that were in conflict with faith, such as Avicenna's teaching on a separate agent intellect, and he insisted on the necessity of divine illumination to reach complete happiness in the *visio beatifica*. Alain de Libera sees the essential project of the Rhineland theology initiated by Albert as a doctrine of conversion that sought to reconcile the two great streams of Christian Neoplatonism, Augustine's understanding of *beatitudo* as residing in the vision of God and the Dionysian view of the universal cycle by which all things flow out from and then return to the God who remains unknown and unseen.[22] What makes it difficult to characterize Albert's philosophy and theology is partly the result of the many streams that flowed into his writings: Augustine, Dionysius, Greco-Arabian Peripateticism, Plato, and Neoplatonism.[23]

Like most medieval thinkers, Albert viewed the world essentially in terms of its relation to God. No created mind can ever know God in Godself (that is, *quid est*), but the mind can know what God is not and it can attain some grasp of how all things flow out from God and return to him. In his late *Summa Theologiae*, Albert says this about theology:

> Theology, by name, says nothing more than argument or speech about God. Speech about God should help explain God, not so much according to his existence and substance, but according to the way that he is the beginning and end of what exists. Otherwise, he would be imperfectly known. He is beginning and end only according to those things that belong to the production of things from him and their return to him. These are the matters that belong to human salvation.[24]

Albert's appeal to the universal paradigm of the production, or *exitus*, of all things from God, and their *reditus*, or return to him, is a commonplace. But the German Dominican was distinctive in helping create a new view of the creative process, or production of the universe, one that Alain de Libera has aptly called "the metaphysics of flow."[25]

In one of his late works, the treatise *The Causes and Procession of the Universe from the First Cause*, probably written about 1264–67, is particularly important for understanding the metaphysics of flow.[26] The second book of this work takes the form of a commentary on the *Book of Causes,* an Arabic reworking of the *Elements of Theology* of the Neoplatonist thinker Proclus.[27] Albert, Thomas Aquinas, Meister Eckhart, and many others, all found this work of profound importance for their thought (see more in the appendix to this chapter).

In book 1 of *The Causes and Procession,* Albert argues for the necessity of a First Principle which has its existence from itself as the being in which there is no difference between what it is (*id quod est*) and its existence (*quo est/ esse*).[28] Central to his understanding of the First Principle is its mode of acting as "an Intellectual Principle like the Intellect acting universally 'by which it makes all things and neither receives nor undergoes' [anything]." Albert's model for such universal action is the dissemination of light: "It is universally understood simply as an Intellect lighting up everything that exists, having nothing before it by which it is illuminated. Its light is the cause of existence for everything that is."[29] Such a Principle, because it is pure Intellect and does not depend on anything else, does not act out of necessity, but is characterized by supreme freedom and perfect will (I.3.1–2). It is also essentially unknown in itself. Because it is beyond both substance and accident, we cannot make predications about it—"No name can define it" (I.3.6).

When Albert seeks to explore just how such an intellectual First Principle acts, he breaks with ordinary Aristotelian categories of causality by distinguishing flow (*fluxus*), that is, formal emanation, from efficient causality: "There is a classification of cause and another of a flowing principle, for nothing flows unless it is one form in that which is flowing and in that from which the flow comes, just as a river is of the same form as the source from which it flows and the water is of the same kind and form in both."[30] The relation involved in flowing, unlike that found in ordinary causality, is based on form. "Since . . . flowing of its very nature means only the procession of form from the simple formal principle itself, it is clear that to flow is not the same as to cause" (I.4.1). *Fluxus* is the transcendental activity by which the First Principle constitutes the universe: "Flow is the emanation of form from the First Source that is the font and origin of all forms."[31] It is neither a necessary emanation, which would be at odds with the Christian doctrine of God's free creation of the universe, nor does it imply any kind of pantheism, because all things receive the divine light according to their own mode of receptive being, or "shade" (*umbra*), as Albert puts it (I.4.5).

The fact that the Dominican developed his teaching on the metaphysics of flow partly on the basis of the *Book of Causes* with its monotheistic and creationist revision of Proclian Neoplatonism helps show that Albert was attempting to frame a new way of speaking about creation based on formal emanation.[32] Because of "the very communicability of the Good" (I.4.1), the First Principle flows into all things, both intelligible beings and corporeal beings. As Albert says: "The First of which we speak penetrates all things because of its excessive simplicity; as everywhere and always existing, there is nothing to which it is lacking."[33] This is especially the case in intellectual beings. Proposition 8 of the *Book of Causes* states, "The stability and essence of every intelligence is through the Pure Goodness that is the First Cause [i.e., First Principle]."[34]

An incisive presentation of Albert's metaphysics of flow can be found in the Dominican's *Treatise on Animals*, book 20, tractate 2, chapter 1, discussing "The Power of the First Cause."[35] Here Albert interjects a discussion of the general formal principles of things into his treatment of corporeal natures, beginning with "the first power, that of the Prime Mover, who is the source of the whole universe." Once again, the Prime Mover is understood not as an efficient cause of motion but as the source of formal emanation or flow. Just as the sun is the source of the light received by bodies in different ways,

> The same is true in the Fontal Cause of the universe from whose overflowing [*ebullitio*] proceed the illuminations and forms of his goodnesses received in distant things and taking different modes of existence according to the different powers of what receives them. Hence, some of these approach the likeness of the First Cause; others are quite distant; others are his obscure effects found in the matter of mixed and animal bodies.[36]

The Universal Cause of all is always "boiling over" forms from itself. All subsequent causation shares in this transcendent activity in a way analogous to how different colors refract pure light because of the diverse media in which light is received. This unified-yet-multiplex flow is Albert's solution to the ancient problem of the relation of the One and the many:

Many repeat but few understand what the ancient philosophers handed down: that the First Form of nature is one. It is one in the First Mover, but according to the procession from which it is active it is more and more multiple in proportion to how far it proceeds through the gradations of things that are moved and move. Therefore, this form is many when compared to beings, but is taken as one in the First Cause.[37]

The Intellect of the First Cause, though multiplied in things, is totally simple in itself. Albert concludes: "In every procession that comes forth from the Intellect, nothing is added to it by means of which a new form of existence might come to be in It. Rather, what is added draws It down to some form of non-existence, as in the case of not-being-simple, not-being-one, not-being-eternal, not-being-stable, and the like. Therefore, it is clear that what is truly the Principle of things is one."[38] Albert's view of the non-being of creatures taken in themselves as the necessary correlative of the flowing out of all things from the Principle was to be taken up by Eckhart among others.

The metaphysics of flow is essentially intellectual in nature. God, the First Principle, is the supreme Intellect universally at work in all things. Albert incorporates many elements of the Greco-Arabian view of the universe as a hierarchical ordering of Intelligences into a Christian doctrine of the creation through the Divine Word and the return of the universe to God through the Word's taking on of flesh. Albert's respect for philosophy, however, led him to avoid any easy assimilationism. Some thinkers, for example, had identified the Intelligences explored by the Peripatetic philosophers with the angels of Christian belief. Albert explicitly denies this.[39] His desire to be true to both reason and revelation was constant throughout his intellectual career, but the precise ways in which he worked out the correlation between faith and reason are not always clear, and this helps account for some of the diverse interpretations of his thought.

Mystical Theology

At the beginning of his commentary on the Dionysian MT, Albert contrasts the science found in this treatise with that presented in the longest text in the Dionysian corpus, the DN. The DN studies the downward movement from the darkness of God to the procession of things into the created universe; the MT moves in the reverse direction back up to the hidden God. Albert also notes the difference between human sciences that proceed from reason's first principles and the mystical science that, he says,

. . . begins rather with a kind of divine light that is not a statement by which something is affirmed; it is a kind of reality which convinces the intellect to adhere to it above all else. And so it raises the intellect to something which transcends it, and this is why the intellect is left with something of which it has no clearly defined knowledge.[40]

Albert's insistence on the supernatural nature of mystical theology must be stressed, especially because he also taught the existence of a natural form of contemplation and union with the First Principle that implies what might be called (though he does not so name it) a philosophical mysticism.

Albert's commentary on Aristotle's *Nicomachean Ethics* 10.16 makes this clear. Here the Dominican first discusses the relation between contemplation and philosophy, noting that contemplation is the goal of all philosophizing, but not all acts of philosophizing are truly contemplative. On this basis, he goes on to distinguish between theological and philosophical contemplation.[41] Theological and philosophical contemplation agree in some things, namely, in being intellectual insight (*inspectio*) of spiritual realities ordered to the supreme happiness of resting in God. But the two differ in the habit that activates them, the goal they aim for, and the way they study their object. Philosophical contemplation is based on the acquired habit of natural wisdom; theological contemplation on a "light infused by God." The philosopher contemplates what can be seen of God in this life, while the theologian is more concerned with the ultimate goal of heavenly contemplation. Neither the philosopher nor the theologian has God's substance as the object, but they differ with regard to the mode in which they consider the divine mystery:

The philosopher contemplates God insofar as he takes him in some kind of demonstrative conclusion, but the theologian contemplates him as he exists beyond reason and understanding. . . . The theologian depends upon the First Truth for its own sake and not because of reason, though he has reason too. Hence, the theologian remains in awe, but not the philosopher.[42]

The fact that philosophical and theological contemplation share much may be the reason why in other places Albert does not advert to the distinction between the two, but cites philosophers along with theologians in speaking of the goal of human felicity. For example, the prologue to his *Summa Theologiae* says that the ultimate aim of theology is the knowledge of what lies above the human heart, so that "this knowledge alone is that which lifts up the heart, purifies what has been lifted up, and establishes it in lasting immortality." As authorities for this elevating function, he cites Alfarabi on the immortality of the intellect that has become attuned to God (*intellectus adeptus*), as well as Dionysius's reference to his teacher Hierotheus on "having learned divine matters by suffering them (*pati divina*)."[43] In his *Commentary on Luke*, treating the text "Blessed are the eyes that see what you see" (Luke 10:23), Albert presents a definition of "contemplative happiness" (*beatitudo contemplativa*) based on Aristotle as an explanation of the biblical text, citing Dionysius for confirmation and without noting any difference between philosophical and theological contemplation.[44] Other texts, however, refer to the need for a supernatural light for the kind of theological contemplation taught by Dionysius in the MT.[45]

The subject capable of receiving this higher light from God is the same subject whose intellectual self-appropriation leads to natural felicity—the intellectual soul.[46] As Albert says in his treatise *The Intellect and the Intelligible*: "Humanity insofar as it is [just] humanity is intellect alone."[47] The intellectual soul is created directly by God as *imago Dei*. Albert's doctrine of the intellectual soul seeks to synthesize Aristotelian and Platonic elements. Considered in itself, the intellectual soul is an independent substance, as Plato taught; considered in its relation to corporeality, it is the individual form of the body, as Aristotle taught.[48] Albert's distinction of two ways of considering the intellect—intellect as independent substance and intellect as informing a material body—was to be developed in significant ways by his followers among the German Dominicans.[49]

To describe how the intellectual soul attains perfection and final happiness Albert sets forth a schema of the stages of the ascent of the intellect to conjunction with divine things, adapting his terminology from a rich mix of Peripatetic sources.[50] As set forth in the second book of *The Intellect and the Intelligible*, the itinerary begins with the action of the agent intellect upon the possible intellect to produce the formal intellect (*intellectus formalis*), which possesses knowledge of terms and principles (II.1–5). The formal intellect in the act of actually knowing things through knowledge of terms and principles is the effective intellect (*intellectus in effectu* [II.6–7]). The effective intellect becomes the adept intellect (*intellectus adeptus*) in the philosopher who studies the sciences to such an extent that his possible intellect has become totally adapted to the agent intellect and is fully self-aware (II.8). Because the philosopher has now become "a likeness of the First Truth," his intellect can rise up to the divine level of the assimilative intellect (*intellectus assimilativus* [II.9–12]). "The assimilative intellect," according to Albert, "is that in which humanity as far as possible or allowable ascends in a proportional way to the Divine Intellect that is the Light and Cause of all things."[51] In order to reach this stage, the intellect must undergo four purifications: first through the study of beauty; then through acquiring illumination; next through separation from continuous matter and time; and finally by "joining with the light of a higher order" (II.10 [518a]). Albert cites Plato, Aristotle, Alfarabi, Ptolemy, Avicenna, Dionysius, and Hermes Trismegistus as witnesses to this divinizing level of intellect: "Therefore, Hermes Trismegistus in the book *The Nature of the God of Gods* says 'Humanity is the link between God and the world,' because through an intellect of this sort it is joined to God, and the other intellects we talked about are the covering of this intellect."[52]

The five levels of the ascent of the intellect to divinization set out here and elsewhere by the German Dominican have been variously evaluated. Loris Sturlese, for example, noting the appeal to Hermes and the prophetic and even miraculous powers ascribed to the perfected knower, denies Albert's teaching has anything to do with Christian mysticism, or even Aristotelian contemplation, but rather emphasizes the divinized man as "a Hermetic prophet and magician."[53] Others, stressing the fact that illumination from above is needed to reach the final stage, read *The Intellect and the Intelligible* as presenting a Christian mystical psychology. Earlier in the treatise, however, Albert distinguishes between two forms of illumination coming down upon the intellect—the inherent natural light of the supreme intelligibles that blinds the intellect unprepared for it, and a "light from elsewhere" (*lumine alieno*), the supernatural illumination by which we accept the higher truths of faith.[54] So it seems that what the treatise is presenting to us is a description of natural contemplation that can perhaps also be conceived of as a parallel, at least in the psychological sense, to the Dionysian account of supernatural contemplation. The exact correlation of the two, however, Albert does not discuss.[55]

The properly supernatural ascent to contemplation and unifying vision of God is set forth primarily in the Dominican's commentary on the MT and to a lesser extent in his comments on the other Dionysian tracts. These works also touch on many of the traditional aspects of Christian mysticism.

Mystical, or hidden, theology differs from other forms of knowledge of God, both those based on reason and those based on faith, not only because it requires a divine light that nonetheless does not reveal anything positive about God, as we saw above, but also because it is essentially experiential and therefore truly known only to someone who has received it. In discussing the attitude of the person wishing to gain this knowledge, Albert says:

> We do not receive the things of God by means of rational principles, but experientially, in a way, by a kind of "sympathy toward them," as Dionysius says of Hierotheus, who learned the things of God "by undergoing them." But if our desire is infected by an unlawful love of things, we shall not feel the

sweetness of divine inspiration, and so, because of the lack of experiential knowledge, we may be able to form syllogisms and utter propositions, but we shall not have that real knowledge which is a part of beatitude.[56]

It is important to note that while Albert insisted on the essentially intellective character of mystical theology, experiencing such knowing involves not only being affectively drawn to God, but also the reception of sweetness in the knowing itself. In his treatment of Dionysius's praise of Hierotheus in DN 2, Albert says: "'He was perfected to a uniting with divine things' through affect and intellect and 'faith,' that is, sure knowledge of spiritual things."[57] A similar message is found in his discussion of Dionysius's praise of Paul's ecstasy (Gal. 2:20) in DN 4.13. Though intellect has a clear preponderance in Albert, "since nothing is loved unless it is known," like all Christian mystics, he sought to correlate the respective roles of loving and knowing in the path to union.[58] There is good reason, then, to agree with Christian Trottmann's assessment of Albert's contemplative wisdom as "a loving intelligence."[59]

The role of faith in Albert's understanding of mystical theology is clear.[60] The mystic begins from faith and, as long as he remains in this life, always needs it, but the light that grants the experiential knowing of mystical theology is a different and higher gift.[61] The dark light of mystical theology is to be seen as part of a process leading to God that involves both positive and negative theology, as well as loving and knowing, though not in equal portions.

Albert discusses many of the traditional headings of mystical theology in his commentary on the MT—contemplation, rapture, union, deification, theophany, etc.[62] In Dionysian fashion, it is the relation between cataphatic (i.e., positive) and apophatic (i.e., negative) theology that is central to his analysis. Although God has nothing in common with his creatures in genus, species, or analogy, cataphatic statements about God are possible, Albert says, because "he has something in common with creatures in the form of an imitative kind of analogy, in as much as other things imitate him to the extent that they are able."[63] Material things imitate him in being formed to an idea in the divine mind and therefore can be predicated of him causally, that is, insofar as he produces them; but immaterial perfections such as wisdom and goodness preexist in him and are therefore predicated both causally and essentially, though in an analogical way.[64] The problem, of course, is that we do not know how these things exist in God, because in him they are one with his infinite being, while we know them only in the limited ways in which they are realized in creatures. God's absolute simplicity means there can be no adequate propositions made of him in human language, which, of its nature, demands the distinction of subject and predicate.[65] Therefore, all affirmations about God are only relatively true, while negations are absolutely true.

Positively, God raises up the intellect toward divine knowledge in two modes: the way of discovery, in which a divine light guides the intellect's own search for God; and by way of the experiential signs that God directs either to the power of love (*affectus*), where they are received as wordless rejoicing (*iubilus*) and inexpressible delight, or to the intellect, where they come as new conceptions of God. (These two are equivalent to what modern investigators often call mystical experiences.) Albert does not deny the usefulness of these ways, but true to his Dionysian negative program, he says, "All these things have to be surpassed, because none of them is the object we seek in contemplation."[66]

In commenting on chapters 2 and 3 of the MT, Albert further explores the different procedures of affirmative and negative theology, emphasizing the superiority of the latter.[67] All our natural ways of understanding fail in relation to God. Even when our mind receives the divine light that elevates it above natural modes of knowing to a vision of God (presumably in this life), it is "only in a blurred and undefined knowledge 'that' he is. This is why it is said that God is seen by not-seeing: he is seen by the absence of natural seeing."[68] Albert often uses such terms as "confused" (*confuse*) and "indeterminate" (*non-determinate*) to describe the non-seeing seeing that is given to the intellect through mystical illumination.[69] He clarifies the negation involved in this mode of seeing by noting that "it is not a pure negation; what is being denied is our natural way of seeing, and what is left is a receiving of a supernatural light, which is, all the same, best indicated by negation. . . ."[70]

Further insight on this issue can be found in Albert's discussion of the knowability of God in one of his late works (after 1270), the *Summa Theologiae*. Again following Dionysius (e.g., CH 2.3 and DN 1.6–8), he says that there are only two ways that God can be known: symbolically, through the comparison of bodily properties to God; and mystically through the transcendental predicates that are truly God's, but that are only known to us through their limited manifestation in creatures. "But because there is no proportion between the infinite and the finite,"[71] both procedures produce the same effect. As Albert puts it: "Proceeding symbolically, we take our stand in the infinite and are diffused into it, grasping no limit"; and, on the mystical side, "Once again, the intellect, proceeding in this manner, takes its stand in the infinite and is diffused into it."[72] Mystical knowing is of its nature the indescribable diffusion of the finite into the infinite. This remains true even in the vision of God enjoyed by the blessed. In his *Question on the Vision of God in Heaven* Albert says: "Therefore, although he is infinite, he will be seen in a finite way, because he will not be comprehended. Nevertheless, he will be understood to be infinite and in this understanding the intellect will reach its goal by knowing the Infinite Itself."[73]

Chapter 4 of the *Super MT* analyzes how the path of negation begins by denying all predications taken from sense knowledge of God. Chapter 5 summarizes Albert's view of Dionysius's teaching on how even immaterial concepts must be denied of the God, who ultimately lies beyond both affirmation and negation. Yet one can apply negations to God that concern denials of specific differences following upon a genus (*negationes in genere*), if only analogically. This restricted mode of negation can help us "locate" the divine nature to the extent that we know what it is not.[74]

Albert's position on the relation between what medieval theologians spoke of as the *via negativa* (denying predicates of God) and the *via eminentiae* (affirming predicates of God, but on a higher level than we can know) makes for interesting comparison with his two most famous students, Thomas Aquinas and Meister Eckhart. Like Thomas, Albert initially grounds his view in the distinction between the substantial signification of terms such as "good" or "true" of God (such terms must belong to God first and foremost), and the way (*modus*) in which we use these terms, something that always implies our mode of conceiving and that therefore must be denied of God.[75] But Albert goes on, and in a direction that is closer to Eckhart, by advancing a second position that says even the reality affirmed by such names as goodness does not justify their ascription to God, because of our composite way of knowing. Thus, he claims that there is no difference at all among attributes in God himself, but only a difference in our way of conceiving them.[76]

At the end of his remarks on chapter 5, Albert argues that in actuality God lies beyond *both* affirmation and negation. The position is Dionysian, but the argument is Albert's. Because all true negation is founded on some affirmation, and since we have no proper affirmation concerning God, there can be no proper negation either. God's position outside the negations of human speaking, however, is founded on his unknowable transcendence, not in any kind of lack. Albert concludes: "The transcendence (*excessus*) of him who is above all transcends all negation. The names which are denied of him are denied because of his transcendence, not because he lacks anything, which is why we deny things of creatures."[77] The same rigorous apophaticism is evident also from Albert's comments on the Dionysian letters, where he says that "God can be seen in no way whatsoever, but he is seen in the very ignorance of him."[78] Though the Dominican does not use the term here, this is clearly a form of *docta ignorantia.*

How does this knowing by ignorance relate to the vision of God in heaven, which, as Albert noted in the commentary on Aristotle's *Nicomachean Ethics,* is the real goal of mystical contemplation? Albert's treatment of this issue is important because of the context within which he wrote his Dionysian commentaries. In 1241 and again in 1244, William of Auvergne, bishop of Paris, along with the authorities of the university, had condemned the view that even in heaven God will never be seen directly, but only through theophanies, or divine manifestations.[79] This denial of direct *visio dei* advanced by some thinkers was the expression of a form of Dionysianism influenced by John the Scot, who had affirmed that no direct gaze upon the hidden incomprehensible God was possible, here or hereafter. Even in heaven "theophanies of theophanies" will be the object of the intellect's beatifying vision.[80] This debate over the nature of the beatific vision was a significant moment in the evolution of medieval scholasticism, and especially in the reception of Dionysian theology.[81] Albert the Great worked out a solution to the problem of the beatific vision, one that adhered to the Paris definition but that also managed to salvage significant aspects of Dionysian apophaticism for the future of German mysticism.

Like all Christian theologians, Albert contrasted the highest forms of contemplative rapture realized here below (*hic*) with the supreme and stable enjoyment to be found in heaven (*ibi*). In order to understand the similarities and differences between the two forms of contact with God and thus to appreciate the true nature of the beatific vision, it is useful to note some distinctions that Albert employs: (1) the difference between vision and comprehension; (2) the distinction between knowledge of God *quid est* and knowledge *quia est;* (3) the meaning of the "face-to-face" vision mentioned in the Bible (e.g., Gen. 32:30; Exod. 33:11; 1 Cor. 13:12); and (4) the role of intermediaries (*media/theophaniae*) in knowing God here and hereafter.

Albert's discussion of "The knowability of God on God's part" (*De cognoscibilitate dei ex parte cognoscibilis*) in question 13 of the third treatise of book 1 of his *Summa Theologiae* is his last and fullest account of these issues.[82] Central to his case is the following claim: "It is one thing to be in contact [with something] through the intellect and to be poured out into the intelligible reality; and it is another to seize or to comprehend that intelligible."[83] On this basis Albert argues, in conformity with the Paris decision, that the created human intellect can directly attain the divine substance "through simple regard" (*per simplicem intuitum*), but that it can never comprehend God.[84] Thomas Aquinas would also distinguish between attaining immediate vision of God and the impossibility for any created intellect to comprehend the divine essence (e.g., STh Ia, q. 12, a. 7). A difference between Albert and Thomas emerges, however, with respect to the understanding of knowledge *quid est* (what God is) and knowledge *quia est* (that God is).

Neither Thomas's STh nor Albert's work of the same name allows for any comprehensive *quid est* knowledge of God here or in heaven.[85] To attain this knowledge would be to know God as God knows God. But what about knowledge *quia est*, knowing that God is? Here Albert differs from his pupil. For Thomas, knowledge *quia est* is a straightforward term—the demonstration *that* a cause exists from knowledge of its effect (STh Ia, q. 2, aa. 2–3); hence the Angelic Doctor's five ways of demonstrating God's existence from his effects in the world. For Albert, on the contrary, knowledge *quia est* is realized in several analogous ways that are not always clearly distinguished. In dependence on Aristotle, for whom knowledge "that it is" is one form of precise philosophical knowledge based on a remote cause or an effect that is "convertible with or proportionate to its cause," in his *Super MT* Albert denies that we can have natural *quia est* knowledge of God in this life, because nothing is really proportionate to God.[86] But in other places the German Dominican seems to hold out the possibility of an imperfect form of *quia est* knowledge of God, even on the basis of natural reason.[87] The clearest treatment of this issue is found in the discussion of the beatific vision in Albert's commentary on the fifth Dionysian letter. Here he argues that although we do attain the vision of God in heaven, we never do so perfectly. Rather, "the created intellect . . . is joined in a kind of confused way to the God who, as it were, goes beyond it. . . ." Thus, there is no knowledge *quid est* of God, because he has no defining feature; nor is there knowledge *propter quid* because God has no cause. There is also no *determined* knowledge *quia* because God has no remote cause or proportionate effect. "Therefore, neither in this life, nor in heaven, do we see more of God than a confused *quia*, although God himself is seen more or less clearly according to the different ways of seeing and of those who see."[88] Albert the Great, therefore, remains deeply apophatic about all knowledge of God, even that in heaven.[89]

The Bible often speaks of "face-to-face" vision, both in this life (e.g., Jacob and Moses) and in the next. The contradiction between such texts and those that denied that any human could ever see God under any cir-

cumstances (e.g., John 1:18) had been a part of Christian mysticism since
the second century. In light of the crisis in the 1240s concerning how to
understand the beatific vision, Albert undertook to work out his own
answer to this seeming contradiction.

The fullest treatment is found in chapter 4 of the treatise on the knowability of God from Albert's *Summa Theologiae* where he takes up not only
the issue of face-to-face vision but also the question of whether such vision
involves any intermediary.[90] Once again, Albert agrees with the 1241 decision that the bare and pure intellect will see the bare essence of God in
heaven. In order to understand this properly, however, it is necessary to
introduce important distinctions about the different ways of understanding
the terms *facies dei* and *medium*. The expression "face of God" can be used
in three ways, according to Albert. The common understanding of the term
points to anything in which God appears and in which he can be known,
that is, potentially anything in the created universe. Second, "[t]he face of
God is used in the proper sense for his evident presence through an effect
of grace aiding or protecting to some purpose. . . . This mode differs from
the first the way nature differs from grace."[91] Finally, "[i]n the most proper
sense the face of God is God's essential presence demonstrated and displayed without an intermediary in the way he shows himself to the
blessed."[92] These qualifications make it easy to show that the face-to-face
visions of God ascribed to Old Testament figures like Jacob and Moses
were different from the vision enjoyed by the blessed in heaven.

To understand the difference between the graced visions of God given in
this life and the beatific vision one must advert to the ways in which God
does or does not use intermediaries or means. There is no need to follow
the details of Albert's distinctions of various intermediaries to grasp the
essentials of his teaching. Visions of God in this life always employ intermediaries, or theophanies, such as the supernatural habits and gifts of the Holy
Spirit.[93] In the case of the most proper understanding of face-to-face vision
in heaven, however, there is no medium or intermediary in the sense of an
instrument God employs to convey or reflect his essence (*medium differens
vel reflectens*); nor is there an intentional medium, nor a *medium coadiuvans*,
something the divine essence needs to make itself visible—God is pure light
in himself. There is, however, need for a medium strengthening and aiding
the soul to see what is infinitely beyond it. "If someone sees by the vision of
glory," says Albert, "he must be perfected by the habits of glory and beatitude. But these intermediaries do not mask or carry away or create distance
between the one seeing and what is seen, but they strengthen the power of
seeing and perfect it in the act of seeing. And to see through an intermedi-

ary in this way is not opposed to immediate vision, but agrees with it."[94] The light of glory, then, is a subjective *medium sub quo* (Thomas's term, though this appears to be what Albert intends). Its function is to help the intellectual soul to receive the vision of God; it is not an objective *medium in quo,* which would create distance between God and the soul.[95]

Albert's doctrine of the *lumen gloriae* was a crucial aspect of his teaching on the immediate and direct nature of the beatific vision, but it is important to note that he continued to use the Dionysian-Eriugenean language of theophany to describe both the *lumen gloriae* itself and the different forms of *lumen divinum* by which God strengthens individual souls in different ways to attain their eternal felicity in the beatific vision.[96] In his explanation of the four kinds of theophanies found in *Super CH* 4, he talks about four kinds of divine light (*lumen divinum*). The first two belong to this life: any seeing of a creature that leads to God, and divinely sent visions. The last two belong to heaven. "The third mode . . . is when in a divine light, which is not God, an object is seen that is truly God, not in the light as in a medium, the way a thing is seen in its image, but along with a light strengthening the intellect [so that] God is seen immediately."[97] The fourth and highest species of theophany is the direct *visio dei* itself. Albert also describes it in Eriugenean language as a theophany:

> Thus God himself is in each of the blessed as an illumination by whose participation he makes him a likeness to himself. In such a likeness the vision of God is called a theophany. In this way the same God will be illumination and object, but object as he is in himself, illumination insofar as he is participated in by the blessed.[98]

Although Albert agreed with the 1241 definition on the direct vision of God in heaven, his intellective Dionysianism did not abandon the Eriugenean language of theophany, even in the case of the beatific vision.

Thomas Aquinas on Contemplation and the Vision of God

Within the vast edifice of the theology of Thomas Aquinas mystical theology plays a more restricted role than it does in Albert.[99] (Thomas wrote no commentary on Dionysius's MT and does not quote it often.) Furthermore, since Thomas never talks about himself, reflections about his interior life remain no more than conjectures, though witnesses at his canonization proceedings testified to his devotion to contemplation.[100] Thomas mentions spirituality fairly often, taking it both in the biblical sense of living in the power of the Holy Spirit bestowed on us through the risen Christ,[101] and in the newer philosophical understanding as the opposite of corporeality. The spiritual center of Thomas's theology has been vindicated by Jean-Pierre Torrell, especially the fundamental role of the Trinity in his teaching on the Christian life. The care with which Thomas treats so many of the fundamental practices of Christian spirituality, such as prayer, provides evidence for both the speculative and practical aspects of his spiritual teaching.[102]

The Dominican doctor was deeply concerned with an issue that was both a doctrinal and a mystical problem in his day—the forms of *visio dei* possible in this life and the next. In addition, many other aspects of mysticism were necessarily involved in Thomas's agenda of presenting "holy teaching" (*sacra doctrina*) in a systematic and accessible way. Among these the nature of contemplative graces, both general and particular, stands out. As a friar fighting for recognition of his order in an often hostile atmosphere, he had to pay particular attention to the relation of action and contemplation in the various forms of specialized religious life. Thomas Aquinas left us no mystical narratives or explicit mystical theology, but his treatment of many significant mystical themes gives him a place in the tradition of Christian mysticism.

The Vision of God

In order to understand what kind of vision of God Thomas holds out as possible both here and hereafter, we must begin with the Angelic Doctor's negative theology. The impact of the apophatic imperative in Thomas's theology has emerged in recent decades with renewed force, particularly as scholars have investigated his indebtedness to Neoplatonism. Thomas was never a pure Aristotelian, for all his use of "the philosopher," any more than he was a follower of Plato, for all his critical remarks about the Platonists.[103] Thomas sought the truth, not labels.

The bedrock of Thomas's doctrine of God is the absolute simplicity of the divine nature, something best conceived of as a formal feature rather than just another divine attribute (STh Ia, q. 3; *De Potentia* q. 7, a. 1).[104] This means that God in Godself is unknowable to the finite human mind and incapable of expression in the categories of human predication, which work by way of composition (i.e., affirming a predicate regarding a subject). "Because we do not know what God is, the proposition [God exists] is not self-evident to us" (STh Ia, q. 2, a. 1). A host of texts across Thomas's works never bend on this key principle. While Thomas consistently rejected the position of Maimonides that language about God is merely negative (STh Ia, q. 13, a. 2; De Pot. q. 7, a. 5), he expressed agreement with the Dionysian program of using negations within a linguistic strategy in which the affirmation that there is something like goodness in God must be negated by the realization that goodness in God is not the goodness we can predicate.[105] Commenting on DN 1, he says: "This is the final point which we can attain concerning divine knowledge in this life, that God is above everything we can know and therefore naming God through negation is especially appropriate."[106] Negation here becomes part of a process of hierarchical ascent to God, a dialectic of presence and absence.[107] Of course, Thomas, following Dionysius, accorded the ultimate place to the language of eminence in speaking about God: "When we say that God is good, or wise, we do not only signify that he is the cause of wisdom or goodness, but that these things pre-exist in him in a higher way" (Ia, q. 13, a. 6c). The problem is that we do not know how they exist there, nor can we express it. As the Dominican put it in his commentary on Boethius's *De Trinitate*: "We can say that at the end of our knowing we know God as an unknown, because the mind has discovered that it has reached the highest point of its knowledge when it knows that his essence is above everything that can be grasped in this life, and thus even though what he is remains unknown, that he is is known."[108] While Thomas gave preeminence to the nonconceptual term *esse* (an infinitive best translated as "is-ing") as the most adequate word to use in relation to God (Ia, q. 3, a. 4; q. 13, a. 11), God as *ipsum esse subsistens* (Subsisting Is-ing Itself) is not an object of knowledge. Our use of the term expresses the mind's judgment regarding the legitimacy of its God-given impetus toward ultimate mystery.[109]

Like Albert, Thomas used the traditional distinction between knowing *quid est* (knowing what something is) and knowing *quia est* (knowing that something is), but in his own way. True to his strategy of turning Aristotle on his head to serve Christian theology, Aquinas adopted an understanding of *quia est* knowledge that enabled him to affirm the possibility of proving God's existence from creatures while maintaining that *quid est*, or comprehensive knowledge of the divine essence, can never be attained, even in heaven. But Thomas also held that human felicity could be found only in the vision of God (STh Ia, q. 12, a. 1; IaIIae, qq. 1–5; SCG III.37–63). So important was seeing God for Aquinas's teaching that he even uses it as his answer to the classic theological question "Cur deus homo?" that is, "Why did God become man?" The Word became man so that man could see God, is Thomas's answer (SCG IV.54). How did Aquinas correlate these seemingly incompatible claims of needing to see God to attain happiness and the impossibility of knowing what God is? The answer to this lies in his teaching about the forms of *visio dei*.

Vision, Aquinas says, properly belongs to the highest form of sensation, but because of its dignity the term is also extended to intellectual knowing (Ia, q. 67, a. 1). In discussing how God is known in q. 12 of STh Ia, Thomas, like Albert, strongly supports the 1241 decision that humans must see God's essence in order to reach beatitude (a. 1). In the remainder of the question he goes on to summarize the conditions of such vision and its difference from seeing in this life. Physical vision and even our natural intellectual powers cannot, by definition, attain the infinite God (aa. 3–4). Since some likeness, or medium, needs to be present in the receptive power of the intellect for any kind of vision, in order for us to attain beatitude in the vision of God, God himself needs to strengthen our intellectual vision by the supernatural gift of the light of glory (*lumen gloriae*). "This light is not required for seeing God's essence as some kind of likeness in which God may be seen, but as a kind of perfection of the intellect. . . . It is not a medium in which God can be seen, but a means by which (*medium sub quo*) he is seen" (a. 5, ad 2).

Two further points presented in q. 12 are of significance for understanding the character of Thomas's teaching on the vision of God. The first is that owing to the divine infinity, seeing God does not mean comprehending him—God will be seen in heaven, but he will nonetheless remain infinitely beyond the human mind (a. 7). Finally, the Dominican insists that despite Old Testament accounts of seeing God face-to-face, "a mere human [Christ is being excepted] cannot see God by essence unless he be separated from mortal life" (a. 11). Neither natural reason (a. 12), nor even the higher lights of faith and prophetic visions (a. 13) provide access to the vision of God's essence. As he put it in the *De Veritate*: "The vision of the blessed is not distinguished from the vision of one still here according to more or less perfect seeing, but through the difference of seeing and not-seeing."[110]

In discussing why not even Adam before the Fall enjoyed the vision of God's essence,[111] Thomas sketches a theory of the various ways of seeing God and the different means or intermediaries employed. The intellect in fallen humanity can attain knowledge *that* God is from the things that God created (see Rom. 1:20), making use of three intermediaries: the means by which (*sub quo*), that is, the natural light of the agent intellect; the means in which (*quo*), the intelligible form of a created thing in the mind; and the means from which (*a quo*), the created thing as a mirror from which we can reason to the God who created it. Adam in the state of innocence did not need the mirror of creatures from which to reason to God, but he utilized a special image of the thing to be seen, that is, "he saw God through a spiritual light divinely influencing a person's mind, which was a kind of expressed likeness of the uncreated light."[112] In heaven, the light of glory functions only as a *medium sub quo*—that is, it is not an image *of* God, but rather a supernatural assistance given to the human mind to enable it to see God directly. While presumably no one in this life can return to the state enjoyed by Adam, Thomas locates contemplative vision in a realm close to that of unfallen humanity:

> In contemplation God is seen through the medium of the light of wisdom that elevates the mind to behold divine things. It is not that the divine essence itself is seen in an immediate way, but this is the way God is seen through grace by a contemplative after the state of sin, though it was realized more perfectly before the Fall.[113]

This is the realm that today we call mysticism.

Contemplation and Wisdom

Contemplatio had a long history in Christian mysticism before Thomas Aquinas dealt with it in the section of STh IIaIIae that treats the gratuitous graces (*gratiae gratis datae*).[114] Thomas treats contemplation, rapture, and related special graces in many places in his writings, but the rich and final summary found in the STh (written about 1271) means that we can concentrate on this presentation.[115]

At the beginning of the IIaIIae (q. 1, a. 8) Thomas says, "Those things directly pertain to faith whose vision will bring us felicity in heaven and by which we are led to eternal life." This teleological principle displays how the Angelic Doctor's treatment of mystical gifts is solidly anchored in his teaching on the role of faith leading to glory. As for contemplation itself, Aquinas gives it a broad definition as whatever belongs to "the simple consideration of truth" (*contemplatio pertinet ad ipsum simplicem intuitum veritatis*—q. 180, a. 3, ad 1).[116] Like Albert, this definition allows for both natural and supernatural forms of contemplation. In his commentary on the first chapter of Isaiah, Thomas explicitly distinguishes the contemplation of the philosophers, that of the saints in this life, and that of the blessed in heaven.[117] Though Thomas's main interest is in supernatural contemplation, Aristotle's analysis of contemplation provided him with many useful insights in the construction of his teaching—grace builds upon nature.[118] As Jean Leclercq pointed out, Thomas's doctrine of the contemplative life was forged within the historical context of the disputes over the status of the mendicants, but on the basis of traditional patristic and medieval teaching on contemplation and through the mediation of his reflections on Aristotle.[119]

Aquinas's teaching on contemplation can be characterized as eschatological, synthetic, nondiscursive and experiential, sapiential, and eminent.

Eschatology for Thomas is the Christian transfiguration of Aristotelian teleology—the nature of a thing or action is determined by its end, in the
Christian sense by its completion in heaven. Thomas's view of contemplation in this life is always geared to the goal, that is, the vision of God's
essence in heaven. As a. 4 of q. 180 puts it: "Now we have imperfect possession of the contemplation of divine truth, 'through mirror and enigma'
(1 Cor. 13:12), but on this basis we gain the first fruits of beatitude, which
begins here in order to find its goal in the future."[120] Second, Thomas's view
of contemplation is synthetic in the sense that he does not limit contemplation to the act of "simple consideration of [divine] truth," but rather views it
analogically, as a process with many components related in primary or secondary ways.[121] In a. 3 Aquinas says that because the human mind knows
by way of process, the contemplative life reaches its perfection and gains its
unity from the nondiscursive consideration of truth itself, but it attains this
goal through many acts that come from both within and without the contemplative subject. In a. 4 he notes that *contemplatio* pertains principally to
the consideration of divine truth, but in a secondary and dispositive way it
includes everything ordered to this: moral virtues (see a. 2); other activities,
such as prayer and meditation (a. 3); and the contemplation of creatures as
God's effects.[122]

The other aspects of Thomas's view of contemplation require more discussion. Describing contemplation as nondiscursive and experiential comes
to the heart of the Angelic Doctor's teaching on the role of knowing and
loving in the contemplative life. In a. 1 Thomas insists that the essence of
contemplation as an activity of knowing pertains to the intellect, but that
the will is also involved both as moving the intellect toward the desired
good and as delighting in the good that is apprehended—"Because a person
delights in gaining what is loved, the contemplative life finds its goal in the
delight that is in the faculty of desire; on the basis of this delight love is also
part of the intention."[123] The role of love is also highlighted in Thomas's
discussion of delight (*delectatio*) in a. 7. Contemplation is delightful both by
reason of its activity, since it is natural for humans to take pleasure in knowing, and also by reason of its object, the beloved attained in contemplation.
"The contemplative life," Thomas concludes, "although it essentially consists in the intellect, has its starting point in the faculty of desire . . . ; and
because the end matches the beginning, even the term and goal of the contemplative life is in the faculty of desire, for as long as someone delights in
seeing the thing that is loved, that delight itself arouses love more greatly."[124]
The contemplative life is ordered to the perfect love of God (q. 182, a. 4,
ad 1).

What kind of nondiscursive knowledge constitutes the essence of contemplation? And how does the loving desire that moves the intellect, as well as the experience of love found in the contemplative act itself, fit in? To answer these questions we need to consider other texts where Thomas takes up such terms as *cognitio experimentalis, connaturalitas,* and above all *sapientia,* understood in its etymological sense as *sapida scientia,* that is, "knowledge by taste."

An important passage from In I Sent. d. 3, q. 4, a. 5, on the presence of God in the soul insofar as it is the image of God distinguishes three kinds of knowing: discerning a thing on the basis of its differences from other things; thinking of a thing discursively according to its properties; and finally the act of understanding taken in its essence. "To understand means nothing else than the simple consideration of the intellect (*simplex intuitus intellectus*) in the intelligible thing present to it." The soul does not always think discursively about God or itself. No, Thomas continues,

> The presence of the thing in any way whatsoever does not suffice for such knowledge; it needs to be present there as an object, and the knower's intention is required. But insofar as to understand means nothing more than consideration, which is nothing other than the presence of the intelligible to the intellect in any way whatsoever, then the soul always understands itself and God, and a certain kind of indefinite love follows upon this.[125]

What Thomas is pointing to here is the natural presence of God in the rational soul, what we might call the precognitive source of the desire for contemplation, whether philosophical or theological.[126] While the structure of the intellectual processes involved in the two forms of contemplation may not be different, the contemplation that proceeds from faith differs from philosophical contemplation with regard to its object; that is, it seeks God as the beatifying goal to be attained in heaven. As such, its source is not the indefinite love (*amor indeterminatus*) that is the effect of the presence of God in the agent intellect insofar as it is created, but rather the specific love that is the Holy Spirit poured out in our hearts (Rom. 5:5).

For the Angelic Doctor the saving grace that comes to us through the missions of the Son and the Holy Spirit being sent into the world involves what he often refers to as a *cognitio experimentalis* (or sometimes *quasi experimentalis*), a form of direct knowing more akin to sensation than discursive reasoning, and one that is primarily affective in the sense that it spurs the recipient on to greater desire for supernatural contemplation.[127] In STh Ia, q. 64, a. 1, for example, Aquinas distinguishes three kinds of knowledge of truth: natural knowledge; graced speculative knowledge; and graced affective knowledge "producing love of God, which properly belongs to the gift of wisdom." What this affective knowing entails is spelled out in q. 43 in the Dominican's discussion of the divine missions. The Holy Spirit, who is Supreme Love, is sent to assimilate us to God through the gift of charity. (The Sentence Commentary speaks of the knowledge gained through this union [*conjunctio*] as "experiential in a sense" [*Unde cognitio ista est quasi experimentalis*].)[128] Here in STh Thomas says that even the mission of the Son in taking on flesh involves not just intellect, but loving intellect. "The Son is sent not according to any form of the perfection of the intellect, but according to that intellectual instruction that bursts forth in the desire of love." The Son is sent to be known and perceived by humans, "but the perception signifies a form of experiential knowing that is properly called *sapientia*, a kind of knowing by taste. . . ."[129] In another text in the STh Thomas illustrates this "affective or experiential knowing of the divine goodness or will" by citing one of the most famous accounts of mystical consciousness in the tradition, Dionysius's description of Hierotheus in DN 2.9 as "learning divine things through his sharing of them." Thomas concludes: "In this way we are invited to experience God's will and to taste his sweetness."[130] These accounts of "a kind of experiential knowledge" of God can be described as relating both to the motive source of the desire for contemplation, and (as the case of Hierotheus shows) to the simple and direct consideration that characterizes the reception of contemplation for the Dominican.[131] Thomas does not describe actual mystical states of consciousness the way, for example, Bernard of Clairvaux did; rather, he wants to locate these states theologically within the process that leads from faith to the vision of God in heaven.

Further light on the nature of such experiential knowledge comes from a consideration of what Aquinas has to say about knowledge by connaturality (*per connaturalitatem*), or knowledge by inclination.[132] A classic text in STh IIaIIae, q. 45, a. 4c, says, "Wisdom, the gift of the Holy Spirit, gives correct judgment about divine matters or God's rules about other things from a kind of connaturality or union with things divine."[133] But what is connaturality? Etymologically, *connaturalitas* indicates any inclination that belongs to something by its nature, as a body, for example, is subject to the law of gravity. In thinking subjects the presence of a good in the appetitive power "causes a kind of inclination, aptitude, or connaturality to the good" (IaIIae, q. 23, a. 4c), so that love itself can be spoken of as a connaturality: "Love is a kind of union or connaturality of the lover and the beloved" (IaIIae, q. 32, a. 3, ad 3). As Inos Biffi has shown, Thomas speaks of knowing by connaturality in three contexts: an intellectual way, signifying how the human mind knows by what is connatural to it, namely, by sense knowledge (Ia,

q. 13, a. 1, ad 2); a moral way in which someone who possesses a virtue knows how to exercise it correctly (IIaIIae, q. 45, a. 2c); and finally in a sapiential way through the reception of the divine gift of Wisdom, as seen above.[134] Discussing how the gift of wisdom is found in the intellect as its subject (IIaIIae, q. 45, a. 2c), Aquinas explains this last form of connaturality in more detail:

> Wisdom brings in a correct judgment according to divine reasons. Correctness of judgment can come about in two ways: one according to the perfect use of reason, the other due to a certain connaturality to the things that are now to be judged. Therefore, to have correct judgment about divine things on the basis of reason's investigation belongs to th⸗ wisdom that is an intellectual virtue, but to have right judgment about them according to a connaturality with them belongs to wisdom insofar as it is a gift of the Holy Spirit.

Thomas goes on to cite once again the example of Hierotheus's passive reception of divine gifts, now invoking the language of mystical union:

> Such a form of sympathy (*compassio*) or connaturality with divine things comes about through charity which unites us to God, according to the text, "He who adheres to God is one spirit" (1 Cor. 6:17). Therefore, the wisdom that is a gift has a cause in the will, namely charity, but its essence is in the intellect whose activity is correct judgment.[135]

Mystical knowing as a form of experiential and connatural knowing, based on the union with God through charity and leading to the reception of the gift of divine wisdom, is the center of Thomas's teaching on contemplation.

A full account of the intricate nexus of themes introduced here—indwelling of the Holy Spirit, and indeed the whole Trinity, through charity;[136] union with God;[137] the respective roles of love and knowledge in union;[138] and the action of divine wisdom[139]—would lead us far afield into the wide reaches of the Angelic Doctor's total theology. While this theology can be said to form the foundation for a distinctive view of mysticism, Thomas himself did not develop one in explicit fashion. These notes, however, may help to show how Thomistic teaching on *contemplatio* is integral to his presentation of *sacra doctrina*.

Several other characteristics of contemplative knowing and loving should be mentioned before closing this section. First of all, the emphasis on the role of grace as gift, from the beginnings in faith to the heights of contemplative contact with God, shows that while the desire to see God and activities conducive to this (such as prayer, reading, meditation) remain important, supernatural contemplation is essentially a gift from God. Second, the nondiscursive knowing received in contemplation does not conflict with the strongly negative view Thomas has regarding knowledge of God, but reinforces it. Contemplation is not any kind of knowledge *quid est* of God. Perhaps it might be described as a stronger and more convincing form of knowledge *quia est*, a knowing that God truly IS in the highest sense because it is based on loving experience. But it can also be seen, perhaps more truly, as a more potent conviction of the impossibility of knowing God. Commenting on DN 7.4, Thomas, like Albert, stresses that the highest form of knowing God is knowing him in ignorance,[140] but he adds a distinctive note by seeing this ignorance as a participation in divine wisdom: "Thus knowing God in this way, in such a state of knowledge, is to be illuminated by the very depth of divine wisdom, which we are not able to investigate."[141]

We can also characterize Thomas's understanding of contemplation as eminent, by which I mean that the Dominican argued for the superiority of the contemplative life over the active, though he admitted, along with tradition, that the obligations of Christian love often made turning to action necessary and more meritorious than remaining in contemplation. Question 181 of the IIaIIae treats of the nature of the active life, while question 182 compares the two forms of life in a way that opts for the traditional superiority of the contemplative life on the basis of both the teaching of Aristotle and the witness of Christian tradition, especially Gregory the Great. In q. 182, a. 1, Thomas presents nine arguments for the superiority of the contemplative life taken in itself, but allows that in some circumstances (*secundum quid*) the active life should prevail.

In his insistence on the priority of the contemplative life, Thomas shows himself as an apologist for the mendicant religious orders (see qq. 184–89), as well as more subservient to tradition than his Dominican successors, notably Meister Eckhart and his followers, who rethought the old paradigms about action and contemplation.[142] Aquinas's thinking here is bound to the categories of the past, preferring Mary (contemplation) to Martha (action), and using Aristotle for philosophical reasons that seem in conflict with the Gospel imperative that Thomas himself expressed in the famous phrase *contemplata aliis tradere*. From the viewpoint of the history of mysticism, this may be the least convincing part of the Angelic Doctor's attempt to integrate a systematic presentation of *contemplatio* with *sacra doctrina*.

One final issue remains to be discussed, because Thomas spent considerable time on it. The Schoolmen often investigated the nature of rapture (*raptus/excessus/exstasis*), especially the question whether or not some biblical figures, such as Moses and Paul, had actually been given the vision of God's essence while still in this life.[143] The question has probably elicited a more extensive literature than it deserves. Whether or not Moses and Paul saw God was scarcely of central significance for those who knew that whatever degree of *contemplatio* they might attain, it could never equal the saints of the biblical past.

Aquinas discusses *raptus* in *De Veritate* q. 10, a. 11, and q. 13, aa. 1–5, as well as in STh IIaIIae, q. 185, aa. 1–6. His basic principle is that the human mind is not able to behold the divine essence in this life, but because both bodies and minds are always subject to divine power, by miraculous exception God could abstract a person's mind from the usual mode of human knowing based on the senses to elevate it to some glimpse of the divine essence. "Those to whom it is granted to see God essentially in this way are totally drawn away from the action of the senses, so that the entire soul is gathered into the vision of the divine essence. Hence they are said to be raptured, and by the power of a superior nature they are drawn away from what belongs to them by nature" (De Ver. q. 10, a. 11c). The key example of this vehement elevation to a transitory vision of God (different from the permanent vision of heaven) is the experience Paul relates in 2 Corinthians 12:2–5 of being taken up to the third heaven. On the basis of the authority of Augustine,[144] Thomas argues that Paul did indeed see God's essence, but through a transient reception of the light of glory (De Ver. q. 13, aa. 2–5; IIaIIae q. 175, aa. 3–6).[145] On the basis of texts like Numbers 12:8 and Augustine's backing once again, Thomas also ascribed such rapture to Moses, as fitting for the lawgiver of the Old Testament.[146] It is hard not to think that tradition here was constraining the Angelic Doctor against the logic of his theology in making these exceptions, especially because he denied vision of God's essence to other Old Testament figures who spoke of seeing God face-to-face, as well as to subsequent saints whose visions had acquired classic status, such as Benedict.[147]

Perhaps the most original aspect of Thomas's theory of rapture comes in q. 175, a. 2, where the Dominican discusses whether rapture belongs more to the appetitive or cognitive power of the soul. Here Thomas introduces important categories taken from Dionysius, especially the notion of the ecstasy of love, into a theological arena that had been dominated by Augustinian theology. As usual, Aquinas solves the question with a distinction. Rapture can be spoken of in two ways. With regard to its goal (i.e., seeing God), rapture must pertain to the cognitive power. The violence that induces it does not belong to innate appetite but comes from above. With regard to its cause, however, rapture can indeed pertain to the appetitive power. Thomas says: "From the fact that the appetite is very strongly drawn towards something it can happen that from the violence of the affection a person is carried away from everything else. It also has an effect on the appetitive power when someone delights in the things he is raptured to" (a. 2c).

In the objections Aquinas distinguishes between ecstasy, a term that merely indicates a going out of self by being placed beyond one's proper order, and rapture, a term that adds the note of violence. Ecstasy, says Thomas citing Dionysius (DN 4.13), can pertain to the appetitive power in the sense that Divine Love causes the human appetite to stretch out toward the Supreme Good. This distinction is based on an important discussion of Dionysius's treatment of the ecstasy of love found in STh IaIIae, q. 28, a. 3.[148] In this article Thomas distinguished ecstasy of the apprehensive or cognitive power from the ecstasy of the appetitive power, which takes place "when someone's appetite is drawn to something else so that a person goes outside himself in some way." Love indirectly prepares for the first form of ecstasy by inducing meditation on the beloved, but it causes the second form, immediately in the case of love of friendship (*amor amicitiae*) that moves us to go outside ourselves to do good to the friend, and indirectly in interested love (*amor concupiscentiae*), insofar as what is outside us becomes the subject of an internal desire.

The invocation of the ecstasy of love in Thomas's treatment of rapture casts light on some of the inbuilt tensions in his treatment of mystical graces. By treating *raptus* along with the other special graces such as prophecy (IIaIIae, qq. 171–79), he clearly wants to distance this phenomenon from the ordinary course of the life of grace leading to *visio dei*. Nevertheless, Thomas does not place rapture in a separate, higher faculty of the soul, the *intelligentia*, as did Albert and others.[149] Furthermore, the invocation of the ecstasy of love seems to draw us back once again to a form of consciousness that is an integral outgrowth of *caritas*, perhaps even an expression of *sapientia*, essential gifts given to all believers in order to be saved and thus attain the beatifying vision of God. To that extent at least we can surmise that the Angelic Doctor believed that all Christians were called to be contemplatives, persons who should at least desire, even in this life, to experience the taste of God in the ecstasy of love.[150]

Thomas Aquinas's teaching on contemplation is among the most systematic in the history of Christian thought. As such, it offers a point of departure for any theological treatment that seeks to locate the mystical element in Christianity within the broad confines of doctrine. While the Neoscholastic view of Thomas that dominated Catholic theology between 1880 and 1960 has passed, Thomas's profound teaching on how *contemplatio* is ordered to *visio dei* was an important source for his Dominican followers and remains a high point of doctrinal reflection on Christian mysticism.

APPENDIX

NEOPLATONIC SOURCES OF DOMINICAN MYSTICISM

Albert the Great, Thomas Aquinas, Meister Eckhart, and many other late medieval thinkers made use not only of traditional sources of Christian Neoplatonism, especially Augustine and Dionysius, but also of a new range of Neoplatonic texts that became available in the twelfth and thirteenth centuries. Three of these are of special significance for mysticism in late medieval Germany: the *Book of Causes* (*Liber de causis*), the *Book of the Twenty-Four Philosophers* (*Liber XXIV Philosophorum*), and what is termed the *Proclus Latinus*, that is, the Latin versions of writings of the last pagan Neoplatonist. Brief comments on these difficult and fascinating texts help fill out the background to the mysticism of Eckhart and his followers.

The Book of Causes
(*Liber de causis*, or *Liber Aristotelis de expositione bonitatis purae*)[151]

This book, which Richard C. Taylor says "played a fundamental role in the formation of the metaphysical thought in the West," is today as little known as it once was famous. Its history reads like a detective story, not least, to cite Taylor again, because its "importance . . . lies not in any intrinsic value it may have, but rather in the philosophical thought it stimulated in its readers, in those who received it and formed their own thought in reaction to it as lovers of wisdom and truth and not as lovers of opinion."[152]

The *Book* (or *Discourse* as its original Arabic name has it) was born in Baghdad probably about the middle of the ninth century among Muslim philosophers engaged with Neoplatonic thought. Most of the material in the thirty-one propositions constituting the short work were adopted from Proclus's *Elements of Theology,* the attempt by the last pagan Neoplatonist to construct a deductive synthesis of Platonic thought about divine reality.[153] However, the *Book of Causes* is more than just a simple translation of parts of the *Elements*. The author adds, subtracts, replaces, and interprets the emanationist system of Proclus to fit the creationist philosophy of his monotheistic Islamic faith—a procedure that also made it welcome to Jews and Christians. Two of the propositions (nos. 8 and 21) have no source in Proclus but are actually adoptions of materials from Plotinus's *Enneads* IV–VI in their Arabic version. So the *Liber de causis* represents in the words of Dennis Brand, "an epitome of monotheistic Neoplatonism."[154] In another twist to the story, however, the book attained much of its importance by being ascribed to Aristotle as the highest part of his metaphysics. Hence, its alternate title, *The Book of Aristotle on the Exposition of the Pure Good.* The work was known to some Islamic and Jewish thinkers, though only three Arabic manuscripts have been identified.[155] Its major impact came through the Latin version made by the energetic Toledan translator, Gerard of Cremona (d. 1187). The book's popularity in the Middle Ages can be judged from the fact that it is found in 238 manuscripts and was the subject of no fewer than twenty-seven commentaries before 1500.

The Latin version was cited by a few late-twelfth-century authors, such as Alan of Lille, but it was not until the thirteenth century that it came into its own. Since its early circulation was under the name of Aristotle, the spread of the work appears to have been curtailed by the 1210 condemnation of Aristotle, but the situation changed toward the middle of the century with the return of the philosopher to importance in the schools. Indeed, in 1255 the University of Paris made the *Book of Causes* a required school text for metaphysics, helping to explain why many of the greatest names in Scholasticism, such as Roger Bacon, Albert the Great, Thomas Aquinas,[156] Giles of Rome, (Ps.) Henry of Ghent, and Siger of Brabant, composed commentaries on it. Other major figures in the history of medieval thought, such as Meister Eckhart and even Dante, knew it well and used it to effect.[157] In his paraphrase and expansion of the book (called *The Causes and Procession of the Universe from the First Cause*), Albert the Great, as we have seen, surmised that the work was a compilation of "Peripatetic" views put together by the Jewish thinker Ibn David, of twelfth-century Spain. When Thomas Aquinas received the first copy of William of Moerbeke's translation of Proclus's *Elements* into Latin, he soon recognized that the *Book of Causes* was based on it. Both Albert and Thomas read the book through the lens of the Dionysian corpus, mining it for their own purposes, but with great respect.

The *Book of Causes* is often described as a form of axiomatic theology, a theological parallel to Euclid's *Elements of Geometry,* but this characterization is not accurate, since the work does not so much presuppose axioms as state propositions from which subsequent truths are deduced.[158] Although Thomas Aquinas worked out a comprehensive logical outline for the book, modern interpreters have found it less systematic, and there is little consensus about the structure of the various propositions.[159] A few comments about some major themes of the book will help explain its role in late medieval mysticism.

The *Book of Causes* is more ontological in outlook than mystical, at least in the sense that with respect to the Proclian paradigm of *monē-proodos-epistrophē* as the three essential moments of reality, it is not God in Godself (*monē*), or God as the goal (*epistrophē*), that is the center of attention, but rather God as the First Cause who produces all things (*proodos*).[160] The position the *Book* takes on the role of divine causation is monotheistic. The Proclian realm of intermediate gods (the Henads) is swept away, and the dignity of the First Cause as direct creator of all things in the universe is resolutely affirmed—"Without doubt the First Being gives being to all effects" (Prop. 17[18].144; see also Prop. 8[9].87). Although the text does not use the term *creatio ex nihilo*, Leo Sweeney is correct in claiming that the First Cause of the *Liber*, "not only causes every thing to be such and such but also and primarily *to be simply.*"[161]

The exact status of being (both *esse* and *ens* are used) is not always clear. The oft-cited proposition 4 states, "Being is the first of created things and before it nothing is created" (*Prima rerum creatarum est esse et non est ante ipsum creatum aliud*). But the Universal First Cause that produces created *esse* is also described as being or existence in an eminent sense, another break with Proclus's thought. Proposition 8(9).90, for example, says: "The First Cause does not have *yliathim* [determination] because it is being only."[162] Of course, being, and even the Pure Goodness (*bonitas pura* [Prop. 8(9).91]) and First True One (*unum primum verum* [Prop. 31(32).217–19]) that the *Liber* ascribes to the First Cause are positive, or cataphatic, predications. One of the reasons that the *Liber de causis* fit so well with much late medieval mysticism was its strongly apophatic view of God. Proposition 5(6) insists that the First Cause is above all speaking, and proposition 21(22).166 proclaims, "The First Cause is above every name by which it is named."

If the *Book of Causes* is creationist in the sense that the First Cause gives all things being, it nonetheless also witnesses to how thirteenth-century theologians could adopt aspects of the language of emanation to express an understanding of creation as a metaphysics of flow. After all, it was in Albert's quasi-commentary on the work, discussed above, that the foundations of this doctrine of flowing creative causality first became explicit. Proposition 1 of the *Book of Causes* provides the leitmotif for the whole work: "Every primary cause exercises more influence (*plus est influens*) upon its effect than does a universal second cause." Analysis of how the causality of the First is necessarily at work flowing into all causation under it is a major theme of the work.[163] Two aspects of the creationist rereading of Proclian theology in the *Liber de causis*, however, created some tension with scholastic understandings of creation from nothing and were to exercise its thirteenth-century commentators greatly. Several texts speak of the First Cause creating Soul and lower realities "by the mediation of Intelligence" (*mediante intelligentia* [Props. 3.32 and 8(9).87]).[164] Christian authors had long debated whether or not God gave the angels power to participate in the act of creation, but by the thirteenth century this view had been rejected.[165] Commentators such as Albert and Thomas gave a benign reading to this suspect teaching of the *Book of Causes*, reading it as a claim not that Intelligence can mediate the created being of a thing (which can only come from the First Cause), but that the Intelligence is involved in the mediation of various "superadded perfections" (e.g., life) to created things.[166]

Dionysius had Christianized the Proclian hierarchical universe by absorbing the First Triad of ideal realities (Being-Life-Intellect) into the trinitarian God.[167] The *Book of Causes* does not explicitly support this absorption (it is, after all, a Muslim work), but its concentration on the creative power of the First Cause tends to marginalize the significance of the Neoplatonic triad in the direction of what has been called a "dyadic view" of the universe according to which, as Vincent Guagliardo puts it, "'all is in all' in a descending order of form of goodnesses, or perfections, where each kind of being receives finitely from the 'richnesses' of the infinite one according to its capacity to receive, and multiplicity is explained by the diverse recipients."[168] This view of the metaphysics of flow helps explain why the *Book of Causes* was so important both to Albert the Great and to Meister Eckhart.[169]

The Book of the Twenty-Four Philosophers
(Liber XXIV Philosophorum)[170]

The *Book of Causes* has yielded most of its secrets to modern research; the same cannot be said of the *Book of the Twenty-Four Philosophers*. This work is one of the more mysterious of the treatises often ascribed to Hermes Trismegistus, the magician-sage of antiquity whose pseudonymous survival over the centuries constitutes a significant and arcane thread in the history of Western thought.[171] The obscurity of the work led to an alternative title in some manuscripts: *Definitiones enigmaticae*, or *Mysterious Definitions*.[172]

Françoise Hudry says of the *Book of the Twenty-Four Philosophers*: "Its content seems sometimes banal, sometimes very original; its very condensed form does not allow it to be easily situated, and finally, precisely for these reasons, it has been very little studied down to the present."[173] The work, ascribed to Hermes in only some of the manuscripts, consists of twenty-four definitions of God supposedly put forth by a similar number of philosophers who met to answer the question "What is God?" (The number twenty-four as signifying high authority is reminiscent of the twenty-four elders of Apocalypse 4:4.) Though not as well known as the *Book of Causes* (Hudry's edition is based on twenty-six known manuscripts, while another ten are lost), the work sometimes circulated with the *Book of Causes* as an authority on the nature of the First Cause that would complement the *Book of Causes* treatment of the hierarchy of lower causes.[174] In the manuscripts the twenty-four enigmatic definitions are often accompanied by a brief commentary that seems to be part of the original text. A subsequent larger supercommentary is included in the new edition.[175] It is difficult to detect any definite structure in the collection.[176]

Because the *Book of the Twenty-Four Philosophers* was first quoted by Alan of Lille about 1165, the standard view of its origin has been that it was created about the middle of the twelfth century in academic circles, perhaps Chartrian, where interest in Neoplatonic and Hermetic texts was cultivated.[177] Alternatively, it may have arisen in Spain, a center for the production and translation of exotic texts. Françoise Hudry, however, has proposed another explanation, namely, that the work, or at least its core, goes back to late antiquity, specifically to Alexandrian school circles in the third century C.E. Hudry holds that the Greek original, also known in Arabic circles, was a part of a longer work entitled the *Book of the Wisdom of the Philosophers* (*Liber de sapientia philosophorum*), which is witnessed to in some medieval catalogues, but has not survived. The details of Hudry's argument cannot be given here, but they thus far have not won broad acceptance.[178]

As Giulio D'Onofrio and Paolo Lucentini have shown, the *Book of the Twenty-Four Philosophers* fits well with the creation of an "axiomatic" theology in the second half of the twelfth century.[179] The work is not only an example of this twelfth-century approach but also a profound expression of Christian Neoplatonism and its desire to show the harmony between ancient thought and revelation. The twenty-four axioms center on the dynamic identity of God as monad and triad—a dialectic that expresses itself not only in the inner mystery of the coincidence of one and three in God, but also in the outward coincidence of divine immanence and transcendence in the created universe.[180] The first axiom expresses the divine inner life in a striking way that was to be often cited by later thinkers: "God is the Monad giving birth to the Monad, reflecting a single flame in itself."[181]

The first two axioms are figural in the sense that they represent the divine mystery by symbols intended, as Paul Ricoeur once put it, "to give rise to thought."[182] The second axiom presents one of the most influential philosophical images in the history of Western thought: "God is the infinite sphere whose center is everywhere and whose circumference is nowhere." Commenting on this, the book says, "This definition is given by way of imagining the First Cause in its own life as a continuum. The term of its extension ends beyond and outside any 'where.'"[183] Much has been written on the history of this image, which was cited by such figures as Meister Eckhart, Nicholas of Cusa, Giordano Bruno, Blaise Pascal, Rabelais, and Jorge Borges, to mention just some.[184] The "infinite sphere" (in some versions "intelligible sphere," and even "infinite intelligible sphere") has precedents in former thinkers, but the image was the creation of the unknown author. Lucentini summarizes:

> If the profundity and beauty of a metaphor rest in the multiple truth of the significations that a single figure offers to the spirit, one can understand the inexhaustible fascination that the image of the infinite sphere has exercised on medieval and modern thought. Together with the figure of the monad [axiom I], it constitutes the bold creation of the philosophical imaginaire and is directed to comprehending a type of thought that wishes to join Christian revelation and Neoplatonic reason.[185]

Other aspects of this enigmatic work also show why it fit so well with the *Book of Causes*. The *Book of the Twenty-Four Philosophers* is deeply apophatic, insisting over and over that the quest to know *quid est deus?* is an impossible task. Axiom XVI says, "God alone is that which words cannot signify because of excellence, nor minds understand because of his unlikeness"; axiom XXIII proclaims the message of Dionysius: "God is what is known by ignorance alone."[186] The book also presupposes the metaphysics of flow, as in the comment on axiom XXIII: "Nothing is known by the soul unless it can receive the idea of the thing and compare it to the exemplar that it has in itself. The only exemplar the soul has is of something that has flowed out from the First Cause into being through the Cause itself."[187]

The obscurity of the enigmatic definitions of the work lent themselves to interpretation according to the proclivities of individual authors. Albert the Great had suspicions about the book; Thomas Aquinas cited it only twice, seeing it as a pagan text dealing with God's relation to the world and not with the Trinity.[188] Meister Eckhart, on the other hand, referred to fourteen of the axioms in his Latin and German works, and was profoundly interested in both the trinitarian and cosmological aspects of the book.[189] Eckhart's fascination with the *Book of the Twenty-Four Philosophers* was continued by many of his followers. The work was extensively mined by another Dominican, Berthold of Moosburg, whose *Commentary on Proclus's Elements of Theology* quotes over half of the mysterious text.[190] Another mystic who cited one of its axioms was Marguerite Porete.[191]

It is difficult today to appreciate the power that a text like the *Book of the Twenty-Four Philosophers* enjoyed in the late Middle Ages and into the early modern period. Perhaps the best way to grasp something of its attraction is to note how its enigmatic definitions fit so well with the apophatic theology of an era when theologians, mystical and otherwise, felt more and more impelled to insist on the infinite difference between our conceptions of God and the God beyond all power of conceiving.

Proclus Latinus

Students of the history of Neoplatonism are sometimes tempted to give too much emphasis to the influence of Plotinus, the great philosopher and mystic who was the fountainhead of Neoplatonism.[192] Plotinus was directly known to Marius Victorinus, Ambrose, and Augustine among late antique ecclesiastical writers, and he was also influential on philosophers like Macrobius who were widely read in the medieval schools. Nevertheless, Plotinus's *Enneads* were not available in translation until the Renaissance. A comprehensive evaluation of medieval Neoplatonism suggests that its Greek roots are more Proclian than Plotinian, thus reflecting a somewhat different Neoplatonic intellectual tradition, one that originated in Iamblichus in the fourth century, was brought to a systematic level in Proclus, and was communicated to the early medieval West through the Dionysian writings and their translation and interpretation by John Scottus Eriugena.[193]

The twelfth and thirteenth centuries saw a new wave of Proclian theology percolate through Europe, one that was to have repercussions in philosophy, in theology, and in the mysticism of those thinkers (notably German Dominicans) who saw no distinction among these linked aspects of human knowing.[194] The indirect Proclianism found in the *Book of Causes* was augmented by a direct influx of Proclus through a series of translations of his writings into Latin by the Dominican William of Moerbeke (d. ca. 1286).[195] William finished his rendering of the *Elements of Theology* in 1268.[196] At a later date, around 1280, he produced a version of three of Proclus's shorter treatises.[197] Around 1286 he also completed a translation of one of Proclus's most significant works, his large *Commentary on Plato's Parmenides* (*Expositio Proclii in Parmenidem Platonis*).[198] Concerning this work, Paul Oskar Kristeller has observed: "Proclus was the chief authority for the view that Plato's dialogue was metaphysical and not merely dialectical in content, and that the first hypothesis (the only one treated in Proclus's commentary) deals with the One, which as the highest principle is above being and above knowledge."[199] Although these texts had a limited diffusion, among the German Dominicans, it is possible to speak of this era of the *Proclus Latinus* as marking a distinctive moment in philosophy and mysticism. As Loris Sturlese put it, "numerous indications concur in leading to the conclusion that for some time in Germany Proclus was a privileged discussion partner."[200]

Thomas Aquinas, as we have seen, made use of his friend William's version of the *Elements of Theology* to decipher the Proclian roots of the *Book of Causes*. The *Elements* were also used by Siger of Brabant. But Proclus's influence diminished in Paris after the 1277 condemnations, becoming restricted and stereotyped. The dialogue with Proclus shifted to Germany and the Cologne Dominican house of studies. Albert the Great did not know Moerbeke's translations, but his devotion to Dionysius and the *Book of Causes* led him to quote Proclus often in his late *Summa Theologiae*.[201] Dietrich of Freiburg, a student of Albert and contemporary of Eckhart, made considerable use of Proclus, whom he praised as a "diligent investigator" (*diligens indagator*) of philosophical matters. Dietrich quotes Proclus about forty times in his writings, largely from the *Elements*.[202]

The relationship of Meister Eckhart to the thought of Proclus has been the subject of some discussion. Eckhart knew and used the *Elements*, often joining them with the witness of the *Book of Causes* (perhaps under the influence of Aquinas). He even refers to Proclus by name about a dozen times. He cites Proclus's support for some key aspects of his mystical thought, such as God as Absolute Unity, the relation of unity and multiplicity, the conversion of the intellect upon itself, the notion of essential cause, the distinction between real being and knowing being (*ens reale/ens cognoscitivum*), and the superiority of the intellect. It is disputed whether Eckhart knew Moerbeke's version of the treatises and the Parmenides commentary. In one place he uses the Proclian phrase "the One of the soul" (*unum animae*) as an alternative for his usual metaphor of the "spark of the soul." The expression *unum animae* is found both in the treatise *On Providence* and in the Parmenides commentary, but Eckhart might have come across the phrase elsewhere.[203] Eckhart's teaching on the One as the negation of negation (*negatio negationis*) has sometimes been seen as a link to Proclus, who uses the expression in the Parmenides commentary, but there is no direct evidence for this, and it is quite possible that the Dominican developed his understanding of the *negatio negationis* out of scholastic sources.[204]

The most Proclian of all the German Dominicans was Berthold of Moosburg, a contemporary of John Tauler. Berthold knew all the Moerbeke translations. He cites the treatises and the Parmenides commentary in his massive exposition on Proclus's *Elements of Theology* composed sometime between 1330 and 1360. This work represents the high point of medieval Proclianism.[205] In his commentary, as Sturlese puts it, "the *Elementatio* had become in a way a symbol of a project and of an international philosophical movement that was an alternative to Parisian Scholasticism. In fact, the spectre of the influence of Proclus extended over the whole movement known as 'German mysticism' and for this reason had a role in determining the nucleus of Dominican intellectuals gathered at the *studium generale* of the order at Cologne."[206] Berthold also had a role in communicating knowledge of Proclus to Tauler, who praised the pagan Neoplatonist highly, as we shall see below.

The impact of Moerbeke's translations should not be overestimated, but they did play a part in the philosophical background of late medieval German mysticism, at least insofar as they enhanced currents already present in the intellective reading of the Dionysian corpus initiated by Albert the Great. The role of the *Proclus Latinus* in the decades before and after 1300 was not to last. But the writings of this pagan Neoplatonist were to have a revival in the fifteenth century in the thought of those eminent Platonists, Nicholas of Cusa and Marsilio Ficino.

CHAPTER 2

Mysticism and Heresy: The Problem of the Free Spirit

T HE AGE OF THE HARVEST OF MYSTICISM was also a time of unprecedented debate over the orthodoxy of certain forms of mysticism. Although fears about dangerous mystical expressions were already smoldering in the second half of the thirteenth century, the conflict between some mystics and the clerical guardians of correct belief did not burst into flame until the first decade of the fourteenth century. The suspicions about mysticism and the inquisitorial investigations directed against some mystics were to be a feature of the history of Western mysticism for the next four hundred years and more. Indeed, it is possible to argue that the growing need to suppress what was seen as mystical heresy was a crucial aspect of the process that eventually led to the decline of mysticism in Western Christendom in the eighteenth century.

The story of the ebb and flow of the tensions between mysticism and magisterium (i.e., authoritative church doctrine) will be featured throughout this volume and those to come in this series. Here, by way of preface, I wish to lay out some historical prolegomena and theological principles to foster a better understanding of this important, and sometimes tragic, strand of the history of Christian mysticism.

Mysticism and Magisterium in Early Christianity[1]

Friedrich von Hügel, in his seminal work, *The Mystical Element of Religion* (1908), argued that religion consists of three essential elements: the historical-institutional element (the Petrine dimension in Christianity); the analytic-speculative element (the Pauline); and the intuitive-emotional element related to will and action (the Johannine).

Expressed as institutionalism, intellectualism, and mysticism, these three aspects have an inherent dialectical relationship. Religion (at least the Christian religion) is always institutional, intellectual, and mystical. If any one element attempts to suppress or minimize the others, however, the harmonious interaction intended to produce a mature spiritual personality will be skewed, both in particular individuals and in the religion as a corporate body.[2]

Von Hügel's model, whatever its general applicability, is helpful for understanding how in Christianity at least, the mystical element has a necessary relation to orthodox teaching as expressed through the developing institutional forms of authority—bishops, councils, creeds, and, in the West, the papacy and its various agencies. It also indicates the dangers attendant upon institutional efforts to exercise undue control over the mystical element, especially by separating it from its intellectual roots in creative theology—the fate of most Catholic mysticism after the Quietist controversy of the seventeenth and eighteenth centuries. A dialectical approach to the relation of the mystical element to the institutional and intellectual aspects of Christianity also allows an insight into the conflicts between mystical piety and institutional authority in the period from roughly 1300 to 1700.

One frequent explanation of the struggles between some mystics and church authority is what could be called the inevitability theory, that is, the notion that the conflict is a foregone conclusion insofar as mysticism is based on the claim to a direct personal relation to God independent of ecclesiastical structures and mediation. Both historians and theologians have adopted this view. For example, Steven E. Ozment, in his *Mysticism and Dissent,* claims that "medieval mysticism was a refined challenge, always in theory if not in daily practice, to the regular, normative way of religious salvation."[3] The English theologian Don Cupitt's *Mysticism and Modernity* has tried to make the case that mysticism's attraction to the postmodern mentality rests in its subversive character—it has always been a protest against dogmatic theology, and more often than not it has also served as a critique by women of male-dominated religion. For Cupitt, mysticism is what saves us from religion.[4]

The story of mystical heresies such as the Free Spirit movement, some Radical Reformers, the Spanish Alumbrados, and the Quietists seems to lend credence to such views, but the theory of inevitable conflict between the mystical element and institutional religion is questionable, if only because so many key mystics in the history of Christianity have also been profound theologians and pillars of the institution—think only of Ambrose, Augustine, Gregory of Nyssa, Gregory the Great, Bernard of Clairvaux, and Bonaventure, among those who have appeared in previous volumes of this history. For this reason, alternative explanations of the connections between mysticism and institution are worth exploring.

A more searching study of the relation of the mystical to the institutional and intellectual elements in Christianity suggests not inherent opposition but complex and dialectical interaction. Helpful in this regard are the writings of the great scholar of Jewish mysticism Gershom Scholem, who laid out elements of a dialectical theory of the relation between mystical contact with God and the established structures of religion, legal, theological, and institutional.[5] Contrary to those who viewed mysticism in a fundamentally anti-institutional way, Scholem argued: "All mysticism has two contradictory or complementary aspects: the one conservative, the other revolutionary."[6]

For Scholem, religion develops in three stages. The first is a mythical one, in which there is no gap between gods and humans; this is succeeded by the classical stage, in which divine revelation creates institutional religion based on the distinction between the human and the divine worlds. In the third stage, mysticism, understood as "direct contact between the individual and God," seeks to revive the original unity of mythical consciousness.[7] Whatever we may think of this model, Scholem employed it to work out a subtle and suggestive view of the relation of the second and third stages, that is, of institutional religion and mysticism. Since mystical contact with God is ineffable ("amorphous" for Scholem), mysticism becomes a historical phenomenon capable of being investigated only when the mystic tries to communicate his or her contact with God to the wider religious community. In order to be understood, the mystic must make use of the language and symbols of the tradition. Thus, Scholem observed, mysticism in the three Western monotheistic faiths has been primarily a conservative force insofar as mystics "seem to rediscover the sources of traditional authority" and thus "try to preserve it in the strictest sense."[8] But because of the amorphous nature of their consciousness of God, the inherited complex of symbols and expressions can never fully capture the experience, but rather needs to be stretched or transformed in the process of communication. This is why Scholem was so attracted to mysticism as the deepest resource for change and development within religion.

Change or adaptation, however, raises the nagging question of how much development a religious tradition can allow without suffering essential deformation or evolution into something different. Here the radical pole of mystical consciousness comes to the fore. Some mystics, although these appear to be relatively rare, seem to have begun from the claim that their contact with God was a new and higher revelation than that mediated by the tradition. Between religious authority and such "innately radical" mystics, as Scholem termed them, conflict is indeed inevitable. More often, however, Scholem thought that mystics had conflict forced upon them by religious authority. In his view, "such conflicts are largely unpredictable and do not hinge essentially on the personality or doctrines of the mystic. They depend entirely on historical circumstances."[9] As evidence he offers the observation that "doctrines which have been expressed with the utmost force at certain times and places without leading to any conflict whatsoever may, under other historical conditions, foment violent struggles," citing the history of Quietism as an example.[10] Thus, for Scholem, it was historical accident that led to situations in which mystics were forced to choose between the truth of their own contact with God and the truth of the tradition.

As useful as Scholem's theory is, it is possible to go beyond the category of historical accident by pointing to certain inherently explosive tendencies in the interaction of mysticism and religious authority, at least in the history of Christianity. These tendencies, or perceived dangers, are relational, that is, they are not so much inherent in mysticism itself as they are expressive of the way in which the mystical aspect of the tradition came to be viewed by the representatives of its institutional life and teaching in the course of history. What follows is an attempt to lay bare some of the most weighty of these developmental tensions in the history of Christianity as a way of understanding the late medieval debates over heretical forms of mysticism.

The obvious starting point is Gnosticism, a debated term that has meant different things to different investigators from the beginning. Given the variety of Gnostic texts and the accounts of their beliefs by their opponents, it is erroneous to speak of Gnosticism as if it were a single movement or system of thought. Nevertheless, to the historian of mysticism, many Gnostic texts of the second through fourth centuries C.E. exhibit a strong mystical character, and experts in Gnosticism have been willing to characterize it as in some ways deeply mystical.[11] In Gnostic writings we find such key mystical themes as the fall and ascent of the soul, negative theology, the importance of contemplation and the vision of God, and unification with the immanent God—all present within a mythic pattern in which salvation is achieved through the special knowledge (*gnōsis*) by which some (not all) believers come to recognize their inherent divinity.

Students of early Christianity continue to disagree about the mechanisms and processes at work in the transition from the first Jesus communities to the church—one, holy, catholic, and apostolic. Few, however, would disagree that the struggle over the meaning of *gnōsis* was a central moment in this evolution. In *The Foundations of Mysticism* I argued that the Gnostic crisis was a defining moment in the development of mysticism. The notion of a teaching authority that was, at least in principle, unified, apostolic, and universal, and therefore applicable to all expressions of belief (something peculiar to Christianity among the religions of the Roman Empire), began to emerge in the second century in the midst of the debates over what it meant to be a Christian, of which the struggle over *gnōsis* was the greatest. Christianity's emphasis on orthodoxy implies an ongoing dialogue between claims for mystical knowledge of God, on the one hand, and public and universal teaching—what later came to be called the magisterium—on the other. This kind of strong conversation is not present, or at least not present in the same way, in the sister religions of Judaism and Islam, which have more diffuse mechanisms for guaranteeing correct belief. One may say that Christian mysticism acquired a necessary relation to magisterium largely because the claims of early Christian Gnostics to esoteric saving knowledge came to be seen as inadmissible in a religion whose success was closely linked with the universality of its teaching and the coherence and solidity of its institutional structure.

Many of the Gnostic texts available to us, as well as the sometimes skewed presentations of Gnosticism found in the fathers of emergent orthodoxy, highlight certain neuralgic issues that were to continue to surface in the subsequent history of mysticism. Among these is the question of whether the soul is naturally divine, a spark fallen from above, or rather something created and only capable of divinization. Another issue is the relation of the three gifts involved in the redemptive process: faith (*pistis*), love (*agapē*), and saving knowledge (*gnōsis*). Different Gnostic texts have different views on the connection of the three, but the insistence that what is attained in *gnōsis* and practiced in *agapē* could not contravene *pistis*, the rule of faith (*regula fidei*), came to be deeply embedded in the orthodox position, as we see in writers like Irenaeus, Tertullian, Hippolytus, and Origen. In subsequent Christian mysticism the relation of love and knowledge to mystical contact with God was to remain a key theme.

The extent to which some Gnostics claimed that their knowledge of God surpassed that of ordinary believers highlights a third issue: the role of esotericism. One aspect of whether saving knowledge was truly open to all is the status accorded to visionary experience and new revelations. To what extent did these grant a higher or different knowing of God available only to a few? A second aspect concerns the interpretation of scripture. All early Christians utilized spiritual exegesis, but what were the limits of reading beneath the surface of the text to uncover deeper wisdom? As a result of the debates over Gnosticism, a general principle emerged in the orthodox church that to the extent that visions and new revelations confirmed the meaning of tradition, they were acceptable and even useful, but insofar as any purported vision or message advanced something at odds with tradition, especially a truth accessible only to the few, they were to be rejected and condemned. The same principle applied to the interpretation of the Bible, which also had to submit to the test of publicly proclaimed orthodoxy, as we can see argued in the exegetical handbooks of writers like Origen and Augustine.[12] What could be reconciled with the *regula fidei* was allowed; what was seen as producing an esoteric message reserved for those inherently capable of receiving it came to be anathematized. Though the victory of nascent orthodoxy was not to be complete for several centuries, the struggles of the second and early third centuries were decisive in this respect.

Suspicion of esotericism marks an important difference between Christian mysticism and the mysticisms of Judaism and Islam. In both these faiths it is striking how many of their forms of mysticism were developed within clandestine circles where specially adept individuals could explore beliefs and engage in practices that went beyond what was expected and sometimes even permitted to ordinary faithful as long as the adepts conducted their public lives according to the required forms of orthopraxy. Although never universal, esotericism was customary, even expected, in Jewish and Islamic mysticism, whereas it was viewed as inherently dangerous in Christianity. To the extent that there were suspicions and persecutions of innately radical mystics in traditions like Judaism and Islam, these seem to have emerged from a different dynamic, perhaps the product more of special historical situations than of fear of esoteric knowledge as such. In the history of Christian mysticism, the struggle against Gnosticism introduced a principle that might be expressed as follows: Insofar as mystics are seen as belonging to secret groups fostering forms of knowledge in conflict with orthodox tradition and not at least potentially accessible to the wider community of faith, such mystics will become subject to suspicion, investigation, and often condemnation.

Closely entwined with the issue of esoteric secrecy is that of illicit sexuality. Religion has always been concerned with sexual regulation. In ancient Rome, at least from the time of the persecution of the Bacchics in 186 B.C.E., secret cults, especially those from the East, were often accused of sexual license by the guardians of social order.[13] Such accusations were also made against Christians from at least the second century C.E., as we know from the Apologists. Athenagoras, writing about 178, rebutted pagan attacks on Christians for indulging in "Thyestian banquets" (i.e., cannibalism), as well as "Oedipean intercourse," or incest.[14] In the second century, bishops and other proto-orthodox writers began to accuse some Gnostic groups, such as the Carpocratians, of secret sexual depravity.[15] The cultural topos that equated secretive religious groups with illicit sexuality, older than Christianity, was to reappear again and again in the debates over mysticism. Individuals or groups that are perceived to be making claims to esoteric higher wisdom lend themselves to being seen as antinomian. Of course, perhaps they were, at least at times; but the inherited topos equating secrecy with sexuality makes it difficult to be sure.

If esotericism and its attendant danger of sexual antinomianism (basically the only antinomianism that ever really counts) became fixed as a neuralgic issue from the second century on, the next major chapter in the history of the tensions between mysticism and magisterium reveals another facet of the story, one that directly concerns Eastern Christianity, but that was also to have analogues in the West. According to Irenée Hausherr, "The great spiritual heresy of the Christian East is Messalianism."[16] The Messalians or Euchites (names that mean "those who pray," one from Syriac, the other from Greek) began to be noted in ecclesiastical documents from the second half of the fourth century.[17] They were anathematized by the Council of Side summoned by Amphilochius of Iconium in 390. Later condemnations followed, including one at Ephesus in 431. Church historians and dogmatic writers, such as Epiphanius (ca. 377), Theodoret (ca. 393–453), Timothy of Constantinople (ca. 600), and John of Damascus (ca. 745), provide us with lists of their errors. Columba Stewart identifies ten key issues of belief and practice that emerge from a comparison of these lists.[18] The central doctrinal problems concern the role of prayer in relation to baptism and Eucharist. The Messalians were accused of claiming that there is a demon indwelling in the human heart (error 1) that cannot be expelled by baptism (error 2), but only by ceaseless prayer (error 3) to the detriment of performing one's duties of work and other Christian practices (errors 7 and 9). Such charges of overdependence on prayer to the neglect of the sacraments and moral effort may be the earliest appearance of the complex of errors that later crystallized under the name of Quietism. Also important, at least for later uses of Messalianism as a term of opprobrium, was the charge that the Messalians thought they could attain physical vision and experience of God through ceaseless prayer. According to John of Damascus, "they say that such is the power of their praying that the Holy Spirit appears perceptibly to them and to those instructed by them."[19]

Who exactly were the Messalians? Some aspects of the language that the orthodox took exception to, if not the most egregious positions themselves, are to be found in the Syriac *Liber graduum* (*Book of Ascents*) from the late fourth century, and also in the contemporary *Fifty Spiritual Homilies* pseudonymously ascribed to Macarius the Great, sermons that were widely read and praised not only in the Christian East but also in the West, especially by the German Pietists and John Wesley.[20] Some have deemed these works Messalian, but if this be the case, we have to admit that Messalianism came in many varieties.[21] In the long run the existence of Messalianism as an actual group or sect is elusive. Columba Stewart notes that "the 'Messalians,' as such, have no recoverable history. But the ideas and texts associated with them certainly do have a history, whoever may have been tagged with them at various points throughout the controversy."[22] Stewart further contends that the attack on the Messalians was primarily the result of a linguistic and cultural misunderstanding between Greek and Syriac forms of spirituality.[23] Be that as it may, Messalianism, like Quietism, was used as a broad brush for smearing any position that seemed to smack of suspect mystical prayer, as well as many other errors. From our perspective, the creation of Messalianism as a category of mystical heresy illustrates another of the neuralgic points at issue in the history of the relation of mysticism and magisterium. Insofar as mystical prayer is seen to be in conflict with the sacramental life of the community and/or the obligations of Christian charity, it becomes automatically suspect.

Mystical Heresy in the Middle Ages:
Origins of the Free Spirit Movement[24]

The history of mystical heresy in medieval Christendom, though historically discontinuous with the quarrels of the early church, is still theologically connected to them, not only because of the influence of patristic writers, but also through the persistence of the issues of esotericism, antinomianism, antisacramentalism, and suspect forms of prayer.[25] There were, however, new dangers that emerged in the Middle Ages, issues that induced continuing suspicions during the long arc of Western mystical heresy in the period between the mid-thirteenth and the mid-eighteenth centuries. Among these, the notion of personal annihilation had a central role, not only because this idea was new to the mystical tradition, but also because it can be seen as the root of many of the other dangers that authorities perceived in mystics of the late Middle Ages and early modernity.

Some medieval mystics have been accused of pantheism. While there are a few pantheistic-sounding statements in inquisitorial records, there is sparse evidence for pantheism in the classic philosophical sense of the identification of all things with God in a direct way.[26] Others have tried to make the key error of medieval heretical mystics more precise by charging them with autotheism, that is, identifying themselves with God to the extent that they share in all the prerogatives of the divine nature, including freedom from law and regulation—*libertas spiritus.*[27] There is certainly an autotheistic element in some late medieval mystical texts, but it may be more helpful to view the mystics' claims for some kind of identity with God in terms of vocabulary they actually used and to see their language of indistinction and annihilation of the created self as forming the essential problem. Indistinction means that one can reach an interior state in which, at least on some level, there is no distinction, or difference, between God and the self—a union of identity deeper than the mystical uniting in love of two entities that maintain their separate substances, the view advanced by most previous Christian mystics, such as the monastic writers of the twelfth century.[28] Mystical identity, however, was not unknown in the earlier Christian tradition, as is evident from the teaching of Evagrius Ponticus and the influential Dionysian corpus.[29]

The emphasis on mystical identity found in many late medieval mystics was rooted, I believe, in the notion of annihilation, especially the annihilation of the created will. This was one of the novel and more dangerous elements in the new mysticism. The need for the fallen will to be cleansed and redirected, a staple of Augustinian theology and mysticism, was not enough for some mystics. For these the will, precisely as created and therefore other than God, must be destroyed. The root of the language of mystical identity and its perceived dangers was planted in the soil of annihilation, the process of interior stripping and decreation intended to produce a situation in which the soul in some way no longer exists, but God himself becomes the place from which divine action flows into the world, as Marguerite Porete, Meister Eckhart, and some others taught. Although there were later mystics, such as Catherine of Genoa, John of the Cross, Benet Canfield, and Pierre de Berulle, who used annihilation language without incurring censure, this was to be a difficult achievement in the centuries from 1300 to 1700.

Given the relational model of the interaction between mysticism and magisterium suggested here, it was not just the emergence of new mystical themes in the thirteenth century, but also changes in the institutional fabric of the church and the ways in which it sought to guarantee orthodoxy that shaped the debates over mysticism stretching out over more than four centuries. Without the organization of inquisitorial pursuit of heresy (*inquisitio hereticae pravitatis*), the story of the conflict would have been quite different.[30] To be sure, it is difficult to recover what "heretics" under inquisition actually believed, because many aspects of late medieval heresy investigations were designed to make the accused admit what the accusers thought they held. Among these were the extract method for the determination of doctrinal error,[31] and the fact that the judges made their decisions based on what *sounded* like heresy (*prout sonat*), regardless of the intention of the defendant.[32] Suspected heretics were investigated on the basis of inquisitional formularies (*interrogatoria*) of what heresy was supposed to be, rather than what they themselves might have said on their own.[33] In cases of mystical heresy the decree *Ad nostrum* issued by the Council of Vienne took on a canonical status as the touchstone for error. Therefore, the inquisitorial sources that form so much of the evidence for the heresy of the Free Spirit must always be read with a strong hermeneutic of suspicion.[34]

The conflicts between mysticism and magisterium after 1300 were rooted not only in increasing mechanisms of control evident in late medieval Christianity, but also in social aspects of the new mysticism that emerged around 1200.[35] The new forms of mysticism were democratized, or open to all, secularized in the sense that they were realizable in the marketplace as much as in the cloister, and they were expressed for the most part in the vernacular, often by women. Paradoxically, although these aspects of the new mysticism would seem to run counter to the suspicion of esotericism inherent in magisterial attitudes toward mysticism, they actually fomented these fears because they were seen as allowing dangerous ideas wider dissemination in strata of society that, unlike enclosed religious men and women, were less subject to everyday supervision. As long as mysticism was largely the purview of monastic elites it was deemed a relatively safe phenomenon. When it moved out into what Pope John XXII called the "uneducated crowd" in his bull of condemnation against Meister Eckhart, it became automatically more dangerous in the eyes of the guardians of correct belief.

The history of the heresy of the Free Spirit is enigmatic and controversial, not least because "freedom of spirit" (*libertas spiritus*) is as old as Christianity, going back to Paul—"Where the Spirit of the Lord is, there is freedom" (*Ubi spiritus Domini, ibi libertas* [2 Cor. 3:17]).[36] The phrase "freedom of spirit" had a long history among Christian mystics.[37] In its decree *Ad nostrum* the Council of Vienne created the Free Spirit as a category of heresy by anathematizing the statement: "Those who are in the state mentioned above [i.e., impeccability, as condemned in article 1] and in the

spirit of liberty are not subject to human obedience nor obliged to any precepts of the church, because, as they say, 'Where the spirit of the Lord is,
there is freedom.'"38 In the twelfth century, however, William of St.-Thierry
in the *Golden Letter* had spoken of how the soul, when all its powers are set
in order by grace, "hastens to burst forth into freedom of spirit and unity, so
that, as has been often said, the faithful person becomes one spirit with
God" (1 Cor. 6:17).39 In the thirteenth century Bonaventure spoke of freedom of spirit in a daring way: "The more someone is established in greater
charity, the more they have of freedom of spirit, and the more they have of
freedom of spirit, the fewer the bonds that obligate them."40 In the fourteenth century, John Tauler, strong opponent of the *freije geiste* as he was,
spoke even more strongly. In a passage in sermon 55 emphasizing that
Christ is the only way to God, he says, "As for those who have followed this
way, the pope has no power over them, because God himself has set them
free. St. Paul says, 'Those who are driven or led by the spirit of God are no
longer under any law'" (Gal. 5:18).41 These statements, taken out of context,
might well have been ascribed to Free Spirit heretics by a zealous inquisitor.

It is true, nevertheless, that traditional mystical language of *libertas spiritus* began to appear in new and questionable contexts in the late thirteenth
and early fourteenth centuries. Errors both old and new were detected
among anonymous suspects, as well as in treatises like Porete's *Mirror*.
Though some scholars have cast the net of the Free Spirit heresy in a broad
chronological frame,42 the earliest clear manifestation of many of the errors
ascribed to the Free Spirits is to be found in the text called the *Compilatio de
novo spiritu* put together by Albert the Great in the 1270s concerning a
group of persons investigated in the Swabian Ries area of Germany.

Various contemporary chronicles and several lists of the errors of these
mysterious figures present us with at least a partial knowledge of the
group.43 Two wandering preachers "in red capes" were said to have spread
dangerous ideas to an undetermined number of women and men. At some
time an investigation was conducted and ninety-seven heretical articles
were collected from what must have been a number of suspects (later more
articles were added). Around 1270–72 the materials were sent to Albert, at
that time living in retirement in Cologne in his old age.44 What we have is
Albert's copy of the list and his comments thereon.

The articles are a mass of heterogeneous, often contradictory, statements. Some of them claim identity with God in formulations similar to
those found in later inquisitorial investigations of the Free Spirits. For
example: "He says in reply that a person is able to be equal to God and
the soul becomes divine"; and "He says that a person can reach the point

that God works all things through him" (a statement hinting at mystical annihilation).[45] One statement that Albert found puzzling, but that was to be repeated by mystics like Eckhart and Marguerite Porete, expresses the need for abandoning God—"Where it says that a person is not good unless he leaves God for God's sake, is likewise Pelagian foolishness."[46] Other passages deny the necessity of Christ, the church, and its sacraments. Yet others speak of erotic union with Christ: "He says that a person can be admitted to the embrace of divinity and then may be given the power of doing what he wants."[47] Many statements are strongly antinomian: "Nothing is a sin except what is thought to be a sin"; or, "A person united to God ought to fulfill the body's pleasure boldly in any way whatsoever, even a religious of either sex."[48] A favorite saying (often retrieved by later heresy hunters) was "What is done below the belt by good people is not a sin."[49] Some articles assert other doctrinal errors, for example, that the soul is as eternal as God (#95), or that Christ did not rise from the dead (#48), or that hell does not exist (#102). A deep anticlericalism based on scorn for book learning and emphasis on personal experience is evident: "They say they ought not to reveal the grace they possess to learned men because they would not know what it is. The learned only know what is on the page, but these folk know through experience by means of which they say they suck from the divine sweetness."[50] This theme too is often echoed in later accounts.

Albert was asked to give a *determinatio,* or judgment, on these errors. He began by noting the danger of secret conventicles, which always tend to go against the faith (the ever-dangerous esotericism). The Dominican proceeds as a learned scholastic would be expected to, trying to fit the mélange of materials into the heretical categories available to him from tradition. He denounces the largest group (thirty-seven) as Pelagian in the sense that they deny the working of grace and the distinction between God and human; others are qualified as Arian, Manichaean, Jovinian, and Nestorian. A few are equated with philosophical errors (e.g., #95, the *haeresis Socratis*). Albert's somewhat puzzled reaction to these lay heretics and their autotheistic, antinomian, and anti-ecclesiastical views presaged much to come.

Albert's *Compilatio,* which appears to have been known to some of the later inquisitors who pursued the Free Spirits, spoke of the "new spirit." The first official appearance of the biblical phrase *spiritus libertatis* to characterize "heretical depravity" occurs in a letter of Clement V. On April 1, 1311, Clement wrote to the bishop of Cremona commanding him to take action against heresy spreading in the valley of Spoleto and elsewhere in Italy. In a letter rich in rhetorical flourishes, the pope says:

> Some ecclesiastics and laypeople, religious and seculars of both sexes,
> accursed folk alienated from the bosom of Mother Church, . . . have taken up
> a new sect and a new rite completely untrue to the way of salvation, hateful
> even to pagans and those living like animals, and far removed from the teach-
> ing of the apostles and prophets and the truth of the Gospel. They call it the
> spirit of liberty, that is, it allows them to do whatever they want. . . .[51]

Clement's letter goes on to provide a proper exegesis of various scriptural
texts on freedom, apparently rebutting what he had heard about these Italian heretics.

What Clement may have heard is reflected in a number of Italian sources
from the early fourteenth century.[52] The Franciscan Spiritual Ubertino of
Casale in his monumental *Tree of the Crucified Life of Jesus*, finished in 1305,
attacked some contemporaries, Franciscans and others, for following "the
pest of that poisonous error—the spirit of liberty, or rather of malignity" by
advancing errors of quietism and antinomianism.[53] The kinds of dangerous
Franciscans Ubertino had in mind appear in the materials collected for the
canonization process of Clare of Montefalco (1268–1308), a female ecstatic
who lived according to the Augustinian rule but who was close to some
Franciscan Spirituals.[54] In 1304 the Franciscan friar Giovannuccio da
Bevagna, and again in 1306 a friar named Bentivenga da Gubbio, said to be
the leader of the sect, tried to convince Clare that "a person can do whatever he wishes, that there is no hell, and that the soul can lose its desire in
this life." Anxious to show the divinely given wisdom of the saint, the canonization *Process* recounts her refutation of Bentivenga in detail. A person
can, indeed, do whatever he wishes, argues Clare, as long as God provides
a perfectly ordered will, so that "the person's will is nothing else but what
God wills." Clare explains the loss of desire (which seems to be a form of
annihilation of the will) as follows:

> The soul loses its desire in this way. It is not that it desires nothing while it is
> in this life, but it can happen that sometimes the soul is absorbed, immersed,
> and placed in the fervor of contemplation through rapture or another kind of
> elevation into God. Joined to its Beloved in a marvelous way, it is at rest,
> because at the point in which the soul exists in that state, it yearns for nothing
> more than what it has.[55]

Clare was so disturbed by her interview with Bentivenga that she arranged
with her friend Cardinal Napoleone Orsini to have him arrested. Bentivenga and his followers were eventually condemned to life imprisonment.
Clare's contemporary, the Franciscan tertiary and mystic Angela of Foligno
(d. 1309), also rebutted Free Spirit errors,[56] and the Franciscan Ugo

Panziera da Prato (d. 1330) wrote a vernacular *Treatise against the Beghards* that attacked their errors.[57]

From his exile in Avignon, Pope Clement summoned a general council in 1308. The council, which met at Vienne from October 1311 to May 1312, confronted a host of problems troubling the Western church: the status of the Templars, who were under attack by Philip IV of France; the perennial issue of the crusade; and questions of church reform and the tensions within the Franciscan order. The troubling news from Italy and elsewhere about the *secta spiritus libertatis* helped spark discussions about the orthodoxy of unregulated religious, especially the beguines and beghards, who had been subject to growing suspicions in the second half of the thirteenth century. The latest weapon in the assault on what was perceived to be dangerous mysticism was the report from the Paris inquisition (1308–10) into the beguine Marguerite Porete's *Mirror of Simple Annihilated Souls*.[58] (Six of the twenty-one theologians who had participated in the beguine's trial were present at Vienne.)[59]

It has been claimed that the Council of Vienne condemned the whole beguine movement along with the mystical heresy of the Free Spirit found among beguines and beghards. The research of Jacqueline Tarrant, however, has qualified this view by showing that it was actually the publication of the Clementine Constitutions, the collection of canons prepared by Clement V (but only published by his successor John XXII in 1317) that brought suspicion on the beguines, and not all beguines at that.[60] The council itself had only touched on the beguines in passing, and although it did condemn mystical heresy, it originally ascribed these errors only to the beghards, the male equivalents of the beguines. Pope Clement himself was responsible for the major changes between the conciliar and the canonical versions of the two decrees that had such powerful effect in later medieval religious history.

The decree against the beguines, *Cum de quibusdam mulieribus,* was primarily disciplinary, banning some aspects of a religious movement that had existed for more than a century, and, at least in its early stages, had won much praise as an authentic way of living the apostolic life.[61] The beguines, however, had always existed in tension with the 1215 decree of the Fourth Lateran Council against new forms of religious life, a ban renewed at the Second Council of Lyons (1274). Suspicion seems to have fallen primarily on the independent beguines and beghards, those who lived a wandering and often mendicant life. The growing regularization of many beguines into court-beguinages, especially in France and the Low Countries, a phenomenon now recognized as beginning quite early, demonstrates how the beguine movement could be made acceptable through institutionalization, if of a somewhat different form from that of traditional religious orders. Those beguines and beghards, like Marguerite Porete, who resisted institutionalization and clerical control were to find increasing opposition.

Cum de quibusdam mulieribus singles out the "women, commonly called beguines who, although they promise no one obedience and neither renounce property nor live in accordance with an approved rule," wear a habit and associate with religious (usually mendicants). The decree goes on to assert that reliable report has it that "some of them, as if possessed by madness, dispute and preach about the highest Trinity and the divine essence and in respect to the articles of faith and the sacraments of the Church spread opinions that are contrary to the Catholic faith." (This could be a reference to Porete.) On the basis of their "perverted view" (*opinione sinistra*), the decree formally condemns the way of life of these evil beguines and excommunicates anyone who continues to practice it and those religious who support them. Although beginning with a general statement about beguines, Clement's rather fuzzy presentation seems to have been directed only at dangerous beguines, an interpretation supported by the final clause of the document, which allows "other faithful women" to live in communal houses (*hospitiis*) and practice penance as God inspires them.[62] In any case, it seems *Cum de quibusdam* was either unclear or seen as going too far. After its promulgation by John XXII, it caused considerable debate, and Pope John soon issued a bull that more carefully distinguished between good (i.e., organized) and bad beguines, approving the former as long as they steered clear of heresy. But the pope left it up to local authorities to make the discrimination between the good and the bad—hence, the ongoing confusion about beguines for the next century.

The second decree of Vienne, *Ad nostrum*, directed against doctrinal error, originally mentioned only beghards, although a number of its eight condemned propositions are close to errors singled out in the investigation of Porete's *Mirror*. Despite the probable connection with Porete's condemnation, the decree also explicitly speaks of Germany as the source of the errors in question, something that may reflect the concerns of important German bishops like John of Strassburg and Henry of Cologne, who were known pursuers of mystical heresy. Given the importance of *Ad nostrum* in the history of mystical heresy, it is worth taking a closer look at its eight anathematized propositions.[63]

The first article contains the error of human impeccability: "That someone in the present life can acquire so great and such a degree of perfection that he is rendered completely without sin and is not able to advance further in grace."[64] The second article is a classic statement of freedom from religious practices and moral obligations: "Upon having attained the degree of this kind of perfection a person does not have to fast or pray, because then sensuality is so perfectly subject to spirit and reason that a person can freely give the body whatever pleases it."[65] The third article, the nodal point of the decree translated above, explicitly mentions the *spiritus libertatis* as the characteristic of this suspect state of perfection. The final five articles, a mix of doctrinal and moral errors, can be seen as further applications of the *spiritus libertatis*. Article 4 is the assertion that a person can attain a degree of perfection in this life fully equivalent to that gained in heaven (a position denied by Marguerite Porete). Article 5 claims that the intellectual nature of the soul itself is sufficient for the beatific vision, a philosophical error that may reflect radical Aristotelianism. Article 6 is close to texts in Porete in its claim that the imperfect person has to exercise acts of the virtues, while the perfect person "gives the virtues their leave" (*licentiat a se virtutes*).[66] The odd seventh article is antinomian, asserting that because nature prompts sexual intercourse it is not a sin, while kissing, since nature does not incline to it, is. The final article is quietistic. The perfect soul should not disturb its contemplation by showing reverence to the Host at mass or even think about the sacrament of the Eucharist or Christ's passion.[67]

When the decree became a part of canon law in 1317, it made sure that not only the "abominable sect of certain evil men called beghards," but also of "some faithless women called beguines" were included. Pope Clement may have intended to distinguish between good and bad beguines, but the effect of *Ad nostrum* was to cement the connection between the Free Spirit heresy and the beguine movement. In the eyes of many in the fourteenth century all beguines and beghards were dangerous heretics. Hence, the period between the Council of Vienne in 1312 and the Council of Constance in 1415 has been characterized by Richard Kieckhefer as "a hundred years' war against beghards and beguines."[68] Nevertheless, the link between the beguines and heresy was never one of complete identity, even in papal documents. Local groups of beguines and beghards, especially those supported by the mendicant orders, although attacked from time to time, continued to flourish, both in Germany and in the Low Countries. While many of those investigated for mystical heresy by inquisitors, both episcopal and papal, were described as beguines and beghards, this is clearly not true in every case. The confusion between the beguine movement, amorphous as it was, and the even more vague notion of the Free Spirit leaves the historian with a situation in which much about the nature and extent of fourteenth-century mystical heresy remains obscure.

Given the extensive recent work on the inquisitorial pursuit of mystical heretics in the late Middle Ages, as well as studies of the treatises written against heresy, it is unnecessary here to summarize every case or document. A brief survey of a few famous examples will suffice to gain a picture of the Free Spirit heresy, at least as it was constructed in official documents.

Pursuing Heresy in the Fourteenth and Fifteenth Centuries

John I, bishop of Strassburg from 1306 to 1328, was one of the most fervent opponents of mystical heresy of the early decades of the fourteenth century.[69] John was especially exercised against mendicant beghards and beguines (Strassburg had a large number of beguine houses),[70] though the papal discrimination between good and bad beguines and the opposition of the mendicants to a blanket condemnation seem to have tempered the scope of his attacks. During 1317 (while Meister Eckhart was resident in Strassburg) Bishop John conducted an investigation of mystical heretics reflected in a number of surviving documents.[71]

Two texts are especially helpful for determining the errors that John found. The first is a letter (called document A here) addressed to his clergy on August 13, 1317, in which the bishop lists forty-two errors gathered under seven headings of "those whom the crowd calls beghards and 'bread-for-God sisters' and who name themselves children, or brothers and sisters, of the sect of the Free Spirit and of voluntary poverty."[72] The second document (B here) is a contemporary list of twenty-four errors, many overlapping with those from the letter, organized under two broad headings.[73] The first group of articles in John's letter (A.I.1–6), as well as the beginning of the error list (B.I.1–7), deal with heretical expressions of mystical identity. It even includes some pantheistic-sounding claims, such as that God is formally everything.[74] Mystical identity is expressed in the language of indistinction: "They say that a person can be so united with God that all his power, will, and action is the same as God's. Again, they believe that they are God by nature without distinction."[75] Such assertions that the perfect are God by nature and not by grace go against traditional teaching (including that of Eckhart), but claiming to be one with God without distinction appears among a number of late medieval mystics. Another interesting statement that seems to occur here for the first time is the claim that those who are united with God created all things. Meister Eckhart also preached this, a point that may help explain why he was later charged with heresy by Bishop John's colleague in Cologne, Henry of Virneburg.[76]

The language of freedom of spirit occurs often in both texts. For example, "Furthermore, some say that on the basis of the perfection of the union some have with God that they are without sin (*impeccabiles*), because they are so free in spirit that whatever they do with the body they never sin."[77] Expressions of antinomian freedom run throughout both lists (e.g., A.I.7, A.II.7, A.III.2; B.I.10–17). The suspect beghards and beguines are also taken to task for mendicancy and their refusal to work (e.g., A.III.4, B.I.15), as were the Messalians before them. The organization of the other headings in the letter demonstrates an attempt at theological coherence, though the contents of the categories sometimes involve contradictory claims not unlike those found in Albert's *Compilatio*, several of whose articles are close to those found in John's letter. The second heading, "Errors against Christ," for example, includes both claims of equality with Christ (A.II.1) and assertions that it is possible to surpass him and therefore not be bound to reverence the God-man (A.II.5). The third and fourth headings, "Against the Church" and "Against the Sacraments," list typical anti-ecclesial and anti-sacramental tenets, some of which seem Waldensian (e.g., "that any layman is as entitled to confer the sacrament of the Eucharist as a sinful priest" [A.IV.1]). "Against the Gospel" upholds the superiority of the inner truth given to the perfect above any external writing (A.VI.2), a theme to reappear often in later mystical heresy. Finally, the heading "Against the Saints" claims that the Free Spirits surpass the saints and are so perfect that they cannot increase or decrease in holiness (A.VII.3). One unusual claim, found in both texts (A.I.8, B.I.6), identifies the perfect soul with the kingdom of God, something also present in Eckhart's preaching. Bishop John's influential letter certainly reflects actual examinations for heresy; how far it also depends on lists such as those of Albert and the discussions at Vienne is difficult to say. It provides one of the most complete pictures of what the opponents of heresy thought they were up against.

Two inquisitorial cases from the 1330s have been seen as witnesses to the communal character of at least some adherents of the *secta spiritus libertatis*. John of Brünn confessed to having been a beghard "free spirit" for twenty-eight years, until he abjured his errors, became a Dominican, and set down the record of his former beliefs for the Dominican inquisitor Gallus of Novo Castro, probably in the late 1330s.[78] John's account is detailed and spicy. Though filled with phrases taken from *Ad nostrum* (especially a constant repetition of *libertas spiritus* and its equivalents), as well as reminiscences of Albert's *Compilatio*, the story has too many particulars to be dismissed as complete fabrication. According to the confession, John was a married layperson, who, like Peter Valdes and others, out of a desire to live a true evangelical life made a settlement with his wife and sold off his possessions. John was convinced to undertake these steps by someone named Nicholas, who introduced him to a beghard community in Cologne where he was instructed and trained in a manner of life designed to lead to true freedom of spirit.

John's account describes the role of beginners in the community as an odd combination of real asceticism and hypocritical subterfuge, but when he reached the level of the advanced (*proficientes*) after twenty years he presents a textbook picture of the antinomianism of those who have attained freedom of spirit. John uses the language of annihilation that appears in many late mystics, but his doctrine of annihilation is an exterior one: "You should exercise yourself in those works that are contrary to you so that your life may be annihilated and brought down and totally subjected to the spirit, because your nature is sterile [i.e., in itself] and contrary to itself in all [its works], and hence it ought to be broken and made subject to the divine will. . . ."[79] The effect of this annihilation is antinomian freedom to engage in any form of sexual license, to steal, lie, cheat, and even murder with impunity. Other themes appearing in lists of heretical mystical errors, such as denial of heaven and hell, opposition to the book learning of clerics, and antisacramentalism, also occur in John's account, as might be expected. In a few places John speaks of mystical identity, even of a corporeal transmutation into God, as the source of the freedom of the adept.[80]

John of Brünn's testimony regarding a heretical beghard house in Cologne in the early decades of the thirteenth century is echoed in another inquisitorial document, the 1332 investigation of a group of "hooded nuns" (*moniales caputiatae*) conducted by the Dominican John Schwenkenfeld in the town of Schweidnitz in Silesia.[81] Again, this account drawn from sixteen witnesses tells a story so filled with detail that it is difficult not to take it as a witness to a house of apostolic poverty gone bad. In the words of Gordon Leff, the Schweidnitz beguinage was a place where "heresy merged with piety, so that the same impulse and many of the same tenets coexisted, even if they were given a new direction."[82] Nevertheless, the fact that so many of the witnesses were novices who might be jealous of the older sisters' strong control,[83] as well as the generally hearsay character of much of the testimony about sexual impropriety and the obvious use of inquisitional formularies to smoke out doctrinal error, leaves us with many doubts about the details.

The severe ascetical practices of the house and the lurid accounts of the antinomian sex that nearby beghards encouraged the sisters to engage in to demonstrate their attainment of freedom of spirit are prominent in several of the testimonies of the young nuns, especially that of Adelheid the *reclusa*, who had been with the community for less than a year.[84] The hypocritical, anti-ecclesial, anticlerical, and antisacramental beliefs testified to in these accounts were to recur in many later inquisitorial documents. Language about indistinct union with God is relatively rare, being found only in reference to one older nun, Gertrude of Civitate, who was also accused of making statements claiming to have co-created the world.[85] It is difficult to be sure about the extent of the errors of the Schweidnitz beguines. In the best-case scenario, the community can be seen as one practicing severe asceticism under a strong internal hierarchy that flaunted church regulation and indulged in a good deal of anticlericalism. In the worst case scenario these beguines were a paradigm of heretical antinomianism.

During the same decades in which these and other inquisitions for "heretical depravity" were being conducted, there is also considerable evidence for the concern of mystics and theologians to discriminate between true and false notions of union, annihilation, and freedom of spirit. We will examine the protests against dangerous mystics advanced by Meister Eckhart, Henry Suso, John Tauler, and several MHG treatises in subsequent chapters. Other noted German theologians, such as the Augustinian Jordan of Quedlinburg, also protested.[86] The spread of such testimony not only indicates the impact of suspicions engendered by *Ad nostrum* and inquisitorial processes, but also points to the concerns of the mystics themselves that the true nature of mystical union was being misunderstood by some of their contemporaries.

Official pursuit of mystical heresy was revitalized in the second half of the fourteenth century through a series of papal decrees and the efforts of the heresy-hunting emperor Charles IV. Again, a few noted cases will suffice to show the perdurance of error, or at least fear of error. The continuing role of *Ad nostrum* as an inquisitional formulary is evident from the process against the beghard John Hartmann conducted in Erfurt in 1367.[87] Hartmann has been seen as one of the most radical of the recorded Free Spirits, owing to the degree to which he was willing not only to admit to the errors condemned in the Clementine Constitutions but also to expand upon them. This beghard comes across as supremely self-confident, even perhaps a bit deranged. Given his refusal to backtrack, he probably went to the stake. Hartmann's frequent expansions on the scenario established by *Ad nostrum* might seem to support the authenticity of his trial record, but some of his admissions echo earlier trial documents, such as those against John of Brünn, so it is again not possible to be sure of all his views. Nevertheless, it would be hypercritical to conclude that the record does not give us some insight into the beghard's strange beliefs.

The inquisitorial process against Hartmann highlights two tendencies in suspicions about late medieval mysticism, suspicions closely intertwined in the minds of the inquisitors. John Hartmann displays a sophisticated language to talk about mystical identity with God at the same that he revels in describing the antinomian practices of those who have arrived at freedom of spirit. A generation before, the "Nameless Wild One" of Suso's *Little Book of Divine Truth* was portrayed as adept at using Eckhartian language about union and lack of distinction, but this mystery figure was not pictured as personally antinomian (see chapter 5, pp. 237–38 below). Hartman's inquisitorial record combines the two.

Hartmann confesses to general antinomianism—not just the usual sexual varieties and lack of obedience to ecclesiastical requirements,[88] but also the freedom to rob, murder, and lie under oath.[89] From the perspective of mysticism, what is most intriguing about this text is what it says about mystical union. In his response to the first article from *Ad nostrum,* for example, Hartmann was willing to accept the language of indistinction in the divine abyss, a theme that will be found in a number of orthodox late medieval German mystics. The report states:

> He was asked by the inquisitor about the first article of the decree on heretics, *Ad nostrum* . . . , namely that a person in the present life, when standing in such contemplation as has been mentioned (that is, in the highest degree of perfection which he had in the Principle, when he was in the abyss of divinity), whether there was any difference between himself and God. He responded that in such perfection at its highest grade he was one with God and God was one with him without any distinction.[90]

This passage seems to suggest that the inquisitor took the lead, thus hinting that the technical language of union without distinction developed by Eckhart and his followers may have been suggested to the accused during his interrogation, rather than springing from his own views.[91]

One of the other central themes of Hartmann's confession is the role of personal experience. Toward the end of the account, Hartmann argues that without the experience of the truth and illumination he has received, all that he says will seem worthless. When asked if he was insane or demented, he replied that neither was the case, but that

> he said these things from his ground, because he found it in himself, and that only someone who had experienced such things from his true ground could express them. The preachers proclaim and teach from books and their concern with the written page leads to forgetfulness of these matters, but those who perceive these things in deepest profundity of the divine abyss are truly able to talk about them.[92]

Again, we are unsure whether the inquisitorial document is providing us with its own view of how a heretic is supposed to appeal to private experience against the objectivity of faith, or Hartmann is being allowed to speak on his own. It may be that both perspectives are at work, though for different purposes.

Strassburg again became a center of pursuit of beguines for heresy in the second half of the fourteenth century. On August 19, 1374, the new bishop, Lambert of Burn, a former advisor of Charles IV, issued a letter against beguines and their supporters among both the Dominicans and Franciscans. One manuscript also contains the formulary (*interrogatorium*) that was to be used to investigate those who came to the bishop's inquisitorial commission—the only surviving example of such a document.[93] This text is largely a pastiche of passages from *Cum de quibusdam mulieribus* and *Ad nostrum,* quoting all eight articles of the latter. What Lambert added was a series of questions related to dress and discipline designed to identify unregulated religious, including third order Franciscans.[94] The final article, however, is new and deals with a well-known vernacular mystical treatise: "It seems expedient that each of them be asked whether they have, or have had, or know anyone to have a certain German book entitled *The Nine Rocks,* in the vernacular *Dz buoch von den nún feilsen,* which is said to contain many things that do not agree with the Catholic faith."[95] This is a reference to the original version of *The Book of the Nine Rocks,* later expanded upon by Rulman Merswin, the leader of the Strassburg Friends of God.[96]

Another example of a late-fourteenth-century Free Spirit is the shadowy figure of Nicholas of Basel, a wandering preacher, probably a beghard, active in the Rhineland and further afield.[97] Nicholas was executed for heresy in Vienna sometime between 1393 and 1397. Though we lack the process against him, documents exist for some of his followers. For example, Martin of Mainz, an ex-monk, was burned at Cologne in 1393 for fifteen antinomian errors that sound much like what John Hartmann admitted to. Another follower of Nicholas, a man named James, when arrested in Basel in 1405 gave a rather different account of his beliefs and did not confess to antinomianism. Once again, it is difficult to determine just what Nicholas may have held, though theologians like Henry of Langenstein pursued him as a dangerous heretic. Other noted theologians and religious leaders of the late fourteenth and early fifteenth centuries, such as Gerard Groot, the founder of the *devotio moderna*, and Jean Gerson, remained deeply concerned about the dangers of mystical heresy.

During the course of the Council of Constance (1414–18) some voices spoke for banning all beguines as heretics, but the movement found supporters among powerful figures. The institutionalized beguines at least had become an accepted part of the religious landscape. While the fifteenth century continued to witness inquisitorial cases against those who were seen as adherents of the *secta spiritus libertatis*, the number declined. A brief glance at three cases, however, shows that worries about mystical heresy still had a broad geographical range.

Among the most-cited cases of late medieval mystical heresy is a movement found in the Low Counties around 1400 called "The Men of Intelligence" (*homines intelligentiae*).[98] In 1410, the bishop of Cambrai, the noted theologian Pierre d'Ailly, commissioned Henry Selle, provost of the canons at Groenendael, to investigate heresy in Brussels. In the following year, on June 12, the episcopal court at Cambrai conducted a trial of a Brussels Carmelite William of Hildernissen on the basis of three lists of errors.[99] The first list comprised the errors attributed to a deceased layman named Egidius Cantor, the leader of the Men of Intelligence. Egidius is described as believing in universal salvation and in a quasi-Joachite third age of the Holy Spirit, now begun with him and his followers. He is said to have asserted identity with the Holy Spirit—"This seducing layman said many times and repeated to many listeners, 'I am the Savior of humans; through me they will see Christ, just as through Christ they see the Father.'"[100] His direct illumination by the Spirit had freed him from all obedience to the church and the constraints of the moral law. Egidius's antinomianism, especially sexual depravity, is described in some detail.[101] He was accused, for example, of practicing a special method of intercourse used by Adam in paradise (we are not told exactly how this worked). Given that Egidius was already dead, and that we have no other names of witnesses to these errors, it is difficult to know just what the Men of Intelligence really believed and practiced.

William of Hildernissen, however, was alive and was willing to confess that he had met Egidius, but he denied that he had ever been a leader of the Men of Intelligence, claiming rather that he had preached against them when he learned of their errors. The Carmelite did, however, admit to a second list of errors, a strange collection that included some anticlerical views, doctrinal errors, such as belief in universal salvation, as well a conviction about a coming third age of the Holy Spirit when "the law of the Holy Spirit and spiritual liberty would be revealed and then the present law will cease."[102] William also confessed to having used pantheistic expressions.[103] Finally, he also abjured a third list of Free Spirit errors drawn from *Ad nostrum* and other standard accusations of mystical heresy. All in all, William appears to have been a confused cleric who confessed to many incautious and erroneous statements, but who also sought to distance himself as far as possible from Egidius and his followers. On the basis of his abject confession William was given the relatively mild sentence of three years imprisonment, after which he seems to have been rehabilitated.

In the decades following the inquisition of the Men of Intelligence, we have evidence of concern with mystical heresy in northern Italy, especially in connection with Marguerite Porete's *Mirror of Simple Annihilated Souls*, available in the Italian peninsula not only in the Latin version, but also in two vernacular renditions.[104] Although Porete's name was not known, her book appears to have circulated fairly widely. The earliest witness is the famous preacher and Franciscan reformer Bernardino of Siena. In his sermon collection the *Quadragesimale de christiana religione*, composed between 1417 and 1429, as well as in the later *Quadragesimale de evangelio aeterno* (1430–37), Bernardino complained several times about those who had fallen into the Free Spirit heresy through reading the *Mirror*. In sermon 6 of the latter work he drew a connection between the *Mirror* and the Vienne condemnations:

> There are some who have fallen into the accursed heresy of the Free Spirit, whose teaching is found in the book usually called *The Simple Soul*. Those who make use of it commonly fall into that heresy, though when they are infected with the deadly disease . . . they say that the book and its mode of life are not understood by its opponents. Thus they judge and damn the church which condemned that teaching in a sacred council, as evident from the decretal on heresy in chapter one of the Clementines.[105]

In sermon 56 Bernardino attacked unnamed persons who neglected grace and Christ's cross in order to attain "wonderful annihilation, as we know through the experience of those who follow the spirit of love, the spirit of liberty, and that heretical book called *Of the Simple Souls*."[106]

Evidence of debate over Marguerite's *Mirror* grew in the 1430s. A General Chapter of the Reformed Benedictine Congregation of Santa Giustina in Padua forbade the reading of the *Mirror* in April of 1433. The major attacks on the book focused on another order, the Gesuati, who were active in the Veneto and other areas in northern Italy.[107] According to Romana Guarnieri's reconstruction of events, the summer of 1437 saw the outbreak of attacks on the *Mirror* across the Veneto. One Antonio Zeno, vicar of Padua, made a list of thirty errors from the *Mirror*, which was sent to the theologians and canonists of the university of Padua for review and condemnation. This list, which survives in a Vatican manuscript, testifies to careful study of Porete's controversial book.[108] On August 8, Pope Eugene IV (the Venetian Gabriel Condulmer) wrote to the Franciscan reformer and friend of Bernardino, John of Capestrano, and also to Lorenzo Giustiniani, the bishop of Venice, commissioning them to investigate the Venetian Gesuati on the charge of Free Spirit heresy and to hunt for copies of Marguerite's *Mirror.* (The action was said to have been initiated on the basis of complaints of an unnamed German member of the order.) Antonio Correr, cardinal of Bologna and a relative of Pope Eugene, also got involved, and soon a circle of significant ecclesiastics of northern Italy were caught up in the investigation. On September 3, Giovanni Tavelli, bishop of Ferrara and friend of Capestrano, testified that he had been a member of the order for twenty-five years and that the Gesuati were "good men, walking rightly in the way of the Lord according to evangelical and apostolic teaching and the traditions of the fathers." Tavelli found it hard to believe that the suspect *Mirror,* read by many servants of God, could contain such manifest errors.[109] Capestrano judged otherwise. After uncovering some copies of the *Mirror,* he pronounced it deeply heretical. Nevertheless, the inquiry cleared the Gesuati of dangerous error, though the decision was apparently not pleasing to all.

Some of those who were unhappy with the verdict appear to have been active in one of the more curious incidents in late medieval pursuit of mystical heresy—the accusation made at the Council of Basel in 1439 that Eugene IV himself was a proponent of mystical error. The confrontation between the revived papacy of Martin V and his successor Eugene and the forces of conciliarism, stewing for almost two decades, reached a point of no return in 1439 when the council fathers gathered at Basel formally deposed Pope Eugene. In the wake of this event, the conciliarist John of Segovia's *Chronicle of the Events of Basel* records the appearance before the council fathers on July 22, 1439, of a strange hermit named James, described as *magister in artibus et medicina.* James is said to have presented a list of thirty heretical articles drawn from the *Mirror* and to have denounced Eugene for defending the book and imprisoning those who attacked its errors. That there was such a list circulating at Basel seems likely, given the existence of the Vatican list, but the rest of the story, even the existence of the mystery hermit, is questionable.[110]

The final representative case from the fifteenth century takes us back to Germany, specifically to Mainz in 1458 for the trial and execution of "a certain beghard by the name of John Becker" (*quidam lolhardus nomine Johannes Becker*), who appears to be one of the more extreme mystical heretics of the late Middle Ages.[111] The Dominican inquisitor Henry Kalteisen organized Becker's confession according to headings, at the end citing five of the eight articles from *Ad nostrum* in confirmation of the heresy. Becker claimed to have been originally obedient to church rules and regulations until one day in May of 1442 when he was in church at Mainz and "heard a sound from the roof of the church which descended on him." In this sound the Holy Spirit entered into his interior with great force so that "afterward he was often raptured in his interior man."[112] The influx of the Holy Spirit freed Becker from the constraints of ecclesiastical and moral law. Throughout the confession, he returns again and again to his status as a true interior man who has been given full unity with the Trinity (Becker used the traditional formula of being made God by grace).[113] Although he does not use the term indistinction, Becker's teaching clearly expresses such a form of identity with God. For example:

> Because he himself is God, he is united with God and made into God through the union of his interior man. He himself is to be adored as God with God, not in a separate way, but he is one with the Most Blessed Trinity, so that while we adore the Father, Son, and Holy Spirit, we ought at the same time to adore him.[114]

Becker's union of identity, like those of Porete and Eckhart, involved annihilation of his own will. He claimed that the inner man is the interior reason, "And concerning this he said that by the fact that he had given himself to the Spirit, he no longer had any will of his own."[115] Becker's total subjection to the Holy Spirit acting within him was the source for his freedom from the moral law and the sacramental life and practices of the church, as well as from all secular authority. "He asserted that those things that are sins to others are not sins for him if he does them from the bidding of his interior man and his Spirit."[116] Although Becker believed that no one had ever received the Holy Spirit more powerfully than he had, he distinguished two groups of people, those subject to the church, and others like himself who were no longer held to adore Christ's humanity, "but only God in his bare divinity."[117] Like Marguerite Porete, he also distinguished two churches: the inferior church of Christendom (*christianitas*), which is "damned and heretical" and the "true catholic church," not of this world, to which he belonged. Becker, who gave his confession freely, was burned along with a book he had written (or books according to one account). It would have been interesting to see the contents of the volume.

Mystical Heresy and Discernment of Spirits

The pursuit of mystical heretics in the late Middle Ages was closely connected to important shifts in the understanding and application of what was traditionally called "discernment of spirits." Within the context of heresy trials themselves inquisitors could make use of the "objective" evidence provided by *interrogatoria*, or lists of errors, but when it came to determining who might be subject to such procedures, especially in relation to those who made claims to visionary contact with God and other special gifts, discernment of spirits was the major, if ambiguous, tool that the orthodox turned to for help.

In the list of charismatic gifts contained in 1 Corinthians 12:4–11, Paul mentions discernment of spirits (*discretio spirituum* [Vg]), and in 2 Corinthians 11:14 he warns that "Satan transforms himself into an angel of light." In 1 John 1:4 the Christian community is told, "Do not believe every spirit, but test the spirits to see whether they are from God." The need for discernment of spirits advanced in these and other biblical texts rooted itself deeply in Christian life from the earliest ages and continues to be important to the present.[118] Discernment was an essential component of a true spiritual life, though the understandings, modalities, and applications of discernment over the centuries have been quite diverse. Mark A. McIntosh has helpfully identified five functions of spiritual discernment in the Christian tradition, often thought of independently, but always interacting in various ways. These are: (1) discernment as a loving and faithful relation to God; (2) discernment as distinguishing between good and evil impulses; (3) discernment as discretion, moderation, and good practical sense; (4) discernment as the desire to pursue God's will; and (5) discernment as a noetic relation to God, a form of contemplative wisdom.[119] The amplitude of this list suggests how intertwined discernment has been with the mystical tradition.

It may be helpful to distinguish discernment broadly understood, which would comprise all the functions identified by McIntosh, with the narrower conception of *discretio spirituum*, which tends to concentrate on the second function, that is, distinguishing between the good and evil impulses that move people. The major mystics themselves, however, rarely adopted the narrow view. Abstracting from the treatment of discernment in the early church, especially among the monastics,[120] it is impressive to note how many medieval mystics developed rich and nuanced understandings of discernment as part and parcel of their teaching. Notable in this respect were Bernard of Clairvaux and Richard of St. Victor in the twelfth century, and in the fourteenth century Catherine of Siena and the anonymous author of the *Cloud of Unknowing*, whose *Treatise of the Discretion of Spirits*, partly based on Bernard, adheres to a basically monastic understanding of the term. The theological meaning of discernment was aptly expressed by Catherine in chapter 9 of her *Dialogue*, where God tells her:

Discernment is nothing else but the true knowledge a soul ought to have of herself and of me, and through this knowledge she finds her roots. It is joined to charity like an engrafted shoot. . . . Discernment and charity are engrafted together and planted in the soil of that true humility which is born of self knowledge.[121]

The aspect of discerning spirits that is important for the history of mystical heresy, however, is of the narrower sort. The visionary explosion that became evident around the year 1200, as well as the growing suspicions about mystical claims of contact with God and deep states of union evident around 1300, led to an increasing concentration on how to discern true from false revelations, and eventually even to formalized handbooks on the topic. Such handbooks in the long run were self-defeating, since even the most skilled scholastic minds were not able to create a coherent set of rules to govern what is, after all, a charism. By isolating one strand of discernment from the others, the authors of these treatises were setting themselves up for failure. It was only when a sixteenth-century mystic of genius, Ignatius of Loyola, reintegrated discernment of spirits into a full spiritual program in his *Spiritual Exercises,* completed in 1541, that discernment once again became a living force in Christian spirituality.

The late medieval fascination with discernment of spirits has recently attracted considerable scholarly attention, so there is no need to try to tell the whole story here.[122] It will be sufficient to take note of aspects of this history that are important for understanding the struggle against mystical heresy, especially as it played itself out in Germany.

The new stage in the story of discernment of spirits, fittingly enough, can be said to begin in 1199 when Pope Innocent III sent a letter to the clergy of Mainz about the dangers of secret conventicles, false preaching, and heresy. This letter, called *Cum ex iniuncto* from its opening words, says that anyone who claims to be sent by God needs to have the witness of scripture or miracles to prove such an assertion. Not surprisingly, Innocent says that the clergy have the obligation to distinguish virtue from vice in such matters, noting that "[t]here is need for greater discernment, because vices can secretly work their way in under the guise of virtues, and Satan's angel can pretend to be and transform himself into an angel of light" (2 Cor. 11:14).[123] Innocent seems to have had Waldensians and their vernacular Bible translations in mind, but his decree was of moment because it was incorporated into the *Decretals* of Gregory IX in the section dealing with heresy and thus provided a legal foundation for clerical discernment as a key factor in investigating heresy.[124]

During the thirteenth century, two controversial movements served to focus attention on the need for discerning the difference between good and bad spirits in practice and not just in theory. The first was the increasing number of people, especially women, who claimed to be possessed by the divine spirit and who frequently manifested this possession in highly somatic ways. But how was one to be sure that the possession was supernatural and not demonic? Many of the excessive and ecstatic female mystics of the thirteenth and fourteenth centuries inspired debates about how to discern the legitimacy of their claims.[125] The more charismatic aspects of the Franciscan movement, especially among the Spirituals, also raised questions about the legitimacy of visions as sources of authority. This is evident, for example, in the life and thought of Peter John Olivi, who was credited with revelations and who also wrote about how to distinguish true from false visions.[126] The German Franciscan David of Augsburg, in his very popular handbook of spirituality called *The Composition of the Interior and Exterior Man*, adopted a negative attitude toward the visionary explosion, both the somatic mystical visions mostly ascribed to women and the apocalyptic visions of the Joachite and Franciscan Spiritual traditions.[127]

The slow growth toward a narrower, more articulated, and legal view of discernment of spirits reached a new stage at the beginning of the fourteenth century when the first specific treatise on the subject was produced. The German Augustinian Henry of Friemar the Elder (ca. 1250–1340) was a contemporary and sometimes even a neighbor of Meister Eckhart, since their home cloisters were both in the city of Erfurt. Like Eckhart, Henry taught as *magister actu regens* in Paris in the first decade of the fourteenth century. He also served on the theological commission that investigated the writings of Marguerite Porete and was a representative at the Council of Vienne. Henry was a prolific author, whose mystical writings will be considered in chapter 8.[128] One of his most popular works was the first formal treatment of discernment of spirits, a *Treatise on the Four Instincts* (*Tractatus de quattuor instinctibus*). The popularity of this work (over 150 manuscripts exist, as well as translations into MHG and several early printed editions) testifies to the increasing role that discerning spirits played in the late Middle Ages.[129]

Henry's treatise does not use the phrase *discretio spirituum*, preferring the broader monastic term *discretio*, but his scholastic systematization of the four forms of instincts or promptings that inspire human action influenced later discernment manuals and practices. The Augustinian's fourfold division appears to be original. "Instinct or interior motion is fourfold," that is, all interior movement is either divine, angelic, diabolical, or natural. "The true cause and reason," Henry avers, "why it is difficult to discern these instincts is the similarity and conformity of natural light to the light of grace."[130] The first half of the treatise deals with the first three instincts, proceeding by way of fourfold lists of the signs of each.[131] Henry's advice is primarily directed at religious persons who wish to analyze their own instincts, but it also contains signs that could be applied to the outward behavior of others, particularly the contrast between the serenity and peace that characterize the good instincts and the tumult and disturbance that accompany the bad. He is not obsessed with claims for visions or revelations, though these too enter into his grid for determining the differences between the good and the bad. Much of what he has to say is traditional, but in organizing his material the way he did, and especially in the context of the growing fear over evil instincts, be they diabolical or merely natural,[132] his treatise broke new ground.

Some of Henry's contemporaries were more worried than he about the danger of proliferating visions. Another Augustinian, Augustine of Ancona, sent his *Treatise against Diviners and Dreamers* to Pope Clement V in 1310. This was a catchall polemic against Spiritual Franciscans, various forms of superstition, and the idea that God would communicate new revelations in this evil age. Augustine also offers a series of negative signs by which one can discern the difference between true and false visions.[133] A generation later, the Dominican Venturino of Bergamo (d. 1346), whose works circulated in Germany, strongly warned against aspiring to "visions, revelations, or experiences that are supernatural or beyond the common ken of those who love and fear God." Venturino even wrote about his own failure to discern the falsity of a young laywoman who had claimed to have received a vision of the archangel Gabriel.[134]

The perceived danger of "Satan transforming himself into an angel of light" (2 Cor. 11:4) greatly increased after the Council of Vienne, as did the growing fears of the Free Spirits who might outwardly seem to live a pious life, but who were inwardly perverse and immoral. Even honored religious men might fall victim to Satan's wiles. In the preface to the 1329 bull condemning Meister Eckhart, John XXII said, "The man was led astray by that Father of Lies who often turns himself into an angel of light." It is scarcely surprising, then, that so many of the mystical authors of the fourteenth and fifteenth centuries, not least in Germany, were concerned with laying out rules for the discernment of spirits so that their audiences could avoid being fooled by false mystics who confused natural impulses with grace and thus left themselves open to diabolical influence.[135] We will see many examples of such advice in the chapters that follow.

The late fourteenth and first part of the fifteenth centuries witnessed another stage in the expansion of the more restricted understanding of *discretio spirituum*. The first treatise to actually bear that title was composed by a German theologian, Henry of Langenstein, in 1383.[136] This work was read at the University of Paris, where Henry had once taught, and the noted master Pierre d'Ailly composed two tracts both named *On False Prophets*, one before 1395, the other shortly after 1410. D'Ailly's even more famous pupil, Jean Gerson, wrote three treatises between 1401 and 1423 on the proper discernment of visions and prophecies. It is clear that the crisis of the Great Schism (1378–1417), as well as the attendant visionaries and prophets whose revelations were thought to have predicted the tragedy and others that purported to offer a way out of Christendom's dilemma, helped fuel this concern on the part of theologians. These treatises aspire to greater accuracy and practical applicability in laying out more precise rules for separating good from evil impulses. They were different in degree but not in kind from what had appeared in the early fourteenth century. Since these works have been studied in detail recently, they need not delay us here.[137] In closing, it is worth noting Mark McIntosh's observation based on his discussion of Gerson, the most famous of the medieval discernment authors. McIntosh says that Gerson's attempt "to order phenomena into discrete categories" results in a subtle shift in which "our attention is being gradually focused more on the *experiences* that discernment examines than on the *truth* that discernment seeks; . . . so that method and analysis begin to dominate the foreground, and the divine agency, calling, and reality slips into the background."[138]

Conclusion

The campaign against mystical heresy that broke out in earnest around 1300 waxed and waned for the next four hundred years. The complaints directed against the Free Spirit heretics, partly inherited from earlier tensions between mysticism and magisterium, but also reflecting suspicions about aspects of the new mysticism of the late Middle Ages—especially the insistence on annihilation of the self and claims to mystical identity—were to reappear often.[139] The history of the construction of mystical heresy is clearly important; the precise nature of such heresy and its extent are more problematic. Nevertheless, a few conclusions can be drawn.

First, there was never a sect of the Free Spirit in the sense of a widespread movement. That there were individuals who made strange and novel claims about their identity with God, and who may well have thought themselves free of all obligations to the church and even to the moral law, cannot be doubted. Some of them attracted followers, as seems to be the case with the Franciscans active in Umbria in the first decade of the fourteenth century, with Nicholas of Basel at the end of the century, and with the Men of Intelligence in Brussels. Early on, there may have been a few beguine and beghard communities who were infected with such views, *if* we can trust figures like John of Brünn and the beguines of Schweidnitz. Other group accusations, such as those against the Gesuati of northern Italy were dismissed by competent judges of heresy. Most of the extreme figures, like John Hartmann and John Becker, appear to have been loners.

The second conclusion that emerges from the cases noted here is that mystical heresy was part and parcel of the new mysticism that emerged in the thirteenth century, at least in the sense that the core suspect points were also taught by some fourteenth-century mystics who were accepted as orthodox. Issues such as indistinct union with God, the need for total interiorization, annihilation of the created will, and the secondary status of outward practices of piety were potential flash points of controversy, though they were capable of being given an orthodox interpretation. Still, the dangers remained. Although Meister Eckhart was never accused of antinomianism or anti-ecclesial views, aspects of his teaching were condemned as heretical by the highest authority in Christendom. Marguerite Porete's *Mirror* was burned along with her. Although Porete's mysticism expresses something of the esotericism that had been a source of suspicion since the Gnostic controversy, and although there are anticlerical expressions in her book, it is difficult to convict her of the antinomianism that her judges found in the *Mirror*. Despite the condemnations, both Eckhart and Porete continued to be read in later centuries.

The testimony of the mystics who came after Eckhart and who will appear later in this volume shows that concern over mystical error was part of their landscape. These teachers and preachers realized how easy it was to go astray in speaking about interiorization, annihilation, union, and other aspects of the mystical path. They also made distinctions between those who held mistaken views but who could be helped by instruction on the one hand, and those who persisted in dangerous error on the other. This type of distinction does not often appear in the inquisitorial records that witness to the creation of the category of mystical heresy.

PART 2

*Meister Eckhart
and His Students*

CHAPTER 3

The Mysticism
of the Ground

N O AREA OF LATE MEDIEVAL EUROPE was as prolific in the production of mystical literature as the German-speaking lands.
Some of the contributions of German writers to the development of Western mysticism during the period 1250–1350 have already
been considered in *The Flowering of Mysticism*, notably those of female
mystics such as Mechthild of Magdeburg, the Cistercian nuns of Helfta
in Saxony, and the Dominican sisters of southern Germany.[1] These
mystical currents, however, represent only one side of the German
contribution. Another, even more powerful, flood of mystical literature first became evident in the teaching and preaching of Meister
Eckhart at the turn of the fourteenth century. It was to flourish for two
hundred years and more in sermons and treatises in the vernacular,
both by noted mystics such as John Tauler and Henry Suso, and by
lesser-known figures and anonymous *gotesfrúnt* (Friends of God). The
forms of mystical consciousness presented by Eckhart and his followers are different from, but not necessarily opposed to, those found in
the women mystics. As the example of Suso shows, rich interactions
of the two streams are evident in the Middle Ages and beyond. But
what was initiated by Eckhart had a distinctive nature and an impact
that shaped the age of the harvest of mysticism.

There are many descriptions and analyses of the mysticism produced in German-speaking lands in the late Middle Ages. Various
attempts to provide a general rubric for this key chapter in the history
of mysticism have been useful for highlighting one or another aspect
of an impressive body of literature and art. One often-employed
description is the term "German mysticism" (*die deutsche Mystik*).[2]
Obviously, it is not incorrect to speak of German mysticism, but when

used of Eckhart and his followers the term has the disadvantage of placing this form of mysticism into such a broad category that its own character does not emerge.

Other accounts have suggested descriptions based on geographical location, affiliation with a particular religious order, or the contrast between affective and speculative mysticisms. An example of the first approach is the term "Rhineland mysticism" to categorize Eckhart and his followers, and even Dutch mystics such as John Ruusbroec.[3] But Meister Eckhart was born and did his earliest vernacular preaching in Saxony, far from the Rhine. The mysticism he initiated spread throughout Germany. Again, since Eckhart was a Dominican and since much of the literature that was influenced by him was produced by fellow Dominicans, other scholars have used the "mysticism of the German Dominicans" as an appropriate rubric.[4] But not all of Eckhart's followers were Dominicans, as texts like the *Theologia Deutsch* demonstrate, and the German Order of Preachers produced a number of forms of mysticism, as evident in the writings of the Dominican nuns.

Given the intellectual nature of Eckhart's preaching and teaching, it has been popular to speak of "speculative mysticism" in connection with the Dominican and his successors.[5] Eckhart and those influenced by him were certainly speculative in the sense that they emphasized the role of the intellect in the return to God; they also often set forth their teaching in deep philosophical language. Nevertheless, insofar as speculative mysticism is often contrasted with so-called affective mysticism (e.g., Bernard of Clairvaux) the term can be misleading. All Christian mystics recognize the importance of both love and knowledge in the path to God, though they interpret the respective roles of the two fundamental powers of the human subject in diverse ways.[6] Categories based on oppositions between knowing and loving, essence and desire, and the like, ultimately tell us little about the nature of particular forms of mysticism.

Given the difficulty of finding appropriate language to describe the mysticism of Eckhart and his contemporaries and followers, the best course might be to eschew general characterizations altogether. But the need for some qualifier to help locate the form of mysticism initiated by Eckhart in relation to other mystical traditions has continued to prompt scholars to propose new descriptive terms to help illuminate the Dominican's teaching.[7] In this volume I will employ the term "mysticism of the ground" (MHG *grunt/grund*) for this purpose.

Throughout the volumes of the *The Presence of God* I have tried where possible to find descriptions for forms of Christian mysticism that originate in the texts of the mystics themselves, rather than from modern terms and methodologies. Powerful new forms of mystical speech came to birth in Eckhart, his contemporaries, and his followers, and it is worth investigating the terms of their own making that shed light on what was distinctive in their thinking. This is also true of other mystical eras and traditions. For example, in *The Growth of Mysticism* I suggested that much of the mysticism of the twelfth century could be described as sharing a concern for the "ordering of love" (*ordo amoris*) based on Song of Songs 2:4.[8] This is not to suggest that the twelfth century invented this theme nor that all mystics of that era gave it equal attention or treated it in the same way, but the ordering of love does help to identify a distinguishing characteristic of much twelfth-century mysticism. In this volume I propose that the mysticism of the ground is an equally useful tool for understanding the message of Eckhart and many who were influenced by him. To be sure, Eckhart and his followers treat many mystical themes, both traditional and innovative, but *grunt* provides a useful lens to bring into focus distinctive elements of their mystical thought.

Grunt is a simple term of spatial and tactile immediacy. Yet it is also an extraordinarily complex word that creates what Josef Quint called "a mystical word-field" (*mystiches Wortfeld*), that is, a new way of using a variety of words and metaphors to express in concrete fashion what cannot be captured in concepts.[9] *Grunt* can be termed a *Sprengmetapher* (explosive metaphor),[10] particularly because of the way it breaks through previous categories of mystical speech to create new ways of presenting a direct encounter with God. When Eckhart says, "God's ground and the soul's ground is one ground," he is announcing a new form of mysticism.

While explosive metaphors like *grunt* can give rise to deep philosophical and theological speculation, their function is more practical, or better, pragmatic, than theoretical: they are meant to overturn and transform ordinary forms of consciousness through the process of making the inner meaning of the metaphor one's own in everyday living. *Grunt* was a term for the preacher, providing Eckhart, Tauler, and other *lebemeister* (literally, "masters of living," or spiritual guides) with an apt tool for inculcating mystical transformation that was as simple and direct as it was profound and polyvalent.[11]

Grunt not only explodes and overturns; it also reorganizes. The return to the imaginal world of the metaphor, the arena of primitive language, can lead to a new creation, that is, new forms of differentiated and "scientific" language. In this sense *grunt* can be described as a master metaphor because of the way it focuses and integrates a whole range of creative language—strategies employed to describe the relationship between God and the human person. *Grunt* is the protean term at the center of Eckhart's mysticism, one that vanishes from our grasp when we try to contain it in any definable scheme or doctrinal system. The consciousness of the ground, a form of awareness different from all other forms of experience and knowing, is central to Eckhart's teaching.[12] Through Eckhart the *grunt* was to play a major role in late medieval mysticism.

Sources and Semantics of *grunt*

Grunt and its substantive relatives (*abgrunt*, abyss; *gruntlôsicheit,* groundlessness) and derived adjectives (*grundelôs, ungruntlich,* etc.) appear frequently in the vernacular works of Eckhart, Suso, and Tauler.[13] The term is important also to the sermons and treatises pseudonymously ascribed to Eckhart,[14] and in many other vernacular mystical texts of the fourteenth century. Its role in Dutch mysticism, especially in Ruusbroec, highlights the affinity, as well as the real differences, between late medieval German and Dutch mysticism.

The distinctively Germanic nature of *grunt* is evident from the fact that there is no real equivalent for the term in the other vernacular mysticisms, or in Latin mystical literature. In the mysticism of Teresa of Avila and John of the Cross, for example, the "center of the soul" (*centro del alma*) plays a somewhat similar role (one that may have been mediated through Latin translations of Eckhart and Tauler), but without the exuberant semantics and distinctive implications characteristic of *grunt* and its cognates.[15] The search for the Latin background to *grunt* reveals much about the dialogue, or conversation, between scholastic Latin and developing vernacular theologies of the late Middle Ages,[16] but it also demonstrates that while there are equivalents for *aspects* of *grunt* in Latin terminology, no single Latin word means *grunt*. The deceptively simple vernacular word has a richer range of significations, offers more subtle possibilities for use, and presents us with a more adequate way to understand a new form of mystical union than any word in the learned but less flexible language of the schools.[17]

Almost everyone who has written on Eckhart has had something to say about the Dominican's teaching on the *grunt*.[18] Discussions of its use in Tauler, Suso, and other mystical texts also exist.[19] In 1929, Hermann Kunisch published a monograph on the use of *grunt* in German mysticism of the fourteenth and fifteenth centuries.[20] Despite these discussions, one can agree with Susanne Köbele that with regard to much of the secondary literature on this central theme "one appears to be left in the lurch, when not led into error."[21] Recent research, however, has begun to reveal something of the complexity and depth of the term, as well as its centrality for understanding Eckhart and his followers.[22]

According to scholars of MHG, the word *grunt* is used in four general ways, two concrete and two abstract.[23] *Grunt* can, first of all, be understood as physical ground, that is, the earth. *Grunt* can also mean the bottom or lowest side of a body, surface, or structure (*basis/profundum/fundamentum/ fundus*). Abstractly, *grunt* is employed to indicate the origin (*origo*), cause (*causa*), beginning (*principium*), reason (*ratio*), or proof (*argumentum*) of something. Finally, *grunt* is employed as what is inmost, hidden, most proper to a being (*intimum, abditum, proprium*), that is, its essence (*essentia*). The semantic richness of this simple German word, especially its spectrum of both concrete and abstract significations, made it a seed ripe for flowering in the age of linguistic creativity that Kurt Ruh has spoken of as the *kairos* (i.e., decisive moment) of the German vernacular in the thirteenth and early fourteenth centuries.[24]

In attempting to show how Eckhart and his followers used the language of *grunt*, it is useful to cast a glance back not only over the uses of the term in previous Germanic mystics but also over the history of the Latin terminology related to it. Mechthild of Magdeburg (ca. 1208–1280) employed *grunt* and related words (*gruntlos/abgrunt*) a number of times, but not as a key term to explore the God–human relationship.[25] A closer parallel to later German uses can be found in the Dutch beguine Hadewijch's employment of the Middle Dutch *gront* and *afgront* (abyss) to describe the mutual interpenetration of God and human in the union of love. For Hadewijch, ground, abyss, and depth (*diepheit*) are terms that can be used both of the unknowable divine nature and of the human soul insofar as it cannot be separated from its exemplary existence in God. In a passage from Letter 18 the beguine speaks of the mutual interpenetration of the "bottomlessness" of the soul "in which God suffices to himself" and God himself is conceived of as "a way for the passage of the soul into its liberty, that is, into his ground that cannot be touched without contact with the soul's depth."[26] This text is close to passages in Eckhart and Tauler, though there is no evidence to suggest that they knew Hadewijch's writings, which were not disseminated until the middle of the fourteenth century.[27] The creation of *grunt/abgrunt* language was not a solitary effort, despite Eckhart's central role, but a response to a widespread yearning to give expression to a new view of how God becomes one with the human person: no longer through mystical uniting, that is, an intentional union between God and human emphasizing the continuing distinction between the two entities, but in a mystical identity in which God and human become truly indistinct, at least on some level.

Consideration of Latin terms that refract aspects of the meaning of *grunt* casts light on how the new master metaphor both absorbed earlier themes at the same time that it exploded and recast them. *Grunt* was often applied to the "innermost of the soul" (*innigsten der sêle*), what Eckhart, Tauler, and others spoke of metaphorically as "spark," "castle," "nobleman," "highest point," "seed," and the like. Much effort has been devoted to studying how *grunt* and its related terms are connected to Latin expressions for the depth of the soul conceived of as *imago Dei*—expressions like *fundus animae, scintilla animae, apex mentis, abditum animae/mentis/cordis, principale cordis/mentis, supremum animae, semen divinum, ratio superior, synderesis, abstrusior memoriae profunditas*, etc.[28] These terms pertain to what has been called the mysticism of introversion whose great source in the West is Augustine of Hippo.[29] Eckhart knew these terms and made use of many of them in his Latin works.[30]

Although these Latin terms cast light on the meaning of the phrase "ground of the soul" (*grunt der sêle*) and show its connection to the tradition exploring the inner nature of subjectivity, they also reveal the limits of the search for sources, because *grunt der sêle* expresses only one side of the range of meaning of *grunt*. It is precisely because these Latin terms are one-sided, signifying only the anthropological aspect of the union of God and the soul, that none of them could function as the master metaphor for the praxis of attaining the dynamic identity that fuses God and the soul in a single *grunt*, what Eckhart, Suso, and Tauler referred to as *ein einig ein*: a Single One.

The other dimension of *grunt* points to the hidden depths of God. The Latin background of this usage has a different semantic field from that of the terms used for the depths of the soul—another indication that *grunt* as a master metaphor is more than just a translation of any single Latin word. Terms like *deitas*,[31] *essentia, fundus divinitatis*,[32] and *principium* are helpful for grasping how references to the *grunt gotes* are illuminated by the technical vocabulary of scholastic theology, but the *grunt götliches wesens* as employed by Eckhart and his followers has a range of meanings and usages that surpasses any of these Latin terms. First of all, *grunt* is not used of God in the sense of *causa*, because God as *grunt* lies at a deeper level than God as efficient cause of the universe.[33] *Grunt*, of course, can be rendered as *essentia* and *deitas/divinitas*, but these abstract terms lack the dynamic character of *grunt* as employed in MHG preaching. In Eckhart's usage the Latin words that stand closest to *grunt gotes* are *principium* ("principle" conceived of as the source of formal emanation) and *unum*, that is, God as Absolute Unity, distinctly indistinct from all things. But again, these terms tend to emphasize one pole of fused identity, this time the theological rather than the anthropological.[34] They lack the simplicity, the tactility, and the versatility of *grunt*.

Choosing *grunt* as the central metaphor is not meant to reduce the importance of other mystical themes, terms, and metaphors characteristic of Eckhart and his contemporaries; rather, it casts new light on aspects of their meaning and helps reveal their inner connections.[35] For example, the emphasis on the absolute unknowability of the divine nature characteristic of the apophatic tradition reached new heights in fourteenth-century German mysticism and gave birth to a range of negative and reduplicative terms based on God's absolute unity (*einicheit*) as the ground, such terms as *gruntlôs grunt* and *ein einig ein*. God as ground and as Absolute Unity is bare, free, empty, pure—totally without distinction (*underscheit*). Indistinction is God's distinguishing characteristic—hence the experimentation with the language of distinction and indistinction in the mysticism of the ground.

The master metaphor of *grunt* also sheds light on many of the metaphors favored by fourteenth-century Germanic mystics. God as *grunt* cannot be understood or adequately expressed but can be manifested through concrete images and symbols suggesting the limitless divine nature. Some of these were traditional, such as the vastness of the ocean (*mer*); others, such as the desert (*einode/wüeste*),[36] and also the abyss (*abgrúnd*),[37] were developed in new ways in MHG mystical texts. Desert and the abyss were used with regard to both the hiddenness of God and the depth of the human soul and thus were synonyms for the *grunt* as the fused identity of God and human.

A second range of language characteristic of the German Dominican thought that gave rise to the mysticism of Eckhart and his contemporaries centered on the investigation of God as pure intellect (*vernunfticheit*) and on human nature as the image (*bild*) of the divine intellect.[38] Pioneered by Albert the Great and his student Dietrich of Freiburg, the intellective emphasis of the German Dominicans employed both traditional language of the agent intellect and the various kinds of illumination present in the stages of knowing, as well as Dionysian language about the superiority of unknowing (*unwizzen*) in the return to God.

A third mystical language field that appears in a new light when seen from the perspective of the metaphor of the ground is the range of terms expressing interiorization, emptying, and decreation: the procedures by which one comes to realization of identity in the *grunt*. The need to turn from the external world of created beings and move into the inner reality of the soul, long a part of Western mystical traditions, received new stress in the fourteenth century. It is within the soul as the true image of God that humans achieve awareness of their union with the inner life of the Trinity, especially the eternal birth of the Word from the Father. Eckhart and others seized upon the birthing theme (*gebern/geburt*) and developed it to an extent not seen in previous Christian mysticism.[39]

More novel was the way in which the mysticism of the ground encouraged expressions of the need for total separation from created things and from the self as created—such terms as *abescheiden* (literally, cutting away, but usually rendered detaching), *gelassen* (letting go), and *durchbrechen* (breaking through), and the substantives derived from these verbs (*abgescheidenheit, gelassenheit, durchbrech*). Such emptying language was closely related to strong terms of annihilation, such as *entbilden* (dis-imaging), *entwerden* (un-becoming), and other expressions for mystical annihilation (e.g., *vernichten*).[40] Only through destruction of the created self can one attain identity in the ground.

These terms reflect only some of the rich vocabulary of the mysticism of Eckhart and his followers, but they suggest how the *grunt* metaphor reveals inner connections that might otherwise be overlooked. From the perspective of semantics and background, we can conclude that the relation of the MHG *grunt* to traditional Latin terms for the depth of the soul and the inner nature of God does help us understand aspects of the term, but such investigation cannot explain its function as a master metaphor exploding previous forms of mystical discourse and organizing mystical themes and terms, old and new, into new configurations. *Grunt* is more than a translation; it is a new creation whose significance can only be appreciated by exploring its contexts and meanings within the world of fourteenth-century German mysticism. As an explosive metaphor, *grunt* continues to break through old categories and invite us to perform our own breakthrough.

Some Masters of the Mysticism of the Ground

Meister Eckhart was the foremost, but by no means the only, master of the mysticism of the ground. To gain an idea of the language and themes of this form of mysticism, as well as to introduce some of its early spokesmen, we can look at the poem known as "The Sayings of the Twelve Masters" ("Sprüche der zwölf Meister"), which appears to date from about 1330.[41]

The fact that we turn to a poem for this access to mystical teaching is of significance.[42] Unlike in Islam, where mysticism and poetry have traditionally been closely allied, the use of poetry as a vehicle for mysticism in Christianity has had an up-and-down history. In Western Europe it is not until the twelfth and thirteenth centuries that we find a significant body of mystical poetry. The "Sayings of the Twelve Masters" (obviously meant to parallel the twelve prophets and twelve apostles as authority figures) is one of a group of over fifty poems of the fourteenth and fifteenth centuries that witness to the spread of the mysticism of the ground, especially in the female Dominican circles in which most of these verses seem to have been produced.[43] The poem is a summary of the teaching of a dozen mystical teachers and preachers, all but one Dominican.[44] We can surmise that it was probably composed by a Dominican nun used to hearing about these preachers.

The poem begins with Eckhart, whose message is summarized as follows:

> Meister Eckhart speaks of pure essence.
> He speaks one simple word, formless in itself.
> This is his meaning, nothing can be added or subtracted.
> Who thus can speak is a good master.[45]

The term *grunt* does not occur here, but the author uses typical Eckhartian language, such as "empty being" *(wesen blosz)* and "without form" *(formlos)*, which belongs to the vocabulary of the mysticism of the ground.

The second master cited is Dietrich of Freiburg (d. ca. 1320), the foremost philosopher among the German Dominicans of the era.[46] Dietrich had considerable influence on Eckhart. His surviving works are technical philosophical treatises,[47] but it is obvious from this poetic summary, as well as from other sources, that Dietrich was a noted preacher on mystical themes, but one whose sermons do not survive.[48] "Meister Dietrich," says the poem, "speaks of self knowledge. He places the soul's image in its selfhood. There it knows God in his self-identity *(isticheit)*."[49] The appearance of the term *isticheit*, a word also found in Eckhart,[50] indicates an important bond between the two thinkers. Dietrich also used the language of the *grunt*, according to another mystical poem:

> The high Meister Dietrich wants to give us a happy glow.
> He speaks in a pure fashion about "in principio" [John 1:1].
> About the flight of the eagle [John] he gives advice so sound.
> He wishes to drown the soul in the ground without ground.[51]

The third and fourth masters cited in the "Sayings of the Twelve Masters" are secondary figures among early fourteenth-century Dominican circles: Henry of Ettlingen, to whom Dietrich dedicated one of his treatises; and John of Dambach (d. 1372), who testified in Eckhart's favor during his trial. Both figures use language typical of the mysticism of the ground, such as the flowing forth of all creatures from God, and the indescribability of the soul as image of God. Some of the other masters cited are hard to identify. The fifth, from Regensburg, is said to speak wonderfully:

> He says that God's goodness is above all essence.
> He holds the highest degree in pure Oneness.
> Life and activity he sets in otherness.[52]

Albert the Great, the father of the German Dominican school of thought, had been bishop of Regensburg, and Berthold of Moosburg (d. ca. 1361) was a lector of theology in the convent there, but neither figure seems identical with this master. Perfectly clear, however, is the reference to the tenth master, the renowned preacher John Tauler (d. 1361):

> The Tauler from Strassburg speaks with simplicity:
> He who gets bare of self and of God, stands free from activity.
> There God acts out of himself; he is without a work.
> Bare is the image of the soul: there is no createdness.[53]

Here the notion of stripping the self of all things to allow God alone to work in the soul, an integral aspect of Tauler's preaching, is brought to the fore.

The word *grunt* itself appears in the verses concerning two of the other masters. Brother John of Müntz is described as young, but praised by all the masters. The poem says of him:

> Now we have heard that he wants to deprive himself;
> For this reason he has taken hold of the ground totally.
> And so he sets both living and working free.[54]

The ground also appears in the account of the eleventh master, the unidentified "Ros of the Bavarians":

> The Ros of the Bavarians speaks sincerely:
> Everything that is created is accidental.
> The spirit stands without accident in its simplicity;
> There it is unified in its self-identity.
> And more, it is free of both sense and desire;
> It is released into the ground, as if it did not exist.[55]

Grasping that all created things are nothing more than accidents of God, the only true reality, was a key aspect of the teaching of Eckhart and his followers. The human spirit as *imago Dei*, however, is identical with God in its inmost reality, self-identity, or *isticheit*. Someone who has come to this realization becomes free and released and sinks into the *grunt* as if no longer having any particular existence.

Several of the other unknown masters are also credited with teaching characteristic of the mysticism of the ground. The verses about "the one from Walthusen" use language similar to Eckhart, but highly controversial after his condemnation:

> He speaks the naked truth in an intellectual way.
> He has lifted himself up into the wild Godhead.
> There he found freedom without distinction.
> He speaks also: There is a light in the soul that cannot be
> Touched by any creature; this is its own way of being.
> There being shines in a similar way in simplicity.
> There he found freedom without distinction.[56]

The "wild Godhead" is reminiscent of the desert motif mentioned above. The light in the soul that cannot be touched by creatures is the Eckhartian spark, the uncreated something. The emphasis on freedom and lack of distinction comes close to the misunderstandings of Eckhartian teaching that Suso, Tauler, and others combatted, as we shall see in subsequent chapters.

"The Sayings of the Twelve Masters" is one of a number of poems dealing with the mysticism of the ground. The way in which the poem summarizes the teaching of a group of mystical teachers reflects the sense that contemporaries had of a distinctive movement, despite individual differences among its exponents. A similar collective approach can be found in other pseudo-Eckhartian literature, such as the prose aphorisms collected in "The Twelve Masters of Paris" ("Sprüche der zwölf Meister zu Paris").[57] It is also evident in the sermon collection known as the *Paradisus anime intelligentis*, which we shall examine more closely in chapter 7. While the mysticism of the ground does not exhaust the contributions of late medieval Germany to the history of mysticism, it forms a central thread in what was new and challenging.

CHAPTER 4

Meister Eckhart: Mystical Teacher and Preacher

I. The Historical and Intellectual Context of Eckhart's Mysticism

EW MYSTICS IN THE HISTORY of Christianity have been more influential and more controversial than the Dominican Meister Eckhart.[1] In his own day Eckhart commanded respect as a Paris *magister*, a high official in his order, and a popular preacher and spiritual guide. But the shock of his trial for heresy and the subsequent condemnation in 1329 of excerpts from his works by Pope John XXII cast a shadow over his reputation that has lasted to our own time.[2] Despite the papal censure, Eckhart, at least in his vernacular works, was widely read in the later Middle Ages.[3] After fading in the wake of the Reformation, interest in Eckhart was revived by German Romantics and Idealist philosophers in the nineteenth century and has grown in remarkable fashion in recent decades.[4] The critical edition of the Dominican's Latin and German works, begun in 1936 and now nearing completion, has provided a sound textual basis for scholarship without, of course, eliminating the conflict of interpretations.[5] The growing host of new translations and studies of Eckhart indicates that the medieval Dominican, for all the controversy surrounding him and the difficulty of understanding his message, continues to be a resource for all who seek deeper consciousness of God's presence in their lives.[6]

Eckhart's Life and Works[7]

Eckhart was born not long before 1260, probably at Tambach in Thuringia, into a family of the lower aristocracy. As with many medieval figures, we know little of his early life before April 18, 1294, when as a junior professor he preached the Easter sermon at the Dominican convent of St. Jacques in Paris.[8] Eckhart would have entered the Dominican order about the age of eighteen, presumably in the mid- to late 1270s. At one point in the Easter sermon he says, "Albert often used to say: 'This I know, as we know things, for we all know very little.'"[9] This reference to Albert the Great suggests that the young friar did part of his early studies of philosophy and theology at Cologne before Albert's death in 1280. At some time he was sent on to Paris for higher theological studies, and he was eventually promoted in the fall of 1293, to *baccalaureus*, that is, lecturer on the *Sentences* of Peter Lombard.[10]

Eckhart's period of study at Paris was a time of turmoil in the world of medieval philosophy and theology. The condemnation of 219 propositions by Stephen Tempier, archbishop of Paris, in 1277, had not only placed Thomas Aquinas's teaching under a cloud,[11] but had also led to a debate over the relation of philosophy to theology. Traditional disputes between Dominican and Franciscan theologians, such as the priority of intellect or will in final beatitude, were now exacerbated by a more fundamental disagreement over the legitimacy of the use of natural philosophy in theology. Throughout his life, Eckhart championed the Dominican position that philosophy and theology did not contradict each other and that philosophy was a necessary tool for Christian theology.[12] Both his historical situation and his own convictions, however, led Eckhart beyond Albert and Thomas Aquinas in claiming that not only was there no contradiction between philosophy and theology, but that, as he put it in his *Commentary on the Gospel of John*:

> What the philosophers have written about the natures and properties of things agree with it [the Bible], especially since everything that is true, whether in being or in knowing, in scripture or in nature, proceeds from one source and one root of truth. . . . Therefore, Moses, Christ, and the Philosopher [i. e., Aristotle] teach the same thing, differing only in the way they teach, namely as worthy of belief, as probable and likely, and as truth.[13]

This conviction is already evident in Eckhart's first works as a *baccalaureus theologiae*.

In the fall of 1294 Eckhart was called back to his Saxon homeland and made prior of his home convent at Erfurt. Eckhart's earliest vernacular work, *The Talks of Instruction* (*Die rede der underscheidunge*), dates from this time (ca. 1295–98).[14] This popular work (fifty-one manuscripts are known), modeled on Cassian's *Collations*, is a series of talks delivered to his Dominican brethren, but probably also intended for a wider audience. It consists of twenty-three chapters falling into three parts: chapters 1–8 deal primarily with denial of self through obedience; chapters 9–17, with various practices of the Christian life; and chapters 18–23 consider a series of questions, concluding with a long treatment of exterior and interior work. Against early views of the *Talks* as an uninteresting youthful work, recently scholars have seen the collection as an important key for understanding Eckhart's development.[15] In emphasizing the metaphysical basis of Christian ethical practice, Eckhart sounds a note that will be constant in his subsequent preaching and teaching. In eschewing all external practices of asceticism in favor of the internal self-denial of radical obedience understood as *abegescheidenheit,* or detachment, the Dominican introduces one of his characteristic themes. Finally, in identifying the intellect as the power in which the human being is informed by God, he announces the centrality of *intelligere/vernünfticheit* in his later mystical thought.

In 1302 Eckhart was called to return to Paris to take up the external Dominican chair of theology as *magister actu regens.* As was customary, his time in this position was brief, but the short *Parisian Questions* that survive from this academic year (1302–3) demonstrate that his thinking on divine and human *intelligere* had already led him to a position beyond those held by Albert, Thomas, and Dietrich of Freiburg.[16] When Eckhart says, "It does not so much seem to me that God understands because he exists, but rather that he exists because he understands,"[17] he has stood St. Thomas on his head in the service of a different form of metaphysics.[18] Eckhart's criticism of ontotheology (i.e., a metaphysic centering on being, or *esse*) marks an important stage in his intellectual development.[19] His teaching is rooted, in part at least, in his distinctive doctrine of analogy, which here appears for the first time. "In the things that are said according to analogy, what is in one of the analogates is not formally in the other. . . . Therefore, since all caused things are formally beings, God will not be a being in the formal sense."[20] Since *esse* here is being treated as "the first of created things," it cannot as such be in God. What is in God is the *puritas essendi,* which Eckhart identifies with *intelligere.* In these scholastic *quaestiones,* however, Eckhart does not yet develop a central theme of his subsequent teaching and preaching, namely, that it is in the human intellect understood as the ground that we find a relation to God that surpasses analogy.

The implications of this understanding of *intelligere* for the divine–human relation became evident in Eckhart's vernacular preaching after the summer of 1303, when he was called back to Germany to take up the position of provincial for the newly created Province of Saxonia, consisting of forty-seven convents in eastern and northern Germany and the Low Countries.

A number of sermons from the period of Eckhart's service as provincial (1303–11) can be found in the collection known as the *Paradise of the Intelligent Soul (Paradisus anime intelligentis)*, which was probably put together ca. 1330–40.[21] One purpose of this collection of sixty-four sermons was to serve as a handbook for learned preachers in their defense of Dominican views, especially that on the priority of intellect over will, against the Franciscans. The thirty-two Eckhart sermons found in the collection set the tone for a daring message about the relation between the human intellect and God. In the key piece, Eckhart's Pr. 9 (Par.an. no. 33), the master once again insists that God is above being and goodness and then goes on to exegete the "temple of God" referred to in Ecclesiasticus 50:7 as the intellect (*vernünfticheit*). "Nowhere does God dwell more properly," he says, "than in his temple, in intellect, . . . remaining in himself alone where nothing ever touches him; for he alone is there in his stillness."[22] Although Pr. 9 does not consider the relation between the intellect and the ground, another sermon in the collection, Pr. 98 (Par.an. no. 55), shows that Eckhart was already employing the term *grunt* in his vernacular preaching. In speaking of the soul's birth within the Trinity, Eckhart says:

> There she is so purely one that she has no other being than the same being that is his—that is, the soul-being. This being is a beginning of all the work that God works in heaven and on earth. It is an origin and a ground of all his divine work. The soul loses her nature and her being and her life and is born in the Godhead. . . . She is so much one there that there is no distinction save that he remains God and she soul.[23]

Thus, the major themes of Eckhart's preaching had clearly emerged in the first years of the fourteenth century.

It is difficult to know how many of Eckhart's surviving vernacular sermons date from this time. Along with the pieces found in the *Paradise of the Intelligent Soul*, Georg Steer has argued that the Christmas cycle of four "Sermons on the Eternal Birth" can be dated to between 1298 and 1305.[24] We know that some of Eckhart's most important Latin works come from his years as provincial, notably the *Sermons and Readings on the Book of Ecclesiasticus* that he delivered to the friars at chapter meetings.[25] This work is important for showing how the Dominican's metaphysics was already being presented in a dialectical way. The *Parisian Questions* had denied that *esse* understood as something creatable could be applied to God. In the *Sermons and Readings*, Eckhart, using the same doctrine of "reversing" analogy (i.e., what is predicated of God cannot be formally in creatures, and vice versa), ascribes transcendental *esse* to God in order to explore the "loaned" character of created *esse*. As he puts it in commenting on Ecclesiasticus 24:29

("They that eat me shall yet hunger"): "Every created being radically and positively possesses existence, truth, and goodness from and in God, not in itself as a created being. And thus it always 'eats' as something produced and created, but it always 'hungers' because it is always from another and not from itself."[26] Toward the end of this comment Eckhart moves into explicitly dialectical language. If hungering and eating are really the same, "He who eats gets hungry by eating, because he consumes hunger; the more he eats the more hungry he gets. . . . By eating he gets hungry and by getting hungry he eats, and he hungers to get hungry for hunger."[27] It is no accident that in this work we also find another keynote of Eckhart's thought, the identification of God as the "negation of negation" (n. 60).

The older view that the surviving parts of Eckhart's attempt at a new form of *summa*, what he called *The Three-Part Work* (*Opus tripartitum*), belonged to his second period as *magister* at Paris (1311–13) has now been abandoned on the basis of the manuscript discoveries of Loris Sturlese.[28] Large parts of what survives of the project must be dated to the first decade of the fourteenth century. Here is how Eckhart describes the work in the "General Prologue" he wrote to introduce it:

> The whole work itself is divided into three principal parts. The first is *The Work of General Propositions,* the second *The Work of Questions,* the third *The Work of Expositions.* The first work contains a thousand or more propositions divided into fourteen treatises corresponding to the number of terms of which the propositions are formed. . . . The second work, that of questions, is divided according to the content of the questions. . . . The third work, that of expositions, . . . is subdivided by the number and order of the books of the Old and New Testaments whose texts are expounded in it.[29]

It seems likely that it was during his service as provincial that Eckhart wrote the following sections: the "Prologue" to *The Book of Propositions* treating the basic term "Existence is God" (*esse est deus*);[30] the first, or literal, *Commentary on Genesis*;[31] and the *Commentary on the Book of Wisdom,* whose dialectical interests reflect the *Sermons and Lectures on Ecclesiasticus.*[32] It is difficult to be sure when the other surviving parts of *The Work of Expositions* were composed. These include the *Commentary on Exodus* with its important discussion of God as *esse* and on the names of God,[33] as well as the great *Commentary on the Gospel of John,* Eckhart's longest work.[34] At some stage the second part of *The Work of Expositions,* called *The Work of Sermons,* was also compiled.[35] This was meant to provide model sermons in Latin, showing young friars how to use scriptural texts for preaching.[36]

Eckhart says that he began the composition of *The Three-Part Work* "to satisfy as far as possible the desires of some of the diligent friars who already for a long time with pressing requests had often asked and compelled me to put in writing what they used to hear from me in lectures and other school activities, and also in preaching and daily conversations."[37] Therefore, Eckhart intended this work for such *fratres studiosi*, that is, those who were eager and able to absorb it.[38] He was well aware that "at first glance some of the following propositions, questions, and expositions will seem monstrous, doubtful, or false." But, as he went on to say, "it will be otherwise if they are considered cleverly and more diligently."[39] Eckhart also insisted that it was only on the basis of the philosophical truths demonstrated in *The Book of Propositions* that the subsequent solutions to disputed questions and the "rare new things" (*nova et rara*) found in his scriptural commentaries could be understood (n. 11).[40]

Eckhart's conviction about the conformity between reason and revelation, philosophy and theology, was the grounding insight of the project. At the beginning of the *Commentary on John* he put it this way: "In interpreting this Word [i.e., *In principio erat Verbum*] and everything else that follows my intention is the same as in all my works—to explain what the holy Christian faith and the two Testaments maintain through the help of the natural arguments of the philosophers."[41] Some would have it that texts such as this show that Eckhart was a philosopher, not really a theologian, and certainly not a mystic whose writings *must* be counter to rationality. Eckhart's life and thought, however, demonstrate that it is possible to be all three at one and the same time.

On May 14, 1311, the General Chapter held at Naples posted Eckhart back to Paris for a second stint as *magister*, a rare privilege hitherto granted only to Thomas Aquinas. Eckhart spent two academic years at Paris (autumn 1311 to summer 1313). Here he lived in the same house with the Dominican inquisitor William of Paris, who had been responsible for the execution of the beguine Marguerite Porete on June 1, 1310. Eckhart's use of Porete's mystical themes shows that he took a very different view of the beguine from that of his Dominican confrère. The stimulus of reading Porete and the encounter with beguines and Dominican nuns in Strassburg and Cologne were doubtless influential on Eckhart's turn toward more intensive vernacular preaching in the final decade and a half of his life, but Eckhart's preaching was always intended for the whole Christian community, not just for a spiritual elite.[42]

This is not to say that Eckhart's reaction to the mystical currents of his time, especially those pioneered by women, was uncritical.[43] His attitude toward many of the ideas put forth by beguines and others, especially their emphasis on visionary experience, expressed a scarcely veiled critique of some of the exaggerations he noted in contemporary mysticism. In addition, some of his later vernacular sermons were critical of the errors of the *secta libertatis spiritus* condemned by the Council of Vienne in 1311.[44] But Eckhart learned much from the women mystics, especially from Porete and probably also from Mechthild of Magdeburg, the German beguine whose visionary collection, *The Flowing Light of the Godhead,* was composed with the assistance of her Dominican confessor, Henry of Halle.[45] Even when he was in disagreement, Eckhart was far from an inquisitor. The purpose of his preaching was not to recriminate and condemn but to show believers, even those who might be in error, how to come to a deeper realization of union with God.[46]

Eckhart left Paris in the summer of 1313. Well over fifty at this time, he did not return to Erfurt, but was called to Strassburg in the Rhineland to serve as a special vicar for the Dominican master general.[47] Strassburg was a center of female piety, not only owing to its seven convents of Dominican nuns, but also for the many beguine houses found in the city and its environs. It was also a flash point for the debates over mysticism that were growing in the aftermath of the condemnation of the beguines at the Council of Vienne and the subsequent publication of a modified version of this decree in the *Clementina* canonical collection of 1317.[48] The bishop of the city, John I (1306–28), was a fierce opponent of heresy.[49]

In Strassburg Eckhart plunged more fully into a life devoted to pastoral care, preaching, and giving spiritual counsel than he had been able to do during his tenure as university professor and official of his order. Although only a few of Eckhart's sermons can be explicitly tied to the pastoral care of religious women (*cura monialium*), there is no reason to doubt that the mystical piety found among women was a significant inspiration for Eckhart during the last decade of his life. Evidence exists for visits to the Dominican convents of Katharinental and Ötenbach in the upper Rhine area during the time of his stay in Strassburg.[50] Eckhart also visited the nearby convent of Unterlinden in Colmar.

A considerable number of Eckhart's surviving MHG sermons appear to come from his time at Strassburg and the last years in Cologne. This fact reflects not only Eckhart's devotion to the care of souls but also a conscious effort to create a new vernacular theology that would, in the words of Thomas Aquinas, "hand on things understood through contemplation to others" (*contemplata aliis tradere*).[51] Marie-Anne Vannier has argued that the theme of the "nobleman," that is, the person who has attained divine sonship through the birth of the Word in the soul, emerged as central in sermons preached at Strassburg.[52]

In one of the sermons that appears to come from the last decade of his life, Eckhart summarized the message of his preaching under four themes:

> When I preach, I am accustomed to speak about detachment, and that a man should be free of himself and of all things; second, that a man should be formed again into that simple good which is God; third, that he should reflect on the great nobility with which God has endowed his soul . . . ; fourth, about the purity of the divine nature, for the brightness of the divine nature is beyond words. God is a word, a word unspoken.[53]

In another sermon, Pr. 6 on the text "The just will live forever" (Wis. 5:16), he put his message more succinctly: "Whoever understands the difference between Justice and the just person, understands everything I say."[54] In his earlier Pr. 9, discussed above, Eckhart was even more parsimonious about the essence of his preaching. Speaking about the nature of the word *quasi* as a *bîwort*, or ad-verb, he says: "I would now like to focus on the little word *quasi* which means 'as.' . . . This is what I focus on in all my sermons."[55] Thus, the essence of Eckhart's preaching can be reduced to understanding that the intellect is nothing but an *ad-verbum*, that is, something that has no existence apart from its inherence in the Word, in the same way that the just person (*iustus*) inheres in divine Justice.

The emphasis in the Strassburg sermons on the noble man and Justice and the just person (that is, the one in whom the birth of the Word has been achieved) suggests that Vannier's contention that the *Commentary on John* was written during this time in Eckhart's life may well be correct.[56] At the beginning of his long treatment of the Prologue to the Gospel, Eckhart once again takes up the issue of analogy. Although "in analogical relations what is produced derives from the source . . . [and] is of another nature and thus not the principle itself; still, as it is in the principle, it is not other in nature or supposit" [i.e., individual subsistence].[57] On the basis of this axiom, the Dominican engages in an extended exploration of the relationship between Unbegotten and Begotten Justice in the Trinity, as well as a further consideration of Divine Justice and the just person. Speaking formally, that is, from the perspective of the just, or noble man, *insofar as* he preexists in Divine Justice, Eckhart can say, "The just man in justice itself is not yet begotten nor Begotten Justice, but is Unbegotten Justice itself": that is, he is identical with God the Father.[58] More than twenty-five times in the course of the commentary Eckhart returns to the exploration of the relations between divine *Iustitia* and *iustus*, the just person.[59]

Loris Sturlese has suggested that Eckhart's move to Strassburg marked a decisive turn in his career. On the basis of the evidence of the new Prologue to *The Work of Expositions* in which Eckhart lays out his parabolic theory of exegesis, as well as the second Genesis commentary (*The Book of the Parables of Genesis*, probably composed during this time),[60] Sturlese claims that Eckhart abandoned the unfinished *Three-Part Work* to concentrate on a new project, *The Book of the Parables of Natural Things*.[61] Not all scholars are convinced that Eckhart totally abandoned the *Three-Part Work*.[62] One can, nevertheless, agree with Niklaus Largier that there was a "hermeneutical turn" in Eckhart's Latin works during the second decade of the fourteenth century, one in which the friar's exegesis began to concentrate more and more on bringing out the parabolical riches of the biblical text to serve as the foundation for his intensified vernacular preaching.[63]

In this period Eckhart also composed at least one further treatise in German, the so-called *Blessed Book* (*Liber Benedictus*), consisting of the *Book of Divine Consolation* and a sermon "On the Nobleman."[64] The *Book of Divine Consolation* tapped into the rich medieval tradition of consolatory literature dating back to Boethius's sixth-century *Consolation of Philosophy*. A manuscript witness in Eckhart's subsequent investigation for heresy connects the book with Queen Agnes of Hungary (ca. 1280–1364); although many scholars have seen it as a work sent to the queen in a time of need, there is nothing to tie the book specifically to Agnes. As Kurt Ruh says, "Eckhart's consolation is the consolation meant for anyone who wants to leave the world behind."[65] There is good reason to think that the book was written about 1318. As a vernacular expression of some of the most daring aspects of the Dominican's teaching, it played a prominent role in the accusations soon to be brought against him. Like the *Talks of Instruction*, the *Book* is divided into three sections. The first deals with "various true sayings" designed to "find complete comfort for all sorrows." The long second part details "thirty topics or precepts" for gaining great consolation, while the third part provides examples of what "wise men" have done and said in the midst of suffering.[66]

This *Book of Consolation* provides evidence concerning Eckhart's teaching and the opposition it was beginning to elicit in an era rife with fear of heresy. At the conclusion of the *Book*, the Dominican addresses possible complaints against his putting forth such deep matters to a general audience. First of all he defends himself (citing Augustine) against those who have already misunderstood him and attacked him. "It is enough for me," says Eckhart, "that what I say and write be true in me and in God."[67] Then he goes on to answer those who argue that such lofty things should not be presented to a general audience. Eckhart's response encapsulates his claim for the necessity of vernacular theology:

And we shall be told that one ought not to talk about or write such teachings to the untaught. But to this I say that if we are not to teach people who have not been taught, no one will ever be taught, and no one will ever be able to teach and write. For that is why we teach the untaught, so that they may be changed from uninstructed into instructed.[68]

Eckhart was soon to have direct experience of those who misunderstood him—and who also had the power to act on it.[69]

In late 1323 Eckhart left Strassburg for the Dominican house at Cologne with its noted *studium generale*, the intellectual home of the order of preachers in Germany.[70] Eckhart's time in Cologne was brief, but filled with activity and controversy. A number of his surviving sermons can be ascribed to the three years between his arrival and spring of 1327, when he left the city for the papal court at Avignon, the last way station of his life.[71] The drama of Eckhart's trial for heresy, initiated at Cologne and partly reconstructable through the documentation that remains to us, has always been a subject of interest and dispute. The critical edition of the *acta* relating to these events has clarified a number of points.[72]

Older suppositions that Eckhart's trial was a result of tensions between the Dominicans and Franciscans have long been put to rest. The accusations against Eckhart make sense within the context of fears concerning the Free Spirit heretics that had been increasing since the turn of the century. Henry II of Virneburg, the archbishop of Cologne (1304–32), was a noted opponent of heresy and a strong ally of Pope John XXII in his struggle against the emperor Lewis of Bavaria.[73] Some of Eckhart's enemies within the Dominican order played a role in the accusations against him, but Archbishop Henry would not have needed prompting to pursue heresy wherever he scented it.

It appears that the Dominican authorities already had qualms about Eckhart's preaching. The Dominican General Chapter held at Venice in the spring of 1325 had spoken out against "friars in Teutonia who say things in their sermons that can easily lead simple and uneducated people into error."[74] In light of these growing clouds, the friars of the Teutonia province tried to forestall a move against Eckhart by conducting their own investigation (ca. 1325–26), during which Eckhart responded to objections against his teaching in a lost document that satisfied his immediate superiors of his orthodoxy. During 1326, however, Archbishop Henry was preparing his own case. A list drawn up by two renegade Dominicans consisting of seventy-four excerpts from Eckhart's Latin and German works was presented to the archbishop sometime during that year.[75] A second list of passages taken from the vernacular sermons was also prepared sometime

before September 1326.[76] On September 26 of that year Eckhart appeared
before the diocesan inquisitorial commission to defend himself against the
charge of heresy.

Eckhart's defense (formerly called the *Verteidigungsschrift*) gives us an
important insight, not only into late medieval heresy trials, but also into his
self-understanding.[77] Eckhart's September rebuttal did not satisfy the
inquisitors. Sometime later that fall a third list, now lost, of extracts from his
Commentary on John was also compiled. Throughout the attack on his reputation and orthodoxy, Eckhart insisted on several premises underlying his
case. The first is that he could not be a heretic: "I am able to be in error,
but I cannot be a heretic, for the first belongs to the intellect, the second to
the will."[78] Thus, he always proclaimed himself willing to renounce publicly
anything found erroneous in his writing or preaching—he did, indeed,
admit that some of the articles were *erronea et falsa*, but never *heretica*. Second, Eckhart said that the often "rare and subtle" passages in his works had
to be explained in light of his good intentions and within the context of the
preaching genre. For instance, in responding to a series of extracts relating
to the birth of the Word in the soul, he says: "The whole of what was said is
false and absurd according to the imagination of opponents, but it is true
according to true understanding. . . ."[79] Eckhart often appealed to his good
intentions in presenting his hyperbolical preaching. For example, in
defending a daring statement from Pr. 6 ("God's being is my life; since my
life is God's being, God's essence is my essence"), he responds: "It must be
said that this is false and an error, as it sounds. But it is true, devout and
morally correct that the entire existence of the just person, insofar as he is
just, is from God's existence, though analogically."[80] The phrase "insofar as
he is just" (*inquantum iustus*) used here is crucial, both for understanding
Eckhart's defense and for the proper interpretation of his preaching and
teaching.

As a scholastic theologian, Eckhart was well aware of the distinction
between speaking of the relation between two things on a material, or
actual, level (i.e., insofar as they are different things) and on a formal level
(i.e., insofar as they possess the same quality). The foundation of his many
discussions of the relation of *iustitia* (Divine Justice or Rightfulness) and the
iustus (the "rightly-directed person") rests on this language of formal speaking, as is evident in the *Commentary on John*. The just person precisely *insofar
as he is just* (not in his total existential reality) must have everything that
Divine Justice possesses. However, when Eckhart presented his teaching
about the meaning of formal predication in the vernacular, the technical
Latin qualifications of the *formaliter/actualiter* distinction were often less

clear (though he does use the phrase "insofar as" in his German preaching from time to time). In his vernacular theology, Eckhart was less concerned with such distinctions precisely because of his recognition of the preacher's role to move and inspire. When taken to task, he tried to show his accusers that the message of his MHG preaching was not different from what could be found in his scholastic writings. It comes as no surprise, then, that the first principle Eckhart invoked in introducing his Cologne defense was that of formal predication. As he put it: "To clarify the objections brought against me, three things must be kept in mind. The first is that the words 'insofar as,' that is, a reduplication, exclude from the term in question everything that is other or foreign to it, even according to reason."[81] Not to understand the *inquantum* principle is not to understand Eckhart.

Apart from the intellectual resources Eckhart called upon to counter his critics, there were also institutional and canonical ones. He announced at the beginning of the Cologne process, "according to the exemption and privileges of my order, I am not bound to appear before you or to answer charges."[82] The Dominicans were a canonically exempt order, that is, free of episcopal control and directly under the pope. Eckhart rightly claimed that only the pope, or the University of Paris as his delegate, had the power to investigate a *magister theologiae* for heresy. To the pope he had appealed, and to the pope he would go.

Throughout the trying months of late 1326 Eckhart had the support of the local Dominican authorities. However, the warnings against dangerous preaching given by the General Chapters of 1325 and 1328 indicate that the international leadership of the order had distanced itself from Eckhart without attacking him personally.[83] Eckhart asked for "dimissory" letters allowing the case to be forwarded to the papal court at Avignon. On February 13, 1327, he also preached a sermon in the Dominican church at Cologne. At the end, he had his secretary read out a public protestation in Latin of his innocence and willingness to retract any errors. Eckhart himself translated the text into German, so that his audience, the vernacular public whom he had served so well, could understand it.[84] This was an important act. By *publicly* proclaiming himself willing to retract any and all errors, Eckhart effectively forestalled any attempt to try him as a heretic. Sometime in the spring of that year, Eckhart, accompanied by other ranking members of the *Teutonia* province, began his journey to Avignon.

Our knowledge of the last year of Eckhart's life is fragmentary. Pope John XXII appointed two commissions to investigate the charges against the Dominican master. We have the names of the commissioners, including Cardinal William Peter de Godino, who was probably a former student of

Eckhart. We also know that the commissions reduced the unwieldy body of some 150 suspect articles down to a modest 28. The important document known as the *Votum Avenionense* gives us, in scholastic fashion, these articles, the reasons why they are judged heretical, Eckhart's defense of each, and the rebuttal of the commissioners. Although it is a summary of his case, rather than his own production, this document (probably dating from late 1327) allows us a final opportunity to hear Eckhart.

Eckhart's Avignon defense summarizes many themes that had been part of his preaching for more than three decades. For example, with regard to what became article 13 of the subsequent bull of condemnation ("Whatever is proper to the divine nature, all that is proper to the just and divine man"), the *Votum* says:

> He defends this article, because Christ is the head and we the members; when we speak, he speaks in us. Also, in Christ there was so great a union of the Word with flesh that he communicated his own properties to it, so that God may be said to suffer and a man is the creator of heaven. To Christ himself it properly belongs to be called "a just person insofar as he is just," for the term "insofar as" is a reduplication that excludes everything alien from the term [being employed]. In Christ there is no other hypostasis save that of the Word; but in other humans this is verified more or less.[85]

The *Votum* makes clear that in the case of the twenty-eight articles still under investigation, the commission was not convinced by the Dominican's explanations. However, it also confirms that a basic shift had taken place in Eckhart's case—he was no longer on trial as a heretic, but was being investigated for the censure of various articles he had once taught, which, *if judged heretical,* he had promised to renounce.

The next secure date in the process comes on April 30, 1328, when the pope wrote to Henry of Cologne to assure him that the case against Eckhart was moving ahead, although the accused was dead. It was long thought that the date of Eckhart's death was lost, but Walter Senner discovered that a seventeenth-century Dominican source noted that Eckhart was remembered in German convents on January 28,[86] so we can surmise that he died on that day in 1328. Finally, on March 27, 1329, Pope John issued the bull "In agro dominico," an unusual step, since Eckhart was already dead and he was not being personally condemned as a heretic.[87] Doubtless the pope's fear of growing mystical heresy and pressure from his ally Henry II had convinced him to bring the case to a definitive conclusion. It has often been said that John XXII tempered the condemnation of Eckhart's articles by restricting the circulation of the bull to the province of Cologne, but Robert E. Lerner has shown that this was not the case—a copy of the document was also sent to Mainz, and there is evidence of a vernacular version in Strassburg.[88] Pope John obviously meant to quash Eckhart's influence decisively, as the defamatory language used in the preface to the text clearly shows.

The bull witnesses to papal fears of Eckhart's vernacular theology by expressly noting that his errors were "put forth especially before the uneducated crowd in his sermons." Strangely enough, although the Avignon *votum* treated all twenty-eight articles as heretical, "In agro dominico" divides the list into three groups: the first fifteen containing "the error or stain of heresy as much from the tenor of their words as from the sequence of their thoughts"; a second group of eleven that are judged "evil-sounding and very rash and suspect of heresy, though with many explanations and additions they might take on or possess a catholic meaning"; and two appended articles, which Eckhart had denied saying (though they in fact reflect passages in his works), also judged heretical. We do not know if the confusing distinction between the heretical and the merely dangerous articles was introduced by the pope himself or at some other stage in the process. Finally, at the end of the bull the pope absolves Eckhart himself of heresy, noting that on the basis of a public document, "the aforesaid Eckhart . . . professed the catholic faith at the end of his life and revoked and also deplored the twenty-six articles, which he admitted that he had preached, . . . *insofar as* they could generate in the minds of the faithful a heretical opinion, or one erroneous and hostile to the faith." So Eckhart, even at the end of his life, maintained his integrity through the invocation of an *inquantum* that the pope either let pass or did not catch.

Perspectives for Reading Eckhart

Eckhart's condemnation is the most serious, but by no means the only, reason why he has been controversial down through the centuries. In the late nineteenth century, Eckhart scholarship shifted the debate away from the question of heresy to the coherence of his philosophical and theological thought in relation to the triumphant Neo-Thomism of post–Vatican I Catholicism.[89] Various judgments were made during the course of the twentieth century about the coherence of his thought, often from alien perspectives. In recent decades there has been increasing effort to try to understand Eckhart on his own terms—what was he trying to do and how successful was he in accomplishing his aims? The attempt to grasp Eckhart from within, however, has by no means led to agreement about the fundamental nature of his teaching.

   Important controversies still divide Eckhart scholarship, such as the
debate about whether the Dominican is to be thought of as a mystic or as a
philosopher-theologian.[90] Over the past four decades a number of interpreters have denied that Eckhart should be called a mystic, insisting that he
should be seen as a only a theologian or philosopher.[91] There are two fundamental problems with the position of those who deny that Eckhart is a
mystic. The first is the either-or mentality that tries to divide what Eckhart
sought to keep together; the second is an inadequate view of mysticism.
Eckhart was both a learned philosopher-theologian and a master of the spiritual life, a *lebmeister*. Although the term "mystic" is a modern creation,[92] as
used in this history its meaning is not far from what was intended by the
MHG *lebmeister*. Furthermore, contemporary scholars of mysticism, whatever their disagreements, do not think of mysticism as a private, emotional,
essentially ecstatic, and irrational mode of religious life, an inadequate view
of mysticism held by those who deny that Eckhart was a mystic. Few
thinkers have valued the unity of truth more than Meister Eckhart.[93] We do
him a real disservice if we try to divide and separate what he sought to keep
together. In order to get a proper perspective for reading Eckhart, then, we
must investigate how the Dominican conceived of the inner harmony of
reason and faith, philosophy and theology, thought and practice.
   All scholastic theologians believed that there could be no *conflict* between
faith and reason because each has its source in the one divine Truth. Eckhart, as we have seen, went further, claiming that Moses, Aristotle, and
Christ "teach the same thing, differing only in the way they teach" (In Ioh.
n. 185).[94] This suggests that there is no difference in the *content* of philosophy and theology, though there is certainly a difference in the way in which
philosophers and theologians grasp the truth of their respective disciplines.
Thus, philosophy as a discipline is not limited to what thinkers like Thomas
Aquinas called natural truths about God (e.g., God's existence), but it
includes teachings like the Trinity and the incarnation, which Eckhart saw
as fully rational because the philosopher could find evidence for them in
the natural world. For Eckhart, creation itself reveals that God is Trinity and
that the Second Person of the Trinity became flesh for our salvation.
   Does Eckhart's statement about Aristotle and Christ teaching "the same
thing" mean that the content of pagan philosophy and what the Christian
philosopher teaches is identical *in all cases*? A number of texts militate
against this view. In these passages Eckhart contrasts the "pagan masters
who knew only in a natural light" with "the words of the sacred masters
who knew in a much higher light."[95] In Pr. 101 he says that those who considered the soul's nobility on the basis of their "natural intelligence"

(*natiurlîche vernunft*) were never able to enter into or to know the ground of the soul, which is attainable only by unknowing.[96] In these passages Eckhart is talking about the naked intellect, which gives access to the ground where the soul is finally satisfied with "the Single One" (*dem ainigen ain*).[97] This suggests that with regard to the core of Eckhart's teaching, that concerning the ground of the soul, the natural light of reason needs the assistance of a higher illumination, a form of not-knowing (*unwizzen*), or learned ignorance (*unbekante bekantnisse*), in order to grasp the deepest truth. But other texts indicate that Eckhart did not exclude all pagan masters from this deeper knowledge. In Pr. 28, for example, he has remarkable praise for "Plato, the great cleric" (*Plâtô, der grôze pfaffe*). Eckhart ascribes to the ancient philosopher knowledge of "something pure that is not of this world," something out of which "the eternal Father derives the plenitude and the depth (*abgrunt*) of all his deity." The Father bears this here [i.e., in us], so that we are the very Son of God, "and his birth is his indwelling and his indwelling is his outward birth."[98] Although Eckhart does not employ the term *grunt* here, it is clear that he is speaking about Plato having an awareness of the unity of ground, something that in Pr. 101 he had denied to other "pagan masters."

These texts raise the question of whether Eckhart thought that there was a realm of theological truth distinct from natural philosophy. More precisely, does his teaching on the *grunt* belong to theology or to philosophy? I believe it belongs to both. The evidence of the passage from Pr. 28, as well as Eckhart's whole way of arguing in the scriptural commentaries, speaks against any essential difference. At the outset of the *Commentary on John*, for example, he says that the purpose of the work is "to explain what the holy Christian faith and the two testaments maintain through the help of the natural arguments of the philosophers."[99] The prologue of the *Book of the Parables of Genesis* echoes this, saying that the second Genesis commentary seeks "to show that what the truth of holy scripture parabolically intimates in hidden fashion agrees with what we prove and declare [i.e., philosophically] about matters divine, ethical, and natural."[100] Eckhart believed that there was no gap or difference between what scripture teaches and what "unknowing philosophy" proves and declares. Nor does the divine light that enables thinkers to grasp *docta ignorantia* need to be restricted to Christians. The highest form of philosophy investigates and shows the full harmony of all three categories of truths: *divina-naturalia-moralia* (i.e., divine matters, or theology, including the Trinity; natural philosophy; and ethics).[101] It also teaches natural reason's insufficiency to attain the ground unless it surrenders itself to the action of the divine light.[102]

Eckhart's notion of the conformability of the Bible and philosophy did not make the Bible into a philosophical book (because its teaching is presented *parabolice* not *demonstrative*), but it did mean that commentary on scripture and preaching the word of God could be presented in philosophical form. For Eckhart philosophy is not the basis of belief, but its employment in exegesis is a vital part of the preacher's calling. In the *Commentary on John* he says: "Just as it would be presumption and recklessness not to believe unless you have understood, so too it would be sloth and laziness not to investigate by natural arguments and examples what you believe by faith."[103] For Eckhart, scriptural commentary serves as the instrument for the creation of a philosophico-theological exposition of the deepest mysteries of God, nature, and ethics, an exposition that, in turn, provides the material for Eckhart's novel form of biblical preaching. Though he had once planned a systematic presentation of his thought in the *Three-Part Work*, the bulk of his surviving writings indicates that he came to the conclusion that his audience was best served through his exegesis and preaching rather than system-building. As Niklaus Largier has argued, this shift suggests that Eckhart believed that the goal of attaining true subjectivity, that is, mystical union, was best realized within a hermeneutical situation in which the exegete-preacher and the attentive hearer "break through" the surface of the biblical word to reach the hidden meaning that negates both ordinary reason and the created self.[104] Like the masters of monastic mysticism, but in his own key, Eckhart believed that mystical consciousness was fundamentally hermeneutical, that is, it is found in the act of hearing, interpreting, and preaching the Bible.

The importance of Eckhart the preacher has long been recognized; deeper investigation of Eckhart the exegete has only recently begun.[105] Like many other biblical interpreters of the patristic and medieval periods, Eckhart was less concerned with presenting a theory of exegesis than in actually doing the work of interpretation, but a brief consideration of some programmatic remarks of the Dominican will highlight his distinctive mode of biblical preaching.

Eckhart's exegesis was both traditional and innovative. The traditional aspect of the Dominican's interpretation is seen in his adherence to spiritual hermeneutics, that is, the conviction that the literal sense of the biblical text is only the starting point for grasping the inner meaning of what God wants to convey to humans.[106] The original character of Eckhart's exegesis (most evident in his practice) resides in the creative way he went about forging a spiritual exegesis that was both philosophical and mystical. The philosophical side of the friar's hermeneutic was deeply indebted to Maimonides, whose *Guide of the Perplexed* in its Latin form (*Dux neutrorum*) provided Eckhart with both a model and a source for many individual readings.[107] The mystical aspect of the Dominican's interpretation was deeply influenced by the great exegetes of the Christian tradition, Augustine above all. Despite his debt to others, Eckhart's form of mystical hermeneutics is very much his own.[108]

For Eckhart, the profundity of the Bible, indeed, of every text in the Bible, means that it contains an inexhaustible fecundity of truths.[109] Citing Augustine, he says that it is the person "who is bare of spirit and seeks the sense and truth of scripture in the same spirit in which it was written or spoken" who will best understand it.[110] To seek for the truth of the Bible in the divine spirit is the first principle of Eckhart's hermeneutics. The truth that is sought is *the Truth*, that is, the Divine Word himself; for Eckhart the entire meaning of the Bible is christological. "No one can be thought to understand the scriptures," he says, "who does not know how to find its hidden marrow—Christ, the Truth."[111] It is only in and through Christ that the verities hidden under the scriptural *parabolae* (i.e., stories and figurative expressions) can be discerned. These truths, as Eckhart lists them in his Prologue to the *Book of the Parables of Genesis*, include the properties of the divine nature which "shine out in every natural, ethical, and artistic work." In other words, what is *intimated* in the parables is also what was to have been *demonstrated* in the other parts of the *Three-Part Work*.

Even those accustomed to the many meanings given to individual biblical texts by earlier exegetes will be surprised at the plethora of readings Eckhart draws out of biblical passages such as the first verse of John's Gospel or Wisdom 8:1.[112] It is not just the number of readings, but the seemingly arbitrary character of many of them that surprises the modern reader. Eckhart himself adverted to this in the General Prologue to the *Three-Part Work* in a text already cited: "Note that some of the following propositions, questions, and interpretations at first glance will appear monstrous, doubtful, or false; but it will be otherwise if they are considered cleverly and more diligently" (Prol.gen. n. 7). The Dominican deliberately adopted a strategy designed to shock the reader, basing his excessive mode of exegesis on the intention of the biblical text itself, which often speaks "excessively." At the end of the *Commentary on John*, noting the hyperbolic claim of John 21:25 that the whole world could not hold all the books that would describe Christ's signs, he says:

> Such a mode of speaking, that is, excessively, properly belongs to the divine scriptures. Everything divine, as such, is immense and not subject to measure.

. . . The excellence of divine things does not allow them to be offered to us uncovered, but they are hidden beneath sensible figures.[113]

In the Latin commentaries, where Eckhart deals with the Vulgate text, the various interpretations he gives are mostly the product of a philosophico-theological impulse to investigate every implication of a word or passage. The same impulse is found in many of the German sermons, but in the vernacular works, because there was no fixed MHG version of the Bible, Eckhart also employs expansions, re-punctuations, and interpretive translations or rewritings in order to bring out the inner meaning of passages.[114] There is a sense in which Eckhart, especially in the MHG sermons, plays with the biblical text.[115] The Dominican consciously adopted this fluid and playful hermeneutic for the use of his audience. In the second prologue to the *Work of Expositions* he says: "The main passages are often expounded in many ways so that the reader can take now this explanation, now another, one or many, as he judges useful."[116] The more multiple and excessive the readings, the more useful: this is the key principle of Eckhart's exegesis.

Eckhart's readings are likely to seem especially strange to modern readers concerned with the narrative development of the biblical story and its historical *Sitz im Leben*. His procedure is the reverse. Even by the standards of traditional spiritual exegesis, Eckhart shows little interest in the biblical story line.[117] Rather, he dehistoricizes and decontextualizes passages into sentences, fragments, or even individual words that he then recombines with other biblical passages in a dense web of intertextuality through a system of cross-referencing that is one of the main characteristics of his hermeneutics.[118] This too was a conscious choice. In one place he says: "In explaining a passage under discussion many other texts of the canon of scripture are often brought forward, and all these passages can be explained in their proper places from this one, just as it is now explained through them."[119] Intertextuality of this sort was not new, but Eckhart's de-historicizing form of it fits his "principial" way of knowing: that is, seeing all things from the divine perspective, the "now" (*nû/nunc*) of eternity in which all words and expressions are one in the eternal Word. For Eckhart such multiplicity does not introduce confusion, because all meanings come from one and the same source.

In line with the traditions of spiritual exegesis, Eckhart insisted that all biblical texts have two levels, one according to "the plain meaning and surface of the letter" (*secundum planum et superficiem litterae*), the other which "is hidden beneath the shell" (*latet sub cortice*).[120] In investigating the *sub cortice* meanings, however, the Dominican shows no interest in the traditional enumeration of three spiritual senses (allegorical, tropological, anagogical), and even though he cites with approval Maimonides' distinction of two kinds of biblical *parabolae*, he does not use it in practice.[121] In his exegesis, as everywhere in his thought, Eckhart is concerned with the basic opposition between inner and outer. Typically, however, Eckhart's seemingly clear distinction between outer shell and inner kernel, between letter and "mystical meaning" (*mystica significatio*),[122] soon becomes unstable and paradoxical both in theory and in practice.

In his comments on exegesis in the prologue to the *Book of the Parables of Genesis* Eckhart takes up the issue of the relation between the literal and the hidden meanings of scripture. Citing Augustine's discussion of the variety of true meanings that an expositor can gather from scripture (even meanings that were not known to the human author), Eckhart advances the claim: "Since the literal sense is that which the author of a writing intends, and God is the author of holy scripture, . . . then every true sense is a literal sense. It is well known that every truth comes from the Truth itself; it is contained in it, derived from it, and is intended by it."[123]

The import of this statement is that the spiritual meaning has become a new form of infinitely malleable letter. The outer and the inner have traded places, or even merged. As Donald Duclow puts it, ". . . when the letter thus fuses with its multiple meanings, the very boundary between text and interpretation becomes indistinct."[124] By means of this procedure we might say that the exegete has become the text in the sense that it is he who provides the meaning adjudged as truly divine. Even more radically, the mystical interpreter has become one with, that is, indistinct from God, the author of the Bible. If the main concern of Eckhart's exegesis, as we have seen, is to "break through the shell" of literalism to reach the infinite inner understandings that become a new letter, exegesis of necessity implodes upon itself. It is the very nature of the Dominican's exegesis and his biblical preaching to encourage such a breaking-through that fuses both the text and the self into divine indistinction.

In sermon 51 Eckhart highlights this self-naughting hermeneutics by proclaiming that "all likenesses must be broken through" (*so muessent die gleychnuss alle zerbrechenn*), that is, all images and discrete meanings must eventually be destroyed as the exegete pursues his task. This sermon contains one of the Dominican's most interesting discussions of the nature of scriptural images and their relation to the Father's "own Image, abiding in himself in the ground." Nature, Eckhart says, teaches us that we must use images and likenesses, "this or that," to point to God. But since God is not a "this or that," in order to plunge back into the divine source and become the one Son, all images must be let go. Eckhart expresses the necessity for this exegetical iconoclasm in a way that subverts the traditional teaching about penetrating the external letter to reach an inner meaning or form of discrete knowledge. As Susanne Köbele has shown, Eckhart is talking here about two stages of movement beyond the surface rather than the traditional single movement from letter to spirit:

> I have said before the shell must be broken through and what is inside must come out, for if you want to get at the kernel you must break the shell. And also, if you want to find nature unveiled, all likenesses must be broken through, and the further you penetrate, the nearer you will get to the essence. When the soul finds the One, where all is one, there she will remain in the Single One.[125]

"Breaking through" and "penetrating into indistinction of the Single One," fundamental motifs of Eckhart's mystical preaching, are also the essence of his hermeneutics. Eckhart is essentially an apophatic exegete.[126]

Eckhart the exegete and Eckhart the preacher are inseparable in the sense that his preaching always took its departure from a biblical text found in the liturgy and therefore must be understood within this biblico-liturgical context. The Dominican's convents at Erfurt, Paris, Strassburg, and Cologne were not isolated monastic communities, but urban houses for preachers charged with the *cura animarum*. In their spacious Gothic churches, such as those that still survive in Erfurt and Cologne, Dominicans like Eckhart served the northern European townfolk in an age when the liturgy played a role in society almost impossible to conceive today.

In recent years Eckhart scholarship has profited from several important investigations of the context, content, and dynamics of the Dominican's mode of preaching.[127] Just as Bernard of Clairvaux's mysticism reached its acme in his *Sermons on the Song of Songs*, Meister Eckhart's place in the history of mysticism is tied to the homilies he preached both to religious and to laity. As Kurt Ruh puts it: "Eckhart's German preaching without a doubt stands at the middle of his creativity. He understood himself more as preacher than as professor and scholar."[128] To be a preacher was not only the essential task of the religious order to which he belonged, but it was a vocation that for Eckhart called for a special relation to Christ: "Thus the preacher of the Word of God, which is 'God's Power and God's Wisdom' (1 Cor. 1:24), ought not exist and live for himself, but for the Christ he preaches."[129]

Eckhart's sermons were liturgical actions presented to worshiping communities, mediated by the texts of the feasts of the church's calendar, and, above all, by the fundamental purpose of the Eucharist itself—uniting

Christ and his body through the re-presentation of the Lord's saving death. Joachim Theisen, whose book *Predigt und Gottesdienst* shows how the liturgical readings of the Dominican missal illuminate the friar's surviving sermons, summarizes Eckhart's preaching program thus: "It is the fundamental intention of his preaching to point out the actuality of the mystery that is being celebrated and to draw the community into this actuality."[130] This helps explain why Eckhart had little interest in the historical reality of the events of Christ's life in his homilies. It is the presence of the Word made flesh *here and now* that is his concern.

Just as the hidden and silent divine mystery present in the Father expressed himself in speaking the eternal Word, so too the preacher takes as his task "re-speaking" the Word of Truth present in the biblical texts of the liturgy so that the community can hear the Word and follow it back into "the simple ground, into the quiet desert, into which distinction never gazed . . ." (Pr. 48). Reiner Schürmann spoke of the "ontological meaning" of Eckhart's preaching: that is, how the very act of preaching, as creation of the word to be heard by others so that they too may find the source from whence the word is formed, mirrors the "event character" of Eckhart's metaphysical view of the God–world relation.[131] Bruce Milem has shown how Eckhart does not so much preach doctrine as seek to involve his audience in a complex interpretive exercise in which "[t]he sermons' self-referential quality opens the door to thinking about the relation between the sermons and the divine truths they articulate."[132]

The preacher, however, cannot convey the message that lies hidden behind all words, and even beyond the Divine Word himself in the depths of deity, unless he has participated in this inner speaking, that is, unless he speaks "out of the ground" of God.[133] In his *Sermons and Lectures on Ecclesiasticus* Eckhart makes this clear in giving his own etymology of Paul's command to Timothy: "Preach the word" (2 Tim. 4:2). "'Preach,' as it were, 'say beforehand,' that is, first say within. Or 'preach,' that is, 'say outwardly,' or 'bring out from within' so that 'your light may shine before men' (Matt. 5:16)."[134] Eckhart invites his audience to hear what he has heard and to become one with him in the one ground—"If you could look upon this with my heart," he once said, "you would well understand what I say; for it is true, and it is Truth's own self that says it."[135] This is a bold claim for any preacher to make, but Eckhart does not advance it on the basis of his individual authority or his own learning; he makes it out of the oneness of divine Truth.[136] In one of the few places where he speaks of his own consciousness of God, Eckhart makes it clear that he thinks of his own union with God as a grace given for all: "I will tell you how I think of people: I try to forget myself and everyone and to merge myself, for them, in Unity. May we abide in Unity, so help us God. Amen."[137]

Eckhart's vernacular preaching has been studied as one of the most interesting examples of how mystical language explores and often explodes ordinary forms of speech. Many insightful studies have been written about Eckhart's use of language.[138] Some reflection on Eckhart's strategies of mystical discourse are important for framing the proper perspective for reading him. The variety of forms of language that Meister Eckhart makes use of in his vernacular preaching defies easy summary. His creativity in using speech to overcome speech and lead it back into the divine ground can be best appreciated by taking sermons as wholes and subjecting them to careful literary and theological analysis.[139] There have also been a number of attempts to summarize Eckhart's basic linguistic techniques. Alois M. Haas, for example, singles out paradox, oxymoron, and negation as general *modi loquendi* of mystical speech and also studies the particular forms these take in what he called Eckhart's *Logosmystik*.[140] On the basis of a treatment of three representative sermons, Burkhard Hasebrink analyzes Eckhart's "appellative speech" (*inzitative Rede*), that is, the way in which his sermons both invite the hearer to become one with the message and yet seek to destroy formal meaning through mystical *gelassenheit*.[141] Michael A. Sells explores Eckhart's apophatic unsaying of a substantialist deity and of gender essentialism in his *Mystical Languages of Unsaying*.[142]

The details, or micro-techniques, of Eckhart's way with language have also been the subject of study. Frank Tobin casts light on many of the particular strategies that made Eckhart's preaching so fascinating to his original audience, and still today, even in translation, make reading him an arresting experience.[143] Just a few of Eckhart's strategies can be mentioned here by way of illustration. For example, he often gives the same word (e.g., *eigenschaft, berüeren*) shifting, or opposing, meanings.[144] Some of these significations were already present in MHG vocabulary; at other times the Dominican was stretching the envelope, creating new fields of meaning, as in the case of *grunt;* or forging neologisms, such as *isticheit*, to express mystical themes in the vernacular. Eckhart's relentlessly apophatic discourse is found not only in the larger semantic structures of his discourse, but in his word formation, with its frequent use of negative particles and prepositions (e.g., *un-/ab-/ent-/über-/-los/âne/sunder*). Tobin notes such procedures as "accumulation, antithesis, parallelism, and hyperbole" that Eckhart frequently employs.[145] Another common trope is chiasmus (i.e., using two or more words or phrases and then repeating them in reversed order), something especially useful for expressing the Dominican's dialectical view of the God–world relationship.[146]

One final issue concerning Eckhart's use of language has been much discussed, namely, the relation of the Latin and German aspects of his mystical discourse.[147] The debate over the relationship between the Latin Eckhart and the German Eckhart shows no signs of going away, though it has become more nuanced in recent years.[148] Older formulations, pitting the Latin scholastic against the German mystic, or Eckhart's Latin "ontological" writings against his German "ethico-mystical" works, no longer hold up; but this has not meant an end to disagreements. On the one hand, there are those who minimize the difference between the German and the Latin.[149] On the other hand, many Germanists maintain a distinctive worth (*Eigenwert*) to Eckhart's German sermons. Thus, Kurt Ruh speaks of "the greater spiritual value [*der spirituelle Mehrwert*] of the vernacular";[150] and Susanne Köbele proclaims, "The new content of mystical expression [in the thirteenth century] is closely bound up with the medium of the vernacular."[151] Burkhard Hasebrink, however, advances the case for a more precise evaluation of the intimate bond between Latin and MHG in Eckhart's writings characterized as a "shifting of boundaries" (*Grenzverschiebung*).[152] We should also remember the sage comment of Alois Haas: "Eckhart has a theology of the Word, not a theology of the German language."[153]

In relating the Latin and the German sides of Eckhart it is important to steer a course between Scylla and Charybdis. On the one hand, we have to avoid any crude opposition between the creativity of the MHG preacher and the more traditional and technical scholastic thinker, if only because Eckhart's mysticism was daring both in Latin and in German. (It is an undisputable fact that in the Cologne and Avignon proceedings Eckhart was taken to task for *both* his Latin and his vernacular works.) On the other hand, we cannot deny the significant opportunity offered to the Dominican by what Kurt Ruh has called the *kairos*, or "decisive moment,"[154] of MHG at the turn of the fourteenth century. Above all, we must try to overhear the conversation between Latin and German within Eckhart himself in order to reconstruct the fullness of his thought. What is often overlooked is the striking fact that Meister Eckhart is the *only* major figure in the history of Christian mysticism in whom we can observe the full dynamics of the interplay between Latin mysticism (almost a millennium old by the time he wrote) and the new vernacular theology (still aborning, despite the achievements of the thirteenth century).

II. Foundations of Eckhart's Mysticism

The Ground as Fused Identity[155]

As argued in chapter 3, the master metaphor of the *grunt* provides a vantage point from which to view the distinctive nature of Eckhart's mysticism and its influence on many mystics who came after him. Although *grunt* had been used by some of the vernacular mystics before him, it was Eckhart who first employed this term to bring to speech a new understanding of mystical identity. But how did the preacher actually use the language of the ground in his MHG works? A study of some of the contexts and meanings of Eckhart's language of the ground is crucial for grasping how this simple word is at the heart of his mysticism.

At the conclusion of Pr. 42, Eckhart addresses his hearers with the following words: "Now know, all our perfection and our holiness rests in this: that a person must penetrate and transcend everything created and temporal and all being and go into the ground that has no ground. We pray our dear Lord God that we may become one and indwelling, and may God help us into the same ground. Amen."[156] In this passage note that Eckhart does not qualify the *gruntlôs grunt* as either God's or the soul's. It belongs to both God and human univocally in fused identity. This is why elsewhere he insists, "If anyone wishes to come into God's ground and his innermost, he must first come into his own ground and his innermost, for no one can know God who does not first know himself."[157]

This fused identity helps us to see why it is preferable to speak of the "mysticism of the ground" rather than the "mysticism of the ground of the soul," though Eckhart often speaks of the *grunt der sêle*.[158] The essential point, as Eckhart put it, is that "God's ground and the soul's ground is *one* ground."[159] It is not because *either* the soul is grounded in its essential reality, *or* God in his, but because they are *both grounded in the same ground* that Eckhart and his followers found the language of the ground so useful.[160] As he expressed it in Sermon 5b: "Here God's ground is my ground and my ground is God's ground. Here I live out of what is mine, just as God lives out of what is his."[161] It is true that Eckhart often speaks of God "penetrating" and "being in" the soul's ground, thus indicating that on one level there is an analogical relationship between the two realities.[162] But, as Otto Langer has shown, texts such as those cited above indicate that on the deepest level, that of fused identity, there is only one univocal *grunt*.[163]

The univocal understanding of *grunt* helps relate this master metaphor to other significant themes in Eckhart's vernacular preaching. For example, within the contours of Eckhart's thought it is clear that the *grunt* is another way of expressing the "uncreated something *in* the soul" (not *of* the soul), a term often linked with metaphors such as the "little spark" (*vunkelîn*) or the "little castle" (*burgelîn*).[164] Central as these metaphors are for understanding the Dominican's teaching about the soul, they are *not* used of the divine nature, and thus they lack the power of *grunt* to express the fused identity of both God and human.

There are also important connections between *grunt* and *geburt/gebern*, the birthing motif that is so widespread in Eckhart's preaching on the birth of the Word in the soul. The mysticism of birthing was not new with Eckhart; it had deep roots in Christianity.[165] However, Eckhart brought the birthing theme to new heights of subtlety and daring. Since the Son's birth can only take place in and out of the *grunt*, these two aspects of Eckhart's mysticism are inseparable. Nevertheless, they are not the same. For Eckhart, the birth of the Son does not exhaust what takes place in the ground. In Pr. 48, for example, he speaks of the "uncreated light" which comprehends God without a medium, a comprehension that "is to be understood as happening when the birth takes place." But this "spark of the soul" is not only not content with creatures, but also "is not content with the Father or the Son or the Holy Spirit . . . so far as each of them persists in his properties." It is not even satisfied with "the simple divine essence in its repose." No, "It wants to go into the simple ground, into the quiet desert, into which distinction never gazed, not the Father, nor the Son, nor the Holy Spirit. . . . For this ground is a simple silence, in itself immovable, and by this immovability all things are moved, all life is received by those who in themselves have rational being."[166] Although there are places in Eckhart's sermons that identify the *grunt* with the divine Paternity,[167] more radical texts speak of going into the *grunt* that lies deeper than the Trinity, beyond the birth of the Word,[168] thus pointing to one of the most difficult aspects of his preaching, but also to what is distinctively Eckhartian.

One of these passages occurs in Pr. 109, a sermon first edited by Franz Pfeiffer (Pfeiffer LVI), which, after some doubts, is now accepted as genuine.[169] This homily is based on the striking language of "God becoming and unbecoming" (*got wirt und entwirt*). Employing a distinction often used in the MHG sermons between God and the Godhead, the preacher says here that as long as he was "in the ground, the depths, the flood and source of the Godhead," no one asked him anything, because while God acts, the Godhead does not. The Godhead *becomes* God in the flowing out of creation;[170] and God *unbecomes* when the mystic is not content to return to the God who acts, but effects a "breaking-through" (*durchbrechen*) to the silent

unmoving Godhead, one that brings all creatures back into the hidden
source through their union in the deconstructed intellect. Eckhart says: "But
when I enter the ground, the bottom, the flood and source of the Godhead,
no one asks me where I come from or where I have been. There no one
misses me, and there God unbecomes."[171] Relying on such texts, we can say
that *grunt* includes the mysticism of the divine birth, but also, at least in
some sense, goes beyond it.[172]

Such expressions show how Eckhart's mysticism of the ground challenged traditional Christian understandings of union with God, which generally preferred the language of mystical uniting, that is, descriptions of an
intentional union of love between God and human that emphasized the
ongoing distinction of the two entities.[173] The monastic tradition of Western
mysticism, especially as set forth by the Cistercians and Victorines, understood union with God as *unitas spiritus*: a loving union of two spirits. (A
favorite biblical proof text for this was 1 Corinthians 6:17: "The one who
cleaves to God is one spirit with him.") Bernard of Clairvaux, the supreme
monastic mystic, was no metaphysician, but he insisted that "the substance
[of the person] remains" (*manebit quidem substantia*).[174] Eckhart knew Bernard well, but he clearly had a different conception of union.[175]

Meister Eckhart is perhaps the purest exponent of what can be called
mystical identity, that is, a union in which, at least on some level, all duality
vanishes. For the Dominican, and some of the anonymous mystical sermons and treatises written under his influence, the goal of the Christian life
was a *unitas indistinctionis* in which there was no difference at all between
God and human: "God's ground and the soul's ground is one ground." Eckhart was not the first mystic to claim that the human person is capable of
attaining indistinction with God. In pagan Neoplatonism, especially in Plotinus, there are equivalent formulations. In Christian antiquity the language
of mystical identity can be found in Evagrius Ponticus and in the Dionysian
corpus.[176] But it was not until the thirteenth century that mystical identity
came to the fore in Christianity. The earliest exponents are found among
female mystics such as Hadewijch and Mechthild of Magdeburg, and indistinct union was richly developed in Marguerite Porete's *Mirror of Simple
Souls*.[177] Eckhart knew Porete's book,[178] but one should not imagine that the
friar developed his form of *unitas indistinctionis* in dependence on the
beguine. Similarly, although Eckhart and his followers made use of Neoplatonic language of union drawn from Christians like Dionysius, and even
from pagans such as Proclus,[179] what emerged in Germany around 1300
was not merely a case of reviving something from the past. Neoplatonism
provided helpful philosophical categories for presenting an understanding

of union that was too widespread to think of as only a learned literary phenomenon. What we find in Eckhart's mysticism of the ground is a new creation designed to express the needs of a late medieval audience avid for
total transformation into God.

If the mysticism of the *grunt* provides a way to understand the distinctiveness of Eckhart's teaching, it is important to observe how the friar actually
used ground-language to get some sense of its power as an explosive metaphor. *Grunt* was employed by Eckhart in a rich variety of ways, but the
basic intention of the semantic field of ground-language always aims at one
goal: achieving indistinct identity of God and human in what Eckhart calls
"a single, or simple, One" (*einvaltigez ein/ein einic ein*).[180] As Susanne Köbele
reminds us, "*grunt* has . . . no other 'meaning' than the identity of the divine
ground with the ground of the soul. This identity is a dynamic identity."[181]
Grunt, therefore, is not a state or condition, but is rather "grounding"—the
event of being in a fused relation.[182]

The relationship of the master metaphor of *grunt* to other images of mystical identity, such as the endless ocean, the bottomless abyss, and the
desert, alluded to in chapter 3, will appear in more detail later in this chapter. The fused identity that is the essential meaning of *grunt* implies so broad
a range of corollaries in Eckhart that only a few can be mentioned here. For
instance, many mystics have insisted that God is ultimately unknowable
and therefore unnameable, so that if the soul in its ground is absolutely one
with God, it too must also be nameless and unknowable. As Pr. 17, one of
the most detailed treatments of the soul's ground, puts it: "Whoever writes
of things in motion does not deal with the nature or ground of the soul.
Whoever would name the soul according to her simplicity, purity and
nakedness, as she is in herself, he can find no name for her."[183] Thus Eckhart, like John Scottus Eriugena, taught a form of negative anthropology in
which God and soul are ultimately one and therefore both radically
unknowable.[184]

Identity without distinction is a paradoxical notion, and Eckhart delights
in creating paradoxes, contradictions, oxymora, and other forms of wordplay in speaking of the ground. These are present even in his earliest vernacular work, the *Talks of Instruction*, which employs ground-language ten
times.[185] Here and in his subsequent works, expressions like the "groundless
ground" (*gruntlôs grunt*), "groundless Godhead" (*gruntlôsen gotheit*), as well as
various uses of *abgrunt*, all provide the Dominican with the opportunity for
word games that are meant to be both playful and serious insofar as they
are part of the practice of deconstructing the self and freeing it from all that
pertains to the created world. Identity in the ground is a wandering, playful

identity in which we are often unsure whether the language used is meant to refer to God, or to the soul, or to both—or maybe even to neither, at least insofar as we usually understand them. Therefore, the commentator or translator should resist adding qualifying terms like "divine" or "human" to *grunt* when Eckhart's text does not contain them.[186] The language of the ground is meant to confuse in order to enlighten.

Although nothing happens in the ground insofar as it is beyond all movement and distinction as we know them (even the dynamic procession that gives rise to the Persons of the Trinity), the ground is transcendentally real as "pure possibility," to use Niklaus Largier's formulation.[187] As the unmoved source of all movement, the ground is the "place" from which the mystic must learn to live, act, and know. In the ground there can be no distinction between knowing and acting, or theory and practice. Nevertheless, as one's actions come forth from the ground into the world of distinction, they have to be expressed in the language proper to that world. Therefore, as Eckhart puts it in speaking of knowledge, "The more someone knows the root and the kernel and the ground of the Godhead as one, the more he knows all things."[188] In the same way, when discussing the relation of life and activity, Pr. 39 advises: "Go into your own ground and there act, and the works that you do there will all be living."[189] So too, Pr. 16b, a homily on soul as *imago Dei,* concludes by telling the hearer: "You should pass through and pass over all virtues and should only take hold of virtue in the ground where it is one with the divine nature."[190] Thus, acting out of a "well-exercised ground" (*wol geübte grunt*), as Pr. 86 says of Martha in Luke 10,[191] is to live and act "without a why" (*sunder/âne warumbe*)—the core of Eckhartian ethics.

One other central aspect of *grunt* should be considered in order to grasp why the mysticism of the ground provides a helpful entry into the Dominican's mysticism: its relationship to Christ. Eckhart claimed that the only way to attain realization of indistinct identity with God is through the action of the Word become man. In the incarnation the Second Person of the Trinity took (or rather is always "taking" on) human nature—not a human person—so that all who possess human nature are absolutely one in Christ. We are identical with Christ *insofar* as we too are God's offspring. Eckhart's functional Christology (to be treated below) implies that the one ground in which we attain identity with God is rooted in the oneness of Christ's own ground. This teaching is explored in Pr. 67, one of Eckhart's most difficult sermons (and one in which *grunt* occurs no fewer than ten times).[192]

Eckhart's theme in Pr. 67 is how God lives in the soul: first, by charity; then by his image, through which we come to share in the life of the Trinity.

According to the preacher, the place of this contact "is the essential understanding of God, of which the pure and naked power is *intellectus*, which the masters term receptive" [i.e., the possible intellect]. He then turns to a higher form of union:

> Above this [the soul] grasps the pure "absolution" of free being that is there without being there, that does not give or receive. It is pure self-identity [*isticheit*] that is there divested of all being and self-identity. There it takes God bare as he is in the ground, there where he is above all being. If there were still being there, the soul would take being in being; there is nothing there save one ground.[193]

Eckhart says that this state is the highest spiritual perfection that can be attained in this life; but he then goes on to speak of a higher perfection to come in heaven, one that is attainable in and through Christ as he exists in the ground. In the difficult lines that follow Eckhart seems to be talking about a union somehow already present in our oneness with Christ, but one that cannot be fully realized because of the unavoidable tension in this life between the "outer man" (*der ûzerster mensche*) and the "inner man" (*der inner mensche*). From the point of view of the ground, however, just as humanity and divinity form "one personal being" (*éin persônlich wesen*) in Christ, losing our self-awareness allows us, even now, some access to this inner unity. "I have the same substrate (*understantnisse*) of personal being—which personal being I myself am—anytime I completely deny my self-awareness, so that in a spiritual way I am one according to the ground, as the ground itself is one ground."[194] Giving up self-awareness, of course, is nothing else than Eckhartian detachment, true poverty of spirit, and the "deconstruction" (*entbilden*) of all images and quotidian forms of consciousness.[195]

Eckhart follows this discussion of the highest form of perfection with a dense section devoted to the relation of the inner and outer man. Basically, he advises the outer man not to become enamored of what we would call mystical experiences—"the flowing in of grace from the personal being in many modes of sweetness, comfort, and inwardness." These are good, but they are not "the best thing," because they may cause the inner man "to be drawn out of the ground where he is one" (*herûzbiegen ûzer dem grunde in dem er ein ist*). Just as the inner man "loses his own being through his ground becoming one ground" (*entvellet sînes eigens wesens dâ er in dem grunde éin grunt ist*), the outer man must lose his own substrate and come to rely on the "Eternal Personal Being" (i.e., Christ). The preacher concludes that "there are two forms of being" in Christ: the "bare substantial being" of the Godhead, and the "personal being" of the Word. But both are one "supposit" (*understôz*), that is, one subsisting individual. However—and here is

Eckhart's decisive point—this same unity is realized in us insofar as we are sons and demonstrate our sonship by "following him in his works." Since we possess human nature (the same nature that the Word united to himself), by grace we are now Christ's "personal being." That means that the *grunt* as identity or fusion of God and human is nothing other than Christ's ground. Eckhart expresses this point in the following convoluted way:

> So since God-Christ eternally dwells within the Father's ground and I in him, one ground and the same Christ [is] a substrate of my humanity. It is as much mine as his in the one substrate of Eternal Being, so that the double being of body and soul will be perfected in the one Christ—one God, one Son.[196]

Although this perfect identity may not be fully attained until after the resurrection of the body, Eckhart's closing prayer leads one to think that he believed the transformation must be begun in this life. If "God became man so that man might become God," then the friar's teaching on the *grunt* must be seen as christological at its core.

The complexity of Eckhart's thought always resists summary. The repetitive themes of his preaching, such as detachment, the role of intellect in the birth of the Son in the soul, and the breakthrough to the hidden God, have long been seen as crucial for understanding the Dominican's message. In recent decades, attention to such underlying metaphysical motifs as the doctrine of analogy, the dialectics of *unum* as distinct-indistinction, and the role of formal predication (e.g., the just man *insofar as* he is just) have helped us better grasp other aspects of his teaching. New investigation of Eckhart the preacher, especially his use of metaphor, "appellative" speech, and deconstructive techniques, have allowed us deeper insight into how in Eckhart's case the medium is indeed the message. For a vantage point on these many perspectives on Meister Eckhart, I suggest that the term *grunt*, at once simple and profound, allows us a new appreciation of the inner coherence of the thought of one of the most remarkable Christian mystics.

Eckhart's Metaphysics of Flow

Eckhart provides us not only with mystical teaching, but also with a metaphysical and theological structure to support his message. It would be a mistake to force a thinker like Eckhart into any rigid system, but in his projected *Work of Propositions,* at least, the friar had intended to create a form of systematics. If there is no surviving Eckhartian system, there is at least a systematic orientation to all his thought.[197]

A good way to approach Eckhart's implied systematics is through the reciprocity of the "flowing-forth" (*exitus-emanatio/ûzganc-uzfliessen*) of all things from the hidden ground of God, and the "flowing-back," or "breaking-through" (*reditus-restoratio/inganc-durchbrechen*) of the universe into identity in the divine source. From this perspective, Eckhart's metaphysics can be described as a form of the "metaphysics of flow."[198] As he once summarized, "I have often said, God's going-out is his going-in" (*Ich han ez ouch mê gesprochen: gotes ûzganc ist sîn inganc*).[199] Here it is only possible to give a survey of the main lines of this speculative teaching—the skeleton, so to speak, on which the Dominican hung the flesh and blood of his mystical preaching. The presentation is under five headings, beginning with Eckhart's treatment of the dynamic activity at the heart of all flowing forth from the divine ground.

Bullitio-Ebullitio

A passage from one of Eckhart's Latin sermons discussing the nature of "image" (*imago/bild*) provides an entry into how the Dominican conceived of *exitus*. Eckhart says: ". . . an image properly speaking is a simple formal emanation that transmits the whole pure naked essence, . . . an emanation from the depths of silence, excluding everything that comes from without. It is a form of life, as if you were to imagine something swelling up from itself and in itself and then inwardly boiling without any boiling over yet understood." On this basis, he distinguishes three stages of *exitus*. The first is "inner boiling" (*bullitio*), the formal emanation that produces a "pure nature" within, one fully equal to its source, "in the way the Good diffuses itself." "The second stage," Eckhart says, "is like the boiling over (*ebullitio*) in the manner of an efficient cause and with a view toward an end [i.e., a final cause], by which something produces something else that is from itself, but not out of itself."[200] Eckhart notes that *ebullitio* is accomplished in two ways: "This production is either out of some other thing (and then it is called 'making' [*factio*]), or it is out of nothing (and then it is the third stage of production which is called 'creating' [*creatio*])."[201]

Other texts in the Latin works show how important emanation understood as comprising both *bullitio* and *ebullitio* is to Eckhart.[202] In his exegesis of the divine self-designation, "I am who am" (Exod. 3:14), Eckhart notes that the repetition found in this phrase

indicates the purity of affirmation excluding all negation from God. It also indicates the reflexive turning back of his existence into itself and upon itself and its dwelling and remaining fixed in itself.[203] It further indicates a "boiling" or giving birth to itself—glowing into itself, and melting and boiling in and into itself, light that totally forces its whole being in light and into light and that is everywhere turned back and reflected upon itself.[204]

Thus, God's inner *bullitio* is the source and exemplar of the boiling over (*ebullitio*) that is creation—the emanation of divine Persons in the Trinity is the prior ground (*ratio est et praevia*) of everything that exists.

Eckhart also refers to boiling and boiling over in S. XXV, a discussion of grace. Putting forth his own understanding of the traditional scholastic categories of "grace freely given" (*gratia gratis data*) and "saving grace" (*gratia gratum faciens*), he identifies the first with the gift of created being that all creatures receive from the goodness of the divine essence. "The second grace," he says, "comes from God as he is understood according to the property of 'personal notion,' and can be received only by intellective creatures." The two types of grace express the difference between *bullitio* and *ebullitio*: "God as good is the principle of the 'boiling over' on the outside; as personal notion, he is the principle of the 'boiling within himself,' which is the cause and exemplar of the boiling over." Eckhart also underlines the implications of the *bullitio-ebullitio* understanding of grace for our return to God. "The first grace," he says, "consists in a type of flowing out, a departure from God; the second consists in a type of flowing back, a return to God himself."[205] In other words, *exitus* comes about through God's creative boiling over *outside* the divine nature, while *reditus*, or deification, takes place through the action of a grace rooted in the trinitarian boiling itself. Only by sharing in the inner activity of the three divine Persons can we attain our goal.

In his sermons Eckhart at times uses the expressive word "break-out" (*ûzbruch*) for *bullitio*: "The first break-out and the first melting-forth is where God liquifies and where he melts into his Son and where the Son melts back into the Father."[206] Wherever we find the language of "breaking out," or its equivalents, in the MHG works, we should bear in mind Eckhart's teaching on *bullitio* and the two forms of *ebullitio* (i.e., creating and making).[207]

Eckhart's *bullitio-ebullitio* dynamic reflects previous Dominican thought but expands on it. The metaphysics of flow, as we have seen in chapter 1, originated with Albert the Great, who used the term *ebullitio* to express how the First Mover flows forth into all things.[208] Dietrich of Freiburg used *ebullitio* for the causative action of the separated intelligences,[209] and *ebullitio* is also found in Berthold of Moosburg's *Commentary on Proclus's Theological Elements*.[210] Non-German authors also employed language of boiling and boiling over. Thomas Aquinas, paraphrasing a passage in Dionysius's CH 7, spoke of how love creates ecstasy, "because it burns, it boils over, and exhales outside itself."[211] Marguerite Porete described the "boiling of love" by which the souls who have died the "death of the spirit" are perfectly united to God and receive "the flower of the love of the Godhead."[212] None of these authors, however, developed the relation between trinitarian *bullitio* and creative *ebullitio* the way Eckhart did.

God as Principle (Principium) and as Trinity

The precondition for the formal emanation, or *bullitio*, in the Trinity is nothing else than the *grunt*; but the active source or origin of emanative inner boiling is what in the Latin writings is mostly referred to as *principium*.[213] The relation between *principium* and *bullitio* is clarified in a passage from the *Commentary on John* where Eckhart says:

> The One acts as a principle [*principiat*] through itself and gives existence and is an internal principle. For this reason, properly speaking, it does not produce something like itself, but what is one and the same as itself. . . . This is why the formal emanation in the divine Persons is a type of boiling, and thus the three Persons are simply and absolutely one.[214]

Eckhart was doubtless drawn to *principium* as a term for the emanative process because of its role in two of the most important texts in the Bible—Genesis 1:1: *In principio creavit Deus caelum et terram*; and John 1:1: *In principio erat Verbum. Principium* is particularly helpful because it implies both *beginning* in the sense of duration and *origin* and *order* in the context of the metaphysics of flow.[215]

Principium first of all refers to the Father as the origin and source of the Son and Holy Spirit. In a passage discussing seven reasons for the sending of the Holy Spirit, Eckhart summarizes his teaching on the two processions in trinitarian emanation, the act of generating (*generare*) by which the Father produces the Son, and the breathing (*spirare*) by which Father and Son give rise to the Holy Spirit. The Son is able to act as a *principium* only through his dependence on the Father:

> The Son is the "Principle from the Principle," the Father is the "Principle without Principle." Therefore, it is necessary that the Son draw near the Father who is the source of the entire deity so that he can receive the power to flow, according to Ecclesiastes 1: "The rivers return to whence they flow, so that they may flow forth again" (Eccl. 1:7).[216]

The Father's fontality in the Trinity is one of the dominant themes of Eckhart's trinitarianism.[217]

Principium also names the triune God as the source of *ebullitio*. Eckhart's two commentaries on Genesis are rich sources for investigating this aspect of his metaphysics of flow. The first, literal, *Commentary on Genesis* presents three understandings of *in principio*.[218] Principle first of all means "Ideal Reason," that is, the *Logos*, Reason, or Son, as "the Image or Ideal Reason" within God in which the essences of all things are precontained in a higher, virtual way. Second, Principle means intellect, indicating that God creates not from necessity of nature, as Avicenna held, but from his own act of understanding and free will.[219] Eckhart's third interpretation of the *principium* of Genesis highlights the duration aspect, one of the chief target of critics of his doctrine of *exitus*. Because *bullitio* and *ebullitio* have only one source, their duration must be one of simultaneity. *Principium*, says the Dominican, "is the very same now in which God exists from eternity, in which also the emanation of the divine Persons eternally is, was, and will be." Thus, "In the one and the same time in which he was God and in which he begot his coeternal Son as God equal to himself in all things, he also created the world."[220] This aspect of *ebullitio* led to the condemnation of three passages concerning the eternity of creation in the papal bull, two of them taken from this comment on the *in principio* of Genesis 1:1.[221]

Augustine, Aquinas, and others had found vestiges of the Trinity in all created things.[222] Eckhart's view of the single source and coeternity of both forms of flowing forth from the Principle meant that he saw all activity as essentially trinitarian. If *ebullitio* has its root in the *bullitio* by which the Father gives birth to the Son and the two Persons emanate the Love that is the Holy Spirit, then *creatio* and even all *factio*, or making, express a trinitarian mode of action. This is the foundation for Eckhart's "a priori" view of the Trinity, that is, that God as Trinity is a truth available not only by faith but also accessible through metaphysical analysis of the forms of *productio*.[223]

Given Eckhart's conviction that the Trinity is a truth that can be demonstrated by a priori arguments, his trinitarianism is an example of what Werner Beierwaltes has termed the "serious game" of the dialogue between philosophy and theology that formed classical Christian speculation on God as three-in-one.[224] In his *Commentary on Wisdom* Eckhart summarizes as follows: "Every action of nature, morality, and art in its wholeness possesses three things—something generating, something generated, and the love of what generates for what is generated and vice versa."[225] Every natural activity, therefore, contains an image of the Trinity. What is distinctive of human nature is its ability to think and thus to produce the trinitarian image in things in a conscious way (Eckhart often uses the Aristotelian example of the carpenter making a chest or box). Such an intellectual appropriation of the inner divine processions of Word and of Love makes human nature an *imago Dei* (Gen. 1:26) in the full and proper sense of image as formal emanation (more on this below).

Eckhart's view of *principium* is spelled out in great detail in the *Book of the Parables of Genesis*,[226] and especially in his lengthy remarks on the second biblical *in principio* text, John 1:1.[227] The nature of God as *principium*, for Eckhart, is always to be understood as the trinitarian God of Father, Son, and Holy Spirit. Eckhart's mysticism, like that of William of St.-Thierry in the twelfth century and Bonaventure in the thirteenth, is pervasively trinitarian.[228] Precisely how the triune God functions in the wider context of his message about attaining indistinct union with God is a central issue in the Dominican's thought.

Because Eckhart's view of mystical identity challenged traditional understandings of the limits of uniting with God, his discussions of how we become one with Father, Son, and Holy Spirit are also controversial. Eckhart's mysticism seems to be both trinitarian and supra-trinitarian in the sense that while he always insists on the necessary role of the Trinity, some of his sermons put in question the ultimacy of the triune conception of God by inviting the believer into the "God beyond God," that is, "into the simple ground, into the silent desert, into which distinction never gazed, not the Father, nor the Son, nor the Holy Spirit" (Pr. 48).[229] One can wonder if Eckhart's teaching on the oneness of *bullitio* and *ebullitio*, by making God's trinitarian life the inner reality of every mode of production, led to a heightened need for an independent realm for God, beyond that of traditional apophatic theology.

Eckhart's teaching on the Trinity appears throughout his works, but a few Latin discussions, such as three mini-treatises in the John commentary and S. IV,[230] provide a good presentation of the doctrine found in the German sermons and vernacular treatises.[231] Eckhart, however, often expressed some of his deepest insights in the MHG sermons. For example, a brief and difficult passage from Pr. 10 reveals how he understands the relation of Trinity and Unity in God. Eckhart says: "Once I preached in Latin on Trinity Sunday and said: 'Distinction comes from Absolute Unity, that is, the distinction in the Trinity.' Absolute Unity is the distinction and the distinction is the unity. The greater the distinction, the greater the unity, for it is the distinction without distinction."[232] What does Eckhart mean by this cryptic statement? The implications seem to be as follows. First, in our experience, distinction (this *is not* that) always involves numeration, while indistinction (this *is* that) implies the possibility of numeration by its very speaking of discrete entities—"this" and "that." But, second, in God there is no number whatsoever. According to S. XI, for example: "In the proper sense God is exempt from all number. He is one without Unity, three without Trinity, just as he is good without quality."[233] God's distinction (what sets him off from all other things) is to be utterly without numeration or any kind of distinction—that is, he alone is indistinct. Third, whatever is God (i.e., the Trinity of Persons) must, by that very fact, be identical with the divine indistinction: "It is the distinction without distinction." Elsewhere Eckhart says this would be true of God even if there were a hundred, or a thousand divine Persons in God (!)—though we know by faith that there are only three.[234] The formulation from Pr. 10 shows that Eckhart believed that the dialectical relationship of God and creation, central to his mysticism, was rooted in the distinct-indistinction in the Trinity itself.

How can there be both absolute oneness in God (i.e., indistinction) and yet a clear distinction of three Persons? The best way to approach this puzzle is from the point of view of the dialectical character of Eckhart's thought, that is, the truth of the opposed propositions can only begin to make sense on the basis of the claim that the more distinct the Trinity of Persons is, the more indistinct, or absolutely one, the three Persons are in their pure potentiality for emanation. This indistinct-distinction is true both of the Trinity and of the soul insofar as it realizes its indistinction in the Trinity. As Eckhart puts it in Pr. 24, speaking of the soul, ". . . in the ground of divine being, where the three Persons are one being, there she is one according to the ground."[235]

The solution rests in Eckhart's view of the *grunt gotes,* that is, the indistinct nonrelative "aspect" of God that is absolutely One precisely in being three and vice versa. In most of the radical MHG texts in which Eckhart speaks of abandoning "God," or going beyond the Trinity of Persons, he also employs the language of penetration to the *grunt.*[236] The fact that *grunt,* as a master metaphor, was not available for Eckhart in his Latin writings, and that he therefore needed to call upon a series of technical terms that could only refract elements of *grunt* in Latin vocabulary (e.g., *essentia-deitas-divinitas*), helps explain why the scholastic works communicate a different tone, though not, I would argue, a different teaching.

From the viewpoint of Aristotelian logic such dialectical predication does not resolve the contradictions present in the various forms of speaking about God, as Eckhart well knew. Its purpose is to jolt the hearer/reader into the recognition of the limits of all language when dealing with God and to remind her of the need to appropriate the deconstruction of all forms of knowing and being into the unknowing and unbecoming that give access to the *grunt.* Eckhart was emphatic about the need for such deconstruction. In

Pr. 109, already mentioned, he says that the Godhead insofar as it is a "sim-ple ground" (*einvaltige grunt*) and "silent desert" (*stille wüeste*) does not act—"God acts, while the Godhead does not act." In the Godhead God "un-becomes" (*entwirt*). Hence, the *grunt* is best described as pure possibil-ity, the unmoving precondition of all activity, even that of *bullitio*.[237] According to this sermon, it is only when we come to the inner boiling by which the three Persons flow forth in the processions characterized by mutual relations that we arrive at the level where "God becomes" (*got wirt*).

The complexities of the relationship between the God who becomes and the God who un-becomes are evident in the ways in which Eckhart applies the transcendental predicates, especially existence (*esse-wesen*), oneness (*unum/unitas–ein/einicheit*), truth (*verum/intellectus–wârheit/bekantnisse*), and goodness (*bonum-güete*) to the Trinity. Following tradition, the friar describes these terms as being appropriated to the Persons, and hence really common to the divine essence as such. Nevertheless, his apophatic doctrine of God effectively does away with any real difference between appropriated and proper properties. All terms are essentially appropriated; transcendental predicates can be used both of the Persons of the Trinity and of the divine nature itself, as we shall see below.

Eckhart employs two patterns in applying transcendental terms to the Trinity. The standard presentation is more traditional. Two of the three treatments in the *Commentary on John* identify indistinct Being (*esse*) with the divine essence, and the One or unity (*unum*) with the Father, the True (*verum*) with the Son, and the Good (*bonum*) with the Holy Spirit. The classic presentation of this model of the Trinity is in the commentary on John 14:8,[238] but this understanding of *esse-unum-verum-bonum* appears frequently in the friar's writings.[239] However, the first of the treatises on the Trinity in the *Commentary on John* sets forth the relation of the transcendentals to the Persons of the Trinity in a different way. Here Eckhart says:

> The works of the three Persons are undivided in the creatures of which they are one principle. Therefore, in creatures the being [*ens*] that corresponds to the Father,[240] the truth that corresponds to the Son, and the good that corre-sponds in appropriated fashion to the Holy Spirit are interchangeable and are one, being distinct by reason alone, just as the Father, the Son, and the Holy Spirit are one and distinct by relation alone.[241]

In this treatment what Eckhart later calls the "term One" (*li unum*), is not ascribed to any particular Person in the Trinity, but denotes the divine sub-stance or essence.[242] Eckhart is not clear about how to relate these different models of the Trinity, but this fact does not really impinge on what is cen-tral in his message: the ineluctably trinitarian nature of mystical identity.

Attaining identity with God in the *grunt* through going-in or "breaking-through" reverses the process by which all things come forth from the hidden Father through his speaking of the Word in the mutual Love that is the Holy Spirit. Just as the Father is the source of the *ûzganc* of all things, within and without the Trinity, so too he is the goal that "suffices," as John 14:8 puts it ("Show us the Father and it is enough for us").

In discussing the First Person of the Trinity, Eckhart recognized that the source of *bullitio* lies beyond all gender language, so the term "Father" needs to be complemented by thinking of God as "Mother." Thus, in Pr. 75 he speaks of God as "eternally pregnant in his foreknowledge" of creation. The same sermon also says that in begetting both his Only-Begotten Son and every soul, the Father "lies in childbed like a woman who has given birth."[243] Pr. 40 reverses the image by speaking of Wisdom, traditionally ascribed to the Son, as "a motherly name" (*ein müeterlich name*), and claiming that both activity (the Father bearing) and passivity (the Son being born) can be ascribed to God.[244] Another sermon (if it is indeed by Eckhart) goes even further in invoking the need for thinking of God maternally.[245] These texts suggesting the need for using maternal as well as paternal language illuminate a passage in Pr. 71 where Eckhart's metaphor of the fused ground is expressed in the image of becoming pregnant with God as if in a "waking dream." Eckhart says: "It seemed to a person that he had a dream, a waking dream, that he was great with Nothingness as a woman with a child. In this Nothingness God was born."[246]

The Father as primordial fullness—the ultimate active source and therefore also in one respect the goal of the return—is so important for Eckhart that he sometimes identifies the Father with the supra-personal and potential *grunt*. Breaking-through (*durchbrechen*) is usually employed in relation to the ground, but in Pr. 26 it refers to how the "soul's highest point" cannot be satisfied with the Persons of the Son or Holy Spirit, or even "God as he is God" with a thousand names (i.e., God as Creator), but rather, "would have him as he is Father" (citing John 14:8 again)."[247] More unusual is a passage from Pr. 51, where Eckhart asserts the primordiality of the Father with regard to both emanation and return. In order to beget the Son, he says, the Father must remain "in himself the ground," where the image is eternally precontained.[248] Perhaps recalling John 14:8 again, Eckhart claims that the "Father is not *satisfied* till he has withdrawn into the first source, to the innermost, to the ground and core of Fatherhood, where he rejoices in himself there, the Father of himself in the Single One." In this text there seems to be no difference between the Person of the Father and the *grunt*, so Eckhart can go on to describe not only his own "captivation" (*ich han mich darinn vertoeret*) with the Father-ground, but also to remark on how all nature desires "to plunge into the Fatherhood, so that it can be one, and one Son, and grow beyond everything else and be all one in the Fatherhood."[249] Such passages help explain what Eckhart meant when he interpreted Paul's promise that "we shall know God as we are known" (1 Cor. 12:13) as referring to the knowledge that God as Father has of himself "in that reflection [i.e., the Son] that alone is the image of God and the Godhead to the extent that the Godhead is the Father."[250]

The Second Person of the Trinity, the Only-Begotten Son, perfect Image of the Father, whose eternal birth is also ours, has always been seen as essential to Eckhart's mysticism. The birth of the Word in the soul will be treated in more detail below, but here a few remarks on the procession of the Word from the Father will help to give us a grasp of the Son's role in the metaphysics of flow—both *bullitio* and *ebullitio*.

Eckhart adhered to the standard Augustinian and Thomistic view of the procession of the Word from the Father as a generation understood according to the model of an intellectual procession within God himself.[251] Hence, the Dominican's teaching on the nature of intellect is ultimately to be "reduced" (i.e., drawn back) to its source in the procession of the Word from the Father.[252] One aspect of this procession, essential for understanding inner boiling as the paradigmatic model and source for creative boiling over, is how Eckhart conceives of the Father's "speaking of the Word" as the total expression of his own hidden divine silence. The relation between silence and speaking was one of the central mysteries for Eckhart, in both his Latin and his German works.[253]

In commenting on John 8:47 ("He who is of God hears God's words"), Eckhart gives a summary of *when, where, what,* and *how* God speaks. While traditional teaching emphasized the beatific *vision* as the fulfillment of all human longing, Eckhart insists that in heaven "seeing and hearing are one" (In Ioh. n. 487). Hence, in order to *see* the God who *speaks,* we must know *when* he speaks, that is (citing Wis. 18:14), "While all things held quiet silence and night was in the midst of its course, your Almighty Word, Lord, came down from heaven."[254] We must also know *where* God speaks, which, Eckhart says, is in the desert, citing another favorite text ("I will lead you into the desert and speak to your heart" [Hos. 2:14]). *What* God speaks is "peace in his people and upon his saints and those converted in their hearts" (Ps. 84:9). Finally, *how* God speaks is answered with a text from Job: "God speaks once and for all and will not say the same thing a second time" (Job 33:14).[255] Thus, it is only by coming into the silent darkness of the desert, where the Father speaks the Word once and for all, that we attain perfect peace. (These themes also appear in Pr. 101.)

This ultimate speaking, of course, is not a word like the words we hear in

everyday speech—"The Word which is in the silence of the fatherly Intellect is a Word without word, or rather a Word above every word."[256] It is
only in and by this Word that all things are spoken—that is, that the universe itself comes to be.[257] "The effect [i.e., the world] is concealed in its
analogous cause, hidden, silent, neither speaking nor being heard, unless it
is said and brought forth in the word conceived and generated within or
brought forth on the outside."[258] Such Latin discussions of the *Verbum* as the
Father's sole communication form the basis for Eckhart's preaching about
the mediation between silence and speaking that is necessary for the breakthrough into the ground.[259]

Eckhart's MHG teaching on the procession of the eternal Word from the
Father is illuminated by a passage in Pr. 9 where the Dominican distinguishes between three kinds of *wort*:

> There is one kind of word which is brought forth, like an angel and a human
> being and all creatures. There is a second kind of word, thought out and not
> brought forth, as happens when I form a thought. There is yet another kind of
> word that is not brought forth and not thought out, that never comes forth.
> Rather, it remains eternally in him who speaks it. It is continually being con-
> ceived in the Father who speaks it, and it remains within.[260]

The Word that "remains eternally in him who speaks it" is, of course, the
Second Person of the Trinity.[261] Though silent, this Word is not totally inaccessible. Indeed, the purpose of the distinction is to emphasize the basic
message of this sermon, that is, the soul must recognize its nature as "an ad-
verb" (*bîwort*), totally dependent on the Word, and therefore able to "work
one work with God in order to receive its happiness in the same inwardly
hovering knowledge where God is happy."[262] In Pr. 53, citing Augustine's
observation on the contradiction of speaking about the ineffable, or
unspeakable, God (*On Christian Doctrine* 1.6), Eckhart discusses how the
divine nature is simultaneously unspeakable and yet spoken. "God is a
Word that utters itself," he says. "God is spoken and unspoken. The Father
is a speaking work, and the Son is the speech working" (*spruch wirkende*).[263]
Therefore, the birth of the Son in the soul comes down to speaking the
Word simultaneously within (i.e., in the eternal silence) and without (i.e., in
creating and sustaining all things).[264]

The frequency with which Eckhart refers to the birth of the Word in the
soul and his discussions about the Word unspoken and spoken have
attracted much attention. Less notice has been given to the Dominican's
teaching on the Holy Spirit proceeding from Father and Son as source of
creation and as the love in which all things are restored to God.[265] Although

he speaks of the Holy Spirit less often than the Word, Pneumatology is no less important than Christology for Eckhart. When the friar discusses the procession of the Holy Spirit in the Trinity, he adopts the standard Latin understanding of this production as an emanation according to love; but, as in much else, he gives this doctrine his own twist.

S. IV provides a summary of Eckhart's trinitarian teaching, as well as an exploration of how existence *in* the Holy Spirit as *nexus*, or bond, of Father and Son, is the ground for our return to the divine source.[266] "All things are from him [the Father], through him [the Son], and in him [the Holy Spirit]," according to Eckhart's reading of Romans 11:36. The Dominican takes the Spirit's "being in" all things as a proper attribute, one that should be understood in a reversible, or dialectical, fashion. "All things are in the Holy Spirit in such a way that what is not in him is nothing," just as "'All things are in him' in such a way that if there is anything not in the Holy Spirit, the Holy Spirit is not God."[267] Thus, the Holy Spirit is treated as the Person of the Trinity who is the root of God's indistinct-distinction in relation to creation. "When we say that all things are in God [that means that] just as he is indistinct in his nature and nevertheless most distinct from all things, so in him all things in a most distinct way are also indistinct."[268] The root of this indistinct presence of all things in the Holy Spirit is his personal property as the bond between the Father and the Son. Eckhart says: "'All things are in him' in such a way that the Father would not be in the Son nor the Son in the Father if the Father were not one and the same as the Holy Spirit, or the Son [also] the same as the Holy Spirit."[269] In a passage in the *Commentary on John* Eckhart explains the traditional description of the Holy Spirit as the bond, *nexus*, between Father and Son by invoking his special language of *in quantum*, the principle of formal reduplication. He says: "The term 'insofar as' is a reduplication. Reduplication, as the word testifies, speaks of the bond or ordering of two things. Reduplication expresses the folding together of two things, a fold or bond of two. Thus the Spirit, the third Person in the Trinity, is the bond of the two, the Father and the Son."[270]

This bond is the mutual love of Father and Son, what Eckhart called the unitive "love of contentment" (*amor complacentiae/amor concomitans*), which is conceptually different from, but really identical with, the "love breathed forth" (*amor notionalis/amor spiratus*), that is, the Holy Spirit understood as proceeding from Father and Son.[271] For this reason, the same love with which the Father loves the Son and the Son loves the Father is the love by which we love God.[272] This is evident in a passage from the John commentary where the fusion language employed in the MHG sermons ("the eye with which I see God is the same eye by which he sees me") is adopted to the role of the Uncreated Love that is the Spirit. Eckhart says: "In the sense that there is one face and image in which God sees us and we him, according to the Psalm text, 'In your light we shall see light,' so too the same Love is the Holy Spirit by which the Father loves the Son and the Son the Father [and] by which God loves us and we him."[273] Therefore, we are united to God because we *are* the Holy Spirit, the very bond of the triune God.

Eckhart's treatment of the Trinity is among the most difficult aspects of his thought. Like all Christian theologians, he held that the Trinity is a mystery. While some theologians concluded that the best way to present the mystery was through reference to accepted creeds and councils and reverent exposition of the dogmatic logic of the terms found therein, Eckhart's trinitarianism was reverent but also experimental. He strove to find more adequate ways to express how God's inner life as a communion of three Persons is both the source of all that is and the way by which we find our way home.

Speaking about God

Eckhart was fascinated by the question of what we think we are doing when we attempt to speak about God. In one sense, his whole surviving corpus is an exploration of this issue. Why is speech necessary when silence is more fitting? What kinds of speech about God are appropriate? The Dominican's experiments and his reflections on these experiments are scattered throughout his writings.

The best way to investigate how Eckhart conceives of using words in relation to God is by distingushing (1) predication, (2) analogy, and (3) dialectic. Like all scholastics, Eckhart was trained in logic, so we must begin at the level of the logic of predication.[274] In his prologues to the *Three-Part Work* and elsewhere, Eckhart adapts the traditional logical distinction between "two-term propositions" (*secundum adiacens*) and "three-term propositions" (*tertium adiacens*). A two-term proposition (e.g., Socrates is) is one in which the verb stands as the second term and denotes that the action is really taking place (the existential *est*), while in a three-term proposition (e.g., Socrates is a man) the verb stands as the copula between two terms indicating their logical compatibility without directly affirming actuality (the copulative *est*, i.e., *if* Socrates exists, he is a man).[275] Thomas Aquinas and other scholastics had used the distinction,[276] but Eckhart adopted it in his own fashion. For Eckhart two-term propositions indicate substantial predication, while three-term propositions signify accidental predication.

Two-term propositions imply the unlimited possession of the predicate: its absolute fullness. Hence, with regard to the transcendentals, two-term propositions, such as "X is," are properly used only of God—"God alone properly speaking exists and is called being, one, true, and good" (i.e., formally speaking, God is-being, God is-good, etc.). Three-term propositions, indicating particular being (X is this), pertain to creatures, because "everything that is being, one, true or good, does not possess this from itself, but from God and from him alone."[277]

This understanding of predication forms the foundation for Eckhart's doctrine of analogy, which, since the time of Vladimir Lossky, has been recognized as central to grasping the peculiar form of the Dominican's teaching about the language used to express the God–world relation.[278] Here again, although Eckhart at times appealed to Thomas Aquinas, analogy for Eckhart is different from what we find in the Angelic Doctor. A key text from the *Sermons and Lectures on Ecclesiasticus* explains why:

> Analogates have nothing of the form according to which they have been given analogical order rooted in positive fashion in themselves, but every created being is analogically ordered to God in being, truth, and goodness. Therefore, every created being radically and positively possesses existence, life, and wisdom from and in God and not in itself. . . .[279]

Therefore, analogy does not indicate some kind of participation by God and creature in a particular predicate (e.g., *esse*), but rather denotes the fact that God alone really possesses the attribute. As Dietmar Mieth puts it: "Analogy is not, as with Thomas, a connective relationship, but a relationship of dependence; analogy does not explain what something is, but where it comes from."[280] The reality of creatures in Eckhart's view of analogy is the reality of a sign pointing to God.[281]

Another characteristic of Eckhart's use of analogy points beyond analogy in the direction of the third and most important level of language about God—dialectic.[282] Eckhart's use of analogy is reversible. If something is affirmed about God, it must be denied of creatures. On the other hand, anything that is affirmed of creatures must be denied of God. This is the root of the kind of formulations about God and creatures that upset the Dominican's inquisitors. In the bull "In agro dominico" examples of both kinds of statements based on reversing analogy come in for attack. Article 26, for example, condemns the statement "All creatures are one pure nothing. I do not say that they are a little something or anything, but that they are pure nothing."[283] This text is based on the predication of *esse* to God and therefore its entailed denial to creatures. The second appended article to the bull cites a passage from Pr. 9 that begins from implied three-term predications of goodness to creatures and boldly proclaims, "God is neither good, nor better, nor best; hence I speak as incorrectly when I call God good as if I were to call white black."[284] Eckhart's doctrine of analogy, then, is one of formal opposition, not the normal scholastic understanding of attribution (i.e., one being possesses a quality which can also be attributed to another) or proportionality (i.e., the way in which one being has a quality has some proportion to the way in which another has it).

The peculiarity of Eckhart's self-reversing analogy leads directly to the passages in his writings where he employs the language of dialectical Neoplatonism, created by pagans such as Plotinus and Proclus and transformed for Christian use by Dionysius among the Greeks and John Scottus Eriugena in the West.[285] By dialectical language I mean: (a) predicating determinations (God is distinct); (b) simultaneously predicating opposed determinations (God is distinct and God is indistinct); and (c) predicating a necessary mutual relationship between the opposed determinations (God is the more distinct the more indistinct he is).[286] Dialectical language of this sort was the linguistic strategy that allowed Eckhart to bring out the higher unity, or deeper "unknowing" (*unwizzen*), of the mutually opposed forms of analogical predications.[287] Though the Dominican was well acquainted with Dionysius and also with texts of Proclus, and had at least some contact with the thought of Eriugena,[288] his form of dialectical Christian Neoplatonism is not reducible to its sources—it is a new rendition of an old theme to fit a changed situation.

Eckhart's use of dialectical language about God as three-and-one, as well as the God–world relation, is found throughout his Latin and MHG works, but in different registers. The friar's favorite way to formulate dialectical language is in terms of distinction and indistinction, but other forms of dialectic can also be found (e.g., similarity/dissimilarity,[289] eating/hungering,[290] height/depth,[291] within/without,[292] mobile/immobile,[293] mine/notmine,[294] etc.). The scholastic writings contain a number of detailed explorations of dialectic;[295] the German sermons and treatises more briefly invoke dialectic when useful for the preacher's purposes.[296] Dialectic is a crucial tool for interpreting Eckhart.[297]

The most detailed of Eckhart's formal treatments on the dialectical character of predicating terms of God comes in his commentary on the transcendental attribute *unum* found in Wisdom 7:27 ("And since Wisdom is one, it can do all things").[298] A full analysis cannot be given here, but it is important to look at how Eckhart's understanding of *unum* as indistinction fuses both negation and affirmation into a higher mode of understanding. Eckhart says: "It should be recognized that the term 'one' is a negative word [= indistinct], but is in reality affirmative. . . . It is the negation of negation which is the purest form of affirmation and the fullness of the term affirmed" (n. 147). The negation of negation is Eckhart's dialectical way of subverting the Aristotelian distinction (both a logical and an ontological one) between "what is" and "what is not." God "negates" everything that we know "is"; but the negation of *all* particular forms of existence opens up a realm in which our distinctions between what "is" and what "is not" no longer pertain. God as *negatio negationis* is simultaneously total emptiness and supreme fullness.

Eckhart analyzes the relation of the divine One to the created many on the basis of his understanding of *unum* as the negation of negation. He continues:

> It [*unum*] signifies the purity and core and height of existence itself, something which even the term *esse* does not do. The term One signifies Existence Itself [*ipsum esse*] in itself along with the negation and exclusion of all nonbeing, which [nonbeing], I say, every negation entails. . . . The negation of negation (which the term One signifies) denotes that everything which belongs to the term is present in the signified and everything which is opposed to it is absent. (n. 148)

Finally, Eckhart is ready to draw together the two poles of understanding *unum*, positive and negative, to show that they are indissolubly linked in a dialectical coincidence of opposites. He begins with distinction. If we conceive of creatures as numerable, then God, since he is beyond all number, must be utterly distinct from all things (n. 154). However, this negation or distinction is founded on and implies the affirmation of God's indistinction. What makes God utterly distinct or different from everything else is that he alone is totally one or indistinct from everything. In the fused mutuality of dialectical predication:

> Everything which is distinguished by indistinction is the more distinct the more indistinct it is, because it is distinguished by its own indistinction. Conversely, it is the more indistinct the more distinct it is, because it is indistinguished by its own distinction from what is indistinct.[299] Therefore, it will be the more indistinct insofar as it is distinct, and vice versa, as was said. But God is something indistinct which is distinguished by his indistinction, as Thomas says in Ia, q. 7., a. 1. (n. 154).

The same kind of argument is then repeated beginning from the side of indistinction (n. 155).

To those unused to dialectical thinking this analysis may seem perverse— a word game. Eckhart probably delighted in the playful quality of the dialectic of *unum*, but his message was a serious one: the transcendental terms, especially *unum* and *esse*, in their very character as words, reveal that God is transcendent in his immanence and immanent in his transcendence—God is the "negation of negation."[300] *Negatio negationis* appears frequently in Eckhart's Latin works, but only rarely in the German sermons.[301] In the MHG writings one can argue that its function is absorbed into the term *grunt*, though in a pastoral and mystical way as a master metaphor for exploring the distinct-indistinction of God's identity with all things, especially the soul.

Dialectical thinking provides a helpful way to approach the controverted question of Eckhart's diverse treatments of the transcendental attributes—*esse, unum, verum/intelligere,* and *bonum*.[302] Unlike Thomas Aquinas, who always gave *esse*, or *ipsum esse subsistens*, priority in speaking about God, Eckhart says different things in different places. In his prologues to the unfinished *Three-Part Work* he presents *esse* as the fundamental transcendental term in a way that sounds much like Thomas Aquinas (though it is important to note that Eckhart reverses Thomas by his formulation *esse est deus*).[303] But in the *Commentary on Wisdom* and elsewhere, he seems to give priority to *unum*: "It [*unum*] signifies the purity and core and height of existence itself, something which even the term *esse* does not do." A variety of texts, both in Eckhart's scholastic works[304] and in his vernacular preaching,[305] make it clear that *unum*, or Absolute Unity, has a special role in the way in which Eckhart speaks of God.

The relation between *esse* and *unum* is further complicated by the fact that in the *Parisian Questions*, as well as in S. XXIX, Eckhart explicitly denies that *esse* is the fundamental transcendental term. In a passage already cited he says: "It is not my view that God understands because he exists, but rather that he exists because he understands. God is an intellect and an act of understanding, and his understanding is the ground of his existence."[306] How, then, is God as *intelligere* related to God as *esse* and *unum*?

Eckhart provides some help for addressing this question in the course of the *Parisian Questions*, particularly when he cites the fourth proposition of the *Book of Causes* (*prima rerum creaturarum est esse,* "Existence is the first of created things"). This indicates that he is not using *esse* in the *Questions* as indistinct being (*esse indistinctum*), but rather as the being of creatures (*ens hoc et hoc*). Furthermore, as he develops his discussion, he admits that although "existence" is not in God, Exodus 3:14 shows us that "purity of existence" (*puritas essendi* [q. 1 n. 9]) can be ascribed to him. Later, in the second of the *Parisian Questions*, he gives a reason why *intellectus/puritas essendi* can be used as a primary name of God—"Intellect insofar as it is

intellect, is nothing of the things that it knows. . . . If therefore intellect insofar as it is intellect is nothing, then neither is understanding some kind of
existence."[307] The second key text, S. XXIX, also elevates *intelligere* above
esse and draws it close to *unum*. For Eckhart, like Thomas Aquinas, understanding must be conceived of in terms of identity and not of confrontation
between knower and known—understanding is becoming one with what is
understood. Hence Eckhart says, "Unity, or the One, seems to be proper to
and a property of intellect alone." Therefore, "the one God is intellect and
intellect is the one God."[308] Here too Eckhart seems to be taking *esse* in its
created sense and thus establishing the priority of *unum-intelligere*.

Thus it appears that when the proper distinctions and qualifications are
made, Eckhart is saying that *esse*, *unum*, and *intelligere* can all be used in
some way as language about God. This helps explain why even in his late
MHG preaching Eckhart often used "pure being" (*lûter wesen*), what the
Latin works refer to as *esse indistinctum*,[309] as a legitimate form of God-
language. As Pr. 91 puts it: "God is nothing but one pure Being, and the
creature is from nothing and also has one being from the same Being."[310]
The places where the Dominican says that God must be thought of as
"beyond being," or as a "being without being,"[311] can be squared with the
esse/wesen formulations *if* we take the former set of texts as referring to the
puritas essendi, and the latter to signal the *esse* that is the first of created
things spoken of in the *Book of Causes*. Although this may be making Eckhart neater than he would want to be, he too tried to regularize his verbal
"flow" when taken to task by the inquisitors.

Although Eckhart has been accused of confusion in his teaching on the
divine attributes, this does not really seem to be the case. As several recent
interpreters have argued, there is no essential opposition between "ontology" and "henology" in Eckhart.[312] From one perspective, *esse* and *unum*, as
well as *intelligere*, are terms that can be appropriately used in speaking
about God, at least to the extent that they are understood dialectically.
From another viewpoint, all language is wanting. Within the context of his
radical apophaticism, that is, the recognition that no human word is *really*
adequate for speaking about God, Eckhart's position is that it is in the play
of language explored through the therapy of preaching and second-order
reflection on naming God that we can begin to understand both what language can do and what its limits are.[313]

In reading Eckhart one is continually brought up short by the apophatic
horizon that limits all forms of knowing and speaking about God. God so
surpasses the measure of our intellect that there can be no real knowledge
of him. Our intellect works by comparing one thing with another (*ens hoc et*

hoc), but nothing can be compared to God because nothing is really distinct from him.[314] We have to make use of genus and species in speaking of things, but God has no genus and species. Hence, these categories are only used "according to our mode of understanding," not according to the reality of God's indistinct Oneness.[315] God, as Eckhart never tired of saying, is strictly speaking "unnameable to us because of the infinity of all existence in him," though, paradoxically, we also can assert that he is "omninameable."[316] Hence, Eckhart qualifies the predicating of any names, even *esse indistinctum, intelligere,* and *unum,* of God with frequent proclamations that God is really "No-thing"—"God is nothing at all"; "God is a nothing and God is a something"; "God is uncreated 'Self-Identity' and unnamed Nothingness."[317]

In Eckhart's preaching the overwhelming force of his desire to "speak" God to his audience (see, e.g., Pr. 60) collides with the impenetrable "unknownness of the hidden Godhead" (Pr. 15 [DW 1:253.1]) to produce many of his most striking and memorable passages. Whole sermons, such as Prr. 22, 52, 71, 80, and 83, are devoted to stripping away concepts and language in a form of intellectual ascesis designed to prepare for the unknowing that alone makes God present to us. Eckhart often uses a form of homiletic shock therapy in which he makes outrageous statements that taken at face value are almost blasphemous in character, as in the treatise on speaking about God in the recently edited Pr. 95b, where he says: "The more a person denies God, the more he praises him. The more one ascribes unlike things to him, the closer one comes to knowing him than if one tried to express a likeness." The goal of this practice is the deconstruction that leads to silent union. "As the soul comes to knowledge that God is unlike every nature, it also comes to a state of amazement and is driven further and comes into a state of silence. With the silence God sinks down into the soul and she is bedewed with grace."[318] The unknowing found in such a state is total. "What is the last end?" Eckhart asks in Pr. 22. "It is the hidden darkness of the eternal divinity, and it is unknown, and it was never known, and it will never be known. God remains there within himself, unknown."[319]

Creation as Boiling Over

Exitus/ûzganc occurs in the God who boils within as Trinity, as well as in God boiling over, or pouring forth into the created universe. ("All things are God over-boiled," as I once read in a student paper.) Eckhart's doctrine of creation helps us grasp how in his mysticism of absolute detachment from all created things lies the only way to be able to really enjoy them. A brief look at Eckhart's view of creation under two headings will help make this clear: (1) the notion of creation itself, especially creation as continuous (*creatio continua*); and (2) the *esse*, or mode of existence, of created being.[320]

Eckhart defines creation in several ways. Most simply, creation is the "giving of existence" (*collatio esse*), or in an expanded formula based on Avicenna, "creation is the giving of existence after non-existence."[321] Eckhart also used the formula, "Creation is the production of things from nothing."[322] Whenever he talks of God as "flowing into all creatures," Eckhart is speaking of creation: creation is the constant activity of God's influx into creatures to give them existence, that is, it is *creatio continua*.[323] This is why Eckhart's understanding of creation centers on *esse*, as both the "ground of creatability" (In Sap. n. 24), and also the purpose, or final cause, for God's action: "He created all things *so that they might be*" (Wis. 1:14).[324]

The function of *esse* in the production of all things from God needs to be understood in light of Eckhart's teaching about the relation of *esse* and *unum*, as well as of God as *principium*. A text from the *Commentary on John* says: "Existence (*esse*) is a principle under the idea or property of the One, and from it procedes the universe and the entirety of all created being."[325] What this means is that God as Creator is to be understood in terms of the one formal cause, that is, the "Ideal Reason" of all things. "You must recognize," as Eckhart says in his *Commentary on Genesis*, "that the 'principle' in which 'God created heaven and earth' is the Ideal Reason."[326] According to Eckhart, the metaphysician does not prove things through efficient and final causes, because these are external, but only through formal causality.[327] In contrast to Thomas Aquinas, whose view of creation was centered on God as efficient cause, Eckhart emphasized God's creative formal causality.

Eckhart's perspective on God as formal cause of the universe is evident in his use of the category *causa essentialis*, a term that had roots in Proclus and Dionysius and that had been developed by Albert the Great and Dietrich of Freiburg.[328] An essential cause, as Eckhart defines it, is an agent "that is a principle in which there is Logos and Idea, . . . an essential agent that precontains its effect in a higher way and exercises causality over the whole species of its effect."[329] An essential cause must be intellectual in nature— "Every true essential agent is spirit and life."[330] It is also a universal agent; not a member of the genus it causes, nor the cause of a particular effect.[331] Eckhart never denied that God was the efficient cause of the universe, but because he defined efficient causality as extrinsic (and nothing can really be extrinsic to God),[332] the notion of *causa essentialis* is more congenial to him than the Aristotelian category of efficient causality.

The ramifications of Eckhart's view of God's causality in creation are far-reaching. Two are evident in the errors concerning creation that Eckhart singles out in his discussion of the production of the universe in S. XXIII. The first is that God creates outside himself, or alongside himself, in nothing. No, says Eckhart, "Everything that happens in nothing, is surely nothing. . . . By creating, God calls all things out of nothing and from nothing to existence."[333] Since he does this "in the Principle," he does it in himself. As the *Commentary on Wisdom* puts it, "He creates all things from himself and in himself."[334] Nothing can be outside of, or distinct from, the *esse indistinctum* that is God. The second false view mentioned in the sermon and taken up in greater detail elsewhere is that "God created and rested from creating in the manner of other workers, according to the superficial sense of the text, 'God rested from all his work on the seventh day.'"[335] Eckhart rebuts this view by insisting that "God created in such a way that he is always creating." If there is no before and after for God in the simultaneous presence of his eternity to all forms of successive duration, then creation must be a continuous activity: *creatio continua.* As he put it in Pr. 30:

> That all creatures should pour forth and still remain within is very wonderful. . . . The more he is in things, the more he is out of things: the more in, the more out, and the more out, the more in. I have often said, God is creating the whole world now this instant. Everything God made six thousand years ago and more when he made this world, God is creating now all at once.[336]

God's continuous act of creation means that creation is eternal, as Eckhart taught in his *Commentary on Genesis* and throughout his works. To think of a time *before* creation is as much of a category mistake as to think of God resting *after* he finished his work.[337] Despite the attacks on his views, Eckhart never wavered in his conviction that the eternity of creation was a necessary implication of Christian faith, one that had been taught by Augustine and other authorities.[338] Of course, this did not mean that Eckhart denied that the universe was also temporal, that is, something made in time. As he once put it, "Exterior creation is subject to the time that makes things old."[339]

How did the Dominican put together these two seemingly contradictory assertions: the universe is eternal, and the universe is temporal? In order to understand this we need to call to mind his teaching concerning the two aspects of created being: virtual existence (*esse virtuale*) and formal existence (*esse formale*).[340] In the *Commentary on Wisdom* Eckhart says, "All things are in God as in the First Cause in an intellectual way and in the mind of the Maker. Therefore, they do not have any of their formal existence until they are causally produced and extracted on the outside in order to exist."[341]

Every creature, therefore, has both virtual existence in its essential cause and formal existence in the natural world.[342] Or, to put it in another way, the *esse* of creatures is both "from another" insofar as it is virtually hidden in its cause, and yet "proper" to itself insofar as it exists in the world.[343] Unlike Thomas Aquinas, for whom formal existence was essential for giving creatures a reality of their own, Eckhart's attention focuses on the virtual, true, that is, the "principial" existence of things in God. This can be seen in the way in which Pr. 57 uses the Neoplatonic symbol of the mirror to describe the nature of *esse formale*.[344] A face, Eckhart says, is always a face, whether or not a mirror is present. The image of a face in a mirror is dependent on the real face, having no existence apart from it and not effecting any change in the face itself. Take away the mirror, and you have an analogy to how the *esse formale* of creatures relates to the *esse virtuale* of created things in God's mind.

Understanding creatures from the perspective of their *esse formale* also helps explain Eckhart's assertions that creatures *taken in themselves* are nothing.[345] "Every created thing of itself is nothing," as Eckhart often repeated both in his scholastic writings and in his preaching. One passage to this effect from Pr. 4, as we have noted, was condemned as heretical. In defending himself at Cologne and Avignon, Eckhart grew indignant: "To say that the world is not nothing in itself and from itself, but is some slight bit of existence, is open blasphemy."[346] He might have appealed to Thomas Aquinas, who once said, "Each created thing, in that it does not have existence save from another, taken in itself is nothing."[347] To say that creatures are nothing for Eckhart is to say that the existence they possess is a pure receiving.[348] Poised between two forms of nothingness, the *nihil* by way of eminence that is God, and the *nihil* that marks the defect of creatures, Eckhart's mystical message is an invitation to the soul to give up the nothingness of its created self in order to become one with the divine Nothing that is also all things.[349]

Humanity as Image of God

Humanity as *imago/bild* occupies a special place in Eckhart's doctrine of the flow of all things from God. Although the universe is one and directed to the One, it is also multiple, hierarchically organized according to the three levels of existence, life, and intelligence. Each of these modalities exists principially in the immediate higher, so that mere being is life in living being, and living being is intellect in intellectual being.[350] The special status of intellectual being, comprising both humans and angels,[351] is that in its Principle it is divine—*imago Dei* in the full sense. Human destiny is to hear and respond to God's speech in creation and thus, as the *principium* in the created universe, to draw all things back to their ultimate source. In one place Eckhart says:

> Thus God speaks in the same way through everything to all that is. He speaks, I say, all things to all. But some hear him and respond under the property of existence by which God is existence and the existence of all things is from him. Others hear him and receive God's Word as it is the first and true Life. These are all living things. The highest beings hear God not only through and in existence, or through and in life, but through and in understanding itself. In that realm understanding and speaking are the same.[352]

Eckhart sets forth his teaching about humanity as intellectual image throughout his Latin and German works.[353] Much of this is standard medieval anthropology dependent on Augustine.[354] For example, in Pr. 83 Eckhart distinguishes three inferior powers of the soul (the power of discretion in the senses, and the irascible and appetitive powers), and three superior powers, the Augustinian triad of memory, understanding, and will.

Like all medieval theologians, Eckhart found the key to understanding humanity in Genesis 1:26, where God says, "Let us make man in our image and likeness." "This was said of the human race," according to the friar, "in relation to the intellect that pertains to the superior reason—that by which it is the 'head' of the soul and 'God's image.'"[355] "Note that humanity is what it is through the intellect," as he put it in another place.[356] Though it was customary in Latin theology to identify the *imago Dei* with the human intellect, Eckhart's understanding of *imago/bild* and *intellectus/vernünfticheit* is distinctive. Image and intellect are essential themes of his preaching.[357]

Eckhart's remarks on Genesis 1:26 in his *Commentary on Genesis* show how he understands humanity's character as *imago Dei*.[358] He says:

> Now recognize that the rational or intellectual creature differs from every creature below it because those below are produced according to a likeness of the thing as it is in God and they have the ideas that are proper to them in God. . . . The intellectual nature as such has God himself as a likeness rather than something that is in God as an idea. This is because "The intellect as such is the power to be all things." It is not restricted to this or that as to a species.[359]

The point is that, as we have seen in speaking of Eckhart's analysis of *imago* in S. XLIX above, "it is of the nature of an image that it fully expresses the entirety of what it images, not that it expresses some determined aspect of it."[360] Therefore, from the perspective of its relation to God, intellect is the image of the *whole* of divinity, while from the perspective of its relation to creatures, intellect, like God, images nothing because it has no determination. As Eckhart said in the *Parisian Questions*: "Intellect, insofar as it is intellect, is nothing of the things that it understands. . . . Therefore, if intellect, insofar as it is intellect, is nothing, then the act of understanding is not any kind of existence."[361] Intellect is not an *ens hoc et hoc.*

Because the intellect is capable of being one with all things in coming to know them, it is more than just the formal existence of some divine idea in the world—it is the presence of God as indistinct One in his creation. The *Commentary on John* takes this perspective even further when it says, "Man is created to the image of the entire divine substance, and thus not to what is similar, but to what is one; . . . [hence] a return to what is similar is not enough, but it must return to the One from which it came forth and this alone satisfies it."[362] Thus, the human intellect is essential to both the *exitus* and the *reditus* that form the dynamic of Eckhart's metaphysics of flow.

Eckhart knew and cited the Pauline texts (e.g., 2 Cor. 4:4 and Col. 1:15) that identify the Only-Begotten Son as the true *imago Dei*. Hence, it is not surprising that he applied the language of both *imago* and of *ad imaginem* to the human intellect, using *imago* to emphasize the indistinction of the divine and human intellect, and *ad imaginem* to express the distinction of our intellect from its divine source insofar as it possesses *esse formale* in this world. Because God's ground and the soul's ground is one ground, the human intellect is not other than the Only-Begotten Image in the Trinity; but it still always remains a created, or as Eckhart sometimes says, "concreated" (*concreatus*), reality. In Pr. 40 the preacher deliberately emphasizes the two perspectives: "In saying that man is one with God and is God according to that unity, one considers him according to [i.e., *inquantum*] that part of the image by which he is like God, and not according to his being created. In considering him as God, one does not consider him according to his being a creature."[363]

What is true of the Son in the Trinity is also realized of the soul *insofar as it is imago Dei*. In Pr. 16b Eckhart says: "You should know that the simple divine image which is pressed onto the soul in its innermost nature acts without a medium, and the innermost and the noblest that is in [the divine] nature takes form in a most proper sense in the image of the soul."[364] Since there is no medium between God and the soul, their relation is one of formal emanation, not creation. The sermon continues: "Here the image does not take God insofar as he is Creator; it takes him, rather, insofar as he is a being endowed with intellect, and what is noblest in [the divine] nature takes its most proper image in this image."[365] When image is understood in this way it is totally dependent on its exemplar: "an image is not from itself, nor is it for itself." Eckhart lists four implications of this: (1) an image is completely from its exemplar and belongs to it totally; (2) it does not belong to anything else; (3) it takes its being immediately from its exemplar; and (4) "it has one being with it and is the same being" (*und hât éin wesen mit im und ist daz selbe wesen* [270.6]). This affirmation of the complete identity of the soul with God—something Eckhart explicitly defends as a truth not just for the university classroom, but for the pulpit "for instruction" (*ze einer lêre*)—was later singled out for attack by the Cologne inquisitors.

The practical applications of Eckhart's teaching on the image of God come to the fore in the second part of Pr. 16b. Here the preacher invites his audience to live according to the inner image: "Be God's, not yours!" Loving God for devotion or for interior consolation is to make God into something to be used for another purpose, like a cow for its milk, as he says. Loving God should be its own reward. Calling upon his language of Justice and the just person, Eckhart continues:

> Only that person is just who has annihilated all created things and stands without distraction looking toward the Eternal Word directly and who is imaged [*gebildet*] and re-imaged [*widerbildet*] in Justice. Such a person takes where the Son takes and is the Son himself. The scripture says: "No one knows the Father but the Son" (Matt. 11:27);[366] and so, if you want to know God, you should not just be like the Son, rather you should be the Son himself.[367]

In three closely related sermons (Prr. 69, 70, and 72) Eckhart discusses the various kinds of images (*bilde*) in order to clarify the difference between knowing things through their created images and knowing God beyond all images in the true *imago Dei*, the Son of God. Prr. 70 and 72 explore how three ways of knowing make use of images. In Pr. 72 Eckhart discriminates (1) bodily knowing by means of the corporeal images the eye sees; (2) mental knowing through the images of bodily things; and (3) "the third [knowing which] is interior in the spirit, which knows without image or likeness, and this knowledge is like to that of the angels."[368] Pr. 70 helps explain this division by noting that the third form of knowing is the knowledge that angels and souls have of themselves, not of other things. It is a knowing without image, likeness, or medium of any kind (Pr. 70 [DW 3:194]). This is the self-presence of intellectual beings, something which for Eckhart is not mediated by any image. Such self-presence provides a hint for how we come to know God without image or medium. "If I am to know God without medium," says Eckhart, "without image, and without likeness, God actually has to become me and I have to become God."[369] In such a union of indistinction we come to know God as he knows himself. Eckhart puts it as follows:

> It is a property of God that he knows himself without a "little bit" (John 16:16) and without this or that. Thus does an angel know God—as it knows itself. . . . But I say: We shall know him just as he knows himself—in that reflection that alone is the Image of God and the Godhead (that is, to the extent that the Godhead is the Father). To the degree that we are like the Image into which all images have flowed forth and have left, and to the degree that we are re-imaged in this Image and are directly carried into the Image of the Father—to the degree that he recognizes this in us, to that degree we know him as he knows himself.[370]

Sermon 69 was also preached on John 16:16 ("A *little bit*," as Eckhart reads it, "and you will not see me").[371] Here the Dominican enriches his teaching on the image by relating it to the nature of the intellect as intellect. The "little bit" that gets in the way of seeing God is every kind of created being, any and all intermediaries. In physical seeing, says Eckhart, we do not see a stone itself, but an image of the stone. However, there is no infinite regress; that is, we do not need an image to see the image; the image itself is the medium. Extending the analogy, Eckhart says that in knowing spiritual things the eternal Word acts as the image without image that enables the soul to know God in that very Word itself (DW 3:168). Only the intellectual creature, however, has this relation to the Word. Eckhart explains: "There is a power in the soul, namely, intellect. From the moment it becomes aware of and tastes God, it has within itself five properties. The first is that it separates from here and now. The second, that it is like nothing. The third, that it is pure and unmixed. The fourth, that it is operating or seeking within itself. The fifth, that it is an image."[372]

The analysis of the meaning of these five properties makes it clear that there is no difference at all "insofar as intellect is concerned" between the divine Intellect and this power in the soul. This is because intellect *inquantum intellectus* is a true image in the sense of a pure formal emanation: "In this you have the whole sermon in a nutshell," says Eckhart. "Image [i.e., the Word] and image [the human intellect] are so completely one and joined together that one cannot comprehend any distinction between them. . . . I say further: God in his omnipotence cannot understand any distinction between them, for they are born together and die together."[373] Furthermore, it is intellect that alone provides access to the ground, as Eckhart says in concluding the sermon:

The intellect looks within and breaks through into every hidden cranny of the Godhead. It takes hold of the Son in the Father's heart and in the ground and places him in its own ground. Intellect penetrates within. It is not satisfied with goodness, or wisdom, or truth, or with God himself. . . . It never rests, it bursts into the ground from which goodness and truth come forth, and takes hold of it *in principio,* in the beginning where goodness and truth are coming forth, before it has a name, before it breaks out. . . .[374]

This view of intellect was at the heart of one of the most controversial aspects of Eckhart's teaching and preaching, his claims about the "uncreated something" in the soul. The first of the two appended articles in "In agro dominico" condemned the friar's teaching on the uncreated something: "There is something in the soul that is uncreated and not capable of creation; if the whole soul were such, it would be uncreated and not capable of creation, and this is the intellect." In his defense Eckhart denied saying precisely this (Proc.Col.I n. 137), though the article is quite close to a passage in Pr. 13.[375] In explaining what he meant, Eckhart again appealed to the difference between the pure Intellect of God, that is, the Word which is "uncreated and has nothing in common with anything," and "the created human being which God made to his image and not [as] the image itself; and he clothed it not with himself, but [only] according to himself."[376]

This uncreated something in the soul is *intellect insofar as it is intellect.* Eckhart characterized it in many ways, as we have seen—spark, castle, nobleman, seed, divine light, height, guardian, temple, etc.[377] Pr. 2 describes it as a "Single One" (*einic ein*: DW 1:43). In S. XXXVI Eckhart used a Latin form of this, taken over from Proclus, the *unum animae*: "Jesus comes to this [city of the soul] to seek the whole, the one of the soul."[378] In grasping what Eckhart meant by these expressions, we need, as always, to be attentive to the formal character of *inquantum* language. The "uncreated something" is *intellect as intellect,* that is as virtual being, not as formal being in the world. It is something *in* the soul (really the soul is in it); it is not *of* the soul, that is, it does not belong to the soul's created nature *ad imaginem.*[379] The uncreated something is not and cannot be a part of any-*thing.* It is another term for *grunt.*

III. The Return to the Ground

Eckhart's teaching about the outflowing of all things from God is a remarkable intellectual achievement, but the preacher did not wish his audience to be content with a merely academic grasp of the dynamism of *bullitio/ebullitio.* His message was designed to rouse his hearers to a new state of awareness that would lead them back into the divine ground. Any separation between *exitus* and *reditus* in Eckhart's works would be artificial, but, just as the preacher can only present one aspect of the divine mystery at a time, so too, for the sake of clarity, I will give an ordered analysis of the major themes of Eckhart's understanding of the return to God, though with the caveat that for Eckhart the "path" to God should not be conceived of as following a series of steps or stages. One must "Go forth without a way" (*genk âne wek*), as the Eckhartian poem called the "Granum Sinapis" puts it (on the poem see chapter 7, pp. 316–18). As Eckhart says in Pr. 5b, "Whoever is seeking God by ways is finding ways and losing God, who in ways is hidden."

We will begin with Christ, because Eckhart's understanding of the return centers on the role of the God-man. Just as creation is an eternal continuous process (*creatio continua*), so too, the Word's taking on flesh is not a past event we look back to in order to attain salvation, but is an ever-present hominification of God and deification of humanity and the entire universe: an *incarnatio continua*.

The Universal Christ[380]

Eckhart's view of Christ has little to do with the new christological currents that shaped the later Middle Ages. The importance of innovative forms of devotion to Christ's humanity that developed in the twelfth and thirteenth centuries is evident in the mention of names like Anselm of Canterbury, Bernard of Clairvaux, and Francis of Assisi.[381] Bernard's "carnal love of Christ" (*amor carnalis Christi*) and Francis's stigmata seen as a literal imitation of Christ's passion effected a revolution in piety.[382] Novel forms of piety were accompanied by a search for better understanding of the person and work of Christ in the theology of the schools. "Faith seeking understanding" pursued more adequate expressions of how God and man are truly one in Christ. Since the early twelfth century, theologians had also explored new ways of understanding redemption. How had Christ redeemed us? How did the effects of his death and resurrection reach the believer? Most thirteenth-century scholastics devoted great effort to exploring the nature of the hypostatic union, as well as to analysis of the meaning of redemptive satisfaction.

Meister Eckhart's writings show almost nothing of this. There are no pictures of the infant Jesus in the crib or meditations on the bleeding Christ on the cross. There is little consideration of the historical events of Christ's life. Eckhart does not discuss different theories of the hypostatic union or of redemptive satisfaction. Only a single MHG sermon gives attention to one of the hotly debated areas of speculative Christology, the question of the modes of knowledge, divine and human, enjoyed by Christ.[383] It is clear that Eckhart's preaching and teaching are exceptions to much late medieval Christology.

But does this mean that Christ is unimportant for Eckhart? Does his emphasis on the birth of the Divine Word in the soul reduce the historical events of Christ's life to a secondary status? If we think that the new spirituality of the *amor carnalis Christi* and the literal *imitatio Christi* is the only form of late medieval devotion to Christ, we must answer yes. Likewise, if analysis of the hypostatic union is essential to Christology, Eckhart has little to offer in this area. Nevertheless, the Dominican's view of Christ and his theology of redemption are both original and essential for understanding his mysticism. Without attention to the role of Christ it is impossible to understand Eckhart's message or to put it into practice.[384]

Eckhart's Christology was practical, that is, it was a "functional Christology."[385] The mystery of the God-man was not meant to be an exercise in making scholastic distinctions, but to be a motive for learning how to live the life of the Incarnate Word. This emphasis on the practical payoff also includes a place for an *imitatio Christi*, though one different from what we usually meet with in the late Middle Ages.

The best place to begin to appreciate Eckhart's Christology is in his commentary on John's Prologue.[386] The remarks on vv. 1–10 explore the relation between the just person and Justice, the theological foundation of Eckhart's preaching about the birth of the Eternal Word in the soul. However, when Eckhart reaches v. 11 ("He came into his own"), he reads the text both as expressing the universal reception of the Divine Word in all reality, and also as indicating the Word's assumption of human nature with all its passibility and mortality. This leads him to an interpretation of v. 12b ("He gave them the power of becoming sons of God") that reveals the core of his Christology, namely, his insistence on the *purpose* of the incarnation. God's intent in sending his Son was that "man may become by the grace of adoption what the Son is by nature" (n. 106). This version of the ancient patristic motto ("God became man that man might become God") was often repeated by Eckhart.[387] "Why did God become man?" he rhetorically asks in Pr. 29: "So that I might be born God himself" is the answer.[388]

The distinction between "Son by nature" and "sons by adoption" to which Eckhart appealed in interpreting John 1:12 was rooted in scripture, especially the Pauline letters, and can be found as early as Augustine.[389] Eckhart uses the distinction in a number of places in his Latin and German works.[390] When his Christology was taken to task in the trials at Cologne and Avignon, it is not surprising that he cited it to explain how his statements could be squared with traditional teaching.[391] For example, his defense of the final article from the second list of extracts culled from his German sermons says: "Don't think that there is one Son by which Christ is God's Son and another by which we are named and are sons; but it is the same and is he himself, who is Christ, born as Son in a natural way, and we, who are sons of God analogically—by being joined to him as heir, we are coheirs."[392]

In commenting on John 1:12, Eckhart explains God's intention in taking on human nature by citing one of his favorite christological texts, 2 Corinthians 3:18 ("With faces unveiled reflecting as in a mirror the glory of the Lord, we are being transformed *in the same image* from glory to glory"). If the distinction of sonships emphasizes the traditional side of Eckhart's theology of the incarnation, the stress on transformation into the *same*, that is, identical, image suggests its more daring aspects.[393] In concluding his reading of John 1:12, Eckhart returns to the first part of the verse and asks who are "the many who received him" and thus gained sonship? Here the Dominican introduces a third essential motif of his Christology, when he says that they are "as many as were empty of every form begotten and impressed by creatures" (n. 110). Total purity, emptiness, detachment—abandoning the *hoc et hoc* of created being—is the condition for receiving the "same image" which is Christ as God and man.

These three motifs are fleshed out in Eckhart's comments on v. 14a ("The Word became flesh and dwelt among us"). The friar says, "It would be of little value for me that 'the Word was made flesh' for man in Christ as a person distinct from me, unless he was also made flesh for me personally so that I too might be God's son."[394] Does this mean that we ourselves become the Second Person of the Trinity? Yes and no, according to Eckhart. Yes, in the sense that there is only one Sonship, which is not other than the Person of the Word; no, in the sense that "we are born God's sons *through adoption*." In his defense at Cologne and Avignon, Eckhart would appeal to the *inquantum* principle to explain this kind of expression. *Insofar as* there is only one real Son of God, if we are sons (as scripture expressly says), we are indeed identically the same Son *insofar as* we are sons univocally speaking. From the perspective of our existence as created beings, however, we are sons by adoption and participation, analogically speaking.[395]

Eckhart interprets the two parts of v. 14 as expressing the indissoluble link between the hominification of God and the divinization of man—"The Word was made flesh" in the incarnation, "'and dwelt among us' when in any one of us the Son of God becomes man and a son of man becomes God."[396] When he turns to v. 14b ("We saw his glory"), the cosmological implications of sonship emerge. Eckhart notes that in *Confessions* 7.9.13 Augustine said that he had found everything John wrote about the eternal generation of the Word in the "books of the Platonists," but he did not find there any reference to the incarnation. Eckhart disagrees with the bishop, claiming that seeing the glory of the Incarnate Word, notwithstanding the truth of the historical birth of Christ, ". . . is contained in and taught by the properties of the things of nature, morality, and art. The Word universally and naturally becomes flesh in every work of nature and art and it dwells in things that are made or in which the Word becomes flesh."[397] Every time a form is generated and comes to perfection in the natural world, and even in the artificial world of human creativity, we catch a glimpse of the glory of the Only-Begotten of the Father taking on flesh.

The explanation for this claim is not given until the comment on v. 17 ("The law was given through Moses, grace and truth were made through Jesus Christ"). In contrasting Moses and the Old Testament with Christ and the New Testament, Eckhart once again speaks ontologically, comparing the Old Law to the imperfection of all forms of change, becoming, and multitude, while the grace and truth of Christ indicate "existence, genera-tion, immutability, eternity, spirit, simplicity, incorruption, infinity, the one or unity" (n. 186). This is so because the incarnation is the necessary link between the eternal emanation within the Trinity and created reality. As he puts it:

> Again, note that because "The Word was made flesh," that he might dwell among us, as expounded above, . . . it seems fittingly added that the Wisdom of God deigned to become flesh in such a way that the incarnation itself, like a medium between the procession of the divine Persons and the production of creatures, tastes the nature of each. This happens in such a way that the incar-nation itself exemplifies the eternal emanation and is the exemplar of the entire lower nature.[398]

This passage expresses a pan-Christic ontology that views the incarnation, the hominification of God, as the purpose and inner reality of creation itself.[399] Eckhart makes the same point with economy in S. XXV: "'I came forth from the Father and came into the world' [John 16:28] through cre-ation, and not only through incarnation."[400]

Thus, Eckhart's functional Christology was not concerned with exploring the mode of the union of God and man in the incarnation. He concen-trated, instead, on the redemptive significance of the Word made flesh. The same message is conveyed in his vernacular preaching. An analysis of two sermons on Christ, as well as some passages in the *Book of Consolation*, will show how the Dominican presented the incarnation to a lay audience.

Pr. 46 is relatively short, but typically Eckhartian.[401] In explaining John 17:3 ("This is eternal life"), the preacher underlines three key points with interjections like *Nû merket* ("Now note well!"). The first is that in order to know God and reach blessednesṣ we must become "one Son, not many sons; rather, one Son," since in God there is only "a single natural flowing out" (*niht wan éin natiurlîcher ursprunc* [DW 2:379.1–2]), namely, that of the Eternal Word. The second point explains how this is possible. Just as Eckhart distinguished between the *ens hoc et hoc*, the *diz und daz* of created reality, and the pure *esse indistinctum* of God, so too the economy of redemption demands that the Word did not assume *this or that* human person, but pure, unformed humanity in itself. It is this humanity, without image or particularity, that the Son takes to himself. Because we too possess this humanity, his Form or Image (i.e., the very Image he eternally receives from the Father) becomes the image of humanity. "Hence," Eckhart says, "it is just as true that man became God as it is that God became man. This is how human nature was transformed [*überbildet*], [namely], by becoming the divine image, that is, the image of the Father."[402]

In order to attain this transformation we must free ourselves from all the "nothing," that is, everything accidental in us. What is accidental causes distinction, and distinction separates us from God. We leave behind every "accident of nature" (*zuoval der natûre*) by reaching the power in the soul that is "separated from nothing" (i.e, indistinct). When we arrive at this power, where God "shines naked," we can realize the status of being the one Son. Having attained this, we will have "movement, activity, and everything," no longer from our individual selves, but from the inner being and nature that the Son takes from the Father. We are now one in the unity of the Father and the Son so that "our" works (which are really now "his") come from within, not from outside, and are thus filled with divine life.[403]

How are we to go about freeing ourselves from the nothing that causes distinction, from our human personality considered as an "accident of nature"? Does the historical life of Jesus Christ play any role in this, or is the process based only on insight into the transcendental meaning of the incarnation? A brief look at a difficult sermon, Pr. 49 on the text "Blessed is the womb that bore you and the breasts that nourished you" (Luke 11:27), will help address these questions.[404] This sermon, as well as a number of other texts in Eckhart's writings, shows that there is definite place for an *imitatio Christi*, even an *imitatio passionis*, in his teaching.

The homily begins with a treatment of the relation between the Virgin

Mary's bearing the Savior and the birth of the Word in the soul of each Christian.[405] Eckhart insisted that it was because Mary was first completely attentive and obedient to God's word (Luke 11:28) that she merited to become the physical Mother of God. In the first part of the sermon, Eckhart makes use of Gregory the Great's description of four things needful for hearing and keeping God's word as a way of beginning the journey toward the one Sonship.[406] This can be described as a general imitation of Christ as "free and poor in all the gifts he gave." But such giving is external, and Eckhart always wants to push into the inner meaning of reality. Hence, in the second part of the sermon, he explores the interior understanding of hearing and keeping God's word.

Here the preacher reverses his consideration of the mutuality of Father and Son considered above in Pr. 46, this time beginning not from how the Son has everything *from* the Father, but rather from how the Father *needs* the Son as his perfect expression: "Whether he would or not, he must speak this Word and beget it unceasingly. . . . So you see the Father speaks the Word willingly but not by will, naturally but not by nature."[407] Echoing what we have seen in the previous sermon, Eckhart claims that in that same necessary speaking God speaks "my spirit and your spirit and every individual human's spirit equally in the same Word."[408] He develops this theme in terms of his teaching on how the soul in its ground possesses the divine power of begetting both the Word and itself in the eternal now. In what follows, however, Eckhart gives this theme a christological thrust by introducing John 12:24, a text that speaks of the grain of wheat falling into the earth in order to bear hundredfold fruit. The grain is the soul of Jesus which falls into the "most glorious humanity of Jesus Christ" (*hôchgelobete menschheit Jêsû Kristi* [439.1]). Eckhart's difficult explanation of how this takes place is not as important as why he invokes the motif of the death of the seed in the first place. Because Christ's fruitfulness comes from his suffering and death, if we too wish to be fruitful, we must follow his example.

In his consideration of the role of Christ's suffering and death in this sermon,[409] Eckhart says that Christ's pain affected only his outer person: "So it is in truth, for when his body died in agony on the cross, his noble spirit lived in this [divine] presence."[410] In affirming a distinction between Jesus' outer suffering and his inner stability in God, Eckhart was presenting his version of a medieval view that modern Christologies have often found problematic—the insistence that even in his suffering Christ somehow never lost the enjoyment of the beatific vision. Eckhart was to return to this theme a number of times in his vernacular works.[411] In this sermon, however, what is important is how Eckhart presents the relation between

Christ's suffering and the central theme of his Christology: God became man so that man can become God.

The grain of wheat that is Christ's human soul perished in the body of the God-man in two senses. First, Christ's human soul possessed an intellectual vision of the divine nature that it continued to enjoy in its ontological ground, but not in the consciousness of its lower powers during his lifetime. (This is the first, or spiritual, death.) Second, Christ's soul gave life to his human body with all that it suffered until he surrendered it in dying on the cross (the second, physical, death). Both modes of dying are significant. Christ's spiritual death meant not turning away from God no matter what the body had to suffer, while his physical death, offering up all his sufferings to the glory of his heavenly Father, "became fruitful . . . to the sanctification of human nature" (444.5–6). Following Christ's example, then, anyone who wishes to cast his soul/grain of wheat into the field of the sacred humanity of Jesus must also die in *both* physical and spiritual fashion.[412] Physical death means accepting willingly what suffering God may send us, regarding all our "suffering as trifling, as a mere drop of water compared to the raging sea, . . . compared to the great suffering of Jesus Christ."[413] Spiritual suffering, however, is inward, nothing less than absolute abandonment to God's will, even if this should involve annihilation or consignment to hell: "You should let God do what he will with you, what he will—just as if you did not exist. God's power should be as absolute in all that you are as it is within his own uncreated nature."[414] According to Eckhart, Christ is the true model for such inner emptying: "Christ our Lord alone is the end to which we must strive and our goal under which we must stay, with whom we shall be united, equal to him in all his glory. . . ."[415]

It is evident from this sermon that Eckhart did not neglect an *imitatio passionis*, though, as we might expect, he had little interest in exterior practices, such as meditation on the blood-drenched Jesus on the cross, let alone physical attempts to inflict such suffering on oneself. Eckhart's reading of the *imitatio passionis* is that enough suffering will come in the course of any life to allow us to imitate the example of Jesus as a way to get beyond our individual wills. We do not need to seek out suffering—we need to transform the way we view suffering. Suffering is not a special way to God, but a way to discover that God is not found in ways.

The role of suffering as imitation of Jesus is featured in the *Book of Consolation*. Here Eckhart takes suffering into the heart of his dialectical understanding of our relationship to God.[416] The *Book of Consolation* is an impressive meditation on the last of the beatitudes, "Blessed are they who suffer persecution for justice's sake" (Matt. 5:10). Beginning from commonplace observations found in standard consolation literature, Eckhart moves on through two deeper levels. The first shows how suffering is really consolation when we recognize it as God's will. The second, typically Eckhartian and based on the identity of the soul's ground and God's ground, asserts that when we accept suffering in this way, God too must be said to suffer: "My suffering is in God and my suffering is God."[417] This claim shows that Eckhart regards divine suffering not as our projection onto God (i.e., from below), but rather as a reality from above: God's desire to suffer is an integral aspect of his eternal will for the Word to become man, and even of the divine decision to create the world. As Eckhart ironically put it in another passage in the treatise: "But God's Son by nature wished by his grace to become man so that he might suffer for you, and you want to become God's son and not man, so that you cannot and need not suffer for God's sake or your own!"[418] Eckhart's view of the mystery of suffering is as challenging as other aspects of his teaching.

The Dominican's understanding of the purpose of the incarnation—God became man so that man can become God—was scarcely new. Nevertheless, Eckhart stands out among his contemporaries in the emphasis he gave to this ancient theological theme, as well as in the variety of ways he presented it.[419] The *exemplum* that Eckhart used in Pr. 22 to illustrate the love that brought the Word down to take on human nature for our sake is particularly striking. He tells the story of a rich man and his wife who had the misfortune to lose an eye. In order to prove the constancy of his love for her, the man gouged out one of his own eyes. Eckhart summarizes the intent of God/the rich man as follows: "'Madam, to make you believe that I love you, I have made myself like you; now I too have only one eye.' This stands for man, who could scarcely believe that God loved him so much, until God gouged out one of his own eyes and took upon himself human nature."[420]

Implied in this functional Christology is Eckhart's unusual teaching about the Word's assumption of universal human nature. To be sure, since the condemnation of Nestorius in the fifth century, it had been common teaching that Christ did not assume a human person, but human nature as such. Eckhart, however, gave this teaching his own spin.[421] Because the Word assumed undifferentiated human nature, not only is divine Sonship open to us only in and through Christ, but, Eckhart claimed, we must be sons in *exactly* the same way that he was.[422] This position was the source of the expressions of the one Sonship for which Eckhart was taken to task in his trials. Several of these excerpts eventually featured in the bull of condemnation, notably articles 11 and 12. Article 11, from Pr. 5a, reads: "Whatever God the Father gave to his Only-Begotten Son in human nature, he gave all this to me. I except nothing, neither union, nor sanctity; but he gave the whole to me, just as he did to him."[423]

Many other issues emerge from Eckhart's functional Christology. Among the most important for the friar's mystical teaching is his view of the relation of time and eternity, an area of some of the Dominican's more controversial speculations. In Galatians 4:4 Paul had said, "In the fullness of time (*plenitudo temporis*) God sent his Son." Eckhart did not read this passage, as was customary, as relating to the course of temporal history, but rather as a reference to the "now" of eternity breaking into each moment of human time. Paul's *plenitudo temporis* is comparable to when the day is "full" (i.e., at an end), because "if it were possible for the soul to be touched by time, then God could never be born in her, and she could never be born in God." Alternatively, the fullness of time can be conceived of as the gathering up of the whole six thousand years of history into the "now of eternity, in which the soul knows all things in God new and fresh and present and joyous as I have them now present."[424] The inherent presentiality of Eckhart's Christology is well brought out in both these readings of Paul—a new way of presenting the incarnation as the meeting place of time and eternity.

Two practical conclusions of Eckhart's functional Christology further emphasize the importance of the God-man for his preaching. The first, already touched on above, concerns the *imitatio Christi*. Eckhart's advice for following Jesus is concerned not with details of moral observance but with intentions—and only the most essential. As noted in the analysis of Pr. 49, the imitation of Christ's passion was significant for Eckhart, but when he considered the passion, he did not retell the story of the death of Jesus, nor did he usually invite his readers to meditate on Christ on the cross. He rather stressed the inner meaning of Matthew 16:24: "If anyone wishes to come after me, let him take up his cross and follow me." For Eckhart, imitation of Christ on the cross was nothing more nor less than total self-denial.[425]

In his treatise entitled the *Talks of Instruction*, for example, Eckhart insisted that to imitate Christ means to be like him in totally surrendering to the Father, and not in trying to follow the particulars of his life, such as his forty-day fast in the desert.[426] The friar's view of self-denial, like his interpretation of poverty in Pr. 52, was radical in the etymological sense of going to the roots. What is essential is to appropriate the inner attitude that Jesus revealed in his suffering and death by becoming totally fixed on God, no matter what the external situations in which we find ourselves.[427] Suffering, as pointed out above, is not a *way* to God, but is actually identical with the goal. If we understand suffering as our opportunity to surrender to the God who totally surrenders himself to us in taking on flesh, then we will grasp that "[i]n order to give himself totally, God assumed me totally."[428]

This view of suffering as detachment and emptying is evident in texts scattered throughout Eckhart's writings. The treatise *On Detachment*, while it may not actually be Eckhart's, is true to his spirit when it says: "The fastest beast that will carry you to perfection is suffering, for no one will enjoy more eternal sweetness than those who endure with Christ in the greatest bitterness."[429] Taken out of context, this sentence might seem to encourage physical forms of passion piety, but whoever wrote the passage proposed these words in light of the declaration already noted from the *Book of Consolation*, "My suffering is God"—and therefore not really *mine*. As long as we consider anything, even suffering, under the rubric of what is "mine," we will always be caught in distinction and be far from God. If, in the midst of suffering, we learn that the pain is his (as he made it in his passion), we are on the way to realizing the one divine Sonship.

Grace and the Means of Salvation

Eckhart's Christology is linked to his teaching on grace. In the *Commentary on John*, as we have seen, he defines the purpose of the incarnation to be "that man may become *by the grace of adoption* what the Son is by nature" (n. 106). In S. LII he expands on this: "God took on our vesture so that he might truly, properly, and substantially be man and man might be God in Christ. The nature taken up is common to all humans, neither more nor less. Therefore, every person can be God's Son, substantially in him, adoptively in self through grace."[430] These texts underline the necessary connection between the incarnation and grace in the return process.[431]

Though grace is important for understanding Eckhart, it is not easy to say exactly what he means by grace. His usage often tends to be general, and traditional formulations appear side by side with distinctive, unusual, and even extreme expressions.[432] Eckhart quoted Thomas Aquinas in expounding grace, but his teaching in its fundamentals is different from that of Thomas.[433] What, then, was grace for Meister Eckhart?

On the most general level, as we have seen in discussing creation, Eckhart holds that grace is every gift we receive from God, from the first grace of our created being (*gratia gratis data*) to the gift of our return to God through intellect (*gratia gratum faciens*).[434] Eckhart takes up this distinction of graces in a passage in the *Commentary on Wisdom* that provides a good introduction to his teaching.[435] Quoting the twentieth axiom from the *Book of*

Causes, he says that all things are a free gift (*gratia gratis data*) from the First which is "rich in itself." More important for his mystical preaching, however, is the *gratia gratum faciens*, which is described as a "divine mode of existence" (*esse divinum*) given to the essence of the soul so that it can work divinely and spiritually. This grace, "which is called supernatural, is in the intellective power alone, but it is not in it as a natural thing, but is there as intellect so that it can taste the divine nature."[436] This is true of intellect "insofar as it is the image or [made to] the image of God" (n. 274). So, truly "supernatural" grace is essential to the return process and is intimately connected to the intellect. But in what way?

This is where Eckhart's teaching on grace grows unusual. Eckhart agrees with Augustine and Thomas that grace is essential for the soul's return to God. He also stands with tradition in insisting that saving grace is the grace made available to us in Christ. The christological character of grace is evident both in the creative grace of *exitus* and the grace of recreation, or return: "And so *every* grace is in God alone, the Wisdom of God, the Son, because all his gifts are unmerited and are of him alone."[437] But Eckhart's teaching on grace departs from Aquinas in at least two ways. First of all, grace has a more intellective cast for Eckhart than it does for Aquinas—for Eckhart grace saves primarily insofar as it activates the intellect to become aware of itself as *imago Dei*.[438] For Aquinas, on the other hand, saving grace (*gratia gratum faciens*) primarily elevates the fallen will, supernaturally enabling it to love God for God's sake alone.[439] Second, the relationship between grace and union is clear in Aquinas but ambiguous in Eckhart. For Thomas Aquinas, union with God in this life takes place only in and through the action of supernatural grace. Eckhart, on the other hand, sometimes affirms that grace unites us to God, but at other times speaks of grace more as a means than as an end: something necessary to attain indistinct union with God, but not constitutive of union itself. These seemingly contradictory statements parallel the clash between passages that speak about the "work of grace" and those that declare "grace performs no works, it is too delicate for this; work is as far from grace as heaven is from earth."[440]

Grace is said to be the necessary means for attaining God in both the Latin and MHG works. For example, Pr. 96 says that every action or work (*ieglich werk*) flows from a particular form of being (*wesen*), as warmth does from fire. Without the grace that makes the soul like God and "God-colored" (*gotvar*), it could do no saving work.[441] Eckhart compares grace to an axe that enables the task of cutting to be done, concluding with the statement: "Grace brings the soul into God and brings it above itself, and it robs it of itself, and of everything that is creaturely, and it unites the soul with God."[442] In this sermon grace seems both active and unitive. S. XXV says the same, describing grace as "a boiling over of the birth of the Son, having a root in the Father's inmost heart." As the highest good, according to Eckhart, such grace "is a confirmation, a configuration, or better, a transfiguration of the soul into and with God . . . ; it makes one have one existence with God, something that is more than assimilation."[443] But elsewhere grace is clearly not unitive. "I say: grace does not unite the soul with God. It is a bringing to [the point of] fullness; that is its function, that it bring the soul back again to God."[444] In other places, such as in Pr. 82, Eckhart clearly distinguishes between two levels of union with God: one in which the soul is raised up by grace and united in a preliminary way; and a second in which grace, because it is something created, must slip away, so that the soul no longer works by grace, but divinely in God as the "mode without mode."[445]

A key for understanding both how grace works and does not work and unites and does not unite can be found in Eckhart's teaching about the difference between the virtual and the formal modes of existence. In S. IX, preached on the text "the God of all grace" (1 Pet. 5:10), the Dominican says that if the grace of any single person is great,

> . . . how great [is the grace] of every human, and of all the different kinds of angels; how great it is to live there, that is, in the very "God of all grace," where already grace is not grace formally, but virtually (just as heat is in the sky)—there where there is neither goodness, nor delight, nor existence, but [only what is] above "in the region and realm of infinite unlikeness."[446]

From this perspective, we can also understand how, as Pr. 43 puts it, grace in its virtual state "has never done any work at all," but formally considered, "it flows forth in the doing of good works."[447]

The uniting with God that formal grace effects is not indistinct union from the perspective of the *ratio gratiae*, that is, the "grace beyond grace" which, in its virtual reality, is identical with the divine nature. This can be seen in Pr. 70, where Eckhart speaks about three forms of progressive illumination that lead the soul back to God. The natural light of the intellect, higher than the sun's light, can attain God in some way, but "intellect is little compared to the light of grace" that transcends all created things. "Yet the light of grace, great as it is, is little indeed compared with the divine light." As long as grace is growing in us, it is still grace in a formal sense and is thus distinct from God. "But when grace is perfected in the highest, it is not grace: it is a divine light in which one sees God. . . . [At that point] there is no access, there is only an attainment."[448] In Pr. 75 a comparable pattern emerges in which Eckhart contrasts the light of the intellect with the stronger light of grace that draws a person into himself. Higher still is the light that is the divine Son being born in the Father's heart. "If we are to enter there," says Eckhart, "we must climb from the natural light into the light of grace, and grow therein into the light that is the Son himself. There we shall be loved by the Father in the Son with the love that is the Holy Spirit. . . ."[449] Despite some ambiguity, there does seem to be an inner coherence to the Dominican's theology of grace behind his at-times-opposed formulations.[450]

In many late medieval mystics an investigation of their doctrine of grace would naturally lead into their views on how Christ's grace is mediated to the community through the means of salvation, that is, the sacramental life of the church. Once again, Eckhart's mysticism appears anomalous, if not exactly subversive. On the surface at least, there is little ecclesiology, sacramentology, or discussion of spiritual practices in Eckhart, although his earliest vernacular work, the *Talks of Instruction*, does offer some reflections on necessary virtues, such as obedience and zeal, as well as on essential practices, such as prayer, repentence, self-abandonment, and detachment. In this treatise the friar also instructs his charges on the role of the Eucharist and the sacrament of penance.[451] But even in this work, as Andreas Schönfeld has shown, Eckhart criticizes the standard goal-oriented understanding of prayer and spiritual exercises, insisting that outward practice means nothing without inward reception and the proper attitude. "What is new in Eckhart's teaching," according to Schönfeld, "rests in the fact that he thinks of God's immediacy not as the goal of an inner development, but in general as the starting-point of the spiritual life."[452] This message was to become more pronounced in his later vernacular preaching. Although the Dominican's homilies were solidly anchored in the liturgical life of the worshiping community, his uncompromising insistence on the inner appropriation of the saving mysteries did not leave much room for discussion of the sacraments and particular practices of devotion.[453]

One exercise of the Christian life that Eckhart does discuss with some frequency is prayer.[454] Here too his teaching is different from what we find in most of his contemporaries. Eckhart's remarks about prayer were unconventional enough that two of them were included in "In agro dominico" as heretical. The first of these, drawn from the *Commentary on John*, expresses the heart of Eckhartian prayer: "He who prays for anything particular prays badly and for something that is bad, because he is praying for the negation of good and the negation of God, and he begs that God be denied to him."[455] Prayer, for Eckhart, should not be a petition for any-*thing* from God—that is the work of those he refers to as "asses" or spiritual "merchants."[456] Rather, it is the continuing dialogue (*confabulatio*) of the detached soul with God alone: a prayer without *eigenschaften* (i.e., personal attachments and concerns); a prayer to and for the Divine Nothing.[457] Both the prayers with which Eckhart the preacher concludes his sermons and the four prayers ascribed to him in manuscript sources amply illustrate his view of the prayer of detachment.[458]

It is important to get Eckhart's stance about practices of piety correct. In spite of his challenging statements about the uselessness of trying to find God in ways, the Dominican never denied the efficacy of the church as the mediator of Christ's saving grace, nor did he attack the sacraments and the other ordinary means by which saving grace is communicated to the faithful. Even his condemned remarks about petitionary prayer need to be seen within the context of his hyperbolical style of preaching *rara et subtilia*. Eckhart was no rebel. Rather, he was fixated on the end, God in Godself, not on means. For him total inner detachment was the only proper attitude for all prayer and practice. One cannot escape the conviction that in taking this stance he was implicitly criticizing much of the preaching and devotion he saw around him in the early fourteenth century.

Detaching/Birthing/Breaking-Through

All of Eckhart's preaching in one way or another is geared to the over-arching theme of helping his audience to return to the ground in which God and human are fully one (*ein einic ein*). We have already touched on some of the major motifs of the return in investigating the *grunt*. What follows is a summary of the process of *reditus* through an analysis of the three central activities Eckhart uses to describe the soul's return to God: detaching (*abescheiden*); birthing (*gebern*); and breaking-through (*durchbrechen*).

Eckhart's notion of return is not a mystical itinerary in the usual sense; it is the attainment of a new form of consciousness, as mentioned above. I have argued throughout the volumes of *The Presence of God* that the consciousness of God's immediate presence provides a flexible and useful framework for understanding the varied teachings of the mystics that are often grouped under the heading of "union." Consciousness of God's presence, even the reverse-awareness that comes from a sense of God's absence, is the formal feature of the various types of mystical language: union, contemplative vision, endless pursuit, divine birth, deification, radical obedience, and so on.

Eckhart makes considerable use of the language of presence in his preaching, though as with many apophatic mystics, the God who becomes paradoxically present is often the "non-God, non-spirit, non-person, non-image" found in silence and darkness (Pr. 83). In his Latin works Eckhart notes scholastic discussions of the ways in which God is present to all things, especially his immediate presence as *esse indistinctum.*[459] The same teaching is found in the MHG sermons, for instance, when the friar says that "All creatures have no being, because their being is suspended (*swebet*) in God's presence (*gegenwerticheit*)."[460] What Eckhart wants his hearers to grasp is not the abstract truth that God is present in all things, but the reality of what it means to live in this awareness.[461] This message is found throughout his teaching and preaching. For example, the sixth of the *Talks of Instruction* speaks of finding God's presence in everything. "He who has God essentially, takes him divinely. . . . God flashes forth in him always, in him there is detachment and turning away, and he bears the imprint of his beloved, present God."[462] The call to be "penetrated with divine presence" (*mit götlîcher gegenwerticheit durchgangen sîn* [208.11]) occurs often in this early work, which roots its teaching in the fact that "God is a God of the present," not of the past.[463] The presentiality of the divine *nû* in which "God is an instanding in himself, an instanding that supports all creatures,"[464] is also found in the later German sermons. An important treatment occurs in Pr. 9, one of Eckhart's most forceful statements of negative mysticism. In this homily the friar uses the planet Venus, which always stands near the sun, like an adverb to the Divine Word, as a figure of "a person who wants to be always near to and present to God in such a way that nothing can separate him from God."[465] Constant awareness of the *gegenwerticheit gotes* is an essential part of Eckhart's message.

How is one to attain this awareness of God's presence in the ground of the soul? Eckhart's attempts to lead his audience to this consciousness defy easy characterization, but we can gain a sense of his strategy by exploring the three essential processes of detaching, or cutting off, birthing, and breaking-through.[466] Although Eckhart used nouns developed from these verbs, it is important to emphasize that he is speaking about activities, not static states of being.

Eckhart's mysticism has often been described as one of detachment, or more literally, of "cutting off, or away."[467] There are few motifs that the Dominican appealed to more often in his vernacular preaching.[468] The ways in which the preacher spoke of the need for separation from all earthly attachments in order to attain the freedom to find God are too varied to be expressed by any single term, so Eckhart employed a range of verbs to convey his strategy for ending possessiveness. These include: detaching or cutting off (*abescheiden*); leaving, letting go, resigning (*lâzen/*

gelâzen); un-forming, or dis-imaging (*entbilden*);[469] un-becoming (*entwerden*). From these action words a series of nouns was formed to express aspects of the deconstruction process, especially *abegescheidenheit* and the rarely used (at least by Eckhart) *gelâzenheit*.[470] A set of adjectives expressing the freedom, emptiness, and nakedness of the dispossessed soul—*ledic, vri, lûter, blôz*—created another semantic range for proclaiming the same message.[471]

Eckhartian detachment is a process that is at once metaphysical, ethical, and mystical. Rooted in the metaphysics laid out in detail in the Latin works, it is present in more ethical and mystical registers throughout the vernacular treatises and sermons. Time and again Eckhart appeals to the principle that a receptive power cannot receive a form unless it is empty and free of other forms—the eye can only see color because it has no color of its own. On a higher level, the intellect can understand all things because it is no-thing in itself, but rather the capacity to know all. Intellect, then, must be empty and free of all created forms and all attachment to forms in order to receive God. The treatise *On Detachment*, though not by Eckhart, summarizes his position concisely: "You must know that to be empty of all created things is to be full of God, and to be full of created things is to be empty of God."[472] Total letting go, following the paradox of the Christian message ("He who would save his soul must lose it" [Matt. 16:25]), is the way to gain all things in the God who is the being of all. "The more a person has left behind and the more poor he is," according to *Commentary on John*, "so much the more he finds; and what he has left behind, he finds in a higher and purer way."[473]

It will not be possible to survey all the ways in which Eckhart preached this message of detachment and deconstruction,[474] but study of a few central texts will suffice to convey Eckhart's message. Detachment was a central part of Eckhart's message from the beginning, as we can see from the *Talks of Instruction*, where three chapters introduce many of the aspects of the detaching process that Eckhart would preach on for the next quarter century. Chapter 3 deals with "Unresigned people (*ungelâzenen liuten*) who are full of self will."[475] Spiritual restlessness, says Eckhart, comes not from things or situations but from our own self-will: "You have to start first with yourself and leave yourself."[476] If we can learn to let ourselves go, we are in effect letting everything go. Here Eckhart cites two of his favorite biblical texts on giving up all things by first giving up self (Matt. 5:3 and 16:24). Such self-abandonment is to be understood as the truest form of self-knowledge: "Take a good look at yourself, and wherever you find yourself, let yourself go; that is the very best."[477] As Alois Haas has shown in his study of self-knowledge in Eckhart, it is only through the grace of Christ who has taken on the whole of human nature that humans can come to know themselves directly and essentially.[478] In perfect self-surrender, God's self-knowing becomes our self-knowing; or better, since there is no distinction in the one ground, there is only a single essential self-knowing. The background for this claim was to be spelled out later on in the Dominican's teaching on intellect and the ground, but the ethico-mystical imperative is already present in his first vernacular work.

The sixth of the talks ("Detachment and Possessing God" [DW 5:200–209]) links letting-go with awareness of the divine presence, as noted above. In this section, Eckhart once again says that only the internal state of being "God-mindful" allows us to have God ever present to us. "This true possessing of God depends on the mind [*gemüete*], and on an inner intellectual turning toward and striving for God, not in a continuous thinking [of him] in the same manner, for that would be impossible for nature. . . ."[479] God is beyond images and concepts, so it is only by "learning to break through things" (*Er muoz lernen diu dinc durchbrechen* [207.8]) and reaching the "inner desert" that we can find him. The teacher compares this awareness of God to a continuous thirst, and also to a skill such as learning to write—at first it takes effort, but with practice it becomes second nature.

The longest consideration of detachment in the *Talks of Instruction* occurs in chapter 21 (DW 5:274–84). Learning to be "free in [doing] works" so that God can be always present to us demands "vigorous diligence" (*behender vlîz*) in keeping free of both outward and inward images. Eckhart's treatment of this inwardness is reminiscent of the teaching found in the Sermon Cycle on the Eternal Birth (Prr. 101–104). Reaching such a condition involves careful and constant training of the intellect and the will: "There is no standing still for us in this life, and never has been for any man, however advanced he might be."[480] When what Eckhart calls the decisive and essential will has attained a constant "well-practiced detachment" (*wolgeüebete abegescheidenheit*), a person can begin to receive gifts from God. Just as individual consciousness vanishes in the true self-awareness that is God, so too the created will itself must be annihilated. "God never gave himself and never will give himself in another's will: he only gives himself in his own will. Where God finds his own will, there he gives himself and bestows himself in it with all that he is."[481] Hence, continues Eckhart, "We must learn to let ourselves go until we retain nothing at all that is ours. . . . We should put ourselves with all that is ours in a pure un-becoming of will and desire into the good and beloved will of God, along with everything we

could will or desire in all things."[482] Here the un-forming and un-becoming
of the created will, to be powerfully proclaimed in Eckhart's later preaching, is already present.

The most famous sermon on the need for annihilating the created will is
Pr. 52, Eckhart's exploration of the three forms of poverty suggested by the
beatitude "Blessed are the poor of spirit for theirs is the kingdom of
heaven" (Matt. 5:3). Although this homily does not use the terms "detaching" or "detachment," its fifteen references to the adjective free (*vrî*) and
three uses of empty (*ledic*), which both refer equally to God and to the soul,
show that it must be ranked among the premier Eckhartian texts on the
need for radical deconstruction of the created self. Edmund Colledge and
others have shown how this sermon contains echoes of the doctrine of annihilation of the created will found in Marguerite Porete.[483] Although this fact
witnesses to the Dominican's respect for this profound mystic, it is clear that
Eckhart had already recognized that without negation of both intellect and
will no real consciousness of God could be attained.

The poverty sermon has often been analyzed.[484] Here I wish only to
highlight how Eckhart's three realizations of poverty of spirit—wanting
nothing, knowing nothing, and having nothing—constitute the absolute
freedom that is the prerequisite for becoming truly aware of the God
beyond God. Any form of attachment, even to our good works, or to our
own will to follow God, must be relinquished, according to Eckhart. One
must strive to become as free of one's created will as one was before creation: an "empty existence" (*ledic sîn*) in which God as creator no longer is
of concern.[485] Becoming free of will, for Eckhart, involves letting go of the
will to be free of will. It means the rejection of all human works. As
Michael Sells has shown, this is not a form of quietism or a lack of produc-
tivity: "The rejection of 'human' work is not a rejection of activity, but of
the identification of the agent with the ego-self. . . . The true actor is the
divine who works in the soul."[486] The return process frees us from God as
Creator and returns us to a blessedness beyond loving and knowing where
"God is free of all things and therefore is all things." It is interesting to note,
however, that in this radical expression of the meaning of freedom and
detachment given to a lay audience, Eckhart recognizes that the message
may well be lost on many: "Whoever does not understand what I have
said, let him not burden his heart with it; . . . for this is a truth beyond speculation that has come immediately from the heart of God."[487]

One of the questions concerning Eckhart's view of detaching from all
created things and desires is how this process relates to the other virtues.[488]
For Eckhart, detachment is not just another virtue, just as it is not just

another type of experience. As Denys Turner puts it, "Detachment and interiority are, for Eckhart, not so much the names of experiences as *practices for the transformation of experience*. . . . 'Detachment,' in short, is the ascetic practice of the apophatic."[489] We must beware, then, of any easy importation of modern psychological categories back into Eckhartian detachment. The treatise *On Detachment*, even if it is not from Eckhart's own hand, is helpful for understanding how detachment, as the relinquishing of possessiveness, is to be understood as a formal feature of all the virtues, rather than just another example of the genus.

The treatise begins by boldly proclaiming detachment as superior to humility, traditionally the foundation of all the virtues, and even more important than love, the summit of the Christian life. The reason for this superiority is that detachment, defined here as the spirit's standing "immovable against whatever may chance to it of joy or sorrow, shame, and disgrace," is actually a fundamental characteristic of the divine nature: "God has it from his immovable detachment that he is God, and it is from his detachment that he has his purity and his simplicity and his unchangeability."[490] It is clear as the treatise proceeds, however, that there can be no detachment without perfect humility and that the love to which detachment is superior is the lower interested love by which we love God as *our* final good.

The higher and purer form of detached love is explored in Pr. 27 preached on the text, "This is my commandment, that you love one another as I have loved you" (John 15:12). In this homily Eckhart says that Christ is enjoining on us "a love so pure, so bare, so detached that it is not inclined toward myself nor towards my friend nor anywhere apart from itself."[491] This love is nothing else than the Holy Spirit. Such detached divine love has no other goal than God and goodness. Because it is one with divine love, it possesses all virtues and virtuous deeds. "If your love is really so pure, so detached, and so bare in itself that you love nought but goodness and God, then it is certain truth that all the virtuous deeds performed by all men are yours as perfectly as if you had performed them yourself."[492] Such loving detachment is the heart of all true virtue.

Many aspects of Eckhart's view of detachment attracted the attention of his opponents, though there is no explicit condemnation of the term in the bull "In agro dominico."[493] It is surprising that one of the most radical corollaries of the apophasis of possessiveness did not arouse more controversy—this is the notion, found in the treatise *On Detachment* and also in places in Eckhart's sermons and other writings, that true detachment "compels" (*twinget*) God to work in us.[494] In the treatise we read that detachment surpasses love because love compels me to love God but detachment compels God to love me. Pr. 48 contains a strong assertion of this notion that absolute self-emptying forces God to fill the vacuum in the soul because it is really nothing else but his own emptiness. Speaking of the person "who has annihilated himself in himself and in God and in all things," Eckhart says that "God must pour the whole of himself into this man, or else he is not God."[495] In order to understand this language we should be mindful of the identity in the one ground that annihilating detachment creates, or perhaps better, borrowing a word from Simone Weil, "decreates." In this ground God *must* be God, and therefore must flood into what is grounded in him.

The process of detaching the soul from all things, especially from the created self, raises the question of the status of the "I" and subjectivity in general in Eckhart's mysticism. This issue has produced disagreement between those who would see Eckhart's thought as the beginning of a trajectory that leads to modern theories of transcendental subjectivity, and others who argue that his notion of the destruction of the created self should be viewed primarily within the context of medieval asceticism and mysticism.[496] In both his Latin and MHG works, Eckhart contended that the pronoun *I* rightly belongs only to God. In Pr. 28, for example, he says, "'Ego,' the word 'I,' belongs to no one save God alone in his oneness."[497] God's absolute self-presence rightly allows him to announce his name as "I am who am" (Exod. 3:14). But in places in his sermons Eckhart also speaks as "I." A good example can be found in Pr. 52, where, toward the end, we find the remarkable sentences: "In my birth all things were born and I was the cause of myself and of all things; and if I would have wished it, I would not be nor would all other things be. And if I did not exist, God would also not exist. That God is God, of that I am a cause. . . ."[498] But here Eckhart is speaking in the voice of the eternal unborn self, not the created corruptible self. The *ego* of our formal being is a false self, a "pseudo-I." It is only by deconstructing this self—a process Eckhart describes using the verbs *entbilden* and *entwerden*—that we can find the true self, the "transcendent-I" who exists virtually in God. "You must un-form [*entbildet*] yourself in such a way," as the *Book of Consolation* says, "that you may be transformed [*überbildet*] in God alone, and be born in God and from God. . . ."[499] *Entbilden*, the process of un-forming the created form of the soul, is what Eckhart elsewhere speaks of as *entwerden*, or un-becoming. God himself "becomes and unbecomes" (*wirt und entwirt*), as Pr. 109 says.

In chapter 21 of the *Talks of Instruction*, following the passage cited above about negating the created will, Eckhart says, "The more we un-become in what is ours, the more truly we become in that [i.e., the divine will]."[500] This process of deconstructing created subjectivity and ordinary forms of consciousness, especially as expressed in the verbs *entbilden* and *entwerden*, as Wolfgang Wackernagel has shown, is one of the dominant metaphors in Eckhart's mysticism, occurring in the *Book of Consolation*, as well as in some of Eckhart's more radical sermons (e.g., Prr. 28, 52, 77). Wackernagel characterizes it as "a vision devoid of reflexive consciousness, [that] opens out into a sort of unknowing of the soul itself in the ground of divinity."[501] As the above passage from the *Book of Divine Consolation* shows, it is in and through the deconstruction of self in detaching, letting go, relinquishing, unbecoming, that the birth of the Word in the soul takes place. Detaching and birthing, therefore, should be seen not as successive stages in a mystical path, but as two sides of the same coin.

The divine birth is among the most frequent themes in Eckhart's preaching, also occuring from time to time in the Latin commentaries.[502] Georg Steer has shown that four sermons (Prr. 101–104) preached for the liturgy of the Christmas season constitute a cycle on the birth of the Word.[503] This cycle, the only such group in Eckhart's preaching, was delivered to his fellow Dominicans most likely early in his time as provincial (ca. 1303–5).[504] Because the eternal birth takes place in the fused identity of the *grunt*, these sermons contain one of the friar's most extensive explorations of the language of the ground (the term and its derivatives appear thirty-three times). In addition, so many other major themes of Eckhart's preaching are evident that these sermons are a vernacular *summa* of his mysticism.

It will not be possible to provide an analysis of the four sermons here, but a look at some key texts in Pr. 101 will illustrate how the birth relates to other themes of Eckhart's preaching. Sermon 101 starts by citing Wisdom 18:14–15, the Introit for the mass of the Sunday within the octave of Christmas. Rather than pursuing the traditional theme of the three births of Christ (from the Father in eternity, from Mary in time, and in the hearts of the faithful today), a characteristic of much Christmas preaching, Eckhart explodes the distinction of births by claiming that the eternal birth of the Word from the Father is actually "now born in time, in human nature." He argues this case on the basis of a distinctive reading of the Introit achieved by adding to it a text from Job 4:12 not found in the liturgy, and then by translating the whole in a way that sets up the three themes of his message about the birth: "When all things were in the *medium*, in *silence*, then there descended down into me from on high, from the royal throne, *a hidden Word*" (my emphasis).[505] To paraphrase: the silencing of the medium, that is, anything between God and the soul, makes possible the birth of the hidden Word in the ground. Eckhart's reading of the Wisdom text illustrates a characteristic of his preaching pointed out by Joachim Theisen—salvation history (the coming down of God at the Exodus as a type of Christ's birth) becomes immanentized in the eternal now through liturgical re-enactment.[506]

As an aid for following the development of the rest of the cycle, the introduction to Pr. 101 briefly sets forth the three issues the preacher will discuss in his first homily before expanding on them in those to come. The first concerns "where in the soul God the Father speaks his Word, where this birth takes place, and where she is receptive of this work."[507] The second has to do with a person's conduct with regard to the birth, especially whether it is better to cooperate with God's action, or "whether one should shun and free oneself from all thoughts, words, and deeds . . . , maintaining a purely God-receptive attitude. . . ."[508] Finally, the third issue concerns the profit that comes to us from the birth.[509]

Eckhart's desire to instruct his audience of fellow Dominicans is evident from the dialogical form he adopts as he begins the treatment of the first question. An imagined interlocutor asks, "But sir, where is the silence and where is the place where the Word is spoken?" The answer is given in terms of the *grunt*. The birth takes place "in the purest thing that the soul is capable of, in the noblest part, the ground, indeed, in the very essence of the soul which is the soul's most secret part," its "silent middle" into which no image or form of activity from outside can enter. According to Eckhart, "This [ground] is by nature receptive to nothing save only the divine essence, without mediation. Here God enters the soul with his all, not merely with a part. Here God enters the ground of the soul."[510] Eckhart contrasts the activity of the soul's powers (memory, intellect, will), which function by means of images of things taken in from the outside through the senses, with the action of God coming into "the ground where no image ever got in, but only he himself with his own being."[511] God's "perfect insight into himself," effected without any image,[512] is the source of the birth of the Son in eternity and also in the ground and essence of the soul. "In this true union lies the soul's entire beatitude."[513] Only in the silence and stillness of the ground can God touch the soul with his own essence and without images.

The motif of interiority and stillness provides the key for the second theme to be explored: the relation between our actions and the consummation of the divine birth.[514] Eckhart insists on the importance of utter passivity as the only possible preparation, though he does warn that this message is only for "good and perfected people" who have absorbed the essence of the virtues and follow the life and teachings of "our Lord Jesus Christ."[515]

This second part also features a discussion of special states of consciousness, what are often called mystical experiences. Here and elsewhere Eckhart uses MHG terms like *geziehen* ("to be drawn up or out of")[516] to describe the inward withdrawal that he contends is a necessary, if not sufficient, precondition for realizing the birth of the Word in the soul's ground. He also cites two biblical examples of such total self-forgetfulness, Paul's ascent to the third heaven (2 Cor. 12:2) and Moses' forty-day fast on Sinai (Exod. 24:18). Robert Forman has argued that Eckhart's use of *geziehen/gezücket* to indicate a state of withdrawal from all sense experience (i.e., a form of contentless pure consciousness) shows that he was not averse to seeing a relation between such states and the path to awareness of the *êwigen geburt*.[517] These passages confirm that Eckhart not only recognized the existence of states of ecstatic withdrawal (he could scarcely not have, given their scriptural warrant), but that he also felt that they could be useful, *if* properly understood. Nevertheless, Eckhart insists that all forms of withdrawal are God's work, not ours, however much we may strive to make ourselves ready for them. Forman himself notes Eckhart's constant opposition to seizing on "ways" to find God,[518] which indicates that there is no necessary connection between ecstasy and mystical oneing.

In the course of investigating our conduct with regard to the birth, Eckhart turns to the third key term embedded in his scriptural-liturgical base text, the "hidden Word" (*verborgen wort*). The "hiddenness" of the Word introduces an exposition of his negative theology. He first paraphrases texts from Dionysius (DN 9.6) about God's lack of all images and the divine "hidden silent darkness" (Pr. 101. lines 137–50), and then frames another rhetorical question from the audience: "What does God do without images in the ground and the essence?"[519] His answer is that he cannot give an answer, because everything we know by ordinary consciousness comes through images (*bilde*), but this is not how God is attained. Knowing God— or more precisely, *striving* to know God—is a constant pursuit of what is by definition unattainable. As he puts it:

> This not-knowing draws her into amazement and keeps her on the hunt, for she clearly recognizes "that he is," but she does not know "what" or "how" he is. When someone knows the causes of things, he tires of them and seeks something else to uncover and to know, complaining and always protesting, because knowing has no resting point. Therefore, this unknown-knowing [i.e., *docta ignorantia*] keeps the soul constant and still on the hunt.[520]

This appeal to the mystical topos of *epektasis*, that is, that the only way to gain God is by constant unfulfilled pursuit, parallels the way Eckhart develops the theme of simultaneous eating and hungering after God in the *Ser-*

mons and Lectures on Ecclesiasticus. (This is another argument for dating these sermons to the first years of the fourteenth century.) The reflection on *epektasis* prompts the investigation of another mystical paradox: how the Word can be both expressed and hidden, a theme Eckhart touches on in other sermons.[521] His treatment here, as elsewhere, is dialectical; that is, he shows how it is the very nature of the Divine Word to be hidden in its revelation and revealed in its hiddenness: the two sides of the coin are inseparable.

As he moves toward the third and final part of the introductory sermon, Eckhart once again marks the transition by introducing an objection, this one expressing a naturalistic view of the soul: "Now, sir, you want to upset the natural course of the soul and go against her nature. Her nature is to take things in from the senses and in images. Would you upset this order?" Eckhart's response is sharp: "No! What do you know of the nobility God has given to the soul, which is not yet fully described; even more, still hidden!"[522] The Dominican attacks those who have written on the soul on the basis of only "natural intelligence," emphasizing that the divine Light shines in the darkness and is received only by its own. This critique of anthropological naturalism returns Eckhart once again to the main theme, the *ewige geburt.* "The use and fruit of this secret word and darkness," as he puts it, is our being born in the same divine darkness as Christ is—"a child of the same heavenly Father." The absolute priority of the dark way to God, taught by the Bible and tradition, receives strong confirmation: "Though it may be called an unknowing, an uncomprehending, it still has more within it than in all knowing and comprehending outside it, for this unknowing lures and draws you from all that is known, and also from yourself."[523] Eckhart concludes the sermon by invoking Christ's teaching about abandoning all things (Matt. 10:37) as confirmation of the need for giving up all externals to retreat into the inner ground where God enters without image in absolute stillness.[524]

In this sermon cycle Eckhart was not content with laying out the essential parameters of the eternal birth, as the following homilies show. While the teaching about the birth of the Word in the hearts of the faithful had deep roots in Christian mysticism,[525] Eckhart must have realized that his form of birthing mysticism, especially its connection with his new teaching on the *grunt,* was unprecedented and controversial. The following three sermons of the Christmas cycle investigate the implications of this radical teaching through a technique of question and answer that invites the hearer to full participation in the task of coming into the ground.

The relations between detaching and birthing, and birthing and the ground, are clear from the Christmas cycle, but other aspects of Eckhart's teaching on the birth of the Word appear in another noted sermon, Pr. 2, a homily on the soul as virgin wife.[526] It was customary in earlier mysticism, given the feminine gender of nouns referring to the soul (*anima/sêle*), for male mystics to adopt a female self-understanding in their descriptions of encounters with God. The combination of physical virginity with spiritual erotics was a powerful motif through much of the history of Christian mysticism.[527] Eckhart rarely makes use of the erotic language of the Song, let alone the new forms of eroticism favored by contemporary women mystics.[528] But the Dominican was fascinated with images of bearing and giving birth, and especially by the paradox explored in Pr. 2 of the virgin who is also a wife.[529] He wants his audience to identify with fruitful femininity through the practice of radical detachment.

According to Luke 10:38, "Jesus went into a village and a woman named Martha received him into her house." Eckhart's rendering of this in MHG already reinterprets the Latin to give a new message: "Our Lord Jesus Christ *went up into* a *little castle* and *was received/conceived* by *a virgin who was a wife*" (the emphasized words indicate the alterations important for Eckhart's teaching).[530] The first part of the homily deals with the paradox of the virgin wife. "Virgin," Eckhart says, "is as much to say as a person who is empty of all foreign images, as empty as he was when he did not exist."[531] Thus, the virgin signifies the utterly detached person. To an imagined questioner who asks how it can be possible to be without images at all, Eckhart responds that it is a matter of attachment or possessiveness (*eigenschaft*)—if we are not attached to any of the countless images in the mind, and also not attached to any of our works, we can be as "empty and free and maidenly" (*ledic und vrî . . . und megetlich*) as Jesus himself and therefore be united to him. But being a virgin is not enough. Eckhart goes on:

> Now mark what I say and pay careful attention. If a person were to be a virgin forever, no fruit would come from him. If he is to become fruitful, he must necessarily be a wife. "Wife" is the noblest word that can be spoken of the soul and is much nobler than "virgin." That a person receive God in him is good, and in the reception he is a virgin. But that God becomes fruitful in him is better, for the only gratitude for the gift is fruitfulness with the gift. The spirit is a wife in the gratitude that gives birth in return, bearing Jesus back again into the Fatherly heart.[532]

In this passage Eckhart fuses the paradox of virgin purity and wifely fruitfulness, especially through the ambiguity of *enphâhen* (meaning both "receive" and "conceive") and the reciprocity of thankfulness and fruitfulness which mirrors the oneness of God and human in the eternal birth of the Word. Since this fruitfulness is nothing else than God's fruitfulness, the virgin wife, unlike ordinary spouses (i.e., those who are attached to their works and practices), can bear fruit a hundred or a thousand times a day "out of the most noble ground, or better said, yes, from that same ground from which the Father begets his eternal Word she is fruitfully bearing along with him."[533]

The second part of the sermon takes up "the little castle" (*bürgelîn*), that is, the ultimate "power" in the soul.[534] Eckhart's treatment is of significance for the proper evaluation of his teaching on the birth of the Word in the soul. First of all, he analyzes the power in the soul that is untouched by time because it is in contact with the eternal now. Although Eckhart does not name it here, this power is obviously the intellect. "For in this power," he goes on to say, "the eternal Father is giving birth to his eternal Son without cease in such a way that the same power is bearing the Son along with the Father and also bearing itself, the same Son, in the one power of the Father."[535] Here we see the identity of Sonship that so troubled Eckhart's inquisitors. Eckhart then briefly discusses the second spiritual power of the soul, the will. Finally, the Dominican turns to the "little castle" itself.

The preacher notes that he has often spoken of "the one power in the soul that alone is free," calling it many names. Now he refuses to name it. "It is neither this nor that; rather, it is a 'something' higher above this and that than the heaven is above the earth. . . . It is free of all names, and stripped of all forms, completely empty and free as God is empty and free in himself."[536] It is as one and simple (*ein und einvaltic*) as God is. Eckhart then briefly returns to "the same power of which I have spoken" (i.e., the intellect) in which the birth takes place in order to set up the most radical part of his message, namely, that the unnamed power lies beyond all powers and even beyond the Persons in the Trinity.[537] Neither intellect nor will can see into this *bürgelîn*. Even God cannot look into it for an instant "insofar as he possesses himself according to modes and personal properties." When it comes to the *grunt* (which is what Eckhart is speaking of here without using the word) God can penetrate only insofar as "He is a simple One, without mode or property: there in the sense that he is not Father, or Son, or Holy Spirit, and yet is a something that is neither this nor that."[538] God's ground and the soul's ground are one and the same ground, and in some way reside deeper even than the birth of the Son in the soul. As Bruce Milem has shown, while Eckhart uses the virgin wife in the first part of the sermon to present a view of trinitarian union with God in the intellect, the analysis of the little castle in the second part undercuts this by showing that "The soul's true identity with God lies within this transcendental singularity represented by this little castle."[539] Such self-subverting language characterizes the dialectical character of Eckhart's mysticism and its avoidance of systematization.[540]

Before turning to the third essential aspect of the return, breaking-through into the ground, we can ask about the historical context of Eckhart's teaching on the birth of the Word in the soul. Given the frequency with which the Dominican preached the *geburt*, it is worth pondering why he made it so central to his message. The theme of God's birth in us, sacramentally and mystically, was old in Christian tradition, rooted in scripture and set forth as early as Origen. Although the birth was taken up by some Latin mystical authors, notably Eriugena and Cistercians like Guerric of Igny, there was little precedent for how Eckhart made *geburt* the focus of his preaching. As Hans Urs von Balthasar put it: "He [Eckhart] melted down the philosophy of every thinker and recast it into the central mystery of the divine birth."[541] The motivation for this smelting process is elusive, though some evidence exists regarding its reception. Eckhart's contemporary, the Augustinian friar Henry of Friemar, as we shall see in chapter 8, wrote two treatises also stressing the importance of the birth of the Word, in which he cautioned against the dangerous conclusions to which some were taking this teaching.[542] If Eckhart had already been preaching on this topic as early as ca. 1300, Henry may well have had him in mind. It is obvious from the Cologne proceedings that Eckhart's teaching on the birth was one of the issues that the opponents seized on. But all this does not help us understand why the Dominican preacher made *geburt* so central. One might hazard the guess that the birthing motif was Eckhart's response to the widespread late medieval devotion to the infant Jesus in the manger, that is, the Dominican wished to redirect his audience's attention to the essential meaning of the Word's taking on flesh, not to peripheral issues.

Meister Eckhart's third dynamic metaphor for the return to God is the "breaking-through" (*durchbrechen*) beyond all conceptions of God "into the silent desert where distinction never gazed" (Pr. 48).[543] No aspect of Eckhart's mysticism is more radical; yet, looking at this language in light of what we have already seen about his teaching on the Trinity and on the *grunt*, one can see that breaking-through, however challenging, is integral to his teaching.

We may begin by asking about the relationship between breaking-through and birthing. Many of Eckhart's formulations give breaking-through an ultimacy that even the birth of the Word in the soul does not have, as suggested in the passage from the end of Pr. 2 on the *bürgelin*. But it is important to think of the three basic activities of the return as having a reciprocal and dialectical relationship—all are simultaneous in the *nû* of eternity and all are simultaneously interdependent.[544] On the one hand, there is no breakthrough without detachment from all possessiveness and the realization of the birth; and, on the other, birthing the Word in the soul and leading a perfectly detached life express the identity in the ground achieved in the breakthrough. The relation between birthing and breaking-through parallels the dialectical relationship between the hidden ground and the "boiling" Trinity.

As we have seen in several texts presented above, Eckhart often uses *durchbrechen* and its equivalents (e.g., *zerbrechen*: Pr. 51 [DW 2:473.5–9]) to express the need of going beyond God conceived of as Creator and as possessed of any attributes, even those of the three Persons of the Trinity. "In the breaking-through," Pr. 52 says, "when I come to be free of will of myself and of God's will and of all his works and of God himself, then I am above all created things, and I am neither God nor creature, but I am what I was and what I shall remain, now and eternally."[545] The power in the soul that effects this breakthrough is the intellect, which is never satisfied with goodness, wisdom, truth, or even God himself; but "forces its way in," "bursts into the ground," and "breaks through to the roots."[546] Other texts speak of the *mutual* breaking-through of God and human. Pr. 26, for example, says that the spirit must transcend all number and multiplicity in order to have God break through it. "And just as he breaks through into me, so I break through in turn into him. God leads this spirit into the desert and into the unity of himself, where he is simply one and welling up into himself."[547] The mention of the desert (*einöde/wüestunge*) introduces another of Eckhart's favorite metaphors for expressing the emptiness of the fused ground.

Moses' encounter with God in the wilderness of Sinai provided a scriptural basis for the use of the desert in Christian mysticism.[548] Although Dionysius never explicitly identified God with the desert, the way in which the *Mystical Theology* links Moses' desert journey to Sinai with apophatic mysticism laid the basis for such identification, which appears first in Eriugena.[549] In the twelfth century, the Cistercians used the desert motif both to signify the inner solitude of the heart stripped and ready to receive God, and also to point to the hidden God. In the thirteenth century, Thomas Gallus, the Victorine commentator on Dionysius and the Song of Songs, identified the desert of Song 3:6 and Exodus 5:3 with "the inaccessible and singular supersubstantial solitude of the eternal Trinity" described by Denys in the *Divine Names* and *Mystical Theology*.[550] As a student of Dionysius, Eckhart need not have known Gallus to make the identification on his own. The Dominican uses the desert motif more than a dozen times to refer to both the uncreated something in the soul and to the inner ground of God.[551]

Eckhart often cites Hosea 2:14, a text in which God proclaims that he will lead rebellious Israel out into the desert to woo her anew. At the end of the sermon "Of the Nobleman," for example, he summarizes how the break-through that is part of the desert journey leads to indistinct union:

> Who then is nobler than he who on one side is born of the highest and the best among created things, and on the other side from the inmost ground of the divine nature and its desert: "I," says the Lord through the prophet Hosea, "will lead the noble soul out into the desert, and there I will speak to her heart," one with One, one from One, one in One, and in One, one everlast-ingly. Amen.[552]

One of Eckhart's most powerful expressions of breakthrough language is found in a MHG sermon on three forms of the soul's death, first edited by Franz Jostes and sometimes referred to under the title "How the Soul Went Her Own Way and Lost Herself,"[553] though it could just as easily be called "The Kingdom of God Sermon."[554] Eckhart scholars such as Alain de Lib-era and Oliver Davies have accepted the sermon as authentic, a supposition strengthened by how it relates to other passages in Eckhart on the theme of *mors mystica*.[555] This homily shows that breaking-through into the God beyond God involves a form of transcendental subjectivity.

After a discussion of trinitarian theology in the first part of the sermon, the preacher turns to the relation between the nobility of the soul's image of God and its divine source. This section, like Pr. 52, is constructed according to a threefold model, namely, three forms of going out from the soul's being (*wesen*): as created being, as being in the Word, and as being pos-sessed "in the overflowing nature active in the Father." Going out from cre-ated being is achieved through self-abandonment, following Christ's command to take up the cross, deny oneself, and follow him. This stage begins with the practice of virtues, seen as modalities of the love that trans-forms us into God. The sermon, like Marguerite Porete, advances the claim that the perfection of virtue is "to be free of virtue" (*Daz ist volkumenheit der tugent, daz der mensche ledik ste der tugent* [92.31–32]). This does not mean that the virtues are destroyed or abandoned; rather, they come to be possessed in a higher way. The spiritual death to our created being is the total aban-donment of self and all things, even God (John 12:24 is cited)—"Here the soul forsakes all things, God and all creatures."[556] Eckhart says that such for-saking of God is not an exaggeration: "As long as the soul has God, knows God, and is aware of God, she is far from God . . . ," so "the greatest honor the soul can pay to God [is] to leave God to himself and to be free of him."[557] Such mystical atheism, however, is only the beginning.

The sermon next turns to the soul's need to go out from the being that it has in the eternal Image in God, that is, "the light of the Uncreated Image, in which the soul finds her own uncreatedness."[558] This "divine death" (*gotlich tot*) is necessary because even though the soul has returned to her uncreated state in the Word as Image of the Father, she still finds herself in the distinction of the Persons of the Trinity. It is at this juncture that the preacher invokes the language of breaking-through: "And so the soul breaks through her eternal Image in order to penetrate to where God is rich in unicity. That is why one master says that the breakthrough of the soul is nobler than her flowing out. . . . This breaking-through is the second death, which is far greater than the first."[559] This "wonder beyond wonders" means the death of God, at least God insofar as he is the Son. When the Son turns back to the divine unity, he loses himself, and hence when the soul "breaks through and loses herself in her eternal Image, then this is the death of the soul that the soul dies in God."[560] Here the soul goes beyond the identity she has with God in the eternal Image. There is no longer any kind of imaging; even the identity that implies two distinct things becoming one is lost. There is only nothingness.

It is hard to see at this stage what kind of death might be left, but the preacher manages a further dying, one that involves the cessation of all work and activity, even in God. This is the attainment of what might be called a unity beyond identity, which is paradoxically also a transcendental self-discovery. This final non-stage involves the Father's "pre-ebullitional" sense of himself as the potential source of the Son and Holy Spirit.[561] Hence, if the soul is to reach "divine union at the highest level" (*gotlich ein-ung . . . in der hohst* [95.14]), it must give up all the "divine activity" (*gotlicher wirkung*) that is associated with the Father as Father. The preacher describes what happens next in terms that go beyond anything found explicitly elsewhere in Eckhart's sermons, but that are extensions of aspects of his preaching. Basically, the third death is getting rid of all the potentiality for activity, within and without God, that is rooted in the Father. The sermon identifies this highest state with the evangelical "kingdom of God" (*daz reich gots*), a term mentioned twenty times in this piece. The exposition of the final death is verbose, though these pages (95.5–98.8) pick up on so many themes present elsewhere in Eckhart that they form a good argument for the authenticity of the piece. What is new in the conclusion of the sermon is the notion that the final death is a transcendental self-realization.

The sermon describes the third death as the necessary corollary of the second. After the second death, when the soul recognizes that she cannot enter the kingdom of God on her own, she must be ready to give up even more. But what is there left to give? In a dark saying, the homily continues,

Then the soul perceives herself, goes her own way and never seeks God; and thus she dies her highest death. In this death the soul loses all her desires, all images, all understanding and all form and is stripped of all her being. . . . This spirit is dead and is buried in the Godhead, for the Godhead lives as no other than itself.[562]

This new place where the soul finds herself is identified as "the fathomless ocean of the Godhead" (*in disem grûndlosen mere der gotheit* [95.38–39]). Here, as "soul loses herself in all ways, . . . she finds that she is herself the same thing which she has always sought without success."[563] Paradoxically, Eckhart says that this is a *new* kind of image, the "highest image in which God is essentially present with all his divinity since he is in his own kingdom" (96.6–7). The fusion of subjectivity, however, remains christological. Eckhart continues, "God became another I so that I might become another he. As Augustine says, 'God became man so that man might become God.'"[564] The homily concludes by insisting that the three deaths can only be attained by the action of grace, and that works based on living in God's kingdom are a single living work performed without distraction or self-interest, the kind of acting "without a why" that is so important for Eckhart's mysticism and will be explored below in relation to Pr. 86. Both the "Kingdom of God Sermon" and the "Martha and Mary" homily (Pr. 86) stretch the limits of sermons generally accepted as authentic works of Eckhart, at least in particulars. But if they are not by Eckhart, who preached them? Was there a mystical preacher more Eckhartian than Eckhart himself?

Mystical Identity

A survey of the three essential activities of *reditus* allows us to summarize Eckhart's view of mystical union, concerning which he once said: "Every desire and its fulfillment is to be united to God."[565] All that Eckhart has to say both about creation and about the return involves the goal of becoming one with God. Eckhart held there are two forms of union: the preexisting essential union that is God's indistinction from all things as their true reality (creative identity); and the union to be achieved by our becoming aware through unknowing of that indistinct presence through detaching, birthing, and breaking-through (re-creative identity).[566]

In one sermon the Dominican describes the latter union as follows: "You should completely sink away from your you-ness and flow into his his-ness and your you and his his shall become one *our* so totally that with him you eternally comprehend his unbecoming Self-Identity and his unnamed Nothingness."[567] In such formulations Eckhart molds language for his own purposes in order to express a union of indistinction. In other places he speaks more simply and directly of mystical identity: "Between man and God there is not only no distinction, there is no multiplicity either—there is nothing but one."[568] Eckhart was uncompromising in his insistence that true union with God was absolute identity, without medium of any kind.[569]

In the history of Christian mysticism, as mentioned previously, we can distinguish two modes of understanding union as re-creative oneing with God: first, mystical uniting, that is, the perfect union of the wills of the divine and human lovers, the *unitas spiritus* suggested by 1 Corinthians 6:17; and, second, mystical identity, the indistinction between God and human expressed in Eckhart's formula *ein einic ein,* "One Single One." For Eckhart, union of wills was not enough. As we have seen in Pr. 52, the friar held that in order to attain true union the created will must become so annihilated that there is nothing left but the divine will working in itself. As Pr. 25 puts it: "When the will is so unified that it forms One Single One, then the heavenly Father bears his only-begotten Son in-himself-in-me. Why in-himself-in-me? Because then I am one with him; he cannot shut me out. And in that act the Holy Spirit receives his being and his becoming from me as from God. Why? Because I am in God."[570] Eckhart did not invent mystical identity, but no mystic in the history of Christianity was more daring in the way in which he explored how real union with God must go beyond the uniting of two substances that remain ontologically distinct in order to reach total indistinction, what Eckhart sometimes called "essential" identity.[571] "God is indistinct," as he once said, "and the soul loves to be indistinguished, that is, to be and to become one with God."[572]

Eckhart has been accused of pantheism. But if pantheism means total identity of God with world and world with God, Eckhart is far from this. God may, indeed, be the reality of all things, but God infinitely surpasses all things too. God is always both distinct and indistinct. Further, the fused identity of the *grunt* of which Eckhart speaks is not reality in its created aspect at all. Although Eckhart realized that his understanding of union with God went beyond what had been customary, he endeavored to show that his teaching was rooted in scripture and tradition. For example, he often appealed to biblical texts like John 17:21, Christ's prayer to his Father for all who will believe in him, "that all might be one, as you, Father, in me, and I in you, that they may be one in us."[573] Eckhart's literal view of such texts is evident in S. XXX, where he says: "All the saints are one thing in God, not [just] one."[574] Finally, we must remember that Eckhart's notion of indistinct union is fundamentally dialectical, that is to say, our union with

God is indeed indistinct in the ground, but we always also maintain distinction from God in our formal being as *ens hoc et hoc.* Even in the ultimate union of heaven, Eckhart insists, this distinction will remain.[575]

The implications of Eckhart's view of indistinct union are many. It may be worthwhile trying to summarize the fundamentals of his position. Indistinct union can be described as a continuous state of nonabsorptive and transformative awareness of the identity of the *grunt.* Eckhart's view of union is nonabsorptive because ecstatic states play at best a preparatory and nonessential role. Furthermore, union is a form of deification or transformation, which, in the last analysis, goes beyond knowing and loving, at least as we experience them in ordinary conscious states.

The dual breaking-through found in Pr. 26 discussed above shows that Eckhart, like the beguine Hadewijch, understood indistinct union as a mutual event. Of course, from the perspective of the soul's *created* being there can be no question of mutuality—pure existence has nothing in common with created nothingness; but from the perspective of the *grunt der sêle* Eckhart often uses the language of mutuality. In Pr. 5b, for example, he says: "Go out of yourself completely through God, and God will go completely out of himself through you. When the two have gone out, what remains is One Single One. In this One the Father bears his Son in the inmost source; out of it the Holy Spirit blossoms forth. . . ."[576] Texts like this, as well as passages from Pr. 52, also declare the limitations of mutuality in the face of absolute identity. What is initally expressed as mutual interpenetration of God and human is only the first stage in a process of unknowing and unbecoming that aims for an identity in which there can be no "mutuality" because all is one: *ein einvaligez ein.*

Among the ways that Eckhart spoke of the identity between God and human in the one ground was through the metaphor of the gaze of a single eye upon itself, a form of specular identity—"The eye in which I see God is the same eye in which God sees me. My eye and God's eye are one eye and one seeing, one knowing, and one loving."[577] Or, as another sermon puts it, "You must know in reality that this is one and the same thing—to know God and to be known by God, to see God and to be seen by God."[578] A lengthy treatment of the identity of knower and known in the act of knowing found in the *Commentary on John* lays out the metaphysical foundations for this teaching in its discussion of how "one is the face and image in which God sees us and we him."[579]

According to Eckhart, our union with God is a continuous state, at least in some way. This is certainly true for the metaphysical indistinction that undergirds awareness of identity, but it should be clear from what has been said about detachment, birthing, and breaking-through that these are meant to be realized in an uninterrupted fashion, though we cannot always advert to this on the level of everyday consciousness. Eckhart explicitly says this in places, such as Pr. 86 to be treated below, as well as in the passage from the sixth of the *Talks of Instruction* cited above: "True possessing of God depends on the mind, and on an inner intellectual turning toward and striving for God, not in a continuous thinking of him in the same manner, for that would be impossible for nature to strive for, very difficult and not even the best thing."[580]

For Eckhart, continuous union with God is not an "experience" in any ordinary sense of the term: it is what happens when a person tries to relate all he or she does to the fused identity of the *grunt*. It is a new *way* of knowing and acting, not any *particular* experience or act of knowing *something*.[581] As we have seen, it is achieved by not-knowing (*unwizzen*), not by knowing as we conceive it. While this not-knowing is reached through the practice of interiority and detachment, as Eckhart insisted throughout his preaching, it is not dependent on our activity; it comes from God, as Eckhart makes clear over and over.

Eckhart's late preaching emphasizes that the capacity to become "unknowingly" aware of the *grunt* is open to all believers and is fully compatible with a life of activity and service. The universalizing of the call to mystical union that was an important aspect of the new mysticism of the thirteenth century appears in a heightened form in Eckhart's preaching.[582] Pr. 66 has a good statement of this. Preaching on Matthew 25:23, "Well done, good and faithful servant, enter into the joy of your Lord," Eckhart invites all in his audience to become "good and faithful servants" by becoming wholly free of self and giving themselves to God. The good and faithful servant is someone who has been faithful over "small things"—the littleness that is the whole of creation. To someone who is faithful in this way God is compelled to give his own inner joy. Eckhart becomes almost rhapsodic:

> But I say yet more (do not be afraid, for this joy is close to you and is in you): there is not one of you who is so coarse-grained, so feeble of understanding, or so far off but that he can find this joy within himself, in truth, as it is, with joy and understanding, before you leave this church today, indeed before I have finished preaching. He can find this as truly within him, live it and possess it, as that God is God and I am a man.[583]

The universality of the call to union helps explain the Dominican's attitude toward states of mystical absorption, rapture, ecstasy, and the like. Eckhart recognized that these forms of special consciousness existed and that they might be useful if properly understood. But they did not pertain to the essence of union, and they could be harmful if they came to be seen as either a necessary way to the goal, or were confused with the goal itself. Eckhart uses Paul's ascent to Paradise described in 2 Corinthians 12 as an example of the kind of raptured realization of the unknown God that is not incompatible with true mystical union.[584] In MHG, as we have seen, Eckhart uses the verbs *gezücket/enzücket* to describe such absorptive states of consciousness.[585] He also recognized that experiences of "enjoyment of God" (*gebrûchenne*) had their place.[586] The danger with such states, however, is the temptation to become attached to them, and therefore to fail in the only necessary practice, complete dying to self in "cutting off" all earthly things and desires in order to concentrate on God alone. In Pr. 41 Eckhart rebukes those who want to "taste God's will" as if they were already in heaven. "They love God for the sake of something that is not God," he continues. "And if they get something they love, they do not bother about God, whether it is contemplation, or pleasure, or whatever you will—whatever is created is not God."[587]

Despite the silence and stillness that characterize it, the highest form of union is not only constant but is also realized in activity, that is, in the transcendental welling-up, or *bullitio*, of life within the Trinity. This is evident in Pr. 6 on the text, "The just will live forever" (Wis. 5:16). This homily is one of Eckhart's most detailed expositions in his vernacular works of the relation between Justice and the just person.[588] In it he puts forth some of his most dangerous formulations on the birth of the Word in the soul and the union of indistinction.[589] Toward the end of the homily, in discussing the activity of the Father in giving birth to the Son, he emphasizes how the union attained in the birth in the soul is a mutual fused "working" (*würken*) and "becoming" (*werden*) in which God and I are one: "I take God into me in knowing; I go into God in loving. . . . In this working God and I are one; he is working and I am becoming."[590]

The mention of knowing and loving in this passage raises another important issue for the understanding of Eckhartian union: the respective roles of intellect and will. It is evident that Eckhart held that union with God takes place in the soul insofar as it is intellective, a position he shared with Maimonides—"In the essence [of the soul], as intellective, it is joined to what is higher than it, God, as Rabbi Moses has it: And thus it is 'offspring of God.'"[591] As S. XXIX puts it: "The one God is intellect and intellect is the one God. . . . Therefore, to rise up to intellect, and to be subordinated to it, is to be united to God."[592] Our earlier treatment of intellect found in Latin texts like *Parisian Questions* qq. 1–2 and S. XXIX, as well as the numerous

MHG treatments in which *vernünfticheit* as necessary for attaining union,[593] make the intellectualism of Eckhart's view of union unmistakable. And yet nothing is ever quite so simple in Eckhart.

First of all, we must remember that Eckhart's view of the intellectual act that makes us one with God involves an unmediated and direct vision of God and the soul as one with God. It is not the kind of reflexive act of understanding that we are accustomed to in knowing something and being able to reflect on what we know. The most detailed discussion of this point comes at the end of the Sermon "On the Nobleman" where Eckhart dis- agees with those who place the ultimate blessedness of heaven (and by extension our direct knowing of God in this life) in a reflex act of knowing by which we know that we know God.[594] He holds that such a reflex act *fol- lows* from the direct, unmediated knowing, but "the first thing in which blessedness consists is that the soul beholds God nakedly." He continues: "From there she takes all her being and her life, and she draws all that she is from God's ground, and she knows nothing of knowledge, of love, or of anything at all. She is totally still and alone in God's being, knowing noth- ing there but being and God."[595] God himself, not my knowledge of God, is true beatitude, though, like the nobleman in the sermon text (Luke 19:12), Eckhart admits that the soul must not only "go out to a distant country to gain a kingdom" (i.e., see God in true felicity), but also "return," that is, "be aware and know that one knows God and is aware of it."[596] The return to awareness, however, is an effect of *beatitudo*, not constitutive of it.

A second problem that confronts a simple intellectualist view of the blessedness of union, both here and hereafter, is the fact that there are pas- sages in Eckhart that (contrary to his usual practice) insist that it is love that brings us to union with God. For example, Pr. 60, a homily on the cosmic eros theme that has many affinities with Dionysius without actually quoting him, accepts the traditional identification of the cherubim with the "under- standing [*bekantnisse*] that brings God into the soul and guides the soul to God, but cannot bring her into God." The highest power, the love identi- fied with the seraphim, "breaks into God leading the soul with understand- ing and all her powers into God and unites her to God. Here God is acting above the power of the soul, not as in the soul, but divinely as in God."[597] One may treat this passage as an anomaly; nevertheless, it suggests that the Dominican's views on union are more complex than often thought. Both knowing and loving unite in one way, though the usual preference is to intellect; but from another perspective, *neither* unites in the ultimate sense *insofar as* they are conceived of as powers of the soul.[598]

Some of Eckhart's sermons make it clear that both love and knowledge must be surpassed to attain mystical identity. Even within the realm of intellect itself, it is important to note—as shown in the sermon cycle on the eternal birth and elsewhere—that it is the passive, not the active, intellect that provides access to God. For example, in Pr. 71 he says that beyond the intellect that seeks, "there is another intellect that does not seek but rather remains in its simple pure being which is enveloped by this [divine] light."[599] Other sermons go further in stressing the limitations of all forms of intellect.[600] Perhaps the most telling text occurs in Pr. 7, where Eckhart initially follows his usual line, claiming that intellect is higher than love because it penetrates beyond truth and goodness to take God as bare being. But then he switches ground: "But I maintain that neither knowledge nor love unites. . . . Love takes God with a coat on [i.e., as goodness]. . . . The intellect does not do this. The intellect takes God as he is known in it, but it can never encompass him in the sea of his groundlessness."[601] Here the friar somewhat surprisingly identifies the unifying force above knowledge and love as "mercy" (*barmherzicheit*), but throughout the sermon, because he equates mercy with what God works "in the groundless ocean" (121.12), and also with "the completely mysterious something [in the soul] that is above the first out-break where intellect and will break out" (123.6–8), it seems that what he is really talking about is nothing else than the *grunt*. Mercy is described as "the soul in its ground" (*diu sêle in ir grunde* [124.102]), the ultimate place of indistinction beyond all knowing and loving. This echoes what we find in Pr. 42: "Where understanding and desire end, there is darkness, and there God shines."[602]

Finally, Eckhart's understanding of union is transformative, that is, divinizing: God became man that man might become God. The friar does not use the terms *divinizatio/deificatio*, preferring *transformatio* (see 1 Cor. 13:12), *transfiguratio*, and other scriptural words.[603] A passage from one of his Latin sermons summarizes transformation as divinization, weaving together a rich range of terms to describe the work of soul leading to vision and union, including the process by which we become identical with the inner eye in which God sees us in the same way we see him. Eckhart says:

> The soul, in order that it may see God, must
> first, be configured to God through transfiguration;
> second, be exalted and purified;
> third, be purified from every imperfection;
> then, be drawn out and transcend itself insofar as it is a [created] nature;
> then, be drawn out from the body and matter, so that it can return upon
> itself and discover God within, in itself.[604]

Living without a Why

How does someone actually live who has attained indistinct union in the *grunt?* How does such a person conduct herself in the world? The answer Eckhart gives revolves around his teaching concerning "living without a why" (*âne warumbe/sunder warumbe/sine cur aut quare*). In the *Commentary on Exodus*, to begin with an example from the Latin, the friar says:

> It is proper to God that he has no "why" outside or beyond himself. There-fore, every work that has a "why" as such is not a divine work or done for God. . . . There will be no divine work if a person does something that is not for God's sake, because it will have a "why," something that is foreign to God and far from God; it is not God or something divine.[605]

Eckhart preached his message of living without a why more often than he commented on it in his scholastic writings, linking this enigmatic phrase to the common themes of his preaching, such as the birth of the Word in the soul: "And so the Son is born in us in that we are without a why and are born again into the Son."[606]

What does it mean to live "without a why"? Where did the expression come from? The notion of pure spontaneous living possibly reflects Gospel injunctions to become like a child (e.g., Matt. 18:1–5). Bernard of Clairvaux had spoken of true spousal love as totally spontaneous. The expression "to live without a why," however, was a creation of thirteenth-century mystics. The earliest use is probably that of Beatrice of Nazareth, whose *Seven Man-ners of Loving* was written between 1215 and 1235.[607] In discussing the sec-ond "manner," Beatrice describes a form of disinterested love, noting that in this state the soul acts "only with love, without any why (*sonder enich waerome*), without any reward of grace or of glory. . . ."[608] The expression "without a why" (*sans nul pourquoy/sine propter quid*) occurs also in Mar-guerite Porete's *Mirror*, a text known to Eckhart.[609] This does not mean that the Dominican merely adopted this motif from Porete and others. His liv-ing "without a why" is a necessary implication of his dialectical apophatic thought. A mysticism based on a "wayless way" to an unknown God of absolute freedom can bear fruit only in a "whylessness" that will seem either empty of meaning or potentially dangerous to those who know noth-ing of it.

Nothing could be simpler to those who have attained true detachment than living *âne warumbe;* nothing will seem stranger to those who are still caught in the toils of attachment. Eckhart does nothing to lessen the para-dox, as a survey of the places where he uses this language indicates.[610] In speaking of life without a why Eckhart can arrest us with concrete analogies, as when he compares God and by extension the person who lives without a why to a frisky horse, gamboling about in a field.[611] But if living without a why is the core of Eckhart's antiteleological ethics, we still can ask exactly what it means to live in such a spontaneous fashion.[612]

A good way to understand the import of Eckhart's "without a why" is to see it as his version of a theme that had a long history in Christian mysticism: the insistence on disinterested love. "He who lives in the goodness of his nature lives in God's love, and love has no why," as he put it in Pr. 28.[613] In a passage that might have been written by Bernard of Clairvaux himself he says: "The lover as such does not seek to be loved. Everything that is not loving is foreign to him. This is all he knows; this is free, and for its own sake. . . . He loves in order to love, he loves love."[614] Eckhart quoted Bernard often, and no text more frequently than the abbot's famous statement that "the reason for loving God is God, and the measure of loving him is without measure" (*sine modo*).[615] All humans have a notion of what it means to be spontaneous. What makes Eckhart's insistence on living *âne warumbe* unusual is how he heightens the stakes by inviting the hearer to aim for *total* spontaneity and freedom in the *nû* of eternity that comprises all moments simultaneously.

Freedom and spontaneity do not rule out intention, at least the interior intention to give up attachment to self and created things and to direct the mind totally to God. Eckhart was unwavering in his insistence that "goodness stands in the interior act," not in any exterior action.[616] Other theologians agreed that interior intention should be the primary motivation of the action of what Eckhart called "a God-loving soul" (*ein gotminnendiu sêle* [Pr. 20b; DW 1:345.9]), but Eckhart took this a step further into dangerous waters by so emphasizing interiority that exterior work of any kind is characterized as "not properly commanded by God," "not properly good or divine," "heavy and oppressive," and "not speaking to God and praising him" as does the interior act.[617] When taken to task for this teaching in the trials at Cologne and Avignon, Eckhart defended himself by citing Thomas Aquinas; but Thomas's doctrine was actually not what Eckhart said it was.[618]

To see how Eckhart conceived of life lived without a why and to understand how, despite his emphasis on inwardness and even on fleeing materiality and the body, his mysticism can be described as a mysticism of everyday life, it will be helpful to look at one of the most difficult sermons ascribed to the Dominican preacher, a homily for the Feast of Mary Magdalene (Pr. 86). In this sermon Eckhart broke through the traditional distinction between the active life and contemplative life represented by Martha and Mary, creating a new model of sanctity: "living out of a well-exercised ground." This sermon, probably preached late in his career, did not represent a departure. In the last of the sermons on the Eternal Birth (Pr. 104), he had already appealed to Martha and Mary in a similar way, arguing that contemplation and action should be fused in the perfected soul: "It is all the same, one nowhere goes further than the same ground of contemplation and makes it fruitful in action, and thus the purpose of contemplation is achieved. . . . And so, in this activity we possess nothing but a state of contemplation in God. The one rests in the other and brings it to fulfillment."[619]

The complexities and problems of Pr. 86 are well known. Lengthy analyses have been devoted to the homily, especially by Dietmar Mieth.[620] Here we will close with some reflections on how the homily helps us see that Eckhart's mysticism taught that true contemplation of God is realized in fruitful action, that is, the only way to proper engagement with the temporal world is through total detachment.

The contrast between the active life and the contemplative life is a part of the Christian inheritance from classical antiquity.[621] From the time of Origen, a number of biblical pairs, notably the sisters Mary and Martha of Luke 10, but also Rachel and Leah (Gen. 29–30) and Peter and John (John 20:1–10), were employed as types for the difference between the contemplative life devoted to love of God and the active life of charitable service to neighbor. Both modes of life were seen as necessary for perfection; but the mystical tradition, beginning with Augustine and carried on by Gregory the Great and Bernard of Clairvaux, insisted on the preeminence of the *vita contemplativa*. Different theories about relating the two were put forward, but in general the mystics taught that in this fallen world there was bound to be a tension between action and contemplation. The best one could hope for was to oscillate between the two, recognizing that the duty of Christian charity would often call the mystic away from the higher delights of contemplation.

Eckhart broke with this model, nowhere more clearly than in Pr. 86. For Eckhart, as Dietmar Mieth put it, "Earthly perfection consists . . . not in the unity of vision, but in the unity of working," so that "here, for the first time, a spirituality of the active life becomes visible."[622] In this sermon on Martha and Mary, as well as in a number of other places,[623] the friar not only abandoned the notion of tension-filled oscillation between action and contemplation but also asserted that a new kind of activity performed out of "a well-exercised ground" was superior to contemplation, at least as ordinarily conceived. Here what Reiner Schürmann called "Eckhart's this-worldliness" clearly contrasts with the "other-worldliness" of many previous Christian mystics.[624] Although Eckhart often speaks of the need for separating from time, multiplicity, and corporality as hindrances to God, the process of detachment from *ens hoc et hoc* is required because it is the only way to overcome selfish attachment to things, which is the necessary prerequisite for discovering a new, nonselfish, free relation to the whole of creation.[625]

Pr. 86 is long and at times obscure.[626] Here I will concentrate on what the sermon says about the value of performing works without a why (though the phrase itself never appears). A brief section introduces the two protagonists, characterizing Mary as filled with "ineffable longing" and "delight" (traditional marks of contemplation), and Martha as possessing "a well-exercised ground" (*wol geübeter grunt*) and "wise understanding" (*wisiu verstantnisse*). After a short excursus on sensual and intellectual satisfaction, the two main parts of the homily take up the roots of Martha's perfection, as well as the value of the works that she does in time. Martha tells Mary to get up and help her (Luke 10:40) not out of a spirit of criticism but from endearment. She believes that Mary is in danger of being overwhelmed by her desire. "Martha knew Mary better than Mary Martha," says Eckhart, "for Martha had lived long and well; and living gives the most valuable kind of knowledge. Life knows better than pleasure or light what one can get under God in this life, and in some ways life gives us a purer knowledge than what eternal light can bestow."[627] This comment introduces the fundamental theme of the sermon: life (i.e., actual practice) gives a higher knowledge than even the light of contemplative ecstasy, which has no relation to actual living (Paul's ecstasy of 2 Cor. 12 is cited as example).[628] Eckhart concludes the first half of part 1 by emphasizing that Martha was worried that Mary not get misled and become stuck in the pleasure of contemplation.

After a second digression, Eckhart comes to the third and most important reason for Martha's superiority to Mary, linking it to the Gospel passage where Jesus names her not once, but twice. "Martha, Martha" indicates that she possesses "everything of temporal and eternal value a creature should have" (484.14–15). Martha is one of the people "who stand in the midst of things, but not in things. They stand very near [the image of eternal light], and yet do not have less of it than if they stood up above, at the rim of eternity."[629] There is much that is puzzling about this section, but the essential message is that Martha makes good use of the two kinds of "means" (*mittel*). The first of these is "work and activity in time" (*werk und gewerbe in der zît* [485.8–9]), something that, Eckhart says, does not lessen eternal happiness. It is even required in order to get to God.[630] "The other means is to be empty of all this" (*daz ander mittel daz ist; blôz sîn des selben* [485:11]), that is, to attain the freedom of detachment.

Eckhart goes on to underline the relation between these two means, insisting that both activity and emptiness are necessary. "We have been put into time," he says, "for the purpose of coming nearer to and becoming like God through rational activity in time."[631] Paul's comment about "redeeming the time" (Eph. 5:16) means that we must continually rise up to God, "not according to different images, but by means of living intellectual truth" (485.13–15). The stripping away of images in favor of finding the pure intellectual truth of unknowing leads us forward toward the eternal light of God. Martha is not there yet: there is still some mediation in her vision of God. But she is praised for standing on the brink of the embrace of the eternal light, "on the rim of eternity" (*umberinge der êwicheit*: 486.5–6).

The Pauline notion of redeeming the time is significant for Eckhart's this-worldly mysticism. Alois Haas and Niklaus Largier have shown that the relationship of time and eternity in Eckhart is not merely one of negation, as some texts taken in isolation might indicate.[632] Rather, eternity should be seen as the fullness of time. The soul as situated between time and eternity must learn by its "rational activity in time" to redeem the times.[633] "Eternity," as Largier says, "is what binds the temporal together in an horizon of origin and end on the one side, and on the other with an embracing presence which grounds the metaphysical model of the unfolding of being. . . ."[634] As Eckhart notes in Pr. 91, through the incarnation God renews himself: "God brings eternity into time, and with himself brings time into eternity. This takes place in the Son, when the Son pours himself out in eternity, then all creatures are poured out with him."[635] Eckhart's Christology requires that someone like Martha who acts from a "well-exercised ground" must work both above time in eternity[636] and also in time through *werk* and *gewerbe*.[637]

In the third part of Pr. 86 Eckhart explains how Martha and "all God's friends" can exist "with care" but not "in care," that is, how they relate to the concerns and troubles of everyday existence. The preacher once again says that a work done in time is as noble as any kind of communion with God save for the highest unmediated vision. A fruitful work has three characteristics: it is orderly, discriminating, and insightful (*ordenlîche, redelîcher, wizzentlîche*). The last characteristic is realized when one "feels living truth with delightful presence in good works" (488.17–18). Eckhart then turns to how a person who has arrived at this state (i.e., a Martha) is able to work undisturbed in the midst of the concerns of the world—traditionally what earlier mystics had held to be impossible, because they conceived of activity as always a distraction from contemplation, not its fulfillment.

Because Martha has attained a "free mind" (*vrîen gemüete*) and lives out of "a splendid ground" (*ein hêrlîcher grunt*), she has found the "one thing necessary" (Luke 10:42), that is, God. Hence, she hopes that Mary will give up consolation and sweetness and become what she is. Two digressions explain what this means. The first is an instruction on virtue, showing that its highest stage is reached when God gives the ground of the soul his eternal will conformed to the loving command of the Holy Spirit (490.3–4). The second excursus explains that this does not mean that a person remains absolutely untouched by pleasure or suffering. Even Christ was sorrowful unto death (Matt. 26:37). As long as suffering does not cause the will to waver in its dedication to God, or to "spill over into the highest part of the spirit," all is well.[638] Thus, Martha "was so essential [*weselich*] that her activity did not hinder her—work and activity led her to eternal happiness."[639] While sitting at the feet of Jesus, Mary is not the true Mary, i.e., the Mary who will one day reach the same status as Martha when she "learns life and possesses it essentially" (*daz si lernete leben, daz si ez weselich besaeze* [491.14]).

In concluding Pr. 86, Eckhart corrects two false understandings of what it means to be a Martha-Mary, or perfect Christian. First of all, we should not aspire to become disembodied spirits, with our senses immune to what is pleasant or unpleasant. It is only the inward will formed to God in understanding that can turn pain and difficulty into joy and fruitful work. Second, we should never imagine that we will attain freedom from external works in this life. Mary herself became active as preacher and teacher (and "washerwoman of the disciples") after Christ's ascension. Christ himself is a model for the necessity of constant activity without a why. According to Eckhart, throughout his life "there was no part of his body that did not practice its proper virtue" (492.16).

Conclusion

Eckhart's model of living *sunder warumbe* is not as impractical or empty of content as it may at first seem. Reading Pr. 86 helps us to understand the implications of his message. As daring, as profound, and sometimes even as obscure as his preaching of the *rara et subtilia* in such MHG sermons were, Eckhart basically was inviting his audience, simple laity as well as pious religious women and learned clerics, to do what Martha had done, that is, to become so dedicated to fulfilling the will of God, so unconcerned with self, that their every action would proceed from the "well-exercised ground" in which God and human are one, in which the Word is ever being born in the soul, and in which "God's ground is my ground, and my ground is God's ground."

Eckhart often closes his sermons with a plea for the recognition of this essential truth. At the end of the *Book of Consolation* he has a particularly effective prayer that can also conclude this long chapter.

> May the loving compassionate God, the Truth,
>   grant to me and to all who read this book,
>   that we may find the truth within ourselves,
>   and become aware of it. Amen.[640]

Henry Suso's Spiritual Philosophy

ENRY SUSO (CA. 1295–1366) is among the most influential, yet elusive, late medieval mystics.[1] Given that there are more than five hundred manuscripts of his works, it is safe to say that no fourteenth-century mystic was more widely read and none was more representative of the many strands of the mysticism of the century than this Dominican friar. Toward the end of his life Suso's concern for his message led him to compile a definitive edition of his vernacular works, which he named *The Exemplar*.[2] *Exemplar* signifies not only the title but also the content and subject of the four texts in the collection. In other words, Suso claims that this four-part work is "*the* exemplar," or model, of mystical transformation. As Jeffrey Hamburger puts it: "*The Exemplar* . . . offers the reader a model of the religious life in the form of an extended meditation on the relation between exemplars and experience construed, in absolute terms, as the relation between the Logos and the self."[3]

The extent to which Suso himself functions as an exemplar is still debated. Given the fact that the first and longest work in the collection, the *Life*, has often been read as an autobiographical, or "autohagiographical," text, many have judged, in the formulation of Michael Egerding, that Suso presents himself as a living metaphor, or "true image" (*war bilde*), of the saving love of Jesus.[4] Although an emphasis on the person and personal experience had not been lacking in the new mysticism that began about 1200,[5] before Suso it had been more evident in women than in men. But Werner Williams-Krapp points out that Suso never names himself in the *Life*. The protagonist is the anonymous "Servant of Eternal Wisdom" (*ein diener der ewigen wisheit* [L Prol.: 7.4]), a figure who shares some biographical

195

details with what we know of the historical Suso, but who cannot be totally identified with him in any simple way.[6] Part of the fascination of Suso and his *Exemplar* rests in this studied ambiguity.

Suso the mystical writer is exemplary in synthesizing (or at least attempting to synthesize) a number of important aspects of late medieval German mysticism: the "spiritual philosophy" (*philosophia spiritualis*) of the monks of the desert handed on through the monastic, and now the mendicant, tradition; *imitatio passionis*, most often understood as a literal following of Christ's sufferings; motifs from courtly literature used to describe the soul's love of God; and, finally, the mysticism of the ground created by Meister Eckhart. All these elements play their role in Suso's thought, though it is not always easy to see how they are related.[7]

Suso is also exemplary as a stylist, both in German and in Latin. Suso's MHG style has been justly praised by students of the German language. As Alois M. Haas puts it: "Among the [German] mystics . . . Suso is certainly the most openly literary, both for the genres he used and also for his stylistic versatility."[8] He is equally impressive in Latin: his exuberant Latin *Clock of Wisdom* is accomplished enough to bear comparison with Bernard of Clairvaux, the master of medieval Latin mystical literature.[9] Yet Suso was also aware of the limitations of language, especially in the still fluid vernacular. The prologue to his *Little Book of Eternal Wisdom* reflects on the difference between "the words that are received in pure grace and flow out of a responsive heart through a fervent mouth," and "these same words written on dead parchment, especially in the German tongue."[10] The reader, Suso avers, needs to have a heart full of love to read *through* the words on the page to find the divine source of the love that also moved the author's heart.

Other aspects of Suso's mysticism reveal further dimensions of his exemplarity. Prominent among these is the use of art as a vehicle for the expression of mystical themes, a trend growing since the thirteenth century. The intersection between the verbal and visual communication of mystical transformation finds one of its major proponents in Suso, who not only offered original reflections on the usefulness and limitations of images (*bilde*) in bringing the believer to an encounter with God, but who also became his own mystical iconographer.[11]

Suso was a remarkable figure, yet one who remains more difficult for us to evaluate, and even to appreciate, than many other fourteenth-century mystics. Although he was a great stylist, his rhetoric is so tied to his era that his works, especially in their repetitions and use of heightened rhetoric (*genus dicendi sublime*),[12] are less accessible today than the more straightforward writings of some of his contemporaries. Aspects of Suso's style (at least for moderns), the ambiguities of his presentation in the *Life*, as well as the difficulty of relating the different strands of his mysticism mentioned above, make him a difficult figure to present in any adequate way. Although I agree with Kurt Ruh that no single formula can capture him, in this chapter I will try to show how Suso's view of what he called *philosophia spiritualis* helps us to grasp the nature of his mystical teaching and the significance of his contributions.

I. Life and Writings[13]

Suso's life is paradoxically both easy and difficult to reconstruct—easy in the sense that we know many of the essential facts; difficult, because the *Life of the Servant* often muddies the waters when we seek to determine the historicity and meaning of many events.

Henry Suso was born in the city of Constance between 1295 and 1297, the child of a pious mother whose name he took and a well-to-do father toward whom he seems to have been disaffected. He entered the Dominican convent in that city at the canonically illegal age of thirteen. Suso believed that this early entry had involved simony in the form of a gift made to the community by his parents. Always given to scruples, he fretted over this issue for some time before being relieved of his worries by Meister Eckhart. In the prologue to the *Life*, Suso tells us that after about five years in the convent the Servant experienced a conversion to a deeper form of religious life through the intervention of Divine Wisdom, something that may reflect his own experience.

After receiving his early training in his native convent, Suso was sent on for further studies in philosophy and theology, probably first at the Dominican house in Strassburg (ca. 1319–21), and then at the *studium generale* at Cologne, the center of German Dominican intellectual life (ca. 1323–27). In both houses he would have come into contact with Eckhart, whom he referred to as "blessed Meister Eckhart" (*der heilige meister Egghart* [L 21:63.4]), and who appeared to the Servant in a dream after his death.[14] There is no question of the deep influence of Eckhart on his life and teaching, but details about Suso's historical relation to the great teacher and preacher are lacking.

When he returned to his home convent (ca. 1327), Suso served as lector, but his teaching aroused criticism, most likely because of his connection with Eckhart in the wake of the master's trial and condemnation. Suso's *Little Book of Truth*, a short defense of Eckhart's teaching, appears to date to

around 1329, while the dispute was in full swing. In 1330 this treatise and
another (most likely the *Little Book of Eternal Wisdom*, or an early version of
it) were denounced as heretical by enemies in the order. Suso journeyed to
the Dominican General Chapter held at Maastricht in 1330 to defend himself. It was probably at this time that he was relieved of his lectorship,
though he was not personally condemned.[15]

We know that at some later time, most likely between 1330 and 1334,
though possibly in the 1340s, Suso served as prior of the Constance convent. If Suso himself ever engaged in the literal *imitatio passionis* ascribed to
the Servant in such gruesome, if hyperbolic, ways in the *Life*, it would have
been in the mid-1330s that he abandoned these in favor of the interior self-
abnegation of true detachment.[16] Suso presents this important transition in
the spiritual life in a striking passage. In chapter 20 of the *Life* he describes
how one day the Servant was sitting in his cell, when an inner voice proclaimed: "Throw open the window of your cell. Look and learn." In the
convent courtyard he saw a dog sporting with a tattered doormat. A voice
then declared to him: "'Exactly this shall happen to you in the mouths of
your fellow friars.' He thought to himself, 'Since it cannot be otherwise, surrender yourself to it. See how without a word the mat lets itself be ill-
treated. Do the same yourself!'"[17] The Servant kept the doormat for years
after, not being able to part with it even when asked by his favorite spiritual
daughter.

It also seems likely, as Pius Künzle suggested,[18] that it was in the years
between 1330 and 1334 that Suso experienced a mystical marriage with
Divine Wisdom, an event whose ramifications are evident in the differences
between the early vernacular *Little Book of Wisdom* (ca. 1328–30) and its
recasting into an expanded and enriched Latin *Clock of Wisdom* (ca.
1334–37). This work was dedicated to the new Dominican master general,
Hugh of Vaucemain, who appears to have been a supporter.

During the eventful years between ca. 1327 and 1334, then, Suso abandoned hopes for the kind of academic career that Eckhart had enjoyed and
turned wholeheartedly to the life of inner devotion and spiritual guidance
of others, especially women, that characterized the remainder of his life.[19]
His criticism of the spiritual deficiencies of training in the various sciences
and also among most theological students is found throughout his works
and echoes a theme that becomes almost universal among fourteenth-
century mystics.[20] Suso witnesses to a growing rift between theology and
mysticism already evident in the thirteenth century that reached epidemic
proportions in the fourteenth. Eckhart was one of the few mystics who
remained above the fray, convinced of the harmony of *good* theology, correct philosophy, and earnest pursuit of God.

In the mid-1330s, during his visits to houses of Dominican nuns and beguines, Suso became acquainted with Elsbeth Stagel, a young woman of aristocratic background who had joined the convent at Töss.[21] Elsbeth, who helped write the Töss *Lives of the Sisters* (*Nonnenbuch*), was pre-eminent among Suso's devoted disciples, a group that included both men and women, especially those connected with the "Friends of God" (*gotesfründe*) movement in the upper Rhine area.[22] The spiritual friendship between the two is evidence of the ongoing cooperation between men and women that was central to much late medieval mysticism. Sometime during these decades of friendship Elsbeth began gathering the materials that Suso eventually put together into his *Life of the Servant.*

The final thirty years of Suso's life were lived out in the midst of the dramatic crises of the mid-fourteenth century: corruption in the church and in the Dominican order; the conflict between Pope John XXII and the emperor-elect Lewis of Bavaria; the Black Death; growing persecution of the Jews—to name but some. Aspects of these tragedies surface in Suso's writings, especially his concern for the state of the church and his order, which is reflected in the "Vision of the Pilgrim" found in the *Little Book of Wisdom* 6 and the *Clock of Wisdom* I.5.[23] The Dominican's message, however, always focuses on the inner transformation that he had experienced in the early 1330s and which he preached and taught to the Friends of God both within and without the order during the last decades of his life.

Suso shared in the exile of the Dominican community from Constance between 1339 and 1346, during the most heated years of the quarrel between the pope and the emperor.[24] We know that he was later transferred to the convent at Ulm about 1348. Here he spent almost two decades of life, dying on January 25, 1366. During his final years, probably about 1361–63, he edited his four main vernacular works into *The Exemplar*. The unusual character of this action deserves to be noted. Suso had a concern for the posthumous dissemination of his writings that would have been foreign to Meister Eckhart, and even strange to Suso's contemporary Tauler, who did allow some communities of nuns to copy collections of his sermons. Suso not only edited the texts himself but also sought official approval for this act, asking the Dominican provincial, the theologian Bartholomew of Bolsenheim, to approve the work. Bartholomew died in 1362, but conveniently appeared to Suso in a vision and encouraged him to finish *The Exemplar*, telling him that "it was God's will that he circulate it among all benevolent people who desired it with right intentions and intense longing."[25] Bartholomew proved a good prophet. Besides the fifteen manuscripts containing all or part of *The Exemplar*, there are no fewer than 232 manuscripts of the *Little Book of Wisdom* and 43 of the *Life*.[26]

Suso's early work, the *Little Book of Truth* (LBT), comprising seven chapters, was probably written about 1329, though it was certainly reworked when edited for *The Exemplar.*[27] There is a consensus that the book was composed to defend Eckhart's teaching against his detractors. Suso even seems to reflect knowledge of the bull "In agro dominico" in his defense of his teacher.[28] As in several of his other writings, Suso adopts the style of a Boethian philosophical dialogue in which the disciple (i.e., Suso) questions Divine Truth about the proper understanding of inwardness, detachment, breaking-through to union with God, and the freedom that flows from this. In chapter 6 there is a noted discussion between the disciple and "the nameless wild one" (*daz namelos wilde*), a figure representing the position of the heretical Free Spirits, who misunderstood and misused Eckhart's thought. Suso's modification of Eckhart will be discussed below, but it should be noted that his Eckhartianism in this treatise is sometimes obscure and difficult to follow (see especially LBT 5).

A debate has emerged in recent scholarship concerning the relation between philosophy and mysticism in the LBT.[29] Is this treatise a philosophical exposition based on Eckhartian metaphysics, or is it a mystical appeal to spiritual transformation? Or is it (to advance what I believe is a more balanced view) fundamentally Eckhartian in its refusal to distinguish between philosophico-theological speculation and insights concerning transformation in God that surpass the level of reason? Loris Sturlese is correct to draw attention to Suso's philosophical acumen in this work, but the speculation set forth in the LBT is not to be thought of as an academic exercise based on Aristotelian reason alone. The LBT is deeply "philosophical," in the root meaning of the love of wisdom, pursuing this goal through an inward mental attitude that breaks through modern distinctions between philosophy, theology, and what we call mysticism, in order to discern the fundamental truth about both being and living. Reason's highest function in such a philosophy is to recognize its own limitations.[30]

The *Little Book of Wisdom* (LBW), which appears to have been written almost contemporaneously with the LBT (ca. 1329–30) is a more ambitious work, and one of a less speculative nature. In his prologue Suso tells us of the occasion of the work. While the Servant was standing before a crucifix one day, he experienced an inability to meditate. Suddenly, he was given an inner illumination of a hundred meditations on Christ's suffering that transformed his insensitivity into "a lovely sweetness" (*ein minneklich suozikeit* [LBW Prol.: 197.5]). He then determined to set out the meaning of these meditations through the medium of an interpretive parable or allegory (*usgeleitú bischaft* in MHG [197.23]; *figurata locutio* in Latin) of intimate conversations between the Servant and Eternal Wisdom, the Second Person of the Trinity, portrayed sometimes as a female, sometimes as a male figure.

The work falls into three parts. Part 1 consists of twenty chapters considering the events of the passion as the supreme manifestation of Wisdom's love for the world. Part 2 has four chapters that deal with the essential exercises for practical living: learning to die;[31] learning to live inwardly; learning how to receive the Eucharist; and learning how to praise God always. Finally, part 3 lists the hundred meditations and the mode of practicing them. (This section may have been written down first, and sometimes circulated independently.)

Apparently a few years later, Suso adopted this MHG work into his Latin *Horologium Sapientiae*, or *Clock of Wisdom*. Although today he is read primarily as a proponent of the vernacular mysticism of the late Middle Ages, Suso's impact through this Latin work was even greater—the number of the manuscripts, translations, and early printings of the *Clock of Wisdom* outweigh even the copies of the LBW, his most popular vernacular work. The *Clock* was also translated into eight vernacular languages. With over four hundred manuscripts in Latin and over two hundred in the translations, as well as many early printings, the *Clock* was second only to the *Imitation of Christ* in popularity among the spiritual writings of the later Middle Ages.[32] Although much of the material of LBW appears in the *Clock*, the Latin version is not so much a translation as a new work, with its rearrangements, expansions, and adaptations of the German treatise. Especially important are the new autobiographical materials, new visions, greater pastoral concerns, and greater emphasis on the mystical marriage with Wisdom.[33]

The vision of the clock decorated with roses presented in the prologue announces the twenty-four-hour pursuit of Wisdom that provides the general structure of the work. The *Clock* is divided into two parts, versus the three in the MHG work: sixteen chapters in the first part, and eight in the second. While the LBW is a fine example of Suso's vernacular style, the success of the *Clock* is due in part to the richness of the Dominican's flowing Latin—an abundance that may at times seem cloying to the modern reader.[34] Since the *Clock* was written in what was still the international language of spiritual instruction, it could serve as a basis for creative adaptations in new linguistic arenas, as the many translations and adaptations demonstrate.

Despite the popularity of the *Clock*, the work for which Suso is most read today is the *Life of the Servant* (*Life*, or *Vita*), a text that is in some sense the joint product of the friar and Elsbeth Stagel, his intimate spiritual friend.

Suso tells us that unbeknownst to him Elsbeth began writing out accounts of his spiritual trials that he had discussed with her. When he discovered this, he destroyed some of the materials, but then was forestalled by a message from God. How much of the final text comes from Elsbeth's pen is probably impossible to know, but it seems clear from the way in which Suso edited his works for *The Exemplar* that he should be thought of as the main author.[35] If it is difficult to think of Elsbeth as a co-author, she can at least be called a co-protagonist, because the role given to the servant's spiritual daughter in the book is essential for its teaching.[36] Hence, this text remains one of the major monuments of the conversations between men and women that were so vital to the new mysticism of the later Middle Ages.[37]

The genre of the *Life* has elicited much discussion. As pointed out above, it has been considered a form of autobiography, and it has indeed been treated as such in classic studies of the genre.[38] In some manuscripts the title of the first part reads: "Here begins the first part of this book, that is called Suso."[39] But this is a scribal addition; Suso speaks only of the "Servant" using the third person, not the first. The *Life* employs autobiographical material, but is scarcely an autobiography. Richard Kieckhefer used the term "autohagiography" to describe this and other late medieval works that adapt some of the devices of hagiographical writings, such as visions and miracles, to present an exemplary life story.[40] Werner Williams-Krapp, however, notes that the *Life* does not hold up Suso himself as an object of saintly veneration. According to Williams-Krapp, the *Life* is "a sophisticated blueprint for exemplary spirituality, aimed primarily at women, related within a narrative that draws upon the exemplary Lives of the Desert Fathers and Mothers,"[41] that is, the *Vitaspatrum* widely read among Dominicans and treasured by Suso.[42]

Suso's *Life* combines so rich a range of genres, materials, and perspectives that it resists any easy characterization.[43] In this context, I will mention only a few aspects of its complexity. Among these we can note the indebtedness of the book to themes from courtly romance literature,[44] though it is scarcely just a courtly tale. Given the friar's acquaintance with Augustine, the influence of the *Confessions* as an exemplary narrative cast in terms of a life story is also obvious. One special problem of the *Life* is the degree to which narrative details, such as the accounts of the Servant's severe asceticism (chapters 13–19), or some of the stories about his trials (e.g., chapter 38, where he is accused of fathering a child), may or may not have an autobiographical foundation. Could the young friar have engaged in severe ascetical acts? Certainly. Could the older wandering preacher have been subject to an unjust accusation of sexual misconduct? Of course. But did these events take place in the manner described? It seems unlikely, even at times impossible. It is the exemplary nature of the stories, not their historicity, that is central to Suso's mystagogy.

According to Alois M. Haas, the *Life* presents an intricate interplay between the purported empirical "I," the subtly-crafted literary "I," and finally the mystical and vanishing "I."[45] The difficulty of sorting out these voices is compounded by Suso's art of presentation, what he calls an "image-giving manner" (*bildgebender wise* [3.3]) in the prologue to *The Exemplar*. As mystagogical strategy, *bildgebender wise/figurata locutio* does not differentiate strongly between event and literary elaboration, as long as the overall strategy of conveying the fundamental spiritual message is attained. As Frank Tobin puts it: "Fiction in the *Vita* is not the opposite of fact but has, rather, a symbiotic relation to it. . . ."[46] The complexity of this symbiosis between what we call fact and fiction, as well as the ambiguity of the "I" being presented, are part of the ongoing fascination and difficulty of reading the *Life*.

The *Life* is composed of two parts. The first (chapters 1–32) narrates the Servant's spiritual progress. After six introductory chapters, three sections recount the growing conformity between the Servant and Divine Wisdom. The first section (chapters 7–12) describes the servant's exercises (*uebunge*), that is, his ritualized following of the life of Christ over the course of the liturgical year. Chapters 13–18 portray his self-imposed torture, the external *imitatio passionis* that reaches a climax in chapter 16, where he literally sees himself as the naked bleeding Christ. The final section, however, transcends external imitation of the passion, stressing the superiority of the internal passion practice of Eckhartian detachment. This interior exercise culminates in an ecstatic inner experience of the passion in which the Servant becomes a co-redeemer with Christ (chapter 31). This transition from outer to inner passion piety shows that Suso was opposed to the more literal forms of *imitatio passionis* found among some contemporary Dominican nuns. Like Meister Eckhart, and in part in dependence on him, Suso engaged in a dialogue with mystical women that was also a corrective critique.[47] Finally, in chapter 32 Suso concludes this Eckhartian section with a discussion of the breaking-through (*durchpruch*) into God.

The second part of the *Life* (chapters 33–53) shifts attention to the master–disciple relation of Suso and Elsbeth Stagel to demonstrate that the Servant is both the *image* of the true way to God and also the *teacher* of how it is to be attained. In the introduction (chapters 33–35), Suso describes Elsbeth's failed attempts to practice Eckhartian teaching before the Servant steps in and undertakes her spiritual education with practices more suitable for beginners. Chapters 36–45 contain a somewhat random series of vignettes in which the Servant recounts his practices and sufferings as models for Elsbeth and his other spiritual daughters. Finally, in a third section (chapters 46–53), which Suso says he completed after Elsbeth's death (ca. 1360), we find a summary of the higher instruction concerning "the heights of contemplative nobility of a blessed life of perfection" (L 46:156.5–6). This "lofty intellectual path" begins negatively with the Servant teaching his daughter to distinguish between true and false mysticism, so much a part of fourteenth-century concerns (chapters 46–49). Chapters 50–53, the positive part, discuss the sublime matters that the daughter asked of her spiritual father. This is a profound summary of Suso's mature, albeit modified Eckhartianism. These chapters demonstrate that while the aged friar explored many forms of mysticism not found in his teacher, he never abandoned the mysticism of the ground as essential to the highest form of consciousness of God.[48]

Several shorter works of Suso's also survive. Elsbeth Stagel collected twenty-eight of his letters in a compilation known as the *Great Book of Letters*. Suso arranged eleven of these into the *Little Book of Letters* (LBL) and included them in *The Exemplar*. These carefully crafted epistles form a practical instruction in the spiritual life from conversion to christological union. Added to the LBL are some stories, prayers, and poems, including the popular "Morgengruss," or "Morning Prayer."[49] A number of vernacular sermons are also ascribed to the Dominican, but only two of these appear to be authentic. Finally, a treatise known as the *Little Book of Love* (*Minnebüchlein*) is sometimes, but probably incorrectly, ascribed to Suso.[50] It is a mélange of texts on devotion to Christ's passion.

II. *Philosophia Spiritualis*

In several places in the *Clock of Wisdom* Suso describes the teaching Wisdom provides as *philosophia spiritualis*. In chapter 9 of part 1, for example, Wisdom contrasts those who study only visible things with the Servant as a student in a higher school:

> But you, who are taught in a different way in our spiritual philosophy, rise up, surpassing all visible things in your mind—"the things that are seen are temporal; those not seen are eternal" (2 Cor. 4:18). . . . Open your mental eyes and see what you are, where you are, and where you are headed. Then you will surely have understanding of all these issues.[51]

The roots of this conception of *spiritualis philosophia* go deep into tradition. Citing Bernard of Clairvaux, who is quoting Paul (1 Cor. 2:2), in Hor. I.14 Suso says, "Meanwhile this is my higher philosophy, 'to know Jesus and him crucified.'"[52] In an autobiographical account in II.3 he tells of the vision that turned him away from worldly learning. A youth appeared to him showing him an old hermit and a small ancient book in which he read the words, "For a spiritual man the source and origin of every good is always to remain in his cell."[53] The author of this teaching, the old hermit, is "the highest philosopher Arsenius," and the book is the neglected *Lives of the Fathers* (*Vitaspatrum*). "This book," concludes Suso, "is little appreciated by many as ancient and outmoded, although it contains the core of all perfection and experience knows with certainty that the true science of Christian philosophy is found therein."[54] For Suso, like the desert fathers, the life of prayer and penance and true philosophy is one. Hence, in one of the readings for the Office (*Cursus de aeterna Sapientia*) that he wrote to accompany the *Clock of Wisdom*, he prays to crucified Wisdom: "Put my philosophy in your wounds, my wisdom in your stigmata, so that from now on I may advance in You, the only book of love, and in your death. . . ."[55]

Coming in the midst of a work chock-full of visions, effusive descriptions of rapture, and meditations on the passion of Christ and the compassion of Mary, the modern reader may be inclined to wonder how these emotionally charged presentations can be described as "philosophy." Nevertheless, the phrase *philosophia spiritualis* provides a clue for understanding how the Dominican's writings connect with a long-standing monastic view of philosophy, as a number of recent studies have suggested.[56] What did Suso intend when he described his teaching as "spiritual philosophy"?

The history of the term *philosophia* (etymologically, "love of wisdom") shows how differing conceptions of what wisdom is have shaped much of the Western tradition. Building on ancient understandings of philosophy as comprising both contemplation and action, that is, the kind of lifestyle committed to pursuing wisdom,[57] the early Christian monks boldly appropriated *philosophia* as a word for describing the wisdom of the desert and the monastic life in general.[58] Good Dominican that he was, Suso was formed by the stories and sayings of the desert monks, the writings of Cassian, and the sermons and treatises of Bernard of Clairvaux.[59] Like the fathers of the desert and their successors, Suso identified *philosophia spiritualis* with *sapientia*, that is, *sapida scientia* (knowledge that knows by taste). It is knowing for living, a "practical philosophy of life," as Philipp Kaiser puts it,[60] but its goal of saving knowledge does not preclude a speculative element. Suso's concern for correcting false understandings of the mystical path is an important part of his practical emphasis on how to live. *Philosophia spiritualis* is a mystical knowing that fuses practice and speculation, action and contemplation into a seamless whole.[61]

Strategies in Presenting Spiritual Philosophy

The complexity of Suso's self-presentation, not only in the *Life* but across his works, has already been noted. Suso was also one of the few late medieval mystics who not only adverted to the role of images in the path to God but also commissioned manuscript illuminations to help convey his message. Both aspects of the Dominican's teaching are too rich to be exhausted in a brief treatment, but they are too important to be totally neglected.

Two dimensions of Suso's literary presentation of the "I" of the Servant that merit notice involve his courtly identity and gender ambiguity. The presence of courtly elements in Suso's corpus has long been noted, and perhaps even exaggerated, by some literary scholars.[62] Nevertheless, the structure of the *Life*, with its intermingling of accounts of suffering and struggle and scenes of rapturous joy, as well as many other themes within the book, betray a conscious attempt to appropriate late medieval courtly motifs in the service of spiritual philosophy. Courtly language and images are most evident in the portrayal of the Servant as a knightly adventurer (*aventúrer* [L 44:149.11]) in faithful service of his lady-love, Eternal Wisdom. This identity allows Suso to show how the spiritual knight, like the worldly one, demonstrates the fidelity of his bond to his lady by his willingness to undergo suffering in her honor (i.e., the struggle to imitate Christ through penance, detachment, and virtuous living). It is especially in chapter 44 that we find the Servant (not so much Suso's own self as the literary "I" of the narrative) as the questing knight of spiritual adventure.[63] But the fact that the courtly self is also prominent in *Life* 20, the chapter that marks the shift from exterior imitation of the passion to the deeper imitation of release-ment (*gelassenheit*),[64] shows that spiritual courtliness is an important element in Suso's mysticism.

The issue of gender-bending has only recently emerged as a significant element in Suso's presentation of the mystical self.[65] Just as mystical states of consciousness break through ordinary ways of knowing and loving to reveal new truths about God and human, so too the liminality of the mystical condition allows for experimentation with gender-identity impossible in ordinary life. God in Godself is beyond gender. Christians usually address the first two Persons of the Trinity in male language, as Father and Son, thus encouraging male humans to take on a female persona in describing their erotic longing for God (in conformity with the feminine gender of *anima*, or soul). However, the wisdom literature of the Old Testament (e.g., Wis. 8:22) contains descriptions of female divine *Sophia/Sapientia* that allow for an alternative possibility in which the male mystic maintains his own gender while exploring a love relationship with a feminine divinity. The ambiguity of gender is further heightened when the feminine divine Wisdom takes on flesh in a male human, Jesus of Nazareth.

Many earlier male Christian mystics were content to cast themselves in the female role, at least in literary projections of the self in their commentaries on the Song of Songs. But from the early centuries, some male mystics experimented with descriptions of masculine love for the feminine Divine Wisdom. Augustine of Hippo, for example, expressed a passionate yearning for Wisdom, marveling at how she offered herself to all her lovers without arousing the ire of jealous males.[66] At times, he even used erotic images for his love for Wisdom, such as the longing to see and embrace her naked beauty.[67] What is unusual in Suso is his deliberate and shifting play with both male and female identities for himself and for the Divine Lover. In the prologue to the *Clock of Wisdom*, speaking in the third person, he says: "Thus he changes his style in different ways according to how it fits the matter. Now he brings on God's Son as the Bridegroom of the devout soul; afterward he introduces the same as Eternal Wisdom betrothed to the just man."[68] This shifting gender identity is especially evident in the early part of the book. Chapter 1 begins by describing the passionate love of *Frater Amandus* (another ambiguous stand-in for Suso) for the beauteous Lady Wisdom. In the midst of the description of Lady Wisdom Suso remarks, "When he already thought of her as a delicate young girl, he at once found her to be a very beautiful young man."[69] The reversing gender polarities, which do not seem to have troubled the Dominican or his large audience, reach a culmination in chapter 4. This chapter begins in the female voice, as the soul laments how she has been false to her male Divine Lover; then it switches to a male persona as the young Christian man speaks of being deceived by a false woman (i.e., *frau wërlt*, or the world); and then it reverts back to the female soul, who proclaims how she has cherished innocence of mind and body. At this point, Wisdom breaks in and the Disciple becomes once again male as he engages in an erotic dialogue with *Sapientia*, who is paradoxically, however, also identified as "brother and Bridegroom" (400.17). In the course of this final part of the conversation, Suso makes use of charged erotic images, such as the naked bloody embrace that he begs from the "Son of the Eternal King" (402.14–

18). The upshot of these dizzying switches has been well summarized by
Barbara Newman, who notes that for Suso "it is the woman Sapientia who
signifies celestial glory, and the man Jesus who embodies suffering flesh."[70]
Hence, Suso is more the male when pursuing Heavenly Wisdom, more the
female in embracing and kissing the bloody Redeemer.[71]

Similar gender ambiguity is found in the *Life*. In chapter 3, where Suso
recounts how he entered into spiritual marriage with Eternal Wisdom following the example of the Wisdom books of the Old Testament, he marvels
at Wisdom's changing identity in a flowery passage that recasts Boethius's
famous picture of Lady Philosophy at the beginning of the *Consolation of
Philosophy*:

> She must be my beloved, and I shall be her servant. O God, if I might just
> catch a glimpse of my dear one! . . . Is he divine or human, man or woman,
> art or knowledge, or what? . . . She was distant yet near, far above yet low,
> present yet hidden. . . . The minute he thought her to be a beautiful young
> lady, he immediately found a proud young man before him. Sometimes she
> acted like a wise teacher, sometimes like a pert young thing. She presented
> herself to him endearingly, and greeted him smiling, saying kindly, "*Prebe, fili,
> cor tuum mihi!* Give me your heart, my child."[72]

For Suso, Lady Wisdom's mutating gender is part of her charm and attractiveness.

Suso lived in a world filled with religious images and statues integral to
his own devotion, as many passages in his writings demonstrate.[73] Furthermore, the highly pictorial character of his style is evident to even a cursory
reader. Suso loves to picture detailed scenes and to present striking images
in words; his mysticism delights in the varied presentation of concrete symbols.[74] But the German Dominican was not content with verbal pictures
alone. Suso is unusual, though not unique, among medieval mystics in the
impulse that led him to become his own mystical iconographer. In chapter
35 of the *Life* Suso tells us that as a youth the Servant had had a picture of
Eternal Wisdom painted on parchment that he carried with him during his
years of study and that he eventually hung in the Dominican chapel in
Constance. Later the Servant commissioned a painter to decorate the
chapel with a series of murals of the fathers of the desert and other devotional materials, copies of which he sent to Elsbeth Stagel.[75] At another time
Elsbeth collaborated with Suso in creating a holy image. The Servant/Suso
describes in elaborate detail how early in his religious life he carved the
name of Jesus in monogram form (IHS) into the flesh over his heart (L 4;
Hor. II.7; Letter 11).[76] His devotion to this image inspired Elsbeth to sew
the monogram in red silk onto a piece of cloth that she could wear to imi-

tate him. She made copies of the monogram, sending them to Suso to place over his living image, and then distributing them to his followers like relics (see illustration 1).⁷⁷

Given this history of using images, it comes as no surprise that toward the end of his life Suso ordered a series of twelve illustrations for *The Exemplar.* As Jeffrey Hamburger has shown, these images are related to the murals in the chapel and hence were meant to encourage the reader to imitate the Servant in using both text and picture in their spiritual praxis. As Hamburger puts it: "In addition to authorizing images as vehicles of mystical ascent no less legitimate than the texts with which they are associated, the drawings identify the viewing and reproduction of images as a model for the process of imitation central to the spiritual life itself."⁷⁸ Hence, for Suso the use of images was not peripheral or secondary, but integral to attaining mystical consciousness. As Niklaus Largier has suggested, the images Suso had made for *The Exemplar* had multiple functions, both as aids to understanding the words of the text, and also as setting them in question due to the way the pictures break through the temporal and linear sequence of the narrative.⁷⁹ Suso's mysticism is both verbal and pictorial.

Suso not only used images, but he also reflected on the necessary impossibility of employing images in the path to God. To adopt a phrase reflecting the Dionysian and Eckhartian side of his mysticism, we can say that the image is always a *dissimilis similitudo* of God.⁸⁰ The image is necessary as a likeness or manifestation (*similitudo*), but impossible as a representation, and therefore always remains more an unlikeness (*dissimilitudo*) than a likeness to God. Images are therefore crucial for the praxis that leads to God, but, like words, images ineluctably fail to capture the hidden divinity. This paradoxical role is rooted in Godself. God, especially in the Person of the Word, is the source of the ideas/images (*bilde*) of all created things (e.g., L 52 [187.1–5]), and yet God is beyond all images and ideas as *die bildlose gotheit* (L 50 [174.8]).⁸¹

Suso mentions the use of "image-giving means" (*bildgebender wise*) in the prologue to *The Exemplar,* and he defends the dozen pictures he ordered for the collection as necessary for drawing the religiously minded person away from the world.⁸² Important discussions of the role of images also occur in the *Clock of Wisdom* and the LBL. In the prologue to the *Clock* Suso says that the visions in the work need not all be taken literally, though many were perceived by him as such. They should rather be considered a form of *figurata locutio,* or "speaking through figures," as found in biblical parables. "The attentive reader," he adds, "will easily note the hidden mysteries of this speaking through figures, if he makes a skillful effort," that is, if he recognizes both the necessity and the limitation of images in mystical praxis.[83] The role of images, as taken up in several later chapters, is rooted both in the difficulty of presenting "the truths of the highest matters" otherwise than "through images and customary likenesses,"[84] as well as in the need to aid weak human memory by exterior signs.[85] Suso analyzes this necessity in similar fashion in Letter 9.[86]

The most penetrating discussion of the need for using images and the limitations of all images, pictorial and verbal, is found in *Life* 53.[87] In this culminating chapter of the work, Elsbeth Stagel requests a summary of the Servant's deepest teaching on Trinity and creation with "pictorial comparisons" (*bildgebender glichnus*) and "brief imagistic language" (*kurzer bildlicher rede* [191.1–4]). Suso obliges by presenting not only linguistic images but also his most famous mystical picture, a synoptic portrayal of the process of *exitus* from the hidden ground of the Godhead and the *reditus*, or return, to it. He also takes time to explain what images (*bilde*), be they verbal or visual, can do. In a famous comment, he says:

> How can one form images of the imageless or describe the mode of what is modeless? Whatever comparisons are made, it is still a thousand times more unlike than like. And yet, so that one may drive out one image with another, I will show it to you here imagistically in the language of pictorial comparisons, as far as this is possible in the case of these meanings beyond images. . . .[88]

To illustrate this observation, Suso commissioned a full-page picture of the inner procession of the Trinity from the *grunt*, its production of spiritual beings, and the stages of their return to the hidden source (illustration 2).[89] Significantly, the picture comes before the lengthy verbal analysis of the stages of emanation and return. As Hamburger puts it, "the picture reminds us that Suso first saw and then read."[90] This image with its attendant didactic captions is a summary of Suso's mystical thought, presenting time and eternity in a single gaze. Starting in the upper left, we see three rings figuring "the modeless abyss of the eternal Godhead without beginning or end" (*der ewigen gotheit wisloses abgrunde daz weder annuang hat noch kein ende* [caption]). The abyss emanates out through a tabernacle-like image to a picture of the three Persons of the Trinity, and then downward through figures representing angels and humans. Death and sinful persons are in the lower right, while the representations of a nun who prays, meditates on the passion, and suffers along with Christ begins the return path that eventually leads back into the modeless abyss. The continuity of the divine outflow and return is shown by the red string connecting all the images, as well as the presence of the divine abyss as *imago Dei* in creatures pictured as small circles that appear in the breasts of the angels and humans (a point merely mentioned in the chapter). While these divergences might be laid to the limitations of the artist, perhaps, given the Servant's view, the slippage between image and text is meant to underline the apophatic horizon that limits both pictures and words. The more images and the more slippage, the more we may begin to grasp how images drive out images, and also how words must unsay themselves in reaching toward the divine mystery.

Toward the end of the chapter, Suso insists that in the highest form of ecstasy no images are possible at all. "This rapture [*inschlag*] takes from him images, forms, and multiplicity; he loses all awareness of himself and all things."[91] As long as the beginning and end of all things (*exitus/reditus*) are conceived of as separate, they can be imagined and imaged; but when the soul is "transported into the One beyond images" (*in daz bildlos ein übersezet* [193.29–30]), beginning and end are one and therefore strictly un-*imageable*. Suso concludes on an Eckhartian note:

> Noble daughter, now note that all these images I have developed, and these thoughts distorted by images I have explained, are as far removed from the truth, which is beyond images and as unlike them, as a black Moor is unlike the sun. And this arises because of truth's formless and unknown simplicity.[92]

The role of images is tied to the centrality of Christ in Suso's mysticism. In one of the ninety-six axioms found in chapter 49 of the *Life* we read: "A released person must be freed from the forms of creatures, formed with Christ, and transformed in the Godhead"[93] The christological dimension of Suso's doctrine of *bild*, both as image and as word, is explicitly set forth in a passage in Letter 10. "True perfection," says Suso, "consists in the union of the highest powers of the soul with the origin of being in sublime contemplation." But due to the weakness of the body, the soul "cannot continually cling to the pure Good in a completely spiritual manner." Therefore, "it must have some kind of image [*etwas biltlichs*] to lead it back to this union. And the best thing for this that I know is the dear image of Jesus Christ." Since he is both God and man, Christ is both the way (physical image) and the goal (imageless image). Echoing Paul (2 Cor. 3:18), Suso continues: "As a person becomes formed according to this image, he is transformed as by God's Spirit into the divine glory of the Lord of heaven, growing brighter and brighter, from the brightness of his humanity to the brightness of his divinity."[94] Elsewhere Suso expresses this state as becoming "a Christ-formed I" (*ein kristfoermig ich* [LBW 4:335.26]).

The Content of Spiritual Philosophy

Imitatio Passionis

Having considered some of the ways in which Suso understands and presents his *philosophia spiritualis,* we can now turn to its content. In several places in his writings the Dominican uses a formula that aptly summarizes his teaching. In chapter 14 of the *Life,* for example, the voice of Christ scolds him, saying: "Don't you know that I am the gate through which all good Friends of God must force their way if they are to achieve true blessedness? You must break your way through by means of my suffering humanity if you are really to come to my pure Godhead."[95] Breaking through Christ's suffering humanity to attain the Son's being in the naked trinitarian Godhead (i.e., being freed of the forms of creatures, reformed in Christ, and transformed in the Godhead) expresses the essence of Suso's mysticism.

In the Middle Ages every branch of knowledge had its textbook. Spiritual philosophy is no different. The scriptures are foundational for *spiritualis philosophia* (Suso cites the Bible about twelve hundred times in his writings), but the Dominican's mysticism is not exegetical in the sense of being tied to narrative exposition of the biblical text.[96] So too Suso's favorite readings in the mystical tradition, especially the sayings and stories of the desert fathers, Cassian, Augustine, and Bernard of Clairvaux, play a role. But the real textbook of spiritual philosophy is nothing else than the book of the cross. Early on in the *Clock,* Wisdom concludes an instruction about compassion by saying: "These, my son, these I say, are the first principles which Eternal Wisdom hands over to you and her other lovers, which, as you see, are written down in this open book, that is, my crucified body."[97] *Philosophia spiritualis,* then, is nothing more nor less than learning to read and live Christ's passion.[98]

Suso, like Eckhart and the other German Dominicans, conceived of reality under the general paradigm of the emanation (*exitus/usfluz*) and return (*reditus/widerfluz*) of all things from their source in God. But, as Philipp Kaiser puts it: "With Suso this going forth and return is made concrete and personal in the Son of God made man."[99] This is clearly expressed in a key text in the LBW where Eternal Wisdom says:

> According to the order of nature, the loftiest flowing forth of all beings from their primal origin proceeds from the highest beings to the lowest; but the return to the origin proceeds from the lowest beings to the highest. And so, if you want to see me in my uncreated Godhead, you should learn to know and love me here in my suffering humanity.[100]

Both Suso and Eckhart emphasized a functional Christology centered on the ancient axiom, "God became man so that man might become God." In Suso, however, this functionalism is centered on a deeply emotional *imitatio passionis*, a gazing on the bloody and suffering God-man that leads to *compassio* (MHG *mitlidunge*), that is, suffering along with Jesus. Suso (or at least the exemplary Servant) at first practiced *compassio* as a literal inflicting on himself of the pains that Jesus endured; he later came to a better understanding. True compassion is inner conformity with Jesus through accepting all adversity in true detachment. "A person who freely suffers adversities for God," we read in the *Clock*, "is made like the suffering Christ, and hence is bound by him in a special, similar bond of love."[101]

Another contrast between Eckhart and Suso concerns the result of compassion. The Servant's compassionate gaze upon the "deformed beauty" (*deformis formositas*) of the Crucified One and his acceptance of suffering in imitation of him leads to the explicitly erotic union of mystical marriage, a form of mysticism marginal in Eckhart and Tauler.[102] In chapter 13 of the first part of the *Clock* (whose whole matter is "the most precious Passion of Christ" [371.18]), the Disciple listens as his soul recounts all the suffering it has endured from its cruel Bride, Holy Wisdom. But sadness then turns to joy. "When the Disciple had heard these things, he understood that it was the mystery of the espousal of Eternal Wisdom, who is accustomed to try her lovers with temporal tribulations and to unite to herself in love those who have passed the test."[103]

Reading in the book of Christ's crucified body, like any form of good exegesis, is a movement from the literal to the spiritual understanding. In the prologue to *The Exemplar,* Suso introduces the *Life* as pictorial example of the progress "from the life of the beginner" through that of "a person making progress," eventually "to the pure truth of a blessed and perfect life."[104] This traditional threefold division of the spiritual path underlies, if not in explicit fashion, what is essential to Suso's mystical teaching in the *Life of the Servant*: the necessity for a transition from the exterior literal imitation of the passion to an interior spiritual appropriation that allows the breakthrough to union in the divine ground.

In the first part of the *Life* (chapters 1–32) we follow this process through a presentation that is at times gripping, at times puzzling, and sometimes even horrifying (at least to the modern reader). It is worth noting that mystical gifts—visions, raptures, unitive moments, and the like—come not at the end of the transition from beginner to perfect, but accompany the entire process. *Life* 2, for example, contains one of Suso's more detailed accounts of a "supernatural rapture" (*úbernatúrlichen abzug* [10:10]) that occured at the beginning of his conversion. In chapter 5 he describes nine different kinds of divine consolations he received while still a beginner. Suso recognized that God often bestows such mystical gifts on beginners to attract them onto the arduous path to perfection. Despite the plethora of such phenomena described in the *Life* and elsewhere, Suso seems to have agreed with Eckhart that they were not essential. What is central is the gradual deepening of one's identity with Christ.

The exterior *imitatio Christi* set forth in the *Life* begins with a ritualization of time and daily conduct designed to keep before the mind Christ's life and saving action. Chapters 7–12 provide examples of these spiritual exercises (*geistliche uebunge* [L 10:30.14]), such as the Servant's eating practices (chapter 7), and how he celebrated certain feasts. Chapter 13 marks a move away from the consolations with which God had "spoiled him" and the beginnings of his direct imitating of the passion, which he found "hard and bitter." Suso describes how the Servant created his own way of the cross by establishing a para-liturgy according to which each night after Matins he walked through the cloister, using the different locations to meditate on the events of the passion.

As a result of the temptations of his "lively nature in his youth," the Servant, in the time-honored tradition of serious ascetics, soon decided to seek "all kinds of rigorous penances to make the flesh subject to the spirit."[105] The description of these self-induced tortures in chapters 15–18 constitutes one of the classic accounts of the human body being made the locus of identity with Christ through severe acts of asceticism (whether or not these are to be taken literally). To give but one example, when the Servant first constructed the cross barbed with thirty iron nails that he fastened to his skin for eight years, he tells us that he lost courage and bent the nails a bit to lessen his pain. The account continues:

> Soon he regretted his unmanly cowardice, and so he sharpened them all again with a file and put it back upon himself. It rubbed his back open where his bones were, making him bloody and torn. Wherever he sat or stood, it seemed to him as though the hide of a hedgehog were covering him.[106]

The limitations of this self-induced torture are evident in chapter 16, where Suso recounts how he took off his clothes and cruelly scourged himself until the whip broke. Looking at himself all bloody reminded him of Christ's sufferings, but, alas, also of himself: "Out of pity *for himself* [my emphasis] he began to weep from his heart."[107]

However real or imagined these accounts may be, there can be little doubt that Suso and other late-medieval mystics engaged in practices that provide rich material to students of abnormal psychology and postmodern theorists of the body. Without denying the possible usefulness of such approaches, from the perspective of the history of mysticism it is important to note that the *Life* presents the bloody agony of literal *imitatio passionis* as an initiatory, and even questionable stage—one more worthy of admiration than of emulation.

Suso's passion practices were a form of *com-passio*, what in MHG is described as *ein cristfoermig mitliden*, that is, learning how to suffer with and for Christ.[108] At the end of chapter 18 he tells us that he gave these practices up when "God made it clear to him that such severity and all these different practices together were nothing more than a good beginning. . . . He instructed him that he must make further progress, but in a different manner, if he were to reach his goal."[109] Later in the *Life* (chapter 35 [107–8]) he cautioned Elsbeth against undertaking such practices, noting that they were particularly dangerous for women.

A more important form of *com-passio* is set forth in *Life* 19–32. Here Suso gradually learns how to bear trials and tribulations in the spirit of "perfect releasement from self" (*volkomnú gelassenheit sin selbs* [L 19:54.2–3]). Like Christ praying at Gethsemane,[110] the Servant becomes the model of accepting God's will in all things, especially in unjust attacks against himself. Finally, in chapter 30, Suso describes what we would call the Servant's near-death experience, imitating Christ's surrender of life on the cross. This leads to the lyrical chapter 31, in which the Servant, rapt in ecstasy, takes all the world's suffering on himself as a co-redeemer, offering it to Christ, who is our model for suffering. "If there were no other advantage or good thing in suffering," he says, "except that we become much more like Christ, our fair shining mirror, it would be well worth it. . . . For love makes love like itself and inclines itself to love wherever at all it can."[111] The same message is summarized in *Clock* I:4, where the Disciple asks Wisdom, "Teach me, I beg, how I may bear your most sweet and delightful wounds in my body." Wisdom responds by setting forth the nature of true imitation of the passion. By abstaining from all excess and even what is permitted, we, like Christ, nail our hands to the cross. By suffering steadfastly we nail our feet; by undergoing "reasonable mortification" we place our back on the cross. "May your heart be ever ready to bear all adversities for my name," concludes Wisdom, "and thus as a faithful disciple, spiritually crucified with his Lord and sprinkled in a way with the blood of compassion, you will make yourself like me in love."[112]

Another insight into the significance of interior *compassio/mitliden* is found in chapter 14 of the *Little Book of Wisdom*. Taking Paul and Bernard as models for the need of contemplating the passion in order to be given a taste of the naked Godhead, Suso tells of his own experience as a beginner when he was sunk in "the bitter affliction of immoderate despondency" (*ungeordneter swermuetikeit* [256.25]), a state that has overtones of both the monastic vice of *acedia* (spiritual sadness and disaffection) and the classical notion of *melancholia*.[113] Then a divine voice addresses him: "Why are you sitting here? Get up and become absorbed in my suffering. Then you will overcome your suffering."[114] By focusing on Christ's suffering Suso was able to let go of his absorption in his own troubles. He never experienced such despondency again. The long speech that Wisdom gives here about the proper way to meditate on the passion to gain forgiveness for sins reveals that compassion is the measure of atonement: "Each person draws this atonement to himself only to the extent that he identifies himself with me by suffering along with me."[115] Such suffering along with Christ is a matter of mental attitude, not physical torture. As Wisdom puts it in LBW 15:

> When, in all the adversity that befalls you because of your neighbor, you are overcome for my sake and you accept the chaotic anger of all men as meekly as a silent lamb, . . . then the true image [*bilde*] of my death is being fashioned in you. Truly, when I find this likeness, what pleasure and what joy my heavenly Father and I experience! Bear my bitter death in the ground of your heart, in your prayers and in the manifestation of your actions.[116]

The importance of *com-passio* casts light on Suso's devotion to the Blessed Virgin. Mary, of course, played a significant role for most medieval mystics, both female and male. There are many facets to the Dominican's devotion to the Virgin, who appears in two of the eleven illustrations in the *Life*. Especially in the twin texts, the *Little Book of Wisdom* (I.16–17, and 20) and the *Clock of Wisdom* (I.16), the Disciple emphasizes both suffering along with Mary during the passion and learning how to engage in *com-passio* by imitating her. The visual character of Suso's mystical piety is once again evident. Speaking to the disciple, Mary says: "O, if in that sad hour you had seen the wretchedness of the mother suffering along with the Son, the sorrow of the Son grieving together with the mother." The imagined gaze is meant to lead to internal appropriation. The Disciple bursts in at this point and says:

> The vehement force of our compassion and the overwhelming flood of so many tears by which we suffer along with you from the inmost depth of our hearts, faithful Virgin, forces us, who cannot listen to these things without groans and tears, to interrupt your speech, Virgin Mother. How hardened the heart which does not suffer along with you in its depths![117]

In the *Little Book of Wisdom* the parallel treatment of Mary's role goes even further. By bringing Jesus into the world, by suffering with him for our redemption, and now as Queen of Heaven, Mary has such an integral place in the whole economy of creation and redemption that the Disciple can praise her with universal cosmological titles: *Du bist der anvang und daz mit-tel, du solt ouch daz ende sin. Ach, zartú reinú muoter*—"You are the beginning and the [mediating] mean; you shall also be the end, O gentle, pure Mother" (LBW 20:278.6–8).

Suso's program of mystical transformation is clearly passion-centered, but in a way that stresses the internalization of the meaning of the cross more than the bloody exterior *imitatio passionis* that the Dominican is often cited for. Like his teacher Eckhart, conversion and inwardness, silence and self-knowledge, detachment and letting go, are the essential practices for finding God. To be sure, Suso's use of images, his Marian devotion, his courtly motifs, the flowery sweetness of his style (Suso revels in flowers, especially the red rose as emblem of the passion),[118] are all different from Eckhart—and typical of his age. But Suso employs these external images and practices to help foster an interiorization that leads into the mysticism of the ground.[119]

Gelassenheit

The word *ker*, which can mean either turning away or turning toward (i.e., conversion), is frequent in Suso. At the beginning of the *Life* he describes how hidden divine grace effected the Servant's "sudden conversion" (*geswinden kere*) and turn away from the things of the world at the age of eighteen.[120] The turn away from the world (*abker*),[121] however, is meant to lead to *inker*, the turn within. In the *Little Book of Wisdom*, Wisdom addresses the soul: "Now listen, my daughter, and look. Incline your ears to me (Ps. 44:11). Make a powerful turn within and forget yourself and all things."[122] The necessity for the proper kind of inward turn is present in all Suso's works. The *Little Book of Truth* begins autobiographically with the picture of the young Suso practiced in the works of the outer man, but with his "inner man without practice in perfect releasement." "One time," the prologue continues, "he experienced a turning-within in which he was thrown back into himself, and a voice spoke within him: 'You should know that inward releasement leads one to perfect truth.'"[123] Chapter 4 of the work is an extended discussion of "the true inward turn which a released person should make through the Only-Begotten Son" (333.2–3). In the *Little Book of Wisdom* Suso also has a whole chapter detailing "How a person should live inwardly," which Wisdom concludes with the lapidary command, "My child, keep yourself inward, pure, free, and directed upward."[124] In the *Life* the same stress on inwardness emerges, for example, in the vision of Meister Eckhart, who instructs the Servant about true detachment (L 6 [23.1–12]). It also features in the ninety-six axioms found in chapter 49.[125] Several of these pithy statements summarize the stress on inwardness that Suso shares with Eckhart. Among these we read:

> Remain in yourself; going out after other things presents itself as a necessity, but it is really an excuse.

> Keep yourself within and be like Nothing; otherwise you shall suffer.

> Enter within yourself again, turn back again to your oneness of purpose and let God be your pleasure.[126]

True inwardness, as well as the silence that should accompany it,[127] are necessary conditions for the detachment (*abgescheidenheit*) and releasement (*gelassenheit*) that Suso, following Eckhart, insisted was the fundamental ascetic-mystical practice. Suso's *kunst rechter gelassenheit*, or "art of true releasement,"[128] might be described as post-Eckhartian in the sense that while its essential message shares much with Eckhart, the attack on Eckhart's mysticism led his disciple to a concern for distinguishing between the true and false forms of releasement not found in his teacher.

Suso speaks of "releasement" more than "detachment" (the terms *gelassenheit* and *gelassen* occur over fifty times, while *abgescheidenheit/abgescheiden* are found about twenty times). However, there appears to be little difference in how he uses these words.[129] Meister Eckhart's teaching on detachment was simultaneously metaphysical, ethical, and mystical. Suso's doctrine of releasement has the same three aspects. Like Eckhart, he thinks of interiority and releasement fundamentally as apophatic practices for the transformation of experience.[130] His constant stress on the need for distinguishing true from false releasement reflects the activity of Free Spirit mystics who had misunderstood the Meister's teaching and whose errors Suso blamed for the attacks on his teacher.

The earliest extended treatment of *gelassenheit* appears in chapter 4 of the *Little Book of Truth*.[131] In setting forth his teaching about the released person, Suso starts by making a significant departure from Eckhart's Christology. Eckhart taught that because Christ assumed not a human person, but the nature that is common to all humans, "Whatever holy scripture says of Christ, all that is also true of every good and divine man."[132] Suso avoids any such language, proclaiming that "human nature taken in itself can make no claim that just because Christ assumed it, and not a human personality, every man therefore should and can be God in the same manner [as Christ]."¹³³ Because Christ's mode of union surpasses that of all others, the proper understanding of the releasement that we can attain requires true discernment (*mit rehtem underscheide*) based on the analysis of five senses of the "self" (*sich*) and two meanings of "leaving," or "releasing" (*laszen*). The self that must be abandoned is not the metaphysical self of being, growing, sensation, and common human nature, but rather the contingent *ego* by which "a person turns outward away from God and toward himself, when he should be returning inward, and he fashions for himself his own self according to what is accidental."¹³⁴ In other words, what we must let go of is the false self that is attached to the things of the world and its own pleasures.

Three insights are needed to let go of this false self, Suso says. The first insight is Eckhartian: the need to recognize that this self and the self of all things "is a nothing" in comparison with God. The second offers the kind of qualification of detachment/releasement that Eckhart eschewed until taken to task by his opponents. Even in the state of "perfect release" (*nehsten gelezse*) the created ego, though not conscious of itself, continues to rest upon "one's own active self identity [*isticheit*]," that is, on the self in the first four meanings of *sich* (i.e., self as being, growing, sensing, and existing as human).¹³⁵ The third insight that emerges as one frees oneself of "creaturely existence in unfree multiplicity" is the growing awareness of becoming one with Christ. "And this released self becomes a Christformed I, about whom the scripture by Paul says, 'I live now, no longer I, Christ lives in me' (Gal. 2:20). And this is what I call a rightly-valued self."¹³⁶ Again, the Christocentric character of Suso's mysticism is evident.

Toward the end of chapter 4 Suso's reflections on the meaning of the verb *lazsen* also demonstrate his desire to qualify Eckhart's views. "To leave," he insists, means to surrender or despise, not to annihilate so that the self becomes absolutely nothing, as Eckhart and Marguerite Porete had proclaimed. When the Disciple asks if anything remains in the "blessed released person," Truth answers with a long discourse that balances the scriptural language of union with and transformation into God both here and hereafter (e.g., 1 Cor. 6:17; 15:28) with the lasting distinction between God and human. Suso is willing to use images that suggest complete absorption, like the drop of water being added to a vat of wine (336.11–18), because he recognizes that the released person, like a drunken man, retains no self-awareness. He is even willing to use the strong verb *entmenschen*, literally "un-humaned" (337.22) to describe the process.¹³⁷ But the qualifications he adds in his discussion show that in this passage at least he is closer to the teaching of Bernard of Clairvaux than to Eckhart. Truth proclaims: "Certainly, his being remains, but in a different form, in a different resplendence, and in a different power. This all comes from his own bottomless releasement."[138]

In the final chapter of the LBT Suso takes up the practical side of *gelassenheit* in discussing how the detached person acts. Like Eckhart, he insists that releasement does not mean abandoning one's usual exercises, but rather changing the attitude out of which they are performed. The released person "exists in an ever-present now, free of selfish intentions and perceives his perfection in the smallest thing as in the greatest."[139] Paradoxically, the released person's passivity is his highest form of activity: "A well-released person's activity is his letting go, and his work is to remain unoccupied because he remains at peace in his acting and unoccupied in his working."[140]

Later, in chapter 48 of the *Life* ("The Right Distinction between True and False Releasement"), Suso returns to the necessity for getting releasement right. He begins by distinguishing three kinds of "withdrawing" (*vergangenheit*): complete ceasing to exist; temporary ecstasy, such as Paul enjoyed (2 Cor. 12:2); and what he describes as "weak releasement" (*kranken gelassenheit*), that is, a withdrawing that is still imperfect. He then differentiates two kinds of releasement, the "preceding releasement" (*vorgendú gelassenheit*) by which we detach ourselves from evil before it happens (i.e., avoiding sin), and the "subsequent detachment" (*nagend gelassenheit*) by which we are sorry for sin committed and become resigned to the weakness of the human condition. The purpose of this distinction becomes clear in the discussion. Suso is combatting those "foolish people" who claim that "a person who wants to achieve perfect releasement must wade through all manner of wrong" in order to gain indifference to evil.[141] The true friend of God (*aller frúmsten gotesfrúnd* [161.32]) holds fast to preceding releasement and practices subsequent releasement when "he puts up with himself as such for the glory of God." Finally, Suso once again insists that "annihilation of spirit, its withdrawal into the simple Godhead . . . , is not to be understood as the changing of its own created nature, or what it is, into the same thing that God is. . . ."[142] No, God and human remain distinct, although in rapture (*entnomenheit*) the spirit does withdraw, forget itself, and see all things as God (162.31–163.8).

Eckhart and Marguerite Porete had presented mystical annihilation as a metaphysical union of indistinction, although the Meister's dialectical way of thinking allowed him to admit, especially when taken to task by his opponents, that from one perspective ontological distinction between God and human always remains. Suso, on the other hand, shifts the ground. Metaphysical distinction is the bottom line for him; mystical identification is a mental state of the mystic.

The *Little Book of Wisdom* also takes up releasement, especially in chapter 9,[143] which is a meditation on the *minne spil,* the game of love that God plays with the soul through the succession of moments of delightful presence followed by painful absence.[144] What is noteworthy here is how the Dominican links this traditional mystical theme with the proper understanding of releasement. The Servant begins by complaining to Wisdom for withdrawing "the sweet intimacy of your sweet presence" (*dem suezen minnekosen diner suezen gegenwúrtikeit* [230.27]). Wisdom replies that she is always present in creatures and in the words of scripture, and then comes back with a question of her own: "What is it of all things that the highest created spirit [i.e., the angels] finds most pleasing?" (232.4–5). The answer is to satisfy the divine will in all things. The lesson drawn is that true releasement is to be free of the desire for consolation, even the consolation of God's presence. The dialogue continues:

> The Servant: "O Lord, . . . you mean to say that I should keep myself free and released in desires and that I should seek your praise alone in difficulty as in sweetness?"

> The response of Eternal Wisdom: "A releasement above all releasement is to be released in releasement."[145]

This pregnant tautology, cited in later mystical texts, reminds one of Eckhart's saying in his sermon on releasement (Pr. 12): "The highest and most perfect thing that a person can let go [*gelâzen mac*] is that he lets God go for God's sake."[146] The remainder of the chapter shows how only constant remaining within allows a person to reach a state beyond the reversals of the game of love, a place where "you do not suffer from either excessive reliance on [God's] presence, nor despondency in letting go."[147]

In the *Life* Suso mentions releasement and detachment often,[148] but not by way of adding new teaching to what is found in the LBT. Rather, Suso wishes to connect this central mystical practice to the broader portrayal of how the Servant functions as the exemplar of seeking God. A key text is chapter 19, entitled "How He Was Directed to the School of the Spirit and Instructed in the Art of True Releasement," because it sets up the transition to the higher life set forth from chapter 20 on. Here the Servant is given a vision in which a youth leads him into "the highest school that exists in this time" where the "chief teacher" (probably the monk Arsenius) says that he can learn this "high art" if he is willing to sequester himself in his cell and have patience. The youth tells the Servant that "[t]he advanced school and its teaching that one reads here is nothing other than complete, perfect releasement from oneself, so that a person stands in such unbecoming . . . that he at all times strives in the same way to be in a state of going out from what is his, . . . and that he looks to God's praise and honor alone, just as dear Christ did with regard to his heavenly Father."[149] The Servant thinks that he is now ready for this, but the youth forbids him by saying, "This art requires a free potentiality—the less one does, the more one has truly done."[150]

The Servant then recognizes that despite his external penances, he still has so much self within that he is "not released enough to accept adversity coming from without." What the Servant will learn in the chapters that follow is the implementation of the message that he has been given in this vision. Toward the end of the work, especially in chapters 47–48 where he summarizes his higher teaching for Elsbeth, Suso again returns to the difference between true and false releasement.[151] Some of the Servant's mystical axioms aptly encapsulate his view of releasement. "What is the goal of a truly released person?" he asks: "A sinking away from the self, and with the self all things sink away." In the inner light of such releasement a person realizes "the presence of the whole divine being in himself and that he is simply its instrument."[152]

Gesiht and Entzogenheit: Vision and Rapture

What are often called mystical experiences, especially those of visions and raptures, play a minor role in Eckhart's mysticism, as we have seen. This is not the case in Henry Suso, who is noted for the frequency of his spiritual (i.e., imaginative) visions,[153] as well as for the many places where he describes experiences of ecstasy and rapture.[154]

Suso does not elaborate a new theory of visions, being content with the Augustinian triple distinction of corporeal, spiritual, and intellectual vision. Nonetheless, a discussion in chapter 51 of the *Life* provides insightful reflections on his use of this traditional paradigm. In this chapter Elsbeth echoes the objections of Free Spirit mystics to Suso's Eckhartianism, averring that God is such a "harmful obstacle" to achieving perfection that a true seeker must be rid of God, of spirit, and of all visions (*und alle vision ze ruggen stossen* [181.28–29]). Suso responds to each error in turn, picking up on Augustinian vision theory in his answer to the third objection. While the third type of vision, that is, the imageless, or intellectual, is more noble, scripture and experience indicate that "visions rich in image" (*bildrich vision* [183.27]), whether given while one is asleep or awake, remain necessary in this life. Such forms of "prophetic vision" are guides to right action in the future. Suso recognizes that it is difficult to discriminate between mere dreams and true imaginative visions. Hence he appeals to the grace of discernment of spirits that Augustine records was given to his mother, Monica, concluding, "The person to whom God has given this same gift can better find his own way in this matter. No one can explain this to another just with words. One knows it by experiencing it."[155]

The Dominican's other treatments of the veracity of visions, an increasingly important issue in late medieval religious life,[156] show that he had other criteria beyond that of the personal grace of discernment. In the prologue to *The Exemplar* he takes pains to insist on the conformity between his collection and the truths set forth in scripture. When Meister Bartholomew read over the most difficult parts of the books, according to Suso, he praised *The Exemplar* as "a secret sweet kernel from sacred scripture for all well-intentioned people" (5.21–22). In other words, the test of the truth of visions is their conformity with the Bible and the church's teaching.

The visions found in *The Exemplar* function as both authentications of the exemplary status of the Servant and didactic tools in setting forth his teaching. As Alois Haas puts it: "The accounts of visions that Suso presents are not pure reports of experience, but are subsequent accounts of spiritual occurrences, stylized in a literary way to serve a distinct didactic purpose."[157] Suso's visions operate between two poles: first, the actual claim to have been given visions/visualizations as confirmation of the Servant's status as the model of the path to perfection; and second, the exemplary teacher's concern for using visionary images (*bilde*) to instruct his spiritual followers in the right path to God.

The dual character of the visionary program in the *Life* helps explain the complicated array of its imaginative showings: dream visions and waking experiences; visions given on earth and raptures described as taking place in heaven; showings presented as direct gifts from God and visualizations of spiritual truths that seem more the product of literary artifice. In order to interpret this confusing proliferation it is important to remember what Suso says of visions in the *Clock*: "The visions contained in what follows are not all to be taken literally, although many did happen literally. . . ." Suso is not much concerned with the modern question of the "reality" of visions, because for him all visionary recitals, whether based on some image experienced as coming from God, or whether a literary construction, are meant to function in the same way, as *figurata locutio*, imagistic ways of presenting divine truth.

The easy access that the Servant has to the heavenly world and its inhabitants is evident throughout the *Life,* where almost half the chapters contain visions of God, the Blessed Virgin, angels, saints, and the dead (some in heaven, some in purgatory or hell). The Servant is depicted as a liminal figure who connects heaven and earth, an intermediary who brings God's message to his followers and who can intercede for them before God. The power of visions to authenticate spiritual authority, however, is not limited to the Servant himself. It is shared by his circle of Friends of God in a way that heightens the Servant's own status, as we can see from how he introduces visions given to others throughout the text. Many of these showings were granted to Elsbeth Stagel, or the holy laywoman, Anna; others are anonymous. Even Suso's mother is portrayed as a visionary.[158] To take but one example, at the end of chapter 5 an unnamed holy person (probably Elsbeth) sees the Servant "in a vision" (*in einr gesiht* [22.3]) as he begins to say Mass. "She saw the dew of divine grace descending into his soul and that he became one with God."[159] Then she beholds many charming children embracing him. When she asks who these are, they reply that they are her deceased sisters in religion, who protect her and reverence the Servant. "He is so very dear to us," they explain, "that we have much to do with him. Know that God performs many marvels in his soul, and whatever he seriously asks of God, God will never deny it to him."[160]

A look at a few of the visions in the *Life* will help flesh out some of the ways Suso employs visionary recitals to enhance the status of the Servant and to set forth his message. In chapter 2, for example, at the very beginning of his conversion, there is a description of an experience of total rapture and intellectual vision of the divine nature with unmistakable accents from Paul's famous account in 2 Corinthians 12. "As he was standing there . . . , his soul was caught up, in the body or out of the body. There he saw and heard what all tongues cannot express (2 Cor. 12:2–4). It was without form or definite manner of being, yet it contained within itself the joyous, delightful wealth of all forms and modes of being."[161] "This overpowering transport" (*dise überswenke zug* [10.28–29]) lasted an hour or half-hour, leaving the Servant's body faint and racked with pain, but his soul and mind full of "flashes from heaven" and its sweet fragrance. Such an experience would ordinarily describe a very high form of vision and rapture, coming at the end of the arduous journey to perfection. Why does Suso put it here at the outset? Possibly to enhance the special status of the Servant; possibly also to indicate that such experiences are not the end in and of themselves. It is also likely that Suso is hinting that spiritual, or imaginative, visions (i.e., most of what is to come) may be lower in themselves, but have a better teaching function.

The limitations and conditions for legitimate use of visions and raptures also appear in an account near the end of the *Life* in chapter 50. Here the Servant tells how once in the chapter house he was in a state of "divine joy of jubilation" (*goetlicher jubilierender froeden* [174.30]), the interior *jubilus* experienced by many late medieval mystics, especially women. The porter informed him that a woman wanted to make her confession to him, but he told the porter that she should find another friar. God then withdrew the grace of jubilation, telling him, "Just as you drove from you the poor woman with her burdened heart without comforting her, so have I withdrawn my divine consolation from you."[162] The Servant then hurried out to confess the woman and God restored the consolation to him. This story is a pictorial presentation of a key theme in Western mysticism: the necessity that contemplation yield to action in behalf of the neighbor's salvation.

Suso, like his contemporary Richard Rolle, is one of the premier male mystics who describe experiences of heavenly sweetness, divine fragrance, celestial song, mystical dancing, and the physical warming of the heart. An example of these highly sensate visions can be found in chapter 41 where the Servant is pictured as sitting in contemplation with his heart on fire after having spoken with his spiritual children. The account continues:

> His senses somehow faded away from him, [and] it seemed to him in a vision that he was led onto a beautiful green meadow. A fine young man from heaven was walking with him and leading him by the hand. The young man began a song in the friar's soul and it resounded so joyously that it chased away all mere sense impressions by its overwhelming sweet sound.[163]

Suso's heart feels ready to burst, so that he puts his hand over it to contain it. His eyes well up with tears. When the song ends, he is given an image to remember it, a picture of Our Lady holding the Christ child, Eternal Wisdom, with the first words of the song written over his head. The writing is secret, but the Servant can read it easily as *herzentrut*—"The heart's Beloved." Looking up at the young angelic guide, the Servant presses Jesus to "the ground of his heart" and sings the song through with the angel. Although this vision lacks the element of the dance, in its combination of Christ, Mary, and angel, as well as in its appeal to song and heat, it demonstrates the affective and sensible elements in Suso's presentations of spiritual showings.[164]

Many of the visions Suso recounts, as might be expected, focus on seeing the events of the passion, especially Christ on the cross. These are often striking in their bloody realism; nevertheless, the didactic character of even the most physically detailed of such showings is always evident, as can be seen, for example, in the visions found in chapter 31 of the *Life*, or the contemplations of the passion in chapters 14–20 of the *Little Book of Wisdom*. The teaching character of Suso's imaginative visions, evident throughout the *Life*,[165] comes even more to the fore in the conversations with Eternal Wisdom and many allegorical showings found in the *Little Book of Wisdom* and the *Clock of Wisdom*. *Figurata locutio*, understood as driving home a saving message through a memorable visionary narrative, is essential to Suso's mysticism.

Meister Eckhart had allowed for the reality of states of ecstasy, though he thought them often dangerous and delusory. While agreeing with his teacher that the goal of the mystical path is not ecstasy in itself but union with God in the ground, Suso shows no suspicion about the significance of extraordinary states of (un)consciousness and/or (supra)consciousness. The *Life* and the *Little Book of Wisdom/Clock of Wisdom* abound in descriptions of the raptures of the Servant and also include accounts of ecstatic experiences enjoyed by his circle of Friends of God.

Suso is not interested in classifying the stages of contemplation and kinds of rapture, as the Victorines had done in the twelfth century. Raptures, like the visions that often accompany them, function in *The Exemplar* as proofs of the Servant's mystical authority and as models for what its readers can aspire to with God's grace. Suso is important, however, for the richness of his language about ecstatic states. The vocabulary of ecstasy was relatively stable in Latin mystical texts, reflecting its scriptural basis in such words as *extasis* (Ps. 30:1; Acts 3:10), *excessus/excessus mentis* (e.g., Ps. 30:23; Ps. 67:28; Acts 10:10 and 11:5), and *raptus* (2 Cor. 12:2–4). These terms, and their expansions and explanations, can be found from time to time in the *Clock of Wisdom*, as would be expected from a theologically well-trained Dominican.[166] Suso even innovates in one passage by creating the term *raptica contemplatio* to describe the union with Christ that can be realized in the reception of the Eucharist.[167]

Suso's real contribution to the vocabulary of ecstasy comes in his MHG works, where the language for describing the cessation of ordinary sense experience and elevation to a higher mode of consciousness was still developing in the fourteenth century. Given his linguistic and stylistic gifts, it is no surprise that Suso shows great creativity in his vernacular descriptions of rapture.

Most of Suso's descriptions of ecstasy occur in the *Life* and in chapter 5 of the LBT, an attack on the false mysticism of the Free Spirit. To simplify, we can say that the Dominican's vocabulary is of two broad types: negative terms to describe the cessation of, and sometimes violent withdrawal from, ordinary modes of consciousness; and positive words, metaphors, and descriptions that try to transpose ordinary language to suggest a higher realm of sensing and knowing. The negative, linguistic field employs a broad range of terms—some common to MHG mystical vocabulary, some apparently Suso's creations.[168] Compounds formed with the prefixes *ver-* and *ent-* predominate, both in verbal and nominal forms. Among the most popular of the former is the verb *verzuken* ("to be drawn out, up, or away"), as when Suso describes his disciple Anna as "one time in her devotion drawn away" (*eins males in ir andaht verzuket* [L 22:63.14–15]).[169] Even more frequent is the use of *vergangen in got* ("to go out, or over, into God") and the noun *vergangenheit*, often appearing as *vergangenheit der sinnen* ("going out, or withdrawing, from the senses"), as, for example, when the Servant is described as "coming into a withdrawal from his outer senses" (*komen in ein vergangenheit der ussren sinnen* [L 22:64.21]).[170] Suso also uses "sinking-away" terms, such as the verb *versinken* and the noun *entsunkenheit*.[171] The word *entgangenheit* ("a going out" from the senses) also occurs relatively frequently,[172] as does the verb *entwurket* ("to be freed, or carried off").[173] Related terms indicating being snatched out of common sense experience appear more rarely.[174]

The positive side of Suso's descriptions of ecstasy is more difficult to summarize. To be sure, it is not hard to list the non-negative nouns that he uses to describe rapture, words such as "pull, or transport" (*zug* [10.29]), or terms indicating a movement of interiorization, such as *inker* (e.g., 168.15) and *inschlag* (e.g., 184.22). Other words stress movement above the ordinary world (e.g., *überflug* [184.2]; *überschal* [112.4]; *übervart* [193.11]). More complex, however, is the determination of what Suso actually meant by these words. A look at two representative texts must suffice to suggest something of the richness of his contribution to the description of rapture. The fifth chapter of the *Life*, in which the Servant recounts nine different experiences of "divine consolation" by which God attracts beginners, provides a good example of Suso's ecstatic narratives.[175] It is interesting to see how he mixes his variety of consolations, not all of which are ecstatic. The first is merely a heartfelt moment of prayer (17.15–24), while the second involves an internal singing "with such a supernatural surge within him that all his inner being was carried along with it" into an experience of "an indescribable embrace."[176] Consolations 3 and 4 (18.10–29) involve his prayers, or greetings to God, and another experience of internal music. The fifth consolation, in which he embraces his guardian angel, is presented as taking place "as in a vision, as if he were somehow led into a foreign land," and thus appears to be a literary vision (19.1–20.10).

The sixth consolation is visionary, ecstatic, and also accompanied by an illustration (20.10–23). The Servant is surrounded by angels in this vision and asks them to see the "hidden dwelling place of God" in his soul. "He quickly looked inside and saw that over his heart his body was as clear as crystal, and he saw in the middle of his heart eternal Wisdom sitting quietly; . . . nearby the soul of the Servant was sitting and longing for heaven" (illustration 3). The soul inclines to Wisdom's heart and is embraced in his arms in a moment of ecstatic love: "There outside itself and immersed in love it lay in the arms of its beloved God."[177] The seventh experience is another audition of heavenly music (20.24–25.5), while the eighth (21.6–22.2) is a sharing in both music and "heavenly dancing" (*himelschlich tanzen*) that bears little resemblance to dancing on earth and brings the Servant into the depths of God—"It was somehow a heavenly flooding out from and an ebbing back into the untamed abyss of the divine mystery."[178] Finally, as is typical with Suso, the ninth experience (22.3–18) is not his, but Elsbeth's vision of his union with God described above.

A lengthy account in *Life* 50 also illustrates how Suso crafted language to portray the indescribable nature of mystical rapture. In teaching his spiritual daughter about the difference between the mirroring, or "speculating" (*speculieren*), knowledge of God gained through creatures and the more direct "jubilating" (*jubilieren*) knowledge,[179] the Servant is described as receiving special mystical graces twice a day for ten years when he was a young friar. Each of these raptures is said to have lasted for the considerable time of two vigils. Their description uses themes both old and new in the mystical vocabulary:

> During this time he sank so completely in God into Eternal Wisdom that he was unable to speak of it. Sometimes he held an intimate conversation with God, sighed in lament, wept with longing, or sometimes he smiled quietly. He often felt as though he were floating in the air and swimming in the deep flow of God's boundless marvels between time and eternity.[180]

The account goes on to emphasize the erotic aspect of the raptures, though coloring the narrative with hints of apophatic language reminiscent of Eckhart. The Servant tells how one day he experienced an exchange between his own heart and the Father's heart, Eternal Wisdom, whom he addresses in spiritual jubilation:

> Come now, my dear Loved One, I shall uncover my heart, and in this simple nakedness of all createdness I embrace your imageless divinity. O you Love surpassing all love! . . . You, infinite Fullness of all love, flow into the heart of the beloved; you pour yourself into the being of the soul, you who are simply

all in all, so that not one simple bit of the lover remains outside, but is lovingly united to the beloved.[181]

Powerful as this text is, Suso does not want to be misunderstood. When Elsbeth asks him whether this jubilation is perfect transport into God, he answers, "No, it is only an enticing preview of entering into a state of essential indwelling" (*weslich ingenomenheit* [174.17–18]), that is, of the union to come in heaven.

Durpruch-Grunt-Vereinung

As we have seen, conformity to the suffering Christ is necessary for breakthrough to the ground of the Trinity. This union, which does not surpass or negate the role of the crucified God-man (who is one of the Trinity), is the goal of Suso's mysticism. This aspect of his thought is dependent on the teaching of Meister Eckhart—some passages are so deeply Eckhartian that they might have come from the pen of the Meister himself. And yet there is need for qualification. Suso uses many of Eckhart's deepest themes and forms of language, yet he also modifies his teacher's mysticism, sometimes in ways that conform to the defense Eckhart himself used when he was challenged, and sometimes in ways that lead to what is a rather different teaching. Nowhere is Suso more difficult to interpret; nowhere does he show more convincingly that despite his abandoning the academic life, he had a subtle and profound mind.

The fundamental texts for this part of Suso's mysticism are the *Little Book of Truth* and the *Life* chapters 50–53, the mini-treatise that closes the book. These complex pages would repay a full exegesis; here I can only try to summarize their teaching and that of some related passages that highlight the adoption and modification of Eckhart's teaching.

Suso, like Eckhart, often speaks of the *grunt*, the inexpressible depths of the divine nature that at least in some sense is beyond, though not other than, the Trinity of Persons.[182] In chapter 2 of the LBT the disciple asks Truth how absolute simplicity can coexist with the Trinity. The answer invokes the ground. Truth says:

> All this multiplicity is, in its ground and foundation, one simple unity. . . . I call the ground that which is the source and origin from which the outflowings arise. . . . That is the nature and being of the Godhead. And in this abyss without out ground the Trinity of Persons sinks into its oneness, and in a certain sense all multiplicity becomes lost. In this same sense nothing at all of outside activity can be perceived, but only a calm, hovering darkness.[183]

The *grunt/abgrunt* that is the Godhead is totally without distinction or action. Divine activity begins with the Father characterized as the "enabling power" (*vermugendú kraft* [330.18]), the source of the primal action of birthing. "In this very instant it becomes pregnant to bear fruit and to act; according to our capacity to understand, the Godhead springs across into God."[184] Like Eckhart, Suso insists that the difference between Godhead/ground and God is merely conceptual, forced on us by the nature of our limited minds.

This teaching on the relation of the *grunt* to the Trinity is pure Eckhart, but differences from the Meister begin to surface in LBT 5, where the term *grunt* occurs a dozen times. In an important section of this long chapter Suso describes the Disciple as being for ten weeks in a state of conscious rapture after which he questions Truth about how far the released person's understanding of the divine mystery can reach. Truth says that someone in this life can come to see himself as one with the nameless Nothing that we call God or Godhead, but the way in which the Divine Nothing knows itself is "mysteriously hidden further within" (*verborgen neiswaz noch inbaz* [342.10–11]). This land of "further within" (think of Marguerite Porete's "Farnear")[185] is the realm beyond speech, forms, and images, the place in which all human language becomes a lie (342.23–343.8). Truth says that "a powerful annihilating bursting into the Nothing removes all difference in the ground, not of essences, but on the part of our perception."[186] In the discussion that follows, Truth tries to clarify how such a transport must be understood dialectically as a state in which a person both remains what he is (a distinct being) and yet becomes indistinct "in the ground that lies hidden in the previously mentioned Nothing." "There one knows nothing about anything," Truth continues, "there nothing is, there is not even a there."[187] Insofar as a person is in the ground, there is none of the activity associated with the eternal birth (349.12–16); there is also no knowledge and no will (349.26–33). Although "such a person is so completely united that God is his ground" (350.19–20), Truth paradoxically also insists that personal distinction remains. Indistinction in the ground is a matter of how one *perceives* things when one is completely divested of self in releasement (350.21–28), not a matter of ontological or supra-ontological identification with God. That is, in such states there is no perception of difference, but in reality there is always a distinction between our created self and the nameless ground. Despite the Eckhartian language, therefore, there is a significant difference between master and pupil. For Eckhart *unitas indistinctionis* is more than just a mental state, however much he also insisted that distinction and indistinction are both dialectically necessary.[188]

Several important passages from Suso's other works fill in further dimensions of his form of the mysticism of the ground. The treatise on God at the end of the *Life* speaks of the ground in chapter 52 in a discussion of how the spirit becomes one with God when it is totally unconscious of itself. While Suso allows that the spirit does take on certain qualities of the Godhead and Trinity of Persons, he again qualifies this by citing the traditional formula that the soul becomes God by grace, not by nature (188.1–4). This psychological transformation takes place in "the naked uncreatedness of Nothingness" (*die blossen ungewordenheit der nihtekeit* [188.19]). The text continues with a wordplay on the groundless ground that cannot be easily reproduced in English: "In this wild mountain of the where beyond God there is an 'Abyssness' full of play and feeling for all pure spirits, and the spirit enters into this secret namelessness and into this wild alienation. This is the deep groundless abyss of all creatures, basic to him alone."[189] The only way to this "where" beyond God, Suso says, is through releasement and mystical death (189.4–11).

Three passages from other texts show how important the metaphor of the *grunt/abgrunt* is in Suso's thought. In the *Little Book of Wisdom* chapter 12 he discusses the difference between the accidental and the essential reward of the soul, which is nothing other than "the contemplative union of the soul with the naked Godhead" (245.5). Detachment is the path to this union with the divine abyss: "The more freely the soul goes out of itself in detachment, the freer is its ascent; the freer its ascent is, the farther it enters into the wild wasteland and the deep abyss of the pathless Godhead into which it plummets, where it is swept along. . . ."[190] Once again, Suso explains that this happens by grace, not by nature.

The ground is the goal of all striving for God, and detachment is the way to it. Suso also makes it clear that love for Eternal Wisdom, so prominent in his own devotion, is needed to turn those smitten with earthly love toward the Divine Lover, who is ultimately one with the ground/abyss. A passage from Letter 5 is typical of Suso's impassioned combination of erotic and abyssal language:

> O eternal Wisdom, dearly Loved One, if all these hearts would see you as my heart sees you, all fleeting love in them would scatter. Lord, it can never again seem strange to me, no matter how strange it seemed to me before, that any bottomlessly-loving heart can have anything but you as its goal, you deep pool, bottomless sea, deep abyss of all loving things.[191]

Although only two of the sermons ascribed to Suso are possibly authentic, it is interesting to note that one of these makes ample use of the language of the ground. He begins Sermon 4 by assuring his audience that all of Jesus' efforts were designed "to teach his beloved friends and lead them inward into the pure ground" (*in den luteren grund* [529.5]). The homily proceeds through an analysis of three classes of people illustrating the three stages of the spiritual life, laying particular stress on the need for total detachment. At the end of the sermon, Suso's message on letting go comes close to Eckhart in its appeal to sink our ground in the divine ground. "You must have a letting go that is bottomless," he advises. "How bottomless?" He continues:

> If a stone were to fall into a bottomless pool, it would have to sink forever because it would never reach bottom. So should a person sink and fall endlessly into the bottomless God and be grounded in him, however serious a thing might befall him. . . . All this should draw a person still deeper into God without his ever sensing, touching, or becoming distressed in his own ground.[192]

For Eckhart the term *grunt* was used both with regard to the depth of the soul and the divine depth—the two are really one in fused identity. Suso concentrates on the divine *grunt/abgrunt*, although he allows some language about the merging of the grounds as the text from Sermon 4 shows. He frequently uses the traditional language of "the ground of the heart,"[193] and also speaks of "a person's own ground,"[194] but it is significant that he generally avoids speaking of the "ground of the soul,"[195] possibly because he felt such language might lend itself to the false views of the Free Spirits.

According to these final chapters of the *Life,* the divine ground, or Godhead, lies beyond all description and all speech, to be hinted at in metaphor and paradoxical unsayings. The God of Christian belief, who is both Unity and Trinity, also remains "above all thought and intellect" (L 50:171.8), and yet this God can be known and expressed, at least partially, by diligent seekers, both philosophers like Aristotle, and Christian believers. Hence, in the final chapters of the *Life* Suso is willing to respond to Elsbeth Stagel's request, "Tell me what is God or where is God and how does he exist, that is to say, how is he one and yet three?" (171.3–5).

The Dominican's answer to "what God is" in chapter 50 begins with a philosophical discourse, the "speculating knowledge" of God as immutable and subsistent intellect (171.17–24),[196] but soon passes on to accounts of "jubilating knowledge" gained in mystical consciousness. The instruction concerning "where God is" in chapter 51 (176.5–178.17) explores the "nameless divine being . . . that supports all divided beings with its presence" (177.4–6). This "being in itself is the negation of negation," that is, the absolute purity of being; but from the perspective of the created "eye of the intellect" it is a "divine darkness," "a Single One in utter nakedness" (*ein einiges ein in ainvaltiger blossheit* [177.27])—all language drawn from Eckhart.[197]

The most developed part of this treatise on the divine nature is the response to "how God is," that is, how in his utter oneness God is also three. Suso works this out in chapters 51 and 52 in three sections: an initial exploration of the processions in God (178.18–181.23); the Servant's response to the three errors of the Free Spirit brought up by Elsbeth (181.24–183.30); and a second analysis of the relation between the divine Abyss and the Trinity (184.2–190.20).

Suso's teaching on the Trinity is a synthesis of traditional elements taken from the Dionysianism of Richard of St. Victor and Bonaventure and combined with the thought of Eckhart. Much of this, of course, is standard trinitarian theology, so the Dominican also appeals to Augustine and Thomas Aquinas. The axiomatic basis is twofold: first, the Dionysian teaching that divine goodness must of its nature overflow perfectly into a Trinity of persons, and then in abundance into creation; and second, the Eckhartian insistence that "the flowing out of the Persons from God is a formal image of the origin of creatures; it is also a prelude of the creatures' flowing back into God."[198] Suso's first discussion of the procession of the Word as the image of the Father and the emanation of the Holy Spirit according to love is a succinct summary of the identity of oneness and threeness in God, reminiscent of Bonaventure's treatise *The Mind's Journey into God* (L 51:179.31–180.4).[199] His doctrine leads Elsbeth to the rapturous statement: "Look! I am soaring in the Godhead like an eagle in the air" (180.5–6).

The second exploration takes up the whole of chapter 53. As suggested above, this chapter is perhaps Suso's most profound treatment of ecstatic sinking into the divine ground; it also represents some of his most challenging attempts to unsay all language about God. In order to attain the "where of the pure divinity of Son" (184.20) the created spirit must lose all that is its own—"In this the spirituality (*geistekeit*) of all spirits ends," he says (185.3–4). The identity of Unity and Trinity in the "where" is beyond all words. In this intellectual realm the de-created spirit, unconscious of itself, exists and shares in the modeless Trinity, which can be described as "the nameless Nothingness itself" (*die istigen namlosen nihtekeit* [187.10–11]), because we can say nothing about what it is or how it is.[200] This is "the silence above all being and above all the learning of the professors" (190.10–11), and as Suso assures his spiritual daughter, "In this where, bereft of all mode, there lies the most sublime happiness" (190.1–2).

How are we to attain this most sublime happiness? In order to grasp Suso's teaching about the path to union we must look at how he understood the dynamic process of emanation and return. Suso's theology of the out-flowing of all things from God is less developed than that of Eckhart and less challenging. Like Eckhart, Suso insists that all things exist eternally, that is, virtually, in God. Unlike Eckhart, however, he holds that "each crea-ture's created nature is nobler and of more advantage to it than the being it has in God."[201] The difference between the two is especially evident in *Life* 46, where Suso, analyzing the distinction between true and false intellect, introduces Eckhart's language of the "just person insofar as he is just." He begins by citing an Eckhartian statement also used by the Free Spirit heretics: "The just one does not have to avoid obstacles," that is, sins (157.8–9). But he goes on to explain the true meaning of the Eckhartian for-mula. While the just person is, indeed, one in God's intellect without any formal difference, and while in this "simple ground" there is no corporality or obstacle, nonetheless, "everyone discovers that outside of this ground he is this or that person. . . . Here one is always in one's frail created nature where one has to avoid all damaging obstacles." To think that a person in this life can perform his material actions as if God were performing them, and therefore never have to be on the lookout for possible sin, "would be a mistake to end all mistakes," he concludes.[202]

Suso's emotional receptivity and deep sensitivity, evident in much of his writing, are the source of his keen appreciation of creation as both a mani-festation of God and also an inspiration for the soul's growing sense of the divine presence. In *The Exemplar* we find passages of a kind of nature mysti-cism reminiscent of St. Francis's "Canticle of Brother Sun," a form of mysti-cism lacking in Meister Eckhart. In chapter 24 of the *Little Book of Wisdom*, for example, there are some beautiful pages praising God in the whole of his creation (304–7), a passage expanded on in the *Clock*.[203] The same nature mysticism is found in *Life* 50 (172–73), and in the "Morgengruss," the prayer ascribed to Suso.

Like the other German Dominicans, Suso's metaphysical outlook was based on the Christian Neoplatonic paradigm of emanation and return. In turning from the flowing out both of Trinity and of creation from the ground to the process of return to the ground, we gain further appreciation of how Suso was both a faithful disciple of Eckhart and yet not afraid to qualify and innovate in presenting his message. Since the activities of birthing, detaching, and breaking-through are central to the way Eckhart conceived of how humans return to the ground,[204] it will be useful to see how Suso understood these mystical processes. The birthing theme seems to have exercised a larger role in Suso's early writings, especially the *Little Book of Truth*, which analyzes both the eternal birth of the Son and the correct form of understanding our "rebirth" (*widergeburt*) in time.[205] In the later works, the erotic attachment to Eternal Wisdom replaces the Eckhartian birth of the Word in the soul as the dominant way to describe our relation to the Second Person of the Trinity.[206] The second major Eckhartian process essential for the return to the ground is "detaching," or, as Suso more usually spoke of it, "releasing" (*gelassen*). In the section above entitled "*Gelassenheit*," I tried to show that Suso's view of releasement was dependent on Eckhart but also differed from him by insisting that the indistinction achieved through detachment is a mental category, not an ontological one.

A similar relationship appears in the way in which Suso used Eckhart's notion of the breakthrough. The terms *durpruch/durchbruch/durchbrechen* occur in a variety of contexts in Suso's writings, mostly in the *Life* and the LBT.[207] Unlike Eckhart, Suso employs breakthrough language to describe our identification with the human nature of the suffering Christ as a necessary preparation for penetrating into the divine mystery. At the beginning of chapter 4 of the LBT, for example, the Disciple says, "I would now like to hear about the breakthrough—how a person through Christ is supposed to return again within and attain his happiness."[208] A few passages go further, coming closer to Eckhart's notion of breaking through into the Godhead beyond the God who creates. These texts connect the breakthrough with absolute releasement and the loss of consciousness of self. In chapter 32 of the *Life*, Eternal Truth instructs the Servant internally about "the breakthrough which one must anticipate by sinking away from oneself and all things." People who have attained this "are so completely lost in God that they somehow have no consciousness of self except by perceiving self and all things in their first origin."[209] They even, Suso says, feel as though God had turned everything over to them, so that heaven and earth serve them and they can feel no sadness and suffering. So, Suso uses the language of breakthrough, but neither as frequently nor as daringly as Eckhart.

Breaking-through into the ground, as well as much of what was discussed in the previous section on ecstasy, points to what modern students of religion usually call mystical union (a term not used by Suso). What was Suso's teaching on union with God?[210] It will suffice here to provide a summary, since many of the key passages that imply *unio mystica* have already been cited in the course of this chapter. First, Suso follows tradition in insisting that there is always a significant difference between the modes of union we can be given in this life and the fullness of union and vision in heaven.[211] Second, Suso, unlike Eckhart, denies that any other person can enjoy the same kind of substantial and personal union with God that Christ does

(LBT 4:333.26–334.13). Third, Suso deliberately mingles the traditional language of *unitas spiritus*, the loving union of the wills of the human and
divine subjects, often expressed in erotic terms, with the new language of
unitas indistinctionis, the union of fused identity found in Meister Eckhart. As
we have seen, however, with regard to indistinct union Suso shifts the Eckhartian metaphysical perspective toward one that emphasizes the mental
state of the mystic and her modeless apprehension of oneness with God.

The whole purpose of *The Exemplar* is to prepare the reader to pursue
what Suso calls "loving union with Eternal Wisdom" (*minneklicher vereinung
mit der ewigen wisheit* [L 3:11.23]). When Suso describes such union, as he
does countless times, we find a wide variety of language. "God-forming
union" (*gotfoermigen vereinunge* [LBT 6:356.11]) is both a matter of becoming
one spirit with God through love (1 Cor. 6:17) and also of uniting with the
ground of God in which there is no distinction. We have already seen many
strong expressions of this Eckhartian union, as, for example, in LBT 6,
where Suso says a person can lose or annihilate his will in God to such a
degree that he "is so completely united that God is his ground" (350.19-20).
Again, in describing the three joys that God gives to those who suffer for
his sake in *Life* 32, Suso uses Eckhart's language of *ein einiges ein.* God
promises: "I shall kiss them so intimately and embrace them so lovingly
that I am they and they are me, and we two shall remain one Single One
for ever and ever."[212] Later chapters in the *Life*, especially 48, 50, 52, as well
as LBT 5, use similar language.

These expressions of *unitas indistinctionis*, however, are qualified in
important ways, as we have seen. First, like Eckhart, Suso insists that all
union is a gift of grace, not the soul's attainment of its own inner divine
nature.[213] The soul is "divinized" (*vergoetet* [L 6:23.3]), not naturally divine.
Where Suso does innovate (although his doctrine bears a striking resemblance to that found in some of the great Sufi mystics whom he could not
have known)[214] is in his insistence that indistinction is essentially the emptiness of mind found in those who have broken through into God. Over and
over again, he repeats the message found in chapter 5 of the LBT: "Being
powerfully transported from self into the Nothing eliminates all difference
in the ground, not of essences but rather in how we perceive."[215]

Gotesfrúnde versus *Geister und Geisterin*

The mysticism of Henry Suso is not only exemplary and didactic but
also polemical. Although Meister Eckhart, Suso's revered teacher, sought to
correct mystical errors, he generally did so with irenicism. Suso was not

allowed that luxury, in large part because the growing fears of dangerous forms of mysticism and the misappropriation of Eckhart's teaching had produced much debate about legitimate forms of presenting union with God, contentions that were to continue through the following centuries. In Suso's case the debate over true mysticism becomes discernible in the opposition between the good "Friends of God" (*gotesfrúnde*) and the false mystics he calls "men and women of the spirit" (*die geister und die geisterin* [L 28:83.14–15]).

The expression "Friends of God," based on John 15:14–15, had emerged in the thirteenth century as a description for persons, both clerical and lay, who were dedicated to the pursuit of more intimate contact with God (see chapter 9). In the fourteenth century, *gotesfrúnde* took on a more sociological form as well. The Friends of God were loose circles of pious folk, clerical and lay, who met together, prayed together, read together, and engaged in other forms of mutual support in their pursuit of mystical transformation. Suso's *Life*, however fictionalized it is, is rooted in this kind of extra-institutional religious movement. (Suso uses the term *gotesfrúnde* more than twenty times to describe his confidants and spiritual advisees.)[216] The position of the Servant of Wisdom in these groups is unique—he is described as the "special friend of the Friends of God" (*aller gotesfrúnden sunder frúnd* [LW 29:85.5–6]).

Suso contrasts the Friends of God, who seek mystical transformation with discretion, humility, and adherence to the teaching of the church, with those misguided and mischievous folk who are devoted to "unrestrained liberty" (*ungeordenter friheit* [LBT Prol.: 327.28]). Suso's teaching about the errors of the Free Spirits is of importance for understanding the disputes about mysticism in the wake of Eckhart's condemnation and growing fear of mystical heresy expressed in the decree *Ad nostrum* of the Council of Vienne (see chapter 2 above, pp. 62–63). The evidence provided by Suso and many of the other mystics of the fourteenth century reveals a situation in which fears about dangerous mystical ideas were on the increase.[217] It also shows that the Free Spirit heresy was at least in part a debate over the heritage of Eckhart and his mysticism of the ground. Suso was one of a group of Dominicans who boldly sought to defend and explain Eckhart's teaching despite the papal condemnation.[218]

The whole of the LBT is concerned with Eternal Truth's teaching about the difference between true and false mysticism: "The power to distinguish well between people whose goal is well-ordered simplicity and those who, as they say, aim at unrestrained liberty."[219] Suso's argument reaches its culmination in chapter 6, which features a debate between the disciple and "the nameless wild one" (*daz namelos wilde* [352.19–20]), a representative of those clever people who were misusing Eckhart because of their lack of humility and inexperience in the spiritual life.

The nameless wild one is portrayed as so devoted to nothingness that he has lost sight of the distinctions necessary for living in the world of creation. Suso first instructs him about the difference between unrestrained freedom and true freedom (352.24–353.9), and then about what separates order from disorder (353.10–354.4). Suso agrees that God is "the Eternal Nothing" (*daz ewig niht* [353.19]), but he seeks to correct his opponent's mistake of thinking that he can reach absolute indistinction in the nothingness of the ground. "A person never becomes so completely annihilated in this nothing that his senses are unaware of the difference of their origin or his reason not aware of its free choice, even if all this is ignored in his primal ground."[220] Suso again cites the difference between the ontological distinction of natures and our perception of this distinction in experiences of breaking into the ground (354.2–4). One can lose the latter, but never the former.

The rest of the LBT 6 is directed to the correct understanding of particular aspects of Eckhart's message, as the nameless one presents five teachings of "a high master" in favor of his view of unrestrained freedom. The first (354.5–355.4) is Eckhart's denial of distinctions in God and between God and human (condemned in "In agro dominico," articles 10, 22, 23). Suso responds by reasserting that God is both indistinct ground and distinct Trinity of Persons, and (contrary to Eckhart) that the lack of distinction in union "describes the human perception of the event, but does not affect the mode of being" (354.13–15). The second, third, and fourth objections (355.5–356.14) deal with Christology, reflecting views of Eckhart that had been condemned in articles 12, 13, and 11 of the papal bull. Suso seeks to clarify Eckhart's teaching by showing the difference between our sonship and that of Christ, using points that are indeed based on Eckhart's writings. Finally, the fifth objection (356.15–26) reiterates Eckhart's doctrine about pure oneness without distinction or similarity. Suso says that his opponent is unable to perceive that some distinction always remains because he works only from the light of nature, not yet being illuminated by the "essential light" (*weslich lieht* [356.21–22]), as Eckhart was. The debate ends on a positive note, however, with Suso's opponent asking for more instruction about this "useful distinction," indicating that there may yet be hope for the nameless wild one.

This open approach agrees with the prologue to *The Exemplar*, where Suso says that he writes for "people whose mind and heart are struggling to achieve what is best and most perfect, but who are lacking in powers of discernment."[221] Thus, the Dominican seems to have distinguished between

those who were well intentioned but confused, and others who were seriously and willfully in error. The fine line that divided the proper understanding of the mysticism of the ground from its counterfeits was often hard
to discern, as *Life* chapter 28 shows by telling the story of the lord who
threatened to kill the Servant because he had been told that he had caused
"his daughter and many others to take up a strange mode of life that is
called 'spirit,'" and thus join "the most perverted group of people on
earth."[222] To some, then, the Servant himself appeared to be a Free Spirit!

Suso carried over his campaign against the "men and women of the
spirit" into the *Life*, which is full of passages that reflect the ongoing debate,
especially in chapters 46, 47, 48, and 51.[223] The Servant picks up on the
issues discussed in the LBT and even expands his attack in relation to positions such the supposed amorality of his opponents. The fundamentals of
his appeal to the necessity for discernment, as well as the qualifications he
covertly introduces into Eckhart's views in the LBT, continue to provide
the basis for this stage in the debate. How far Suso's characterizations of
Free Spirits may actually reflect the views of those he met and talked with is
hard to say, but it is clear that *The Exemplar* as a whole is a valuable witness
to the fourteenth-century debate over the heritage of Eckhart.

Conclusion

Henry Suso was the most widely read of the mystics of the late Middle
Ages in his own time. This fact alone merits him a detailed treatment in any
history of medieval mysticism. We need to try to discern what there was in
his teaching that stimulated such a broad readership, while also investigating his more lasting contributions to Western mysticism. I hope that this
account has helped to reveal that for all the peculiarities of his writings and
self-presentation, and despite a certain lack of coherence in his attempt to
bring so many mystical currents together, Suso was more than just an emotional follower of Meister Eckhart, as some have treated him. Rather, he
must be ranked among the foremost mystics of the Middle Ages. His
philosophia spiritualis has deep roots in monastic mysticism, as well as in
Eckhart's mysticism of the ground, but it is ultimately the product of the
personality and outlook of the passionate Dominican from Constance.

CHAPTER 6

John Tauler the Lebmeister

Dear children, the great clerics and masters of learning dispute about whether knowledge or love is greater and nobler. But here we want to speak about the masters of living [*lebmeistern*]. When we come there [i.e., heaven], then we shall have a good view of the truth of all things. Our Lord says: "One thing is necessary" (Luke 10:42). What is this one thing that is necessary? The one thing is that you know your own nothingness—that is what is yours, what you are, and who you are from yourself.[1]

THIS IS THE VOICE of John Tauler (ca. 1300–1361): preacher, teacher, moralist, and mystic. Though Tauler himself was a man of great modesty and humility (he once said that he would have been just as happy being a shoemaker as a preacher [V 42 (177.23–25)]), there is no doubt that he was one of the most famous *lebmeistern* of the late Middle Ages.[2]

Tauler, in the words of David Blamires, "enjoys the distinction of being the only medieval German mystic whose work has been known and valued in both manuscript and print in a virtually unbroken sequence from his own lifetime through to the present day."[3] Like Suso, Tauler was a student of Meister Eckhart, at least in the broad sense of having known and admired Eckhart and being influenced by his thought. His mysticism, like Suso's, is comprehensible only within the context of Eckhart's innovative and challenging thought. Again like Suso, Tauler qualified a number of the teachings for which Eckhart had been condemned. It would be quite wrong, however, to see Tauler as merely Eckhart simplified, or as a secondary figure.[4] In the early fourteenth century the German Dominicans produced three closely related, yet distinct, mystical writers of genius—a true harvest of mysticism.

240

I. Tauler's Life and Writings

Life[5]

Tauler rarely spoke about himself. Outside documentation about his life is also sparse. He was born about 1300 in a well-to-do Strassburg family and entered the Dominicans probably about the age of fifteen. He went through the normal theological education for a Dominican preacher, which would have lasted about eight years, but he did not do advanced studies. In this regard he contrasts with Meister Eckhart, who achieved the highest academic ranks, and even with Henry Suso, who aspired to these but whose academic career was blocked. Tauler was typical of the broad range of Dominicans who received a good theological education but never aspired to the status of *lesmeistern*, that is, academic theologians. Indeed, Tauler's view of theology professors was not a positive one, but this does not mean that he was a shallow thinker.

During his time as a young friar, Tauler most likely came into contact with Eckhart, who was active in Strassburg ca. 1313–26, though we lack any details about their personal relations. How far the tensions within the German Dominicans in the early fourteenth century affected him is difficult to say. The wider crises of the era certainly had an impact. Men like Suso and Tauler lived through one of the most troubled periods of the Middle Ages—the time of the Black Death, economic stagnation, and endemic warfare. The papal domination of the Western church, seemingly so secure in the thirteenth century, began to crack in the fourteenth century, as the ambition and avarice of the papacy in exile at Avignon spread disaffection throughout Europe. From time to time Tauler's sermons reflect these situations, though the brunt of his message is not social or political.

Around 1330 Tauler began his preaching career in Strassburg, a city that contained eight convents of Dominican nuns and perhaps as many as seventy smaller beguine communities.[6] As with Eckhart and Suso, much of Tauler's preaching was directed to holy women, the *cura monialium* that had been part of the pastoral duty of the friars since the mid-thirteenth century.[7] Tauler doubtless preached to mixed congregations of laity, but most of his nearly eighty sermons that survive seem to reflect a convent situation, the context in which such homilies were more likely to be written down and preserved to be read and reread.

The major ecclesio-political event of Tauler's preaching days was the conflict between Pope John XXII and Lewis of Bavaria. The pope's insistence on maintaining rights over the examination and consecration of the emperor (already outmoded in the thirteenth century) led to a standoff that did grave harm to the church in Germany and elsewhere. Pope John put the territories supporting Lewis under interdict in 1324. The Dominican order remained true to the pope, so after the city of Strassburg came down on the imperial side, Tauler and his community were exiled in 1338 or 1339. Tauler spent his exile in Basel farther down the Rhine (ca. 1339–43), where he became acquainted with the circles of devout clergy and laity known as the "Friends of God" (*gotesfründ*).[8]

Tauler mentions the Friends of God often in his sermons. Evidence for his connection with these circles of mystical piety is found in the letters exchanged between the secular priest Henry of Nördlingen and his spiritual friend, the Dominican nun Margaret Ebner (d. 1353).[9] Through Henry, Tauler also became acquainted with the masterpiece of thirteenth-century German mysticism, Mechthild of Magdeburg's *Flowing Light of the Godhead.* Later at Strassburg, Tauler also came to know and to advise another friend of God, the pious banker turned bankroller of a new religious community, Rulman Merswin (1307–82). The significance of the Friends of God for the church in a time of troubles became more and more important for Tauler as he sought to make sense of the turmoil he saw all about him. The Strassburg Friends of God were responsible for a treatise of importance to Tauler's later reputation, though modern scholarship has proven the *Masterbook (Meisterbuch)*, or *History of Tauler's Conversion,* is neither by Tauler nor about him.[10]

Lewis of Bavaria died in 1347, but Tauler had already returned to Strassburg by about 1343. The late 1340s were years of disasters and crises piled one atop the other. Strassburg experienced a devastating earthquake and fire in 1346. From late 1347 through 1349, the city, like much of Europe, underwent massive mortality due to the Black Death. Crowds of flagellants, itinerant penitents seeking to appease divine anger by ritual scourging, began to visit the city from June of 1348. In a few places (e.g., V 41 [170.16–25]; V 68 [374.20–24]), Tauler's sermons indicate that he saw these events as indications of the fleetingness of the world, possibly even signs of its coming end, though Tauler is not a thoroughgoing apocalyptic thinker.[11]

Strassburg witnessed yet more horrors. In the wake of the plague, Jews were often accused of having caused the epidemic. One of the worst pogroms of the Middle Ages occured in the city in February of 1349. The entire Jewish population of about two thousand was marched outside the walls and given the choice of conversion or death by fire. Most were burned to death. Tauler is silent about the pogrom, and we have no evidence that he sought to protect the Jews (which might have cost him his life). Nevertheless, in one sermon the Dominican insists that there are good and bad Jews, just as there are good and bad Christians (V 13 [62.18–30]).[12] This indicates that he was opposed to the regnant late medieval conception of Jewish collective guilt.

Tauler traveled fairly extensively in the last two and a half decades of his life. He made several trips to Cologne. A number of his sermons were delivered there, as their survival in the "Ripuarian" (i.e., the Cologne) dialect of MHG indicates. There is a credible, if not secure, tradition that he visited John Ruusbroec at his retreat at Groenendaal sometime in the 1350s. The translation of Ruusbroec's *Spiritual Espousals* into MHG may bear witness to this contact between two of the major figures of late medieval mysticism. Finally, Tauler and his friend John of Dambach are said to have visited the Dominican community at Paris sometime around 1350. Tauler's negative comments on school theologians demonstrate that he did not think much of what went on in Paris.

Hints in some of his sermons indicate that John Tauler was not a robust and healthy man. According to tradition, he contracted a mortal illness and died on June 16, 1361, in Strassburg, under the care of his sister Gertrude, a Dominican nun. He was buried in the Dominican church in that city with an incised gravestone that still survives. On it appears the figure of the properly emaciated friar holding the Lamb of God in his left hand while the letters T (Tau = the Cross) and the monogram IHC (= Jesus) surmounted by the crown of life (see Apoc. 2:10) appear over his right hand. Further to the right is a column supporting the beginning of the inscription IN CHRISTO IESU. This most likely refers to the preacher's view of the true Friends of God as the pillars of the church. The monument fits the man and his message.

Sermons

Tauler differs from Eckhart and Suso in leaving no Latin writings and no formal treatises, either in the language of the schools or the vernacular.[13] He was a preacher pure and simple. This is not to say that Tauler was ignorant of philosophy and theology, even aspects of the Neoplatonism favored by the Dominican school at Cologne.[14] His praise for Proclus and ability to quote from this Neoplatonic *meister* are evidence against those who would see him as nothing more than a pious preacher and moral guide. Still, there is no denying that Tauler is less theological in the school sense than Eckhart or Suso.

Tauler's sermons began to be collected in his own lifetime, especially after his return to Strassburg from exile in Basel. Three fourteenth-century manuscripts date from this time, one of which (MS Engelberg 124) may have corrections in Tauler's own hand. The many later manuscripts that survive testify to the popularity of the gifted preacher.[15] Nevertheless, the modern student of Tauler's sermons confronts several problems, notably the absence of a good critical edition with scholarly apparatus.[16] In English, the reader is even worse off, because of the lack of a complete and accurate translation of the roughly eighty sermons of the Strassburg *lebmeister*.[17] Excellent scholarly discussions of Tauler exist in German, but the relevant literature in English is sparse.[18]

Tauler's sermons follow the course of the liturgical year and have a distinctive tone that reflects his role as a mystical moralist.[19] In general, these homilies have not received the kind of close rhetorical and stylistic analysis that has been given to Eckhart's sermons.[20] Tauler's manner of preaching is relatively more simple than that of Eckhart, and he is not the creative stylist that Suso was. His sermons often combine the homily form of a commentary on scriptural passages from the feast of the day with a thematic approach characteristic of more learned scholastic preaching. Tauler's use of scripture tends to focus on the moral and mystical application of the text to the lives of his audience, not on doctrinal readings.[21]

The structure of Tauler's sermons is generally loose, with transitions between sections often being made by means of an address to the audience—*liebes kint, kinder, vil lieben schwesteren*. The introduction (*exordium*) tends to be brief, citing the text to be commented upon in Latin and translating, or paraphrasing it in German. After announcing the main theme, Tauler usually constructs the central part of the sermon (*tractatio*) fairly freely, developing the ascetical and moral aspects of his teaching as the basis for the soul's movement inward to the detachment and self-negation that leads to mystical contact with God. The preacher mingles his message with direct address to his audience, criticism and warnings, and often strong appellations and exhortations. The summary (*conclusio*) is typically quite brief. While most of Tauler's sermons touch on a number of issues, some are more closely structured around the development of a single theme (e.g., V 5, 11, 26, 29, 37, 40, 47, 54, 55, 60, 76), or provide an extended allegorical exegesis of a text from the liturgy (e.g., V 8, 36, 41, 62, 75).

Sources and Influences[22]

Tauler was widely read in the traditional classics of Latin mysticism. According to the figures compiled by Louise Gnädinger, he cites Augustine about forty times, Gregory the Great twenty times, and Dionysius about fifteen times. He makes use of important aspects of the mysticism of *der minnende Bernhardus* ("the loving Bernard" [V 43 (188.8)]), as well as of Hugh of St. Victor and Richard of St. Victor. Like all Dominicans, for whom the *Lives of the Fathers* (*Vitaspatrum*) and *Sayings of the Fathers* (*Verba seniorum*) were daily reading, Tauler praised the desert fathers and introduced sayings and incidents from them into his sermons.[23] All of this is to be expected.

Tauler also had a good working knowledge of the theology of the order of preachers. Thomas Aquinas had been the official theologian of the order since 1309, and Tauler cites him by name nine times. But Tauler was not afraid to disagree with Thomas, as will be seen below. Thomas's teacher, Albert the Great, is also named and quoted in a number of places. The generic term *die meister* that the preacher employs from time to time refers to a broad range of the Dominican philosophers and theologians who distinguished the German order of preachers between ca. 1250 and 1350.[24]

The most intriguing issue regarding Tauler's sources is the question of his relationship to the teaching of Meister Eckhart and the Neoplatonic tradition that Albert, Dietrich of Freiburg, Eckhart, and others had revived.[25] A brief look at two sermons dealing with the ground of the soul will provide information on this aspect of Tauler's background.

In a sermon for the Second Sunday after Trinity (V 29 = V 60d) Tauler discusses how the image of the Trinity dwells in the soul: "For God is in this image, and is this image, though he is without image." The preacher identifies three views of the *imago Trinitatis*, in ascending order of adequacy. First, he notes that "all the masters" teach that the image is in the soul's higher powers, the Augustinian triad of memory, intellect, and will; but he asserts that this is the lowest aspect of the mystery, that which pertains to the natural order. The second position is that of Thomas Aquinas, who "says that the perfection of the image rests in the activity of the image, in the working of the faculties, and so in active memory, active intellect, active love. And this is as far as he will go."[26] For Tauler, Thomas's view, while not incorrect, is not sufficient. He continues:

> But now other masters speak (and this view is incomparably better and higher), and they say that the image lies in what is most interior, in the completely hidden deepest ground of the soul, where God is present essentially, and actively, and substantially. Here God acts and exists and rejoices in himself, and God can be no more separated from this than from himself.[27]

This break with the Augustinian and Thomistic position on the image of God is based on the teaching of Dietrich of Freiburg and especially Meister Eckhart, the *ander meister* of the text. Even more surprising is what comes

next, as Tauler explains his position by quoting not a Christian authority
but a pagan one, Proclus. The lengthy passage from the pagan philosopher's treatise *On Providence,* which Tauler cites, insists on the necessity of
abandoning images, multiplicity, and all rational methods in order to concentrate attention totally within and thus "to become one with the One"
(*unde wirt eins mit dem einen* [300.35]).[28] Tauler specifically appeals to Proclus, it seems, because of his witness to a knowledge of the One that few
Christians have attained:

> And he [Proclus] speaks of the One in this way—"A darkness, still, silent, at
> rest, divine, beyond the senses." Children, it is disgraceful and a great shame
> that a heathen has understood and arrived at this truth and that we are so far
> away and so unlike it. Our Lord expressed this when he said: "The kingdom
> of God is within you" (Luke 17:21). It is to be found only within, in the
> ground, beyond the activity of the faculties.[29]

The extent to which Proclus's attainment of the One is like or unlike the
union that Tauler preached to his Christian audience will be taken up later,
but it is remarkable to see a pagan author cited as corroborating Christ's
teaching in a way that surpasses Augustine and Aquinas.

Tauler's respect for pagan Neoplatonic teaching on the ground can also
be seen in V 64, a sermon for the Thirteenth Sunday after Pentecost, the
only place where Tauler mentions Eckhart by name. The sermon deals with
essential topics in Tauler's thought, such as the soul's relationship to God in
the *grunt,* and the nature of the *gemuete,* what can be called the soul's essential inclination (more on this later). In introducing his discussion of the
grunt, Tauler says:

> About this inner nobility that lies hidden in the ground, many masters have
> spoken, both old and new—Bishop Albert, Meister Dietrich, Meister Eckhart.
> The one [Eckhart] speaks of it as a spark of the soul; the other as a foundation
> or a crowning point: a single origination. And Bishop Albert calls it an image
> in which the Holy Trinity is represented and in which it is present.[30]

It is not surprising to see Tauler cite the three main voices of German
Dominican speculation to support his view of the ground, but once again
he goes further, setting forth the witness of pagan philosophers:

> The masters who have spoken about this have followed hard upon it in life
> and in thought, and they have now [i.e., in heaven] found it in all truth. They
> have received it from the great saints and teachers of Holy Church who spoke
> about it. And before God's birth [i.e., the Incarnation] many masters spoke
> about it: Plato, and Aristotle, and Proclus. This greatly attracts good folk and

makes them turn in and toward this high nobility of close relationship [to God]. But also false people use it for their eternal harm.[31]

The fact that Tauler refers to three groups of people who strive to attain the ground of the soul is significant. The first are the best Christian teachers, whom he praises. The second are the good philosophers, who put many Christians to shame, and, be it noted, he does not criticize. The third, "the false people," are the Free Spirit heretics whom he attacks in many other places. This indicates that the pursuit of the ground is part of the natural capacity of human nature, something that can be used for good or bad purposes.

Sermon V 64 is the only place where Tauler mentions Eckhart by name, but there is no question that he often uses him, either without any identifying marker, or with the commonly generic title, *ein meister*. Two texts are especially revealing. In a sermon preached on the eve of Palm Sunday (V 15) Tauler treats of the interior prayer of union in which the Uncreated Spirit and the created spirit melt into each other, capping this with a defense of Eckhart. "One loving master," he says, "taught you and told you about these matters, and you did not understand him. He spoke from eternity, and you took it as referring to time."[32] This shows that Tauler had grasped the importance of the divine, or what has been called the principial, perspective for understanding Eckhart's message. In V 56 we find Tauler again breaking with Thomas Aquinas and agreeing with Eckhart on a disputed issue. Here too the prime concern is with the *grund*, the essence of Eckhart's teaching that Tauler recognized had implications not found in Thomistic theology. Tauler notes that theologians disagreed whether a soul that had committed a mortal sin and lost its acquired virtues and merits would have to start from scratch again after its return to the state of grace. Aquinas and the main tradition held to the rigorist view—the soul would have to start all over again. Tauler disagrees and sides with Eckhart: "A great noble teacher says: 'As soon as a person returns with his essential inclination (*gemuete*) and with his whole will, and draws his spirit into God's Spirit above time, so he will instantly regain everything that he lost.'"[33]

The full ramifications of Tauler's relation to Meister Eckhart are only suggested by these texts. Many of the links between the two will be taken up below, but the sermons in which Tauler combines the witness of Eckhart, Dietrich, and Albert with that of the pagan Neoplatonists, especially Proclus, deserve one further comment. Tauler was neither an academic theologian nor a trained philosopher, as were Dietrich of Freiburg and Berthold of Moosburg. Nevertheless, he was more deeply influenced by the Neoplatonism of the German Dominican school than has been previously realized. Tauler's interest in Neoplatonism, however, was not for its own sake, but rather as a confirmation of some essential features of his preaching. This is especially true in relation to his teaching on the *grunt*, where he found Proclus's teaching on the *unum animae* (the one of the soul) a powerful witness to his own more pastoral version of the Eckhartian mysticism of the ground.[34] A brief survey of Tauler's relation to his sources does not alter the picture of the *lebmeister*, but does show that even masters of living cannot do without deep and careful thinking.

II. Theological Foundations

It would not be helpful to try to create a Taulerian theological system, something at which the preacher would have probably looked aghast.[35] He thought of himself as a humble witness to Christian belief, handing on what he had received. Where he wanted to have an effect was not in theory but in the application of the message, even its more challenging aspects, such as Gospel teaching about total emptying of self (i.e., becoming "poor in spirit" [Matt. 5:3]). Like Eckhart, Tauler believed that such poverty was necessary to attain the inner ground of God and human expressed in Christ's saying, "The kingdom of God is within you" (Luke 17:21). Despite Tauler's avoidance of theological systematization, however, his sermons reveal important underlying assumptions about the relation of God and the human person that help clarify the preacher's moral-mystical message.

It is important to stress the practical character of Tauler's preaching. Tauler, even more than Suso, felt himself at odds with the academic theology of his time.[36] The growing rift between scholastic theology and mystical piety meant that one of the characteristics of fourteenth-century mysticism was an increasing suspicion of, and even opposition to, the theology of the schools. This rift seems to have affected clerical mystics, like Suso, Tauler, and the author of *The Cloud of Unknowing*, as much as it did lay mystics. In the course of the fourteenth century, the professionalization of scholastic theology and its increasing obsession with technical debates concerning epistemology and language had clearly come to seem counterproductive for believers who sought more than just discourse about God. One of the reasons Tauler was such an effective preacher was that his audience could appreciate that his message not only had a deep foundation in Christian faith, but that it was also directly related to the lived concerns of his hearers. As he put it in V 29: "It is better to experience the Trinity than to talk about it."[37]

Tauler's preaching was rooted in two fundamental areas of Christian theology: the doctrine of God and theological anthropology. He does not give us a full-fledged treatment of the divine nature, or a detailed consideration of the problem of speaking about God, as Eckhart does. But the Strassburg preacher does address such topics as the divine attributes, the trinitarian emanations, and the absolute simplicity of the divine nature as *ein einig ein*—a Single One.[38]

A short text found in a few manuscripts and entitled "Dis ist ein guote lere" ("This is good teaching") is somewhat of an anomaly among Tauler's sermons, if it is a sermon at all.[39] Commenting on Exodus 6:4 ("Hear, O Israel, your God is one"), the text is really a short treatise or meditation on the common attributes (*eigenschaften*) of God. The piece is important for demonstrating how much Tauler shared the apophaticism of Eckhart. It begins with a treatment of positive names: God as being (*luter wesen*) and goodness (*wesen der guoten*). Sinking into this being in contemplation, says Tauler, enables our nothingness to be received into the divine being and then to "gaze on the attribute of the simple unity of the essence" (*sehe der mensche an die eigenschaft der einiger einikeit des wesens* [277.14–15]).

The three final divine properties discussed in the text are all negative. The first two are Eckhartian. "Truly, you are a hidden God" (Isa. 45:15) was a favorite biblical passage of Eckhart.[40] Tauler uses it here to indicate God's deepest hiddenness "in the soul's ground, hidden to all feeling and totally unknown in the ground" (277.23–24). Next, the preacher invokes the Eckhartian view of the divine desert ("Then the person can consider the attribute of the divine desert in silent solitude" [277.31–32]), citing Eckhart's signature text for the desert motif, Hosea 2:14: "I will lead you out into the desert and speak to your heart."[41] Tauler concludes with a consideration of the Dionysian attribute of divine darkness, making use of his distinctive term for divine incomprehensibility, the abyss (*abgrunt*). But for Tauler, unlike Dionysius, the abyss is mutual: both divine and human. As he puts it:

> It is there that you must bring your own abyssal darkness, bereft of all true light and lacking all light, admitting that the abyss of divine darkness is known to itself alone and unknown to all else. That abyss, the unknown and unnamed, the holy, is more loved and more enticing to souls than all that can be known about the divine being in eternal blessedness.[42]

This brief text demonstrates Tauler's ability as an apophatic preacher.

Another Eckhartian theological term that Tauler uses is *das* or, *ein einig ein*, the replicating phrase Eckhart employed to signify the absolute simplicity of the divine nature. For example, in a Sermon for the Fifth Sunday after Trinity (V 39), speaking of pure interior prayer, Tauler says that at the highest stages it is possible to join interior and exterior prayer in the way activity and rest are one in God:

> There the highest form of all activity and the purest delight of all is a Single One (*ein einig ein*) without hindrance–each exists in the highest degree and they do not hinder each other. The activity is in the Persons [of the Trinity], and the delight belongs in the simple essence.[43]

In two texts Tauler uses *das einig ein* in combination with a text from Psalm 41:8 ("Abyss cries out to abyss") to point to the absolute oneness that characterizes the melding together of the divine and human abysses at the deepest stage of union.[44] While the Strassburg preacher has nothing like Eckhart's extended dialectical explorations of the *unum/einig ein*, his employment of the term indicates how much his doctrine of God was influenced by Eckhart.

In several places Tauler cautions against any rational discussion of the divine mystery itself: "When you come together, you should speak about God and the life of virtue and not dispute about the Godhead in another way according to reason."[45] But this warning does not negate the need for *supernatural* meditation upon the mystery of the God as one and three.[46] Several sermons contain brief summaries of the doctrine of the trinitarian processions (e.g., V 13 [62.35–64.7], V 29 [299.3–14], V 39 [156.23–29], and V 76 [412.12–14]). One of Tauler's longer treatments of the Trinity is typically practical and pastoral. In V 27 (110–14) he allegorizes the parable of the Good Shepherd and the sheepfold (John 10:1–18) as teaching about our return to the Trinity. The Shepherd is the Eternal Word, while the door is Christ's humanity; the doorkeeper is the Holy Spirit. The sheepfold itself is read as the heart of the Father. Thieves (i.e., our tendencies to possessiveness) and murderers (our harsh judgments on our neighbors) prevent us from entering into final joy, but if we let them kill each other off (i.e., if we judge our own evil tendencies), "the doorkeeper will open up and let a person into the fatherly Abyss, and . . . he would sink with unspeakable joy into the Godhead and he would go forth full of love in the holy, divinized, loving humanity [i.e., of Christ] in full happiness and joy."[47]

The area of theology that Tauler spends the most time on, not surprisingly, is anthropology.[48] The proper understanding of humans as *imago Trinitatis*, including a survey of the technical terms for the soul and its powers, is a crucial basis for his mysticism. Tauler's view of human nature is essentially Pauline (we should remember that the fourteenth century was marked by deepened study of Paul, both among the mystics and the scholastic theologians). The Apostle to the Gentiles had contrasted the inner and the outer person (2 Cor. 4:16; Eph. 3:16) and had also put forth a tripartite view of human nature as consisting of body, soul, and spirit (1 Thess. 5:23). Both these schemas, richly developed in the history of Christian anthropology with considerable help from Platonic thought, are foundational for Tauler.

Tauler's anthropology, read superficially, may seem dualistic. Therefore it is important at the outset to insist that the preacher's distinction between the inner and the outer person is not that between body and soul. Rather, the outer person represents the attitude we take toward the world around us, while the inner person concerns our relation to God and the soul.[49] In our present fallen situation, the contrast between the inner and the outer person is often characterized by the language of tension and opposition. In V 6, for example, Tauler exegetes Jesus' statement "My yoke is sweet and my burden light" (Matt. 11:30) as referring to the yoke of "the inner noble man who has come forth from the noble ground of the Godhead" (V 6 [25.19–20]), and the burden as indicating the outer man who is afflicted by various sufferings.[50] This tension, however, is the result of Adam's sin. The goal of the spiritual life is to restore, as far as possible in this life, the lost harmony between the inner and the outer person. Toward the end of a sermon for the Sixteenth Sunday after Trinity (V 67) Tauler says, "Do not submit your inner person to anyone save God. As for the outer person submit it in true humility to every creature. . . . The outer person should be attentive in an inner way to the commands of the inner person in order to satisfy them in every way and act."[51]

Language of the inner and outer person implies a more fundamental tripartite understanding of humanity found in Tauler. In a sermon for the Thirteenth Sunday after Trinity (V 64) he lays this out as follows:

> The human person is quite correctly [described] as if it were three people and yet it is one person. The first is the outer, animal, and sense-knowing person; the second is the rational person with his rational powers. The third person is the essential inclination [*gemuete*], the highest part of the soul. These all are one person, although there are also many ways of willing in a person, each having its own manner.[52]

In the sermon for the Sixteenth Sunday cited above, Tauler expands upon the relationship of the three levels of the person. The outer person is meant to be brought to a state of releasement (*gelossenheit*) so that it may be drawn inward and under the control of the rational person. When the rational person attains the releasement that allows it to recognize its own nothingness and complete dependence on God, then the third person is unhindered and "can turn itself to its origin and its uncreated state, where it has been eternally, and where it exists without image and form in perfect passivity." This condition brings fruition to all three persons and their powers: "There God gives to him according to the riches of his glory (Eph. 3:16). So greatly is he rewarded that from this richness all the lower, the middle, and the higher powers are enriched and strengthened in a perceptible and effective way."[53] Tauler often appeals to this tripartite anthropology, a view of humanity that has its roots in Paul, but that had been developed by a number of earlier Christian mystics, notably William of St.-Thierry, whose thought seems to be Tauler's immediate source.[54]

The outer and inner persons have different faculties that offer both dangers and possibilities on the mystic path (the highest aspect of the soul, or third person, is beyond all faculties). Sermon 2 for the Feast of the Nativity of John the Baptist (V 61) spells this out. In order for us to become a witness to the divine light of Christ, such as John was, we need to detach our lower and higher faculties from all that is worldly.[55] The two lower faculties belong to the outer person: the concupiscible faculty that moves us to seek pleasure (*begirliche kraft*) and the irascible faculty (*zúrnende kraft*) that contends against what is harmful. The former must eschew sensual pleasure, and the latter must be redirected to give us the strength and perseverance to live a life of detachment (V 61:329.33–330.21). The three higher faculties of the inner person—reason, will, and love (*vernunft/wille/minne*)—must also receive the witness. Reason is a prophet, that is, one who sees far. But it must recognize that it cannot gaze into the ground, the *grundelos abgrund* (331.4) that lies beyond all faculties. At this point, Tauler launches into a digression on the role of the *grund* (331.1–333.6). In essence, this section demonstrates the gap between the Strassburg preacher's anthropology rooted in *grund* and *gemuete* and the traditional Augustinian-Thomistic doctrine of humanity. Important divergences appear, for example, in the way in which Tauler, like Eckhart, emphasizes the pre-creational, or virtual, existence of the ground of the soul in God, and in how (contrary to Thomas) he is willing to ascribe knowledge of the Trinity to ancient philosophers, such as Plato and Proclus, who had penetrated to the *grund*, which in essence is the *imago Trinitatis* in human nature.[56]

After the digression on the ground, Tauler returns to the soul's faculties, specifically to the way in which "the faculty that enables us to love and to will" (333.7–8) also witnesses to the light of Christ. Tauler appeals to the four degrees of violent love of Richard of St. Victor to show how the joint faculty of will and love leads beyond itself into the ground, that is, into the realm of the inmost uncreated *mensche*. Wounding love (*wundende minne*) drives us into the ground, and binding love (*gevangene minne*) keeps us totally imprisoned there, "where you have no command over yourself;

where there is no thought, no exercise of the faculties, no work of the virtues."[57] Agonizing love (*qwelende minne*) and frenzied love (*rasende minne*) are activities within the ground—the love madness well known to the female mystics of the late Middle Ages, and obviously not strange to Tauler and his audience. This is the love that "consumes your marrow and blood" (334.3). When caught in these storms of love (*in disem sturme der minne* [335.9]), we should give up all practices and devotions, as well as thoughts of our sins and failings. "One should have constant and burning desire," Tauler says, "a full and sure confidence, and attach yourself strongly to love, and your experience will be as powerful and as overwhelming as ever anyone had in life."[58]

Similar descriptions of four or five faculties appear in a number of other sermons, sometimes in association with the *imitatio passionis* theme so dear to Tauler and his contemporaries.[59] In Sermon 52, the preacher discusses the relation between four faculties and four faults that hinder the soul's return to the inner ground (236.24–237.28). The concupiscible faculty, or appetite for pleasure, is inclined to delight in exterior things, while the irascible faculty, good in itself, is often wrongly used in a spirit of anger and condemnation of others. Reason leads us astray by letting us suppose that we possess some truth or virtue when humility would show us the opposite. Finally, the interior pleasure that we take in the spirit can also be a danger when we mistake this joy for God himself. Tauler warns, "Know that where God is not the object of intention, there will be neither end nor reward."[60] This sermon shows that Tauler's interest in anthropology, while informed by speculation, always had a practical aim.

One of Tauler's most structured sermons deals with the soul and the names for its different functions. The text for the sermon for the Nineteenth Sunday after Trinity (V 56), "Be renewed in your mind's spirit" (*Renovamini spiritu mentis vestri* [Eph. 4:23]), doubtless prompted this anthropological mini-treatise. Tauler translates the Vulgate *mens* by the MHG *gemuete*, one of the most important terms in his vocabulary (translated here as "essential inclination").[61] The homily begins practically: renewal in the *gemuete* means avoiding lying, anger, and theft, each of which Tauler intreprets not in terms of individual bad actions, but of the bad tendencies that block our path to God (V 56 [259.15–261.28]). The second, more theoretical part of the sermon (261.29–262.28) deals with the various names that are given to the "spirit of man according to its activities and different aspects" (*Der geist des menschen hat manigen namen, das ist nach der wúrklicheit und nach dem wider gesichte* [261.30–31]). It is called soul (*sele*) insofar as it gives life to the body and spirit (*geist*) as expressing its close kinship with God. Because both God and the soul are *geist,* "the soul has an eternal inclination and attentive gaze back into the ground of its origin." This close similarity (*gelicheit*) that always attracts the soul to its divine source, something that can never be extinguished even in the damned, bears the name *gemuete,* or essential inclination. Tauler describes it as follows:

> The *gemuete* is a wonderful thing! All the faculties are gathered up into it—reason, will—but it is itself superior and has something more. It has an inner, essential direction beyond the activity of the faculties,[62] and when the *gemuete* is in order and directed the right way, everything else is right; but when it is turned aside, so is everything else, whether this is known or not. Now, it is also called the *mens.* Children, this is the *grunt* where the true image of the Holy Trinity is hidden within. It is so noble that no one could ever give it a proper name.[63]

This important passage highlights the central reality (*gemuete/grunt*) of Tauler's theological anthropology, and, indeed, of his mystical message as a whole.

III. *Gemuete* and *Grund/Abgrund*

Meister Eckhart was the creator of the mysticism of the ground, a new form of teaching centered on the fused identity of God and human. Eckhart used the term *grunt* and its derivatives about 140 times; his disciples Suso and Tauler employed the terms even more often—in Tauler's case well over four hundred times![64] While there are significant differences among the three Dominicans, the role they give to attaining the ground within—the "place" beyond time, beyond distinction, beyond being—shows how closely they are related in the fundamental thrust of their message about mystical transformation.

If Tauler's mysticism, like Eckhart's, is a form of mysticism of the ground, this does not mean that the Strassburg preacher merely followed the Meister in his message about how God and human become one. Tauler's view of the *grunt,* when compared to Eckhart's, shows developments, adaptations, and sometimes qualifications of what we find in the Meister.[65] The development is evident, first of all, in the relation between the terms *gemuete* and *grund* as seen in V 56 and in many other texts—a feature not present in Eckhart.[66] Much has been written about these key terms of Tauler's teaching;[67] the number of places where these words appear is legion.[68] A full treatment of all these passages cannot be given here, but a synopsis of Tauler's view of *gemuete* and *grund* is foundational for understanding his mysticism.

Gemuete was a term familiar to medieval German mystics, one with a broad range of meanings within which individual authors had considerable freedom to mold their own understandings. Tauler, for example, distinguishes *gemuete* from both the *herze* (the heart as the faculty of affective sensibility)[69] and from *wille* (the inner faculty of particular acts of willing and loving). As we have seen in V 56, he treats *gemuete* as the MHG equivalent of the Latin *mens*, a term with its own rich history, but that in its Augustinian usage signified what was supreme in the soul: the source of the faculties of knowing and loving.[70] Thus, when the preacher translates the familiar definition of prayer as "the ascent of the mind to God," he renders it as *ein ufgang des gemuetes in Gotte.*[71] But Tauler goes even further. Augustine had spoken of the *abditum mentis*, the hidden core of the mind, which he identified with *memoria*, the soul's self-presence as the source of all acts of knowing and loving.[72] Tauler translated this as *das verborgen des geistes* and equated it both with the "indwelling ground" (*indewenigen grunt* [V 24:101.4]) and, in another sermon, with the "hidden essential inclination" (*verborgen gemuete*).[73] This represents a break not only with Augustine but also with Dietrich of Freiburg, who had identified the Augustinian *abditum mentis* with Aristotle's agent intellect.[74]

The third sermon for the Thirteenth Sunday after Trinity (V 64), already noted above, reveals more about the relation of the MHG *gemuete* and Latin *mens*, as well as the mutuality of *gemuete* and *grund*. After discussing the soul's noble relationship to God in the ground (346–48), the second part of the sermon (349–53) turns to how we can love God as the Gospel commands with our whole heart, soul, faculties, and mind (Matt. 22:37). Richard of St. Victor and Albert the Great are cited for their teaching on how to love with heart, soul, and faculties, but since the mind (*gemuete*) contains all the other powers of the soul, it needs more extensive treatment. Tauler begins from the familiar Latin etymology of *mens/gemuete* from *mensura* (measure). "It is called a measure, because it measures all the others [i.e., faculties]. It gives them their form, their stability, their weight. It penetrates all things round about—*habitus mentis.*"[75] One may consider this as Tauler's bow to tradition, his willingness to see the *gemuete* as encompassing what Augustine ascribed to the *mens*. What follows is his own teaching, which goes beyond Augustine, as the new introductory formula seems to indicate. Tauler says:

> Now we ought to consider what the *gemuete* is. It is much higher and more inward than the faculties, because the faculties receive their power of acting from it; they are within it and have flowed forth from it. It is in all of them, but is much higher; it is totally simple, essential, and formal [i.e., pure form,

like God]. One master speaks of this more than the others. The masters say
that the *gemuete* of the soul is so noble that it is always at work, whether a person sleeps or wakes, and whether he is aware of it or not. It has a divinely-
formed, ineffable, eternal inclination back to God.

The "one master" may be Meister Eckhart. The other "masters" would
probably include Dietrich of Freiburg. "These masters," Tauler summarizes,
"say it always beholds, loves, and enjoys God without cease. How that is,
we leave go for now. What is more, the *gemuete* knows itself as God in God,
and yet it is created."[76]

Here the *gemuete* takes on something of the nature of what the scholastics
called the *synderesis*, that is, "the natural habit of the first principles of
actions," to quote Thomas Aquinas (STh Ia, q. 79, a. 12); and yet it is more
than this.[77] As the essential inclination of the human person, the *gemuete*
looks outward in the sense that it motivates and controls all the actions of
the faculties. But it can only serve this controlling function because it
always looks back to its source in God (*ewig wider kaffen in Got*). In this
activity it sees itself as God, that is, it beholds its virtual existence in God,
though in its actual existence it remains something created.

From this perspective *gemuete* looks the same as the *grunt der sêle*, which
in its deepest reality is one with the divine ground. What Tauler goes on to
say seems to confirm this. Once again, as in V 29, the preacher surprisingly
cites the authority of a pagan, not a Christian, teacher. "Proclus, a pagan
master, calls it a sleep, a silence, a divine repose, and says: 'We have a hidden pursuit of the One that is far beyond knowledge and understanding.'"[78]
When the soul turns toward this inner mystery, it becomes divine; when it
turns outward, it cannot even believe that the inner reality exists. Tauler
goes on to identify the essential inclination and the ground: "This *gemuete*,
this *grunt*, is so planted in us that the plant has an eternal impulse and
attraction, and the *gemuete*, the *grunt*, has an eternal inclination, a ground-
inclination back to the source."[79] He concludes by saying that it can never
be lost, not even in hell, where it exists as the greatest punishment of the
damned.[80]

This text, and others like it,[81] link the *gemuete* so closely to the *grunt* that
some investigators have seen no difference at all in the two. Paul Wyser
says, "The *Gemüt* is the ground of the soul itself."[82] Certainly, *gemuete* and
grunt cannot be separated: in one sense they are two aspects of the same
reality. Yet from another perspective, they are *two* aspects; that is, *grunt* is
not precisely the same as *gemuete*. Two essential differences in the way the
words are used demonstrate this. First, *grunt* is a term that can be used not
only of what its deepest in the human, but also of the depths of God: *der edel*

grunt der gotheit.[83] *Gemuete,* however, is never used of God. Second, as C. Champollion notes, *gemuete* is a word used primarily in relation to verbs of action, while *grunt* mostly appears as the terminus of an action.[84] Third, the activity of the *gemuete* has a relation not only to the powers of the soul and to the divine nature, but to the *grunt* itself. In a sermon for the Sunday after All Saints (V 77), Tauler preached about the true way to happiness, saying: "This way of life in which a person finds all truth, joy, and peace in every situation, action, and place, can only be learned and found in inwardness, in the turning of the *gemuete* to the *grunt,* which requires first of all free passivity, inactivity, [the right] time and place."[85] The *gemuete,* taken by itself, expresses activity both outward to the working of the faculties and backward, self-reflexively, to the ground where the soul is one with God.[86] *Grunt* in itself, as the "place" where the *imago Trinitatis* is found, however, speaks more of presence and potentiality. In those texts where *grunt* and *gemuete* are joined (e.g., V 56 and 64) this joint activity is described as a "seeking" (350.21) and an "eternal turning back" (350.28). So, while *grunt* and *gemuete* are inseparable in Tauler, there are significant differences between these two aspects of the deepest reality of the human being.

When we turn to Tauler's use of the term *grunt* itself, many of the essential features of his view correspond to what we have seen in Eckhart. Like the Meister, Tauler uses *grunt* as a master metaphor, a term capable of being employed in many ways and one which can be used in conjunction with other metaphors that suggest the inmost reality of the human as image of God. Thus, Tauler occasionally speaks of the divine spark of the soul (*gotvar fünckelin*),[87] or of the soul's base (*boden*) or crown (*tolden*),[88] though these terms are not central to his preaching. Making use of the image of the Temple, a rich tradition in Christian mysticism, he sometimes speaks of the journey within to find God in the soul's ground as entry into God's house and the holy of holies.[89] Like Eckhart, Tauler also insists that the *grunt* is the source and goal of all things in the most basic sense. In a sermon for the Ascension (V 21) he tells his audience: "Bring everything back into the ground from which it flowed out, and do not be concerned with the nothingness [of creation], but [let] yourself flow along with all things. There is where true praise of God is born and truly brings forth fruit in the ground."[90] *Grunt* as source and goal, of course, means that the ground is nothing other than God, an understanding made explicit in the passages that speak of the *grunt Gottes* mentioned above.

The majority of the Strassburg preacher's uses of ground language, however, deal with the *grunt* as the core of the human, the *imago Dei: grunt der sele* (29 times), *grunt des herze* (9 times), *grunt des mensche* (143 times), or the various uses of *grunt* without modifier (193 times) that most often have an anthropological connotation.[91] Like Eckhart, Tauler is especially interested in linking the soul's ground and God's ground, though he prefers to express this in his own language of the abyss (*abgrunt*).

Like Eckhart, Tauler teaches that it is only by gaining our own ground in pure humility that we will be able to attain God's ground (e.g., V 38 [149.33–36]). Also in agreement with Eckhart, the Strassburg preacher insists that the human ground, like God's ground, is unnameable and unknowable: "This is the ground where the true image of the Holy Trinity lies hidden within, and it is so noble that one cannot give it a proper name."[92] This implies an apophatic anthropology that Tauler does not develop in detail in this sermon. If the ground is nameless, it is also evident that it is beyond the temporal realm, beyond movement and rest as we experience these in time, beyond distinction, and even beyond being, though Tauler does not enter into metaphysical discussions. The *grunt*, Markus Enders notes, is the place where God works in us and therefore must be free of all particularity and activity, "a nothing in the sense of form-lessness itself."[93]

Tauler makes use of other forms of Eckhartian language to illustrate the *Sprengmetapher* of the ground, especially the equation of the *grunt* with the desert. Eckhart spoke in a dozen or so places of the *grunt*, both divine and human, as the desert or wild wilderness. Tauler uses the same language about ten times. We have already noted the use of desert language in the discussion on God found in V 60 (277.35–278.8), a text where Tauler, like Eckhart, employs the desert both with regard to the divine emptiness and to the "empty deserted ground" (*italen wuesten grunt* [278.6]) of the soul.[94] These, and many other aspects of Tauler's incessant invitation to go into our own ground to find God's ground, show us how deeply Eckhartian his mysticism was.

Other aspects of Tauler's use of the metaphor of the *grunt*, however, reveal differences from Eckhart. In speaking of the ground of the soul, Tauler distances himself from the Meister by sometimes speaking of the ground as created, language he also uses about the abyss (*abgrunt*).[95] Tauler also speaks about "working" and experiencing the ground in a way foreign to Eckhart, for whom the *grunt* lies beyond anything we might think of as experience. In V 24, for example, comparing the activity of the farmer working the earth in spring and the soul seeking God he says: "In the same way with great energy a person should turn himself over and look into the ground and turn to working it over. . . ."[96] In other sermons Tauler speaks of this working as revealing our true loves and desires. In V 77 we read:

"Every day a person shall pay attention to the ground of his soul and see what its inscription is [the image is of the soul as a coin]. That is to say, what it loves the most, what it intends, what it seeks—how it may be completely consoled, delighted, touched."[97] These passages, be it noted, deal with love and seeking, not with the intellect, which for Eckhart is the faculty that alone gives access to the ground.[98]

Another difference probably reflects the situation after Eckhart's condemnation: Tauler's emphasis on the *grunt* as the *imago Trinitatis* and his avoidance of Eckhartian expressions that suggest a ground beyond the Persons of the Trinity. In Tauler there is no hint of the "God beyond God" motif that remains such an enigmatic aspect of Eckhart's thought. Finally, a fourth non-Eckhartian aspect of Tauler's thought is the Strassburg preacher's distinctive way of emphasizing the mutual identity in the ground: his teaching about the dual abyss of God and human. Eckhart spoke about the *abgrund* rarely; it is central in Tauler.

The way in which the Strassburg preacher put his mark on the mysticism of the ground can be appreciated by a close look at several sermons. Two homilies that are helpful for seeing how Tauler prepared his audience for finding the path to awareness of the ground are the third sermon for Epiphany (V 5), and a sermon for the Monday before Pentecost (V 24).[99]

The text for the Epistle for the Feast of the Epiphany, "Rise up, Jerusalem, and be illuminated" (Isa. 60:1), introduces Tauler's central message in the first section, the need for our active consent in freeing ourselves from everything worldly so that God can shine forth "in the lovely ground and work there" (22.12–13). "From this rising up," Tauler continues, "the ground is moved by a burning desire to be stripped and purified of all unlikeness [to God]. The more that is left behind, the greater the desire grows and one transcends the self; and often when the naked ground is touched, the desire [flows over] to flesh, and blood, and marrow."[100] Tauler distinguishes two kinds of reactions to this touch: some people approach it with natural reason, seeking to figure out for themselves what is happening. This approach leads to disaster. But "noble people" (*edeln menschen*) "allow God to prepare the ground, leaving themselves totally to him" (23.9–10). This releasement allows them to deal with temptation and the experience of darkness and desolation. They are raised up to a supernatural level in which "they themselves no longer work, but God works in them." Tauler says they are "lovely people who bear the whole world; they are the world's noble pillars" (24.2–4). The attitude of all who wish to follow this path must be a constant "uplifting of the essential inclination (*gemuete*) to God and a purification of the inner ground" (24.20–21: note again the distinction between the two). The preacher concludes by emphasizing the inexpressibility of such direct experience of God in the ground: "No one can speak of it and no one can ever tell another about it. He alone knows it who has experienced it, but he can tell you nothing about it, because God has truly taken possession of this ground."[101]

The sermon for the Monday before Pentecost is a fine example of the attractiveness of Tauler's preaching. The first part of the homily (97.19–98.24) is structured around a comparison between the farmer preparing his ground for planting and our need to prepare ourselves for God's action in our ground by purifying the inner and the outer person. Just as the sun shines upon the earthly ground to bring forth the harvest, "the tender divine sun begins to shine into the ground" to bring about "great joy that arises in the spirit" (98.6–12). However, this sweetness given by the Holy Spirit can be deceptive, either for those who take too much pleasure in it, or those who seek in it a "false freedom," that is, the dangerous Free Spirits whom Tauler and Suso both combatted. The central part of the sermon (99.2–101.6) consists of practical advice about how to use mystical consolations without becoming entrapped by them. The basic point, one on which Tauler and Eckhart agree, is that all attachments need to be transcended. God's gifts "are to be used, but God alone is to be enjoyed" (100.11–12). The final part of the sermon deals with the relation between prayer and the ground (101.7–102.29). Reading and vocal prayer are meant to help us achieve true prayer, which is defined as a lifting up of the spirit and essential inclination to God without intermediary (101.17–19). This heavenly form of prayer "is a true ascent to God that rightly draws the essential inclination upward so that God may in truth enter into the purest, most inward, most noble, most interior ground, where true unity alone exists." St. Augustine spoke of this as "a hidden abyss [*ein verborgen appetgrunde*] which has nothing to do with time or with the whole world, and which reaches far beyond the part [of the soul] that gives life and movement to the body."[102]

Tauler concludes with some remarkable reflections on the prayer of those who have attained "this noble and delightful abyss" (*edeln wunneclichen abgrunde*). The soul becomes silent, "essential" (*wesenlich* [102.2]), detached, "released in all things" (*gelossen in allen dingen*). Having attained a divine life, "the spirit melts entirely and sinks itself into all things and is drawn into the hot fire of love which is essentially and by nature God himself." From this divine location, such persons can see the needs of all, so that their prayer embraces the whole of Christendom in a simple and wise way. Tauler concludes:

Just as at a glance I see you all seated before me, so too they embrace all in the same abyss, the same furnace of love, and in a contemplative manner. And they turn their gaze back again to the abyss of love, into the furnace of love, and there they rest. Again, they plunge into the lovely hot fire, and again they descend down to all who are in need in Holy Christendom, before again [returning] to rest in the lovely dark silence in the abyss. Thus they go out and in and yet always remain in the lovely silent abyss.[103]

For Tauler, like Meister Eckhart, the *grunt* and not any faculty of the soul is the seat of the *imago Trinitatis.* This is especially clear in the sermon for the Second Sunday after Trinity (V 29), a central part of which has already been treated above. We can now return to this important sermon, not only because it is one of Tauler's most detailed treatments of the *grunt,* but also because it demonstrates how he sought to avoid Eckhartian language of the ground as in some sense beyond the Trinity. Tauler hails the Feast of the Holy Trinity as the consummation of the church's calendar. His brief review of the theology of the trinitarian processions (299.3–17) is followed by the comment that we should seek to experience the Trinity rather than to discourse on it: "See that it is born in you in the ground, not according to reason, but in an essential way, in the truth; not in words, but in reality."[104] This introductory section is followed by the treatment of the "divine image" (*goetliche bilde*) as residing not in the faculties, as Augustine and Thomas taught, but according to the "other teachers," including Proclus, in the inmost ground beyond the activity of the soul's faculties (300.1–301.17: see the treatment above).

The final section of the sermon (301.17–303.29) returns to the core of Tauler's message—the necessity for personal witness to the *grunt.* Christ's bearing witness to what he has seen (John 3:11) Tauler reads as the witness "in the imageless ground" (*in dem grunde unbiltlichen* [301.19]), where the Father eternally and instantly is always giving birth to the Son. In order to experience this, we must turn within, beyond the faculties and imagination, "and sink and melt into the ground" (301.25). "Then," continues the preacher, "the Father's power will come and call the person into himself through his Only-Begotten Son, and just as the Son is born of the Father and flows back into the Father, so too will this person be born in the Son from the Father and will flow again into the Father and will be one with him."[105] All this might have come from one of Eckhart's sermons on the birth of the Son in the soul. Also Eckhartian is the attention given to the role of the Holy Spirit, which, Tauler says, pours himself out with love and joy, "inundating and saturating the person's ground with his loving gifts"

(301.31–34). The three who bear witness within the soul that it is truly a child of God are the Persons of the Trinity illuminating the human subject in the ground (302.14–16). The final paragraphs of the sermon continue the appellative style so characteristic of Tauler, inviting the soul to come into the ground and providing sound advice for the kind of preparation needed (303.5–27). However much may be said about the *grunt*, Tauler insists that it remains a mystery: "It is an utterly simple, super-essential, hidden desert and free darkness. The paths of sense knowledge will not discover it."[106] This sermon demonstrates that while Tauler shares with Eckhart a profound doctrine about the *grunt* as the place in which we come to partake of the inner life of the Trinity (Eckhart's *bullitio*), he avoids any language suggesting a ground beyond the Trinity of Persons.

Eckhart, as we have seen, claimed that at the deepest level the ground of the soul and God's ground were one and the same, a claim that some of his contemporaries misunderstood as indicating total equality with God. Such Eckhartian formulae are lacking in Tauler, but the Strassburg preacher has his own way of pointing to an inexpressible identity between God and human through the metaphor of the fusion of the divine and human abyss. The term *abyssus* (from the Greek *a-byssos*, i.e., without bottom) occurs in the Latin Vulgate to express the depths of the underworld, of the sea, or of the judgments of God. A particularly significant text is found in Psalm 41:8: *Abyssus abyssum invocat in voce cataractarum tuarum* ("Abyss calls out to abyss in the voice of your cataracts").[107] By the twelfth century some Cistercian mystics, such as Bernard and William of St.-Thierry, had begun to interpret this text as describing the relation between the fullness of the divine abyss, or mystery, and the neediness, or abyss, of the human spirit. In the thirteenth century, emphasis on the soul's insatiable desire for God, especially as found among female mystics such as Beatrice of Nazareth, Hadewijch, and Angela of Foligno, shifted the connotation of the human abyss from a negative to a positive valence, at the same time that the divine abyss came to be more and more seen as the Abyss of Love. The beguine Hadewijch seems to have been the first to speak of the mutuality of the abyss, or bottomlessness, of God and the soul in mystical union.[108]

Meister Eckhart employed *abgrunt* rarely and not in the service of expressing the identity of the divine and human. Tauler, on the other hand, uses *abgrunt* often and with connotations that go beyond what is found in Eckhart.[109] Many texts use *grunt* and *abgrunt* as synonyms (e.g., V 15 [67.28–68.2], V 28 [92.23–25], V 26 [109.15–20]), but in other places *abgrunt* seems to indicate a deeper region of total ungraspability. For example, in

V 9 on the Canaanite woman, Tauler describes how Jesus' dismissal of her request drove her further on in suffering humility so that she could reach a more profound level of union. "How could he tempt her and prove her like this, driving her and pressing her the more?" Tauler asks. "What did she do, when harassed like this? She endured his driving and drove herself still deeper than he was able to drive her. With this driving she went into the *grunt*, and she went yet deeper into the *abgrund*."[110] Later in the sermon Tauler invites his hearers to imitate the experience of a contemporary "Canaanite woman," still alive, who four years before had been enraptured in an experience of hell-like suffering in which she was rejected by Christ, Mary, and the saints. Her total abandonment to God's will, even in such suffering, brought her the reward of abyssal absorption: "She abandoned herself down to the ground for eternity. She was so abandoned that she was straightaway drawn far above every intermediary and drawn completely into the divine abyss; she was truly swallowed up in the wondrous divinity! O what a wondrous chasm that is!"[111] (The wordplay *grunde-abgrunde-slunt* in this passage is difficult to bring out in English.)

Tauler's explorations of the dynamic qualities of *abgrunde* and *grunde* indicate that he seems to prefer the former term for the replicating unsayings that are typical of his version of apophatic mysticism. Most of these expressions are paradoxical in the original MHG and therefore difficult to translate into English. For example, speaking of the depth of God (Eph. 3:18) in V 67, he says: "A person should pursue and meet this depth [i.e., God's] with the depth that is a boundless abyss [*grundelos abgründe*] of his own self-annihilation that is without ground."[112] This passage reveals the most interesting aspect of Tauler's abyssal language—its status as the favored metaphor for the mystery of the identity of God and human.

Tauler's full teaching on mystical union carefully delineated the continuing differences between God and the human person in union, but such qualifications exist alongside expressions of absolute identity that are often linked to the melting together of the divine and human abysses. Three times Tauler explicitly appeals to Psalm 41:8 and its invocation of the abyss calling out to the abyss. For example, in a sermon for the Fifth Sunday after Trinity he says:

> Here the word the prophet spoke in the psalter becomes true: "Abyssus abyssum invocat, the abyss draws the abyss into itself." The abyss that is created draws the uncreated Abyss into itself, and the two abysses become a Single One (*ein einig ein*), a pure divine being, so that the spirit is lost in God's Spirit. It is drowned in the bottomless sea.[113]

An equally powerful passage using similar language is found at the end of V 45, where Tauler crowns a discussion of how self-annihilation leads us into the "divine inner abyss" (*goetlich innerlich abgründe*). "Children, there one loses oneself totally in true loss of self. *Abyssus abyssum invocat*—the abyss calls the abyss into itself." Again the created abyss, by its total annihilation, invites, even compels, the divine Abyss to take over completely: "The created abyss draws its depth within for this purpose. Its depth and its recognition of its nothingness draws the uncreated open Abyss into itself, and there the one abyss flows into the other abyss and there is a Single One—one nothing in the other nothing."[114] Tauler concludes by citing the authority of Dionysius on the nothingness of God.

Tauler was original in using Psalm 41 and the "abyss calling out to the abyss" as a biblical basis for his teaching on the fused abyss. He puts forth the same teaching about union of indistinction in other places in his sermons without the scriptural appeal, often using both *grunt* and *abgrunt.* The fourth sermon for the Ascension (V 21), for example, allegorizes the three locations of Judea, Jerusalem, and Samaria as stations on the soul's progress to God, reading Samaria as "union with God" (87.19–21). Tauler describes two forms of union: the first a state in which the higher and lower faculties of the soul are raised up into bliss; the second a raising up to a higher heaven in which the soul "completely loses itself and sinks away" (87.30–33) into the divine being (*goetteliche wesen*). The spirit that is united with God in this way "is so submerged in the divine abyss that it knows nothing, feels nothing, tastes nothing but a single, pure, empty, unified God."[115]

It is useful to remember that the fusing of the two abysses suggested in these and other passages, while they may seem to be the action of the abyss within the soul, can be more truly understood as the action of the divine Abyss making itself receptive to itself *within* the totally annihilated soul. Preaching on Pentecost (V 26) Tauler says that in order to be received in the soul the Holy Spirit "must prepare the place, create the receptiveness in the soul, and also dwell there to receive himself; it is the ineffable abyss of God that must be his dwelling and the place where he is received, not that of creatures."[116]

Tauler's use of the language of *grunt/abgrunt* forms a flexible field of metaphors for helping his audience to attain the deepest union with God possible in this life. Though obviously inspired by Eckhart, and also assisted by his knowledge of Neoplatonic sources, such as Proclus, Tauler's preaching of the ground and abyss had its own originality and power, as well as qualifications not found in Eckhart.

IV. Tauler's Mystical Praxis

Tauler's mysticism is experiential and practical.[117] It is experiential not in the modern sense of emphasizing psychological analysis of inner states, but in the Bernardine sense of appealing to the hearer to inscribe within the depths of her soul the objective truth of the relation between God and human revealed in scripture and taught by the church. It is practical in the sense that the Strassburg preacher relates his teaching to the daily life of his hearers in a way that is different from what we find, for example, in Meister Eckhart.

The MHG verb *bevinden* (to get to know, to become sensible of, to experience) is a key word in Tauler's vocabulary.[118] In V 13, speaking of the need to penetrate into the interior Temple or ground, he says:

> It is when a person with all his faculties and his soul turns within and goes into this Temple that he truly finds [*vindet*] God within living and working. He finds him in an experiential way [*in bevindender wisen*], not by sensation or by reason, or as something heard or read about, or as something that comes in from the senses, but by tasting in an experiential way [*in bevindender smackender wisen*], as something that wells up out of the ground as from its own source and spring. . . .[119]

Similar language about the need to experience, to taste, to become aware of, rather than to feel by sensation, or know by rational reflection, peppers Tauler's sermons.[120] But what is the nature of this ground-experience that Tauler constantly appeals to? The issue is problematic, because in a noted passage Tauler denies that he himself has actually enjoyed the highest form of such experience, while at the same time defending his right to preach about it. In V 41, in the midst of a reflection on the deiform souls who have become the very heaven in which God dwells and through whom he directs the universe, he says: "Don't think that I pretend to have reached this state. No teacher should give instruction about what he himself has not experienced. But if necessary, it is sufficient that he love and intend what he speaks about and puts up no obstacle."[121] Is Tauler, then, a mystic or not? Is he perhaps best thought of as just a mystical preacher?

It has been my contention throughout this history that the choice between mystic and mystical preacher is a misleading one. If we think of mysticism as an ongoing element within the broader Christian tradition, the decisive question is whether or not a preacher, like Tauler, made a significant contribution to this tradition concerning transformative contact with God, not what his own "experience" might have been. There can be no question that Tauler did make an important contribution. His emphasis, like so many others, is not on himself, but on his message. How far Tauler went along the path to union with God in the ground (note that he is here speaking of the very highest mystics, the hidden "pillars of the universe") was not vital to him, and probably not to his audience either. His ability to convey correct teaching about the path, and to love and intend it, to inspire and guide others to reach it, were the essential criteria.

Tauler's admission of a certain lack of experience, as scholars such as Alois M. Haas, Josef Schmidt, and Michael Egerding have argued, can paradoxically be seen as a significant aspect of his theology of experience. The only way to allow God to enter into the soul, Tauler always claimed, was to recognize one's own nothingness in total humility. As he says in V 67: "A person ought to bow down before God in all his capacities; . . . from the ground up he ought to recognize his natural nothingness and his sinful nothingness. The natural nothingness is that we are nothing in ourselves, and the sinful nothingness is what has brought us to nothing."[122] Such self-negation, what Haas called "the experience of apophatic self-knowledge,"[123] must involve indifference to, even the denial of, anything that might be claimed as "my own." Only our admission of nonpossession makes God's gift possible.[124] What is important for the preacher is to convey the living faith of the church as the source of the message about the possibility of transformation in the abyss, here or in the hereafter. The preacher serves the message, not himself. As Josef Schmidt put it: "Nonexperience is thus thematized as mystic faith expressed in faithful preaching."[125] The mystical sermon, therefore, is not a teaching that a master condescends to present to novices, but is rather an invitation to the experience that both the preacher and the listener may receive *if* they truly can recognize their own nothingness.

Essential Attitudes

At the outset, it may be helpful to distinguish between essential attitudes, or the underlying states of mind present in all forms of mystical praxis, and the specific day-to-day activities in which these are concretized.[126] Three essential attitudes that Tauler constantly preached can be summarized as *turning, releasing,* and *receiving.* These are not to be thought of as discrete or different virtues, nor as stages in a journey, but rather as continuous, co-present aspects of the mystical path. Although they appear linguistically most often as substantives (*inker–gelossenheit–lidikeit*), it is best to understand these nouns as signifying processes whose developments and nuances cannot be fully captured by concepts or definitions.

The importance of *turning,* especially turning within, is evident in the Strassburg preacher's frequent use of the MHG *ker,* or "turn."[127] "Anyone who wishes to taste this ground," says the preacher, "must necessarily have turned his heart and his love from everything that is not purely God and whose true cause is not God."[128] The life of penance, as Tauler preached to a community of Dominican nuns, "is nothing other than a totally true turning away from everything that is not God and a totally true turning toward the pure true good that is called and is God."[129] As Tauler teaches in V 33, the more powerful the turning, or conversion, the more effectively it removes sin (125.23–29). Conversion is the key to the beginning of the spiritual life: "Children, we must be brave and make a powerful turn; otherwise we will come to nothing."[130]

While Tauler's use of *ker* begins with the necessity for *abker,* the turn away from the world, his real stress is on the *inker,* or turn within, that leads to what he called the *weselich ker,* the essential turn into the *grunt/abgrund.* Turning within is closely tied to the need for self-knowledge, which, as Alois Haas has shown, is both an ascetical practice and a form of mystical insight for Tauler.[131] *Kerent úch in úch selber mit bekentnisse úwer selbes* (V 58 [275.1])—"Turn in to yourself with self-knowledge."[132] This turning within, which is described in terms of specific meditative practice in V 71, fosters the inwardness in which we realize our nothingness and total dependence on God, the precondition for the essential turn (*weselich ker*).[133] This deepest form of turning is indistinguishable from mystical union. In V 39, for example, Tauler equates it with the third and highest stage of mystical consciousness: "The third stage is a lifting up into a godlike being in oneness of the created spirit in the very Spirit of God, which one can call an essential turning."[134] In the first sermon for the Nativity of John the Baptist (V 40) Tauler describes two forms of the essential turn of mystical union. The first is found in the inner experience of darkness and desolation which one endures in the spirit of releasement (*gelossenheit*). "This," Tauler avers, "is called the essential turn to which the essential reward corresponds; the other turns correspond to the accidental reward"[135] (here he cites the authority of Thomas Aquinas and Dionysius). But Tauler also admits that it is possible to speak of even external conversion as in some way essential, an important clue to the way in which his unified anthropology overcomes the distinction between inner and outer. "Another turning, even one in a generally exterior manner, can be called essential. That is in every turn by which a person looks to God and nothing else in a pure and simple way, without any why other than God in and of himself."[136]

Turning within implies *releasing/detaching,* the removal of desire and possessiveness that are essential to the mysticism of the ground. Like Eckhart and Suso, Tauler was a constant proponent of the necessity of letting go of all that is "ours" in order to gain God. With Suso, Tauler preferrred the term *gelossenheit* (releasement) to *abgescheidenheit* (detachment, cutting-off), though there seems to be little difference in the way he employs the words.[137] Tauler's conception of releasement has more of a sense of process than what we find in Eckhart, according to Walter Haug,[138] but both Dominicans would agree with the summation of Louise Gnädinger that releasement signifies "removal and freeing from the too-narrow desires, demands, and needs of the ego."[139] Although the consideration of emptying and releasing in Eckhart and Suso in chapters 4 and 5 have revealed many dimensions of these terms, it will be useful to look at how Tauler used *gelossenheit* in two representative sermons.

Tauler's first sermon for Pentecost (V 25) takes as its theme the importance of emptying of self in order to receive the Holy Spirit. The preacher begins by comparing the outpouring of the Spirit to the Rhine in flood, drowning everything in its path. The initial argument concerns the double work of the Spirit: "The first is that he empties; the second that he fills what is empty as far and as much as he finds it empty." The point is that the emptying process is just as much the work of the Spirit, that is, the work of grace, as is the filling. As Tauler puts it: "The measure of our emptiness is the measure of our receptivity. . . . If God is to go in, the creature of necessity must get out."[140] Tauler presses the message of abandonment, insisting that we must let go of creatures, even of the animating soul, and that, finally, "A person must let the self be taken captive, emptied, and made ready, and [a person] ought to lose everything—even the losing of self ought to be let go of."[141] Only then can we arrive at our own "pure nothingness" (*sin luter nicht*). This is the true poverty of spirit (*die woren armen des geistes* [306.18]) spoken of in the Sermon on the Mount. Allowing ourselves to be prepared by the Holy Spirit, not interfering with God's work, is the essence of the emptying that is "true releasement" (*rechter gelossenheit* [308.7]). Toward the end of the sermon Tauler makes the important point that it is not enough for us to sit back and wait for the Holy Spirit to act. We must do nothing to hinder the Spirit as we continue to do all our required tasks "in peaceful releasement" (*in fridelicher gelossenheit* [309.32]). It is not activity in itself, but disordered activity (*unordenunge in den wercken* [309.33]) that prevents the Spirit from flooding the soul.

The following second sermon for Pentecost (V 26) deals with what the Holy Spirit pours into the empty soul: the seven gifts. Tauler connects the fifth gift, counsel (*der rat*), with the acceptance of interior suffering, even the sense of being abandoned by God. When God allows us to sink down so we no longer have any knowledge of him or feeling of consolation, then there is need for true counsel. "Then a person is stripped of self in true and correct releasement, and he sinks into the ground of the divine will, so that if God wished, he would remain in this same poverty and emptiness not a week or a month, but a thousand years or forever. . . . Children, this would be true releasement."[142] Tauler describes this gift as the beginning of our divine life—a releasement that sets one foot in heaven (108.34–109.7).

In V 23, a sermon for the Sunday after Ascension, Tauler makes use of the related term *abgescheidenheit*, connecting it with the third of the inner attitudes: *lidikeit*, or receiving in empty passivity. In this thematic sermon the preacher announces, "It is true detachment and receiving and inwardness and oneness—this is the nearest and the best preparation, and the person who has these and in whom they grow has the greatest possible capacity for receiving the Holy Spirit." He goes on to define true detachment as what occurs "when one turns away and detaches from all that is not God pure and simple; and [when one] examines with the light of his discretion all his actions, words, and thoughts with a tranquil essential inclination to see if there is anything in the ground that is not purely God."[143] Tauler says that such detachment is necessary if we wish to receive the Holy Spirit, but that it is realized in different ways by different people (92.16–93.3). Later in the sermon he again discusses the experience of anxiety and alienation, proposing the same message found in V 26: "When this trouble comes, a person should ignore it until he has found peace, and should bear himself in releasement and in passive releasement [*lidiger gelossenheit*] and wait upon God in the anguish."[144] After a discussion of following Christ, the model of poverty, detachment, and patience, at the end of the homily Tauler once again returns to the message of accepting all things from the hand of God, whether they are pleasant or painful, "in inwardness and in true detachment" (96.23).

Tauler does not define *lidikeit* in V 23, though it is significant that he uses it in close connection with *abgescheidenheit* and *gelossenheit*. Nowhere is there an extended definition of this word, which appears to be Tauler's neologism and bears both the connotation of MHG *ledic* (free, empty) and *lidec* (receptive, or passive, in the sense of the Aristotelian distinction between the active and passive aspects of motion).[145] It might be translated into English as "empty passivity." In a sermon for Corpus Christi (V 31) Tauler appeals to the Aristotelian teaching that two beings or two forms, such as heat and cold, cannot coexist in one being—"If God is really to perform his works in you, you must be in empty passivity [*lidekeit*], and all your powers must abandon all their own activities and preoccupations and stand in pure self-denial."[146] Because God is essential activity (*wúrcken*), our ontological relation to him is always one of empty reception, or passivity (*liden*), whether we recognize it or not. Hence, as Tauler insists in this sermon and in other places: *wan es ist besser liden denne wúrcken* ("It is better to be passive than to act" [315.30–31]).

Elsewhere, however, Tauler speaks about the need for activity, at least in the sense of a "work" of preparation. In the same V 25 mentioned above, for instance, he speaks of two little points to remember if we wish to grow in holiness. The first is to make ourselves "empty and free" (*italent und lidig machent* [308.22]) of all created things and observe due order in everything so as not to hinder the work of the Holy Spirit. The second is to accept everything that comes our way, the good and the bad, as coming directly from God (V 25 [308.20–29]). In V 5, the third sermon for the Epiphany, Tauler says that external works are of no value to "noble souls," but then reflects on the command of Isaiah's *surge*. "Now the text says this word '*surge*' which means arise; that is always a work. Yes, it is the one work that belongs to them and that they should perform without ceasing as long as they live." He goes on to describe this one work and its characteristics as follows:

> A person can never come to perfection unless he always lifts himself up and directs his essential inclination up to God and sets his inmost ground free. . . .
> If God wishes such people to be passive, they will be passive; if he wishes them to work, work they will; [if he wishes them] contemplation or rapture, they will enjoy it. Their ground bears witness in itself that it is God who has prepared and purified it. . . .[147]

Tauler's teaching about passivity is complex, subtle, and consistent, as Richard Kieckhefer has shown.[148] Ontologically, it is based on the theological perspective that ascribes all our being, as well as all saving action, to God. But Tauler also recognizes that this truth must come alive in the believer's mode of life in two ways. First, by adopting a fundamental attitude of *lidikeit*, that is being totally open to God, allowing him to act on us and in us, recognizing our total dependence on him. This fundamental attitude, however, does not preclude preparation and even activity, when that is God's will. What it does reject is any notion of dependence on ourselves, something always rooted in pride. The only thing that is actually in our power is to interfere with God's work, something we are always tempted to do, especially when we concentrate on performing *our* good works.

In making his case for the centrality of *receiving*, Tauler based himself on truths deeply enshrined in scripture and in the mystical tradition. The Epistle to the Hebrews spoke of Jesus learning obedience "through what he suffered" (*quae passus est*), and Dionysius praised his teacher Hierotheus, who "not only learned, but also underwent [i.e., suffered, or received] divine things."[149] For Tauler, the entire mystical life is a deepening realization of that inner *turning* to God which is the *releasing* from all created things that makes possible the *receiving* of God in the ground.

The Following of Christ

These essential attitudes could appear speculative and abstract were it not for the fact that Tauler always presents them in relation to a concrete model, the following of Christ. The role of Christ, both as Eternal Word, and especially as Incarnate God-man, is pervasive in Tauler's preaching.[150] Few Christian mystics have been as Christocentric, yet the Strassburg preacher's teaching on the role of Christ in the return to God has been controversial and at times misunderstood. Some have argued that while Tauler finds Christ necessary as a preparation to mystical union, his mysticism does not have much room for historical Christology and eventually moves beyond Christ in its emphasis on union in the ground.[151] However, as much recent literature has shown, imitation of Christ is essential for all stages of Tauler's view of our progression to union with God, though it is realized in different ways.[152] As the Strassburg preacher himself once put it, "No one can ever go beyond the image of Our Lord Jesus Christ" (V 15 [71.7–8]).[153]

Like Eckhart, Tauler's Christology is fundamentally functional, that is to say, he shows no interest in scholastic disputes about the nature of the union between God and human in Christ, nor such controversial issues as the knowledge of Christ. He too cites the traditional formula, "He became man so that man could become God": *Wan dar umb wart er mensche, das der mensche Got wúrde* (V 30 [293.33–34]). Tauler's concern is with Christ as Redeemer: Christ the Light of the World (V 10), Christ the Door to the Father's Heart (V 17), Christ the Good Shepherd (V 36), and especially Christ on the Cross drawing all to himself (V 51). Tauler's form of *imitatio Christi*, like many of his contemporaries, centered on the *imitatio passionis*.[154] While Tauler often speaks of the events of Christ's life as he preaches on the Gospels of the liturgical year, his concern is not with the past, but with making present the saving action of Jesus as both effective cause of redemption and model for imitation in his hearers' path to God.[155]

Tauler's sermon for the Feast of St. Matthew (V 55), on the text "Follow me! And he left all things and followed him" (Luke 5:27–28), provides rich evidence for how following Christ is crucial to progression toward union.

This homily begins by emphasizing how we, like the sinner Matthew, must give up all things to follow after Christ. Tauler then specifies six virtues needed for this following: humility, mildness, and patience in the lower faculties; and faith, hope, and charity in the higher (254.12–16). These virtues are realized by imitating "the lovely model of Our Lord" (*dem minneklichen bilde unsers herren* [254.18]); but there is a more direct way to reach the goal: "An inner, entirely released, still silence within an inward turned essential inclination where we wait simply upon what God wishes to work in us. . . ."[156] Here we see once again the emphasis on releasing and receiving, but we can wonder how this more direct way is connected to the model of Christ.

With regard to external works, Tauler continues, we must always try to separate the natural contentment we take in performing good works (something that cannot be avoided) from self-satisfaction in doing such works. Such pleasure must be directed to God alone (254.23–255.3). He emphasizes that Christ's "Follow me" should be understood both with regard to the outer person concerned with the exercise of the virtues and love for all, and with regard to the inner person in true and total releasement (255.4–9). Tauler enforces this by a rare personal comment, emphasizing his willingness to give up his status as priest and preacher if that were God's will as expressed through ecclesiastical authority (a passage that may reflect his experience of the papal interdict in Germany). Then Tauler presses home the message that since we have received everything from God, we should be equally ready to give up everything in "true releasement," though he admits that the full realization of this ideal may only come to "some special people who should follow the dark way" (255.35–36). But even when we perform actions in the faculties, we must strive to do these "without any possessiveness" (*sunder alle eigenschaften* [256.3]).

The middle part of this sermon appears to be influenced by one of Meister Eckhart's most famous homilies, Pr. 52 on the meaning of poverty of spirit as wanting nothing, knowing nothing, having nothing.[157] Tauler employs this triple formula to study how the lower and upper faculties fade away in the process of releasement. "It is in the nature of humanity to possess, to know, and to will; these are the operations of the faculties."[158] This is where the six virtues mentioned above come into play as the forces that enable the lower and upper faculties to divest themselves of their own operations. Tauler describes this operation beginning from above, noting how faith robs reason of its own way of knowing and renders it blind, while hope takes away our sense of self-security and possessiveness, and charity deprives the will of its egotism (256.11–15). Just as important, however, is the action of the other three virtues on the outer faculties. Humility sinks us in the abyss; mildness takes away possessiveness, and then sinks into name-lessness, along with the virtue of patience (256.16–24). The effect of this emptying action is a total and deeper "sinking into your nothingness." "Everything," he continues, "rests in this: in a bottomless sinking into the bottomless nothing."[159] To explain this mysterious nothingness Tauler launches into one of his most challenging investigations of the dark way of alienation and suffering on the path to God (256.36–258.6), appealing to the figures of Job and Elijah as Old Testament models, in dependence on Gregory the Great (more on this below). This sinking is described as a going into the "unknown and unnamed abyss beyond all modes [of being], images, and forms, . . . where there remains in this state of loss only one ground that is essentially self-sustaining—one being, one life, one above all."[160]

By this stage, V 55 seems to have left the historical Christ far behind, and therefore to confirm the suspicions of Tauler's critics. But the opening sentence of the last part of the sermon belies this: "The road that leads to this goal must be through the adorable life and suffering of Our Lord Jesus Christ, for he is the way along which a person must pass, and he is the truth that illuminates this way, and he is the life to which we must come."[161] By means of Christ as the door (see V 17) we break through our nature through works of humility, meekness, and patience, whereas without him we go astray and are reduced to blindness (258.10–15). Those who follow this inner way, says Tauler in daring fashion, are beyond the power of the pope himself because God himself has freed them. In the higher part of their being they are already beyond time; in the lower part they are freed and released into "essential peace" (*weselichen friden* [258.24]).

This sermon on following Christ shows us that Tauler insisted that the path to the deepest union with God was always the path of Christ, but it does not explain how. Other sermons, however, shed more light on the role of the *imitatio Christi* in the Strassburg preacher's teaching. The key to understanding the constant yet developing role of Christ in the path to God is to grasp the difference between meditation on the events of Christ's life as an external model and the internalization of Christ's own essential inten-tion, so that we *become* Christ, both in suffering the alienation he experi-enced at Gethsemane and on the cross,[162] and in participating in the inner life of the trinitarian processions that he as Son of God incarnate always enjoys.

The transition from carnal love to spiritual love of Christ was traditional in Western mysticism. It was a central motif in the mysticism of one of Tauler's favorite authorities, Bernard of Clairvaux. Like Bernard, Tauler read Christ's announcing to the apostles that he must depart from them physically so that the Holy Spirit could come upon them (John 16:7) as a declaration of the need to pass from carnal to spiritual enjoyment of his presence.[163] Many texts in his sermons speak of the need to pass from meditation on Christ's humanity, necessary as that is, to a higher recognition of his divinity and full equality with the Father.[164] For instance, in his sermon for the Twenty-Second Sunday after Trinity (V 76) he distinguishes between two forms of love: the spiritual sweetness the apostles experienced while Jesus was still with them, and the higher love he promised them after his departure at the Ascension. "This love is nothing else than a loss of self; there is no affirmation. It does not consist of a possession, as the apostles had before, but it is a privation." He continues: "In it there is ignorance and unknowing; it is far above understanding, above all essence and modes of being." This love tortures the created subject so that it can die to self and all images "in order to enter into the realm where God loves himself and is his own intended one."[165] Tauler identifies this love with the Dionysian "hidden divine darkness" (*verborgen goettelich vinsternisse* [411.26]), and yet, "It is also the day of Jesus Christ of which Saint Paul spoke" (Phil. 1:6). This is the day in which we receive full redemption. The harvest of Christ's passion "is now received more purely and nobly, not in sensible ways or in images taken in from the senses, or as we have in the imagination, but inwardly, nobly, divinely, hiddenly, not as it was in the former mode of love."[166] Tauler concludes by alluding to the example of Mary Magdalene, who washed Christ's feet in a bodily way before his death, but could touch him only spiritually after his resurrection (412.4–14).

The message is clear. Christ and Christ's passion are not lost sight of, though meditation on the physical aspects of the Savior's life and death are transcended in the higher states. The necessity for the continued presence of both forms of participation in Christ is evident from V 23, where Tauler compares the Christian who is admonished to be as wise as a serpent in gaining salvation (Matt. 10:16) to the snake who sloughs off its old skin by rubbing between two rocks, that is, the eternal truth of Christ's divinity, and the adorable humanity of the God-man, the essential way to God (95.1–16). The same teaching about the ongoing role of Christ's humanity, especially in his suffering and death, though expressed in different registers, is found in a number of other sermons, as Richard Kieckhefer has shown.[167]

Tauler is explicit throughout his preaching that *imitatio passionis* is never surpassed, though *how* we imitate Christ's passion and death is subject to growing intensification and interiorization. In V 31, preaching on the proper reception of the Eucharist, he cites Paul's command to proclaim the

Lord's death until he comes (1 Cor. 11:26), noting "You do not make this proclamation with words and thoughts, but with dying and unbecoming in the power of his death."[168] One is reminded of the words of one of Tauler's great admirers, Martin Luther, who once said: "By living, yet more by dying and being damned, you become a theologian, not by understanding, reading and speculating."[169] In V 40 he explicitly responds to an objector who says that the inwardness he preaches will make us forget Christ's passion. "No, dear children," he says, "you should go into the ground where grace alone is truly born and with that grace look upon the suffering and the life of Our Lord in complete love and simplicity, and with a simple regard."[170] Such a synthetic gazing at Christ in one glance, and the identification with the suffering and yet glorified Lord that it leads us toward, is the heart of Tauler's christological mysticism.

Ecclesial Mysticism

Although Tauler was critical of the scholastic theology of the day, bewailed the decline in morality he saw around him, and may even hint at dissatisfaction with the overly politicized fourteenth-century papacy, this never led him to question the role of the church as Christ's Body, the necessary instrument of salvation.[171] Tauler's preaching always had a deep ecclesial dimension, especially in the way in which he tied his message to the life and practice of his audience, mostly nuns and religious immersed in the daily round of Dominican observance. Still, Tauler's advice was meant not just for religious, but for all Christians striving toward deeper devotion and searching for God in the ground. His connection with the Friends of God showed him that it was not any form of life as such, but the degree of one's releasement and self-negation that is the measure of progress. In one sermon he says that the holiest person he ever knew was a simple man who had never heard more than five sermons in his life (V 73 [396.24–27]).[172]

The virtues and devotional practices that Tauler preached were frequent objects of medieval sermonizing, but few preachers were more insightful and original in presenting them. Especially important for him was the inculcation of the virtues, among which humility, discretion,[173] patience, obedience, poverty of spirit, and universal love stand out. In several sermons he lists essential virtues and discourses on them at length.[174] Humility is particularly praised by Tauler, because it is the virtue that is most necessary for self-negation.[175] Just as earth, because it is the lowest element, draws down heaven's power into itself to become fruitful, so too the humble person will be filled by God (V 45 [200.26–34]).[176] Humility is closely related to, indeed necessary for, sinking into the ground. In V 57 the Strassburg preacher says this about their relation:

> Before everything else a person shall set himself in his nothingness. In order to attain the crown of perfection, there is nothing more important than to sink down into the deepest ground and into the root of humility. Just as a tree's height comes out of its deepest root, so too everything that is high in this life comes from the ground of humility.[177]

Closely allied with humility is the poverty of spirit that Jesus spoke of in the Sermon on the Mount (Matt. 5:3) and to which Eckhart devoted much attention. In his sermon for the First Friday in Lent (V 8) Tauler allegorizes the account of Jesus's cure of the lame man, who represents humanity, at the pool of Bethesda. The pool itself signifies "our dear Lord Jesus Christ," while the moving of the waters is the flowing of his precious blood by which we are redeemed. The five porticoes are Christ's five wounds, or alternatively the five virtues we must practice. The first is humility; the second "a constant remaining in the ground" (*ein flissig bibliben bei dem grunde* [35.32]). The third is true repentance, and the fourth is voluntary poverty— not outward poverty, which is a matter of chance, but the inward poverty that is essential for all. Tauler says it means "that God alone should possess our ground and that we should not be possessed by anything but him and that we should own our possessions as God would have us own them, in poverty of our spirit."[178] Finally, the fifth virtue is our offering back to God everything that we have received from him. Tauler often returns to the theme of poverty of spirit, especially in his sermon for the Feast of All Saints, edited by Dick Helander and considered authentic today.

The All Saints' Day Sermon begins with a description of the kinds of saints and goes on to give a commentary on the eight beatitudes, which includes a distinction of four kinds of poverty of spirit, the virtue which Tauler says is "a head and origin of all perfection" (*ein houbet und ein begin aller vollekomenheit* [Helander, 354]). In ascending order these forms of poverty are: involuntary poverty; the poverty of the religious life, which allows a sufficiency in life without concern for earning a living; interior poverty, by which a person loves God so much that nothing exterior is a hindrance; and finally, the fourth and highest degree, which combines interior and exterior poverty. Tauler describes it as follows:

> The fourth form of pure poverty is to be pure within and without from love, through love for the lovely image of Our Lord Jesus Christ, to imitate his pure empty poverty with real and true love, to be unencumbered and unattached, inwardly and outwardly, [having] only a pure, empty, unmediated reflux and return of our essential inclination ceaselessly into its source and principle.[179]

This passage shows that poverty of spirit for Tauler is another way of expressing the constant need for imitating Christ in the depths of the ground. Poverty of spirit, humility, and love go together for Tauler. At the end of V 29 he says that if everything he has spoken about were to be forgotten, it would be enough to remember *zwei púntelin*, "two little points": the first is to be humble, within and without; the second, to be sure our love of God is true, existing not in the emotions, but in the whole intent of our *gemuete*, the way an archer aims at his target (303.18–27).

Tauler, like other Christian mystics, insisted there could be no salvation without the action of the three supernatural virtues of faith, hope, and charity (*minne*) in the depths of the soul, especially charity, which according to Paul (1 Cor. 13:13), is "the greatest of these." The preacher speaks of the love of charity in an almost scholastic way in V 64, defining its form, matter, and goal. "The matter of love is our heart, soul, and powers; its form is love [itself]; its activity is loving totally; its goal and intention is God without intermediary. The essence of love is love, because love loves for the sake of loving."[180]

Love originates in God: it is God (1 John 4:14). Tauler says that everything that God sends us, whether of happiness or suffering, comes from "the depths of his inexpressible love" (V 3 [17.26]). Our response must be a burning love for God and a universal love for all our neighbors, the "operative love" (*wúrkliche minne*) that the preacher often spoke about.[181] In preaching on Corpus Christi (V 34), Tauler says that the banquet to which God invites us is within the ground of the soul and that God measures the banquet according to the measure of our love (318.8–9). If love is the measure of all things (see also V 62 [338–39]), this means that we should do all things in love (V 24 [309.29–32]). We will take up below Tauler's analyses of the various stages in the progression of love, since these are a part of his teaching on union, but any treatment of his message needs to emphasize the relation between humility and love.

An important practical implication of Tauler's view of humility and the need for universal love is his opposition to judging others. The Strassburg preacher condemns contemporary scribes and pharisees, that is, those who practice an external, prideful, and self-sufficient form of religion (see, e.g., V 9, 10, 19, 54, and C LXXXIII). The pious practices of these pharisees seem no different from those of the Friends of God, but there is a way to tell them apart: "They have this difference from the true Friends of God on the exterior; they are full of judgment about other people and God's Friends and never judge themselves, while God's true Friends judge no one except themselves."[182] Tauler's conviction that the only way to attain God is by beginning with self-condemnation necessarily implies that those who delight in judging others are headed in the wrong direction, no matter how holy they seem.

Tauler's teaching makes it clear that it is only by imitating Christ's poverty, chastity, and obedience that we become open to the action of the three theological virtues (faith, hope, and charity) and the seven gifts of the Holy Spirit (V 23 [96.1–8]). Since the time of Gregory the Great, the Latin mystical tradition had seen these ten charisms as essential for the return to God.[183] Tauler was particularly interested in the operation of the seven gifts (based on Isa. 11:2), detailing their role in the believer's progress in three sermons. The most important treatment is in the second sermon for Pentecost (V 26), treated above, in which the first three gifts (fear of the Lord, gentleness, knowledge) prepare the soul for perfection, while the final four (divine strength, counsel, wisdom, and understanding) "bring it to the highest, purest, and most enlightened state of true perfection" (106.3–4).[184]

Tauler's sermons have much to say about the role of the sacraments in the life of devotion.[185] All the sacraments were given to us to help us escape the hindrances we face in our fallen condition (V 10 [49.29–50.2]), but the preacher naturally concentrates on the sacraments that were foremost in medieval practice. He devotes several homilies to the proper use of the sacrament of penance (see V 46, 57, 58), but his greatest concern is with the Eucharist. The five sermons that Tauler preached for the Feast of Corpus Christi (V 30–34) rank among his most important, not least for their detailed treatment of the role of the Eucharist in the mystical life. It is not possible here to give a full account of Tauler's teaching on the Eucharist, but a brief summary will be helpful.

Again and again, Tauler praises the greatness of the sacrament as the place where God meets us in an unmediated fashion (V 32 [118]) and as our daily source of the saving fruits of Christ's death (V 34 = 60g [318]). It is God's humility that brings him down to be our brother and our food (V 30 = 60c [293]). Building on a tradition begun by Augustine and furthered by Bernard of Clairvaux,[186] Tauler reverses the digestion model of our relation to the sacrament. When we receive the Eucharist we do not eat God so much as he devours us. This process begins when we allow conscience to eat at us and confess our sins so that we can worthily receive the sacrament (V 30 [294–95]). More importantly, the Eucharist helps to realize the destruction, or "unmaking" of the old self (*entwerden* appears six times in V 30 [295–96]).[187]

Tauler discusses the conditions for worthy reception of the Eucharist (e.g., V 31 = 60f [311]), as well as the obstacles, our "daily sins" (V 33 [126–29],

V 34 [319–20]), that prevent a fruitful reception. Above all, he is concerned to emphasize frequent, even daily, communion, if one has the correct attitude (V 30 [297], V 32 [122–23], V 51 [232–33], and V 57 [267–72]). Of course, the preacher's high regard for the Eucharist also leads him to stress the dangers of unworthy reception (e.g., V 30 [297–98] and V 31 [313]). A peculiarity of the Dominican's eucharistic teaching is one exception he makes to the practice of frequent reception, advising against it when a person is experiencing the pangs of inner abandonment by God (*getrenge*; see V 31 [315]). Tauler also advises frequent spiritual reception of the sacrament (e.g., V 33 [125–26, and 129]), a growing practice in the late Middle Ages.

With regard to the other practices of religious life, Tauler is especially emphatic on the role of prayer. His teaching is based not only on the definition of prayer as the "raising up of the *gemuete* to God," mentioned above, but also on the distinction between outer, or verbal, prayer, and the interior prayer of union.[188] Tauler condemns two opposed errors about prayer in V 50 (224.17–225.8). On the one hand, there are those who say that we should never pray, but leave everything in God's hands; on the other, some are constantly petitioning God, but according to their own will and desire. Tauler excuses the former, but says they are mistaken because the church and Christ himself in the Our Father instruct us how to make right petition; the latter need to learn how to pray in the spirit of true releasement. He also counsels his hearers, especially the religious, about their obligation to fulfill the community round of the divine office, but he notes that there will be times when an individual is so rapt in interior prayer that external prayer, as long as it is not the obligatory prayer of the liturgical hours, would be a dangerous interruption and therefore can be dispensed with.[189] He becomes incensed at those who wish to force "their own methods" on souls who are seeking the inner life of prayer, saying they are worse than Jews and pagans (V 29 [303.1–6]). Only three things are needed: keeping our attention focused on God alone; keeping a close watch on our external activities and being mindful of our nothingness; and ignoring what goes on around us (303.6–12).[190] More will be said below on interior prayer, because of its association with mystical union.

Finally, we should note how Tauler shows concern for the daily life of religious men and women. V 57 (266–74), for example, deals with life in community, especially observance of the rule, confession, communion, and the exercise of charity. V 12 discusses the essential purpose of the way of life undertaken by nuns. Other sermons now and again are interrupted by pieces of concrete advice: how to perform meditation on the *grunt* after Matins (V 70 [382]); physical practices for remembering Christ's passion

(V 47 [211]); the usefulness of spending at least an hour a day in spiritual exercises (V 42 [179]); and Tauler's advice that when one is in doubt about which of two choices is closer to God's will, "Look into your own self and then do what is less pleasing to your nature" (V 33 [130.23–24]). Tauler was clearly a gifted spiritual adviser.

Union with God

Like most Christian mystics (though unlike Eckhart), Tauler viewed the path to union with God as a process that could be sketched out in terms of a mystical itinerary. Such itineraries are primarily pedagogic; that is, they provide a variety of maps, or guidebooks, to help understand a journey that will be realized in different ways by each soul. The various stages can be seen as different modalities of God's presence, revealed and concealed in great variety.

The ability to discern God's presence within the common practices of the spiritual life and more deeply in the ground of the soul is fundamental to how Tauler views the path to union. In a sermon preached to Dominican nuns (V 12) he speaks of seeking God's presence in every moment as the goal of their lives in community. "This is the time that is always ours, that we seek God out and pursue his presence in all our actions, and our life, will, and love. We should always lift ourselves above ourselves and above all that is not God, willing and loving him alone in all purity, and nothing else. This moment is every moment."[191] It is true, Tauler admits, that we often do not perceive the divine presence, but we should strive to do everything we do knowing that "he is necessarily present; even though it be in a hidden manner, he is still there" (57.23–24). In other sermons where Tauler speaks of realizing the divine presence, he sometimes speaks of the process of directing our inner "face" (*antlit*), or sometimes our essential inclination (*gemuete*), toward God's face. In V 71 he draws on the language of the Psalms. "Turn your ground to him and say with the prophet, 'My face has sought you out, I long for your face; Lord, my face seeks your face, do not turn your face from me' (Ps. 26:8). And so turn your face, your ground, toward the divine face in total emptiness."[192] Commenting on 1 Peter 3:8, he says, "When St. Peter says we should be single-minded, he means that the essential inclination should cling to God entirely and exclusively, and that a person should actually (*gegenwertlichen*) turn the face of his ground and inclination entirely to God." In the midst of community prayer, we can still maintain single-minded prayer by drawing ourselves into the inner ground with uplifted inclination and faculties, "inwardly gazing at God's presence and with inner desire for everything that is dearest to God's will."[193]

The growing awareness of God's mysterious presence in everything we do is realized in three broad stages comprised of beginners, advanced, and perfect—the threefold itinerary that was pioneered by Origen and that had been popular in Christian mysticism since the time of Dionysius. Tauler mentions this general pattern in several sermons. In V 11, for example, he speaks of the action of the Holy Spirit within the soul as producing desire for God that can be seen in three kinds of people who differ greatly: "The first are the beginners, the second are the advanced, the third are those called perfect, insofar as perfection is possible in this life."[194] Using the mystical Psalm 41, which speaks of the deer's desire for fountains of water, Tauler joins earlier mystics like Augustine in reading the deer as the soul longing for God. The beginners are souls who have turned away from the world, but who are still pursued by temptations the way that deer are hunted by dogs (V 11 [51.14–37]). The remainder of this important sermon—one of Tauler's richest expositions of the path to mystical union—does not clearly distinguish what sets off the beginners from the advanced, or the advanced from the perfect, indicating that this threefold pattern, useful in itself, was not the major focus of the Strassburg preacher's teaching.[195]

More important to Tauler's presentation of the mystical journey, as is evidenced by the frequency and length of his treatments, are two other itineraries: first, the various stages in the progress of love, where Tauler takes over patterns from Bernard of Clairvaux and Richard of St. Victor, but gives them new content; and second, a mystical itinerary of his own making to describe the higher stages of God's presence: the progression from ecstatic joy (*iubilieren*), through alienation and inner dereliction (*getrenge/arbeit der nacht*), to the goal of union of indistinction (*heimliche einekeit sunder alle underscheit* [V 7 (33.28)]).

Late medieval mystics often debated the relative roles of love and knowledge in the path to God. Tauler shows his practicality and disdain of scholastic quarrels by deliberately sidestepping the question.[196] We have already glanced at his teaching about the necessity of love as a virtue. The role of love as a dynamic force and the importance of the stages of love in the path to mystical union emerge in many of Tauler's sermons.[197] This is especially clear in V 76, a sermon for the Twenty-Second Sunday after Trinity, which is Tauler's most impassioned homily on the need for love. The preacher begins by claiming that "The noblest and most wonderful thing that can be spoken about is love; there is nothing more useful to learn about."[198] Jews and pagans display great gifts of mind, but love alone saves. Love makes all pious practices worthy; it separates the good from the bad.

Tauler's teaching on love is based on an initial distinction between interior love of God and exterior love of neighbor. Both are necessary. Following tradition, he insists that "[t]rue divine love that you have within can be known and understood from the exterior love that you have for your neighbor" (408.20–21). Practically, this means sharing as much as we can with others, showing acts of kindness to them, bearing with their shortcomings, and refraining from judging them. The quality of our brotherly love demonstrates whether our inward love is properly directed to God, just as the knowledge (*kunst*) found in inner love enables it to set the proper order between the inner and outer (408.32–409.19). The quality of inner love, Tauler says, can be measured by our reaction to suffering. When we find ourselves in the midst of suffering, begging God's mercy and praying for eventual salvation is certainly a good reaction, "but a person who has true love casts himself, and his judgment and faults, into God with a loving sinking into his well-pleasing good will, [and] in true rejection of one's self-will; true divine love causes renunciation of self and all self-will."[199] Inner love, then, is really absolute releasement.

The love that causes us to sink into the Beloved encounters two things in the process: first, hindrance to love in the form of sin and the temptation that leads to it; and second, the joy and delight that we take in God. Tauler's emphasis on self-naughting leads him to reverse what we would expect here. Temptation, though not sin itself, should be welcomed out of love for God, because the suffering we endure in conformity to God's will is important for our purification. With regard to delight in God, if he chooses to withdraw it from us, we should accept this in perfect detachment and rejoice in this deprivation (410.10–411.9). In the final part of V 76 Tauler says he will speak of "another love that is higher above this love than the heaven is above the earth" (411.10–11). This is a form of totally apophatic love reminiscent of the annihilating love of Marguerite Porete, or of what Eckhart says about "unspiritual love" (see Pr. 83). We have already examined this final part of the homily above. It suffices here to underline the fact that this section (411.9–412.26) demonstrates that love, from its positive exterior form to its most interior, annihilated, nonexistent form as emptiness, unknowing, and divine darkness, is the dynamism that powers the entire process of sinking into indistinct union in the ground.

In a number of sermons Tauler employs some of the itineraries of love created by the mystics of the twelfth century to give sharper relief to the stages in the advance to the dark love of union. Richard of St. Victor, in his treatise *The Four Degrees of Violent Charity*, had set forth an itinerary of four stages: wounding love (*amor vulnerans*), binding love (*amor ligans*), languishing love (*amor languens*), or the love that makes ill, and dying love (*amor deficiens*).[200] Tauler adopts this schema in several sermons, notably V 61, the second sermon for the Nativity of John the Baptist. (This sermon has been discussed above for its teaching on the ground and mutual abyss.) In analyzing how we can bear witness to the light of Christ in the faculty that enables us to love and to will, Tauler introduces an extended discussion of Richard's four kinds of violent love (333.7–335.31). "It is wounding love (*wundende minne*) that leads you into the ground, . . . but when you come into the deep hidden abyss in binding love (*gevangene minne*), you must let love have its way."[201] Picking up on the intensity and violence that Richard had described so effectively, Tauler insists that in this state one must be a slave to love. Any space given to our own thoughts will result in our declining back to the stage of wounding love. "After this comes agonizing love (*qwelende minne*), and in the fourth place frenzied love (*rasende minne*)." (Tauler's translation slightly alters Richard's terms.) Richard had understood the fourth stage both subjectively, as a state of permanent desire, an *epektasis* in which the soul "thirsts and drinks, but its drinking does not extinguish its thirst,"[202] and objectively, as a love so insane that it gives up erotic union with God (stage 3) in order to return to the saving work of love of neighbor. Tauler is not interested in stage 3, and he interprets stage 4 in terms of his own teaching on passivity. Frenzied love "makes him disturbed in all the faculties; he longs after love and does not know that he has it; it consumes his very marrow and blood." Tauler insists that in this attack of love, external works would only be a distraction—"all human activities must give way." "Our Lord comes and speaks a word right through us, a word that is more noble and more telling than a hundred thousand human words."[203]

At this point Tauler refers to Dionysius's teaching about the Eternal Word spoken in the ground of the soul that is one with God, in union though not in its essence (334.13–18).[204] He cites other key authorities on total transformation in God: Christ's prayer, "Father, may they be one as we are one" (John 17:11); and God's word to Augustine, "You must be changed into me" (*Conf.* 7.10.16). It is clear, therefore, that Tauler believes that the fourth degree of violent love (he continues to emphasize the violent and ravishing nature of this inner assault [e.g., 335.9–17]) is identical with union with God in the ground. Tauler's other appeals to Richard's four degrees, while not as richly developed, suggest the same.[205]

In his second sermon for the Thirteenth Sunday after Trinity (V 54)

Tauler turns to Bernard of Clairvaux for help. The abbot had distinguished sweet love (*suesse minne*), wise love (*wise minne*), and strong love (*starke minne*) in his *Sermons on the Song of Songs* 20.3. Tauler sees in these three types another itinerary of love leading to union. God pours sweet love into the senses and imagination to attract the soul to himself. We should humbly accept this gift, recognizing that it is only by means of images and outer practices that we eventually penetrate into the ground where we find the kingdom of God (248.13–31). Wise, or rational, love is much more wonderful (248.32–249.27). Tauler describes it as a form of union with God in which the essential inclination turns to eternal things, specifically to the eternal birth in which the Son proceeds from the Father and the Holy Spirit flows from both Father and Son. In this state, contemplation of the vast divide between time and eternity leads "love to elevate itself into detachment and become equal to wise love and to surpass all images, forms, and likenesses, through images passing beyond images."[206] This form of love involves both the birth of the Word in the soul, and sinking down and melting away in the divine darkness as God's light shines in the soul's ground (249.27–250.6). At this point, Tauler digresses to attack the "Free Spirits" (*die frijen geiste*), who bask in their own false light and mistaken passivity.

At the end of V 54 (251.1–253.23) Tauler turns to strong love. Although the treatment of wise love might be thought to express full union with God, Tauler considers it only the entryway into the total annihilation that he identifies with strong love. In the final stage of love, "the soul has no support and must sink and drown in the divine abyss in which it loses itself. . . ."[207] Tauler appeals to the example of the prophet Elijah's (3 Kgs. 19:12–13) becoming aware of God's presence at the entrance to the cave and covering his head to mask all his faculties, "so that God must do everything in him, knowing in him, loving in him, because when he is plunged in this strong love into the Beloved in whom he is lost, he is like a drop of water in the deep sea, and is become more one with him than the air is united with the sun's brightness at noonday."[208] Tauler goes on to describe some of the aspects of this deepest union, especially the way in which it makes Christ's passion more dear to the soul than ever (251.33–252.2), and how it provides the person with a seemingly whole new way of living in which things great and small become equal. Strong love is both ecstatic and apophatic: "And so strong love exerts its force. It compels and draws the soul so that it makes a leap above and wants to go beyond itself in an unknowing that restrains it for a time in a state of unconsciousness and then brings it again into a consciousness of its own nothingness."[209]

In surveying Tauler's view of love's role in union, it is obvious that the

Strassburg preacher was not interested in many contemporary issues, such as the relation of love and knowledge. Likewise, although most of his sermons were delivered to nuns and beguines, his references to bridal language and use of the Song of Songs is relatively rare.[210] What Tauler did preach was the role of violent, strong divine love in driving the soul to total self-denial, and even further into the annihilation of the ground. Though he used the categories of Richard and Bernard, his apophatic view of love's power is different from theirs.

Tauler's originality in dealing with the stages leading to union is most evident when we turn to his teaching on the three forms of union that mark the height of the mystical path: ecstasy-affliction-identity. Toward the end of V 39 Tauler introduces these three stages in the following words:

> Now we want to speak about three stages, a lowest, a middle, and highest stage. The first stage of an inward, virtuous life, which can lead us to lofty nearness to God, is when a person turns himself totally to God's wonderful works and the manifestations of the inexpressible gifts and outflowings of God's hidden goodness. From this is born the state called "jubilation." The second state is poverty of spirit, when in strange way God withdraws himself from the soul, leaving it in a painful deprivation. The third is a transformation [*übervart*] into divine being in the union of the created spirit with the self-existent Spirit of God, which can be called an essential conversion.[211]

This passage summarizes a triple pattern that appears elsewhere in the Dominican's sermons, though all three stages are not always given full treatment.

Tauler was aware, both from scripture (e.g., Paul's rapture in 1 Cor. 12) and from the lives of contemporary mystics, of the role of rapture in mystical consciousness. In V 67 he speaks of a young married woman he knew "whose essential inclination launched itself to a height where her own ground was uncovered and revealed. There she beheld in ineffable clarity the unattainable infinite height [of God's love], and its endless length, and breadth, and depth—all without ground."[212] In a number of places Tauler employs the technical vocabulary of ecstasy, not only the term *jubilacio/ jubilieren*,[213] but also such verbs as *entzücken, entziehen/erziehen, geziehen*, and the like.[214] As the discussion of the first stage in V 39 shows, Tauler seems to think of jubilation as open to many who undertake the spiritual life. He says that it is attained by reflection on God's gifts, both in nature and in salvation history.[215] This is the means by which God attracts us and draws us out of ourselves. "When a person reflects on all this with love, a great active joy will be born in her, and if she looks upon this with true love, she will overflow with so much inner joy that the weak body cannot contain it, and it breaks out in its own wonderful way."[216] Tauler speaks of this state as "an inner embrace in experiential union" (*ein innerlich umbevang in bevintlicher vereinunge* [160.25–26]). Pleasant as the experience is, he goes on to praise a brother who voluntarily gave up God's offer of a divine kiss in order to be free to pray for sinners and the souls in purgatory (160.33–161.7). This suggests the superiority of the second stage, that of mystical dereliction.

Tauler was by no means the first to see *getrenge* (distress, anguish, desolation, affliction) as crucial for attaining union with God.[217] Gregory the Great had a deep appreciation for the role of anguish and inner suffering in the mystical life, as can be seen from his *Moral Commentary on Job*. Exegeting Job 4:13, Eliphaz's account of seeing God "in the horror of a vision by night" (*in horrore visionis nocturnae*), he said: "The human soul is lifted high by the engine of contemplation so that the more it gazes on things higher than itself the more it is filled with terror."[218] Tauler also sees Job as an exemplar of mystical dereliction and explictly cites Gregory's Job commentary several places in describing the role of suffering.[219] Meister Eckhart emphasized divine hiddenness, but not the anguish of the believer in the face of the mystery of God who seems to draw away and abandon his lovers. Many thirteenth-century female mystics, however, experienced estrangement, suffering, and a sense of desolation in their mystical journey, even to the extent of feeling totally abandoned by God in the pains of hell.[220] Some of these women, such as Angela of Foligno, Tauler could not have known; but he had read *The Flowing Light of the Godhead*, Mechthild of Magdeburg's collection of mystical visions and narratives. Mechthild's accounts of how she endured estrangement from God (*gotesvremedung*), as well as a sense of rejection (*verworfenheit*), are among the most powerful in mystical literature.[221] These texts, and doubtless the experiences of many of his spiritual charges, helped Tauler to see the importance not just of physical suffering but of the inner torture of being abandoned by God.

Returning to V 39, this is how Tauler describes the second stage of the mystical three steps. After a person has been fortified by the milk of spiritual sweetness, he is ready for stronger food. Tauler continues:

> He is led along a very wild path, totally dark and foreign. On this road God takes away from him everything that he ever gave him. The person is left so much alone that he knows nothing of God, and he comes into such distress [*getrenge*] that he is not sure if he was ever right, or if he ever had a God or not, even whether he really exists or not. He is so strongly afflicted that the wide world seems too narrow for him.[222]

This form of "dark night," to use a later but not inappropriate term, Tauler expects to be the lot of all those who really seek God down to the ground. Like Mechthild before him, he counsels the soul caught in such straits to welcome the estrangement—"Sit down and say, 'Welcome, Bitter Affliction'" (161.23–24). In conformity with John of the Cross after him, he says that during this trial we must cling to the rock of faith (161.25–26). Like some of the women mystics who endured similar experiences of dereliction, Tauler tries to give a sense of what it is like by a concrete comparison. "It is as if a person were hemmed in between two walls with a sword behind him and a sharp spear in front" (161.20–22).

Again and again Tauler dwells on the experience of mystical affliction. We are not told how much this may have reflected his own life of prayer, but it is clear that he felt the message was essential for his audience. It was also important for later readers, not least Luther, who found in Tauler's *getrenge* an analogue for his own sense of the torturous absence that God imposes in order to bring prideful humans to the proper sense of their own absolute neediness. The reformer's comments on a number of Tauler's sermons indicate how much sympathy he had with this side of the Dominican's message.[223]

It would scarcely be possible to survey the dozens of sermons where Tauler expatiates on *getrenge*, what he once tellingly called the "night-work" (*arbeit der nachte* [V 63 (345.12)]). Brief comments about several sermons will provide some sense of the richness of his teaching. In V 3 for the Feast of Epiphany the preacher distinguishes three forms of myrrh: the myrrh of detachment from the world; the myrrh of inner and outer suffering; and "the very bitter myrrh that God gives, inner anguish and darkness" (*indewendig getrenge und indewendig vinsternisse* [19.5]). No one knows this suffering who has not experienced it. It must not be resisted inwardly or outwardly, because such a trial is worth more than all consolations (19.5–33). In V 9 Tauler uses the Canaanite woman (Matt. 15:21–28), who refused to be put off by Jesus' rejection, as a model for the soul who is driven and harassed by God but continues to cry out to God in humility (43.22–45.10). In the second sermon for Corpus Christi (V 31) Tauler describes three degrees of worthiness that prepare one for the reception of the sacrament. The first is to suffer all assaults from the world in true releasement and silence (313.14–17). This is certainly adequate, but there are two higher stages. The first, which is attained by knowledge and experience, is renunciation and annihilation of self (*entsetzen und entwerdende* [314.2–3]). The second, which is attained by experience without knowledge, is "inward anguish which is born from renunciation" (*das inwendige getrenge das geborn wurt von der entsetzunge* [314.3–4]). Later in the sermon Tauler gives an extended analysis of this dereliction as our way of proclaiming the death of the Lord until he comes (314.30–315.25).

One of Tauler's most powerful presentations of mystical dereliction is found in V 37, a homily on the parable of the woman with the ten drachmas (Luke 15:8–10).[224] The woman signifies God's divinity, the lost drachma is the soul imprinted with God's image, and the lantern with which she searches for it is Christ's human nature. Divine Wisdom lights the lantern of love and turns the house upside down in search of the lost coin, but the lantern of love is not experienced as delight but rather as torturing love. Tauler says:

> This is love, that a person is on fire in seeking and in lacking, and in a feeling of being abandoned. One remains in constant torment, but content to be tormented. In this torment a person is melted and consumed by the fire of desire, yet is in equal contentment. This is love; it is not what you imagine it to be. It is the lighting of the lantern.[225]

The preacher quotes Christ's command "If anyone wants to follow me, let him deny himself and come to me" (Matt. 16:24) as a model for the self-denial we must practice in the face of affliction sent by God (145.26–146.6).

One other example must suffice here.[226] In V 47 Tauler discusses three paths to God. The first is to live without vainglory and to come to the aid of our neighbor. The second is to use the loving image of Christ as the model for all our actions, following Christ crucified in all things (209.22–211.24). The third path is beyond all images. Tauler describes it as follows:

> [It is] a way that is rapid, direct, dark, unknown, foreign. . . . On it women become men and every man who does not follow God becomes nothing. This path is certainly very dark, because everything we spoke about previously is taken away and has no more attraction. Where it leads is not known; then everything is in great anguish, and the path for those on it is totally covered in darkness, as St. Gregory says on this passage [i.e., Job 3:23], a person finds himself deprived of knowing.[227]

The analysis of the third way that follows (212.4–214.5) is one of Tauler's longest accounts of mystical dereliction. It is especially interesting for showing how this "small narrow path" (*smale enge weg* [213.6]) treads the middle way between knowledge and ignorance by means of simple faith, between security and insecurity by hope, between peace of spirit and unrest of nature by releasement, and between presumption and fear by humility (212.13–213.10). The distress and disquiet found in this state cause many to seek for external aid, such as going on pilgrimage, or some other good work, but Tauler says only patience and following in Christ's footsteps will allow us to endure it (213.21–214.5).

The way of dereliction would be unbearable without Christ. Although

Job is an exemplar of this dark night, he functions as a type for Jesus, who sweated blood in the Garden and experienced dereliction on the cross. Tauler paraphrases Paul's passage about having the knowledge (*kunst*) of Christ (Eph. 3:19) to indicate the experience of dereliction. "He was the most forsaken of all although he was the most pleasing to the Father, when he cried out, 'God, God, my God, why have you forsaken me!' (Matt. 27:46). He was at that moment more forsaken and more bitter than any saint ever was."[228] We can note one final characteristic of the stage of dereliction, one not unexpected. In this hellish state, true releasement means that the soul is willing to suffer forever in hell itself, should that be God's will—the *resignatio ad infernum* motif (see Rom. 9:3) found in many late medieval mystics.[229]

Both ecstatic *jubilacio* and (paradoxically) terrible *getrenge* are progressive stages of union with God, who remains present within the ground of the soul. They lead to the deepest form of union, what V 39 spoke of as "a transformation into divine being in the union of the created spirit with the self-existent Spirit of God" (160.3–4). Tauler describes this relatively briefly toward the end of the sermon (161.34–162.22). The terrible trials of the second stage are the necessary preparation for the third stage, which is like the passage from death to life (162.3–4). The preacher continues:

> In this stage the Lord lifts a person up out of self and into him. He consoles him for all his suffering and heals his wounds. God raises him from a human mode of life to a divine one, out of all sorrow into divine security, and a person becomes so divinized that everything that he is and does, God is and does in him. He is lifted up so far beyond his natural mode of being that he becomes by grace what God is by nature. In this state a person feels himself lost; he neither knows, nor feels, nor experiences himself. He knows nothing beyond one simple essence.[230]

In this form of union, says Tauler, up and down lose all sense, because the deeper we penetrate into the depths of humility, the higher we climb— "deep and high mean the same thing" (162.17–18).

This passage is typical of Tauler's attempts to describe the supreme form of union. Three things should be noted. First, the Strassburg preacher uses traditional language of divinization, as well as expressions of a union of identity, or indistinction, found in Eckhart. Second, Tauler emphasizes that this union is totally the result of divine activity and grace, not something that can be achieved by human effort and awareness.[231] Third, like Suso, Tauler held that in this state the mystic is *unaware* of self, but he does not deny that some distinction remains between God and the self in an objective, ontological sense.

Tauler's accounts of the third stage of union are so many and so varied there can be no question of trying to survey them all.[232] A look at a few of the most important will flesh out the three points just mentioned. For example, in V 7 Tauler has a rich description of the lack of distinction that the mystic experiences when all practices and intermediaries fall away in the deepest and sweetest union. "The spirit," he says, "is sunk in God into divine unity so that it loses all distinction. Everything that it brought there—its humility, its intention, its very self—loses its name, and there is only a bare, silent, mysterious unity without any distinction."[233] A similarly Eckhartian expression of *unitas indistinctionis* is found in V 11 (54.27–55.16), where the language of the ground and the desert is prominent. Tauler's use of the Eckhartian phrase *ein einig ein,* noted above, speaks to the same sense of being united to God as truly and as deeply as the Son and Spirit are united to the Father (like Eckhart, Tauler sometimes cites Christ's prayer for unity in John 17:21 in this connection).[234] Following other fourteenth-century German mystics, Tauler uses a wide variety of verbs for hinting at what happens in this indescribable state: *vereinen* (to be united), *sich-verlieren* (to lose oneself), *versinken* (to sink down), *ertrinken* (to drown), *verschmolzen* (to melt), *verwandeln* and *überformen* (to be transformed).[235]

Many of Tauler's expressions of the union of indistinction, especially those relating the melting of the two abysses into one, are quite as daring as those of Eckhart. In V 56, shortly after quoting Eckhart, he says: "Who then could make a separation in this divine and supernatural union in which the spirit is pulled and drawn into the abyss of its origin? Know that if it were possible to see the spirit in the Spirit, one would without doubt see it as God himself."[236] Nevertheless, while human vision could not help but see the divinized soul as God—*if it could see it at all,* and while human consciousness has no awareness of anything but indistinction in this third stage, Tauler insists that the substances of God and human remain distinct on the ontological level. In V 15, commenting on Jesus' prayer of union in John 17:21, Tauler says that the union is not something accidental in God, but it remains beyond all understanding (69.11–22). In V 32 he again says that the union surpasses all understanding, and vehemently rejects the heretical view of union as being changed into God without qualification. He says:

> Some silly fools take this in a fleshly way and say that they will be changed into the divine nature, but this is wicked, false heresy. In the highest, most inward, closest union with God, his divine nature and his being are still infinitely high above every height. This is in the divine abyss where no creature ever was or will be.[237]

This is the sense in which Tauler understands a standard tag from the mystical tradition he often cites. "In this union," he says, "the soul becomes totally God-hued, God-like, divine. By grace she becomes everything that God is by nature."[238] Everything we gain in union comes from God's grace. This overwhelming gift leads to a state in which, from our perspective, we can see no difference between the self and God. But God still remains far beyond what we can see or understand in his unfathomable abyss.[239] Difference always remains along with—and higher than—identity.[240]

In presenting the difference between true and false understandings of mysticism, Tauler contrasts the Friends of God who are the pillars of the church with the false mystics who pretend to have attained freedom and union, but who are actually still caught in their own self-will. In the wake of Eckhart's condemnation, and the confused appeals that many were making to his deep speculation, Tauler, like Suso, felt compelled to rebut those who misunderstood and misused the Meister.[241] Though modern scholarship has undermined the concept of an international and widespread heretical sect of the Free Spirit, the evidence provided by Tauler and other mystics indicates that they were deeply concerned about those, however many or few, who mistook their satisfaction in their own inner states for the self-negation and releasement that would provide the emptiness that only God could fill.

Tauler distinguished between those, on the one hand, who were in error, or led astray, about mystical states of consciousness, and on the other hand, the "free spirits" (*frije geiste* [219.1 and 250.4]), who were dangerous heretics. A number of his comments deal with the former, such as when he counsels some people to remember that only God and no creature can effect inner freedom (V 2 [14.11–19]), or when he talks about the dangers of depending on reason and not following Christ when one has a strong longing for anni- hilation (V 5 [22.21–23.8]).[242] Four passages explicitly single out pernicious error and heresy. The first is the sharp comment already noted about those who claimed that in mystical union we are physically changed into God (V 32 [121.26–28]). A brief but equally stinging remark in V 54 (250.4–8) attacks the "free spirits" for their dependence on their own "false illumina- tions" and "false passivity."

Tauler explains his position in more detail in sermons V 40 and V 48. A fundamental concern in these discussions is the difference between true and false freedom.[243] In V 40 the Dominican emphasizes, once again, the need to pass beyond our own possessive delight in the natural light of reason if we would learn to appreciate God's true workings in the ground of the soul. Those who cannot get beyond reason will neglect the virtues, reveling in a false passivity that is not combined with active charity. According to Tauler, the devil then can easily lead them further astray into unchastity, avarice, or pride—the false freedom in which they follow their natural inclinations and think they are serving God (167.6–25). The discussion of erroneous mysticism in V 48 (218.11–219.4) expands on this, noting that for forty years heretics who have fallen into false freedom and passivity and claimed to go beyond the practice of the virtues have been a nuisance and danger. This passage displays Tauler's knowledge of the condemnation of the beghards and beguines at the Council of Vienne in 1311; it probably also reflects his own pastoral experience.

For the proper understanding of the deepest form of mystical union Tauler returned to biblical models. If Job was a good exemplar of the second stage of mystical union, Tauler, like Gregory the Great, found the prophet Elijah a model for the deeper encounter of indistinction. In the Third Book of Kings (3 Kgs. 19:11–13) the word of the Lord came to the prophet as he dwelt in a cave on Mount Horeb, instructing him to await a divine visitation. First came a great wind, breaking the rocks; then an earthquake, and a fire. But God was in none of these. Finally, when Elijah heard the whistling of a gentle breeze, he covered his face with his mantle, knowing that the Lord was present. Gregory the Great used this incident in his *Moralia* to indicate the secret nature of God's coming to the soul.[244] Tauler follows Gregory's allegorization of the passage at length in V 50, and more cursorily in three other sermons,[245] to show the passivity, brevity, and incomprehensibility of mystical union. "The Lord came like a flash of lightning," he says. "The flash was beyond all measurement. It was so intense that Elijah stood in the entrance to the cave and drew his mantle over his eyes." According to Tauler, the cave signifies human incapacity, and the entrance is the moment of seeing God. "The reason he drew the mantle over his eyes, brief and rapid though it was," Tauler says, "is because it is a flash surpassing all natural things and mere nature cannot bear or conceive of it."[246]

The final and deepest stage of union, like a prism, reflects many of the distinctive themes of Tauler's teaching, some already studied, and a few that can be added now. As we have seen, union is divinizing, and the Strassburg preacher often uses this kind of language.[247] Union also implies annihilation of the self, a basic theme of all Tauler's preaching. Verbs signifying "self-denial" (e.g., *ein gantz verloeucken sin selbes* [24.31]), and even stronger terms, such as *vernúten* (annihilate), *entbilden* (dis-image), *entformen* (un-form), and especially *entwerden* (un-become) are frequent in these sermons, especially in descriptions of union.[248] "If you want to become God, you must un-become yourself" (*Solt du in Got gewerden, so muost du din selbes entwerden*

[295.33–34]). Such annihilation is the fusing of our own created and there-fore deficient nothing with the transcendent Nothing that is God. "So sinks the created nothing in the Uncreated Nothing," as V 41 puts it.[249] The sink-ing into indistinct union is characterized as a state of unknowing (*unwissen/ unbekentnisse*) whose description Tauler, like many others, took from Diony-sius.[250]

Tauler also uses positive metaphors to help understand whatever can be understood of union and the path to it. He rarely makes use of the language of "breakthrough" (*durchbruch*) that had been popular with Eckhart. When he does employ the word, it is generally not in terms of union with God, as when he speaks of breaking through our nature, and the like (48.14–15, 86.16, 258.11, 417.8). Only one sermon seems to use the term more mysti-cally. In V 54 he speaks of breaking through into the ground (248.29) and breaking through by means of the life of Jesus Christ (250.19–20).[251] A posi-tive metaphor for mystical consciousness that Tauler employed more often was the notion of the *blik*, or "divine lightning flash," seen in V 50 above. Mystical illuminations, often understood as flashes, had a background in scripture and in tradition. Tauler seems to have used the image because it emphasized the divine initiative in suddenly lifting up a person to final union after a period of trial and distress.[252] Another metaphor Tauler employs, one also found in Eckhart,[253] is the identification of union in the ground with the kingdom of heaven, particularly with the use of the text, "The kingdom of heaven is within you" (Luke 17:21).[254] V 66, preached on the text "Seek first the Kingdom of God and his justice" (Matt. 6:33), is devoted to seeking God hidden in *der grund der sele*.[255]

A more pervasive Eckhartian theme, which we have also seen in Suso, is describing union in terms of the inner birth (*geburt*). Although Tauler does not use the motif of birthing as frequently as Eckhart did, it still appears in about twenty of his sermons, though usually not as the main theme.[256] At times, Tauler speaks of the birth in a trinitarian way that is virtually identi-cal to what we find in Eckhart, as in V 29 where he says:

> This witness one finds in the ground without images; certainly in this ground the Heavenly Father gave birth to his Only-Begotten Son a hundred thousand times quicker than the blinking of an eye. . . . The paternal power comes and calls a person into himself through his Only-Begotten Son, and just as the Son is born from the Father and flows back into him, so too a person is born of the Father in the Son and flows again into the Father with the Son and becomes one with him.[257]

More often, however, Tauler speaks in a general way of the birth that takes place in the soul through the action of the Holy Spirit. V 28, for example,

exegetes John 3:5 (being born again of water and the Spirit) as the acceptance of our own water of unlikeness (*ungeliche*) gradually leading us
through the likeness (*geliche*) of the Holy Spirit to eventual absorption in
God where all likeness and unlikeness disappear (116.27–117.20).[258]

One way that Tauler speaks of the deepest form of union with God in the
ground is to describe it as pure, interior prayer. Tauler discusses inner
prayer in a number of homilies,[259] and it forms the theme for one of his
most impressive sermons, the first sermon for the Fifth Sunday after Trinity
(V 39) on the text "Beloved, be single-minded in prayer" (1 Pet. 3:8). While
the second part of this sermon (159–63) lays out the three stages of mystical
advance considered above, the first part (154–59), detailing the nature of
true prayer, shows the close connection between union and prayer.

Tauler begins the homily by setting out four themes: what is prayer; its
essence; its method; and where one ought to pray (154.14–15). Prayer is
defined as the raising of the essential inclination (*gemuete*) to God, and we
are told to pray in the spirit with all our attention focused on God, the
single-mindedness of the Petrine text (154.19–155.12). The preacher's main
concern is the proper method for true prayer, which consists not in exterior
devotions, which can often get in the way, but in "self-recollection and turning into the inward ground with the essential inclination lifted up and elevated faculties, inwardly gazing upon God's presence" (155.26–28). All
external practices should serve this end, the way the many workers on a
cathedral all strive to one purpose, building God's house, which is the
house of prayer (155.31–156.11). True spiritual prayer is far superior to
external prayer, but Tauler says there are people so well practiced (*wol geue-
bet*) that they can combine the two without hindrance. He adds:

> It belongs to a truly essential, inward, and transfigured person that activity
> and [inner] delight are one, and the one does not hinder the other, just as it is
> in God. There the highest form of all activity and the purest delight of all is a
> Single One one without hindrance—each exists in the highest degree and they
> do not hinder each other. The activity is in the Persons, and the delight
> belongs to the simple essence.[260]

For Tauler, then, true prayer is a form of union with God that allows the
mystic to combine action and contemplation, to unify inner and outer
prayer, and to share in the supreme activity of the trinitarian processions at
the same time as one delights in the essential unity of the Single One (*ein
einig ein*).

This possibility is rooted in humanity's nature as *imago Dei*. All our faculties have a proper object in the created universe, but when they are turned
totally toward God, then "action will also be godlike" (*des werk würden also*

goetlich [157.13]). The exemplar for this supreme gift of unifying inner contemplation with outward godlike action is "our Lord Jesus Christ," whose higher faculties were always blessed with the vision of God while his lower powers were active in doing and suffering (157.12–23). The "noble intimate friends of God," those who best imitate Christ, are the ones who truly realize humanity's likeness to God in uniting action and inner enjoyment. "This is an interior desire to gaze on God's presence. In its inwardness it possesses a delight [in God], while outwardly, from the same and into the same intention, it turns itself actively to the benefit and usefulness of all."[261] Tauler compares this process to the master builder who plans and organizes everything through his apprentices, although he does not do the actual work himself (158.8–16). Such perfect harmony of inner and outer characterizes holy church as the Mystical Body of Christ (158.24–159.28). This final point makes clear once again that Tauler's understanding of mystical union is thoroughly ecclesial.

Conclusion

John Tauler's mysticism was not concerned with Meister Eckhart's philosophico-theological explorations of the divine nature and the metaphysics of the ground. Nevertheless, if we can characterize Eckhart's mysticism as centered on the explosive metaphor of the *grunt*, the fused identity of God and human, then it is correct to say that Tauler's mysticism was in many ways Eckhartian, though this does not lessen the originality and lasting influence of the Strassburg preacher.

Tauler's originality is evident on several fronts. For one thing, he rooted his mysticism in the life of the church, especially its sacramental practice, far more deeply than had Eckhart. For another, Tauler filled out Eckhart's radical view of a this-worldly mysticism in which there was no essential conflict between action and contemplation in a more concrete way than the Meister had. Further, Tauler is perhaps the most consistently christological of the great German mystics—the following of Christ pervades the entire path to union. As his sermon on Jesus' call to Matthew puts it: "When a person has left all things and himself in all things, he should follow upon God-Christ above all things with his outer person in the exercise of all the virtues and in universal love, and also with his inner person in complete releasement of self in everything that happens to him, however God acts upon him within and without."[262] Tauler understood the following of Christ as including an experience of mystical dereliction foreign to Eckhart, but present in other late medieval mystics, especially women. Beyond the stage of anguish and dereliction, on the level of indistinct union, Tauler both used Eckhart's language and also sought to qualify the more daring ways in which the Meister had expressed the union of indistinction.[263]

While John Tauler was deeply influenced by Eckhart, he is and remains John Tauler, the Strassburg *lebmeister*. His place in the history of Christian mysticism is assured, as those who have profited from reading his sermons over the centuries will attest. Tauler's message, repetitive as it can sometimes be, has a steadiness and humaneness that make him one of the most accessible of all Christian mystics.

PART 3

Mysticism for the Many
in Late Medieval Germany

CHAPTER 7 🔲

Spreading the Message: The Diffusion of Mysticism in Late Medieval Germany

I T IS NOT POSSIBLE to give a full survey of all aspects of late
medieval German mysticism. The sheer amount of evidence pre-
cludes any brief attempt at total coverage. Other problems also
impede a synoptic presentation. Many texts exist only in old editions
from the nineteenth and early twentieth centuries; others have not
been edited. Aside from major works, such as the *Theologia deutsch*,
only a few texts are available in languages other than their original
MHG. Although the *Verfasserlexikon* (VL) of German literature in the
Middle Ages provides a valuable tool for introducing this broad
stream of mystical literature,[1] detailed studies of many texts are lacking. Furthermore, many of the mystical sermons, treatises, and poems
are anonymous and difficult to date.

The wealth of mystical texts from late medieval Germany is
impressive both for quantity and often for quality. Even in comparison with Eckhart, Suso, and Tauler, many of these texts hold their
own as significant monuments in the history of mysticism, not only to
what I have called the mysticism of the ground, but also to other
forms of mystical expression—erotic, didactic, monastic, and more.[2]
Furthermore, it has become increasingly clear that the investigation of
medieval mysticism cannot be confined to prose works, or even to the
realm of written evidence. From early centuries, there has been an
important relation between spirituality and art in Christianity, especially because in the economy of the incarnation God took on visibility as a man. Even in the case of mysticism, with its claims to make

A special word of thanks to my friend Frank Tobin for valuable assistance with this
chapter, particularly with regard to translations of MHG texts.

contact with the invisible and unknowable God, there were images from the patristic and early medieval periods that can be read as having a connection, at least implicitly, with mystical traditions. The expansion of explicitly mystical images and programs in the late Middle Ages, many of great originality, make the study of art an integral part of the investigation of mysticism. Images were more than just illustrations for texts, but were themselves independent modes of communicating mystical teaching, though image and text often went together. The first section of this chapter, therefore, will look at some examples of the interaction of art and mysticism from the fourteenth and fifteenth centuries. Although this topic has already been touched upon in considering Henry Suso, the Dominican's role as a mystical iconographer is symptomatic of a broader movement in which mystics turned to art to invoke the transformation into God that is the goal of the mystical path.

The second and longer section of this chapter will consider select examples of a variety of literary genres employed by late medieval German mystics, such as poems, sermons, letters, dialogues, saints' lives, and visionary accounts. (A survey of some important mystical treatises will be given in chapter 8.) One of the reasons that Germany in the fourteenth and fifteenth centuries witnesses what I have called a harvest of mysticism can be found in the profusion of literary forms in which mystical consciousness was communicated to a broad, and increasingly lay, audience. The notion of genre in the Middle Ages, of course, was quite fluid. Many mystical texts come down to us in manuscripts that the Germans call *mystische Sammelhandschriften*, that is, mystical collections that contain several genres.[3] Nevertheless, an analysis of select examples of different, if often intermingling, forms of dissemination of mystical teaching illustrates how widespread the hunger for spiritual literature actually was.

Despite the presence of important works in Latin, by the fourteenth century it is clear that the vernacular had become the language of choice for writing about mysticism. Much of this literature continued to be written by clerics and religious, but there was an increasing production of literature for a distinctly lay audience. As Georg Steer puts it, "Book learning became popularized for a lay audience; it was laicized, . . . not secularized."[4] The desire of the laity for spiritual teaching fostered the growth of a sense, at least on the part of some, that lay people, male and female, were as fully capable of mystical insight as the learned clergy—perhaps even more so. Finally, while the fourteenth century was the age of greatest creativity, it was the fifteenth century that saw the real explosion of the copying and dissemination of mystical texts. According to Werner Williams-Krapp, 80 percent of the manuscripts written in German and Dutch during this century

contain religious literature, and 80 percent of the copies of the texts of Eckhart, Suso, Tauler, and the other major fourteenth-century mystics come
from this era.[5] These numbers provide ample reason for speaking of these
centuries as a harvest of mysticism.

Art and Mysticism in Late Medieval Germany[6]

Late medieval culture was intensely visual. The prevailing Gothic art
involved both a saturation of space by images and a new way of seeing,
according to art historian Michael Camille.[7] From the thirteenth century on
the prevailing theory of seeing was by intromission, according to which the
object sends out rays that enter the eye to be processed by the mind, thus
assuring both the object and the viewer "a dynamic role in perception."[8]
Within this new cultural situation, the relation of the visual and the visionary became more intense and reciprocal. External images could be used to
trigger internal states of consciousness of God.[9] Images were even created
to portray contemplative experiences that by definition were beyond
images, such as participation in the inner life of the Trinity. The paradox
implicit in creating images of what is beyond all image is no greater than
that of using human words to try to express what is above words—parallel
examples of the impossible yet necessary task of the mystic. Even in the
case of Meister Eckhart, as we have seen in chapter 4, the image (*imago/bild*)
remains an important, if ultimately insufficient, expression of mystical states
of awareness.

The use of images to help induce contact with God was not new in the
fourteenth century. The role of images in meditational techniques, especially as a way to excite affective empathy, is explicit from at least the
twelfth century.[10] Jeffrey Hamburger has sketched apects of the history of
"speculation," that is, seeing the invisible things of God through the visible
creation (Rom. 1:20), which, he argues, "occupies an intermediary position
in a progression of mystical perception leading from the natural to the
supernatural."[11] Mystics of the twelfth century were aware of the role of
images and the imagination in contemplation. Richard of St. Victor, in *The
Twelve Patriarchs*, says that Rachel (i.e., reason) must first have children from
her handmaid Bala, that is, imagination, before she can have offspring of
her own. "It is sweet for her [Rachel] to retain, at least by means of imagination, the memory of those things whose understanding she is not yet
capable of grasping by a reasoning process. . . . No one is ignorant that this
is the first way for all those who enter into contemplation of invisible things.
. . ."[12] Even Bernard of Clairvaux, so often seen as an enemy of art and
images, recognized that the internal "sacred image" (*sacra imago*) of the

302 The Harvest of Mysticism

events of Christ's life played an important role in binding the soul to love of virtue and hatred of vice.[13] For both Richard and Bernard, however, the use of images, external or internal, was a lower stage, at best a preparation for imageless contemplation. It was meant to be surpassed, especially by monastics, as trained experts in the higher stages of prayer.

While imageless contact with God remained an ideal for many late medieval mystics, the relation between images and states of mystical consciousness became more complex, more interactive, and less hierarchical. The case of Henry Suso discussed in chapter 5 provides one example. The shift is also evident in other mystics of the thirteenth and fourteenth centuries. An early example of the significant role of external images appears in Thomas of Celano's account found in the *First Life* of Francis's construction of the Christmas crib at Greccio. Francis summoned the pious nobleman John to make ready the tableau of the birth of Jesus with a command expressing his desire to see in the most concrete way: "I wish to enact the memory of that babe who was born in Bethlehem: to see as much as is possible with my own bodily eyes the discomfort of his infant needs. . . . " After recounting how Francis and the crowds were "overcome with wondrous joy" at the scene, Celano describes how the *poverello* preached to the people during Mass with such fervor that "a virtuous man [probably John] sees a wondrous vision," in which Francis approaches the child lying asleep in the manger and awakens him, a visualization of how the saint awakens Christ in the hearts of his listeners.[14] Here the external seeing triggers an interior, or spiritual, vision (in Augustine's terms), which in turn produces an intellectual perception of the meaning of the mission of St. Francis.

In *The Flowering of Mysticism* I noted the degree to which the late thirteenth-century Cistercian nuns of Helfta, such as Gertrude the Great, made use of devotional images in their mystical practices.[15] The distinctive biblical-liturgical mysticism created at Helfta expressed itself in visualizations, or imaginative creations, of the inner meaning of both liturgical actions and sacred images, such as statues of the Virgin, or John the Beloved resting his head on Christ's bosom, or pictures of the crucifixion and the bleeding heart of Christ. A good example of how liturgy and the reception of the Eucharist, together with visual meditation on a picture, worked together to produce a direct inner visualized contact with Christ can be found in the second book of Gertrude's *The Herald of Divine Love*. She recounts:

> After I had received the life-giving sacrament, on returning to my place to pray, it seemed to me as if on the right side of the Crucified One painted on the page, that is to say, from the wound in the side, a ray of sunlight like a sharp arrow came forth and spread itself out for a moment, drew back, and

then spread itself out again. It continued like this for a while, tenderly drawing my love.[16]

A few days after this vision/visualization, Christ appeared to Gertrude and inflicted a similar wound on her heart.

Gertrude herself wondered about the concrete and visual nature of so many of the communications she received from God. In one passage in the *Herald* she puzzles over why the Lord had instructed her with "so corporeal a vision." But the nun boldly puts the defense of such images directly in Christ's mouth. The Savior declares that just as he had instructed the prophets of old about his coming "by mystical [i.e., hidden] images and similitudes of things," so now spiritual realities can only be explained to humans "by means of similitudes of things perceived by the mind." Christ concludes: "That is why no one ought to despise what is revealed by means of bodily things, but ought to study anything that would make the mind worthy of tasting the sweetness of spiritual delights by images of bodily things."[17] Clearly, Gertrude does not consider images as an inferior mode of communication with God the way her twelfth-century predecessors did, however much she may cite them as authorities.

The proliferation of images of devotion (*Andachtsbilder*) in the late Middle Ages was an integral part of the new mysticism.[18] Designed to produce what Erwin Panofsky called "contemplative immersion" (*kontemplative Versenkung*),[19] such images depicted both the historical source of devotion in the life of Christ (especially scenes relating to the passion) and the emotional experience it sought to stimulate in the viewer's response.[20] Although not all these responses need be seen as mystical in the sense of fostering a direct and transformative encounter with God, many images were doubtless employed to this effect, as we can see from the texts in Gertrude. Passion images in particular, such as portrayals of the crucified Jesus, the *arma Christi* (instruments of the passion), the Man of Sorrows image (*Schmerzensmann*), and the *Pietà*,[21] can often be seen as pertaining to what Ewert Cousins called "the mysticism of the historical event."[22]

Other forms of religious images found in the late Middle Ages also were used to stimulate mystical transformation of consciousness. Among the most significant were portrayals of the erotic relation of Christ and the soul, whether based directly on the Song of Songs or on other forms of love imagery, such as that of the courtly tradition. Marian images could also be given mystical meaning, insofar as the viewer was encouraged to identify with Mary as supreme lover of Christ and therefore worthy to become Mother of God. Not all images of Mary need call to mind the possibility of giving birth to God in the soul (*Gottesgeburt*), but some surely could. Identi-

fication with saints, most notably John the Beloved as a model of deification, was also a feature of mystical iconography.[23] Finally, there are even
fascinating examples of images inviting the mystic into the inner life of the
Trinity.[24]

The manuscript known as the Rothschild Canticles was produced in
Flanders or the Rhineland around 1300, probably for a nun. We do not
know who the theological consultants or the artists were, but they display
remarkable genius. The Canticles, as Jeffrey Hamburger has shown,[25] is a
stunning example of the profundity and variety of late medieval mystical
art. Stylistically, the book is close to the Franco-Flemish art of the beginning
of the fourteenth century, but the Latin texts that accompany its illustrations
bring it within the ambit of the mysticism of Eckhart and his followers.

Hamburger identifies six cycles of images in the manuscript.[26] Three of
these can be directly related to aspects of late medieval mysticism. The two
cycles of scenes illustrating the Song of Songs are particularly revealing of
the role of images in late medieval mysticism. Illustrations of the Song of
Songs were not new in Western art, having begun in the eleventh century.
Up to around 1200, however, manuscript miniatures based on the Song
tend to be static and didactic, largely allegorical portrayals of Christ and the
church (e.g., pictures of Christ kissing a crowned bride), or more rarely
Christ and the individual soul portrayed as an uncrowned female figure.[27]
In the later Middle Ages, however, the hieratic and didactic elements, while
never totally abandoned, tend to diminish in relation to a narrative, more
detailed, and often more erotic mode of presentation. Though it is not possible to draw direct connections, this new iconography of mystical erotics
may be seen as an analogue to the shift from the insistence on a sharp distinction between inner and outer sensation in interpreting the Song to the
late medieval breakdown of this bifurcation in the direction of an embodied
language of sensation to describe the union of Christ and the soul.[28]

The Rothschild Canticles scenes illustrating the Song display a narrative
mode emphasizing the direct erotic potential of the biblical text.[29] The
numerous descriptive elements seem designed to help the reader take an
active part in the game of love between the Divine Bridegroom and the
love-smitten bride played out in the Song. As Hamburger puts it, "The
Song of Songs is no longer treated as a pretext for allegory," but rather "as a
dramatic account of inner experience."[30] The bold literalism of the scenes
helps elide the distinction between inner spiritual senses and outer physical
senses in the direction of what Gordon Rudy has called "spiritual sensation," that is, a unified sensorium in which direct contact with Christ is the
goal.[31] This new mode of reading the Song, pioneered by Bernard of Clairvaux, was strong in many of the women mystics studied in *The Flowering of*

Mysticism, such as Hadewijch, Mechthild of Magdeburg, and Angela of Foligno. Such direct experience was not without its critics. The thirteenth-century Franciscan spiritual writer David of Augsburg complained about visions of Christ involving quasi-physical embraces and kisses, and, as he put it, "being caressed by other less decent deeds and acts, so that just as the interior spirit is consoled by Christ or Mary, so too the exterior flesh is consoled in a physical way and carnally by a sensation of delight fitted to it."[32]

The first set of scenes from the Rothschild Canticles illustrating the Song of Songs contains five of what were originally seven illustrations. Folio 17v has a catena of verses from the Song along with several other texts (e.g., Rev. 3:20), but lacks a facing image on f. 18r (it probably would have illustrated the mystical kiss). The next opening (ff. 18v–19r: illustration 4) portrays images based on the opening catena of texts, with the upper left register illustrating first Song 2:6, the embrace of the lovers, and then Revelation 3:20, Christ inviting the bride into his dwelling place.[33] In the lower left of f. 18v we see the seated soul, like a female Longinus, wounding Christ with "one of her eyes" (Rev. 4:9). On f. 19r opposite is a daring full-page picture of a totally naked Christ showing the instruments of the passion and emphasizing the side wound through which the loving gaze of the bride can penetrate into the depths of his saving love. This accords well with a passage in a familiar Pseudo-Bernardine text, the *Mystical Vine,* which says: "Let us see through the visible wound the invisible wound of love."[34] This illustration is a potent visual version of the ancient theme of the wound of love (*vulnus amoris*).

The following four openings continue the program, though illustrations survive in only three cases. In each opening the left side contains a small anthology of texts, mostly from the Song of Songs, and the right side features illustrations of the different aspects of the encounter between the Bridegroom and the bride. Obviously, the user of the book was meant to employ both pictures and text in a meditative practice designed to lead to deeper personal appropriation of loving union with Christ. Bernard of Clairvaux had once invited his readers into a new kind of intertextuality in which the book of the Bible and the book of experience were meant to mutually illuminate each other in the quest for deeper consciousness of God.[35] In the Rothschild Canticles this is carried a step further. Here sacred texts, from both the Bible and elsewhere, are used in conjunction with original, often unprecedented, illustrations to induce states of mystical rapture that are suggested by the frequent appearance of figures in the miniatures that gaze toward and point to the illustrations with gestures of amazement.

A second set of illustrations to the Song of Songs, found at folios 65v–73r, consists of five openings and four surviving sets of pictures. These scenes also illustrate a personal erotic encounter with Jesus. Folio 66r (illustration 5A), for example, has a full-page picture of the bride awakening on her bed to welcome the descent of the Bridegroom from heaven, a scene illustrating a number of Song texts about the bride's flight and rest at midday (Song 1:6; 8:14), as well as Hosea 3:3, a text Bernard of Clairvaux had used to indicate the Word's taking on of flesh and coming into the world.[36] The catena on the facing page emphasizes the need for personal experience of union with the Incarnate Word, citing a passage from Augustine's *Confessions* that notes that the desire for mystical encounter is a result of God's grace, not our own effort: "My God, I summon you into my soul, which you prepare to grasp you from the desire you breathe into her."[37] The following group of texts and pictures (ff. 67v–68r) illustrates passages from the Song of Songs in a literal fashion, showing the bride adorned with flowers lying in the garden, sick with love for the Bridegroom (Song 2:5). Below this is a picture of the Groom inviting the bride into his wine cellar to enjoy mystical inebriation (Song 2:4). On ff. 69v–70r two scenes in three registers illustrate Song 2:7 and related texts, while f. 71v contains a series of passages from Proverbs and the Song of Songs, but without a facing illustration. Finally, ff. 72v–73r have a catena of passages mostly drawn from the Song facing a full-page picture of the mystical goal, Christ's crowning of the soul based on the popular imagery of the coronation of the Blessed Virgin. In other words, the user of the book is encouraged to aspire to the same heavenly reward as Mary in her identity as virgin, lover, and mother of Jesus.

Another area where the Rothschild Canticles made an original contribution to mysticism is in its unusual trinitarian miniatures.[38] All Christian mysticism is at least implicitly trinitarian because faith in God as Father, Son, and Holy Spirit is the foundation of prayer and practice. Some mystics, however, can be described as explicitly trinitarian owing to their emphasis on the role of the three persons in mystical transformation. Trinitarian mysticism became strong in the West in the twelfth century with William of St.-Thierry, and it reached new heights in the late Middle Ages in figures like Hadewijch, Bonaventure, Marguerite Porete, Eckhart, and Ruusbroec, to name but a few. Given the invisibility of the Father (John 1:18),[39] and the belief that neither Son nor Spirit was visible before their salvific missions to the world, it would seem that the Trinity precisely as Trinity must be beyond all representation. Many theologians, among them St. Augustine, argued this case forcefully (see Letter 120). But not all Christians agreed.

There has been a rich tradition of trinitarian iconography, both in Eastern and Western Christian art, as well as an ongoing debate over what kinds of images are acceptable. In the Christian East, the Old Testament Trinity icon, the depiction of the appearance of the three angels to Abraham at Mamre (Gen. 18), was viewed as a symbolic presentation of the three-in-one God and acquired a canonical status.[40] This image was also known in the West, but there was a great variety of Western images of the Trinity created in the medieval period, some of them of a clearly mystical cast in so far as they were intended to help realize the presence of the three persons in the soul in some direct way.

Attempting to create images of the invisible Trinity may be described as a limit situation in mystical art: something that is clearly impossible, but that seems imperative, at least for some. The Rothschild Canticles' nineteen surviving Trinity miniatures appear in two sections of the manuscript and are unique.[41] They do not make use of any of the traditional forms of trinitarian iconography, such as the Mamre scene, or the popular image of the Throne of Grace (*Gnadenstuhl*) in which God the Father holds Christ on the cross with the dove representing the Holy Spirit hovering between them.[42] Rather, the patrons, planners, and executors of the work created an almost totally new iconography, which can be described as a series of texts and pictures exploring a fundamentally Dionysian program, suggesting how the mystery of the Trinity is concealed in its very revelation. Symbolic presentations, as Dionysius taught, are necessary as manifestations of God, even God as Trinity, but they are impossible as representations, being consumed in the very act of using them as instruments of contemplative practice. As Hamburger observes, there is a double paradox involved in this program— not only that of the representation of the mystery at the heart of Christian faith but also the paradox of attempting to enact the process of mystical vision. "The real subject," as he puts it, "is the climactic encounter between the viewer and the image as a simulacrum of the encounter between God and the soul."[43] The Canticles depict this latter paradox not only by introducing images of prophets, seers, and evangelists on the text pages in a manner similar to what we saw in the Song of Songs cycle, but also by depicting figures of angels and humans around the Trinity images themselves, figures expressing a variety of reactions from praise and humble faith to awestruck wonder.[44]

The text units that face the trinitarian miniatures in the Rothschild Canticles are anthologies of scriptural passages, liturgical antiphons, and theological extracts, mostly from Augustine's *On the Trinity*.[45] Occasionally, some unidentified citations appear. The texts emphasize the invisibility and

incomprehensibility of the mystery of the Trinity; several also stress the
need for allegorical understanding of scriptural passages describing God (ff.
80v, 95v, 101v). The images follow a triple pattern (though not in a linear
way in the manuscript), incorporating: (1) basically anthropomorphic
images; (2) pictures that begin to undercut or problematize such direct presentations through techniques of veiling and unveiling, and unusual employment of suns, rays, and tongues of flame; and (3) geometrical mandalas
without any hint of a human figure (there are only two of these: ff. 44r and
106r). The images of the second and third types often display an extraordinary energy and invention as they explode or implode on the page in their
attempt to manifest the Trinity as the dynamic source of all reality. Since
exitus and *reditus* are one and the same in God, to manifest the outflowing
source is also to invite the beholder back into the inner dynamism of the
Trinity. The Rothschild Canticles perform this task with remarkable subtlety and skill. These images had little precedent in previous art; nor do
they appear to have found real successors.

   Jeffrey Hamburger has analyzed the Rothschild Trinity images in detail.
Here, I wish only to make a few remarks on one example of each form. An
example of an anthropomorphic image can be found at the beginning of
the second series on f. 77r (illustration 5B). Here the Father and the Son are
portrayed as similar figures seated facing each other and grasping the dove
of the Holy Spirit, the bond of their mutual love. All three figures are surrounded by a circular cloth expressive of the divine unity and the whole
image is superimposed on a large flame burst whose tongues of fire pass
beyond the divine realm, penetrating the picture's frame and suggesting the
Trinity's role as the dynamic source of all reality. The facing text page contains a quotation from Saint Augustine.

   The last two Trinity miniatures in the manuscript illustrate the transition
from veiled presentation of the mystery to completely symbolic manifestation. On f. 104r (illustration 6) a kind of circular screen of originally golden
light rays seems to implode upon a gold starburst in the center (possibly a
representation of the Godhead). The screen is upheld by three figures
partly visible behind it with the dove of the Holy Spirit above, and figures
representing the Father and Son on the sides, who strangely touch each
other's feet to indicate their unity in the three-personed divinity. The facing
text is of interest, especially for its quotation adapted from the definition of
God first found in the *Book of the Twenty-Four Philosophers*, "My center is
everywhere; my circumference nowhere," an axiom that fascinated Eckhart
and other late medieval mystics, as we have seen.[46]

   The final trinitarian image is among the most unusual (illustration 7).[47]

The veils that ordinarily conceal the mystery are here drawn back, hanging from the clouds in an almost surrealistic fashion. Concentric circles of light and cloud flash back and forth upon the same gold starburst seen in the previous image. No human form appears, just the constant interplay of pulsating energy expressed in three broad fields but with no fewer than nine subsections. One is reminded of the three circles of Dante's final vision of the Trinity in the *Paradiso,* though the differences are as great as the similarities. This is a bold expression of the coincidence of opposites at the heart of Christian mystical Neoplatonism. The text that accompanies this impressive mandala emphasizes the apophatic nature of the teaching found in the Rothschild Canticles. It begins with three scriptural passages often used by mystics about divine transcendence (Exod. 3:14; John 1:18; and Isa. 55:9), and concludes with two unidentified prayers, making use of themes found in the mysticism of the ground. The first is the divine desert: "O Lord, lead me into the desert of your deity and the darkness of your light, and lead me where you are not."[48] The final prayer is put in St. Bernard's mouth: "Bernard prayed, 'O Lord, lead me where you are.' God said, 'Bernard, I will not do it, because if I were to lead you where I am, you would be annihilated, both to me and to yourself.'"[49] The desire for annihilation, scarcely an aspect of Bernard's mysticism, was very much present in thirteenth- and fourteenth-century mystics, as we have seen. This enigmatic text might be taken as a criticism of such mystical annihilation. But might it not also be seen as the expression of the mystic's desire to be one with God whatever the consequences?

The Rothschild Canticles is unique for the richness of its mystical iconography, but there are many other examples of mystical images from the fourteenth and fifteenth centuries. It is no accident, given what we know about late medieval mysticism, that some of this art was not only used by, but also produced by women.[50] In portraying the secrets of the love encounter between Christ and the soul, male and female mystical artists were not restricted to illustrations of the Song of Songs, but turned to a variety of ways of expressing the love relation between God and human in both word and image. An example of such a fusion of text and image can be found in the MHG poem "Christus und die minnende sele" ("Christ and the Loving Soul"), composed in the late fifteenth century in the Lake Constance area, probably by a woman.[51] Hildegard Keller has shown how this didactic poem and its accompanying illustrations form an intriguing, even troubling, example of carrying "the nuptial model to extremes."[52] The disconcerting aspect of "Christus und die minnende sele" appears in the way in which the author adopted medieval portrayals of what today would be called an abusive marriage in which the husband tyrannizes his wife, both mentally and physically, as an analogue for the manner in which the Divine Bridegroom disciplines his earthly bride through ascetical practice to prepare her for mystical union. Both text and picture render the abusive nature of the relationship with considerable realism.

The poem begins with a prologue in which Christ appears to the sleeping soul and in time-honored fashion warns about the evils of human marriage. In part 1, consisting of sections 2–10, Christ is portrayed as a cruel husband, chastising the soul through deprivation of food and sleep, keeping her prisoner in the house, and even scourging her for her faults.[53] Finally, he takes the drastic step of hanging her on a gallows, a scene that is at once an imitation of the passion, a mystical death (*mors mystica*), and a strong parallel to other accounts of mystical dereliction, such as the abandonment experience related by Angela of Foligno, in which she feels as if she "remains dangling on the gallows and yet lives, with no help, no support, no remedy, swinging in the empty air" (illustration 8A).[54] It is at this point in the poem that the transition to mystical experience takes place, as Christ releases the bride and says to her: "Go down from here, for it is time; I will no longer allow this suffering in you" (*Nu gang her ab, won es ist zit,/diss liden ich nit lenger an dir lid* [lines 1024–25]).

If the first part of the poem and its pictures employ an abusive marriage as a model for ascetical training, in part 2 (sections 11–21) we find an allegory of courtly love with a heavy dose of the Song of Songs guiding a presentation of mystical erotics. Here the tables are turned, as the bride rather than Christ does much of the speaking and takes the initiative in the love affair (in one of the manuscripts she also changes into religious garb). The note of mutuality between the mystical soul and Christ comes to the fore— a theme found in the Song itself and well developed by many late medieval female mystics. The bride now promises Christ her total fidelity: "O Lord, I will never fail you again, / I promise you that with body and soul."[55] When Christ hides himself in the game of love, the bride pursues him and wounds him with the arrow of love. She then takes him prisoner and leads him away (illustration 8B). After consenting to a true spiritual marriage with Christ, she gladly dances with him as he plays music like a wandering minstrel (*varend man*). In section 17 Christ and the soul exchange gestures of intimacy in a location well known from courtly romance, the garden of love (*locus amoenus*). In section 19 Christ once again leads the soul in a dance of love, invoking deeply erotic language:

> I would want to nestle close to you,
> And press you affectionately to my heart,

> And draw you into my soul.
> You would have to be always within.[56]

Finally, the soul is crowned, just as the bride was in the Rothschild Canticles Song of Songs sequence. At this point of full union Christ says to her, "My love, you and I are all one; thus from the two of us there comes forth one" (*Lieb, ich und du sind all ain, / alsus wirt ains us uns zwain* [lines 2045–46]). The bride responds echoing the full mutuality of the lovers: "O Lord, you are mine, as I am yours; / This loyal love will be constant forever" (*O herr, du bist min, so bin ich din; / Die trúw sol iemer stat sin* [lines 2049–50]) (illustration 9).[57] However much "Christ and the Loving Soul" may trouble us with its acquiescence to violence in marriage, the poem and its illustrations display considerable originality in its version of mystical erotics.

Because of its appearance in a devotional handbook with accompanying texts, the trinitarian cycle of the Rothschild Canticles is unique as an explicit portrayal of mystical trinitarianism. In the absence of such direct evidence it is often difficult to know how far the many Trinitarian images of the late Middle Ages may or may not have been used within contemplative practices to lead to inner participation in the life of the Trinity. For example, the Hours of Catherine of Cleves, produced for a pious noblewoman around 1440, contains a series of nine illuminations for the hours of the Office of the Blessed Trinity, forming one of the most complete collections of traditional forms of picturing the three persons. While the accompanying prayers of the Trinity Office testify to the importance of private devotion to the Trinity, they offer no direct evidence of mystical participation.[58]

Among traditional images of the three persons none was more popular than the Throne of Grace (see Heb. 4:16) noted above. Created around 1100, this image originally appeared in missals in connection with the eucharistic prayer, which emphasized the role of the Trinity in the offering of Christ for the salvation of the world. In the later Middle Ages and beyond, it came to be used more as an *Andachtsbild* and took many forms.[59] An even more popular but non-trinitarian image was the picture of the suffering Christ known as the Man of Sorrows, a standing half-figure usually of the dead Christ displaying the wounds of the passion.[60] Originating in a Byzantine icon that combined the standard half-portrait of Christ as triumphant Pantocrator with the image of the suffering Savior (thus picturing the fundamental paradox of the Gospel, glory achieved through suffering and death), the image became popular in the West around 1300. One of the earliest appearances, in a Franciscan prayerbook from Genoa dated 1293, is accompanied by a Pseudo-Bernardine prayer beginning, "With what a strong embrace you have embraced me, good Jesus, when the blood drained from your heart!" The prayer and image could be used together to induce a sense not only of sorrow but also of mystical identity with the suffering Christ. The prayer continues: "O man, Christ shows you his hands so that you may do what he did; his side so that you may feel what he felt; his feet so that you may walk on the path he trod."[61]

Around 1400 a new form of the Man of Sorrows appeared, a trinitarian one sometimes referred to as the *Notgottes* (Distress of God), because it combined the portrayal of the dead or dying Christ with the traditional Throne of Grace.[62] Around 1430, the Swabian master Hans Multscher (ca. 1400–1467) created one of the most evocative examples of this form in a small alabaster relief in which both an angel and the sorrowing figure of the Father support the dying Christ as the dove of the Holy Spirit breathes into his ear, an image hinting at the resurrection and new life achieved through death on the cross.[63] Medieval passion piety and the role of the Trinity in salvation history are fused in a striking way in this example of late Gothic realism. That such a private image was an object of intense devotion can be shown from the reverse, where a devout admirer carved the words: "Herrgott las mich nit"—"Lord God, do not abandon me!" This kind of image of "undoubted sacral power," in Wolfgang Braunfel's terms, witnesses to the role of the Trinity in late medieval devotional and mystical life.[64]

Some illustrations of the Trinity allow for a directly mystical reading. In *Nuns as Artists,* Jeffrey Hamburger studied a series of works of art produced by the nuns of Saint Walburg convent near Regensburg around 1500. The manuscript illuminations from Saint Walburg feature many of the characteristic images of late medieval mystical piety, such as the rose as a symbol of both suffering love and joyful celebration.[65] Another dominant image is that of the house of the heart, a many-sided symbol of divine domesticity, the mutual indwelling of God and the soul.[66] Among the four heart images surviving from Saint Walburg is an illustration of the heart as house with a door and large picture window through which we can gaze upon the soul embraced by Christ her divine Lover, who is enveloped by both the Father and the Holy Spirit in the form of a dove. The presence of the eucharistic altar and a series of accompanying captions and figures spell out the meaning of this image of mystical union with the Trinity achieved through the reception of the Eucharist. The inscription that begins from within the embrace between bride and Bridegroom highlights marital mysticism: "Here is Jesus embracing the soul in the arm of his great ineffable love," while the caption that begins under the dove's wing and circles up around the Father expresses the assumption of this love into the source of all love, that is, the Spirit as the *caritas* binding the three persons into one: "The Holy Spirit binds love together with the loving bond of eternal union" (*ewiger verainnigung*).[67]

The ingenuity that late gothic artists brought to these experiments in picturing the erotic union between Christ and the soul and even union with the ineffable Trinity is evident also in the extraordinary proliferation of art illustrating the passion in the late Middle Ages and the Renaissance.[68] Much of this art involved narrative expansions of the details of Christ's sufferings based not only on the Gospel accounts and apocryphal writings but also on Old Testament typologies of the passion. It is difficult to determine how much of the passion-saturated piety of the fourteenth and fifteenth centuries can be described as mystical, both in its literary and artistic remains. Certainly, any image or account of Christ's passion offered an occasion for meditation on the significance of redemption, and (implicitly at least) invited interior identification with the suffering Lord. Some images reveal mystical possibilities in a more direct fashion. One master symbol of late medieval passion-centered mysticism was blood—the blood of Christ as the redeeming fluid with the power to save, cleanse, nourish, and inebriate the devoted worshiper.[69] The role of blood in attaining union with Christ is evident in many of the major mystics of the fourteenth and fifteenth centuries, such as Henry Suso in Germany, Catherine of Siena in Italy, and Julian of Norwich in England. Blood is omnipresent in passion art, and sometimes with a possible mystical emphasis expressed through concentration on blood as the redemptive presence of Christ himself. An illustration of this nature can be found in a dramatic fourteenth-century German drawing now in the Schnütgen Museum in Cologne (illustration 10). In this image the nun artist has portrayed herself, along with Bernard of Clairvaux, kneeling and embracing the cross upon which the totally bloody body of the dead Christ, like a single wound, spouts streams of blood that fall around but not upon the two worshipers, suggesting that outward contemplation of the passion should lead to inward bathing in the blood of Jesus.[70] No text accompanies the scene, nor is one needed.

The crude but forceful image of contemplation of the passion in the Schnütgen Museum can be compared with a more sophisticated and subtle picture of the suffering Christ painted in the 1420s by the Dominican artist known as Meister Francke. In this version of the Man of Sorrows the infantilized and strangely feminine body of Christ displays his side wound as supporting angels thrust the instruments of the passion into his hands.[71] Christ's gaze directly meets that of the viewer, inviting by expression and gesture compassionate meditation upon the blood-seeping wound in his side. As Michael Camille puts it: "Francke's Christ . . . asks that we return his gaze, that we look upon him as piteously as he looks upon us"—that is, that we experience a form of deep *com-passio*.[72] The painting reminds the onlooker that Christ is still suffering, asking the faithful to identify with him in his ongoing pain, as many mystics did. As a "work of spiritual performance" (Camille's term), the painting invites us to be transformed by Christ's love into the image of the suffering Beloved.[73]

This sampling of some images created in late medieval Europe is intended to underline what has become increasingly evident in the past two decades: the necessity of recognizing that the image can be as potent as the word in providing insight into the varieties of mysticism.

Genres of German Mysticism

Previous attempts to survey the proliferation of mysticism in late medieval Germany have adopted various procedures, beginning with Wilhelm Preger's three-volume historical narrative, whose first volume was published in 1874.[74] Other works have surveyed the mystics of a particular religious order, such as the Dominicans,[75] Franciscans, and Augustinians. All these models have both advantages and disadvantages. Given the dissemination of mystical literature to such a broad audience, both clerical and lay, in fourteenth- and fifteenth-century German lands, the approach adopted here will be through a selective study of examples of major genres used to effect this dissemination. There was, to be sure, considerable fluidity of genre in MHG literature, especially perhaps in mystical literature. Some mystical treatises began as sermons, and sermons often take on a didactic character that brings them closer to tracts than to living preaching. A few mystical texts were written specifically as dialogues, but the dialogue form, or at least scholastic-style question and answer, is present in many treatises and sermons. Many letters were written and sent, but letters were also absorbed into other works, such as treatises, or even visionary narratives and hagiographical texts. Poems were mixed into prose works (prosimetrum). Although we must always keep this malleability in mind, a genre-based approach does have the advantage of demonstrating the many-sidedness of the harvest of medieval German mysticism.

Mystical Poetry

The relation between poetry and mysticism has inspired considerable literature, both theoretical and historical.[76] How poetic inspiration relates to mystical contact with God is not easy to determine. It is clear, of course, that not all religious poetry need be thought of as mystical, but what constitutes a poem as mystical has been subject to differing interpretations. I do not intend to try to take up this issue, but if we adopt a simple criterion for mystical poetry, taking it as verse produced by authors generally accepted as mystics, or anonymous poems that feature themes and language found in contemporary mystical prose texts, it is clear that the era of the new mysticism from ca. 1200 on witnessed an unusual growth of mystical poetry.

Some of this literature has already been considered in *The Flowering of Mysticism*, such as Francis of Assisi's "Canticle of the Sun" (1225–26), and the poems of Hadewijch, Mechthild of Magdeburg, Marguerite Porete, and Jacopone da Todi. The thirteenth century saw the production of MHG poetry that can be described as mystical, not only in the case of Mechthild but also arguably in the long allegorical poem known as the "Tochter Syon" ("Daughter of Sion"), based on the Song of Songs and composed by the Franciscan Lamprecht of Regensburg around 1250.[77] Hildegard Keller has drawn attention to how Lamprecht's poem serves as a link between various treatments of the bridal relationship in texts such as Mechthild's *Flowing Light of the Godhead* and other forms of medieval literature, such as didactic allegory and narrative epic. Lamprecht's poem provides a detailed study of the interpenetration of devotion to the passion and the power of bridal love,[78] and the poem's closing portrayal of the love union between the Divine Groom and the bride features too many of the characteristic themes of bridal mysticism to exclude the work from the history of German mysticism.[79]

Here I will concentrate on poems produced between ca. 1300 and ca. 1375 that can be connected with the mysticism of the ground. Although only a percentage of the hundreds of religious verses produced in late medieval Germany can be described as mystical (perhaps fifty in all), they include some striking examples of mystical verse, especially owing to their witness to the struggle to find poetic expression for complex theological concepts.[80] I will specifically look at two poems. One is surely among the masterpieces of late medieval mysticism, the MHG sequence known as the "Granum Sinapis" ("The Mustard Seed" [see Matt. 13:31]). The second, "Vom Überschall" ("On the Ecstatic Song") is less accomplished as a poem, but is a fascinating witness to some of the major themes of fourteenth-century mysticism. The importance of these two poems is evident from the fact that they were both given learned commentaries, a Latin one for the "Granum Sinapis," and a vernacular explanation for "Vom Überschall"—a sign of how significant the poems were judged for the communication of mystical teaching.

The "Granum Sinapis" is found in nine manuscripts, while its Latin commentary survives in three.[81] It appears to date from the early years of the
fourteenth century. A number of experts, such as Kurt Ruh and Alois M.
Haas, have defended its Eckhartian authorship, while others, such as Walter
Haug, have questioned whether the poem could have come from Eckhart's
pen, not only because the Meister was not known as a poet, but also
because of some significant differences from Eckhartian views.[82] If the
poem is not by Eckhart, it testifies, as do a number of sermons of doubtful
Eckhartian provenance, that some authors sought to "out-Eckhart" Eckhart,
that is, use his insights in ways that tried to equal the Meister's profundity.

The sequence, modeled on a popular Latin form, contains eight stanzas
of ten lines each, rhyming according to the scheme of *aabbc, ddeec.* The first
three stanzas, dealing with the inner emanation of the Trinity of Persons,
constitute a poetic summary of Eckhart's doctrine of the inner "boiling"
(*bullitio*) of the divine nature, beginning with an appeal to the notion of
principium/begin (i.e., both beginning and principial source):

> In the Beginning,
> High above understanding,
> Is ever the Word.
> O rich treasure,
> There the Beginning always gave birth to the Beginning.[83]

The presentation is deeply apophatic, characterizing the trinitarian mystery
as a "depth without ground" (*hîr ist ein tûfe sunder grunt*).

The second three stanzas explore intellect as the power capable of leading into the divine depth, or up to divine height (mountain). Here the poet
turns to another favorite Eckhartian motif, the divine desert that lies
beyond all affirmation and negation. As stanza 4 puts it:

> The mountain of this point
> Ascend without activity,
> Intellect!
> The way leads you
> Into a wondrous desert,
> So wide, so broad,
> It extends without measure.
> The desert has
> Neither time nor place,
> Its mode of being is unique.[84]

After a detailed exploration of the coincidence of opposites of the mystical
desert in stanzas 5 and 6, the final two stanzas abandon objectively descrip-

tive language to highlight personal appropriation of the mystery, first with a second-person adjuration emphasizing mystical annihilation: "Become like a child / Become deaf, become blind! / Your own something / Must become nothing; / Drive away all something, all nothing!"[85] The last stanza switches to a mixture of self-address and direct appeal to God, merging Eckhartian expressions with Augustinian and Dionysian ones—a melding that shows why the authorship of the poem remains under contention:

> O my Soul,
> Go out, let God in!
> Sink all my something
> Into God's Nothing,
> Sink in the groundless flood!
> If I flee from You,
> Then You come to me [Augustine, *Conf.* 5.2 et al., using
>   Ps. 138:7].
> If I lose myself,
> Then I find You,
> O Goodness beyond being! [Dionysius, DN 3.1][86]

The Latin commentary on the poem is unusual, a reversal of the expected direction from learned Latin to vernacular explanation for a broader audience. The readers of this work would have been largely clergy. The purpose of the comment appears to have been as much apologetic as explanatory: to defend the poem's vernacular theology by showing its conformity with established theological and philosophical authorities.[87] The sequence itself, as the basic *auctoritas,* is exegeted line by line through the invocation of a rich range of philosophical, theological, and mystical resources, especially the Dionysian corpus and Thomas Aquinas, but also a good deal of Proclus (both the *Elements of Theology* and the adapted Proclianism of the *Book of Causes*),[88] as well as Maximus's glosses on Dionysius, Eriugena,[89] Hugh of St. Victor, Alan of Lille, and Thomas Gallus,[90] among others.[91] The presence of Gallus gives away one aspect of the apologetic program—not only to defend Eckhartian mystical theology,[92] but also to try to show the compatibility of the two major forms of late medieval Dionysianism, the affective interpretation of Gallus and his followers, and the intellective Dionysianism of Albert the Great as reinforced by the *Proclus latinus* popular among the German Dominicans. How successful the anonymous author was in this endeavor is less important than what his attempt has to tell us about the relation between vernacular and scholastic theology in the early fourteenth century, as well as about the endeavors to come to the defense of Eckhart's mysticism.

Aspects of the teaching of this fascinating commentary, particularly its rich exploration of the "mystical desert" (*desertum mysticum, hoc est esse divinum* [98.18–19]),[93] give it a special place in the story of late medieval mysticism. But its teaching on mystical union, for all its deep Neoplatonic background, is more cautiously put than what we find in Eckhart. Commenting on the verse *sink al min icht,* the commentator explains that this state is reserved for heaven:

Here the poet desires his whole reality to be transformed into God, which is only possible in the future life. So great is the excellence of divine power in the future life that will be manifested to all who are worthy to contemplate it that nothing else but it will be visible to them whether in bodies or in intelligible things, as is explained more fully in the book of *The Fourfold Division of Nature.*[94]

The second poem to be considered is known as "Vom Überschall," a word that in modern German means supersonic, and here may be translated as "About the Ecstatic Song." This poem survives in ten manuscripts, and in several is accompanied by a MHG commentary, the "Gloss on 'The Ecstatic Song.'"[95] Kurt Ruh thinks that the poem was composed by a nun who was a follower of Henry Suso and therefore cannot be dated earlier than 1330. It may well be some decades later. The prose commentary for the most part consists of passages drawn from chapter 52 of Suso's *Life of the Servant,* the text that contains the Dominican's profoundest reflections on the Trinity (the rare word *überschal* also occurs in the *Life*).[96] It was once thought that Suso might have copied from the anonymous gloss, but Ruh has shown that the relationship is actually the other way, so that the "Gloss" probably dates to after the publication of the edition of the *Life* in Suso's *Exemplar,* that is, after 1362.

Although the poem does not reach the artistic level of the "Granum Sinapis," it is still a profound meditation on the mysticism of the ground, making use of much of the vocabulary created by Eckhart and carried on by his disciples. The two major foci are the mystery of the Trinity (stanzas 1–8) and the way in which the soul is drawn into indistinct union with God (stanzas 9–17). The first section presents the relation of the Trinity of Persons to the hidden divine source through a variety of apophatic meditations centering on how the unmanifested mystery is made manifest. Stanza 5, for example, says:

The river takes its origin where the Unity exists;
The Simple One is without need, hovering in itself
In a dark stillness: no one can understand it.
Although in its own self it is manifest.[97]

This apophatic approach is presented both in terms of traditional mystical paradoxes, as well as Eckhart's new language of the ground and abyss, as we see in stanza 8:

> O bottomless deep Abyss, high in your depth,
> Low in your height; how can this be?
> This is hidden from us in your deep ground.
> Yet St. Paul tells us we shall know it.[98]

The second part of the poem explores the way in which the human spirit comes to be drawn into the triune God by dying to self through decreation, thus reaching indistinction in the divine Unity (*einikeit*). Here the poet makes use of the language of the dual abysses of God and human first found in Hadewijch, but also present in Tauler. As is customary in intellective Dionysianism, it is the mind, or intellect, that enables the passage to indistinction. Stanzas 15 and 16 make this evident. Stanza 15 says:

> The mind that I am talking about, it is without word;
> One and one united, there shines forth bare being to
>   bare being
> In the unknowability of the high Unity
> That annihilates all things in their forms of existence.

This passage introduces the apophatic merging of God and human described in stanza sixteen:

> There the two abysses [Ps. 41:8] hover in a single likeness,
> Both filled with spirit and stripped of spirit: that is the height
>   of life.
> Where God strips himself of spirit, there is darkness
> In an unknown, yet still known Unity.[99]

The final stanza, 17, one of the most obscure of this dark poem, says that the hidden mystery of divine–human fusion is something that we must learn to love and hasten toward, because it is nothing other than "the ecstatic song" (*daz ist der überschal*).

Both the "Granum Sinapis" and "Von Überschall" test the limits of what poetry can do to communicate mystical teaching. The contraction of language characteristic of some forms of lyric may well conflict with the exuberant plethora with which many mystics have attempted to point to the "always-more" nature of contact with God through forms of rhetorical excess characteristic of their ages, but longer forms of lyric, especially those based on liturgical poetry such as the sequence, are also amenable to use and adaptation, as shown by the "Granum Sinapis." The fact that both these intriguing poems attracted commentaries casts interesting light on the differences between prose and poetry as linguistic vehicles for conveying transformation into God.

Sermons and Sermon Collections[100]

Meister Eckhart was one of the greatest preachers of his, or of any, era. His more than a hundred surviving sermons are the chief source for his mysticism, if not his total theology. Eckhart's follower, John Tauler, left us only sermons as the vehicles of his message. The vernacular sermon was arguably the most widespread and potent genre for the communication of mystical teaching in late medieval Germany, though it is often difficult, as mentioned above, to distinguish between treatise and sermon.[101]

Mystical preaching in Latin did not end at 1300, though many of the sermons that survive in Latin may have been originally delivered in the vernacular. Nevertheless, the bulk of preaching, mystical or not, shifted to the mother tongue in the last centuries of the Middle Ages.[102] Of the thousands of MHG sermons known today, both anonymous and the product of known figures, many hundreds are mystical in the sense that their main message concerns transformative contact with God rather than doctrine, moral practice, or that pervasive theme of late medieval preaching, fear of hell.[103] If the fourteenth century was the most creative era of preaching and the production of religious and mystical literature, the fifteenth century featured a transmission explosion.[104]

Despite the efforts of editors and students of mysticism for a century and a half, much work still remains to be done on medieval German mystical sermons. For example, Franz Pfeiffer's 1857 edition of Eckhart's sermons included 110 sermons, and more were discovered by later investigators. After a time in which there was a tendency to reduce the number of authentically Eckhartian pieces (for Josef Quint there were only 86), newer research has been cautiously but convincingly expanding the tally of real Eckhart pieces against the category of "pseudo-Eckhart." Many of the pseudonymously Eckhartian homilies are also of considerable interest, though they have rarely been given in-depth analysis. Recent editions of important mystical preachers (e.g., Hartwig of Erfurt, Marquard of Lindau) are welcome additions to our knowledge, but other important preachers remain unedited and little known. Any *full* study of mystical preaching in late medieval Germany is far off.

As the *ordo praedicatorum*, the Dominicans constitute the largest group of mystical preachers of the fourteenth century. Kurt Ruh points out, however, that in comparison with the "big three" of Eckhart, Suso, and Tauler, the other Dominicans have been relatively neglected.[105] Ruh's presentation of nine of these figures in the third volume of his *Geschichte der abendländische Mystik* provides a helpful survey of the range of Dominican mystical preaching and shows how much still remains to be done, even on the essential level of critical editions.[106]

A number of these Dominicans contributed to the important sermon collection known as the *Paradisus anime intelligentis (Paradis der fornunftigen sele)*, that is, the *Paradise of the Intellectual Soul*.[107] Although this collection is known today in only two copies, its sixty-four homilies (half by Eckhart) have been the subject of considerable study because the *Paradise* sermons constitute one of the most important monuments to fourteenth-century mystical preaching.[108] Along with Eckhart, we find the Dominicans Eckhart Rube, Giseler of Slatheim, Johannes Franke, Florentius of Utrecht, Hermann of Loveia, Albrecht of Treffurt, Helwic of Germar, Brother Erbe, and Thomas of Apolda. In addition, a Carmelite Magister named Hane contributed three sermons, and there is one sermon by an anonymous Franciscan.[109] The sermons fall into two groups with the first thirty-one organized according to the feasts of the liturgical calendar (*de tempore*) and the last thirty-three devoted to the feasts of the saints (*de sanctis*).

The place of origin and purpose of the *Paradisus anime intelligentis* remain under dispute. Kurt Ruh argued for the Dominican house at Erfurt (Eckhart's own convent), dating the collection to around 1340, although many of the sermons appear to come from the first decade of the fourteenth century and thus may indicate an earlier redactional stage. Georg Steer, on the other hand, thinks that the collection was put together at Cologne about 1330 by followers of Eckhart eager to defend his orthodoxy in light of the papal condemnation. This dispute has implications for the way in which the content and purpose of the collection are evaluated.

As its name indicates,[110] the *Paradise of the Intellectual Soul* argues for the traditional Dominican position that ultimate *beatitudo*, the vision of God in heaven, rests in the interior paradise of the intellect, not in the will and love. As Thomas Aquinas said, "Thus the essence of beatitude consists in an act of the intellect, but the delight following upon blessedness belongs to the will" (STh IaIIae, q. 3, a. 4). The lone Franciscan sermon in the collection serves as a deliberate counterposition, one explicitly rebutted by Giseler of Slatheim in Sermon 41. The tendentious comments by the redactor in the *tabula* introducing the collection make this purpose evident. In respect to Giseler's homily, the redactor says, "In this sermon Brother Giseler of Slatheim, lector at Cologne and Erfurt, disputes the Franciscans and proves that the action of the intellect is nobler than the action of the will with respect to eternal life, and he destroys the Franciscan arguments with authority."[111]

If the *Paradise of the Intellectual Soul* originated in Erfurt, it may have functioned, as Kurt Ruh has argued, as an "Erinnerungsbuch," that is, as a memorial volume commemorating the famous Dominican preachers associated with the Erfurt convent in the time of Meister Eckhart.[112] But Ruh's claims that the Eckhart sermons in the volume mostly date from the Meister's time as vicar at Erfurt (1303–11) and thus reflect his early position on the priority of the intellect as found in the *Parisian Questions* have been shown to be incorrect by Ria van den Brandt. Only about eleven of the Eckhart sermons concentrate on the role of the intellect,[113] and these and the remaining sermons seem to span Eckhart's preaching career from perhaps as early as 1294 to 1326, his last years in Cologne. Even the sermons on the intellect reflect a typically Eckhartian variety of viewpoints, whether or not these can be given chronological precision. Hence, if the *Paradise of the Intellectual Soul* comes from Cologne, which seems more likely, a desire to defend Eckhart in the light of the papal condemnation of 1329 can be seen as important, something suggested also by the way the redactor edited Eckhart's sermons, partly to make his complex doctrine of the overcoming of both will and intellect in the path to ultimate blessedness more compatible with standard Dominican views.[114] A careful study by Burkhard Hasebrink of the redactional process at work in the collection reveals another purpose—the desire to create a handy compendium for preachers, model sermon materials that the learned friars could adopt for their vernacular preaching.[115] This goal was in line with Eckhart's own intentions, as shown by the Meister's collected Latin sermons.

The *Paradise of the Intellectual Soul* is a witness to the continuing importance among the German Dominicans of the intellective Dionysianism created by Albert the Great. Nevertheless, as Niklaus Largier has shown, the competing views of the role of intellect in the ascent to God among the fourteenth-century Dominicans make it difficult to speak about a single position, or "Dominican School."[116] The most crucial divide was on the question whether beatitude resides in the active intellect conceived of as a natural power and identified with the Augustinian *abditum mentis*, as Dietrich of Freiburg taught, or, as Eckhart and those influenced by him held, beatifying union is attained through the passive reception of divine action in the possible intellect—the birth of the Word in the soul. For Eckhart, the active intellect as a power of the soul is different from the essence of the soul, which, in its deepest ground, after all created reality has been put aside, is where the joy of indistinct union is realized in the single ground. This conception of intellect dominates the *Paradise of the Intellectual Soul*, both in the sermons by Eckhart and in those of his confrères.[117] Largier has also taken the Dionysian context further, arguing that the *Paradise* collection reflects a particular contextualization of Eckhart's notion of the birth of the Word in the soul that sought to connect his atemporal Christology and immanent eschatology to the general intellective Dionysianism of the German Dominicans.[118] It is obvious that this sermon collection is a rich mine for the study of speculative theology and mystical preaching in the first half of the fourteenth century.

Rather than entering into the varying theories about the shape and purpose of the collection and its place in the history of Eckhartianism, here I wish only to examine a few of the non-Eckhart pieces to provide some sense of the richness of Dominican preaching in Eckhart's wake. Hermann of Loveia, a Thuringian like Eckhart, was a lecturer in theology at Erfurt. He has three sermons in the *Paradisus anime* collection. No. 17, preached on the Gospel for Sexagesima Sunday ("To you is given to know the mysteries of the kingdom of God"), begins with a distinction of three kinds of life: the animal life of the senses; the active life; and the contemplative life through which we are given the mysteries of God's kingdom. Hermann distinguishes reason (*redelichkeit*), which knows by discursive activity, from intellect (*forstentnisse*), that is, direct intuitive knowing. "What reason has brought together," he says, "intellect looks into with its utter simplicity; the master calls this the 'flower of intellect,' because so too the flower precedes the fruit and is a pledge of the true knowledge of God which follows it. The more one it is, the better; the more divided and defective, the worse."[119]

Hermann goes on to emphasize the working of grace as necessary for every virtuous action before returning to the issue of knowledge of God. Coming to know the mysteries of the kingdom is a gift of grace and the action of the Eternal Word. A thing can be known either from its cause, from its action, or in itself. God, however, cannot be truly known in the first two ways—"If he is to be known, it must come about from himself in his own nature" (*daz mûiz geschehin an ume selber an sinir nature* [43.13]). To analyze this last possibility, Hermann discusses four powers by which the soul obtains knowledge (43.14–35). The first is physical sensation which by definition cannot know God. The second is the imagination, which brings far things near, but is still tied to physical images. The power of reason also cannot know God, because there is no concept of God. Surprisingly, even the "insight of the intellect" (*inblickin des forstentnisses*) cannot know God because while intellect can attain the essential being of things (*bestende wesin*), God is beyond all being. Hermann concludes: "So we have it that God cannot be known in the four ways because everything we conceive or know is not God. . . . Nothingness is the highest knowledge that we can have of God here on earth."[120]

If knowledge of God cannot be attained by the activity of our powers of knowing, the final part of the homily (43.36–44.31) explores how some knowledge of God can still be granted us in accord with the Gospel text "to you is given." Hermann insists that true knowledge, that is, the kingdom of God understood as "the complete enjoyment of all good and what belongs to it in this life and at the end" (44.29–30), belongs to the next life; but he employs the Dionysian distinction between positive and negative theology to describe mystical knowing. "There is a twofold knowledge," he says, "by which God is known. The first is 'removing knowledge' by which one removes from God everything that may be ascribed to him. The second is 'enriching or ascribing knowledge' by which we give to God all the nobility we find in everything, though this is an incomplete knowledge."[121] Hermann proceeds to locate this basic Dionysian teaching within a broad consideration of the relation of the vision of God here below and in heaven. If God is to be known, it must happen through a double light. "The first is a natural light, not the natural light of the soul [this against Dietrich of Freiburg], but the light that is God. The other is a supernatural light and this is the light of illumination, which, though we said it was double, is really one."[122] Hermann explains by describing the supernatural light, whether of the positive or negative kinds, as a "prevenient light" (*forgenclich licht*) in the sense that it is a foretaste of heaven that takes away all normal sensation and knowing, illustrating this by Paul's ascent to the third heaven in 2 Corinthians 12. He explicitly distinguishes this light from the eternal light of God to be enjoyed in heaven, the light referred to in Exodus, "No one can see me in this light and live" (Exod. 33:20). Knowledge of the first causes is open to all, even God's enemies, by way of natural knowing. "But the things that God has kept as proper to himself—that is the three Persons—this is the hiddenness that he promised to his own."[123] Hermann of Loveia's sermon compares with better-known homilies of Eckhart and Tauler as an exploration of the modes of knowing God both in this life and in the next.

Johannes Franke, a lecturer at the Cologne Dominican *studium*, contributed five sermons to the *Paradise* collection. He is also the author of a widely disseminated mystical treatise known under the name of its biblical base text, *Ego sum via, veritas, et vita* (John 14:6).[124] Sermon 35, preached for the Feast of the Assumption of the Blessed Virgin, exegetes the text "In all things I sought rest" (Eccl. 23:11), applying it both to Mary and to each holy soul. Johannes's homily treats themes typical of Dominican mysticism, such as the need to attain rest, imitation of Christ, and the soul as image and likeness, but in a simpler way than Eckhart or Hermann of Loveia.

The sermon falls into two parts. The first (80.3–30) considers how the Holy Spirit seeks to find rest in all things, that is, in humans considered as all things (i.e., man as microcosm). Because humanity has a double nature, that is, flesh and spirit, it is necessary that the flesh be brought under control by following the way of the virtues through imitation of Christ in order to receive the "graces and gifts of the Holy Spirit" that restore our likeness to God. "Where there is likeness, there is rest; the more like we are to Eternal Wisdom, the more at rest" (*wo glicheit ist, da ist ruwe: ie glicher der ewigin wisheit, ie me ruwe* [80.21]). The second part of the sermon (80.30–81.11) explores a second type of rest, how Eternal Wisdom "seeks rest in the city, namely in the soul that stands in God's presence" (80.31–32). For Johannes Franke this is the realm of contemplation, of mystical gifts. "Although the soul is not able to remain in a state of persistent rest all the time, still from time to time, as God shall flow into her, so she must rest, because his influx requires rest. The soul must rest in order to receive his influx, for he has a greater richness in flowing out than the soul has the capacity to receive him."[125] This receptiveness is characteristic of Mary and needed by Martha (Luke 10). Johannes closes with the insistence that we must never look for rest in created things, but seek only God in all things in order to find our repose.

A third example of a preacher from the Paradise circle is Helwic of Germar, a lecturer in theology at Erfurt.[126] His two sermons in the *Paradise of the Intellectual Soul* are among the most theologically accomplished of the collection. No. 43, a homily on John 14:9–10, deals primarily with the vision of God possible in this life. Helwic emphasizes that "the active intellect cannot know God either from nature or from grace" (95.29–30), again taking issue with Dietrich. For Helwic it is the possible intellect's reception of a divine influx that enables it to know God in some way here below. The rest of this relatively long sermon is a detailed treatment of the forms of knowing ascribed to the three persons of the Trinity.

Helwic's theological expertise takes a more mystical turn in no. 52, a short piece devoted to the theme of the birth of the Word in the soul. Although the birthing motif was widespread among the Dominicans, Helwic develops this in his own way on the basis of an exegesis of the Pauline text "Preach the word," which he interprets in an Eckhartian manner as "Bring forth the word" (2 Tim. 4:2).[127] Helwic starts from the accepted view that in saying the Word the Father expresses both himself and all things. "In order to enable the soul to receive the Word, he has given her the same capability to possess all things in their nobility."[128] The soul has this ability not from nature but as a result of the Father's special action. In order to form any image within, the soul must be free, as the eye must be empty of images in order to see (a favorite example of Eckhart). God works in the soul in three ways to help it remove created images (115.25–28). As the result of this process the soul is prepared for the birth of the Son, which takes place, not as with Eckhart in the ground, or the uncreated something, but in the highest power (*craft*) of the soul. Helwic says:

> The soul has a power that is without matter and that works outside time and place. When the soul stands alone in this power, then the Father speaks a word in the power and bears his Son in the power and receives himself in himself in this power. And so the Eternal Word is received in the soul; this is the child and Word that we should bring forth.[129]

As with Eckhart, the birth can take place only when the soul is pure and empty, "drawn out of all transitory things into God's eternity" (116.2). Contrary to most of the sermons in the *Paradise of the Intellectual Soul,* Helwic's sermon ends on a strong appellative rather than didactic note: "Well now, noble soul, if you have the Word in you, speak it out! When will the Word be brought forth? When the light of truth shines upon it in the spirit, and through the spirit into the powers of the soul, and into its actions, and into its manner and modes of living."[130]

There are important Dominican mystical preachers of Eckhart's time who do not appear in the *Paradisus anime intelligentis.* It is surprising that John of Sterngassen, whose few but powerful sermons at times challenge those of Eckhart, is not in the collection, especially because he and Eckhart must have known each other.[131] John came from Cologne and was active at the Dominican house in Strassburg from as early as 1310, so he would have been there during Eckhart's stay (1313–23). Like Eckhart, he had studied in Paris. His commentary on the *Sentences of Peter Lombard* shows that he was a spokesman for the Thomist position, as contrasted with the anti-Thomism of Dietrich of Freiburg and his followers. John's surviving sermons and sermon fragments provide evidence that many of the themes favored by Eckhart were also found in his contemporaries. A glance at John's MHG sermons serves to deepen our appreciation of the rich vein of mystical preaching of the early fourteenth-century Dominicans.

John's sermons emphasize the need for detachment from created reality (*abgescheidenheit*) and attaining a state of empty purity (*lûterkeit*), which echoes Eckhart's teaching but seems even closer to the pseudo-Eckhartian treatise "On Detachment."[132] This practical apophaticism of desire coexists with a deeply negative view of the divine nature and the hidden Trinity. A sermon on the story of Mary and Martha (Luke 10:40–42), for example, explores the role of silence in the path to *beatitudo*.[133] In order to attain happiness, we must be able to hear God, according to John. The preconditions for hearing God are, first, the silencing of all creatures, and then our inner silencing of ourselves (Senner 2:262.6–263.6). John goes even further:

> All creatures must be silent in the Godhead. The Trinity itself must be silent in me. In the Eternal Word the Father is not speaking; in the Eternal Word nothing speaks except pure being. If the divine person were removed, he would still remain as pure being. My blessedness is that I gaze upon God with God. God, you shall speak, I shall listen. You shall give form to things in the Eternal Word, I shall behold them.[134]

Like Meister Eckhart and Johannes Franke, John of Sterngassen preached on the text for the Epistle of the Feast of the Assumption, "In all things I have sought rest" (Eccl. 24:11), a sermon that Kurt Ruh described as his most significant and best organized.[135] This homily picks up on many themes found in Eckhart, such as the nothingness of the naked Godhead and the eternal birth of the soul in God. It also contains the kind of startling statements about the divine nature of the soul in God that were the source of so much difficulty for Eckhart. In one place, for example, John says: "My soul is god-formed in its being. Therefore, it is capable of all and its work is eternal. Everything that God can do, the soul can receive. . . . All our Masters cannot determine whether God's power or the soul's receptivity is greater."[136]

Equally impressive is the short sermon beginning, "The wise man says in the Psalter, 'All creatures ask me, Who is God?'" (probably referencing Ps. 148:7–12). In this homily John uses the Eckhartian language of annihilation and the ground to convey his message about attaining union.[137] In response to the question "Who is God?" the preacher goes within himself to consider that all creatures are nothing in themselves but are "faultless splendor" in God. It is in this inner undisturbed rest that annihilation of the created reality of the soul can be achieved. John expresses this in first-person language with a string of negative verbs:

> And there came upon me a "diapsalma," that is, a complete silence of all outward things, and a rest of all inward things, and I experienced a sweet heavenly sighing. My understanding was stripped of images; my spirit was deprived of all mediation, and my devotion was disrobed, and my very mind was brought down. Then there came upon me a forgetfulness of all things, a loss of self, and a knowing of you alone, God.

This dissolution allows the soul to be led into the ground and to become one with the Trinity. John describes it thus:

> There came upon me a forgetting of self in you so that my reason was filled with your Spirit. Then I was led by the Holy Spirit into the ground where the Son is formed within. There I came to understand God in God, that is, the Father's nature in the Son and the person of the Son in the Father and the person of the Holy Spirit in the Father and in the Son.[138]

This absorption into the inner life of the Trinity leads to an ecstatic state of self-forgetfulness framed in hyperbolic language:

> There came upon me a beyond-seeing, a beyond-desire, and a beyond-understanding. I found in myself a forgetfulness of all things, and a self-forgetfulness: a knowing of you alone, God. There came upon me a vision of your eternity and a discovery of your blessedness. I found myself fixed on you alone. I came out of myself and found myself in you and you in me. I found myself one being with you.[139]

This sermon differs from Eckhart not in its appeal to annihilation and indistinct union, but in its expression of these themes in highly personal language. More study is needed before we can assess the relation between John of Sterngassen and Eckhart, but this brief look has at least suggested that Eckhart's confrère was a powerful mystical preacher in his own right.

The Dominican friars of the first half of the fourteenth century were not the only mystical preachers in Germany, but their contemporaries and successors in other orders are less well known. The Franciscans were widespread in Germany, but they did not have an intellectual center to challenge the Dominican *studium generale* in Cologne. Kurt Ruh's research has uncovered many aspects of the transmission into MHG of classics of Franciscan mystical thought, especially works by and ascribed to Bonaventure.[140] If Franciscan theology did not challenge the preeminence of the Dominicans, there is no question the *barfusser* ("barefoot religious") were important for spreading the gospel in urban environments. Some Franciscans also attained a reputation for mystical preaching. The *Postills* and other sermons ascribed to Hartwig of Erfurt (d. ca. 1340), a contemporary of Eckhart, have begun to be edited and studied.[141] Hartwig may not have made any original contributions to mystical preaching, but given the number of manuscripts that survive of his preaching, he is representative of the broad spread of mystical themes in the first half of the fourteenth century.

By 1350 the great age of German Dominican philosophy and theology was over, though Tauler and Suso continued their mystical preaching and writing for another decade and a half. During the second half of the fourteenth century other religious orders made greater contributions to preaching on mystical themes than did the Dominicans. The Augustinian friar Jordan of Quedlinburg (sometimes referred to as Jordan of Saxony) was among the most important writers and preachers of the period after 1350.[142] Jordan was born in 1299, studied in Bologna and Paris, and served as lector in the Augustinian cloisters in Erfurt and Magdeburg. In his later years he devoted himself to writing. In 1357 he produced a well-known account of the order, *The Life of the Brethren (Vitasfratrum Liber)*; he also completed several massive collections of sermons before his death in ca. 1370. Jordan was influenced by the most important Augustinian theologian and spiritual writer of the older generation, Henry of Friemar (see the following chapter); he also knew Eckhart's writings. The Augustinian's *Opus Postillarum et Sermones* of ca. 1365 contains well over a thousand sermons divided into several collections. A number of these Latin sermons, such as those for the Advent season that discuss the birth of the Word in the soul, show Jordan's use of Eckhartian themes and testify to the wide dissemination of aspects of the Meister's mysticism in the late fourteenth century. Although many of Jordan's sermons received early printings, only a few have appeared in modern critical editions. When Jordan's sermons are edited we will be better able to assess his place in medieval German mysticism.[143]

In the period after 1350 the most interesting mystical writer and preacher was the prolific Franciscan Marquard of Lindau.[144] Nothing is known about Marquard's early life, though he was presumably born around 1330. He served as the lector of the Franciscan house of studies in Strassburg in 1373 and was a figure of importance in the order and in the late fourteenth-century ecclesiastical world. Marquard's frequent use of the term "Friends of God" (*vriunde gottes*), as well as his unedited letter "The Rule for all Prelates," show his connection with the Strassburg circles of the Friends of God under the leadership of Rulman Merswin (see chapter 9).[145] His attacks on the false mysticism of the Free Spirits tie him to contemporary debates. He died on August 13, 1392.

Marquard, like Eckhart, wrote in both Latin and MHG. Many of his works were translated from one language into the other—proof that the ongoing conversation between Latin and vernacular mysticism did not die with Eckhart.[146] One good example of this interchange is to be found in the Franciscan's largely unedited *Commentary on the Prologue of John*. Written originally in Latin, it was later anonymously translated into MHG. This work makes frequent use of Eckhart's John commentary, though it mounts a strong attack against the Dominican's teaching on the eternity of the world.[147]

The Franciscan's works are found in about 450 manuscripts, strong testimony to his popularity. Marquard's corpus includes twenty-seven authentic treatises, ten originally written in MHG and seventeen in Latin. Many of these tracts, which adopt a scholastic question-and-answer form, may have been based on his preaching and composed to provide his confrères materials for their own sermons, further emphasizing the fluid relation between sermons and treatises. While Marquard's treatises can be described as primarily doctrinal and spiritual in nature, some of the tracts contain material of a mystical nature, such as those that are loose renderings of works from the Victorine tradition.[148] Among the Latin works *The Reparation of Humanity (De reparatione hominis)* of 1374 is a survey of fall and redemption, a Franciscanized *Cur Deus Homo*.[149] The first of its thirty articles, dealing with "The Formation or Creation of Humanity," lays out Marquard's theology of human nature as made in the image of the Trinity, a key element in his preaching.[150] Among the vernacular works, the popular tract *The Explanation of the Ten Commandments*, is described by Nigel F. Palmer as "a detailed Christian account of how to live, expanded through mariological and mystical teachings."[151] Only a few of these prose tracts have received modern editions. While the treatises doubtlessly will repay study for their mystical content, in this context I will concentrate on Marquard's collection of forty-one sermons, which he published in 1389.[152]

Marquard's sermons are scholastic in form, each homily consisting of three points subdivided into six parts and often with accompanying *quaestiones*. While the format is monotonous in comparison with Eckhart or Tauler, the content demonstrates a form of mystical preaching that combines a wide range of sources, both traditional and contemporary. Along with much use of expected figures, like Augustine, Dionysius, Gregory the Great, Bernard of Clairvaux, and the Victorines, we find an extensive, if critical, appropriation of Eckhart within the overall perspective of a form of Franciscan mysticism based on personal devotion to Christ and the affective Dionysianism pioneered by Thomas Gallus and taken up by Bonaventure and other followers of Francis.[153] Marquard also uses other contemporary mystics, such as Suso, Tauler, Ruusbroec, and especially the anonymous *Book of Spiritual Poverty* (see chapter 8), from which he quotes large sections. This melding of traditions was not new, as can be seen from the Latin commentary on the "Granum Sinapis," but Marquard gave the mixture his own imprint.

While there is a greater ascetical and moral element in Marquard's preaching than in that of Eckhart, his attempt to balance mysticism with the common practices of Christian living is not unlike Tauler. Like Eckhart and

Tauler, the Franciscan's sermons are liturgically based, designed to provide his hearers and readers with the deeper meaning of the pericopes for the feasts of the church calendar—a point that needs to be emphasized for modern readers who so often think of mysticism as a private aspect of religious life. Marquard used (and misused, or at least reinterpreted) Eckhart for his own purposes, as he did with many of his other sources.[154] His mystical preaching, however, should not be measured by alien standards, but on the basis of his own attempt to describe the transformation into divine life that is the goal of Christian belief and practice.

Marquard's sermon collection allows us an overview of his mysticism, though one in need of further qualification on the basis of ongoing research into his whole corpus. Like Eckhart, the Franciscan's mystical teaching about the path to God can be best understood by beginning with his doctrine of God and creation. The apophatic character of Marquard's view of God is obvious throughout his sermons. For example, in dependence on Meister Eckhart's treatment of Paul's conversion, where the apostle is described as seeing nothing (Acts 9:8), Marquard says that "And in the light he saw nothing, because he saw God."[155] This negative theology is often presented in Dionysian terms with frequent quotations from the DN and MT. Outlining six kinds of knowledge of God in Sermon 19, for example, Marquard describes the highest form as a *docta ignorantia* characterized by "taking holy scripture and drawing it up to the modes of knowing above intellect and over images and all light and pointing humans beyond themselves in total ignorance of all things, as Saint Dionysius says in the *Mystical Theology*. . . . In this unknowing one sees in blindness and knows in unknowing."[156]

Marquard makes use of specifically Eckhartian negative language about God, as in Sermon 16 when he says, "in the essential reward one sees the groundless sea of the Godhead in its self-identity (*istikait*) and purity, as it is without image or form."[157] In Sermon 2 he surveys the apophatic names of God, like Eckhart finding the name Tetragrammaton the highest and worthiest, "because it is God's name as he is perceived in his naked detached nature itself."[158] Such emphasis on the "imageless nameless Godhead" (*bildlovsen namlovsen gotthait* [264.48]) was, of course, usual among many fourteenth-century German mystics. Although Marquard's negative language may have been commonplace among Dominicans, his adherence to the preeminence of apophatic theology is important for the history of Franciscan mysticism.

Marquard's ability to combine theological speculation and mystagogical teaching is evident in the way in which he roots his preaching in an original treatment of the Trinity. Sermon 32 for Trinity Sunday is one of his most impressive homilies.[159] He begins the sermon by claiming that if there were only one person in the Godhead the soul could not reach true blessedness, because it would have to give up "contemplation of the loving birth of the Eternal Word and the immeasurably sweet outflow of the Holy Spirit" (221.6–7). Although God can never be truly known or praised, the preacher says he must honor the feast by preaching on three points: (1) why it is necessary that there be three persons in the Godhead; (2) how the Trinity shines in all things; and (3) what pertains to the trinitarian light in the soul.

The first part of the sermon (221.17–225.144) is a presentation of claims for necessary proofs (*rationes necessariae*) for the Trinity. Marquard marshals six arguments from respected authorities, such as Augustine, Richard of St. Victor, Hilary of Poitiers, and Ambrose. The second part of the sermon (225.145–228.262) sets forth another six-part discussion, this time on the trinitarian light in all creation. In the first two points (225.147–226.177) Marquard shows how the Trinity is revealed in scripture, not only in the New Testament but also in the Old. The third point (226.178–227.199) discusses the pagan witnesses for the Trinity, citing Plato, Pythagoras, Aristotle, Porphyry, and the *Book of the Twenty-Four Philosophers*. This shows that the Franciscan, like the Dominican theologians of the first half of the fourteenth century, had a high regard for pagan witness to the Trinity.[160] The fourth and fifth points of the second part (227.200–218) note Anselmian and Augustinian teaching about trinitarian analogies in created things.

The sixth mode of the presence of the Trinity in creation (227.219–228.262) expresses a central theme of Marquard's theology, the image of the Trinity in the human soul. He says: "For the sixth point the Holy Trinity shines in the image of the intellectual soul in that there are three powers in which God has impressed his image in such noble fashion that St. Augustine says that to one who sees this image the Holy Trinity is as evident as the sun is seen coursing in the heavens."[161] This presence, Marquard argues, is especially dear to God and therefore far superior to any other.

In the last part of the sermon (228.263–230.320) Marquard analyzes the nature of the presence of the Trinity in the soul with the help of Eckhart's theology of the image. The aim of divine love in impressing its image in the soul is the birth of the Word in the soul: "God has displayed unmeasurable love in that he has impressed his noble image in the soul so that he might bear his Only-Begotten Son in her. . . ."[162] In order to understand the character of the *bild gottes* in the soul, Marquard uses the example of a painting of a king on a wall, an image that can be taken in two ways: in its essence in which it is only paint; or in its function as an image (*navch bildlicher wis*). To explore the latter he cites a passage from Eckhart's *Commentary on John* concerning four aspects of any image in relation to its archetype—an image takes its total reality from what it images; an image takes no reality from another source; an image takes the whole of the reality of its archetype; and finally the image and the archetype exist in each other.[163] Paraphrasing Eckhart, Marquard says, "The fourth point is that the image is always in God and God in the image just as Christ, who was an image of the Father says, 'The Father is in me and I in the Father' [John 14:11]."[164] It might seem that the Franciscan is in full agreement with Eckhart's image theology, but such is not the case. Marquard cites the Dominican when useful, but also draws back from those aspects of his teaching that went against tradition and had been attacked. Specifically, at the end of this sermon, he raises the debated question whether the image resides in the essence of the soul (*wesen der sele*), or in the three powers of memory, intellect, and will. Here, as elsewhere, he parts company with Eckhart, agreeing with Augustine (and Bonaventure and Aquinas) that the image resides in the powers.[165]

Marquard's teaching on the *imago Trinitatis* is found throughout his sermons,[166] but its exact relationship to other aspects of the Franciscan's teaching about God's presence in the depths of the soul needs further research. In Sermon 31, for example, he again turns to the nature of the image, this time identifying it, quoting one of Eckhart's sermons, with the *synderesis*, that is, "an image of divine nature that is related to God; it is a light that without intermediary is always enflamed by the Holy Spirit."[167] A number of sermons use the Eckhartian language of the "ground of the soul" (*grund der selen* [71.108]), or "ground of the mind" (*grund des gemuetes* [152.32; 305.137]). Marquard uses the latter term with a trinitarian meaning, as can be seen in Sermon 25, where, citing the authority of Augustine (probably *On the Trinity* 15.20.39), he says that gazing down upon "the golden plaque of one's mind" a person can behold and contemplate "God and the blessed Trinity gleaming in the ground of its mind."[168] Presumably, these uses of the term *grund* are not meant to indicate an uncreated something beyond all the soul's powers, as in Eckhart, but are a mode of expression for the soul's created nature whose three powers form the image of the Trinity.

Marquard of Lindau's doctrine concerning the path to union with God emphasizes many of the central themes of medieval mysticism: the cultivation of the virtues, particularly humility, poverty, and charity; the importance of silence and inwardness; devotion to Jesus, especially in his passion; the need to achieve releasement (*gelassenhait*) and inner freedom (*ledikait*); the birth of the Word in the soul; and rapture and loving union with God achieved in an *apex affectus* that surpasses all understanding. None of these themes was new, but Marquard's ability to present them in an effective way in MHG testifies to the power of his mystical preaching. A brief look at some of these cornerstones of medieval mysticism will help to show why Marquard can be considered the last great mystical preacher of the era.

In conformity with long tradition, Marquard identifies three stages on the path to God: "The first is outward virtuous exercise. The second is turning inward and meditation with images. The third is without images in pure unification and contemplation."[169] In practice, however, he does not dwell on overt itineraries. Like other mystics, Marquard insisted that love was the essential virtue. Sermon 31 preached for the Monday in Pentecost week begins with a six-point consideration of "the love of the Eternal Father," which is the source of creation and the power that draws all things back to himself. Following Augustine, Marquard insisted that love (*caritas/minne*) is the form of all the virtues, so that advance in every kind of goodness is possible only through the power of burning love.[170] In Sermon 8 Marquard allegorizes the two days that Jesus remained in the Samaritan village (John 4:40) as the two kinds of love necessary for salvation: "One day is pure love of God, the other is pure godly love of our fellow humans" (76.292–93). Sermon 39, preached on the Feast of St. Lawrence, has an extended treatment of how the fire of divine love enflames the mind and makes us like Christ.[171] It is no surprise that love is the dominant theme in Marquard's preaching, but the Franciscan does not neglect other essential virtues necessary for attaining the heights of contemplation, especially the humility that is the foundation of all the virtues,[172] as well as the poverty so much discussed among Franciscans and by Eckhart and his followers.[173] In practicing these virtues, Marquard says, we are achieving conformity to Christ.

Sermon 2 for the Feast of the Circumcision gives a good idea of the importance of Jesus in Marquard's preaching.[174] The first part of the sermon briefly lays out six reasons why the Savior voluntarily shed his blood at the circumcision, but Marquard's major interest, as shown in the question at the end of the first part (13.37–14.66), concerns our appropriation of this mystery through the spiritual circumcision by which a person is cut off from all superfluous images, thought, and desires, "so that the simple form of God may be reflected in him as in a pure mirror."[175] The second part of the sermon emphasizes the devotion to the name of Jesus, which had been strong in medieval mysticism since the time of Bernard of Clairvaux, who is liberally cited. (Marquard also mentions St. Francis's devotion to the Holy Name [17.164–67]). The preacher begins the second part by reviewing the various negative names of God found in the Old Testament as a way of highlighting the special positive revelation of the name of Jesus when God became man (14.67–15.105). The five letters of "Jesus" reveal five essential marks of the saving name—inwardness, oneness, strength, joy, and sweetness (15.105–18.180). Finally, part 3 (18.193–21.281) deals with the renewal that the faithful should embrace at the beginning of each new year.

Marquard's preaching about the imitation of Christ centers on following Jesus' example of burning love for God and neighbor. In his discussion of six ascending kinds of schools in Sermon 30, it is noteworthy that the Franciscan ranks the "school of Jesus Christ" third (204.70–205.98), below the school of the angels and the school of the Holy Spirit. This is because the third school is conceived of as involving *outward* following of the crucified Christ ("How a person finds all delight in the cross and in the suffering of our Savior Jesus Christ" [204.88–89]), while the school of the angels deals with "the inner spiritual life," and the school of the Spirit with unknowing and supreme affectivity. Sermon 23 expands on the role of the passion in a typically Franciscan way, treating how the five "signs of love of our Lord," that is, Christ's five wounds, become the object of the meditation of the God-seeking soul as it follows the Savior in the path of the virtues (155.144–158.234). However, the school of Christ and the school of the Holy Spirit are really the outer and inner dimensions of the same supreme love, as a discussion of the "divine fire" in Sermon 39 indicates (298.215–299.242). The fire of Holy Spirit that "makes the soul one love with him" (298.226) produces the Christlike person: "The more a person is like Christ, the more he has true divine love, because the life of Christ is the true rule of divine love. . . ."[176]

All this is very Franciscan. Where Marquard strikes a note different from usual Franciscan themes is in his use of the Eckhartian language of releasement, inner purity, silence, and the birth of the Son in the soul. He occasionally uses the language of detachment (*abegeschaidenhait*), but he favors releasement (*gelassenhait*) to describe the cutting off of desire by which a person becomes free (*ledic*) and empty (*blovss*) of all created things and thereby capable of being filled by God.[177] Sermons 5 and 41 contain treatments of this aspect of the Franciscan's mysticism. Sermon 5, preached for the Annunciation,[178] uses Mary as an exemplar of "a pure release of her heart to the divine will" (42.51–52). The third part of the sermon (45.157–47.230) analyzes six ways by which we can attain releasement into God's will, as shown by Mary and the Apostle Paul. True releasement, says Marquard, grants us "likeness to the sweet life of Jesus Christ" (45.168–69). Such releasement enables God to work in us "without a medium" (*sunder mittel*); it produces a state of dependence on God in all things so that "the person's spirit becomes so peaceful, quiet, and at rest in all accidental things that one remains always undisturbed in all things in peace of heart and equal thankfulness in everything" (46.182–84). This total dependence has a christological dimension as a form of self-surrender to Christ on the cross (46.204–7). It does not think of God as a source of sweetness or reward, but is rather directed to the divine being alone, thus "allowing God to be God" (*vnd got lavssen got sin* [47.217]).[179]

Silence is another theme that Marquard shares with Eckhart. In his Sermon 1 for the Feast of the Nativity, the Franciscan even cites the Dominican to make his point. Commenting on Wisdom 18:14 ("When quiet silence was in all things and the night had reached the mid-point, then your Almighty Word came down from the royal throne"), Marquard paraphrases passages from Eckhart's sermon cycle on the birth of the Son in the soul (Prr. 101–4), saying:

> If the Son of God is to come into a person's heart and mind there must be a stilling of every breaking in of the senses and a stillness of every creaturely image in the human intellect. And if a person remains in this kind of stillness, he will come to an unknowing and forgetting of himself and of all creatures, and then the Eternal Word will be spoken in the soul. . . . For this reason, if no creature bears itself in the soul, the Eternal Word will come from the royal throne and God the Father will speak his Eternal Word in the soul with all delight and bliss.[180]

Inner stillness is a necessary condition for the birth of the Word in the soul, both for Eckhart and for Marquard of Lindau.[181]

If Eckhart and Marquard were in agreement on the need for inwardness, silence, and the stripping away of all created reality to prepare for the birth of the Son, they differed on the role of the soul's powers in achieving birthing and union with God. Meister Eckhart developed the intellective Dionysianism of Albert in his own way, while Marquard can be described as the most effective German preacher of the affective Dionysianism initiated by Thomas Gallus. Marquard's dependence on the Victorine is evident in his description of the "School of the Holy Spirit" in Sermon 30 (205.100–206.132). This school is open only to "humble, empty, god-receptive people" (205.102), those who have chosen the most difficult and narrowest path. Quoting Paul and Dionysius (DN 7.1), Marquard emphasizes how this path goes beyond all knowing and naming, all intellect, thought, and speech. What is not surpassed is love:

> Because intellect and every power are there divested of their activity and are in a silence of unknowing concerning themselves and all things, as Saint Dionysius says, the apex of the power of love alone seeks union with God.

And in the apex of the loving power God is praised in a superessential way with overpowering love which there sweetens the activity of all the other powers and is nakedly turned toward God, as the abbot of Vercelli says.[182]

This stress upon *der spicz der minnenden kraft*, the *apex affectus* of Gallus and Bonaventure, is a characteristic note of affective Dionysianism. In other passages where Marquard does not use this technical term, he still clearly reflects the affective Dionysian stress on "the fire of love" (*fúr der minn*) as the only power capable of bringing the soul to union.[183] In Sermon 36 devoted to a presentation of the Dionysian theology of the angels, following Gallus, Marquard identifies the action of the Seraphim on the soul as the purification by the fire of love that produces union with God:

> Then come the burning Seraphim and they enkindle your inward mind so ardently that all dissimilarity is there burned away and in this sweet fire the mind is melted away and is united with God. Hence a person is made into "an angelic person" and is placed in such great nobility that no one can express it.[184]

The term *engelscher mensch* reflects both the Dionysianism of Gallus and its Franciscan appropriation by Bonaventure.

Marquard's stress on love fits in with the Franciscan view on the question of the nature of the beatific vision. Despite his appropriation of elements of Meister Eckhart, Marquard rejected the Dominican view of the priority of the intellect here and hereafter. In Sermon 16 he lays out the various characteristics of the "essential reward" (*daz wesenlicher lon*) of heaven in the first two parts (119.7–120.52), using language that is similar to Eckhart, but when he takes up the *quaestio disputata* of whether intellect or will shall enjoy the greater blessedness in heaven, he breaks with the Dominican, responding, "The loving power of the will shall have the greatest blessedness of all, because since a person does not earn the reward with the intellect but with the will's love, so should that power receive the greatest reward. Certainly, the intellect will enjoy blessedness insofar as it sees God within itself, but the will enjoys blessedness in that it finds itself in God, and that is much more noble."[185]

Marquard believed that uniting with God is the goal of the whole creative process, given humanity's status as microcosm.[186] In Sermon 16, as mentioned, he gives an Eckhartian-sounding analysis of the characteristics of the final union of heaven. This suggests that, like the anonymous author of the Latin commentary on the "Granum Sinapis," he thought that union of identity could take place only in heaven, not on earth.[187] But what kind of union can be enjoyed in this life? How are union and the vision of God, both here and hereafter, related?

While Marquard often speaks of union and vision, he does not present any full theory of union, as did some contemporaries like John Ruusbroec. Nonetheless, a survey of passages on mystical rapture and uniting with God in this life can help us understand Marquard's perspective.[188] Citing the examples of David in the Old Testament and Paul in the New, Marquard claims that it is possible to attain some direct vision of God in this life, but this must always be distinguished from the perfect vision to come.[189] In describing the various kinds of Christians in Sermon 37, he presents the sixth and final form in a way reminiscent of Eckhart's preaching about totally detached and poor persons, "who stand as nakedly as when they flowed out from God and as empty as when they did not exist."[190] It is significant that Marquard follows this presentation of the highest contact with God possible in this life not with a description of indistinct union, but with a discussion of whether or not the "divine, grace-filled presence of God" in the soul can ever be received so emphatically as to guarantee eternal blessedness. Using the example of Paul, who, despite his rapture to the third heaven castigated his body lest he fall away (2 Cor. 12; 1 Cor. 9:2), Marquard answers in the negative. Therefore, the Franciscan's view of the union with God possible in this life always stresses the difference between union here and union in heaven. The uniting that can be attained during this life is an interior transformation in love that takes place above the realm of intellect.[191] The union to come in heaven is expressed in the Eckhartian language of indistinct identity, as in the first part of Sermon 16, though Marquard always insists that it is achieved primarily through love and not intellect.

Marquard's fascination with forms of "being drawn away" (*gezuken*) and rapture (*zug*) are evident in many of his homilies. Sermon 8, for example, closes with a description of two forms of experience—an inner light that breaks out into the body and a sense of absolute inner truth—both signs of the presence of God (78.325–35). Sermon 41, preached for the Feast of the Conversion of St. Paul, features an extended discussion of Paul's rapture, discussing what the Apostle saw in the third heaven (315.180–316.212), as well as a comment on the nature of the three heavens and the differences between Paul's rapture and those of Adam and the evangelist John (316.226–317.255).[192] In order to get some idea of how Marquard presented the higher forms of contact with God possible in this life, expressed in terms of transforming love and rapture rather than of indistinct union, we can close by looking at one more of his sermons, Sermon 41, a homily preached for the Feast of St. Mary Magdalene, the archetypal image of the loving soul.[193]

Although the Virgin Mary was often seen as the model for mystical piety, her sinless status created problems for fallible humans who sought to imitate her to attain deeper contact with God. Hence, the other Mary, Mary Magdalene, converted sinner, single-minded lover, ascetic, apostle, model of the contemplative life, often emerged as a more accessible exemplar of total love for God. Commenting on the text from Luke 10:42 about Mary choosing the better part, Marquard begins his sermon by laying out six reasons for Mary's election of the better part, expounding on the purity of her love for Jesus, her wisdom in directing her efforts to divine infinity rather than creaturely finitude, and the superiority of contemplation over action (301.14–304.127).[194] Marquard sees Mary's devotion as aiming toward union with Jesus: "And so her mind at all times was turned to her Beloved and she was united with him alone without any intermediary."[195] The Franciscan's description of the contemplative person in the *quaestio* he appends to this first section of the sermon (304.117–27) centers on the issue of attaining "freedom of mind" (*frihait des gemútes*), which we may take as an expression of releasement.

The second part of the sermon is occupied with describing the six ways in which the Magdalene heard God's word while sitting at Jesus' feet. Here again Marquard shows his interest in what was typical of much fourteenth-century mysticism, that is, physical accounts of the action of God in both soul and body. For example, the fourth mode in which God speaks and Mary hears is described as one in which "God so pours his own sweetness into the soul that she receives the intellectual joy and is so overwhelmed by it that she cannot keep it within her but it must break forth from her in marvelous ways."[196] Marquard emphasizes Mary Magdalene as a model for attaining the heights of the rapture, union, and birth of the Word in the soul that God grants his true lovers in this life. God, he says, worked in her soul to form "a pure union between himself and the soul without any medium, without form or image, but only speaking his Eternal Word in the soul in the pure naked union. . . ."[197] Finally, in the third part of the sermon, Marquard considers what the Magdalene did in her legendary thirty years in the desert as the model contemplative, commenting not only on her "rich rapture and many exalted visions of the Godhead and the eternal mirror" (307.208–9), but also taking the opportunity for an attack on the erroneous mysticism of the Free Spirits, who are guilty of a "false emptiness" and therefore cannot recognize the ongoing need for human cooperation even with the exalted graces of mystical union.[198] Marquard uses some language of indistinction in talking about Mary Magdalene's union with God, but the weight of his affective Dionysianism tends to emphasize the ongoing difference between the divine Lover and the beloved.

Marquard of Lindau marks the last peak of the great age of German mystical preaching. Although the fifteenth century saw a broad dissemination of mystical literature, it is harder to find originality among its mystical preachers, though the sermons of Nicholas of Cusa (see chapter 10) may be an exception to this generalization. To be sure, there were many preachers who used mystical themes. An example can be found in the secular priest John Geiler of Kaysersberg (1445–1510), perhaps the most famous preacher at the end of the fifteenth century.[199] Geiler was a nominalist theologian and moral reformer deeply influenced by the writings of the chancellor of Paris, Jean Gerson (d. 1429). At Augsburg in 1488 and in several other venues he preached a series of sermons based on Gerson's popular vernacular treatise the *Mountain of Contemplation.* He reworked these homilies in treatise form in 1492 and eventually had the work printed in 1508. A survey of this text, as well as some of Geiler's other numerous treatises and sermons, shows his interest in mysticism, but Geiler's contributions are scarcely original.[200]

Letters

Although Bernard of Clairvaux wrote more than five hundred surviving letters, these epistles are not generally seen as essential sources for his mystical theology. There are, however, letters both by Bernard and by other twelfth-century figures that touch on aspects of mystical teaching.[201] By the thirteenth century, mystical letter collections had come into existence, as we see in the case of the beguines Hadewijch of Antwerp and Christina of Stommeln. This form of the dissemination of mystical teaching grew in the fourteenth century, as in the case of Henry Suso, whose *Great Book of Letters* and *Little Book of Letters* are underutilized sources for understanding his mysticism.[202]

The Flowering of Mysticism has already treated the *Revelations* of Margaret Ebner (1291–1351), a Dominican nun of the convent of Maria Medingen. Margaret's spiritual diary was composed about 1344–48 with the help of her confessor and spiritual friend, the secular priest Henry of Nördlingen. Henry's wanderings meant that much of the contact between the two took place by way of letters, "the earliest example of an edifying correspondence of an intimate and personal character in German," according to Manfred Weitlauff.[203] Unfortunately, since the collection was put together at Maria Medingen, it includes fifty-six letters that Henry sent to Margaret, but only one of hers.[204] Henry nurtured and helped publicize Margaret's mystical gifts in the manner similar to the many learned clerics of the late Middle Ages who saw ecstatic women as special channels of access to God. His letters display a knowledge of the vocabulary characteristic of the mysticism of the ground, with references to the birth of the Word in the soul, the hiddenness of God, the Friends of God, and the divine abyss (*abgrunt*). In one letter, for example, Henry echoes language typical of Eckhart and Tauler when he says of St. Paul's ascent to the third heaven: "There he was deified in God, unified in the Only One, bound with love, surrounded by light, totally penetrated with peace, shot through with pleasure. . . ."[205] Henry's acquaintance with mystical themes doubtless helped shape Margaret's visionary accounts, but he made no major contribution to mystical literature of his own. Exchanges of letters between other early fourteenth-century female mystics and their male advisors also exist, such as the letters of Christine Ebner (1277–1356) to John Tauler and Konrad of Füssen,[206] and the letters of Adelheid Langmann (1312–1375) and her spiritual friend, the Cistercian Ulrich of Kaisheim.[207]

These letters testify to the frequency of epistolary interchanges between clerics and female mystics. Other mystical epistles of the fourteenth and fifteenth centuries, mostly anonymous, give us a further perspective on the role of letters in the spread of mysticism.[208] A look at a few examples of this literature can serve to show that letters were not always derivative or second-rate sources of mystical teaching.

One example of an anonymous mystical letter of great power is the brief epistle known by its beginning phrase as "From the Hidden God to the Naked God" (*Vom verborgenen Gott zum blossen Gott*).[209] The letter, only a fragment, appears to be from a spiritual director to a penitent, probably a woman, who has taken up the life of inner releasement meant to lead into the deepest recesses of God. The content and vocabulary reflect the intellective Dionysianism of Eckhart (e.g., Pr. 52) and his pupil Henry Suso, whose terminology is evident in several places. The first lines announce the mysterious nature of *gelassenheit*: "Learn how to let go of God through God, the hidden God through the naked God,"[210] that is, even the God of negative theology must be removed if we would find the empty God beyond God. The first part of the letter, presented in strongly rhythmical prose, is a series of maxims concerning the need for total detachment and letting go, such as, "Be willing to lose a penny in order to find a gulder; pour out the water, so that you can draw wine." A christological dimension is also present: "If you want to catch fish, learn to wade; if you want to see Jesus on the shore [John 21:4, a resurrection reference], first learn to sink down into the sea" [Matt. 14:30].[211] The advice soon takes the form of direct commands— "Listen! Look! Suffer and be still! Release yourself into the light!" and the like, leading to the reaffirmation of releasement into the immanent presence of God. "My child, be patient and release yourself, because no one can dig God out from the ground of your heart."[212] Finally, the third part of the letter features a series of ecstatic praises of the divine mystery:

> O deep treasure, how will you be dug up? O high perfection, who can attain you? O flowing fountain, who can exhaust you? O burning Brilliance; out-bursting Power; simple Return; naked Hiddeness; hidden Security; secure Confidence; simple Silence in all things; manifold Good in single silence. You silent Cry [*du styles geschrey*], no one can find you who does not know how to release you.[213]

This brief epistle ranks among the most potent statements of the mysticism of the ground.

Other anonymous letters illustrate different aspects of late medieval mystical teaching. For example, a letter edited by Wilhelm Preger summarizes the mystical life with particular attention to divine love.[214] This anonymous epistle, described as being sent from one friend of God to another, begins with an elaborate address invoking the love of the three persons of the Trinity:

> With the burning seriousness of the truth of grace, which all the friends of God ever have possessed, I wish for you that the message of the Eternal Father that he sent to us through his Eternal Son in the love of his Eternal Spirit . . . begin in you and draw you into him, so that your outer person may be reflected in the humanity of our Lord Jesus Christ and your inner person in the Eternal Word, and you may respond to the dear will of the Father.[215]

All the Redeemer's works of love, says the author, have no other purpose than that the Word may speak in our hearts, though there are few that listen. The appeal to the birthing motif is reinforced by an unusual MHG rendering of Ecclesiasticus 24:26: "Come to me, all you who desire me, and be filled by my births."[216]

The second part of the letter provides a brief summary of how to begin the mystical path. The loving soul must first take leave of the world, the flesh, and even itself, and ". . . then first will you be ready to hear the message of all the works of love of our Lord Jesus Christ." The letter closes with an appeal to one of the archetypes of mystical consciousness, at least since the time of Gregory the Great, the prophet Elijah standing at the mouth of the cave and covering his face with his mantle at the passing by of the Lord (3 Kgs. 19:11–13). The divine message is the whisper of air heard by the prophet as he stood with heart uplifted to God, "that is, directed with all his desire to listen to God passing by, although with covered face, that is, with knowledge of his own unworthiness that made him ashamed and timid before the brightly illuminating Glory of God."[217]

Letters of mystical teaching remained popular in the fifteenth century, as a glance at Wilhelm Oehl's *Deutsche Mystikerbriefe* shows. The letters concerning the mid-century debate over the respective roles of love and knowledge in which Nicholas of Cusa became involved will be taken up in chapter 10. Other important letters from this period are still unedited. For example, Werner Williams-Krapp has studied a letter treatise that the Dominican Eberhard Mardach (d. 1428), prior of the Nuremberg convent, directed against the Free Spirit heretics.[218] This *Letter on True Devotion (Brief von rechtem warem sicherem andacht)* demonstrates not only the importance of the ongoing discussion of the distinction between true and false forms of mysticism that haunted late medieval Germany, but also shows that acquaintance with Eckhart and Suso continued among fifteenth-century Dominicans. Eberhard was involved in efforts to reform the Dominican order, both in male and female branches.[219] His unedited letter, found in at least twenty-one surviving manuscripts, probably dates to about 1420. It is highly suspicious of ecstatic experience, especially among women, an opposition that relies in part on Eckhart, but that also speaks to the growing tension over female visionaries in late medieval Europe. Mardach's answer to these dangers is in the form of a doctrine of *gelassenheit*, conceived of more as traditional obedience to the will of God than as a total metaphysical and ethical orientation in the style of Eckhart.[220] Mardach's letter was influential among the reform Dominicans, as can be seen in the case of his confrère, John Nider (d. 1438), and in other letters and treatises attacking false mysticism found in some female ecstatics.[221] Such opposition was quite different from the position of many Dominicans of the thirteenth and fourteenth centuries.

Dialogues

The use of dialogue was a common teaching tool in the Middle Ages, doubtless encouraged by the centrality of the *quaestio* in scholastic theology. Mystical sermons and treatises often make use of some form of question and answer ascribed to master and disciple to present their message in a clear and even memorizable form. Other short mystical texts, such as the stories about Eckhart (*Eckhart-Legenden*), also often adopt a dialogue or polylogue format.[222] The use of true dialogue, in which the voices actually add to the narrative presentation and the character of the message of the text, is rare, though it is found in parts of Mechthild of Magdeburg's thirteenth-century *Flowing Light of the Godhead*. At least one treatise from the fourteenth century demonstrates how effective an actual dialogue, rather than mere didactic question and answer, could be in setting forth mysticism. This text is usually known as *Sister Katherine* (*Schwester Katrei*), but more correctly entitled *About the Confessor's Daughter*. This discussion between an unnamed friar confessor and a female mystic, probably a beguine, is also famous, even notorious, because it has been seen as an example of the heresy of the Free Spirit.

Sister Katherine survives in seventeen manuscripts and several versions, including a Latin translation.[223] The language links the piece to Strassburg, and it was produced in the first half of the fourteenth century (ca. 1330?). Because it uses Eckhartian themes, it has also been linked with Eckhart, though his name is never mentioned and he cannot have been the author.[224] Since its first edition by Franz Pfeiffer, *Sister Katherine* has been much discussed among students of mysticism and heresy. The critical edition by Franz-Josef Schweitzer has cleared up many questions about this fascinating text,[225] but there is still disagreement about how far the text may be said to be the product of the Free Spirit heresy.[226]

Unlike Marguerite Porete's *Mirror of Simple Annihilated Souls, Sister Katherine* was never condemned. Many of its views, not only those it shares with Eckhart but others that are non-Eckhartian, are strange and challenging, perhaps even in some particulars unorthodox; but I find it difficult to think of the dialogue as essentially a Free Spirit text, as the following analysis will attempt to show. Rather, we must approach *Sister Katherine* as a witness to the spread of a variety of mystical views in fourteenth-century Germany and a good example of the ongoing debate about mystical authority. While not denying the role of the church and its clergy and sacraments (and also attacking heresy along the way!), *Sister Katherine* is one of the boldest examples of a new type of tract that elevates illuminated laity, in this case a woman, over learned clerics when it comes to attaining direct contact with God. This was certainly daring, but need not have been heretical.

On the basis of the peculiar views of the dialogue about the last things (death, judgment, heaven, and hell), as well as the role of the body in heaven (see ed., 340–44), F.-J. Schweitzer has argued that the text originated in the Free Spirit group in Strassburg, which between 1317 and 1319 was attacked for various errors.[227] But rather than directly denying the existence of heaven and hell (which is apparently what the Strassburg group did according to the inquisitorial documents), *Sister Katherine* spiritualizes the afterlife in ways not unlike those found in Eriugena's *Periphyseon*, a text known in a number of mystical circles in fourteenth-century Germany.

A second argument for the Free Spirit connection has been based on the passage in which the confessor invites the beguine who has attained establishment in God to "enjoy all creatures, . . . because any creature you enjoy you bring back to its origin,"[228] a statement that has been described as a classic expression of Free Spirit antinomianism. Taken in isolation, perhaps; but in the context of the whole work the passage constitutes a test by the friar of the mystic's authenticity—a test she passes with flying colors, insisting that she will not act this way, but will "never diverge from the path of our Lord Jesus Christ" (346.7–8). In other words, *Sister Katherine* is giving a lesson on what kind of mysticism to avoid. This is confirmed by a later passage that attacks as "true heretics" (*recht keczer* [348.31]) those who do not "take sin for sin," and who do not follow "the example of our Lord Jesus Christ."[229] Finally, much has been made of the passage where the woman boldly announces, "Father, rejoice with me, I have become God!" (*Herre, fröwent üch mitt mir, ich bin gott worden* [334.13–14]). For many interpreters this is a statement of the autotheism of the Free Spirits. Yet the language of deification is found in many mystics of the fourteenth century, even the most orthodox. Admittedly, it is unusual to put such a claim in the first person, but the genre of this work, a dramatic dialogue, helps explain this procedure. Furthermore, shortly afterward the mystic explains such language by appealing to the theological topos so often used to qualify divinization language when she says, "I am granted my everlasting bliss. I have attained by grace what Christ is by nature."[230] So, while *Sister Katherine*, like Eckhart, raises questions about its more daring statements, it is hard to see it as a Free Spirit tract.

The mini-drama that constitutes *Sister Katherine* is remarkable, not only for the interplay between the two protagonists, but also for the richness and at times obscurity of its teaching. It will not be possible here to give more than an introduction to the text and to highlight some of its more significant claims about the mystical life. Although there are no divisions or subtitles in the manuscripts, for the sake of clarification I will follow the divisions of the English translation into seven sections. The first four sections (ed. 322–31) contain dialogues in which the friar confessor instructs the God-seeking woman about the best path to mystical union in a style reminiscent of descriptions of other priest-penitent relationships, such as that between Suso and Elsbeth Stagel.[231] At the end of section 4, however, the woman, following the guidance of the Holy Spirit, asserts her independence and her desire to go off on her own to suffer for Christ. She says: "I will go into exile and to all the places where I can be persecuted. You must understand that I have found more good in the least humiliation than in all the sweetness that was ever done to me by creatures" (330.39–331.4). The friar cannot gainsay this apostolic intention (he cites Matt. 10:22–23), so he closes by telling her, "Come to me where you find me," as she goes off into exile (*die tochter enweg jn das ellend* [331.14]). The theme of exile had also been used by Eckhart in his sermon "On the Nobleman" to describe a person who went off into a far country to gain a kingdom (Luke 19:12), that is, the inner person who departs from the created world, all images, and even the self, in order to find God in the desert within.[232]

The fifth section (331.15–335.18) constitutes the dramatic center of the dialogue. Here the description of the changing relationship of the two protagonists achieves a rare subtlety. When the daughter returns from the distant lands of her journey within, the friar at first does not recognize her; but when she tells him that this is because he does not know himself, he admits the charge. After hearing her confession, he announces to his brethren, "I have listened to the confession of a person and I'm not sure if she is a human being or an angel. . . . She knows and loves more than all the people I have ever known" (331.34–332.7). In their second encounter she informs him of who she is, and he begs her to tell him "about the life and labor you have had since I last saw you," setting the stage for the second half of the dialogue, in which the woman for the most part instructs the cleric. However, just as in the first part the female often made her voice and views known, in the second part the cleric remains an important interlocutor who makes his own contributions, at least at times, to the presentation of the message.

Before that can happen, however, the daughter needs to "gain a permanent place" (*ein stetes bliben* [333.9–10]), or "become permanently established in eternity" (*bestettet jn der steten ewikeit* [333.12]). Although such a form of permanent union with God goes beyond the boundaries of classic monastic mysticism, as found in the Cistercians and Victorines, who insisted that all union with God in this life was temporary and partial, the mysticism of Eckhart, as well as later mystics such as Teresa of Avila, allowed for the possibility of states of lasting union. It is also interesting to note that the beguine achieves this state with the confessor's help, even though he is less spiritually advanced than she (another proof that the text is not anticlerical). In good Eckhartian fashion, the friar tells the daughter that she must get rid of the desire for establishment in God in order to attain it. The narrative goes on: "And she puts herself into a state of emptiness. There God draws her into a divine light so that she thinks she is one with God as long as it lasts."[233] When she tells him what she experienced in this state, he responds by advancing an observation crucial to the remainder of the dialogue:

> HE: Realize that this is foreign to all people. Were I not so learned a priest that I had myself read about this divine wisdom, it would also be foreign to me.

SHE: I'm sorry about that. I wish you had learned it with your own life!

HE: ... I admit to you it grieves me that I did not learn it through life.[234]

In other words, the female mystic has arrived at what Cardinal Newman would centuries later call real knowledge, while the friar still only has notional knowledge of the mysteries of God. He must turn to her for the higher instruction that will eventually lead him to union.

It is at this point that the daughter goes off into another ecstasy in God, after which she makes the claim noted above to have become God. Finally, she retreats into a corner of the church and enters into a three-day ecstasy, during which the other friars think she must be dead (recall Christ's three days in the tomb). When she awakens, she is conformed in grace as joint heir with Christ and ready to begin her instruction of the confessor. The Christocentric nature of the mystical transformation is essential, as the daughter exclaims at the end of this section: "Praised and honored be the name of our Lord Jesus Christ, because he has revealed to me that I can know and love God in him. He has been the example through which I found my salvation."[235]

The long sixth section (335.19–369.33), comprising over half the tract, features a series of dialogues sometimes fading into monologues, in which the daughter instructs the friar confessor about a wide variety of topics mystical and theological. The first of these dialogues (335.22–339.28) is important for the text's Eckhartian notion of union. The daughter begins by speaking of ten external things that have assisted her to reach perfection. More important are the internal aids, which are distinguished between practices before she became established and those after. The pre-establishment union was a dwelling within the Trinity insofar as the three persons remain distinct and the source of all distinct creatures. "When I looked into myself," she says, "I saw God within me and everything he has ever created in heaven and on earth" (337.8–10), as in the mirror of truth (*spiegel der warheit*). But after her establishment she has nothing to do with any creature or anything that was ever spoken. She speaks of being "established in the pure Godhead in which there never was form or image" (337.26–27), explaining:

I am where I was before I was created; that place is purely God and God. There are neither angels nor saints, nor choir, nor heaven, nor this nor that. . . . Realize that in God there is nothing but God. You must understand that no soul may come into God before it has become God as it was God before it was created. No one may come into the naked Godhead except the one who is as naked as he was when he flowed out from God.[236]

The similarity of this presentation to Eckhart's view of indistinct union and returning to one's pre-creational state, as expressed, for example, in Pr. 52, is striking. A few lines later the friar even quotes "one master" on the need to love God in God's self and not as "our God," an Eckhartian point, though one not found word for word in Eckhart's surviving texts. The daughter praises this statement—"Blessed be the master who said that."[237] This section closes on an equally Eckhartian note, as the daughter explains how the highest power, or "man," in the soul enters into the origin: "It is the soul, naked and empty of all expressible things, which stands as one in the One, so that it can go forward in the naked Godhead, just like oil on a cloth flows on and on."[238]

The second instruction concerns the four last things and the status of the body in heaven (339.29–344.10). As mentioned above, this part of the dialogue advances a highly spiritualized, immanentized, and often rather obscure view of the last things reminiscent in some particulars of John Scottus Eriugena. The three following dialogues are instructions on living the Christian life. In the first of these (instruction 3: 344.10–346.8) the daughter asks the friar how she should conduct her life. This is where the confessor tests her authenticity by inviting her to take her ease and enjoy all creatures, and she refuses in her desire to never abandon the model of Christ. Instruction 4 (346.9–347.21) deals with the imitation of Christ, while instruction 5 (347.22–349.21) features the attack on false mysticism noted above.

The final instructions (which I number as 6–9) contain a somewhat confusing mélange of materials. Instruction 6 (349.22–351.31) deals with the nature of the soul. Instruction 7 (351.32–356.41) analyzes the "least, or lowliest people" (Matt. 25:45), which the daughter interprets as the saints, especially those to whom "God is indebted" for their pure apostolic lives. Here there is a treatment of Mary Magdalene, the archetype of lovers of Christ, who is an example of the necessity of moving from the natural love of Christ's physical presence to the spiritual love by which the Magdalene came to recognize the Father in the Son. (The transition from carnal to spiritual love had been an important topos in mysticism at least since the time of Bernard of Clairvaux.) The long eighth instruction (356.42–367.20) is really a monologue by the daughter on the danger of serving God for the sake of reward. In it the author mounts what is perhaps the most powerful critique of the desire for physical and even spiritual visions of God in late medieval mysticism. Using stories and unusual reflections on the apostles (including an as yet untraced apocryphal story about Bartholomew [360.23–361.19]), the author underlines that it is only when Christ physically departed that the apostles were able to recognize the Father in the Son and to receive immediate union with the three persons of the Trinity. "Because all exterior comfort was taken from them," says the daughter, "their souls raised themselves internally with all their strength, into the Creator. Then the Holy Spirit flowed from the Father and the Son into their souls. . . . They saw and recognized the Father in the Son and the Son in the Father and knew the Holy Spirit that flowed from the two persons into their souls."[239]

The ninth and final instruction (367.21–369.33) summarizes the teaching of the daughter and marks a second culmination of the text as the confessor himself achieves mystical rapture. The daughter again stresses the need to overcome all mediation and shows her pity "for the people who claim to see God with exterior eyes" (367.29–30). God can only be seen in and through Christ the mediator. Here the author even attacks those who claim to have had physical visions of Christ in the Eucharist (a widespread phenomenon among beguines). The recognition of the body of Christ on the altar as true God and true man "takes place only in right belief, and in understanding and in love" (368.43–45). This section closes with the overpowering of the confessor's senses: "The daughter told him so much about the greatness, power and providence of God that he lost his outer senses and had to be helped to a sheltered cell where he lay a long time before regaining consciousness."[240]

That this was a mystical ecstasy becomes clear in the brief seventh part of *Sister Katherine* (369.34–370.27). When the confessor awakes he calls the daughter and thanks God that she has guided him to eternal salvation, saying: "I was drawn into a divine manifestation (*götlich beschöwede*) and have been given proof of everything I have heard from your mouth" (369.40–43). The text ends with the daughter cautioning him that he is just at the beginning of the mystical life. He must be persistent in his journeys up and down, eventually learning the difference "between God and the Godhead," and the more mysterious difference "between the Spirit and spirituality" (*vnderscheid zwischent dem geiste vnd der geistlichait* [370.13–14]). He should also seek activity with creatures so that he can gather his strength and avoid madness (perhaps another reference to false mysticism). The *Sister Katherine* conceives of the mystical life as one of ongoing commitment and perseverance.

Hagiography and Visions

Saints' lives had been a favorite way of expressing mystical teaching since at least the fourth century. Hagiographical literature as exemplary, catechetic, inspiring, and (yes) entertaining was as central to medieval culture as motion pictures have become to contemporary society. From 1200 on, traditional hagiographical narrative models interacted with the explosion of visionary accounts often presented in the first person that were an important feature of the new mysticism of the late Middle Ages. This was an international phenomenon, but we will consider it here only from a German perspective.

Lives of saints, especially of holy women, concentrating on mystical gifts and visionary revelations began to spread in thirteenth-century German-speaking lands, though they were still written in Latin.[241] One noted mystical text, Mechthild of Magdeburg's vernacular *Flowing Light of the Godhead*, mixes many genres, not least collections of visions, to authenticate the saint and her message. In the fourteenth century, German-language experiments with new hagiographical forms for spreading mystical teaching began to appear. One trend eschewed traditional biographical narrative and emphasis on the acquiring of virtues and the performance of public miracles to concentrate instead on stories concerning special gifts of grace—visions and revelations, as well as ecstasies and other miraculous somatic manifestations (e.g., inedia, stigmata, levitations).

German scholars created the term *Gnadenviten* ("Grace-Lives") to describe this form of narrative theology presenting models of sanctity through accounts centered on mystical visions and unusual graces.[242] Such collections were most often, though not exclusively, devoted to women. The most noted examples are the *Sister Books* (*Schwesternbücher/Nonnenleben*) produced by German Dominican nuns mostly between ca. 1300 and 1350.[243] These collections of accounts of holy women of particular communities, such as the convents of Engelthal, Unterlinden, and Töss, were based on older genres, remotely the collections of stories about the desert fathers, and proximately the accounts of the early Dominican friars compiled by Gerald of Frachet in the *Lives of the Brethren* (*Vitasfratrum*) of ca. 1260. Nevertheless, there was novelty, too, not only because of the move into the vernacular, but also because of the intent to foster the identity and fame of particular convents. As literature written by and for women, these collections brought an original dimension to the variety of genres that spread mystical doctrine in late medieval Germany. Individual *Gnadenviten*, often largely collections of visions, continued to be produced through the fourteenth century, as we can see both from the accounts of female visionaries such as the Viennese beguine Agnes Blannbekin (d. 1315),[244] and also in the case of exceptional males, such as the priest Friedrich Sunder (d. 1328), who served as the chaplain for the Dominican convent at Engelthal.[245]

The third-person accounts of saintly lives, either more traditional hagiographies or the newer *Gnadenviten*, were complemented by first-person narratives of the reception of mystical gifts, mostly featuring visions and revelations from Christ, Mary, and the angels and saints. Such accounts often appear in texts designed to testify to the sanctity of a holy person. It has become fashionable to speak of such works as "autohagiography."[246] Although the term has been used somewhat loosely, it does point to a new dimension in the relation between hagiography and mysticism in the later Middle Ages: the way in which first-person descriptions of contact with God were used to claim religious status and teaching authority. "Autohagiography" might be best described as a technique or new didactic mode of presentation rather than a genre. It is found in texts that present personal narratives of what are purported to be real events and experiences, although, in the words of Kate Greenspan, "an individual's experience was always ancillary, valuable only insofar as it could teach, inspire, or provide a model."[247] As a mode of presentation, it was used in narratives like Suso's *Life of the Servant*, as well as in the visionary diaries and journals of fourteenth-century women such as Elsbeth of Oye (d. 1340), Margaret Ebner (d. 1351), Christine Ebner (d. 1356), and Adelheid Langmann (d. 1375).[248]

Traditional hagiography, the stories of holy men and women, especially the classic figures of Christian tradition, remained a very popular genre in late medieval Germany, reaching its peak in the fifteenth century.[249] Interestingly enough, the hagiographers of late medieval Germany show less concern for producing the official Latin *vitae* necessary for a canonization process than for experimenting with vernacular forms of presenting local models of mystical holiness.[250] Although this was the era of what André Vauchez has called the "mystical invasion" (ca. 1370–1430), during which women gifted with mystical and prophetic gifts were pushed for canonization,[251] German hagiographers concentrated on obtaining a local cult or disseminating effective mystical models rather than gaining Rome's approbation. The varied forms of mystical hagiography continued to be employed in the late fourteenth century and through the early fifteenth century.

By far the best-seller of fifteenth-century mystical hagiography was the German version of Raymond of Capua's *Legenda major* of Catherine of Siena (d. 1380) written between 1384 and 1395 and translated in Nuremberg around 1400.[252] As Master General of the Dominicans, Raymond was the initiator of the reform movement within the order, a reform for which Catherine was an inspiration and model. The reform spread to Germany in the 1390s and was an important force in the religious life of fifteenth-century Germany.[253] Similar reform movements were found among the male and female orders of the Franciscans, as well as the Augustinians.[254] The role of these reform movements, as Werner Williams-Krapp has shown, was vital for the spread of the reputation of some women as exemplars of mystical sanctity. In his words, "Mystical piety could either be excluded as error or incorporated into the work of reform, domesticated and, should the occasion arise, even used instrumentally."[255] In an age that was increasingly suspicious of female visionaries and ecstatics, all too ready to denounce them as deceived by the devil or filled with heretical depravity, women could still be put forward as saintly mystics if their lives and revelations supported religious reform movements. While the increasingly formalized application of rules of discernment of spirits (*discretio spirituum*) for the most part weighed against women,[256] some of the reformers who generally were hostile to female claims to direct contact with God were ready to make exceptions in the case of nuns whose lives could be used to demonstrate divine approbation for more rigorous observation of the religious life.

Dominican nuns had dominated the hagiography of fourteenth-century Germany. Their numbers were fewer in the fifteenth. Margaret of Kenzingen (d. 1428), wife of a wealthy merchant, joined the reformed Dominican convent at Unterlinden after the death of her husband in 1411, sending her five-year-old daughter to another reformed house, that of the Franciscan Clarisses at Freiburg. Margaret was associated with the reform of the Dominican nuns at Basel, at least in the presentation of her life by the friar John Meyer, a leader of the observantine Dominicans. John credits her with the usual extreme forms of asceticism and numerous raptures, as well as the virtues of a good reformed nun.[257]

Margaret's daughter, Magdalena of Freiburg (d. 1458), also known as Magdalena Beutler or Beutlerin, was not to be outdone by her mother. This controversial Franciscan nun provides a test case for the debates over acceptable forms of female mysticism in the fifteenth century.[258] It is difficult not to think of her as something of a fraud (whether pious or not).[259] Certainly, many contemporaries, such as John Nider (d. 1438), another key figure in the Dominican reform and the early stages of the persecution of witches, did. Nider's noted *Formicarius* is most often seen as an opening salvo in the war against witches, and two of the five books of the prolix collection are devoted to distinguishing good revelations from evil ones. John uses the case of Magdalena's mystical death of 1431 as an example of the kind of "deceptive illumination" (*phantastica luminaria*) to which women were especially prone.[260]

Magdalena announced that she had received a message from God that she would die on the Feast of the Epiphany. Her nuns and crowds from

Freiburg and nearby cities assembled on the appointed day. She went into ecstasy, but doctors felt her pulse and determined that she was still alive. Nevertheless, she cried out that she should be laid in the coffin that had been prepared for her. After a period there, she arose and asked for something to eat, apparently claiming a mystical death (*mors mystica*), not a physical one. A near riot ensued. Magdalena lost her chance for the kind of popular and clerical following that might have allowed her eventual acceptance as a revered mystic, though her community continued to believe in her and to preserve her writings and accounts of her claims. The *vita* produced by her convent, the still-unedited *Magdalenen-Buch,* which contains some material written by her, tries to turn the failed prediction of death into another sign of her absolute submission to the hidden will of God, though admitting that "Her holy, blessed life was scoffed at and denied by many sinful people, and it was often taken as a sign that she was a sorceress."[261]

Another reformed Franciscan nun of the fifteenth century received some attention as a holy ecstatic, Ursula Haider (ca. 1413–1498).[262] The hagiographical materials about Ursula, as well as some of her own writings, unfortunately survive only in a much later collection, the *Chronicle of the Bickencloister at Villingen,* put together by the prioress Juliana Ernestin in 1637–38. More contemporary is the life of the Franciscan tertiary Elsbeth Achler of Reute (1386–1420), compiled by her Augustinian confessor and sponsor, Konrad Kügelin. She alone of the mystical religious of fifteenth-century Germany maintained a popular cult as Elisabeth Bona, "die gute Beth." Kügelin's *vita* taps into themes made popular in the life of Catherine of Siena, especially excessive asceticism, devotion to the passion, stigmata, and numerous raptures. Kügelin also paints Elisabeth as a model of reform.[263]

Perhaps more interesting for the hagiographical presentation of mysticism in late medieval Germany are the materials relating to women who tried to achieve contact with God in the world rather than behind cloister walls.[264] Such lay mystics, both women and men, provide a new dimension to traditional hagiography.[265]

The mass of materials produced to further the canonization of the Prussian married woman and later anchoress Dorothy of Montau (1347–1394) is the best-known example. Dorothy has received a good deal of attention in recent decades, not only because the Vatican finally recognized her sanctity in 1976 (the cause began shortly after her death in 1394!), but also because she features, though not favorably, in Günther Grass's novel *The Flounder.*[266] Due largely to the efforts of her last confessor, John Marienwerder (1343–1417), a canon of the order of Teutonic Knights, we have a large, if repetitious and tendentious, mass of information about her life and mystical gifts.[267] Her mode of sanctity as a married woman attempting to live a life of contemplative piety is emblematic of a new style of holy woman of the late Middle Ages, as we see in figures who eventually won canonization, such as Birgitta of Sweden (d. 1373),[268] and those who did not, like the English mystic Margery Kempe (d. ca. 1440). John Marienwerder composed his Latin lives to further Dorothy's canonization. His German life, however, was aimed at the kind of lay audience avid for mystical literature characteristic of the fifteenth century. At the beginning of the chapter "On her praiseworthy marriage," John comments: "Not only virgins and those who live chastely enter the kingdom of heaven but also married people who with true faith and good works earn God's grace."[269]

We can recover a surprising amount about Dorothy's fascinating life from John's writings, even though his interpretive viewpoint as a hagiographer interested in the "really real," that is, the exemplary more than the factual, is scarcely that of modern biography. Born into a middle-class family, Dorothy is portrayed as remarkably pious from an early age. Married at age seventeen to an older and well-off craftsman, she bore nine children, only one of whom survived to eventually become a nun.[270] It appears that it was only after the death of most of her children between 1378 and 1384 that she was able to devote herself increasingly to a life of ascetical and mystical practices. Though her husband, Adalbert, is pictured as a pious man who accompanied her on her early pilgrimages to Aachen and the hermitage at Finsterwald in 1384, he became angry and abusive toward her because of the raptures that interfered with her household duties. In 1385 Dorothy experienced a mystical turning point, the extraction of her human heart by Jesus and its replacement with a new heart. As might be expected, John Marienwerder makes much of the tension between Dorothy's sexual obligations to her husband and her desire to devote herself fully to Christ. Like Margery Kempe, she eventually convinced her now elderly husband to live in chastity,[271] but it was only after his death in 1390 while she was away on pilgrimage in Rome that Dorothy was able to devote herself fully to a religious way of life. She did this by pulling up stakes, leaving Danzig and migrating to Marienwerder. The acts of Dorothy's canonization process hint that she was a controversial figure in her native Danzig, attacked by some as a heretic and seen by others (again like Margery Kempe) as eccentric and disruptive.[272] It was only in the last four years of her life at Marienwerder that she found real recognition as a holy woman.

This acceptance was due in no small part to the interest that John Marienwerder and his friend the canonist John Reyman took in the recent widow. In the vernacular life Dorothy describes her initial encounter with John as an example of love at first sight:

> As he heard my confession for the first time, I immediately conceived a greater love for him than for any other person. At once I loved him as sincerely as a brother and trusted him so explicitly that then and there I would have revealed all the secrets of my heart to him had the Lord taught me how to phrase them properly at that very moment.[273]

Such highly charged relationships expressed in quasi-marital terms were not unknown in earlier times, as the example of the Dominican Peter of Dacia and the beguine Christina of Stommeln shows.[274] But while Peter's account (which includes letters from Christina) gives the impression of a young friar in awe of the spectacular and often bizarre experiences of his spiritual beloved, John Marienwerder's writings emphasize control, that is, the total obedience that Christ, the invisible Bridegroom, commands Dorothy to give to her confessor and new, though nonsexual, husband, Canon John. For example, the German life speaks for Christ ordering her as follows: "You shall subordinate your will entirely to his. Whatever he asks you to do, do, and whatever he prohibits you from doing, do not do."[275] John, however, was nothing if not a faithful surrogate spouse, as his heroic efforts to gain her canonization show.[276] Through the efforts of John and her other supporters at Marienwerder Dorothy did finally gain a recognized religious status at the end of her earthly life, being accepted as an anchoress, or recluse, in May of 1393, thirteen months before her death on June 25, 1394.

Such close relations between pious and theologically well-educated clerics and illiterate lay female ecstatics were an important feature of late medieval mysticism. In *The Flowering of Mysticism* I investigated a number of examples of these forms of interdependence and conversation between men and women, beginning with Jacques de Vitry and Mary d'Oignies, the archetypal beguine. These cases of what Dyan Elliott has called "double authorization" were typical of the new mysticism.[277] The learned cleric had much to gain: not only a direct channel to God but also prestige for his order, his local church, and himself as the spokesman of the saint. The female mystic acquired clerical support and advice (especially in the sacrament of penance), as well as the possibility of disseminating her message through the writings of her confessor and friend. In some cases, as in that of Angela of Foligno and her Franciscan scribe, we are able to discern a real collaboration. In other cases, such as that of Dorothy and John, it is difficult to determine how much of the woman's voice filters through. Although John does describe the mutuality of the writing process in several places,[278]

the canon's extensive writings about Dorothy, perhaps because of their pro-
lixity and artificiality, give the impression of a great degree of stage-
management. More detailed comparison between the surviving examples
of Dorothy's German dictations and John's versions of Dorothy's revelations are needed before we can say how much access we have to the saint's
own voice.[279] Though we need not doubt the general accuracy of many of
the events described by John, the theological screen through which he presents them reflects his own obsessive agenda for securing Dorothy's canonization. Our knowledge of Dorothy's mysticism is largely what a learned
cleric thought a lay female mystic should be—something in itself highly relevant for the communication of mysticism in late medieval Germany.

John makes his didactic purpose clear at the outset of his vernacular life
of the recluse. Appealing to "all inhabitants of Prussia and all believers in
Christ," he defends the length of the work because the richness of Dorothy's
ascetical practices and miraculous graces cannot be briefly described.
Though much of her example was doubtless more the object of admiration
than of imitation, John says that all devout people can enter into Dorothy's
life, "as into a winsome meadow, to gather there, with God's help and the
strength of individual discernment, the flowers of virtue which she produced with such abundance that they were sufficient to secure not only her
own salvation but the salvation of all lovers of virtue."[280]

Richard Kieckhefer has shown how John's picture of what he calls
Dorothy's "strongly affective piety" is based on three essential themes of
late medieval hagiography: the practice of pilgrimage; severe asceticism as
a form of *imitatio Christi*; and an emphasis on forms of mystical experience,
often of an excessive character.[281] While the first two are of importance,[282] it
is obvious from the hundreds of pages of John's often cloying prose (especially in the Latin writings) that he put his greatest emphasis on Dorothy's
mystical gifts as a paragon of all the modalities of divine *caritas* and a perfect example of a bride of Christ. In constructing this picture of the widow,
John brought to bear a good knowledge of the mystical tradition,[283] as well
as a late medieval scholastic penchant for meticulous organization and verbal overkill.

As mentioned above, the pivot of John's account of the development of
Dorothy's mysticism is the 1385 extraction of her heart. This mystical
grace, which John bases on Ezekiel 36:26, was also ascribed to Catherine of
Siena.[284] At the beginning of book 2 of the vernacular life John describes
the event and its consequences in detail. On Candlemas day Dorothy went
to the Marian church in Danzig early in the morning and prayed devoutly.
During Mass,

Our Lord Jesus Christ, her mighty lover, came, pulled out her old heart and pushed into its place a new hot one. The blessed Dorothy felt very well that her old heart was being extracted and that in place of that heart an extremely hot piece of flesh was shoved into her. In receiving this piece of flesh or new heart she experienced such rapture and joy that she could never fully express it to anyone.[285]

This form of somatic experience with distinct sexual overtones, typical of many late medieval women mystics, is meant to highlight a central theme of John's picture of Dorothy's mysticism—the growth of divine *caritas* in all its varied manifestations in the body as well as in the soul of the Prussian woman. John insists that the extraction event was a physical as well as a spiritual change (*mutacio substancie* in VL III.1), citing biblical examples like Eve's formation from Adam's rib, and even the transsubstantiation of the Eucharist. Although Dorothy is described as being privileged with raptures and other mystical gifts prior to this,[286] after the extraction and renewal of her heart the frequency and quality of her mystical gifts greatly increases (DL II.2). The heart replacement strengthens her desire for the Eucharist and grants her more intense forms of piercing by the Divine Lover, "who daily wounded her soul and heart, now with the arrows of love, now with love's steel spears." John continues: "And in the injuries caused by these projectiles she now felt pain, now sweetness, now love and longing."[287] The physical heat of the new organ, according to John, subsequently provided Dorothy with miraculous imperviousness to cold (see DL III.13). Two years later she received another special gift, the grace of a self-transparency that allowed her "to see herself through and through as if she were gazing through a crystal with healthy eyes."[288]

In enumerating the gifts following upon the heart transplant, John begins to discuss the kinds of love that God granted Dorothy, not only the "wounding love" already noted, but also such modes as "overflowing love" (*obirv-lutige libe*). This introduces one of the more original aspects of John Marienwerder's theology of mysticism, his enumeration of the thirty-six or thirty-seven modalities of divine love active in Dorothy.[289] This rather cumbersome presentation appears to be John's own creation, and apparently a controversial one, given his defense of it in the *Septililium.* (The reason for the two slightly different enumerations is not clear.)[290] In explaining his position, John argues that divine love is, of course, single in itself, but capable of infinite forms of reception in its recipients. Nevertheless, he claims that his distinction of loves is an accurate reflection of the graces given to Dorothy.[291]

There is no need to outline John's enumeration of all the forms of love, especially because he himself says that some types are more important to the contemplative life than others.[292] At the beginning of the treatise on contemplation in the *Septililium,* he says that the Lord told Dorothy that although the contemplative needs all the modes of charity, "such a person ought especially to have inebriating love and violent love through which the soul is raised and raptured above itself to gaze upon heavenly things."[293] In the course of the German version of the life it becomes clear that inebriating love, violent love, and its cognate wounding love are central to Dorothy's excessive life, just as what John calls "heartbreaking love" (*hertczbrechende libe/caritas effractiva*) is the mode of love characteristic of Dorothy's dying into Christ.

The incunable edition (1492) of John's vernacular life of Dorothy portrays the saint in widow's garb holding a bookbag and rosary beads with five arrows piercing her, one directly into her heart. The theme of the wound of love, one of the most ancient in Christian mysticism, has had few more ardent exponents than Dorothy of Montau. DL II.36 describes how these spiritual wounds, more intense than any physical piercing, spill over into the external senses, a point made later by Teresa of Avila.[294] The lifelong wounding process reaches its culmination in her last hours as "wounding love" (*vorwunte libe/vulnerans caritas*) passes over into the "heartbreaking love" that kills Dorothy. In her last conversation with Canon John a few hours before her death she says:

> I feel excruciating pain because the Lord has wounded my heart and limbs through and through with the rays and arrows of his love, which he shot without ceasing into my heart, arms, back and shoulders, and all about my heart. I move like a woman about to give birth and can find neither rest nor leisure. . . . The time has now come of which I spoke to you earlier, the time when I am to deliver my soul into eternal life.[295]

An equally ancient theme in mysticism, one predating Christianity, is that of spiritual inebriation. On the basis of texts from the Psalms, and especially the image of the wine cellar from Song of Songs 2:4, divine drunkenness had featured in many forms of mystical erotics. Inebriated love (*trunckene libe/inebrians caritas*) plays a large role in Dorothy's mystical states, appearing frequently in the DL and other texts. Most of these descriptions can be paralleled in other mystics. One new twist, however, is the distinction John introduces between two kinds of spiritual inebriation, an initial "sufficient drunkeness" (*genuglichen trunckenheyt/contentativa ebrietas*) in which the soul attains rapture, which is followed by a new "strong drink" given during rapture through which the soul experiences endless thirst for God. This "insufficient drunkenness" (*ungenugeliche trunckenheyt/non-contentiva ebrietas*) is John's version of mystical *epektasis*, the fusion of enjoyment and endless desire. John claims that Dorothy sometimes experienced drunkenness for a month, and even three months running.[296]

John Marienwerder's accounts of Dorothy's mysticism are deeply erotic and ecstatic.[297] Although the descriptions of her relationship to Jesus do not have the direct erotic potency found in Mechthild of Magdeburg's *Flowing Light of the Godhead*, they reveal many of the same bridal themes. Even during her actively married years "God entertained sweet dalliance with her soul" (*got der herre hilt eyn liblich kosin mit irer selen* [DL I.26; ed., 224]). She is pictured as "the bride of the Eternal Bridegroom" (III.5), capable of enjoying daily familiarity with Jesus, as well as all the delights of the highest form of marriage. The spousal character of Dorothy's life reaches a culmination in the elaborate wedding ceremony recounted in DL III.27–32 (ed., 311–18; trans., 184–93).[298] John describes how Dorothy was adorned for marriage with the clothing of the virtues and courted by messengers from heaven. After having "wept in wounded love" for a long time, she finally sees her most beautiful Beloved approach with his mighty host for the marriage ceremony (III.27). The Lord tells her that marriage means complete union, saying,

> "From now on I will come to you more graciously than ever before. . . . We will melt together into one ball to be united and alone with one another." As the Lord said this, the fire of divine love melted Dorothy's soul to resemble the liquid ore used for casting bells, flowing with God into one mass. And Dorothy's soul felt clearly how she was united with God and totally immersed in him.[299]

Later Dorothy told John about the celestial banquet that followed in which she was led into the King's wine cellar and "inebriated by the liquor of divine sweetness" (III.29). She describes the gifts that she received, as well as "sweet whisperings" (*susse oerrawmen/blanditia*) that the bride and Groom exchange in the bed chamber, a form of speech that can be heard, though not understood nor remembered (III.31). This notion of secret mystical discourse is summarized by Christ, who tells Dorothy, "Whenever I want to reveal a secret to your soul that is to remain a secret, I first intoxicate your soul before I reveal my secret to you. That way your soul can neither remember nor repeat what I whisper. At times the soul hears my whispers but still cannot deal with them rationally."[300]

Although Dorothy of Montau's mysticism is clearly Christocentric and love-centered, the Holy Spirit plays an important role. As a good theologian, John knew that grace is the action of the Spirit, so that all the mystical gifts bestowed on Dorothy are described as manifestations of the one Spirit.

In the kind of enumeration dear to him, he counts the number of times the Spirit visited Dorothy with special graces each day—from a high of ten times to a low count of three![301] In a few places John notes that Dorothy's union with God is actually the work of the whole Trinity in her soul,[302] but, unlike many fourteenth-century mystics, Dorothy's life and graces are not deeply trinitarian. In his desire to present Dorothy as a suitable candidate for canonizaton, John also shies away from discussion of controversial issues, such as the relation of love and knowledge in attaining God, though he does emphasize that among Dorothy's most important mystical graces were "pure illumination of her intellect and the burning flame of love and desire for God."[303]

Among the themes that mark out the Prussian anchoress as typical of late medieval female ecstatics is the deeply sacramental nature of her relation to Jesus. Dorothy's obsessive reception of confession (it receives a whole treatise in the *Septililium*) is no more or less excessive than that of other female mystics, such as Catherine of Siena.[304] Its purpose is both to highlight her sense of sin and the ongoing need for purification, and also to show her submission to the authority of her confessor and obedience to the church. Like so many medieval female mystics, however, confession is primarily an access to the central religious ritual, the reception of Christ in the Eucharist. John depicts Dorothy's desire for the Eucharist as continually growing during the course of her life as she approaches the ultimate manifestation of heartbreaking love that causes her death and passage to heaven (e.g., DL II.17 and 27; III.17 and 40; IV.3.1–2). Union with Christ is essentially a uniting realized in and through the Eucharist.[305] Among the most touching moments of John's account of Dorothy's last days is his portrayal of their final conversation. Dorothy had already received communion early that morning, but she begs John in the evening to give her the sacrament again. He replies that he can only do so after midnight when the "Te Deum" of Matins is being sung. She responds, "'I don't know how I will be able to wait that long,' as if to say: 'Waiting that long is too hard for me, too bitter.'" When he returns at matins, she has already gone to her final union through the force of heartbreaking love.[306] Dorothy of Montau is thus idealized as a martyr for love.[307]

Dorothy's mystical piety is encapsulated within the genres of traditional hagiography, though of an excessive nature typical of much of the late Middle Ages. Two texts from the early fifteenth century are more original presentations of female lay mystics living in the world. Though shorter and less well known, they deserve comparison with the mystical autohagiography of their English contemporary, Margery Kempe.

Katharina Tucher (ca. 1375–1448) was married to a wealthy merchant of Neumarkt. After his death in 1419, she moved to neighboring Nuremberg, which may have been her native city. Between 1418 and early 1421 she wrote down a diary of her mystical revelations, ninety-four in all, a unique text for its era in Germany.[308] In 1433 she entered the Dominican convent in Nuremberg as a lay sister, bringing with her a remarkable library of at least twenty-six books largely of spiritual and mystical literature, including the diary. The breadth of Katharina's spiritual reading and her desire to record her revelations are a potent indication of the role of mysticism in the lay culture of late medieval Germany.[309]

Katharina's *Revelations* are the only surviving autograph of the first stage of what might have become a *Gnadenvita*. Although relatively artless, the widow's diary of her showings was clearly shaped by her extensive knowledge of mystical texts. The dialogue form she uses, reminiscent of Birgitta of Sweden, includes many types of holy conversation. Generally Christ talks to Katharina, but there are also dialogues with Mary, and polylogues with Christ, Mary, and St. John. At times Katharina reports conversations among heavenly figures without joining in (no. 60 is a dialogue between Mary and the devil). There are some self-addresses, and one revelation features a debate between body, soul, and intellect (no. 7). Katharina's unnamed confessor occasionally is introduced (nos. 50, 62, 87). The form in which the revelations are presented is also unusual. They invariably begin with a word of praise to Jesus, most often "Praise to Jesus in his five lovely wounds" (*Iesv zv lob sein lieplichen fvnf bvnden*). They often include the brief introduction "there was present to me" (*mir wart gegenbvrtig*), a formula that makes it difficult to say if we are dealing with visions accompanying auditions, or only auditions. A few obscure revelations (e.g., nos. 24 and 44) seem to be based on dreams.[310]

Much of what we meet with in the collection is customary, especially the bridal nature of Katharina's relation to Jesus,[311] as well as the strong emphasis on the passion.[312] Other aspects, however, are unusual. It is surprising, for example, that reception of the Eucharist plays so small a part, though it is mentioned in no. 19.[313] Unlike Dorothy of Montau, Katharina Tucher did not center her relation with Christ on communion. In the revelations in which Katharina is upbraided by Christ for her many failings (a feature of many mystical dialogues), it is peculiar to find the visionary's addiction to wine singled out (nos. 55, 79). On the basis of the Song of Songs 1:1 many mystics aspired to the kiss of Christ's mouth, but in no. 86 Jesus forbids her to kiss his mouth, saying this belongs only to his mother. Katharina, like Mary Magdalene, should kiss his feet.

Katharina's devotion to the passion is particularly strong. It was not unusual for medieval mystics, both women and men, to display intense emotional response to texts or images representing Christ's sufferings and to pass from these to visions/visualizations of the Man of Sorrows crucified or standing immediately before them. This is true of Katharina. Revelation no. 14 centers on a common late medieval mystical motif, drinking the blood flowing from the Savior's heart. Christ begins by addressing her:

> "Gaze upon me, nourish the soul with the body if you want to drink from my heart. It is warm not cold. Give me a drink upon the cross where my hands have been nailed."

> "Dear Lord, how will I give you a drink?"

> "With an attentive released mind and with submission in obedience you will give me to drink. In this way I want to give you a drink from my own heart that takes its origin in eternal life."[314]

This direct connectedness allows the visionary to place herself within the events of Christ's life in a manner that recalls what Ewert Cousins has described as the mysticism of the historical event, a form of immediate identification with the major saving moments of the life of Jesus in which the mystic becomes a direct participant. Revelation no. 15 (ed., 36–37), for example, is a mini-passion play in which Katharina interacts with the Blessed Virgin and St. John during the time after Christ's death.[315] In no. 16 she is present at Christ's birth and in the days of his infancy, not unlike Birgitta.

Katharina extended this direct participation in biblical events even further. For example, in Revelation 28 she becomes the adulteress pardoned by Christ (John 8:1–11), while in no. 29 she is the Samaritan woman of John 4. In the last recorded revelation (no. 94) she becomes Mary Magdalene in conversation with Christ. Katharina's ability to reenact female roles within scripture, rather than using the liturgical and sacramental forms of identification found in cloistered women, may reflect her status as a well-read lay woman denied frequent access to communion.

Many of the details of Katharina's visions need further study. Here, I wish only to stress how a widowed laywoman was able to claim for her own a wide range of the motifs of bridal mysticism usually restricted to cloistered nuns. Revelation 25, for example, describes the marriage between Jesus and Katharina, if in less detail than John Marienwerder's account of Dorothy's wedding. Revelation 8 is especially interesting for the intensity of its use of language taken from the Song of Songs. Jesus begins by addressing Katharina's soul, "My dove, my bride, my spotless one, come, I want to be united to you." He promises her a wedding ring, Solomon's beautiful clothes, fine shoes, and a crown of pearls. He will make music and sing to her, and surround her with roses, lilies, and other flowers. The vision closes with a description of the love-game played between the human and divine lovers:

> Then he hides himself and I seek him. He sees very well, but I do not see him. When I spy him again I become happy and say, "O my beautiful Love, stay with me! Do not leave me!" . . . The game of love, the fondling, the loving conversation in amicable presence surpasses all earthly love and joy of this world.[316]

The reference to loving union with the Beloved in this passage echoes other revelations where Katharina expresses her desire to become one with Jesus and with God.[317]

Contemporary with Katharina Tucher was an anonymous woman of Basel who attempted something even more difficult by late medieval standards. Like Dorothy of Montau, she sought mystical contact with God while still bound to sexual obligations in marriage.[318] This "Holy Visionary" has been called a beguine because she was opposed to the campaign against beguines carried on by the Dominicans in Basel, especially John Mulberg, in the first decade of the fifteenth century.[319] But the anonymous seer was a beguine only in the broad sense of a woman who elected to devote her life to special religious practices and was allowed to wear quasi-religious garb. Beguines were not allowed to live with their husbands. The holy visionary, like Dorothy of Montau and Margery Kempe, testifies to the attempts of some women to break through the barriers the medieval church had erected between marriage and mysticism.

The anonymous visionary appears to have belonged to the merchant class. Her confessor, an important figure in the text, was a Franciscan, the order that supported the beguines and tertiaries in the city against their Dominican detractors. He certainly had a hand in the production of this *Gnadenvita*, though it is difficult to say how much. Hans-Jochen Schiewer holds that the text "originally was a pro-Franciscan propaganda piece of the Basel Beguine controversy."[320] The visions and other divine manifestations found in the story make for an interesting comparison with those of Dorothy of Montau and Katharina Tucher. The anonymous woman is even more deeply eucharistic in her mysticism than was Dorothy, and she was far more independent of her confessor. Much of the central part of the account revolves around the struggle between her and the confessor about how often she can receive communion. As in the case of Katharina, the account of the anonymous's visions, for all its use of traditional mystical motifs, has an air of freshness, providing a sense that we can overhear something of the woman's own spiritual story.

The text has a narrative form and is therefore a true "grace-life" rather than a spiritual diary or collection of visions. Much of the story is couched in dialogue form, detailing the visionary's conversations with Christ or her discussions with her confessor. It begins with a conversion account: *Es lag ein moensch in sterbender not* ("A person lay dying"). In the midst of this suffering, "There came a voice in a great light saying to her: 'In order to have God clothe your soul with his sufferings, you must come elegantly and nobly and be well dressed before him.'" The soul begs Christ's forgiveness for her sins and asks to be clothed with the Lord's sufferings. "Then again came the voice in the light to her and said, 'You are assured of eternal life through the merits of our Lord.'"[321] Surviving a diabolical temptation, the woman pledges her life to the Lord. The text notes that she was a married woman, so that she had to ask her husband if he would permit her to lay aside worldly clothes and adopt a poorer style of life.

The anonymous visionary, however, was not allowed to adopt a life of chastity. According to church regulation, she could not receive communion the day after having sexual relations, and her confessor advises her not to deprive her husband of his marital rights. She obeys this injunction, but much of the story of the holy visionary (ed., 307–12) is taken up with her struggle to receive communion as often as possible. When her confessor attempts to restrict her to three times a week, for example, she reacts by becoming deathly ill and getting support from her celestial voice. Eventually the confessor gives in and allows her to receive as often as she desires within the accepted boundaries (312.231–32 [*Vnd der bihter verseite ir dar nach nit me daz heilge sacrament*]).

The reason for the visionary's intense desire for the sacrament is that her immediate contact with the suffering Christ is realized in the reception of communion. Like so many late medieval mystics, it is the bloody Jesus on the cross, and more specifically drinking the blood that flows from his heart, that is the center of her mystical devotion.[322] This experience is physically realized in communion, though it can also happen through spiritual communion.[323] The account tells how one day she heard her confessor preaching in the Franciscan church about "receiving the flesh and blood of Our Lord spiritually" (307.58–308.85). At that point she has a vision of the cross that St. Francis saw suspended in the air with Christ's five wounds visible. Four streams of blood flow from the five wounds into her mouth and "she was greatly strengthened and made glad by the drink of blood" (308.72–73). One Pentecost when she cannot receive she meditates on the sacrament. The account continues:

She beheld the worthy sufferings of our dear Lord and she was raptured and her soul sat by the cross of the Lord under his heart. And our Lord broke his heart and the worthy blood flowed from his heart into her mouth. And when she came to herself again she thought, "Great things have happened to you. You have drunk from the heart of our Lord. This also happened to Saint John. . . . What have you drunk? I have drunk the will of God. I sink myself down totally into his will."[324]

Such experiences are repeated in the text, especially in the long last part (312.233–317.423), which features fourteen different visions given to the holy woman. Unlike Katharina Tucher, the anonymous beholds the gospel scenes as an outsider rather than becoming a direct actor in them. Many of the visions are passion-centered; others involve Jesus' birth and infancy. Some of these showings involve a direct encounter with Christ. Like Dorothy of Montau and Catherine of Siena, she exchanges hearts with Jesus (316.366–79), and in another vision Christ kisses her on the mouth and congratulates her on her devotion to the Eucharist, even when she gave it up in obedience to her confessor. "By the kiss with which our Lord kissed her," continues the text, "and by the words he spoke to her, she observed that she should not let the sacrament go and that our Lord wanted to have a concord and a union with her soul."[325] The life concludes by informing the reader that "this holy woman" died on June 1, 1409 (317.425–26).

Conclusion

Throughout the history of Christianity mystical teaching has been communicated in a variety of ways, many of which have left little historical record, such as the private conversations of mystics with their followers, or the living examples provided by the holy men and women of every century. What I have tried to show in this lengthy chapter is that the mysticism of late medieval Germany provides us with a special opportunity to observe a time and place in which the hunger for direct contact with God spread broadly to all levels of believers, including lay men and women. For this reason, and also due to the increasing literacy of the late medieval society, we have a larger body of surviving evidence regarding mysticism from fourteenth- and fifteenth-century Germany than perhaps ever before. The variety of forms of mysticism in German-speaking lands between 1300 and 1500 is as remarkable as the many ways and different genres in which the message was disseminated.

CHAPTER 8

Three Treatises
on the Mystical Life

T HE TWELFTH AND THIRTEENTH CENTURIES witnessed the production of a number of treatises devoted to the nature of contemplation and the mystical path to God. In the twelfth
century the Victorine canons Hugh and Richard pioneered such summaries, but some were also written by Cistercians and Carthusians.
Latin treatises continued to be produced in the thirteenth century.
One of the best known, coming from the pen of the German Franciscan David of Augsburg in the 1240s, has a cumbersome title that is
revelatory of the purpose of these works—*The Composition of the Interior and Exterior Man according to the Triple State of Beginners, Proficient,
and Perfect.*[1] A decade or so later the Franciscan "prince of mystics,"
Bonaventure, wrote a series of widely read summaries of mystical
teaching, especially *The Mind's Road into God* and *The Threefold Way.*[2]

The turn of the fourteenth century saw the production of formal
mystical manuals, attempts to summarize and harmonize a variety of
mystical authorities and traditions into scholastically organized handbooks for the use of confessors and spiritual guides to instruct their
charges. One of the most popular was composed by a German Franciscan, Rudolph of Biberach (ca. 1270–ca. 1330), around 1300.
Rudolph's *Seven Roads of Eternity* survives in about a hundred manuscripts and was translated into MHG about 1350.[3] About 1290 a
French Carthusian, Hugh of Balma, wrote an even more popular treatise called *The Roads to Sion Mourn,* which often circulated under the
title *The Threefold Way* and was ascribed to Bonaventure.[4] The genre of
mystical treatise, including both formally structured works and looser
examples, was widely known by the end of the thirteenth century.

There can be no hard and fast definition of what constitutes a mystical treatise. Nevertheless, the growth of works characterized by the desire to organize and synthesize, often in an articulated way that owes much to scholastic theology, the basic teachings about the preparation for, the path to, and the characteristics of union with God, was an important feature of late medieval mysticism, not least in German-speaking lands. While the many forms of both literature and art studied in the last chapter provide a window on new developments in the spread of mysticism in Germany between 1300 and 1500, the continued production of mystical treatises is important for showing the links between this harvest and what had gone before.

The number of works from late-medieval Germany that could be described as mystical treatises is large. No full survey or list is available.[5] In his ground-breaking Eckhart edition of 1857, for example, Franz Pfeiffer edited seventeen treatises he ascribed to Meister Eckhart, though only two of these are considered authentic today.[6] This chapter, like the last, will adopt a representative approach by studying three important examples in detail, rather than merely trying to mention as many works as possible. Four principles have guided my choice of tracts. The first is the somewhat arbitrary one of value: Which works seem, to me at least, to offer insights into what was distinctive and significant in the German mysticism of the late Middle Ages? The second criterion is that of variety of affiliation with respect to the religious orders that were such an important part of the medieval spiritual landscape. Although the Dominicans had a special role in late medieval German mysticism, there were many other orders that made significant contributions—Benedictines, Carthusians, Augustinians, and Franciscans,[7] to name but some. Because so much consideration has already been given to Dominican mystics, I have avoided treatises that seem to have a definite Dominican connection. In considering these works I will not try to identify a distinct form of mysticism characteristic of the various orders (a line of research that has been attempted by others); rather, I wish to highlight, once again, the variety and diffusion of mysticism in late medieval Germany. Third, I have chosen treatises that try to provide a general survey of the mystical life rather than those that investigate one or another aspect of mysticism, interesting as that might be. Finally, I think it is important to consider both Latin and MHG works. While the forms of mystical literature studied in the former chapter, most intended for a lay audience, were vernacular in nature, this is less true of the treatises, which often (not always, of course) were aimed at clerics who needed systematic information, both for themselves and for those who came to them for spiritual guidance.

The three treatises considered in this chapter stretch over the fourteenth century: (1) the Augustinian Henry of Friemar's Latin *The Word's Coming into the Mind* (early fourteenth century); (2) the *Book of the Poor of Spirit*, a work whose authorship is disputed and which appears to date ca. 1350–70; and (3) the *Theologia Deutsch*, written late in the second half of the fourteenth century by an anonymous priest of the Order of Teutonic Knights. I will close with a few remarks on some fifteenth-century treatises. The two MHG works treated here achieved subsequent fame; Henry's Latin treatise was less widely read. Nevertheless, each of these treatises provides us with a distinctive window on the various ways in which late medieval German mystical authors sought to organize and present their spiritual teaching.

Henry of Friemar the Elder (ca. 1250–1340)

The Order of the Hermits of St. Augustine (to give them their full title) developed from twelfth- and thirteenth-century Italian communities of hermits. By the time of the formal recognition of the order in 1256, however, the group, which followed the malleable *Rule of St. Augustine*, had taken on the characteristics of the popular mendicant orders of Dominicans and Franciscans. Like the other mendicants, the Augustinians recognized the need for a solid theological education in order to preach and instruct souls in urban environments. They soon established houses of study in some of their convents and began to send their best men to the universities for higher education. The writings of Augustine remained the foundation for both their theology and their spirituality, but they also acquired a specific theological authority for the order, the friar Giles of Rome (d. 1316), who at one time had studied with Thomas Aquinas. The order's spirituality can be characterized as broadly Augustinian, with an emphasis on the centrality of love (Giles described theology as neither speculative nor practical, but essentially affective), the prevenience and necessity of God's grace, and the primacy of the will over the intellect.[8]

The Augustinians flourished in the German cities of the thirteenth and fourteenth centuries. Beginning with a single province in 1256, by 1300 there were four provinces and almost eighty convents. The fourteenth century also witnessed the creation of important works on spirituality and mysticism by the German Augustinians. The central figure is Henry of Friemar, called the elder, to distinguish him from a younger friar of the same name.[9] Henry was born in Friemar near Gotha in Saxony around 1250. He entered the community in Erfurt, studied at Bologna and Paris, and served as provincial in Erfurt from 1291 until about 1300. He then went on to Paris, where he was promoted as *magister* in 1305 and taught for some years. Henry was a member of the theological commission that investigated Marguerite Porete and served as a theological advisor at the Council of Vienne. By about 1315 he was back in Erfurt, where he directed the Augustinian *studium generale* until his death in 1340. As is evident from this brief history, Henry must have known Meister Eckhart. His writings give evidence of this as well, though naturally Eckhart is not named. Henry also had considerable influence on the other Augustinian spiritual writers of the era. These include the younger Henry of Friemar (d. 1354), Hermann of Schildesche (d. 1357), and especially Jordan of Quedlinburg (d. 1370), whose sermon collections include mystical material.[10]

Henry's writings were extensive (about thirty works) and quite popular. As we have seen in chapter 2, he wrote the earliest treatise explicitly devoted to the discernment of spirits, a topic of growing importance in late medieval mysticism.[11] He also penned several ethical manuals, as well as works on liturgy, Latin sermons, and some scholastic commentaries. His treatise *On the Ten Commandments* survives in about three hundred manuscripts. Henry wrote only in Latin, but several of his more popular works were translated into MHG. The three Latin treatises edited by Adolar Zumkeller were not among his best-known works, but they demonstrate his contributions to mystical theory. These are a theological tract *On the Incarnation of the Word*, and two mystical works, *The Word's Coming into the Mind (De adventu Verbi in Mentem)* and a *Treatise on the Lord's Coming (Tractatus de adventu Domini)*.[12] Both mystical tracts employ allegorical interpretations of scriptural texts to create an articulated scholastic presentation of mystical theology. Here I will concentrate on *The Word's Coming into the Mind*, occasionally referring to the *Treatise on the Lord's Coming* to expand on some issues.[13]

The Word's Coming is particularly interesting because it seems to have been produced early in the first decade of the fourteenth century as Henry's version of the mystical theme of the birth of the Word in the soul that was so important to Meister Eckhart. The Dominican was preaching about how the Word is born in the soul from the 1290s on in Erfurt, where Henry lived just a few blocks away. Eckhart was also teaching in Paris some of the years when Henry was there. The Augustinian, like the Dominican, sees the birthing motif as essential to Christian mysticism: "The mental conception of the Eternal Word seems to be the greatest and highest grace of all the gifts that in this life are conferred on the devout soul by grace in accordance with God's usual law."[14] Although it is interesting to see that Henry and Eckhart agree in their attempts to revive and update this ancient theme of Christian mysticism, it is more revealing to observe where they part company.

The first and most obvious difference is that Henry devoted a scholastic Latin treatise to the theme, one designed to present the doctrine as clearly as possible. He also supported his case with a wide range of authorities, both biblical and theological, and took care to correct possible misunderstandings of the Word's birth. Eckhart too could present his understanding of the birth of the Word in the soul in an organized way, as in the noted Christmastide cycle of four sermons (Prr. 101–4), possibly preached at Erfurt ca. 1303–5, which I have elsewhere described as "a vernacular *summa* of his mysticism."[15] (These sermons seem to have been delivered to his Dominican brethren and not to a general audience.) There are also a few texts in Eckhart's Latin writings that concern this central aspect of his mystical thought, but the Dominican's usual practice was to preach about the Word's birth in the vernacular and in a far from systematic way, inserting it here and there in the course of many sermons side by side with other significant aspects of his message, the practice that Burkhard Hasebrink has called "paradigmatic substitution," by which the preacher shifts back and forth between different but correlative paradigms of his exploration of contact with God.[16] The second major difference between the Augustinian and the Dominican concerns the content of the teaching. Henry of Friemar identifies the *mentalis conceptio Verbi* as the high point of "divine union" (*divina unio*), but he understands this union in a traditional way as the loving union of wills (*unitas spiritus*) between God and human that leaves both beings distinct in essence or being. He also expends considerable effort to relate the birth to traditional mystical themes, such as the three stages of the itinerary to God, rapture and ecstasy, and the erotic language of the Song of Songs. Eckhart, on the other hand, understands the birth of the Word as part of the process that allows the soul to recognize and live its indistinction from God in the Trinity of persons. He has less interest in relating the birth to more traditional mystical themes.

The differences between the two forms of birthing mysticism become even more striking as one investigates the artificial way that Henry presents this teaching in a handbook characterized by scholastic triple articulations within articulations so typical of the "arborizing," or "tree-building," constructions of late medieval preaching and teaching.[17] Although modern readers may find this procedure irritating, it was designed to present doctrine in a clear and memorizable way. *The Word's Coming into the Mind* is reminiscent of other mystical treatises of the time (those of John Ruusbroec come to mind) in the way in which its abstract schematization uses the

Bible. Monastic mystical texts often followed the sequence of the scriptural narrative; scholastically influenced mystical writings use biblical proof texts as points of origin for their own constructions.

Henry's *The Word's Coming* is among the most systematic medieval presentations of mysticism. If mysticism, as I have argued, involves the preparation for, the consciousness of, and the effects that follow from some form of immediate contact with the divine presence, it is interesting to observe that all three moments appear in the structure of Henry's work and that the Augustinian makes the divine presence (*divina praesentia*) into an explicit and central category.[18] Almost all of the traditional themes of Western mysticism are invoked and their relation to the main motif of the birth of the Word explored.[19] The range of Henry's sources is impressive and largely traditional. Augustine has pride of place (explicitly cited thirty times), followed by Bernard of Clairvaux (fourteen citations, some to pseudonymous works), and Gregory the Great and Dionysius (each seven times). The Pseudo-Origenistic sermon on Mary Magdalene (also used by Eckhart) is quoted, and Proclus appears once.

Henry of Friemar's presentation of the birth of the Word in the mind differs from Eckhart's in many ways, not least in how it is rooted in Augustine's theology of operative grace, the *inspiratio divina* that alone makes possible all movement back to God on the part of fallen humans.[20] Henry's Augustinianism appears early in the treatise in an exegesis of Song 5:4 ("My beloved put his hand through the opening and my belly shuddered at his touch"). This is given the following allegorical reading: "Through the Beloved's hand understand the inspiration of grace; through the opening understand the consent of free choice, because no gift is conferred on us in a divine way unless it is proclaimed through this opening. Hence, the insertion of this hand through the opening is the lifegiving inspiration of divine grace through the will's free choice."[21] In this context Henry obviously does not need to spell out how grace and free choice are related in detail. In the fourteenth century, when many theologians gave the fallen will's turn to God a key role, his stress on the prevenience of grace emphasizes a distinctively Augustinian view.

More surprising, however, is the Proclian conception that Henry employs to illustrate grace's activity, since the use of Proclus is usually associated with the Dominicans. Reflecting on the ontological light of grace as "an unlike participation of the uncreated light" (*quaedam difformis participatio luminis increati*), he invokes Proclus's view of the three essential processes of Neoplatonic metaphysics to explain the action of grace.[22] Since every effect remains within its cause, proceeds from it, and returns to it, this dynamism must be true of grace in an exemplary fashion. Hence, Henry says, the soul informed by grace has a threefold relation to its source in the uncreated divine image: first, it should remain within the cause by its conformity to God's will in all its actions; second, it should go forth in the good example it shows to others; and third, it should return to the cause through its recognition of the graces and gifts it has received from God. What is noteworthy here is how Henry has taken a metaphysical paradigm, and even a scriptural text (Eccl. 1:7) that Eckhart and others used to illustrate the metaphysical flow out from and back to God, and adapted them for moral and mystical purposes.

Although the first part of *The Word's Coming* deals with the preparation for the conception of the Word in the soul, it contains important discussions of how grace draws the soul on to the experience of "the embrace of the divine presence" (*amplexus divinae praesentiae*) through four special gifts. First, the gift of gracious inspiration (*inspiratio gratiosa*) leads to virtuous uplifting (*sublimatio virtuosa*). In this stage Henry discusses an important mystical theme that again brings him close to Eckhart. This is what he calls *abstractio.* "Virtuous uplifting is perfected in the withdrawal (*abstractio*) of the mind from all created forms in every way, which is aptly hinted at in the name 'Galilee' [Luke 1:26] which is interpreted as transmigration and signifies a mind that is withdrawn and emptied of every created form. . . . The mind which is capable of conceiving the Eternal Virginal Word must be virginal and not pregnant with any created form."[23] This *abstractio,* and even the language of virginal emptiness in which it is expressed, is much like Eckhart's detachment (e.g., Pr. 2).

Under this same heading of virtuous uplifting Henry also discusses how the Holy Spirit's presence in the soul brings about the "full fruitfulness" (*plenaria fecundatio*) of the virtues and divine anointings, using the image of the "little flowery bed" of the Song of Songs ("Come, my Beloved; behold, our little bed is flowery," combining Song 7:11 and 1:15). This potent erotic image had been favored by Cistercian mystics, such as William of St.-Thierry.[24] Henry cites Bernard and others as he describes how the image reveals different aspects of the Bridegroom's presence in the bed, which is "the pure conscience and rational image brought to perfect purity and safe interior quiet" (19.135–36). The third of these aspects introduces an Augustinian theme that will reappear later—"How the Eternal Spouse rests in three ways in this little bed of conscience, insofar as through his presence he inhabits the three powers belonging to the rational image." This is a reference to Augustine's teaching about how God dwells in the memory by his majesty, in the intelligence by his truth, and in the will by his love.[25]

The final two modes of preparation, "vigorous zeal" (*aemulatio vigorosa*) and "gleaming illumination" (*illustratio radiosa*), illustrate further aspects of Henry's mystical theory. The vigorous zeal for greater gifts of grace and growth in virtue, according to Henry, is motivated by three reasons based on the active life and three on the contemplative. The three contemplative motives include the "strength of love" that moves the mind to continue to penetrate its inmost depths and move forward "to interior divine union," the "verdure of attention" that causes it to flower in virtues, and the "sweetness of desire" illustrated by the bride of the Song of Songs (25.108–27.149). These typical triple analyses also appear in the discussion of the final stage of preparation, gleaming illumination.

Henry begins his discussion of illumination by analyzing what he calls the *vita tripharia*, that is, the traditional division of souls into beginners, advanced, and perfected (*incipientes/proficientes/perfecti*). Each stage has a different kind of mind or mental state, from the beginners who recognize their weakness and need for God, through the advanced, who struggle against vice, to the perfect who are enflamed by divine love through their "perception of the sweetness of divine consolation" (29.57–59). The Blessed Virgin Mary, whose name is interpreted as "illuminated," is the exemplar for each stage. As the model for the perfect, those who possess "a devout mind illuminated by the light of contemplation and are finally ready for the spiritual conception of the Eternal Word" (27.8–10), the story of her conception of the Word at the Annunciation provides an exegetical hook on which Henry hangs his analysis of the gifts of grace that prepare for union with God. The inflammation, elevation, and simplification of the mind, following Mary's example, eventually yield a threefold fruit, which Henry describes by linking Mary to another noted scriptural locus for mystical teaching, the Transfiguration account of Matthew 17. The splendor of Jesus' garments signifies "the purity of the interior mind and the perfect attainment of the beauty of virtue" so evident in Mary. The bright cloud that overshadowed the apostles is interpreted as the interior colloquy between God and the soul abstracted from all created things—"secret words that are revealed to the devout mind in the light of contemplation and are so ineffable that no tongue or any perceptible word could declare them."[26] Mary heard such inexpressible divine words at the Annunciation, according to Bernard of Clairvaux. Finally, Christ's shining face signifies the deifying transformation of the rational image of the soul into its uncreated image spoken of by Paul in 2 Corinthians 3:8. This too was fulfilled in Mary whose mind was fully conformed to the eternal image by grace so that "in a singular way she is called the seal of the divine likeness and the noble resting place of the whole Trinity" (*ipsa singulariter appellatur signaculum divinae similitudinis et nobile reclinatorium totius Trinitatis* [33.174–75]).

The second part of Henry of Friemar's *The Word's Advent* takes up the actual mechanism by which the Word is born in the well-disposed soul, once again through the creation of at times tedious triple distinctions. The first principal point (34–48), the longest of the treatise, deals explicitly with the "three processes by which the Word is conceived in the mind through grace." Using the canticle of Simeon from Luke 2:29–32, Henry says this conception and birth first takes place "through the mode of sweetness of ineffable delight," figured in Simeon's mention of peace and salvation. Second, it is effected "through the mode of light shining upon the mind" as noted in the words "a light to enlighten the gentiles" (Luke 2:32); and third, "through the mode of radiance beatifying eternally" illustrated by the glory mentioned at the end of the canticle. The section on divine sweetness cites Bernard, as might be expected (Sermon 6 for the Ascension), for its presentation of how God's gift of sweetness induces a state of mystical consciousness. The actual link to the motif of birthing is made clear only when Henry again refers to Mary at the Annunciation as the exemplar for how the experience of divine sweetness drives out all other desires and needs. Henry summarizes: "The devout mind should long for this conception of the Eternal Word with the highest desire, because through such presence of the Eternal Word the mind is ignited by a form of divine love. This love is rightly called 'consuming' (*consumptivus*) in that its fervor burns up in the soul every desire or inclination" that might lead to sin.[27]

The second process addresses more directly why it is the Second Person of the Trinity who comes to birth in the devout soul. The Eternal Word is born "through the mode of light shining in the mind" because this is proper to the Word insofar as he proceeds from the Father in the Trinity as "he knows himself in a personal way and through the act of generation calls forth a personal action and produces a person formally distinct from himself."[28] It is also fitting that the Word is born in us because this expresses the generosity of the Father's communication, giving us a pledge of our eternal inheritance as sons of God in the Eternal Son. Here Henry takes up the motif of sonship (*filiatio*) that was important to Eckhart and was later to be used by Nicholas of Cusa. He distinguishes two modes in which the pledge of the birth gives us a right to the eternal reward: "First, by right of the filiation by which he adopts us as sons of God through grace; second, by right of the brotherly participation by which the Eternal Word assumed our nature and wished to be our flesh and our brother."[29]

At this point Henry once again adverts to Mary "full of grace" (Luke

1:28) as a model for the plenitude of graces and charisms that accompany the birth of the Word. He then adds a telling comment on the proper way to understand the birth that appears to be a criticism of Meister Eckhart. The text begins as follows:

> It is certain that anyone who receives the presence of divine goodness in a real form of existence in another being [*inexistenter*] ought for that reason receive the whole treasury of grace which is born as flowing from the divine goodness. This is just like someone who receives the sun's presence in an essential way and has communicated to him the effect of light, of brightness, and all the other effects which are born as flowing from the sun. But it is evident that through the spiritual conception of the Word the Word itself is given to the mind in a present mode and as existing in another.[30]

The main puzzle about this passage is what Henry means by *inexistenter* (his neologism based on the scholastic *inexistentia*). Though it could mean "inexistent" in some contexts, here it must signify a "mode of existing in another," that is, a real, present, and even essential, mode of communication signifying that the sonship received by the soul shares in all the essential formal characteristics of the Sonship of the Word, but not by way of becoming the same personal hypostasis possessed by the second person in the Trinity. Henry goes on to explain that the union achieved through the birth of Word is a participatory union by which we are transformed into God through becoming one spirit with him (1 Cor. 6:17)—not one essential being.[31] He concludes: "This kind of unity is not to be understood according to a really existing identity, as some erroneously suppose, but rather according to a kind of similarity of conformity and transformation as we read in the third chapter of 1 John, 'We know that when he appears we will be like him, because we will see him as he is'" (1 John 3:2).[32] It is hard not to imagine that Henry had Eckhart's notion of indistinct union in mind here. The Augustinian ends this section by identifying this second mode of birthing as the wounding love (*amor vulnerativus*) so well known in erotic mystical traditions (44.296–45.314).

The third and final process of birth Henry describes as being achieved by the mode of beatifying radiance. This section is largely concerned with summarizing materials from the history of Christian mysticism to support the author's view of the birth of the Word. The basic point is that the birth provides a mental refreshment and intellectual joy that can be perceived in three ways in this life, as illustrated by appropriate biblical types. The first is cognitive. Paul was "illuminated in a temporary rapture by intuitive contemplation of the divine essence" (46.340–41), while David represents a foretaste of the enjoyment of divine sweetness. Finally the Queen of Sheba illustrates fainting away in ecstasy through a vision of the divine glory and magnificence.[33] In his *Treatise on the Lord's Coming* Henry says more about the nature of rapture and ecstatic experience. Citing the Song of Songs and Dionysius (MT 1), he notes that the excessive light of the divine essence can overshadow and enflame the rational mind to the point of mystical death and annihilation. "Sometimes it happens that the mind is fervently snatched up and led into an ecstasy and loss of itself. This ecstasy is called annihilation. Because the mind which is placed in ecstasy completely dies to itself and to all creatures insofar as it is deprived of self-consciousness, it forgets itself and everything else."[34] This mystical death, for which Henry uses a variety of the usual terms (*annihilatio/defectio mentis/liquefactio*) is ascribed to Paul in the famous text from 2 Corinthians 12. This third mode of birth is also characterized by its own type of love, the *amor constrictivus* that binds the soul indissolubly to God (48.381–86). Henry closes this section with a brief discussion of the transformation of the soul as created image into the uncreated image in the Trinity.

By now the advantages and disadvantages of Henry's treatise should be evident. Replete with learning and carefully structured, the work is as much compilation as creation. The Augustinian's desire to be inclusive of so much material results in some confusion about how the themes cohere, as well as in a certain sense of artificiality. These traits are also evident in the final two principal points of the second part. The second *principale* treats the maternal fecundity by which the Word is spiritually born in the mind, that is, the divine charity that serves as the mother of the Word in all three of his births, eternally from the Father's mind, corporally in human nature from the Virgin Mary, and spiritually in the devout mind (49.23–26). Henry's presentation of the universal role of *materna caritas* testifies to his powers of theological organization, but the remainder of this section is a somewhat labored survey of three kinds of people crowned by charity and the three forms of crowns they are granted (51.78–55.188). Finally, the third principal point takes up the spiritual fruits, or effects, that result from the mind's contact with the presence of the Word. Here Henry summarizes several themes that had already appeared in the treatise, notably his teaching on the restoration of the trinitarian image in the soul's three powers that is effected by the birth of the Word.

True to his scholastic mode of proceeding, Henry says that there are three fruits that follow from the Word's presence in the mind. The first is the foretaste of divine sweetness that comes from the mind's internal contemplation of its three highest powers as the true image of the Trinity (56.15–58.85). The second fruit is "the complete transformation of the rational image to its uncreated image." Here Henry, once again citing 2 Corinthians 3:8, reprises Augustine's teaching on how the Father rests in the memory through his majesty, the Son rests in the intelligence "through the gleaming contemplation of divine truth," and the Holy Spirit rests in the will "through an embrace of divine charity and through the honeyed taste of divine sweetness" (58.86–59.121). Finally, the treatise closes with a consideration of the third effect, what Henry calls "the constant renewing of interior devotion and the foretaste of eternal joy." The Augustinian, like other mystical teachers, insists that the life of grace here below never remains still, but always progresses to new forms of delight in its journey toward the perfect enjoyment of God to be given in heaven.

Henry of Friemar's treatises present a distinctive form of mysticism, one of the many options available in late medieval Germany. Although he employs a number of themes also found in Eckhart, the Augustinian is true to the traditions of his order, using the bishop of Hippo and the twelfth century mystics who built upon him for the foundation of his mystical edifice. What moved Henry of Friemar to compose his treatise precisely on the theme of the birth of the Word in the soul? It is difficult to believe that the Augustinian's efforts were sparked mainly by opposition to Eckhart, despite the differences that separate the two perceptions of the birth of the Word. Henry develops his view of this major theme of Christian mysticism so much in his own way that we can surmise that birthing mysticism saw a general and as yet unexplained revival around the year 1300. Henry's mysticism is a valuable witness to a broad phenomenon that we can recover only in part.

The Book of Spiritual Poverty

Henry of Friemar's *The Word's Coming into the Mind*, at least from the perspective of its manuscript survival, cannot be described as a work that had a major impact on later mystical traditions. This is not the case with the anonymous tract generally known today as *The Book of Spiritual Poverty (Das Buch von geistlicher Armut)*, the title given to it by its editor, Heinrich Denifle (d. 1905), the great Dominican scholar of mysticism.[35] Although the text survives in only thirteen manuscripts (one from the Green Isle community of the Friends of God), it was used by important contemporary mystical writers, such as Marquard of Lindau (d. 1392), and later was widely diffused. Several late medieval Latin texts appear to be versions of the book. Like the *Masterbook* (see chapter 9, pp. 420–23), this treatise came to be associated with the name of Tauler and was often ascribed to him under the

378 *The Harvest of Mysticism*

title *The Imitation of the Poor Life of Jesus Christ.* In 1548 it was translated into Latin by Lawrence Surius, the indefatigable Carthusian collector, editor, and translator of spiritual works.[36] Daniel Sudermann, another collector of mystical and spiritual literature, published the first German edition in 1621 under Tauler's name.[37] Many other editions followed, as well as a French translation in 1693. The book was known and used by both Protestants and Catholics, including mystics like Francis de Sales and Augustine Baker. Denifle's edition of 1877, while not fully critical, showed that the work could not be by Tauler, though most scholars recognize a strong Taulerian influence.

The beatitude "Blessed are the poor in spirit for theirs is the kingdom of Heaven" (Mattt. 5:3) played a key role in the mysticism of Eckhart (e.g., Pr. 52). *The Book of Spiritual Poverty* takes poverty, both outer and inner, as its main subject. The treatise's presentation of poverty of spirit as a category at once ethical, metaphysical, and mystical shows a deep dependence on Eckhart and Tauler, but the book also develops their thought in distinctive ways, such as in its insistence that external poverty of goods is a necessary precondition for internal poverty of spirit.[38] The book tries to summarize a wide range of material, but it does so in a way that makes an original contribution to late medieval mysticism.

The Book of Spiritual Poverty uses so many of the terms and themes that had been introduced by Eckhart that it might almost be described as the textbook of the mysticism of the ground.[39] (The word *grunt* appears about thirty times, though its use differs somewhat from Eckhart, as we will see below.) The closely allied notions of detachment and emptying, abandonment and annihilation, inner silence and the birth of the Word in the soul, pure love and acceptance of suffering are all integral to the treatise. Many characteristics of the rigorous apophaticism of the mysticism of the ground also appear, such as the need for removing all images (*entbilden*), the notion of the soul's losing its name, divine nothingness,[40] and the use of the term "the single One" (*daz einige ein*).[41] There is even one Eckhartian mention of the "desert of inner oneness" where God speaks to the soul.[42] Like Eckhart, *The Book of Spiritual Poverty* features expressions of mystical indistinction, and it makes frequent appeal to how the poor in spirit attain divinization.

There are, to be sure, teachings of the *Book* that are not prominent in Eckhart, such as the emphasis on contemplation of Christ's passion not only as preparation for, but also as necessary to the deepest states of union. There is far more use of erotic language based on the Song of Songs than we find in Eckhart. The motifs that depart from Eckhart, however, are mostly compatible with the mysticism of Eckhart's followers, particularly

John Tauler, whose influence on the book is evident in many ways.[43] Further reflecting Tauler and the situation after Eckhart is the section attacking mystical heresy entitled, "The Difference between Freedom under God and Unordered Freedom" (*Underscheit under goetlicher friheit und ungeordenter friheit* [16–20]). Also reflecting the time after Eckhart is an attack on academic theology (136.28–29)

What does all this tell us about the author and date of the work? It is generally agreed that *The Book of Spiritual Poverty* was produced in the second half of the fourteenth century between ca. 1350 and 1380, probably toward the earlier part of this span. Denifle thought that it was written by a moderate member of the Strassburg Friends of God movement, but this does not seem likely. Nor does the hypothesis of Robert E. Lerner that the book is a product of Free Spirit beguine circles seem convincing, given the broad audience intended and the care the book takes to avoid Free Spirit errors.[44] The author was certainly a cleric. Learned authorities are invoked, though sparingly (Aristotle, Dionysius, Augustine, Gregory, Bernard, etc.), and there is a discernible structure and organization of a somewhat scholastic character, though it is not rigorously articulated in the manner of Henry of Friemar. At times the tract assumes a quasi-dialogical form to advance the argument.[45] Given the influence of Eckhart and Tauler, many have supposed that one of their Dominican followers was responsible for its composition. But one passage says "the will is the highest power of the soul" (*der wille ist der oberste kraft der sele* [78.32]). The relation of the will and intellect is not a major concern of the book, but it is difficult to imagine a Dominican adopting this Franciscan position. Could a Franciscan be the author? Given the evidence at our disposal and without a new critical edition, there is no way of proving or disproving either Franciscan or Dominican authorship. Nor can we exclude the possibility that a learned and spiritually gifted priest from some other religious order might have seen fit to try to summarize the mystical currents of the time.

The Book of Spiritual Poverty is an ample treatise (194 closely packed pages in Denifle's edition), too long to think of trying to study it fully here. A look at the general plan of the work will show how the book presents the relation between poverty of spirit and contemplation, its two major themes. I will also analyze some passages that illustrate the treatise's view of several other basic aspects of mysticism, especially the role of Christ's passion, the birth of the Word in the soul, and union with God.

Denifle's edition divides *The Book of Spiritual Poverty* into two large parts.[46] The structure of the work is rather digressive, like many MHG tracts, with a good deal of circling back to examine issues from different perspectives. Nevertheless, there appears to be an overall coherence to the presentation of the main ideas. The title provides a summary of the contents of the book's teaching: how a person can follow the suffering life of Jesus Christ; how to live an inward life; how to come to true perfection; and how to understand "many lovely distinctions of divine truth" (3.1–8). The presentation of part 1 comprises three chapters of increasing length. The first chapter (3–8) deals with the definition of true poverty as detachment and inner freedom. The second chapter (8–20) concerns poverty and freedom and contains a discussion of the difference between true and false conceptions of freedom. The long third chapter (20–90) takes as its basic theme the relation between poverty and "pure working," or activity.[47] Crucial to this chapter is the distinction of three kinds of human working: natural, grace-filled (i.e., supernatural), and divine (22.29–32). These provide the skeleton on which the development of the chapter hangs. The treatment of pure working itself serves as the introductory section 1 (20–22). Section 2 (22–27) deals with the activities of nature—bodily, sensible, and intellectual. Section 3 (27–34) treats the action of grace as it encourages virtue and teaches the dangers of sin. This leads into a digression on the discernment of spirits in section 4 (34–44), one based on Henry of Friemar's distinction of four kinds of spirits that act in us: evil spirit, natural spirit, angelic spirit, and divine spirit.[48] The treatment of the divine spirit leads into a long second digression in section 5 (44–54) on the nature of friendship and of being a friend of God, which the book uses in a traditional biblical way, not to describe a particular movement or group.

The third kind of working or activity, divine action, occupies section 6 (55–64). What divine working means is analyzed primarily through a consideration of contemplation of Christ's passion, which here emerges as a central topic. For *The Book of Spiritual Poverty* consideration of the passion and of the Eckhartian birth of the Word in the soul are correlative aspects of attaining union with God, as section 7 on "How the Spirit of God speaks to the Soul without Image" shows (64–79). This section features a powerful analysis of such mystical themes as speaking and silence, light and darkness, and the difference between what happens in the soul's essence and in its powers. No less impressive is section 8 of part 1 (79–90), which deals with how the perfect will which has abandoned all things is ready to perform the "essential work where two things are one and have only one action" (80.1–2), that is, where our working and God's become one working. Here we find analyses of such mystical topics as the nature of resignation of will (*gelassener wille*), as well as a dialectical view of the relation between God and the soul reminiscent of Eckhart. Concerning the paradox of how perfect souls continue to advance, or "rush" (*louffet*), into God at the same time that they find their immovable rest in the divine goal, the author says:

> This advancing is not in the manner of creatures, and therefore it is not considered to be a movement. Rather, it takes place in a divine way, and hence is unmoved, for the will in no way moves itself outside God. Rather, it always remains in God. And so, its remaining within is its advancing, and its advancing is its remaining within. Hence, the more it remains within, the more it advances into God, and the more it advances into God, the more it is totally silent and completely unmoved.[49]

This is a succinct presentation of the dialectical mysticism that might have come from Eckhart.

Part 2 of *The Book of Spiritual Poverty* takes up many of the same mystical themes found in the first part, but with new insights and observations. The author's initial remarks on the topic might suggest a more practical presentation in this part, but it would be artificial to separate theory and practice in the treatise. At the outset, the book announces that this part will deal with four ways of arriving at the perfection of the poor life. The first is following the teaching and life of Jesus Christ (chap. 1:93–104). This chapter features general observations on the imitation of Christ, and a more specific treatment of the role of meditation on the passion. These christological reflections include an exploration of how the mind (*gemuete*) "loses itself in the hidden darkness of the unknown God" (*und da verluret es sich selber in dem verborgen dunsternisse des unbekanten gottes* [99.25–26]). Like Tauler, the author seeks to show how the imitation of the passion and sinking into the unknown God are two sides of the same coin. The second way to the perfection of the poor life is the perfection of the virtues (chap. 2:104–5); the third is dying to self and to creatures (chap. 3:106–12).

Up to this point the second part of the treatise has added little that had not appeared in the first. When the author turns to the fourth way of attaining perfect poverty, however, he receives a new impetus that carries on through to the end of the tract—"the perfection of the contemplative life" (*vollekomenheit eines schovwenden lebens* [112.5–6]). Contemplation, of course, is one of the central themes in the history of Christian mysticism. The anonymous author employs it in this last long part of his handbook (112–93) as a lens for reconsidering many of the aspects of mysticism he has already treated. Once again, he begins with an introductory chapter 4 (112–19), which sets forth the general meaning of the contemplative life and its relation to poverty and love of God. Then, to further his analysis, he provides a second fourfold distinction, this time of four ways the soul can attain a poor and perfect contemplative life (119.19–24). This final distinction organizes the last third of the work.

The first mode of attaining perfect contemplation is by giving up all that is opposed to God, in other words, detachment (chap. 5:119–21). The second is following in Christ's footsteps, because it is "through his humanity [that we come] to his divinity" (*daz ist durch sine menscheit in sine gotheit* [121.26–27]). This chapter 6 (121–38) includes discussions of union and divinization. The third mode of gaining the height of contemplation features a long consideration of how to deal with suffering (chap. 7:138–69). Suffering, both in the sense of actively induced ascetic practices and inner conformity to the trials sent by God, was an important feature of Christian mysticism, not least that of late medieval Germany. *The Book of Spiritual Poverty* sides with Eckhart and Tauler in emphasizing that patient and detached acceptance of suffering, rather than self–torture, is the key to advancing in the contemplative life. The organizational impetus lurking throughout the treatise is illustrated in the lengthy discussion that follows concerning the four ways in which the Friends of God deal with suffering (152–69)—in actions, in will, in spirit, and finally in God himself. The last three of these feature extended treatments of mystical union. After a brief digression (chap. 8 on avoiding sin), *The Book of Spiritual Poverty* concludes with two chapters that consider the fourth mode for attaining perfect contemplation: "A careful watch over everything that can happen to someone, bodily or spiritual, so that he can accept it in such a way that his spirit is not disturbed."[50] In other words, we are still talking about the detachment, releasement, and inner peace that are the essence of true poverty of life. Chapter 9 (176–83) concentrates on how we must remove created images to attain God, while chapter 10 (183–93) forms a fitting conclusion to the whole in its attempt to summarize how silencing all the faculties and drawing the soul into "the ground of the soul" (*in dem grunde der selen* [191.12]) leads to the final union in which the soul "should love God for God's sake, and should leave behind all pleasures, and should depend on God alone without any why whatever" (*ane alles warumb*).[51] A truly Eckhartian conclusion.

This survey of the text helps to show why it is not incorrect to see *The Book of Spiritual Poverty* as a handbook of the mysticism of the ground. Of course, there is something of a paradox or contradiction involved in attempting to capture the shifting perspectives of Eckhart's mysticism into a kind of teaching manual. But the inner dynamism of the mysticism of the ground was not totally quenched by its reconfiguration in a didactic work, as a look at a few passages may demonstrate. In what follows, I will begin with a consideration of two important structural sections, Chapters 1 and 2 of part 1, where the anonymous author sets out the meaning of poverty, detachment, and freedom, and then chapter 4 of part 2, in which the contemplative life, the overarching theme of this part, is introduced and its relation to poverty and detachment analyzed.

The Book of Spiritual Poverty starts with an implied syllogism: "What is poverty? [Major] Poverty is likeness to God. What is God? [Minor] God is a being detached from all creatures, a free power, a pure activity. [Conclusion] Therefore, poverty is a being that is detached from all creatures." The next question proceeds from this. To the query "What is detachment?" comes the response, "That which clings to nothing; poverty clings to nothing and nothing clings to it."[52] The chapter follows this dialogical procedure through a series of about a dozen questions and answers, a kind of simplified scholastic *quaestio*. The first of these shows that clinging to nothing really means clinging only to God. In explaining this, the author steps back from the most extreme claims of Eckhart's Pr. 52 on the nature of true poverty. "Some say that the highest poverty and the most intimate detachment is that a person should be as he was before he came to be; when he understood nothing; when he willed nothing; when he was God with God."[53] If this were possible, it would be true, according to the author, but because we possess created being, we must continue to exercise the works of knowing and love that lead to blessedness. It is difficult to decide here whether the author is disagreeing with Eckhart, or only cautioning the unwary reader that the Dominican's extreme formulations about poverty and union are true only *insofar as* we lose our created being in God's existence and not insofar as we also remain creatures. The basic point, however, is an Eckhartian one: in order for a person to be poor, or detached, in knowing and loving, "He must know God by means of God, and love God by means of God" (3.31–32).

The remainder of the chapter explores the relation between spiritual poverty and reason, virtue and grace, and how these all relate to external poverty. Reason, or "rational discernment through images and forms," is important by way of preparation, but when inner poverty is attained, "a person must leave behind all discernment by images and must draw himself with one into the One without any discernment."[54] The relation between total interior stripping and the life of virtue had been a debated topic since the early fourteenth century and the condemnation of Maguerite Porete's view of "saying goodbye to the virtues."[55] *The Book of Spiritual Poverty* advances a view of virtue's role that is not essentially different from Porete's, though more carefully expressed. Virtue and grace as created realities, or accidents, are important by way of preparation, but the perfect soul becomes "poor" in both virtue and grace when it goes beyond time and the manifold nature of creation and "dwells in eternity and unites herself to the single One" (4.34–35). Such a soul possesses grace and virtue in a divine and essential way, that is, insofar as they are nothing other than God. Since true perfection depends on being empty and detached, not only in the inner person but also in the outer person (6.9–17), the first chapter closes with a practical discussion of how the poor person is to use riches, especially the gifts that might be given him or her (6.19–8.5). This shows that the book was intended for actual poor practice with regard to external goods, not just a theoretical understanding.

The second chapter explores the relation between poverty and the freedom that was a mark of detachment and among the other greatly contested notions of late medieval mysticism. "God is a free power, and so too poverty is a free power bound by no one, because its nobility is freedom." To the question "What is freedom?" the author responds, "Freedom is true purity and detachment which always seeks Eternity. Freedom is the detached being that is God, or that depends totally on God."[56] What emerges here is that the key terms of the first chapters (*armuot/friheit/ abgescheidenheit*) are all really synonyms for separation from created reality and absolute dependence on God. Adopting Eckhartian language, the treatise says that the soul who can attain this state "attains God by violence; God cannot withhold himself; he must give himself to her," because that is his nature (8.24–28). Again, the author is willing to use some of the more daring language of the mysticism of the ground, but within the context of a treatise that tries to explain and sometimes qualify the meaning of the terms. This freedom is not something that the soul attains on its own; rather, "Real freedom is so noble that no one gives it except God the Father" (9.4–5). The Father's gift is mediated by the action of the Holy Spirit, illuminating the soul to enable her to give up her own free will and become one with the divine will. At this point, the treatise quotes 1 Corinthians 6:17: "He who is joined to the Lord becomes one spirit." This form of union of the created spirit with the Divine Spirit allows the soul to do all things freely. Here another Pauline text appears, "Where the Spirit of the Lord is, there is liberty" (2 Cor. 3:17), the passage that was the battle cry of the Free Spirit heretics.

In the context of fourteenth-century debates over mysticism no phrase was in need of more careful understanding than "freedom of spirit." The rest of chapter 2 takes up this task (9.36–20.11). Three topics are treated in detail. The first is the relation between obedience and freedom—doesn't someone who promises obedience to another compromise or lose freedom? In a scholastic manner the treatise distinguishes four modes of obedience, showing that forms of obedience which involve the need for instruction, for ascetical training, and for gaining humility, as well as obedience to the commandments of the church, are necessary for beginners. When it comes to the truly poor, however, the situation is different. Here *The Book of Spiritual Poverty* skates on thin ice, using language that borders on what would later be called Quietism (10.12–11.35). The spiritually poor person has become so interiorized that he or she no longer needs to be obedient externally for instruction or for ascetic practice. He need not abandon himself to creatures, though he always abandons himself to God (10.36–37). For such a person interior detachment is more important than demonstrating his virtues to others. More dangerously, the author says, "A free poor person is also not bound to take all that is legally prescribed in Holy Christianity in an external way, as another person would who is not free, because what Holy Christianity performs in an external manner the poor person performs inwardly and essentially."[57] Citing another often misunderstood Pauline text here ("The law is not made for the just man" [1 Tim. 1:9]) only compounds the ambiguity of this language, which could be easily read, at least by medieval inquisitors, as encouraging freedom from ecclesiastical obligations. But the section concludes by trying to avoid any such interpretation, affirming that "all that Holy Christianity has prescribed is good," and that one who is poor in spirit is always obedient and submissive.

The next section (11.36–16.11) takes these issues further, exploring how "a poor person may abandon himself in three ways" to external works. Here *The Book of Spiritual Poverty* is traditional in emphasizing that the contemplative, or the person who has attained poverty of spirit, is bound to perform acts of charity for his neighbor who is in need. If one has achieved true freedom and detachment, external works, such as weaving, and aiding one's neighbor, do not hinder a person, but actually increase freedom. However, it is important to use discernment to determine whether the external work is prompted by an evil spirit, by nature, or by God. Even the evil spirit can promote works of charity when it serves his purpose, as in the case of the desire for excessive asceticism that might induce mental imbalance or physical illness. The treatise will return to the theme of the discernment of spirits in more detail later.[58]

The third and final topic for the proper understanding of freedom of spirit is also framed as a question: "How is unordered freedom (*ungeordenter friheit*) to be understood, and how is a person to discern if his freedom is ordered to God or not?" (16.14–16). This issue, as we have seen, was a burn-

ing question since the condemnation of the Free Spirits at the Council of
Vienne in 1311. The treatise's handling of these issues is generally in agreement with what we have seen in Tauler, but with interesting reflections on
the dangers of a purely natural practice of inner emptying that bear comparison with another contemporary mystic, the Dutch John Ruusbroec. The
key difference between good and bad freedom, here as in Tauler, is the difference between humility and pride. This is most easily seen in times of difficulty. When someone who has poverty of spirit is troubled or assailed, he
is humble, patient, and silent, while those who have disordered freedom
become angry and seek revenge. True to its didactic intent, the book goes
on to distinguish two kinds of unordered freedom, one bodily and the other
spiritual (17.16–17). Bodily misdirected freedom comes from attachment to
temporal goods and honors. (The anonymous author thought that wealth
and power were at best compatible with only an inferior kind of freedom.)
More dangerous is unordered spiritual freedom, which comes in three
forms. The first is found in those who practice a merely external form of
religion and yet think that they have attained perfection. The second is
found in a person who turns away from external works into the mind in a
purely natural way. The author says of such a one, "In this inner remaining
a natural light springs up in him, and this reveals to him the distinction of
natural truth, and this distinction produces great pleasure in him." This
intellectual illumination is only from nature, but it leads people to think that
they know all truth and are so free that they need not submit to anybody.
Their pride leads them to judge others and to pay no heed to virtues and
good works. "And from this," the author goes on, "springs up an unordered
freedom so that he spurns the laws of Holy Christianity."[59] This spiritual fall
is like that of Lucifer. Concerning those who have fallen into this trap the
author says: "These are called the Free Spirits" (*Und dis heissent die frien
geiste* [19.32]). Finally, a third form is briefly mentioned, the unordered freedom that comes from visions, which all too often are misleading or induce
pride. Both in his analysis of the errors of the Free Spirits, and in his suspicion of visions, the author of *The Book of Spiritual Poverty* shared much with
Tauler.

As mentioned above, contemplation and the nature of the contemplative
life play an organizing role in the second part of the treatise similar to that of
the terms poverty, detachment, and freedom in the first part. A look at the
fourth chapter of this second part will show how the author of *The Book of
Spiritual Poverty* integrated this important mystical theme into his handbook.
Contemplation is introduced as the fourth way to attain a poor life.
Although the active life (*wurckende leben*) is necessary as long as a person is

bound to temporal things, the contemplative life (*schovwende leben*) goes beyond all that is temporal and attains detachment from creatures. Those who reach this state are called "the hidden Friends of God" (*die verborgen gottesfreunde* [112.29–30]); they practice "a perfect contemplative life, that is, a free poor life freed from all temporal things" (113.4–5). Such people would have to abandon contemplation and succor their neighbor in need, if they still possessed temporal things, but the author presumes that they no longer possess anything. Such detached free souls are passive to God's action, which is described here in the accents of the erotic mysticism of the Song of Songs 1:2, "He has kissed me with the kiss of his mouth." The anonymous author explains: "God inclines his countenance to her and kisses her, and the kissing is the uniting of love with love, and one gazes at the other and each one is so bound to the other that one cannot act without the other, so completely are they bound together with love."[60] Bernard of Clairvaux and Augustine are cited as authorities for this loving union. Worldly folk, who do not act from "the ground of divine love" (*uz dem grunde goetlicher minne* [114.7]), can never love in this way. At this point the tract sets out an itinerary of the levels of poverty, beginning from letting go of superfluous goods, through shunning the self, to conclude with forgoing all forms of bodily or spiritual mediation between God and human (115.18–23). This stress on lack of mediation, presented in a practical and moral way, was one of the leitmotifs of the mysticism of the ground. The conclusion is that "poverty and contemplation stand on the same level," insofar as they express knowing and loving God "without the mediation of creatures" (116.15–19).

The second section (116.21–118.23) of the consideration of the relation between contemplation and poverty of spirit features an enumeration of eight forms of usefulness of the contemplative life, the kind of list typical of medieval treatises, mystical or otherwise. Many of these uses are traditional. Contemplation performs its works effortlessly, essentially, totally, and in a heavenly manner. The treatise goes on to claim that a "real contemplative life" (*einem rehten schovwende leben* [117.19]) guarantees eternal possession of glory, a startling statement, but one found in some of the most orthodox mystics, such as Bernard of Clairvaux. The sixth and seventh forms of usefulness express the author's understanding of *epektasis*, the constant progression of the contemplative soul into ever deeper reaches of the divine mystery, "because the divine being is so groundless that the creature can never reach its ground." Hence, "the spirit hovers in God as a fish in the sea and a bird in the air," comparisons that had become commonplaces in mystical literature (117.33–118.5). The final usefulness, however, expresses the language of the mysticism of the ground more directly. The truly contemplative soul loses all unlikeness to the extent that "she loses her name so that she is called God rather than spirit. Not that she is God, but rather she is godly, and so she is described more in relation to God than to spirit."[61] Here the author cites one of the prime scriptural proof texts for divinization (Ps. 81:6), but with the customary qualification that we are "gods" through the action of grace, while Christ is God's Son by nature. After a brief reference to the birth of the Word in the soul, the process which allows us to be truly called gods and children of God, the chapter closes by bringing the themes of the first and second parts of the treatise together through an invocation of the divine presence. "Hence, the person who is empty and removed from all mediation has God present to him, and in this presence he gazes on God, for God is present in all things." But not everyone who claims to be poor in spirit is so: "Only the person who works as a poor person is a poor person, and he is also a contemplative person."[62] This section of part 2 of the book makes evident the author's desire to show the conformity between an Eckhartian understanding of poverty of spirit and the traditional view of the supremacy of the contemplative life.

These two organizing sections of *The Book of Spiritual Poverty* give a sense of the arrangement of the guidebook and how it argues its case. Many of the main themes and their interaction are also evident in these pages. It will be helpful, however, to consider several passages that display these and other significant motifs in more detail.

In the middle of part 1 of the book (59–64) there is a treatment of the inward work that draws us to God based on a distinction between three objects needed for proper inner contemplation. The first is preliminary, the need for self–knowledge, especially "correct knowledge of our failings" (59.16). The second object is knowledge of the sufferings of our Lord, which is indispensable since it is the channel by which God pours his divine love into the heart to draw it to the goal. "As God the Father," he says, "gives birth to the Son in himself and in all things, so with the same birth he draws people into himself through the sufferings [of Christ] and through all virtues. Just as God's birth is eternal, so too is the drawing within with which people are led inside through his sufferings."[63] So, a person who gives himself totally to consideration of the passion becomes "a second Christ" and is united in love with the Lord. The anonymous author insists that perseverance in consideration of Christ's passion is the only way to attain God. Self-inflicted penance apart from the passion is useless, and natural knowledge of truth has no saving value. "If a person wants the divine truth that alone is blessed, he must seek it in the sufferings of Jesus Christ" (61.32–33). Here the treatise uses another popular image of late medieval passion piety, that of drinking from the wounds of the crucified one, citing John 4:14. This is the road that leads to the kingdom of heaven, which *The Book of Spiritual Poverty* (as we have also seen in Eckhart) identifies not with the heaven above, but with the interior heaven of the divinized soul (62.22–29).

The necessity for consideration of the passion leads to a discussion of two inadequate forms of turning within. The first is that of the pagan philosophers of old. "The pagans," he says, "sought the bare being of the soul, but they could not arrive at it without Christ. Therefore, they could not fully know God nor attain blessedness, though they wished to be blessed."[64] Eckhart and Tauler had thought that philosophers like Plato and Proclus had attained some measure of the vision of God in the naked being of the soul. The author of *The Book of Spiritual Poverty* is more critical, not only here, but in other passages where he discusses the pagans.[65] Second, he also criticizes "all those who seek the bare essence of the soul apart from Christ's sufferings" (63.23–24), presumably another reference to the Free Spirits.

The third and final object of contemplation is "God according to his naked Godhead" (*got nach siner blossen gotheit* [63.35–36]). The person who has overcome his faults and been conducted through all the virtues by his meditation on the passion is ready to be led into God himself and united with him. As in many other mystical authors of the time, this writer uses language that reflects both the union of indistinction found in Eckhart and the traditional erotic language of the loving unity of spirits. "So [the poor person] has an eternal entry into God, and he is so completely enveloped by God that he loses himself and knows nothing save God alone. He is drowned in the bottomless ocean of divinity and swims in God like a fish in the sea."[66] Immediately after these merging images, however, the text invokes the language of Song of Songs 4:9 about the bride wounding the Bridegroom with one of her eyes. "The eye is the penetrating love that the soul has for God. With love she forces God to do what she wants. . . . She draws the bow of her heart; she draws it, shoots into God with enflamed desire, and she hits her mark right on."[67]

The author of *The Book of Spiritual Poverty* is not overly concerned to make careful discriminations between different forms of mystical union. What he does stress is that there can be no union without inner identification with the suffering Christ. Here, as well as in the other passages where he talks about the need for contemplation of the passion,[68] the author does not present realistic, blood-drenched meditational practices or imitations of Christ in the manner of Suso's *Life*, but adheres to Tauler's attitude toward the passion as both the ontological center of Christ's saving work and the archetype of full acceptance of the divine will. It is worth noting that in one of its discussions of the continuing need for consideration of the passion such meditation is seen as the basis for the praiseworthy desire for frequent reception of the Eucharist.[69]

The birth of the Word in the soul, briefly mentioned in the discussion of the inward work that draws the soul to God in part 1, receives a more extended treatment in other places in *The Book of Spiritual Poverty*. This is further evidence for how the anonymous author sought to weave together in handbook form many significant strands of late medieval German mysticism. A look at a section dealing with the distinction between inner and outer work in part 2 (101–4) provides a sense of how important the motif of birthing is to the treatise.[70] Although *The Book of Spiritual Poverty* does not contain much metaphysical speculation, it is founded on a sound grasp of the philosophical and theological implications of the mysticism of the ground. This section of the text begins by identifying inward working as God's being and nature, and outward working as creation. And so, the author remarks, "In the way that the creature flowed forth from God, so in the same way shall it again flow back into him."[71] But this flowing back cannot be accomplished by the creature on its own; it can only be prepared for by our becoming free of all our own forms of working and letting God work in us (101.26–27). On the basis of this emptying, God works in us in two ways. The first work is that of grace; the second work is "essential and divine" (*wesenlich und goetlich* [102.16]). The presentation of the latter is deeply Eckhartian. The work of grace that helps us overcome sin and attain individual virtues prepares for the essential work, which is identified as the birth of the Word in the soul, embracing all the virtues in an essential way. It takes place when "the Father gives birth to the Son in the soul and this birth lifts the spirit up above all created things to God."[72] This work is above, but not contrary to, grace and reason. It is described as a work of the light of glory (*lieht der glorien*), that is, it is identical with whatever kind of activity is performed in heaven. The "divinized person" (*vergoetteter mensche* [102.40]) is described as "working all things with God in an essential way," because "when two are one there is a single work" (103.1–4). Such language reflects Eckhart's teaching about the inner identity of God and human, but how far the author of this treatise is willing to push such a position is not clear. He does, however, emphasize how this elevation into God must go beyond all created images, the process of dis-imaging (*entbilden*) also found in Eckhart (103.13–20).[73] The language used here expresses the learned ignorance of the apophatic tradition:

The effort that the intellect makes to follow after the divine work is nothing else than to empty itself of all created images and with the uncreated light to penetrate into the darkness of the hidden Godhead. There intellect becomes free of knowledge by knowing and free of love by loving, that is, it no longer knows in a creaturely fashion, but rather in a divine way; and it does not love with its own love, but with God's love.[74]

The section closes with a typically sober reminder that even the soul who attains such a vision of the divine reality above all grace and reason needs to be reminded that it can only be realized by following Christ.

The metaphor of the *grunt*—the detonator of Eckhart's mystical explosions whose reverberations resound in usually less disruptive ways among his successors—plays a significant role in *The Book of Spiritual Poverty*. Although the treatise uses the term quite often, its presentations are less daring than Eckhart's. *Grunt* is not a metaphor of mystical fusion here, as it is in Eckhart. The treatise does speak of God as *grundlos*, using the image of the soul as a stone sinking into the bottomless divine sea (e.g., 99.23–100.1, and 117.35–39). It also uses the phrase "the ground of divine love" (114.6–40). But the author prefers more traditional Dionysian language for the divine mystery, such as the phrase "the hidden darkness of the naked divine being" (*die verborgen dunsternise des blossen goetlichen wesens* [164.15–16]). The term *grunt* is primarily used of the innermost level of the soul, where the birth of the Word takes place.[75] This is evident in a passage at the end of the tract where the term *grunt* appears more often than in any other place in the work.

The theme in this final section (191.5–194.5) is the mystical paradox of the "poor inner dead life" (*arm innerlich erstorben leben*). A person must die to all sinfulness and gain all virtue so that God can speak his Word in the soul's ground (191.7–12). The unity of pure being is realized in three correlatives: "True dying is unity, and true unity is inwardness, and true poverty is unity" (191.14–15). This inner unification, or poverty of spirit, allows the soul to receive "the influx of divine light" (*indruck des goetlichen liehtes* [191.33.34]). "Because that light is simple, so too there must be a simple ground in order to reflect its brilliance."[76] This mention of *grunt* introduces a discussion of the importance of the "simple pure ground" (*einvaltigen lutern grunde*) in the mystical life (192.5–36). It is only by being fixed on this inner simple ground that we can avoid the illusions of the imagination and the deceptive visions sent by the devil. (The author, like Eckhart, is strongly opposed to visionary experiences.) He summarizes: "Now God is invisible and beyond all images. Therefore, they are deceived who accept visions, because what comes to birth in a simple pure ground is so subtle and so simple that no one can grasp it with images and no one can speak about it."[77] Desire for visions, says the author, has more in common with Antichrist than Christ! Avoiding all images even extends to what are here termed "pure distinctions of god-formed truth" (*lutern underscheide gotfoermiger warheit* [192.38–39]), apparently the kind of theological concepts that the poor in spirit would use to teach others. These too are other than God and are therefore a form of distraction from absolute resting in the divine simplicity (192.37–193.12).

The last word in *The Book of Spiritual Poverty* is fittingly given to love (193.13–194.5). In this life even weaker souls can turn to God with the words of Song of Songs 2:5, "Speak, my Beloved, I am sick with love." This plea brings on the active love (*wurckende minne*) of the Holy Spirit that burns away all imperfections and forms of unlikeness to God until the sweet passive love (*suesse lidende minne*) springs up in which the soul loses its own activity and God alone works in it. "Then," continues the text, "the soul is in an eternal entering into God. With himself God draws her into himself and makes the soul one love with him" (193.27–30). The two now have one name—*minne*. Here the treatise again turns to the language of the ground, this time applying it to God: "This is brought about by the simple pure ground out of which simple divine love springs. The greatest joy that exists in time is found in this."[78]

The *Theologia Deutsch*

The most widely known of all the late medieval MHG mystical treatises is customarily called the *Theologia Deutsch* (sometimes *Theologia Germanica*), the title given it by Martin Luther, whose editions and praise of the book did much to guarantee it a wide readership, especially among Protestants, though some Catholics continued to vindicate the book for their own.[79] In the words of Alois M. Haas, "It becomes ever more clear that the *Theologia Deutsch* is not only a key text for the so-called German mysticism, but is also a central instructional manual of the Reformation."[80] The *Theologia Deutsch* (TD) is known in only eight manuscripts, all from the second half of the fifteenth century, so it did not have a wide diffusion for close to a century after its composition. Luther produced a partial edition first in 1516, where his preface cautions the reader not to pass by the anonymous work because of its seeming lack of learning, but says that it came forth "from the depths of the Jordan by a true Israelite whose name is known to God." At that time Luther thought the work might have been written by Tauler. In 1518 he issued a more complete edition on the basis of a new manuscript that had come to his attention, this time with more fulsome praise, arguing that along with the Bible and Augustine, the TD proves that his own "German theology" is really the ancient teaching of the church. "Let anyone who wishes read this little book, and then let him say whether theology is original with us or ancient, for this book is not new." Although, as Steven Ozment has shown, there are many aspects in which Luther's theology was different from that of the TD, Luther found much that was congenial to him in this late medieval text.[81] Luther's praise, as well as the innate qualities of the work, gave it immense cachet in the Lutheran and Spiritualist tradition (though Calvin and the Reformed tradition rejected it). A 1528 edition circulated with comments by the Radical Reformer Hans Denck. Another radical, Sebastian Franck, composed a Latin paraphrase in 1542. The work was also translated by Sebastian Castellio and studied by Valentin Weigel.[82] Orthodox Lutherans also continued to read the book. The mystic John Arndt reedited an earlier printing based on Luther in 1597; his version had over sixty later printings. The German Pietists had a particular affection for the work.

The warm embrace that so many Protestants gave to the TD naturally led to some suspicions among Catholics. Castellio's Latin version was put on the *Index* of forbidden books by Paul V in 1612, but seventeenth-century Catholic mystics continued to read the book, which was available in many languages (Latin, Dutch, French, English, Swedish, etc.). It has been calculated that between Luther's first version of 1516 and the year 1961 one hundred and ninety editions appeared in a growing list of languages![83] Twentieth-century manuscript discoveries led to some discussion about the original form of the book, but the critical edition published by Wolfgang von Hinten in 1982 has cleared up most disputes. New translations based on this edition,[84] as well as recent studies,[85] have helped us toward a better understanding of this important treatise.

The prologue of the work, written by a later redactor, ascribes it to "a wise, judicious, truthful, just man, God's friend, who in earlier times was a member of the Teutonic Order, a priest and warden in the house of the Teutonic Order in Frankfurt." Hence the name given the treatise in some manuscripts, "The Frankfurter." The prologue provides a window on the historical context of the book, noting, "It teaches many valuable aspects of the divine truth and particularly how and in what way one can distinguish between the true, just Friends of God and the unjust, false, Free Spirits who are so harmful to the Holy Church."[86] Attempts to identify this member of the Teutonic Order have been in vain. Although some scholars tried to date the tract to the fifteenth century, there is general agreement that it probably comes from the last quarter of the fourteenth.

The most authentic surviving form of this relatively short work contains fifty-three chapters of varying length. The longer chapters may have been based on talks or addresses given to members of the order, but many chapters are too short for that. Luise Abramowski has convincingly argued that not only the prologue and chapter headings but also the important final two chapters come from the hand of a redactor, but a very skilled one given the quality of the added chapters.[87] Although the work shows evidence of scholastic organization and modes of arguing, the TD is a less academic treatise than those previously discussed, one that may have had at least a partly lay audience in mind. The Bible is the main source, cited more than forty times. (The deeply biblical nature of the book doubtless helped its popularity among Protestants.) There are only five other explicit references (Boethius, Dionysius, Tauler, and twice to pseudonymous Eckhartian texts), but the author seems to have had a good theological education.[88] The organization of the TD is difficult to determine. Some have supposed that the mention of the three-stage itinerary of the purgative, illuminative, and unitive ways in chapter 14 provides a structure, at least to the core chapters 14–38. It is not evident, however, that the text tries to follow the three stages of the mystical path in any real way. There does not seem to be a consistent structure. It is more important to understand the author's fundamental vision, which plays itself out in various ways in the treatise.

The anonymous author of the TD has a distinctive literary style,[89] as well as an original theological vision. Although he makes use of many terms and themes created by Eckhart and frequent in the mysticism of the ground,[90] he had his own way of presenting a christological path to divinizing union with God.[91] A key to his vision can be found in the biblical foundation on which he builds. The TD is unusual in citing the Old Testament only twice (both times from Isaiah). The more than forty citations from the New Testament are integral to the argument, not mere extraneous proof texts. They fall into two groups. The first is a series of nine Pauline quotations stressing Paul's gospel, that is, the contrast between the old, fallen Adam, and the new risen Christ. The tract starts, for example, by citing 1 Corinthians 13:10, "When the perfect comes, then one destroys the imperfect and what is in part." Strong, almost dualistic, contrasts between good and evil, old and new, perfect and imperfect, whole and part, self-will and divine will, obedience and disobedience, and the like, pervade the treatise.[92] The second and even larger group are quotations from the Gospels, especially from

Matthew, also stressing the contrast between the old and the new, but now including the note of movement away from what is bad toward the good through the following of Christ: "If you wish to come to me, then let go of yourself and follow; whoever does not let go, abandon and lose himself and everything is not worthy of me and cannot be my disciple" (Matt. 16:24–25).[93] The TD reconfigures themes common to late medieval German mysticism within the perspective of a biblical view of obedience and discipleship.

What we might call the bipolarism of the TD creates a mode of address directed to the necessity of making a fundamental choice between good and evil forms of life, that is, between the true freedom of the Friends of God and the false liberty of the Free Spirits.[94] Just as Adam's disobedience is the essence of the sinful condition, so Christ's humility, detachment, and poverty of life are the expression of his total obedience to his Father. In imitating him we regain our true status as pure expressions of the divine will. This stark contrast between the opposed positions gives the TD a directness not found in many other mystical treatises of the late Middle Ages. We should not, however, confuse directness with simplicity. The treatise argues its case with considerable subtlety, some unusual theology, and not a few obscure and difficult passages.[95] These too may be seen as signs of an original perspective struggling to find expression.

The doctrine of God found in the TD has affinities with the mysticism of Eckhart and his followers, along with some special elements. The text does not show much interest in the inner life of the Trinity, but rather focuses on the essential divine attributes. In Dionysian fashion, the book emphasizes that God is "the one true Good," the source of all things. There is also frequent repetition that God is beyond all knowing and naming. A passage from chapter 9 says of the one reality that will bring happiness to the soul, "It is the Good or has become the Good, and yet it is neither this nor that good that one can name, recognize or point out, but it is everything and above everything; it does not need to come into the soul either, for it is already there, but unrecognized."[96] The unknowable Good that is God is also spoken of as the One, "For God is one and must be one, and God is all and must be all" (chap. 46: 140.4–5). This supreme reality is also being (*wesen*). Chapter 1, for example, says, "The perfect is a being that has comprehended and included everything in itself and in its being. Without it and apart from it no true being exists. In it all things have their being, because it is the being of all things. . . ."[97] The TD summarizes the total dependence of all things on God in chapter 36, saying, "God is the being of all beings, and the life of everything living, and the wisdom of all knowledge, since all things have their being more truly in God than in themselves."[98] This is the virtual existence (*esse virtuale*) stressed by Eckhart. Throughout the treatise we also find the Eckhartian contrast between created being, the "this and that" of particularity, with the perfect, absolute, and yet unknown, reality of God.

These traditional forms of speaking about God's transcendence and immanence, however, coexist with an unusual presentation of divine presence in the human person. Chapters 31–32 (114–17) contain a complicated, and not always clear, analysis of the divine nature. Chapter 31 (114.15–115.29) analyzes a distinction of three levels in God: (1) "God as Godhead," lying beyond all knowing, natural or revealed; (2) "God as God," the level of the distinction of persons in the Trinity; and (3) "God as man, or as God lives in a godly person, or in a divinized person." The passage continues by saying that this last level, that of the incarnation and the divinization of humans in Christ, belongs to God (not to creatures) in a special way: "It is in him apart from the creature in an originating and essential way, but not in a formal or actual way."[99] This is not easy to interpret, but I take it to mean that God's coming to exist in Christ, as well as in those who achieve divinization through him, is an essential aspect of the divine reality, though God is not the form of creatures in their actual existence in the world. The author then tries to explain his view in a dense passage at the end of the chapter, claiming that because God wants "it [i.e., the third level] to be practiced and carried out," he needs creatures (*Nu dar got wil das gevbet vnd gewircket han, vnd das mag an creatur nicht gescheen, das es also seyn solle* [115.30–31]).

What this third level of God needing creatures as an "essential" aspect of his being may mean is illuminated by a text in the following chapter and other passages in the work. The divine need for humans is expressed in chapter 32 in terms of an analysis of the proper names for God. Because God is pure good, beyond all this and that, he can both be everything and be beyond everything. He is also light and understanding in an essential way, not as a mere activity. All God's attributes are identical with his being—a teaching that goes back at least as far as Augustine. But what follows is new. The author says, "Nothing can ever be brought about or practiced without creatures, for without creatures there is nothing in God but one essence and one source and not action. And yet where the one thing that is nonetheless everything [i.e., God] takes one creature to itself [i.e., in the incarnation and divinization] and takes control over it and molds it to itself, it seems as if it can recognize itself fully there."[100] In other words, God needs incarnation and divinization in order to recognize his nature in action. What this recognition involves becomes clearer in other places where the TD says, for example, that God needs creation in order to be able to express order, rule, and measure (chap. 39: 124.1–8). The most striking of the passages about God's need for creation, especially for human beings, is found in chapter 51, where a lengthy consideration of the divine will concludes by claiming that God needs to create humans so that his eternal willing can be realized in a created will that has the freedom to choose the divine goodness above all things. God's eternal will, says the author, exists apart from deeds and reality, so it would be fruitless if it were to have no expression. He continues: "This cannot take place without the creature. The creature therefore exists, and God wants to have the creature, so that this will, which is and must be without outward expression in God, expresses itself in action."[101] This unusual view of God's need to create raises questions that cannot be pursued here.

The *Theologia Deutsch* presupposes but does not discuss the flowing out of all things from the overflowing Good that is God. The text has little interest in cosmology as such; it concentrates on the nature and destiny of humanity. Here too, the TD goes its own way, largely bypassing traditional anthropology based on the human person as image and likeness of God to focus its attention on humanity's existential situation as fallen and living in disobedience. A series of strongly worded chapters explores the opposition between Adam's disobedience and Christ's obedience. Chapter 15 sets the theme: "Everything that perished and died in Adam, arose again in Christ and came alive. Everything that arose in Adam and became alive, perished in Christ and died. What, however, was and is that? I say it is true obedience and disobedience."[102] True obedience (*war gehorsam*) is being as free of oneself as if one did not exist, so that one can be totally fixed on the One (89.5–14). In other words, it is nothing else than spiritual poverty (*geistlich armut*),[103] letting go or releasement (*gelassen*),[104] and abandoning the will in detachment (*abgescheiden*).[105] All these terms, as well as the related language of the soul becoming empty, naked, and free, appear frequently throughout the TD.

The obedience owed by the creature to its Creator perished at the Fall. In its place came "disobedience, and selfhood, and I-ness (*icheit*), and the like" (chap. 16; 90.2–3). The major opponent blocking access to God is self-centeredness, our obsession with "I, me, mine, and the like" (*ich, mir, mich vnd des glich* [126.17–18]).[106] Over and over again the TD repeats its message that the essence of sin is disobedience and the root of disobedience is our concern for self—"Disobedience and sin are one" (*Vngehorsam vnd sunde ist eyns* [93.75]). One of the strongest statements of the equivalence of these negative forces comes in chapter 43, which says: "Whenever and wherever one speaks about Adam, disobedience, the old man, selfishness, one's own will and willfullness, self-will, I, mine, nature, falsehood, devil and sin, it is all one and the same. It is all opposed to God and without God."[107] The mention of nature in this passage highlights another aspect of the TD that doubtless appealed to Luther. The anonymous author of the text has an essentially negative rather than a neutral concept of nature; for him nature means fallen nature—"Therefore the devil and nature are one" (*Dar vmmb ist der tufel vnd natur eyns* [137.87–88]). Hence, like Luther, he insists that of ourselves we can do nothing good: "All who will without God's will are acting out of self-will, and whatever happens out of self-will is sin."[108]

In a daring way at the end of the treatise the author heightens this pessimistic view of humanity's situation by interpreting both hell and the account of the Fall as realized in our present existence. Hell is nothing else than present disobedience (chap. 49). Paradise is God's good creation, meant to be a precinct of heaven in which all creatures point us to God. In this paradise all things are allowed, except the eating of the forbidden fruit, which is "one's own will, or wishing something different from what the eternal will wishes" (chap. 50: 143.12–13). This emphasis on the role of the will leads into the final and longest chapter of the original composition (chap. 51: 143–48), which seeks to answer the question why God created free will and placed it in the paradise of the world. The first response is not to question God's decisions, but the real answer is to be found in the fact that reason and will belong together as God's noblest creation. Indeed, as noted above, there is a sense in which God needs to create the will in order to have outward expression of his hidden will. God's purpose, of course, is that the created will should recognize its total dependence on him and therefore become identical with his own will now active in a new way. But because the will is free, the devil and Adam, or false nature (*die falsch natur*), can rob God of what is rightfully his, the noble freedom of the will. We are now placed between the hell of self-centeredness and the heaven of abandoning everything to follow Christ. The author summarizes: "Whoever wants to follow him must abandon everything else, for in him everything was as completely abandoned as was ever abandoned among creatures, or could happen. Also, whoever wants to follow him must take up his cross upon himself, and the cross is nothing other than Christ's life."[109]

The *Theologia Deutsch* explores the fundamental option of taking up the cross and following Christ in loving obedience in many ways, calling upon ideas and forms of language characteristic of late medieval German mysticism. The treatise does not organize these themes into any sequence, but sees them as correlative aspects of the Christic redirection of the will. Following Christ here means not so much to undertake a journey, as to realize the need for abandonment and annihilation of self-will. The dominant practices, if such they may be called, are internal, involving emptying the self through detachment, abandonment, poverty of spirit, essential humility (*wesenliche demutikeit*), and the radical obedience that sums them all up. We are called upon to cooperate with God's grace in the work of preparation,[110] but the goal is to achieve an interior state in which one passively allows God to act.[111] Exterior acts of virtue and practices are not condemned. In one place, the TD says that whoever receives the Eucharist has really received Christ and increased Christ's hold on him (chap. 45: 139.18–20).[112] Furthermore, the book condemns the false mystics who advise people to disregard the ordinances, practices, and sacraments of the church (see chaps. 25, 39, and 40, and the discussion below). But the treatise is not really fixated on external religious practices.

The program of following Christ that the TD sets forth is spelled out in detail in a number of chapters. As might be expected, the book lays great stress on Christ as the model of perfect obedience. "Humanity was created for true obedience and owes it to God," as we read in chapter 15. "This obedience perished and died in Adam and arose and became alive in Christ. . . . In his humanity Christ was and existed entirely free from himself, and so free from every created thing and was nothing but a house or dwelling place for God."[113] Christ's willingness to suffer, in this sense actual physical suffering, is also a part of the model we must follow to attain divinization and union with God.[114] Like Eckhart, the TD sees Christ as the exemplar of a universal love shown equally to all human beings—to love anyone more than another is to distance oneself from the Christ model (chap. 33). Above all, the TD insists that Christ is the one and only way to attain the Father (chap. 50). We can never go beyond Christ (chap. 29), or try to shake off Christ's life, as the false mystics attempt to do (chap. 31). Christ's life is the perfect life (chaps. 43 and 45). In language dear to Eckhart, the TD says that there is no "why" in Christ, because everything that is divine and belongs to God "wills and works and desires nothing but the good as good and for the sake of the good; there is otherwise no why."[115]

According to chapter 11, the christological model is to be lived out through two modes of participating in Christ's life of total obedience. The chapter begins with the statement "Christ's soul had to go to hell before it came to heaven, so the human soul must do the same." Our descent begins with self-knowledge as we come to see ourselves from within and recognize that our wickedness makes us worthy of damnation. This prepares for a divine action that actually casts the soul into hell. Such a person "is neither willing nor able to desire any consolation or salvation either from God or from created things" (84.11–12), knowing that it is in accordance with God's will that he is worthy of damnation. The experience of hell and mystical dereliction, of course, was not new. We have seen it in John Tauler, whose sermons the author of the TD certainly knew.[116] God in his mercy does not leave the soul in hell, however, but at his pleasure takes the person once again to himself and gives him an overwhelming awareness of the eternal good. The text continues: "This hell and heaven are two good, sure ways for a person in this life, and he is happy who experiences them, for this hell passes away, but heaven remains."[117] The two forms of experience are the work of God; we can neither make them come, or avoid them. One can slip from one to the other often, both by day and by night. In chapter 40 (127.42–61), combatting the views of the false mystics, the author brings out what is implicit here. In this life we can never go beyond Christ's bodily life and its suffering. Only in heaven shall we experience the total freedom of the resurrected Christ.

Fundamental to the teaching of the TD is the message that to follow Christ is to become divinized and to attain union with God. Few medieval works have put more emphasis on how the soul attains the status of "a divinized or godlike person" (*eyn vorgotter ader eyn gotlich mensch* [chap. 41: 130.1]). The treatise's doctrine of the three levels of divine reality, mentioned above, helps explain why divinization is so central a motif of this mystical guidebook. (The prevalence of divinization language may also help qualify generalizations that Protestant Christianity was always resistant to the concept of divinization.) Although there are some discussions of divinization in the early chapters,[118] the expression *vergotter mensch* becomes more frequent after chapter 32. The divinization spoken of in these late chapters so stresses the reality of our partaking of the nature of the God-man that it often borders on a kind of identity. At the end of a discussion in chapter 32 about the purity of the divine nature, for example, the author applies this purity to the divinized person. God's love is totally unselfish, because the "I-ness" (*icheit*) and the "selfness" (*selbheit*) characteristic of creatures are not found there, save insofar as they have a transcendent source in the persons of the Trinity. The same must also be true of the divinized person: "This must be so and true of a godlike person or of a true divinized person, for he would not otherwise be godlike or divinized."[119] In other words, the absolute unity of the three persons in the Trinity is also realized in the divinized human.

In chapter 41 there is a detailed discussion of the characteristics of the divinized person. The chapter begins by saying, "Someone may ask what a divinized or a divine person is. The answer: Someone whom the eternal or divine light shines through and illuminates and who is set on fire with an eternal and divine love. That is a godlike or divinized person."[120] The author employs these two aspects of divine light and divine love to underline the fact that it is not enough to claim to know God in some exalted way; the only proof of divinizing union is love. "A person may know much of God and what belongs to God, and think he knows what God is, but if he does not have love, he will not be godly or divinized. But if true love is there, a person must adhere to God and leave everything that is not God, or does not belong to God." The passage closes by emphasizing the power of love to effect permanent union with God: "This love unites a person to God so that he can never again be separated."[121]

For the author of the *Theologia Deutsch,* divinization is another way of speaking about union with God. The treatise often mentions union and becoming one with God, though formal discussions are rare. One penetrating analysis of union is found in chapter 24. After a presentation in chapter 23 about how acceptance of God demands releasement, obedience, and "silent resting within the ground of the soul," the author turns to what constitutes union. Becoming one with God is conceived of in a primarily christological way. The many paths that lead to Christ are realized "whenever God and man have been so united that it is said in truth (and the truth is evident) that the one reality is true, perfect God, and true, perfect man, and yet the man has so completely yielded to God that God himself is the man."[122] What this means is further explained as the chapter proceeds. When we divest ourselves of all "I, me, and mine," we become, like Christ, a pure channel of divine activity. When that happens there is nothing but God acting. "Since God in that place is that same man, he can also apprehend things and experience pleasure and pain. . . . That is the case when God and man are one and yet God is man."[123] A metaphor that the TD uses twice in other places for this mode of activity is becoming the hand by which God acts.[124] At the end of the chapter this absorption is couched in terms of the creature losing "what is its own and its selfhood" (*seyn eigen vnnd seyne selbheit* [103.26]), and the created selfhood being replaced by the divine selfhood. This involves the annihilation of the human—"The person becomes nothing and God is everything" (*do selbs der mensch czu nicht wirt vnd got alles ist* [103.15–16]).

Expressions of annihilation are frequent in the TD, often concentrating on the total erasure of the created will, another aspect of the text that brings it close to the radical view of mystical oneing found in mystics like Mar-

guerite Porete and Meister Eckhart.[125] Among the strongest passages is a
text in chapter 27, where the following description of union appears: "For it
[union] to exist, a person should in the truth be purely, singly, and entirely
single with the single, eternal will of God, or indeed be completely without
will, after the created will has flowed into the eternal will and been merged
with it and become nothing, so that the eternal will alone can act or not act
in that place."[126] On the basis of such accounts it is not surprising to find the
TD using the expression "essential union" (*eynunge wesenlich* [chap. 28:
110.1]). Nonetheless, the TD is less interested in theoretical analyses of
union than in drumming home the message about what is left after total
effacement of the fallen selfish will—an existential state of pure obedience.

The single-mindedness of the *Theologia Deutsch*, especially with regard to
destroying self-will, helps explain the work's polemical edge. In the view of
the anonymous priest who composed the book, there was no greater error
in the spiritual life than striving to attain union with God on the basis of
prideful self-will. Although it would be a mistake to describe the TD as primarily an attack on the false mysticism of the Free Spirit heretics, the fact
that the tract discusses false mystics in fifteen of its fifty-three chapters says
much about the situation of mysticism at the time. All the treatises we have
examined have had something to say about the dangers of aberrant mytics,
but none more than the TD.

The TD occasionally speaks of its opponents anonymously ("Some people say . . ." [chaps. 1 and 17]), but more often it identifies the enemy as "the
evil false Free Spirits" (*bose falsche freyen geiste* [125.18, 31–32; 128.74–75]),
who advocate a "useless free life" (*ruchlos frey leben* [95.3; 97.7–8]), or "false
disordered freedom" (*falsch ungeordent freyheit* [130.126; 149.35; 153.97]). In
conformity with its strongly oppositional mode of presentation, the book
shows how two contrasting forms of life are rooted in the difference
between the true light of God and the true freedom and love it fosters, as
contrasted with the false light of reason, which gives rise to disordered freedom and misguided love of self (especially chaps. 40 and 42–43). The fundamental errors of the Free Spirits appear again and again: the spiritual
pride which allows them to be deceived by the false light (chaps. 25 and
40); their mistake in thinking they are equal to God (chaps. 20, 40, and 42);
their disregard for Christ's humanity and attempt to live without the suffering that marked his life (chaps. 17, 18, 29, 40, 42, and 53); their false conception of freedom (chaps. 5 and 25); and their rejection of order, law, and
conscience itself (chaps. 25, 30–31, 39, and 40).

Along with *The Book of Spiritual Poverty*, the TD is suspicious of internal
states in which reason "climbs so high in its own light and in itself that it

imagines that it is the eternal true light and claims to be the same."[127] In other words, the root of the Free Spirit error is placed in what might be called natural mystical experience. Given the author's strongly negative view of fallen human nature, any attempt at inwardness that is separated from the humility and obedience of Christ must necessarily be a deception of the devil, who himself was also deceived into thinking that he could equal God.[128] With considerable psychological acuity the anonymous priest describes how a person becomes so enamored of his knowing ability that he fixates on the knowing itself, not on what is known, and thus he comes to love his ability so inordinately that he thinks it divine and equal to God—the autotheism so often identified with the Free Spirit heresy. Chapter 40, which lays out ten helpful instructions concerning the false light and its characteristics, says that the "excessive cunning" (*vbrigren kundickeit*) of the rational mind "mounts and climbs to such a height that it imagines it is above nature and that it is impossible for nature or any creature to get so high." The author continues, "In this way it imagines it is God, and as a result it lays claim to everything that pertains to God, and especially to God as he is in eternity and not as he is human."[129] This root error of neglecting the suffering humanity of Christ is mentioned often. Such inflated natural light is wrong, concludes chapter 42, "because it does not want to be Christ, but wants to be God in eternity" (*wan ess wil nicht Cristus seyn, sundern ess wil got seyn yn ewikeit* [133.42]).

From this root in the false light come all the other errors of the Free Spirits—the familiar list that we have seen in other mystical writings. The Free Spirits do not wish to imitate Christ in his suffering, but always choose "the easy light life" (chaps. 17–18). In their pride they disregard and scorn scripture and all the practices and sacraments of Holy Church (chap. 25: 105.31–40). They say that a person should become so detached that he no longer knows or loves God, not recognizing that pure and perfect understanding and loving of God always continue, but as the Eternal Word knowing and loving in us (chap. 5: 75.1–9). The TD also recounts with horror the tale of "a certain false Free Spirit" who claimed he was so free of conscience that he would kill ten people with the same impunity he would kill a dog (chap. 40: 128.74–76).

In chapters 30 and 31 the TD does give a careful answer to one of the neuralgic points in the debate over the difference between true and false mysticism: To what extent can virtues, rules, ordinances, and laws be put aside? To those who make the claim they can, the author answers with a scholastic distinction, "This is partly true and partly untrue" (*Hie ynne ist etwas wares vnd etwas vnwares* [113.3–4]). He then makes a careful enumeration of three senses in which it is true that virtues and laws can be abandoned. First, Christ was above all virtues and laws because he did not need them. Second, the children of God (Rom. 8:14 is cited) do not need external laws since the Spirit within them instructs them always to do good and avoid evil (113.13–22). Finally, those who are established in this state do not need laws to acquire or gain something for themselves, because they already possess all that they need for eternal life (113.23–114.29). The untrue side of the distinction is taken up in the first part of chapter 31. Here the author flatly rejects as a lie the statement that "one should reject and cast off Christ's life and all commandment, laws, rules, ordinances, and so on" (114.1–4). His answer once again appeals to the difference between the true light and the false. Such a statement proceeds from the false light and is therefore untrue. As he puts it at the end of chapter 40: "Where the false light is, people become heedless of Christ's life and every virtue, seeking and loving what is comfortable to nature. From this there arises a false, disorderly freedom."[130]

The *Theologia Deutsch* stands out as one of the most original mystical treatises of the late Middle Ages. It would be a mistake to view it as in some way a forerunner of the Reformation, but it is easy to see why Luther and later generations of Protestants valued it so highly. Looked at from the perspective of its situation in late medieval Germany, what makes the treatise striking is the way in which it was able to take so much from the mystical tradition that had been initiated by Eckhart and carried forward by figures such as Tauler and recast these mystical themes into a new view of union achieved through obedience to the model of Christ.

The Fifteenth Century

The production of mystical treatises did not end with the close of the fourteenth century. In the fifteenth century there seems to have been something of a shift back to Latin, particularly in works produced by the monastic orders of Benedictines and Carthusians, but until further research is done it is difficult to generalize. Certainly, all over Europe the fifteenth century saw the appearance of learned, often massive, Latin handbooks of mystical theology. This literature was important for communicating the riches of patristic and medieval mysticism to the world of the sixteenth and seventeenth centuries, the era of the great split in Western Christendom. Most of these works were more witnesses to tradition than new departures, but we must remember that the value of a treatise or handbook is a function not only of its originality of thought (of more importance to moderns perhaps than to medieval folk), but also of the work's character as representative of tradition. Mystical teaching, as I have insisted throughout this study, is the product both of remarkable personalities and thinkers, like Meister Eckhart, and of the wisdom of tradition.

In the first decade of the fifteenth century, Jean Gerson (1363–1429), the noted chancellor of the University of Paris, conciliar theorist, and theological polymath, wrote two treatises on mystical theology, one in French and one in Latin, which will be considered in the next volume of this history.[131] In the Low Countries the amazingly prolific Denys the Carthusian (Denys Rijkel, ca. 1402–1471) composed a number of works touching on mystical themes, as well as a major Latin treatise in three volumes *On Contemplation*.[132] His contemporary, the Franciscan Hendrik Herp (Harphius, ca. 1400–1477), wrote a popular work called *The Mirror of Perfection* (*Spieghel der volcomenheit*) that was translated into Latin, German, Italian, Portuguese, Spanish, and French. *The Mirror* was among the most read and influential of the medieval handbooks. This too I hope to take up in more detail in the next volume.[133]

German-speaking lands also continued to produce mystical guidebooks and *summae*, as well as polemical treatises on the nature of mystical theology and the role of love and reason in the path to union. In treating Nicholas of Cusa in chapter 10, I will touch on some of the tracts produced by Benedictines and Carthusians during the mid-century debate over mysticism in which Cusa took part. Earlier in the century the Benedictine John of Kastl (ca. 1360–ca. 1430) made a significant contribution to the ongoing task of summarizing the traditions of monastic mysticism.[134] John's writings show an impressive command of the medieval tradition, but not much interest in the themes characteristic of the mysticism of the ground. Josef Sudbrack has provided a detailed analysis of John's mystical writings, the most popular of which was the treatise usually called *Cleaving to God* (*De adhaerendo Deo*), but more correctly named *The Goal of Religious Perfection* (*De fine religiosae perfectionis*).[135] This treatise, which circulated under the name of Albert the Great, is found in fifty-five manuscripts.[136]

During the late Middle Ages, both in Germany and throughout Western Europe, the Carthusian order played a special role in preserving, copying, and at times composing mystical literature. The charter houses served as publishing houses for the dissemination of spiritual and mystical writings. Almost from their origins, the Carthusians had been engaged in writing surveys of contemplative and mystical theology, as we have seen beginning from the twelfth century.[137] The interest of Denys the Carthusian in mystical literature was echoed among some of the learned German Carthusians active from the mid- to the late fifteenth century. Jacob of Paradise, or of Jüterbock (1381–1465), composed four treatises on mystical theology toward the middle of the century.[138] Chapter 10 will look briefly at his contemporary, Vincent of Aggsbach, who wrote several treatises against Cusa and his Benedictine sympathizers in the mid-century debates over the nature of mystical theology. The research of Dennis Martin has done much to recover another late medieval German Carthusian, Nicholas Kempf (ca. 1417–1497), who penned a *Treatise on Mystical Theology*, as well as some other mystical works, in the 1450s.[139]

These learned Latin works of the end of the Middle Ages were meant mainly for the clergy, but their proliferation makes it clear that confessors and spiritual guides, both in the monastic and the mendicant orders, were avid for sound knowledge about the nature of mystical theology, not only for their confrères, but also for the laity, whose thirst for vernacular mystical wisdom I have tried to document, if only in part, in this chapter and its predecessor.

CHAPTER 9

The Friends of God

T HE FOURTEENTH CENTURY saw the creation of two movements of spiritual reform that broke with the standard categories of religious observance to try to live the gospel in new ways. The first of these, the Friends of God (*gotesvriunde*, spelled in various ways), took shape as a distinct, if amorphous, movement in the Rhineland in the 1330s and 1340s; the second, the *devotio moderna*, began in the diocese of Utrecht in the 1370s with the preaching of Master Geert Grote of Deventer. The Friends of God grew out of the preaching and teaching of Eckhart, and especially his spiritual heirs Henry Suso and John Tauler, and therefore put mysticism at the center of its spirituality. Although the movement achieved a nascent institutional form through the activities of a wealthy layman, Rulman Merswin, and the religious house he sponsored at Strassburg, it did not long survive Merswin's death in 1382, thus lasting for only two generations. The "new devout," on the other hand, or "brothers and sisters of the common life" as they are commonly known, were more interested in a broad program of ascetical and moral reform within the context of new forms of community life, both for laity and clerics. They were not originally much concerned with mysticism, though the movement later fostered some mystical writing. The new devout had great impact on late medieval religious life into the sixteenth century, not only in the Low Countries, but also in Germany, and to a lesser extent in France and Italy. The mystical aspect of the *devotio moderna* will be taken up in the next volume of this series. Given the strong mystical emphasis of the Friends of God, this amorphous and to some extent mysterious group deserves its chapter in the story of the harvest of mysticism in late medieval Germany.

The history of the Friends of God is not easy to unravel, given the deliberate obfuscation found in some of the texts relating to the movement. Its role in late medieval mysticism has also been controversial. Some older accounts made large claims for the significance of the *gotesvriunde* in fourteenth-century mysticism.[1] These assertions are difficult to support today, not only because of the derivative and often second-rate character of its mystical literature, but also because the geographical extent of the movement and its impact on the range of medieval literature in German was relatively modest given the variety of mystical expression in Germany at the time. Nevertheless, as a type of reform pietism with a strong emphasis on mystical themes, the Friends of God have a role in the harvest of mysticism.[2]

The term "friends of God" (*amici dei*) has its roots in the Bible.[3] Both Abraham (Judg. 8:22; Jas. 2:23) and Moses (Exod. 33:11) are described as friends of God; and Psalm 138:17 (Vg) says, "Your friends, O God, have been made exceedingly honorable to me." The term also occurs in Wisdom 7:27. In the New Testament the title of "friend" is used especially in the Gospels of Luke (e.g., 12:4ff.) and John. The most famous passage is in John 15, where Christ addresses the apostles with the words, "You are my friends, if you do what I command you. I shall no longer call you servants, because a servant does not know the master's business; I call you friends, because I have made known to you everything I have learnt from my Father" (15:14–15). Colored by the classical idea of friendship (e.g., Cicero, *De amicitia*), the notion of friendship, even friendship with God, played a role in patristic thinking of both the East (e.g., Basil) and the West (Augustine). Friendship on the human level was also a significant element in monastic spirituality.[4] In the twelfth century, the Cistercian Aelred of Rievaulx incorporated monastic friendship into a distinctive mystical practice in his treatise *De spirituali amicitia*.[5] In the thirteenth century Thomas Aquinas provided a classic analysis of the concept of *amicitia* as a fitting way to present intimacy between God and human.[6] The notion of being a friend of God went deep into the Christian tradition before it emerged as a distinctive mystical term and eventually a social description in fourteenth-century Germany.

The emergence of the *gotesvriunde* as a distinctive form of mystical life is tied, in part at least, to the social and religious context of late-medieval Germany. The fourteenth century was a grim time that witnessed disasters both natural (the Black Death) and political. Furthermore, the crisis of the church beset by the Avignon captivity of the papacy, the struggle between Pope John XXII and Lewis of Bavaria, the evident corruption of many clergy and religious, and the failure of movements for church reform produced a situation in which even those loyal to ecclesiastical authority tended to look for real religious meaning more in the personal than in the institutional sphere. An emphasis on the importance of inner contact with God allowed pious religious and laity to enter into free associations that did not challenge so much as bypass traditional structures and the strong division between clergy and laity that had been central to medieval Christianity since the Great Reform of the eleventh century.

Challenges to clericalism, as we have seen in chapter 2, often moved in dangerous and heterodox directions, but the Friends of God and the later *devotio moderna* struggled hard, and generally with success, to keep their implicit alternative to late medieval ecclesiastical structures free from heresy, if not from all suspicion. In an era of tribulation and religious uncertainty, the notion that God had graced the world with special friends who not only kept true religion alive but who also interceded for the world and church becomes quite understandable.

The use of the term "Friends of God" in medieval German mystical literature began in the thirteenth century, when it appears in the Franciscan David of Augsburg and especially in Mechthild of Magdeburg's *Flowing Light of the Godhead.*[7] However, it was not until the fourteenth century that *gotesvriunde* began to be widely used among mystical authors.[8] Meister Eckhart did not use the term frequently, though the idea of friendship with God does appear in his writing and preaching in several significant contexts. In chapter 15 of the *Talks of Instruction,* the Dominican speaks of two kinds of certainty of eternal life, the second and better form being perfect love for God without distinction in all things. "There is no need," according to Eckhart, "to say anything to the lover and the beloved, for once he [God] knows that he is his friend (*daz er sîn vriunt ist*) at once he knows all that is good for him and that belongs to his blessedness."[9] The most important appearance of friendship in Eckhart occurs in Pr. 27, where quoting John 15:15, he says: "In the same birth where the Father gives birth to his only begotten Son and gives him the root and all his Godhead and all his blesssedness, and holds back nothing, in that same birth he calls us his friends."[10] Thus, friendship with God is another way of speaking about the eternal birth. The only place where Eckhart (if indeed it is Eckhart) uses the term *vriunde gotes* (three times) is in Pr. 86, the famous homily on Mary and Martha.[11] These appearances are important, however, because the way in which this sermon emphasizes the figure of Martha as the mystic active in the world provided a model for later presentations of the "true Friends of God."[12]

The denomination *gotesvriunde* begins to appear more often among Eckhart's followers. In the *Sister Katherine* dialogue studied above (chapter 7, pp. 344–49), "Friends of God" (usually as *die fründe vnsers herren*) is used nine times to describe perfect souls, primarily the apostles and other saints such as Mary Magdalene, but not excluding people still on earth.[13] Since this text is an example of the kind of mystical literature that presents an illumined lay figure as guide to mystical union (without, however, denying the need for the clergy, sacraments, and institutional church), we may take it that the beguine who is the heroine is being portrayed as among these "Friends of our Lord." Both Henry Suso and John Tauler use the term Friend of God often. With them and their contemporary, the secular priest and spiritual guide Henry of Nördlingen, this originally generic theological term began to take on a concrete social meaning, indicating circles of devout religious and laity in the Rhineland, especially in the cities of Basel, Strassburg, Cologne, and neighboring towns and religious houses.

Henry Suso employs the form *gotesfründ* mostly in the *Life of the Servant.*[14] The appearances of the term in his letters, as well as in the *Life*, show that Suso not only used it generically to describe what advanced souls should be like, but that he also employed it as a concrete designation for persons named and unnamed that he had encountered in his travels. In chapter 18, for example, Christ appears to "a saintly Friend of God" carrying a box containing fresh blood that he will use to anoint the Servant (ed., 51.17–26), while chapter 22 features the visions and raptures of "a chosen Friend of God named Anna, who is one of his spiritual daughters."[15] The term can also be applied to the Servant himself, at least insofar as he is a representative of those who have reached the higher stages of the mystical life. In chapter 33 the Servant writes to his spiritual daughter Elsbeth Stagel, giving her advice about the progress of "this or that Friend of God" (ed., 98.12), though obviously the reference is meant to be concretized in the model of the Servant himself. The caption above the picture of the Servant as "Eternal Wisdom's Suffering Servant" accompanying chapter 38 reads, "This next piteous picture shows the severe afflictions of certain chosen Friends of God"—it is an image of the Servant as the exemplar of imitation of the passion.[16]

John Tauler provides even more information about the circles of Friends of God in the 1330s and 1340s, especially in Basel and Strassburg.[17] The preacher, as noted in chapter 6 above, served as spiritual adviser and supporter to Henry of Nördlingen and the pious religious and laywomen he served. He also was familiar with other devout contemporaries who sought to achieve the union of inner and outer prayer that was essential to his conception of the mystical life. In his sermons Tauler dwells at length on the nature and significance of the Friends of God, more than once with reference to contemporary, if unnamed, figures of his acquaintance.[18] With Tauler, Friend of God emerges as the term of choice for living the mystical life.

As Dietmar Mieth has shown, Tauler, following Eckhart, broke with the ancient model of the tension between action and contemplation and the need for an oscillation between the two to advance the view of an integrated existence of both contemplation and action in the world as the ideal form of Christian life.[19] As in Eckhart's Pr. 86, this mode of living is described as characteristic of the Friends of God. The Strassburg preacher also makes it clear that the deepest form of union with God, the experience of the mutual merging of the divine abyss and the human abyss into "one simple One,"[20] was open not only to clergy and religious, but was a universal call that he had seen realized in young and old, noble and commoner, married and religious.[21] In V 32 he chides those who think that they must take up some extraordinary life of penance and devotion to find God, "because," he says, "if you try really hard, you can attain God and the noble pure Good in every mode of life and all the states in which you are."[22] In one sermon he notes that the holiest person he ever met was a simple man who had never heard as much as five sermons in his life. He also speaks of "one of the greatest Friends of God," a farmer for more than forty years, who asked God if he should spend all his time in church and was told instead that he should go on earning his bread in the sweat of his brow in honor of Christ's precious blood (V 42 [179.20–24]). Such folk showed Tauler that mystical union could be granted to anyone who practiced self-emptying and was ready to undergo the ordeal of mystical dereliction for the pure love of God.

Tauler talks about the Friends of God in some twenty of his eighty sermons. *Gottes fründe* keeps its biblical meaning for him, as descriptive of all those, known and unknown, whose deep union with God and inner prayer life make them essential to the life of the church, just as the apostles were. (Tauler, of course, was no rebel, implicit or explicit, against the institutional church of his day, whatever its manifest failings.[23]) His deeply realized sense of the church as Christ's body, in which each member must seek to fulfill his or her task for the common good, is remarkable (see especially V 42). But it is important to note that the Dominican believed that the survival of the church depended not so much on pope, bishops, and clergy as on the mystical Friends of God.

One can get a sense of Tauler's conception of the Friends of God through V 10, the sermon in which the term appears more often than in any other. This homily deals with Christ as the light of the world (John 8:2), showing the difference between those who seem to follow the Lord but who are really serving themselves (i.e., the pharisees), and the true followers, or Friends of God, who annihilate themselves and live for God alone. The clearest external sign of difference between the two groups is that the pharisees are always judging others, while the Friends of God judge only themselves (V 10:47.35–48.15). But how does one attain the status of a Friend of God? Tauler emphasizes the great effort needed to overcome self-love and our natural phariseeism. Above all, we must follow the light of Christ, not the light of natural reason; we must also practice "true self-denial" (*war verloucken der mensche sin selbes* [48.31]), and we must direct our love and intention purely and totally to God. "This separates the true Friends of God from the false ones," he concludes. "The false ones turn everything back to themselves; they refer [God's] gifts to themselves, and they do not direct them back to God in a pure manner with love and thanksgiving in self-denial and total pure entering into God. He who does all this is the most complete Friend of God" (*der allergantzeste frúnt Gottes*).[24] The test of whether or not one has attained this state lies in the response to suffering. In the midst of suffering, "God's true friends take refuge in him and accept all sorrow freely for his sake" (49.9–10), while the false friends are confused, break down, and fall into despair. In everything, the Friends of God turn to and depend on Jesus as their model of virtue, their support in suffering, and especially as the light of the world. His power, communicated through the sacraments, is what brings them back to their origin (49.29–50.2).

Tauler does not conceive of the Friends of God as isolated individuals, or as some elite esoteric group. True Friends of God are active in the world as models of the oneness of love of God and love of neighbor. In V 76 he speaks of "a great Friend of God and wonderfully holy man" who desired the kingdom of heaven more for his neighbor than for himself. He exclaims—"This is what I call love!" (*dis hies ich minne* [410.31]). While the Friends of God should avoid those who might tempt them to sin, they are not meant to separate themselves from the world. Rather, their love should overflow even into their lower faculties and in how they relate to others in their external actions (410.39–411.6). The Friends of God, both clerical and lay, serve as the best spiritual guides: "People should seek out an experienced Friend of God a hundred miles away, one who knows and can direct them in the right path."[25] At the end of V 41 Tauler speaks about the character of those who have merged their own inner abyss in the divine Abyss.

Although he does not use the term *Gottes frúnt* here,[26] what he says is a good description of the true mystical Friend of God. According to Tauler:

> Such a person becomes so essential, so united, so virtue-filled, so good, and loving in his way of acting toward all people in community and friendship, that one can never see or find fault in him. These folk are trustful and merciful toward all; they are not severe or hard-hearted, but full of graciousness. One cannot think that such a person can ever be separated from God.[27]

These are powerful claims.

The importance of the mystical Friends of God is heightened by what Tauler says in a few places about their status as "pillars of the world." In V 5, for example, Tauler uses the Eckhartian expression "noblemen" (*edele menschen* [23.8]) rather than "Friends of God" to describe those who depend on God in all things, but it is clear that the two terms have much the same meaning. Such perfected souls allow God to work in their ground without mediation. They are raised to a supernatural level so that they no longer work of themselves, but God works in them (24.1–3, another Eckhartian motif). Tauler summarizes their status by saying: "Oh, these lovely people who bear up the whole world and who are the world's noble pillars! To find oneself in such a state would be a blessed and delightful thing!"[28] The idea of perfect mystics as pillars of the universe was found in Islamic mysticism.[29] In Christian scripture, the apostles are called pillars (Gal. 2:9), and in Apocalypse 3:12 Christ promises, "Anyone who proves victorious I will make into a pillar in the sanctuary of my God, and it will stay there forever." Tauler appears to be the first in Christian history to see perfected mystics as the church's true pillars.[30] This fits with the almost extravagant language he uses in other places, such as in V 41, where he speaks of the "true Friends of God" as being an abyss beyond understanding and as the very heaven in which God dwells (174.26–31). In V 40 they are called the people on whom the entire church depends, because without them it could not survive for an hour (169.28–31).

The letters that Henry of Nördlingen sent to Margaret Ebner in the 1330s and 1340s are further witness to the emergence of the Friends of God as a distinctive movement. As noted in chapter 7, Henry was a secular priest with a strong interest in mystical piety, though no mystic himself. He met the Dominican nun Margaret Ebner (1291–1351) in 1332 and for the last two decades of her life was her spiritual advisor, though most often from a distance.[31] From 1335 to 1337 Henry was at the papal court at Avignon. As a supporter of the papal party in the conflict with the emperor Lewis, he had to live in exile in Basel from 1339 to 1349. Here this noted preacher became acquainted with Tauler, as a number of his letters to Margaret show. In 1345 he visited Strassburg, where he met the banker Rulman Merswin, who later became the central figure among the Friends of God in that city.[32] He also knew Henry Suso.[33] After Margaret's death, we lose sight of Henry, who presumably died about 1360.

Margaret hails Henry in her *Revelations* as "a true Friend of God" (*warhaften friund gotez*).[34] Henry's letters to her often speak of the circles of fervent believers he was in contact with in Basel and elsewhere in the Rhineland. In Letter 45, for example, he commends himself "and the many friends whom God gives him" to Margaret so that she may take them into her heart and carry them "into the merciful heart of Jesus Christ."[35] A number of these Friends of God are featured in the letters. For example, the pious widow Eufemia Frickin traveled to Basel to consult with Henry. In Letter 47 he says: "My lady Frickin has come to Basel with great joy in her heart, pleased with both the teaching and the Friends of God, and that she can receive the holy sacraments with Christian obedience. She wishes to stay for a while with the holy followers of the spiritual community (*gaistlicher geselschaft*), of whom there are many in Basel."[36] Henry mentions Tauler several times in connection with these Basel circles, as in Letter 32, where he tells Margaret, "Our dear Father Tauler and the other Friends of God desire that you write us everything that your beloved Jesus reveals to you, especially about the state of Christendom and about his friends who suffer much from this situation."[37] This reminds us that the Friends of God movement was born in the midst of a particularly troubled time in the fourteenth century.[38]

Henry reports on the mystical experiences, especially the raptures, given to some of the Friends of God, both within convents and without.[39] His letters also provide us with information about how the Friends of God nourished their spirituality through the dissemination of mystical literature. A key text was Mechthild of Magdeburg's *Flowing Light of the Godhead*, the most prominent MHG mystical treatise of the thirteenth century.[40] Henry tells us that he spent two years (ca. 1343–45) translating the book from its original Middle Low German (he calls it "a foreign German": *fremden tützsch*).[41] He not only recommends the book very warmly to Margaret, but also quotes sections of it in several letters, referring to the author in one place as belonging to the "great Friends of God who show us the spiritual ascent to heaven of the inner person—your and my God speaks in them."[42] Henry also knew the Latin version of the *Flowing Light* (see Letter 44), and he refers to copy of Suso's widely diffused Latin work the *Clock of Wisdom*, which Tauler gave him and which he sent to the prior of the monastery of

Kaisheim to be copied so that Margaret and her nuns might have access to it.[43] Furthermore, we know that the Flemish mystic John Ruusbroec sent a copy of his treatise the *Spiritual Espousals* to the Strassburg Friends of God about 1350, where it was translated and in part adopted in some of Rulman Merswin's writings. The Friends of God were nurtured on such mystical writings. The movement was soon to produce its own body of vernacular texts.

Rulman Merswin and the Green Isle Community

In the midst of these loosely connected groups of clerics, religious women, and male and female laypersons that constituted the *gotesvriunde* emerged one of the more interesting, but also problematic, figures in the history of late medieval mysticism, the wealthy banker Rulman Merswin. Born into a patrician family of Strassburg in 1307, Merswin had a successful business career prior to experiencing a conversion that turned him from worldly pursuits. His conversion played itself out between 1347 and 1352, and constitutes the first stage of his religious career, one in which he adopted the life of an urban hermit, a devout Friend of God in retreat from the world.[44] (This was not at all unknown in late medieval urban society, though more usually realized by women.) The autohagiographical text known as the *Little Book of the Four Years of his Beginning Life (Büchlein von den vier Jahren seines anfangenden Lebens)*, purportedly written in 1352, tells this story in some detail.[45]

The *Four Year Book* may owe something to Suso's popular *Life of the Servant*, but it differs from the Dominican's autohagiography in its constant use of the first person. Merswin tells of his decision in 1347 to do penance for his sins by making "a beginning conversion" (*aller ersten ker*). After ten weeks, he enjoyed an ecstatic experience while walking in his garden on the evening of Martinmas (Nov. 11). In the midst of deep feelings of repentance Merswin looked up to heaven and promised to give up all his possessions if God had mercy on him. The reward for this traditional act of conversion is described as follows:

> Then it happened that a very clear light suddenly appeared and surrounded me and I was taken up and was led hovering above the earth, being carried in every direction hither and yon through the garden. As I was being carried in this way it seemed, I know not how, as if exceedingly sweet words were spoken to me, but what the light, the carrying, and the sweet words were I did not know; God knows it well [2 Cor. 12:2], because it was all beyond my under-

standing. When this happy short hour was over and when I had come to myself again, I found that I was standing alone in the garden.[46]

After this garden experience (remember Augustine's account in the ninth book of the *Confessions*), Merswin dedicated himself to extraordinary asceticism for a year, until he took John Tauler, who commanded him not to practice such austerities, as his confessor.

Although the pious layman had frequent experiences of God's sweet presence in his heart (ed., 7.19–30), God allowed the devil to tempt him sorely in these early years of his converted life. These temptations involved issues of faith (doubts about the Trinity), but especially temptations against chastity that Merswin will not even describe. Like many other late medieval mystics, he experienced inexpressible joy in receiving the Eucharist, and even a miraculous cure from something that might have been the plague (wounds and swellings in the lower part of his body). Rulman continued to suffer during the second and third years of his new life. During this time he tells us that illness prevented him from going to Rome for the Jubilee Year of 1350 (ed., 14.19–29). In the fourth year, however, he says that God took infinite pity on his sufferings, both externally and internally. In this year Merswin describes a supernatural enjoyment of God that lasted "for about eight or fourteen days" (ed., 19.19–30). He also recounts his desire to suffer for the will of God (not unlike his English contemporary Julian of Norwich), as well as a missionary impulse to go preach God to the heathen. But the most decisive event of the last of the beginning years was the sudden appearance of God's emissary, the mysterious "Friend of God from the Land Above." As Merswin narrates: "Then one day God commanded a man from the Land Above to come down to me. And when he came God told me to speak with him about all this. This man was a perfect stranger to the people, but he became my secret friend."[47] This mystery man immediately assumed authority over Merswin, commanding the ex-banker to write down his religious development, because he himself had given Merswin an account of the first five years of his own spiritual journey.[48] Merswin claims that he was promised that if he fulfilled the Friend of God's command, he would never be forced to write down any more of his experiences (ed., 27.16–25)—a promise that seems ironic given the many pages that the banker was to pen under his own name and that of his pseudonym, the dear Friend of God from the Land Above (*der liebe gottes fründ in oeberlant*).

The Friend of God from the Land Above seems to have been accepted as a real figure by at least some of Merswin's contemporaries, and there were attempts among nineteenth-century students of mysticism to uncover his historical identity. Since the thorough research of the Dominican scholar of mysticism Heinrich Denifle,[49] however, it has been generally accepted that the Friend of God is a literary creation of Rulman Merswin and his followers, however much the figure may include the traits of some real people.[50] Much has been made of the lay status of the fictional Friend of God. Rulman Merswin is often seen as creating an imaginary mystic to underline a new kind of specifically lay mysticism for late medieval Germany. But Georg Steer has pointed out that Merswin, like Eckhart, Tauler, and Henry of Nördlingen saw the Friends of God as including both clergy and laity, and that the converted banker's writings were intended for such a mixed congregation.[51] The emphasis in a number of late medieval mystical texts on the higher authority of a lay figure should be viewed primarily as a critique of the pretensions of learned theologians in contrast to the higher knowledge that God could grant to anyone, cleric, or even unlearned laymen and women.[52] Once again, the split between theology and mysticism so evident in late medieval religion comes to the fore.

In 1364 Merswin purchased a derelict monastery on what had originally been an island on the river Ill passing through Strassburg, a house known as the "Green Isle" (*grünenwörth*). He restored the buildings, converting them into the first institutional center of the Friends of God. For the first few years the Green Isle was under the control of four secular priests nominated by Merswin, but this arrangement did not work out. In 1371 Merswin gave the house to the Order of the Knights of St. John of Jerusalem, the Hospitalar order (*Johanniter* in German). Merswin, however, kept real power over the community, attempting to create a religious house in which both clergy and laity would be welcome. Several of those who joined the Green Isle are known to us, notably the priest Nicholas of Louvain (d. 1402), who served as Merswin's secretary and literary executor. Nicholas had an important, if difficult to determine, role in the production of the Memorial Books of the house that contain the writings discussed here. The Green Isle community, however, was largely a function of the vision and resources of its owner, which helps explain why its importance for the history of mysticism was short-lived.[53]

What did Rulman Merswin hope to achieve by establishing this religious foundation? His intentions are expressed in the narrative known as the *History of the House of St. John*, where the community is described as "a house of refuge for the retreat of all honest and pious men, lay or ecclesiastics, knights, squires, and burgers who desire to flee the world and consecrate themselves to God without entering a monastic order."[54] Thus, Merswin sought to create an institution that would facilitate a deep religious life—the ideal of the Friends of God—without respect to clerical status, though one of a notably patrician cast.[55] His 1364 decision also indicates a new stage in the ex-banker's spiritual career, that of a religious founder.

Merswin appears to have struggled with several forms of his new conception of religious life for the next decade and a half. Finally, in 1380, he gave up his public role, retiring to live as a recluse within the Green Isle community, adding to and editing his literary output. From this large collection of texts we can gain some idea of the achievements, real and imagined, of the Friends of God, at least as envisaged by Rulman Merswin.

In the history of medieval mysticism, the story of the Green Isle community is less impressive than the wealth of literature the community (i.e., mostly Merswin himself) produced in the half-century between the beginning of his writing career in 1352 and the death of his editor Nicholas in 1402.[56] According to legend, at Merswin's death a casket was discovered in his room with a collection of texts both by himself and also by "the dear Friend of God from the Land Above."[57] Nicholas of Louvain copied and edited these materials into several compendia, or "Memorial Books," such as the *Great Latin Memorial* (now lost), the *Great German Memorial,* and the *Book of Letters.* Within the surviving collections there are texts relating to the foundation and history of the Green Island community, accounts of the conversions of both Rulman Merswin and the Friend of God, and other mystical and hagiographical treatises. There is also a group of twenty-one letters supposedly written by the Friend of God.[58] Seven of these writings are ascribed to Merswin himself, while seventeen are said to come from the Friend of God.[59] This material can be described as literature for the community (*Hausliteratur*) whose purpose, as Georg Steer puts it, was "to legitimate the concept of a special notion of Friend of God and to provide ideological assurance for the spiritual distinctiveness of Merswin's foundation that sought to unite under one roof the Hospitalar brothers and laity who had renounced the world."[60] A good deal of this mass of spiritual pedagogy incorporates older texts that had come to Merswin's attention. If little of it is really original or equal to the best mystical writing of late medieval Germany, Merswin's works are not without narrative skill, and he must be given credit for creating the fascinating fiction of the Friend of God from the Land Above.

Pseudonymity has a long history in mystical literature, at least from the time of the writings ascribed to Macarius around 400 C.E. and those circulated under the name of Paul's first-century disciple Dionysius, around 500. What makes the case of Rulman Merswin interesting is that perhaps for the first time we find an author who created both himself as an exemplary mystic and a fictional mentor to provide a heightened heavenly authority for his message. Like his English contemporary, the hermit Richard Rolle, Merswin was a layman. Nicholas Watson has shown how assiduously Rolle as a layman strove to gain authority for his mystical writings.[61] Merswin needed to defend his status not only as teacher but also as the founder of a new form of religious community. He hit upon a solution of some genius—the creation of an imaginary and mysterious higher mystic, as well as a hidden holy community that provided a model for and defense of his own career and actions. Ingenious as his solution was, there is a sense in which, to use Alois Haas's phrase, his invention threatened to turn mysticism into mystification.[62]

In the Green Isle collection there are three autohagiographical accounts that the Friend of God purportedly sent to Rulman Merswin. These are the basis for the mystical "legend" (in the etymological sense) created by Merswin. The banker's own conversion account mentions that the *gottes frúnt* supposedly gave him a text shortly after they met in 1350–51. This appears to be the tract known as the *Book of the Two Fifteen Year Old Boys.* The work provides an imaginative, almost novelistic, presentation of the early life of the Friend of God. Born the only son of a rich merchant, the Friend grows up the close friend of the son of a knight. When they reach the age of fifteen, both fall in love with noble young ladies, but they also begin to go their separate ways. The young merchant eventually succeeds in winning permission to marry above his station, but he then rejects his long-desired bride after having a vision of Christ on the cross asking him to convert to a life of devotion. After many temptations and trials, the young man gains the status of a true Friend of God, converts his old friend the knight, who had fallen into evil ways, and becomes a pillar of the church and a guide to others. Interestingly, he is not called upon to give up his wealth, but rather to use it in trust for God.[63]

Further information about Merswin's alter ego is provided in the *Book of the Five Men.*[64] This mystical fiction describes a later stage in the story of the Friend of God, a narrative that he was supposed to have sent to the Green Isle house describing his life between 1365 and 1374. Here the *gottes frúnt* is portrayed as a great, though hidden, authority in the church, controlling a network of secret Friends of God throughout the world. To escape notoriety, he flees to the mountains with four companions: his old friend the knight; another knight who had taken up a life of poverty after the death of his family; a converted Jew; and a canon lawyer. In their high retreat this small group of Friends of God lead a life of strict penance and interior prayer that illustrates the ideal mystical community—the archetype of what Merswin was trying to realize in the Green Isle. Other texts add more detail to the legend of the influence of the Friend of God. In 1377 he is said to have gone to Rome to advise Pope Gregory XI . During the meetings, or diets, held by the group and the other Friends of God who come to the mountain retreat, supernatural events take place. In 1380 a heavenly letter descends to them predicting the end of the world, but the crisis is delayed for three years through the prayers of the Friends of God. Mystification has indeed taken over.

The most influential of all the stories about *der lieber gottes fründ in oeberlant* is found in what is called the *Masterbook (Meisterbuch)*, or in later printed versions, the *History of the Reverend Doctor John Tauler*. The work is a conversion narrative of ten chapters in the form of a dialogue originally between a unnamed *meister* (doctor of theology) and an equally unnamed *laie*, or layman. It also contains the texts of five sermons preached by the master, one before and four after his conversion. Like many of the texts from the Green Isle scriptorium, it is based on earlier materials. The scope of Merswin's efforts in the composition and redaction is still unclear in the absence of a critical edition. The version found in the *Great German Memorial Book* from the Green Isle identifies the layman with "our founder Rulman Merswin's faithful companion, the dear Friend of God from the Land Above."[65] The earliest printing of the work (Leipzig, 1498) identified the master with John Tauler—clearly an error, but one that was to have a long history.[66] The identification with Tauler, as several scholars have pointed out, is not without reason, since a number of themes of the *Masterbook* reflect aspects of his teaching.[67] With at least thirty manuscripts and four early printings, the *Masterbook* was the best known and the most influential of the texts from the Strassburg Friends of God.

The *Masterbook*, as Michel de Certeau has suggested,[68] is an important witness to a theme that was not new (as a look at female mystics of the thirteenth century shows), but that was to gain power in the late Middle Ages and early modern period—narratives involving an unlearned layperson enlightened by heaven as the instructor for clerical professionals whose knowledge was merely human and often prideful. It is necessary to remember, however, that the story, like the *Sister Katherine* dialogue, centers not on opposition between laity and clergy so much as on the process of conversion in which the holy layperson serves as the instrument of the grace of the Holy Spirit moving the cleric to become what he was meant to be—a master of life (*lebmeister*) rather than a mere master of learning (*lesmeister*).[69] At the beginning of chapter 5 of the *Masterbook*, the Friend of God even observes that he has no more real work to do, because the converted master is now under the direct guidance of the Holy Spirit: "Now, Master, as things stand with regard to you, it is no longer necessary for me to speak to you as a teacher as I have done. I now greatly desire to be taught by you, and I will also stay here until I have heard a good deal of your preaching."[70]

The *Masterbook*, despite its compilatory nature, tells an engaging tale with two strongly etched main protagonists. The manuscripts introduce the tale as beginning in either 1340 or 1346 when the Friend of God comes from his own country to the city (presumably Strassburg) to be confessed by the learned Master and to hear him preach. The Master's sermon on attaining the highest state of life (chap. 1; ed., 3–7) is interesting because of its generally Eckhartian nature, ending with twenty-four conclusions drawn from scripture about how souls are to strive for emptiness and freedom from willing to attain God. The fact that this style of preaching is put to the test because it proceeds from mere learning rather than true experience of God is significant. It points to a critique of exalted "Eckhartian" preaching in Germany after 1350.[71] Chapter 2 (ed., 7–18) presents a series of conversations between the Master and the Friend of God in which the Master first protests that it would be unlikely that a mere layman could instruct a learned cleric, but then gradually comes to accept the Friend of God's accusations that he is a pharisee who has allowed the letter of the Bible to kill its spirit within his preaching. The basic issue is that one must practice what one preaches. Finally, the Master accepts the Friend of God as his "spiritual father" (*geistlicher vatter* [ed., 10]). From then on the Friend of God instructs the Master on the basis of his own experience of seven years of spiritual training. First of all, the Master must give up preaching and restrict himself to the exercises prescribed by the Friend of God (chaps. 2–4). These are not essentially different from those found in Tauler's sermons. The fundamental religious attitude to be cultivated is that of deep humility,[72] but also important is moderate asceticism as a form of imitation of Christ, as well as willingness to undergo intense internal suffering (Taulerian terms like *getrenge* appear). The Master must become willing to accept disrespect and loss of public reputation for Christ's sake.

The Master, who is said to have been about fifty when his conversion began, gradually absorbs these painful lessons, beginning with learning the simple ABC's of true piety that the Friend of God gives him to contrast with the twenty-four deep counsels found in his own initial sermon. At times the counsel of the *gottes frúnt* is itself tinged with Eckhartian themes, as in the long advice about how to attain the birth of God though humble releasement (*demuetigen gelossenheit*) in chapter 3 (ed., 20–22). The Master suffers the loss of his friends and spiritual charges, as well as the respect of his brethren in the monastery, before he is ready to give himself totally to God without any reserve of selfishness. Then, in the midst of a spiritual crisis in his cell on the Feast of the Conversion of St. Paul, he finally achieves total self-abandonment and receives a divine illumination that gives him confirmation in grace and an inner knowledge of the meaning of the Bible (chap. 4, ed., 25). Finally, he is ready to preach again, though God has one more test in store for him. After announcing that he is ready to preach, his first public sermon is a disaster, since all he can do is weep and beg the forgiveness of his audience who depart in disgust. But just when his fortunes seem at the lowest, the Master's training in humility is about to see fruit.

The Friend of God counsels him to spend five days meditating on Christ's wounds (a devotion recommended by Tauler too). At the end of this period, the Master preaches a sermon not to the general public but to a cloister audience on the text "See the Bridegroom comes; go out to meet him" (Matt. 25:6).[73] This sermon is a classic example of late medieval mystical preaching, showing how the bride, who is identified with human nature (*menschliche nature ist die brut*, ed., 29), through imbibing three cups of suffering offered her by the Heavenly Bridegroom finally achieves total surrender to God and is rewarded with an experience of mystical marriage within the Trinity. This section of the homily has a dialogical form. First, the Son praises the now spotless bride, and then the Father addresses her: "Get up with joy and come to church." The text continues: "He then takes the Bridegroom and the bride and leads them to church, gives them to each other in marriage, and binds them together with the greatest marital love, . . . so that they can never be separated in time or in eternity." When the Bridegroom asks the Father for a wedding gift, he gives them the Holy Spirit. "He fills the bride with the total overflowing of great love so that the bride overflows with love and totally flows back into the Bridegroom. She completely comes out of herself and is totally drunk with love. She forgets herself and all creatures, both those in time and in eternity."[74] This description of the "joy beyond joy" (*froeide úber froeide*) of mystical marriage has a powerful effect on the audience. One member of the congregation cries out, "It is true, it is true, it is true!" He then falls down as if dead. When the preacher finally concludes after a description of the bride's return to ordinary consciousness, he says Mass. Afterwards, a dozen other members of the audience are found so enraptured by the sermon that they need to be cared for by the nuns of the community. Literary fiction though it be this account of the Master's sermon is meant to suggest what the Friends of God hoped to hear from the mystical preachers of late medieval Germany.

The remainder of the *Masterbook* is less dramatic. Chapters 7–9 give three more examples of the Master's preaching, less mystical in tone. The final chapter recounts his last conversations with the Friend of God as death approaches. The text preserved by the Green Isle community says that after nine years of successful preaching the Master senses death is near and summons the Friend of God, giving him his notes about his conversion and asking him to write it all up without using real names. Again, Merswin's skill at creating a plausible fictional narrative is evident. The Master is described as undergoing a difficult death agony, after which the Friend of God flees lest he be given any honor in the city. Three days into his journey, as promised, the Master's voice addresses him at night in a supernatural audition, telling him that his last struggle was a divine gift to allow him to skip Purgatory and enter heavenly bliss ahead of time. The mystical narrative ends with the Friend of God sending a letter to the prior and community of the Green Isle with this information.

Rulman Merswin's other writings did not have the broad dissemination of the *Masterbook*. Several, however, give us a good sense of the way in which this energetic and pious layman used mystical themes to propound his version of the search for God. The longest and most noted text bears the title of the *Book of the Nine Rocks*. This mystical treatise is available in shorter and longer MHG versions, and also in a Latin translation. The original short text must date from the time of the Black Death (ca. 1347–50); it was mentioned as a suspect work in the inquisition of beguines in Strassburg in 1374. In 1352 Merswin adopted this text and expanded it for the purposes of the Green Isle community.[75]

The *Book of the Nine Rocks* is a visionary dialogue whose purpose, as described in the preface, is to teach "the true road that leads up to the Origin" (*die rechte strose . . . die do ufgat zuo sime ursprunge* [1.13–14]). It is divided somewhat awkwardly into four discourses: first, by way of preface, how the anonymous protagonist was compelled to write the book; second, the strange visions shown to the man; third, a digression on the sins of the various classes of Christians; and fourth, the actual vision of the nine rocks and its analysis.[76] To these is appended another discourse on the vision of the Origin. The preface tells how during Advent a man went off to a secret place to pray, turned inwardly to Eternal Truth (reminiscent of Suso), and was given "great, wonderful, strange images" (*grose wunderliche froemede bilde* [2.28]) that threw him into fear and confusion. Eternal Truth, also called the Beloved, tells the visionary not to be afraid, because "these images are nothing more than a likeness of other things that God will let you see and that are much more wonderful than these" (3.37–4.3). The use of imaginative visions as the basis for allegorical exposition and mystical pedagogy is typical of Merswin's dossier.[77] The rest of the preface has a rather stilted debate in which Eternal Truth compels the visionary to agree to write down what he has seen. The purpose, as in other mystical texts written by laymen or laywomen, is to provide authority for the visionary and his text.[78]

The brief second discourse (11.32–18.8) presents a vision of a high mountain with a lake on the top filled with fish. The water flows down the mountain, carrying the fish along with it to another lake in the valley below. The desire of the fish is to re-ascend the mountain to get back to their source. This vision is revealed to be a "symbol or likeness" (*bizeihen odder gelichnisse* [16.24]) of how people live so badly in the current state of Christendom. This showing sets up the long third discourse (18.9–73.12), which consists of speeches made to eighteen estates of Christians, beginning with popes and ending with women and the married, detailing their sinful lives and commanding them to reform. Much of this is dreary moralizing, contrasting the good old days and the corrupt present, but two sections are more interesting. The first is the address to the burgers and merchants (43.30–47.27), which shows a strong sense of social justice; the second is the rather surprising positive attitude toward good Jews and pagans. In a time and place that saw so many terrible pogroms, the Beloved tells the visionary, "God is more pleased with some Jews and heathens nowadays than with many Christians who live against all Christian ordinances."[79] The explanation is that the God-fearing Jew or pagan who does not know any faith better than the one he is born into can be saved by God "in many secret ways unknown to Christendom" (63.9). This is especially true at the time of death when God illumines the good heathen or Jew from within to desire baptism (something later called the baptism of desire).

The fourth discourse (73.13–139.21) finally takes up the vision of the nine rocks, or rocky plateaus, that lead to the top of the mountain. These nine rocks constitute a spiritual itinerary leading the fish, or souls, who originally were seen pouring down the mountainside, now striving to leap back up to the divine source, like salmon going upstream. The first four stages are largely ascetical; the last five are increasingly mystical in stressing surrender of self-will and growing conformity with God. The ascent process is marked by the rapidly declining numbers of those who achieve each stage, until on the ninth level there are only three people! From this perspective, the *Book of the Nine Rocks* has been described as "an apocalyptic parable, in that it describes the separation of the saved few from the many damned."[80] Rock 1 holds those who have confessed their sins, but who remain in danger of falling back. Rock 2 features those who turn from the world and wish "to be obedient to a Friend of God who knows the true way."[81] On rock 3 we find those who accept from God "severe exercises" (*strenge uebunge* [98.20]), but who do so on the basis of their own wills. The fourth rock contains those who try to put down their own human natures and strive to be as obedient to God's will as they can be.

The fifth rock marks the beginning of more mystical forms of spirituality, because the answer the visionary gets from the divine voice at this point declares: "He who comes to this fifth rock and is able to remain there constantly has just come to the correct beginning of the true road that leads up to the Origin."[82] On the sixth rock are those who have "let themselves go into God, and who have given up their wills to the Friends of God in God's place. They have a steadfast will to be obedient and constant and to remain so unto death."[83] On the seventh rock we find the even smaller number of those who have totally surrendered themselves to God and are obedient to God in all things. (By now the distinction between the different stages begins to be artificial with the same descriptions appearing over and over again.) Those on rock 8, though described as far beyond rock 7, are once again portrayed as totally obedient, though they still have a bit of hidden self-will. One new note does emerge in a plethora of repetitions, when the visionary says, "At times they are given a small glimpse at the Origin, one that cannot be expressed with either image or word."[84]

The description of the ninth rock (123.14–139.21) reveals how the writings of Rulman Merswin can be seen as a form of mysticism becoming an elite mystification in support of his vision for the Green Isle community. This section of the treatise is rich in the language of the mysticism of the ground pioneered by Eckhart, but in restricting it to three people (124.6–7) Merswin has adapted these motifs in such a way that union with God seems to be no longer an option for many good Christians to aspire to, but only a distant vision for those who are willing to submit to the Friends of God, the only true (and few) mystics. The democratic vision of mystical union put forth by Eckhart and Tauler has become a new form of elitism for Merswin.

The ninth rock is portrayed as "the gate to the Origin from which come all created things in heaven and on earth" (126.6–8). The very few who are found there (now including the visionary) are sick and meagre in outward appearance as a result of their asceticism, but inwardly illuminated by divine love. They are the true Friends of God, the pillars of Christendom, as Tauler and others had noted. "As few as they are," Truth tells the visionary, "for their sake God permits Christendom to continue. You see, if these men were gone, God would immediately let Christendom perish."[85] The people on the rock are completely humble, having totally surrendered their wills to God in imitation of Christ. Since they are still in this life, they are only given "a small glimpse of the Origin" from time to time (128.24–24; cf.

137.26–138.8). Eckhartian themes are used to describe these perfected souls. They "love all persons equally in God" (130.12–13); "they live in unknowing (*unwissende*) and they do not even desire to know" (130.26–27). However, status on the ninth rock is not guaranteed. It is possible for someone to fall from it, and such renegades become the most harmful people in Christendom because of their ability to lead people astray (134.22–31). Merswin may have had the Free Spirit heretics in mind here (see also 148.37–150.17).

At the end of the fourth discourse, the visionary asks to be allowed to remain on the ninth rock, but the Beloved promises him even more than this. Because "his heart and soul are full of humility and loving releasement" (*minnender gelosenheithe* [139.18]), he is granted a vision of the Origin in his inner eye. The description of this constitutes the fifth discourse (139.22–166.34). The visionary is reluctant to behold the Origin, but is obedient to the divine command. "At these same words, as soon as the man surrendered his will completely to God (*zuo gruonde gotte*), in the same instant he was led to the gate of the Origin and was allowed to see into the Origin."[86] The brief vision grants him immeasurable joy, and although he is commanded to write about it, the Origin is totally inexpressible. "The more he thought about it the less he knew, because it was greater than anything he had ever seen or heard of" (140.33–34). The vision is further described using many of the themes of the mystical tradition—it is a mystical marriage (144.23–26); it is attending the great school of the Holy Spirit (144.26–31); it allows the visionary to express *resignatio ad infernum*, that is, the desire even to be damned if that would be God's will (146.15–20). In several later passages the language of union with God is also used, sometimes expressed in Eckhartian terms: "The Answer was given: 'I say to you you should know that these persons have lost their names and have become nameless and have become God.'" When the visionary is surprised over this divinization language, however, a traditional explanation is given: "Someone who in time is allowed by God to see into the Origin becomes by grace what God is by nature."[87] The fifth discourse closes with a long dialogue between the Beloved and the visionary now elevated to the company of the "true Friends of God" (*geworen gottes fründe* [160.29]) about the sinful state of Christianity and the need to turn to the Friends of God rather than the pharisees to stave off the impending judgment. The disturbing tone of divine vengeance that pervades the *Book of the Nine Rocks* is far from Eckhart and Tauler, and its repetitive style makes it often tedious reading. The book expresses both the vision of Green Isle community and its limitations.

Several of the shorter works from Merswin's dossier are also revealing about the status of mysticism among the Friends of God, especially in the Green Isle. Once again, we should note that reading these texts as either forerunners of the Reformation (as was often done a century and more ago), or as the birth of a new form of lay piety (still prevalent today), is anachronistic. These texts are typical of much of the mystical literature of the fourteenth century. This can be seen, for example, in their concern over the dangers of false mysticism. This fear appears in the *Book of the Nine Rocks*, and is even more evident in the text known as the *Book of the Banner of Christ (Bannerbüchlein)*.[88] This programmatic work highlights the opposition between those who march under the banner of Christ and the supporters of false freedom who follow the banner of Satan. These "free false people" (*frigen valschen menschen*) claim they have arrived at a state where they no longer need to suffer or to die. They deny the humility taught by Christ and belittle his sufferings; they also misuse scripture. The tract cries out for all to flee such people and to take refuge in Christ—"I know nothing more secure in this time than to flee to the crucified Christ. Anyone who flees to Christ with total trust should have complete confidence that he will never abandon him."[89] Under Christ's blood-red banner, in the company of the true Friends of God, all Christians must continue to struggle against such errors.

Two of the more interesting mystical texts found in the Green Isle dossier are the *Book of the Three Breakthroughs (Buoch von den dreien durchbrüchen)*, and the *Book of the Spark in the Soul (Buch von dem fünkelin in der selen)*, which Bernard Gorceix describes as one of "the two spiritual pearls of the dossier" (the other being the *Neunfelsenbuch*).[90] The *Book of the Three Breakthroughs*, like much of the Green Isle literature, depends on an earlier anonymous treatise called the *Three Questions (Von den drîn fragen)*, a work in the style of Eckhart (he is even named four times). This mid-fourteenth century text survives in no fewer than forty-two copies (more than any authentic work of Eckhart) and had considerable influence in Germany and the Netherlands into the sixteenth century.[91]

The tract begins in an Eckhartian mode, setting three questions that pertain to all three stages of the itinerary to God—the beginners, the advanced, and the perfected:

> The first question is: What is the quickest breakthrough that a person can make so that he can come to the highest and most perfect life? The second question is: What is the surest step that a person in time can stand upon after this first breakthrough? The third question is: What is the closest union with which a person in time can be united to God?[92]

The answers are those that Eckhart would have given. A free humble "withdrawal (*abegang*) in spirit and in nature" is the quickest way to the breakthrough. We must leave behind all created external things and even the "overflowing sweetness of the spirit" in order to achieve "great humble divine releasement" (*grosser demuetiger goettlicher gelossenheit* [216]). At this point Meister Eckhart speaks, condemning those who mistake the reality of God's being for the mere appearance of spiritual sweetness—"God is the reality, but spiritual sweetness is the appearance" (*Wanne got der ist das wesen; aber geistliche sússikeit ist der schin* [216]).

As the questions are further analyzed the text adopts a dialogue form. An unnamed person questions a great teacher (Eckhart?) about the truest form of releasement. The teacher praises "a true resigned releasement (*gelossene gelossenheit*) in spirit and in nature . . . so that a person with all his natural powers can totally release God at all times." Another teacher is then cited who continues to speak in the same paradoxical language dear to Eckhart about the relation of releasement and union: "A releasement above all releasement is to release him [God] in releasement. A person should stand in such releasement and oneness with God that outside himself he finds nothing that discontents him."[93] A person must break through both nature and intellect in total releasement in order to attain union, which the tract describes by quoting Paul: "As the beloved Saint Paul says, 'Who adheres to God becomes one spirit with him' (1 Cor. 6:17), and in this same becoming free the spirit is lost and becomes a simple one in the One."[94] The first part of the treatise concludes with a delineation of six grades or stages of withdrawal and with another speech from Meister Eckhart, who says that in order to realize the birth of the Son in the soul, we must attain a level where we can stand as we were before we existed, free of all images (ed., 219-20).

The second part of the *Book of the Three Breakthroughs* (ed., 220–27) takes a rather different view of Meister Eckhart. This section presents a dialogue between Eckhart and a young priest who is described as a great master of scripture. In a manner not unlike what we have seen in the *Masterbook*, the anonymous young priest admonishes Meister Eckhart, showing him that his preaching is too advanced for beginners and progressives and is not really needed by the perfect. The priest says: "Dear Meister Eckhart, you speak publicly in your sermons about very high intellectual and high-flown matters that very few people can understand or that are useful, and bring forth very little fruit."[95] Eckhart admits the accusation, saying that he has not heard so pleasing a speech in many years and that he recognizes that the young priest is speaking out of "a living ground" (*usse eime lebenden grunde* [222]). Eckhart then asks the priest to tell his life story. The young man obliges by recounting another typical Friend of God conversion narrative (ed., 222–27), whose basic message is abandoning the learned theology of the schools and committing oneself to a life of devotion and imitation of Christ. At the end, the *Book of the Three Breakthroughs* returns to a more Eckhartian mode, emphasizing (unlike the *Book of the Nine Rocks*) the universality of God's call to conversion and salvation (ed., 227–28). The final paragraphs show the influence of Tauler, especially his characteristic theme of the double abyss of the soul and God (see chapter 6, pp. 249–50). At this point the treatise attains a depth of expression that rivals Eckhart and Tauler on the ground:

> There is a hidden abyss in the soul, which continuously echoes the divine abyss without cease and with a wild, groundless, and concept-less voice. . . . The highest, the noblest, and the most useful thing that can happen to it here in time is that it draws all valuable desires, all thoughts, and all divine love into the soul, so that it sinks itself at every moment and drowns itself in the deep groundless ground of the Godhead.[96]

However much Merswin's adaptation of this Eckhartian source was intended to express his own agenda of abandoning speculation for the sake of simple piety, this short treatise contains fine expressions of an Eckhartian mysticism that highlight the ambiguity of the relation of the Strassburg Friends of God to the mysticism of the ground.

The *Book of the Spark in the Soul* witnesses to the interest of Merswin and his followers in itineraries of ascent to God,[97] as well as in another of the key themes of the mysticism of the ground, the inner divine spark (*fünkelin*) whose cultivation leads to union. This text too makes use of an earlier source, a treatise whose ideas were deeply imbued with Tauler's thought. Once again, the teaching takes the form of a short tale and a dialogue. A young brother comes to a "holy old father" and complains that he feels little heavenly love despite his pious practices. The ancient tells him: "I tell you, dear son, fifty years ago, when I was a boy and in the world, in those days there was a proverb people used to use—'The cat would like to eat fish, but it doesn't want to get its feet wet.'"[98] The teacher explains that the only way to feel divine love is not just to long for it, but to make a real spiritual effort. The youth asks for his advice, and the old man tells him that he has received an illumination from the Holy Spirit that he will pass on to him if he agrees to keep it secret. The old man then commands him to go away for three days. When the young man returns, he tells him to depart for another three days while he writes out the message. Finally, the old man reads out his teaching about how to find "divine supernatural love" (*goetteliche übernatúrliche minne* [ed., 23.33]).

Since the Holy Spirit himself is "the true sweet burning love," it is only by the Spirit's action that "the little spark hidden in the soul" can be enkindled (ed., 24.5–33). The text is not interested in speculative exploration of the nature of the spark and its relation to God, but in the practical steps needed to bring the cold *fünkelin* to life. This demands dying to our natural life, following the suffering Christ, and practicing the virtues "in great humility and in divine releasement and love" (ed., 25.33–38). The wise old teacher sketches out an ascetic and contemplative program with care. Although the stages are not numbered in the text, there appear to be seven in all.[99] The first step, turning away from the world and turning toward the Holy Spirit, brings a feeling of joy, but it is just the beginning. Perseverance on the path is essential to spiritual progress. The second and third stages deepen these experiences of love. The end of the third stage, however, is marked by Tauler's emphasis on the role of suffering and dereliction. Here, "one is sent and given by the Holy Spirit the greatest horrifying and unspeakable sufferings" (ed., 26.31–27.1). The Holy Spirit withdraws, leaving the soul in agony so that she may learn the virtue of perseverance and to trust in God alone. At a time the Spirit determines, however, the trial ends and the soul advances to the final stages of increasing enflamed love and devotion to Jesus.

The fourth stage sees the return to a state of being able to practice the virtues in joy. The fifth and sixth steps highlight illumination and enkindling. First, the Spirit acts upon the soul by fanning its inner spark, and then "out of the light and of the shining spark stream forth very clear rays of light" (ed., 29.1–6). The soul has become a source of illumination for others and is ready for the final enkindling of love on the seventh level. Here the soul loves God alone and gives itself totally to him. The Holy Spirit "comes to such a person with full force in a fiery flaming flood of love and shines all around and envelops such a one, drawing him to himself and into himself and hiding him in the wounded heart of our Lord Jesus Christ."[100] The last pages of the treatise are rich in many of the main motifs of late medieval mysticism: the play of love between God and human that lies beyond all forms and images; unmediated union with God; and ecstatic experience after the model of St. Paul. At the conclusion, the old father tells his student that this is how the Holy Spirit "works in and with his friends" (ed., 34.37–39).

The story of the Green Isle community illustrates something that might have been, namely, a successful institutionalized form of devout life aiming at mystical contact with God, a way of life open to both clergy and laity. This Strassburg experiment, however, was not fated to succeed, perhaps as much because of the personality of its founder as because of accidents of time and context. Although this community centered its attention on a particular conception of the Friends of God, we should not imagine that the term *gottes vriunde* was totally commandeered by Rulman Merswin and his followers. The use of "Friend of God" as a denomination for advanced mystical believers continued to be found in other writers, notably Franciscans. Marquard of Lindau used the term in his sermons (see chapter 7, p. 329). Otto of Passau, lector at the Basel Franciscan convent, published a massive work entitled *The Twenty-Four Elders, or the Golden Throne of the Loving Soul* in 1386, just four years after Merswin's death.[101] (There is no modern edition of this popular work.) Using the twenty-four elders of the Apocalypse to mark out the number of stages in the path to God, the treatise discusses friendship with God as the eighteenth stage. Although the notion of Friends of God remained popular both inside and outside the Green Isle congregation in the late fourteenth century, as a social phenomenon, and even as a description for mystical aspirants, it faded rapidly after 1400.

Did the Friends of God really contribute anything of importance to the history of medieval mysticism? The contribution was probably less than what is suggested by the community's propaganda. Whether or not Rulman Merswin himself was a mystic cannot be answered—and is not really of significance. What is clear is that this lay patron did dedicate his life and fortune to the support of a community designed to encourage devout persons, both clerical and lay, to seek deeper contact with God, an important option in an era of natural calamities, clerical corruption, and pervasive institutional malaise. Merswin's greatest literary achievement was the creation of an enduring mystical fiction, the legend of the Friend of God from the Land Above. His other writings, mostly unoriginal, mediocre, and based on earlier mystical texts, relegate him to the status of a second-rate figure at best.[102] Nevertheless, Rulman Merswin and the literature produced by his community have their place in the story of mysticism in the second half of the fourteenth century, especially for their witness to the conviction that only real saints, true Friends of God, might be able to save a church so mired in corruption and conflict.

CHAPTER 10

Nicholas of Cusa
on Mystical Theology

OR THOSE WHO VIEW MYSTICISM as primarily a matter of personal accounts of ecstatic experiences of God, Nicolas of Cusa
can hardly merit more than a footnote in its story. From this
perspective, Nicholas (by self-confession) appears to have been a
failed mystic. If, however, mysticism is more than purportedly autobiographical accounts of such a kind, but rather involves serious intellectual consideration of how contact between God and human
transforms the awareness of the human subject—from the data of
external and internal perception, through the subject's attempt to
understand and evaluate what these mean in terms of affirmation of
truth and commitment to action—then mysticism takes on a different
character, and Cusa may merit the kind of treatment attempted here.
The German cardinal believed that the desire to plumb the meaning
of mystical theology and to make it available to others was the essential goal of all pursuit of knowledge. *Theologia mystica* was not
restricted to the experiential categories so popular in modern treatments, nor to the imaginative visions found among many of his contemporaries, but was a total commitment to contemplating and loving
the supreme and unknowable mystery that is God. The purpose of
this chapter is to investigate how Nicholas of Cusa presented the
meaning of this highest aspect of human unknowing-knowing, or *docta
ignorantia*. Few thinkers have been more persistent in their exploration of the meaning of mystical theology or more innovative in discerning its implications.[1]

Cusa's Life and Works

Nicholas Krebs was born in 1401 in Kues on the Mosel river, the
son of a well-to-do boatman.[2] In 1416 he matriculated at the university

of Heidelberg as a cleric of the diocese of Trier. From 1417 to 1423 he studied canon law at Padua, where he made the acquaintance of several Italian humanists. He also briefly studied philosophy and theology at Cologne under Master Heimerich de Campo. By 1427 Nicholas had abandoned the world of the universities to begin a career in church administration at Trier. The young priest and canon lawyer was sent to the council meeting at Basel in 1432 to represent Ulrich von Manderscheid, one of the claimants in a disputed election for the diocese of Trier. Here he entered into the larger world of ecclesiastical politics and soon became an adherent of the conciliar party. His first work, *The Catholic Concordance (De concordantia catholica)* of 1433, was a defense of conciliarism based on the Dionysian notion of the concord found in all hierarchy as a created manifestation of the triune God.[3] In the same work Cusa laid down the outline of a program of reform of church and society that was to take up much of his energy for the next three decades.[4]

The growing tensions between the council fathers at Basel and Pope Eugenius IV, who resisted the council's decrees and calls for reform, eventually led to a split among the representatives. Cusa sided with the minority party, those conciliarists who tried to work out a compromise with the pope. Between the summer of 1437 and early 1438 Cusa was a member of the delegation sent to Constantinople with the pope's approval to bring back the Byzantine emperor and his representatives to a new papally summoned council at Ferrara and Florence in 1439, a meeting that achieved the long-awaited reunion of the Eastern and Western churches—alas, a very short one. By this time Cusa had changed camps and had become a strong supporter of the papal party. For the next ten years he labored strenuously to advance the cause of Eugenius in Germany against the remnant of the Basel fathers who had deposed the pope and nominated an antipope. Nicholas's shift of allegiance has remained controversial. Did he act from careerist motives (he was awarded the red hat for his efforts in 1449)? Or did he come to the conclusion that hopes for reform could be achieved only under papal leadership? As in many lives, his motives were probably mixed.

During this same decade Nicholas began to produce the speculative works that were to guarantee his fame as philosopher, theologian, scientist, and humanist, especially his most noted work, *On Learned Ignorance (De docta ignorantia*; hereafter DDI), a treatise in three books. Cusa's return from Constantinople had been a long and hard voyage of more than two months, ending on February 4, 1438. Two years later, on February 12, 1440, he records finishing *On Learned Ignorance* during a brief stay in his native

Kues. Given his frequent travels and political activity, it is remarkable that he was able to write this original synthesis of dialectical Neoplatonism in so short and harried a time. Equally remarkable is his claim that the work was based on a divine illumination given him while at sea during his return from Constantinople. In the dedicatory letter to his patron Cardinal Giulio Cesarini postfaced to the work Cusa wrote:

> Worthy Father, now receive what I have desired to attain already for so long a time by various forms of teaching, but which I could not before now. This was until I was returning from Greece by sea, when I believe by a heavenly gift from the Father of Lights from whom comes every best gift [Jas. 1:7], I was brought to be able to embrace incomprehensible realities in an incomprehensible manner in learned ignorance through surpassing the incorruptible truths that are open to knowing in a human way.[5]

This text is both suggestive and puzzling, like learned ignorance itself. Marjorie O'Rourke Boyle has shown how claiming an illumination at sea connects Cusa with a Neoplatonic theme of divine enlightenment given in the midst of the sea of materiality and confusion.[6] But if Cusa's use of maritime illumination as a form of Renaissance epideictic rhetoric is unmistakable, as is his later reference to Christ as the mountain of truth (DDI 3.11.246), this does not rule out the possibility that some such moment of mystical insight may actually have taken place. What is evident, though, is that Cusa saw this illumination in ways quite different from the visions typical of much late medieval mysticism. It was, first of all, no imaginative appearance of God or Christ; and it also seems to be rather different from Augustine's understanding of an intellectual vision, that is, an internal conviction of some truth about God. Cusa's illumination surpasses all human forms of reception of incorruptible truths, plunging him into the paradoxes of the "non-seeing seeing" introduced by Dionysius and explored by such Christian Neoplatonists as Eriugena and Eckhart. Nicholas of Cusa's account of his illumination at sea still leaves us staring out from the shore more than six centuries later.

On Learned Ignorance introduced a quarter-century of feverish literary activity. In 1441–42 Cusa produced a companion piece to his investigation of *docta ignorantia* in the *On Conjectures (De coniecturis;* hereafter DC), an analysis of how the human mind constructs its own mental universe through intelligible likenesses in a manner analogous to the unfolding of the universe from the mind of God. His conclusion is at once traditional in the medieval sense of conceiving humans as made in the divine image, yet also striking in its expression: "Man is God, but not absolutely, since he is also man; he is therefore a human God. Man is also the world, but he is not all things in a contracted fashion, since he is also man. Man is therefore a microcosm and a human world. . . . All things exist in their own way within the power of human nature."[7] A spate of shorter works also soon appeared between 1444 and 1447: *On the Hidden God* (*De deo abscondito*); *On Seeking God* (*De quaerendo Deo*); *On Divine Sonship* (*De filiatione Dei*); *On the Gift of the Father of Lights* (*De dato patris luminum*); and *On Genesis* (*De genesi*). In 1449 Cusa wrote a response to an attack on his work on learned ignorance penned by the theologian John Wenck of Heidelberg, entitled *On Unknown Learning* (*De ignota litteratura* [ca. 1443]). He called this rebuttal *The Defense of Learned Ignorance* (*Apologia doctae ignorantiae*).

The year 1450 found Cusa in Rome receiving his cardinal's red hat from Pope Nicholas V, a famous humanist. Here the new cardinal wrote a dialogue *The Layman on Mind* (*Idiota de mente*), in which a layman shows himself a better student of learned ignorance than an orator and a philosopher—a theme found in many late-medieval mystical works. In the same year Cusa was appointed bishop of Brixen in the Tyrol and commissioned to travel through German-speaking lands as papal legate to spread the message of reform. During this "Great Legation" of 1450–52 Cusa travelled almost three thousand miles, preaching, teaching, and reforming, though also meeting with considerable resistance. Cusa met even greater opposition when he took up his role as bishop in Brixen. His period at Brixen (1452–58) saw much conflict with his feudal overlord, Archduke Sigismond, as well as the local nobility and monastic houses who resisted reform. Cusa's actions were not always politically astute or even consistent. During these years, however, the cardinal continued to preach extensively and to write mathematical, theological, and mystical works. *On the Peace of Faith* (*De pace fidei*) of 1453 was a work of what could be called ecumenical theology, written in response to the news of the fall of Constantinople to the Turks. *On the Vision of God* (*De visione Dei*; hereafter DVD), written in the same year, was his most important mystical text, while *On the Beryl* (*De beryllo*) of 1458 is another speculative work.[8]

Nicholas's friend, the humanist Aeneas Sylvius Piccolomini, became Pope Pius II in 1458 and brought the beleaguered bishop of Brixen back to Rome, where he appointed him to a reform commission. In 1459 Nicholas wrote a treatise on the general reform of the church (*Reformatio generalis*). But Pius and the other cardinals were not really interested in reform, and the pope tells the story of how Nicholas reacted in 1461 when Pius tried to win his vote for approving a group of new cardinals (something Pius had sworn not to do). The pope's autobiographical memoirs, the *Commentaries*, tell us that Cusa reproached Pius in the following way:

> You are preparing to create new cardinals without any pressing reason merely at your own whim, and you have no regard to the oath you swore to the Sacred College. If you can bear to hear the truth, I like nothing that goes on in this Curia. Everything is corrupt; no one does his duty. All are bent on ambition and avarice. If I ever speak in a consistory about reform, I am laughed at. Allow me to withdraw; I cannot endure these ways. I am an old man and need rest.

According to Pius, "with these words he burst into tears."[9] Nicholas of Cusa did not have long to wait to be relieved of his earthly cares, dying at Todi on August 11, 1464. During his final trying years in Rome he produced some important, though usually brief, treatises. Two short works of 1459, *On the Principle* (*De principio*) and *On Equality* (*De aequalitate*), were designed to introduce his sermons.[10] Many of the works written after 1460 are in dialogue form, exploring again and again the main themes of Cusa's theology, especially the best way of speaking about God.[11] Among these are the 1460 *Conversation on Actualized Possibility* (*Trialogus de possest*); *On the Not-Other* (*Directio speculantis seu de non-aliud*) of 1462;[12] two works written in 1463, *The Game of Spheres* (*De ludo globi*) and *The Hunt for Wisdom* (*De venatione sapientiae*); and finally, *The Summit of Contemplation* (*De apice theoriae*), of 1464.[13] The brief *Compendium* may also date from this last year of his life. These treatises show that despite his age and disappointments, Nicholas of Cusa remained as committed to the exploration of the mystery of God at the end as he had been throughout his life.

The German cardinal, like Meister Eckhart before him,[14] was largely forgotten for centuries but rediscovered in the 1800s and has been the subject of much study for the past two hundred years. Cusa's range of learning and interests, as well as the difficulties of his thought, have led to quite diverse interpretations of his significance. Was he a conciliarist or a papalist? A careerist or a devoted reformer? A philosopher or a theologian? Should he be seen as standing in fundamental continuity with medieval thought, or does his contribution mark an important stage in the birth of modernity (however defined)?[15] I cannot hope to take up these debates explicitly here, though any interpretation naturally implies a position. Nor will I try to pay attention to the full range of Cusa's writings. I will also avoid entering into the much-disputed question of the consistency of Cusa's thought as it developed over three decades. My concerns are restricted to the cardinal's role in the history of mysticism. How did Cusa view mystical theology? What contribution did he make to late medieval mysticism?

Faith, Reason, and the Forms of Theology

Theology in the etymological sense of a logos, or word, about God was central to all Cusa's intellectual endeavors. Yet Cusa has been more studied by philosophers than theologians, and in recent years debate has emerged as to whether the cardinal should be seen primarily as a philosopher *or* a theologian.[16] Of course, such a dichotomy would never have entered into Cusa's own mind—like Eckhart, he was both a philosopher and a theologian, and a mystical theologian at that. He would have insisted that there can be no essential difference between the love of wisdom, or philosophy, and the true word about God that is theology. As he put it in his treatise *On Divine Sonship*: "There is one thing that all who do theology or philosophy are trying to express in their many modalities," despite the different forms of language that often "seem incompatible." "Thus, all possible modes of speaking in theology are trying to express that which is ineffable in any way they can."[17]

If theology and philosophy aim at bringing to speech the same mystery, we can still inquire about the respective roles of reason and faith in constructing adequate philosophico-theological teaching. Nicholas of Cusa discussed the relationship between reason and faith and the consequent differences between philosophers and theologians in a number of places, especially in *The Hunt for Wisdom*.[18] What ties great thinkers together, both the pagan philosophers, such as Plato, Aristotle, and Proclus, and the Christian theologians, such as Augustine, Dionysius, and Thomas Aquinas, as the cardinal insists, is that they all were deeply engaged in pursuing wisdom. In this late treatise he endeavors to show how much agreement there has been among the philosophers and the theologians, especially when viewed from the perspective of the higher truth given by revelation. For example, he concludes a chapter on how Plato and Aristotle conducted the hunt for wisdom by saying, "But our divine theologians, on the basis of revelation from above, learned that the First Cause, that which is called the One and the Good by Plato, and Intellect and the Being of beings by Aristotle, since it is tricausal (namely, efficient, formal, and final), in the estimation of all is one in such a way that it is three and three in such a way that it is one."[19] Thus, the philosophers intimated but did not gain clear knowledge of the Trinity. Revelation, however, allows the theologian to see the trinitarian dimension of their thinking. Later, in discussing his new name of God as actualized possibility (*possest*) he says, "It is evident how the philosophers, who did not enter into this field, have not tasted of this most pleasing form of hunting."[20] Such contrasts between philosophy and theology occur throughout the treatise.[21] The higher role of theology based on faith is emphasized across

Cusa's works, as well as in his preaching.[22] A passage in Sermon CCXXVI preached for the Feast of the Annunciation in 1456, in which Cusa discusses the soul's espousal to the Word, is revealing. This homily engages in an allegorical reading of Song of Songs 6:7–9. Solomon, the true Wisdom who is Christ, had sixty queens, eighty concubines, innumerable young girls, but only one perfect and chosen dove. The young girls are the grammarians, who are just beginning their studies; the concubines, a more select number, are those who move on to dialectics. The even smaller number of "honored queens . . . are perfect in the study of philosophy." "But one is the dove who is true theology."[23] This text reminds us that although Cusa did not write long exegetical works in the style of Eckhart, a christological and spiritual reading of the biblical text, especially evident in his sermons, was a crucial foundation for his thought.[24]

Cusa's position on the relation of faith and reason, like much else in his thought, seems to invite interpreters to extremes. Between the Scylla of seeing him as a philosopher who merely adopted Christian theological language as a mode for exploring metaphysics, and the Charybdis of viewing him as a late medieval nominalistic fideist who despaired of any real knowledge of God without the aid of revelation,[25] the cardinal fits into the broad middle ground of varying attempts in the Middle Ages to do justice to both faith and reason in the pursuit of God. Cusa staked out his own distinctive view of the traditional Augustinian conception of theology as "faith seeking understanding" (*fides quaerens intellectum*). Like the bishop of Hippo, Cusa often cited the proof text from Isaiah 7:9 to describe the relation between faith and understanding. A noted passage occurs in chapter 11 of book 3 of *On Learned Ignorance*:

> Our ancestors all agreed in asserting that faith is the beginning of understanding. . . . It is necessary for everyone who wants to ascend to doctrinal science to believe in those things without which ascent is impossible, for Isaiah says, "If you do not believe, you will not understand." Therefore faith enfolds in itself everything intelligible; intellect is the unfolding of faith. Hence the intellect is directed by faith and faith is drawn out further [*extenditur*] through intellect.[26]

Cusa's version of what Werner Beierwaltes has termed the "dialectical view" of the relation of faith and reason can be summarized under five headings: (1) there can be no real conflict between reason and faith, since both forms of knowing come from God; (2) reason, as exemplified in the philosophers' search for wisdom, had attained significant truth about God, both explicitly and implicitly; (3) given humanity's fallen state, the revelation given by Christ is needed to acquire true saving knowledge; (4) for the theologian, faith and reason have a dialectical relationship since faith requires human thinking to attain its self-realization;[27] and (5) this intellectual self-attainment is most fully realized in the mystical theology that is also *docta ignorantia.*[28] Let me comment briefly on each of these points.

On the basis of the texts already cited, I hope the first two points are already clear. First, Cusa, like most medieval theologians, was convinced that there could be no real (as opposed to *seeming*) conflict between *fides* and *ratio/intellectus,*[29] given that both had their source in the supreme divine *veritas.*[30] Second, human knowing as exemplified by the ancient philosophers had attained partial truth in its pursuit of wisdom. Natural knowledge of the world and especially the mind's reflexive grasp of its own mode of knowing provides access to the truth that God is (*quia est*).[31] The lifelong study that Cusa devoted to the ancient philosophers showed him that the hunt for wisdom was essential to being human, but pure reason and natural intellect alone were not sufficient to attain the saving knowledge conveyed by the Incarnate Word.

In the third place, Cusa, like other medieval thinkers, believed that human nature and its powers of knowing and willing had suffered grave harm through the Fall and therefore needed divine assistance if it was to attain salvation.[32] The incarnation, for Cusa, was certainly a remedy for sin, though primarily the Word's taking on of flesh was the central intention of the divine plan for the perfection of the universe. However much Cusa developed his notion of truth in ways that challenged the standard medieval worldview, there is no question that, like John Scottus Eriugena and Meister Eckhart before him, he understood the source of truth as Eternal Wisdom, the Logos made flesh in Jesus, active both in creation and in redemption. As the treatise *On Equality* (an Augustinian-Chartrian term for the Word) makes clear,[33] the Word is responsible for all knowing, both in heaven and on earth—"The Word is that without which neither Father, nor Son, nor Holy Spirit, nor angels, nor souls, nor all intellectual natures can understand anything."[34] Throughout his life, Cusa insisted that true knowledge of God, both theological and philosophical, is fundamentally christological.[35] His last work, *The Summit of Contemplation*, written the Easter before he died, concludes with the words: "The three and one God . . . whose most perfect manifestation is Christ (because no manifestation could be more perfect) leads us to the clear contemplation of the possible itself by word and example. This is the happiness that alone can satisfy the mind's highest longing."[36]

The very structure of Cusa's most noted work, *On Learned Ignorance*, demonstrates the christological core of his theology. Book 1 deals with God

as the absolute maximum and book 2 with the created universe as the contracted maximum. But since there is no proportion between the finite and
the infinite, no kind of analogy,[37] how does Cusa arrive at his new theology
of the coincidence of opposites that provides the learned ignorance set forth
in these two books? The answer becomes clear in book 3, which treats of
"Jesus Christ, . . . the maximum that is both absolute and contracted." Here
Cusa cites the archetypal mystic Paul, rapt into learned ignorance (2 Cor.
12:2), as the exemplar for all those who have been illuminated by Christ:
"And this is that learned ignorance by which the very blessed Paul, as he
ascended, saw that as he was being lifted higher, he was then unknowing of
the Christ, whom at one time he had only been aware of [i.e., humanly]."[38]
Cusa goes on to invoke the experience of Moses, the other biblical model
of ascent to mystical darkness:

> We who have faith in Christ are led into learned ignorance to the mountain
> that is Christ and that we are forbidden to touch with the nature of our ani-
> mality. And when we endeavor to look on this mountain with the intellectual
> eye, we fall into a darkness, and we know that within that very darkness is the
> mountain on which only all the living who have intellect may dwell. If we
> approach it with a greater constancy of faith, we will be snatched away from
> the eyes of those who live by the senses. . . . And there we behold God more
> clearly, as if through a more transparent cloud.[39]

Without Christ there is no adequate theology, but Cusa's position is
scarcely fideistic. So, in the fourth place, he holds that revelation completes
the search for wisdom rather than canceling or overriding it. Cusa's view of
the dialectical relationship between faith and reason holds that both are co-
determinants in the pursuit of wisdom. He frames their mutual interaction
nicely in a text from Sermon IV, where he compares faith to our right eye,
which is like a "mirror grasping great things, because the divine majesty is
reached through faith," while reason is like the left eye, "which judges only
of natural things."[40] The comparison goes on to state that someone who
loses a right eye cannot prevail in combat, because the left eye is always
covered by the shield, but this observation suggests that the two-eyed man
has a better time of it, both in battle and in life. For Cusa, as for Augustine,
Anselm, and others, the application of reason to further the understanding
of the truths revealed in faith, or *speculatio* in Cusa's terms,[41] is not just a secondary phenomenon, a kind of icing on the cake. The mind's exploration
of revealed truth is necessary not only to defend faith against its enemies,
but also, and more importantly, to help the believer come to deeper self-
awareness of the dynamics of the inexhaustible truth revealed by Christ.
Fides quaerens intellectum is a necessity, not an entertainment.

The fifth point, namely, that faith's self-realization is attained in *theologia mystica*, introduces us to the cardinal's conception of the modes of theology and the role of the mystical theology first set forth explicitly by Dionysius, whom Cusa once referred to as "the sharpest of thinkers, who in his search for God discovered that contrary attributes are truly joined in him and that non-existence is excellence."[42] Important as are Cusa's explicit discussions of *theologia mystica*, it is worth noting with Hans Gerhard Senger that the role of mystical theology as a fundamental category is more widespread, being presupposed throughout his writings in the treatment of such key terms as *visio/theoria, docta ignorantia,* and *coincidentia oppositorum.*[43]

In a sermon preached on Christmas 1456 Cusa briefly defined mystical theology: "God revealed means the following, namely that God exists and that he is not visible, and this is mystical theology."[44] Cusa had investigated and preached about divine hiddenness from the beginning of his career. His earliest sermon from 1430 insists that "God is so immense that he remains unnameable, inexpressible, and fully unknowable by all creatures."[45] The treatment of the divine names given here does not use Dionysius, but depends heavily on Jewish sources, especially Maimonides. We do not know precisely when Cusa began studying the Dionysian corpus. His *Catholic Concordance* already shows profound knowledge of the ecclesiastical writings of the Areopagite. If we accept the shipboard revelation of the winter of 1437–38 as a turning point in Cusa's career, then it was presumably during the following eighteen months that he began to search for authorities that would enable him to extend this revelation into a full-blown new theology, the first stage of which was completed with *On Learned Ignorance.* There is evidence that at this time Cusa was not only involved in intensive study of Dionysius, but that he had also begun reading Eckhart, as several sermons given in the winter of 1438–39 demonstrate.

In these homilies (Sermons XIX–XXI) we can see Cusa beginning to explore the role of Dionysian positive and negative theology in the path to learned ignorance.[46] No human language can properly describe God's essence (Sermo XIX), and even the revelation of the name of Jesus at his circumcision (Luke 2:21) does not provide real knowledge of the nature of God (Sermo XX). In Sermon XX Cusa explicitly cites Dionysius's triple path of ascent to God by way of the language of causality, of eminence, and by way of remotion "so that the defect which we find in the thing caused we remove from the eminence of the Cause."[47] His clear preference is for the names that are ascribed to God by remotion, such as invisible and immortal, as well as for names that give him a perfection that is not found in creatures, such as omnipotent and eternal (S. XX, nn. 8–9). Here we see

Cusa feeling his way toward the more systematic and original use of Dionysius that emerges in *On Learned Ignorance*. In short, during these years Cusa
was working out a new form of the intellective Dionysianism that had been
so powerful in Germany a century and a half earlier.

In book 1 of Cusa's DDI his new theology of the coincidence of opposites as a key to the pursuit of wisdom emerges with clarity. Here Cusa
explores the understanding of the maximum, as "that beyond which there
can be nothing greater . . . which the indubitable faith of all nations believes
to be God" (1.2.5). A maximum of this sort is beyond all oppositions of
affirmation and negation, as chapter 4 argues:

> Because the absolutely maximum is absolutely and actually all that can be,
> and it is without opposition to such an extent that the minimum coincides
> with the maximum, it is above all affirmation and negation. It both is and is
> not all that is conceived to be, and it both is and is not all that is conceived not
> to be. But it is "this" in such a way that it is all things, and it is all things in
> such a way that it is none of them, and it is a "this" maximally in such a way
> that it is also a "this" minimally.

Cusa concludes, "Absolute maximumness could not be actually all possible
things, unless it were infinite and the limit of all things and unable to be
limited by any of them."[48] My purpose here is not to analyze the *coincidentia
oppositorum* in detail (a task undertaken in many studies),[49] but rather to
examine how Nicholas integrates his new approach into the categories of
theology inherited from Dionysius.

In the latter part of book 1 Cusa relates his teaching on the coincidence
of opposites to the Dionysian modes of theological ascent. After providing
a geometrical example to illustrate the coincidence, in chapter 16 he concludes that because "the maximum infinitely and completely transcends all
opposition . . . we can deduce as many negative truths about the maximum
as can be written or read."[50] This principle is the source of all theology, he
avers, citing a series of texts from the Dionysian writings about how theology, as speech about God, is both "greatest and least," and thus goes
beyond both affirmation and negation.[51] Chapter 24 explicitly takes up the
role of affirmative theology, once again showing how no name can properly be ascribed to the maximum because it has no opposite (24.74). Reason cannot leap over the wall of contradictories (24.76), cannot grasp the
infinite unity of the maximum, and therefore positive names can say nothing about God in Godself; they only "apply according to God's infinite
power in relation to creatures" (24.79). This is true even of the names of the
Trinity. Cusa's teaching here, which quotes Maimonides, appears to be

based on the citations from the Jewish sage found in Meister Eckhart's *Commentary on Exodus.*

The purpose of affirmative theology is described at the beginning of chapter 26, which deals with the meaning of negative theology—"All religion in its worship has to ascend by means of an affirmative theology." But if affirmative theology is not tempered by the learned ignorance of negative theology, worship may turn into idolatry by treating the infinite God as no more than another *being* (i.e., a creature). The key term here, as later in the *On the Vision of God,* is infinity. Infinity is a name common to all three Persons, in that sense lying beyond the Trinity. "According to the theology of negations," says Cusa, "nothing other than infinity is found in God. Consequently, negative theology holds that God is unknowable either in this world or the world to come, . . . but God is known to God alone" (26.88). Therefore, what Cusa calls the "precision of truth" (*praecisio veritatis*) shines out in the darkness of our admission of ignorance.[52] This hard-won admission is the basis for the *docta ignorantia* that Cusa had been searching for (26.89). While Cusa characterizes it here as a negative theology, it is in fact a negation that surpasses the mere activity of denying this or that attribute of God; it is the affirmation (paradoxical as that may be) that God as the coincidence of the infinitely large and infinitely small can be praised but not known.

In *On Learned Ignorance* Cusa did not explicitly describe the coincidence of opposites and the *docta ignorantia* it elicits as "mystical theology." But he did affirm precisely this in his response to John Wenck's attack on his book in the treatise *On Unknown Learning.* At one point the Heidelberg theologian exclaimed, "I ask how ignorance can teach, since teaching is a positive act of conveying doctrine?"[53] In his *Apology for Learned Ignorance,* Cusa defended learned ignorance forcefully, claiming, "The Aristotelians prevail today, who think that the coincidence of opposites, acceptance of which is the beginning of the ascent to mystical theology, is heresy. Hence, for those raised in this camp this approach is completely idiotic. . . ."[54] He went on to buttress his defense of the negative approach to God by citing the authority of Dionysius and by noting the difference between the kind of knowledge (*scientia*) that delights in self-inflating verbal conflict and "mystical theology [which] leads to emptiness and silence, where resides the vision granted to us of the invisible God."[55] In this passage the coincidence of opposites has become the necessary beginning of mystical theology, though perhaps not its end.

Other texts from the decade 1440–1450 express the same link between mystical theology and the coincidence of opposites. In *On Divine Sonship*

(1445), Cusa affirmed that all the modes of theology, which he here names
as affirmative, negative, dubitative, disjunctive, and unitive, are really one
(5.88), as we have noted above. He goes on to say that the recognition of
the one truth at the basis of all modes of speaking about God is part of the
pursuit of deification. The scholar who does theology in a true way (*vere the-*
ologizans scholaris) finds nothing to be concerned about in the variety of theological conjectures, because he or she "knows that God is ineffable,
beyond every affirmation and negation, whatever anyone might say. . . ."[56]
At the start of the second book of his treatise *The Layman on the Mind* (1450),
Cusa has a discussion of "the theology of discourse" (*theologia sermocinalis*),
in which the wise layman leads the orator to the recognition that asking a
question about God is different from other kinds of questions. All questions
presuppose something about the answer, but because God is the coincidence of opposites (in this place expressed as absolute facility coinciding
with absolute incomprehensibility), the most precise way of talking about
God goes beyond both affirmative and negative theology. "There is a treatment of God insofar as neither positing or removing belongs to him," he
says, "but rather insofar as he is beyond every affirmation and negation. In
this case the response denies affirmation, and negation, and the conjunction
[of the two]."[57] In this passage Cusa does not name the mode of theological
discourse that is beyond all others, but his writings of the early 1450s make
it clear that he is referring to mystical theology.

In the 1450s Cusa returned to the relation between his "coincident theology" and the mystical theology of the Dionysian tradition.[58] In the context
of the emerging debate over the nature of mystical theology (to be discussed in more detail below), he expatiated on the relation between coincidence and mystical theology in a letter sent to the Benedictine community
at Tegernsee of September 14, 1453. Here Cusa notes that in the MT
Dionysius teaches that the cloud where God is encountered lies beyond
both affirmative and negative theology. He explains as follows:

> In this little book [the MT] where he wants to show mystical and secret theol-
> ogy in a likely way he leaps above the disjunction [of positive and negative]
> up to combining and coincidence, that is, the most simple union, which is not
> one-sided but directly above all remotion and positing. Here remotion co-
> incides with positing and negation with affirmation. This is that most secret
> theology to which no philosopher had access nor could have as long as the
> principle common to all philosophy is in force, that is, that two contradictories
> do not coincide. And so it is necessary that someone doing theology in the
> mystical manner place himself in the cloud beyond all reason and intellect,
> even leaving self behind.[59]

Cusa goes on to say that this self-abandonment of the intellect in which we come to taste "necessity in impossibility and affirmation in negation" cannot be perfectly realized in this life, but it is nonetheless the goal toward which we must strive.

This teaching remained constant throughout the last decade of the cardinal's life. It undergirds the treatise on the vision of God (DVD), his major contribution to mystical theology, a text he was working on in the last months of 1453, and which he sent to the same monks to whom the letter was directed. We shall treat of this in detail below. The same combination of *speculatio* and mysticism (or perhaps better the *speculatio* that is mysticism) surfaces again in the *Trialogus de possest,* written in 1460. This conversation explores Paul's claim in Romans 1:20 that the invisible things of God can be understood from the things of the world. The Pauline text had long been a cornerstone of philosophical proofs for God's existence, but Cusa takes the argument in a different direction, away from discursive proof to an exploration of the coincidence of absolute actuality and absolute possibility in God named as *possest* or actualized possibility. Once again, it is not my purpose to follow the analysis of this new version of naming God based on the coincidence of opposites,[60] but rather to underline the fact that the cardinal sees the recognition of this name not so much as an academic exercise, but as a necessary step in the mind's preparation for the revelation that provides mystical sight of the invisible God. As he says in chapter 15: "Therefore this name [*possest*] leads the one engaged in *speculatio* above all sense, reason, and intellect into mystical vision where there is the end of the ascent of every cognitive power and the beginning of the revelation of the unknown God. When he has left all things behind, the seeker after truth ascends above himself and discovers that he still has no access to the invisible God." Here the seeker waits "in very devout desire" for God to manifest himself. So, concludes Cusa, what Paul meant is that "when we understand that the world is a creature and when we seek its Creator by transcending the world, he manifests himself to those who seek him as their Creator with the most profoundly formed faith."[61]

The Debate over Mystical Theology

Nicholas of Cusa's Dionysian emphasis on mystical theology as the goal of the Christian life led him into controversy, not least because, as we have seen, there was considerable debate in the late Middle Ages over how Dionysius was to be read. The dispute had deeper roots in the quarrel over the legitimacy of forms of mysticism developed on the basis of Neoplatonic

dialectical thinking. Two of Cusa's predecessors and prime sources, Eriugena and Eckhart, had run afoul of ecclesiastical authority on these issues.
Cusa was spared any condemnation by church authority, but he too was
attacked for mystical heresy.

The controversy over Cusa's view of mysticism evolved in two stages.
The first centered on the attack of the Heidelberg theologian John Wenck
(ca. 1395–1460) on Cusa's *On Learned Ignorance.* Wenck was a conciliarist
who opposed Cusa as a turncoat, but there was also a deep divide between
the two men over how theology was to be done.[62] Along with the personal
and academic aspects of their animosity, the quarrel was also one about the
nature of mystical contact with God because, as Jasper Hopkins put it:
"Nicholas's reflections on mystical theology were an extension of his doctrine of learned ignorance."[63] Wenck's attack on Cusa's doctrine of *coincidentia oppositorum* was the basis for his rejection of what he claimed was
Cusa's teaching about the formal identity of God and human, as well as his
adherence to the errors of the condemned beghards and of Meister Eckhart.[64]

Although Wenck was not an original theologian, his attack on Cusa represents one of the most forceful late medieval polemics against the dangers
of forms of mysticism, like those of Eckhart and Cusa, that aim at attaining
indistinction with God. Wenck structures his argument in scholastic fashion
according to ten false theses and their corollaries, rebutting these by
appeals both to scripture and to the rules of logic. He has little trouble
showing that Cusa's coincidence of opposites flouts the laws of Aristotelian
logic used in late medieval scholastic theology.[65] In his response, as noted
above, Cusa freely admitted this accusation. Throughout his career, he
never denied the validity of Aristotelian logic in dealing with the realm of
discrete entities; but he insisted that the principle of contradiction is wanting when it attempts to go beyond its proper limits to investigate what lies
beyond distinction—the God who is not *some-thing* distinct from other
things, but rather the ground of all things simultaneously enfolded in himself in a transcendental way while also unfolded in the multiplicity of real
existences.[66]

Wenck also noted a connection between Cusa's treatment of the coincidence of opposites and the condemned views of Eckhart and of the beguines
and beghards, thus connecting his attack to the late medieval debates on
the dangers of mysticism. According to Wenck, the views found in Cusa's
treatise are "incompatible with our faith, offensive to pious minds, and
vainly repelling of obedience to God."[67] At the start, he criticizes Cusa's reference to the shipboard illumination at the origin of *On Learned Ignorance,*

seeing it as an example of the false visions mentioned by the apostle John, who cautioned Christians to "test the spirits" (1 John 4:1). Wenck, like many other fourteenth- and fifteenth-century theologians, appealed to the discernment of spirits to cast doubt on his opponent's claims. "For," as he says, "the spirit from whence this learned ignorance proceeds has already been shown some while ago from the Waldensian, Eckhartian, and Wycliffite teachings."[68] Wenck's linking of Cusa and Eckhart is a major theme of his polemic. The Heidelberg theologian shows knowledge of the Dominican's Latin and German writings apparently gained through the trial documents. The attack on the coincidence of opposites in the first thesis provides the most detailed example. Wenck claims that saying that nothing is opposed to God and therefore no name is appropriate to him (passages from DDI 1.2 and 24 are cited) is equivalent to Eckhart's teaching about the identity of God and the soul (he cites texts from the *Book of Divine Consolation* and Pr. 2). This kind of learned ignorance and "most abstract understanding" (*abstractissima intelligentia*), he says, led to the errors of the beghards and sisters (i.e., beguines) who were condemned by John of Strassburg in 1317 for holding "that God is formally everything that is and that they were God by nature without any distinction."[69] A corollary of this position is Eckhart's view of the eternity of creation, which Wenck rebuts by attacking passages from the Dominican's commentaries on Genesis and Exodus (DIL 26.1–14).

Wenck continues this line of attack through the treatise, sometimes citing Eckhart texts expressly and by name (e.g., DIL 30.17–20), and sometimes anonymously summarizing Eckhartian teaching (e.g., 35.19–22). Perhaps the most interesting example of his antipathy to the Eckhartian-Cusan understanding of mysticism is shown in his rebuttal of the fourth thesis, where the Heidelberg professor links Cusa's learned ignorance to Eckhartian detachment. He says: "From this it is clear how much poisoning of knowledge and morals this most abstract understanding, called learned ignorance, or in the vernacular 'detached living,' has caused."[70] Wenck concludes that Cusa's notion of divine unity, like Eckhart's, destroys the Christian doctrine of the Trinity and that his view of the universal Christ, also like Eckhart's, is incompatible with the proper understanding of the incarnation. For Wenck, the root of the errors of Cusa (and Eckhart) is that they do not "know anything at all about the different unions of things."[71] In other words, their notion of mystical union is totally askew. On this basis, he ends with a ringing rejection—"I don't know if in my time I have ever seen a single author as detestable as this one on the question of God and the Trinity of Persons, on the question of the world, Christ's incarnation, the theological virtues, and the church."[72]

Wenck's attack apparently did not come to Cusa's attention until 1448 or 1449. His response, though also quite polemical, gives us insight into his developing thought on how we should strive toward God in this life. Wenck had attacked the vision/illumination that Cusa in his letter to Cardinal Cesarini claimed had been the source of his new theology. In response Cusa does not give any detailed "discernment of spirits" defense of his illumination, but he does insist that he had received "the conception from on high," before he had recourse to the authorities, especially Dionysius and Augustine, to whom he appealed to confirm and explain his insight (*Apologia* 12.19–13.3). Invoking the authority of Dionysius becomes a main motif in the treatise—he cites the *divinissimus Dionysius* more than any other figure. Cusa does not back down on the use of Eckhart, admitting that he had read a considerable amount of the suspect author, including a document (probably what today is known as the *Processus Coloniensis*) in which Eckhart showed how his attackers had misunderstood him (*Apologia* 25.1–7). Cusa's third person account continues:

> The teacher [i.e., Cusa] said that he had never read that Eckhart thought that the creature was [the same as] the Creator. He praised his genius and zeal, but he wished that his books might be removed from public places because the common folk were not ready for the things he often mixed into them that were beyond the manner of speaking of other teachers, though intelligent people would find much that was subtle and useful in them.[73]

Cusa constantly returns to several essential points throughout his rebuttal: (1) the necessity to go beyond the Aristotelian principle of contradiction in dealing with divine matters; (2) the proper understanding of *coincidentia oppositorum*;[74] and (3) the ways in which Wenck has completely misunderstood *On Learned Ignorance*, such as his claim that the text says that creatures actually coincide with God (see, e.g., *Apologia* 16.8–11; 22.17–23.14). A number of other aspects of his defense are important for the mature mystical theology that Cusa was to develop in the following years. First of all, Cusa sees his new approach as fundamentally an issue of what it means to see God: "This approach differs from other ways as much as sight differs from hearing."[75] The concentration on *visio dei* will reach maturation in the 1453 treatise *On the Vision of God*. Second, in this treatise, unlike *On Learned Ignorance*, Cusa says that God lies *beyond* the coincidence of opposites itself,[76] another teaching that reflects the view to be advanced in *On the Vision of God*. While the *Apologia* is a work of controversy, not of mystical teaching, it is a significant defense of the foundations of the mystical Neoplatonism of Cusa and his predecessors.

The second chapter in the mid-fifteenth century debate over mysticism into which the new cardinal plunged also concerned Dionysius, specifically the clash between affective and intellective readings of Dionysius that had emerged two centuries earlier. In order to appreciate the issues at stake, it is necessary to take a glance backward.

The relation between knowing and loving, the essential powers of the human subject, in the path to God is one of the central themes in the history of Christian mysticism.[77] Given the scriptural identification of God with love (e.g., 1 John 4:16), as well as the insistence on how God surpasses all knowledge, most Christian mystics have privileged the role of love, though without denying a significant place for cognition, both in the path to God and in the enjoyment of God's presence, imperfectly in this life and fully in the world to come. The ways of relating loving and knowing over the course of the history of mysticism have been so varied and subtle that it is misleading to contrast affective and speculative, or intellective, forms of mysticism in any simple way. Nevertheless, certain strands of mysticism have not incorrectly come to be associated more with knowing or with loving.

In the decades between 1230 and 1250, as we have seen (chapter 1, pp. 12–14), two contrasting interpretations of the Dionysian writings emerged that can be described as affective Dionysianism and intellective Dionysianism. Thomas Gallus, or Thomas of Vercelli, who created the former, never denied that knowing, especially the knowing symbolized by the cherubim, was an important part of the ascent described by Dionysius, but he interpreted the *superintellectualis cognitio* of the Dionysian writings in terms of the burning love of the seraphim—"This superior wisdom is by way of the human heart."[78] The *apex affectus*, or supreme point of affectivity, was understood by Gallus as a vaulting beyond all forms of knowing. He also used language that emphasized how intellectual operations need to be cut away at the height of union, thus breaking the link between knowing and loving at the summit of the mystical ascent. In the 1240s Albert the Great also commented on the Dionysian corpus. His reading, however, stressed intellect over will and affect: "It is necessary to be united to God through intellect and to praise him by word." This is not to say that Albert did not give love a role both in preparing for union and as a concomitant of supraintellectual union. Commenting on the figure of the mystical teacher, Hierotheus, as described in DN 2, Albert says, "He was perfected to a uniting with divine things through affect and intellect and faith."[79] Nicholas of Cusa studied Albert's Dionysian commentaries carefully, and he was also aware of Gallus whom he called the *abbas vercellensis*.[80]

Gallus's commentaries on Dionysius were widely read, influencing many late medieval mystical writers, such as Bonaventure and the author of the Middle English masterpiece *The Cloud of Unknowing*.[81] A key work in the tradition of affective Dionysianism, and one that was important to the debate into which Cusa entered, was the mystical handbook entitled *The Roads to Sion Mourn (Viae Sion Lugent)*, often ascribed to Bonaventure in the later Middle Ages but known today to have been written by the Carthusian monk Hugh of Balma, who was active in the late thirteenth century.[82] Hugh's popular work, like Bonaventure's *Threefold Way*, is organized according to the three classic stages of spiritual progress, the purgative, the illuminative, and the unitive ways. Pride of place and space is given to the long analysis of the unitive way, and the work closes with an appended scholastic "Difficult Question" (*quaestio difficilis*) on "Whether the soul in her *affectus* by means of aspiration and yearning can be moved into God without any of the intellect's cogitation leading the way or keeping her company."[83] In the course of exploring arguments on this issue, Hugh makes considerable use of Gallus's reinterpretation of Dionysius as teaching a supercognitional contact with God in the *apex affectus*. He writes: "Only what the *affectus* feels in relation to God does the intellect most truly apprehend."[84] Hence, it is not surprising that the question concludes by affirming, "It is clear that the soul that loves truly is able to rise up to God through an *affectus* set afire by yearning love without any prior thinking."[85] Coming as it does at the end of a lengthy treatment of the path to mystical union, Hugh's position can easily be read as an even more forceful separation of knowledge and love than Gallus had affirmed. Dennis D. Martin, however, has claimed that this is actually a misreading, because a look at the whole of Hugh's treatise indicates that he had a far more nuanced understanding of the interdependent roles of loving and knowing. Martin argues that the "Difficult Question" is speaking not so much about a stage in the mystical life as an act of ejaculative prayer in which a sudden upsurge to love of God need not depend on meditation or other forms of cogitation.[86] Cusa and his allies, however, read Hugh as claiming that the state of union with its flaming love might grant a knowledge of God that had no need for any prior intellectual activity.

One other important mystical writer also needs to be mentioned to help understand the quarrel that erupted around 1450—Jean Gerson (1363–1429), the chancellor of the University of Paris and a voluminous author on many subjects, not least on mysticism. Gerson was a great student of Dionysius, and he also knew both Gallus's commentaries and Hugh of Balma's treatise. (A more complete account of Gerson's place in Western mysticism will appear in the next volume in this history.) The chancellor's popular two-volume handbook on mystical theology had a considerable role in the mid-century debates. About 1402 Gerson completed a work entitled *De theologia mystica speculativa*, an academic summary of the Western mystical tradition, and in 1407 a companion piece, the *De mystica theologia practica*, a more how-to account of the right way of going about mystical practices, including the dangers to be avoided.[87] These were not Gerson's only writings on mysticism, but this double treatise had popularity in learned circles. It is not surprising that it was known to Cusa and his correspondents and opponents.

Treatise 8, nn. 40–42 of the *Speculative Mystical Theology* contains an analysis of the true and false understandings of union (what Wenck accused Cusa of neglecting). This leads up to Gerson's famous definition of mystical theology:

> Experiential knowledge of God through the joining of spiritual *affectus* with him, so that the Apostle's statement is fulfilled, "The person who adheres to God, is one spirit" [1 Cor. 6:17]. This adherence, as blessed Dionysius says, happens especially through ecstatic love. Again, the same mystical theology is called wisdom in terms of its location among the gifts [of the Holy Spirit]. . . . The divine Dionysius calls it irrational and insane wisdom because it surpasses reason and mind, leaping up into *affectus*, not of any old sort, but a pure love matching the mental understanding and by means of which God is seen by the pure of heart [Matt. 5:8].[88]

So Gerson gives the priority to love, as so many other commentators had, but he is also anxious to maintain a place for mental understanding. In the *Practical Mystical Theology* Gerson returns to the point: "Mystical theology has the property of being located in affectivity, while all other forms of knowledge are found in intellect."[89]

The writings of Gallus, Hugh of Balma, and Gerson (as well as Bonaventure), all seen as interpreters of Dionysius, were important in the second stage of Cusa's engagement in debates about mystical theology, a controversy that stretched from about 1450 to the early 1460s.[90] While these disputes are today accessible to us only in the records of learned contributors, the flurry of letters and treatises points to a broad interest in issues relating to mysticism among the monastic communities of southern German lands, both Benedictine and Carthusian. The letters that Cusa exchanged with the abbot and prior of the Benedictine monastery at Tegernsee in Bavaria show that the whole community was involved. His treatise *On the Vision of God* is further proof that this was more than a battle of the books. The debate centered on the respective roles of love and knowledge in attaining mystical theology, but many other issues were implied—the nature of contemplation and its relation to mystical theology, the proper interpretation of the Dionysian corpus, and the meaning of seeing God, especially the face-to-face vision mentioned in some biblical texts. Cusa gave his own answers to these questions, but other writers were involved, both in agreement and disagreement with his views.

The ancient Benedictine monastery of Tegernsee, fallen on hard days from the thirteenth century on, had undergone a vigorous reform under the influence of the famous abbey of Melk, beginning in 1426 with the appointment of Kaspar Ayndorffer as abbot.[91] Prior John Keck (1400–1450), who had attended the Council of Basel, was interested in mystical literature and may have been responsible for bringing different texts on mysticism into the community.[92] In any case, when Cusa visited Tegernsee during his great legation (June 22–27, 1452), he found a monastic community open to his ideas. Indeed, the new prior, Bernard of Waging (ca. 1400–1472), had read *On Learned Ignorance* and in 1451 had even written a brief work entitled *The Praise of Learned Ignorance*.[93] Between 1452 and 1458 Cusa remained in close contact with the Tegernsee community, exchanging many letters and at one time even expressing the hope that he could retire there to devote his last days to the contemplative life.[94] He was also called upon by the monks of Tegernsee to answer their questions about how to understand and practice mystical theology. Sometime in the summer of 1452 Abbot Ayndorffer wrote to Cusa, asking "whether without intellectual knowledge, or even any prior or accompanying thinking, a devout soul can attain God by *affectus* alone, or through the highest point of mind that they call *synderesis* and to be immediately moved or carried up into him."[95]

This letter shows the kinds of questions under discussion in the Tegernsee community. It also demonstrates that monks in several abbeys had been reading Cusa's *On Learned Ignorance* and had questioned how its views conformed to their own understanding of mystical theology. Cusa's foremost opponent was a Carthusian, another strong conciliarist, Vincent of Aggsbach (ca. 1389–1464), who had at one time been prior of his community.[96] Vincent had studied Hugh of Balma and on this basis reacted vigorously against not only Cusa's views, but also those of Gerson. He was friendly with John Schlitpacher (1403–1482; also known as John of Weilheim), a Benedictine reformer of Melk.[97] Many of Vincent's attacks on Gerson and Cusa were addressed to Schlitpacher, who shared at least some of his views, although Schlitpacher also seems to have served as a kind of middleman. On the other side, the prolific Bernard of Waging and the Tegernsee community found an ally in Marquard Sprenger (ca. 1395–1474), a secular priest and master of theology resident in Munich.[98] The conflict produced a mass of polemical writings, not all of which have been adequately studied or even edited. Nicholas of Cusa's role is what is of particular concern here.

Cusa's most direct contribution came in the form of two letters to Ayndorffer and the monks at Tegernsee. The first of these, written on September 22, 1452, gives a brief reply to the issue raised by Ayndorffer, noting that the power of loving (*affectus*) can only be moved by love of the good and that this demands some knowledge of the good. "In every kind of love by which one is carried into God," he says, "a form of knowledge [*cognicio*] is present, although it is ignorant of the essence that it loves. It is therefore a coincidence of knowing and ignorance, or learned ignorance." Being moved to love the infinite Good that is God is possible only through the faith given by Christ, which proves itself through observance of the commandments. This saving knowledge explains how even the simple but fervent believer can be rapt up to God as Paul was. Cusa expresses caution, however, noting: "But many are deceived in rapture by clinging to images and thinking a fanciful vision is true. But truth is the object of the intellect and is seen only in an invisible way, an issue that for now needs much more discussion, and perhaps it can never be fully explained."[99]

On June 12, 1453, Vincent of Aggsbach sent a letter-treatise to his friend John Schlitpacher in which he attacked Gerson's understanding of Dionysius, particularly his interpretation of the command Dionysius gave to Timothy, *ignote consurge*, that is, "rise up in an unknowing way" (MT 1:997B).[100] The Tegernsee monks apparently had quick access to this work and once again turned to Cusa for his opinion. Vincent was a literalist and something of a fundamentalist when it came to mystical theology. For him, Paul was the first mystic and he had handed on his teaching to his pupil Dionysius, so that mystical theology was what Denys said it was. The text of the MT, of course, was difficult, so Vincent consulted various translations and the best commentators, among whom he had once included Gerson, but now, on the basis of the interpretations of Gallus, Grosseteste, and Hugh of Balma (as practioner as well as theorist), he saw how mistaken, even self-contradictory, Gerson was, because he had fudged on the essential point, namely, "the main author of this art [i.e., Dionysius] says plainly and openly that the willing person rises up in an unknown fashion and ought to rise up without knowing, that is, without any accompanying form of knowledge [*cogitacione concomitante*]."[101] Interpreters who try to find both intellective and affective aspects to mystical theology are missing the boat. Without a firm foundation in Dionysius (i.e., in Gallus's version of Dionysius), each such investigator, such as Gerson and Cusa, will make up his own mystical theology and schism and chaos will result.

Vincent's view of mystical theology, narrow as it is, reveals important points about the situation of mysticism in the late Middle Ages. First of all, the Carthusian insists that mystical theology has nothing to do with scholastic theology, the latter being a purely academic practice, while mystical theology "is a certain kind or act of devotion, or a special mode of a mental reaching out into God."[102] Thus, the gap between school theology and mystical theology that had become more and more evident after the condemnation of Eckhart, despite the efforts of men like Gerson and Cusa to close it, was self-evident to the Carthusian. Second, Vincent also wishes to distinguish between the traditional monastic term *contemplatio* and *theologia mystica* in the proper sense, here following Hugh of Balma.[103] Vincent admits that older authors, such as Richard of St. Victor, seem to have used the terms interchangeably, so that contemplation is mystical theology in a broad sense, but the differences are greater than the similarities, he insists. The first of the differences he notes marks a significant divide between the Carthusian and Cusa, helping us to understand why seeing God was such a central theme for the cardinal. For Vincent, mystical theology cannot involve any seeing by definition—"Contemplation takes its name from contemplating or seeing, but mystical theology is named from the act of hiding. Certainly there is a great difference between vision and hiding."[104] Cusa did not think so. For Vincent, contemplation involves both love and intellect, indeed all the soul's powers; mystical theology, on the other hand, "exists only in the *affectus*" (i.e., in a reception, or being drawn by God).[105] This is why it can be received by the unlearned, the simple, even women (!), while contemplation belongs to the learned. The two cannot exist at one and the same time in one person, and, Vincent concludes, if mystical theology were to be apprehended, defended, or expressed by human reason, it would lose its very name.

Vincent of Aggsbach wrote six more polemical treatises against his opponents, especially Gerson, Cusa, and Marquard Sprenger, whom he saw as forming a single Cerberus-like monster of mystical error—the beast Gerchumar![106] His letter to John Schlitpacher of December 19, 1454, shows that he had kept up with Cusa's contributions, since he denounced the cardinal's *De visione dei* with its use of an image (*eycona*) to help attain mystical theology as an idol that might be useful for the illuminative way, but not for the unitive.[107]

Nicholas of Cusa mentioned Vincent's attack on Gerson at the beginning of his response to the Tegernsee monks about the meaning of Dionysius's "ascend in an unknown manner." This letter of September 14, 1453, is a succinct statement of his view of mystical theology, as well as a classic presentation of the alternative to Vincent of Aggsbach's affective Dionysian mystical theology. Cusa subtly undercuts Vincent's argument by resting his case on the Greek text of the Dionysian corpus and the new translation of his friend Ambrose Traversari, not on the commentarial tradition. More significantly, he shifts attention away from the secondary question of love and knowledge to the primary issue of what it means to see God and be united to him—"Dionysius intends nothing more than to show Timothy how the speculation that concerns the rational ascent of our spirit to union with God and that vision which is without veil will not be completed as long as it understands whatever it judges to be God."[108] In other words, the mind needs to recognize its own limitations when it comes to God; it must enter into the darkness and cloud of the intellect, not of some other power, in order to find God.

Cusa now takes a further step, but one in line with the Dionysian text, noting that the cloud of which Dionysius speaks is more than just making denials about God. In the MT, "where he wishes to show mystical and secret theology in an accessible way," Dionysius goes beyond the opposed categories of the positive and negative approaches into the coincident theology that surpasses the philosophical principle of noncontradiction (see the passage cited above on p. 444). After once again criticizing Vincent's reading of Denys' *ignote consurge*, Cusa ends this important letter with two points that announce his forthcoming treatise, *On the Vision of God*. The first was already adumbrated in the DDI, that is, the role of infinity. "It seems to me," he says, "that the whole of mystical theology is to enter Absolute Infinity itself, for infinity expresses the coincidence of contradictories, that is, the end without end, and no one can see God mystically save in the cloud of coincidence which is infinity."[109] Finally, he notes how he has been using a pictorial image of the all-seeing Christ as an "experimental practice" (*praxis experimentalis*) for leading to mystical theology. Thus, the stage was set for Cusa's major contribution to mystical theology.

The controversy over seeing God, mystical theology, love and knowledge, and related issues did not end with Cusa's treatise. This is not the place to follow the war of pamphlets and the understandings and misunderstandings involved in this debate on mysticism. For our purposes it is worth noting how several of the subsequent letters between Cusa and Ayndorffer and Bernard of Waging cast light on how *On the Vision of God* was read. Writing to the cardinal in the early months of 1454, Ayndorffer thanked him for this book, which was designed to help "loving minds to be always borne upwards by enflamed acts of love" (*mentes amorosas affectibus flammigeris iugiter evehere sursum*), waxing eloquent on the paradoxes of Cusa's notion of seeing God: "But what a goal it is, namely to see God and to inhere in him in joyful fashion by means of the love that gives fruition! O vision, O fruition, that is the more the less it is, that is the nearer the further away it is, that is more present the more absent it is, that is the clearer the more obscure it is!"[110] Responding to Ayndorffer on February 12, Cusa introduced the notion of the hunt for God that he was later to expand in the treatise *On the Hunt for Wisdom*, emphasizing that the love that drives the pursuit strives to go beyond the coincidence of opposities. "Perfect charity," he says, "is above the coincidence of contradictories of what contains and what is contained. Therefore, the divine hunt is on the heights above this coincidence of opposites, to which nevertheless none can reach. I have written a few things about it to try to raise myself above myself."[111] Bernard of Waging, writing to Cusa shortly after, spoke of this driving force as an *amor misticus*, which still has to include "some kind of knowledge of God" (*Dei qualicumque cognicione*).[112] Finally, we can note Cusa's letter to Bernard on March 18, in which he declares how the "taste of divine sweetness" is ambiguous to many because they do not recognize the necessity for both knowing and loving in the path to the vision of God. The focus is once again on seeing God as revealed by Christ:

> Christ, who revealed to us that happiness resides in the vision of God [Matt. 5:8], also revealed to us that just as we desire to see everything that comes to us from any of the senses (as if seeing is the ultimate perfection of the senses in beings with sensation), so too seeing God enfolds in itself every mode of attaining God as their ultimate perfection. Seeing is like their form and perfection.[113]

Cusa's Mysticism of Seeing God

In order to get a better grasp of why Nicholas of Cusa put seeing God at the center of his thought on mystical theology, especially as laid out in his treatise *On the Vision of God*, once again it will be helpful to step back into Christian tradition—far back, since the issue of what it means to see God begins in the Bible.[114]

In Exodus 33:20 God tells Moses, "You cannot see my face, for no one will see my face and live." But in Genesis 32:30 Jacob names the place where he wrestled with a divine adversary "Phanuel," claiming "I have seen God face-to-face and my soul has been saved" (cf. Exod. 24:10; Num. 12:8). Similarly, after his vision of "the Lord sitting upon a high and lofty throne" in the Temple, Isaiah announces, "with my own eyes I have seen the King, the Lord of hosts" (Isa. 6:5); but in Deutero-Isaiah 45:15 we find the proclamation: "Truly, you are a hidden God, the Savior God of Israel."[115] Equally contradictory texts about whether or not God can be seen in this life are found in the New Testament. Some passages announce that God will be seen by the justified, such as the beatitude "Blessed are the pure of heart for they shall see God" (Matt. 5:8; see also Heb. 12:14). 1 Timothy 6:16, however, speaks of God "dwelling in unattainable light" as he whom "no one sees or can see." The Prologue to John's Gospel announces, "No one has ever seen God; the Only-Begotten Son, who is in the Father's bosom, has revealed him" (John 1:18; see John 6:46, 1 John 4:12, and Matt. 11:27). The Johannine emphasis on the Son as the only one who sees the Father and can therefore reveal him is evident also in the passage where Philip asks Jesus, "Show us the Father," and Jesus responds, "Who sees me, sees the Father. How can you say, 'Show us the Father'?" (John 14:8–11). Finally, texts in both the Pauline and Johannine letters stress the eschatological character of the vision of God. 1 Corinthians 13:12 is based on a contrast: "We see now mysteriously through a mirror, but then face-to-face; now I know in part; then I will know as I am known" (see 2 Cor. 3:18). 1 John 3:2 also stresses the eschatological nature of the vision of God, adding an important reference to filiation: "Beloved, now we are God's sons and it has not yet been revealed what we shall be; but we know that when he has appeared, we will be like him, because we will see him as he is."

Faced with these conflicting texts, one might expect the history of Christian thought to show a Hamlet-like hesitation—"To see or not to see, that is the question." On the contrary, there has been well-nigh universal agreement that the vision of God in heaven, however understood, is the goal of human life. A broad stream of Christian thought and practice, especially among the mystics, also held that some kind of seeing of God is possible in this life as preparation for and foretaste of what is to come. Precisely why early Christians found the notion of seeing God usually unproblematic may reflect their cultural location in a society that privileged the visual in so many ways. This is certainly the case with regard to Platonic philosophical spirituality, which placed seeing God (*theôria theou*) as the ultimate human fulfillment.[116]

The brief autobiographical fragment that the converted philosopher, Justin, narrates at the beginning of his *Dialogue with Trypho* (ca. 160) gives us a window on this encounter. Justin speaks of his restless intellectual journey through the schools of Stoics, Peripatetics, and Pythagoreans, until he finally begins to make progress in "the contemplation of ideas" under the guidance of the Platonists. "I expected quite soon," he says, "to look upon God, for this is the goal of Plato's philosophy."[117] But an old sage convinced him that while the Platonists were right about the goal, they could not really show him the way to that end. The mind (*nous*) begotten by God can, indeed, come to see its Unbegotten Creator, but only as a gift given by the Holy Spirit in reward for a virtuous life, not as an innate capacity of its nature.[118]

It would be impossible to give a brief treatment of the role of *visio Dei* in Christian mysticism. Even classic books like those of K. E. Kirk and Vladimir Lossky,[119] or the recent work of Christian Trottmann on scholastic disputes on the *visio beatifica*,[120] only provide a part of the story. Nevertheless, the problem of seeing God is central to Christian mysticism, and it also provides us with a vantage point to consider Nicholas of Cusa's contribution to the mystical tradition. The cardinal's involvement in the debate on the relation of love and knowledge in the path to union with God helped him realize that an adequate solution to the issue demanded a broader perspective, one based on an investigation of what it means to see God. The result was his central mystical text, the *De visione Dei*, or *De Icona*, composed in late 1453.[121] Many Christian thinkers, especially the scholastic theologians, had discussed *visio Dei*, but Cusa had few predecessors in composing a distinct treatise on the problem of seeing God in this life.[122] In that sense his *De visione* was a novel work, however much it was influenced by the rich range of sources typical of his wide reading.[123] Of course, Cusa did not discover the importance of seeing God in the 1450s.[124] Major treatments can be found in two treatises of 1445, the *De quaerendo Deo* and the *De filiatione Dei*, as well as in later texts, such the *De beryllo* and the *De apice theoriae*. If Cusa's decision to compose a treatise on the topic of seeing God was unusual, the centrality of the theme of *visio Dei* in his writings and in the mystical tradition at large was not.

Clement of Alexandria is a good starting point for considering the problems involved in seeing and not-seeing God, because it is with the Alexandrian catechist of the late second century that we get the first real encounter between Platonic philosophical mysticism and Christian spiritual teaching. Clement introduced three of the essential themes of Christian mysticism that helped form the basis for Cusa's discussion almost thirteen centuries later: (1) the attempt to understand the scriptural vision of God in terms of Platonic contemplation; (2) the exploration of the relation between seeing God and divinization; and (3) the use of categories taken from Hellenistic philosophy to express biblical teaching about God's invisibility and unknowability.[125] Clement's thought raised, for the first time in Christian theology, the fundamental *aporia* with which Cusa wrestled: How can the utterly invisible God become visible in a divinizing vision that is the goal of Christian faith?

Clement and his contemporaries Theophilus and Irenaeus provide evidence for a concerted effort on the part of the leaders of nascent Orthodox Christianity to defend the goal of seeing God for their own understanding of belief in Jesus against the varieties of Gnostic Christianity.[126] In the course of his writings Clement uses the term *theôria* some eighty-five times, linking it with the true *gnôsis* (saving knowledge) that he sought to rescue from Valentinian understandings of the word. For him, biblical texts on the eschatological vision of God (e.g., Matt. 5:8, 1 Cor. 12:13) demonstrate that *theôria* is the fruit and goal of true *gnôsis*. In book 7 of his *Stromateis*, for example, he says that gnostic souls "keep always moving to higher and higher regions, until they no longer greet the divine vision in or by means of mirrors [1 Cor. 12:13], but with loving hearts feast forever on the uncloying, never-ending sight. . . . This is the apprehending vision of the pure of heart [Matt. 5:8]."[127] While the final goal of such *theôria* is in heaven, it begins in this life and progresses through "mystic stages" (*Strom.* 7.10.57) that involve both contemplation and action.[128] Their aim is divinization (Clement introduced the verb *theopoiein* into Christianity). In his *Protrepticus* we find him using the famous formula, which first occurs in his contemporary Irenaeus: ". . . the Logos of God became man so that you may learn from man how man may become God."[129] Clement, however, never explicitly analyzed the problematics of just how the invisible God comes to be seen. A closer analogue to how Cusa confronted the aporia of seeing what cannot be seen can be found in Neoplatonic mystics, both those directly utilized by the cardinal and others who had a role in providing insights that were passed on to him through tradition, both pagan and Christian.

Cusa did not have direct contact with the texts of Plotinus; but, as Werner Beierwaltes has shown, there are fascinating analogies between the two thinkers, especially when they discuss the intellectual vision of the First Principle.[130] A transcendent First cannot be seen, but if that First is also immanent in all things, it must somehow be present in the very act of seeing. Plotinus explored this issue in a number of texts that analyzed how *nous*, or Pure Intellect, can be said to see the invisible One, or Good. In *Ennead* V.5.7–10, for example, Plotinus begins from an analysis of physical seeing, moving upward through an exploration of how *nous* sees objects, to finally explore the mysterious inner light that grounds vision both in us and in *nous* insofar as it is directed toward the First Principle.[131] A second passage, found in *Enneads* VI.7.35–36, discusses how, when soul becomes one with *nous* and sees "the god, at once it lets everything go." This act of "true contemplation" (*tês ontôs theas*) fuses the see-er and the seen. "By the continuity of his contemplation," Plotinus says, "he no longer sees a sight, but mingles his seeing with what he contemplates, so that what was seen before has now become sight in him, and he forgets all other objects of contemplation."[132]

Late antique Christian authors also took up the issue of how we can be said to see God, both in this life and in the next. Augustine devoted much attention to the scriptural texts about seeing and not-seeing God,[133] as well as to the underlying theoretical issues.[134] His insistence that the intellectual vision of God is the essence of beatitude carried great weight in the later Latin theological tradition. Cusa knew and cited many of Augustine's treatments.[135] Nevertheless, the cardinal's solution to the problem of how we come to see the invisible God in this life was based on a version of Neoplatonic dialectical thinking not found in Augustine.

Cusa's major predecessors in this form of dialectical Neoplatonism were Dionysius, John Scottus Eriugena, and Meister Eckhart. Dionysius's MT is a key text for Cusa, especially because of the way in which it emphasized the absolute invisibility of God.[136] Moses, the archetypal mystic, cannot contemplate the God who cannot be seen, but only the place where he dwells (MT 1: 1000D). He must break free of all that can be perceived by the eyes of the body and of the mind, "away from what sees and is seen, and plunge into the truly mysterious darkness of unknowing" in order to be "supremely united to the Wholly Unknown by an inactivity of all knowing . . ." (1001A). This removal of all knowing and all seeing, however, leads to a paradoxical higher vision that Dionysius describes as seeing "above being that darkness concealed from all the light among beings" (MT 2: 1025B).[137] Dionysius, however, does not engage in any extended analysis of this "not-seeing seeing," nor does he explicitly relate it to the other fundamental mysteries of Christian faith, as Cusa will.

The influence of Eriugena on the thought of Cusa has become evident in recent scholarship.[138] The Irishman's thought displays a fundamental affinity with Cusa's view of *visio Dei* in the way in which it identifies God's seeing with his creative action: "God's seeing is the creation of the entire universe, for it is not one thing for him to see and another to make, but his seeing is his will and his will is his working."[139] In exegeting John 1:18, Eriugena, like Dionysius, presents a strong case for God's absolute invisibility.[140] Citing both Dionysius and Augustine he concludes: "If anyone says he has seen him, namely God, he has not seen him, but rather something made by him. For he is altogether invisible, 'who is better known by not-knowing,' and 'ignorance of whom is true wisdom.'"[141] What we do not find in Eriugena, though, is a treatment of the way in which human seeing both reveals and conceals the divine *visio absoluta*. This aspect of the Neoplatonic dialectics of vision, however, was available to Cusa in Meister Eckhart.

Eckhart's emphasis on the birth of the Word in the soul out of the *grunt*, the fused identity of God and human,[142] is a reworking of the ancient Christian understanding of divinization achieved through filiation—our becoming God by realizing our essential oneness in the Son of God who took on flesh.[143] "Whatever God the Father gave to his Only-Begotten Son in human nature," said Eckhart, "he gave all this to me. I except nothing, neither union, nor sanctity; but he gave the whole to me, just as he did to him."[144] Eckhart's writings contain a number of discussions of the meaning of *visio dei*, both here and in the world to come.[145] Eckhart, like Dionysius and Eriugena, held that in reality God cannot be seen, or, if he is said to be seen, he must be seen as Absolute Nothingness. His Pr. 71, interpreting Acts 9:8 ("Saul rose from the ground and opening his eyes saw nothing"), is a good example of this visionary apophasis.[146] Perhaps the most important link between Eckhart and Cusa on *visio dei*, however, concerns the mutuality, even identity, of the gaze between God and human. Eckhart's dialectical view of fused-identity ("God's ground is the soul's ground, and the soul's ground is God's ground") led him to preach that insofar as we can be said to see God, this cannot be other than God seeing himself. He expresses this ocular identity in Pr. 12: "The eye in which I see God is the same eye in which God sees me. My eye and God's eye are one eye and one seeing, one knowing, and one loving."[147] The mutuality of *visio* suggested by Paul's text in 1 Corinthians on face-to-face vision was not exactly a new theme in Christian mysticism, having been used by William of St.-Thierry in the twelfth century.[148] What is new with Eckhart was understanding this as a form of fused identity, that is, there is only one eye and one act of seeing. This was also the view to be advanced by Cusa.

Cusa's DVD has often been analyzed.[149] The treatise is a true classic, so, like Augustine's *Confessions*, the *De visione* resists closure or any final interpretation. Part of the richness of the work rests in its mystagogical character. Throughout his writings Cusa loved to employ "similitudes"—mathematical, geometrical, mechanical examples—to illustrate his teaching; but the *De visione* is different in the way in which it integrates not only similitudes, but also exercises of seeing, hearing, and speaking into a praxis designed to lead his monastic audience, by experience (*experimentaliter*), into what he calls "ready access to mystical theology" (*facilitas mysticae theologiae*). Just how far each practitioner of his method will be able to advance in this *facilitas* is not up to any outsider to judge, as the cardinal emphasizes in chapter 17 with his remarks on his own practice:

Trusting in your infinite goodness, I tried to undergo a rapture so that I might
see you who are invisible and the unrevealable vision revealed. How far I got,
you know, not I. And your grace, by which you assure me that you are incomprehensible, is sufficient for me [2 Cor. 12:9]; and by it you raise up a firm
hope that under your guidance I may come to ultimate delight in you.[150]

In the preface, Cusa begins his mystical handbook by creating a para-
liturgy around the *eicona*, the image of the omnivoyant face of Christ, probably of the Veronica, or "Suffering Christ" type, he sent to the Tegernsee
monks.[151] Michel de Certeau has provided a stimulating analysis of the
dynamics of the gaze set forth by Cusa in the *praxis devotionis* described in
the preface.[152] As in the normal monastic liturgy, this ritual commences
with a procession by the community.[153] Each monk first stands observing
the icon's a-temporal gaze seemingly directed to him alone. Then each
moves from his original location to the opposite side, in amazement at the
"change of the unchangeable gaze" that introduces temporality and muta-
bility into the experience. The crucial part of the experiment, however, is
the transition from the visual realm to the audible, the speaking and hearing that form the believing community—that is, faith is what enables the
aspirant to begin to move beyond a particular perspective toward a more
universal viewpoint. The simultaneous omnivoyance, or infinity, of Christ's
gaze begins to be revealed only when each brother asks the other as they
meet coming from opposite directions whether the icon's gaze has moved
simultaneously with him too. As de Certeau notes, willingness to share
wonder and to *believe* one's brother expressed in the implied question, "You
too?" is at the root of Cusa's mystagogical exercise.[154] As the cardinal puts
it, echoing Augustine's *fides quaerens intellectum*, "He will believe him, and
unless he believed, he would not grasp that it is possible."[155] The exercise
also implies another key feature of Cusa's mystagogy—recognizing the difference between seeing and illusion. Each brother sees the icon looking at
him, but the image has no real eyes. It does not look; we look at it and
imagine it is looking at us. The reverse is true, however, with regard to
God's seeing. We think that it is we who actually see, but Cusa will show
how our seeing is really God's seeing in us.[156]

It is only on the basis of such asking, hearing, and believing that we, i.e.,
each member of the community of faith, begin to grasp with amazement
(not rational understanding) the experience of being seen by an infinite and
omnipresent gaze. Since in God there is no difference between seeing and
speaking ("I realize, O Lord, that your gaze speaks, for your speaking is the
same as your seeing," as chapter 10 puts it),[157] we can also understand that
what we have learned about God's seeing holds true for God's speaking to
us. This realization is effected through a second experiment, one of medita-

tive prayer on the meaning of the liturgical praxis introduced in the preface. During the course of this extended *oratio/meditatio* that comprises the remainder of the treatise, Cusa introduces other *similitudines* to help advance his argument (e.g., clock and mirror), and also encourages other verbal practices (e.g., praying the Our Father in chapter 8), but he continues to return to the master symbol of the *eicona*.[158]

The first three chapters of the DVD form an introduction to the mystagogy, laying down the premises for what follows. They are meant to be read and studied, whereas the remainder of the work is also an exercise to be put into practice. This is evident from the way in which in these first three chapters Cusa speaks in his own voice as teacher, but beginning in chapter 4, he asks the *frater contemplator* to gaze once again upon the *eicona dei* so that "a contemplation (*speculatio*) will arise in you, and you will be stirred up and speak."[159] With few exceptions, the rest of the treatise is in the form of a prayer, not in Cusa's own voice but in the voice of the brother speaking for Cusa (though Cusa is actually speaking for the brother). Thus, the *ego* of the author and the *tu* of the one addressed are here fused through their shared calling out to the divine *tu* in uplifting prayer. The shifting perspectives of the *De visione* function on many levels, for, as H. Lawrence Bond has noted, the text is both an iconography, or explanation of the meaning of the image, and "an icon, picturing by its own form, with words or other symbols, so as to signify, convey, and transpose the reader from one state of awareness or experience to another."[160]

The originality of Cusa's verbal-audial transpositions becomes evident from a comparison with a work that Cusa knew well. In the *Confessions* Augustine had created a new kind of mystical text in which he made his confession, that is, gave his testimony, to God in his own voice, while God responded to him in the words of scripture that the bishop himself quoted so liberally throughout the book (about a third of the total text). Although Cusa uses scriptural citations fairly often, he does not employ the Bible as the "other voice" as Augustine did. Is God then silent in the *De visione*? Yes, in the sense that the appeal to silence is an essential part of Cusa's message;[161] but, from another perspective, God's speaking is as omnipresent as his gaze—and just as immanent. If seeing God is the same as being seen by him (and vice-versa), and God's seeing is his speaking, then the outpoured prayer of the *contemplator* speaking for and with Cusa is itself God's hidden Word continuously breaking forth in human voice. Thus, the content of Cusa's message of what it means to see God—a seeing that is being-seen and a speaking that is hearing oneself being-spoken—is already inscribed in the dynamics of the text's voices.[162]

The remainder of the DVD falls into three sections. In section 1 (chapters 4–16) there is an extended analysis of *visio Dei*, understood as both God's own seeing (subjective genitive) and our vision of him (objective genitive). Central to this part are the themes of *visio facialis*, the *murus paradisi* (or *murus coincidentiae*), and God as *infinitas absoluta*. The essential conclusion, as Bond puts it, is that "Our seeing is a being seen. God is never the object of our sight; God is the eternal subject of seeing."[163] The brief section 2 (chapters 17–18) shows why a proper understanding of seeing God reveals God as a loving Trinity. Finally, section 3 (chapters 19–25) demonstrates that our only access to vision of the *unitrinus deus* is through the filiation, or sonship, bestowed on us by the union of the divine and human natures in Jesus.[164] A consideration of key elements in light of the trajectory of thought sketched above will help show how Cusa was able to provide, perhaps for the first time in the history of Christian mysticism, an account that integrated divine invisibility, the face-to-face vision promised in scripture, and divinization understood as filiation.

As the reader proceeds through the pyrotechnics of Cusa's experiments with thought and language in the first section, it is often difficult not to lose the way—to become mystified about how one chapter relates to another.[165] The structure of the argument is not linear but prismatic, in the sense that different facets of the problematics of seeing the unseeable are held up to our mental gaze in such varied ways that their very profusion helps deepen the amazement that is essential to the mystagogic exercise. In order to prevent dazzlement from becoming mere confusion, however, it is useful to look at this first section in the light of its conclusion in chapter 16 before we proceed through it in order. In this conclusion to section 1 Cusa summarizes his dialectics of vision by affirming that the more we comprehend that God is incomprehensible, the more we attain the goal of our own infinite desire (16.69). The *contemplator* who recognizes this can thus say, "I see you, O Lord my God, in a kind of mental rapture, because if sight is not satisfied with seeing, nor the hearing with hearing, then how much less the intellect by understanding."[166] The mental rapture that Cusa speaks of here is not a loss of consciousness in the manner of ecstatic mystics, or even a new insight into *a* truth, but, to adopt the language of Bernard Lonergan,[167] a kind of transcendental reverse insight—that is, a sudden awareness by which we understand that our drive toward total understanding can only be understood as the affirmation of the existence of an *incomprehensible* Truth that is both within us as infinite desire and outside us on the other side of what Cusa calls "the wall of paradise."

The operative identity that fuses our infinite desire with God's Absolute Infinity described in this passage had been explored by Cusa since the early pages of the treatise in terms of his analysis of vision. In Chapter 5, for example, he says, "In seeing me, you who are the hidden God [Isa. 45:15] give yourself to be seen by me. . . . To see you is not different from your seeing the one who sees you."[168] Recognizing that seeing God is really participating in God seeing himself and all things in one single act of vision (what the *De li non aliud* was to call the *visionum visio*, the "vision of visions") is at the heart of Cusa's message.[169] But our desire to see God and to love God is nothing more nor less, as chapter 7 tells us, than the actualization of the freedom God's creative gaze bestows on each of us as *contemplator*: "When I thus rest in the silence of contemplation, you, O Lord, respond in the depths of my heart and say, 'You be yours and I too will be yours.' . . . This rests in my power, not in yours, O Lord. . . ."[170] Lest some unwary Augustinian literalist conclude that this smacks of Pelagianism, Cusa adds the plea, "But how will I be mine, if you do not teach me, Lord?"[171] From the perspective of the cardinal's dialectical Neoplatonism, God's transcendent otherness is identical with his absolute immanence, and the more transcendent he is, the more immanent he is. The intellect, as Cusa concludes in chapter 16, is not satisfied by understanding some "thing," because any act of understanding a thing by its nature is finite, not infinite. He also insists that intellect cannot be satisfied by something intelligible of which it is totally ignorant. Rather, "only the intelligible which it knows to be so intelligible that it can never be fully understood can satisfy the intellect."[172] The intellect embraces the ignorance that comes from excess, not deficiency. Cusa closes his summary with an appeal to a dialectical understanding of hunger and satiation based on Eckhart. Our never-ending desire for God is like a hunger that can only be satisfied by a meal, "which, although continually eaten, can never be fully consumed, because being infinite, it is not diminished by being eaten."[173]

The multiple facets of Nicholas of Cusa's argument in chapters 4–16 make ample use of the coincident theology that Cusa had first developed in his *De docta ignorantia*.[174] The DVD, however, extends this into the further dimension that Cusa, following Dionysius, calls mystical theology.[175] If coincident theology expresses the space where the cataphatic and apophatic approaches to God fuse into the paradoxical unity of the coincidence of opposites, then mystical theology, as found on the other side of the wall of paradise, represents a kind of hyperspace, a dimension beyond any realm of language. Mystical theology is like a black hole into which even coincidences of opposites vanish in order to be transformed in ways that cannot be conceptualized, though they can be said to be "seen" in a not-seeing seeing.

The relation between coincident theology as developed in the DDI and the mystical theology set forth in the DVD emerges more clearly as one studies the three sections of the cardinal's mystical treatise in greater detail. On the basis of the three premises put forth in the introductory chapters,[176] Cusa begins the long first section (chaps. 4–16) on the contemplation of *visio facialis dei* with two chapters in which the prayer of the *frater contemplator* explores the relation between the divine gaze and the other affirmations made about God in positive theology. God's seeing, Cusa argues, is the same as his love, his existence, his maximum goodness, indeed, his absolute maximality itself (*absoluta maximitas*) (4.10–12). As the exercise of meditating on the mutuality of the gaze extends itself to the affirmation of identity of see-er and seen in chapter 5, the contemplative also experiences the gaze as the biblical "tasting and seeking of God," as well as God's having mercy on and working in all things from within.

These considerations set up the investigation of the *facies Dei* that commences in chapters 6 and 7.[177] Here Cusa's coincident theology makes an explicit appearance, but in the service of a negative theology based on scripture and thematized by Dionysius. "Your gaze, Lord, is your face," says Cusa, transferring the eschatological vision of the face of God promised in 1 Corinthians 13:12 into the face that gazes upon each of us here and now. God is the *facies facierum*, the exemplar of all faces, or what we might call all modes of attention. Therefore, every face that looks toward the divine face sees itself, that is, it sees its own transcendent truth in the divine exemplar (6.18–20). This form of seeing is one that cannot be conceived by the mind (i.e., it has no human *conceptus*); it can only be experienced in darkness and unknowing, since it takes place "under a veil and in a mystery," in "a secret and hidden silence" (6.21). The fruit of this *visio facialis*, as explained in chapter 7, is found through realizing our freedom to love God in learned ignorance and the cloud of unknowing (7.23–26).

After this exploration, Cusa returns to the positive pole of his theology, introducing a new exercise (praying the Our Father), as well as a new series of visual similitudes—the book, the eye, the mirror, and the infinite ocular sphere—to further his exploration (8.29–30). Positive theology and coincident theology, however, once again are put in question by the limit situations expressed in negative theology. This is evident from how chapter 9 begins, for the first time, to explore two new ways of using limits to go beyond them—the language of *infinitas*, and the image of the *murus paradisi*.[178] All contracted forms of existence are found in God, the Absolute Form and "essence of essences," in a simple and infinite way (9.33–34). Thus motion and rest and all opposites are found in "a face absolute from

these conditions, because it exists above all standing and motion, in sim-
plest and most Absolute Infinity" (9.35). This is the coincidence of opposites,
the cloud above reason, where "impossibility coincides with necessity."
Cusa calls it the wall of paradise whose gate is guarded by reason, just as
sinful Adam and Eve were excluded from paradise by the angel with the
fiery sword (Gen. 3:24). "It is on the other side of the coincidence of contradictories," he says, "that You will be able to be seen, and nowhere on this
side" (9.36–37).[179] God both embraces the coincidence of opposites and also
goes beyond it.[180]

The cardinal continues the exploration of the *murus paradisi* in chapter 10
with a series of comments on the coincidences of seeing and being seen,
hearing and being heard, earlier and later, now and then, and the like, that
are found at the entrance of paradise. "But you, my God, who are Absolute
Eternity, exist and speak beyond the now and then."[181] In chapter 11 he
explores many different aspects of the dialectic of enfolding (*complicatio*)
and unfolding (*explicatio*), while chapter 12 examines the Eriugenean paradox of how God both creates and is created. This brings him once again to
the seemingly insurmountable barrier he now calls the *murus absurditatis*
(12.49), and to the first discussion of how it may be possible to "leap over
(*transilire*) that wall of invisible vision where you are to be found" (12.47).
Here the cardinal advances a three-stage mystical journey. As long as we
think of the Creator as creating, we are at the first stage, that is, our side of
the wall of paradise, the world of reason and distinction. When we come to
see the coincidence of opposites, the identity of enfolding and unfolding in
the paradox of "Creatable Creator" (*creatorem creabilem*), we have arrived at
the wall itself. "But when I see you as Absolute Infinity to whom neither the
name of Creating Creator nor Creatable Creator applies, then I begin to
gaze at you in an unveiled way and to enter into the garden of delights."[182]
This is the gaze of mystical theology, begun in this life but not to reach its
fulfillment until the permanent possession of paradise.[183] In his late treatise
De possest, as we have seen, Cusa describes such forms of speculation as
leading into "mystical vision where there is an end of the ascent of every
cognitive power and the beginning of the revelation of the unknown
God."[184]

The notion of Absolute Infinity introduced here, one which Cusa analyzes in detail in chapter 13, has rightly been seen as central to his entire
treatise.[185] The first part of this chapter is a dialectical argument similar to
what Meister Eckhart set forth in his exploration of divine Oneness as distinct indistinction.[186] Cusa's wall is the limit of all conceptual naming, but
infinitas is not really a name at all—it is the recognition of a "necessary

impossible." We cannot see, in the sense of understand, *how* "an end with-out end is an end" (13.53), but we must assert *that* God as infinite essence is the end without end, namely, the necessary end of all things. Such an assertion goes beyond just affirming a coincidence of contradictories, because when we speak of God's absolute infinity we admit a coincidence of contradictories *without contradiction,* that is, "the opposition of opposites without opposition" (13.54).[187] This is true *docta ignorantia,* a seeing that is not seeing.

In the remaining three chapters of the first part of the *De visione* Cusa shows how infinity is the key that unlocks earlier aspects of his argument. It also provides a launching pad for other dialectical terms that he was to explore in his subsequent writings. God enfolds all things without the other-ness that makes one thing different from another in the unfolded realm (chapter 14). Divine infinity is "the absolute and infinite power to be," the *potentia absoluta* that he would later analyze in his *Trialogus de possest* (15.61–62). Chapter 15 returns to the image of God as mirror, something already mentioned in chapters 4, 8, and 12, concluding that as the "living mirror of eternity," God acts in a way opposite to our mirrors that reflect the image of a form—"What one sees in this mirror of eternity is not an image, but what one sees is the truth of which the one who sees is an image."[188] He also reprises the notion of face-to-face vision, once again locating it in our pre-sent existence rather than in heaven. The dialectical mutuality of face-to-face vision means that "according to the changing of my face your face is equally changed and unchanged" (15.65). That is to say, God's face changes insofar as his infinite goodness never abandons the truth of our changeable faces; but as Absolute Goodness God's face can never change.

The introduction of divine goodness and love at this point, further explored in chapter 16, forms a bridge to the treatment of the Trinity and the incarnation in the remaining two sections of the *De visione.* It also serves as a foundation for the cardinal's summary analysis of the relation of love and knowledge, the question debated among German monks in the early 1450s. Much of the discussion found in the first part of the DVD had dealt explicitly with cognitional aspects of mystagogical practice—what does it mean to see God? But, because "Your loving is your seeing" (*Amare tuum est videre tuum* [8.27]), coming to understand better what it means to see God cannot be separated from the love that God has implanted in the human person, a love that drives the soul on its hunt. Thus, the identity of seeing and being seen is not other than the coincidence of loving and being loved, both absolutely, that is, supra-coincidentally, in God, where Love (i.e., the Holy Spirit) enfolds both Filial and Paternal Love, as well as mediately in our face-to-face relation to God. "O Loving Kindness beyond explanation, you offer yourself to someone gazing upon you," says Cusa, "as though you receive being from him, and you conform yourself to him so that he may love you more the more you seem like him."[189] Therefore, if our self-love is a *true* love of self (i.e., love of the Truth of which we are an image), we are really loving God. In chapter 16, as noted above, Cusa concludes this whole discussion by showing that the infinite nature of our love and desire for God is the root of the *docta ignorantia* that brings us to ever-deepening union with God here and in eternity.

The return to the theme of love and desire in chapters 15 and 16 shows why Cusa could not be satisfied with setting forth his case for the proper understanding of how the invisible God comes to be seen in chapters 4–16 alone. For Cusa, such a treatment by itself would be incomplete. The face-to-face vision of the kind he has presented is realizable only by our coming to see the God who is trinitarian love revealed to us in Jesus Christ. In other words, mystical theology is essentially trinitarian and christological. While the concluding chapters of the *De visione* have been somewhat less studied than the earlier ones, they are no less vital to Cusa's mysticism.[190]

Trinity and Christology in Cusa's Mysticism

From the human perspective, knowledge of the Trinity is accessible only through Jesus Christ, God and man. There is no philosophical demonstration of the Trinity, although Christian faith reveals the hints of the Trinity that ancient thinkers had uncovered in their hunt for wisdom. Although Christ's revelation is necessary for our knowledge of this article of faith, the origin of the Word from the Father and of the Holy Spirit from Father and Son has essential priority in the world of existence. Hence, it is not surprising that in the DVD Cusa first considers how seeing God is seeing God as loving Trinity before he turns to consider in closing how such a vision becomes accessible to us through Christ the Mediator.

The two chapters devoted to the Trinity in the *De visione dei* provide an entrance into the cardinal's distinctive trinitarian theology. Cusa's trinitarianism, like much of his thought, has been subject to differing evaluations, not least because of his constant experimentation with analogies for the triune God.[191] John Wenck, as we have seen, put Cusa's teaching about the "the divinity and the Trinity of the Person" at the head of his list of errors. Cusa responded in his *Apologia* that only someone who has attained *docta ignorantia* can recognize that "the coincidence of supreme simplicity and indivisibility and of unity and trinity" and will thus be able to affirm that "when the Father is said to be a person, and the Son another person, and the Holy Spirit a third person, otherness cannot maintain its usual meaning, since this way of speaking is imposed to signify an otherness that is distinct and separate from unity."[192] In God there is no number; he is beyond all modes of being as "distinctly indistinct" (*discretum indiscrete*). Cusa had already expressed this view in *On Learned Ignorance*, when he said, "Join together what seems to be opposite, . . . and you will not have one and three and the reverse, but rather 'one-in-three,' or 'three-in-one' (*unitrinum seu triunum*)—this is the absolute Truth."[193]

Cusa's understanding of what it means to describe God as *unitrinum seu triunum* went through many variations dependent on diverse sources. His fundamental perspective, however, as in much of his theology, goes back to Augustine, though he develops Augustinian themes in his own way. As might be expected, the cardinal made use of the two forms of analogy found in Augustine's *On the Trinity*. In this work Augustine presented introspective analogies for the Trinity based on the soul's nature as the created image of God. In book 8 he argued that in order to see God we must desire him, and in order to desire him we must know him, at least in some fashion. Faith gives us this incipient knowledge, and we know that we love and desire God through the love that we have for our neighbor (8.7.10). In what sense is the love of God displayed in our love of neighbor trinitarian? Augustine presented several analogies for the three Persons based on our experience of love, such as the triad of loving love, loving something that loves, and the love we have for it because it loves.[194] But Augustine apparently was not satisfied with analogies based on love alone. In books 9–14 he went on to explore a series of models that placed love in the wider perspective of the total activity of the mind as *imago Trinitatis*. Since we cannot love unless we know, and we cannot know unless we are spiritual subjects capable of knowing and loving, then our whole inner activity presents an image of the Trinity insofar as mind or memory (*mens/memoria*), that is, intellectual self-presence, gives rise to understanding (*notitia/intelligentia*) through the production of the inner word, and such self-knowledge produces love for truth in the will (*voluntas*). Augustine considered a number of forms of this inner analogy. For example, toward the close of book 9 he says: "There is an image of the Trinity—the mind itself; and its knowledge which is its offspring and the word that comes from it. Love is the third; and these three are one and one substance" (9.12.18).

Augustine's theology, however, also explored other analogies for the triune God. In book 1 of *On Christian Teaching* (396 C.E.) he presented a quasi-mathematical analogy. Discussing the Trinity as the one reality that should be truly loved and enjoyed for its own sake, Augustine reflected on the difference between the attributes common to all three persons and those that are proper to the individual persons. "The same eternity, immutability, majesty, and power are common to the three," he says. "In the Father there is unity, in the Son equality, in the Holy Spirit the agreement of unity and equality. And all three are one because of the Father, equal because of the Son, and connected because of the Holy Spirit."[195] Augustine abandoned the *unitas-aequalitas-conexio* analogy in his later writings, but the Latin tradition, especially in those thinkers open to henology, or the Neoplatonic metaphysics of the One, did not.[196] Transcendental trinitarian mathematical analogies based on Augustine were richly developed in the twelfth century, especially by Thierry of Chartres, a master who taught at Paris and Chartres ca. 1130–50. Nicholas of Cusa was inspired not only by Augustine but also by Thierry. He read at least one of the Chartrian master's commentaries on Boethius, which feature this form of trinitarian theology and praised him (anonymously) as "a man easily the foremost in genius of those I have read."[197] Cusa was especially drawn to Thierry because he had used the Augustinian formula within the context of a negative theology of a Dionysian cast and an understanding of the God–world relation in terms of the model of *complicatio* and *explicatio*, the dialectical understanding of how God enfolds all things in himself in absolute simplicity at the same time as he unfolds all things in their created particularities. Thierry, however, did not draw out the mystical implications of the Augustinian formula. While hints of this can be found in Meister Eckhart, it was Cusa who first realized its potential, especially when used along with the more familiar introspective trinitarian analogies whose mystical dimensions had already been explored by such figures as William of St.-Thierry.

Nicholas of Cusa used a wide variety of triadic formulae, or *rationes* based on faith, to present the mystery of the Trinity.[198] As he said in Sermon XXI, "Today, for those who hold the Trinity through faith, it is not hard after the coming of faith to find *rationes* for the Trinity, as Richard of St. Victor says at the beginning of his *The Trinity*, just as he does there, and as Anselm, Augustine, John of Damascus, and others sought out *rationes*."[199] These *rationes* are not to be thought of as demonstrations, or a-priori proofs, that provide real comprehension of the unknown God, but rather as a-posteriori conjectures, or transcendental reductions, based on faith and designed to lead us back to God. As helpful similitudes, they pertain to this side of the wall of paradise. Among these triadic reasons the Augustinian mathematical formula played a large role. A survey of over fifty trinitarian passages in the cardinal's treatises reveals him explicitly using *unitas-*

aequalitas-conexio in twenty passages, while many other presentations can be reduced to, or are the equivalent of, this formula. Cusa had already used the mathematical *ratio* in sermons before he gave it an important place in *On Learned Ignorance*. The stress on God as "absolute unity" (*unitas absoluta* [1.5.14]) in this treatise reveals why this analogy so appealed to the cardinal.

In chapter 7 of the first book of the DDI Cusa begins to investigate why absolute and eternal unity must also be triunal. If otherness, inequality, and division are characteristic of our world, and if otherness, inequality, and division require a ground in what is not-other, not-unequal, and not-divided, such a ground must be both eternal (because otherness, inequality, and division are temporal) and also an eternity that is both one and three. Cusa concludes: "Because unity is eternal, equality too is eternal, so too is connection; hence unity, equality and connection are one. This is that triunal unity which Pythagoras, the first of all philosophers and the glory of Italy and Greece, taught was to be adored."[200] In the following three chapters, Cusa analyzes the relation between triune eternity and the Christian doctrine of the Trinity in language that echoes Thierry of Chartres. In chapter 9 he notes that "our holiest doctors" have ascribed *unitas* to the Father, *aequalitas* to the Son, and *conexio* to the Holy Spirit, though these terms are only a "very distant likeness" (*distantissima similitudo*) drawn from creatures (1.9.26). Finally, in chapter 10 he reflects on how intellect attains to the realm of the coincidence of opposites, where it affirms that "maximal unity will never be understood unless it is understood as three" (1.10.27). In book 2 Cusa goes on to explore how the triune reality of God is expressed in a contracted mode in the "trinity of the universe" (DDI 2.7.130). In this early work, however, he does not deal with the mystical aspects of his trinitarian theology.

The *De coniecturis* of 1441–43 provides an example of a more mystical use of the triadic formula that helps us understand chapters 17–18 of the *De visione dei*.[201] The main theme of this exercise in epistemology is the analogy between how the divine mind creates all things and the human mind constructs the conceptual world of its "conjectures," understood as "positive assertions participating in the truth in otherness" (1.11.57). Cusa's analysis of knowing, like Augustine's, is not meant to be a purely abstract or academic exercise. As he says, "The more we plumb the depths of our mind, whose single living center is the Divine Mind, the more closely we are raised up to become like it."[202] The understanding of the mind as "the principle of conjectures" reveals it as "a unitrinal principle," whose "unity enfolds in itself all multitude, and whose equality enfolds all magnitude, and whose connection enfolds all composition."[203] What Cusa has done here is to make the mathematical and originally extramental Augustinian trinitarian analogy into an interior and introspective one allows it to be linked to Augustine's intramental analogies found in *The Trinity*. This produces a personal, even mystical, appropriation of the *unitas-aequalitas-conexio* of the mind as image of the Trinity, as is clear from the appeal that Cusa makes to his patron, Cardinal Giulio Cesarini.

Nicholas tells Cesarini that self-knowledge will enable him to realize that "the humanity that is individually contracted in otherness [in him] is the otherness of a more Absolute Unity [i.e., God]."[204] By means of the conjectural example of light, Cusa shows Cesarini how his own unity as a knowing subject participates in the light of divinity in which unity, equality, and connection are all one and that it does so in an appropriate manner on each of the three levels of apprehension—intellect, reason, and sense knowing (2.17.172–76). This participation is actualized not only in grasping how the self participates in a contracted fashion in the unitrinal light of God, but also in understanding the human drive to construct the speculative sciences, and indeed, in every form of human knowing (2.17.177–78). The aim is not just knowing more things, but in coming to realize the meaning of knowing, that is, grasping how knowing makes one the "likeness of God," that is, a unitrinal contraction of Absolute Unity, Equality, and Connection. This is nothing more nor less than learning how to love God truly and to live the equality of his Justice (2.17.179–84). Cusa summarizes:

> From yourself you can behold the godlike elections. For you see that God, who is the Infinite Connection [i.e., the Holy Spirit], is not to be loved as some kind of contracted lovable thing, but as the most Absolute Infinite Love. In that love in which God is loved the Most Simple Unity [i.e., the Father] and the Infinite Justice [i.e., Equality, or the Son] must also exist. . . . You also know that to love God is to be loved by God, for he is charity. The more that anyone loves God, the more he participates in divinity.[205]

This passage, with its Eckhartian overtones, especially the stress on the Son as justice and the Holy Spirit as the connection of love in God and in us, summarizes the core of Cusa's trinitarian mysticism.

The chapters dealing with the Trinity in the DVD are part of a careful linking of the first, second, and third parts of the treatise. Chapter 16 deals with human desire that can only be satiated by an infinite goal. In chapter 17 God is revealed as an infinitely lovable Trinity, while in chapter 18 Cusa shows that only a triune God can bestow human felicity. This chapter also introduces the notions of union and sonship, which are dominant themes of the remaining christological chapters. The trinitarian section in the DVD does not use the *unitas-aequalitas-conexio* triad explicitly, though an equivalent formula appears in speaking of the Trinity as *unitas uniens-unitas uni-*

bilis-utriusque unio (17.71). The central focus is on a form of love analogy based on Augustine's *On the Trinity*, though Cusa also notes an equivalent intellectualist triad.[206] However, it is now evident that Cusa's description of God as infinitely lovable, that is, an absolute oneness of "loving love, lovable love, and the love that is the bond of loving love and lovable love,"[207] is perfectly compatible with the interiorized understanding of the mathematics of the Trinity.

Cusa first turns his attention to the paradoxical coincidence of opposites in the loving God. "Therefore," he says, "these things that seem to me to be three, namely the lover, the lovable, and the bond, are the very simple and absolute essence itself."[208] This coincidence is found at the wall of paradise (17.74), where we count "one" three times, but do not say "three." But when we begin to realize that the plurality we see in God is "an otherness without otherness, because it is the otherness which is identity" (17.75), we begin to move from the second to the third stage of the mystical path, that is, to go beyond the wall. Cusa describes the move this way:

> I see that the distinction of the lover and the lovable exists inside the wall of the coincidence of oneness and otherness. That is why this distinction which is inside the wall of coincidence where what is distinct and what is indistinct coincide precedes every form of otherness and difference that can be understood. For the wall closes off the power of all intellect, although the eye gazes out beyond into paradise where what it sees can neither be understood nor spoken about.[209]

So, mental exercise can begin to reveal that all loving participates in, but can never fully attain, the infinite divine love that resides beyond the wall of coincidence. The transcending eye that gazes beyond the wall is nothing else than the eye of loving desire stretching out toward the Absolute Infinity that will always continue to elude it.

Cusa then shows how our own experience of contracted love can give us a sense of this mystery. If our seeing God is really being seen by him, then our act of loving is nothing other than our being loved by God. The cardinal emphasizes that this takes place essentially in the inner act of self love, not in love that proceeds to another subject (Richard of St. Victor thought differently). Cusa introduces the argument by saying: "O Lord, you give me to see that I see love in myself, and I see myself loving, and because I see that I love myself, I see myself as lovable and I also see that I am a perfectly natural bond of both—I am love, and am lovable, I am the bond."[210] These three aspects of love as accidents of his being are present in Cusa's love of self, and he still is one in person. Were his love his essence, and not merely an operation of his being, Cusa too would be a perfect coincidence of one and three, rather than merely a contracted likeness of the triune God. The same, however, is not true for love directed outside the self, for the subject does not become lovable to itself in loving an object that may or may not return its love (17.77).

From this section of the DVD it is evident that Cusa allied himself with the dominant tradition of Christian mysticism that held that while intellect had a necessary role to play in the path to God, love was the power that led to union.[211] Both intellect and love are necessary in the pursuit of God, as he had affirmed in his earlier letters to the Tegernsee community; but in the DVD he framed the disputes that disturbed the German monastics of his time within a more capacious treatment of the nature of mystical theology. Hence, his explicit treatment of the relation of love and knowledge in chapter 18 has an added systematic force. Insofar as both intellect and love bear the image of the Trinity, Cusa affirms, both are needed for bringing us to God, though in different ways. We are not united to God insofar as he is *intelligens* and *amans* in himself, because the divine mode of understanding and loving is beyond us. But insofar as God has planted in us an infinite desire to know and love him, he has become for us *deus intelligibilis* (the God to be understood) and *deus amabilis* (the God to be loved). Hence, he concludes, "I behold rational human nature as very capable of being united to your intelligible and lovable divine nature; and someone, in the act of receiving you, crosses over into a bond with you so close that it can be named 'filiation.'"[212]

A similar dialectical development of Augustine's introspective analogies from *On the Trinity* with the transcendental mathematical similitudes originating in the bishop's *On Christian Teaching* can be found in later treatises, such as *On Equality*, where Cusa concentrates on the intellectualist triad of *memoria-intelligentia-voluntas* rather than the love analogies.[213] Cusa continued to experiment with analogies for the Trinity in the final five years of his life, though they were often based on, or reducible to, older models. For Cusa, seeing God was always seeing the triune God who reveals himself in Christ.

The christological dimension of Cusa's thought, especially his mysticism, is evident in the final chapters of the DVD. The appeal to filiation at the end of chapter 18 is crucial, because *filiatio* is the rubric under which the cardinal discusses mystical union. In the final section of the *De visione dei* (chaps. 19–25) Cusa describes how such sonship, the maximum bond of union, is made available to humans in the person of Jesus Christ.[214] Cusa's Christology appears throughout his writings, especially his sermons, and has attracted even more study than his treatment of the Trinity.[215] Here I will restrict myself to some remarks on the general character of his doctrine of the God-man and a brief analysis of crucial issues in these final chapters of the cardinal's mystagogical manual.[216]

One way to open up a broad perspective on Cusa's doctrine of Christ is to see it in light of the medieval debates over the motive of the incarnation—*cur deus homo*? As in the case of seeing God, the scriptural witnesses varied. One set of New Testament texts clearly tied the incarnation to overcoming the effects of the Fall, such as Luke 19:10, "The Son of Man has come to seek out and save what was lost" (cf. 1 Tim. 1:15; Titus 2:13–14). On this soteriological foundation, Augustine had argued, "If man had not sinned, the Son of Man would not have come."[217] Other passages, however, emphasized the broader anthropological and cosmological dimensions of the incarnation, such as the christological hymn from Colossians, which speaks of Christ as "the image of the unseen God, the firstborn of all creation, for in him were created all things in heaven and on earth. . . . He exists before all things, and in him all things hold together" (Col. 1:15–17). The task of Christology is not so much to choose between the more soteriological and the more universalistic texts as to seek to reconcile them in some coherent way. During the High Scholastic period, the issue of the motive for the incarnation was much debated.[218] The mature view of Thomas Aquinas, expressed in STh IIIa, q.1, a.3, held that "it is more fittingly (*convenientius*) said that the work of the incarnation was ordained by God as a remedy for sin, so that had sin not existed, the incarnation would not have happened." Duns Scotus, however, constructed a logical argument based on an analysis of predestination (using Rom. 1:4) that said that since anyone willing something in an ordered way must first will what is closer to the goal intended, the divine will's first intention outside itself is directed to the glory ordained for the incarnate Word.[219] According to this view, often termed that of the absolute predestination of Christ, Christ would have become incarnate even if Adam had not sinned, "even if no one else were to be created but Christ alone" (*Reportatio Parisiensia* 3.7.4).

Nicholas of Cusa was aware of these divergent viewpoints and tried to be true to both aspects of the scriptural message. In doing so he created a new form of what I call the third option for the motive of the incarnation, that is, a christological ontology that emphasized the Christic reality of the whole of creation, as suggested by Colossians and other texts. Cusa believed that this was the proper context within which to understand why and how the Word became flesh to redeem humanity by his death and resurrection. Cusa was working his way toward this kind of Christology in some of his early sermons, but it first emerged clearly in *On Learned Ignorance*.

The very structure of the DDI reveals the need for a christological ontology. The analysis in book 1 of the absolute maximum, that is, the triune God, leads to the consideration of the universe in book 2 as the contracted maximum. What allows the believer to grasp the meaning of the universe as the unfolding of the divine reality is the treatment in book 3 of the "maximum that is at once both contracted and absolute, Jesus, the ever blessed" (DDI 3, praef. 181). In other words, without the Christology of book 3 Cusa's whole effort to rethink the relation of God and universe would be in danger of collapsing.[220] The first four chapters of this book, which set up the faith-based hypotheses for Cusa's argument, cite the text of the Colossians hymn five times. Cusa begins by arguing that in the created universe as the contracted maximum nothing can equal God, the absolute maximum, or even any other thing, since all things are distinguished by degrees. Nor can any genus, species, or individual be considered as maximally perfect or imperfect by attaining the limits assigned to it, since these always admit of more or less. If, however, it were possible that the absolute maximum could be contracted to a genus or species, such a union of "creator and creature without confusion and without composition" would have to be realized in "the being that is more common to the whole company of beings," that is, in man, because humanity, "the middle nature, which is the means of the connection of the lower [i.e., material] and the higher natures [i.e., spiritual], is the only one that can be fittingly raised to the maximum by the power of the Infinite Maximum God."[221] This argument is hypothetical. In what follows Cusa turns to scripture to show how this hypothesis fits the biblical witness concerning the incarnation.

Because humanity embraces all created things (man as microcosm), Cusa argues that one human being (humans exist only as individuals) could be brought to God so as "to be human in such a way as to be God and God in such a way as to be human." This human being then "would be the perfection of the universe, holding primacy in everything" (Col. 1:18). Cusa does not frame his argument for the necessity of the God-man either on a purely soteriological basis, or on an abstract consideration of predestination, but rather on the basis of the ontological (or better, hyper-ontological) system laid out in *On Learned Ignorance.* Understanding God as the *maximum absolutum* and the universe as the *maximum contractum* demonstrates to the believer the necessity that Jesus Christ precisely as this human being (not just in his eternal state as the Word) is the reason for and the means of both the *exitus* of all things from God and their *reditus* back to him. Cusa summarizes:

> Through this human being all things would receive the beginning and the end of their contraction, so that through this human, who is the contracted maxi-

mum, all things would come forth from the absolute maximum into contracted being and would return to the absolute through the same intermediary, so to speak, through the one who is the beginning of their emanation and
the end of their return.[222]

Thus for Cusa, creation is inherently christological both in its production
and in its consummation—cosmogenesis is Christogenesis. Here Nicholas
joins a long tradition in the history of Christian thought, featuring both
Eastern theologians such as Maximus the Confessor and Western thinkers,
including Hildegard of Bingen and Meister Eckhart. It is important to recognize the status of the argument that Cusa has advanced. The necessity of
the God-man is not an object of purely rational exposition; it is only
through *docta ignorantia* based on faith that we can hypothesize the maximum humanity of Jesus as the fullness of the meaning of finite reality.[223]

Beginning with the fourth chapter of book 3, Cusa moves from the level
of theological hypothesis to that of concrete affirmation and analysis, showing how this model is fulfilled in Jesus, in whom "we have every perfection
and the redemption and remission of sin" (3.4.203). The soteriological
aspect of the incarnation does not get forgotten (though it appears more
powerfully in Cusa's sermons), but it is incorporated into a broader view of
anthropological and cosmological primacy of the God-man.[224] In the chapters that follow (3.5–10) Cusa shows how the fundamental mysteries of
Christ's life—conception, birth, death, resurrection, ascension, and coming
judgment—realize the incarnational primacy argued in the first four chapters. Cusa's interest here, like Eckhart's, is not so much in the historical
aspects of the life of Jesus as in the intellect's grasp of the inner significance
of Christ's saving acts. Chapter 11 goes on to deal with the relation between
the mysteries of faith and learned ignorance, as we have seen above. Chapter 12 concludes the book with a treatment of the church as the Body of
Christ in this world and the world to come—the necessary mediator of
Christ's universal primacy to our concrete historical existence.[225]

In turning to the christological section of the DVD, we see that although
Cusa does not provide an explicit discussion of *cur deus homo?* as he had in
the DDI and in some of his sermons, he does root the necessity for the
incarnation in the divine loving-kindness that is the major theme of the
later part of the book.[226] "You, God, who are Goodness itself, cannot satisfy
your infinite kindness and your generosity unless you give youself to us.
And this could not come about in a more fitting and more accessible way
for us than that you should assume our nature because we are not able to
approach yours. So you have come to us, and you name yourself Jesus,
ever-blessed Savior."[227]

The Father, as loving God (*deus amans*), gives birth to the *deus amabilis*, that is, the Son, with whom he is indissolubly united through the act (*actus*), or connecting bond, that is the Holy Spirit (19.83). The *deus amabilis* is both the divine reason, or concept, enfolding all things, and also the object of desire that makes possible our own union with God. In order to attain that union, we must first of all accept that the Second Person in the Trinity is "the intermediary (*medium*) of the union of all things, so that all things take their rest in you through the mediation of your Son." This act of faith is meant to lead on to the enrapturing vision "that the blessed Jesus, as Son of Man [Mark 2:10 et al.], was most profoundly united to your Son, and that the Son of Man could not be united to you, God the Father, except by the mediation of your Son, the Absolute Mediator."[228] Jesus as *filius hominis* is maximally united to the Absolute Intermediary, the Second Person and the *filius Dei*, not to the point of the absorption of the human nature into the divine nature, but as the exemplar of filiation. "Because you are the Son of Man," says Cusa, "human filiation is most profoundly united to divine filiation in you, Jesus, so that you are rightly called Son of Man and Son of God." Continuing the prayerful address, Cusa says, "Your human filiation, Jesus, is supremely united in the Absolute Filiation that is the Son of God, which enfolds every form of filiation."[229]

The importance of filiation for expressing the mystery of the God-man, as well as for understanding our deifying union with Christ, was a new development in Cusa's Christology that goes back to two treatises of 1445, *On Divine Sonship* and *The Gift of the Father of Lights*.[230] In these two works, as David Albertson has shown,[231] Cusa deepened his christological ontology by showing both how the Word made flesh descends into the created world of manifestations, or theophanies, as the supreme theophany that enfolds all creation,[232] and by sketching out the main lines of an ascensional Christology in which study of the world spurs the intellect to realize its potential as a "living image" (*viva imago*) of the Word as Son of God, thus attaining the filiation that is *theosis*. Because "creation unfolds incarnation, and incarnation enfolds creation," in Albertson's words,[233] our becoming one with the Son of God made flesh demonstrates that mystical union, or what Cusa calls filiation, is the realization of both human and cosmic destiny. Obviously, the details of this new stage in Cusa's Christology cannot be followed here, nor its relation to the thought of Eckhart,[234] but a brief look at how Cusa understands the relation between filiation and deification in the *De filiatione Dei* (DF) is significant for the background of the mystical Christology found in the DVD.

Cusa begins his treatise with a reference to a key Johannine text on filiation ("But as many as received him, he gave power to them to be made children of God" [John 1:12]) in order to advance his main theme that sonship is to be identified with deification, "which in Greek is also called *theosis*" (DF 1.52). The road to filiation is rooted in faith, but as deification it exceeds every "mode of intuition." The remainder of the tract advances various mental conjectures that allow some approach to this mystery. These experiments ring the changes on many of Cusa's fundamental paradoxes about the impossibility, but necessity, of striving to reach the ineffable God by means studying the "effable" contracted modes of his unfolding. For our purposes, two issues stand out: the nature of *filiatio/theosis* and its relation to vision. After extended conjectural discussions of intellect's exercise of creating concepts through study of the world, Cusa ventures several provisional definitions of filiation. The third section, for example, uses the analogy of the mirror to argue that while all things reflect God in distorted ways, the distortion grows less in the mirror of the intellect as it approaches the exemplary and perfect mirror of the Word of God, that is, insofar as it partakes of filiation (DF 3.65–68). On this basis Cusa defines filiation as "nothing more than the transformation from the dense remnants of images to union with Infinite Reason itself."[235] But Cusa goes deeper in what follows. Because all otherness and distinction are below filiation, the treatise advances a quasi-Eckhartian view in which every intelligible thing within the intellect becomes identical with intellect itself so that in the ideal sense intellect, truth, and life itself are completely one. From this perspective, the most proper meaning of filiation is "the removal of every form of otherness and diversity and the bringing back of all things into one, which is also the pouring out of the one into everything. And this is *theosis* itself."[236] This is Cusa's lapidary formulation of the dynamic identity-in-distinction of Christian dialectical Neoplatonism.

This filiational identity can also be conceived of in terms of a mental sight that fuses God and intellect, as shown by a passage toward the end of the DF. Here Cusa discusses the relation between God as the actual essence of all things and the intellect as the "living likeness of God" when it is separated from all things and brought back into itself after having been extended outward in its hunt for understanding the things of the world. In this return, or conversion, to itself the intellect knows itself both as a likeness of God and as a likeness of all things. What is more, it comes to see itself in God as God himself becomes its seeing. Cusa expresses this in a dense but striking text that foreshadows the analysis of *visio dei* in the DVD:

> Since the intellect is a living intellectual likeness of God, when it knows itself it knows all things in itself as one. But the intellect knows itself when it gazes

at itself as it is in God. This, however, happens when God in the intellect is the intellect itself. Therefore, knowing all things is nothing else than seeing itself as God's likeness–this is filiation. It beholds all things in a single simple cognitive intuition.[237]

In the *De filiatione Dei,* Cusa had presented an original understanding of filiation, but with limitations, first because he had concentrated on our sonship with the Word more than on our union with the incarnate Christ, and second because his analysis was developed only in terms of the intellectual appropriation of sonship. This treatment receives its completion in the DVD, where the cardinal turns to the incarnate Son and the way in which both knowing and loving attain their goal in filiation. Chapter 20 of the *De visione* presents Cusa's rather idiosyncratic understanding of the Chalcedonian teaching of the union of God and man in Jesus. First of all, he distinguishes this union from the union of the persons in the Trinity. Although the union between the human nature and the divine in Jesus is maximum (i.e., no greater union between God and human is possible), it is not infinite. In gazing at the loving Jesus (as in the icon of the face of the suffering Christ), we see the Son of God and through him also the Father, because Jesus is a human son in such a way as to be Son of God (20.88). In this chapter Cusa is so concerned with mediation and union between the human and divine natures and modes of filiation that he fails to emphasize, though he never denies, the hypostatic character of the union of God and human in the person of the Word, thus giving his presentation the quasi-Nestorian tone that some critics have noted.[238]

If it is the Son as "lovable love" that attracts us to Jesus as both God and man, this attraction also involves the truth conveyed to us by Jesus whose human intellect is supremely united to the divine intellect, "just as the most perfect image to its exemplar Truth" (20.89). Because Jesus is both God and man, truth and image, infinite and finite, he is seen to be within the wall of paradise, not outside it (20.89). This recognition sets up chapter 21, which returns to the theme of felicity. Just as we cannot be happy save in the triune God (chap. 18), so too happiness is impossible outside "Jesus, the end of the universe, in whom every creature rests as in the ultimacy of perfection" (21.91). Like John Scottus Eriugena,[239] Cusa identifies Jesus as the tree of life planted in paradise (Gen. 2:8) which provides the food of heaven— nothing other than the meal of insatiable satiation referred to in chapter 16. Here Cusa cites John 1:18 and other classic scripture passages on seeing God (1 Tim. 6:16 and 1 Cor. 13:12) to buttress his insistence that Jesus alone makes the Father visible, grants humans true happiness, and leads them to divinizing union. Ultimate felicity is possible only inside paradise with

Jesus. "Every happy spirit sees the invisible God, and in you, Jesus, is united to the unapproachable and immortal God [1 Tim. 6:16]. Thus in you the finite is united to the infinite and to what cannot be united, and the incomprehensible is seized by eternal fruition, which is the most joyful happiness, never to be exhausted."[240]

Before concluding, Cusa explores several related issues. The most important of these is found in chapters 22–23. Given the theme of the treatise, Cusa obviously wished to make clear to the monks of Tegernsee how Jesus sees and how this relates to our own *visio dei*. For the last time he invites the monks to return to the gaze of the omnivoyant icon and conjecture about the wonderful and astonishing gaze of Jesus (22.94). Jesus used eyes of flesh like ours, but because of the "noble discerning power in his spirit" he was able to see into the inward motives of people far more effectively than anyone else (22.95–96). Since his human sight was united to the absolute and infinite divine seeing, Jesus was even able to perceive the substance of things (22.97). Cusa explores this unique way of seeing by summarizing an argument he had already made in the third book of the DDI.[241] Just as in us physical seeing is enfolded in the higher seeing of the intellect, so too in Jesus all forms of seeing, from the physical to the intellectual, are enfolded the absolute seeing of God. This is why Jesus is truly the fountain of life that enlightens every intellect (John 1:9). Chapter 23 describes the different ways in which we see Christ inside the wall of paradise as "the Word of God humanified and the human deified" (*verbum dei humanatum et homo deificatus* [23.101]). This is not seeing a coincidence, or mingling of creature and creator, nor some kind of intermediary third thing between God and human; it is seeing "a sensible and corruptible nature subsisting in an intellectual and incorruptible nature" as "one person" (*suppositum*).[242]

Chapters 24 and 25 provide a prayerful summary for the long mystagogic exercise that the cardinal laid out for his Tegernsee audience. He advises them to imitate the apostles, who recognized that Jesus possesses the words of life and has sowed the seeds of new life in us through his saving death (24.107–9). Hence, just as all the powers of the body and soul should be harmonized with the higher action of the intellect, the intellect itself can be perfected by submitting itself in faith to the Word of God (24.109–12). Christ teaches only two things, says Cusa: the faith by which the intellect approaches God, and the love by which it is united to him (24.113). Love and the knowledge gained through faith are the two essential components of Christ's teaching: "You urge nothing else than believing; you command nothing else but loving."[243] The final chapter on Jesus as consummation thanks God for sending the Holy Spirit into our intellects to enkindle the process that leads to perfection by the warmth of its love. Returning to the visionary motif, God is compared to a painter who depicts myriad images of himself in the intellectual spirits he creates because his infinite power is unfolded more perfectly in many figures. This allows Cusa to stress the mutuality of the mystagogical exercise with which he started, emphasizing that each spirit sees in God "something that must be revealed to the others if they would attain you in the best possible way." "The spirits filled with love," he says, "reveal their secrets to each other, and the knowledge of the Beloved is increased, as well as desire for him, and the sweetness of joy blazes forth."[244] True *visio dei* always involves both knowledge and love.[245]

Nicholas of Cusa's place in the history of Christian mysticism has perhaps not been fully appreciated. He lived toward the end of a period (ca. 1300 to 1500) that witnessed both new forms of vernacular mysticism, often of a highly personal and deeply emotional character, and attempts to create a form of scholastic mysticism, that is, organized treatises and handbooks on the nature of mysticism for the use of confessors and spiritual guides. The *De visione Dei* fits into neither of these categories, though it does inculcate actual spiritual practices designed to lead to union, and it is a structured summary of *theologia mystica* that takes positions on some of the key issues under dispute at the time. What I have tried to show is that the cardinal's treatise and his mystical theology in general surpassed its times. The *De visione* not only rethought and reformulated the fundamentals of the dialectical Neoplatonic mysticism developed by Dionysius, Eriugena, and Eckhart, but it also sought to bring coherence to issues about God's invisible visibility that were rooted in scripture and that had been present in Christian mysticism since its earliest encounters with Hellenic philosophy. Cusa "coincidated" the opposing scriptural positions on seeing God into a new synthesis on the basis of the necessary interdependence of both love and knowledge in the path to union, or filiation, as he termed it. However we may wish to judge his effort, it was more than a mere summary of what had gone before. It was a new creation.

1. Suso and Elsbeth distribute the IHC monogram. *Exemplar* from
   Ms. 2929: Photo et Collection de la Bibliothèque Nationale et
   Universitaire de Strasbourg, f. 68v.

2. The Mystical Path. *Exemplar* from Ms. 2929: Photo et Collection de la Bibliothèque Nationale et Universitaire de Strasbourg, f. 82r.

3. Vision of Wisdom and the Servant's Soul. *Exemplar* from Ms. 2929:
Photo et Collection de la Bibliothèque Nationale et Universitaire de
Strasbourg, f. 8v.

Chapter 7

4. Song of Songs Illustrations: (a) Embrace of the Lovers; (b) The Bride wounds Christ. *Rothschild Canticles.* New Haven, Yale University, Beinecke Rare Book and Manuscript Library, MS. 404, ff. 18v-19r.

5B. Trinity Illumination. *Rothschild Canticles.* New Haven, Yale University, Beinecke Rare Book and Manuscript Library, MS 404, f. 77r.

5A. Song of Songs Illustration: The Bridegroom descends on the Bride. *Rothschild Canticles.* New Haven, Yale University, Beinecke Rare Book and Manuscript Library, f. 66r.

6. Trinity Illumination. *Rothschild Canticles.* New Haven, Yale University, Beinecke Rare Book and Manuscript Library, MS 404, f. 104r.

7. Trinity Illumination. *Rothschild Canticles*. New Haven, Yale University, Beinecke Rare Book and Manuscript Library, MS 404, ff. 105v–106r.

8A. Christ hangs the Bride. *Christus und die minnende Seele.*
Badische Landesbibliothek Karlsruhe, Cod. Donaueschingen
106, f. 19r.

8B. The Bride takes Christ Prisoner. *Christus und die minnende Seele.*
Badische Landesbibliothek Karlsruhe, Cod. Danaueschingen
106, f. 29r.

9. Christ and the Bride embrace. *Christus und die minnende Seele.*
   Badische Landesbibliothek Karlsruhe, Cod. Donaueschingen,
   f. 34r.

10. St. Bernard and Nun at Crucifixion. Cologne, Schnütgen Museum, Inv. Nr. M340. Photo courtesy of Rheinisches Bildarchiv.

Notes

Introduction

1. On the history of the creation and reception of Huizinga's book, see the perceptive essay of Edward Peters and Walter P. Simons, "The New Huizinga and the Old Middle Ages," *Speculum* 74 (1999): 587–620. There are two English versions of Huizinga's book, the abbreviated translation of Fritz Hopman first published in London in 1924 under the title *The Waning of the Middle Ages*, and the more recent and more complete, but still problematic version of Rodney J. Payton and Ulrich Mammitzsch entitled *The Autumn of the Middle Ages* (Chicago: University of Chicago Press, 1996).

2. Margaret Aston, "Huizinga's Harvest: England and the Waning of the Middle Ages," *Mediaevalia et Humanistica*, n.s. 9 (1979): 1–24. On p. 2 Aston says, "'Waning' is a bleaker word than 'Harvest,' since it allows neither for the fullness of autumn nor the promise of a new spirit."

3. Werner Williams-Krapp estimates that at least 80 percent of the surviving manuscripts of the works of Eckhart, Suso, Tauler, and other fourteenth-century mystical writers date from the fifteenth century; see "The Erosion of a Monopoly: German Religious Literature in the Fifteenth Century," in *The Vernacular Spirit: Essays on Medieval Religious Literature*, ed. Renate Blumenfeld-Kosinski, Duncan Robertson, and Nancy Bradley Warren (New York: Palgrave, 2002), 251–55.

4. Heiko A. Oberman, *The Harvest of Medieval Theology: Gabriel Biel and Late Medieval Nominalism* (Cambridge, Mass.: Harvard University Press, 1963). In the introduction, Oberman notes, "Deeply indebted as we are to Johan Huizinga's *The Waning of the Middle Ages*, the image of 'harvest' in our title is intentionally opposed to the connotation of 'decline' carried by the French and English titles of the Dutch 'Herfsttij,' which literally means "harvest-tide" (p. 5).

5. See, for example, the interesting book of Gordon Leff, *The Dissolution of the Medieval Outlook: An Essay on Intellectual and Spiritual Change in the Fourteenth Century* (New York: Harper & Row, 1976), which argues that it was the collapse of the accepted medieval ways of thinking initiated in the fourteenth century that made possible the emergence of the modern world. Among these new ways of thinking Leff gives some prominence to mysticism (see pp. 118–30), which he calls "the most pervasive spiritual force of the fourteenth century" (p. 121).

6. A humorous aside made in the "Introduction," in *Handbook of European History, 1400–1600: Late Middle Ages, Renaissance, and Reformation*, ed. Thomas A. Brady, Jr., Heiko A. Oberman, and James D. Tracy, 2 vols. (Grand Rapids: Eerdmans, 1996), 2:xx.

7. The 1400–1600 position is presented in the aforementioned *Handbook*. In his fine book of essays entitled *The Dawn of the Reformation: Essays in Late Medieval and Early Reformation Thought* (Edinburgh: T & T Clark, 1986), Oberman "arbitrarily" set forth the later Middle Ages as "ranging from about 1350–1550" (p. 20). Oberman's student, Steven Ozment, entitled his major and influential survey *The Age of Reform 1250–1550: An Intellectual and Religious History of Late Medieval and Reformation Europe* (New Haven: Yale University Press, 1980).

8. On the character of the new mysticism, see Bernard McGinn, *The Flowering of Mysticism: Men and Women in the New Mysticism (1200–1350)*, vol. 3 of *The Presence of God: A History of Western Christian Mysticism* (New York: Crossroad, 1998), 12–30.

9. Huizinga, *Autumn of the Middle Ages*, 264–65; see the larger discussion on 257–65.

10. See Oberman, *Harvest of Medieval Theology*, chapter 10, "Nominalistic Mysticism" (pp. 323–60). In the next volume I hope to take up the issue of the relation of nominalism and mysticism in relation to the figure of Jean Gerson.

11. Oberman (*Dawn of Reformation*, 126–54) reprints as chapter 6 his essay, "*Simul Gemitus et Raptus*: Luther and Mysticism," first published in 1967 in German. For more on Oberman's view of mysticism, see chapter 1 in the same collection.

12. The latest large-scale history of the late Middle Ages is to be found in *The New Cambridge Medieval History*, vol. 6, *c. 1300–c. 1415*, ed. Michael Jones (Cambridge: Cambridge University Press, 2000); and vol. 7, *c. 1415–c. 1500*, ed. Christopher Allmand (Cambridge: Cambridge University Press, 1998). Mysticism, alas, comes in for only a rather truncated and erroneous treatment in 6:58–65.

13. On lay piety in the late Middle Ages, see the papers in *Laienfrömmigkeit im späten Mittelalter: Formen, Funktionen, politisch-soziale Zusammenhänge*, ed. Klaus Schreiner (Munich: Oldenbourg, 1992), especially Klaus Schreiner, "Laienfrömmigkeit—Frömmigkeit von Eliten oder Frömmigkeit des Volkes? Zur sozialen Verfasstheit laikaler Frömmigkeitspraxis im späten Mittelalter" (pp. 1–78); and Volker Honemann, "Der Laie als Leser" (pp. 241–51).

14. On medieval Germany during the fourteenth and fifteenth centuries, see *New Cambridge Medieval History*, vol. 6, chapter 16 (a) and (b) (pp. 515–69); and vol. 7, chapter 17 (pp. 337–66).

15. Ivan Hlaváček ("The Luxemburgs and Rupert of the Palatinate, 1347–1410," in *New Cambridge Medieval History*, 6:567) estimates that in the first half of the fourteenth century the population of Germany was about fourteen million, and that the plague killed almost half, so that even by 1470 when the population was rebounding there may have been only ten million inhabitants.

16. As in so many disasters in human history, there also appear to have been some positive effects of the plague, such as those argued for in the provocative posthumous volume of David Herlihy, *The Black Death and the Transformation of the West*, ed. with an introduction by Samuel K. Cohn, Jr. (Cambridge, Mass.: Harvard University Press, 1997).

17. For a fine introduction to the late medieval church, see Francis Oakley, *The Western Church in the Later Middle Ages* (Ithaca: Cornell University Press, 1979). The differing perspectives on late medieval Christianity and its relation to the Reformation presented in Oakley's book and in Ozment's *Age of Reform* are insightfully set forth by Mark U. Edwards in a review essay in *Religious Studies Review* 7 (1981): 124–28.

18. On late medieval calls for reform, see Gerhard Strauss, "Ideas of *Reformatio* and *Renovatio* from the Middle Ages to the Reformation," in *Handbook of European History 1400–1600*, 2:1–30.

19. Huizinga, *Autumn of the Middle Ages*, 34–35.

20. Jean Gerson, *Trilogus in materia schismatis*, in *Jean Gerson: Oeuvres Complètes*, 10 vols. (Paris: Desclée, 1960–73), 6:81: Neque praeterea latet vos potestatem papalem datam esse in aedificationem Ecclesiae, non in destructionem.

21. Brian Tierney, *Foundations of the Conciliar Theory: The Contributions of the Medieval Canonists from Gratian to the Great Schism* (Cambridge: Cambridge University Press, 1955).

22. "Haec sancta" can be found in *Conciliorum Oecumenicorum Decreta*, ed. Josephus Alberigo et al. (Bologna: Istituto per le Scienze Religiose, 1973), 409: . . . potestatem a Christo immediate habens, cui quilibet cuiuscumque status vel dignitatis, etiam si papalis existat, obedire tenetur in his quae pertinent ad fidem et exstirpationem dicti schismatis, ac generalem reformationem dictae ecclesiae Dei in capite et membris.

23. For an overview of the history of the church in this period, see John Van Engen, "The Church in the Fifteenth Century," *Handbook of European History 1400–1600*, 1:305–30.

Chapter 1

1. For introductions to Dominican spirituality, see Simon Tugwell OP, "The Spirituality of the Dominicans," in *Christian Spirituality: High Middle Ages and Reformation*, ed. Jill Raitt et al. (New York: Crossroad, 1987), 15–31; and especially *Early Dominicans: Selected Writings* (New York: Paulist Press, 1982). A recent introduction is Richard Woods OP, *Mysticism and Prophecy: The Dominican Tradition* (London: Darton, Longman & Todd, 1998).

2. Hans Urs von Balthasar, "The Gospel as Norm and Test of All Spirituality in the Church," *Spirituality in Church and World* (New York: Paulist Press, 1965), 7–23.

3. Woods discusses four key strands in the Dominican charism: community, prayer, study, and mission (*Mysticism and Prophecy*, 23–26).

4. For Thomas as a mystic, see James A. Weisheipl, "Mystic on Campus: Friar Thomas," in *An Introduction to the Medieval Mystics of Europe*, ed. Paul Szarmach (Albany: SUNY Press, 1984), 135–59.

5. Jean-Pierre Torrell OP, *Saint Thomas Aquinas,* volume 2, *Spiritual Master* (Washington, D.C.: Catholic University of America Press, 2003), viii.

6. For a sketch of the life and works of Albert, see Simon Tugwell OP, "Albert: Introduction," in *Albert and Thomas: Selected Writings* (New York: Paulist Press, 1988), 3–129.

7. Loris Sturlese, *Die deutsche Philosophie im Mittelalter: Von Bonifatius bis zu Albert dem Grossen 748–1280* (Munich: C. H. Beck, 1993), 326.

8. For a sketch of the introduction of Aristotle, the condemnations, and the movement that reversed them, see Fernand Van Steenberghen, *Aristotle in the West: The Origins of Latin Aristotelianism* (Louvain: Nauwelaerts, 1955). For more recent information, see Peter Schultheiss and Ruedi Imbach, *Die Philosophie im Mittelalter: Ein Handbuch mit einem bio-bibliographischen Repertorium* (Düsseldorf: Artemis & Winkler, 2000), chapters 4 and 5.

9. For a survey of recent literature on Albert, see Hendryk Anzulewicz, "Neuere Forschung zu Albertus Magnus: Bestandsaufnahme und Problemstellungen," *Recherches de théologie ancienne et médiévale* 66 (1999): 163–206. Two major evaluations are those of Sturlese, *Die deutsche Philosophie im Mittelalter*, chapter 12, "Der philosophische und naturwissenschaftlicher Rationalismus Albert des Grossen"; and Alain de Libera, *Albert le Grand et la philosophie* (Paris: J. Vrin, 1990). A number of excellent recent studies can be found in *Albertus Magnus: Zum Gedenken nach 800 Jahren: Neue Zugänge, Aspekte und Perspektiven*, ed. Walter Senner OP (Berlin: Akademie, 2001).

10. Quoted in Loris Sturlese, "Albert der Grosse und die deutsche philosophische Kultur des Mittelalters," *Freiburger Zeitschrift für Philosophie und Theologie* 28 (1981): 147.

11. Albert's large corpus is available in two editions: (a) the old complete edition, *Alberti Magni Opera Omnia*, ed. Augustus Borgnet, 38 vols. (Paris, 1890–99; hereafter abbreviated as *Op.Par.*); and (b) the ongoing critical edition of the Cologne Albert Center, *Alberti Magni Opera Omnia* (Münster: Aschendorff, 1951–; hereafter abbreviated *Op.Col.*). I will use the Cologne edition where available.

12. For a brief sketch of Dionysian mysticism and an introduction to the literature on it,

see Bernard McGinn, *The Foundations of Mysticism: Origins to the Fifth Century,* volume 1 of *The Presence of God: A History of Western Christian Mysticism* (New York: Crossroad, 1991), 157–82.

13. The Dionysian corpus comprises four treatises and ten letters (in the Middle Ages an eleventh, inauthentic, letter also circulated): CH, EH, DN, MT, and Epp, in the medieval order. On the Paris glossed version of the corpus, see H. F. Dondaine, *Le Corpus Dionysien de l'université de Paris au XIIIe siècle* (Rome: Edizioni de Storia e Letteratura, 1953), especially 72, which lists the contents of the corpus as comprising three parts:

I. Opus majus
    (a) "Compellit me"—Eriugena's translation of CH along with the scholia of Max-
        imus the Confessor and Anastasius and the commentaries of Eriugena, Hugh of
        St. Victor, and John Sarrazin
    (b) Opus alterum—Eriugena's translation of EH, DN, MT, and Epp, along with the
        glosses of Maximus and Anastasius, as well as Pseudo-Maximus glosses, which
        are actually extracts from Eriugena's *Periphyseon.* Another gloss (E') is also found
        here.
II. The new translation of John Sarrazin
III. The *Extractio* paraphrase of Thomas Gallus

Albert began his systematic interpretation while at Paris, following the order of books in the Paris corpus. He completed the *Super CH* in 1248. Next in order and worked at in Cologne would have been the *Super EH* (1249–50); the *Super DN* was written ca. 1250–52; and finally the *Super MT* and *Super Epp* also date to about 1252. One of the copies of these texts is in the hand of Thomas Aquinas (Naples, Biblioteca Nazionale I. B. 54).

14. Thomas Gallus's *Extractio* can be found in part in Philippe Chevalier, *Dionysiaca,* 2 vols. (Paris: Desclée, 1937), 1:673–717. The long *Explanatio* remains for the most part unpublished. It is worth noting that between 1238 and 1243 the aged Robert Grosseteste also turned to the Dionysian corpus, producing a new translation and commentary, on which see James McEvoy, *The Philosophy of Robert Grosseteste* (Oxford: Clarendon Press, 1982), chapter 2.

15. For brief summaries of Gallus's affective Dionysianism, see Bernard McGinn, *The Flowering of Mysticism: Men and Women in the New Mysticism (1200–1350),* volume 3 of *The Presence of God: A History of Western Christian Mysticism* (New York: Crossroad, 1998), 78–87; and Kurt Ruh, *Geschichte der abendländische Mystik* (Munich: Beck, 1985), 3:59–81. The term "affective Dionysianism" should not be taken to mean that there is no role for cognitive states in Gallus's thought, just as it would be a mistake not to recognize the essential role of love in the Dionysian writings. Ecstatic love or yearning (*erōs*) serves as a fundamental ontological category for Dionysius, the explanation for God's creation of the universe and the motive power drawing all things back to the divine source. But Dionysius does not give love any constitutive role in mystical union, and he has no room for anything like the more psychological category of *apex affectionis/scintilla apicis affectualis* found in Gallus.

16. *Super MT* 2 (*Op.Col.* XXXVII.2: 465.8–9): . . . quomodo scilicet oportet per intellectum uniri deo et voce laudare ipsum. Albert also speaks of *unitio intellectiva* (460.74). For other texts on the intellective nature of union with God, see *Super MT* 1 (460.49–50 and 462.22–25) and *Super Ep* 5 (*Op.Col.* XXXVII.2, 493.64–68).

17. There is no fully adequate account of the history of medieval Dionysianism. The most detailed treatment, that found in the multiauthor article "V. Influence du Pseudo-Denys en Occident," in DS 3:318–429, treats Albert on cols. 343–49. See also Walther Völker, "Abschluss: Die Auslegung von Cap. 1 der 'Mystischen Theologie' in den Kommentaren des Mittelalters und der neueren Zeit als Beispiel für das Fortwirken und die Umformung der Areopagitischen Gedanken," in *Kontemplation und Ekstase bei Pseudo-Dionysius Areopagita* (Wiesbaden: Franz Steiner, 1958), 218–63 (for Albert see 241–45). Newer essays can be found in *Die Dionysius-Rezeption im Mittelalter: Internationales Kolloquium in Sofia vom 8. bis 11 April 1999,* ed. T. Boiadjiev, G. Kapriev, and A. Steer (Turnhout: Brepols, 2000), which contains an article by Henryk Anzulewicz, "Pseudo-Dionysius und das Strukturprinzip des Denkens von Albert des Grossen" (pp. 252–95). In English, see Paul Rorem, *Pseudo-Dionysius:*

A Commentary on the Texts and an Introduction to Their Influence (New York: Oxford University Press, 1993), Afterword.

18. On Albert's understanding of mystical theology, especially as based in the *Super MT*, see Edouard Henri Wéber, "L'interprétation par Albert le Grand de la Théologie Mystique de Denys le Ps.-Aréopagite," in *Albertus Magnus: Doctor Universalis 1280/1980*, ed. Gerbert Meyer and Albert Zimmermann (Mainz: Matthias Grünewald, 1980), 409–39; and William J. Hoye, "Mystische Theologie nach Albert dem Grossen," in *Albertus Magnus: Zum Gedenken nach 800 Jahren*, 587–603. There is a large literature on Albert's commentary on the DN, especially Francis Ruello, *Les "Noms divins" et leur "Raisons" selon Albert le Grand commentateur du "De Divinis Nominibus"* (Paris: J. Vrin, 1963).

19. Martin Grabmann, "Der Einfluss Alberts der Grossen auf das mittelalterliches Geistesleben: Das deutsche Element in den mittelalterlichen Scholastik und Mystik," in *Mittelalterliches Geistesleben*, 2 vols. (Munich: Max Heuber, 1936) 2:325–412. See the judgment of Kurt Ruh in *Geschichte*, 3:121: "Die Frage, ob Albertus zu den Vätern der sogenannten 'Deutschen Mystik' gehört, ist mit einem eindeutigen Ja zu beantworten."

20. Ruh, *Geschichte,* 3:129: ". . . dass Albertus der Ausgangspunkt eines stark neuplatonisch orientierten Denkens ist, das zu einer neuen Metaphysik geführt hat."

21. E.g., Sturlese, *Die deutsche Philosophie*, 332–42, 346, 356–57, 376, etc.

22. A. de Libera, *La mystique rhénane d'Albert le Grand à Maître Eckhart* (Paris: Éditions du Seuil, 1994), 36, 41–46, 53–56.

23. For an overview of Albert's use of Plato, see Henryk Anzulewicz, "Die platonische Tradition bei Albertus Magnus: Eine Hinführung," in *The Platonic Tradition in the Middle Ages: A Doxographical Approach*, ed. Stephen Gersh and Maarten J. F. M. Hoenen (Berlin: Walter de Gruyter, 2002), 207–77. There is a large literature on Albert's relation to Neoplatonism; see, e. g., Maria-Rita Pagnoni-Sturlese, "A propos du néoplatonisme d'Albert le Grand, *Archives de philosophie* 43 (1980): 635–54.

24. *Summa Theologiae*, Liber I, tr. 1, q. 2, ad 3 (*Op.Col.* XXXIV.1:9): . . . theologia nomine ipso non dicit nisi rationem vel sermonem de deo, sermo autem de deo debet esse declarativus dei, non secundum esse et substantiam tantum, sed secundum quod est principium et finis eorum quae sunt, quia aliter imperfecte cognoscitur. Non autem est principium et finis nisi per ea quae ad exitum rerum ab ipso et ad reductionem rerum ad ipsum pertinent. Et haec sunt quae pertinent ad salutem hominis.

25. A. de Libera, *Albert le Grand*, chapter 4, "La métaphysique du flux" (pp. 116–77). On pp. 143–45 de Libera provides a summary of seven theses basic to Albert's metaphysics of *fluxus*. For the roots of Albert's metaphysics of flow, see also chapter 5 in Edward Booth OP, *Aristotelian Aporetic Ontology in Islamic and Christian Thinkers* (Cambridge: Cambridge University Press, 1983).

26. *Alberti Magni: De causis et processu universitatis a Prima Causa* (hereafter *De causis*); the work is found in *Op.Col.* XVII.2. De Libera (*La mystique rhénane*, 158–61 n. 106) provides a summary of the teaching of the treatise.

27. In *De causis* II.1.1 (XVII.2:59) Albert claims that the *Liber de causis* is a compilation "quae ante nos David Iudaeus quidem ex dictis Aristotelis, Avicennae, Algazelis et Alfarabii congregavit, per modum theorematum ordinans ea quorum ipsemet adhibuit, sicut et Euclides in Geometricis fecisse videtur."

28. *De causis* I.1.8. Albert understands the distinction between *id quod est* and *quo est* in Boethian terms, not according to the metaphysics of *esse* pioneered by Aquinas.

29. *De causis* I.2.1 (25.72–74): Erit ergo intellectuale principium sicut intellectus universaliter agens, "quo est omnia facere et pati nihil vel recipere . . ." (a quotation from Aristotle's *De anima* 3.5 [430a15]); and I.2.1 (26.51–54): Sed intelligitur universaliter simpliciter sicut intellectus illustrans super omne quod est, nihil ante se habens, quo illustretur. Illius enim lumen causa est existendi omne et quod est.

30. *De causis* I.4.1 (42.37–41): Alia est enim divisio causae et alia divisio fluentis principii. Non enim fluit nisi id quod unius formae est in fluente et in eo a quo fit fluxus. Sicut rivus

eiusdem formae est cum fonte, a quo fluit, et aqua in utroque eiusdem est speciei et formae. The eight chapters of the fourth treatise of the first book deals with "De fluxu causatorum a Causa Prima et causarum ordine."

31. _De causis_ I.4.1 (43.1–3): Ex his patet, quod fluxus est simpliter emanatio formae a primo fonte, qui omnium formarum est fons et origo.

32. On the creationist perspective of Albert's _De causis_, see de Libera, _Albert le Grand_, 139.

33. _De causis_ I.4.1 (43.53–56): Primum enim, de quo locuti sumus, propter suam nimiam simplicitatem penetrat omnia; et nihil est, cui desit ubique et semper existens.

34. _Liber de causis_, Prop. 8: Omnis intelligentiae fixio et essentia est per bonitatem puram quae est causa prima. For the text and editions of the _Liber de causis_, see the appendix to this chapter.

35. _Albertus Magnus: De Animalibus Libri XXVI_, ed. Hermann Stadler, 2 vols. (Münster: Aschendorff, 1920), Book XX, tract. 2, cap. 1 (2:1306–8). Written ca. 1258–62.

36. _De Animalibus_ XX.2.1.n. 64 (1307.5–10): . . . et sic est in fontali universitatis causa, a qua ebullitione procedunt bonitatum ipsius luces et formae quae in rebus distantibus receptae diversum esse accipiunt secundum diversam recipientium potestatem: et ideo quaedam sunt accedentes ad similitudinem causae primae, quaedam autem longe distantes sunt, quaedam obscurae resultationes ipsius in materia mixtorum et animalium corporum. On the term _ebullitio_ to characterize creation (it will also be found in Eckhart), see Pagnoni-Sturlese, "A propos du néoplatonisme d'Albert le Grand," 644–48.

37. _De Animalibus_ n. 66 (1308.8–14): Et patet iam quod a multis quidem dicitur sed a paucis intelligitur quod prima forma naturae est una sicut quidam antiquissimorum tradiderunt. Est enim in motore primo una, sed secundum processum ab ipso agitur in multitudinem plus et plus secundum quod ab ipso longius procedit per gradus eorum quae movent et moventur: et ideo haec forma comparata entibus est multa et accepta in prima causa est unica.

38. _De Animalibus_ n. 67 (1308.22–26): Cum autem in omni processu quo procedit ab ipso, nichil addatur sibi per quod novum esse fiat in ipsa, sed potius addita trahunt ad quoddam non esse, sicut est non esse simplex, non esse unum, non esse perpetuum, non esse stans et huiusmodi, patet quod illud quod est vere principium rerum, est unicum . . . .

39. E.g., _De causis_ I.4.8 (58.19–29). On the importance of this denial, see Sturlese, _Die deutsche Philosophie_, 355–57.

40. _Super MT_ 1 (455.15–20): . . . sed potius ex quodam lumine divino, quod non est enuntiatio, per quam aliquid affirmetur, sed res quaedam convincens intellectum, ut sibi super omnia adhaereatur. Et ideo elevat intellectum ad id quod excedit ipsum, propter quod remanet intellectus in quodam non determinate noto. The supernatural character of this light is also evident from a later passage in Cap. 1 (462.36–38): . . . _super mentem cognoscens_, idest supra naturam suae mentis, lumine divino desuper infuso, quo mens supra se elevatur. For translations of Albert's _Super MT_ I will generally make use of Tugwell, _Albert and Thomas: Selected Writings_ (I have slightly adapted Tugwell's translation from p. 139 here). It should be noted that Albert's view of _theologia ut scientia_ differs from that of his student Aquinas. Albert adhered to the Augustinian view that theology is fundamentally affective rather than speculative; see _In I Sent._, d. 1, a. 4 (_Op.Par._ XXV:18): . . . ista scientia proprie est affectiva; and _Summa Theologiae_, Lib. I, tr. 1, q. 2 (1:8).

41. On the distinction between philosophical and mystical contemplation in Albert, see Christian Trottmann, _La vision béatifique: Des disputes scolastiques à sa définition par Benoît XII_ (Rome: École Française de Rome, 1995), 292–302.

42. _Super Ethicam ad Nichomachum_, Liber X, lectio XVI (_Op.Col._ XIV.2:775.3–13): . . . in objecto etiam non quantum ad substantiam, sed quantum ad modum, quia philosophus contemplatur deum, secundum quod habet ipsum ut quandam conclusionem demonstrativam, sed theologus contemplatur ipsum ut supra rationem et intellectum existentem . . . sed theologus innititur primae veritatis propter se et non propter rationem, etiamsi habeat ipsam, et ideo theologus miratur, sed non philosophus.

43. _Summa Theologiae_, Lib. I, Prologus (1.57–59): Sola autem illa est quae cor elevat et ele-

vatum purificat et in aeterna fundat immortalitate. The prologus continues to quote equally from both theologians and philosophers (Aristotle several times, Averroes, and Alfarabi again).

44. Albert the Great, *Enarrationes in Secundam Partem Evangelii Lucae* (*Op.Par.* XXIII: 46b): . . . beatitudo contemplativa, quae est secundum actum perfectum virtutis intellectualis in summo contemplationis: quae consistit in actu contemplationis mirabilissimorum, purissimorum et certissimorum: non retracta, et non impedita, retenta in contemplando delectatione non habente contrarium. He goes on to treat such contemplation as the *beatitudo divina* intended for the intellect insofar as it is the image of God.

45. E.g., *In II Sent.*, d. 35, a. 1 (*Op.Par.* XXVIII:643–46) treats the nature of the gift of wisdom (i.e., supernatural wisdom) as "quoddam lumen divinorum sub quo videntur et gustantur divina per experimentum" (645a). The emphasis on experiencing and tasting the sweetness of God in a gift of light that is superior to faith is once again illustrated by Dionysius's reference to Hierotheus (DN 2.9 [648B]).

46. For an overview of Albert's teaching on the soul, see A. de Libera, *Albert le Grand*, chap. 6, "Psychologie philosophique et théologie de l'intellect," 215–65.

47. *De intellectu et intelligibili* (hereafter *De intell. et intellig.*) II.8 (*Op.Par.* IX:515b): . . . eo quod homo in quantum homo solus est intellectus. Cf. I.1 (478b): . . . et proprie homo scit quid proprie ipse est, cum sit solus intellectus, sicut dixit Aristoteles in X *Ethicorum*. . . .

48. See *Summa Theologiae*, Liber II, tr. 12, q. 69, c. 2, a. 2 (*Op.Par.* XXXIII:17); and *De intell. et intellig.* I.1.6–7 (486–89).

49. See Sturlese, *Die deutsche Philosophie*, 371–77.

50. For the sources for Albert's stages of the intellectual soul, see de Libera, *Albert le Grand*, 251–66.

51. *De intell. et intellig.* II.9 (516a): Est autem intellectus assimilativus, in quo homo quantum possibile et fas est proportionabiliter surgit ad intellectum divinum, qui est lumen et causa omnium.

52. *De intell et intellig.* II.9 (517b): Et ideo dicit Hermes Trismegistus in libro de *Natura Dei deorum*, quod "homo nexus est Dei et mundi": quia per hujusmodi intellectum conjungitur Deo, et stramentum hujus intellectus sunt alii intellectus de quibus diximus . . . . On the role of the Hermetic writings in Albert's thought, see Loris Sturlese, "Saints et magiciens: Albert le Grand en face d'Hermès Trismégiste," *Archives de Philosophie* 43 (1980): 615–34; and "Proclo ed Ermete in Germania da Alberto Magno a Bertoldo di Moosburg: Per una prospettiva di ricerca sulla cultura filosofica tedesca nel secolo delle sue origini (1250–1350)," in *Von Meister Dietrich zu Meister Eckhart*, ed. Kurt Flasch (Hamburg: Felix Meiner, 1984), 22–33. The work that Albert refers to as the *Natura Dei deorum* is the Hermetic treatise *Asclepius* (the reference here appears to be a summary of *Asclepius* 6a).

53. Sturlese, *Die deutsche Philosophie*, 381–88.

54. *De intell. et intellig.* I.3.2 (500a): Quaedam [intelligibilia] autem luce sua nostrum intellectum qui cum continuo et tempore est, vincentia sunt, sicut sunt manifestissima in natura quae se habent ad nostrum intellectum, sicut lumen solis vel fortissime scintillantis coloris ad oculos noctuae vel vespertilionis. Quadam autem non manifestantur nisi lumine alieno, sicut ea quae ex primis et veris accipiunt fidem. On the issue of Albert's shifting treatments of illumination, see Mark Führer, "Albertus Magnus' Theory of Divine Illumination," in *Albertus Magnus: Zum Gedenken nach 800 Jahren*, 141–55.

55. A. de Libera (*La mystique rhénane*) sees the two as correlative: "Le théorie avicenienne des degrés de l'intellect a ainsi pour corrélat naturel la doctrine dionysienne de la déification."

56. *Super MT* 1 (458.54–62): Dicendum, quod divina non accipiuntur per principia rationis, sed quodam experimento per "compassionem ad ipsa," sicut de Hierotheo dicit Dionysius, quod didicit divina "patiendo divina." Sed affectus infectus illicito rerum amore non sentit dulcedinem divinae inspirationis, et ideo deficiente cognitione, quae est per experimentum, potest quidem formare syllogismos et dicere propositiones, sed realem scientiam non

habet, quae est pars beatitudinis. On the role of Hierotheus as a model for mystical knowing, see the comments in Wéber, "L'interprétation par Albert le Grand de la Théologie mystique," 98.

57. _Super DN_ 2 (_Op.Col._ XXXVII.1:91–92) commenting on DN 2.9 (648B). The text cited here is 92.20–23: _Perfectus est ad unitionem ipsorum,_ idest divinorum, per affectum et intellectum, _et fidem,_ idest certam cognitionem spiritualium. . . . Albert also adds the useful point that such a _passio_ is really a _perfectio._ On the role of _cognitio_ and _affectus,_ see Wéber, "L'interprétation par Albert le Grand de la Théologie mystique," 420–21 and 436–37.

58. The discussion of Paul's ecstasy is found in _Super DN_ 4 (219.31–221.60). Here (220.40–41) Albert ascribes the axiom _nihil diligitur nisi cognitum_ to Augustine, probably thinking of _De spiritu et littera_ 36.64 (PL 44:423). Albert differs from Aquinas in denying that, properly speaking, there can be ecstasy in loving (220.50–70), though he admits that love can be a disposing cause for the ecstasy of the intellect. For more on the relation of love and knowledge, see the discussion of prayer as the affective instrument predisposing the soul for the reception of superior illumination in _Super DN_ 3 (104.61–92).

59. Trottmann, _La vision béatifique,_ 294. See also the account of the relation of love and knowledge in Tugwell, "Albert: Introduction," in _Albert and Thomas,_ 72–73.

60. Wéber, "L'interprétation par Albert le Grand de la Théologie mystique," 409–14. Hoye ("Mystische Theologie nach Albert dem Grossen," 595) is wrong in claiming that natural light is sufficient.

61. Albert does speak of faith as involving a kind of ecstasy insofar as it takes us outside our usual ways of knowing; see _Super DN_ 7 (364.26–40).

62. I cannot give attention to all these topics here. For example, in _Super MT_ 1 (462.46–463.33) there is an interesting discussion of the relation between _contemplatio_ and _raptus,_ in which Albert argues for the view that sees rapture as a higher dimension of contemplation. See also his _Quaestio de raptu_ in _Op.Col._ XXV.2:85–96.

63. _Super MT_ 1 (459.29–31): . . . communicat tamen quadam analogia imitationis, secundum quod alia imitantur ipsum, quantum possunt. In the comment on Cap. 2 Albert returns to this link between God and creatures, calling it a _communitas imitationis_ (467.53–60).

64. Albert appeals to what he calls the _regula Anselmi_ (cf. Anselm of Canterbury, _Proslogion_ 5) in _Super DN_ 7 (348.33–37): . . . sed omnia huiusmodi quae simpliciter et melius est esse quam non esse, secundum regulam Anselmi dicuntur analogice de deo et creaturis et primo inveniuntur in deo; ergo non debent de deo dici per privationem.

65. See _Super MT_ 5 (474.7–28). For Thomas Aquinas's teaching on the absolute simpleness of God as beyond all predication, see STh Ia, q. 3, especially a. 7.

66. _Super MT_ 1 (461.29–30): . . . et haec omnia oportet transcendere, quia nullum eorum est obiectum, quod quaerimus contemplatione.

67. For a survey of Albert's teaching on the supremacy of negation in the search for God, see Edouard Wéber, "Langage et méthode négatifs chez Albert le Grand," _Revue des sciences philosophiques et théologiques_ 65 (1981): 75–99.

68. _Super MT_ 2 (466.67–69): . . . confuse tamen et non determinate cognoscens "quia." Et ideo dicitur, quod per non-videre videtur deus, scilicet per non-videre naturale.

69. For some uses in the _Super MT,_ see, e.g., 454.82, 455.20, 464.1–3, 474.85–87.

70. _Super MT_ 2 (466.78–81): . . . quia non est pura negatio, sed negatur modus naturalis visionis et relinquitur susceptio supernaturalis luminis, quod tamen magis notificatur per negationem. . . .

71. _Summa Theologiae,_ Lib. I, tr. 3, q. 13, cap. 1 (39.21–2): Infiniti autem accipiendi ad finitum accipiens non est proportio. This axiom was later to be foundational to the thought of Nicholas of Cusa.

72. Ibid. (40.58–60 and 77–78): . . . procedendo symbolice stamus in infinito et diffundimur in illo, nullum terminum comprehendentes; . . . et ideo iterum intellectus sic procedens stat in infinito et diffunditur in illo.

73. _Quaestio de visione dei in patria_ (_Op.Col._ XXV.2:100.63–66): Licet sit ergo infinitus, finite

videbitur, quia non comprehendetur, tamen infinitus esse intelligetur, et in hoc finietur intellectus, scilicet cognoscendo ipsum infinitum.

74. The distinction between *negatio in genere* and pure negation (*negatio extra genus/per se negatio*) was well known to medieval philosophers. Albert describes the difference as follows in *Super DN* 13 (449.86–450.3): Dicendum, quo negatio, secundum id quod est per se negationis, non certificat neque coniungit; sed accidit negationi, quae est in genere, quod certificat et coniungit nos alicui cognoscibili, in quantum restringit ipsum genus, et talis est negatio, qua negamus aliquid de deo, quia relinquit ipsum esse, et inquantum removet ipsum ab uno oppositorum, relinquet ipsum in altero, et sic quousque ab omnibus removeatur et in esse proprio relinquatur. See also *Super DN* 4 and 7 (195.39–52, 358.88–359.5). On the significance of this distinction, see Wéber, "Langage et méthode," 92–94.

75. *Super MT* 5 (473.49–474.6). See Aquinas, STh Ia, q. 13, a. 3, for a comparable position.

76. *Super MT* 5 (474.7–28). Aquinas held that our diverse predications of God have a real foundation in the plenitude of the divine essence (STh Ia, q. 13, a. 4). In his In Ex. n. 58 (LW 2:64), Eckhart sides with Albert and advances a position that included a passage condemned as art. 23 in the papal bull "In agro dominico." This point, technical though it be, reflects an important difference between the rigorous apophaticism of the German heirs of Albert and the negative theology of Aquinas.

77. *Super MT* 5 (475.34–39): . . . et *excessus* eius qui est super omnia, excedit omnem negationem, ideo dicit, quod nomina, quae negantur ab ipso, negantur propter excessum et non propter defectum, sicut est in creaturis, et ideo excessus suus superat omnem negationem.

78. *Super Ep 1* (482.38–40): Et sic patet, quod non vult, quod nullo modo videatur deus, sed quod in ipsa sui ignorantia videtur. Cf. *Super Ep 5* (493.61–68). For a discussion, see Tugwell, "Albert: Introduction," 89–95.

79. Ten articles were condemned, the first of which was: *Primus* [error], quod divina essentia in se nec ab homine nec ab angelo videbitur. Hunc errorem reprobamus et assertores et defensores auctoritate Wilhermi episcopi excommunicamus. Firmiter autem credimus et asserimus, quod Deus in sua essentia vel substantia videbitur ab angelis et omnibus sanctis et videbitur ab animabus glorificatis. See the *Chartularium Universitatis Parisiensis*, ed. Henry Denifle OP (Paris: Delalain, 1889), Vol. 1, #128.

80. For Eriugena's teaching, consult Dominic J. O'Meara, "Eriugena and Aquinas on the Beatific Vision," in *ERIUGENA REDIVIVUS: Zur Wirkungsgeschichte seines Denkens im Mittelalter und im Übergang zur Neuzeit,* ed. Werner Beierwaltes (Heidelberg: Carl Winter, 1987), 224–36. As O'Meara points out, both Aquinas and others misunderstood Eriugena's position in viewing these theophanies as mediums for the vision of God. For the Irish thinker, theophanies are God, but God manifested.

81. See Trottmann, *La vision béatifique*, chapter 2, "Du *quid* au *quomodo* de la vision béatifique: Autour des condamnations de 1241–44" (pp. 115–208). Trottmann treats Albert's solution in chapter 4, "La solution intellectualiste d'Albert le Grand et de Thomas d'Aquin: le *lumen gloriae*" (pp. 282–302 on Albert). See also William J. Hoye, "Gotteserkenntnis per essentiam im 13. Jahrhundert," in *Die Auseinandersetzungen an der Pariser Universität im XIII. Jahrhundert,* ed. Albert Zimmermann (Berlin: Walter de Gruyter, 1976), 269–84, who treats Albert on 274–79.

82. *Summa Theologiae*, Lib. I, tr. 3, q. 13 (38–50). Two other important treatments are *De resurrectione ex parte bonorum tantum,* q. 1, a. 9 (*Op.Col.* XXVI:326–29); and the *Quaestio de visione dei in patria* (*Op.Col.* XXV.2:96–101).

83. *Summa Theologiae*, Lib. I, tr. 3, q. 13 (40.39–41): Aliud est contingere per intellectum et diffundi in intelligibili, et alius est capere sive comprehendere intelligibile.

84. Ibid. (41.3–45). For a similar argument, see *De resurrectione* q. 1, a. 9 (328.49–74).

85. A succinct text is found in Albert's *De resurrectione* (329.22–25): . . . "perfecta ignorantia" dicitur ignorantia perfecti, id est ignorantia eius quod est "quid est"; est enim perfectissima cognitio dei visio esse ipsius cum recognitione impotentiae attingendi "quid est." See also *Super DN* 1 (10.64–66): Dicimus, quod substantiam dei, "quia est," omnes beati videbunt;

"quid" autem sit, nullus intellectus creatus videre potest. This formula "non quid est, sed quia est," stems from Eriugena's *Periphyseon* 5 (PL 122:919C). On Albert's denial of *quid est* knowledge here and in heaven, see Trottmann, *La vision béatifique*, 193.

86. *Super MT* 1 (463.76–464.3), in dependence on Aristotle, *Posterior Analytics* 1.13 (78a22–38). See also *Super MT* 5 (475.12–17). In his commentary Albert seems to hold that faith and mystical illumination grant some form of *quia est* knowledge (e.g., 436.72–74, 456.72–74, 463.45–47, 464.1–3).

87. E.g., *Super DN* 7 (357.43–44), and *Summa Theologiae*, Lib. I, tr. 3, q. 14 (51.78–90). For a consideration of these texts and the ambiguity of *quia est* knowledge in Albert, see Hoye, "Mystische Theologie," 598–99.

88. *Super Ep* 5 (495.33–43): . . . intellectus creatus . . . sub quadam confusione iungitur ei quasi excedenti . . . ; . . . et ideo nec in via nec in patria videtur de ipso nisi "quia" confusum, quamvis ipse deus videatur clarius vel minus clare secundum diversos modos visionis et videntium. From these diverse treatments it seems (although he nowhere says so explicitly) that Albert distinguished at least three progressive modes of *cognitio quia confusa* in relation to God: (1) a minimal one available to natural reason; (2) an advanced form given in faith and enhanced by mystical illumination; and (3) a strong form given in heaven by the direct vision of God. A passage from *Super DN* 1.26 (13.52–57) says: . . . cognitio nostra perficietur non alia cognitione "quid" vel "propter quid," sed alio modo cognoscendi, quia videbimus "quia" [corrected from the reading "quid" as found in *Op.Col.*] sine medio, quod nunc in aenigmate et speculo et velate videmus.

89. For a good appreciation of this, as well as Albert's proximity to Eriugena, see Tugwell, "Albert: Introduction," in *Albert and Thomas*, 83–95. See also Wéber, "Langage et méthode," 80–81 and 785–87, on the influence of Eriugena on Albert.

90. The importance of this text for understanding Albert's doctrine of mystical knowing and the beatific vision was first noted by Giles Meersseman OP, "La contemplation mystique d'après le Bx. Albert est-elle immédiate?" *Revue Thomiste* 36 (1931): 408–21.

91. *Summa Theologiae*, Lib. I, tr. 3, q. 13 (46.26–38): Proprie dicitur facies dei praesentia evidens per effectum gratiae adiuvantis ad aliquid vel protegentis. . . . Et ille modus differt a primo, sicut natura differt a gratia.

92. Ibid. (46.46–48): Propriissime autem dicitur facies essentialis praesentia dei sine medio demonstrata et exhibita, hoc modo quo se exhibet beatis.

93. Ibid. (47.19–21): Si videt visione gratuita, oportet eum esse perfectum habitibus gratiae, sicut sunt sapientia et intellectus et gratia et fides.

94. Ibid. (47.21–27): Si videt visione gloriae, oportet eum esse perfectum habitibus gloriae et beatitudinis. Haec tamen media non tegunt vel deferunt vel distare faciunt videntem et visibile, sed visivam potentiam confortant et perficiunt ad videndum. Et ideo sic per medium videre non opponitur ad immediate videre, sed stat cum ipso. This enables Albert to give the following definition of the most proper meaning of face-to-face vision: ". . . et ideo propriissime facie ad faciem non videt nisi nudus intellectus nudam essentiam divinam, hoc est sine medio differente vel reflectente vel intentionaliter significante et sine medio coadiuvante videntem . . ." (47.51–57).

95. On this point, see Hoye, "Mystische Theologie," 599–601; and "Gotteserkenntnis per essentiam," 274–75. Albert stresses the partly subjective nature even of the divine lights we receive in this life (*Super MT* 1 [461.7–11]). They are given to us not so much as objects in which we inhere, but as aids to strengthen us on the way to God.

96. In his *Summa de creaturis*, tr. IV, q. 32, a. 1, "De theophania quid sit" (*Op.Par.* 34:507–10) Albert gives the following definition: Theophania est ostensio alicujus cognitionis de Deo per illuminationem a Deo venientem: et haec potest esse dupliciter, scilicet in symbolis, et facie ad faciem sive per speciem (509). Albert speaks of the *lumen gloriae* as *theophania*, for example, in *Super DN* 13 (448.31–49), and in the *Quaestio de visione dei in patria* (99.26–36). On the different ways in which God "meets" the blessed, that is, strengthens their individual

natures to see what of his infinity they are capable of seeing, *Super DN* 1 (11.12–25). See the discussion of the relation between *lumen gloriae* and *theophania* in Trottmann, *La vision béatifique*, 295–302.

97. *Super CH* 4 (*Op.Col.* XXXVI.1:71.20–25): . . . tertio modo, ut est in usu loquentium, quando in lumine divino, quod non est deus [i.e., a created light] videtur obiectum, quod vere est deus, non in lumine sicut in medio, sicut videtur res in sua imagine, sed sub lumine confortante intellectum videtur immediate deus. This seems to correspond to what in other places he calls the *lumen gloriae.* Albert criticizes Hugh of St. Victor for not recognizing the existence of this third type. Trottmann (*La vision béatifique,* 299–302) discusses the ambiguity of the third form and opts for the kind of Thomistic reading also suggested here. He states (p. 301), along with E. Wéber ("L'interpretation par Albert le Grand de la Théologie Mystique," 438–39), that some form of the third theophany may be accessible to mystics in this life.

98. *Super CH* 4(71.24–31): . . . sic deus ipse est in quolibet beato ut lumen quoddam, participatione sui faciens eum sui similitudinem, et in tali similitudine dei visio dicitur theophania; sic enim idem deus erit lumen et objectum, sed objectum prout in se, lumen vero, prout est participatus a beatis.

99. The texts of the works of Aquinas can be found in the old Parma edition and in the still ongoing Leonine edition (Rome, 1884–), as well as in many individual volumes and series. For the most part I will cite by work and section, rather than by edition.

100. William of Tocco, in the *Processus canonizationis S. Thomae Neapoli,* chap. 58, said: Tota vita eius fuit aut orare et contemplari, aut legere, predicare et disputare, aut scribere aut dictare (Antonio Ferrua, *Thomae Aquinatis vitae fontes praecipui* [Alba: Edizioni Dominicane, 1968], 287). Hagiographical tradition credits Thomas with a famous vision on December 6, 1273, in which a manifestation of God convinced him that everything he had written "was like straw," an experience that led to his abandoning further work on the STh. This incident and Thomas's devotion to contemplation are discussed in the most recent life of the Angelic Doctor, Jean-Pierre Torrell OP, *Saint Thomas Aquinas,* volume 1, *The Person and the Work* (Washington, D.C.: Catholic University of America Press, 1996), 283–95.

101. According to the *Index Thomisticus,* Aquinas uses the term *spiritualitas* about seventy times and *vita spiritualis* some 280 times. Thomas expresses the biblical conception of *spiritualitas* clearly when he says: "Sanctificatio gratiae pertinet ad spiritualitatem" (STh IIIa, q. 34, a. 1, obj. 1). His view is also deeply christological: because Christ had *perfecta spiritualitas* from the moment of the incarnation (IIIa, q. 34, a. 1, ad 1), all our *spiritualitas* flows from him (In 1 Cor. 15, lect. 7).

102. On Thomas's theology of prayer, see STh IIaIIae, q. 83, and other texts translated in Tugwell, *Albert and Thomas,* 363–523.

103. The literature about Thomas's relation to Aristotle, Plato, and especially Neoplatonism has grown exponentially in the past half-century. An older work that remains helpful for the Dominican's attitude toward Platonism is R. J. Henle, *Saint Thomas and Platonism* (The Hague: Martinus Nijhoff, 1956). The current view of Thomas's sources reveals him as far more Neoplatonic than would have been admitted fifty years ago, without making him less dependent on Aristotle.

104. See David B. Burrell, *Aquinas: God and Action* (Notre Dame: University of Notre Dame Press, 1979), 14–19; and *Knowing the Unknowable God: Ibn-Sina, Maimonides, Aquinas* (Notre Dame: University of Notre Dame Press, 1986), 38–50. In a slightly different vein, see Mark D. Jordan, "The Names of God and the Being of Names," in *The Existence and Nature of God,* ed. Alfred J. Freddoso (Notre Dame: University of Notre Dame Press, 1983), 161–90.

105. On Thomas's attitude toward the apophaticism of Maimonides as contrasted with that of Dionysius, see Jordan, "Names of God and the Being of Names," 165–67, 174–75. Thomas, like almost all scholastics and following Dionysius (DN 7.3 [872A]), distinguished three ways of predicating things of God: the way of causality; the way of eminence; and the way of negation (STh, q. 13, a. 1c).

106. *In Librum B. Dionysii De Divinis Nominibus Expositio* (hereafter: In DN), cap. 1, lect. 3, n. 83: Hoc est enim ultimum ad quod pertingere possumus circa cognitionem divinam in hac vita, quod Deus est supra omne id quod a nobis cogitari potest et ideo nominatio Dei quae est per remotionem est maxime propria. . . . Cf. *Scriptum super Libros Sententiarum I* (In I Sent.) d. 8, q. 1, a. 1, ad 4; *Summa contra Gentiles* (SCG) I.14; *In Boethium De Trinitate* (In De Trin.) q. 6, a. 2; *De Veritate* (De Ver.) q. 8, a. 1, ad 8; and *Super Evangelium S. Iohannis* (Super Io.) 1:18, lect. 11, n. 211; etc.

107. For an example of Thomas's use of the Dionysian dialectic of presence and absence, see, In DN cap. 7, lect. 1, nn. 701–2.

108. In De Trin. q. 1, a. 2, ad 1: Ad primum ergo dicendum quod secundum hoc dicimur in fine nostrae cognitionis deum tamquam ignotum cognoscere, quia tunc maxime mens in cognitione profecisse invenitur, quando cognoscit eius essentiam esse supra omne quod apprehendere potest in statu viae, et sic quamvis maneat ignotum quid est, scitur tamen quia est.

109. See David B. Burrell, "Aquinas on Naming God," *Theological Studies* 24 (1963): 183–212.

110. De Ver. q. 18, a. 1: Non igitur visio beati a visione viatoris distinguitur per hoc quod est perfectius et minus perfecte videre, sed per hoc quod est videre et non videre. For a detailed treatment of why it is impossible to see the divine essence in this life, see De Ver. q. 10, a. 11. Thomas treats *visio dei* in many places; see, e. g., SCG III.51–63; *Quaestiones Quodlibetales* (Quod.) VIII, q. 9, aa. 1–2. The literature on the topic is large; for a brief introduction, see Trottmann, *La vision béatifique*, 302–20.

111. For Aquinas's treatments of this issue, see In II Sent. d. 23, a. 1; De Ver. q. 18, a. 1; and STh Ia, q. 94, a. 1. For discussion, see Lucien Roy SJ, *Lumière et Sagesse: La grace mystique dans la Théologie de saint Thomas d'Aquin* (Montréal: Studia Collegii Maximi Immaculatae Conceptionis, 1948), 118–23.

112. De Ver. q. 18, a. 1, ad 1: Indigebat autem medio quod est quasi species rei visae; quia per aliquod spirituale lumen menti hominis influxum divinitus, quod erat quasi similitudo expressa lucis increatae, Deum videbat.

113. De Ver. q. 18, a. 1, ad 4: . . . in contemplatione Deus videtur per medium, quod est lumen sapientiae, mentem elevans ad cernenda divina; non autem ut ipsa divina essentia immediate videatur: et sic per gratiam videtur a contemplante post statum peccati, quamvis perfectius in statu innocentiae.

114. See STh IIaIIae, qq. 171–89. The treatise is divided into three parts: (a) the diversity of gratuitous graces, dealing primarily with prophecy and rapture (qq. 171–78); (b) the different modes of life, treating the contemplative and active lives (qq. 179–82); and (c) the various religious states of life (qq. 183–89). The first two sections are the subject of the excellent commentary of Hans Urs von Balthasar, *Thomas und die Charismatik: Kommentar zu Thomas von Aquin Summa Theologica Quaestiones II II 171–182; Besondere Gnadengaben und die zwei menschlichen Lebens* (Freiburg: Johannes Verlag, 1996). For a translation with notes of qq. 179–82, see Tugwell, *Albert and Thomas*, 534–85. Although Thomas treats contemplation here in association with the *gratiae gratis datae*, there is a sense in which contemplation is also a prolongation of the grace of sanctification (*gratia gratum faciens*). This tension in Thomas's thought is noted and discussed both by Roy (*Lumière et Sagesse*, 51–54, 284–90) and von Balthasar (*Thomas und die Charismatik*, 282–84, 469–71). Thomas seems to want to have it both ways (e.g., STh IIaIIae, q. 45, a. 6c) without being clear on the relation of the two categories of grace to *contemplatio*.

115. For some other treatments of contemplation, see, e.g., In III Sent. d. 34, q. 1, a. 2, and d. 35, q. 1, a. 2; *Expositio super Isaiam* (In Is.) Cap. 1 and Cap. 6; *Expositio super Matthiam* (In Mt.) Cap. 5, lect. 2 (Aquinas's comment on Matt. 5:8: "Blessed are the pure of heart for they shall see God"); and In DN, Cap. 4, lect. 7. On St. Thomas's doctrine of contemplation, besides von Balthasar and Roy, see Joseph Maréchal, *Études sur la psychologie des mystiques*, 2 vols. (Paris: Alcan/Desclée, 1924–37), "Le sommet de la contemplation d'après Saint

Thomas" (2:193–234); and Inos Biffi, *Teologia, Storia e Contemplazione in Tommaso d'Aquino* (Milan: Jaca Book, 1995). See also the treatment of Aquinas in Ruh, *Geschichte,* 3:130–63.

116. I translate the word *intuitus* here not by "intuition" but by "consideration," because I believe modern understandings of intuition tend to misperceive Thomas's intellectualist epistemology. Knowing for Aquinas takes place not by way of confrontational gaze, but by an identification of knower and known—perfection, act, identity. A *simplex intuitus* is a knowing identity that is not discursive in nature. It should also be noted that *intuitus* is an analogical term, since the fullest form of *intuitus* is found in God: *praesens intuitus Dei fertur in totum tempus* (Ia, q. 14. a. 9c). My approach to Thomas's epistemology is based on Bernard J. Lonergan, *Verbum: Word and Idea in Aquinas* (Notre Dame: University of Notre Dame Press, 1967); see also William E. Murnion, "St. Thomas Aquinas's Theory of the Act of Understanding," *The Thomist* 37 (1973): 88–118.

117. In Is. Cap. 1: Est enim quaedam visio ad quam sufficit lumen naturale intellectus, sicut est contemplatio inuisibilium per principia rationis; et in hac contemplatione ponebant philosophi summam felicitatem hominis. Est iterum quaedam contemplatio ad quam eleuatur homo per lumen fidei sufficienter, sicut sanctorum in uia. Est etiam quaedam beatorum in patria, ad quam eleuatur intellectus per lumen gloriae, uidens Deum per essentiam in quantum est obiectum beatitudinis. . . .

118. Thomas explicitly cites Aristotle's famous text on the contemplative life (*Nicomachean Ethics* X.7 [1177a–78a]) several times in STh IIaIIae (e.g., q. 180, a. 2c; a. 7, ad 3). See Aquinas's commentary on this passage in his *In Ethicorum Aristotelis ad Nichomachum* X (In Eth.), lect. 10–11. On the Aristotelian element in Thomas's doctrine of contemplation, consult von Balthasar, *Thomas und die Charismatik,* 538, 571–72; and Biffi, *Teologia, Storia e Contemplazione,* 49–50, 70, 76.

119. Jean Leclercq, "La vie contemplative dans S. Thomas et dans la tradition," *Recherches de théologie ancienne et médiévale* 28 (1961): 251–66. The main authorities that Thomas cites are Gregory the Great, Cassian, Augustine, Bernard, Dionysius, and Richard of St. Victor.

120. STh IIaIIae, q. 180, a. 4c. The same perspective is evident in aa. 5, 6, and especially 8, where Thomas discusses the nature of contemplation as *diuturna,* or lasting, not only because it concerns incorruptible things but also because the incorruptible intellect lasts beyond this life.

121. Thomas's treatment of contemplation as a synthesizing process is evident also in the fact that q. 180 treats the contemplative life, not the act of contemplation per se. This approach of Thomas to the meaning of contemplation bears a resemblance to the case made in these volumes for the broad meaning of mysticism as a process.

122. Q. 180, a. 6, extends this by defending a text from DN 4.7 on the threefold contemplative motion of the soul. The soul needs to use rectilinear and oblique motion in order to attain the circular motion which is the image of "the simple contemplation of intelligible truth."

123. Q. 180, a. 1c: Et quia unusquisque delectatur cum adeptus fuerit id quod amat, ideo vita contemplativa terminatur ad delectationem, quae est in affectu: ex qua etiam amor intenditur.

124. Q. 180, a. 7, ad 1: . . . vita contemplativa, licet essentialiter consistat in intellectu, principium tamen habet in affectu: . . . Et quia finis respondet principio, inde est quod etiam terminus et finis contemplativae vitae habetur in affectu: dum scilicet aliquis in visione rei amatae delectatur, et ipsa delectatio rei visae amplius excitat amorem. See the comment on this article in von Balthasar, *Thomas und die Charismatik,* 558–61. For another text on the role of love in contemplation, consult In III Sent. d. 35, q. 1, a. 2, sol. 1. L. Roy (*Lumière et Sagesse,* 280) summarizes nicely: "La contemplation est intellectuelle dans sa ligne essentielle, mais affective dans le plan existentiel, sous son aspect de vie."

125. In I Sent. d. 3, q. 4, a. 5: Intelligere autem dicit nihil aliud quam simplicem intuitum intellectus in id quod sibi est praesens intelligibile. . . . Ad talem enim cognitionem non sufficit praesentia rei quolibet modo; sed oportet ut sit ibi in ratione objecti, et exigitur intentio

cognoscentis. Sed secundum quod intelligere nihil aliud dicit quam intuitum, qui nihil aliud est quam praesentia intelligibilis ad intellectum quocumque modo, sic anima semper intelligit se et Deum, et consequitur quidam amor indeterminatus.

126. This is not the only place where Thomas speaks of such an innate presence of God in the soul; see, e.g., De Ver. q. 10, a. 7, ad 2. On these texts, see Lonergan, *Verbum,* 91–93.

127. On *cognitio experimentalis,* see Torrell, *Saint Thomas,* vol. 2, *Spiritual Master,* 94–98, and the literature cited there.

128. In I Sent. d. 14, q. 2, a. 2, ad 2; see also d. 16, q. 1, a. 2, sol.

129. STh Ia, q. 43, a. 5, ad 2: Non igitur secundum quamlibet perfectionem intellectus mittitur Filius: sed secundum talem instructionem intellectus, qua prorumpat in affectum amoris . . . . Quod Filius mittitur, *cum a quoquam cognoscitur etque percipitur* [Augustine, *De Trin.* 4.10]: perceptio enim experimentalem quandam notitiam significat. Et haec proprie dicitur *sapientia,* quasi *sapida scientia* . . . . For a comparable passage, see In I Sent. d. 15, q. 2, ad 5.

130. STh IaIIae, q. 97, a. 2, ad 2: Alia est cognitio divinae bonitatis seu voluntas affectiva seu experimentalis, . . . sicut de Hierotheo dicit Dionysius, . . . quod *didicit divina ex compassione ad ipsa.* Et hoc modo monemur ut probemus Dei voluntatem et gustemus eius suavitatem. Thomas discusses the affective character of Hierotheus's union in In DN, Cap. 2, lect. 4, n. 191. For other passages on the experience of divine sweetness, see especially the Dominican's commentary on the Psalms, e.g., In Psalmos 24.7, 30.16–17, and 33.9. For background on the role of experience in Thomas, see Pierre Miquel, "La place et le rôle de l'expérience dans la théologie de saint Thomas," *Recherches de théologie ancienne et médiévale* 39 (1972): 63–70.

131. For both Albert and Thomas, Dionysius's description of Hierotheus "suffering, or receiving, divine things" through "compassion with them" became a classic example of mystical consciousness. Dionysius wrote: . . . *ou monon mathôn alla kai pathôn ta theia* (DN 2.9 [648B]), emphasizing both the passivity and the immediacy of the divine action on Hierotheus. This was variously translated into Latin: (1) *non tantum discens sed et patiens divina* (Hilduin, Sarrazin, Grosseteste); (2) *non solum discens sed et affectus divina* (Eriugena); and (3) *sive per divinam inspirationem et divinorum experientiam* (Thomas Gallus). For a treatment of this Dionysian text and its interpretation with useful remarks on Aquinas, see Ysabel de Andia, "'*pathôn ta theia,*'" in *Platonism in Late Antiquity,* ed. Stephen Gersh and Charles Kannengiesser (Notre Dame: University of Notre Dame Press, 1992), 239–58.

132. The most detailed treatment of *iudicium per connaturalitatem,* or *per modum inclinationis* is in Biffi, *Teologia, Storia e Contemplazione,* 89–127; see also Roy, *Lumière et Sagesse,* 261–63.

133. For another mention of connaturality and judgment by inclination, see Ia, q. 1, a. 6.

134. Biffi, *Teologia, Storia et Contemplazione,* 94–98.

135. STh IaIIae, q. 45, a. 2c: . . . sapientia importat quandam rectitudinem iudicii secundum rationes divinas. Rectitudo autem iudicii potest contingere dupliciter: uno modo, secundum perfectum usum rationis; alio modo, propter connaturalitatem quandam ad ea de quibus iam est iudicandum. . . . Sic igitur circa res divinas ex rationis inquisitione rectum iudicium habere pertinet ad sapientiam quae est virtus intellectualis: sed rectum iudicium habere de eis secundum quandam connaturalitatem ad ipsa pertinet ad sapientiam secundum quod donum est Spiritus Sancti . . . . Huiusmodi autem compassio sive connaturalitas ad res divinas fit per caritatem, quae quidem unit nos Deo: secundum illud I ad Cor. 6, 17: *Qui adhaeret Deo unus spiritus est.* Sic igitur sapientia quae est donum causam quidem habet in voluntate, scilicet caritatem; sed essentiam habet in intellectu, cuius actus est recte iudicare. . . . For a comparable text, see In III Sent. d. 35, q. 2, a. 1, sol. 3c.

136. For charity as the greatest of the theological virtues, see STh IaIIae, q. 66, a. 6. Torrell (*Saint Thomas,* vol. 2, *Spiritual Master,* chapter 14) has a good treatment of Aquinas's view of charity. On the indwelling or inhabitation of the Trinity, see, e.g., In I Sent. d. 14, q. 2, a. 1; and d. 15, q. 4, a. 1; STh Ia, q. 43, a. 3c; and SCG IV.23. The indwelling of the Trinity is a major theme of Torrell's book; see also the older works of Francis L. B. Cunningham OP, *The*

Indwelling of the Trinity: A Historico-Doctrinal Study of the Theory of St. Thomas Aquinas (Dubuque: Priory Press, 1955); and Noel Molloy OP, "The Trinitarian Mysticism of St. Thomas," *Angelicum* 57 (1980): 373–88.

137. Thomas speaks of union with God relatively often, sometimes citing the standard biblical proof text for loving union of wills (1 Cor. 6:17). For some representative texts in STh, see Ia, q. 43, a. 5, ad 2; IIaIIae, q. 82, a. 2, ad 1; IIIa, q. 6, a. 6, ad 1. See also In DN 13.3, n. 996.

138. Although beatitude consists essentially in the intellect, there is a key role for the will and love, as we have seen. The same is true with regard to contemplation of God in this life. On the necessary roles of both knowing and loving, see, e.g., STh Ia, q. 43, a. 5, ad 2; q. 82, a. 3; IaIIae, q. 27, a. 2, ad 2; q. 27, a. 4; q. 28, a. 1; q. 62, a. 3; q. 175, a. 2; and q. 180, aa. 1 and 7, discussed above.

139. Aquinas discusses *sapientia*, both natural and supernatural, in many places. The most important treatment is in IIaIIae, q. 45; other useful texts can be found in Ia, q. 1, a. 6; Ia IIae, q. 57, a. 2; SCG II.24 and IV.12; In De Trin. q. 1, a. 2; etc. For a full treatment of the role of wisdom, see Roy, *Lumière et Sagesse*, part 3.

140. In DN 7.4, n. 731: . . . et iterum cognoscitur *per ignorantiam* nostram, in quantum scilicet hoc ipsum est Deum cognoscere, quod nos scimus nos ignorare de Deo quid sit.

141. In DN 7.4, n. 732: Et sic cognoscens Deum, in tali statu cognitionis, illuminatur ab ipsa profunditate divinae Sapientiae, quam perscrutari non possumus.

142. See Dietmar Mieth, *Die Einheit von Vita Activa und Vita Passiva in den deutschen Predigten und Traktaten Meister Eckharts und bei Johannes Tauler* (Regensburg: Pustet, 1969), and the discussions in chapters 4 and 6 (190–93, and 269–70 and 294).

143. For a treatment of the disputes, both in the tradition and among the scholastics, see von Balthasar, *Thomas und die Charismatik*, 429–54, and the literature cited there. Von Balthasar comments exhaustively on Thomas's treatment in IIaIIae, q. 175 on pp. 454–99. For other classic treatments, see Joseph Maréchal, "Note d'enseignement théologique: La notion d'extase, d'après l'enseignement traditionnel des mystiques et des théologiens," *Nouvelle revue théologique* 63 (1937): 986–98; and his *Études sur la psychologie des mystiques* 2:204–8, 237–50. The lengthy article devoted to "Extase" in DS 4:2045–2190 treats Thomas on 2126–30.

144. Augustine, *De Trinitate* 12.26, and 28 (PL 34:476, 478); and Ep. 147.13 (PL 33:610). STh IIaIIae, q. 175, a. 3, says that Augustine's view is *convenientius*. Aquinas also discusses Paul's rapture In 2 Cor., Cap. 12, lect. 1–2.

145. Many details of Thomas's treatment of Paul's rapture, interesting as they are, will not be taken up here. See, for example, the discussion of the relation of vision of the essence of God to the Apostle's later memory of the event in De Ver. q. 13, a. 3, ad 4.

146. For a treatment of the vision given to Moses, see, e.g., In IV Sent. d. 49, a. 7, ad 4.

147. In Quod. q. 1, a. 1, Thomas denies that Benedict saw God's essence in the famous vision recounted by Gregory the Great (*Dialogi* 2.35), because Benedict was not alienated from his senses.

148. For a treatment of the ecstasy of love in Dionysius, see McGinn, *Foundations of Mysticism*, 179–80. I discuss Thomas's treatment of this passage in his DN commentary (In DN, Cap. 4, lect. 10, nn. 426–41) in my article "God as Eros: Metaphysical Foundations of Christian Mysticism," in *New Perspectives on Historical Theology: Essays in Memory of John Meyendorff*, ed. Bradley Nassif (Grand Rapids: Eerdmans, 1996), 204–7. For another passage on the ecstasy of love citing DN 4.13, see In III Sent. d. 32, a. 1, ad 3.

149. These two points are noted by von Balthasar, *Thomas und die Charismatik*, 455–56, 462–63.

150. The term "mystics" would, of course, have been foreign to Thomas; he refers to *spirituales, sancti, perfecti*, and even *contemplativi*, throughout IIaIIae, q. 180.

151. There are two recent editions of the Latin version of the *Liber de causis*, along with

studies and German translations. See Alexander Fidora and Andreas Niederberger, *Von Bagdad nach Toledo: Das "Buch der Ursachen" und seine Rezeption im Mittelalter* (Mainz: Dieterich'sche
Verlagsbuchhandlung, 2001); and [Anonymous] *Liber de causis: Das Buch von den Ursachen,*
with an introduction by Rolf Schönberger (Hamburg: Felix Meiner, 2003). There is an English translation of the *Liber de causis* by Dennis J. Brand, *The Book of Causes [Liber de Causis]*
(Milwaukee: Marquette University Press, 1984). This is based on the earlier edition of Adri-
aan Pattin, *Le LIBER DE CAUSIS: Édition établie à l'aide de 90 manuscrits avec introduction et
notes* (Leuven: Uitgave "Tijdschrift voor Filosophie," 1966). For a treatment of the role of the
Liber de causis among medieval mystics, see Ruh, *Geschichte,* 3:19–32.

152. Richard C. Taylor, "A Critical Analysis of the Structure of the *Kalām fī mahd al-khair
(Liber de causis),*" in *Neoplatonism and Islamic Thought,* ed. Parvis Morewedge (Albany: SUNY
Press, 1992), 21.

153. The *Liber* originally consisted of thirty-one propositions (subdivided into 219 sections
by modern editors). Somewhat confusingly, one manuscript tradition split proposition 4 into
two parts. Since this was the version known to most scholastics, it will be reflected in the citations used here (e.g., Prop. 5(6).57). Thus, the book was much shorter than Proclus's text,
which contained 211 propositions. (It has been calculated that the *Liber* uses material from
thirty-seven of Proclus's propositions, so about a sixth.) See *Proclus: The Elements of Theology; A
Revised Text,* with translation, introduction, and commentary by E. R. Dodds, 2nd ed.
(Oxford: Clarendon Press, 1963).

154. Brand, *Book of Causes,* 7.

155. Richard C. Taylor, "The *Kalām fī mahd al-khair (Liber de causis)* in the Islamic Philosophic Milieu," in *Pseudo-Aristotle in the Middle Ages: The "Theology" and Other Texts,* ed. Jill
Kraye, W. F. Ryan, and C. B. Schmitt (London: Warburg Institute, 1986), 37–52.

156. Aquinas's commentary, written in 1272, is important for understanding his relation to
Neoplatonism. See the edition by Ceslaus Pera OP, *S. Thomae Aquinatis: In Librum de causis
Expositio* (Turin: Marietti, 1955). There is an English translation with helpful introduction and
notes, *St. Thomas Aquinas: Commentary on the Book of Causes,* trans. Vincent A. Guagliardo OP,
Charles R. Hess, and Richard C. Taylor (Washington, D.C.: Catholic University of America
Press, 1996).

157. The most detailed treatment of Eckhart's use of the *Liber* is Werner Beierwaltes, "Primum est dives per se: Meister Eckhart und der 'Liber de causis,'" in *On Proclus and His Influence in Medieval Philosophy,* ed. E. P. Bos and P. A. Meijer (Leiden: Brill, 1992), 141–69.

158. On the distinction between axiomatic treatises like Euclid and deductive treatises, see
Charles Lohr, "The Pseudo-Aristotelian *Liber de causis* and Latin Theories of Science in the
Twelfth and Thirteenth Centuries," in *Pseudo-Aristotle in the Middle Ages,* 53–62.

159. Richard C. Taylor ("Critical Analysis of the Structure," 15–17) outlines the work as
follows: (A) General Principle (Prop. 1); (B) True Being (Props. 2–5); (C) The Intelligence
(Props. 6–10); (D) Epistemological Considerations (Props. 11–14); (E) Infinity (Props. 15–16);
(F) The First Cause (Props. 17–23); (G) Substances (Props. 34–31). For another view, see
Cristina D'Ancona Costa, "Sources et Structure du *Liber de causis,*" in her *Recherches sur le Liber
de causis* (Paris: J. Vrin, 1995), 23–52.

160. For a brief sketch of this and some of the main lines of Proclus's thought that influenced Dionysius and other Christian mystics, see McGinn, *Foundations of Mysticism,* 57–61.

161. Leo Sweeney SJ, "Doctrine of Creation in the *Liber de causis,*" in *An Etienne Gilson
Tribute,* ed. Charles J. O'Neil (Milwaukee: Marquette University Press, 1959), 289. See also
D'Ancona Costa, "Sources et Structure," 52.

162. Prop. 8(9).90 (ed. Fidora-Niederberger, 66): Et causae quidem primae non est
yliathim, quoniam ipsa est esse tantum. On this passage and the Arabic term *yliathim,* see
D'Ancona Costa, "'Causae primae non est yliathim': *Liber de causis,* prop. 8(9): les sources et
la doctrine," in *Recherches sur le Liber de causis,* 97–119. In another chapter in this work, "La
doctrine néoplatonicienne de l'être entre l'antiquité tardive et moyen âge: Le *Liber de causis*
par report à ses sources" (pp. 121–53), D'Ancona Costa argues that the book's ascription of

being to the First Cause may come from the Syriac version of the Dionysian corpus, specifically DN 5.

163. For example, Prop. 1.17 (ed. Fidora-Niederberger, 38): Quod est quia causa secunda quando facit rem, influit causa prima quae est supra eam super illam rem de virtute sua, quare adhaeret illus rei adhaerentia vehementi et servat eam. The language of *fluxus* is particularly strong in the later propositions, e.g., Props. 19(20).157; Prop. 20(21).165; Prop. 21(22).169–70; Prop. 22(23).173 and 179.

164. See D'Ancona Costa, "La doctrine de la création 'mediante intelligentia' dans le *Liber de causis* et dans ses sources," in *Recherches sur Le Liber de causis*, 73–95.

165. Thomas Aquinas, In II Sent. d. 1, q. 1, a. 3, denounces the creation by intermediate intelligence view of Avicenna as heretical, though he allows Peter Lombard's position that God could have shared creation with the angels (but did not). By the time of STh Ia, q. 45, a. 5, he rejects even the Lombard's view.

166. See *Thomas Aquinas: Commentary on the Book of Causes*, Prop. 3 (24), and Prop. 8(9) (69–70). Meister Eckhart holds the same doctrine in dependence on Thomas in Pr. 8 (DW 1:130.9–131.5).

167. For the triad in Proclus, see, e.g., *Elements of Theology*, Prop. 103; for the Dionysian re-reading, see DN 5.1–2.

168. Vincent A. Guagliardo OP, "Introduction," *Thomas Aquinas: Commentary on the Book of Causes*, xix.

169. There are many other aspects of the teaching of the *Liber de causis* that influenced the mysticism of Eckhart and his followers. See, for example, the principle of reciprocal omnipresence (Prop. 11[12].103 and 106, Prop. 23[24].176–77); the *reditio completa* involved in essential knowing (Prop. 14[15]); the notion that the First is superabundant richness (*primum est dives per se*: Prop. 20[21]); and the discussion of the relation between time and eternity in Props. 29–31(30–32).

170. The critical edition of the work and the commentaries on it is by Françoise Hudry, *Liber Viginti Quattuor Philosophorum* (CCCM 143A; Turnhout: Brepols, 1997). There is a discussion of its significance and influence, along with an edition and translation, in Paolo Lucentini, *Il libro dei ventiquattro filosofi* (Milan: Adelphi, 1999). Ruh (*Geschichte*, 3:33–44) has remarks on its role in late medieval mysticism, especially its treatment by Eckhart.

171. On the medieval Hermetica, see K. H. Dannenfeldt et al., "Hermetica Philosophica," in *Catalogus Translationum et Commentariorum: Medieval and Renaissance Latin Translations and Commentaries*, ed. P. O. Kristeller et al. (Washington, D.C.: Catholic University of America Press, 1960), 1:137–56. Attention was drawn to the importance of the Hermetic tradition by A.-J. Festugière OP, *La révélation d'Hermes Trismégiste*, 4 vols. (Paris: Gabalda, 1950–54); and Frances A. Yates, *Giordano Bruno and the Hermetic Tradition* (Chicago: University of Chicago Press, 1964). See also Garth Fowden, *The Egyptian Hermes: A Historical Approach to the Late Pagan Mind* (Cambridge: Cambridge University Press, 1986), on the origins of Hermetism; and *From Poimandres to Jacob Böhme: Gnosis, Hermetism and the Christian Tradition*, ed. Roelof van den Broek and Cis van Heertum (Amsterdam: In de Pelikaan, 2000), for the later influence.

172. The work has various titles and is ascribed to different figures in the manuscript tradition. The customary modern title of *Liber XXIV philosophorum* occurs in Meister Eckhart; e.g., In Gen. I n. 155 (LW 1:305), and In Ex. n. 91 (LW 2:94–95).

173. Hudry, "Introduction," *Liber Viginti Quattuor Philosophorum*, vi.

174. Hudry, "Introduction," xxxi. It is interesting to see Bonaventure, In I. Sent. d. 37, q. 1, a. 1, ad 3 (*Opera Omnia* 1:638–39) bringing the two texts together to show how divine simple immobility and total diffusion are not contradictory.

175. Hudry ("Introduction," xlviii–l) suggests that the English Dominican Nicholas Trivet may be the author of the larger commentary and that he was possibly inspired to undertake the task by Eckhart, whom he could have met in Paris during the German's second magistral period (1311–13).

176. Hudry ("Introduction," viii–ix) divides the twenty-four definitions in three: I–VII on the divine nature; VIII–XX on God and the world; and XXI–XXIV on God and the soul.

177. This was the view of the original editor, Clemens Baeumker, "Das pseudo-hermetische 'Buch der vierundzwanzig Meister' (Liber XXIV philosophorum)," in *Studien und Charakteristiken zur Geschichte der Philosophie insbesonder des Mittelalters* (Münster: Aschendorff, 1927), 194–214; and also Marie-Thérèse d'Alverny, "Un témoin muet des lottes doctrinales du XIIIe siècle," *Archives d'histoire doctrinale et littéraire du moyen âge* 24 (1949): 223–48.

178. For Hudry's case, see "Introduction," ix–xxii. For doubts about the argument, see Lucentini, *Il libro,* 43–46; Alexander Fidora and Andreas Niederberger, *Vom Einen zum Vielen: Der neue Aufbruch der Metaphysik im 12. Jahrhundert* (Frankfurt: Klostermann, 2002), xxxi–xxxiv; and Ruh, *Geschichte,* 3:34–36.

179. Giulio D'Onofrio, *Storia della teologia nel Medioevo,* volume 2, *La grande fioritura* (Casale Monferrato: Piemme, 1996), 353–56; Lucentini, *Il libro,* 13–14, 43–46.

180. The ternary nature of the supreme *monas* is strong in axioms I, IV, VII, X, XII, XV, and XXII. Two of these also contain implied scriptural references (John 14:6 in axiom XV, and Rom. 11:36 in axiom XXII)—another sign of a Christian origin.

181. *Liber Viginti Quattuor* (ed. Hudry, 5): Deus est monas monadem gignens, in se unum reflectens ardorem. The trinitarian implications are evident in the language of generation and the reference to the love that is the Holy Spirit. On the background of the axiom and its later influence, see Lucentini, *Il libro,* 21–29, 111–24. Hudry ("Introduction," ix–x) sees the use of *monas* and other Greek terms as proof of a Greek original, but many of these words were well known in the Latin tradition. On God as *monas,* see, e.g., Augustine, *Confessiones* 4.5.24; and Macrobius, *Commentum in Somnium Scipionis* I.6.7–8.

182. Paul Ricoeur, *The Symbolism of Evil* (New York: Harper, 1967).

183. *Liber Viginti Quattuor* (ed. Hudry, 7): II. Deus est sphaera infinita cuius centrum est ubique circumferentia nusquam. Haec definitio data est per modum imaginandi ut continuum ipsam primam causam in uita sua. Terminus quidem suae extensionis est supra, ubi et extra terminans.

184. The best account remains Dietrich Mahnke, *Unendliche Sphäre und Allmittelpunkt: Beiträge zur Genealogie der mathematischen Mystik* (Halle: Max Niemeyer, 1937). See also the discussion in Lucentini, *Il Libro,* 30–37, 124–50.

185. Lucentini, *Il Libro,* 36–37.

186. An apophatic note is found in the axioms or comments on II, VIII, XI, XVI, XVII, XXI, and XXIII.

187. *Liber Viginti Quattuor* (ed. Hudry, 31): Nihil cognoscitur ab anima nisi cuius speciem recipere potest et ad exemplar eius quod est in ipse comparare. Nullius enim habet anima exemplar nisi illius quod per ipsam a prima causa fluit in esse. The meaning is that there is no exemplar of God in the mind, but only of the things that flow from God. For more on *fluxus,* see axiom VI (12.9): . . . substantia diuina est ut substantia propria quae non fluit; and axiom XIV (21.3–6): . . . sphaera diuina . . . a quo per exuberantiam suae bonitatis uocauit in esse rem quae est quasi circa centrum.

188. Aquinas cites axiom I in STh Ia, q. 32, a. 1, arguing that the saying does not refer to the Trinity, but to God's production of the world. De Ver. q. 2, a. 3, obj. 11, cites axiom II as known through Alan of Lille.

189. On Eckhart's use of the *Liber XXIV,* see Ruh, *Geschichte,* 3:38–44; and Lucentini, *Il Libro,* 121–22 and 130–34.

190. Loris Sturlese, "Proclo ed Ermete in Germania da Alberto Magno a Bertoldo di Moosburg," in *Von Meister Dietrich zu Meister Eckhart,* 28.

191. *Marguerite Porete: Le mirouer des simples ames,* ed. Romana Guarnieri and Paul Verdeyen (CCCM 69; Turnhout: Brepols, 1986), chapter 115 (308.8–9), paraphrases axiom I to describe the love that annihilated souls have for God: Hee, Unité, dit l'Ame sourprinse de divine Bonté, vous engendrez unité, et unité reflecist son ardour en unité. Whether Mar-

guerite knew the text directly, or became aware of this axiom through independent citation, is difficult to ascertain.

192. For a sketch of the history of medieval Platonism that has retained much value despite its age, see Raymond Klibansky, *The Continuity of the Platonic Tradition during the Middle Ages* (London: Warburg Institute, 1939).

193. Two stimulating approaches to this intellectual tradition are Stephen Gersh, *From Iamblichus to Eriugena: An Investigation of the Prehistory and Evolution of the Pseudo-Dionysian Tradition* (Leiden: Brill, 1978); and Edward Booth OP, *Aristotelian Aporetic Ontology in Islamic and Christian Thinkers* (Cambridge: Cambridge University Press, 1983).

194. For an overview of the influence of Proclus, see Paul Oskar Kristeller, "Proclus as a Reader of Plato and Plotinus, and His Influence in the Middle Ages and Renaissance," in *Proclus: Lecteur et interprète des anciens* (Paris: CNRS, 1987), 191–211. A number of useful studies can be found in *On Proclus and his Influence in Medieval Philosophy*; and *Proclus et son influence: Actes du Colloque de Neuchâtel*, ed. G. Boss and G. Seel (Zurich: Éditions du Grand Midi, 1987).

195. On Moerbeke as translator, see especially Lorenzo Minio-Paluello, "Moerbeke, William of," *Dictionary of Scientific Biography* (New York: Scribners, 1974), 9:334–40. A number of studies have been devoted to the role of these translations in late medieval thought. See Ruedi Imbach, "Le (Néo-)Platonism médiévale, Proclus latin et l'école dominicaine allemande," *Revue de théologie et philosophie* 110 (1978): 427–48; Loris Sturlese, "Proclo ed Ermete in Germania da Alberto Magno a Bertoldo di Moosburg," in *Von Meister Dietrich zu Meister Eckhart*, 22–33; "Il dibattito sul Proclo latino nel medioevo fra l'università di Parigi e lo Studium di Colonia," in *Proclus et son influence*, 261–85; and de Libera, *La mystique rhénane*, 30–33, 278–79.

196. *Proclus: Elementatio theologica translata a Guillelmo de Moerbecca*, ed. Helmut Boese (Leuven: University Press, 1987).

197. *Procli Diadochi Tria Opuscula (De Providentia, Libertate, Malo)*, ed. Helmut Boese (Berlin: Walter de Gruyter, 1960).

198. *Proclus: Commentaire sur le Parménide de Platon; Traduction de Guillaume de Moerbeke*, ed. Carlos Steel, 2 vols. (Leuven: University Press, 1982). The edition is based on seven manuscripts, indicating a relatively modest diffusion (one of the manuscripts was owned by Nicholas of Cusa). This edition also contains the fragments of Moerbeke's translation of Proclus's commentary on the *Timaeus*. There is a translation of this key monument of Neoplatonic thought, *Proclus' Commentary on Plato's 'Parmenides,'* trans. Glenn R. Morrow and John M. Dillon with introduction and notes by John M. Dillon (Princeton: Princeton University Press, 1987).

199. Kristeller, "Proclus as a Reader," 208.

200. Sturlese, "Proclo ed Ermete," 24.

201. Sturlese ("Il dibatitto," 268–69) studies the roughly twenty references to Proclus in Albert's *Summa Theologiae.*

202. On Dietrich's use of Proclus, see Sturlese, "Proclo ed Ermete," 24–26; and "Il dibatitto," 279–81; see also Imbach, "Le (Néo-)Platonisme médiéval," 235–37.

203. Eckhart, S. XXXVI n. 364 (LW 4:313.9–10): Et ut totum, quod est animae unum, quaerat in hac, venit Iesus . . . . The *unum animae* appears in the *De Providentia* 8.31 (ed. Boese, 139–40), as well as in the *Expositio Procli in Parmenidem* 6.1071–72 (ed. Steel 2:364.53–71). On the importance of this notion in Proclus, see Werner Beierwaltes, "Der Begriff des 'Unum in Nobis' bei Proklos," in *Die Metaphysik im Mittelalter: Ihr Ursprung und ihr Bedeutung*, ed. Paul Wilpert (Berlin: Walter de Gruyter, 1963), 255–66.

204. Werner Beierwaltes (*Proklus: Grundzüge seiner Metaphysik* [Frankfurt: Klostermann, 1965], 395–98) notes the differences between Proclus's and Eckhart's understandings of negation without deciding on the question of textual contact. Carlos Steel ("Introduction," in *Proclus: Commentaire sur le Parménide de Platon* I:34*–35*) denies that Eckhart could have known the commentary. Wouter Goris (*Einheit als Prinzip und Ziel: Versuch über die Ein-*

heitsmetaphysik des Opus tripartitum Meister Eckharts [Leiden: Brill, 1997], 197–206, 215–18) contends that Eckhart developed his understanding of the *negatio negationis* from Henry of Ghent.

205. *Berthold von Moosburg: Expositio super Elementationem theologicam Procli*, ed. Maria Rita Pagnoni-Sturlese, Loris Sturlese, Burkhard Mojsisch, et al., Corpus Philosophorum Teutonicorum Medii Aevi 6 (Hamburg: Meiner, 1984–). Thus far the commentaries on Props. 1–107, and 160–83 have been published. There is also an edition of the final propositions nn. 184–211 in Loris Sturlese, *Bertoldo di Moosburg: Expositio super Elementationem theologicam Procli* (Rome: Edizioni di storia e letteratura, 1974). On the Platonic features of this work, see Stephen E. Gersh, "Berthold of Moosburg and the Content and Method of Platonic Theology," in *Nach der Verurteilung von 1277: Philosophie und Theologie an der Universität von Paris im letzten Viertel des 13. Jahrhunderts; Studien und Texte*, ed. Jan A. Aertsen, Kent Emery Jr., and Andreas Speer (Berlin: Walter de Gruyter, 2001), 493–503. Other studies include Kurt Flasch, "Einleitung," in *Expositio super Elementationem*, Vol. VI.1: XI–XXXVII; de Libera, *La mystique rhénane*, chapter 7; and Loris Sturlese, "'Homo divinus': Der Prokloskommentar Bertholds von Moosburg und die Probleme der nacheckhartischen Zeit," in *Abendländische Mystik im Mittelalter*, ed. Kurt Ruh (Stuttgart: Metzler, 1986), 145–61.

206. Sturlese, "Il dibatitto," 282.

Chapter 2

1. This section is based in part on Bernard McGinn, "'Evil-sounding, rash, and suspect of heresy: Tensions between Mysticism and Magisterium in the History of the Church," *Catholic Historical Review* 90 (2004): 193–212.

2. Von Hügel lays out his philosophy of religion in chapter 2 of *The Mystical Element of Religion as Studied in Catherine of Genoa and her Friends*. For a discussion, see Bernard McGinn, *The Foundations of Mysticism: Origins to the Fifth Century*, volume 1 of *The Presence of God: A History of Western Christian Mysticism* (New York: Crossroad, 1991), 293–96.

3. Steven E. Ozment, *Mysticism and Dissent: Religious Ideology and Social Protest in the Sixteenth Century* (New Haven: Yale University Press, 1973), 1.

4. Don Cupitt, *Mysticism and Modernity* (Oxford: Blackwell, 1998), chapters 9–10.

5. Gershom Scholem, "Religious Authority and Mysticism," in *On the Kabbalah and Its Symbolism* (New York: Schocken Books, 1965), 5–31; and "Mysticism and Society," *Diogenes* 58 (1967): 1–24. The following account is based on my "Foreword" to the 1996 reprint of *On the Kabbalah and Its Symbolism*, x–xiii.

6. Scholem, "Religious Authority and Mysticism," 7.

7. Ibid., 9–11; Scholem, "Mysticism and Society," 9, 15–16.

8. Scholem, "Religious Authority and Mysticism," 7.

9. Ibid., 24. See the whole discussion on pp. 23–25, as well as Scholem, "Mysticism and Society," 8–13.

10. Scholem, "Religious Authority and Mysticism," 24–25.

11. Among the accounts of Gnosticism that stress its mystical character, see especially Bentley Layton, *The Gnostic Scriptures: A New Translation with Annotations and Introductions* (Garden City, N.Y.: Doubleday, 1987); and Robert M. Grant, "Gnostic Spirituality," in *Christian Spirituality: Origins to the Twelfth Century*, ed. Bernard McGinn, John Meyendorff, and Jean Leclercq (New York: Crossroad, 1986), 44–60. For more on my view of the relation of Gnosticism to the history of Christian mysticism, see *Foundations of Mysticism*, 89–99.

12. On the role of the *regula fidei* as a norm for exegesis, see Origen, *De principiis* 4.2.2; and Augustine, *De doctrina christiana* 3.10.14.

13. In 186 B.C.E. the Roman authorities instituted a persecution of clandestine bacchics said to have numbered seven thousand. The *senatus consultum* accused the bacchics of much the same sexual and homicidal practices that were later ascribed to early Christians and

medieval heretics. See Livy, *Roman History* 39.8–19; and the study of Adrien Bruhl, *Liber Pater, origine et expansion du culte dionysiaque à Rome et dans le monde romain* (Paris: E. de Boccard, 1953), 82–116.

14. *Athenagoras: Legatio and De Resurrectione*, ed. and trans. William R. Schoedel (Oxford: Clarendon Press, 1972), 3.1 and 31–34.

15. On accusations of illicit sexuality among the Gnostics, see Irenaeus, *Adversus haereses* 1.6.3–4, and 1.13.3–6; Clement of Alexandria, *Miscellaneae* 3.2.5–10, 3.4.27–28, and 3.6.54; and Epiphanius of Salamis, *Panarion* 26. For a discussion, see Stephen Benko, *Pagan Rome and the Early Christians* (Bloomington: Indiana University Press, 1986), 65–73.

16. Irenée Hausherr, "L'erreur fondamentale et la logique du messalianisme," *Orientalia Christiana Periodica* 1 (1935): 328.

17. The most recent account is Daniel Caner, *Wandering, Begging Monks: Spiritual Authority and the Promotion of Monasticism in Late Antiquity* (Berkeley and Los Angeles: University of California Press, 2002), chapter 3. See also Columba Stewart OSB, *"Working the Earth of the Heart": The Messalian Controversy in History, Texts, and Language to AD 431* (Oxford: Clarendon Press, 1991); and Antoine Guillaumont, "Messaliens," DS 10:1074–83.

18. Stewart, *"Working the Earth of the Heart,"* 52–69. Stewart also gives the Greek texts, translations, and a synoptic comparison of the lists of errors in his "Appendix 2" (pp. 244–79).

19. John of Damascus, *De haeresibus* 80.10, as cited in Stewart, *"Working the Earth of the Heart,"* 269. At times this physical presence of God is expressed in sexual terms, such as in 80.8: "That it is necessary for the soul to feel such communion with the heavenly Bridegroom as a woman feels in being with a man" (Stewart, 253). Such anthropomorphite views were also found among the early monastics of Egypt.

20. On the relation of these two texts to Messalianism, see Caner, *Wandering, Begging Monks*, 107–17. On the mysticism of the Macarian Homilies, see *Foundations of Mysticism*, 142–44.

21. John Meyendorff ("Messalianism or Anti-Messalianism? A Fresh Look at the 'Macarian' Problem," in *KYRIAKON: Festschrift Johannes Quasten*, ed. Patrick Granfield and Joseph Jungmann, 2 vols. [Munster: Aschendorff, 1970] 2:585–90) argues that ". . . if 'Macarius' is a Messalian, this entire tradition [i.e., Eastern Christian spirituality] is Messalian as well" (p. 586).

22. Stewart, *"Working the Earth of the Heart,"* 43.

23. Ibid., 234–40.

24. In the literature on the Free Spirit heresy there is a split between older accounts that tend to trust the inquisitorial sources and thus see the Free Spirit as a widespread heretical *movement* and more recent studies that stress the constructed view of the heresy and thus question whether there was ever a Free Spirit heresy in the sense of a real social group. The essential book for the latter view is Robert E. Lerner, *The Heresy of the Free Spirit in the Later Middle Ages* (Berkeley and Los Angeles: University of California Press, 1972). (Lerner's excellent study, however, restricts its account to northern Europe and does not discuss the Free Spirit in Italy.) Representatives of the older historiography can be found in Ernest W. McDonnell, *The Beguines and Beghards in Medieval Culture with Special Emphasis on the Belgian Scene* (New Brunswick: Rutgers University Press, 1954); and Gordon Leff, *Heresy in the Later Middle Ages*, 2 vols. (New York: Barnes & Noble, 1967), vol. 1, chap. 4. A mass of useful, if disorganized, materials can be found in Romana Guarnieri, "Il Movimento dello Libero Spirito dalle Origini al Secolo XVI," *Archivio Italiano per la Storia della Pietà* 4 (1965): 353–708. Guarnieri also wrote the article "Frères du Libre Esprit," in DS 5:1241–68. An important essay on the inquisitorial processes for mystical heresy is Herbert Grundmann, "Ketzerverhöre des Spät-mittelalters als quellenkritisches Problem," *Deutsches Archiv für Erforschung des Mittelalters* 21 (1965): 519–75. See also the overview of Eleanor McLaughlin, "The Heresy of the Free Spirit and Late Medieval Mysticism," *Mediaevalia et Humanistica* n.s. 4 (1973): 37–54. More recently, see Walter Senner, "Rhineland Dominicans, Meister Eckhart and the Sect of the Free Spirit,"

in *The Vocation of Service to God and Neighbour: Selected Proceedings of the International Medieval Congress, University of Leeds, 14–17 July 1997,* ed. Joan Greatrex (Turnhout: Brepols, 1998), 121–33; and Martina Wehrli-Johns, "Mystik und Inquisition: Die Dominikaner und die sogenannte Häresie des Freien Geistes," in *Deutsche Mystik im abendländischen Zusammenhang,* ed. Walter Haug and Wolfram Schneider-Lastin (Tübingen: Niemeyer, 2000), 223–52.

25. There is a vast literature on heresy in the Middle Ages. For an overview, see Alexander Patschovsky, "Was Sind Ketzer? Über den geschichtlichen Ort der Häresien im Mittelalter," in *Eine finstere und fast unglaubliche Geschichte? Mediävistische Notizen zu Umberto Ecos Monchsroman 'der Name der Rose,'* ed. Max Kerner (Darmstadt: Wissenschaftliche Buchgesellschaft, 1988), 169–90.

26. Dermot Moran ("Pantheism from John Scottus Eriugena to Nicholas of Cusa," *American Catholic Philosophical Quarterly* 64 [1990]: 131–52) shows how pantheism is an inaccurate term to describe important Christian Neoplatonic mystics.

27. On autotheism, see Lerner, *Heresy of the Free Spirit,* 1–3, 5, 82–84, 115, 126, 178–79, 194–95, 203–4, 218–20, etc.

28. On the two forms of *unio mystica,* see Bernard McGinn, "Mystical Union in Judaism, Christianity, and Islam," in *The Encyclopedia of Religion,* 2nd ed. (forthcoming).

29. See Evagrius Ponticus, *Letter to Melania* 6 and 12, Pseudo-Dionysius, MT 1.3. See the discussion of these texts in *Foundations of Mysticism,* 154, and 177–78.

30. For a general account, see Edward Peters, *Inquisition* (New York: Free Press, 1988). Also useful is H. Ansgar Kelly, "Inquisition and the Persecution of Heresy: Misconceptions and Abuses," *Church History* 58 (1989): 439–51. On the suppression of mystical heresy, see Richard Kieckhefer, *Repression of Heresy in Medieval Germany* (Philadelphia: University of Pennsylvania Press, 1979), chapter 3, "The War against Beghards and Beguines." For a summary of the procedures against learned heresy, see J. M. M. H. Thijssen, *Censure and Heresy at the University of Paris 1200–1400* (Philadelphia: University of Pennsylvania Press, 1998), chapter 1.

31. On the method of investigating heresy by compiling lists of extracts or articles taken out of context, which goes back at least as far as the case against Abelard, see Josef Koch, "Philosophische und theologische Irrtumslisten von 1270–1329," in *Kleine Schriften,* 2 vols. (Rome: Edizioni di Storia e Letteratura, 1973), 2:423–50. The method of taking extracts out of context was a source of dissatisfaction even in the medieval period, as can be seen from Thijssen, *Censure and Heresy,* 25–30.

32. On the *prout sonat* principle in academic heresy trials, see Thijssen, *Censure and Heresy,* 25–33. Learned defendants, such as Meister Eckhart, strongly protested this approach, insisting on the importance of the intention of the author of the suspect texts.

33. On the use of formularies, see Kieckhefer, *Repression of Heresy,* 30–32.

34. Sources for the Free Spirit heresy fall into three broad groups: inquisitorial records; contemporary chronicles and other historical records, such as antiheretical treatises; and texts produced by Free Spirit heretics themselves. Marguerite Porete's *Mirror* is the only *sure* document in the third group, because it comes from someone formally executed for heresy. Other texts said to be of the Free Spirit, such as the *Schwester Katrei* (see chapter 7 below), were never formally condemned and are often no less orthodox than many other mystical texts.

35. On the characteristics of the new mysticism, see Bernard McGinn, *The Flowering of Mysticism: Men and Women in the New Mysticism (1200–1350),* volume 3 of *The Presence of God: A History of Western Christian Mysticism* (New York: Crossroad, 1998), 12–30.

36. Many other New Testament texts stress the freedom granted the Christian; e.g., Gal. 5:18, and Jas. 1:25.

37. For a sketch of the early history, see M.-A. Dimier, "Pour la fiche *spiritus libertatis,*" *Revue du moyen age latin* 3 (1947): 56–60.

38. The text of *Ad Nostrum,* art. 3, can be found in Joseph Alberigo et al., *Conciliorum Oecumenicorum Decreta* (Bologna: Istituto per le Scienze Religiose, 1973), 383: Tertio, quod illi, qui

sunt in predicto gradu perfectionis et spiritu libertatis, non sunt humanae subiecti obedien-
tiae, nec ad aliqua praecepta ecclesiae obligantur, quia, ut asserunt, *ubi spiritus Domini, ibi libertas.*

39. William of St.-Thierry, *Epistula ad fratres de Monte Dei* n. 286, in J.-M. Déchanet, *Guillaume de Saint-Thierry: Lettre aux Frères du Mont Dieu (Lettre d'or)* (SC 223; Paris: Éditions du
Cerf, 1975), 372: . . . erumpere festinat in libertatem spiritus et unitate, ut, sicut iam saepe dictum est, fidelis homo unus spiritus efficiatur cum Deo.

40. Bonaventure, *In III Sent.* d. 30, q. 3, art. unica, 3 sed contra (*Opera omnia* 3:661): . . .
quanto magis aliquis est in maiore caritate constitutus, tanto plus habet de libertate spiritus, et
quanto plus habet de libertate spiritus, tanto paucioribus vinculis obligatur.

41. *Die Predigten Taulers,* ed. Ferdinand Vetter (reprint, Zurich: Weidmann, 1968), Pr. 55
(258.16–18): Mer die die disen weg gont, über die lúte enhat der babest enkeinen gewalt, wan
Got hat si selber gefriget. S. Paulus spricht: "die von dem geiste Gotz getriben oder gefuert
werdent, die ensint under enkeinem gesetzde."

42. A number of studies have tried to connect the 1210 condemnation of the Paris Master
Amaury of Bene for pantheism with the later Free Spirit, but evidence for a clear historical
link is lacking and the errors involved have many differences.

43. On the heretics of the Swabian Ries, see Herbert Grundmann, *Religious Movements in
the Middle Ages* (Notre Dame: University of Notre Dame Press, 1995), 170–87; Leff, *Heresy in
the Later Middle Ages,* 1:311–14; and Lerner, *Heresy of the Free Spirit,* 13–19.

44. The most accessible edition of the *Compilatio de novo spiritu* is that of Wilhelm Preger
in *Geschichte der deutschen Mystik im Mittelalter,* 3 vols. (Leipzig, 1874–98), 1:461–71. I will use
the improved edition in the rare work of Joseph de Guibert, *Documenta ecclesiastica christianae
perfectionis studium spectantia* (Rome: Gregorian University Press, 1931), 116–25.

45. *Compilatio* #27 (de Guibert, 119): Ad idem redit dicere hominem posse fieri aequalem
Deo vel animam fieri divinam; #56 (de Guibert, 122): Dicere quod ad hoc perveniat homo
quod deus per eum omnia operetur. . . . See also, e.g., ##7, 13, 14, 15, 23, 28, 30, 36, 37, 58,
77, 84, 96, etc. A few texts express true pantheism; e.g., #76 (de Guibert, 123): Dicere quod
omnis creatura sit Deus, heresis Alexandri est.

46. *Compilatio* #19 (de Guibert, 119): Quod dicitur, quod homo non est bonus, nisi dimit-
tat Deum propter Deum, similiter de Pelagii stultitia est.

47. *Compilatio* #72 (de Guibert, 123): Dicere quod ei qui admittitur ad amplexus divinitatis, detur potestas faciendi quod vult. . . . See also #90 (de Guibert, 125) on the experience
of suckling Christ (well known among medieval nuns). Albert qualifies this as *fatuitas* rather
than outright error.

48. *Compilatio* #61 (de Guibert, 122): Dicere quod nihil sit peccatum nisi quod reputatur
peccatum . . . ; #106 (de Guibert, 126): Item quod unitus deo audacter possit explere
libidinem carnis per qualemcumque modum, etiam religiosus in utroque sexu. See also ##6,
21, 41, 43, 53, 69, 74, 87, 94, 100, 113, 114, 117, etc.

49. *Compilatio* #63 (de Guibert, 122): Dicere quod hoc quod fit sub cingulo a bonis non sit
peccatum. Albert's only reference to the "New Spirit" heretics in his own works focused on
their sexual errors. See *Summa theologiae* II Pars, tract. xviii, q. 122, mem. 1, art. 4 (*Opera
Omnia,* ed. Borgnet 33:399): Quaeritur de tactibus immundis, et osculis, et amplexibus, quae
quidam dicunt non esse peccatum: qui se dicunt esse de novo spiritu. Et est novella haeresis
ex antiqua Pelagii haeresi orta est.

50. *Compilatio* #116 (de Guibert, 126): Item quod non debeant revelare viris litteratis gratiam quam habent, quia nesciant quid sit, non recognoscentes nisi per pellem vitulinam, ipsi
vero per experientiam, qua sugere [text reads: surgere] se dicunt de dulcedine divina. See
also #17 (de Guibert, 118).

51. *Regestum Clementis Papae V* (Rome: Tipographia Vaticana, 1887), 5:424 (#7506): . . .
nonnulli ecclesiastici et mundani, religiosi et seculares utriusque sexus viri pestiferi, qui alien-
ati ab utero matris ecclesie . . . , novam sectam novumque ritum a via salutis omnino
degenerem etiam ipsis paganis et animaliter omnino viventibus odiosum et ab apostolica et

prophetica doctrina et evangelica veritate remotum, quem libertatis spiritum nominant, hoc est, ut quicquid eis libet, liceat, assumserunt. . . .

52. Most of the sources for the Italian manifestations of the Free Spirit heresy can be found in the scarce volume of Livarius Oliger, *De secta Spiritus Libertatis in Umbria saec. XIV: Disquisitio et Documenta* (Rome: Edizioni di Storia e Letteratura, 1943). Some of the early notices are also available in Guarnieri, "Il Movimento dello Libero Spirito," 404–8.

53. This text is from the *Arbor Vitae Crucifixae Jesu*, with an introduction and bibliography by Charles T. Davis (Turin: Bottega d'Erasmo, 1961; reprint of 1485 ed.), bk. 4.37 (389b). See *Flowering of Mysticism*, 125.

54. On Clare of Montefalco, see David Burr, *The Spiritual Franciscans: From Protest to Persecution in the Century after Saint Francis* (Philadelphia: University of Pennsylvania Press, 2001), 316–23, who discusses the saint's relations with the Free Spirits (pp. 320–22). Detailed studies on Clare can be found in *S. Chiara da Montefalco e il suo tempo*, ed. Claudio Leonardi and Enrico Menestò (Perugia-Florence: "La Nuova Italia," 1985).

55. These texts from the *Legenda B. Clarae* can be found in Guarnieri, "Il Movimento dello Libero Spirito," 405–6: (a) Bentivenga's claim: . . . quod homo potest facere quicquid vult, et quod infernus non est et quod anima potest perdere desiderium in hac vita. (b) Clare's response: Et tunc talis persona potest facere quicquid vult, quia velle ipsius aliud non est nisi quod Deus vult. . . . Anima vero perdit desiderium isto modo: non quod nichil appetat in hac vita existens, sed est possibile et contingit interdum quod anima in contemplationis fervore per raptum vel aliam elevationem in Deum absorpta, immersa et reposita, coniunctione mirabili in dilecto quiescit, quod in illo puncto quo anima in illo statu consistit, nil aliud appetat quam quod habet.

56. For an account of Angela's mysticism, see *Flowering of Mysticism*, 142–51. Her attack on the Free Spirit is noted on p. 150.

57. For some excerpts from Ugo's *Tractatus contra Begardos*, written about 1319, see Guarnieri, "Il Movimento dello Libero Spirito," 425–27.

58. For a summary of Marguerite's mystical teaching, see *Flowering of Mysticism*, 244–65. Marguerite's book in both the French and Latin versions has been edited by Romana Guarnieri and Paul Verdeyen, *Marguerite Porete: Le Mirouer des Simples Ames* (CCCM 69; Turnholt: Brepols, 1986). The materials regarding her trial can be found in Paul Verdeyen, "Le procès d'Inquisition contre Marguerite Porete et Guiard de Cressonessart (1309–1310)," *Revue d'histoire ecclésiastique* 81 (1986): 48–94. That the beguine's book tested the limits of medieval orthodoxy, especially when passages were taken out of context, is unquestionable. But in every issue about dangerous mysticism (e.g., esotericism, autotheism, antinomianism, quietism, anti-sacramentalism, anti-ecclesialism, etc.) Marguerite's subtle presentations offer qualifications to easy characterizations of her views as manifestly heretical. On the issue of mystical annihilation, however, she was uncompromising, though she was also convinced that her teaching was in harmony with Christian belief. My point here is not to enter once again into the theoretical question of whether or not Marguerite's views were heretical, but to insist that heresy is a historically constructed category whose parameters are always fluid. It is clear, however, that Marguerite's condemnation was a crucial moment in defining mystical heresy.

59. Lerner, *Heresy of the Free Spirit*, 80.

60. Jacqueline Tarrant, "The Clementine Decrees on the Beguines: Conciliar and Papal Versions," *Archivum Historiae Pontificiae* 12 (1974): 300–308.

61. The origins of the beguines and many of the early beguine mystics are discussed in the *Flowering of Mysticism*, especially chapters 1, 4, and 5. Along with the literature cited there, see two important new books, Saskia Murk-Jansen, *Brides in the Desert: The Spirituality of the Beguines* (London: Darton, Longman & Todd, 1998); and Walter Simons, *Cities of Ladies: Beguine Communities in the Medieval Low Countries, 1200–1565* (Philadelphia: University of Pennsylvania Press, 2001).

62. For the text of *Cum de quibusdam mulieribus*, see Alberigo, *Conciliorum Oecumenicorum*

Decreta, 374. There is a translation without the final clause in McDonnell, *Beguines and Beghards*, 524. The interpretation of *Cum de quibusdam mulieribus* as not intending a blanket condemnation of all beguines is made by Tarrant, "Clementine Decrees," 304.

63. The text of *Ad nostrum* can be found in Alberigo, *Conciliorum Oecumenicorum Decreta*, 383–84.

64. Alberigo, *Conciliorum Oecumenicorum Decreta*, 383: Primo videlicet, quod homo in vita praesenti tantum et talem perfectionis gradum potest acquirere, quod reddetur penitus impeccabilis et amplius in gratia proficere non valebit. As noted by Lerner (*Heresy of the Free Spirit*, 83), this article is close to #94 of Albert's *Compilatio* (de Guibert, 125): Dicere quod homo sic proficere possit ut impeccabilis fiat—mendacium est in doctrina veritatis. The error of impeccability appears elsewhere in the *Compilatio*; e. g., ##21, 24, and 100.

65. Ibid.: Secundo, quod ieiunare non oportet hominem nec orare, postquam gradum perfectionis huiusmodi fuerit assecutus, quia tunc sensualitas est ita perfecte spiritui et rationi subiecta, quod homo potest libere corpori concedere quidquid placet. The *Continuatio* of the *Chronicle of William of Nangis* notes that among the articles of Marguerite Porete singled out for condemnation was the statement: . . . quod anima annihilata in amore conditoris sine reprehensione conscientiae vel remorsu potest et debet naturae quidquid appetit et desiderat [concedere] . . . (Verdeyen, "Le procès," 88). In several places in her book Marguerite does speak of "giving nature its due," though always with qualifications that avoid antinomianism. The passage that seems closest to the *Ad nostrum* article, because it too expresses indifference to fasting and praying, is found in *Mirouer* chap. 9 (33.15–18): Talis anima . . . non appetit nec despicit paupertatem, tribulationem, missas, sermones, ieiunium uel orationem, et semper dat naturae quidquid petit absque omni remorsu conscientiae. See also chaps. 13 and 17 (55.24–27, 69.51). Denial of the need to fast and pray also is found in Albert's *Compilatio*, e.g., ##44, 50, and 110.

66. This parallels the first article of the process against Porete (Verdeyen, "Le procès," 51): Quod anima adnichilata dat licentiam virtutibus nec est amplius in earum servitute, quia non habet eas quoad usum, sed virtutes obediunt ad nutum. That the perfect soul says goodbye to the virtues (*anima accepit licentiam a virtutibus* [*Mirouer* chap. 21 (79.2)]) is a constant teaching of the *Mirror*, e.g., chaps. 6–9, 21, 56, 66, 82, 88, 94, 105, 121–2, but once again Porete always explains this in a way that avoids antinomianism.

67. This article could reflect a number of passages in Marguerite Porete, including one of the articles known from the process (Verdeyen, "Le procès," 51): Quod talis anima non curet de consolationibus Dei nec de donis eius, . . . quia intenta est circa Deum, et sic impediretur eius intentio circa Deum. There is no mention here, however, of the Eucharist. Albert's *Compilatio*, however, does have several articles about not paying proper reverence to the Eucharist or meditating on the Passion (e.g., ##28, 42, 65, 109, 118, 120), though none of them is an explicit match for what we find in *Ad nostrum*.

68. Kieckhefer, *Repression of Heresy*, 19.

69. The Strassburg cases of mystical heresy have been the subject of considerable study. See especially Alexander Patschovsky, "Strassburger Beginenverfolgerung im 14. Jahrhundert," *Deutsches Archiv für Erforschung des Mittelalters* 30 (1974): 56–198, which discusses bishop John's attack on the beguines (pp. 92–109) and publishes a critical edition of the relevant documents (pp. 126–61). In English, there is a treatment in Lerner, *Heresy of the Free Spirit*, 85–95.

70. See Dayton Phillips, *Beguines in Medieval Strassburg: A Study of the Social Aspect of Beguine Life* (Stanford: Stanford University Press, 1941).

71. Patschovsky ("Strassburger Beginenverfolgerungen") distinguishes three periods of John I's pursuit of mystical heresy during 1317–19.

72. The letter is edited by Patschovsky ("Strassburger Beginenverfolgerungen," 126–42) from fourteen manuscripts. This text is found at 134.21–23: . . . quos vulgus Bêghardos et swestriones Brot durch got nominat, ipsi vero et ipse se de secta liberi spiritus et voluntarie paupertatis pueros sive fratres vel sorores vocant. . . . That mendicant beguines and beghards begged food with the formula "brot durch got" is mentioned in many sources. The seven

510 Notes to Pages 64–66

headings of A are: (I) 11 errors against God (*divinitas*); (II) 7 errors against Christ; (III) 5 errors against the church; (IV) 6 errors against the sacraments; (V) 5 errors about heaven and hell; (VI) 4 errors against the gospel; and (VII) 4 errors against the saints. On this letter, see also Éric Mangin, "Le *Lettre du 13 Août 1317* écrite par l'Évêque de Strasbourg contre les disciples du Libre Esprit," *Revue des sciences religieuses* 75 (2001): 522–38.

73. Patschovsky edited this list on the basis of three manuscripts ("Strassburger Beginenverfolgerungen," 144–48).

74. A.I.1 (ed., 135.31–32): Dicunt enim, credunt et tenent, quod deus sit formaliter omne quod est. See also B.I.9 (ed., 146): Item, dicunt aliqui, quod deus sic est in omnibus, quod omnia sunt deus, et, quod non est deus, nichil est. . . . Even both these pantheistic-sounding statements might be explained in a dialectical sense, because to say that God is the reality of all things is not the same thing as to claim that all things (the universe) exhaust the reality of God.

75. A.I.2–3 (ed., 135.33–35): Item dicunt, quod homo possit sic uniri deo, quod ipsius sit idem posse et velle et operari quodcumque, quod est ipsius dei. Item credunt se esse deum per naturam sine distinctione.

76. A.I.5 (ed., 135.36–37): Item dicunt se omnia creasse, et plus creasse quam deus (see B.I.4). Eckhart, to be sure, never spoke of humans creating *more* than God. See the discussion of Pr. 52 (chapter 4, pp. 168–69) for the Dominican's statements on humans as co-creators with God in the ground.

77. B.I.10 (ed., 146): Ulterius ex hac perfectione unionis aliquorum cum deo dicunt aliqui, quod sint impeccabiles, quod adeo sint liberi quoad spiritum, quod, quidquid faciunt cum corpore, numquam peccant. . . .

78. John of Brünn's confession, as well as that of his brother Albert, can be found in Leff, *Heresy in the Later Middle Ages,* 2:709–16. For studies, see ibid., 1:371–77; and Lerner, *Heresy of the Free Spirit,* 108–12.

79. Leff, *Heresy in the Later Middle Ages,* 2:711: Item tu debes te exercere in illis operibus, que sunt tibi contraria, ad hoc quod vita tua anichiletur et diminuatur et spiritui totalier [*sic*] subiciatur, quia natura tua est sterilis et sibi ipsi in omnibus operibus adversatur [ms.: anichilatur], et ideo frangi debet et subici divine voluntati. . . . A subsequent passage also refers to annihilation: . . . nam necesse est, ut natura exterior, (que) in Christo servicio est annichilata.

80. Leff, *Heresy in the Later Middle Ages,* 2:713: Item dicti fratres in spiritu viventes, cum ad perfectum statum libertatis pervenerint, ita totaliter et corporaliter transmutantur, quod unum cum Deo efficiuntur, et Deus totaliter et corporaliter est cum eis, quod angeli in speculo Trinitatis non possunt discernere inter Deum et animum, que in libertate spiritus vixerit, propter prefatam unionem ipsorum. This teaching on corporeal transformation into God sounds much like the view of union condemned by John Tauler; see chapter 6, pp. 290–91.

81. The text, edited from a manuscript in Krakow by B. Ulanowski, is reprinted in Leff, *Heresy in the Later Middle Ages,* 2:721–40, who also discusses the group in 1:386–95. Lerner (*Heresy of the Free Spirit,* 112–19) makes use of the original Vatican manuscript of the investigation in his account. The Schweidnitz house appears to have been part of a wider network of beguine communities, since the superior, Heylwig of Prague, is described as visiting other houses (see Leff, 2:736). We are not told if these other houses were involved in the same beliefs and practices.

82. Leff, *Heresy in the Later Middle Ages,* 1:389.

83. The first group of sisters questioned on September 7, 1332, were all novices, most at the community less than a year. On September 11, five senior sisters were examined. Their confessions are notably shorter; their admissions much milder and not antinomian.

84. For Adelheid's testimony, see Leff, *Heresy in the Later Middle Ages,* 2:723–28. Adelheid herself does not admit any errors, but only what she heard, including the classic statement of antinomianism from *Ad nostrum*: Item dicit iurata, quod Capuciate dicunt, quod se exercere in actibus virtutis est hominis imperfecti, perfecta autem anima licenciat a se omnes virtutes (p. 727).

85. Leff, *Heresy in the Later Middle Ages,* 2:725: . . . quod audivisset de ore Gertrudis de Ciuitate . . . ista verba: Quando deus omnia creauit, tunc ego concreavi sibi omnia uel creavi omnia cum eo, et sum deus cum deo, et sum Christus, et sum plus. Gertrude herself was investigated in the second group and answered the accusation thus: . . . audivi predicare, sed non multum vlterius docui (p. 738). Gertrude might have read Eckhart, and indeed she appears to have known some theology, as witnessed by her admission that she had taught that Christ would have become incarnate even if Adam had not sinned (a Scotist position that would not have sat well with her Dominican inquisitors), but such a view was scarcely heresy. The other strong expression of indistinct union language was also ascribed to Gertrude: Sicut deus est deus, ita ipsa esset deus cum deo; et sicut Christus numquam separatus est a deo, sic nec ipsa (p. 723).

86. Jordan of Quedlinburg (1300–ca. 1380) wrote a lost treatise entitled *De spiritu libertatis.* He also attacks Free Spirit errors in several of his surviving sermon collections. For extracts, see Guarnieri, "Il Movimento dello Libero Spiritu," 444–50.

87. Hartmann's *processus* before the noted inquisitor Walter Kerlinger OP, took place at Erfurt in December 1367. The text is edited in Martin Erbstösser and Ernst Werner, *Ideologische Probleme des mittelalterlichen Plebejertums, Die freigeistige Häresie und ihre sozialen Wurzeln* (Berlin: Akademie, 1960), 136–49. For accounts of Hartmann, see Leff, *Heresy in the Later Middle Ages,* 1:377–79; and Lerner, *Heresy of the Free Spirit,* 134–39.

88. The sexually antinomian aspects of Hartmann's account are especially evident in Erbstösser and Werner, *Ideologische Probleme,* 144–48.

89. On the freedom to murder and steal, see the reply to article 3 (ed., 140); on lying under oath, the response to article 8 (ed., 150).

90. Ed. 138: Et sic interrogatus a predicto inquisitor de primo articulo in Clementina de haereticis "ad nostram" [*sic*] . . . , Quod homo in presenti vita etc. quando ipse stetit in tali contemplatione, de qua prius dictum est, videlicet in summo gradu perfectionis quem ipse in principio habuit, quando in abysso divinitatis fuit, an sit aliqua differentia tunc inter deum et se. Respondit, quod in tali perfectione et summo gradu unus est cum deo et deus cum eo unus absque omni distinctione. . . .

91. In the response to article 4 (ed., 142) again it is the inquisitor who introduces the technical term by asking Hartmann if his mode of union is without intermediary (*sine medio*). In article 5 (ed., 142), however, a sophisticated expression of mystical union (*nobilitas spiritus ex effluxu divinitatis et refluxu in deitate essencialiter est unus cum deo*) and its relation to the *lumen gloriae* is put directly in Hartmann's mouth. I do not wish to deny that lay theologians may have speculated about such issues, but their appearance in inquisitorial documents leaves us with the problem of guessing how much came from the inquisitor and how much from the accused.

92. Ed., 148–50: . . . sed ex fundo suo talia dixit, quia sic in se invenit et iste solus talia exprimere potest ex vero fundamento qui est expertus talia in se ipso et quod predicatores predicant et docent ex libris, et studio pellium obliuiscuntur eorum, sed qui in intima profunditate diuina abyssus talia perspiciunt illi verissime talia dicere possunt. . . .

93. See the treatment and edition of the two documents in Patschovsky, "Strassburger Beginenverfolgerungen," 78–92, 171–85; see also Lerner, *Heresy of the Free Spirit,* 97–101.

94. Interrogatorium no. 4 (Patschovsky, "Strassburger Beginenverfolgerungen," 182): Item si dicant se professas regulam tercii ordinis sancti Francisci, quaeratur ab eis, quis sit modus vivendi earum, et an et qualiter et per quem ad huiusmodi regulam sint recepte. Naturally, the Franciscans and Dominicans protested Lambert's attempt not only to quash approved beguine houses, but also third order groups.

95. Interrogatorium no. 21 (Patschovsky, "Strassburger Beginenverfolgerungen," 184): Item expedire videtur, ut quaeratur a qualibet, an habeat vel habuerit vel sciat habentem quendam librum theotunicum, qui intitulatur "De novem rupibus"—vulgariter dicendo dz buoch vin den nún feilsen—in quo dicuntur multa fidei katholice dissona conineri. See the discussion in Patschovsky, 118–25.

96. On the *Book of the Nine Rocks*, see chapter 9, pp. 423–26.

97. On Nicholas of Basel, see Lerner, *Heresy of the Free Spirit*, 151–54; and Guarnieri, "Il Movimento dello Libero Spirito," 461.

98. On the *homines intelligentiae*, see McDonnell, *Beguines and Beghards*, 502–4; Lerner, *Heresy of the Free Spirit*, 157–63; and Leff, *Heresy in the Later Middle Ages*, 1:395–99. Leff's contention that the group was connected to the activities of one Bloemardinne, a woman attacked by Ruusbroec sixty years before, is very unlikely.

99. The notarial record of this inquisition edited from a Paris manuscript can be found as document 249 in Paul Fredericq, *Corpus documentorum inquisitionis haereticae pravitatis Neelandicae*, 2 vols. (Ghent: J. Vuylsteke, 1889–1906), 1:267–79. Lerner makes use of a superior manuscript version from Wolfenbüttel ms. Helmst. 279, ff. 264r–269v. The document available in Fredericq only provides the twenty-one articles in List I and eighteen in List II, along with William's responses.

100. List I, no. 1 (Fredericq, 271): Item dictus laicus seductor dixit pluries repetendo pluribus audientibus: Ego sum salvator homunum; et per me videbunt Christum, sicut per Christum patrem.

101. See List I, nos. 8–14 and 20.

102. List II, no. 10 (Fredericq, 274): . . . et quod instabit tempus quo revelanda erit illa lex Spiritus Sancti et libertatis spiritualis et tunc praesens lex cessabit. . . .

103. List II, no. 13 (Fredericq, 274): Tertiam decimam, quod Deus est ubique in lapide, in membris hominis et in inferno, sicut in sacramento altaris. . . . William appears to have been unable to make simple scholastic distinctions about the various forms of God's presence.

104. On the Latin and Italian versions of the *Mirror*, see Guarnieri, "Il Movimento dello Libero Spirito," 504–9. My account is based largely on Guarnieri's discussion in "Il Movimento," 466–77. She also edits important documents concerning the Italian debates on the *Mirror* in her "Appendice," 645–63.

105. Bernardino da Siena, *Quadragesimale de evangelio aeterno*, sermon 6, as cited in Guarnieri, "Il Movimento dello Libero Spirito," 467: . . . quidem qui lapsi sunt in damnatam haeresim de spiritu libertatis, quae doctrina ponitur in libro qui *de anima simplici* intitulari solet, quo qui utuntur in illam haeresim communiter prolabuntur, licet tales, quando tali pestifero morbo infecti sunt . . .dicant talem librum et statum non intelligi ab impugnatoribus suis, et sic iudicant et damnant Ecclesiam, que talem doctrinam in sacro Concilio condemnavit, sicut patet Extra, De Haereticis, unico capitulo in Clementinis.

106. Guarnieri, "Il Movimento dello Libero Spirito," 468: . . . devenit in admirabilem annihilationem, sicut per experientiam patet in his qui sequuntur spiritum amoris, spiritum libertatis, aut librum haereticum qui dicitur *Animarum simplicium*. . . .

107. The Gesuati, or "Little Poor of Christ," were founded in the 1360s by Giovanni Colombini, a converted merchant-banker of Siena. Originally a lay penitential group, they were soon clericalized. The order was suppressed in 1668. See Romana Guarnieri, "Gesuati," in *Dizionario degli Istituti di Perfezione*, ed. Guerrino Pelliccia and Giancarlo Rocca (Rome: Edizioni Paoline, 1977), 4:1116–30.

108. The list, edited by Guarnieri in "Il Movimento dello Libero Spirito," 649–60, deserves further study. Though drawn only from the first part of the *Mirror*, it deftly isolates the main points of contention—e.g., (1) mystical identity: arts. 13–16, 20, 30; (2) annihilation of the will: arts. 6, 18, 22; (3) indifference and quietism: arts. 3, 7, 8, 10, 11, 26, 29; (4) strong apophaticism, which is seen as denying the beatific vision: arts. 2, 9; (5) leaving the virtues behind: arts. 5, 28; and (6) the idea of two churches: art. 17. Each suspect article is countered by citations and arguments drawn from scripture and a broad range of authorities. There are no Dominicans cited, so the work seems to reflect a Franciscan and/or Augustinian theological background.

109. See Guarnieri, "Il Movimento dello Libero Spirito," 473: De libro miror valde, quod si in illo sunt errores de quibus dicitur, quod per plures servos Dei legatur, nec percipiant tam

manifestos errores. Tavelli was a major figure in the Gesuati, having been central in the creation of the first rule for the order.

110. Here I agree with the conclusions of Edmund Colledge, "Introductory Interpretive Essay," in *The Mirror of Simple Souls* (Notre Dame: University of Notre Dame Press, 1999), lxii–lxiv.

111. The text of Becker's examination and confession is studied and edited by Grundmann, "Ketzerverhöre des Spätmittelalters," 551–61, 566–75. There are treatments of Becker in both Leff, *Heresy in the Later Middle Ages,* 1:383–86; and Lerner, *Heresy of the Free Spirit,* 177–81. Lerner (pp. 179–80) questions whether Becker was really a beghard because he seems to have lived as an artisan.

112. Grundmann, "Ketzerverhöre des Spätmittelalters," 566: . . . audivit in summitate ecclesie sonitum, qui descendit super eum. Et in illo sonitu recepit spiritum sanctum. Et ille spiritus sanctus pressit eum adeo, quod magnum dolorem sensit interius. Et quod postea sepius raptus sit in suo interiori homine.

113. Grundmann, "Ketzerverhöre des Spätmittelalters," 571: Tenet inprimis, quod homo potest effici per graciam illud, quod est deus per naturam, probans per illud Johannis, ubi ait salvator: *Oro, pater, ut ipsi sint unum nobiscum, sicut unum sumus* (John 17:21). It is worth noting that Eckhart used the same text to defend his teaching on mystical identity (see chapter 4, p. 182).

114. Grundmann, "Ketzerverhöre des Spätmittelalters," 571: Secundo quia ipse deus est, deo sit unitus et deus factus per unionem sui hominis interioris, quod ipse sit cum deo adorandus ut deus, non separatim, sed ipse cum beatissima trinitate, ita quod, dum adoramus patrem et filium et spiritum sanctum, debemus simul cum hoc adorare ipsum. See also p. 570: Quarto credit, quod ipse propter unionem, qua cum deo unitus est sit sanctior Christo ea sanctiate, qua Christus sanctus est secundum humanitatem.

115. Grundmann, "Ketzerverhöre des Spätmittelalters," 572: Et circa hoc asserit, quod ex quo se spiritui dedit, non habet amplius propriam voluntatem.

116. Grundmann, "Ketzerverhöre des Spätmittelalters," 570: Ex eodem asserit, quod illa, que sunt aliis hominibus peccata, non essent sibi peccata, si faceret eadem ex instinctu interioris sui hominis et sui spiritus procedere. The account does not accuse Becker of the usual sexual antinomianism, though it is specific about his failure to observe church regulations.

117. Grundmann, "Ketzerverhöre des Spätmittelalters," 570.

118. For a historical account, see the multi-author "Discernement des esprits," DS 4:1222–91. For a recent theological analysis that also surveys key figures in the history, see Mark A. McIntosh, *Discernment and Truth: The Spirituality and Theology of Knowledge* (New York: Crossroad, 2004).

119. McIntosh, *Discernment and Truth,* 5. McIntosh spells out these five moments in more detail in chapter 1, pp. 8–22.

120. On discernment in the patristic period, see Joseph T. Lienhard, "On 'Discernment of Spirits' in the Early Church," *Theological Studies* 41 (1980): 505–29; and the sketch in McIntosh, *Discernment and Truth,* chapter 2.

121. *S. Caterina da Siena: Il Dialogo,* ed. Giuliana Cavallini (Rome: Edizioni Cateriniane, 1968), IX (22–24): Chè discrezione non è altro che un vero cognoscimento che l'anima debba avere di sè e di me: in questo cognoscimento tiene le sue radici. Ella è un figliuolo che è innestato e unito con la carità. . . . [P]erchè elle sono legate ad innestate insieme, e piantate nella terra della vera umiltà, la quale esce del cognoscimento di sè. On Catherine's understanding of discernment, see Diana L. Villegas, "Discernment in Catherine of Siena," *Theological Studies* 58 (1997): 19–38; and McIntosh, *Discernment and Truth,* 54–61.

122. See especially Wendy Love Anderson, "Free Spirits, Presumptuous Women, and False Prophets: Discernment of Spirits in the Late Middle Ages" (Ph.D. diss., University of Chicago, 2002). Nancy Caciola, *Discerning Spirits: Divine and Demonic Possession in the Middle Ages* (Ithaca: Cornell University Press, 2003), is a mine of information and interesting insights,

but I cannot share the author's view that the investigation was almost invariably directed against women, or that "discernment of spirits was always really a discernment of bodies" (p. 86). In addition, the debates over Joan of Arc have cast light on discernment of spirits. See Deborah A. Fraioli, *Joan of Arc: The Early Debate* (Woodbridge: Boydell Press, 2000); and Dyan Elliott, *Proving Women: Female Spirituality and Inquisitorial Culture in the Later Middle Ages* (Princeton: Princeton University Press, 2004), chapter 7.

123. "*Cum ex iniuncto*" can be found in the *Corpus iuris canonici*, ed. E. Friedburg after the second Leipzig edition of A. L. Richter, 2 vols. (Leipzig: B. Tauchnitz, 1881), Lib. V. Tit. VII De Haereticis, cap. xii (784–87). This text is at c. 785: Tunc autem opus est discretione maiori, quum vitia sub specie virtutum occulte subintrat, et angelus Satanae se in angelum lucis simulat et transformat.

124. On the role of *Cum ex iniuncto*, see Anderson, *Free Spirits, Presumptuous Women*, 63–67.

125. For a survey, see Barbara Newman, "Possessed by the Spirit: Devout Women, Demoniacs, and the Apostolic Life in the Thirteenth Century," *Speculum* 73 (1998): 733–70; and Caciola, *Discerning Spirits*, chapters 1–3. I have considered some of these women in *Flowering of Mysticism*, especially chapter 4, as well as in my essay, "Visions and Critiques of Visions in Late Medieval Mysticism," in *Rending the Veil: Concealment and Secrecy in the History of Religions*, ed. Elliot R. Wolfson (New York: Seven Bridges Press, 1999), 87–112.

126. For a survey of the contribution of Olivi, his followers, and the debates they engendered, see Anderson, *Free Spirits, Presumptuous Women*, 75–102. On Olivi as mystic, see *Flowering of Mysticism*, 120–22.

127. For an account of David's invocation of the need for *discretio spirituum*, see Anderson, *Free Spirits, Presumptuous Women*, 70–75. On David's interest in mysticism, see *Flowering of Mysticism*, 113–16.

128. For an introduction to Henry and his thirty writings, see Robert G. Warnock, "Heinrich von Friemar der Ältere," VL 3:730–37. For more on Henry and the literature about him, see chapter 8, pp. 368–77. Henry's teaching on discernment of spirits is treated in Anderson, *Free Spirits, Presumptuous Women*, 105–15; and Caciola, *Discerning Spirits*, 215–22.

129. There is an edition of the treatise by Robert G. Warnock and Adolar Zumkeller, *Der Traktat Heinrichs von Friemar über die Unterscheidung der Geister* (Würzburg: Augustinus Verlag, 1977). Warnock and Zumkeller believe the work dates to the first decade of the fourteenth century, since it shows no knowledge of *Ad nostrum*.

130. *Tractatus* (ed., 152): . . . quadruplex est instinctus sive motio interior. . . . Causa vero et ratio, quare sit difficile praedictos instinctus discernere, est similitudo et conformitas naturalis luminis et luminis gratuiti.

131. There are four lists of signs applied to the first three instincts: four signs of divine instincts; four signs of angelic instincts; four signs for discerning the difference between diabolical and divine instincts; and four signs for discriminating diabolic and angelical instincts.

132. Henry was most concerned with discerning the difference between the natural and the grace-inspired instincts. The fourth and longest section of the *Tractatus* deals with these questions in detail. Henry shows a particular interest in distinguishing between inquiries inspired by nature and those inspired by grace, noting that the natural instinct often leads to pride, while the *instinctus gratiae* fosters humility (*Tractatus*, 198). Observations like this are reminiscent of later mystics who attack the false Free Spirits for trusting in their own inner natural light rather than in divine grace.

133. Augustine's treatise is available in Pierangela Giglioni, "Il *Tractatus contra divinitores et sompniatores* di Agostino d'Ancona: Introduzione e edizione del testo," *Analecta Augustiniana* 48 (1985): 24–37. For accounts of his contribution, see Anderson, *Free Spirits, Presumptuous Women*, 94–100; and Caciola, *Discerning Spirits*, 221–22.

134. For an account of Venturino and the source of this quotation, see Caciola, *Discerning Spirits*, 218–21.

135. Anderson (*Free Spirits, Discerning Women*, chapter 3) studies much of this literature.

136. The Latin and MHG versions of the treatise have been edited by Thomas Hohmann,

Heinrichs von Langenstein 'Unterscheidung der Geister' Lateinisch und Deutsch: Texte und Untersuchungen zu Übersetzungsliteratur aus der Wiener Schule (Munich: Artemis, 1977).

137. See Anderson, *Free Spirits, Presumptuous Women*, chapters 5–6; Caciola, *Discerning Spirits*, chapter 6; and Elliott, *Proving Woman*, chapter 7.

138. McIntosh, *Discernment and Truth*, 61–62.

139. Investigators of the history of heresy have long realized that fourteenth-century debates set the standard for subsequent determinations of mystical error. Although it is hard to reduce this standard to one set of accusations, there is broad agreement about central issues. Some of these were carried over from antiquity, especially esotericism, antinomianism, quietism (i.e., indifference to moral and spiritual practice), and freedom from church control. Others, as I have argued here, were new, such as annihilation of self and mystical identity. For another look at this problem, see Kent Emery, "Foreword," in *Margaret Porette: The Mirror of Simple Souls*, xxiv, who lists six basic themes of the fourteenth-century debates that were later used to test spiritual teaching.

Chapter 3

1. See Bernard McGinn, *The Flowering of Mysticism: Men and Women in the New Mysticism (1200–1350)*, volume 3 of *The Presence of God: A History of Western Christian Mysticism* (New York: Crossroad, 1998), 222–44 on Mechthild; 267–82 for Helfta; and 292–317 for the female Dominicans.

2. According to Alois M. Haas ("Meister Eckhart und die deutsche Sprache," in *Geistliches Mittelalter* [Freiburg, Switzerland: Universitätsverlag, 1984], 218–19), "die deutsche Mystik" was first used in 1831 by Karl Rosenkranz. This term was also employed by Wilhelm Preger in his classic work, *Geschichte der deutschen Mystik im Mittelalter: Nach den Quellen untersucht und dargestellt*, 3 vols. (Leipzig: Dörffling & Franke, 1874–93). Joseph Bernhart used "Die deutsche Mystik" to describe Eckhart and his followers in his *Die philosophische Mystik des Mittelalters von ihren antiken Ursprüngen bis zur Renaissance* (Munich: Reinhard, 1922), chapter 8. For a more recent summary under the same heading, see Alois Maria Haas, "Deutsche Mystik," in *Geschichte der deutschen Literatur III/2: Die deutsche Literatur im späten Mittelalter 1250–1370*, ed. Ingeborg Glier (Munich: C. H. Beck, 1987), 234–305.

3. The term appears most often in French literature, e.g., Jeanne Ancelet-Hustache, *Master Eckhart and the Rhineland Mystics* (New York: Harper, 1957; French original: Paris, 1956). See also *La mystique rhénane: Colloque du Strasbourg 16–19 mai 1961* (Paris: Presses universitaires de France, 1963), and the recent survey of Alain de Libera, *La mystique rhénane d'Albert le Grand à Maître Eckhart* (Paris: Éditions du Seuil, 1994). "Rhineland mysticism" has sometimes been expanded into the rather cumbersome French term, "rhéno-flamand," as in Louis Cognet, *Introduction aux mystiques rhéno-flamands* (Paris: Desclée, 1968).

4. Carl Greith, *Die deutsche Mystik im Prediger-Orden (von 1250–1350)* (Freiburg-im-Breisgau: Herder, 1861); and Kurt Ruh, *Geschichte der abendländische Mystik*, Band 3, *Die Mystik des deutschen Predigerordens und ihre Grundlegung durch die Hochscholastik* (Munich: C. H. Beck, 1996).

5. This characterization also goes back into the nineteenth century. Josef Bach, in dependence on Franz von Baader, entitled his book on Eckhart, *Meister Eckhart: Der Vater der deutschen Spekulation* (Vienna: Braumüller, 1864). Another early use of the term was that of Henry Delacroix, *Essai sur le mysticisme spéculatif en Allemagne au XIVe siècle* (Paris, 1899). In the twentieth century the term was used by many, such as Josef Quint, "Mystik und Sprache, Ihr Verhältnis zueinander, insbesondere in der spekulativen Mystik Meister Eckeharts," in *Altdeutsche und altniederländische Mystik: Wege der Forschung XXIII*, ed. Kurt Ruh (Darmstadt: Wissenschaftliche Buchhandlung, 1964), 113–51.

6. On the relation of love and knowledge in Western mysticism, see Bernard McGinn, "Love, Knowledge and *Unio mystica* in the Western Christian Tradition," in *Mystical Union in*

Judaism, Christianity, and Islam: An Ecumenical Dialogue, ed. Moshe Idel and Bernard McGinn (New York: Continuum, 1996), 59–86.

7. E.g., Alois M. Haas's argument for the term *Fundamentalmystik* in "Die Aktualität Meister Eckhart: Ein Klassiker der Mystik (ca. 1260–1328)," in *Gottes Nähe: Religiöse Erfahrung in Mystik und Offenbarung; Festschrift zum 65. Geburtstag von Josef Sudbruck SJ*, ed. Paul Imhoff SJ (Würzburg: Echter, 1990), 84.

8. Bernard McGinn, *The Growth of Mysticism*, volume 2 of *The Presence of God: A History of Western Christian Mysticism* (New York: Crossroad, 1994), 154–57.

9. Josef Quint, "Mystik und Sprache," 141–51, with a treatment of *grunt* on pp. 141–43. According to Quint (p. 141): "Und so wächst denn, aus innersten Denk- und Sprachnot hervorgetrieben, zur adäquaten Benennung des innersten Seinsgrundes der Seele wie des göttlichen Urgrundes ein mystisches Wortfeld, das weithin durch *metaphorische*, bildliche Ausdrücke das sprachlich auszusagen versucht, was begrifflich nicht zu fassen ist.

10. For the notion of *Sprengmetapher*, see Hans Blumenberg, "Paradigmen zu einer Metaphorologie," *Archiv für Begriffsgeschichte* 6 (1960): 7–142; "Beobachtungen an Metaphern," *Archiv für Begriffsgeschichte* 15 (1971): 161–214; and "Ausblick auf eine Theorie der Unbegrifflichkeit," in *Theorie der Metapher*, ed. Anselm Haverkamp (Darmstadt: Wissenschaftliche Buchgesellschaft, 1983), 438–54. For applications to Eckhart, see Susanne Köbele, *Bilder der unbegriffenen Wahrheit: Zur Struktur mystischer Rede im Spannungsfeld von Latein und Volkssprache* (Tübingen and Basel: Francke, 1993), 17–18, 66–67, and 181–91; and Alois M. Haas, "The Nothingness of God and its Explosive Metaphors," *The Eckhart Review* 8 (1999): 6–17.

11. On the importance of the *Grunderfahrung* as demanding communication to others, see Erwin Waldschütz, *Denken und Erfahren des Grundes: Zur philosophischen Deutung Meister Eckharts* (Vienna/Freiburg/Basel: Herder, 1989), 328–29.

12. This point has been emphasized by Waldschütz, *Denken und Erfahren des Grundes*, especially part 3, chapter 4 (pp. 324–49) on the *Grunderfahrung*.

13. The most recent survey of the terminology of *grunt* and related words in selected German mystics can be found in Michael Egerding, *Die Metaphorik der spätmittelalterlichen Mystik*, 2 vols. (Paderborn: Schöningh, 1997), 2:279–309. Egerding lists ninety-two appearances of *grunt* in Eckhart, but a survey of eighteen of the eventual twenty-six sermons to appear in DW 4 provides another thirty-seven appearances for a total of 129. Given other possibly authentic works, and some uses missed by Egerding, we can surmise that Eckhart used *grunt* and related terms 140 to 150 times. Suso employs the term seventy-nine times according to Egerding, while Tauler uses it no fewer than 414 times. These numbers too are probably on the low side of the total uses.

14. For example, in the thirty-two sermons not included in DW that appear in Franz Pfeiffer, *Meister Eckhart* (Leipzig: Röder, 1857; reprint, Göttingen: Vandenhoeck & Ruprecht, 1924), *grunt* appears at least thirty times. Particularly important are Pf. LXI (ed., 194–95) with ten appearances; Pf. LXXI (ed., 224–26) with five; and Pf. XCIII (ed., 303–05) with eight.

15. On the *centro del alma* in the Spanish mystics, see Léonce Reypens, "Âme (structure)," in DS 1:461–63; and especially Edward Howells, *John of the Cross and Teresa of Avila: Mystical Knowing and Selfhood* (New York: Crossroad, 2002), chapter 2 and *passim*. John of the Cross occasionally uses the term *fondo* as the equivalent of *centro*, e.g., "la intima sustancia del fondo del alma" (*Llama*, str. 3, v. 3); "en el centro y fondo de mi alma" (*Llama* c.4, vv.1–2, t.2).

16. On the conversation between Latin scholastic theology and vernacular mystical theologies, see Bernard McGinn, *The Flowering of Mysticism: Men and Women in the New Mysticism (1200–1350)*, volume 3 of *The Presence of God: A History of Western Christian Mysticism* (New York: Crossroad, 1998), 22–24.

17. The point is emphasized by Köbele, *Bilder*, 176–80, against the views of previous treatments of the meaning of *grunt* that sought to reduce it to its Latin equivalents.

18. Among older discussions of *grunt* in Eckhart, see Benno Schmoldt, *Die deutsche Begriffssprache Meister Eckharts: Studien zur philosophischen terminologie des Mittelhochdeutschen* (Heidel-

berg: Quelle & Meyer, 1954), 49–62; Bernward Dietsche, "Der Seelengrund nach den deutschen und lateinischen Predigten," in *Meister Eckhart der Prediger*, ed. Udo Nix (Freiburg: Herder, 1960), 200–258; and Heribert Fischer, "Fond de l'Âme: I, Chez Maître Eckhart," in DS 5:650–61.

19. A classic study of Tauler's use of *grunt* is Paul Wyser, "Taulers Terminologie vom Seelengrund," in *Altdeutsche und Altniederländische Mystik*, 324–52. Several more recent works have also addressed the use of *grunt* in Tauler; e.g., Louise Gnädinger, "Der Abgrund ruft dem Abgrund: Taulers Predigt Beati oculi (V 45)," in *Das "Einig Ein": Studien zur Theorie und Sprache der deutschen Mystik*, ed. Alois M. Haas and Heinrich Stirnimann (Freiburg, Switzerland: Universitätsverlag, 1980), 167–207; and Loris Sturlese, "Tauler im Kontext: Die philosophischen Voraussetzungen des 'Seelengrundes' in der Lehre des deutschen Neoplatonikers Berthold von Moosburg," *Beiträge zur Geschichte der deutschen Sprache und Literatur* 109 (1987): 390–426; and Louise Gnädinger, *Johannes Tauler: Lebenswelt und mystische Lehre* (Munich: Beck, 1993), 181–93, 241–51.

20. Herman Kunisch, *Das Wort "Grund" in der Sprache der deutschen Mystik des 14. und 15. Jahrhunderts* (Osnabrück: Pagenkämper, 1929). Kunisch's work remains valuable for its collection of materials, but is insufficient in many ways, most notably for its overemphasis on courtly language of the *grund des herzens* as a source for mystical uses (see pp. 11–14) and its failure to appreciate the central role of Eckhart (e.g., 1, 15, 42–43, and 93).

21. Köbele, *Bilder*, 173.

22. Recent helpful analyses include Burkhard Mojsisch, *Meister Eckhart: Analogie, Univozität und Einheit* (Hamburg: Felix Meiner, 1983), 131–44; Otto Langer, "Meister Eckharts Lehre vom Seelengrund," in *Grundfragen christliche Mystik*, ed. Margot Schmidt and Dieter R. Bauer (Stuttgart/Bad Cannstatt: frommann-holzboog, 1987), 173–91; Waldschütz, *Denken und Erfahren des Grundes;* Burkhard Hasebrink, "GRENZVERSCHIEBUNG: Zu Kongruenz und Differenz von Latein und Deutsch bei Meister Eckhart," *Zeitschrift für deutsches Altertum und deutsche Literatur* 121 (1992): 369–98; Köbele, *Bilder*, 171–91; and Michael Egerding, *Die Metaphorik der spätmittelalterlichen Mystik* 2:279–309.

23. What follows is based on the summary found in Köbele, *Bilder*, 174–75, citing appropriate MHG dictionaries.

24. Ruh's term as cited in Köbele, *Bilder*, 13 and 51.

25. Egerding (*Die Metaphorik*, 279–82) discusses thirty-nine uses of these words in Mechthild's *Das fliessende Licht der Gottheit*. These texts can be found in Hans Neumann, *Mechthild von Magdeburg: Das fliessende Licht der Gottheit*, 2 vols. (Munich: Artemis, 1990, 1993).

26. Joseph Van Mierlo, *Hadewijch: Brieven*, 2 vols. (Antwerp: N.V. Standaard, 1947), Letter 18.69–70 (1:154–55): Siele ist een wech vanden dore vaerne gods in sine vriheit, Dat es in sinen gront di niet gheraect en can werden, sine gherakene met hare diepheit. . . . See the discussion in *Flowering of Mysticism*, 211–19.

27. See Ruh, *Geschichte*, 2:161–63.

28. See Martin Grabmann, "Die Lehre des hl. Thomas von Aquin von der *scintilla animae* in ihre Bedeutung für die deutsche Mystik des Predigerordens," *Jahrbuch für Philosophie und spekulativen Theologie* 14 (1900): 413–27; Hieronymus Wilms, "Das Seelenfünklein in der deutschen Mystik," *Zeitschrift für Aszese und Mystik* 12 (1937): 157–66; Endré von Ivanka, "Apex mentis: Wanderung und Wandlung eines stoischen Terminus," *Zeitschrift für katholischen Theologie* 72 (1950): 129–76; and Hans Hof, *Scintilla Animae: Eine Studie zu einem Grundbegriff in Meister Eckharts Philosophie* (Lund: Gleerup; Bonn: Hanstein, 1952). For a treatment in English on the spark of the soul, see Frank Tobin, *Meister Eckhart: Thought and Language* (Philadelphia: University of Pennsylvania Press, 1986), 126–40. Surveys of terminology relating to the soul and its structure can be found in the DS, notably Léonce Reypens, "Âme (structure)," DS 1:433–69; and Aimé Solignac, "NOUS et MENS," DS 11:459–69; and "Synderesis," DS 14:407–12.

29. Reypens, "Âme (structure)," DS 1:434: . . . le père de l'introversion et le grand théoreticien de l'image de Dieu dans l'âme, saint Augustin.

30. For example, in S. XLIX.1, n. 507 (LW 4:422:12–13) Eckhart says that the *imago Dei* resides *in supremo animae.* In the same sermon Eckhart speaks of the "superius in anima, ubi vertex animae nectitur lumini angelico" (n. 505 [LW 4:421.10–11]). In a text from In Io. n. 679 (LW 3:593.4–7) Eckhart uses both *abditum mentis* and *supremus animae* jointly, citing Augustine's *De Trinitate.* Another passage, this one from In Gen. II n. 149 (LW 1:606.1), identifies this "high point" with intellect: Supremum autem animae in nobis intellectus est.

31. See Hélène Merle, *"DEITAS:* quelques aspects de la signification de ce mot d'Augustin à Maître Eckhart," in *Von Meister Dietrich zu Meister Eckhart,* ed. Kurt Flasch (Hamburg: Felix Meiner, 1984), 12–21, who argues that Gilbert of Poitiers' logical distinction between *deus (quod est)* and *deitas (quo est)* is helpful for understanding Eckhart's doctrine of the *deus absconditus.*

32. Wyser ("Taulers Terminologie vom Seelengrund," 334) suggested the use of *fundus* in Dionysian writings as a source for *grunt* language. Dionysius uses the phrase *puthmên pantokratikos* in DN 4 (700B) and 10 (937A). These passages were translated in a variety of ways, including *fundus,* but *fundus* does not occur in Eckhart, despite his knowledge of Dionysius.

33. On the relation of *grunt* to the Latin terms *causa, principium,* and *ratio,* see Schmoldt, *Die deutsche Begriffssprache Meister Eckharts,* 49–54.

34. In some texts, however, both *principium* and *unum* are used in ways similar to *grunt* as expressing mystical identity. In Pr. 69, for example, *principium* is used in relation to *grunt:* Vernünfticheit . . . brichet in den grunt, dâ güete und wârheit ûzbrichet, und nimet ez *in principio,* in dem beginne . . . (DW 3:179.2–6). See also Pr. 18 (DW 1:302.6–7): . . . und der sun treit sie [the soul] vürbaz ûf in sînen ursprunc [= *principio*], daz ist in dem vater, in den grunt, in daz êrste, dâ der sun wesen ine hât. . . . For *unum* as expressing fused identity in Eckhart, see, e.g., the analysis of the relation between *unum* and *intelligere* in S. XXIX (LW 4:263–70), as well as the passage on union in S. IV (LW 4:28.5–8). In the MHG sermons *ein* is also used correlatively with *grunt* in some contexts; see, e.g., Pr. 13 (DW 1:219.3–5).

35. The literature on the mystical vocabulary of MHG is large so only a few classic works can be listed here: Grete Lüers, *Die Sprache der deutschen Mystik des Mittelalters im Werke der Mechthild von Magdeburg* (Munich: Reinhardt, 1926); Kurt Kirmsee, *Die Terminologie des Mystikers Johannes Taulers* (Engelsdorf/Leipzig: Vogel, 1930); Kurt Berger, *Die Ausdrücke der Unio mystica im Mittelhochdeutschen* (Berlin: E. Ebering, 1935); Benno Schmoldt, *Die deutsche Begriffssprache Meister Eckharts;* Kurt Ruh, "Die trinitarische Spekulation in deutscher Mystik und Scholastik," in *Kleine Studien II* (Berlin: Walter de Gruyter, 1984), 14–45; and Egerding, *Die Metaphorik der spätmittelalterlichen Mystik.*

36. Bernard McGinn, "Ocean and Desert as Symbols of Mystical Absorption in the Christian Tradition," *Journal of Religion* 74 (1994): 155–81.

37. For the development of mystical meanings of *abyssus,* see Bernard McGinn, "The Abyss of Love," in *The Joy of Learning and the Love of God: Studies in Honor of Jean Leclercq,* ed. E. Rozanne Elder (Kalamazoo: Cistercian Publications, 1995), 95–120.

38. On *imago/bild* in Eckhart, see especially Mauritius Wilde, *Das neue Bild vom Gottesbild: Bild und Theologie bei Meister Eckhart* (Freiburg, Switzerland: Universitätsverlag, 2000).

39. The classic history of the birthing motif in Christian mysticism is Hugo Rahner, "Die Gottesgeburt: Die Lehre der Kirchenväter von der Geburt Christi aus den Herzen der Kirche und der Gläubigen," in *Symbole der Kirche: Die Ekklesiologie der Väter* (Salzburg: Müller, 1964), 7–41.

40. Some representative studies of these words include: Shizuteru Ueda, *Die Gottesgeburt in der Seele und der Durchbruch zur Gott: Die mystische Anthropologie Meister Eckharts und ihre Konfrontation mit der Mystik der Zen Buddhismus* (Gütersloh: Mohn, 1965); Ludwig Völker, "'Gelassenheit': Zur Entstehung des Wortes in der Sprache Meister Eckharts und seiner Überlieferung in der nacheckhartschen Mystik bis Jacob Böhme," in *'Getempert und Gemischet'* *für Wolfgang Mohr zum 65. Geburtstag,* ed. Franz Hundsnurscher and Ulrich Müller (Göppingen: A. Kümmerle, 1972), 281–312; Alois M. Haas, ". . . 'Das Persönliche und eigene ver-

leugnen': Mystische *vernichtigkeit und verworffenheit sein selbs* in Geiste Meister Eckharts," in *Individualität: Poetik und Hermeneutik XIII*, ed. Manfred Frank and Anselm Haverkamp (Munich: Fink, 1988), 106–22; Wolfgang Wackernagel, *YMAGINE DENUDARI: Éthique de l'image et métaphysique de l'abstraction chez Maître Eckhart* (Paris: J. Vrin, 1991); Niklaus Largier, "Repräsentation und Negativität: Meister Eckharts Kritik als Dekonstruktion," in *Contemplata aliis tradere: Studien zum Verhältnis von Literatur und Spiritualität*, ed. C. Brinker, U. Herzog, et al. (Frankfurt: Lang, 1995), 371–90; and Denys Turner, *The Darkness of God: Negativity in Christian Mysticism* (Cambridge: Cambridge University Press, 1995), chapter 7.

41. The text can be found in Adolf Spamer, *Texte aus der deutschen Mystik des 14. und 15. Jahrhunderts* (Jena: Diedrichs, 1912), 175–77. For studies, see Kurt Ruh, "Mystische Spekulation in Reimversen des 14. Jahrhunderts," in *Kleine Schriften* II:183–211; Loris Sturlese, "Alle origini della mistica tedesca: Antichi testi su Teodorico di Freiburg," *Medioevo* 3 (1977): 36–44; idem, "Sprüche der zwölf Meister" in VL 9:197–201; and Ruth Meyer, "'Maister Eghart sprichet von wesen bloss': Beobachtungen zur Lyrik der deutschen Mystik," *Zeitschrift für deutsche Philologie, Sonderheft Mystik* 113 (1994): 63–82. In English there is a translation and commentary by Wolfgang Wackernagel, "Some Legendary Aspects of Meister Eckhart: The Aphorisms of the Twelve Masters," *Eckhart Review* (Spring 1998): 30–41. Since Tauler is already mentioned as one of the masters it is difficult to date the poem to ca. 1320, as Sturlese contends.

42. For more on mystical poetry, see chapter 7, pp. 314–20.

43. Ruh ("Mystische Spekulation in Reimversen") lists twenty-six poems characterized as "mystisch-spekulativ." Meyer ("Maister Eghart sprichet von wesen bloss," 66–69) lists fifty-one mystical poems divided into two classes: "mystisch-aszetisch" and "mystisch-spekulativ." This total is a small percentage of the hundreds of religious lyrics of the period, but still a significant one.

44. The masters named are (1) Meister Eckhart; (2) Meister Dietrich of Freiburg; (3) Henry of Ettlingen; (4) John of Dambach; (5) a master of Regensburg (unidentified); (6) Binderlin of Freiburg (otherwise unknown); (7) the one from Waldthusen (also unknown); (8) John of Müntz; (9) Brother John the Younger, who testified at Eckhart's trial; (10) John Tauler; (11) Ros of the Bavarians (unknown); and "the one from Talhain," who is probably Henry of Talhain, a Franciscan provincial in Germany 1316–26.

45. Maister egghart sprichet von wesen blosz. / Er sprichet ain ainiges wörtlin, das selb ist formloz. / Das ist sin selbes sin; im gat weder zow noch abe. / Es ist ain guoter maister, der da sprechen chan (Spamer, *Texte aus der deutschen Mystik des 14. und 15. Jahrhunderts,* 175).

46. For an introduction to Dietrich, see Loris Sturlese, "Dietrich von Freiburg," in VL 2:127–38. Useful studies of Dietrich's thought and its implications for mysticism include Sturlese, "Alle origini della mistica speculativa tedesca"; de Libera, *La mystique rhénane*, chapter 5; and Ruh, *Geschichte*, 3:184–212.

47. One of these is available in English, *Dietrich of Freiburg: Treatise on the Intellect and the Intelligible,* translated from the Latin with an introduction and notes by M. L. Führer (Milwaukee: Marquette University Press, 1992).

48. Because Dietrich's mystical sermons are lost, he will not be given lengthy treatment in this volume. This is not meant to detract from his significant role in the intellectual world that gave birth to the mysticism of the ground.

49. Maister Dietrich sprichet von sinnekeit. / Er seczt das bild der sele in seines selbeshait; / da bekennet es got in seiner isticheit (Spamer, *Texte aus der deutschen Mystik des 14. und 15. Jahrhunderts,* 175). Recent work has shown important links between Dietrich and Eckhart, especially on the soul's formal procession from God as a pure image. See Kurt Flasch, "Procedere ut imago: Das Hervorgehen des Intellekts aus seinem göttlichen Grund bei Meister Dietrich, Meister Eckhart und Berthold von Moosburg," *Abendländische Mystik im Mittelalter,* ed. Kurt Ruh (Stuttgart: Metzler, 1986), 125–34.

50. On *istikeit*, see especially Alessandra Beccarisi, "Philosophische Neologismen

zwischen Latein und Volkssprache: 'istic' und 'isticheit' bei Meister Eckhart," *Recherches de théologie et philosophie médiévales* 70 (2003): 329–58. Among older studies, see Meinrad Morard, "Ist, istic, istikeit bei Meister Eckhart," *Freiburger Zeitschrift für Philosophie und Theologie* 3 (1956): 169–86. Wackernagel ("The Aphorisms," 33) suggests that the word could be rendered in English as "is-me-ness" (*ist-ich-keit*).

51. From the poem "Ich wil uch sagen mer," as cited in Ruh, *Geschichte*, 3:197: Der hohe meister diderich der wil uns machen fro. / er sprichet luterlichen al in principio. / des adeles flucke wil er uns machen kunt. / dy sele wil er versencken in den grunt ane grunt (my trans. with an attempt to convey the rhyme). This poem, like the "Sprüche," also features a list, in this case of three mystical teachers.

52. Der von regenspurg spricht so wunderleich. / Er sprichet, das götlich güti sei über wesentlich. / Er halt den höchsten grad in blosser ainichait. / Leben und würcken seczt er in anderheit (Spamer, *Texte aus der deutschen Mystik des 14. und 15. Jahrhunderts,* 176).

53. Der tauler von strasburg sprichet ainualticlich:/ der sich sein selbes vnd gotes enblösset, der stat würckens frey. / Da würcket got sich selber; des werckes ist er frey. / Enbloset ist das bilde der sele: da ist chain geschaffenhait (Spamer, *Texte aus der deutschen Mystik des 14. und 15. Jahrhunderts*, 177).

54. Nun haben wir vernomen, er welle sich sprechen ab. / Des hat er den grund besessen alzemal. / Leben vnd würcken seczt er zemale frey (Spamer, *Texte aus der deutschen Mystik des 14. und 15. Jahrhunderts,* 176).

55. Der ros von den baiern, der sprichet lauterlich: / alles, das da ist geschaffen, das ist zuouallig. / Der gaist stat sunder zwoual in seiner ainualtichait: / da stat er veraint in seiner istichait. / Ain anders: sin vnd begert, der stat er baider frey; / zegrund ist er gelassen, als ob er nit ensey (Spamer, *Texte aus der deutschen Mystik des 14. und 15. Jahrhunderts,* 177).

56. Der von walthusen ist ain pfaffe grosz. / Er sprichet vernünfticlich die warhait also blosz. / Er hat sich uf erswungen in die wilden gothait. / Da hat er freyhait funden an allen vnderschaid. / Er sprichet och: ain liecht ist in der sele, das vnberürlich ist / von allen creaturen; das ist sein aigen art. / Da laüchtet gleich wesen in ainualtichait. / Da hat er freyhait funden an allen vnderschaid (Spamer, *Texte aus der deutschen Mystik des 14. und 15. Jahrhunderts,* 176).

57. See Volker Honemann, "Sprüche der zwölf Meister zu Paris," VL 9:201–05. There is a translation in Wackernagel, "Some Legendary Aspects of Meister Eckhart," 34–37.

Chapter 4

1. Most of the material for this chapter comes from Bernard McGinn, *The Mystical Thought of Meister Eckhart: The Man from Whom God Hid Nothing* (New York: Crossroad, 2001). These pages represent a condensed and in some cases altered and improved version of that account.

2. Since 1980, the Dominican order, as well as interested groups such as the International Eckhart Society, have sought to obtain an official declaration from the papacy to acknowledge "the exemplary character of Eckhart's activity and preaching." Most recently, the foundation of the "Meister-Eckhart-Gesellschaft" in April of 2004 has furthered the task of making Eckhart and his writings better known. The Gesellschaft maintains a Web site at www .meister-eckhart-gesellschaft.de.

3. Over three hundred manuscripts containing Eckhart's German sermons, both authentic and pseudonymous, survive. Some Eckhart sermons that were ascribed to his follower, John Tauler, were printed in the early Tauler editions and were widely read, by Martin Luther among others.

4. Niklaus Largier (*Bibliographie zu Meister Eckhart* [Freiburg, Switzerland: Universitätsverlag, 1989]) lists 1491 items. Largier also provides introductions to recent research on Eckhart in two articles: "Meister Eckhart: Perspektiven der Forschung, 1980–1993," *Zeitschrift für deutsche Philologie* 114 (1995): 29–98; and "Recent Work on Meister Eckhart: Positions, Prob-

lems, New Perspectives, 1990–1997," *Recherches de Théologie et Philosophie médiévales* 65 (1998): 147–67.

5. *Meister Eckhart: Die deutschen und lateinischen Werken herausgegeben im Auftrag der deutschen Forschungsgemeinschaft* (Stuttgart/Berlin: Kohlhammer, 1936–). The Latin works (hereafter LW) will eventually comprise six volumes of which five are largely complete (vol. 6 will contain indices). The MHG works (hereafter DW) are in five volumes. Work continues on the final volume of the MHG sermons in DW 4. Texts will be cited by volume, page, and line numbers for direct quotations. The most accessible version of Eckhart's MHG sermons (hereafter Pr. and Prr. for plural), treatises, and some selections from his Latin works, can be found in Niklaus Largier, *Meister Eckhart Werke*, 2 vols. (Frankfurt: Deutsche Klassiker Verlag, 1993), which contains modern German translations, as well as an excellent commentary and bibliography. The first modern edition of Eckhart sermons and treatises was by Franz Pfeiffer, *Deutsche Mystiker des vierzehnten Jahrhunderts,* volume 2, *Meister Eckhart* (Leipzig, 1857; reprint, Göttingen: Vandenhoeck & Ruprecht, 1924; hereafter abbreviated Pfeiffer).

6. There are many English translations of Eckhart. Specially to be noted are *Meister Eckhart: The Essential Sermons, Commentaries, Treatises, and Defense*, translation and introduction by Edmund Colledge OSA and Bernard McGinn (New York: Paulist Press, 1981) (hereafter *Essential Eckhart*); and *Meister Eckhart: Teacher and Preacher*, ed. Bernard McGinn with the collaboration of Frank Tobin and Elvira Borgstadt (New York: Paulist Press, 1986) (hereafter *Teacher and Preacher*). Almost all of Eckhart's MHG works have been translated by M. O'C. Walshe, *Meister Eckhart: Sermons & Treatises*, 3 vols. (London/Dulverton: Watkins & Element Books, 1979–87). Another important translation is Oliver Davies, *Meister Eckhart: Selected Writings* (London: Penguin, 1994). All translations from the Latin are my own; translations from the MHG works will vary and be noted in all cases.

7. The documents relating to Eckhart's life, the "Acta Eckhardiana," are now being edited by Loris Sturlese in LW 5. Among the accounts of Eckhart's life and works, see especially Josef Koch, "Kritische Studien zum Leben Meister Eckharts," *Archivum Fratrum Praedicatorum* 29 (1959): 1–51; and 30 (1960): 1–52; Kurt Ruh, *Meister Eckhart: Theologe, Prediger, Mystiker* (Munich: C. H. Beck, 1985); and "Kapitel XXXVI. Meister Eckhart," in Kurt Ruh, *Geschichte,* 3:216–353. A useful short account is Loris Sturlese, *Meister Eckhart: Ein Porträt*, Eichstätter Hochschulreden 90 (Regensburg: Pustet, 1993), part of which is available in English as "A Portrait of Meister Eckhart," *Eckhart Review* (Spring 1996): 7–12.

8. This *Sermo paschalis* (LW 5:136–48) already shows Eckhart's mastery of philosophical sources and impressive rhetorical skills.

9. *Sermo paschalis* n. 15 (LW 5:145.5–6): Et Albertus saepe dicebat: "hoc scio sicut scimus, nam omnes parum scimus." On Eckhart's use of Albert, see Bernhard Geyer, "Albertus Magnus und Meister Eckhart," in *Festschrift Josef Quint anlässlich seines 65. Geburtstages überreicht,* ed. Hugo Moser et al. (Bonn: E. Semmel, 1964), 121–26.

10. Eckhart's brief *Collatio in Libros Sententiarum*, a sermon prologue to his commentary, can be found in LW 5:17–26. There is still debate over whether an anonymous *Sentence* commentary found in a Bruges manuscript may belong to Eckhart, or at least to his circle. See Andreas Speer and Wouter Goris, "Das Meister-Eckhart-Archiv am Thomas-Institut der Universität zu Köln: Die Kontinuität der Forschungsaufgaben," *Bulletin de philosophie médiévale* 37 (1995): 149–74.

11. About twenty of the 219 condemned propositions could be found in Aquinas's writings. For an introduction to the condemnation and the debate over its meaning and effect, see John F. Wippel, "The Condemnations of 1270 and 1277 at Paris," *Journal of Medieval and Renaissance Studies* 7 (1977): 169–201.

12. For a comparison of Eckhart's view of the relation of philosophy and theology with that of Bonaventure on the one hand and Albert and Thomas on the other, see Bernard McGinn, "*SAPIENTIA JUDAEORUM*: The Role of Jewish Philosophers in Some Scholastic Thinkers," in *Continuity and Change: The Harvest of Late Medieval and Reformation History; Essays*

Presented to Heiko A. Oberman on his 70th Birthday, ed. Robert J. Bast and Andrew C. Gow (Leiden: Brill, 2000), 206–28.

13. In Ioh. n.185 (LW 3:154.14–155.7): Secundum hoc ergo convenienter valde scriptura sacra sic exponitur, ut in ipsa sint consona, quae philosophi de rerum naturis et ipsarum proprietatibus scripserunt, praesertim cum ex uno fonte et una radice procedat veritatis omne quod verum est, sive essendo sive cognoscendo, in scriptura et in natura. . . . Idem ergo est quod docet Moyses, Christus et philosophus, solum quantum ad modum differens, scilicet ut credibile, probabile sive verisimile et veritas.

14. The RdU is edited in DW 5:137–376. An important recent study is Andreas Schönfeld, *Meister Eckhart: Geistliche Übungen; Meditationspraxis nach den "Reden der Unterweisung"* (Mainz: Matthias-Grünewald Verlag, 2002).

15. Sturlese, "Portrait of Meister Eckhart," 8–10; Ruh, *Geschichte*, 3:258–67.

16. The Qu.Par. can be found in LW 5:29–71. There is an English translation by Armand Maurer, *Master Eckhart: Parisian Questions and Prologues* (Toronto: PIMS, 1974). In addition, from the same year at Paris we have Eckhart's *Sermo die b. Augustini Parisius habitus* (LW 5:89–99).

17. Qu.Par. 1 n. 4 (LW 5:40.5–6): . . . quod non ita videtur mihi modo, ut quia sit, ideo intelligat, sed quia intelligit, ideo est. . . .

18. Much has been written on the relation between Thomas and Eckhart. On the issue of their respective understandings of the role of intellect, see Ruedi Imbach, *DEUS EST INTELLIGERE: Das Verhältnis von Sein und Denken in seiner Bedeutung für das Gottesverständnis bei Thomas von Aquin und in den Pariser Quaestionen Meister Eckharts* (Freiburg, Switzerland: Universitätsverlag, 1976); and Bernard McGinn, "Sermo XXIX: 'Deus unus est,'" in *Lectura Eckhardi II. Predigten Meister Eckharts von Fachgelehrten gelesen und gedeutet,* ed. Georg Steer and Loris Sturlese (Stuttgart: Kohlhammer, 2003), 205–32.

19. On the context and significance of the Qu.Par., see *Maître Eckhart à Paris: Une critique médiévale de l'ontothéologie; Les Questions parisiennes no. 1 et no. 2* (Paris: Presses universitaires de France, 1984). For the historical background, Edouard Wéber, "Eckhart et l'ontothéologisme: Histoire et conditions d'une rupture," in ibid., 13–83.

20. Qu.Par.1 n. 11 (LW 5:46.7–10): Item: in his quae dicuntur secundum analogiam, quod est in uno analogatorum, formaliter non est in alio . . . . Cum igitur omnia causata sunt entia formaliter, deus formaliter non erit ens.

21. On the *Paradisus anime intelligentis (Paradis der fornunftigen sele),* see the treatment in chapter 7, pp. 321–26, below.

22. Pr. 9 (DW 1:150.3–7): Niergen wonet got eigenlîcher dan in sînem tempel, in vernünfticheit, . . . diu dâ lebet in sîn aleines bekantnisse, in im selber aleine blîbende, dâ in nie niht engeruorte, wan er aleine dâ ist in sîner stilheit (*Teacher and Preacher,* 257). For a general interpretation of the homily and the literature on it, see Largier, *Meister Eckhart,* 1:834–55. An insightful study of the major theme can be found in Susanne Köbele, *"BÎWORT SÎN: 'Absolute' Grammatik bei Meister Eckhart," Zeitschrift für deutsche Philologie* 113 (1994): 190–206.

23. Pr. 98 (DW 4:244.38–43): Dâ wirt si sô lûterlîchen ein, daz si kein ander wesen enhât dan daz selbe wesen, daz sîn ist, daz ist daz sêle-wesen. Diz wesen ist ein begin alles des werkes, daz got würket in himelrîche und in ertrîche. Ez ist ein urhap und ein grunt aller sîner götlîchen werke. Diu sêle engât ir natûre und irm wesene und irm lebene und wirt geborn in der gotheit. . . . Si wirt sô gar ein wesen, daz dâ kein underscheit ist, dan daz er got blîbet und si sêle (my trans.). Georg Steer, the editor of DW 4, notes the many parallels between Pr. 98 and Pr. 17, a key text on the *grunt.* Eckhart had already used the term *grund/abgrund* ten times in his RdU.

24. Georg Steer, "Meister Eckharts Predigtzyklus *von der êwigen geburt:* Mutmassungen über die Zeit seiner Entstehung," in *Deutsche Mystik im abendländischen Zusammenhang: Neue erschlossene Texte, neue methodische Ansätze, neue theoretische Konzepte,* ed. Walter Haug und Wolfram Schneider-Lastin (Tübingen: Niemeyer, 2000), 253–81.

25. The In Eccli. is found in LW 2:231–300. On the dating of this work, see Acta n. 33 (LW 5:179).

26. In Eccli. n. 53 (LW 2:282.3–6): Igitur omne ens creatum habet a deo et in deo, non in se ipso ente creato, esse, vivere, sapere positive et radicaliter. Et sic semper edit, ut productum est et creatum, semper tamen esurit, quia semper ex se non est, sed ab alio.

27. In Eccli. n. 58 (LW 2:287.1–4): Qui ergo edit, edendo esurit, quia esuriem edit, et quantum edit, tantum esurit. . . . Edendo enim esurit et esuriendo edit et esurire sive esuriem esurit. On this text, see Donald F. Duclow, "The Hungers of Hadewijch and Eckhart," *The Journal of Religion* 80 (2000): 421–41.

28. Loris Sturlese, "Un nuovo manoscritto delle opere latine di Eckhart e il suo significato per la ricostruzione del testo e della storia del Opus tripartitum," *Freiburger Zeitschrift für Philosophie und Theologie* 32 (1985): 145–54; "Meister Eckhart in der Bibliotheca Amploniana: Neues zur Datierung des 'Opus tripartitum,'" in *Der Bibliotheca Amploniana: Ihre Bedeutung im Spannungsfeld von Aristotelismus, Nominalismus und Humanismus*, ed. Andreas Speer (Berlin/New York: Walter de Gruyter, 1995), 434–46; and "Meister Eckhart: Ein Porträt," 16–19.

29. The *Opus tripartitum* (Op.trip.) survives only in its prologues edited in LW 1: (a) Prol.gen. in LW 1:148–65; (b) Prol.op.prop. in LW 166–82; and (c) Prol.op.expos. in LW 1:183–84. This text is from Prol.gen. nn. 3–6 (LW 1:149.3–151.12): Distinguitur igitur secundum hoc opus ipsum totale in tria principaliter. Primum est opus generalium propositionum, secundum opus quaestionum, tertium opus expositionum. Opus autem primum, quia propositiones tenet mille et amplius, in tractatus quattuordecim distinguitur iuxta numerum terminorum, de quibus formantur propositiones. . . . Opus autem secundum, quaestionum scilicet, distinguitur secundum materiam quaestionum. . . . Opus vero tertium, scilicet expositionum, . . . subdividitur numero et ordine librorum veteris et novi testamenti, quorum auctoritates in ipso exponuntur. On the Op.trip., see Wouter Goris, *Einheit als Prinzip und Ziel: Versuch über die Einheitsmetaphysik des "Opus tripartitum" Meister Eckharts* (Leiden: Brill, 1997), as well as Ruh, *Geschichte*, 3:290–308.

30. The treatment of the proposition *esse est deus* can be found both in Prol.gen. nn. 12–22 (LW 1:156–65) and Prol.op.prop. nn. 1–25 (LW 1:166–82). There is a translation of these texts in Armand Maurer, *Master Eckhart: Parisian Questions and Prologues* (Toronto: PIMS, 1974), 77–105. Although the prologues are the only parts of the Op.prop. to survive, Eckhart's references to other treatises, e.g., *De bono, De natura superioris*, etc., indicate that some other propositions were probably written down, at least in a preliminary way.

31. In Gen. I is edited in LW 1:185–444.

32. In Sap. is in LW 2:303–634.

33. In Ex. is edited in LW 2:1–227. Eckhart's extensive use of Maimonides in this commentary may argue for a date in the second decade of the fourteenth century when he seems to have begun using the Jewish sage more extensively.

34. The massive In Ioh. takes up the whole of LW 3.

35. The fifty-six Latin *sermones* (hereafter given Latin numeration and the abbreviations S. and SS. to distinguish them from the vernacular Prr.) are edited in LW 4.

36. In a number of places, Eckhart refers to other parts of the *Opus expositionum* (Op.ex.), especially to commentaries on the Pauline Epistles. It is likely, as Ruh suggests (*Geschichte*, 3:291), that Eckhart lectured on these texts, but did not have time to commit his commentaries to writing.

37. Prol.gen. n. 2 (LW 1:148.5–9): Auctoris intentio in hoc opere tripartito est satisfacere pro posse studiosorum fratrum quorundam desideriis, qui iam dudum precibus importunis ipsum impellunt crebro et compellunt, ut ea quae ab ipso audire consueverunt, tum in lectionibus et aliis actibus scholasticis, tum in praedicationibus, tum in cottidianis collationibus, scripto commendat. . . .

38. Goris, *Einheit als Prinzip und Ziel*, 12–14 and 46.

39. Prol.gen. n. 7 (LW 1:152.3–5): Advertendum est autem quod nonnulla ex sequentibus propositionibus, quaestionibus, expositionibus primo aspectu monstuosa, dubia aut falsa apparebunt, secus autem si sollerter et studiosius pertractentur.

40. Ruh (*Geschichte,* 3:293) notes the close interconnection of the three parts demonstrated in the parallel between the first proposition (*esse est deus*), the first question (*an deus est?*), and the first commentary dealing with *In principio creavit deus caelum et terram* (Gen.1:1).

41. In Ioh. n. 2 (LW 3:4.4–6): In cuius verbi expositione et aliorum quae sequuntur, intentio est auctoris, sicut et in omnibus suis editionibus, ea quae sacra asserit fides christiana et utriusque testamenti scriptura, exponere per rationes naturales philosophorum.

42. For an introduction to Eckhart's preaching, see Alois M. Haas, "Meister Eckharts geistliches Predigtprogramm," in *Geistliches Mittelalter* (Freiburg, Switzerland: Universitäts-verlag, 1984), 317–37.

43. On Eckhart's encounter with women mystics, see Otto Langer, *Mystische Erfahrung und spirituelle Theologie: Zu Meister Eckharts Auseinandersetzung mit der Frauenfrömmigkeit seiner Zeit* (Munich/Zurich: Artemis, 1987); and the papers in *Meister Eckhart and the Beguine Mystics: Hadewijch of Brabant, Mechthild of Magdeburg, and Marguerite Porete,* ed. Bernard McGinn (New York: Continuum, 1994).

44. See especially the remarks in Pr. 29 (DW 2:78–79), a sermon probably given at Cologne ca. 1324–26. A number of Eckhart's other sermons witness to his response to Free Spirit errors; e.g., Pr. 12 (DW 1:195), Pr. 37 (DW 2:211), and Pr. 51 (DW 2:468, 471). For more on Eckhart's reaction to false mysticism, see Walter Senner, "Rhineland Dominicans, Meister Eckhart, and the Sect of the Free Spirit," in *The Vocation of Service to God and Neighbour,* ed. Joan Greatrex (Turnhout: Brepols, 1998), 121–33.

45. See Frank Tobin, "Mechthild of Magdeburg and Meister Eckhart: Points of Comparison," in *Meister Eckhart and the Beguine Mystics,* 44–61. For an introduction to these women mystics, see Bernard McGinn, *The Flowering of Mysticism: Men and Women in the New Mysticism (1200–1350),* volume 3 of *The Presence of God: A History of Western Christian Mysticism* (New York: Crossroad, 1998), 222–65.

46. As Senner puts it ("Rhineland Dominicans, Meister Eckhart," 132): "In reasoning with the members of the Free Spirit Eckhart exposed himself to the danger of appearing to ignore certain important distinctions. . . ."

47. The earliest witness for Eckhart's presence at Strassburg is in a document dated April 14, 1314 (Acta n. 38 [LW 5:182–84]).

48. Jacqueline Tarrant, "The Clementine Decrees on the Beguines: Conciliar and Papal Versions," *Archivum Historiae Pontificiae* 12 (1974): 300–307. For the wider context of the Free Spirit heresy, see chapter 2 and the literature cited there.

49. Ruh, *Meister Eckhart,* 112–14; and *Geschichte,* 3:242–43.

50. See Acta nn. 41–42 (LW 5:187–88).

51. In Pr. 104A (DW 4:579.155–80.159) Eckhart cites Aquinas (STh IIIa, q.40, a.1, ad 2) on *contemplata aliis tradere*: Meister Thomas sprichet: dâ sî daz würkende leben bezzer dan daz schouwende leben, dâ man in der würklicheit ûzgiuzet von minne, daz man îngenomen hât in der schouwunge.

52. Marie-Anne Vannier, "L'homme noble, figure de l'oeuvre d'Eckhart à Strasbourg," *Revue des sciences religieuses* 70 (1996): 73–89; and "Eckhart à Strasbourg (1313–1323/24)," in *Dominicains et Dominicaines en Alsace XIIIe-XXe S.,* ed. Jean-Luc Eichenlaub (Colmar: Éditions d'Alsace, 1996), 197–208.

53. Pr. 53 (DW 2:528.5–529.2): Swenne ich predige, sô pflige ich ze sprechenne von abegescheidenheit und daz der mensche ledic werde sîn selbes und aller dinge. Ze andern mâle, daz man wider îngebildet werde in daz einvaltige guot, daz got ist. Ze drittem mâle, daz man gedenke der grôzen edelkeit, die got an die sêle hât geleget, daz der mensche dâ mite kome in ein wunder ze gote. Ze dem vierden mâle von götlîcher natûre lûterkeit—waz klârheit an götlîcher natûre sî, daz ist unsprechelich. Got ist ein wort, ein ungesprochen wort (*Essential Eckhart,* 203).

54. Pr. 6 (DW 1:105.1–2): Swer underscheit verstât von gerechticheit und vom gerehtem, der verstât allez, was ich sage (my trans.). Ruh (*Meister Eckhart,* 155–57) treats this sermon as a late production, without assigning any definite date.

55. Pr. 9 (DW 1:154.7–9): Ich meine daz wörtelîn 'quasi', daz heizet 'als', daz heizent diu kint in der schuole ein bîwort. Diz ist, daz ich in allen mînen predigen meine (*Teacher and Preacher*, 259). Eckhart explains what he means in more detail in 158.4–8.

56. Vannier, "L'homme noble," 77 and 81–83.

57. In Ioh. n. 6 (LW 3:7.12–8.1): . . . licet in analogicis productum sit descendens a produ-cente, . . . Item fit aliud in natura, et sic non ipsum principium, ut est in illo, non est aliud in natura, sed nec aliud in supposito.

58. In Ioh. n. 19 (LW 3:16.10–11): Rursus duodecimo: iustus in ipsa iustitia iam non est genitus nec genita iustitia, sed est ipsa iustitia ingenita. This first discussion of *iustitia* and *ius-tus* stretches from nn. 14–22 (LW 3:13–19).

59. See In Ioh. nn. 46, 85, 119, 169–72, 177, 187–92, 196, 225, 252–53, 256, 316, 340–41, 416–17, 426, 435–36, 453–55, 458, 470–71, 477, 503–04, 511, 601, 620, 640, 643–44, 659–60, 731.

60. In Gen. II can be found in LW 1:447–702. The *prologus* to this work (nn. 1–7 [447–56]), especially because it mentions "this book and others in the holy canon," can be taken as a second *prologus* to the whole Op.expos.

61. Sturlese, "Meister Eckhart in der Bibliotheca Amploniana"; and "Meister Eckhart. Ein Porträt," 16–19.

62. E.g., Ruh, *Geschichte,* 3:301–3; Goris, *Einheit als Prinzip und Ziel,* 49–51.

63. Niklaus Largier, "*Figurata locutio:* Philosophie und Hermeneutik bei Eckhart von Hochheim und Heinrich Seuse," in *Meister Eckhart: Lebenstationen—Redesituationen,* ed. Klaus Jacobi (Berlin: Walter de Gruyter, 1997), 328–32; and "Recent Work on Meister Eckhart," 150–51.

64. The *Liber Benedictus* appears in DW 5:1–136, with *Daz buoch der goetlichen troestunge* (BgT) on 3–61, and the sermon *Von dem edeln menschen* (VeM) on 109–19. For a treatment of the issues connected with the book, see Ruh, *Geschichte,* 3:308–23, and the literature discussed there.

65. Ruh, *Meister Eckhart,* 135.

66. BgT (DW 5:8.9–9.2).

67. BgT 1 (DW 5:60.13–14): Mir genüeget, daz in mir und in gote wâr sî, daz ich spreche und schrîbe (*Essential Eckhart*, 239).

68. BgT 1 (DW 5:60.27–61.1): Ouch sol man sprechen, daz man sôgetâne lêre niht ensol sprechen noch schrîben ungelêrten. Dar zuo spriche ich: ensol man niht lêren ungelêrte liute, sô enwirt niemer nieman gelêret, sô enmac nieman lêren noch schrîben. Wan dar umbe lêret man die ungelêrten, daz sie werden von ungelêret gelêret (*Essential Eckhart*, 239).

69. The BgT raises the question about the other vernacular treatises ascribed to Meister Eckhart. Early Eckhart editions had no fewer than seventeen of these, but most have been judged inauthentic, however much they resonate with Eckhartian language and themes. Debate still continues about the short tractate *On Detachment* (*Von abegescheidenheit,* abbrevi-ated Vab). Although Josef Quint, the editor of Eckhart's MHG works, included this penetrat-ing investigation of one of Eckhart's major mystical themes in DW 5:400–434, most recent investigators seem to be negative toward its authenticity; see, e.g., Ruh, *Meister Eckhart,* 165–67; and *Geschichte,* 3:349–51, and 355–58.

70. See Walter Senner OP, "Meister Eckhart in Köln," in *Meister Eckhart: Lebenstationen— Redesituationen,* ed. Klaus Jacobi (Berlin: Walter de Gruyter, 1997), 207–37.

71. Joachim Theisen (*Predigt und Gottesdienst: Liturgische Strukturen in den Predigten Meister Eckharts* [Frankfurt: Peter Lang, 1990], 121–22) provides a list of fifteen sermons that he dates to 1325–26. These include Prr. 1, 11, 12, 13, 14, 15, 18, 19, 25, 26, 37, 49, 51, 59, and 79. Senner ("Meister Eckhart in Köln," 226–28) also includes Prr. 16, 22, 28, 29, and 80. Ruh (*Meister Eckhart,* 158) argues that Eckhart's sermon on poverty of spirit (Pr. 52) is one of his last and therefore a product of the Cologne years. If all these ascriptions are correct, at least twenty-two of Eckhart's surviving MHG sermons come from these three years.

72. The *Acta Echardiana: Secunda Pars. Processus contra Mag. Echardum* is edited as nn. 46–48

in LW 5:197–354. This consists of two lists of errors against Eckhart and his responses (Proc.Col.I and Proc.Col.II). For a theological treatment, see Bernard McGinn, "Eckhart's Condemnation Reconsidered," *The Thomist* 344 (1980): 390–414. Further precision about issues of dating, context, and the status of the documents has been enhanced by scholarship of the past two decades; see, e.g., Ruh, *Meister Eckhart,* 168–86; Winfried Trusen, *Der Prozess gegen Meister Eckhart: Vorgeschichte, Verlauf und Folgen* (Paderborn: Pustet, 1988); and "Meister Eckhart vor seinen Richtern und Zensoren," in *Meister Eckhart: Lebenstationen,* 335–52. Also useful are Oliver Davies, "Why Were Eckhart's Propositions Condemned?" *New Blackfriars* 71 (1990): 433–45; Jürgen Miethke, "Der Prozess gegen Meister Eckhart im Rahmen der spätmittelalter Lehrzuchtverfahren gegen Dominikanertheologen," in *Meister Eckhart: Lebenstationen,* 353–75; and especially the papers in *Eckardus Theutonicus, homo doctus et sanctus: Nachweise und Berichte zum Prozess gegen Meister Eckhart,* ed. Heinrich Stirnimann and Ruedi Imbach (Freiburg, Switzerland: Universitätsverlag, 1992). Most recently, see Ruh, *Geschichte,* 3:243–57; Robert E. Lerner, "New Evidence for the Condemnation of Meister Eckhart," *Speculum* 72 (1997): 347–66; and Susanne Köbele, "Meister Eckhart und die 'Hunde des Herrn': Vom Umgang der Kirche mit ihrem Ketzern," *Beiträge zur Geschichte der deutschen Sprache und Literatur* 124 (2002): 48–73.

73. For a sketch of Henry II and the background to the trial, see Davies, "Why Were Eckhart's Propositions Condemned?"; as well as his *Meister Eckhart: Mystical Theologian* (London: SPCK, 1991), 31–45. See also Friedrich Iohn, *Die Predigt Meister Eckharts* (Heidelberg: Carl Winter, 1993), 157–68.

74. See *Monumenta Ordinis Praedicatorum Historica. Tomus IV. Acta Capitulorum Generalium,* volume 2, ed. Benedict Maria Reichert (Rome: Propaganda Fidei, 1899), 160.25–161.5. The key passage reads: . . . quod in ipsa provincia [Theutonia] per fratres quosdam in praedicacione vulgari quedam personis vulgaribus ac rudibus in sermonibus proponuntur, que possint auditores faciliter deducere in errorem, idcirco damus vicariam super istis diligencius inquirendis et censura debita puniendis ac coerecendis. . . . A similar reprimand was issued by the General Chapter of Toulouse on May 28, 1328, when Eckhart's case was still *sub judice* (*Monumenta* IV:180.1–5).

75. Proc. Col.I (Acta n. 46, in LW 5:197–226).

76. Proc. Col.II (Acta n. 47, in LW 5:226–45).

77. The critical edition by Loris Sturlese (Acta Echardiana n. 48, in LW 5:247–354) has an important introduction and is followed by a facsimile of the ms., Hs. Soest, Stadtarchiv und wissenschaftliche Stadtbibliothek, Cod. Nr. 33 (LW 355–509).

78. Acta n. 48 (Proc.Col.I n. 80, LW 5:277.4–5): Errare enim possum, hereticus esse non possum. Nam primum ad intellectum pertinet, secundum ad voluntatem. Eckhart repeats the point often.

79. Acta n. 48 (Proc.Col.II n. 99, LW 5:341.24–26): Solutio. Totum, quod dictum est, falsum et absurdum secundum imaginationem adversantium. Verum est tamen secundum verum intellectum. . . .

80. Acta n. 48 (Proc.Col.II nn. 91–92, LW 5:340.1–5): . . . 'Vivere meum est esse dei, vel vita mea est essentia dei, quidditas dei quidditas mea.' Dicendum quod falsum est et error, sicut sonat. Verum quidem est, devotum et morale quod hominis justi, inquantum justus, totum esse est ab esse dei, analogice tamen.

81. Acta n. 48 (Proc.Col.I nn. 80–81, LW 5:2776–8): Ad evidentiam igitur premissorum tria notanda sunt. Primum est quod li 'inquantum', reduplicatio scilicet, excludit omne aliud, omne alienum etiam secundum rationem a termino.

82. Acta n. 48 (Proc.Col.I n. 76, LW 5:275.12–14): . . . quod juxta libertatem et privilegia ordinis nostri coram vobis non teneor comparere nec objectis respondere. . . .

83. Ruh, *Geschichte,* 3:246–47.

84. Acta n. 54 (not yet edited in LW 5). The present edition is that of M.-H. Laurent, "Autour de procès de Maître Eckhart," *Divus Thomas,* ser. III, 13 (1936): 344–46.

85. The *Votum,* Acta n. 57, has not yet appeared in LW 5. The current edition is Franz

Pelster, "Eine Gutachten aus dem Eckehart-Prozess in Avignon," in *Aus der Geisteswelt des Mittelalters: Festgabe Martin Grabmann* (Münster: Aschendorff, 1935), 1099–1124. The text in question deals with XXIIIus articulus (1120): Istum articulum verifficat, quia Christus caput et nos membra, cum loquimur, in nobis loquitur. Item in Christo tanta fuit unio verbi cum carne, quod communicat sibi ydiomata, ut Deus dicatur passus et homo creator celi et ipsi Christo proprie competit quod dicatur iustus, inquantum iustus; li inquantum reduplicacio excludit omne alienum a termino. In Christo autem non esse aliud ypostaticum nisi verbi, in aliis autem hominibus verifficatur plus et minus.

86. Senner, "Meister Eckhart in Köln," 233.

87. The critical text of the papal bull has not yet appeared in LW 5, but a text may be found in Laurent, "Autour du procès," 435–46.

88. Lerner ("New Evidence," 363–66) provides an edition of the Mainz copy.

89. This period began with the publication of Heinrich Denifle OP, "Meister Eckeharts lateinische Schriften und die Grundanschauungen seiner Lehre," *Archiv für Literatur- und Kirchengeschichte des Mittelalters* 2 (1886): 417–615.

90. For surveys of this debate, see Ruh, *Geschichte,* 3:227–31; and Largier, "Meister Eckhart: Perspektiven der Forschung," 52–59. For an earlier treatment of the issue, see Frank Tobin, *Meister Eckhart: Thought and Language* (Philadelphia: University of Pennsylvania Press, 1986), 185–92.

91. The denial of Eckhart's status as a mystic seems to have begun with Heribert Fischer, "Grundgedanken der deutschen Predigten," in *Meister Eckhart der Prediger: Festschrift zum Eckhart-Gedenkjahr,* ed. Udo M. Nix and Raphael Öchslin (Freiburg: Herder, 1960), 55–59; and "Zur Frage nach der Mystik in den Werken Meister Eckharts," in *La mystique rhénane* (Paris: Presses universitaires de France, 1963), 109–32. After Fischer, similar claims have been made by C. F. Kelley, *Meister Eckhart on Divine Knowledge* (New Haven: Yale University Press, 1977), 106–13; and Kurt Flasch, "Die Intention Meister Eckharts," in *Sprache und Begriff: Festschrift für Bruno Liebrucks,* ed. Heinz Röttges (Meisenheim am Glan: Hain, 1974), 292–318, especially 299–302; and "Meister Eckhart: Versuch, ihn aus dem mystischen Strom zu retten," in *Gnosis und Mystik in der Geschichte der Philosophie,* ed. Peter Koslowski (Darmstadt: Wissenschaftliche Buchgesellschaft, 1988), 94–110. These views have been countered by other Eckhart scholars, such as Ruh, *Geschichte,* 3:227–31; Alois M. Haas, "Aktualität und Normativität Meister Eckharts," in *Eckhardus Theutonicus, homo doctus et sanctus,* 203–68; and *Meister Eckhart als normative Gestalt geistlichen Lebens,* 2nd ed. (Freiburg: Johannes, 1995); and Largier, "Meister Eckhart: Perspektiven der Forschung," 52–59.

92. Words like "mysticism," and "mystic," although modern, can still be useful for revealing important aspects of the religious world of medieval Christianity. For more on this issue, see Bernard McGinn, "*Quo vadis?* Reflections on the Current Study of Mysticism," *Christian Spirituality Bulletin* (Spring 1998): 13–21, especially my response to Simon Tugwell (p. 17).

93. A good expression of this unity can be found in a passage from In Ioh. n. 444 (LW 3:381.4–7): Patet ergo, sicut frequenter in nostris expositionibus dicitur, quod *ex eadem vena* descendit veritas et doctrina theologiae, philosophiae naturalis, moralis, artis factibilium et spectabilium et etiam iuris positivi, secundum illud Psalmi: 'de vultu tuo iudicium meum prodeat' (my emphasis).

94. In Ioh. n. 185 as cited above. On this point, see Robert J. Dobie, "Reason and Revelation in the Thought of Meister Eckhart," *The Thomist* 67 (2003): 409–38.

95. Pr. 9 (DW 1:152.2–5): . . . noch sint ez allez heidenischer meister wort, diu hie vor gesprochen sint, die niht enbekanten dan in einem natiurlîchen liehte; noch enkam ich niht ze der heiligen meister worten, die dâ bekanten in einem vil hoehern liehte (*Teacher and Preacher,* 258). See also Pr. 15 (DW 1:251.10–13): Dis luter bloss wesen nemmet Aristotiles ain 'was'. Das ist das hoechst, das Aristotiles von naturlichen kunsten ie gesprach, vnd uber das so enmag kain maister hoeher gesprechen, er sprach dann in dem hailgen gaist.

96. Pr. 101 (DW 4:365.195–99, and 366.207–09).

97. Pr. 15 (DW 1:251.15).

98. Pr. 28 (DW 2:67.1–68.3): Nû sprichet *Plâtô,* der grôze pfaffe, der vaehet ane und wil sprechen von grôzen dingen. Er sprichet von einer lûterkeit, diu enist in der werlt niht; . . . her ûz drücket im got, der êwige vater, die vüllede und den abgrunt aller sîner gotheit. . . . [U]nd sin gebern daz ist sîn inneblîben, und sîn inneblîben ist sîn ûzgebern (Walshe 1:145 modified). In the notes on this passage in DW 2:67–68, Quint discusses what particular teachings of Plato Eckhart may have had in mind. Aquinas's summary of Plato's treatment of *ens/ unum/summum bonum* in STh Ia, q.6, a.4 is certainly a text that Eckhart would have known, but this does not seem a likely source for the point Eckhart makes here. Others have thought that Eckhart may actually be referring to Proclus rather than Plato. Hans Hof (*Scintilla animae: Eine Studie zu einem Grundbegriff in Meister Eckharts Philosophie* [Lund: Gleerup, 1952], 213–15) saw the influence of the doctrine of the *unum animae* found in Proclus's *De providentia et fato,* a supposition considered "séduisant" by Alain de Libera in *La mystique rhénane d'Albert le Grand à Maître Eckhart* (Paris: Éditions du Seuil, 1994), 310 n. 156. Similar teaching is found in Proclus's *Expositio in Parmenidem Platonis,* translated into Latin by William of Moerbeke. See Carlos Steel, *Proclus. Commentaire sur le Parménide de Platon: Traduction de Guillaume de Moerbeke,* 2 vols. (Leuven: University Press; Leiden: Brill, 1982–85); Steel (*Commentaire* 1:34*–35*) denies that Eckhart knew the work.

99. In Ioh. n. 2 (LW 3:4.4–6): In cuius verbi expositione et aliorum quae sequuntur, intentio est auctoris, sicut et in omnibus suis editionibus, ea quae sacra asserit fides christiana et utriusque testamenti scriptura, exponere per rationes naturales philosophorum.

100. In Gen. II n. 4 (LW 1:454.6–10): Primum est, quod non est putandum, quasi per talia parabolica intendamus probare divina, naturalia et moralia ex parabolis; sed potius hoc ostendere intendimus, quod his, quae probamus et dicimus de divinis, moralibus et naturalibus, consonant ea quae veritas sacrae scripturae parabolice innuit quasi latenter. See also In Ex. n. 211 (LW 2:178).

101. This triple division, which appears often in Eckhart's works, may have been taken from Thomas Aquinas (*In De Anima* I, lect. 1.7), though it is also suggested by Jerome (*Epistola* 30. 1 in PL 22:441–42), as well as in Avicenna and Albert the Great. Eckhart uses it especially in the prologue to In Gen. II, the introduction to his later exegetical writings (see nn. 1, 2, 4, and 7 [LW 1:447.8, 451.3, 454.7–9, and 456.4]). It also frequently appears in the John commentary; e.g., In Ioh. nn. 2–3, 125, 186, 441, 444, 477, and 509 (LW 3:4, 108, 156, 378, 381, 410, 441).

102. From this perspective, Eckhart's view bears an analogy to a position like that of Hugh of St. Victor, or Bonaventure, who argued for a special form of Christian philosophy over and above the "fallen philosophy" of natural reason. But Eckhart arrives at his position in a different way, and uses it differently. He does not criticize the failings of the philosophy of natural reason, but rather absorbs it into the higher synthesis of the apophatic Christian philosophy of *unwizzen.*

103. In Ioh. n. 361 (LW 3:307.1–4): Sicut enim praesumptionis est et temeritatis nolle credere, nisi intellexeris, sic ignaviae est et desidiosum quod fide credis, rationibus naturalibus et similitudinibus non investigare. . . .

104. Niklaus Largier, "Intellekttheorie, Hermeneutik und Allegorie: Subjekt und Subjektivität bei Meister Eckhart," in *Geschichte und Vorgeschichte der modernen Subjektivität,* ed. Reto Luzius Fetz, Roland Hagenbüchle, and Peter Schulz (Berlin/New York: Walter de Gruyter, 1998), 462–64, and 474–82.

105. Among the older works devoted to the topic are Josef Koch, "Sinn und Struktur der Schriftauslegungen," in *Meister Eckhart der Prediger,* 73–103; and Konrad Weiss, "Meister Eckharts biblische Hermeneutik," in *La mystique rhénane,* 95–108. In recent scholarship this gap has been redressed by treatments such as those of Donald F. Duclow, "Hermeneutics and Meister Eckhart," *Philosophy Today* 28 (1984): 36–43; and "Meister Eckhart on the Book of Wisdom: Commentary and Sermons," *Traditio* 43 (1987): 215–35; Frank Tobin, "Creativity and Interpreting Scripture: Meister Eckhart in Practice," *Monatshefte* 74 (1982): 410–18; and *Meister Eckhart,* 23–29. Important recent work in German includes Susanne Köbele, *"PRIMO*

ASPECTU MONSTRUOSA: Schriftauslegung bei Meister Eckhart," *Zeitschrift für deutsches Altertum und deutsche Literatur* 122 (1993): 62–81; Niklaus Largier, *"FIGURATA LOCUTIO:* Hermeneutik und Philosophie bei Eckhart von Hochheim und Heinrich Seuse," in *Meister Eckhart: Lebensstationen—Redesituationen,* 303–32; "Intellekttheorie, Hermeneutik und Allegorie," in *Geschichte und Vorgeschichte der modernen Subjektivität,* 460–86; and Wouter Goris, *Einheit als Prinzip und Ziel,* chapter 1.

106. Eckhart went against the program of Thomas Aquinas, who, although he did not deny the importance of the spiritual interpretation, argued that *sacra doctrina* should depend on the Bible's literal sense (see STh Ia, q. 1, a.10).

107. The most recent work on the relation of Eckhart and Maimonides is by Yossef Schwartz; see "'*Ecce est locus apud me':* Maimonides und Eckharts Raumvorstellung als Begriff des Göttlichen," in *Raum und Raumvorstellungen im Mittelalter,* ed. Jan A. Aertsen and Andreas Speer (Berlin: Walter de Gruyter, 1998), 348–64; and "Metaphysische oder theologische Hermeneutik? Meister Eckhart in Spuren des Maimonides und Thomas von Aquin" (unpublished). Niklaus Largier (*"FIGURATA LOCUTIO,"* 326–32) has advanced the case for a hermeneutical turn in Eckhart's thinking under the influence of Maimonides during the second decade of the fourteenth century. Though Eckhart may have shifted toward a more parabolical mode of interpretation at this time and have begun to use Maimonides more extensively, he was certainly familiar with the *Dux neutrorum* from his days as a student in Paris.

108. Duclow ("Hermeneutics and Meister Eckhart," 42) aptly uses the phrase "mystical hermeneutics" to characterize Eckhart's approach to scripture.

109. See, e.g., Pr. 22 (DW 1:381.3–5): "Mich wundert," sprach ich, "daz diu geschrift alsô vol ist, daz nieman daz allerminste wort ergründen enkan." See also Pr. 89 (DW 4:38–39) and Pr. 51 (DW 2:465–66).

110. BgT 1 (DW 5:42:21–43.1): Sant Augustinus sprichet, daz der allerbest die geschrift vernimet, der blôz alles geistes suochet sin und wârheit der geschrift in ir selben, daz ist: in dem geiste, dar inne si geschriben ist und gesprochen ist: in gotes geiste (Walshe 3:86). The text from Augustine is *De doctrina christiana* 3.27.38 (PL 34:80).

111. In Gen. II n. 3 (LW 1:453.5–6): Nec enim aliquis scripturas intelligere putandus est, qui medullam, Christum, veritatem, latitantem in ipsis nesciet invenire. Largier (*"FIGURATA LOCUTIO,"* 318–19) points out that the centrality of the christological principle distances Eckhart from Maimonides in decisive fashion, however much he learned from the Jewish sage.

112. John 1:1 (*In principio erat verbum*) is given an initial fifteen interpretations in In Ioh. nn. 4–12, another seven in nn. 28–39, and a moral reading in n. 51 (LW 3:5–12, 22–33, and 41–43). Wisdom 8:1 (*Attingit a fine usque ad finem fortiter et disponit omnia suaviter*) receives twenty-two interpretations in In. Sap. nn. 167–200 (LW 2:502–35). On this text as a paradigm of Eckhart's philosophical mysticism, see Erwin Waldschütz, "Probleme philosophische Mystik am Beispiel Meister Eckharts," in *Probleme philosophischer Mystik: Festschrift für Karl Albert zum siebigsten Geburtstag,* ed. Elenor Jain and Reinhard Margreiter (Sankt Augustin: Academia Verlag, 1991), 71–92.

113. In Ioh. n. 745 (LW 3:649.3–10): Adhuc autem notandum quod talis modus loquendi, excessive scilicet, proprie competit divinis scripturis. Omne enim divinum, in quantum huiusmodi, immensum est nec ad mensuram datur. . . . Divinorum etiam est excellentia nobis ea non nude praeponi, sed sub figuris rerum sensibilium occultari. . . .

114. For an example of this type of rewriting by translation, see the remarks on Pr. 30 dealing with the Our Father in Köbele, *"PRIMO ASPECTU MONSTRUOSA,"* 68–79. Eckhart also engaged in similar reinterpretations through re-punctuation and unusual translations at times in his Latin works. For example, rather than reading John 1:3 (*sine ipso factum est nihil*) as the traditional "without him nothing was made," he translates it as "without him what was made [*factum* as participial noun] was nothing" (In Ioh. n. 53 [LW 3:44]).

115. On Eckhart's delight in word games, biblical and nonbiblical, throughout his works, see Tobin, *Meister Eckhart*, 171–79.

116. Prol.op.expos. n. 5 (LW 1:184.16–18): Quinto notandum quod auctoritates principales plerumque multis modis exponuntur, ut qui legit, nunc istam rationem, nunc aliam, unam vel plures accipiat, prout iudicaverit expedire. See also In Ioh. nn. 39 and 225 (LW 3:33 and 189).

117. There are, to be sure, a number of places where Eckhart does follow the narrative structure of the text. For example, in Pr. 71 (DW 3:219–22 and 230) he uses Sg. of Sgs. 3:1–4 as an account of the soul's progress to God.

118. On this aspect of Eckhart's hermeneutics, see Goris, *Einheit als Prinzip und Ziel*, 37–51.

119. Prol.op.expos. n. 1 (LW 1:183.1–184.2): Primo quod in expositione auctoritatis, de qua tunc agitur, plurimae et plerumque adducuntur aliae auctoritates canonis, et illae omnes auctoritates possunt in locis suis exponi ex ista, sicut nunc ista per illas. The same point is made in Prol.gen. n. 14 (LW 1:159.9–12).

120. In Ioh. n. 433 (LW 3:371).

121. For the two kinds of *parabolae*, see In Gen. II, prol. n. 5 (LW 2:454–55), and In Ioh. nn. 174–76 (LW 3:143–45).

122. In Gen. II, prol. n. 1 (LW 1:448.17–449.1): Quando ergo ex his quae leguntur intellectum alicuius mysticae significationis possumus exsculpere. . . . Eckhart also uses the terms *mystice exponere* (ibid., n. 2 [452.8–9]) and *mystice consonare* (In Ex. n. 222 [LW 2:185.6]).

123. In Gen. II, prol. n. 2 (LW 1:449.5–9): Cum ergo "sensus" etiam "litteralis, quem auctor scripturae intendit, deus autem sit auctor sacrae scripturae," ut dictum est, omnis sensus qui verus est sensus litteralis est. Constat enim quod omne verum ab ipsa veritate est, in ipsa includitur, ab ipsa derivatur et intenditur. The embedded quotation here is from Thomas Aquinas, STh Ia, q.1., a.10, but Eckhart's notion of the multiplicity of true meanings is actually drawn from Augustine as the succeeding quotations from *Confessiones* 12.31.42, 12.18.27, and 13.24.37 make clear (see PL 32: 844, 835–36, and 861).

124. Duclow, "Meister Eckhart on the Book of Wisdom," 234.

125. Pr. 51 (DW 2:473.5–9): Ich han gesprochenn etwan me [probable reference to DW 1:212.3–6]: die schal muoz zerbrechen, vnnd muoz sa, dass darinn ist, herauss kommen; Wann, wiltu den kernen haben, so muostu die schalen brechen. Vnd also: wiltu die natur bloss finden, so muessent sich die gleychnuss alle zerbrechenn, vnnd ye das es me darin trittet, ye es dem wesen naeher ist. So wenn das sy dass ein findet, da es alles eyn ist, da bleibet sy <in> dem einigen <ein> (trans. Walshe 2:252 modified). See the analysis in Köbele, *"PRIMO ASPECTU MONSTRUOSA,"* 64–67; cf. Duclow, "Meister Eckhart on the Book of Wisdom," 40–41; and Largier, *"FIGURATA LOCUTIO,"* 323–26.

126. In the apophatic character of his exegesis, Eckhart bears comparison with John Scottus Eriugena. On Eriugena's exegesis, see Bernard McGinn, "The Originality of Eriugena's Spiritual Exegesis," in *Iohannes Scottus Eriugena: The Bible and Hermeneutics*, ed. Gerd Van Riel, Carlos Steel, and James McEvoy (Leuven: University Press, 1996), 55–80.

127. On Eckhart the preacher, see Joachim Theisen, *Predigt und Gottesdienst*; Burkhard Hasebrink, *Formen inzitativer Rede bei Meister Eckhart: Untersuchungen zur literarische Konzeption der deutschen Predigt* (Tübingen: Niemeyer, 1992); Friedrich Iohn, *Die Predigt Meister Eckharts: Seelsorge und Häresie* (Heidelberg: Carl Winter, 1993); Bruce Milem, *The Unspoken Word: Negative Theology in Meister Eckhart's German Sermons* (Washington, DC: Catholic University of America, 2002). See also the treatment of individual sermons in *Lectura Eckhardi I: Predigten Meister Eckharts von Fachgelehrten gelesen und gedeutet*, ed. Georg Steer and Loris Sturlese (Stuttgart: Kohlhammer, 1998); and *Lectura Eckhardi II*, also edited by Steer and Sturlese (Stuttgart: Kohlhammer, 2003). Although Eckhart's sermons do not survive as *corpora* or in groups, several references to "my book" (*mîn buoch*: e.g., Pr. 28 [DW 2:62.3]) argue that he originally organized the sermons into a collection that probably followed the liturgical year,

both *de tempore* (the Sundays and main feasts) and *de sanctis* (the saints). Loris Sturlese is developing this argument and I thank him for the information.

128. Ruh, *Geschichte,* 3:324.

129. Eckhart analyzes three essential characteristics of the preacher (*vitae puritas, intentionis sinceritas, opinionis aut famae odoriferae suavitas*) in his In Eccli. nn. 2–5 (LW 2:231–34). The passage cited here is from n. 4 (233.3–4): Sic praedicator verbi dei, quod est 'dei virtus et dei sapientia', non debet sibi esse aut vivere, sed Christo quem praedicat. . . .

130. Theisen, *Predigt und Gottesdienst,* 550.

131. Reiner Schürmann, *Meister Eckhart: Mystic and Philosopher* (Bloomington: Indiana University Press, 1978), 89, 106–7. The same point is made by Duclow, "Hermeneutics and Meister Eckhart," 38–39. See also Hasebrink, *Formen inzitativer Rede,* 57–58.

132. Milem, *Unspoken Word,* 4.

133. Ruh (*Geschichte,* 3:352–53) analyzes how Eckhart's preaching strives to identify both the speaker and the audience in the oneness of the ground.

134. In Eccli. n. 69 (LW 299.2–3): 'Praedica' quasi praedic, id est prius intus dic; vel 'praedica', id est prodic vel produc extra, ut 'luceat coram hominibus'. A comparable interpretation is found in Pr. 30 (DW 2:93–94 and 97–98).

135. Pr. 2 (DW 1:41.5–7): Möhtet ir gemerken mit mînem herzen, ir verstüendet wol, waz ich spriche, wan ez ist wâr und diu wârheit sprichet ez selbe (*Essential Eckhart,* 181).

136. Eckhart claims to be speaking out of, or in the name of, divine Truth in a number of places. For example, in Pr. 48 (DW 2:415.4–5): Ich spriche ez bî guoter wârheit und bî êwigen wârheit und bî iemerwerdender wârheit . . . (repeated in 420.5–6). Such formulas are especially evident in Pr. 52 (DW 2:487.5–7, 490.6, 491.9, and 506.1–3). In a passage in Pr. 66 (DW 3:113–14) he invites his hearers to realize the divine Truth within each of them.

137. Pr. 64 (DW 3:90.4–7): Ich wil üch sagen, wie ich der läute gedenck: ich fleiss mich des, das ich mein selbs vnd aller menschen vergesse, vnd füge mich für sy in ainicheit. das wir in ainicheit beleiben, des helf vns got. Amen (Walshe 2:226). Alois M. Haas ("Schools of Late Medieval Mysticism," in *Christian Spirituality: High Middle Ages and Reformation,* ed. Jill Raitt et al. [New York: Crossroad, 1987], 147) puts it well: "The speaker [Eckhart] understands himself as a witness to the unity to which he directs others."

138. Erich Auerbach devoted some pages to Eckhart's language in his *Literary Language & Its Public in Late Latin Antiquity and the Middle Ages* (Princeton: Princeton University Press, 1965), 330–32. Among the most important contributions of the 1980s were two essays of Alois M. Haas in his *Geistliches Mittelalter* (Freiburg, Switzerland, 1984): "Meister Eckhart und die Sprache: Sprachgeschichtliche und sprachtheologische Aspekte seines Werkes" (pp. 193–214), and "Meister Eckhart und die deutsche Sprache" (pp. 215–37). See also Walter Haug, "Das Wort und die Sprache bei Meister Eckhart," in *Zur deutschen Literatur und Sprache des 14. Jahrhunderts: Dubliner Colloquium 1981,* ed. Walter Haug, Timothy R. Jackson, Johannes Janota (Heidelberg: Carl Winter, 1983), 25–44. In English the comments of Frank Tobin, *Meister Eckhart,* chapters 3 and 5, summarize and expand on his earlier papers in this field. Literature of the 1990s will be mentioned below.

139. An older example of such analysis of entire sermons can be found in Schürmann, *Meister Eckhart,* which studies Prr. 2, 17, 26, 16b, 71, 76, 30, and 52. For recent examples, see Hasebrink, *Formen inzitativer Rede* (Prr. 12, 30, and 49); Iohn, *Die Predigt* (Prr. 1 and 6); and Milem, *Unspoken Word* (Prr. 52, 2, 16b, and 6). Susanne Köbele (*Bilder der unbegriffenen Wahrheit: Zur Struktur mystischer Rede im Spannungsfeld von Latein und Volkssprache* [Tübingen/ Basel: Francke, 1993]) compares the parallel Latin and MHG sermons, Pr. 21 and SS. XXXVII and XXXVIII, and Pr. 20a and S. VIII. See also Ruh, *Geschichte* 3 (treating Prr. 22, 2, 39, 6, and 52); and the sermons presented and commented on in *Lectura Eckhardi I* (Prr. 4, 12, 16b, 17, 18, 19, 48, 52, 63, 71, 101, and S. IV); and *Lectura Eckhardi II* (Prr. 1, 6, 10, 37, 72, 86, and SS. XXV and XXIX).

140. Alois M. Haas, "Mystische Erfahrung und Sprache," in *Sermo mysticus,* 18–36. See

also Haas, "Das mystische Paradox," in *Das Paradox: Eine Herausforderung des abendländische Denkens*, ed. Paul Geyer and Roland Hagenbüchle (Tübingen: Stauffenberg, 1992), 273–89.

141. On the "appellative text function" that invites the hearer to identify himself as the subject of the thematized divine knowledge set forth in the sermon, see Hasebrink, *Formen*, 36–48; and *Lectura Eckhardi I*, 240. On the way in which Eckhart's sermons effect their own transcendence or self-destruction, see *Formen*, 134–36 and 265–68.

142. Michael A. Sells, *Mystical Languages of Unsaying* (Chicago/London: University of Chicago, 1994), chapters 6 and 7.

143. Tobin, *Meister Eckhart*, especially chapter 5. Tobin summarizes: "In reading his works we sense the appropriateness of the adage that in recognizing the boundaries of language and human thought one can in some sense transcend them" (p. 87; cf. vii, 89, 158–59). See also the reflections of Haug, "Das Wort und die Sprache bei Meister Eckhart," 34–35.

144. See Frank Tobin, "Eckhart's Mystical Use of Language: The Contexts of *eigenschaft*," *Seminar* 8 (1972): 160–68.

145. Tobin, *Meister Eckhart*, 158–67.

146. See ibid., 167–71. For an example of a chiasmic text in the German works, see, e. g., Pr. 30 (DW 2:94.6–7): Got ist in allen dingen. Ie mê er ist in den dingen, ie mê er ist ûz den dinge: ie mê inne, ie mê ûze, ie mê ûze, ie mê inne.

147. On the relation between Latin and vernacular languages in general in late medieval mysticism, see McGinn, *Flowering of Mysticism*, 22–24.

148. Two important recent discussions of the relation of German and Latin in Eckhart are Burkhard Hasebrink, "GRENZVERSCHIEBUNG: Zu Kongruenz und Differenz von Latein und Deutsche bei Meister Eckhart," *Zeitschrift für deutsches Altertum und deutsche Literatur* 121 (1992): 369–98; and Köbele, *Bilder der unbegriffenen Wahrheit*, chapter 2.

149. For example, W. Haug, "Das Wort und die Sprache," 39: ". . . im Prinzip könnte man sich seine Predigten genausogut lateinisch wie deutsch denken. . . ."

150. Ruh, *Meister Eckhart*, 45: "Es ist, um es auf eine Formel zu bringen, der spirituelle Mehrwert der Volkssprache, der Eckhart deren Gebrauch in den 'Reden der Unterweisung' aufdrängte." See also pp. 192–95.

151. Köbele, *Bilder*, 10.

152. Hasebrink, "GRENZVERSCHIEBUNG," 379–98, as illustrated through an analysis of parallel German and Latin sermons (Pr. 25–27 and S. VI.1; Pr. 18 and S. XXXVI; and Pr. 17 and S. LV.4). The interchanges between Latin and German, evident both within Eckhart's oeuvre, and in the later Latin translations of German sermons and German versions of Latin works, is evidence for this exchange of boundaries.

153. Haas, "Meister Eckhart und die deutsche Sprache," 168.

154. Köbele (*Bilder*, 13, 51) uses this term, thanking Ruh for suggesting it to her.

155. Much of this first section is drawn from chapter 3 in *The Mystical Thought of Meister Eckhart*.

156. Pr. 42 (DW 2:309.3–7): Nû wizzet: alliu unser volkomenheit und alliu unser saelicheit liget dar ane, daz der mensche durchgange und übergange alle geschaffenheit und alle zîtlicheit und allez wesen und gange in den grunt, der gruntlôs ist. Wir biten des unsern lieben herren got, daz wir ein werden und innewonen, und ze dem selben grunde helfe uns got. Âmen (my trans.). Eckhart often insists that only the power of "intellect" (*vernünfticheit/ bekantnisse*) can penetrate into the ground; see, e.g., Pr. 7 (DW 1:122.10–123.5), and Pr. 66 (DW 3:113.1–3).

157. Pr. 54b (DW 2:565.13–566.2): Wan swer komen wil in gotes grunt, in sîn innerstez, der muoz ê komen in sînen eigenen grunt, in sîn innerstez, wan nieman enmac got erkennen, er enmüeze ê sich selben erkennen (my trans.). See the parallel in Pr. 54a (DW 2:550.4– 551.2): Suln wir iemer komen in den grunt gotes und in sîn innerstez, sô müezen wir ze dem êrsten komen in unsern eigenen grunt und in unser innerstez in lûterer dêmüeticheit. The relation between humility and *grunt*, must be understood in an ontological way, as pointed out by Erwin Waldschütz, *Denken und Erfahren des Grundes: Zur philosophischen Deutung Meister Eckharts* (Freiburg/Vienna: Herder, 1989), 184–85.

158. On the *grunt der sêle*, see, e.g., Pr. 17 (DW 1:281–93), and Pr. 101 (DW 4:344.45–346.55).

159. E.g., Pr. 15 (DW 1:253.5–6): . . . da gottes grund vnd der sele grund ain grund ist. It is interesting that Eckhart could use the same formula to express ultimate beatitude; see, e.g., Pr. 39 (DW 2:257.2–3): . . . wan des gerehten saelicheit und gotes saelicheit ist éin saelicheit, wan dâ ist der gerehte saelic, dâ got saelic ist. For more on the relation between *grunt* and *saelicheit* in Eckhart, see Pr. 45 (DW 2:363.3–7, and 373.4–7).

160. Such fused identity, of course, has been expressed by other mystics; see, e.g., Michael Sells on Plotinus in *Mystical Languages of Unsaying*, 22–27.

161. Pr. 5b (DW 1:90.8–9): Hie ist gotes grunt mîn grunt und mîn grunt gotes grunt. Hie lebe ich ûzer mînem eigen, als got lebet ûzer sînem eigen (*Essential Eckhart*, 183). There are a number of other such fused-identity formulas in the German sermons; e.g., Pr. 28 (DW 2:67.1–69.4), using both *grunt* and *einicheit*; Pr. 48 (DW 2:415.4–9); Pr. 80 (DW 3:378.2–5); Pr. 98 (DW 4:243.35–244.44); etc. In the sermons edited by Pfeiffer, see especially LXI (194–95), and LXXI (225.34–226.13).

162. This form of relation between God and the soul is found especially in those Latin texts that use the word *illabor* to indicate God's movement into the soul's depth (e.g., S. IX, n. 98 [LW 4:93.6]). But similar formulae can also be found in German sermons, e.g., Pr. 10 (DW 1:162.4–6); Pr. 76 (DW 3:252.1–6).

163. See Langer, "Eckharts Lehre von Seelengrund," 183–90, arguing against the view of B. Mojsisch.

164. A classic account of the *vunkelîn*, or uncreated something, remains that of Hans Hof, *Scintilla Animae*.

165. See Hugo Rahner, "Die Gottesgeburt: Die Lehre der Kirchenväter von der Geburt Christi aus den Herzen der Kirche und der Gläubigen," in *Symbole der Kirche: Die Ekklesiologie der Väter* (Salzburg: Müller, 1964), 7–41; for a general analysis, see Dietmar Mieth, "Gottesschau und Gottesgeburt: Zwei Typen Christlicher Gotteserfahrung in der Tradition," *Freiburger Zeitschrift für Theologie und Philosophie* 27 (1980): 204–23.

166. Pr. 48 (DW 2:420.7–421.3): . . . ez wil in den einvaltigen grunt, in die stillen wüeste, dâ nie underscheit îngeluogete weder vater noch sun noch heiliger geist; . . . wan dirre grunt ist ein einvaltic stille, diu in ir selben unbeweglich ist, und von dirre unbewegelicheit werdent beweget alle dinc und werdent enpfangen alliu leben, diu vernunfticlîche in in selben sint (*Essential Eckhart*, 198). On this sermon, see the commentary by Burkhard Mojsisch in *Lectura Eckhardi I*, 156–62.

167. E.g., Pr. 51 (DW 2:470.3–6).

168. E.g., Pr. 69 (DW 3:178.2–180.2). In Pr. 52, especially in the third section (DW 2:499.9–505.9), similar language is used with regard to *durchbrechen*, though *grunt* is not employed. Another daring expression of indistinct union beyond the Persons of the Trinity without *grunt* language can be found in Pr. 83 (DW 3:448).

169. Pr. 109 (DW 4:748–74). Originally rejected by Josef Quint for inclusion in the DW, the homily was later translated in Quint's own *Meister Eckhart: Deutsche Predigten und Traktate* (Munich: Carl Hanser, 1963), 271–73. It has been translated into English by both Walshe 2:79–82, and Davies, *Meister Eckhart*, 232–34.

170. Pr. 109 (DW 4:771.56–772.59): Dô ich stuont in dem grunde, in dem boden, in dem rivier und in dem quellenne der gotheit, dô envrâgete mich nieman, war ich wölte oder waz ich taete. Dô enwas nieman, der mich vrâgete. Dô ich ûzflôz, dô sprâchen alle crêatûren got. As Burkhard Mojsisch has shown, in his "'Ce moi': La conception du moi de Maître Eckhart," *Revue des sciences religieuses* 70 (1996): 27–28, *got* as used by Eckhart is a relational term employed of the Creator, and therefore not an adequate name for the hidden divinity. Thus, *got* must be left behind (see, e.g., Pr. 52) in the releasement that some have spoken of as Eckhart's "mystical atheism." On "mystical atheism," see Schürmann, *Meister Eckhart*, 213.

171. Pr. 109 (DW 4:773.66–68): Swenne ich kume in den grunt, in den boden, in den rivier und in daz quellen der gotheit, sô envrâget mich nieman, wannen ich kume oder wâ ich sî gewesen. Dâ envermiste mîn nieman. Dâ entwirt got (trans. Davies, 234).

172. The dialectical character of Eckhart's thought means that from different perspectives any of the major themes of his thought can be given a certain priority. Thus, Waldschütz (*Denken und Erfahren des Grundes,* 351) is not incorrect in claiming "Gottesgeburt ist höchster und letzter Vollzug der Grunderfahrung," without necessarily contradicting my insistence that in another sense identity in the *grunt* is deeper than the *gottesgeburt.*

173. For a sketch of Christian understandings of union, see Bernard McGinn, "Love, Knowledge, and *Unio mystica* in the Western Christian Tradition," in *Mystical Union in Judaism, Christianity, and Islam: An Ecumenical Dialogue,* ed. Moshe Idel and Bernard McGinn (New York: Continuum, 1996), especially 71–80 on Eckhart and his contemporaries and followers. For the distinction between *mystical uniting* and *mystical identity,* see Bernard McGinn, "Mystical Union in Judaism, Christianity, and Islam," in *The Encyclopedia of Religion,* 2nd ed. (forthcoming).

174. Bernard of Clairvaux, *De diligendo Deo* 10.28 (*S. Bernardi Opera,* 8 vols. [Rome: Editiones Cistercienses, 1957–77] 3:143.15–24).

175. On Eckhart's use of Bernard, see Bernard McGinn, "St. Bernard and Meister Eckhart," *Cîteaux* 31 (1980): 373–86.

176. See Bernard McGinn, *The Foundations of Mysticism: Origins to the Fifth Century,* volume 1 of *The Presence of God: A History of Western Christian Mysticism* (New York: Crossroad, 1991), 154–55, and 175–78.

177. For a treatment of Porete and her teaching on union, see McGinn, *Flowering of Mysticism,* 244–65; and Sells, *Mystical Languages of Unsaying,* chapters 5 and 7.

178. On the historical contacts, see Edmund Colledge and J. C. Marler, "'Poverty of Will': Ruusbroec, Eckhart and the Mirror of Simple Souls," in *Jan van Ruusbroec, the Sources, Content, and Sequels of His Mysticism,* ed. Paul Mommaers and N. de Paepe (Leuven: Leuven University Press, 1984), 14–47; as well as the papers of Maria Lichtmann, Amy Hollywood, and Michael Sells in *Meister Eckhart and the Beguine Mystics,* 65–146.

179. On the role of Proclus in German medieval thought, see chapter 1, pp. 45–47 above.

180. E.g., Pr. 5b (DW 1:93.7–8): . . . ein einvaltigez ein (see the note on this text in Largier, *Meister Eckhart,* 1:803–07); Pr. 25 (DW 2:11.1): . . . ein einic ein. These threefold repetitive formulas of absolute unity (*ein-ein-ein*) are among Eckhart's characteristic ways of expressing the fused identity of God and human. As Burkhard Hasebrink has shown, they were developed from metaphors used in medieval love literature, both secular and mystical; see his *"EIN EINIC EIN:* Zur Darstellung der Liebeseinheit in mittelhochdeutscher Literatur," *Beiträge zur Geschichte der deutschen Literatur und Sprache* 124 (2002): 442–65.

181. Köbele, *Bilder,* 187. To claim that *grunt* has a special ability to express Eckhart's indistinct union is not to deny that he often uses other terms, such as *wesen* and *isticheit,* in comparable ways (e.g., Prr. 6, 52, 77, 83 [DW 1:106.1–3; DW 2:492.3–7 and 504.2; DW 3:340.8–10 and 447.5ff.]). Identity formulas using birthing language also occur; e.g., Prr. 4, 22, 38 (DW 1:72.8–73.1; DW 1:382.3–383.1; DW 2:228.1–3).

182. Mojsisch refers to this fused identity as a "univocal-transcendental relationship of correlation" (*Meister Eckhart,* 135). Waldschütz equates *Grund-Sein* with *In-Beziehung-Sein* (*Denken und Erfahren des Grundes,* 173, 201, 215, and especially 342–48), stressing the event-identity of the *grunt* (e.g., 139–40, 164–66). See also Bernhard Welte, *Meister Eckhart: Gedanken zu seinem Gedanken* (Freiburg: Herder, 1979), 110–26.

183. Pr. 17 (DW 1:281.12–282.3): . . . swer dâ schrîbet von beweglîchen dingen, der enrüeret die natûre noch den grunt der sêle niht. Swer nâch der einvalticheit und lûterkeit und blôzheit die sêle, als si in ir selber ist, nennen sol, der enkan ir enkeinen namen vinden (Walshe 1:171). Cf. Pr. 17 (DW 1: 284.5); Pr. 77 (DW 3:337–38); Pr. 83 (DW 3:440.5–6); and Pr. 98 (DW 4:236.11–237.13). Pr. 17 parallels S. LV.4 (LW 4:458–65), which treats the same verse from John 12:25. For a discussion of the two homilies, see Hasebrink, "GRENZVERSCHIEBUNG," 393–97; and Loris Sturlese, "Predigt 17: 'Qui odit animam suam'," in *Lectura Eckhardi I,* 75–96. In several sermons Eckhart says that the soul in its essence, like God, has

no name; e.g., Prr. 3, 7 (DW 1:53–56, 123–24); Pr. 38 (DW 2:237). See also the discussion of the unnameable ground of the soul as a desert in Pr. 28 (DW 2:66.2–7).

184. For the negative anthropology of Eriugena, see McGinn, *Growth of Mysticism*, 104–6.

185. See, e.g., RdU 23 (DW 5:293.5–7): . . . sunder diu hoehste hoehe der hôchheit liget in dem tiefen grunde der dêmüeticheit. Wan ie der grunt tiefer ist und niderr, ie ouch diu erhoeunge und die hoeher und unmaeziger ist. . . . The RdU speaks of the *abgrunde gotes* (238.4–5) and the *grunde der sêle* (219.8, 255.8, 256.7), but does not yet use fused identity formulae.

186. This seconds the point made about translations of Pr. 52 by Sells in *Mystical Languages of Unsaying*, 187–90.

187. Largier, "Negativität, Möglichkeit, Freiheit," 158–62.

188. Pr. 54a (DW 2:560.6–7): Ie man die wurzel und den kernen und den grunt der gotheit mê erkennet ein, ie man mê erkennet alliu dinc (my trans.).

189. Pr. 39 (DW 2:256.3–4): Und dar umber ganc in dînen eignen grunt, und dâ würke, und din werk, diu dû würkest, dui sint alliu lebendic. See also Pr. 5b (DW 1:90.6–12). On working "out of the ground," see Waldschütz, *Denken und Erfahren des Grundes*, 140–42, and 173–85.

190. Pr. 16b (DW 1:276.3–5): Dû solt alle tugende durchgân und übergân und solt aleine die tugent nemen in dem grunde, dâ si ein ist mit götlîcher natûre (my trans.). On this sermon, see Susanne Köbele, "Predigt 16b: 'Quasi vas auri solidum,'" in *Lectura Eckhardi I*, 43–74; and Mauritius Wilde, *Das neue Bild vom Gottesbild: Bild und Theologie bei Meister Eckhart* (Freiburg, Switzerland: Universitätsverlag, 2000), 298–309. The same insistence on taking virtue "in the ground" is found in RdU 21 (DW 5:282.4). *Grunt* has a special relation to the virtue of humility. For example, in Pr. 55 Eckhart says: "Ie mê der mensche in den grunt rehter dêmuot gesenket wirt, ie mê er gesenket wirt in den grunt götlîches wesens" (DW 2:582–3–4). For Eckhart's teaching on the relation of virtues to the *grunt*, see Dietmar Mieth, "Die theologische transposition der Tugendethik bei Meister Eckhart," in *Abendländische Mystik im Mittelalter*, ed. Kurt Ruh (Stuttgart: J. B. Metzler, 1986), 63–69.

191. Pr. 86 (DW 3:481.11). See the treatment below.

192. Pr. 67 makes the connection between *grunt* and Christ more explicitly than any other Eckhartian homily. In Pr. 24, however, a discussion of the soul's oneness in the ground of the Trinity leads into a treatment of Christ's assumption of total humanity through the Incarnation (DW 1:419–20).

193. Pr. 67 (DW 3:133.2–8): Ez ist diu wesenlich vernünfticheit gotes, der diu lûter blôz kraft ist *intellectus*, daz die meister heizent ein enpfenclîchez. . . . Dar obe nimet si êrste die lûter *absolûcio* des vrîen wesens, daz dâ sunder dâ, dâ ez ennimet noch engibet; ez ist diu blôze isticheit, diu dâ beroubet ist alles wesens und aller isticheit. Dâ nimet si got blôz nâch dem grunde dâ, dâ er ist über allez wesen. Waere dâ noch wesen, sô naeme si wesen in wesene; dâ enist niht wan éin grunt (my trans.).

194. Pr. 67 (DW 3:134.5–8): . . . daz ich in dem selben understantnisse habe des persônlîche wesens, daz ich daz persônlich wesen selber sî, alzemâle lougenlîche mîn selbes verstantnisses alsô, als ich nâch geistes art éin bin nâch dem grunde alsô, als der grunt selbe ein grunt ist . . . (my trans.). Part of the difficulty of this sermon is trying to undertand what Eckhart means by the technical terms he is creating: *persônliche wesen* (12 times); *understantnisse* (5 times); *persônlicheit* (twice); *understôz* (3 times).

195. On the importance of *entbilden*, see Wolfgang Wackernagel, *YMAGINE DENUDARI. Éthique de l'image et métaphysique de l'abstraction chez Maître Eckhart* (Paris: J. Vrin, 1991).

196. Pr. 67 (DW 3:135.11–15): Wan denne got [= Christ, a common MHG use] in dem grunde des vaters êwiclîche inneblîbende ist und ich in im, ein grunt und der selbe Kristus, ein understandicheit mîner menscheit, sô ist si als wol mîn als sîn an einer understandicheit des êwigen wesens, daz beidiu wesen lîbes und sêle volbrâht werden in éinem Kristô, éin got, éin sun (my trans.).

197. In this connection, see Jan Aertsen, "Der 'Systematiker' Eckhart" (forthcoming).
198. See chapter 1, pp. 14–17, above.
199. Pr. 53 (DW 2:530.3–4).
200. *Ebullitio* involves formal, or exemplary, causality along with efficient and final causality; *bullitio* is purely formal.
201. Sermo XLIX.3, n. 511 (LW 4:425.14–426.12): *IMAGO.* Nota quod imago proprie est emanatio simplex, formalis transfusiva totius essentiae purae nudae, . . . Est ergo emanatio ab intimis in silentio et exclusione omnis forinseci, vita quaedam, ac si imagineris rem ex se ipsa et in se ipsa intumescere et bullire in se ipsa necdum cointellecta ebullitione. . . . Primus, . . . quo quid producitur a se et de se ipso et in se ipso naturam nudam . . . , eo siquidem modo quo bonum est diffusivum sui. . . . Secundus gradus est quasi ebullitio sub ratione efficientis et in ordine finis, quo modo producit quid a se ipso, sed non de se ipso. Aut ergo de alio quolibet, et dicatur factio; aut de nihilo, et est tertius gradus productionis, qui dicitur creatio. The most detailed study of Eckhart's image theology is Wilde, *Das neue Bild vom Gottesbild.* On this sermon, see Donald F. Duclow, "'Whose Image is This?' in Eckhart's *Sermones*," *Mystics Quarterly* 15 (1989): 29–40; and Bernard McGinn, "Sermo XLIX: 'Cuius est imago haec et superscriptio?'" in *Lectura Eckhardi III* (forthcoming).
202. On the importance of *bullitio-ebullitio* in Eckhart, see Vladimir Lossky, *Théologie négative et connaissance de Dieu chez Maître Eckhart* (Paris: J. Vrin, 1960), 116–20; and Lyndon P. Reynolds, "*Bullitio* and the God beyond God: Meister Eckhart's Trinitarian Theology," *New Blackfriars* 70 (1989): 169–81, 235–44.
203. The *reditio completa* of the divine nature upon itself was central to Eckhart's dynamic view of the *emanatio* within God (i.e., *bullitio*). It occurs in many places in his Latin works; e.g., here in In Ex. nn. 16–17 (LW 2:22–23), and also In Ex. n. 74; In Eccli. n. 10; In Sap. n. 5 (LW 2:77, 239, 326–27); In Ioh. n. 222 (LW 3:186); and S. XLIX.2 and S. LII (LW 4:425 and 438). Eckhart often cited the *auctoritas* of the *Liber de causis* 15: "Omnis sciens qui scit essentiam suam [i.e., substantia divina] est rediens ad essentiam suam reditione completa." The notion is ultimately derived from Proclus's *Elements of Theology,* prop. 83 (see *Proclus: The Elements of Theology,* ed. E. J. Dodds, 2nd ed. [Oxford: Clarendon Press, 1963], 76–79).
204. In Ex. n. 16 (LW 2:21.7–22.1): . . . puritatem affirmationis excluso omni negativo ab ipso deo indicat; rursus ipsius esse quandam in se ipsum et super se ipsum reflexivam conversionem et in se ipso mansionem sive fixionem; adhuc autem quandam bullitionem sive parturitionem sui—in se fervens et in se ipso et in se ipsum liquescens et bulliens, lux in luce et in lucem se toto se totum penetrans, et se toto super se totum conversum et reflexum undique.
205. S. XXV.1, nn. 258–59 (LW 4:236.2–237.2): Secunda gratia procedit a deo sub ratione et proprietate personalis notionis. . . . Rursus deus sub ratione boni est principium ebullitionis ad extra, sub ratione vero notionis est principium bullitionis in se ipso, quae se habet causaliter et exemplariter ad ebullitionem. . . . Adhuc prima gratia consistit in quodam effluxu, egressu a deo. Secunda consistit in quodam refluxu sive regressu in ipsum deum. On this sermon, see Niklaus Largier, "Sermo XXV: 'Gratia dei sum id quod sum,'" in *Lectura Eckhardi II,* 177–203.
206. Pr. 35 (DW 2:180.5–7): Der êrste ûzbruch und das êrste ûzsmelzen, dâ got ûzsmilzet, dâ smilzet er in sînen sun, und dâ smilzet er wider in den vater (Walshe 1:249 modified). For comparable passages, see, e.g., Prr. 3 and 7 (DW 1:54, 123).
207. For other appearances of *bullitio-ebullitio,* see, e.g., S. XXV n. 263 (LW 4:239–40); and In Sap. n. 283 (LW 2:615–16). For an introduction to Eckhart's MHG terminology on the Trinity as the source of all emanation, see Kurt Ruh, "Die trinitarische Spekulation in deutscher Mystik," in *Kleine Schriften,* Band II, *Scholastik und Mystik im Spätmittelalter,* ed. Volker Mertens (Berlin: Walter de Gruyter, 1984), 33–36. Key terms are also treated in Michael Egerding, *Die Metaphorik der spätmittelalterlichen Mystik,* 2 vols. (Paderborn: F. Schöningh, 1997), vol. 2, especially under *brechen* (129–33), *brunne* (139–42), *smelzen* (524–25), and *vliessen* (633–43).
208. See chapter 1, p. 16.

209. For Dietrich of Freiburg's use of *ebullitio*, see de Libera, *La mystique rhénane*, 196–97. Sample texts can be found in his *De intellectu et intelligibili* 1.5.2 and 1.8.2. See *Dietrich von Freiberg: Opera Omnia*, ed. Burkhard Mojsisch et al. (Hamburg: Felix Meiner, 1977-), 1:139, 142.

210. See Berthold, *Expositio super Elementationem theologicam Procli*, ed. Loris Sturlese, Maria Rita Pagnoni-Sturlese, and Burkhard Mojsisch (Hamburg: Felix Meiner, 1984–), Prop. 18B (47.123–28), with reference to *Honorius Augustodunensis: Clavis physicae*, ed. Paolo Lucentini (Rome: Edizioni di Storia et Letteratura, 1974), 126–27. For more on Berthold's use of *ebullitio*, see de Libera, *La mystique rhénane*, 353–56, 362–64, and 384.

211. See Thomas Aquinas, *In III Sent.* d. 27, q. 1, a. 1, ad 4: . . . dicitur amor extasim facere et fervere, quia fervet, *extra se ebullit*, et exhalet, commenting on DN 4.13 (PG 3:711A) and CH 7.1 (205C).

212. Marguerite Porete, *Le Mirouer des simples ames*, ed. Romana Guarnieri and Paul Verdeyen (CCCM 69; Turnhoult: Brepols, 1986), chapter 64 (186–87): Haec sola dongeria amoris, dicit Amor, dant sibi profundationem et cumulationem et attingentiam bullitionis amoris [French: boillon de amour], iuxta testimonium ipsiusmet amoris.

213. For treatments of *principium* and the role of "principial knowing" (i.e., seeing all things from the divine perspective), see C. F. Kelley, *Meister Eckhart on Divine Knowledge*; and Erwin Waldschütz, *Denken und Erfahren des Grundes*, Part II.

214. In Ioh. n. 342 (LW 3:291.4–8) Unum autem per se principiat et dat esse et principium est intra. Et propter hoc proprie non producit simile, sed unum et idem se ipsum. . . . Hinc est quod in divinis personis emanatio est formalis quaedam ebullitio [sic], et propter hoc tres personae sunt simpliciter unum et absolute. The use of *ebullitio* here goes against all Eckhart's other formulations, and hence I consider it a scribal error and translate as *bullitio*.

215. In Eccli. n. 12 (LW 2:241–42).

216. In Ioh. n. 656 (LW 3:570.13–571.2): Item secundo: filius est principium de principio, pater 'principium sine principio'; oportet ergo filium adire patrem qui fons est totius deitatis, ut ibi accipiat quod fluat, secundum illud Eccl. 1: 'ad locum unde exeunt flumina, revertuntur, ut iterum fluant'. The characterization of the Father as *principium sine principio* and the Son as *principium de principio*, comes from Augustine, *Contra Maximinum* 2.17.4 (PL 42:784).

217. This is discussed at length in Eckhart's commentary on John 18:8 ("Lord, show us the Father and it is enough for us"). See In Ioh. nn. 546–76 (LW 3:477–506).

218. In Gen. I nn. 3–7 (LW 1:186–91). Eckhart– also analyzes the verse in the Prol.gen. nn. 14–22 (LW 1:159–65).

219. Eckhart agrees with Thomas Aquinas's teaching on creation as found, for example, in STh Ia, q. 46, a. 1, especially ad 6, and ad 9.

220. In Gen. I n. 7 (LW 1:190.1–12): Rursus tertio principium, in quo *deus creavit caelum et terram*, est primum nunc simplex aeternitatis, ipsum, inquam, idem nunc penitus, in quo deus est ab aeterno, in quo etiam est, fuit et erit aeternaliter personarum divinarum emanatio. . . . Simul enim et semel quo deus fit, quo filium sibi coaeternum per omnia coaequalem deum genuit, etiam mundum creavit.

221. "In agro dominico" arts. 1 and 3, both drawn from In Gen. I n. 7 (LW 1:190–91). The second article, taken from In Ioh. n. 216 (LW 3:187), also deals with the eternity of the universe.

222. E.g., Augustine, *De Trinitate* 6.10.12 (PL 42:932); and Thomas Aquinas, STh Ia, q. 46, a. 7.

223. On the a priori aspect of Eckhart's trinitarianism, see Reynolds, *"Bullitio* and the God beyond God," 170–71, 240–41. See also Dobie, "Reason and Revelation in Meister Eckhart," 423–34.

224. Werner Beierwaltes, "Unity and Trinity East and West," in *Eriugena East and West*, ed. Bernard McGinn and Willemien Otten (Notre Dame: University of Notre Dame Press, 1995), 211.

225. In Sap. n. 28 (LW 2:348.9–11): Sic ergo omnis actio naturae, moris et artis habet de

sui integritate tria, puta generans, genitum et amorem gignentis ad genitum et geniti ad gig-nentem. . . . A more detailed development can be found In Ioh. nn. 361–67 (LW 3:306–12).

226. Eckhart's comment on Gen. 1:1 takes up In Gen. II nn. 8–40 (LW 1:479–507), treat-ing three themes: (1) "productio sive emanatio filii et spiritus sancti a patre aeternaliter"; (2) "item productio sive creatio generalis totius universi ab uno deo temporaliter"; and (3) "et plura quantum ad proprietates tam creatoris quam creaturarum" (n. 8 [LW 1:479.4–7]). For other texts dealing with *principium* in this work, see In Gen. II nn. 49–50 and 111–12 (LW 1:517–18, 576–78).

227. The comment on John 1:1 takes up In Ioh. nn. 4–51 (LW 3:5–43). The key passages are nn. 4–14, 19–21, and 28–51. For a commentary with references to secondary literature, see Largier, *Meister Eckhart* 2:835–67.

228. For Eckhart's view of the Trinity, see Bernard McGinn, "A Prolegomenon to the Role of the Trinity in Meister Eckhart's Mysticism," *Eckhart Review* (Spring 1997): 51–61; and the longer German version, "Sermo IV," in *Lectura Eckhardi I*, 289–316. See also R.-L. Oechs-lin, "Eckhart et la mystique trinitaire," *Lumière et vie* 30 (1956): 99–120; and "Der Eine und Dreieinige in den deutschen Predigten," in *Meister Eckhart der Prediger*, 149–66; Reynolds, "*Bullitio* and the God beyond God"; Alain de Libera, "L'Un ou la Trinité," *Revue des sciences religieuses* 70 (1996): 31–47; and Rainer Haucke, *Trinität und Denken: Die Unterscheidung der Einheit von Gott und Mensch bei Eckhart* (Frankfurt: Peter Lang, 1986).

229. Bernard McGinn, "The God beyond God: Theology and Mysticism in the Thought of Meister Eckhart," *Journal of Religion* 61 (1981): 1–19.

230. The three treatises on the Trinity are in In Ioh. nn. 358–67, 511–18, and 546–76 (LW 3:303–12, 442–48, and 477–506); S. IV can be found in LW 4:22–32. There are many other passages in the Latin works of importance for Eckhart's trinitarianism. These occur not only in the John commentary (e.g., nn. 4–27, 32–36, 40–50, 56–60, 82, 160–66, 187–98, 411–14, 422–25, 437–38, 468–69, 641, 656), but also in Eckhart's other biblical expositions and ser-mons; e.g., In Gen. II nn. 9–20, 44, 48–51, 179–80, 214–17; In Ex. nn. 16, 28, 56, 62–65, 70–72); In Eccli. nn. 11–12, 23; In Sap. nn. 27–29, 64–67, 89, 192; see also SS. II nn. 3–18, XXXV nn. 357–63, XXXVI nn. 366–67, and XLIX n. 512.

231. At least thirty-four of Eckhart's MHG sermons contain discussions of the Trinity. Among the most important are Pr. 10 (DW 1:173); Prr. 35, 47, 49 (DW 2:180–81, 394–96, 433–35); Prr. 67, 83 (DW 3:132–34, 446–48); and BgT 1.1 (DW 5:30–34, 41–42).

232. Pr. 10 (DW 1:173.1–5): Ich predigete einest in latîne, und daz was an dem tage der drîvalticheit, dô sprach ich: der underscheit kumet von der einicheit, der underscheit in der drîvalticheit. Diu einicheit ist der underscheit, und der underscheit ist diu einicheit. Ie der underscheit mêr ist, ie diu einicheit mêr ist, wan das ist underscheit âne underscheit (my trans.). Quint in his note to this passage suggests Eckhart has S. II n. 14 in mind, but the same teaching is also found in S. IV.

233. S. XI n. 118 (LW 4:112.5–6): Deus autem est ab omni numero proprie eximitur. Est enim unus sine unitate, trinus sine trinitate, sicut bonus sine qualitate, ... There are many parallels in the Latin texts, and also in the MHG sermons, e.g., Pr. 38 (DW 2:234). God's freedom from all number is part of the aseity that frees him from place (*locus*) and time (*tem-pus*). Because God is *illocalis* (e.g., In Sap. n. 133 [LW 2:471]), he can be described as the *locus omnium* (e.g., In Ioh. nn. 199–205 [LW 3:168–73]; S.V n. 51 [LW 4:48]). Eckhart's thought on God as the *locus* of all things makes for interesting comparisons with the thought of Maimoni-des; see Schwartz, "'*Ecce est locus apud me*': Maimonides und Eckharts Raumvorstellung als Begriff des Göttlichen."

234. Pr. 38 (DW 2:234) speaks of the Godhead having distinction without number or quantity even if there were a hundred Persons there. See also In Sap. n. 38 (LW 2:360.1–3): Hinc est quod tres personae in divinis, quamvis sint plures, non tamen multa, sed unum, etiam si essent personae mille; cf. In Sap. n. 112 (LW 2:449).

235. Pr. 24 (DW 1:419.4–5): . . . wan in dem grunde götlîches wesens, dâ die drîe persô-nen éin wesen sint, dâ ist si ein nâch dem grunde (Walshe 2:313).

236. For example, in Pr. 2, Eckhart uses the language of "looking into the *einic ein*" beyond the three Persons (DW 1:43–44). Pr. 48 explicitly speaks of the "simple ground" into which the distinct Person never gazed (DW 2:420–21). Pr. 69 (DW 3:178–80) and Pr. 109 (DW 4:772–73) talk of getting rid of "God" by breaking through into the ground. Only two sermons contain radical breakthrough formulae without explicitly using *grunt*—Pr. 52 (DW 2:499–505) and Pr. 83 (DW 3:447–48).

237. Eckhart's notion of God as "pure possibility," what Pr. 48 describes as the "simple silence, in itself immovable, and by this immovability all things are moved" (DW 2:421), is different from Aquinas's notion of the divine nature as pure act, *ipsum esse subsistens.*

238. In Ioh. nn. 546–76 (LW 3:477–506). Attributing *unitas/unum* to the Father, as Eckhart notes (nn. 546, 556–57, 562), was approved by saints and teachers, especially by Augustine, who is the source of the trinitarian triad of *unitas-aequalitas-connectio/nexus* (*De doctrina christiana* 1.5.5 [PL 34:21]). Eckhart often appeals to this form of trinitarian language by ascribing *unitas* to the Father; e.g., In Gen. II nn. 12, and 215 (LW 1:483, 691); In Ioh. nn. 360, 513, 668 (LW 3:305–06, 444, 581). For a history of the development of the triad, see Bernard McGinn, "Does the Trinity Add Up? Transcendental Mathematics and Trinitarian Speculation in the Twelfth and Thirteenth Centuries," in *Praise No Less Than Charity: Studies in Honor of M. Chrysogonus Waddell* (Kalamazoo: Cistercian Publications, 2002), 237–64.

239. See, e.g., In Ioh. nn. 512–13 (LW 3:443–45); In Gen. II nn. 12–15 and 215 (LW 1:483–86, 690–91); BgT 1 (DW 5:30).

240. The ascription of *ens* to the Father also occurs in the third trinitarian treatise in the John commentary (In Ioh. n. 568 [LW 3:496]). This is a sign that Eckhart was not really concerned about consistency in applying the transcendentals to the three Persons.

241. In Ioh. n. 360 (LW 3:304.14–315.4): . . . quod indivisa sunt opera horum trium in creaturis, quarum sunt unum principium. Propter quod in creaturis ens respondens patri, verum respondens filio, bonum respondens appropriate spiritui sancto convertuntur et unum sunt, distincta sola ratione, sicut pater et filius et spiritus sanctus sunt unum, distincta sola relatione. What Eckhart seems to mean here is that *insofar* as he is efficient cause, God is one principle, so that the differing terms *ens-verum-bonum* in creatures are distinct by reason alone (*sola ratione*), that is, they are really one in the concrete creature and are distinguished only by different concepts in the mind. There is an (imperfect) parallel between this and the three divine Persons, who are really one in the divine essence, but who are also distinct by relation alone (*sola relatione*), that is, *really* distinct insofar as they are different Persons.

242. In Ioh. n. 360 (LW 3:305.9–306.2): Nec obstat quod ab Augustino unitas patri appropriatur ratione quidem prioritatis sive fontalis diffusionis et originis, quia has rationes positivas, scilicet prioritatis et huiusmodi, non significat li unum. Here Eckhart seems to distinguish between two kinds of oneness: (a) *li unum*, or "the absolute, and totally indeterminate term One," which has no relation to positive predication or to any mode of production and therefore can be used of the divine essence; and (b) the prior, productive, and implicitly determinate oneness (*unitas*) that Augustine had in mind when he ascribed the term to the Father in *On Christian Doctrine.*

243. Pr. 75 (DW 3:293.5–294.2, and 299.3): . . . und alsô liget er kindes als ein vrouwe, diu geborn hât. . . . Pr. 29 (DW 2:86.4–5) uses similar language.

244. Pr. 40 (DW 2:278).

245. This is Pfeiffer CIII (ed., 335–37), where Eckhart (?) discusses how the Fatherhood can have a motherly name (*muoterlîchen namen*) (336.22–29).

246. Pr. 71 (DW 3:224.5–7): Ez dûhte einen menschn als in einem troume—ez was ein wachender troume—wie ez swanger würde von niht als ein vrouwe mit einem kinde, und in dem nihte wart got geborn; dér was diu vruht des nihtes (my trans.).

247. Pr. 26 (DW 2:31.3–8): Si [die oberste teile der sêle] enwil nit got, als er der heilige geist ist und als er der sun ist, und vliuhet den sun. Si enwil ouch nit got, als er got ist. War umbe? Dâ hât er namen, und waerent tûsent göte, si brichet iemermê durch, si wil in dâ, dâ er niht namen enhât: si wil etwaz edelers, etwaz bezzers dan got, als er namen hât. Waz wil si denne? Si enweiz: si wil in, als er vater ist.

248. Pr. 51 (DW 2:469.9–10): . . . so muoss er geberen sein bild bleibende in im selber grund, das bilde, also als es ewigklich ist gewesen in im (forme illius), daz ist sein form bleybend in im selber (my trans.).

249. Pr. 51 (DW 2:470.3–10): . . . vnd doran benueget den vater nit, er ziehe wider in die erstekeit, in das innestes, in den grund vnnd in den kernen der vetterlicheit, da er ewigklich ist inne gewesen in im selber in der vatterschaft vnnd da er gebraucht sein selbs in dem, der vatter als der vatter sein selbs in dem einigen ein. . . . Diss ist das aller best, vnd ich han mich darinn vertoeret. Darumb: alles, das die natur geleisten mag, das schlüsset sy darzuo, daz stürtzet in die vatterschaft, das sy ein sey vnd ein sun sey vnd entwachse allem dem andern vnd al ein sey in der vaterschafft . . . (my trans.).

250. Pr. 70 (DW 3:197.4–6): Nû spriche ich: 'wir suln in bekennen rehte, als er sich selben bekennet' in den widerbilde, daz aleine bilde gotes ist und der gotheit, niht der gotheit dan als vil, als si der vater ist (my trans.). On this passage, see the comments in Largier, *Meister Eckhart*, 2:680–81.

251. E.g., S. II n. 8 (LW 4:9.11–12): . . . quia processus ille est ad intra, tum quia intellectualis, tum quia nihil est deo extra . . . . On Thomas Aquinas's teaching regarding the *emanatio intelligibilis* in God, see STh Ia, q. 27, a.1. The difference between *generatio* and all forms of *alteratio*, or change, is important for Eckhart (see, In Ioh. n. 409 [LW 3:348]).

252. Much has been written on Eckhart's teaching on the procession of *verbum*; see especially, Émilie Zum Brunn and Alain de Libera, *Métaphysique du Verbe et théologie négative* (Paris: Beauchesne, 1984).

253. Eckhart's teaching on silence is prominent in the sermon cycle on the eternal birth (Prr. 101–104). An important passage on silence can be found in Pr. 95 (DW 4:192–95).

254. In Ioh. n. 488 (LW 3:420.11–421.3). Eckhart also quotes Job 33:15–16, and Augustine, *Confessiones* 9.10.24 to confirm God's speaking in the midst of darkness and silence. For a similar MHG use of Wis. 18:14, see Pr. 73 (DW 3:266).

255. In Ioh. n. 488 (LW 3:421.3–8).

256. In Gen. I n. 77 (LW 1:239): . . . verbum, quod est in silentio paterni intellectus, verbum sine verbo aut potius super omne verbum.

257. See the comment on *dixitque deus* (Gen. 1:3) in In Gen. II nn. 48–51 (LW 1:516–20), where Eckhart shows that God's creative speaking must be understood in light of John. 1:1. The same teaching is found in the MHG works; e.g., Pr. 53 (DW 2:535.1–2): Alle crêatûren sint ein sprechen gotes.

258. In Gen. II n. 49 (LW 1:519.11–13): Effectus enim in sua causa analoga latet, absonditur, tacet, non loquitur nec auditur, nisi dicatur et producatur verbo intus generato et concepto vel extra prolato.

259. For Eckhart's teaching on silence, see Karl Albert, "Meister Eckhart über das Schweigen," in *Festschrift für Lauri Seppänen zum 60. Geburtstag* (Tampere: Universität Tampere, 1984), 301–9; Marco Vannini, "*Praedica Verbum:* La *generazione* della parola dal silenzio in Meister Eckhart," in *Il Silenzio e La Parola da Eckhart à Jabès*, ed. Massimo Baldini and Silvano Zucal (Trent: Morcelliana, 1987), 17–31; Kurt Ruh, "Das mystische Schweigen und die mystische Rede," in *Festschrift für Ingo Reiffenstein zum 60. Geburtstag* (Göppingen: Kümmerle, 1988), 463–72; and Andreas Schönfeld, *Meister Eckhart: Geistliche Übungen* (Mainz: Matthias-Grünewald Verlag, 2002), 18–22, 44–46, and especially 96–116.

260. Pr. 9 (DW 1:157.3–8): Ez ist ein vürbrâht wort, daz ist der engel und der mensche und alle crêatûren. Ez ist ein ander wort, bedâht und unvûrbrâht [not *vûrbrâht* as in Quint], dâ bî mac ez komen, daz ich mich bilde. Noch ist ein ander wort, daz dâ ist unvürbrâht und unbedâht, daz nimer ûzkumet, mêr ez ist êweclich in dem, der ez sprichet; ez ist iermermê in einem enpfâhenne in dem vater, der ez sprichet, und inneblîbende (*Teacher and Preacher*, 259). Both Tobin (*Teacher and Preacher*, 261 n. 23) and Walshe (2:156 n. 13) argue for the "unvürbrâht" given above as the better reading because it indicates the nature of the human *verbum interius* as contrasted with the divine.

261. The Word that remains eternally within is equivalent to what Eckhart speaks of as

"the eternal Word [being] the medium and image itself that is without medium and without image" in Pr. 69 (daz êwic wort ist daz mittel und daz bilde selber, daz dâ ist âne mittel und âne bilde [DW 3:168.8–10]). For a discussion, see Zum Brunn and de Libera, *Métaphysique du Verbe*, 172–94.

262. Pr. 9 (LW 1:158.5–7): Dâ sol diu sêle sîn ein bîwort und mit gote würken ein werk, in dem înswebenden bekantnisse ze nemenne ir saelicheit in dem selben, dâ got saelic ist (*Teacher and Preacher*, 260).

263. Pr. 53 (DW 2:529.6–530.1): Got ist ein wort, daz sich selber sprach. . . . Got ist gesprochen und ungesprochen. Der vater ist ein sprechende werk, und der sun ist ein spruch würkende (Walshe 1:177). Eckhart's teaching on the Father's speaking of the *wort*, and the relation of the Word and silence, is found throughout his sermons; see, e.g., Prr. 1 and 19 (DW 1:15–17, 312); Prr. 30, 36a, and 49 (DW 2:97–98, 189–91, 433–38); and Pfeiffer CIII (ed., 335–36).

264. It is on this basis that Eckhart can speak of the human soul as co-creator with God; see Pr. 52 (DW 2:502–04). Robert Forman, *Meister Eckhart*, 166, has rightly spoken of the "dynamization of silence" as a crucial aspect of Eckhart's mysticism, but we should remember that this dynamization is not ours—it is essentially God's own.

265. The discussions of the Holy Spirit in the Latin works are too numerous to list here, but it is instructive to note how often the Spirit's role also comes up in the vernacular sermons (e. g., Prr. 1, 10, 11, *15*, 18, 20b, *23*, *27*, 29, 37, 41, 53, 65, 69, 76, 81, *82*, 85, 92, with the more important treatments italicized). De Libera (*La mystique rhénane*, 287–95) stresses the importance of Eckhart's doctrine of the Holy Spirit.

266. On S. IV and the Holy Spirit, see McGinn, "A Prolegomenon to the Role of the Trinity," 57–58; and the longer version, "Sermo IV: 'Ex ipso, per ipsum et in ipso sunt omnia'," in *Lectura Eckhardi I*, 289–316.

267. S. IV nn. 22–23 (LW 4:24.5–11): . . . nota primo quod in ipso spiritu sancto sic sunt omnia, ut quod in ipso non est, necesse sit esse nihil. . . . Secundo nota quod sic *in ipso sunt omnia*, ut si aliquid sit non in ipso spiritu sancto, spiritus sanctus non est deus. In the first form Eckhart takes John 1:3 (*sine ipso factum est nihil*) as referring to the Spirit and not to the Word.

268. S. IV n. 28 (LW 4:27.10–28.1): Ubi notandum quod cum dicimus omnia esse in deo, sicut ipse est indistinctus in sui natura et tamen distinctissimus ab omnibus, sic in ipso sunt omnia distinctissime simul et indistincta.

269. S. IV n. 24 (LW 4:25.3–5): Tertio, quod sic *in ipso sunt omnia*, ut pater in filio non sit nec in patre filius, si pater non sit unum, id ipsum cum spiritu sancto, aut filius id ipsum quod sit spiritus sanctus.

270. In Ioh. n. 438 (LW 3:376.2–5): Li inquantum autem reduplicatio est; reduplicatio vero, sicut ipsum vocabulum testatur, dicit nexum et ordinem duorum; dicitur enim reduplicatio duorum replicatio, plica et nexus duorum. Sic spiritus, tertia in trinitate persona, nexus est duorum, patris et filii.

271. The distinction between *amor concomitans* and *amor spiratus* is discussed in several places, e.g., In Ioh. nn. 165–66 and 364 (LW 3:136–37 and 308–10), and In Sap. n. 28 (LW 2:348–49).

272. See, e. g., S. IV n. 25 (LW 4:26); In Ioh. n. 506 (LW 3:437–38); Pr. 41 (DW 2:287.7–8); etc.

273. In Ioh. n. 506 (LW 3:437.12–438.2): . . . eo quod una sit facies et imago in qua deus nos videt et nos ipsum, secundum illud: 'in lumine tuo videbimus lumen.' Sic enim et idem amor est spiritus sanctus quo pater filium diligit et filius patrem, quo deus nos diligit et nos deum.

274. For what follows, see McGinn, "Meister Eckhart on God as Absolute Unity," 130–35; and Alain de Libera, "À propos de quelques théories logiques de Maître Eckhart: Existe-t-il une tradition médiévale de la logique néo-platonicienne?" *Revue de théologie et de philosophie* 113 (1981): 1–24.

275. Eckhart's most detailed discussion of *secundum adiacens* and *tertium adiacens* predica-

tion occurs in the Prol.op.prop. nn. 1–8 and 25 (LW 1:166–70, 181). See also In Ex. n. 15 (LW 2:20); In Sap. n. 20 (LW 2:341–42); In Ioh. nn. 97, 377 (LW 3:83–84, 321). For a history of the distinction, though one that does not mention Eckhart, see Gabriel Nuchelmans, *Secundum/tertium adiacens: Vicissitudes of a logical distinction* (Amsterdam: Koninklijke Nederlandse Akademie, 1992).

276. E.g., STh Ia, q. 13, a. 5; and In *Perihermeneias* bk. 2, chap. 10, lect. 2, nn. 2–5.

277. Tabula prologorum in op.trip. n. 4 (LW 1:132.4–6): Primum est quod solus deus proprie est et dicitur ens, unum, verum et bonum. Secundum est quod omne quod est ens, unum, verum aut bonum, non habet hoc a se ipso, sed a deo et ab ipso solo.

278. Among the treatments of Eckhart on analogy, see Lossky, *Théologie négative et connaissance de Dieu*, "Index des thèmes," 426; Josef Koch, "Zur Analogielehre Meister Eckharts," in *Mélanges offerts à Etienne Gilson* (Paris: J. Vrin, 1959), 327–50; Fernand Brunner, "L'analogie chez Maître Eckhart," *Freiburger Zeitschrift für Philosophie und Theologie* 16 (1969): 333–49; Alain de Libera, *Le problème de l'être chez Maître Eckhart: Logique et métaphysique de l'analogie* (Geneva: Cahiers de la Revue de théologie et de philosophie, 1980); B. Mojsisch, *Meister Eckhart*, chapter 3; and Reiner Manstetten, *Esse est Deus: Meister Eckharts christologische Versöhnung von Philosophie und Religion und ihre Ursprünge in der Tradition des Abendländes* (Munich: Karl Alber, 1993), 284–302.

279. In Eccli. n. 53 (LW 2:282.1–5): . . . analogata nihil in se habent positive radicatum formae secundum quam analogantur. Sed omne ens creatum analogatur deo in esse, veritate et bonitate. Igitur omne ens creatum habet a deo et in deo, non in se ipso ente creato, esse, vivere, sapere positive et radicaliter. Among the other discussions of analogy in Eckhart, see In Gen. I n. 128 (LW 1:282–83); In Ex. n. 54 (LW 2:58–60); In Sap. n. 44 (LW 2:367); In Ioh. nn. 5–6, 86, 97, 182–83, 492 (LW 3:7, 74, 84, 150–52, 405); and Qu.Par. 1, n. 11 (LW 5:46–47). Analogy is often employed in the MHG works, but rarely reflected upon in a formal way.

280. Dietmar Mieth, *Die Einheit von Vita Activa und Vita Passiva in den deutschen Predigten und Traktaten Meister Eckharts und bei Johannes Tauler* (Regensburg: Pustet, 1969), 136.

281. Tobin, *Meister Eckhart*, 64; and de Libera, "À propos de quelques théories," 15.

282. The pioneering character of Lossky's *Théologie négative* is nowhere more evident than in its recognition of the importance of Eckhart's dialectic (see "Index des thèmes" under "Dialectique," on p. 431). Also significant was the early article of Maurice de Gandillac, "La 'dialectique' du Maître Eckhart," in *Le mystique rhénane*, 59–94; and the reflections in Schürmann, *Meister Eckhart*, 176–92.

283. "In agro dominico," art. 26, drawing on a passage in Pr. 4 (DW 1:69–70).

284. "In agro dominico," appended art. 2, drawn from Pr. 9 (DW 1:148).

285. Ultimately, dialectical langauge is based on Plato's *Parmenides*, but for the history of mysticism the story begins with Neoplatonic developments from Plato. For reflections on this component of the history of Western mysticism, see McGinn, *Foundations of Mysticism*, 44–61 (on Plotinus and Proclus), and 157–82 (on Dionysius); as well as McGinn, *Growth of Mysticism*, 88–118 on Eriugena.

286. For this notion of dialectical language, see Hans Georg Gadamer, "Hegel and the Dialectic of the Ancient Philosophers," in *Hegel's Dialectic: Five Hermeneutical Studies* (New Haven: Yale University Press, 1976), 20–27.

287. For some reflections on Eckhart's place in the history of Platonic dialectic, see McGinn, "Meister Eckhart on God as Absolute Unity," 136–39.

288. On Eckhart's use of these and other thinkers, see "Appendix: Eckhart's Sources" in *Mystical Thought of Meister Eckhart*, 162–82. See also Ruh, *Geschichte*, 3:17–56, 280–90, building on his earlier studies "Dionysius Areopagita im deutschen Predigtwerk Meister Eckharts, Perspektiven der Philosophie," *Neues Jahrbuch* 13 (1987): 207–23; and "Neuplatonische Quellen Meister Eckhart," in *Contemplata aliis tradere: Studien zum Verhältnis von Literatur und Spiritualität*, ed. Claudia Brinker, Urs Herzog, Niklaus Largier and Paul Michel (Frankfurt: Peter

Lang, 1995), 317–52. On Eckhart's relation to Proclus, the best study is Werner Beierwaltes, "Primum est dives per se: Meister Eckhart und der 'Liber de causis,'" in *On Proclus and His Influence in Medieval Philosophy*, ed. E. P. Bos and P. A. Meijer (Leiden: Brill, 1992), 141–69.

289. E.g., In Ex. nn. 112–19 (LW 2:110–17). The use of similarity/dissimilarity is where Eckhart is closest to Dionysius, who employs the same language in DN 9.6–7 (PG 3:913C–916A).

290. In Eccli. n. 58 (LW 2:286–87).

291. Pr. 14 (DW 1:237); RdU 23 (DW 5:293–94).

292. In Eccli. n. 54 (LW 2:283); In Ioh. n. 12 (LW 3:11); Pr. 30 (DW 2:94).

293. In Sap. n. 132 (LW 2:469–70).

294. In Ioh. n. 425 (LW 3:360–61).

295. The three most important are: (1) In Ex. nn. 113–19 (LW 2:110–17); (2) In Eccli. nn. 42–61 (LW 2:270–90); and (3) In Sap. nn. 144–57 (LW 2:481–94). For other appearances, see In Gen. I n. 173 (LW 1:318); In Ex. nn. 40, 102, 104–7 (LW 2:45, 104, 106–7); In Sap. nn. 38–39, 52, 60, 282 (LW 2:359–60, 379, 388, 614–15); In Ioh. nn. 99, 103, 197, 562, 634 (LW 3:85, 88–89, 166–67, 489, 551–52). Distinction/indistinction language also appears in Eckhart's Latin sermons; e.g., SS. II, IV, X, XXIX, XXX, XXXIV, XXXVII, XLIV (LW 4:9, 27–28 and 31, 98–100, 265, 278, 299, 320–21, 368).

296. See Prr. 10, 13b, 14 (DW 1:173, 225, 237); Prr. 28, 30, 36a, 50 (DW 2:67–68, 94, 189, 459–60); Prr. 63, 77 (DW 3:82, 338 and 340); VeM and RdU 23 (DW 5:115 and 293–94).

297. Many students of Eckhart have recognized the importance of this aspect of Eckhart's thought, though not all have given it the same name. Hof (*Scintilla animae*, 155–58) preferred the term "Analektik" (i.e., speech that leads "above"); Mojsisch (*Meister Eckhart*, 86–87) speaks of Eckhart's "objektive Paradoxtheorie."

298. In Sap. nn. 144–57 (LW 2:481–94). In what follows I will make use of the translation in *Teacher and Preacher*, 166–71. On this text, see McGinn, "Meister Eckhart on God as Absolute Unity," 132–34; and Goris, *Einheit als Prinzip und Ziel*, 209–28. Other treatments include Lossky, *Théologie négative*, 261–65; Mojsisch, *Meister Eckhart*, 86–95; and Manstetten, *Esse est Deus*, 218–24.

299. In the LW edition this key sentence reads: Et e converso, quanto distinctius, tanto indistinctius, quia distinctione sua *distinguitur* ab indistincto (In Sap. n. 154 [LW 2:490.5–6]). But, as Goris has effectively argued (*Einheit als Prinzip und Ziel*, 224–28), if the subject is God, as it appears is the case, then the verb should be *indistinguitur*. Hence, the translation given here.

300. In Ex. n. 73 (LW 2:75–76) says that the truth of an affirmative proposition subsists in the identity (= indistinction) of terms, while the truth of a negative one stands in the distinction of terms. The *negatio negationis* fuses both forms of predication into one, a formally negative expression of positive fullness, or "what the One signifies when expressed negatively" (In Ex. n. 74). Eckhart affirms this In Eccli. n. 63 (LW 2:293.1–2): . . . unum transcendens in voce quidem negatio est sed in significato, cum sit negatio negationis, est mera affirmatio.

301. On the *negatio negationis*, see Prol.op.prop. nn. 6, 12, 15 (LW 1:169, 172, 175); In Gen. I n. 158 (LW 1:306, in the form *privatio privationis*); In Ex. nn. 16, 74 (LW 2:21, 76–78); In Eccli. nn. 60, 63 (LW 2:289, 293); In Sap. n. 147 (LW 2:485–86); In Ioh. nn. 207–8, 556, 611, 692 (LW 3:175–76, 485, 533, 608); SS. X n. 111, XXXVII n. 375 (LW 4:104, 320). In the MHG sermons we find it explicitly featured in Pr. 21 (DW 1:361.10 and 363.1–7), and implicitly appearing in Pr. 44 (DW 2:348.1–2). The extent to which Eckhart may have been aware of Proclus's use of *negatio negationis* is disputed. Thomas Aquinas (e.g., *Quodlibet* X, q.1, a.1, ratio 3) and Dietrich of Freiburg also used the term, but only to express a being of reason, not the inner nature of God. Goris (*Einheit als Prinzip und Ziel*) correctly describes *negatio negationis* as the "operator" of the transcendentals in Eckhart's thought—". . . kann die *negatio negationis* hier als Operator der Gottesattributen auftreten: Sie negiert jene Dimension der Vielheit und legt die *perfectiones* in ihrer *göttlichen* Reinheit frei" (p. 376). See his discussions

on pp. 197–206, 215–18, which contend that Eckhart adapted his metaphysical understanding of the term from Henry of Ghent's *Summa quaestionum ordinarium* a. 25, q. 1, and a. 73, q. 11, ad 2.

302. The role of the transcendentals in Eckhart's thought has been often discussed. For a brief analysis, see Werner Beierwaltes, *Platonismus und Idealismus* (Frankfurt: Klostermann, 1972), 37–67. More detailed considerations can be found in Lossky, *Théologie négative;* and especially Goris, *Einheit als Ziel und Prinzip;* and Manstetten, *Esse est Deus.*

303. Eckhart gives priority to *esse* as a divine predication in other texts besides the Prol.op.prop. The Dominican's teaching on *esse* has been the subject of considerable study; see especially Karl Albert, *Meister Eckharts These vom Sein* (Saarbrücken: Universitäts-und Schilbuchverlag, 1976); and Manstetten, *Esse est Deus.*

304. Without attempting to provide an exhaustive list of the other discussions of God as *unum* in the Latin works, see (1) In Gen. I nn. 10–13, 84, 158 (LW 1:193–97, 243–44, 306); (2) In Gen. II nn. 10–12, 73–74, 179, 215 (LW 1:481–83, 538–40, 649, 690–91); (3) In Ex. nn. 57–61, 74, 91, 101, 134, 138 (LW 2:62–66, 77–78, 94, 103, 123, 126); (4) In Eccli. nn. 60, 63 (LW 2:289, 293); (5) In Sap. nn. 38, 99, 107, 110, 219, 287, 293 (LW 2:359–60, 434–35, 443, 446–47, 553–54, 620–21, 628–29); (6) In Ioh. nn. 24, 67, 114, 195, 207–8, 320, 329, 342, 360, 513–18, 526, 546–65, 692 (LW 3:20, 55–56, 99–100, 164, 75–76, 268, 278–79, 291, 305, 444–48, 456–57, 477–93, 608); (7) SS. X n. 103–7, XXIX, XXXVII n. 377, XLIV nn. 438–39, XLVIII n. 503 (LW 4:98–101, 263–70, 322–23, 367–69, 419).

305. For some of the sermons in which Eckhart speaks about the divine *einicheit* and *einig ein,* see, e.g., Prr. 13, 15, 19, 21, 23 (DW 1:219, 245, 314, 361–68, 401–2); Prr. 28, 29, 51 (DW 2:63, 76–77 and 88, 472–73); Prr. 64, 67, 71, 83 (DW 3:88–90, 130, 221–24, 442 and 447–48). There are also important passages in the BgT (DW 5:30–31, 34, 46–47) and in the VeM (DW 5:114–15 and 119).

306. Qu.Par.1 n. 4 (LW 5:4–7): Tertio ostendo quod non ita videtur mihi modo, ut quia sit, ideo intelligat, sed quia intelligit, ideo est, ita quod deus est intellectus et intelligere et est ipsum intelligere fundamentum ipsius esse. On *esse* and *intelligere* in Eckhart and their relation to Aquinas, besides Imbach, *Deus est intelligere;* and McGinn, "Sermo XXIX: 'Deus unus est,'" in *Lectura Eckhardi II,* 205–32; see also John Caputo, "The Nothingness of the Intellect in Meister Eckhart's 'Parisian Questions,'" *The Thomist* 39 (1975): 85–115; and Emile Zum Brunn, "Dieu n'est pas être," in *Maître Eckhart à Paris,* 84–108.

307. Qu.Par. 2 n. 2 (LW 5:50.1–5): Prima est, quia intellectus, in quantum intellectus, nihil est eorum quae intelligit, . . . Si igitur intellectus, in quantum intellectus, nihil est, et per consequens nec intelligere est aliquod esse. The logic of the argument would be: (a) *esse* is the first of creatures and God cannot be a creature; (b) but *intellectus/intelligere* is nothing of the creatures it knows; therefore (c) God can be said to be *intellectus.*

308. S. XXIX nn. 300 and 304 (LW 4:266.11–12, 270.1–2): Ubi nota quod unitas sive unum videtur proprium et proprietas intellectus solius. . . . Deus enim unus est intellectus, et intellectus est deus unus. Another important text on the relation of *esse* and *intelligere* is S. XI (LW 4:105–15), on which see Zum Brunn, "Dieu n'est pas être," 105–8.

309. The distinction between God as the *esse* that is *indistinctum/absolutum/simpliciter* and creatures as *esse hoc et hoc* is one of the most frequent themes in Eckhart. Karl Albert counts sixty-five appeals to it in the course of the Op.trip. alone; see his "Die philosophische Grundgedanke Meister Eckharts," *Tijdschrift voor Philosophie* 27 (1965): 321 n. 5. Thomas Aquinas had spoken of the difference between the *esse universale* of God and the *esse hoc vel tale* of creatures (e.g., STh Ia, q. 45, a. 5c), a passage that may have provided a source for Eckhart.

310. Pr. 91 (DW 4:92.7–9): Got enist niht wan ein lûter wesen, und diu creâtûre ist von nihte und hat ouch ein wesen von den selben wesene (my trans.). For some other appearances, see Prr. 3, 7, 8, 23 (DW 1:55–57, 122, 131, 397); Prr. 37, 39, 45, 54a (DW 2:216, 262, 372, 553–54); Prr. 67, 77, 86 (DW 3:135, 339–41, 488); and BgT (DW 5:28–29).

311. To choose just a few examples from Eckhart's preaching. In the Latin sermons, God is said to be beyond being in SS. XI, XXIV, and XXIX (LW 4:112, 226, 270). In the MHG

sermons we find such formulations as that in Pr. 9 (DW 1:146.1–2): Ich spraeche als unrehte, als ich got hieze ein wesen, als ob ich die sunnen hieze bleich oder swarz. In Pr. 71 God is *wesen âne wesen* (DW 3:231.1–3); in Pr. 82 he is *wesen weselôs* (DW 3:431.3–4); and in Pr. 83 *ein vber swebende wesen und ein vber wesende nitheit* (DW 3:442.1–2).

312. E.g., Goris, *Einheit als Prinzip und Ziel*, 52–53, 376–78. J. A. Aertsen ("Ontology and Henology in Medieval Philosophy [Thomas Aquinas, Meister Eckhart and Berthold of Moosburg]," in *On Proclus and his Influence in Medieval Philosophy*, 132–39) agrees, arguing that Eckhart unifies the Aristotelian position of the "transcendentality of the first" with the Platonic notion of the "transcendence of the first."

313. De Libera (*La mystique rhénane*, 286) puts it well: "Si aucune *pré*-sence ne nous livre Dieu, l'entrée dans l'unique-Un nous délivre de la présence."

314. In Ex. nn. 39–40 (LW 2:44–46).

315. In Gen. I n. 270 (LW 1:409).

316. S. VIII n. 84 (LW 4:80): Nota primo quod dicit *homo quidam* [Luke 14:16] sine nomine, quia deus est nobis innominabilis propter infinitatem omnis esse in ipso. Characterizing God as *innominabilis* goes back to Dionysius (DN 1.6 [PG 3:596]), a passage that Eriugena translated as "mirabile nomen, quod est super omne nomen, quod est innominabile" (PL 122:1117). The affirmation of the unnameability of God (*innominabilis-indicibilis/namelôs-âne name*) is found often in Eckhart's preaching; e.g., SS. IV n. 30, IX n. 96, LV n. 547 (LW 4:31, 92, 458); Prr. 7, 16, 17, 20a (DW 1:122, 253, 284, 328–30); Prr. 26, 36a, 38 (DW 2:31, 188–89, 237); Prr. 71, 77, 80, 82, 83 (DW 3:221–22, 337, 380–83, 431, 441); Pr. 95 (DW 4:189–91). Conversely, taking a term from the Hermetic treatise *Asclepius* III.20a, Eckhart also spoke of God as *omninominabilis*; e.g., In Gen. I n. 84 (LW 1:243–44), In Ex. n. 35 (LW 2:41–42), S. VIII n. 88 (LW 4:84), Pr. 71 (DW 3:222). For a study of this aspect of Eckhart's God-language, see Lossky, *Théologie négative*, 17–26, 60–64.

317. Pr. 23 (DW 1:402.2): Er ist nihtes niht; Pr. 71 (DW 3:223.1–2): Got ist ein niht, und got ist ein iht; and especially Pr. 83 (DW 3:443.7): . . . got ist vngewordene istikeit vnd sin vngenanten nitheit. . . . On Eckhart's neologism *isticheit*, see especially the careful analysis of Alessandra Beccarisi, "Philosophische Neologismen zwischen Latein und Volkssprache: 'istic' und 'isticheit' bei Meister Eckhart," *Recherches de Théologie et Philosophie médiévales* 70 (2003): 329–58, who shows that contrary to earlier views which understood *isticheit* as *esse existentiae*, the term is developed from *istic* and therefore signifies the intellect's self-identity, or *reditio completa*. Meinrad Morard ("Ist, istic, istikeit bei Meister Eckhart," *Freiburger Zeitschrift für Philosophie und Theologie* 3 [1956]: 169–86) lists fourteen uses of *istikeit*, and three of *ist* and seven of *istic*.

318. The treatise on naming God can be found in the comment on the word *aperuit* of the base text "Os suum aperuit" (Prov. 31:26) for Pr. 95b (DW 4:185.106–198.290). The tract is structured around three questions: (1) Do you know what God is? (2) Why does scripture give God so many names? and (3) Is God to be praised or should we keep silence? The passage cited comes from the answer to this third question (193.220–24): Ie man sîn mê luogent, ie man in mê lobet. Ie man im mê unglîches zuoleget, ie man sînem bekantnisse naeher kumet, als ich ein glîchnisse sagen wil. See also 194:237–195.242: Als diu sêle in daz bekantnisse kumet, daz got alsô unglîch ist allen natûren, sô kumet si in ein wunder und wirt wider getriben und kumet in ein swigen. Mit der stille senket sich got in die sêle, und mit der gnâde wirt si begozzen. . . (my trans.).

319. Pr. 22 (DW 1:389.6–8): Waz ist daz leste ende? Ez ist diu verborgen vinsternisse der êwigen gotheit und ist unbekant und wart nie bekant und enwirt niemer bekant. Got blîbet dâ in im selber unbekant . . . (*Essential Eckhart*, 196).

320. Eckhart's major discussions of creations are (1) Prol.gen. nn. 12–22 (LW 1:156–65); (2) In Gen. I nn. 1–28 (LW 1:185–206); (3) In Gen. II nn. 8–40 (LW 1:479–507); and (4) In Sap. nn. 19–40 (LW 2:339–62). For analyses of Eckhart's teaching on creation, see Bernard McGinn, "Do Christian Platonists Really Believe in Creation?" in *God and Creation: An Ecumenical Symposium*, ed. David B. Burrell and Bernard McGinn (Notre Dame: University of

Notre Dame Press, 1990), 197–223; and Alois M. Haas, "Seinsspekulation und Geschöpflich-keit in der Mystik Meister Eckharts," in *Sein und Nichts in der abendländischen Mystik,* ed. Wal-ter Strolz (Freiburg: Herder, 1984), 33–58.

321. E.g., Prol.gen. n. 16 (LW 1:160); In Gen. I n. 14 (LW 1:197); In Sap. n. 19 (LW 2:340). See Avicenna, *Metaphysica* VI.2.

322. E.g., Prol.gen. n. 12 (LW 1:157); In Gen. II n. 9 (LW 1:480); In Sap. n. 25 (LW 2:345); In Ioh. n. 56 (LW 3:47). This definition is also found in Aquinas.

323. To cite but one example, Pr. 71 (DW 3:217.6–7): Got vluizet in alle crêatûren, und blîbet er doch unberüeret von in allen.

324. In Sap. nn. 25–26 (LW 2:345–46). Eckhart often says that the granting of *esse* is the purpose of creation, but, since *esse* contains all other qualifications, he could use other formu-lations to express the divine intent. For example, In Sap. n. 197 (LW 2:531) describes the unity of the universe as God's intent, while Pr. 60 (DW 3:11–12) says that God created all things so that they can attain final rest (*ruowe*).

325. In Ioh. n. 514 (LW 3:445.3–4): Restat ergo videre quomodo esse sub ratione sive pro-prietatis unius principium est et ab ipso procedit universitas et integritas totius entis creati. The linking of *esse* and *unum* to understand creation is also evident in In Ex. n. 97 (LW 2:100), where Eckhart cites Maimonides concerning the two fundamental beliefs (*duae princi-palitates*): "scilicet quod creator est et quod unus est."

326. In Gen. I n. 3 (LW 1:186.12–87.1): De primo sciendum est quod principium, in quo *creavit deus caelum et terram,* est ratio idealis. Et hoc est quod Ioh. 1 dicitur: 'in principio erat verbum'—graecus habet logos, id est ratio. . . .

327. In Gen. I n. 4 (LW 1:187–88).

328. On *causa essentialis,* see Burkhard Mojsisch, "'Causa essentialis' bei Dietrich von Freiburg und Meister Eckhart," in *Von Meister Eckhart zu Meister Dietrich,* ed. Kurt Flasch (Hamburg: Meiner, 1984), 106–14; and *Meister Eckhart,* 24–29.

329. In Ioh. n. 31 (LW 3:25.8–10): Et tale agens, principium scilicet in quo est logos, ratio, est agens essentiale nobiliori modo praehabens suum effectum, et est habens causalitatem super totam speciem sui effectus. Eckhart often returns to the *causa essentialis* in the commen-tary; see, e.g., nn. 38, 45, 139, 195, 239 (LW 3:32–33, 37–38, 117, 163, 200). See also In Gen. II n. 47 (LW 1:515); In Sap. nn. 21, 71, 132 (LW 2:342, 400–401, 470).

330. In Gen. II n. 45 (LW 1:512.13–14): . . . quia omne verum agens essentiale semper est spiritus et vita. . . .

331. S. II n. 6 (LW 4:8.4–9) distinguishes two kinds of *causae essentiales:* "the primal-prime causes," better characterized under the term *principium* (i.e., the way the Father is principle of the Son); and the "second-prime essential causes" which deal with the created realm.

332. In Sap. n. 170 (LW 2:505.10–11): . . . agens enim sive efficiens secundum genus causarum est causa extrinsica, forma vero est causa rei intrinseca.

333. S. XXIII n. 223 (LW 4:208.5–11): Non est ergo imaginandum quod deus creavit extra se et quasi iuxta se caelum et terram in quodam nihilo. Omne enim quod fit in nihilo, utique fit nihil. . . . Sed e converso creando vocat cuncta ex nihilo et a nihilo ad esse.

334. In Sap. n. 122 (LW 2:459.1–2): Non enim imaginandum, sicut plurimi autumnant, quasi deus extra se et a se, non in se creaverit aut produxerit omnia, sed a se et in se creavit. . . . Cf. Prol.gen. n. 17 (LW 1:160.13–62.12); In Eccli. n. 49 (LW 2:207.11–08.11).

335. S. XXIII n. 222 (LW 4:208.1–2): . . . secundo quod creavit et quievit a creando ad modum aliorum artificum, secundum planum litterae quae dicit: 'requievit deus die septimo ab universo opere' (Gen. 2:2)."

336. Pr. 30 (DW 2:94.3–9): . . . daz alle crêatûren ûzvliezent und doch inneblîbent, daz ist gar wunderlich; . . . Ie mê er ist in den dingen, ie mê er ist ûz den dingern: ie mê inne, ie mê ûze, und ie mê ûze, ie mê ine. Ich hân ez etwenne mê gesprochen, daz got alle dise werlt schepfet nû alzemâle. Allez, daz got ie geschuof sehs tûsent jâren und mê, dô got die werlt machete, die schepfet got nû alzemâle (Walshe 1:147). *Creatio continua* is spoken of in both the MHG works, e.g., Pr. 38 (DW 2:231–32), and BgT (DW 5:44), and also in the Latin writ-

ings: e.g., Prol.gen. nn. 18 and 21 (LW 1:162–63 and 165); In Gen. I n. 20 (LW 1:201); In Sap. nn. 33 and 292 (LW 2:354, 627); In Ioh. nn. 411–12 and 582 (LW 3:349–50, 510).

337. See especially In Ioh. nn. 213–19 (LW 3:180–84), which makes use of Augustine, *Confessiones* 11.10–13, to rebut this error.

338. Along with the passages from *Conf.* 11, in the Cologne trial Eckhart also cited *Conf.* 1.6.3 (PL 32:665). He also quotes this passage in In Ioh. nn. 580, 638 (LW 3:508, 554).

339. In Ioh. n. 323 (LW 3:271): Adhuc autem, quia creatio exterior subiacet tempori quod facit vetus. . . . See also In Gen. II n. 62 (LW 1:529); In Ex. n. 85 (LW 2:88); and S. XV n. 155 (LW 4:147–48).

340. For a brief summary on *esse virtuale/esse formale*, see Tobin, *Meister Eckhart*, 59–62.

341. In Sap. n. 21 (LW 2:342.9–12): Omnia autem sunt in deo tamquam in causa prima intellectualiter et in mente artificis. Igitur non habent esse suum aliquod formale, nisi causaliter educantur et producantur extra, ut sint.

342. Eckhart appeals to the *esse virtuale/esse formale* distinction often in his Latin writings; see In Gen. I nn. 77, 83 (LW 1:238–39, 242); In Gen. II nn. 35, 45, 52, 62 (LW 1:503, 512, 520, 528–30); In Ex. n. 175 (LW 2:151); In Sap. nn. 22, 32, 127 (LW 2:343, 352–53, 465); In Ioh. nn. 37–38, 45, 342 (LW 3:31–33, 37, 290–91); SS. VIII nn. 89–90, IX n. 102 (LW 4:84–87. 96–97); Qu.Par. I nn. 8–11 (LW 5:45–47).

343. See, e.g., In Gen. I nn. 2 and 14 (LW 1:186, 197–98).

344. Pr. 57 (DW 2:600–02). On the history of the mirror as a mystical image, see Margot Schmidt, "Miroir," DS 10:1290–1303. On the use of the mirror in Eckhart, see Wilde, *Das neue Bild vom Gottesbild*, chapter 3.

345. See Prol.op.prop. n. 22 (LW 1:178); In Ex. nn. 29, 40, 135 (LW 2:34, 45, 124); In Sap. n. 34 (LW 2:354); In Ioh. nn. 215, 308 (LW 3:181, 256); S. XXXI n. 323 (LW 4:283). In his sermons Eckhart sometimes uses neologisms to express the nothingness of created being, such as *nulleitas* (S. XV n. 158 [LW4:150.5]) and *nihileitas* (S. XXXVII n. 375 [LW4:321.1]).

346. Proc.Col.II n. 153 (Acta n. 48, LW 5:354.8–9): Praeterea, dicere mundum non esse nihil in se et ex se, sed esse quid modicum, manifesta blasphemia est. See also Proc.Col.I n. 150 (LW 5:304.4–10).

347. Aquinas, STh IaIIae q. 109, a. 2, ad 2: Unaquaeque autem res creata, sicut esse non habet nisi ab alio, et in se considerata est nihil.

348. See In Gen. I n. 146 (LW 1:299). In Tobin's insightful formulation, "creatures . . . exist at the non-dimensional intersection of nothingness and infinity" (*Meister Eckhart*, 188).

349. See Annick Charles-Saget, "Non-être et Néant chez Maître Eckhart," in *Voici Maître Eckhart*, ed. Emilie Zum Brunn (Grenoble: Jérôme Millon, 1994), 301–18. On Eckhart's differing uses of *nihil/niht*, consult Beverly Lanzetta, "Three Categories of Nothingness in Meister Eckhart," *Journal of Religion* 72 (1992): 248–68; and Burkhard Mojsisch, "*Nichts* und *Negation.* Meister Eckhart und Nikolaus von Kues," in *Historia philosophiae medii aevi: Studien zur Geschichte der Philosophie des Mittelalters*, ed. Burkhard Mojsisch (Amsterdam: G. R. Grüner, 1991), 2:675–93.

350. On the three levels of created being, see In Ioh. nn. 63–64, 83, 89 (LW 3:144–45, 153, 155–56).

351. Eckhart often talked about the angels, especially in his MHG sermons; see Frank Tobin, "Meister Eckhart and the Angels," in *In hôhem prîse: A Festschrift in Honor of Ernst S. Dick*, ed. Winder McConnell (Göppingen: Kümmerle, 1989), 379–93; and Thomas Renna, "Angels and Spirituality: The Augustinian Tradition to Eckhardt," *Augustinian Studies* 16 (1985): 29–37.

352. In Gen. II n. 151 (LW 1:621.5–11): . . . sic eodem modo per omnia deus loquitur omnibus quae sunt. Loquitur, inquam, omnibus et omnia. Sed alia ipsum audiunt, ipsi respondent sub proprietate esse, qua scilicet deus est esse et ab ipso esse omnium. Alia vero ipsum audiunt et suscipiunt verbum dei, ut est vita prima et vera; et ista sunt viventia omnia. Suprema vero in entibus ipsum audiunt deum non solum per esse et in esse, aut per vivere et in vivere, sed per intelligere et in ipso intelligere. Intellectio enim et locutio illic idem.

353. Two central expositions of Eckhart's anthropology are: (1) the account of the Fall, exegeting Gen. 3:1 (In Gen. II nn. 135–65 [LW 1:601–35]); and (2) Pr. 83 (DW 3:437–48).

354. For a brief sketch of Western medieval doctrine of humanity as *imago Dei*, see Bernard McGinn, "The Human Person as Image of God: II, Western Christianity," *Christian Spirituality I: Origins to the Fifth Century*, ed. Jean Leclercq, Bernard McGinn, John Meyendorff (New York: Crossroad, 1985), 312–30.

355. In Gen. II n. 153 (LW 1:623.11–12): Hoc dictum est de homine ratione intellectus quantum ad rationem superiorem, qua est 'caput' animae et 'imago dei'.

356. In Gen. II n. 113 (LW 1:579.6): Notandum quod homo id quod est per intellectum est.

357. Not even the birth of the Word in the soul appears more frequently than *bild* and *vernunft* in Eckhart's sermons. (A) *Bild* comes in for discussion in Prr. 1, 2, 3, 5b, 6, 9, 10, 16a, *16b*, 17, 20a, 20b, 22, *23*, 24, 30, 32, *40*, *43*, *44*, 45, 50, *51*, 57, 67, *69*, *70*, *72*, 77, 78, 83, 89, *101*, 102 (I have italicized the more important treatments). In addition, Pfeiffer LXXVII (249–51) has a significant commentary on Gen. 1:26. (B) *Vernunft* is treated even more often; see Prr. *1*, 3, 4, 6, 8, *9*, 10, 13, *15*, 16b, 17, 18, 19, 20b, 21, 22, 23, 26, 32, 34, 36a, 36b, *37*, 38, 42, 43, 45, 52, 53, 54a, 59, *61*, 66, 67, *68*, *69*, 70, *71*, 72, *73*, 75, 76, *80*, 83, *90*, *101–4*. Both motifs have attracted a large literature. Besides Wilde, *Das neue Bild vom Gottesbild*, see Alois M. Haas, "Meister Eckhart. Mystische Bildlehre," in *Sermo mysticus*, 209–37; Loris Sturlese, "Mysticism and Theology in Meister Eckhart's Theory of the Image," *Eckhart Review* (March 1993): 18–31; and Wackernagel, *YMAGINE DENUDARI*, chapters VI–X. Eckhart's teaching on the relation of intellect and *imago* has been the subject of several important treatments, especially Kurt Flasch, "Procedere ut imago: Das Hervorgehen des Intellekts aus seinem göttlichen Grund bei Meister Dietrich, Meister Eckhart und Berthold von Moosburg"; and Burkhard Mojsisch, "'Dynamik' der Vernunft bei Dietrich von Freiberg und Meister Eckhart" (both in *Abendländisches Mystik*, 116–44). See also Mojsisch, *Meister Eckhart*, 74–81; de Libera, *La mystique rhénane*, 250–77; and N. Largier, "'intellectus in deum ascensus': Intellekt-theoretische Auseinandersetzungen in Texten der deutschen Mystik."

358. The key texts on *imago* in the Latin works are (1) In Gen. I nn. 115–20 (LW 1:270–76), exegeting Gen.1:26, *faciamus hominem ad imaginem et similitudinem nostram*; (2) In Sap. n. 143 (LW 2:480–81) on Wis. 7:26, *imago bonitatis illius*; (3) In Ioh. nn. 23–26 (LW 3:19–21) on Col. 1:15, *imago dei invisibilis*; (4) S. XLIX nn. 505–12 (LW 4:421–28) on Matt. 22:30, *Cuius est imago haec et superscriptio?*

359. In Gen. I n. 115 (LW 1:270.4–13): Quantum ad nunc autem sciendum quod creatura rationalis sive intellectualis differt ab omni creatura quae citra est, quod ea quae citra sunt producta sunt ad similitudinem eius quod in deo est et habent ideas sibi proprias in deo, . . . natura vero intellectualis ut sic potius habet ipsum deum similitudinem quam aliquid quod in deo sit ideale. Ratio huius est quod "intellectus ut sic est, quo est omnia fieri," non hoc et hoc determinatum ad speciem. The quotation is from Aristotle, *De anima* 3.18 (430a14). On this passage, see Goris, *Einheit als Prinzip und Ziel,*, 245–51.

360. In Gen. I n. 115 (LW 1:272.1–2): De ratione enim imaginis est quod sit expressiva totius eius plene, cuius imago est, non expressiva alicuius determinati in illo. Cf. S. XLIX nn. 505, 509–12 (LW 4:421, 424–28).

361. Qu.Par. 2 n. 2 (LW 5:50.1–5): Prima est, quia intellectus, in quantum intellectus, nihil est eorum quae intelligit. . . . Si igitur intellectus, in quantum intellectus, nihil est, et per consequens nec intelligere aliquod esse. The same point is made in the MHG sermons; e.g., Pr. 69 (DW 3:171.1–2).

362. In Ioh. n. 549 (LW 3:479.3–480.1): Homo autem creatus est ad imaginem totius substantiae dei, et sic non ad simile, sed ad unum. . . . Non sufficit recursus ad simile, sed recurrit ad unum unde exivit, et sic solum sibi sufficit.

363. Pr. 40 (DW 2:277.7–10): Und dar umbe: als man sprichet, daz der mensche mit gote ein sî und nâch der einicheit got sî, sô nimet man in nâch dem teile des bildes, an dem er gote glîch ist, und niht nâch dem, und er geschaffen ist (*Teacher and Preacher*, 301).

364. Pr. 16b (DW 1:268.3–6): Ir sult wizzen, daz daz einvaltic götlîche bilde, daz in die sêle gedrücket ist in dem inigsten der natûre, âne mittel sich nemende ist; und daz innigste und daz edelste, daz in der natûre ist, daz erbildet sich aller eigenlîchest in daz bilde der sêle . . . (*Teacher and Preacher*, 276). Pr. 16, preached for the Feast of St. Augustine, exists in two forms, 16a and 16b (DW 1:257–76). As one of Eckhart's most important treatments of *bild*, it has often been commented upon; see especially Susanne Köbele, "Predigt 16b: 'Quasi vas auri solidum,'" in *Lectura Eckhardi I*, 43–74; Wilde, *Das neue Bild vom Gottesbild*, 298–309; and Milem, *Unspoken Word*, chapter 4.

365. Pr. 16b (DW 1:268.9–11): Hie ennimet daz bilde niht got, als er ein schepfer ist, sunder ez nimet in, als er ein vernünftic wesen ist, und daz edelste der natûre erbildet sich aller eigenlîchest in daz bilde (my trans.).

366. Eckhart used this text often, citing it seventeen times in the John commentary and another eight times in the LW and DW according to the indices published thus far.

367. Pr 16b (DW 1:272.11–273.6): Her umbe ist daz aleine ein gereht mensche, der alliu geschaffeniu dinc vernihtet hât und an einer glîchen linien âne allez ûzluogen in daz êwige wort gerihtet stât und dar în gebildet und widerbildet in der gerehticheit. Der mensche nimet, dâ der sun nimet und ist der sun selber. Ein geschrift sprichet: "nieman bekennet den vater dan der sun," und dâ von, wellet ir got bekennen, sô sult ir niht aleine glîch sîn dem sune, sunder ir sult der sun selber sîn (my trans.). There are similar expressions of identity with the Son as *imago Dei* elsewhere; see, e.g., Pr. 44 (DW 2:328–44, and 349), Pr. 51 (DW 2:472), and Pr. 70 (DW 3:197–98).

368. Pr. 72 (DW 3:243:1–2): Daz dritte ist inwendic in dem geiste, daz bekennet sunder bilde und glîchnisse, und diz bekantnisse glîchet sich den engeln (my trans.). For a commentary on this sermon, see Walter Haug, "Predigt 72: 'Videns Iesus turbas,'" in *Lectura Eckhardi II*, 111–37.

369. Pr. 70 (DW 3:194.13–195.2): Sol ich got bekennen âne mittel und âne glîchnisse, sô muoz got vil nâhe ich werden und ich vil nâhe got, alsô gar ein . . . (*Teacher and Preacher*, 318).

370. Pr. 70 (DW 3:197.2–198.2): Gotes eigenschaft ist, daz er sich selben bekennet sunder 'kleine' und sunder diz und daz. Alsô bekennet der engel got, als er sich selben bekennet. . . . Nû spriche ich: 'wir suln in bekennen rehte, als er sich selben bekennet' [cf. 1 Cor. 13:12] in dem widerbilde, daz aleine bilde ist gotes und der gotheit, niht der gotheit dan als vil, als si der vater ist. Rehte als vil wir dem bilde glîch sîn, in dem bilde alliu bilde ûzgevlozzen und gelâzen sint, und in dem bilde widerbildet sîn und glîche îngetragen sîn in daz bilde des vaters, als verre als er daz in uns bekennet, als verre bekennen wir in, als er sich selben bekennet (*Teacher and Preacher*, 318–19 modified). A similar teaching is found in Pr. 72, where Eckhart also preaches the necessity of going beyond all images of this and that to "the Son . . . as an image of God above all images, . . . an image of his concealed Godhead" (DW 3:244.4–245.1). The perfect mutuality of the knowledge between God and the soul at this level is expressed in Pr. 10 (DW 1:162.2–4): Daz selbe bekantnisse, dâ sich got selben inne bekennet, daz ist eines ieglîchen abegescheidenen geistes bekantnisse und kein anderz.

371. Pr. 69 (DW 3:159–80). For literature on this sermon and a commentary, see Largier, *Meister Eckhart*, 2:666–75.

372. Pr. 69 (DW 3:169.1–5): Ein kraft ist in der sêle, daz ist vernünfticheit. Von êrste, sô diu gotes gewar wirt und gesmecket, sô hât si vünf eigenschefte an ir. Daz êrste ist, daz si abescheidet von hie und von nû. Daz ander, daz si nihte glîch enist. Daz dritte, daz si lûter und unvermenget ist. Daz vierde, daz si in ir selber würkende oder suochende ist. Daz vünfte, daz si ein bilde ist (*Teacher and Preacher*, 313).

373. Pr. 69 (DW 3:176.4–17.5): . . . in dem hât ir die predige alzemâle: bilde und bilde ist sô gar ein und mit einander, daz man keinen underscheit dâ verstân enmac. . . . Ich spriche mê: got mit sîner almehticheit enmac keinen underscheit dâ verstân, wan ez wirt mit einander geborn und stirbet mit einander (*Teacher and Preacher*, 314).

374. Pr. 69 (DW 3:178.3–179.7): Vernünfticheit diu blicket în und durchbrichet alle die winkel der gotheit und nimet den sun in dem herzen des vaters und in dem grunde und setzet

in in irn grunt. Vernünfticheit diu dringet în; ir engenüeget niht an güete noch an wîsheit noch an wârheit noch an gote selber. . . . Si engeruowet niemer; si brichet in den grunt, dâ güete und wârheit ûzbrichet, und nimet ez *in principio*, in dem beginne, dû güete und wârheit ûzgânde ist, ê ez dâ deheinen namen gewinne, ê ez ûzbreche (my trans.).

375. See Pr. 13 (DW 1:220.4–8): Ein kraft ist in der sêle, von der ich mêr gesprochen hân—und waere diu sêle alliu alsô, sô waere si ungeschaffen und ungeschepflich. Nû enist des niht. An dem andern teile sô hât si ein zuosehen und ein zuohangen ze der zît, und dâ rüeret si geschaffenheit und ist geschaffen—vernünfticheit: dirre kraft enist niht verre noch ûzer. Note that Eckhart's qualifications expressed in the sermon text did not make it into the condemned article. In the Cologne proceedings this text is found in Proc.Col.I n. 59 (LW 5:218). Many other texts in the MHG sermons have similar language about an uncreated something or power in the soul; see, e.g., Prr. 2, 7, 10, 11, 12, 22, 24 (DW 1:32–35 and 39–45, 123–24, 171–73, 182–84, 197–98, 380–81, 417–18); Prr. 26, 27, 28, 29, 30, 40, 42, 46, 48, 50 (DW 2:30 and 34, 52–53, 66, 88, 95–97, 277, 306–08, 382, 418–20, 459–60); Prr. 68, 76, 84 (DW 3:141, 315–16, 462); Pr. 95 (DW 4:186). The same teaching is propounded in the Latin works; see In Sap. n. 24 (LW 2:344.6–345.1): Si quid esset vivens aut intelligens, non habens esse aliquod praeter et extra vivere et intelligere, ipsum esset ut sic increabile. Cf. In Gen. I n. 112 (LW 1:267), In Sap. nn. 32, 94 (LW 2:353, 428); S. XXIX nn. 301, 304 (LW 4:267–68, 269–70).

376. Eckhart's response can be found in Proc.Col.I n. 137 (Acta n. 48, LW 5:298.13–299.4): Falsum est et error. Nam, sicut dicit alius articulus, supremae potentiae animae 'sunt creatae in anima et cum anima'. . . . Filium quidem suum unigenitum quem generat, qui est imago, vestivit se ipso, non secundum se ipsum, ut esset increatus, immensus, qualis et pater; hominem autem, utpote creatum, fecit ad imaginem, non imaginem, et 'vestivit' non se ipso, sed 'secundum se' ipsum. In the sermon that he preached in his defense at Cologne on February 13, 1327, Eckhart gave a similar argument, invoking the term *concreatum* to describe the soul as *ad imaginem*. On this text, see Tobin, *Meister Eckhart*, 133.

377. Most of these terms are taken up in Tobin, *Meister Eckhart*, 126–40. Other studies include Hof, *Scintilla Animae;* and Klaus Kremer, "Das Seelenfunklein bei Meister Eckhart," *Trierer theologische Zeitschrift* 97 (1988): 8–38.

378. S. XXXVI n. 364 (LW 4:313.9–10): Et ut totum, quod est animae unum, quaerat in hac, venit Jesus. On the role of the *unum animae* in Eckhart's preaching and its connection with Proclus, see de Libera, *La mystique rhénane*, 278–84.

379. Mojsisch, *Meister Eckhart*, 131–32; and Wackernagel, *YMAGINE DENUDARI*, 45–48, 131–32.

380. On Eckhart's Christology, see Bardo Weiss, *Die Heilsgeschichte bei Meister Eckhart* (Mainz: Matthias Grünewald Verlag, 1965), chapters 2–4; Richard Schneider, "The Functional Christology of Meister Eckhart," *Recherches de théologie médiévale* 35 (1968): 291–32; Dietmar Mieth, *Christus—Das Soziale im Menschen* (Düsseldorf: Patmos, 1972); Alois M. Haas, "Jesus Christus—Inbegriff des Heils und verwirkliche Transzendenz im Geist der deutschen Mystik," in *Epiphanie des Heils: Zur Heilsgegenwart in indischer und christlicher Religion* (Vienna: Institut für Indologie der Universität Wien, 1983), 193–216; and his *Meister Eckhart als normative Gestalt geistlichen Lebens*, 2nd ed. (Freiburg: Johannes Verlag, 1995), especially chapter 4; and de Libera, *La mystique rhénane*, 250–59. Specifically on Eckhart's soteriology, see Irmgard Kampmann, *"Ihr sollt der Sohn selber sein": Eine fundamentaltheologische Studie zur Soteriologie Meister Eckharts* (Frankfurt: Peter Lang, 1996).

381. See Ewert Cousins, "The Humanity and Passion of Christ," in *Christian Spirituality: High Middle Ages and Reformation*, 375–91.

382. For an overview of the history of *imitatio Christi*, Giles Constable, *Three Studies in Medieval Religious and Social Thought* (Cambridge: Cambridge University Press, 1995), part 2.

383. Pr. 90 (DW 4:43–71). In DW 4:66–70 Eckhart adopts Aquinas's teaching on the four modes of Christ's knowledge (see STh IIIa, qq. 9–10) as a springboard for a treatment of what Christ teaches us through our participation in these modes.

384. There are many treatments of Christology in the MHG sermons, for example (with

emphasis on the most important texts): Prr. 1, 5a, *5b*, 20a, 20b, *22*, 23, *24*, 25, *29*, 30, 40, 41, *47*, *49*, 55, 59, *67*, 78, 86, 87, *90*. In the MHG treatises, see BgT (DW 5:48–49); RdU (DW 5:246–49, 253–54, 259, 270–72). Christology is also a frequent topic in the Latin works, especially the John commentary, as we shall see.

385. See Schneider, "Functional Christology of Meister Eckhart"; and Haas, "Jesus Christus."

386. See the commentary on John 1:1–18 in In Ioh. nn. 4–198 (LW 3:5–167).

387. The earliest appearance of the axiom "God became man so that man might become God" is in Irenaeus, *Adversus haereses* 3.19.1 (PG 7:939AB); but it appears in many fathers; e.g., Athanasius, *De incarnatione* 8 (PG 25:110). Eckhart may have been familiar with it through texts in Augustine (e.g., Sermo 13 [PL 39:216]). The related formula used here (*homo est per gratiam quod Deus est per naturam*) is based on a passage found in Maximus Confessor, *Ambigua* (PG 91:1088C) paraphrased by Eriugena, *Periphyseon* 5 (PL 122:880A): Animadverte, quod ait [i.e., Maximus], totus homo manens secundum animam et corpus per naturam, et totus factus Deus secundum animam et corpus per gratiam.

388. Pr. 29 (DW 2:84.1–2): Warumbe ist got mensche worden? Dar umbe, daz ich got geborn würde der selbe. See also Prr. 25, 30, 46 (DW 2:14–16, 98, 378–83); Pr. 67 (DW 3:134–35).

389. The formula *filius per naturam/filius per gratiam* occurs in Augustine's *Tractatus in Ioannem* 75.1 (PL 35:1829): Quamvis ergo nos Filius Dei suo Patri adoptaverit filios, et eumdem Patrem nos voluerit habere per gratiam, qui ejus Pater est per naturam. . . . For a more detailed exposition of the distinction in the commentary on the Prologue, see n. 123 (LW 3:107). Similar appeals to the distinction of sonships can be found In Ioh. nn. 117, 368, and 455 (LW 3:101–02, 312–13, and 389).

390. E.g., BgT 1 (DW 5:37–38), and Prr. 40 (DW 2:277) and 59 (DW 2:378). In the Latin writings, see SS. XLII n. 422, LII n. 523 (LW 4:355, 437–38). The same theme is implied when Eckhart discusses how we are co-heirs with Christ in In Eccli. n. 41 (LW 2:269–70), S. XII n. 126, and S. LV n. 556 (LW 4:120 and 465).

391. E.g., Proc.Col.I n. 61 (LW 5:219) and Eckhart's response in Proc.Col.I n. 139 (LW: 299–300). Eckhart defends his Christology and the birth of the Son in the soul often in his responses to the second list of errors; see Proc.Col.II, especially the long response to article 27 in nn. 59–74 (LW 5:330–37); also nn. 15–16, 31–32, 55–58, 98–99, 126, 134–36, and 139–45 (LW 5:321, 325, 329–30, 341–42, 348, 349–50, and 351–52). See also Votum Theologicum from Avignon, art. XVII-XVIII, and XXI-XXIII (Pelster ed., 1117, 1119–21). On these texts, see Karl G. Kertz, S.J., "Meister Eckhart's Teaching on the Birth of the Divine Word in the Soul," *Traditio* 15 (1959): 339–63, though Kertz misses the import of the distinction of sonships by failing to see that they represent only one pole of Eckhart's dialectical thought about our relation to Christ.

392. Acta n. 48 (Proc. Col.II n. 145, LW 5:352.21–24): Non est ergo putandum quod alius sit filius, quo Christus ejus filius est, et alius, quo nos nominamur et sumus filii dei, sed id ipsum et is ipse, qui Christus filius est naturaliter genitus, nos filii dei sumus analogice cui cohaerendo, utpote haerenti, coheredes sumus.

393. The 2 Corinthians text is used three more times in the commentary on v. 14 (In Ioh. nn. 119–120 [LW 3:103–05]). It is cited frequently elsewhere: e.g., In Gen. I n. 301 (LW 1:440); In Gen. II nn. 130, 141, 219 (LW 1:596, 609–10, 697–98); In Sap. n. 45 (LW 2:368); In Ioh. nn. 155, 505, 575 (LW 3:128, 436, 504); S. XLIX nn. 507–08 (LW 4:423); Prr. 6 and 23 (DW 1:110, 397–98); Pr. 41 (DW 2:296); BgT 1 (DW 5:32); RdU 20 (DW 5:266).

394. In Ioh. n. 117 (LW 3:101.14–102.2): Parum enim mihi esset *verbum caro factum* pro homine in Christo, supposito illo a me distincto, nisi et in me personaliter, ut et ego essem filius dei.

395. Besides its frequent presence in the defense documents, Eckhart also used the *inquantum* principle in sermons discussing Christ's Sonship and ours; e.g., Pr. 22 (DW 1:381–82) and Pr. 40 (DW 2:272–81).

396. In Ioh. n. 118 (LW 3:103.12–14): Ait ergo: *verbum caro factum est* in Christo, *et*

habitavit in nobis, quando in quolibet nostrum filius dei fit homo et filius hominis fit filius dei. Eckhart emphasizes the necessary connection between the two sonships by appealing to Jn. 16:2 ("I will see you *again*"), arguing that the first "seeing" is the incarnation and the second is the Son's dwelling in us (see nn. 117 and 119).

397. In Ioh. n. 125 (LW 3:108.9–13): . . . *plenum gratiae et veritatis* inclusive, supposita veritate semper historiae, continere et docere rerum naturalium, moralium et artificialium proprietates. Notandum ergo quod universaliter et naturaliter in omni opere naturae et artis verbum caro fit et habitat in illis quae fiunt sive in quibus verbum caro fit.

398. In Ioh. n. 185 (LW 3:154.8–14): Rursus notandum quod, quia 'verbum caro factum est', ut habitaret in nobis, ut supra expositum est, . . . congrue subiciendum videtur quod dei sapientia sic caro fieri dedignata est, ut ipsa incarnatio quasi media inter divinarum personarum processionem et creaturarum productionem utriusque naturam sapiat, ita ut incarnatio ipsa sit exemplata quidem ab aeterna emanatione et exemplar totius naturae inferioris.

399. For a sketch of the history of cosmic Christologies centering on Nicholas of Cusa, see Bernard McGinn, "*Maximum Contractum et Absolutum*: The Motive for the Incarnation in Nicholas of Cusa and Some of His Predecessors," in *Nicholas of Cusa and His Age: Intellect and Spirituality*, ed. Thomas M. Izbicki and Christopher M. Bellitto (Leiden: Brill, 2002), 149–75. See also Haas, *Meister Eckhart als normative Gestalt*, 94–96.

400. S. XXV n. 253 (LW 4:232.2–3): . . . Ioh. 16: 'exivi a patre et veni in mundum' per creationem, non tantum per incarnationem. This notion of what was later called the absolute predestination of Christ is also found in Pfeiffer LXXVII (ed., 250.22–26): Ez stêt in dem buoche Moysi geschriben, daz Âdam wêre der êrste mensche, den got ie geschuof. Und ich spriche, daz Kristus wêre der êrste mensche, den ie got geschuof. Alse wie? Ez sprichet ein meister: daz êrste in der meinunge ist daz beste von den werken.

401. Pr. 46 (DW 2:378–86). For a commentary, see Largier, *Meister Eckhart*, 1:1031–33.

402. Pr. 46 (DW 2:380.5–381.2): Wan als daz wâr ist, daz got mensche worden ist, als wâr ist daz, daz der mensche got worden ist. Und alsô ist diu menschlîche natûre überbildet in dem, daz si worden ist daz götlîche bilde, daz dâ bilde ist des vaters.

403. The sermon concludes (DW 3:384–86) with a fourth point illustrating the transformation by means of an examination of the relation between the just person and Justice.

404. Pr. 49 (DW 2:427–51). I will use the translation found in Walshe 2:285–97. There is a detailed commentary on the sermon in Hasebrink, *Formen inzitativer Rede*, 196–258.

405. For other treatments of the relation between Mary's birth and our own, see, e.g., Prr. 22, 23, 78, etc.

406. The four conditions that Eckhart advances (DW 2:429–31) are based on Gregory's *Homilia in Evangelia* I.18.1 (PL 76:1150B).

407. Pr. 49 (DW 2:435.6–8): Sehet, her umbe sprichet der vater diz wort williclîche und niht von willen, und natiurlîche und niht von natûre.

408. Pr.49 (DW 2:435.8–9): In disem worte sprichet der vater mînen geist und dînen geist und eines ieglîchen menschen geist glîch dem selben worte.

409. On suffering in Eckhart, see Donald F. Duclow, "'My Suffering is God': Meister Eckhart's *Book of Divine Consolation*," *Theological Studies* 44 (1983): 570–86; and Alois M. Haas, "'trage Leiden geduldiglich': Die Einstellung der deutschen Mystik zum Leiden," *Zeitwende* 57, no. 3 (1986): 154–75.

410. Pr. 49 (DW 2:440.10–11): Daz ist in der wârheit; wan dô der lîchame von pîne an dem kriuze starp, dô lebete sîn edel geist in dirre gegenwerticheit.

411. For another discussion of Christ's external suffering, see RdU 20 (DW 5:270–72). In the pseudo-Eckhartian VAbe (DW 5:411–22), we find the helpful analogy of the moving door (= outer powers) and the immobile hinge (= inner ground) to help explain why Christ did not suffer within (DW 5:421–22).

412. Eckhart often proposes Christ's suffering and death as the example for Christians, using Matt. 10:37 ("Deny yourself and come follow me") and Matt. 16:24 ("If anyone wishes to come after me, let me take up his cross and follow me"), as well as related texts in Luke

9:23 and 14:27. The most extended treatment is in S. XLV nn. 459–68 (LW 4:380–87), but see also S. LV nn. 545–46 (LW 4:456–57). For some appearances in the vernacular works, see, e.g., Prr. 10, 15 (DW 1:170, 224); Pr. 59 (DW 2:628, 630); Pr. 76 (DW 3:326); and BgT (DW 5:45). There are other texts that propose Christ's suffering as a model without citing these specific biblical verses; e.g., S. XIII n. 149 (LW 4:140).

413. Pr. 49 (DW 2:445.7–9): . . . und alles sînes lidennes sol in dünken als kleine, rehte als ein tropfe wazzers gegen dem wilden mer. Als kleine solt dû ahten alles dînes lidennes gegen dem grôzen lîdenne Jêsû Kristî.

414. Pr. 49 (DW 2:446.5–7): . . . sunder er sol got lâzen mit im würken allez, daz er wil, oder als dû niht ensîst: alsô gewaltic sol got sîn in allem dem, daz dû bist, als in sîner eigenen ungeschaffenen natûre. The motif of utter surrender to God even if he should damn us (*resignatio ad infernum*), based on Rom. 9:3, was a popular one with late medieval mystics. Eckhart makes use of it often: In Ex. n. 270 (LW 2:217); In Ioh. n. 79 (LW 3:67); S. VI n. 67 (LW 4:65); Prr. 4, 6, 12 (DW 1:63–64, 100 and 103, 195–97); Pr. 25 (DW 2:10–11); RdU 10 (DW 5:223); and especially BgT 1 (DW 5:14–15, 21, 25, and 40).

415. Pr. 49 (DW 3:449.3–5): Kristus, unser herre, der ist aleine unser ende, dem wir nâchvolgen suln, und unser zil, under dem wir blîben suln und mit dem wir vereinet werden suln glîch aller sîner êre, als und diu einunge zuogehoeret.

416. On the BgT, see Duclow, "My Suffering is God," especially 575–82. Suffering is a major theme of Eckhart's preaching; see, e.g., Prr. 2, 4, 6, 8, 11, 12, 13 (DW 1:36–38, 61–64, 103, 127–28, 188, 200–201, 214); Prr. 30, 49, 51, 59 (DW 2:106, 430–47, 476, 630–31); Prr. 62, 68 (DW 3:63, 145); Pr. 94 (DW 4:142–45). There are also important considerations in RdU (DW 5:225, 229, 257–58, 271–72).

417. BgT (DW 5:54.3): . . . mîn leit in gote ist und mîn leit got ist.

418. BgT (DW 5:49.6–8): Gotes sun von natûre wolte von gnaden, daz er durch lîden möhte, und du wilt gotes sun werden und niht mensche, daz du niht enmügest noch endürfest lîden durch got noch durch selben (Walshe 3:91) There is a similar passage in DW 5:48.5–8.

419. Among Eckhart's sermons, we find frequent discussion of the purpose of the incarnation; see, e.g., Prr. 5a, 25, 29, 30, 38; S. XII; Pfeiffer LXXV; etc.

420. Pr. 22 (DW 1:377.12–379.1): "Vrouwe, daz ir nû gloubet, daz ich iuch liep hên, sô hân ich mich iu glîch gemachet; ich enhân ouch niht dan éin ouge." Diz ist der mensche, der kunde gar kûme glouben, daz in got sô lip hâte, biz als lanc daz got im selber ein ouge ûz stach und an sich name menschlîche natûre (*Essential Eckhart*, 193). Eckhart tells the same story in In Ioh. n. 683 (LW 3:598–99).

421. For discussions of Christ taking on common human nature and not a human person, beside the texts utilized above, see, e.g., Prr. 5b, 24, and 41. In the Latin writings, see Prol.op.prop. n. 19 (LW 1:177); In Ioh. nn. 288–91 (LW 3:241); and SS. XX n. 199, XXV n. 263, and LII n. 523 (LW 4:184, 240, and 437).

422. See Pr. 2, and the other vernacular sermons cited below. The theme is frequent in the Latin sermons; e.g., SS. XX, XXII, XLII, XLIV.1, and LII.

423. "In agro dominico," art. 11, as drawn from Pr. 5a (DW 1:77.10–13). Article 12 is taken from Pr. 24 (DW 1:421–22). A number of other articles, especially 13 and 20–22, deal with the related question of the identity between the Eternal Word and the just person, though they do not explicitly mention the incarnate God-man.

424. Pr. 38 (DW 2:231.3–232.1): Waere aber, daz zît diu sêle berüeren möhte, sô enmöhte got niemer in ir geborn werden, und si enmühte niemer in gote geborn werden. . . . Daz ist daz nû der êwichkeit, dâ diu sêle in gote alliu dinc niuwe und vrisch und gegenwertic bekennet und in der lust, als diu ich iezuo gegenwertic hân (Walshe 1:216). The same interpretation of Gal. 4:4 is found in Prr. 4, 11, and 24 (DW 1:74, 177–78, 422–23). See also In Ioh. n. 293 (LW 3:245).

425. See, e.g., Prr. 1, 49, and 86; and RdU 16–18. In the Latin works, S. LV.3 is important.

426. RdU 17 (DW 5:253–55).

427. While the essence of the *imitatio passionis* rests in complete abnegation and stripping off of all created reality, the most detailed treatment of Matt. 16:24, that found in S. XLV (LW 4:374–87), also has much to say about how "devout remembrance of the Lord's Passion" in a concrete and practical sense can help lead us to this goal.

428. S. XLVII n. 485 (LW 4:400.14): Unde ut daret [Deus] totum se, assumpsit totum me.

429. Vab (DW 5:433.1–3): Daz snelleste tier, iuch treget ze dirre volkomenheit, daz ist lîden, wan ez niuzet nieman mê êwiger süezicheit, dan die mit Kristô stânt in der groesten bitterkeit (*Essential Eckhart*, 294).

430. S. LII n. 523 (LW 4:437.7–11): Deus assumpsit vestem nostram, ut vere, proprie et per substantiam sit homo et homo deus in Christo. Natura autem assumpta communis est omni homini sine magis et minus. Ergo datum est omni homini filium dei fieri, per substantiam quidem in ipso, in se autem adoptive per gratiam.

431. On grace in Eckhart, see Edouard-Henri Wéber, "La théologie de la grâce chez Maître Eckhart," *Revue des sciences religieuses* 70 (1996): 48–72; Lossky, *Théologie négative*, 175–97; Tobin, *Meister Eckhart*, 105–15; Goris, *Einheit als Prinzip und Ziel*, 249–51, and chapter 8 *passim*; and Niklaus Largier, "Sermo XXV: 'Gratia dei sum id quod sum,'" in *Lectura Eckhardi II*, 177–203.

432. Treatments of grace occur in many places in Eckhart. *I. Latin Works*: In Gen. II n. 145 (LW 1:613); In Ex. nn. 13, 275 (LW 2:19, 222); In Sap. nn. 214, 272–74 (LW 2:550, 602–04); In Ioh. nn. 179, 326, 500–501, 521, 544, 592–94, 709 (LW 3:147–48, 274, 431–32, 449–50, 474–75, 516–17, 621); SS. II nn. 15–18, IX nn. 96–102, XV n. 159, XVII n. 179, XX n. 200, XXV, XXXII n. 328, XLIV n. 437, XLIX n. 508, LII n. 523 (LW 4:16–20, 92–97, 151–52, 167–68, 185, 230–44, 286–87, 367, 423, 437). *II. German Works*: Prr. 7, 11, 21, 24 (DW 1:124, 177, 366–67, 419); Prr. 33, 38, 43, 44, 52 (DW 2:151, 241–45, 325–27, 346–47, 501–2); Prr. 66, 67, 70, 73, 75, 76, 80, 81, 82, 86 (DW 3:109–10 and 118, 134, 196, 262–63 and 267, 297–98, 318–20, 381, 398–404, 428–30, 490); Prr. 96, 103 (DW 4:213–19; and 485–86). See also RdU (DW 5:265, 272, 307–8).

433. See Tobin, *Meister Eckhart*, 107–8, 111.

434. S. XXV n. 258 (LW 4:237–38).

435. In Sap. nn. 272–74 (LW 2:602–4).

436. In Sap. n. 273 (LW 2:603.7–9): . . . quod gratia gratum faciens, quae et supernaturalis dicitur, est in solo intellectivo, sed nec in illo, ut res est et natura, sed est in ipso ut intellectus et ut naturam sapit divinam. . . . On grace as supernatural, see also S. XXV nn. 264 and 268. In his MHG works Eckhart also insists that grace is given only to the soul's essence; see, e.g., Pr. 11 (DW 1:177.4–8). The supernatural, but still created, status of grace is emphasized in Pr. 81 (DW 3:400.12–13).

437. S. II n. 18 (LW 4:20.6–7): Sic ergo in solo deo, sapientia dei, filio, est omnis gratia, quia sine merito sunt eius dona omnia et sui solius. The entire S. II.2 nn. 16–18 speaks of the double gratuity of grace, both of creation (*gratia gratis data*) and re-creation (*gratia gratum faciens*).

438. S. XXV n. 266 (LW 4:241–42) says that the soul can receive grace only insofar as it is an *imago* ordered to God, not in its created status as *ens hoc et hoc*. Although grace is received in the essence of the soul as intellect, in Pr. 33 (DW 2:152–54) and elsewhere Eckhart allows that grace overflows to work in all the powers—will, reason, and the irascible power.

439. See STh IaIIae, q. 109, aa. 2–8; q. 111, aa. 2–3. Of course, in q. 109, a.1 Aquinas also recognizes the necessity of grace in elevating the mind to know supernatural truths. For Aquinas's doctrine of grace, see Bernard J. F. Lonergan, S.J., *Grace and Freedom: Operative Grace in the Thought of St. Thomas Aquinas* (New York: Herder & Herder, 1971).

440. Pr. 38 (DW 2:244.6–8): Gnâde enwürket kein werk, si ist ze zart dar zuo; werk ist ir als verre, als der himel ist von der erden (Walshe 1:221).

441. Pr. 96 (DW 4:215.33–35): Daz ander, daz si die sêle machet gote glîch und drücket gotes glîchnisse in die sêle und machet sie gotvar, daz si sich den den tiuvelen erbiutet vür

einen got, daz ist von der edelkeit der gnâde. The adjective *gotvar* is also used in Prr. 43, 54b (DW 2:328–29, 568), and Prr. 81, 82 (DW 3:400, 429).

442. Pr. 96 (DW 4:218.51–52): Alsô bringet diu gnâde die sêle in got und bringet die sêle über sich selber und beroubet sie ir selbes und alles des, daz crêatûre ist, und vereinet die sêle mit gote (my trans.). The axe example (DW 4:217–18) is adapted from Aristotle, *De anima* II.1 (412b).

443. S. XXV n. 263 (LW 4:239.10–240.4): Nota primo quod gratia est ebullitio quaedam parturitionis filii, radicem habens in ipso patris pectore intimo. . . . Item respectu suscipientis gratiam gratia est confirmatio, configuratio sive potius transfiguratio animae in deum et cum deo. Secundo dat esse unum cum deo, quod plus est assimilatione.

444. Pr. 21 (DW 1:367.3–5): Ich spriche: gnâde eneiniget niht die sêle mit gote, si ist ein volbringen; daz ist ir werk, daz si die sêle wider ze gote bringet (*Teacher and Preacher*, 282). See also Pr. 52 (DW 2:501–2), where Eckhart speaks about Paul as going beyond the work of grace.

445. Pr. 82 (DW 3:427–31).

446. S. IX n. 102 (LW 4:96.8–97.2): Nota, si tantum bonum est gratia unius hominis, quantum bonum omnis hominis, omnium angelorum tot specierum, quantum bonum ibi vivere, immo in ipso *deo omnis gratiae*, ubi iam gratia non gratia formaliter, sed virtualiter sicut calor in caelo, ubi iam nec bonum nec suave nec esse, sed supra "in regione et regno dissimilitudinis" infinitae. Eckhart's reversal of the famous Platonic-Augustinian phrase of the *regio dissimilitudinis* (*Confessiones* 7.10.16 [PL 32:742]), which had always been applied to the sinful realm of fallen humanity, is striking.

447. Pr. 43 (DW 2:326.1–2): Gnâde engeworhte nie dehein guot werk, daz ist: si engeworhte nie dehein werk; si vliuzet wol ûz an üebunge einer tugend (Walshe 2:232).

448. Pr. 70 (DW 3:196.2–12): Daz lieht der sunnen ist kleine wider dem liehte der vernünfticheit, und diu vernünfticheit ist kleine wider dem liehte der gnâde. . . . Daz lieht der gnâde, swie groz ez ist, ez ist doch kleine wider dem götlîchen liehte. . . . Wenne aber diu gnâde wirt volbrâht ûf daz hoehste, sô enist ez niht gnâde, ez ist ein götlich lieht, dar inne man got sihet. . . . Dâ enist kein zuoganc, dâ ist ein dar komen (Walshe 1:289–90 modified). For more on the superiority of the light of grace over the light of natural intellect, see Pr. 73 (DW 3:262–63).

449. Pr. 75 (DW 3:299.9–300.3): Suln wir dar în komen, sô müezen wir klimmen von natiulîchem liehte in daz lieht der gnâde und dar inne wahsen in daz lieht, daz der sun selber ist. Dâ werden wir geminnet in dem sune von dem vater mit der minne, diu der heilige geist ist . . . (Walshe 2:282 modified).

450. Eckhart does not use the language of created and uncreated grace, so I have avoided it in this presentation. However, his insistence on the virtual existence of grace in God is not unlike what other scholastics referred to as uncreated grace. See Wéber, "La théologie de la grace," 57–60.

451. On the Eucharist, see RdU 20 (DW 5:262–74); on confession, RdU 21 (DW 5:274–75).

452. Schönfeld, *Meister Eckhart Geistliche Übungen*, 37.

453. To be sure, Eckhart was not totally silent on the sacraments. See, for example, the reflections on the Eucharist in Prr. 20a and 20b (DW 1:326–45), and SS. V, and XL n. 402 (LW 4:33–49, 343). (S. V is largely a summary of Aquinas's eucharistic theology.) Eckhart also sometimes preached on exercises of devotion; e.g., the *collatio* on bearing the cross in S. XLV nn. 464–68 (LW 4:384–87). Mieth, *Die Einheit von Vita Activa und Vita Contemplativa*, 159–64, 173, 178, suggests that both the strength and something of the weakness of Eckhart's spirituality lies in this lack of attention to the concrete forms of piety.

454. For Eckhart's teaching on prayer, see Freimut Löser, "*Oratio est cum deo confabulatio:* Meister Eckharts Auffassung vom Beten und seine Gebetspraxis," in *Deutsche Mystik im abendländischen Zusammenhang*, 283–316; and Schönfeld, *Meister Eckhart Geistliche Übungen*, chapters III-V, and VII. In English, there are remarks in Ian Almond, "How *Not* to Decon-

struct a Dominican: Derrida on God and 'Hypertruth,'" *Journal of the American Academy of Religion* 68 (2000): 338–40. Almond concludes: "Eckhart's prayers do not 'direct,' they *de-limit*; they do not 'determine,' they *empty*. Far from invoking the very concept of the God Eckhart deemed idolatrous, Eckhart's prayers initiate the breakthrough to the nameless, silent darkness of the Godhead" (p. 340).

455. "In agro dominico" art. 7: Item quod petens hoc aut hoc, malum petit et male, quia negationem boni et negationem Dei petit, et orat deum sibi negari. This is an adaptation of In Ioh. n. 611 (LW 3:534.2–4). The other condemned article relating to prayer concerns not taking or asking anything from God. See art. 9 drawn from Pr. 6 (DW 1:112.6–9).

456. On "asses," e.g., Pr. 52 (DW 2:489); on "merchants," e.g., Pr. 16b (DW 1:272–74).

457. Discussions of prayer can be found in both the Latin and the MHG sermons. See SS. XIII nn. 147–50, XXIV nn. 231–33, and XLVII n. 409 (LW 4:138–41, 215–17, and 404–5); and Prr. 53 and 59 (DW 2:543, 624–26); Prr. 62, 63, 65, 67, and 68 (DW 3:60–61, 81, 102, 131, and 145); and RdU (DW 5:188, 190–91). Eckhart also wrote a commentary on the "Lord's Prayer," probably an early work, that can be found in LW 5:109–29. In addition, there is an extensive discussion in the doubtfully authentic Vab (DW 5:414–16, and 426–27). For a more complete listing and discussion of texts, see Löser, "*Oratio est cum deo confabulatio.*"

458. On these four prayers, see Löser, "*Oratio est cum deo confabulatio,*" 302–9.

459. On God's presence as *esse*, see, e.g., In Ex. n. 163 (LW 2:143) and In Ioh. n. 97 (LW 3:84).

460. Pr. 4 (DW 1:70.2–3): Alle crêatûren hânt kein wesen, wan ir wesen swebet an der gegenwerticheit gotes (my trans.).

461. Tobin, *Meister Eckhart*, 144, puts it this way: "One who merely has an intellectual grasp of all this is still far from the truth. We have to be like this truth to understand it. . . . Paradoxically, it is only by living in such a way that we become the truth do we understand the truth."

462. RdU 6 (DW 5:205.10–211.1): Der got alsô in wesenne hât, der nimet got götlîchen, und dem liuhtet er in allen dingen; . . . In im blicket got alle zît, in im ist ein abegeschieden abekêren und ein înbilden sînes geminneten gegenwertigen gotes (Walshe 3:18).

463. RdU 12 (DW 5:234.5–7): Got ist ein got der gegenwerticheit. Wie er dich vindet, alsô nimet er und enpfaehet dich, niht, waz dû gewesen sîst, sunder waz dû iezunt bist (Walshe 3:29). For more on presence, see RdU 7 and 21 (DW 5:210–12, 276).

464. Pr. 13a (DW 1:224.12–13): Got ist vber ellu ding ein instan in sich selber vnd sin instan enthaltet alle creaturen (my trans.). See Pr. 3 (DW 1:56).

465. Pr. 9 (DW 1:155.9–10): . . . meinet einen menschen, der hie zuo komen wil, der sol got alle zît bî und gegenwertic sîn . . . (*Teacher and Preacher*, 259). In the same sermon see also 156.11–157.7. Many other sermons deal with the presence theme, e.g., Prr. 5b, 24 (DW 1:93, 418–19 and 423); Prr. 42, 49, 56 (DW 2: 301, 437, 589); Pr. 68 (DW 3:142); and Pr. 97 (DW 4:228).

466. For Eckhart's use of these terms, see the materials gathered in Egerding, *Die Metaphorik der spätmittelalterlichen Mystik*, vol. 2, specifically *abescheiden* (pp. 24–28), *brechen* (pp. 129–33), and *gebern* (pp. 219–29).

467. Among the many treatments of detachment in Eckhart, see especially Denys Turner, *The Darkness of God: Negativity in Christian Mysticism* (Cambridge: Cambridge University Press, 1995), chapter 7. Also helpful are Alois M. Haas, "'. . . DAS PERSÖNLICHE UND EIGENE VERLEUGNEN': Mystische *vernichtigkeit und verworffenheit sein selbs* im Geiste Meister Eckharts," in *Individualität: Poetik und Hermeneutik XIII*, ed. Manfred Frank and Anselm Haverkamp (Munich: Fink, 1988), 106–22; Niklaus Largier, "Repräsentation und Negativität: Meister Eckharts Kritik als Dekonstruktion," in *Contemplata aliis tradere: Studien zum Verhältnis von Literatur und Spiritualität*, ed. C. Brinker, U. Herzog, et al. (Frankfurt: Lang, 1995), 371–90; and "Penser la finitude: Création, détachement et les limites de la philosophie dans la pensée de maître Eckhart," *Revue des sciences religieuses* 71 (1997): 458–73; Marie-Anne Vannier, "Déconstruction de l'individualité ou assomption de la personne chez Eckhart?" in *Indi-*

viduum und Individualität im Mittelalter, ed. Jan A. Aertsen and Andreas Speer (Berlin: Walter de Gruyter, 1996), 622–41; and Robert Dobie, "Meister Eckhart's Metaphysics of Detachment," *The Modern Schoolman* 80 (2002): 35–54.

468. Detachment, or cutting off (*abescheiden*), appears in many MHG sermons; see, e.g., Prr. *2, 7, 10,* 11, *12,* 15, 21, 23, *27,* 28, 29, 30, 38, 42, 43, 44, 46, 48, *52,* 53, 54a, 57, 60, 61, 67, 68, 69, 73, 74, 75, *77, 103, 104* (with the more significant appearances emphasized). Both the RdU and the BgT also offer treatments (e.g., DW 5:28–29, 114, 194–98, 200, 205–6, 224–31, 244–45, 275–76, 280–84, 290–309). In addition, there is the pseudo-Eckhartian treatise *Von abegescheidenheit* (Vab) edited in DW 5:377–437. Even if not by Eckhart himself, the work, at least in large part, is close to his teaching. The parallels in Eckhart's Latin works are not in terms of terminology, but in content: the oft-repeated message of *abnegatio sui,* following the model of Christ. See, e.g., In Ioh. n. 290 (LW 3:242.4–6): . . . volens filius dei fieri, verbum caro factum in se habitare debet diligere proximum tamquam se ipsum, hoc est tantum quantum se ipsum, abnegare personale, abnegare proprium.

469. On the importance of *entbilden,* see Wackernagel, *YMAGINE DENUDARI.*

470. These terms (*abegescheidenheit* and *glâzenheit*) appear as synonyms in RdU 21 (DW 5:283.8). In RdU 2 (DW 5:194.3–9) Eckhart uses the verbal form *sich lâzen*: Er sol sich selber lâzen ze dem êrsten, sô hât er alliu dinc gelâzen. Such verb forms are more common in his sermons.

471. Mieth (*Die Einheit von Vita Activa und Vita Contemplativa*) says: "So ist die Abgeschiedenheitslehre nichts anders als eine Lehre von der Freiheit . . ." (p. 152).

472. Vab (DW 5:413.3–4): Und dû solt wizzen: laere sîn aller crêâtûre ist gotes vol sîn, und vol sîn aller crêâtûre ist gotes laere sîn (*Essential Eckhart,* 288).

473. In Ioh. n. 397 (LW 3:338.10–11): Secundo patet quod quanto quid reliquerit plura et est pauperior, tanto invenit plura; et quod reliquerit, invenit nobilius et purius. Cf. S. XXXVII n. 375 (LW 4:320–21).

474. The relation of Eckhart's "deconstruction" to contempoary philosophies of deconstruction, especially that of Jacques Derrida, has received attention lately. See John D. Caputo, "Mysticism and Transgression: Derrida and Meister Eckhart," in *Derrida and Deconstruction,* ed. Hugh J. Silverman (London: Routledge, 1989), 24–39; Largier, "Repräsentation und Negativität"; Marius Buning, "Negativity Then and Now: an Exploration of Meister Eckhart, Angelus Silesius and Jacques Derrida," *The Eckhart Review* (Spring 1995): 19–35; and most recently Ian Almond, "How *Not* to Deconstruct a Dominican: Derrida on God and 'Hypertruth,'" *Journal of the American Academy of Religion* 68 (2000): 329–44.

475. RdU 3 (DW 5:191–96).

476. DW 5:193.3: Dar umbe hebe an dir selber an ze dem êrsten und lâz dich (my trans.).

477. DW 5:196.4: Nim dîn selbes war, und swâ dû dich vindest, dâ lâz dich; daz ist daz aller beste (my trans.).

478. Alois M. Haas, *NIM DIN SELBES WAR: Studien zur Lehre von der Selbsterkenntnis bei Meister Eckhart, Johannes Tauler und Heinrich Seuse* (Freiburg, Switzerland: Universitätsverlag, 1971), chapter 1, especially pp. 20–75. Haas shows how Eckhart's view conflicts with that of Thomas Aquinas, who denied that the soul can know itself *per essentiam* (STh Ia, q. 87, a. 1, and *De veritate* q. 10, a. 8).

479. DW 5:205.2–4: Diz waerlîche haben gotes liget an dem gemüete und an einem inniclîchen vernünftigen zuokêrene und meinenne gotes, niht an einem staeten anegedenkene in einer glîchen wîse, wan daz waere unmügelich der natûre . . . (my trans.).

480. DW 5:279.7–8: Ze keiner wîse enist unsers stânnes in disem lebene, noch nie menschen enwart, swie verre er ouch ie kam (Walshe 3:47).

481. DW 5:281.5–8: Got gegap sich nie noch engibet sich niemer in deheinen vremden willen. Niht engibet er sich dan in sîn selbes willen. Swâ got sînen willen vindet, dâ gibet er sich în und laezet sich in den mit allem dem, waz er ist (Walshe 3:48).

482. DW 5:282.11–283.4: Als lange lerne man sich lâzen, biz daz man niht eigens enbeheltet. . . . Man sol sich selber und mit allem dem sînen in einem lûtern entwerdenne willen

und begerennes legen in den guoten und liebesten willen gotes mit allem dem, daz man wellen und begern mac in allen dingen (my trans.).

483. On the relation between Porete and Eckhart's Pr. 52, see Colledge and Marler, "'Poverty of Will': Ruusbroec, Eckhart, and *The Mirror of Simple Souls*"; Ruh, *Meister Eckhart*, 99–104; Sells, *Mystical Languages of Unsaying*, chapter 7; Hollywood, *Soul as Virgin Wife*, chapter 7; and the papers of Lichtmann, Hollywood, and Sells in *Meister Eckhart and the Beguine Mystics*.

484. The text of Pr. 52 can be found in DW 2:486–506. For a commentary and bibliography, see Largier, *Meister Eckhart* 1:1050–60. The most recent commentaries are those of Kurt Flasch, "Predigt 52: 'Beati pauperes spiritu,'" *Lectura Eckhardi I*, 163–99; and Milem, *Unspoken Word*, chapter 2.

485. On the soul becoming free of God compare Pr. 52 (DW 2:492.7, and 493.8) with Porete's *Mirouer* chapter 92 (ed., 258–60).

486. Sells, *Mystical Languages of Unsaying*, 193.

487. Pr. 52 (DW 2:506.1–3): Wer dise rede niht enverstât, der enbekümber sîn herze niht dâ mite. Wan als lange der mensche niht glîch enist dirre wârheit, als lange ensol er dise rede niht verstân: wan diz ist ein unbedahtiu wârheit, diu dâ komen ist ûz dem herzen gotes âne mittel (*Essential Eckhart*, 203).

488. For a treatment of the virtues in Eckhart, see Dietmar Mieth, "Die theologische Transposition der Tugendethik bei Meister Eckhart," in *Abendländische Mystik im Mittelalter*, 63–79.

489. Turner, *Darkness of God*, 179.

490. Vab (DW 5:411.12–412.6): Hie solt dû wizzen, daz rehtiu abegescheidenheit niht anders enist, wan der geist alsô unbeweglich stande gegen allen zuovellen liebes und leides, êren, schanden und lasters. . . . Wan daz got ist got, daz hât er von sîner unbeweglîchen abegescheidenheit, und von der abegescheidenheit hât er sîne lûterkeit und sîne einvalticheit und sîne unwandelbaerkeit (*Essential Eckhart*, 288).

491. Pr. 27 (DW 2:43.6–44.1): . . . daz diu minne, mit der wir minnen, diu sol sîn alsô lûter, alsô blôz, alsô abegescheiden, daz si niht ensol geneiget sîn weder ûf mich noch ûf mînen vriunt noch neben sich (Walshe 1:104). The triple formula (*lûter-blôz-abegescheiden*) occurs eight times in the sermon.

492. Pr. 27 (DW 2:45.10–46.2): Und ist, daz dîn minne alsô lûter, alsô abegescheiden, alsô blôz ist in ir selber, daz dû niht anders enminnest dan güete und got, sô ist daz ein sicher wârheit, daz alle tugende, die alle menschen ie geworhten, die sint dîn alsô volkomenlîche, als ob dû sie selber geworht haetest . . . (Walshe 1:104–5).

493. Three of the condemned articles (nos. 7, 8, and 9) can be said to be conclusions from pure detachment insofar as they are expressions of the detached person's inability to desire or pray for any reward.

494. On compelling God in the MHG sermons, see, e.g., Prr. 14, 20a (DW 1:235, 328); Prr. 25, 26, 40, 41, 43, 51 (DW 2:8–9, 29 and 34–35, 280–81, 296–97, 319, 476); Prr. 63, 65, 73 (DW 3:81–82, 97–98, 269); Prr. 93 and 103 (DW 4:132, 484).

495. Pr. 48 (DW 2:415.1–3): Ze glîcher wîs alsô spriche ich von dem menschen, der sich selben vernihtet hât in im selben und in gote und in allen crêatûren: der mensche hât die niderste stat besezzen, und in den menschen muoz sich got alzemâle ergiezen, oder er enist niht got (*Essential Eckhart*, 197).

496. On the "I" in Eckhart, see Mojsisch, *Meister Eckhart*, 118–20; and "'Ce moi': La conception du moi de Maître Eckhart: Une contribution aux 'Luminaries' du Moyen-Age," *Revue des sciences religieuses* 70 (1996): 18–30; Haas, ". . . DAS PERSÖNLICHE UND EIGENE VERLEUGNEN'"; Largier, "Intellekttheorie, Hermeneutik, Allegorie: Subjekt und Subjektivität bei Eckhart von Hochheim"; and Marie-Anne Vannier, "Déconstruction de l'individualité ou assomption de la personne chez Eckhart?" in *Individuum und Individualität im Mittelalter*, ed. Jan A. Aertsen and Andreas Speer (Berlin and New York: Walter de Gruyter, 1996), 622–41.

497. Pr. 28 (DW 2:68.4–5): "Ego," daz wort "ich," enist nieman eigen dan got aleine in sîner einicheit (my trans.). See also Pr. 77 (DW 3:341); In Ex. nn. 14 and 264 (LW 2:20 and 213); and S. XXII n. 213 (LW 4:197–99).

498. Pr. 52 (DW 2:503.6–504.3): In mîner geburt, dâ wurden alliu dinc geborn, und ich was sache mîn selbes und aller dinge; und haete ich gewolt, ich enwaere niht, noch alliu dinc enwaeren niht; und enwaere ich niht, sô enwaere ouch got niht. Daz got got ist, des bin ich ein sache . . . (*Essential Eckhart*, 203, modified). Milem (*Unspoken Word*, 23–48) has penetrating reflections on the ambiguity of the "I" in this sermon. For a comparable text, see Pr. 83 (DW 3:44.4–8). In the same Pr. 28 in which Eckhart says that *ich* belongs only to God, he goes on to say: 'Vos', daz wort sprichet als vil als 'ir', daz ist ir ein sît in der einicheit, daz ist: daz wort 'ego' und 'vos', 'ich' und 'ir', daz meinet die einicheit (68.5–69.2). For more on the transcendental "I" in this sermon, see 63.3–7.

499. BgT 1 (DW 5:11.12–14): . . . sô müezen sie ir selbes entbildet werden und in got aleine überbildet und in gote und ûz gote geborn werden (my trans.). For other appearances of *entbilden* in the BgT, see DW 5:12.22, 21.8, 27.6, 112.19, and 116.16. See Wackernagel, *YMAGINE DENUDARI*, 66–78.

500. RdU 21 (DW 5:281.8–9): Und ie wir mêr des unsern entwerden, ie mêr in disem gewaerlîcher werden (my trans.). Eckhart also uses *entwerden* in 283.3.

501. Wackernagel, *YMAGINE DENUDARI*, 78.

502. Many of Eckhart's MHG sermons mention the birth of the Word, and more than a few make it their major theme. Among the treatments (with more important analyses emphasized), see especially Prr. *2*, 3, *4*, 5a, 5b, *6*, *10*, 11, 12, 13, 14, 16b, 18, 19, *22*, 24, *25*, 26, 28, *29*, 30, 31, 37, *38*, *39*, 40, 41, 42, *43*, 44, 46, 49, 50, 54b, 59, *75*, 76, 84, 86, *87*, 91, 98, 91, and *101–104*. In addition, the BgT has a number of important considerations (e.g., DW 5:9–11, 26, 33, 35, 41–46, 114–14). The birthing motif is less prevalent in the Latin works, but still found in such passages as In Gen. II nn. 180, 191 (LW 1:650, 663); In Sap. nn. 55, 67, *279–88* (LW 2:383, 395, 611–22); In Ioh. nn. 118–19, 341, 573 (LW 3:103–04, 290, 500); SS. VI nn. 57–59, *XL n. 405*, XLII nn. 422–23, XLIV n. 441, LI n. 518, LV n. 544 (LW 4:56–59, 344–45, 355–56, 43, 455–56). The literature on this aspect of Eckhart's mysticism is too extensive to be summarized. An older study that still is helpful is Shizuteru Ueda, *Die Gottesgeburt in der Seele und der Durchbruch zur Gott: Die mystische Anthropologie Meister Eckharts und ihre Konfrontation mit der Mystik der Zen-Buddhismus* (Gütersloh: Mohn, 1965).

503. Prr. 101–04 (DW 4:279–610). These sermons were first edited by Pfeiffer as nos. I–IV of his edition (*Meister Eckhart*, 3–30). There is a translation of Pfeiffer's version in Walshe 1:1–47. Steer analyzes the cycle in "Meister Eckharts Predigtzyklus *von der êwigen geburt*: Mutmassungen über die Zeit seiner Entstehung," in *Deutsche Mystik im abendländische Zusammenhang*, 253–81. See also Steer, "Predigt 101: 'Dum medium silentium tenerent omnia,'" in *Lectura Eckhardi I*, 247–88. What follows here is an abbreviated version of my analysis of this cycle in chapter 4 of *The Mystical Thought of Meister Eckhart*.

504. During the cycle Eckhart several times adverts to speaking to a learned and pious audience (e.g., Pr. 101; Pr. 104A [DW 4: 336–37 and 354–55; 607]). The sermons' affinities with the RdU and the Wisdom commentary argue for an early date.

505. The Introit from the the Old Latin version of the Bible reads "Dum medium silentium tenerent omnia et nox in suo cursu medium iter haberet, omnipotens sermo tuus, Domine, de caelis a regalibus sedibus venit." Eckhart silently added Job 4:12: "Porro ad me dictum est verbum absconditum." He then translated this into MHG as: . . . 'dô alliu dinc wâren enmitten in einem swîgenne, dô kam von oben her nider von dem küniclîchen stuole' 'in mich ein verborgen wort' (Pr. 101 in DW 4:338.11–12; my trans.).

506. Theisen, *Predigt und Gottesdienst*, 552.

507. Pr. 101.15–16 (DW 4:338.15–339.16): Daz êrste ist, wâ got der vater spreche sîn wort in der sêle und wâ dirre geburt stat sî und wâ si dises werkes enpfenchlic sî (my trans.). This part will be treated in Pr. 101 (DW 4:343.36–353.106) and taken up in more depth in Pr. 102.

508. Pr. 101.28–30 (DW 4:340.28–341.30): . . . oder daz man sich entziehe und ledic

mache von allen gedenken und von allen worten und werken . . . , und daz man sich zemâle halte in einem lûtern gotlîdenne . . . (Walshe 1:2 modified). This question is treated in Pr. 101 (DW 4:354.107–366.202) and explored in more detail in Prr. 103 and 104.

509. Issue 3 takes up the least space; see Pr. 101 (DW 4:366.203–367.224) and Pr. 103 (DW 4:478.39–486.106), but it is also touched upon in other places in the cycle.

510. Pr. 101 (DW 4:343.37–346.54): Ach, herre, wâ ist daz swîgen und wâ ist diu stat, dâ diz wort îngesprochen wirt? . . . Ez ist in dem lûtersten, daz diu sêle geleisten mac, in dem edelesten, in dem grunde, jâ, in dem wesene der sêle, daz ist in dem verborgensten der sêle. . . . Wan daz enist von natûre nihtes enpfenlich dan aleine des götlîchen wesens âne allez mittel. Got gat hie in die sêle mit sînen allen, niht mit sînem teile. Got gât hie in den grunt der sêle (Walshe 1:3).

511. Pr. 101 (DW 4:350.82–84): Got würket in der sêle âne alle mittel, bilde oder glîchnisse, jâ in dem grunde, dâ nie bilde înkam dan er selber mit sînem eigenen wesene (Walshe 1:5). Because the soul can have images of things outside it, but no image of itself, in this context Eckhart also reaffirms his negative anthropology: Und dar umbe sô ist der sêle kein dinc als unbekant als ir selber (Pr. 101 [DW 4:348.65]).

512. As Steer points out ("Pr. 101," 275–76), Eckhart differs markedly from Thomas Aquinas here in denying any form of *species intelligibilis* in the procession of the Son from the Father (e.g., STh Ia, q. 14, a. 2).

513. Pr. 101 (DW 4:352.92): Und in der wâren einunge liget alliu iriu saelicheit.

514. Eckhart makes the transition by means of a second interjection, an objection put by a questioner representing Avicenna (see *Metaphysica* 9.7), who claims that there is nothing in the soul but the images that enable it to become a *saeculum intellectuale/vernünftigiu werlt*. Eckhart decisively rejects this, because it would make true beatitude (i.e., union with God) impossible. See also In Gen. I n. 115 (LW 1:270.13–271.1), Pr. 17 (DW 1:289.1–8), and the discussion in Steer, "Pr. 101," 276–77.

515. Pr. 101 (DW 4:354.112–355.117). Eckhart's caution here, especially with regard to absorbing *aller tugenden wesen*, is reminiscent of Marguerite Porete's teaching about "saying goodbye" to the virtues while preserving their inner meaning (see *Flowering of Mysticism*, 253–54).

516. Pr. 101 (DW 4:355.118–21): Als dâ alle die kreft sint abegezogen . . . sô dû alle dîne krefte ie mê maht *geziehen* in ein vergezzen aller dinge und ir bilde. . . .

517. Robert K. C. Forman, *Meister Eckhart. Mystic as Theologian* (Rockport: Element Books, 1991), chapter 5. Forman discusses nine passages from the German works and two from the Latin, including these texts from Pr. 101 (see 98–101).

518. Forman, *Meister Eckhart*, 115–25.

519. Pr. 101 (DW 4:360.151): Nû möhtest dû sprechen: swaz got würket âne bilde in dem grunde und in dem wesene.

520. Pr. 101 (DW 4:361.155–60): Daz unwizzen ziuhet sie in ein wunder und tuot sie disem nâchjagen, wan si bevindet wol, daz es ist und enweiz aber niht, wie noch waz ez ist. Wenne der mensche weiz der dinge sache, alzehant, sô ist er der dinge müede und suochet aber ein anderz ze ervarne und ze wizzene und quilet und jâmert iemer mê alsô nâch wizenne und enhât doch kein bîblîben. Dar umber, diz unbekante bekantnisse daz enthaltet sie bî disem blîbende und tuot sie disem nâchjagen (my trans.). This may be the earliest vernacular appearance of *docta ignorantia*, a phrase that goes back to Augustine (Ep.130.14.28 [PL 33:505]). The importance of unknowing/not-knowing is a constant throughout Eckhart's works; see Pr. 52 (DW 2:494–97) and Pr. 83 (DW 3:448).

521. See, e.g., Pr. 9 (DW 1:157–58) on the three kinds of *wort*; and the discussion in Pr. 53 (DW 3:528–31).

522. Pr. 101 (DW 4:364.192–365.196): . . . Eyâ, herre, ir wellet der sêle irn natiurlîchen louf umbekêren und wider ir natûre tuon. Ir natûre ist, daz si durch die sinne neme und in bilden. Wellet ir den orden umbekêren? Nein! Waz weist dû, waz adels got geleget habe in die natûre, diu noch niht alliu geschriben ensint, mêr: noch verborgen? (my trans.)

523. Pr. 101 (DW 4:366.209–12): Swie daz ez doch ein unwizzen heize und ein unbekantheit, sô hât ez doch mê inne dan allez wizzen und bekennen ûzwendic disem. Wan diz unwizzen daz reizet und ziuhet dich von allem wizzenden dinge und ouch von dir selber (my trans.).

524. Pr. 101 (DW 4:367.212–20). Rather daringly, Eckhart asserts that a person who has attained this form of "establishment" (*der hie inner rehte stüende*) can never be separated from God, either by mortal or venial sin.

525. Rahner, "Die Gottesgeburt." For twelfth-century uses, see McGinn, *Growth of Mysticism*, 283–84, and 331–32.

526. Pr. 2 is found in DW 1:21–47 (translations are my own unless otherwise noted). Much has been written on this sermon; see, e.g., Schürmann, *Meister Eckhart*, 3–47; Ruh, *Meister Eckhart*, 143–49; Sells, "Pseudo-Woman and the Meister," in *Meister Eckhart and the Beguine Mystics*, 136–40; Hollywood, *Soul as Virgin Wife*, chapter 6; and most recently Milem, *Unspoken Word*, chapter 3. See also the comments and notes on further literature in Largier, *Meister Eckhart,* 1:759–72.

527. Bernard McGinn, "The Language of Love in Jewish and Christian Mysticism," in *Mysticism and Language*, ed. Steven T. Katz (New York: Oxford University Press, 1992), 202–35.

528. One exception is Pr. 22, where Eckhart speaks of the Son's penetration into the hidden chamber of the Fatherhood using the language of the Song (DW 1:387–88).

529. Eckhart was not the first to give attention to the virgin wife, a theme that can be found as early as Origen (see McGinn, *Foundations of Mysticism*, 125).

530. Pr. 2 (DW 1:24.4–6): . . . 'unser herre Jêsus Kristus der gienc ûf in ein bürgelîn und wart enpfangen von einer juncvrouwen, diu ein wîp was.' Here Eckhart surpresses the name of Martha, although in this sermon, as in Pr. 86, she serves as the type of the person who has combined action and contemplation and thus is superior to her purely contemplative sister. Similarly, the Virgin Mary is not named, although she is the exemplar of the motif of the fruitful virgin and the sermon was preached for the Feast of the Assumption. The failure to mention the names may be Eckhart's way of suggesting that each of his hearers should become a Martha and a Virgin Mary.

531. Pr. 2 (DW 1:24.8–25.2): Juncvrouwe ist alsô vil gesprochen als ein mensche, der von allen vremden bilden ledic ist, alsô ledic, als er was, dô er niht enwas.

532. Pr. 2 (DW 1:27.1–9): Nû merket und sehet mit vlîze! Daz nû der mensche iemer mê juncvrouwe waere, sô enkaeme keine vruht von im. Sol er vruhtbaere werden, sô muoz daz von nôt sîn, daz er ein wîp sî. Wîp ist daz edleste wort, daz man der sêle zuo gesprechen mac, und ist vil edeler dan juncvrouwe. Daz der mensche got enpfaehet in im, daz ist guot, und in der enpfenclicheit ist er maget. Daz aber got vruhtbaerlich in im werde, daz ist bezzer; wan vruhtbaerkeit der gâbe daz ist aleine dankbaerkeit der gâbe, und dâ ist der geist ein wîp in der widerbernden dankbaerkeit, dâ er gote widergebirt Jêsum in daz veterlîche herze.

533. Pr. 2 (DW 1:31.1–3): . . . ûz dem aller edelsten grunde; noch baz gesprochen: jâ, ûz dem selben grunde, dâ der vater ûz gebernde sîn êwic wort, dar ûz wirt si vruhtbaere mitgebernde.

534. On the second part of the sermon, see the analysis of Milem, *Unspoken Word*, 71–85.

535. Pr. 2 (DW 1:32.6–9): Wan der êwige vater gebirt sînen êwigen sun in dirre kraft âne underlâz, alsô daz disiu kraft mitgebernde ist den sun des vaters und sich selber den selben sun in der einiger kraft des vaters.

536. Pr. 2 (DW 1:39.4–40.3): . . . ez enist weder diz noch daz; nochdenne ist ez ein waz, daz ist hoeher boben diz und daz dan der himel ob der erde. . . . Ez ist von allen namen vrî und von allen formen blôz, ledic und vrî zemâle, als got ledic und vrî ist in im selber.

537. "Diu selbe kraft dar abe ich gesprochen hân," discussed in 40.4–41.7, must be intellect and not the nameless power, as the parallels of language to the previous discussion of intellect show.

538. Pr. 2 (DW 1:43.9–44.2): Sunder als er ist einvaltic ein, âne alle wîse und eigenschaft:

dâ enist er vater noch sun noch heiliger geist in disem sinne und ist doch ein waz, daz enist noch diz noch daz. This passage was excerpted in the Cologne list; see Proc. Col.I n. 69 (LW 5:223–24), and Eckhart's response in Proc.Col.I n. 147 (LW 5:303). See also Proc.Col.II n. 121 (LW 5:346–47).

539. Milem, *Unspoken Word*, 78.

540. Ibid., 79–85.

541. Hans Urs Von Balthasar, *The Glory of the Lord. A Theological Aesthetics*, volume 5, *The Realm of Metaphysics in the Modern Age* (San Francisco: Ignatius, 1991), 33.

542. See the discussion in chapter 8, pp. 368–77.

543. Eckhart uses the verbal form *durchbrechen*, though his followers, like John Tauler, often employ the noun *durchbruch*. Breaking-through language is less frequent in the MHG sermons than the motifs of detaching and birthing (I count sixteen sermons in which it appears). The essential treatments, including those in which the verb does not appear, but the concept is present, are Pr. 2 (DW 1:43–44), Pr. 7 (DW 1:122), Pr. 12 (DW 1:196–97, on "leaving God for God"), Pr. 22 (DW 1:388, on "going into the secret chamber"), Pr. 26 (DW 2:31–32), Pr. 29 (DW 2:76–77), Pr. 31 (DW 2:121, 144), Pr. 48 (DW 2:420–21, on going into the desert), Pr. 49 (DW 2:448–50), Pr. 51 (DW 2:473), Pr. 52 (DW 2:504–05), Pr. 60 (DW 3:60), Pr. 69 (DW 3:178–80), Pr. 81 (DW 3:401), and Pr. 109 (DW 4:773). There is also an important appearance in a homily that many Eckhart scholars accept as genuine, Sermon Jostes 82 (Franz Jostes, *Meister Eckhart und seine Jünger: Ungedruckte Texte zur Geschichte der deutschen Mystik* [Freiburg, Switzerland: Universitätsbuchhandlung, 1895], 94). Davies has translated this sermon in *Meister Eckhart: Selected Writings*, 241–51.

544. John D. Caputo, "Fundamental Themes of Eckhart's Mysticism," *The Thomist* 42 (1978): 224.

545. Pr. 52 (DW 2:504.6–505.1): Mêr: in dem durchbrechen, dâ ich ledic stân mîn selbes willen und des willen gotes und aller sîner werke und gotes selben, sô bin ich ob allen crêatûren und enbin weder got noch crêatûre, mêr: ich bin, daz ich was und daz ich blîben sol nû und iemermê (*Essential Eckhart*, 203). Similar passages can be found in Prr. 2, 22, 49, etc. One rather different formulation, noted above, is the passage in Pr. 26 (DW 2:31–32) where Eckhart speaks of breaking-through into the Father *insofar as* he is the ground.

546. Pr. 69 (DW 3:179.2–180.1): Vernünfticheit diu dringet în; ir engenüeget niht an güete noch an wîsheit noch an wârheit noch an gote selber. . . . Si brichet in den grunt, dâ güete und wârheit ûzbrichet, und nimet ez *in principio*, . . . Aber vernünfticheit diu scheidet diz allez abe und gât în und durchbrichet in die wurzeln . . . (Walshe 1:298–99).

547. Pr. 29 (DW 2:76.2–77.2): Dirre geist muoz übertreten alle zal und alle menige durchbrechen, und er wirt von gote durchbrochen; und alsô, als er mich durchbrichet, alsô durchbriche ich in wider. Got leitet disen geist in die wüestunge und in die einicheit sîn selbes, dâ er ein lûter ein ist und in im selben quellende ist (Walshe 1:136).

548. See Bernard McGinn, "Ocean and Desert as Symbols of Mystical Absorption in the Christian Tradition," *Journal of Religion* 74 (1994): 155–81. Also useful are Belden C. Lane, *The Solace of Fierce Landscapes: Exploring Desert and Mountain Spirituality* (New York-and Oxford: Oxford University Press, 1998); and Andrew Louth, *The Wilderness of God* (Nashville: Abingdon, 1991).

549. On God as desert, see *Jean Scot: Commentaire sur l'évangile de Jean*, ed. Édouard Jeauneau (SC 180; Paris: Cerf, 1972), 140.

550. *Thomas Gallus: Commentaires du Cantique des Cantiques*, ed. Jeanne Barbet (Paris: J. Vrin, 1967), 67: Desertum est invia et singularis eterne Trinitatis supersubstantialis solitudo, de quo *Exo.* 5: *Deus Hebraeorum vocavit nos ut eamus viam trium dierum in desertum; De div. nom.* 13f.

551. See McGinn, "Ocean and Desert," 167–72, especially on the MHG Sequence "Granum Sinapis," which will be discussed below in chapter 7, pp. 316–18.

552. VeM (DW 5:119.2–7): Wer ist danne edeler wan der einhalp geborn ist von dem hoehsten und von dem besten, daz crêatûren hât, und anderhalp von dem innigsten grunde

götlîcher natûre und des einoede? Ich, sprichet unser herre in dem wîssagen Osee, wil die edeln sêle vüeren in ein einoede, und ich wil dâ sprechen in ir herze ein mit einem, ein von einem, ein in einem und in einem ein êwiclîche. Amen (*Essential Eckhart*, 247). For a comparable passage in the Latin works, see In Gen. II n. 149 (LW 1:618.12–619.1).

553. Here I shall treat only the second part of this sermon, Jostes no. 82 (ed., 91–98), using the translation of O. Davies. This homily, like Pr. 52, has a number of resonances with Marguerite Porete's *Mirror*, including the motif of the three deaths of the soul (see *Mirror* chaps. 54, 60–64, 73, 87, 131; and the discussion in *Flowering of Mysticism*, 257–59). For a translation and commentary of this sermon, see Curzio Cavicchioli, "Meister Eckhart e la morte dello spirito: Un sermone apocrifo," *Rivista di Ascetica e Mistica* 21 (1996): 181–206.

554. Several other sermons of Eckhart treat the kingdom of God, notably Pr. 68 (DW 3:138–52, especially 143.1–144.3 and 151.1–3) on Luke 21:31 (Scitote, quia prope est regnum dei); and S. XXXIV.3–4 (LW 4:302–07) on Luke 17:21 (Quaerite ergo primum regnum dei). See also Pr. 38 (DW 2:233.3–4).

555. A. de Libera, *La mystique rhénane*, 242–48. On *mors mystica*, see Alois M. Haas, "MORS MYSTICA. Ein mystologisches Motiv," in *Sermo mysticus*, 392–480, treating Eckhart on 449–58 (though without mention of this sermon). For other passages on the *mors mystica* in Eckhart, see Prr. 49 and 56 (DW 2:445–46, 589); Pr. 84 (DW 3:462–65); Prr. 95 and 97 (DW 4:195–96, 234–36).

556. Jostes 82 (93.15): Hie verlust die sele all dink, got und all creaturen.

557. Jostes 82 (93.20–26): . . . wann als lang als di sele got hat und got bekent und got weiz, so ist si verre von got. . . . Und daz ist die meist ere, di die sele got tut, daz ist, daz si got im selbe lazze und ste (si) sein ledik.

558. Jostes 82 (94.2–3): . . . so leuhtet ir daz ungeschaffen bild, in dem sich di sele vindet noch ir ungeschaffenheit. . . .

559. Jostes 82 (94.13–18): . . . so durchbricht di sele ir ewigen bild, uf daz si kum, da got ist reich in einikeit. Dar um spricht ein meister, daz der sele *durchbruch* edeler sei denn ir aufluz. . . . Diz durchbrechen daz ist der ander tot dez geistes, der ist vil mer denn der erst. The quotation from "ein meister" (Eckhart himself?) is also found in Pr. 52 (DW 2:504.4), though in Pr. 52 the more usual verbal form of breaking-through is employed: Ein grôz meister sprichet, daz sîn *durchbrechen* edeler sî dan sîn ûzvliezen. . . .

560. Jostes 82 (94.28–30): Als di sele durchbricht und sich verleust in irm ewigen bild, daz ist daz sterben, daz die sele stirbet in got.

561. This is my reading of the obscure passage (Jostes, 95.5–12) in which it seems that the term *natur* should be understood as the Father's personal property, while *wesen* signifies the divine nature or Godhead.

562. Jostes 82 (95.28–36): . . . so enphint di sele ir selbs und get ir eygen weg und ensucht got nimmer; und allhie so stirbet si iren hohsten tot. In disem tot verleuset di sele alle begerung und alle bild und alle verstentnuzz und alle form und wirt beraubt aller wesen. . . . Wann diser geist ist tot und ist begraben in der gotheit, wann di gotheit enlebt nieman anders dann ir selber.

563. Jostes 82 (96.4–5): Als nu di sele also sich verleuset in aller weis, als hie gesagt ist, so vindet di sele daz, daz si daz sel ist, daz si gesucht hat sunder zugank.

564. Jostes 82 (97.4–6): Got ist dor um worden ein ander ich, uf daz ich wurd ein ander er. Also spricht sant Augustinus: Got ist mensch worder, uf daz der mensch got wurd (my trans.). The reference to Augustine is probably Ep. 342 (PL 39:1534), as noted by Davies.

565. In Ioh. n. 547 (LW 3:477.10–11): . . . omne autem desiderium et eius quies est uniri deo. . . .

566. Most treatments of Eckhart discuss his teaching about mystical union, but few studies take this as their focus. See, however, Richard Kieckhefer, "Meister Eckhart's Conception of Union with God," *Harvard Theological Review* 71 (1978): 203–25.

567. Pr. 83 (DW 3:443.5–7): Dv solt alzemal entzinken diner dinisheit vnd solt zer fliesen in sine sinesheit vnd sol din din vnd sin sin éin min werden als genzlich, das dv mit ime ver-

standest ewiklich sin vngewordene istikeit vnd sin vngenanten nitheit (my trans.). On this text, see Morard, "Ist, istic, istikeit bei Meister Eckhart," 172–75.

568. Pr. 40 (DW 2:274.10–12): Aber zwischen dem menschen und gote enist niht aleine niht underscheit, sunder dâ enist ouch kein menige; dâ enist niht wan ein (*Teacher and Preacher*, 301). There are many such passages in Eckhart; e.g., Pr. 9 (DW 1:106.1–3); Prr. 58, 59 (DW 2:614–16, 631–32).

569. Eckhart repeats constantly that union must be *sine medio/âne mittel*. For a few typical expressions, see In Gen. II n. 146 (LW 1:615); In Sap. nn. 282–84 (LW 2:614–16); Prr. 62, 76, 81 (DW 3:64, 323–24, 400–401).

570. Pr. 25 (DW 2:11.1–4): Swenne der wille alsô vereinet wirt, daz ez wirt ein einic ein, sô gebirt der vater von himelrîche sînen eingebornen sun in sich in mich. War umbe in sich in mich? Dâ bin ich ein mit im, er enmac mich ûzgesliezen niht, und in dem werke dâ enpfaehet der heilige geist sîn wesen und sîn werden von mir als von gote. War umbe? Dâ bin ich in gote (Walshe 1:93 modified).

571. Although indistinction goes beyond ordinary ontology, Eckhart occasionally speaks of union as "substantial" or "essential" (*weselîch*, etc.); see, e.g., Pr. 76 (DW 3:320.5–6): . . . âne allen underscheit werden wir daz selbe wesen und substancie und natûre, diu er [got] selber ist; and Pr. 76 (DW 3:327.3–4): Und ich bin wol übergesast in daz götlich wesen, sô wirt got mîn und swaz er hât.

572. In Sap. n. 282 (LW 2:614.13–615.1): Deus autem indistinctus est, et anima amat indistingui, id est unum esse et fieri cum deo.

573. Eckhart employs John 17:21 to ground his teaching on indistinct union in In Sap. n. 44 (LW 2:366); In Ioh. nn. 130, 383, 548 (LW 3:112, 326, 478); Pr. 46 (DW 2:383, 388); Prr. 64, 65 (DW 3:88–90, 100–101); BgT 1 (DW 5:33).

574. S. XXX n. 314 (LW 4:276.7–8): Unum autem, non unus, omnes sancti in deo. See S. XLIV n. 441 (LW 4:369.12–13): . . . omnes tamen 'in eandem imaginem' transformantur et in ipso filio deo unum sunt.

575. Eckhart does distinguish from time-to-time between the perfect union to come in heaven and what is attainable in this life (e.g., Pr. 86 [DW 3:486.3–9]). On the union to come in heaven, see Pr. 7 (DW 1:118) and Pr. 39 (DW 2:265–66). As Tobin puts it (*Meister Eckhart*, 114) in commenting on the latter text: ". . . even in heaven the human spirit exists in a condition including both the birth as a state implying utter oneness with the divine existence, and the birth as an incomplete and ongoing process."

576. Pr. 5b (DW 1:93.6–94.1): Ganc dîn selbes alzemâle ûz durch got, sô gât got alzemâle sîn selbes ûz durch dich. Dâ disiu zwei ûzgânt, swaz dâ blîbet, daz ist ein einvaltigez ein. In disem ein gebirt der vater sînen sun in dem innersten gequelle. Dâ blüejet ûz der heilige geist (my trans.).

577. Pr. 12 (DW 1:201.5–8): Daz ouge, dâ inne ich got sihe, daz ist daz selbe ouge, dâ ine mich got sihet; mîn ouge und gotes ouge daz ist éin ouge und éin gesiht und éin bekennen und éin minnen (*Teacher and Preacher*, 270). See also Pr. 69 (DW 3:175.5). In Pr. 10 the same formula is applied to knowledge (DW 1:162.2–4) and to love (168.4–7). A basis for this formulation in Aristotelian theory of vision is often mentioned in the Latin works; see, e.g., In Gen. II n. 33 (LW 1:501); In Ex. n. 125 (LW 2:116–17); In Ioh. nn. 107, 505 (LW 3:91–92, 436). On the use of the eye in Eckhart's works, see Gudrun Schleusener-Eichholz, *Das Auge im Mittelalter*, 2 vols. (Munich: Fink, 1985), 1:116–28; and Jeffrey F. Hamburger, *St. John the Divine: The Deified Evangelist in Medieval Art and Theology* (Berkeley: University of California Press, 2002), 192–95.

578. Pr. 76 (DW 3:310.3–4): Ez ist ze wizzenne, daz daz ein ist nâch dingen: got bekennen und von gote bekant ze sîne und got sehen und von gote gesehen ze sînne (Walshe 1:63).

579. In Ioh. n. 506 (LW 3:437.12–13): . . . eo quod una sit facies et imago in qua deus nos videt et nos ipsum . . . . See the whole passage in nn. 506–9 (LW 3:437–41) and the parallel texts noted there.

580. RdU 6 (DW 5:205.2–5; Walshe 3:17–18 modified).

581. See Mieth, *Die Einheit von Vita Activa und Vita Contemplativa*, 215; Turner, *Darkness of God*, 171–72; Tobin, *Meister Eckhart*, 186–92; and Kieckhefer, "Meister Eckhart's Conception of Union," 211–14.

582. McGinn, *Flowering of Mysticism*, 13–14.

583. Pr. 66 (DW 3:113.8–114.2): Ich spriche aber mê—erschricket niht, wan disiu vröude diu ist iu nâhe, und si ist in iu—ez enist iuwer keinez sô grop noch sô kleine von verstantnisse noch sô verre, er enmüge dise vröude in im vinden in der wârheit, als si ist, mit vröude und mit verstânne, ê daz ir tâlanc ûz dirre kirchen komet, jâ, ê daz ich tâlanc gepredige; er mac ezals waerlîchen in im vinden und leben und haben, als daz got got ist und ich mensche bin! (Walshe 2:93 modified). Eckhart repeats this almost word-for-word later in the sermon (118.13–119.6).

584. Paul's rapture, described as an *exstasis mentis*, is mentioned in one of Eckhart's earliest works, e.g., *Sermo in die B. Augustini* n. 6 (LW 5:94–95). He gives it an extended treatment in S. XXII nn. 213–16 (LW 4:197–203), quoting Thomas Aquinas. In the vernacular sermons, Eckhart refers to the rapture a number of times: Pr. 23 (DW 1:404–07); Prr. 61, 80, 86 (DW 3:36–40, 381, 483 and 486–87); Prr. 101, 102, and 104 (DW 4:362–63, 412–13, and 573–76). In addition, Eckhart discusses the rapture of St. Benedict in Pr. 73 (DW 3:259).

585. On the uses of the terms *gezücket/enzücket*, see the fifteen passages studied by Forman, *Meister Eckhart*, 95–125. Other appearances can now be added; e.g., Pr. 87 (DW 4:22.22). A comparable term is *gerucket/ergerucket* as used in Pr. 75 (DW 3:297–98).

586. The term *gebrûchenne/gebrûchunge* occur a number of times, for example, in Prr. 49, 52, 59 (DW 2:447, 492 and 493 and 497, 626); Prr. 84, 86 (DW 3:465, 487); Pr. 90 (DW 4:62). It also appears in RdU 20 (DW 5:270).

587. Pr. 41 (DW 2:291.9–292.1): Sie minent got umbe iht anders, daz got niht enist. Und eht in wirt, daz sie dâ minnent, sô enruochent sie umbe got niht. Ez sî andâht oder lust oder swaz dir wol kaeme; ez enist allez got niht, swaz dâ geschaffen ist (Walshe 2:4 modified).

588. Pr. 6 (DW 1:99–115). This sermon has the distinction of being the one from which the largest number of incriminating articles were taken during the Cologne proceedings. For recent commentaries, see Kurt Flasch, "Predigt 6: 'Iusti vivent in aeternum,'" in *Lectura Eckhardi II*, 29–51; and Milem, *Unspoken Word*, chapter 5. The theme of *justitia* occurs less often in the MHG texts than in the Latin, but see Prr. 10, 16b, 24 (DW 1:161 and 174, 272–73, 421–22); Prr. 28, 29, 39, 41, 46 (DW 2:62–63, 82, 251–63, 288–89, 384–85); and BgT 1 (DW 5:9–13, 18).

589. "In agro dominico" arts. 8, 9, and 10, all condemned as heretical, are taken from Pr. 6 (DW 1:100.4–6, 112.6–9, and 110.8–111.6). In addition, art. 22, said to be rash, etc., is taken from 109.7–110.2: Der vater gebirt sînen sun âne underlâz, und ich sprich mêr: er gebirt mich sînen sun und den selben sun. Ich spriche mêr: er gebirt mich niht aleine sînen sun; mêr: er gebirt mich sich und sich mich und mich sîn wesen und sîn natûre. In dem innersten quelle dâ quille ich ûz in dem heiligen geiste, dâ ist éin leben und éin wesen und éin werk. Allez waz got würket, daz ist ein; dar umbe gebirt er mich sînen sun âne allen underscheit.

590. Pr. 6 (DW 1:113.7–114.5): Got und ich, wir sint ein. Mit bekennenne nime ich got in mich, mit minnenne gân ich in got. . . . Got und ich wir sint ein in disem gewürke; er würket, und ich gewerde (my trans.). For more on union as an activity in which God works and the soul passively receives the working, see Pr. 48 (DW 2:416–17) and Pr. 83 (DW 3:447). Eckhart summarizes the essence of *beatitudo* realized in the birth of the Son in the soul in S. IX n. 100 (LW 4:95.3–4) as follows: Quae gloria sive beatitudo consistit in uno eodem active in deo, passive in anima. In Pr. 21 Eckhart seems to contradict the notion that union is an activity by saying that love does not really unite us to God, because it unifies in work but not in being (*minne eneiniget niht; si einiget wol an einem werke, niht an einem wesene*: DW 1:360.3–4). The contradiction disappears if we think of Eckhart as talking about a human work here, not as the divine work done in us when we are unified in the God in whom there is no distinction between *wesen* and *werke*.

591. S. XI n. 115 (LW 4:109.1–2): . . . in essentia, ut intellectiva, sic copulatur sui supremo deo, secundum Rabbi Moysen, sic est 'genus dei'. The reference to Maimonides is to *Guide* 3.53. On intellect and union, see also In Ioh. nn. 673, 697 (LW 3:587–88, 612).

592. S. XXIX n. 304 (LW 4:270.1–5): Deus enim unus est intellectus, et intellectus est deus unus. . . . Ascendere igitur ad intellectum, subdi ipsi, est uniri deo.

593. On knowledge rather than love as uniting us with God, see Prr. 7, 9, and 21 (DW 1:122–23, 152–53, 360–63). In S. VI n. 64 (LW 4:62–63) Eckhart analyzes the relation between *voluntas/caritas* and *intellectus/beatitudo* as that between a *dispositio* and a *forma substantialis*, asserting: Iterum per ipsam solam [caritatem] boni sumus, intellectu autem nudo et supernudo non boni, sed beati sumus (62.4–5). Cf. In Ioh. n. 697 (LW 3:612).

594. Eckhart's opponents, who placed true *beatitudo* in reflexive knowing, seem to have included John Quidort and Durandus of St. Pourçain. See Alain de Libera, "On Some Philosophical Aspects of Meister Eckhart's Teaching," *Freiburger Zeitschrift für Philosophie und Theologie* 45 (1998): 160–63; and Largier, *Meister Eckhart,* 2:786–88.

595. VeM (DW 5:116.28–117.2): . . . wan daz êrste, dâ saelicheit ane geliget, daz ist, sô diu sêle schouwet got blôz. Dâ nimet si allez ir wesen und ir leben und schepfet allez, daz si ist, von dem grunde gotes und enweiz von wizzenne niht noch von minne noch vin nihte alzemâle. Si gestillet ganze und aleine in dem wesen gotes, si enweiz niht dan wesen dâ und got (my trans.).

596. VeM (DW 5:118.23–24): . . . und herwider komen daz ist wizzen und bekennen, daz man got bekennet und weiz. Eckhart also insisted on the direct nature of the vision of beatitude in In Ioh. nn. 108, 678–79 (LW 3:93, 594).

597. Pr. 60 (DW 3:22.2–23.1): Cherubîn bezeichent die wîsheit, daz ist die bekantnisse; diu treget got in die sêle und leitet die sêle an got. Aber in got enmac si sie niht bringen. . . . Sô tritet diu oberste kraft her vür—daz ist diu minne—und brichet in got und leitet die sêle mit der bekantnisse und mit allen irn kreften in got und vereinet si mit gote; und dâ würket got obe der sêle kraft, niht als in der sêle, sunder als in gote götlich (Walshe 2:15 modified). There is a comparable passage in S. VI n. 52 (LW 4:51).

598. De Libera (*La mystique rhénane*, 278–79 and 312 n. 176) argues for two conceptions of union in Eckhart, an earlier intellectualist view, and a later "Proclian" view centering on the One, but it is not evident that the difference is chronological.

599. Pr. 71 (DW 3:215.9–11): . . . ein ander vernünfticheit, diu dâ niht ensuochet, diu dâ stât in irm lûtern einvaltigen wesene, daz dâ begriffen ist in dem liehte (*Teacher and Preacher*, 321).

600. Prr. 39, 43 (DW 2:265.1–266.3, 329.3–330.3); Pr. 52 (DW 2:495.6–496.5); and Pr. 83 (DW 3:448.1–9).

601. Pr. 7 (DW 1:122.8–123.3): Ich spriche: noch bekantnisse noch minne eneiniget niht. . . . Minne nimet got under einem velle, . . . Des entuot vernünfticheit niht; vernünfticheit nimet got, als er in ir bekant ist; dâ enkan si in niemer begriffen in dem mer sîner gruntlôsicheit (*Teacher and Preacher*, 254 modified).

602. Pr. 42 (DW 2:304.1–2): Dâ diu verstantnisse und diu begerunge endet, dâ ist ez vinster, dâ liuhtet got (Walshe 2:236).

603. Eckhart used the example of the transformation of the bread and wine into the eucharistic body and blood of Christ as a model for this process. See Pr. 6 (DW 1:110.8–111.7), a passage condemned as heretical in art. 10 of "In agro dominico." See also RdU (DW 5:265–66, 268–69).

604. S. LIV n. 532 (LW 4:448.3–8): Sic anima, ut deum videat, debet primo deo configurari per transfigurationem. . . . Secundo debet exaltari et depurari. Tertio eximi ab omni imperfecto. . . . Item debet eximi et transcendere se ipsam, ut natura est, ... Item eximi a corpore et materia, ut possit super se redire et deum intus in se ipsa invenire. See also In Sap. n. 64 (LW 2:392). MHG sermons also take divinization as a theme; e.g., Prr. 6, 40, 44, etc.

605. In Ex. n. 247 (LW 2:201.7–11): Adhuc autem secundo proprium est deo, ut non habeat quare extra se aut praeter se. Igitur omne opus habens quare ipsum ut sic non est div-

inum nec fit deo. . . . Qui ergo operatur quippiam non propter deum, non erit opus divinum, utpote habens quare, quod alienum est deo et a deo, non deus nec divinum. For comparable passages, see S. IV n. 21 (LW 4:22–23), and In Ioh. n. 50 (LW 3:139).

606. Pr. 41 (DW 2:293.1–2): Alsus sô wirt der sun in uns geborn: daz wir sî sunder warumbe und werden wider îngeborn in dem sune (my trans.).

607. On Beatrice, see McGinn, *Flowering of Mysticism*, 166–74.

608. *Beatrijs van Nazareth. Seven Manieren van Minne*, "Dander maniere der minnen" (7.4–6): . . . allene met minnen, sonder enich waeromme ende sonder eneghen loen van gratien van glorien . . . (my trans.).

609. Marguerite Porete, *Mirror*, chapters 81, 93, 134, and 135 (ed., 232–33, 260, 394, 397), and the discussion in McGinn, *Flowering of Mysticism*, 257, 264.

610. The language of *âne warumbe* and cognates is more often employed in the MHG works, but is also found in the Latin writings: (I) MHG: Prr. 1, 5a, 5b, 6, 12 (DW 1: 9, 80–81, 90 and 92, 113 and 115, 199–200); Prr. 26, 27, 28, 29, 39, 41, 59 (DW 2:26–27, 45–46, 59, 77 and 80, 253–54 and 266, 289 and 293, 625–26); Pr. 62 (DW 3:66–67); Bgt 1 (DW 5:43–44); RdU 21 (DW 5:282); (II) Latin: In Ex. n. 247 (LW 2:201); In Eccli. n. 59 (LW 2:287–88); In Sap. n. 187 (LW 2:523); In Ioh. n. 50 (LW 3:41); SS. IV n. 21, VI n. 59 (LW 4:22–23, 58). On this aspect of Eckhart's thought, see John D. Caputo, *The Mystical Element in Heidegger's Thought* (Athens: Ohio University Press, 1978), chapter 3, "The Rose Is Without a Why."

611. Pr. 12 (DW 1:199–200). See In Eccli. n. 59 (LW 2:287.12–13): Exemplum posset poni, si dicatur aliquis currere propter currere.

612. For an analysis of living without a why as an anti-teleological ethic, see John M. Connolly, "Teleology as the (frustrated) Pursuit of Happiness: Meister Eckhart on 'living without a why'" (unpublished). My thanks to the author for sharing this paper with me.

613. Pr. 28 (DW 2:59.6–7): Wer nû wonet in der güete sîner natûre, der wonet in gotes minne, und diu mine enhât kein warumbe (my trans.).

614. In Ioh. n. 734 (LW 3:641.3–7): Amans enim ut sic non quaerit amari. Alienum est ipsi omne quod non est amare. Hoc solum novit, liberum est, sui gratia est. . . . Amat, ut amet, amorem amat. This is close to Bernard's *Super Cantica* 84.4 (*Opera* 2:300.5–6): Amo, quia amo; amo, ut amem. See also S. VI n. 75 (LW 4:71.9–10): Amans vere et verus amor nisi amare nescit.

615. Bernard, *De diligendo Deo* 1.1 (*Opera* 3:119.19): Causa dilgendi Deum, Deus est; modus, sine modo diligere. Eckhart cites this five times: In Ioh. nn. 369, 414 (LW 3:314, 351); Pr. 9 (DW 1:144); Pr. 82 (DW 3:430–31); and in Proc.Col.II n. 84 (LW 5:339). On the influence of Bernard on Eckhart, see Bernard McGinn, "St. Bernard and Meister Eckhart," especially 382–84; and Georg Steer, "Bernhard von Clairvaux als theologische Authorität für Meister Eckhart, Johannes Tauler und Heinrich Seuse," in *Bernhard von Clairvaux: Rezeption und Wirkung im Mittelalter und in der Neuzeit*, ed. Kaspar Elm (Wiesbaden: Harrassowitz, 1994), 249–59.

616. In Ioh. n. 307 (LW 3:255.2–3): Bonitas autem principaliter et formaliter ut moralis consistit in actu interiori. . . . See In Gen. II nn. 131, 165–66 (LW 1:596, 634–36); In Eccli. n. 26 (LW 2:253); In Sap. nn. 117, 224 (LW 2:453–54, 559); In Ioh. nn. 380, 583–86 (LW 3:323–24, 510–13). The same teaching can be found in BgT 1 (DW 5:38–40) and RdU 16 (DW 5:247–48).

617. These are the four conclusions that Eckhart reaches in his longest treatment of the relation of interior and exterior act, In Gen. II n. 165–66 (LW 1:634–66). This passage was the source for two of the four condemned articles on the relation of the interior and exterior work: "In agro dominico" arts. 16 and 17.

618. In Proc.Col.I n. 124 (LW 5:292) Eckhart incorrectly cites STh IaIIae, q. 20, a .4, as holding the same view he had advanced.

619. Pr. 104A.159–73 (DW 4:580.159–581.173): Dâ enist niht dan einez, wan man engrîfet niergen dan in dem selben grunde der schouwunge und maht daz vruhtbaere in der würkunge; und dâ wirt diu meinunge der schouwunge volbrâht. . . . Alsô in dirre würklicheit enhât man anders niht dan eine schouwelicheit in gote: daz eine ruowet in dem andern unde volbringet daz ander (my trans.).

620. Mieth, *Die Einheit von Vita Activa und Vita Contemplativa;* and more recently, "Predigt 86: 'Intravit Iesus in quoddam castellum,'" *Lectura Eckhardi II,* 139–77. See also Largier, *Meister Eckhart* 2:739–47, as well as Alois M. Haas, "Die Beurteilung der Vita contemplativa und vita activa in der Dominikanermystik des 14. Jahrhunderts," in *Gottleiden-Gottlieben,* 97–108. In English, see Blake R. Heffner, "Meister Eckhart and a Millennium with Mary and Martha," in *Biblical Hermeneutics in Historical Perspective,* ed. Mark S. Burrows and Paul Rorem (Grand Rapids: Eerdmans, 1991), 117–30.

621. For aspects of the early development, see Bernard McGinn, "Asceticism and Mysticism in Late Antiquity and the Middle Ages," in *Asceticism,* ed. Vincent L. Wimbush and Richard Valantasis (New York: Oxford, 1995), 58–74.

622. *Die Einheit,* 190 and 201. On the ways in which Eckhart broke with what Mieth calls *Kontemplationmystik,* see 154–64, 171–84, 191–98. On Eckhart's model as one of integration, 207–18.

623. Other important texts on the relation between action and contemplation include RdU 23 (DW 5:290–309, esp. 291); Pr. 75 (DW 3:302); and Pr. 104A (DW 4:579–81).

624. Schürmann, *Meister Eckhart,* 47.

625. Mieth puts this well (*Die Einheit,* 131): "Kreatur ist kein Weg zu Gott; sie ist zugleich der einzige Weg zu Gott."

626. Pr. 86 is found in DW 3:481–92. I will generally use Tobin's translation (*Teacher and Preacher,* 338–45), but with some modifications. Mieth (*Die Einheit,* 188 n. 224) provides a helpful outline. See also the outline in McGinn, *Mystical Thought of Meister Eckhart,* 264–65 n. 239.

627. Pr. 86 (DW 3:482.17–483.1): Marthâ bekante baz Mariên dan Marîa Marthen, wan si lange und wol gelebet hâte; wan leben gibet daz edelste bekennen. Leben bekennet baz dan lust oder lieht allez, daz man in disem lîbe under gote enpfâhen mac, und etlîche wîs bekennet leben lûterer, dan êwic lieht gegeben müge.

628. Along with Paul, Eckhart mentions *heidenishen meister* (483.4) as proving this.

629. Pr. 86 (DW 3:485.5–7): . . . und die liute stânt bî den dingen und niht în den dingen. Sie stânt vil nâhe und enhânt es nit minner, dan ob sie stüenden dort oben an dem umberinge der êwicheit.

630. Eckhart says that *werk* means the external practice of the virtues, while *gewerbe* indicates their internal rational observance (485.9–11).

631. Pr. 86 (DW 3:485.11–13): Wan der umber sîn wir gesetzet in die zît, daz wir von zîtlîchem vernünftigem gewerbe gote naeher und glîcher werden.

632. Alois M. Haas, "Meister Eckharts Auffassung von Zeit und Ewigkeit," in *Geistliches Mittelalter,* 339–69 (see pp. 363–69 on *plenitudo temporum*); Niklaus Largier, *ZEIT, ZEIT-LICHKEIT, EWIGKEIT: Ein Aufriss des Zeitproblems bei Dietrich von Freiburg and Meister Eckhart* (Frankfurt: Peter Lang, 1989).

633. On the soul as created between time and eternity, see Pr. 23 (DW 1:404–05); Prr. 32, 47 (DW 2:133–34, 404–05); and Pr. 95 (DW 4:180).

634. Largier, *ZEIT, ZEITLICHKEIT, EWIGKEIT,* 123–24.

635. Pr. 91 (Dw 4:96.102–05): Dar zuo hât got einen heimlichen rât vunden und hât sich selber verniuwet dâ mite, daz er die êwicheit hât brâht in die zît und mit sich hât brâht die zît in die êwicheit. Daz ist geschehen an dem sune, wan dô sich der sun entgôz in die êwicheit, dô wurden alle crêatûren mite entgozzen (my trans.).

636. See, e.g., Pr. 39 (DW 2:261–62); Pr. 77 (DW 3:335–36).

637. On the value of works done in time, see also Pr. 5b (DW 1:91–92 and 94–95). On the christological character of Eckhart's view of the relation between time and eternity, see Haas, "Meister Eckharts Auffassung," 355–56.

638. In this section Eckhart speaks of a man accused of heresy (*der kaeme und spraeche, er waere ein ketzer.* 490.18), who still experiences a flood of grace that leaves him indifferent to either joy or suffering. This may reflect Eckhart's situation in Cologne in late 1326 and after.

639. Pr. 86 (DW 3:491.6–7): Marthâ was sô weselich, daz sie ir gewerp niht enhinderte; werk und gewerp leitte sie ze êwiger saelde.

640. BgT 1 (DW 5:61.10–12): Der minnclîche, milte got, diu wârheit, gebe mir und allen den, die diz buoch suln lesen, daz wir die wârheit in uns vinden und gewar werden. Âmen (Walshe 3:102).

Chapter 5

1. For introductions to Suso, see Alois M. Haas, "Heinrich Seuse," in *Geschichte der deutschen Literatur: Die deutsche Literatur im späten Mittelalter, 1250–1370*, ed. Ingeborg Glier (Munich: Beck, 1987), 275–91; Alois M. Haas and K. Ruh, "Seuse, Heinrich OP," VL 8:1109–29; Kurt Ruh, *Geschichte der abendländische Mystik* (Munich: Beck, 1985), 3:415–75; and J.-A. Bizet, "Henri Suso," DS 7:234–57. See also Bizet's posthumously published, "Le Mysticisme de Henri Suso: Texte inédit de Jean Baruzi," *Revue d'Histoire de la Spiritualité* 51 (1975): 209–66. Important studies can be found in two collections: *Heinrich Seuse: Studien zum 600 Todestag, 1366–1966*, ed. Ephrem M. Filthaut (Cologne, 1966; hereafter abbreviated as HS); and *Heinrich Seuses Philosophia spiritualis: Quellen, Konzept, Formen und Rezeption*, ed. Rüdiger Blumrich and Philipp Kaiser (Wiesbaden: Ludwig Reichert, 1994). Also valuable are the collected papers of Alois M. Haas, *Kunst rechter Gelassenheit: Themen und Schwerpunkte von Heinrich Seuses Mystik* (Bern: Peter Lang, 1995). I wish to thank Prof. Frank Tobin for a number of helpful suggestions regarding this chapter.

2. *The Exemplar*, which survives in seven complete and eight partial manuscripts, was edited by Karl Bihlmeyer, *Heinrich Seuse: Deutsche Schriften* (Stuttgart, 1907; photomechanical reprint, Frankfurt: Minerva, 1961). It comprises four works:

A. *Seuses Leben, or Vita (Suso's Life)*: abbreviated here as L and cited by chapter number and page and line when appropriate;

B. *Büchlein der Ewigen Weisheit (Little Book of Eternal Wisdom)*: abbreviated as LBW and cited by chapter with page and line when needed;

C. *Büchlein der Wahrheit (Little Book of Truth)*: abbreviated as LBT and cited by chapter, page, and line;

D. *Briefbüchlein (Little Book of Letters)*: abbreviated LBL and cited by number with page and line.

In addition, Bihlmeyer's edition contains:

A. *Die grosse Briefbuch (Large Book of Letters)*;

B. Four Sermons of which two are generally considered authentic;

C. *Das Minnebüchlein (Little Book of Love)*, which is probably not by Suso.

The best English version of *The Exemplar* is that of Frank Tobin, *Henry Suso: The Exemplar with Two German Sermons* (New York: Paulist Press, 1989). I will use this translation unless otherwise noted.

Suso's one Latin work, the *Horologium Sapientiae*, was extremely popular. It has been edited by Pius Künzle, O.P., *Heinrich Seuses Horologium Sapientiae* (Freiburg, Switzerland: Universitätsverlag, 1977). It will be cited as Hor. according to part, chapter, page, and line where appropriate (e.g., Hor. I.5 [407.3–15]). There is an English version of this by Edmund Colledge, O.S.A., *Bl. Henry Suso: Wisdom's Watch upon the Hours* (Washington, D.C.: Catholic University of America Press, 1994), but I have preferred to make my own translations.

3. Jeffrey F. Hamburger, "Medieval Self-Fashioning: Authorship, Authority and Autobiography in Seuse's *Exemplar*," in *Christ among the Medieval Dominicans*, ed. Kent Emery, Jr., and Joseph P. Wawrykow (Notre Dame: University of Notre Dame Press, 1998), 430. Hamburger goes on to speak of it as "a discourse on the nature of imitation, understood in terms of the right relationship between models and their copies" (p. 431). See also the concluding remarks on pp. 448–49.

4. Michael Egerding, *Die Metaphorik der spätmittelalterlichen Mystik*, 2 vols. (Paderborn: Schöningh, 1997), 1:154–58 ("Die Person 'Seuse' als existentielle Metapher").

5. See Bernard McGinn, *The Flowering of Mysticism: Men and Women in the New Mysticism (1200–1350)*, vol. 3 of *The Presence of God: A History of Western Christian Mysticism* (New York: Crossroad, 1998), 18–19, 24–30.

6. Werner Williams-Krapp, "Henry Suso's *Vita* between Mystagogy and Hagiography," in *Seeing and Knowing: Women and Learning in Medieval Europe 1200–1500*, ed. Anneke B. Mulder-Baker (Turnhout: Brepols, 2004), 35–47.

7. Ruh, *Geschichte*, 3:420: "Seuse ist nicht auf eine Formel zu bringen."

8. Haas, "Heinrich Seuse," 290. On Suso's vernacular style, see also Ruh, *Geschichte*, 3:472–75.

9. On Suso's Latin style, see Benedikt K. Vollmann, "Stil und Anspruch des 'Horologium Sapientiae,'" in *Heinrich Seuses Philosophia spiritualis*, 83–93, who also notes important affinities with Boethius.

10. LBW Prol. (199.16–19): . . . als unglich sint dú wort, dú in den lutren gnade werdent enpfangen und usser einem lebenden herzen dur einen lebenden munt us fliezent gegen den selben worten, so sú an daz tout bermit koment, und sunderliche in tútscher zungen. . . . On the importance of this discussion, see Egerding, *Die Metaphorik*, 1:151–54.

11. Studies on Suso's use of images include Edmund Colledge, O.S.A., and J. C. Marler, "'Mystical' Pictures in the Suso 'Exemplar' *Ms Strasbourg 2929*," *Archivum Fratrum Praedicatorum* 54 (1984): 293–354; Jeffrey F. Hamburger, "The Use of Images in the Pastoral Care of Nuns: The Case of Heinrich Suso and the Dominicans," *The Art Bulletin* 71 (1988): 20–46; and "Medieval Self-Fashioning: Authorship, Authority, and Autobiography in Seuse's *Exemplar*," in *Christ among the Medieval Dominicans*, 430–61; Niklaus Largier, "Der Körper der Schrift: Bild und Text am Beispiel einer Seuse-Handschrift des 15. Jahrhunderts," in *Mittelalter: Neue wege durch einen alten Kontinent*, ed. Jan-Dirk Müller and Horst Wenzel (Stuttgart/ Leipzig: S. Hirzel, 1999), 241–71; Stephanie Altrock and Hans-Joachim Ziegeler, "Vom *diener der ewigen wisheit* zum Autor Heinrich Seuse: Autorschaft und Medienwandel in den illustrieten Handschriften und Drucken von Heinrich Seuses 'Exemplar,'" in *Text und Kultur: Mittelalterliche Literatur 1150–1450*, ed. Ursula Peters (Stuttgart: Metzler, 2001), 150–88; and Bernard McGinn, "Theologians as Trinitarian Iconographers," in *The Mind's Eye: Art and Theological Argument in the Medieval West*, ed. Jeffrey F. Hamburger and Anne-Marie Bouché (Princeton: Princeton University Press, 2005), 186–207.

12. Vollmann ("Stil und Anspruch," 84–87) correctly notes that the dominant style of the Hor. is the *genus medium*, but that this does not prevent appearances of the *genus sublime*.

13. Fundamental studies for Suso's life are those of Bihlmeyer (*Deutsche Schriften*, 63*–163*) and Künzle (*Horologium Sapientiae*, 1–6). There is an English account in Tobin, *Henry Suso*, 19–26. See also Walter Senner, O.P., "Heinrich Seuse und der Dominikanerorden," in *Heinrich Seuses Philosophia spiritualis*, 3–31.

14. For Eckhart's role in relieving the Servant of his scruples, see L 21 (62–63); for the Servant's dream about Eckhart in glory, see L 6 (22–23). There has been some question as to whether the Eckhart who appeared to the Servant was his "beloved Master," or another of the Dominicans named Eckhart, but I see no solid reason to doubt that the soul in glory was, indeed, that of Meister Eckhart.

15. Suso speaks of the crisis and his removal from his position as lector in allegorical form in Hor. I.13 (480–81). Chapter 23 (68–69) of the *Life* contains a somewhat obscure account of an attack on the Servant that seems to reflect this event.

16. The *Life* describes the exterior penitential practices of the Servant as lasting roughly from his eighteenth until his fortieth year in L 18 (52–53).

17. L 20 (58.5–13): . . . "tuo uf den celle venster, und luog und lern." . . . und ward in ime gesprochen: "reht also wirst du in diner bruoder munde." Er gedaht in im selb: "sid es anders nút mag gesin, so gib dich dar in, und luog eben, wie sich daz fuosstuoch swigende úbel lat handlen; daz tuo och du!" The analogy with Augustine's famous account of his conversion in the garden at Milan (*tolle, lege* of *Confessiones* 8.12) is unmistakable. It has been noted that the image of absolute obedience portrayed in the form of trampling on a cloth occurs in the stories of the desert fathers so beloved by Suso; see, e.g., *De vitis patrum* VII.9 (PL 73:1032–33).

18. Künzle, *Heinrich Seuses Horologium Sapientiae*, 50–53.

19. On Suso's pastoral concerns, see Ephrem Filthaut, "Heinrich Seuse in dominikanisch-priestlich-seelsorgerlicher Sicht," HS, 267–304; and Hamburger, "Use of Images in the Pastoral Care of Nuns."

20. Suso's criticism of school theology is most evident in his allegorical vision of the "golden ball" in Hor. II.1 (519–26), but is also found in other places in his writings.

21. On Stagel, see Haas, *Kunst rechter Gelassenheit*, 25–29.

22. For Suso and the Friends of God, see below and also in chapter 9, pp. 410.

23. LBW 6 (217–22); Hor. I.5 (404–12). On Suso's reform program, see Haas, "Civitatis Ruinae—Heinrich Seuses Kirchenkritik," in *Kunst rechter Gelassenheit*, 67–92.

24. Many Franciscans supported Lewis, but the Dominicans generally were on the papal side. John XXII's interdict (i.e., forbidding of ordinary Christian worship) in the lands controlled by Lewis caused great hardship. Many cities, like Constance, eventually confronted the Dominicans with the choice: "singen oder us der stadt springen," that is, "Either sing [the Mass], or get out of town!" (see Senner, "Heinrich Seuse und der Dominikanerorden," 11).

25. Prol. (6.7–10): . . . und der vorgenand maister der erschain im vor in ainer liehtricher gesiht und tet im kund, daz es gotes guoter wille were, daz es fúrbaz wúrdi gemainsamet allen guotherzigen menschen, dú mit rehter meinung und jamrigen belangung sin hetin ein begeren.

26. Rüdiger Blumrich ("Die Überlieferung der deutschen Schriften Seuses: Ein Forschungsbericht," in *Heinrich Seuses Philosophia spiritualis*, 189–201) notes some 331 manuscripts containing Suso's MHG works.

27. Besides the edition in Bihlmeyer, there is a recent new version, *Heinrich Seuse: Das Buch der Wahrheit; Daz buechli der warheit*, ed. Loris Sturlese and Rüdiger Blumrich (Hamburg, 1993). Unlike Suso's other works, the LBT had little dissemination outside *The Exemplar* (only six mss.).

28. LBT 6 defends Eckhart's views on a number of the positions condemned in the papal bull (e.g., articles 23–24, 13, and 11). It is difficult to think that Suso chose these points without knowing the text of the condemnation. On the relation of the LBT to Eckhart there is a detailed study in Herma Piesch, "Seuses 'Büchlein der Wahrheit' und Meister Eckhart," HS, 91–133, who sees the LBT as Suso's attempt to rework Eckhart's VeM.

29. Loris Sturlese has advanced an antimystical reading of the text in his article "Seuses 'Buch der Wahrheit': Versuch einer 'vernünftigen' Interpretation," in *Heinrich Seuses Philosophia spiritualis*, 32–48, and in the introduction to his edition of the work, IX–LXIX. Haas contests this view in *Kunst rechter Gelassenheit*, 50–66. The debate echoes the disputes about whether Eckhart should be considered a philosopher and/or a mystic.

30. For remarks on Suso's understanding of philosophy, see Niklaus Largier, "*FIGURATA LOCUTIO:* Hermeneutik und Philosophie bei Eckhart von Hochheim und Heinrich Seuse," in *Meister Eckhart: Lebensstationen-Redesituationen*, ed. Klaus Jacobi (Berlin: Akademie Verlag, 1997), 303–15.

31. LBW 21 (278–87), entitled "Wie man sol lernen sterben, und wie ein unbereiter tovt geschaffen ist," is perhaps the earliest explicit *ars moriendi* treatise and another proof of Suso's contribution to late medieval piety. See Haas, "Heinrich Seuses Sterbekunst," in *Kunst rechter Gelassenheit*, 223–45.

32. Künzle (*Horologium Sapientiae*, 105–249) discusses 233 surviving manuscripts, 88 lost manuscripts, and 144 manuscripts of excerpts, for a total of 465 whole or partial witnesses! In addition, the Hor. was translated into Middle French (70 MSS); Middle Dutch (93 MSS); Italian (28 MSS); Middle English (14 MSS); Czech (8 MSS); and Swedish, Danish, and Hungarian, for roughly another 220 manuscripts. Surely, a medieval best-seller.

33. For discussions of the differences between the LBW and Hor., see Künzle, *Horologium Sapientiae*, 53–54; and Colledge, *Wisdom's Watch*, 14–15 and 17–30. For remarks on the differing styles of the two works, see Claire Champollion, "Zum intellektuellen Wortschatz Heinrich Seuses OP," HS, 77–89.

34. Colledge aptly characterizes Suso's Latin as "mellifluous, emotional, hortatory" (*Wisdom's Watch*, 21).

35. The authorship question has been much discussed. A classic treatment is that of Julius Schwietering, "Zur Autorschaft von Seuses Vita," in *Mystik und höfische Dichtung im Hochmittelalter* (Tübingen: Niemeyer, 1960), 107–22. For a balanced recent summary, see Frank Tobin, "Henry Suso and Elsbeth Stagel: Was the *Vita* a Cooperative Effort?" in *Gendered Voices: Medieval Saints and Their Interpreters*, ed. Catherine M. Mooney (Philadelphia: University of Pennsylvania Press, 1999), 118–35.

36. I take the term "co-protagonist" from Paul Lachance, who used it to describe the collaboration of Angela of Foligno's Franciscan scribe with the mystic; see *Angela of Foligno: The Complete Works* (New York: Paulist Press, 1993), 51.

37. For the theme of conversation, see McGinn, *Flowering of Mysticism*, 15–24.

38. Georg Misch, *Geschichte der Autobiographie*, vol. IV.1 (Frankfurt: G. Schulte-Bulmker, 1967), 113–310; and Karl Joachim Weintraub, *The Value of the Individual: Self and Circumstance in Autobiography* (Chicago: University of Chicago Press, 1978), 197–209.

39. L Prol. (7.1): Hie vahet an daz erste tail dizz buoches, daz da haisset der Súse.

40. Richard Kieckhefer, *Unquiet Souls: Fourteenth-Century Saints in Their Religious Milieu* (Chicago: University of Chicago Press, 1984), 6.

41. Williams-Krapp, "Henry Suso's *Vita*," especially 38 and 45 (quotation here).

42. On the role of the *Vitaspatrum* in the *Life*, also see Werner Williams-Krapp, "'*Nucleus totius perfectionis*': Die Altväterspiritualität in der *Vita* Heinrich Seuses," in *Festschrift für Walter Haug und Burghart Wachinger*, 2 vols. (Tübingen: Niemeyer, 1992), 1:405–21. This ancient work of monastic spirituality was available in MHG; see the edition of Ulla Williams, *Die Alemannischen 'Vitaspatrum': Untersuchungen und Edition* (Tübingen: Niemeyer, 1996).

43. Helpful for the literary richness of the text is Walter Blank, "Heinrich Seuses 'Vita': Literarisches Gestaltung und pastorale Funktion des Schriftens," *Zeitschrift für deutsches Altertum und deutsche Literatur* 122 (1993): 285–311.

44. See, for example, L 3, 20, 36, 41, and 44.

45. See Alois M. Haas, *NIM DIN SELBES WAR: Studien zur Lehre der Selbsterkenntnis bei Meister Eckhart, Johannes Tauler und Heinrich Seuse* (Freiburg, Switzerland: Universitätsverlag, 1971), 154–55, 168–69, 192–95, 206–8.

46. Tobin, "Henry Suso and Elsbeth Stagel," 133. See also Haas, *Kunst rechter Gelassenheit*, 65–66.

47. See the remarks in Williams-Krapp, "Henry Suso's *Vita*," 41–47.

48. Chapter 52 has parallels with an anonymous mystical poem "Vom Überschall" and the MHG commentary on it. For more on this work, see chapter 7, pp. 318–19 below.

49. The "Morgengruss" can be found in both MHG and Latin forms in Bihlmeyer, 395–96. This text has affinities with the prayer found in LBW 24 (313–14), and Hor. II.5 (583–84). On the "Morgengruss," see Heinrich Stirnimann, "Seuses Morgengruss," in *Homo Medietas: Aufsätze zu Religiosität, Literatur und Denkformen des Menschen vom Mittelalter bis in die Neuzeit; Festschrift für Alois Maria Haas zum 65. Geburtstag*, ed. Claudia Brinker-von der Heyde and Niklaus Largier (Bern: Peter Lang, 1999), 317–21.

50. The *Minnebüchlein* is edited in Bihlmeyer, 536–54.

51. Hor. I.9 (453.5–10): Tu autem in nostra spirituali philosophia aliter institutus consurge,

cuncta visibilia mente supergradiendo; *quae enim videntur, temporalia sunt, quae autem non videntur, aeterna sunt.* . . . Aperi oculos mentales, et vide quid sis, ubi sis, et quo tendas; tunc profecto horum omnium rationem habere valeas. The parallel passage in LBW 10 (236.28–237.6) does not use the phrase. For another appearance of *philosophia spiritualis,* see 547.2. Suso employs a number of equivalent terms: *nostra philosophia* (447.25), *vera et summa philosophia* (520.2, 526.11); *sublimior philosophia* (493.21); *utilissima scientia* (526.12); and *vera scientia christianae philosophiae* (547.14).

52. Hor. I.14 (493.21–22): Haec mea interim sublimior philosophia, *scire Iesum, et hunc crucifixum.* The passage is from Bernard's *Sermo super Cantica* 43.4 (*Sancti Bernardi Opera* 2:43.21–22).

53. Hor. II.3 (546.2–3): Fons et origo omnium bonorum homini spirituali est in cella sua iugiter commorari. The dictum reflects the teaching ascribed to Abba Theodore in Cassian, *Conlationes* VI.15, and no. 11 of the sayings of Arsenius in the Alphabetical *Apophthegmata Patrum* (PG 65: 90C), but the formula itself is not in these texts.

54. Hor. II.3 (547.11–15): . . . vitae sanctorum patrum et eorum collationes, qui liber a plerisque tamquam antiquus et abolitus parum curatur, licet nucleus totius perfectionis, et vera scientia christianae philosophiae in ipso esse certissima experientia cognoscatur.

55. "Cursus de aeterna Sapientia" (608.3–5): Pone meam in tuis vulneribus philosophiam, in tuis stigmatibus sapientiam, ut ulterius in te, solo caritatis libro, et morte tua proficiam. . . .

56. Some of the essays in *Heinrich Seuses Philosophia spiritualis* are helpful here, especially those of Rüdiger Blumrich, Philipp Kaiser, Peter Ulrich, and Markus Enders. See also Peter Ulrich, *Imitatio et configuratio: Die philosophia spiritualis Heinrich Seuses als Theologie der Nachfolge des Christus passus* (Regensburg: Pustet, 1995).

57. Pierre Hadot, *Philosophy as a Way of Life: Spiritual Exercises from Socrates to Foucault,* ed. with an introduction by Arnold I. Davidson (Oxford: Blackwell, 1995).

58. See Jean Leclercq, "Chap. II. Philosophia," in *Études sur le vocabulaire monastique du moyen age* (Rome: Herder, 1961), 39–79.

59. Rüdiger Blumrich ("Die *gemeinú ler* des "Büchleins der ewigen Weisheit': Quellen und Konzept,"in *Heinrich Seuses Philosophia spiritualis,* 49–70) discusses Suso's use of the monastic tradition and includes a list of the sources cited in the LBW, showing that Bernard outnumbers all others (eighteen uses).

60. P. Kaiser, "Die Christozentrik der *philosophia spiritualis* Heinrich Seuses," in *Heinrich Seuses Philosophia spiritualis,* 109–23, especially 109–12.

61. See M. Enders, "Das mystische Wissen Seuses: Ein Beitrag zu seiner theologischen Relevanz," in *Heinrich Seuses Philosophia spiritualis,* 139–72, summarizing the author's published dissertation, *Das mystische Wissen bei Heinrich Seuse* (Paderborn: Schöningh, 1993). Enders's account of Suso's mysticism is thorough and impressive, though his tendency to divide the speculative from the practical side according to particular works masks the constant interplay between the two in the Dominican's teaching.

62. See, for example, Schwietering, "Zur Autorschaft von Seuses Vita"; and Maria Bindschedler, "Seuses Begriff von Ritterschaft," HS, 233–40. For an English summary, Tobin, "Introduction," 43–44.

63. L 44 (149–53). For some other important passages, see LBW 7, and Hor. I.6 and 13.

64. L 20 (55–57). The knightly ideal of struggle for Christ, of course, taps into the ancient motif of the *athleta Christi,* as evidenced here by the quotation of Job 7:1, "Militia est vita hominis." Nevertheless, aspects of Suso's presentation, such as his stress on the proper knightly attire, shows that his is a specifically late-medieval adaptation of the theme.

65. See Vollmann, "Stil und Anspruch," 91–92; Hamburger, "Medieval Self-Fashioning," 435–37; Williams-Krapp, "Henry Suso's *Vita,*" 41; and especially Barbara Newman, "Henry Suso and Medieval Devotion to Christ the Goddess," *Spiritus: A Journal of Christian Spirituality* 2 (2002): 1–14.

66. Augustine, *De libero arbitrio* 2.14.37 (PL 32:1261).

67. Augustine, *Soliloquiae* 1.13.22 (PL 32:881). Love language used in relation to female

Sapientia is not just found in the early Augustine, but also occurs in later texts, such as *Enarrationes in Psalmos* 32.2.7, 33.2.6, and 35.5 (PL 38:282, 310–11, and 344).

68. Hor., Prol (366.16–19): Et sic diversimode stilum vertit secundum quod tunc materiae congruit. Nunc etiam Dei Filium ut devotae animae sponsum inducit; postea eundem tamquam aeternam sapientiam viro iusto desponsatam introducit. It should be noted that in the LBW, while Wisdom is feminine, there is little gender experimentation.

69. Hor. I.1 (379.26–380.1): Cum iam putabatur haberi velut delicata iuvencula, subito ut iuvenis pulcherrimus inveniebatur.

70. Newman, "Henry Suso and the Medieval Devotion to Christ the Goddess," 7.

71. The most powerful presentations of Suso as the male courtly lover revealing how Lady Wisdom has wounded his heart can be found in the love-scenes portrayed in Hor. I.6 (417–33). On the *vulnus amoris,* see specifically Hor. I.6 (426.10–13) and LBW 7 (226.15–18).

72. L 3 (14.3–23): . . . "gewerlich, ez muos recht sin, si muos reht min liep sin, ich wil ir diener sin." Und gedahte: "ach got, wan moehti ich die lieban núwan einest geshehen, . . . weder ist es got ald mensch, frow oder man, kunst ald list, oder waz mag ez sin? . . . si waz verr und nahe, hoh und nieder, si waz gegenwúrtig und doch verborgen. . . . So er iez wande haben ein schoen jungfrowen, geswind vand er einen stolzen jungherren. Si gebaret etwen als ein wisú meisterin, etwen hielt si sich als ein vil weidenlichú minnerin. Sie bot sich zuo im minneklich und gruozte in vil lechelich und sprach zuo ime gútlich: 'Prebe, fili, cor tuum mihi! Gib mir din herz, kind mins!'"

73. E.g., L 8, 20, 23, 34 (26, 60, 66–67, 103); LBW 18 (273–74); LBT 5 (342); LBL 11 (391–93).

74. On Suso's use of symbols, see Jean Baruzi, "Le Mysticisme de Henri Suso," 212–20.

75. L 20 and 35 (60, 103–7). On these pictures, see Hamburger, "Use of Images in the Pastoral Care of Nuns," 29–42.

76. On the importance of this scene in L 4 for an approaciation of Suso's visual imagination, see Hildegard Elisabeth Keller, "Kolophon im Herzen: Von beschrifteten Mönchen an den Rändern der Paläographie," *Das Mittelalter* 7 (2002): 157–82. Keller shows how this incident functions as a living "colophon" of the heart as the medium of the Servant's bond with Jesus. See also Bettina Spoerri, "Schrift des Herzens. Zum vierten Kapitel der 'Vita' Heinrich Seuses," in *Homo Medietas,* 299–315.

77. L 45 (153–55) with accompanying image. See also Letter 11 in the LBL (391–93). Hamburger ("Medieval Self-Fashioning," 443–46) comments on this proliferation of images. See also Keller, "Kolophon im Herzen."

78. Hamburger, "Medieval Self-Fashioning," 432; see p. 440 on the relation of the images in Suso's oratory to those in *The Exemplar.*

79. Largier, "Der Körper der Schrift," especially 266–71.

80. On the symbol/image as both *similis* and *dissimilis,* see Pseudo-Dionysius, DN 9.7 (916A), CH 2.2–3 (137D–141C) and 15.8 (337B).

81. For an analysis of Suso's use of *bild* and related terms, see Heinrich Stirnimann, "Mystik und Metaphorik: Zu Seuses Dialog," in *Das "einig Ein": Studien zu Theorie und Sprache der deutschen Mystik,* ed. Alois M. Haas and Heinrich Stirnimann (Freiburg, Switzerland: Universitätsverlag, 1980), 230–43. Suso shows surprisingly little interest in traditional mystical speculation on man as the *imago dei/trinitatis,* mentioning it only rarely in the twin texts, LBW 6, 10, and 19 (219.28–30, 237.7–8, 277.10–12), and Hor., I.9 (453.10–14).

82. *The Exemplar,* Prol. (3.2–9, 4.24–28). See also L 46 (155.15–20).

83. Hor., Prol. (367.12–14): Porro huius figuratae locutionis occulta mysteria diligens lector faciliter poterit advertere, si tamen sollertem curam studerit adhibere. On the importance of *figurata locutio* in Suso, see Largier, "*FIGURATA LOCUTIO.*"

84. Hor. I.6 (422.23–26): SAPIENTIA: Rerum altissimarum veritates in sua simplicitate acceptas intellectus humanus capere non potest; et ideo necesse est eas tradere per imagines et consuetas similitudines. See also the following discussion of the *prudens pictor* (423.10–424.13).

85. Hor. II.7 (597.18–598.3). For reflections on images in the LBW, see chaps. 9 and 18 (235.14–20, 273.18–20).

86. Letter 9 (387.7–16).

87. There are a number of other passages in Suso's writings that reflect on the limitations of images. See, e.g., L 33 (97.13, 98.15–16), 47 (158.23–27), 49 (164.12–16); and LBW 22 (288.12–13). In L 51 (183.3–30) Suso also has an interesting discussion of discernment of spirits, that is, how to distinguish true from false visions.

88. L 53 (191.6–11): . . . wie kan man bildlos gebilden unde wiselos bewisen, daz úber alle sinne und úber menschlich vernunft ist? Wan waz man glichnust dem git, so ist es noh tusentvalt ungelicher, denn es glich sie. Aber doch, daz man bild mit bilden us tribe, so wil ich dir hie biltlich zoegen mit glichnusgebender rede, als verr es denn múglich ist, von den selben bildlosen sinnen . . . (my trans.).

89. For more on this picture and the literature on it, see McGinn, "Theologians as Trinitarian Iconographers," 200–201.

90. Hamburger, "Medieval Self-Fashioning," 441.

91. L 53 (193.18–20): Der inschlag entschleht im bild und form und alle menigvaltikeit, und kunt in sin selbs und aller dingen warnemenden unwússentheit. . . .

92. L 53 (193.31–194.2): Fro tohter, nu merk eben, daz disiú ellú entworfnú bild und disiú usgeleiten verbildetú wort sind der bildlosen warheit als verr und als ungelich, als ein swarzer mor der schoenen sunnen, und kunt daz von der selben warheit formlosen, unbekanten einvaltekeit (Tobin translation modified). This comparison is reminiscent of Meister Eckhart's statement that calling God good is as wrong as calling the sun black (Pr. 9 in DW 1:148.6–7). A similar discussion of the impossibility of presenting God can be found in LBT 5 (342.23–343.8). On L 53, see Stirnimann, "Mystik und Metaphorik," 241–43.

93. L 49 (168.9–10): Ein gelassener mensch muoss entbildet werden von der creatur, gebildet werden mit Cristo, und úberbildet in der gotheit. An alternative translation would be: "A released person must be freed of the image of the creature, re-imaged in Christ, and trans-imaged in the Godhead."

94. LBL 10 (390.24–391.10): Und in dem entspringet warú volkomenheit, dú da lit an der vereinunge der hoehsten kreften der sele in den ursprung der wesentheit in hohem schowene. . . . Wan aber dú sele von dez sweren libes krankheit dem lutern guot in entbiltlicher wise nit mag blosseklich alle zit an gehaften, so muesse si etwas biltlichs haben, daz si wider in leite. Und daz beste dar zuo, daz ich verstan, daz ist daz minneklich bilde Jesu Cristi. . . . Und so er in daz selb bilde wirt gebildet, so wirt er denne als von gotes geist in die goetlichen guenlichi dez himelschen herren úberbildet von klarheit zu klarheit (2 Cor. 3:18), von klarheit siner zarten menschheit zuo der klarheit siner gotheit (Tobin modified). On this passage and the christological character of Suso's teaching on *bild,* see Stirnimann, "Mystik und Metaphorik," 249–53; and Egerding, *Die Metaphorik,* 1:200–207.

95. L 13 (34.9–12): . . . weist du nit, daz ich daz tor bin [Mt. 7:13–14], dur daz alle die waren gotesfrúnd muessent in dringen, die zuo rechter selikeit son komen? Du muost den durpruch nemen dur min geliten menscheit, solt du warlich komen zuo miner blossen gotheit (Tobin modified). For similar formulations, see L 52 (184.11–19); LBW 1 and 2 (203.7–10, 205.1–11); Hor. I.2 and 3 (384.1–9, and 388.19–21). In LBW 14 (254.11–16) and Hor. I.14 (492.24–493.5) Paul is taken as a model for this, because he not only was rapt into God (2 Cor. 12:2), but also based his life on the crucified Christ (1 Cor. 2:2). These passages express Suso's understanding of a traditional theme in Western spirituality, going back at least as far as Augustine—"Per Christum hominem ad Christum Deum . . ." (e.g., *Tractatus in Joannis Evangelium* 13.4 [PL 35:1494]).

96. For Suso's understanding of scripture, see the Prol. to *The Exemplar* (4.10–16 and 5.20–23), which affirms the harmony between the collection and the biblical message, as well as LBW Prol., and chapter 9 (197.12–21 and 231.7–11). In Hor. II.1 (525.27–526.11) Suso briefly discusses three ways of reading the Bible. For a study of his exegesis, see Paul Michel, "Heinrich Seuse als Diener des göttlichen Wortes: Persuasive Strategien bei der Verwendung von Bibelzitaten im Dienste seiner pastoralen Aufgaben," in *Das "einig Ein",* 281–367.

97. Hor. I.3 (393.26–29): Haec sunt fili mi, haec sunt, inquam, prima principia, quae tibi ceterisque amatoribus suis tradit aeterna sapientia, quae in hoc libro aperto, videlicet corpore meo crucifixo, sicut vides, sunt exarata. According to LBW 13 (393.15–23), the contemplation of Christ's suffering turns a simple person into a learned master because "It is a living book where one discovers all things" (es ist doch ein lebendes buoch, da man ellú ding an vindet . . .). See the parallel passage in Hor. I.14 (494.10–15). The image of the *librum crucis Christi* had been used by Bonaventure in the *Legenda major* 4.3 (*Opera omnia* 8:513). On the relation between *philosophia spiritualis* and *imitatio passionis*, see Ulrich, *Imitatio et configuratio*, 119–89.

98. Accounts of the *imitatio passionis* in Suso are many. For a good summary, see Haas, *Kunst rechter Gelassenheit*, 125–77.

99. P. Kaiser, "Die Christozentrik der *philosophia spiritualis* Heinrich Seuses," in *Heinrich Seuses Philosophia spiritualis*, 113. Kaiser's essay is a helpful summary of Suso's Christology.

100. LBW 1 (203.4–9): Den hoehsten usfluz aller wesen von ir ersten ursprunge nimet man nach natúrlicher ordenunge durch dú edelsten wesen in dú nidersten; aber den widerfluz zuo dem ursprunge nimt man durch dú nidersten in dú hoehsten. Dar umb, wilt du mich schowen in miner ungewordenen gotheit, so solt du mich hie lernen erkennen und minnen in miner gelitnen menschiet. . . . See the parallel in Hor. I.2 (384.1–9).

101. Hor. I.13 (488.18–20): Qui adversa libenter pro Deo patitur, Christo passo assimilatur, et ideo ab eo tamquam a consimili nexu dilectionis praecipuo constringitur.

102. Hor. I.2 (386.11–22) contains a discussion of the *deformis formositas* of the crucified Christ. For the use of this theme by Suso, see Paul Michel, *'Formosa deformitas': Bewältigungsformen des Hässlichen in mittelalterlichen Literatur* (Bonn, 1976), 177–243. For the differences between Eckhart's and Suso's Christologies, see Alois M. Haas, *Nim din selbes war*, 166–71.

103. Hor. I.13 (481.18–20): Haec cum discipulus audisset, intellexit mysterium esse desponsationis aeternae sapientiae, quae suos amatores temporalibus consuevit tribulationibus probare, et probatos sibi in amicitia copulare. . . . The mystical marriage is described especially in Hor. II.7 (590–95) and in L 41 (139–40).

104. Prol. (3.3–18): . . . von eim anvahenden lebene . . . von aim zuonemenden menschen . . . zuo der blossen warheit eins seligen volkomen lebens. . . . Suso also uses the triple path motif in chapter 36 (113), as well as in Letter 10 (390–91) and Sermon 4 (529).

105. L 15 (39.3–6): Er hate gar ein leblich natur in siner jugende. . . . Er suochte mengen list und gross buossen, wie er den lip macheti undertenig dem geiste.

106. L 16 (41.20–24): Dú unmanlich zagheit gerow in balde, und machet sú alle andrest wider spizzig und scharpf mit einer viln, und nam es wider auf sich. Es riflet im uf dem ruggen, da es beinoht was, und machet in bluotig und verseret. Wa er sass oder stuond, da waz ime, wie ein igelhut uf ime lege. . . .

107. L 16 (43.25–26): Er ward von erbermde úber sich selb als reht herzklich weinende.

108. There are many discussions of *compassio*, especially in the Hor.; see, e.g., I.3 (388–90, 392–93), I.4 (403), I.14 (494–95, 498), and I.15 (499–506). The MHG phrase *ein cristfoermig mitliden* is from L 13 (34.17). For other appearances of *mitliden* in the MHG works, see, e.g., 41.4, 142.25, 206.3, 258.27, 260.22–23. L 40 (134.5–7) says: Aber daz edelst und daz best liden, daz ist ein cristfoermig liden, ich mein daz liden, daz der himelsch vater sinem einbornen sun und noh sinen lieben fründen git. On the role of *compassio* in Suso, see Markus Enders, "Das mystische Wissen Seuses: Ein Beitrag zu seiner theologischen Relevanz," *Heinrich Seuses Philosophia spiritualis*, 162–65, and 170. On the development of the notion of *compassio* in medieval spirituality down to the twelfth century, see Rachel Fulton, *From Judgment to Passion: Devotion to Christ and the Virgin Mary, 800–1200* (New York: Columbia University Press, 2002).

109. L 18 (52.10–53.4): . . . und ward ime von got gezoeget, daz dú strenkkeit und die wisen alle sament nit anders weri gewesen, denn ein guoter anvang . . . , er muesti noch fúrbaz gedrungen werden in einer anderley wise, soelti im iemer reht beschehen.

110. For parallels with Christ's abandonment at Gethsemane, see L 20 and 23 (57–58, 69).

There are many other allusions in these chapters to the Servant's growing identification with Christ, such as the way in which he applies the passion Psalm 22 to himself in chapters 25 and 30 (78, 87).

111. L 31 (92.1–7): Wan weri nit anders nuzzes noch guotes an lidene, wan allein, daz wir dem schoenen klaren spiegel Cristus so vil dest glicher werden, es weri wol angeleit. . . . wan lieb glichet und húldet sich liebe, wa es kan ald mag.

112. Hor. I.4 (403.7–31): . . . o aeterna sapientia, doce me, obsecro, qualiter tua stigmata dulcissima et suavissima in corpore meo deferam, . . . Cor promptum tibi sit ad sustinenda omnia adversa pro nomine meo: et sic tamquam fidelis discipulus cum domino suo spiritualiter crucifixus et quodam modo sanguine compassionis respersus, mihi similis amabilisque efficieris.

113. LBW 14 (254–56; see the parallel in Hor. I.14 [495.25–496.8]). In L 21 (62.1–5) the same temptation appears as *ungeordnetú trurkeit.* For a study of the term *swermuetikeit,* which was to have a long history in later mystical discourse, see Haas, *Kunst rechter Gelassenheit,* 93–123.

114. LBW 14 (256.33–257.2): ". . . wes sitzest du hie? Stant uf und vergang dich in min liden, so úberwindest du din liden!"

115. LBW 14 (258.25–27): . . . und doch so zúhet ieder mensch der besserunge als vil zuo im, als vil er sich mir mit mitlidenne gelichet. On the significance of this chapter, see Haas, *Kunst rechter Gelassenheit,* 128–35, 152–59.

116. LBW 15 (261.26–262.5): Swenne du denne in aller widerwertikeit, dú dich von dem nechsten an gat, von minne durch mich siglos wirst, und du aller menschen ungestuemen zorn, wannen er wejet, . . . als senfmuetklich enphasest als ein swigentes lembli, . . . so wirt daz war bilde mins tovdes in dir us gewúrket. Eya, da ich dis glicheit vinde, waz hab ich da in dem lusts und wolgevallens mir selber und minem himelschen vatter! Trage minen bittern toud in dem grunde dins herzen und in dinem gebette und in erzoeigunge der werke. . . . See also LBW 18 (273.28–274.28) on modelling all our suffering after that of Christ.

117. Hor. I.16 (516.1–2, 23–27): O si vidisses in hora illa lamentabili miseriam matris Filio compatientis, dolorem Filii matri condolentis. . . . . Porro nos, qui haec non sine gemitu et fletu audire potuimus, interrumpere sermonem tuum, virgo mater, cogit compassionis nostrae vehementia et exuberantia tantarum lacrimarum, quibus tibi, o virgo pia, compatimur ex intimis visceribus cordium nostrorum. O quam induratum est cor, quod tibi ex intimis non compatimur.

118. The role of roses and other flowers in Suso's mysticism is striking. See the remarks in Jeffrey F. Hamburger, *Nuns as Artists: The Visual Culture of a Medieval Convent* (Berkeley: University of California Press, 1997), 64–66; and especially Hildegard Elisabeth Keller, "Rosen-Metamorphosen: Von unfesten Zeichen in der spätmittelalterlichen Mystik; Heinrich Seuses 'Exemplar' und das Mirakel 'Marien Rosenkranz,'" in *Der Rosenkranz. Andacht–Geschichte– Kunst,* ed. Urs-Beat Frei and Fredy Bühler (Bern: Beuteli Verlag, 2003), 48–67. Roses are particularly prominent in the Hor. (e.g., 389.11–12, 396.25–397.2, 398.16–19, 400.19–21, 418.14–419.4, 427.12–17, 433.14–15, 490.8–10, 491.4–6, 492.11–15, 498.12–16, 517.22–24, 557.25–28, 558.22–23, 604.19–25, etc.).

119. For an analysis of how Suso's view of suffering relates to the Eckhartian aspects of his mysticism, see P. Ulrich, "Zur Bedeutung des Leidens," in *Heinrich Seuses Philosophia spiritualis,* 133–35.

120. L Prol. and 1 (8.8–17, 9.23–25).

121. L 9 (29.2–4): Den ruoft ich und mir selb uf ein getúrstiges wagen unser selbs mit einem ganzen abker von uns und von allen creaturen.

122. LBW 7 (223.20–22): Nu hoer, min tohter, und sihe, neige ze mir dinú oren, tuo einen kreftigen inker und vergiss di selbes und aller dinge. For other uses of *inker* and *inkeren,* see 168.15, 169.35, 289.20, 309.12, 326.11, 335.6, 431.14, 435.14, and 470.4. On the importance of *inker* in Suso, see Haas, *Kunst rechter Gelassenheit,* 50–63.

123. LBT, Prol. (326.11–14): . . . do wart im eins males ein inker, in deme er wart getriben

zuo im selben, und ward in im gesprochen also: du solt wissen, daz inrlichú gelazenheit bringet den menschen zuo der nehsten warheit (my trans.).

124. LBW 22 (288–90); see the parallel in Hor. II.3 (542–45). The quotation is at 290.1–2: Min kint, halte dich inrlich, luterlich, ledklich und ufgezogenlich.

125. L 49 (163–70). Eighteen of these axioms deal with true *gelassenheit* and no fewer than twenty-two concern inwardness: nos. 8, 13, 25, 26, 33, 34, 35, 42, 46, 50, 55, 59, 61, 70, 75, 85, 86, 90, 91, 92, 94, and 95.

126. L 49 (166.15–16; 156.5–6; 170.17–18): Blib in dir selb; ursach ander dingen zoeget sich als ein noturft, es ist aber ain behelfen./ Hab dich inne und erzoeg dich dem nút glich, anders du wirst lidende./ Gang wider in, ker aber und och wider in in din ainmuot, und gebruche gotes (Tobin modified).

127. Suso's teaching on silence is found throughout his works. For some key treatments, see, e.g., L 14 (37–38), 49 (170.1–2), and especially 52 (186.22–25; 187.7–8; 190.9–16). See also LBW 12 (245.16–20) and Letter 2 (366.15–17).

128. This phrase occurs in the title to L 19 (53.6–7). *Gelassenheit*, a term created by Eckhart based on Matt. 19:29, was to have a long history, not only in Suso and Tauler, but down to Heidegger and beyond. For two studies, see Haas, *Kunst rechter Gelassenheit*, 247–69 (pp. 262–67 on Suso); and Ludwig Völker, "'Gelassenheit': Zur Entstehung des Wortes in der Sprache Meister Eckharts und seiner Überlieferung in der nacheckhartschen Mystik bis Jacob Böhme," in *'Getempert und Gemischt' für Wolfgang Mohr zum 65. Geburtstag*, ed. Franz Hundsnurschen and Ulrich Müller (Göppingen: Kümmerle, 1972), 281–312 (pp. 285–88 on Suso).

129. For a list and discussion of *abgescheidenheit/abgescheiden* in Suso, see Egerding, *Die Metaphorik*, 2:30–32.

130. The expression is from Denys Turner, *The Darkness of God: Negativity in Christian Mysticism* (Cambridge: Cambridge University Press, 1995), 179.

131. There are a number of other considerations of releasement in the LBT. See, e.g., Prol. (326.6–14); and chapters 5, 6, and 7 (339.13–24, 353.7–9, and 358–59).

132. This is article 12 of "In agro dominico," drawn from Pr. 24 (DW 1:421–22).

133. LBT 4 (333.17–21): Unde dar umbe so hat menschlichú nature an ir selben genomen kein solich recht—wan si Cristus hatte an genomen und nit persone—daz ieder mensche dar umbe súl und múg in der selben wise got und mensch sin.

134. LBT 4 (335.5–7): . . . da der mensch den usker nimet von gotte uf sich selb, da er wider in solte keren, und im selb nach dem zuoval ein eigen sich stiftet. . . .

135. This is my reading of an admittedly difficult passage (335.14–18): Der ander inblik ist, daz da nit übersehen werde, daz in dem selben nehsten gelezse iedoch sin selbs sich alwegent blibet uf siner eigen gezoewlicher istikeit nach dem usschlage, und da nút male vernihtet wirt.

136. LBT 4 (335.25–26): Und dis gelassen sich wirt ein kristfoermig ich, vom dem dú schrift seit von Paulo, der da sprichet: 'ich leb, nit me ich, Cristus lebt in mir.' Und daz heiss ich ein wolgewegen sich (Tobin modified).

137. Suso uses a number of the verbs of annihilating introduced by Eckhart, especially in the last chapters of the *Life*, such as *entwerden*, i.e., un-become (e.g., 164.10–11, 166.6), *entbilden*, or dis-image (e.g., 160.28, 168.9), *entgeisten*, i.e., de-spirit (e.g., 182.14, 183.1, 189.21), and *entgoetet*, or un-god (e.g., 181.28, 182.9). Radical as these terms are, they need to be read in the light of the modifications that Suso brought to Eckhart's teaching. For a survey of the differences between Eckhart and Suso on mystical transformation, see Egerding, *Die Metaphorik*, 1:91–95.

138. LBT 4 (336.21–24): Da blibet wol sin wesen, aber in einer anderú forme, in einer anderú glorie und in eime andern vermugenne. Und daz kumet alles von ir selbs grundlosen gelazsenheit (Tobin modified). The other issue Truth discusses in this passage is the relation of the partial transformation possible in this life to the full state in heaven. In this section Suso makes extensive use of Bernard's *De diligendo deo* 10 and 15 (*Sancti Bernardi Opera* 3:142–44, 152–54); he also refers to Thomas Aquinas, STh IaIIae, q. 61, a. 5.

139. LBT 7 (357.19–20): Er stat in einem gegenwúrtigen nu ane behangnen fúrsaz, und nimt sin nehstes in dem minsten als in dem meisten.

140. LBT 7 (358.22–24): Eines wolgelazsenen menschen tuon ist sin laszen, und sin werk ist sin muessig bliben, wan sines tuonnes blibet er ruwig und sins werkes blibet er muezsige (Tobin modified).

141. L 48 (161.28–29): . . . als etlichú torohtú menschen sprechent, daz man dur alle gebresten muess waten, der zuo volkomenr gelassenheit wil komen (Tobin modified).

142. L 48 (162.26–28): . . . wan dez geistes vernihtkeit, sin vergangenheit in die ainvaltigen gotheit und aller . . . ist ze nemene nút na verwandlung sin selbes geschafenheit in daz, also daz daz selb, daz er ist, got sie (Tobin modified).

143. The LBW contains other discussions of both *abgescheidenheit* (e.g., 218.6, 219.11, 232.26, 245.9–10, 296.26–28) and *gelassenheit* (e.g., 246.7–9, 250.3–4).

144. The game of love features in many of the authors known to Suso, especially Bernard of Clairvaux; see, e.g., *Sermo super Cantica* 32.2 (*Sancti Bernard Opera* 1:227–29). The treatment of presence and absence in LBW 9 is expanded upon in Hor. I.8 (436–48).

145. LBW 9 (232.13–17): Der diener: Ach herre, . . . Wan du meinest, daz ich mich halte ledklich und gelazenlich an luste, und din lob allein suoche in hertikeit als in suezikeit. Entwúrt der Ewigen Weisheit: Ein gelazenheit ob aller gelazenheit ist gelazen sin in gelazenheit. On this text, see Haas, *Kunst rechter Gelassenheit*, 265–66. The parallel in Hor. I.8 (441.29–442.2) is weaker: Tanta deberet esse absolutio affectus probati discipuli, ut non solum corporalibus delectationibus non esset alligatus, sed neque pro spiritualibus tantum inhiaret, ut eas carius quam ipsum summum bonum in seipso acceptum quaerendo appeteret.

146. Eckhart, Pr. 12 (DW 1:196.6–7): Daz hoehste und daz naehste, daz der mensche gelâzen mac, daz ist, daz er got durch got lâze. This sermon, one of Eckhart's most daring, also discusses releasement at 193.5–8 and 201.9–203.5. Since the same sermon includes a treatment of the angels' perfect desire to complete the divine will in all things, echoing what we have seen above in LBW 9, Suso is likely to be reflecting this homily. A parallel passage is found in L 6, where Suso is given a vision of the dead Brother John "der Fuoterer," who tells him that the most painful and profitable exercise is "that a person go out from God in releasement with patience toward himself and thus leave God for the sake of God" (. . . denn da der mensch in gelassenheit von got im selber gedulteklich us giengi und also got dur got liessi [23.18–20]).

147. LBW 9 (235.3–4): . . . so enkan dir weder úbermuetikeit in der gegenwúrtikeit, noch schwarmuetikeit in gelazenheit geschaden (my trans.).

148. For some appearances of *abgescheidenheit*, see, e.g., 15.6, 59.29–31, 138.18–19, 183.11, 185.31, 192.18. Both *abgescheidenheit* and *gelassenheit* occur in the other works, e.g., Letter 2 (364.2, 365.2), Letter 3 (367.11–14), Letter 9 (388.22–26), and Sermon 4 (530–36 passim).

149. L 19 (54.1–8): "Dú hohe schuol und ir kunst, die man hie liset, daz ist nit anders denn ein genzú, volkomnú gelassenheit sin selbs, also daz ein mensch stand in soelicher entwordenheit, . . . saz er alle zit stand glich in einem usgene des sinen, . . . und allein gotes lob und ere sie ansehende, als sich der lieb Cristus bewiste gen sinem himselschen vatter" (my trans.).

150. L 19 (54.12–14): . . . "disú kunst wil haben ein ledig muessikeit: so man ie minr hie tuot, so man in der warheit ie me hat getan . . ." (my trans.).

151. See L 47 (160.1–10) and especially 48 (160–63), discussed above. In chapter 49 (163–70) nineteen of the axioms relate to *gelassenheit* (nos. 12, 27, 29, 45, 63, 67, 70, 71, 73, 74, 75, 77, 83, 84, 85, 89, 90, 91, 93). See also the treatment of releasement in chapter 38 (127.5–20).

152. L 49 (168.21–2 and 169.3–5): Waz ist eins reht gelassen menschen gegenwurf in allen dingen? Daz ist ein entsinken im selb, unt mit ime entsinkend im ellú ding. . . . Und sol denn in dem lieht merken die gegenwúrtikeit dez allichen goetlichen wesens in ime, und daz er dez selben allein ist ein gezoew (Tobin modified).

153. Suso uses the term *gaisliche gesiht* in L 37 (116.8). The "Glossar" in Bihlmeyer lists thirteen appearances of the word *gesiht*, noting that there are many others; the equivalent

MHG word adapted from Latin, *vision*, is noted three times, but also appears more frequently. Suso's teaching on visions has been studied by Alois Haas, "Seuses Visionen—Begriff der Vision," in *Kunst rechter Gelassenheit*, 179–220; and Ernst Arbman, *Ecstacy or Religious Trance*, 2 vols. (Uppsala: Svenska Bokförlaget, 1963), 1:58–75, who gives a psychoanalytic reading. For the wider background on medieval visions, with some references to Suso, see Peter Dinzelbacher, *Vision und Visionsliteratur im Mittelalter* (Stuttgart: Hiersemann, 1981), as well as Barbara Newman, "What Did It Mean to Say 'I Saw'? The Clash between Theory and Practice in Medieval Visionary Culture," *Speculum* 80 (2005): 1–43.

154. For a history of ecstasy in mysticism, see the multi-author article "Extase" in DS 4:2045–2189, which briefly treats Suso on col. 2134.

155. L 51 (183.28–30): Und welem menschen got die selben gabe git, der kan sich dest bas hier inne berihten. Es kan nieman dem andern wol mit worten geben, denn der merkt es, der es enpfunden hat. The immediately preceding mention of Monica refers to *Confessiones* 4.13.

156. On discernment of spirits, see the discussion in chapter 2 above, pp. 73–78.

157. Haas, *Kunst rechter Gelassenheit*, 218: "Die Berichte von Visionen, die er gibt, sind keine reinen Erfahrungsnotizen, sondern literarisch stilisierte Niederschriften seelischer Ereignisse, die einem bestimmten didaktischen Ziel dienen." See also Haas's discussion of the "didaktischer Wert" of Suso's visions (pp. 204–5).

158. Examples of such third-person confirmatory visions can be found in eleven chapters in the *Life*: Chapters 5 (22), 16 (44), 18 (50–51, 51–52), 20 (59), 22 (63–65), 23 (70), 34 (101), 37 (117), 42 (142–44, including visions relating to Suso's mother), 44 (150), 45 (152). They occur more rarely in the other works, e.g., LBL 8 (384), and Hor., Prol. (371).

159. L 5 (22.5–6): . . . und sah, daz dú goetlich gnade her ab towete in sin sele, und daz er ward eins mit gote.

160. L 5 (22.15–18): . . . "do ist er uns als herzeklich liep, daz wir vil tuenes mit im haben, und wússist, daz got unsaglichú wunder wúrket in siner sele, und waz er got ernschlich hat ze bitene, dez wil im got niemer versage."

161. L 2 (10.15–19): Und so er also stat . . . , do ward sin sel verzuket in dem libe neiss uss dem libe. Da sah er und horte, daz allen zungen unsprechlich ist: es waz formlos und wiselos und hate doch aller formen und wisen froedenlich lust in ime. The same rapture is described in more detailed theological language in Hor. I.1 (380.22–381.18).

162. L 50 (175.9–11): . . . "luog, als du die armen frowen mit einem geladen herzen hast von dir getriben ungetroestet, also han ic minem goetlichen trost von dir gezuket."

163. L 41 (139.24–29): Und do im in der betrahtunge die sinne neiswi entsunken, do duht in in einer gesiht, er wurdi gefueret uf ein schoen, gruenen heide, und gie ein stolzer himelscher jungling bi ime und fuorte in an siner hand. Also erhuob der selb jungling in dez bruoder sele ein lied, und daz erschal als froelich, daz es im alle sin sinne verflogte von úberkraft des sussen gedoenes. . . .

164. For another passage on the warming of the heart, see Hor. I.1 (383.1–4). For some texts containing descriptions of the Servant joining in heavenly singing and dancing, see, e.g., L 5 (20–22), 11 (31), 23 (69), 35 (109), and 36 (111–12, and 114). See also LBL 8 (385–86), and the psaltery vision in Hor. I.13 (478–79).

165. One of the most interesting of the more didactic visions of the passion in the *Life* occurs in chapter 43 (144–45), where the Servant, in imitation of St. Francis, is given a vision of the Crucified One in the form of a Seraph. The account does not expatiate on any possible physical effect on the beholder, but is content to list the messages on the captions that appear on the three pairs of wings: "Receive suffering willingly"; "Bear suffering patiently"; and "Learn to suffer as Christ did."

166. See the indices in Künzle's edition, especially under *excessus, exstasis*, and *rapere*.

167. Hor. II.4 (558.8).

168. For Suso's contributions to MHG vocabulary, see Ruh, *Geschichte*, 3:473–75. Ruh's

judgment is worth citing: "Wenn mich nicht der Eindruck täuscht, so ist der Wortschatz Seuses der reichste und differenzierste von allen Mystikern."

169. For other appearances of *verzuken*, see L 10.16, 20.22, 64.3, 90.18, 102.6, 115.14, 160.27, and 174.15. The term is also found in Eckhart; see chapter 4, p. 185.

170. For other uses of *vergangenheit*, see 90.23, 101.8, 152.11, 159.16, 160.16f.—discussed above, 188.5, 189.12, 193.26, and 338.18. For *vergangen in got* and related uses, see 94.12 and 28–29, 95.1, 160.29, 161.6, 185.2, 189.2, 193.13, 194.27, 335.22, 336.12, 344.13, and 345.12.

171. For *versinken*, see 173.20 and 336.18; for *entsunkenheit*, 90.19, 93.6–8, 109.15, 139.25, 182.26, 187.24, and 192.3. On these terms, see Egerding, *Die Metaphorik*, 2:490–92.

172. For *entgangenheit*, see 94.27, 113.13, 162.31, 168.16 and 19, 189.16–17, and 344.12.

173. For *entwurket*, see 160.29, 165.20, 168.18, 189.21, 192.31, and especially 341.18–23.

174. For example, *entzogenheit* (127.34), *entnomenheit* (163.1, 349.28), *ufgezogenheit* (196.7, 290.2), and the verb *erzogen* (112.7).

175. L 5 (17–22). The term *goetlich troste* used in the title here is equivalent to what is elsewhere called *goetliche gebruchunge* (334.2). Both terms have a rich history.

176. L 5 (17.25–18.9). The passage cited is clearly ecstatic: Dis gesang erhal als úbernatúrlich wol in ime, daz im alles si gemuet verfloeget ward. . . . Do ward im ein unsaglicher umbvang . . . (Tobin modified).

177. L 5 (20.16–23): Geswind sah er dar und sah, daz der lip ob sinem herzen ward als luter als ein kristalle, und sah enmiten in dem herzen ruhelich sizen die ewigen wisheit . . . , und bi dem sass des dieners sele in himelscher senung; . . . und lag also verzogen und versofet von minnen under dez geminten gotes armen.

178. L 5 (21.28–29): . . . ez waz neiswi ein himelsche uswal und ein widerinwal in daz wild abgrúnd der goetlichen togenheit.

179. On the role of such *speculieren* knowledge, that is, knowledge of God as revealed in the mirror of creation (Rom. 1:20), see Jeffrey F. Hamburger, "Speculations on Speculation: Vision and Perception in the Theory and Practice of Mystical Devotion," in *Deutsche Mystik im abendländische Zusammenhang*, ed. Walter Haug and Wolfram Schneider-Lastin (Tübingen: Niemeyer, 2000), 353–68. According to Hamburger: "Speculation defines the procedure by which the one form of perception is linked to the other, in other words, the process by which the perception of the natural leads to the perception of the supernatural" (364).

180. L 50 (173.20–25): Er versank die wil als gar in gote die ewigen wisheit, daz er nút konde dur von gesprechen. Underwilent hat er ein minneklich einreden mit gote, denn ein jamriges suefzen, denn ein senliches weinen, etwen ein stillswigendes lachen. Im waz dik, als ob er in dem luft swepti, und enzwischen zit und ewikeit in dem tiefen wage gotes grundlosen wundern swummi.

181. L 50 (174.6–13): . . . "nu dar, min liepliches liep, so enbloez ich min herz, und in der einvaltigen blossheit aller geschafenheit umbvah ich din bildlosen gotheit. Owe, du úbertrefendes liep alles liebes! . . . du, alles liebes grundlosú vollheit, du zerflússet in liebes herzen, du zergússet dich in der sel wesen, du bloss al in al, daz liebes ein einig teil nit uss blibet, den daz es lieplich mit lieb vereinet wirt" (Tobin modified).

182. Suso uses the terms *grunt/abgrunt/grundelos* a little over two hundred times—even more than Eckhart. For a helpful survey, see Egerding, *Die Metaphorik* 2:302–08.

183. LBT 2 (330.3–14): Disú menigheit ellú ist mit dem grunde und in dem bodme ein einveltigú einikeit. . . . Ich heisse den grund den usqual und den ursprung, us dem die usflússe entspringent. . . . Daz ist dú natur und daz wesen der gotheit; und in disem grundelosen abgrúnde siget dú driheit der personen in ire einikeit, und ellú mengi wirt da ir selbs entsetzet in etlicher wise. Da ist ovch nach diser wise ze nemenne nút froemdes werkes, denne ein stillú inswebende dúnsterheit (Tobin modified).

184. LBT 2 (330.20–23): . . . und da in dem selben ougeblicke ist es swanger berhaftikeit und werkes, wan also hat sich in der nemunge únserre vernunft gotheit ze gotte geswungen.

185. For Porete's conception of the *Loingprés*, see McGinn, *Flowering of Mysticism*, 253.

186. LBT 5 (343.18–19): . . . daz der kreftiger entwordenliche inschalg in daz niht entschlecht in dem grunde allen underscheid, nút nach wesunge, mer nach nemunge únser halb, . . . (my trans.).

187. LBT 5 (346.2–4): Sol er dar komen, so muoz er sin in dem grunde, der verborgen lit in dem vor genemten nihte. Da weis man nút von núte, da ist nit, da ist ouch kein da. . . .

188. Suso's most detailed discussion of indistinction is found in LBT 6 (354.5–355.4), where he refers to Eckhart's passage on the One as indistinct-distinction (*In. Sap.* nn. 144–57 [LW 2:481–94]). However, Suso's transposition of Eckhart's *indistinctus* into the MHG *inniges* (355.3), as well as his claim that "this distinction in the proper sense is not in God but rather from God" (355.1–2), demonstrates that his teaching is not the same as Eckhart's.

189. L 52 (188.20–189.3): In disem wilden gebirge des úber goetlichen wa ist ein enpfintlichú vorspilendú allen reinen geisten abgrúntlichkeit, und da kunt si in die togen-lichen ungenantheit und in daz wild enpfroemdekeit. Und daz ist daz grundlos tiefes abgrúnd allen creaturen und im selber grúntlich . . . (Tobin modified). Whereas Eckhart only used the term *abgrund* six times, Suso employs it and its derivatives twenty-nine times.

190. LBW 12 (245.9–12): . . . und ie abgescheidner lediger usgang, ie vrier ufgang, und ie vrier ufgang, ie neher ingang in die wilden wuesti und in daz tief abgrúnde der wiselosen gotheit, in die sú versenket, verswemmet und vereinet werden. While there is no real Latin equivalent for *grunt*, the term *abyssus* (= *abgrund*) had a long history in Western mysticism. Suso uses the word nineteen times in the *Horologium*. The most interesting passage is in Hor. I.6 (432.20–21) where he employs the text from Psalm 41:8 to describe the relation of God and human: Ecce nunc *abyssus abyssum* reperit. Abyssus desideriorum abyssum introivit omnium gratiarum et perfectionum. On this mystical theme, see Bernard McGinn, "The Abyss of Love: The Language of Mystical Union among Medieval Women," in *The Joy of Learning and the Love of God: Essays in Honor of Jean Leclercq*, ed. E. Rozanne Elder (Kalamazoo: Cistercian Publications, 1995), 95–120. In the Hor. Suso also makes use of the term *fontale principium* from time to time as a Latin analogue to *grund* (e.g., 380.29, 462.2, 554.30, and 579.9).

191. LBL 5 (377.4–9): Ach, ewigú wisheit, minnekliches lieb, wan sehin dich ellú soelichú herzen, als dich min herze siht, so zerstube in in ellú zerganglichú liebi! Herr, mich kan niemer verwundren, swie froemd es mir och hie vor waz, daz kein grundlos minnendes herz in úte denn in dir, tiefer wag, grundloses mer, tiefes abgrúnd aller minneklicher dingen gelen-den mag (Tobin modified).

192. Sermon 4 (534.7–15): Duo muost haben eyn grundelois lazen. Wie grundelois? Were eyn stein und viel in eyn grundeloiz wazzer, der muoste ummer vallen, wan he inhielte niet grundes. Also sulde der mensche haben eyn grundeloiz versinken und vervallen in den grun-delosen got und in in gegrundet sin, wie swere eynich dink uf in vile. . . . Dir sulde allez den menschen ye difer in got senken, und insulde sines grundes nummer da an gewar werden noch ruren noch bedruben . . . (Tobin modified).

193. The term *grunt des herzens* appears some eighteen times.

194. Terms like *menschegrund* and *eigen grund* occur about ten times.

195. The only appearance of *grund siner sele* in *The Exemplar* is in L 38 (124.24–25). The phrase *grund mines herzen und miner sele* occurs in 214.26 and 294.17, and one of the poems ascribed to Suso uses *der sele grund* twice (400.10 and 21). This sparse usage contrasts with the approximately twenty times Eckhart refers to the *grunt der sele*.

196. The exploration of God as intellect, so prevalent among the German Dominicans, plays a role in Suso, but certainly not to the extent found in Eckhart and others. For other passages on God as *vernunftikeit*, see, e.g., 160.21–22, 192.2, 329.9–17.

197. The "negation of negation" (176.12–13) is a major theme of Eckhart (see chap. 4, pp. 139–40). Divine darkness (*goetlichen vinsterheit*: 177.19), a Dionysian expression, is used fifteen times by Suso (see the "Glossar" in Bihlmeyer, 619). The Eckhartian expression *ein einig ein*

(177.27) occurs also at 93.20, 106.35, 159.6, 164.3, 225.16, 294.23–24, 313.1, 330.1, and 477.18.

198. L 51 (179.9–11): . . . wan als daz usfliessen der personen usser got ist ein foermliches bilde des ursprunges der creatur, also ist es och ein vorspil des widerfliessens der creatur in got.

199. On Bonaventure's *Itinerarium mentis in deum*, see McGinn, *Flowering of Mysticism*, 105–12.

200. Suso discusses the divine Nothingness in a number of passages; see, e.g., L 49 and 52 (167.5–6, 184.20–26); LBT 1 and 6 (329.6, 342.23–343.11 and 347.7–12). The Divine Nothing is nameless, but is nonetheless fruitful (". . . daz geberlich niht, daz man got nemmet [343.9–10]). On Suso's doctrine of Nothingness, see Minoru Nambara, "Die Idee des absoluten Nichts in der deutschen Mystik und seine Entsprechungen im Buddhismus," *Archiv für Begriffsgeschichte* 6 (1960): 201–8.

201. LBT 3 (332.17–18): . . . aber die kreaturlicheit einer ieklicher kreature ist ir edeler und gebruchlicher, denne daz wesen, daz si in gotte hat. Virtual existence is also mentioned in the Latin *Hor.* I.1 (382.1–4).

202. L 46 (157.26–158.5): Aber ein ieklicher mensch bevindet, daz er dise ald der mensch ist ussrent dem selben grunde, . . . und da ist er iez in siner gebresthaftigen geschafenheit, da er wol bedarf ellú schedlichú mitel ze miden. . . . daz weri gebrest ob allen gebresten.

203. See *Hor.* II.5 (572–79); see also I.6 (423–24). On Suso's appreciation of nature, see Hamburger, "Speculations on Speculation," 360–65.

204. See chapter 4 above.

205. LBT 2 (330.25–26), 5 (340.19–19, 347.25–349.11), and 6 (355.5–356.5). See also LBW 21 (279.3–8). A careful study of these passages would show Suso's intent was to modify some of the more daring aspects of Eckhart's teaching on the birth of the Word in the soul. H. Piesch ("Seuses 'Büchlein der Wahrheit' und Meister Eckhart," 131) notes that Suso prefers the term *widergeburt* to Eckhart's *gotesgeburt*, just as he uses *gelassenheit* more than *abgescheidenheit*.

206. The major passages that deal with the *geburt* theme in the *Life* concern the eternal birth of the Son from the Father; see L 51 (179.13–22, 181.11–13), and 53 (191.21–29), though Suso does use the birthing metaphor for our union in God in two places: L 48 (162.9–10); and L 52 (186.13–16).

207. Suso at times uses "breakthrough" in an ascetical sense of a "breakthrough of one's unmortified nature" (3.11–12, 53.2, 333.28–29, 497.2–3). On Suso's use of various terms based on the verb *brechen*, see Egerding, *Die Metaphorik*, 2:134–36.

208. LBT 4 (333.5–7): Ich horti nu gerne von dem durchbruche, wie der mensche durch Cristum sol wider in komen und sin selikeit erlangen. See also 34.11–12.

209. L 32 (94.9–14): . . . luog, dien menschen, dien reht beschiht in dem durpruch, den ein mensch voran hin muoss nemen mit einem entsinkene im selben und allen dingen, dero doch nit vil ist, dero sin und muot sind als gar vergangen in got, daz sú neiswi umb sich selber nút wússen, denn sich und ellú ding ze nemene in ire ersten ursprunge (Tobin modified). See also L 33 (97.8–9), which uses the phrase *durpruch zuo gote*; and Letter 28 in the *Grosses Briefbuch* (474.7–18).

210. A detailed treatment of Suso's understanding of union can be found in Egerding, *Die Metaphorik*, 1:197–207, who emphasizes the differences between Eckhart and Suso.

211. For a summary text on how the union begun in this life will be perfected in heaven, see LBW 12 (245.4–15). See also *Hor.* II.3 (543.19–544.6) and II.4 (563.5–13).

212. L 32 (93.18–20): Daz drit ist: ich wil sú als inneklich durkússen und als minneklich umbvahen, daz ich sú und sú ich, und wir zwei ein einziges ein iemer me eweklich súlin bliben.

213. This teaching is found in many texts, e.g., *Hor.* I.11 (465.17–20): Et quanto plus se actibus mancipaverit spiritualibus, tanto illic felicius absorbebitur in abyssum divinissimae claritatis, et unus cum eo spiritus efficietur, ita ut hoc, quod Deus est per naturam, ipsa fiet per gratiam. Cf. LBW 12 (245.1–15), L 50 (188.1–7).

214. Sufi mystics, such al-Ghazzali, sought to explain the autotheistic statements of figures like al-Hallaj by showing how these statements expressed the loss of the consciousness of self in mystical *fana*, not the ontological dissolution of the created person. See al-Ghazzali's *The Niche for Lights (Mishkat al-Anwar)*, chapter 6, as found in *Four Sufi Classics*, introduction by Idries Shah (London: Octagon, 1980), 120–23. See Annemarie Schimmel, *Mystical Dimensions of Islam* (Chapel Hill: University of North Carolina, 1975), 141–48.

215. LBT 5 (343.17–19); in the same chapter see 345.20–24, 350.23–28. See LBT 6 (353.34–354.15, 356.18–23).

216. For the uses of the term, see Bihlmeyer's "Glossar," 581. MHG *gottesfründe* and its equivalents appear more rarely in the other works; see, e.g., LBW 7 (227.25), and Letters 9 and 11 (388.13, 391.20), as well as some texts in the *Grosses Briefbuch* (421.2, 429.5, 431.21, and 469.17).

217. On the relation between Suso and the Free Spirit, see especially Georg Hofmann, "Die Brüder und Schwestern des freien Geistes zur Zeit Heinrich Seuses," HS, 9–32; and Robert E. Lerner, *The Heresy of the Free Spirit in the Later Middle Ages* (Berkeley: University of California, 1972), 186–88.

218 On the Dominican defense of Eckhart, see Loris Sturlese, "Die Kölner Eckhartisten: Das Studium generale der deutschen Dominikaner und die Verurteilung der Thesen Meister Eckharts," in *Die Kölner Universität im Mittelalter*, ed. Albert Zimmermann (Berlin: Walter de Gruyter, 1989), 192–211, where Suso is listed among the group on p. 208.

219. LBT Prol (327.25–28): . . . daz sú im guoten underscheid gebi, als verre es muglich were, enzwúschent dien menschen, die da zilent uf ordenlicher einvalikeit, und etlichen, die da zilent, als man siet, uf ungeordenter friheit. . . .

220. LBT 6 (353.27–31): Der mensch wirt niemer so gar vereinet in disem nihte, sinen sinnen blibe dennoch underscheit ir eigenes urspringes und der vernunft dez selben ir eigen kiesen, wie daz alles in sinem ersten grunde unangesehen blibet. On LBT 6, see Wolfgang Wackernagel, "Maître Eckhart et le discernement mystique: A propos de la rencontre de Suso avec 'la (chose) sauvage sans nom,'" *Revue de Théologie et de Philosophie* 129 (1997): 113–26.

221. Prol. (3.13–15): Wan ouch etlichú menschen sind, dero sin und muot na dem aller nehsten und besten ze erfolgen ringet und in aber underschaides gebristet . . . ; see also 4.9–17.

222. L 28 (83.12–16): . . . ir habent im sin tohter als och vil ander menschen verkeret in ein sunder leben, daz heisset der geist, . . . daz daz sie daz verkertest volg, daz uf ertrich lebt.

223. See L 46 (156–58), 47 (158–60), 48 (160–63), and 51 (181–83).

Chapter 6

1. Tauler's sermons will be cited from the edition of Ferdinand Vetter, *Die Predigten Taulers* (Berlin: Weidmann, 1910; photomechanical reprint, 1968). Texts will be cited by sermon number, page, and line. This passage is V 45 (196.28–197.2):

> Lieben kinder, die grossen pfaffen und die lesmeister die tsipitieren weder bekentnisse merre und edeler si oder die minne. Aber wir wellen nu al hie sagen von den lebmeistern. Als wire dar komen, denne súllen wir aller dinge worheit wol sehen. Unser herre sprach: 'eins ist not'. Weles ist nu das eine des als not ist? Das eine das ist das du bekennest din nivht, das din eigen ist, was du bist und wer du bist von dir selber.

Since there is no full or adequate version of Tauler in English, all translations are my own unless otherwise noted. I have tried to stay as close to the MHG as is compatible with readable English. I would like to thank Prof. Oliver Davies for helpful suggestions regarding both the presentation and translations of Tauler.

2. The best recent account of Tauler is Louise Gnädinger, *Johannes Tauler: Lebenswelt und mystische Lehre* (Munich: Beck, 1993). See also Kurt Ruh, *Geschichte* 3:476–526. An important collection of essays is *Johannes Tauler: Ein deutsche Mystiker. Gedenkschrift zum 600. Todestag*, ed. Ephrem Filthaut, O.P. (Essen: Hans Driewer, 1961). Useful monographs include Ignaz Weilner, *Johannes Taulers Bekehrungsweg: Die Erfahrungsgrundlagen seiner Mystik* (Regensburg: Pustet, 1961); Christine Pleuser, *Die Benennungen und der Begriff des Leides bei J. Tauler* (Berlin: Schmidt, 1967); Gösta Wrede, *Unio Mystica: Probleme der Erfahrung bei Johannes Tauler* (Uppsala: Almqvist & Wiksell, 1974); Stefan Zekorn, *Gelassenheit und Einkehr: Zu Grundlage und Gestalt geistlichen Lebens bei Johannes Tauler* (Würzburg: Echter, 1993); and Thomas Gandlau, *Trinität und Kreuz: Die Nachfolge Christi in der Mystagogie Johannes Taulers* (Freiburg: Herder, 1993). Two important studies comparing Tauler and Eckhart are Dietmar Mieth, *Die Einheit von Vita activa und Vita contemplativa in den deutschen Predigten und Traktaten Meister Eckharts und bei Johannes Tauler* (Regensburg: Pustet, 1969); and Alois M. Haas, *Nim din selbes war: Studien zur Lehre von der Selbsterkenntnis bei Meister Eckhart, Johannes Tauler und Heinrich Seuse* (Freiburg, Switzerland: Universitätsverlag, 1971). For the seven hundredth anniversary of Tauler's birth, two volumes of essays appeared: Marie-Anne Vannier, ed., *700e Anniversaire de la naissance de Jean Tauler* (*Revue des sciences religieuses* 75, no. 4 [2001]); and *Cheminer avec Jean Tauler: Pour le 7e centenaire de sa naissance* (*La vie spirituelle* 155 [March 2001]).

3. David Blamires, "Introduction," in *The Book of the Perfect Life* (Walnut Creek, Calif.: AltaMira Press, 2003), 14.

4. Mieth (*Die Einheit*, 275–81) is insightful on Tauler's originality, especially in relation to ecclesiology, Christology, and social ethics. Zekorn (*Gelassenheit und Einkehr*, 195–208, 227–34) also speaks to Tauler's originality in relation to Eckhart. Tauler's large and continuing influence testifies to his significance. There are a number of essays on his posterity in *Johannes Tauler: Ein deutsche Mystiker*, 341–434. See also Maarten J. F. M. Hoenen, "Johannes Tauler (d. 1361) in den Niederlanden: Grundzüge eines philosophie- und rezeptionsgeschichtlichen Forschungsprogramms," *Freiburger Zeitschrift für Philosophie und Theologie* 41 (1994): 389–444; Marco Vannini, "Le posterité de Tauler: La théologie allemande, Luther et les autres," in *Cheminer avec Jean Tauler*, 115–32; and Gérard Pfister, "La posterité de Jean Tauler," in *700e anniversaire de la naissance de Jean Tauler*, 465–78.

5. The most complete account of Tauler's life is Gnädinger, *Johannes Tauler*, 9–103. In English, see Oliver Davies, *God Within: The Mystical Tradition of Northern Europe* (London: Darton, Longman, and Todd, 1988), 71–78.

6. On the Dominicans in Strassburg, see Heribert Christian Scheeben, "Der Konvent der Predigerbrüder in Strassburg—Die religiöse Heimat Taulers," in *Johannes Tauler: Ein deutscher Mystiker*, 37–74; and Francis Rapp, "Le couvent des dominicains de Strasbourg à l'époque de Tauler," in *Cheminer avec Jean Tauler*, 59–74.

7. On the relation between Tauler and religious women, see the section in Zekorn, *Gelassenheit und Einkehr*, "Tauler und die Nonnenmystik," 203–18.

8. For Tauler's relations with the Friends of God, see chapter 9 below, pp. 410–13.

9. The letters between Margaret and Henry have been edited by Philipp Strauch, *Margaretha Ebner und Heinrich von Nördlingen: Ein Beitrag zur Geschichte der deutschen Mystik* (Freiburg im Breisgau: Herder, 1882; reprint 1966). This collection includes Tauler's only surviving letter, a brief missive sent to the prioress of the convent of Maria Medingen, Elisabeth Scheppach, and Margaret Ebner shortly before Lent of 1346 with a present of cheeses (see Letter LVII in Strauch, 270–71). For accounts of the references to Tauler in other letters in the correspondence, see Gnädinger, *Johannes Tauler*, 34–43. For more on Henry and Margaret Ebner, see chapter 9 below.

10. Carl Schmidt, *Nicolaus von Basel: Bericht von der Bekehrung Taulers* (Strassburg, 1875; photomechanical reprint, Frankfurt: Minerva, 1981). For an account of the *Meisterbuch* and its affinities with Tauler's teaching, see chapter 9 below, pp. 420–23.

11. On Tauler's view of the approaching end, see Gnädinger, *Johannes Tauler*, 46–49; and Ruh, *Geschichte*, 3:481 and 485.

12. Tauler often attacks the pharisees as examples of merely external religion (e.g., V 9 [41.6–22 and 42.17–22]; V 10 [47.35–48.10]; V 54 [246.12–27]), but it is clear that the pharisee for him is a general type, not one restricted to Jews. In V 13 (62.34–63.1) the evil Jews (*boese juden*) who attacked Jesus are read as present-day Christians who oppose the friends of God. In two sermons (V 42 [177.1–3]; V 75 [405.39–406.9]) Tauler says that Jews and pagans often have more faith and lead better lives than Christians. For Tauler's view of the Jews, see Gnädinger, *Johannes Tauler*, 56–60.

13. The "Tauleriana," that is, the pseudonymous works attributed to Tauler, will not be taken up here. The most important of these, *The Book of Spiritual Poverty* and the *Masterbook*, will be treated below in chapter 8, pp. 377–92, and chapter 9, pp. 420–23, respectively. A number of songs have also been attributed to Tauler. For discussions, see Gnädinger, *Johannes Tauler*, 426–31; and Ruh, *Geschichte*, 3:515–26.

14. On Tauler's relation to the Dominicans of his age, see Ephrem Filthaut, "Johannes Tauler und die deutsche Dominikanerscholastik des XIII./XIV. Jahrhunderts," in *Johannes Tauler: Ein deutscher Mystiker*, 94–121.

15. On Tauler manuscripts, see Johannes Gottfried Mayer, *Die 'Vulgata'-Fassung der Predigten Johannes Tauler* (Würzburg: Königshausen & Neumann, 1999).

16. The edition of Vetter is based on only a few manuscripts and does not adhere to the proper liturgical order of the sermons. It does list variant readings and has a useful word index, but it lacks any apparatus of sources. Several of the sermons are not authentic (V 1 [= Eckhart], 59, 79 [= Ruusbroec], 80). An edition based on two Vienna manuscripts was made by A. L. Corin, *Sermons de Jean Tauler et autres écrits mystiques: I, Le Codex Vindobonensis 2744; II, Le Codex Vindobonensis 2739* (Liége/Paris: Bibliothèque de la Faculté de Philosophie et Lettres de l'Université de Liége, 1924–29). This rare edition restores the proper order of the sermons and contains many improved readings, but it is not a full critical text. The translation into modern German of Georg Hofmann, *Johannes Tauler: Predigten* (Freiburg: Herder, 1961; reprint, Einsiedeln, 1979) makes use of readings both from Vetter and Corin and thus provides a good modern version, but not a critical MHG one. Also useful is the complete French translation made by É. Hugueny, G. Théry, and A.-L. Corin, *Sermons de Tauler: Traduction faite sur les plus anciens mss. allemands*, 3 vols. (Paris: Éditions de la Vie Spirituelle, 1927–35), hereafter abbreviated C with sermon number in Roman numerals and appropriate volume, page, and line when cited. This version will be used at times below, because it contains an important introduction, many improved readings, and useful footnotes. This translation also accepts as authentic three other sermons: two sermons from Strassburg, MS 3885, edited by Dick Helander, *Johann Tauler als Prediger: Studien* (Lund: Almqvist & Wiksell, 1923), 346–61 (= C LX and LXXI); and a sermon for the Third Sunday of Advent (= C LXXXIII) ascribed by Karl Bihlmeyer to Suso and found in his *Seuse: Deutsche Schriften*, 509–18.

17. Older English translations of Tauler include inauthentic pieces and were often made from the Latin version of Laurentius Surius. Two partial more recent translations exist. Eric Colledge and Sister Mary Jane, O.P., *Spiritual Conferences by Johann Tauler, O.P. (1300–1361)* (New York: Herder, 1961; reprint 1978). This rather loose translation of sermons and excerpts of sermons from Vetter was done with consultation of the French translation and includes some helpful notes. Its disadvantage is that it rearranges the passages according to theological headings rather than keeping the order of the sermons themselves. Maria Shrady, trans., *Johannes Tauler: Sermons* (New York: Paulist Press, 1985) translates twenty-three sermons, but from the modern German of Hofmann, not from the MHG of Vetter or Corin. Given this fact, plus the version's omissions, errors, and lack of notes or apparatus, it is quite deficient.

18. There are three general accounts in English: James M. Clark, *The Great German Mystics: Eckhart, Tauler and Suso* (Oxford: Blackwell, 1949), 36–54; O. Davies, *God Within*, 73–98;

and Josef Schmidt, "Introduction," in *Johannes Tauler: Sermons*, 1–34. Some helpful essays will be mentioned below.

19. Like Eckhart, Tauler's sermons always must be seen in the context of the church's year and the liturgical readings of its feasts. On this, see Joachim Theisen, "Tauler und die Liturgie," in *Deutsche Mystik im abendländischen Zusammenhang*, ed. Walter Haug and Wolfram Schneider-Lastin (Tübingen, Niemeyer, 2000), 409–23.

20. An exception is the comparative study of Gabriele von Siegroth-Nellessen, *Versuch einer exakten Stiluntersuchung für Meister Eckhart, Johannes Tauler und Heinrich Seuse* (Munich: W. Fink, 1979), who finds Tauler more free and spontaneous than the other two. For brief remarks on Tauler's preaching style and further literature, see Gnädinger, *Johannes Tauler*, 104–9; and Schmidt, "Introduction," in *Johannes Tauler: Sermons*, 9–22.

21. Tauler's exegesis has not been given great attention. See Helander, *Johann Tauler als Prediger*, 310–27; and Raymond Alexis, "Die Bibelzitate in Werken des Strassburger Prediger Johannes Tauler: Ein Beitrag zum Problem der vorlutherischen Bibelverdeutschung," *Revue des langues vivants* 20 (1954): 397–411.

22. The most detailed studies of Tauler's sources are by Gnädinger, in *Johannes Tauler*, 370–410, and "Das Altväterzitat im Predigtwerk Johannes Taulers," in *Unterwegs zur Einheit. Festschrift für Heinrich Stirnimann*, ed. Johannes Brantschen and Pietro Selvatico (Freiburg, Switzerland: Universitätsverlag, 1980), 253–67.

23. Among the sermons that contain such stories, see V 6 (27.3–10), V 29 (302.29–32), V 41 (174.8–14), V 67 (370.32), V 74 (399.3–6), and V 80 (425.17–29). For a discussion of these sources, see Gnädinger, *Johannes Tauler*, 403–10.

24. For Tauler's use of scholastic authors, see Gunther Müller, "Scholastikerzitate bei Tauler," *Deutsche Vierteljahrsschrift für Literaturwissenschaft und Geistesgeschichte* 1 (1923): 400–418.

25. Besides Filthaut ("Johannes Tauler und die deutsche Dominikanerscholastik des XIII./XIV. Jahrhunderts," in *Johannnes Tauler*, 94–121), the question of Tauler's use of Neo-platonism, especially through Dietrich of Freiburg and Berthold of Moosburg, has been investigated by Loris Sturlese, "Tauler im Kontext: Die philosophischen Voraussetzungen des 'Seelengrundes' in der Lehre des deutschen Neuplatonikers Berthold von Moosburg," *Beiträge zur Geschichte der deutschen Sprache und Literatur* 109 (1987): 390–426. The most extensive treatment of Tauler's relation to Eckhart is in Zekorn, *Gelassenheit und Einkehr*, 194–203, and 233, who summarizes the Strassburg preacher's approach as "eine Art 'Meister Eckhart für die Praxis'" (203).

26. V 29 (300.14–17): Meister Thomas sprach daz vollekomenheit dis bildes lige an der würglicheit dis bildes, an der uebunge der krefte, also an gehugnisse gegenwúrklich und wúrklich verstentnisse und an minnen wúrklich; do lat er das ligen in disem sinne. Thomas's view is set forth in STh Ia, q. 93, a. 7.

27. V 29 (300.17–22): Aber nu sprechent ander meister, und daz ist unzellichen vil und verre harúber, und sprechent das es lige in dem allerinnigsten, in dem allerverborgensten tieffesten grunde der selen, do sú daz in dem grunde hat Got wesentlichen und wúrklich und isteklich, in dem wurket und weset Got und gebruchet sin selbes in dem, und man moehte Got also wenig dannan abe gescheiden also von ime selber. . . .

28. Three of Proclus's treatises, including the *De providentia*, were translated into Latin by William of Moerbeke. The passage Tauler summarizes comes from *De providentia* 8.31–32, as found in *Procli Tria opuscula (De providentia, libertate, malo)*, ed. Helmut Boese (Berlin: Walter de Gruyter, 1960), 139–40. Loris Sturlese has argued that Tauler's use of Proclus is mediated through his contemporary Berthold of Moosburg, the most Proclian of all the German Dominicans; see "Tauler im Kontext," especially 399–409 on this sermon.

29. V 29 (300.35–301.5): . . . und er nemmet dis eine alsus: 'eine stille swigende sloffende goetteliche unsinnige dúnsternisse.' Kinder, das ein heiden dis verstunt und darzuo kam, das wir dem also verre und also ungelich sint, das ist uns laster und grosse schande. Dis bezúgete

unser herre do er sprach: 'das rich Gottes ist in úch'. Das wurt alleine indewendig in dem grunde obe allen werken der krefte.

30. V 64 (347.9–14): Von disem inwendigen adel der in dem grunde lit verborgen, hant vil meister gesprochen beide alte und núwe: bischof Albert, meister Dietrich, meister Eckhart. Der eine heisset es eine funke der selen, der ander einen boden oder ein tolden, einer ein erstekeit, und bischof Albrecht nemmet es ein bilde in dem die heilige drivaltikeit gebildet ist und do inne gelegen ist. This important sermon is permeated with the teaching of the German Dominican masters. A lengthy passage from Albert's commentary on Luke is quoted (349.17–36), and another long citation is given on 351.14–29. The *ein meister* cited at 350.13 ff. is probably Eckhart.

31. V 64 (347.17–24): Dise meister die hannan ab gesprochen hant, die hant es mit lebende und mit vernunft ervolget, und si hant es nu in der worheit befunden, und dise hant es genomen us den grossen heiligen und lerern der heiligen kilchen die hinnan ab gesprochen hant, und vor Gotz gebúrte vil meister die hinnan ab sprachen: Plato und Aristotiles und Proculus. Und also als dis die guoten groeslich reisset und tuont einen swinden in ker und zuo ker von disen hohen adel in der naher sibschaft: also tuont die valschen iren ewigen schaden hie mitte. Tauler again refers to Proclus by name and quotes him directly later in the sermon (350.20–22). The reference to Aristotle holding a doctrine of the ground of the soul is possibly explained on the basis of the conviction of many medieval thinkers that Aristotle was the author of the *Liber de causis* whose teaching on *intelligentia* and its mode of knowing was deeply Proclian. (See *Liber de Causis*, Prop. VI-XII.) L. Sturlese, however, thinks that Tauler is here influenced by Berthold of Moosburg, who equated Proclus's *unum animae*, Augustine's *abditum mentis*, and Aristotle's *intellectus agens* ("Tauler im Kontext," 415–16 and 422–26). With regard to Plato, we can note that Meister Eckhart also praised Plato, "that great cleric," for his teaching about the *grunt* (Pr. 28 [DW 2.67.1–68.3]).

32. V 15 (69.26–28): Usser diseme lert úch und seit úch ein minnenclich meister, und das enverstont ir nút; er sprach uss der ewikeit, und ir vernement es noch der zeit.

33. V 56 (263.1–4): Aber ein gros edel meister sprach: 'also schiere als sich der mensche wider kert mit sinem gemuete und mit gantzem willen, und sinen geist in treit in Gotz geiste úber die zit, so wirt alles das wider bracht in dem ougenblicke das ie verloren wart'. The passage from Eckhart that Tauler is summarizing here is from Pr. 5b (DW 1:94.8–95.3). For the opposing view of Aquinas, STh IIIa, q. 89, a. 6.

34. Along with the passages from V 29 and V 64 mentioned above, Tauler also cites Proclus in V 61 (332.21–26) and V 65 (358.14–16). Tauler quotes a passage from the Neoplatonist Porphyry (referred to as *ein heidenscher kúnig*) in V 69 (378.33–36).

35. The attempt to sketch a Taulerian systematics (curiously called philosophical) by Dietrich M. Schlütter ("Philosophische Grundlagen der Lehren Johannes Tauler," in *Johannes Tauler: Ein deutsche Mystiker*, 122–61) collects much information, but its rigid form militates against usefulness as a general presentation of Tauler's thought.

36. For Tauler's critical comments on academic theology, see, e.g., V 18 (287.32–288.14), V 19 (77.23–27), V 29 (299.18–34), V 45 (196.28–30), and V 78 (420.35–421.9). For a discussion, see Maurice De Gandillac, *Valeur du temps dans la pédagogie spirituelle de Jean Tauler* (Paris/Montréal: J. Vrin, 1956), 12–17, 83–87.

37. V 29 (299.18): Hinnan ab ist besser ze bevindende wan ze sprechende.

38. The summary of Tauler's doctrine of God by Alfons Hufnagel ("Taulers Gottesbild und Thomas von Aquin," in *Johannes Tauler: Ein deutsche Mystiker*, 162–77) attempts to make Tauler more of a Thomist than he actually was.

39. V 60 (276–78). The text has been little studied and would repay a detailed comparison with Eckhart and Suso, as well as Dionysius.

40. Eckhart uses Isa. 45:15 eight times. His treatment in Pr. 15 (DW 1:252.1–253.6) is quite close to this Tauler text. For a history of some uses of Isa. 45:15, see Bernard McGinn, "*Vere tu es Deus absconditus*: The Hidden God in Luther and Some Mystics," in *Silence and the*

Word: Negative Theology and Incarnation, ed. Oliver Davies and Denys Turner (Cambridge: Cambridge University Press, 2002), 94–114, especially 103–4 on Eckhart.

41. On Eckhart's use of the desert motif and Hosea 2:24, see chapter 4 above, pp. 178–79.

42. V 60 (278.14–19): Dar engegen trag din abgrúndig vinsternisse beroubet von allem woren liechte und darbende alles liechtes und la das abgrúnde des goetlichen vinsternisses im selber allein bekant und allen dingen unbekant. Das abgrúnde, das unbekant und ungenant, das selig, ist me gemint und reisset me die selen denne alles das si bekennen múgen in der ewigen selikeit, an dem goetliche wesende.

43. V 39 (156.19–22): Do ist das aller oberste wúrken und das aller luterste gebruchen ein einig ein ane hinderen und ein ieklichs in dem aller hoechsten, und das ieklichs ane des anderen hinderen. Das wúrken ist in den personen, das gebruchen git man dem einvaltigen wesende.

44. V 41 (176.6–11), and V 45 (201.1–7). For another use of *ein einig ein,* see V 53 (245.17). In several places Tauler uses phrases that are the equivalent of *ein einig ein*; e.g., V 54 (249.9: ein einvaltig luter einikeit); V 60 (277.16–17: in dem einigen ein wesende); V 64 (347.12: einer ein erstekeit); and V 67 (366.22: in einer einveltiger einvaltiket).

45. V 25 (309.5–7): . . . daz ist wenne ir zuo ennander kummet, so súllent ir reden von Gotte und von tugentlich leben und nút disputieren von der gotheit in ander wise noch der vernunft. . . .

46. The terms "supernatural" and "superessential" (*úbernatúrlich* and *úberweselich*) occur often in Tauler. He even speaks of *úberweselicheit* (superessentiality; see 143.6, 238.36, 411.16).

47. V 27 (113.30–34): . . . und dem tete der torwerter uf und liesse in rechte in in daz vetterliche abgrund, und . . . er versúnke mit unsprechenlicher weide in der gotheit und gienge mit minnen us an die heilige vergoettete minnenkliche menscheit in voller weiden und wunnen. . . .

48. A number of studies of Tauler's anthropology exist. See, for example, E. Hugueny, "La doctrine de Tauler," in *Sermons de Tauler,* 1:74–89; Steven E. Ozment, *Homo spiritualis: A Comparative Study of the Anthropology of Johannes Tauler, Jean Gerson and Martin Luther (1509–16) in the Context of their Theological Thought* (Leiden: Brill, 1969), 15–46; Wrede, *Unio Mystica,* Teil II. *Mensch* (93–202); Zekorn, *Gelassenheit und Einkehr,* Erster Teil, *Gott und Mensch* (32–74); Gnädinger, *Johannes Tauler,* 129–36 and 241–51. There are also important analyses of Tauler's anthropology in Mieth, *Die Einheit,* 235–331; and Haas, *Nim din selbes war,* 76–153. Michael Egerding's essay, "Johannes Taulers Auffassung vom Menschen," *Freiburger Zeitschrift für Philosophie und Theologie* 39 (1992): 105–29, deals not so much with Tauler's view of the soul and its powers as with the preacher's attitude toward human destiny.

49. See Mieth, *Die Einheit,* 254–57.

50. On the conflict between the inner and the outer person, see also V 9 (42.28–43.5) and V 57 (266.5–19).

51. V 67 (370.22–28): Dinen innewendigen menschen den ensolt du under nieman legen denne under Got; sunder dinen uswendigen menschen den leg in wore demuetikeit under alle creaturen. . . . Also sol der usser mensche innewendig warten was im der inwendig mensche gebiete, das er dem in allen wisen und werken genuog si. For other texts on the need for harmony and cooperation of inner and outer person, see, e.g., V 11 (56.12–23), V 15 (71.14–17), and V 24 (98.3–9).

52. V 64 (348.22–26): . . . wan der mensche ist rechte als ob er drú menschen si und ist doch ein mensche. Das eine das ist der uswendig vihelich sinneliche mensche; der ander das ist der vernúnftige mensche mit sinem vernúnftigen kreften; der dritte mensche das ist das gemuete, das oberste teil der selen. Dis alles ist ein mensche. Als ist och maniger kúnne wille in den menschen, ieklichs nach siner wise.

53. V 67 (366.4–9): . . . und mag sich keren in sinen ursprung und in sin ungeschaffenheit, do er ewiklich gewesen ist, und stet do sunder bilde und forme in rechter ledikeit [following the reading of Corin]; do git im Got nach dem richtuom sinre ere. Also groeslichen wirt er do

begabet das von der richeit alle die nidersten und die mittelsten und die obersten krefte werdent begabet und gesterket in bevintlicher wise und gebruchlichen.

54. Tauler would have known William's *Epistola aurea*, which is organized according to the tripartite anthropology, though he read it under the name of Bernard of Clairvaux. On William's doctrine of man, see Bernard McGinn, *The Growth of Mysticism*, vol. 2 of *The Presence of God: A History of Western Christian Mysticism* (New York: Crossroad, 1994), 229–34. For other texts in Tauler that make use of the tripartite schema, see, e.g., V 65 (357.15–358.10—an allegorical development based on the sacrifice of Isaac), V 68 (373.9–12, 376.18–22), and V 70 (382.4–26). Tauler also expresses his tripartite anthropology in terms of three powers: the sense powers that receive images; the rational powers; and the hidden *grund* that receives God directly without images; see V 10 (50.15), V 15 (68.1–2), V 23 (92.20–26), V 24 (101.1–4), and V 66 (363.7–11).

55. The generic distinction between higher and lower powers appears in a number of sermons; e.g., V 11 (54.20–28) and V 21 (88.7–15).

56. V 61 (332.19–27). On this contrast, see Sturlese, "Tauler im Kontext," 407–9. In STh Ia, q. 32, a. 1, Aquinas denies any knowledge of the Trinity apart from revelation.

57. V 61 (333.18–20): . . . do bist du in ungewalt din selbes: do ist weder gedanke noch uebunge der krefte noch werk der tugende. It can be noted that the final phrase about losing the work of the virtues is precisely the kind of statement, taken out of context, that was one of the objections against Marguerite Porete (see Bernard McGinn, *The Flowering of Mysticism: Men and Women in the New Mysticism (1200–1350)*, vol. 3 of *The Presence of God: A History of Western Christian Mysticism* [New York: Crossroad, 1998], 245 and 254).

58. V 61 (335.14–16): . . . und hab stete emzeklich begerunge und ein gantz sicher getrúwen, und halt dich hert zuo der minne, und du solt als gros und als vil bevinden als ie mensche in der zit bevant.

59. In V 51 (233.32–234.19), the third sermon for the Feast of the Exaltation of the Holy Cross, four faculties of the soul are crucified with Christ in order to be reborn—the higher powers of *vernunft* and *willen*, and the lower powers of *uswendunge gelusticheit* and *zúrnende kraft*. In V 71 (388.6–25) five powers are associated with Christ's five wounds: the *begirliche kraft* to the wound in the left foot, the *zornliche kraft* to the wound in the right foot; the *eigenwille* to the wound in the left hand; the *vernunft* to the wound in the right hand; and the *minnende kraft* to the wounded heart.

60. V 52 (237.23–24): Wissent: wo Got nút gemeint enwirt, des sol er och kein ende noch kein lon sin.

61. In translating *mens* as *gemuete*, Tauler is following Eckhart, who began his sermon for the Nineteenth Sunday after Trinity the same way: *Renovamini spiritu*. 'Ir svnt ernúwet werden an vwerme geiste, der do mens heiset,' das ist ein gemúte (Pr. 83 [DW 3:437.1–3]).

62. The word translated as "direction" is MHG *vúrwurf*, which can have both the connotation of "object," and also a kinetic aspect, i.e., "being thrown ahead." I take it in the latter sense and thank Prof. Hildegard Keller for the suggestion.

63. V 56 (262.4–13): Das gemuete das ist ein wunneklich ding; in dem sint alle die krefte versament: vernunft, wille; aber es ist an im selber dar úber [following C LXX in 3:160] und hat me dar zuo. Es hat einen innigen weselichen fúrwurf úber die wúrklicheit der krefte, und wanne dem gemuete recht ist und es wol zuo gekert ist, so ist allem dem andern recht, und wo das ab gekert ist, so ist alles ab gekert, man wisse oder enwisse nút. Nu heisset si och ein mens [C LXX in 3:160]. Kinder, das ist der grunt do dis wore bilde der heiligen drivaltikeit inne lit verborgen, und das ist so edel das man dem enkeinen eigenem namen enmag gegeben.

64. Among Tauler's authentic sermons, I can find only two that do not mention *grund*: V 4 and V 78 (which replaces the *grund* with a treatment of the inner *tempel Gotz*). For some major treatments, see, e. g., V 5, 9, 20, 24, 29, 35, 38, 43, 54, 60, 61, 67, 70, and 71.

65. On the relation between Eckhart and Tauler, and especially Tauler's "critical revision" (*kritische Umformulierung*) of Eckhart, see Walter Haug, "Johannes Taulers Via negationis," in

Die Passion Christi in Literatur und Kunst des Spätmittelalters, ed. Walter Haug and Burghart Wachinger (Tübingen: Niemeyer, 1993), 76–93.

66. Eckhart used the word *gemuete* at times, like Tauler employing it as a MHG equivalent of *mens*; but he did not dwell on its relation to *grunt*. Mieth (*Die Einheit*, 251–52) suggests that in Eckhart the term *intellectus*, i.e., *vernunfticheit*, functions in much the way that *gemuete* does for Tauler.

67. Studies of *gemuete* and *grunt* in Tauler include: Hugueny, "La doctrine de Tauler," in *Sermons de Tauler*, 1:75–82; Kurt Kirmsee, *Die Terminologie des Mystikers Johannes Tauler* (Leipzig: Vogel, 1930), especially 32–38 (*grunt*) and 54–57 (*gemuete*); A. Walz, "'Grund' und 'Gemüt' bei Tauler," *Angelicum* 40 (1963): 328–69; Paul Wyser, "Taulers Terminologie vom Seelengrund," in *Altdeutsche und Altniederlandische Mystik*, ed. Kurt Ruh (Darmstadt: Wissenschaftliche Buchgesellschaft, 1964), 324–52; Claire Champollion, "La place des termes 'gemuete' und 'grunt' dans le vocabulaire de Tauler," in *La mystique rhénane* (Paris: Presses Universitaires de France, 1963), 179–92; Haas, *Nim din selbes war*, 140–45; Ozment, *Homo spiritualis*, 15–20; Wrede, *Unio Mystica*, 153–59, 191–202; Sturlese, "Tauler im Kontext," 422–26; Gnädinger, *Johannes Tauler*, 125–26, 241–51; Zekorn, *Gelassenheit und Einkehr*, 43–61; Michael Egerding, *Die Metaphorik der spätmittelalterlichen Mystik* 2:289–302; and Markus Enders, "Selbsterfahrung als Gotteserfahrung: Zum Individualitätsbewusstsein bei Johannes Tauler," in *Individuum und Individualität im Mittelalter*, ed. Jan A. Aertsen and Andreas Speer (Berlin: Walter de Gruyter, 1996), 642–64, especially 653–60.

68. According to Champollion ("Le vocabulaire," 183), Tauler uses *gemuete* 132 times, and *grunt* a staggering 427 times (*vernunft* only appears 84 times). Egerding (*Die Metaphorik* 2:289–91) lists 414 appearances of *grund*, 55 uses of *abgrund*, and 44 uses of *grundelos/ungruntlich*.

69. See, for example, V 38 (150.17–18): . . . und die widerwertigen gebresten die du wieder din gemuete und herze liden muost dich pingende. . . . See also V 54 (246.9–10).

70. In *De Trinitate* 15.7.11 (PL 42:1065) Augustine says: Non igitur anima, sed quod excellit in anima, mens vocatur. A useful survey of the history of *mens* and other terms for the soul and its faculties can be found in Léonce Reypens, "Âme (son fond, ses puissances, et sa structure d'après les mystiques)," DS 1:433–69, which treats Augustine on 436–41, and Tauler on 452–53. See also Aimé Solignac, "'NOUS' et 'MENS,'" DS 11:459–69.

71. See V 3 (20.6–7); the definition is repeated in V 24 (101.13–14), V 39 (154.16–17), and V 78 (421.20). It is significant for a key difference between Eckhart and Tauler that the former interprets this standard definition of prayer from John of Damascus in terms of intellect, not *gemuete*. Eckhart renders "oratio est ascensus mentis in Deum" (*De fide orthodoxa* 3.24) as "ein vernünftic ûfklimmen in got, daz ist gebet" (Pr. 19 [DW 318.12–319.1]) and "intellectus in deum ascensus" (S. XXIV, n. 247 [LW 4:225.13–14]).

72. On *abditum mentis/abstrusior profunditas memoriae*, see, e.g., Augustine, *De trinitate* 14.7.9 and 15.21.40 (PL 42:1043, 1088).

73. V 65 (357.27–30): . . . den uswendigen menschen ze ziehende in den innewendigen menschen und von den bildelichen dingen und gesichtlichen in die ungesichtlichen: das ist in dem grunde das S. Augustinus nemt: 'abditum mentis'. Also 358.6–8: Gib do dich al zemole uf und ging do in und verbirg din verborgen gemuete, das S. Augustinus also nemt, in die verborgenheit des goetlichen abgrundes. . . . On these texts, see Wyser, "Taulers Terminologie vom Seelengrund," 337–41.

74. For Dietrich's teaching, see his *De visione beatifica* in *Dietrich von Freiberg Opera omnia* I:14.45–46. On the significance of this break, see Sturlese, "Tauler im Kontext," 405, 422–24. Eckhart preferred the term *abditum animae* to *abditum mentis* and used it fairly broadly in relation to the soul's essence; see Bernard McGinn, *The Mystical Thought of Meister Eckhart* (New York: Crossroad, 2002), 204 n. 38.

75. V 64 (350.2–4): Es wirt genant ein mosse, wan es misset das ander alles. Es git im sine forme, sine swere, sin gewicht. Es teilet al umbe und umbe. Habitus mentis. The passage goes on to cite Augustine on the nature of habit. The sense in which *habitus* is being used here is not exactly clear. Haas (*Nim din selbes war*, 142–43) understands it as the soul's habitual self-

knowledge *per essentiam*, knowledge that becomes actual in deification in the *grund*. Sturlese ("Tauler im Kontext," 424–25) takes it in a more general way.

76. V 64 (350.9–19): Nu súllen wir alhie merken was dis gemuete si. Das ist verre hoher und innerlicher wan die krefte; wan die krefte nement al ir vermúgen dannan us und sint do inne und dannan us geflossen und ist in allen doch ob sunder mosse. Es ist gar einvaltig und weselich und formelich. Ein meister sprichet von disem und och me denne die meister. Die meister sprechent das dis gemuete der selen das so als edel, es si alwegent wúrkent, der mensche slaffe oder wache, er wisse es oder enwisse es nút, es hat ein gotformig unzellich ewig wider kaffen in Got. Aber dise sprechent, es schouwe alwegen und minne und gebruche Gottes ane underlos. Wie das si, das lossen wir nu ligen; mer dis bekent sich Got in Gotte, und noch denne ist es geschaffen.

77. On *synderesis*, see Heinrich Appel, "Die Syntheresis in der mittelalterlichen Mystik," *Zeitschrift für Kirchengeschichte* 13 (1892): 535–44; and Aimé Solignac, "'Synderesis,'" DS 14:1407–12.

78. V 64 (350.20–22): Proculus, ein heidenscher meister, nent es ein slaf und ein stille und ein goetliche rasten [C LIII in 2:361] und sprichet: 'uns ist ein verborgen suochen des einen, das ist verre úber die vernunft und verstentnisse'. On the use of Proclus in this sermon, see Sturlese ("Tauler im Kontext," 409–15), who provides an analysis of the parallels with Proclus's *De providentia* and *De decem dubitationibus*.

79. V 64 (350.26–28): Dis gemuet, diser grunt das ist als in pflanzet das die pflanze hat ein ewig reissen und ziehen nach ir, und das gemuete, der grunt hat ein ewig neigen, ein grunt neigen wider in den ursprung.

80. For some other important treatments of the *gemuete*, see, e.g., V 23 (96.8–29), V 25 (310.1–5), V 52 (239.16–34), V 57 (270.23–271.7), V 70 (382.16–18), and V 77 (414.32–415.16, 416.1–5).

81. E.g., V 39 (155.5), V 52 (238.10), and V 56 (262.4–13).

82. Wyser, "Taulers Terminologie vom Seelengrund," 346. The same view is found in Zekorn, *Gelassenheit und Einkehr*, 43–50.

83. See V 6 (25.20). Although Tauler prefers the term *abgrunt* to characterize the inner reality of God and the Godhead, he also uses *grunt* in several places; see, e.g., V 27 (113.27), V 38 (149.34), and V 52 (235.9). In addition there are a number of texts where it is obvious that the *grunt* being spoken of cannot be the *grunt der sele*, but must be the divine ground; e.g., V 56 (261.34–262.1).

84. Champollion, "Le vocabulaire de Tauler," 188–89.

85. V 77 (416.1–5): Dise wisen in den der mensche alle truwe, froeude und fride vindet in allen wisen, wercken und stetten, daz wurt alleine gelert und funden in indewendigkeit, in zuogekerheit des gemuetes in den grunt, und daz bedarf in dem ersten lidekeit und muessekeit, zit und statte. See also V 56 (262.20–21) and V 74 (402.8–9). On the reflexive activity of the *gemeüte*, see Haas, *Nim din selbes war*, 140–45.

86. Wyser, "Taulers Terminologie vom Seelengrund," 345, puts it well: "Dieses Neigen des Gemütes in sich selbst hinein ist also nichts anderes als das Streben zum Göttlichen in uns."

87. Tauler speaks of the spark nine times according to Egerding, *Die Metaphorik* 2:680–83. Most of these uses concern *sele* or *mensche* (e.g., 46.20, 74.28, 80.13, 137.1–3, 322.14, 347.11–15), but in one unusual text Tauler also uses the term in relation to the divine abyss: V 28 (117.17–18): . . . so kummet das goettliche abgrunde und lat do sine funken stieben in den geist. . . . For the relation between *grunt* and *funke*, see Wyser, "Taulers Terminologie vom Seelengrund," 346–48. Wrede (*Unio Mystica*, 169–72, 184) notes that Tauler, unlike Eckhart, does not identify the spark with the intellect.

88. V 56 (262.13–14), and V 64 (347.10–12). See Wyser, "Taulers Terminologie," 349–51.

89. On the soul as the Temple, or House (of God), see, e.g., V 13 (61.3–27), V 37 (144.8–32), and V 78 (418–21). On this metaphor, see Gnädinger, *Johannes Tauler*, 143–46; and Zekorn, *Gelassenheit und Einkehr*, 51–53.

90. V 21 (87.14–17): Trage es rehte wieder in den grunt do es usgeflossen ist, und merre du niht uf nichte, sunder flús selbe mit in mit allen dingen. Do wurt der wore lop Gottes geborn und bringet in der worheit fruht in deme grunde. . . . Other texts echo this; e.g., V 8 (37.15–16), V 20 (81.10–14, a christological text), and V 33 (127.35–36).

91. These figures are based on Egerding, *Die Metaphorik* 2:289–90.

92. V 56 (262.11–13): . . . das ist der grunt do dis wore bilde der heiligen drivaltikeit inne lit verborgen, und das ist so edel das man dem enkeinen namen enmag gegeben . . . (see also 262.16–18).

93. Enders, "Selbsterfahrung als Gotteserfahrung," 657: ". . . muss der 'Grund' der Seele reine Empfänglichkeit und Bestimmbarkeit und deshalb frei von jeder eigenen Bestimmtheit und Wirksamkeit, muss er ein Nichts im Sinne des selbst Formlosen sein."

94. For other uses of desert language in Tauler, see V 11 (54.29, 55.4), V 15 (68.13), V 29 (302.33–35), V 32 (121.9–10), V 61 (330.7, 331.21–22), and V 75 (406.12–13). On the mutual desert in Eckhart, see Pr. 28 and 29 (DW 2:66.6–8 and 76.2–77.4), and the discussion in Bernard McGinn, "Ocean and Desert as Symbols of Mystical Absorption in the Christian Tradition," *Journal of Religion* 74 (1994): 167–72. Like Eckhart, Tauler rarely uses the symbol of the sea or ocean, though he does speak of the "storm of the Godhead" as a *mer das grundelos ist* (V 18: 291.10–12).

95. In Tauler the *geist* and *sele* are always created, and such language is occasionally used of *grunt*; e.g., V 29 (300.20–25), V 61 (334.13–18, a quote from Dionysius), and V 65 (358.10–14). On *abgrunt,* see below.

96. V 24 (97.23–24): . . . also sol der mensche mit vil grossem flisse sich selber umbe-graben und sehen in sinen grunt und keren rechte den wercken den grunt. . . .

97. V 77 (417.19–21): Und des sehe ein iegliches in sinen grunt tegeliche und dicke waz sin úberschrift si, was von ime allermeist geminnet und gemeinet und gesuochet si, was in allermeist troesten, erfrovwen, bewegen múge. . . . Other passages in this vein include V 12 (59.7–9) and V 13 (62.19–28).

98. The point is stressed by Wrede, *Unio Mystica,* 192–202, 222–25.

99. Haug ("Johannes Taulers Via negationis," 79–86) sees Tauler's emphasis on ethical process in the path to the ground as an important difference from Eckhart's notion of absolute "waylessness." He sumarizes: "Die spekulative Weglosigkeit Eckharts ist von Tauler also ebenso dezidiert wie vehement in den Bereich der sittlichen Erfahrung übertragen wor-den. Er hat die Negation des Weges in einen Weg der Negativierung verwandelt" (p. 86).

100. V 5 (22.15–20): . . . und vom disem ufstonde so wurt diser grunt berueret mit einem swinden begerungen und in der inblostikeit und inblosende aller ungelicheit, und so die ie me ist abegelacht [reading C 5; 1:199], so die begerunge ie me wehsset und hoeher úber sich selber gat, und gat dicke an dem beruerende des blossen grundes durch fleisch und bluot und durch das marg.

101. V 5 (24.29–32): . . . dovon enkan nieman gesprechen noch kein mensche enmag dem andern dovon gesagen, sunder der es weis, hat dis befunden alleine, aber er enkan dir selber nút darabe gesagen, wanne das Got disen grunt in der worheit besessen hat. . . .

102. V 24 (101.26–32): . . . das ein worer ufgang ist in Gotte, das treit rechte das gemuete zuomole uf, also das Got in der worheit múge eigentliche ingon in daz luterste, in das innig-ste, in daz edelste, in den innerlichesten grunt, do wore einikeit alleine ist, von dem sancte Augustinus sprichet das die sele habe in ir ein verborgen appetgrunde, daz enhabe mit der zit noch mit aller diser welte nút zuo tuonde, und es ist verre úberhaben úber das teil das dem licham leben und bewegunge git.

103. V 24 (102.15–22): . . . also ich úch all hie vor mir sehe sitzen mit eime angesicht, also zúhent sú als mit in in, in daz selbe abgrunde, in den selben minnengluot und in ein anschovwelichen wisen und widersehet aber wider in der minnen abgrunde, in der minnen gluot und rastent do; und denne aber so dovwent sú in daz minnenkliche heisse fúr, und aber hernider uf alle die in noeten sint in der heiligen cristenheit, und aber wider in das minnen-kliche dunster stille rasten in dem abgrunde. Alsus gont sú uz und in, und blibent doch

allewegent inne in dem minnenklichen stillen abgrunde. . . . This is the only use of the term *minnen abgrunde* in Tauler, though he employs *grunt der mine* in 17.26 and 350.8.

104. V 29 (299.32–34): Aber sehent das es in úch geborn werde in dem grunde, nút in vernúnftiger wise, sunder in weselicher wise, in der worheit, nút in redende, sunder in wesende.

105. V 29 (301.25–29): Denne kummet die vetterliche kraft und ruoffet den menschen in sich durch sinen eingebornen sun, und also der sun wirt geborn uz dem vatter und widerflússet in den vatter, also wurt dis mensche in dem sune von dem vatter geborn und flússet wider in den vatter mit deme sune und wurt eine mit ime.

106. V 28 (302.32–34): Dis ist ein einveltig úberwesenliche verborgene wueste und frie dúnsternisse; daz wil mit sinnelicher wisen nút funden werden.

107. On the history of the abyss motif and Ps. 41:8 in Christian mysticism, see Bernard McGinn, "The Abyss of Love," in *The Joy of Learning and the Love of God: Studies in Honor of Jean Leclercq*, ed. E. Rozanne Elder (Kalamazoo: Cistercian Publications, 1995), 95–120.

108. On Hadewijch's teaching, see McGinn, "Abyss of Love," 106–8; and *Flowering of Mysticism*, 216–18.

109. On the use of *abgrund* in Tauler, see Wrede, *Unio Mystica*, 64–67; Louise Gnädinger, "Der Abgrund ruft dem Abgrund. Taulers Predigt *Beati oculi* (V 45)," in *Das 'einig Ein'*, 167–207; Egerding, *Die Metaphorik*, 2:296–301; McGinn, "Abyss of Love," 97–99; and Haas, *Nim din selbes war*, 150–52.

110. V 9 (44.15–18): Wie moehte er sú me versuochet und bekort han, und sú naher gejaget und getriben haben? Waz tet sú zuo allem disem jagen? Sú lies sich jagen und jagete sich selber noch tieffer dan er sú gejagen moehte, sú ging mit dem jagen in den grunt, noch naher trang sú hinin in daz abgrunde. . . .

111. V 9 (45.33–46.4): Und aldo lie sú sich zuo grunde in ein ewikeit; sú wurde do alzuohant gezogen verre úber alle mittel und wart alzuomole in das abgrunde Gottes gezogen, sú wart rehte von der wunderlichen gotheit ingeslunden, O wie ein wunneclich slunt ist diz! This is Tauler's only use of the evocative term *slunt* as an equivalent for *abgrunde*.

112. V 67 (367.32–368.1): Diser tieffi sol der mensche volgen in diser wise und begegen mit der tieffi, das ist ein grundelos abgrúnde eins vernichtendes irs selbes sunder grunt; . . . . Another example is in V 61 (331.4–5): . . . denne es its ein grundelos abgrúnde swebende in im selber sunder grunt. *Abgrúnde* is characterized as *grundlos* in many texts; e.g., 228.15, 331.4, 407.3.

113. V 41 (176.6–11): Hie wirt das wort wor das in dem salter der prophete sprach: 'abyssus abyssum invocat, das abgrúnde das inleitet das abgrúnde.' Das abgrúnde das geschaffen ist, das inleit in sich das ungeschaffen abgrúnde, und werdent die zwei abgrúnde ein einig ein, ein luter goetlich wesen, und do hat sich der geist verlorn in Gotz geiste; in dem grundelosen mere ist er ertrunken. For another text combining the metaphors of the abyss and the ocean, see V 38 (152.35–153.2): Do tuot der geist einen úberswank in das goetlich abgrúnde. Er gússet sich us und blibet doch vol; als der ein klein krusen stiesse in das grundelose mer; das wúrde bald vol und gienge úber und blibe doch vol.

114. V 45 (201.2–7): Kinder, da verliessent si sich al ze mole in rechter worer verlornheit ir selbs. 'Abyssus abyssum invocat, das abgrúnde das in leitet das abgrúnde'. Das geschaffen abgrúnde das in leitet von siner tieffe wegen. Sin tieffe und sin bekant nicht das zúhet das ungeschaffen offen abgrúnde in sich, und do flússet das ein abgrúnde in das ander abgrúnde und wirt do ein einig ein, ein nicht in das ander nicht und nicht. The third passage in which Tauler appeals to Ps. 41:8 is in V 61 (331.1–31). In both this text and that from V 41 just cited it is significant to note that Tauler insists that the human *abgrúnde* is created.

115. V 22 (88.1–4): Der geist enweis es selber nút, wanne er ist also versmoltzen in das goetteliche abgrúnde das er nút enweis, enfuelet noch ensmacket dan einen einigen lutern blossen einvaltigen Got. See also V 26 (109.22–23) and V 32 (120.17–24); etc.

116. V 26 (103.21–25): . . . wo der heilige geist enpfangen sol werden, do muos er selber die stat bereiten unde die enpfenglicheit selber machen mit ime selber und enpfahen ouch

sich selber. Das unsprechenliche abegrunde Gottes das muos sins selbes stat und der enfenglicheit sin und niht [C XXVI; 2:39] der creaturen. Here I make use of the translation of Shrady, *Johannes Tauler. Sermons*, 91.

117. Zekorn (*Gelassenheit und Einkehr*, 161–64), analyzing V 42, speaks of Tauler's "Spiritualität des Tätigseins," or spirituality of everyday existence.

118. See Kirmsse, *Die Terminologie*, 78–81, for a survey of the usage of *bevinden*.

119. V 13 (61.10–16): . . . wenne der mensche mit allen sinem kreften und ouch mit sinre selen inkert und inget in disen tempel, do er Got in der worheit inne vindet wonende und würkende, und er me hie vindet in bevindender wisen, nút in sinnelichen wisen noch in vernúnftiger wisen, obe [C XIII; 1:279] also man gohoert oder gelesen [C XIII; 1:279] het oder durch die sinne ist inkummen, sunder in bevindender smackender wisen, also es uz dem grunde heruz ist quellende also us sime eigenen burnen und us der fonténien. . . . Another sermon, V 34 (317.30–318.1), speaks of "die smeklichen bevintlicheit des grundes . . . ." According to V 29 (299.18): Hinnan ab ist besser ze bevindende wan ze sprechende.

120. To note just a few other texts on *bevinden*, see V 3 (19.8–9), V 13 (62.19–25), V 24 (99.2–6), V 29 (301.22–25), V 38 (151.17–21), V 54 (248.16–19 and 251.24–25, based on Bernard of Clairvaux, SC 85.14 [*Bernardi Opera* 2:316.15]), and V 78 (421.30–31).

121. V 41 (175.4–7): Nút wenent das ich mich dis út anneme das ich út her zuo komen si, allein enkein lerer nút ensúlle leren das er selber von lebende nút enhabe. Doch ist ez ze noeten genuog das er es minne und meine und nút do wider entuo. Another passage in V 50 (226.6–9), without being quite so autobiographical, reflects a similar view.

122. V 67 (365.18–22): . . . also sol der mensche alles sin vermúgen búgen fúr Got; . . . und sol gruntlich bekennen sin natúrlich nicht und sin gebrestlich nicht. Das natúrlich nicht das ist das wir von naturen nicht ensint, und das gebrestlich nicht das ist das uns ze nichte gemacht hat. See also V 35 (322.23–30). Recognition of this double nothingness is the essential starting-point for Tauler's teaching on self-knowledge; see Haas, *Nim din selbes war*, 121–30; Zekorn, *Gelassenheit und Einkehr*, 76–79 and 92; and Gnädinger, *Johannes Tauler*, 121–29.

123. Haas, *Nim din selbes war*, 79.

124. M. Egerding, "Johannes Taulers Auffassung vom Menschen," 126, puts the point well: "Für Tauler bedeutet das Bekenntnis seiner mangelden Erfahrungskompetenz, dass er in Hinblick auf seiner Rolle als Prediger nachvollzieht, was er generell vom jedem Menschen fordert: dass er sich als ein Nichts erkennt und damit umgeht."

125. Schmidt, "Introduction," in *Johannes Tauler. Sermons*, 31. Schmidt appeals to the longer discussions by Alois M. Haas, "Johannes Tauler," in *Sermo mysticus: Studien zu Theologie und Sprache der deutschen Mystik* (Freiburg, Switzerland, 1979), 278–82; and "Sprache und mystische Erfahrung nach Tauler und Seuse," in *Geistliches Mittelalter* (Freiburg, Switzerland, 1984), 240–42.

126. For a slightly different form of presenting Tauler's underlying attitudes, see the "Zweiter Teil" in Zekorn, *Gelassenheit und Einkehr*, 75–93, which studies *vernúten sin selbes*, *lidikeit und gelassenheit*, and *liden und demuete*.

127. Over half of Tauler's sermons specifically address the need for such *ker* in the life of the Christian. A number of studies of Tauler's use of "turning" exist; see Gnädinger, *Johannes Tauler*, 136–47; and Weilner, *Johannes Taulers Bekehrungsweg*, especially chapters 6–7.

128. V 34 (318.9–10): Aber wer disent grunt smacken sol, der muos von not sin herze und sine minne gekert haben von allem dem das nút luter Got enist noch got ein wore sache enist.

129. V 12 (59.30–33): Was ist daz leben der penitencien in dem wesende und in der worheit? Daz enist anders nút denne ein gantz wor abeker von allem dem [for this reading, see Gnädinger, *Johannes Tauler*, 138] daz Got nút enist, und ein gantz wor zuokeren zuo dem luteren woren guote daz Got ist und heisset. Similar formulae occur in many sermons; e.g., 36.12–14, 104.4–12, 128.27–37, 216.24–27, 235.8–11, and 325.27.

130. V 33 (130.11–12): Kinder, wir muessent man werden und tuon einen kreftigen ker, oder do enwurt nút usser uns.

131. Haas, *Nim din selbes war*, 83–153.

132. For some other examples, see V 53 (243.11–12), V 71 (384.31), and V 77 (415.1–2). An important sermon on self-knowledge is V 35 = 60h (321–28).

133. V 71 (386.14–20). For more practical advice on *inker*, see V 63 (342.5–8).

134. V 39 (160.3–5): Das dritte das ist ein úbervart in ein gotformig wesen in einikeit des geschaffenen geist in den istigen geist Gotz, das man einen weselichen ker mag heissen.

135. V 40 (169.3–4): Das heissent weseliche kere, den aller weselich lon antwúrtet. Andern keren den antwúrtet zuo vallender lon. This *ker* is further described in the language of *unitas indistinctionis* in 169.16–19. For more on *weselich ker*, see 117.20–30, 174.14–18, 263.1–4 and 25–26, 344.7–8, and 406.10–13.

136. V 40 (169.12–15): Ein ander ker mag och wol in einer gemeiner usserliche wise weselich heissen, das ist in allen den keren do der mensche Got luterlichen und bloeslichen meint und nút anders, noch enkein warumbe, denne Got durch sich selber und in im selber. This is the only appearance in Tauler of the expression "without a why" (*noch enkein warumbe*), used by Eckhart and thirteenth-century woman mystics.

137. My own rough count has *gelossenheit* featured in forty-two sermons and *abgescheidenheit* in sixteen. Among the sermons that feature discussions of *gelossenheit*, see especially V 6, 13, 19, 25, 26, 31, 36, 37, 47, 55, 63, 67, 73, 81, and 83.

138. Haug, "Johannes Taulers Via negationis," 85.

139. Gnädinger, *Johannes Tauler*, 231: ". . . Loslösung und Freiwerden von den zu kleinen Ichwünschen, Ichansprüchen und Ichbedürfnissen." For *gelossenheit* in Tauler, see Gnädinger, *Johannes Tauler*, 275–86; and Zekorn, *Gelassenheit und Einkehr*, 83–88.

140. V 25 (305.22–30): Das ein ist: er itelt. Das ander: das er fúllet das ital als verre und als vil als er ital vindet. . . . Wan recht als verre und als vil der mensche geitelt ist, als vil und als vil me ist er enphengklich. . . . Sol Got in, so muos von not die creature us.

141. V 25 (306.1–3): Also muos sich der mensche lossen vahen und italen und bereiten und al lossen und des selben lossendes also gar und ze mole us gon. . . .

142. V 26 (108.12–17): Do wurt der mensche berovbet sin selbes in rechter worer gelossenheit und versincket in den grunt des goettelichen willen, nút in diseme armuote und blosheit zuo stande ein wochen oder ein manot, mere, obe Got wil, tusent jor oder eweklichen, . . . kinder, dis were gelossenheit.

143. V 23 (92.1–9): . . . daz ist wore abgescheidenheit und lidikeit und innigkeit und einikeit; dis ist die allernehste und die woreste bereitunge, und wer dis het und me an diseme zuonimmet, der ist allermeist und aller enpfenglichest der enpfenglicheit des heiligen geistes. Was ist nu wore abgescheidenheit, . . . ? Das ist daz sich der mensche abekere und abescheide von allem dem das nút Got luter und blos enist, und mit dem liehte siner bescheidenheit alle sine werg, wort und gedenke durchsehe mit eime versaistme [C XXIII; 2:5] gemuete, obe út do si in dem grunde das Got nút luterlich ensi. . . . (I have adopted several phrases from the translation of Colledge, *Spiritual Conferences*, 108.)

144. V 23 (93.30–32): Wenne denne dise bekorunge kummet, so sol er also werlich entwichen bitz er vil wol besast wurt, und sol sich liden in gelossenheit und in lidiger gelossenheit und warte Gottes in dem getrenge.

145. See Haas, *Nim din selbes war*, 133 n. 146, on *lidekeit*. The MHG verb *liden*, like the Latin *pati*, bears both the meaning of undergoing pain and the more general sense of receiving, that is, being passive to some action. Zekorn, *Gelassenheit und Einkehr*, 80–83, stresses the "emptying" aspect over the "receptive," but it seems to me difficult to separate the two.

146. V 31 (314.12–15): . . . sol Got eigentliche in dir wúrken, so muostu sin in einer lutern lidekeit und muessent alle dine krefte also gar entsast sin aller ir wúrklicheit und angenomenheit und ston in einem lutern verlouckenen ir selbes. . . .

147. V 5 (24.16–26): Nu sprichet doch dis wort surge und heisset sú daz sú ufstont, daz ist

iemer ein werg; ja ein werg gehoert in zuo, daz súllent sú allewegent tuon on underlos die wile sú iemer gelebent, das der mensche niemer zuo der volkomenheit enmag kummen, er ensúlle allewegent ufston und ein ufrihtunge des gemuetes in Got und in ein entlidigen des innewendigen grundes. . . . Git in Got in lidender wise, so lident sú, git er in in wúrckender wise, so wúrckent sú, in schovwen oder in gebruche wise, so gebruchent sú. Diser grunt git des selber gezúgnis in in selber daz in Got bereit und gelutert hat. . . .

148. Richard Kieckhefer, "The Notion of Passivity in the Sermons of Tauler," *Recherches de théologie ancienne et médiévale* 48 (1981): 198–211. Kieckhefer's three-point summary (p. 210) is worth quoting: "First, that the sanctity which a soul possesses is at every stage *de facto* God's work and not the result of human striving; second, that sanctification *may* be frustrated by freely chosen interference; and third, that sanctification is indeed thwarted by those various forms of activity which (whether freely chosen or not) inhibit a proper stance of submission to God."

149. DN 2.9 (448B): . . . ou monon mathôn, alla kai pathôn ta theia [Latin translation of Eriugena: . . . non solum discens, sed et affectus divina; (PL 122:1124C)].

150. Christ is mentioned in almost all Tauler's sermons. Here is a partial list with some of the more significant sermons emphasized: V 6, 7, 8, 9, 10, 11, 13, *15*, 17, 20, *21*, 23, 25, 27, 28, 30, *31*, 35, 36, 37, 39, *40*, 41, *45*, 46, *47*, 48, *50*, 51, 52, 53, *54*, *55*, 57, 65, *66*, 67, 69, 70, 71, 72, 73, 75, 76, 77; and C LX (Helander ed.), and C LXXXIII (Bihlmeyer ed.).

151. This view was found in older Protestant scholarship on Tauler, and is still present, though in more qualified fashion, in Ozment, *Homo spiritualis*, e.g., 30, 45.

152. In English see the essay of Richard Kieckhefer, "The Role of Christ in Tauler's Spirituality," *The Downside Review* 96 (1978): 176–91. The same argument appears in recent German studies, notably Gandlau, *Trinität und Kreuz*; Gnädinger, *Johannes Tauler*, 286–97; Alois M. Haas, "Jesus Christus—Inbegriff des Heils und Verwirklichte Tranzendenz im Geist der deutschen Mystik," in *Epiphanie des Heils*, ed. Gerhard Oberhammer (Vienna, 1982), 209–12; and M. Egerding, "Johannes Taulers Auffassung vom Menschen," 120–29. For a survey of Tauler's texts on Christ, see Adolf Hoffmann, "Die Christusgestalt bei Tauler," in *Johannes Tauler: Ein deutsche Mystiker*, 208–31.

153. Other passages to this effect include V 21 (88.16–17), V 47 (210.19–22), and V 53 (243.23–29).

154. Tauler's devotion to the passion is especially evident in the five sermons he preached for the Feast of the Exaltation of the Holy Cross (Sept. 14). The correct order of these is V 50, 52, 51, 65, and the sermon "Von dem heiligen crúze" found in Helander, 346–51. Two specific aspects of Tauler's passion devotion that cannot be taken up here are: (1) the role of meditation on Christ's five wounds (see, e.g., V 8 [35–37], V 46 [206], and V 71 [387–88]); and (2) the equation of the four dimensions of the love of God (see Eph. 3:18) with the four arms of the cross (e.g., V 52 [238–39], and C LX [ed. Helander, 348–50]).

155. Haas (*Sermo mysticus*, 264) says that for Tauler, "Die Heilsgeschichte einst hat nur Sinn, wenn sie zur Heilsgeschichte jetzt wird."

156. V 55 (254.20–22): . . . ein inwendige gantz gelossen stilles swigen in einem in gekerten gemuete und Got luterlichen ze wartende was er in im wúrken welle. . . .

157. Eckhart's Pr. 52 appears in DW 2:486–506; see the treatment in chapter 4 above, pp. 168, 178.

158. V 55 (256.5–6): Nu ist aller menschen nature geneiget uf das si haben und das si wissen und wellen. Dis sint die werk der krefte.

159. V 55 (256.27–31): . . . das du noch tieffer versinkest in din nicht. . . . Hie lit es alles an, an einem grundelosen entsinkende in ein grundelos nút. This language reflects Eckhart.

160. V 55 (257.32–35): . . . ie tieffer versinken in das unbekante und ungenante abgrúnde úber alle wise, bilde und formen, . . . so enblibt nút in diser velornheit denne ein grunt der weselichen uf im selber stot, ein wesen, ein leben, ein úber al.

161. V 55 (258.6–9): Dise weg zuo disem ende ze komende, das muos sin durch das hoch

wurdige leben und liden unsers herren Jhesu Christi, wan er ist der weg und er ist durch den man gon sol. Und er ist die worheit die in disem wege lúchten sol. Und er ist das leben zuo dem man komen sol.

162. For a particularly powerful passage on this, see V 67 (371.12–26).

163. E.g., V 24 (100.24–101.6) and V 38 (152.17–25, using Phil. 3:14).

164. A number of these are discussed by Kieckhefer in "Role of Christ in Tauler's Spirituality," 180.

165. V 76 (411.12–25): . . . in der minne enist nút denne ein verloeucken, nút ein verjehen, es enist nút in eime habende also di jungern zuo vorderste hattent, sunder sú ist in eime darbende; in diseme ist ein unwissen, ein unbekentnisse, und ist verre úber redelicheit in ein úberwesenlicheit und úberwislicheit. . . . [W]an Got minnet sich selber hie und ist hie sin selbes fúrwurf. For a study of the doctrine of love in this sermon, see Markus Enders, "La compréhension mystique de l'amour humaine chez Jean Tauler," in _700e anniversaire de la naissance de Jean Tauler_, 438–43.

166. V 76 (411.39–412.4): . . . mer in uns, das wir sú hie luterlicher und edellicher nemen, nút in sinnelicher wisen und biltlichen, also es durch die sinne ist ingetragen, also man es hat in der fantasien, nút also, sunder innerlichen und edellichen und goetlichen und verborgenlichen, nút also hie vor in der ersten wisen.

167. Kieckhefer, "Role of Christ," 180–87, studies V 15 (69–71), V 47 (207–14), V 53 (240–46), and V 54 (246–53), along with other texts. His conclusions (pp. 187–91) are a helpful presentation of the nuances of Tauler's view of the role of _imitatio Christi_. As he puts it, "At the highest level, devotion to the humanity of Christ focuses on the totality of his life, seen in a single glance" (p. 190).

168. V 31 (314.36–315.2): Das kúnden ist nút mit worten noch mit gedenckende, sunder ez ist mit sterbende unde entwerdende in der kraft sines todes. For other passages on taking up the cross and following Christ, and the _imitatio passionis_ in general, see V 21 (85.12–14), V 38 (149.17–24), V 45 (199.8–28), V 47 (210.19–22), V 50 (229.19–28), V 51 (230.24–232.7), V 52 (237.29–34), V 54 (251.33–252.3), V 65 (353–57), V 67 (371.12–26), V 73 (296.3–10), and C LX (Helander, 346–51). Occasionally, Tauler recommends various forms of physical practices of _imitatio passionis_; e.g. V 47 (211.11–24).

169. Luther, _Operationes in Psalmos_ (_Weimarer Ausgabe_ 5:163.26–29).

170. V 40 (166.8–11): Nein, lieber kinder, ir súllent úch in keren in den grunt do die gnade allein geborn wirt in der worheit, und mit der blicket dir das liden und das leben unsers herren in in einer gevoellicher minne und einvaltikeit und in einem einvaltigen angesicht. . . .

171. See Mieth, _Die Einheit_, who treats Tauler's ecclesiology on pp. 266–70. Mieth emphasizes the treatment of the church as Body of Christ found in such sermons as V 21 (85), V 39 (158–59), and especially V 42 (176–81). See also Adolf Hoffmann, "Taulers Lehre von der Kirche," in _Johannes Tauler: Ein deutscher Mystiker_, 232–40.

172. On sanctity as open to Christians in all walks of life, see Mieth, _Die Einheit_, 293–94; and Zekorn, _Gelassenheit und Einkehr_, 169–72. As Zekorn points out, virginity, often seen as necessary for mystical contact with God in monasticism, has no such role in Tauler.

173. Reasons of space preclude a more detailed treatment of discretion (MHG _bescheidenheit_). See the analysis in Zekorn, _Gelassenheit und Einkehr_, 227–34, who aptly states: "Obwohl sie von Tauler nur selten namentlich genannt wird, sind seine Predigten grundlegend von dieser _discretio_ geprägt."

174. For example: V 35 (321–23) treats humility (_demuetikeit_), love of God (_wore goetteliche minne_), and discretion (_bescheidenheit_); V 47 (212) discusses faith, hope, releasement, and humility; C LX (Helander, 347–50) has the four arms of the cross signifying love of God, deep humility, inner purity, and complete obedience; V 67 (365–66) speaks of the three necessary dispositions, or sister virtues—releasement, passivity, and lack of self-seeking (_unannemlicheit_); and V 55 (254–56), as we have seen, discusses six virtues purifying the inner and outer powers.

175. On humility, see Gnädinger, *Johannes Tauler,* "Mystik des Sinkens: Demut," 251–61, who notes that Tauler's teaching on humility is especially developed in his Pentecost sermons, V 25, 26, and 27. For other texts on the necessity of humility, see, e.g., V 35 (323.16–324.13), V 38 (149.33–36), V 40 (164.14–24), and V 65 (347.25–29).

176. For other discussions of humility, see, e.g., V 38 (148.30–36) and V 40 (164.14–24).

177. V 57 (274.9–13): Alsus sol der mensche vor allen dingen sich setzen in sin nút. Wenne der mensche kumet uf den tolden aller volkomenheit, so enwart im nie so not nider ze sinkende in den aller tiefsten grunt und an die wurzele der demuetikeit. Wan also als des bovms hoehi kumet von den tiefsten der wurzelen, also kumet alle hoehin dis lebens von dem grunde der demuetikeit.

178. V 8 (36.26–28): . . . das ist das Got uns alleine besitze unsern grunt und daz wir von keinen dingen besessen anders ensint und das wir alle ding also haltent also sú Got in uns wil gehalten haben in armuete unsers geistes. . . .

179. C LXXI (ed. Helander, 355): Die vierde wise die lutern armütes daz ist von minnen arm sin ussewendig und innenwendig, von minnen umb das minnencliche bilde unsers herren ihu xri, sime lutern blossen, armüte nochzuofolgende von rehter worer minnen, und unbekúmbert und unbehangen sin innewendig und ussewendig, denne alleine ein blos luter unmittelich widerflus und widergang des gemütes on onderlos in sinen ursprung und in sinen begin. . . . For some other passages on poverty of spirit, see V 25 (306.18–24), V 48 (215.8–15), V 56 (264.24–265.32), and V 63 (345.4–10).

180. V 64 (349.8–11): Der minne materie das ist unser herze, sele, krefte. Ir forme das ist minne. Ir wirklichkeit das ist das man minne von al. Ir ende und ir fúrwurf das ist Got sunder mittel; minne wesen ist minne; wan minne minnet umbe minne. The final phrase echoes a passage in Bernard's *Sermo super Cantica* 83.4 (*Sancti Bernardi Opera* 2:300.24–26). On Tauler's teaching on love, see Wrede, *Unio Mystica,* 144–52 and 222–25.

181. On *wúrkliche minne* and its universality, see, e.g., V 44 (193.11–18) and V 57 (273.1–7).

182. V 10 (46.7–10): Aber ein underscheit hant sú von den woren frúnden Gottes ussewendig; dise sint vol urteiles ander lúten und der Gottes frúnt und urteilent sich selber nút, aber die waren Gottes frúnt enurteilent nieman danne sich selber. For other comments against judging others, see V 16 (74.12–13), V 18 (287.22–25), V 27 (112.22–31), V 38 (147.24–25, 148.31–32), V 57 (268.5–6), V 62 (336.8–12, and 339.25–27), V 75 (405.3–8), and V 76 (408.32–409.39).

183. See McGinn, *Growth of Mysticism,* 54–56.

184. The full treatment of the seven gifts in V 26 extends from 105.32 to 110.3. The other treatments are more brief; see V 29 (301.35–302.5) and V 44 (194.1–21). On the role of the seven gifts in Tauler, see Gnädinger, *Johannes Tauler,* 302–07.

185. For Tauler on the sacraments, see Adolf Hoffmann, "Sakramentale Heilswege bei Tauler," in *Johannes Tauler: Ein deutscher Mystiker,* 247–67; Gnädinger, *Johannes Tauler,* 336–47; and Zekorn, *Gelassenheit und Einkehr,* 149–60.

186. In V 30 (294.18–24) Tauler first cites a passage from Augustine, *Conf.* 7.10.16, in which God says to him: Nec tu me in te mutabis, sicut cibum carnis tuae; sed tu mutaberis in me (PL 32:742). He follows this with a paraphrase of a text from Bernard of Clairvaux, *Sermo super Cantica* 71.5 (*Sancti Bernardi Opera* 2:217.15–17): Nolite mirari hoc: et manducat nos, et manducatur a nobis, quo arctius illi adstringamur. See also V 32 (121.6–8), and V 33 (125.20–21).

187. Tauler also mentions the destruction of the old self in V 31 (314) and V 32 (121).

188. See, e.g., V 17 (278–83), V 24 (101–02), V 28 (115), and V 29 (302).

189. See V 15 (68.8–28).

190. Earlier in this sermon (302.8–11) Tauler says that one prayer for our friends that takes place in the ground is worth more than reciting a hundred thousand psalters!

191. V 12 (57.7–11): . . . das ist die zit die unser allewegent ist, das wir Got suochent und sine gegenwertikeit meinent in allen unsern werken und lebende, willen und minnen; und

alsus súllent wir ufgon úber uns selber und úber allez das Got nút enist, in alleine wellende und minnende luterlichen und anders nút; dise zit ist alle zit. This sermon mentions God's presence a dozen times.

192. V 71 (386.17–21): Kere dinen grunt in zuo ime; sprich mit dem propheten: 'Exquisivit te facies mea; faciem tuam requiram, herre, min antlit suochet din antlit; nút enkere din antlit von mir'; also bloeslichen kere din antlit, dinen grunt engegen dem goetlichen antlit. The use of the biblical "face" to signify the divine presence is found in a number of earlier mystics, such as William of St. Thierry and Hadewijch.

193. V 39 (155.3–6 and 25–29): Das S. Peter heisset das es einmuetig súlle sin, das ist das dis gemuete an Gotte alzemole und alleine klebe und das der mensche das antlit sines grundes und gemuetes alzemole an Got gegenwertlichen gekert habe. . . . Er sol sich samnen zuo im selber und in sinen inwendigen grunt keren mit uferhabenem gemuete und ufgetenten kreften, mit einem innerlichen angesicht der gegenwúrtikeit Gotz und mit inwendiger begerunge vor allen dingen des aller liebsten willen Gotz. . . . This sermon also speaks of God's presence on 158.6–7 and 159.31–35. For other sermons that discuss the presence of God, see, e.g., V 24 (98.12–15, 100.24–26, and 102.4–5), V 52 (239.16–20), V 53 (244.28–245.3), V 54 (251.9–17), V 56 (264.13–15), V 61 (331.7–12), V 77 (413.22–24 and 414.3–6), and V 78 (421.13–15).

194. V 11 (51.11–14): Dise begerunge ist drier leige in drier leige lúten und sint vil ungelich. Die erste ist in anhebenden lúten, die ander ist in zuonemenden lúten, die dritte in den die volkommen lúte heissent, also hie múgelich ist in diseme lebende.

195. The most detailed treatment of the triple pattern is in V 15 (69.33–71.24), where Tauler illustrates it by three ways in which Christ drew St. John the Beloved. The pattern is also mentioned in V 54 (234–35) and V 53 (241), but again does not form the basis for the exposition of the itinerary. For a study of the threefold pattern in Tauler, see M. Engratis Kihm, "Die Drei-Weg-Lehre bei Tauler," in *Johannes Tauler: Ein deutscher Mystiker*, 268–300; and Gnädinger, *Johannes Tauler*, 147–60.

196. In V 45 (196.28–32), as we have seen, Tauler says this is a question for *die grossen pfaffen und die lesmeister*. In V 64 (349.1–6) he says that he will not discuss the debate, but that there is no question that love is more meritorious and useful than knowledge (*bekentnisse*) in this life, because "love goes in where reason must remain without" (*Wan die minne die get do in do das bekenntnisse muos husse bliben*). Tauler goes on to insist that no subtle knowledge is needed, but only simple faith. Here, Tauler's distance from Eckhart's stress on the role of intellect is once again obvious.

197. For Tauler's teaching on love, see Markus Enders, "La compréhension mystique de l'amour humain chez Jean Tauler," in *700e anniversaire de la naissance de Jean Tauler*, 429–43.

198. V 76 (407.33–34): Das edelste und daz wunnenclichste do man abe gesprechen mag, das ist minne, man enmag nit nútzers geleren.

199. V 76 (409.29–32): . . . aber der wore minne hette, der viele mit sime urteile und mit allen sinen gebresten in ein minnencliche insinckende in Got in sinen wolgevellichen guoten willen, in eime woren usgange alles eigens willen; wanne wore goetliche minne die tuot den menschen verloeuckende sin selbes und alles eigens willen. . . .

200. Gervais Dumeige, ed., *Ives Épitre à Severin sur la Charité: Richard de Saint-Vistor. Les quatres degrés de la violent charité* (Paris: J. Vrin, 1955), 129–45. For a study, see McGinn, *Growth of Mysticism*, 415–18.

201. V 61 (333.14–18): Das ist die wundende minne, die sol dich in disen grunt fueren. . . . Aber kumest du in die gevangene minne in disem tieffen verborgenen abgrúnde, so muost du dich lossen der minne nach irem willen. . . .

202. *Les quatre degrés*, chapter 14 (141.2).

203. V 61 (334.1–12): . . . si machet in ungestuoem in allen sinen kreften: er qwilt nach der minne, und das er si hat, des enweis er nút. Si verzert dir das marg und das bluot . . . so get das menschlik werk under: so kumet denne unser herre und sprichet ein wort denne

durch den menschen: das wort das ist edeler und nützer denne hundert tusent wort die alle menschen mügent gesprechen.

204. This passage from Dionysius has not been identified.

205. See V 18 (290.16–291.26), in which only the first two degrees are discussed; and V 31 (316.22–26), which mentions the first two again. He also refers to Richard's teaching on love in V 64 (349.7–16).

206. V 54 (249.16–19): Und alsus zúhet sich die minne bas uf in ein abgescheidenheit und wirt der wisen minne gelich und kumet über alle bilde und formen und gelichnisse und kumet alsus durch die bilde über die bilde. This last phrase about using images to go beyond images is remarkably close to a major aspect of Suso's mysticism studied above (chapter 5, pp. 210–11). For Tauler's teaching on the use of images (*bild*) and the necessity of stripping them away (*Bildlosigkeit*), see Zekorn, *Gelassenheit und Einkehr*, 132–36.

207. V 54 (251.12–14): Und denne enhat der geist enkein enhalt denne das er versinke und ertrinke in das goetlich abgründe und in dem sich verliere. . . .

208. V 54 (251.19–24): . . . und Got muos alle ding do in ime würken, in im bekennen, in im minnen, wan er ist im selbe in diser starken minne entsunken in den geminten in dem er sich verlorn hat als der trophhe wassers in dem tieffen mere, und ist verre me mit im eins worden denne der luft si vereiniget mit der klarheit der sunnen, als die schint an dem liechten tag. These two metaphors for mystical union, used by Bernard of Clairvaux (*De diligendo Deo* 10.28), have a long history in mystical literature. The most complete treatment is Jean Pepin, "'Stilla aquae modica multo infusa vino, ferrum ignitum, luce perfusus aer': L'origine de trois comparisons familières à la théologie mystique médiévale," *Miscellanea André Combes (Divinitas 11)* (Rome, 1967), 1:331–75.

209. V 54 (252.16–19): Alsus recht tribt dise starke minne: si tribet und zühet den geist, das er tuot einen überswank und wil ze male us im selber in ein unwissen, das haltet in denne in ein unbekentnisse, und denn her wider in ein bekentnisse sines nichtes. Immediately after this Tauler expands on the negativity of "strong free love" by specifying three characteristics (252.20–33): (1) it suspends the activity of all the faculties; (2) it plunges the spirit so deeply in the ground that it loses its own name (another echo of Eckhart); and (3) it makes the spirit completely essential (*weselich*) and gives it tranquil repose in which it waits upon serving God.

210. Erotic language apears in some of Tauler's sermons. See V 11 (55.34–56.9), a passage on the wine cellar (Sg 2:4) and the game of love as taking place in the ground; and V 53 (245.13–18) on the kiss of Christ the King. Tauler also occasionally speaks of the soul's marriage to God (e.g., V 12 [12–14], V 46 [207.5–7], V 48 [216.19–23], V 74 [398.6–16], and especially V 81 [431.23–432.10]).

211. V 39 (159.29–160.5): Nu wellen wir sagen von drin greten, die mag der mensche haben in dem nidersten, in dem mittelsten, oder in dem obersten grate. Der erste grat eins inwendigen tugentliche lebens die do die richten leitent in die hochste nacheit Gotz, ist das der mensche kere ze mole sich in die wunderlichen werk und bewisunge der unsprechlicher gaben und der usflüsse der verborgener guotheit Gotz, und dannan us wirt geborn ein uebunge, die heisset jubilacio. Der ander grat das ist ein armuote des geistes und ein sunderlich in ziehen Gotz in einer qwelender berovbunge des geistes. Das dritte das ist ein übervart in ein gotformig wesen in einikeit des geschaffenen geistes in den istigen geist Gotz, das man einen weselichen ker mag heissen.

212. V 67 (369.9–13): Dis gelich bevant ein mensche, ein junge frovwe die in der e was: der gemuete erswang sich in die hoehi, und in dem wart ir ir eigen grund enteket und erzoeiget und sach den in unwordelicher clorheit und sach den in unervolgenlicher hoehi, die was ane ende und in einer endeloser lengi und breiti und tieffi, alles sunder grunt.

213. The term *iubilus* and its cognates is based on the language of the Psalms (e.g., Pss. 46:2, 80:2). In medieval mysticism it generally refers to the ecstatic singing found mostly among mystical women. Tauler appears to be using it a broader sense of all forms of overwhelming mystical joy, as the long description in V 39 (160.7–161.7) shows. For other uses,

see V 11 (53.18), V 41 (171.23), and V 42 (185.10). This more general sense may reflect an Augustinian influence; see M. Benedetta Zorzi, "*Melos* e *Iubilus* nelle *Enarrationes in Psalmos* di Agostino: Una questione di mistica agostiniana," *Augustinianum* 42 (2002): 383–413.

214. See, e.g., V 6 (27.10–16), V 9 (45.14), V 11 (54.4), V 39 (159.11), V 40 (169.23–25), V 41 (175.16–18), and V 81 (432.27). Tauler appears to use the noun *zuk* (rapture) only in V 15 (71.12), as shown by Ruh, *Geschichte,* 3:512. Tauler is also aware of some of the physical characteristics of ecstatic states. In V 50 (227.17–30) he speaks of two men who experienced inner and outer manifestations of the heat of divine love, in the manner of Richard Rolle.

215. V 39 (160.7–18). There is an element of cosmic piety in Tauler, though not as strong as in Suso. See, e.g., V 16 (75.14–15), V 39 (156.30–157.2), V 46 (202.28–29), and V 49 (221.23–28).

216. V 39 (160.18–23): Und als dis dirre mensche mit einem minneklichem durch sehen wol durch gat, so wirt in im geborn grosse wirkliche froeide, und wirt der mensche der dise ding in rechter minne an sicht, als úber gossen mit innerlicher froeide das der kranke licham die froeide nút enthalten enmag und bricht us mit eigener sunderlicher wise. In V 41 (175–76) Tauler used the image of the breaking of the nets in the account of the miraculous draught of fishes (Luke 5:6) to indicate how the body is sometimes physically afflicted in mystical union.

217. Tauler's teaching on suffering has been much studied. For an account of forms of suffering in Tauler, see Pleuser, *Die Benennungen und der Begriff des Leides bei J. Tauler,* especially 191–204 on mystical suffering. For more on mystical suffering in particular, see Alois M. Haas, "'Trage Leiden geduldiglich': Die Einstellung der deutschen Mystik zum Leiden," *Zeitwende* 57 (1986): 154–75; and "'Die Arbeit der Nacht': Mystische Leiderfahrung nach Johannes Tauler," in *Die dunkle Nacht der Sinne,* ed. Gotthard Fuchs (Düsseldorf, 1989), 9–40. See also Gnädinger, *Johannes Tauler,* 162–69; and Bernard McGinn, "*Vere tu es Deus absconditus*" in *Silence and the Word,* 110–13.

218. Gregory, *Moralia in Iob* 5.31.55 (CC 143:258.80–82). For an account of this side of Gregory's mysticism, see McGinn, *Growth of Mysticism,* 66–69; and "*Vere tu es Deus absconditus,*" 101–2.

219. Tauler mentions Gregory's teaching on suffering explicitly in V 44 (192.29–193.3). He appeals to the figure of Job as a model of mystical dereliction in a number of texts. For example: (1) Job 17:12 (*noctem verterunt in diem et rursum post tenebras spero lucem*) in V 41 (172.7–8); (2) Job 17:16 (*in profundissimum infernum descendent omnia mea*) in V 46 (205.13–17); (3) Job 4:15 (*et cum spiritus me praesente transiret inhorruerunt pili carnis meae*) in V 49 (222.8–32), with an explicit citation from Gregory, *Moralia* 5.33, and V 50 (226.10–15) and V 52 (238.12–14); finally, (4) Job 3:23 (*quia timor quem timebam evenit mihi*) in V 47 (211.25–30), and V 55 (257.2–13).

220. McGinn, "*Vere tu es Deus absconditus,*" 104–10.

221. One passage that brings Tauler close to Mechthild is found in V 46 (205.13–31). The preacher begins by citing Job's experience of being plunged into the abyss of hell and confirms this with a reference to the Dominican *bruoder Wigman,* who was buried under Lucifer until he heard a voice calling him to heaven. The same incident is mentioned in Mechthild's *Das fliessende Licht der Gottheit* 5.4, ed. Hans Neumann (Munich: Artemis, 1990) 1:158.50–52.

222. V 39 (161.13–19): . . . und er wirt gefuort einen gar wilden weg, der gar vinster und ellent ist. Und in dem wege benimet im Got alles das er im ie gegab. Und al do wirt der mensche als gar ze mole zuo im selber gelossen das er von Gotte al zemole nút enweis, und kumet in alsolich getrenge das er nút enweis ob im ie recht wart und ob er einem Got habe oder nút habe und ob er es si oder nút si, und wirt im do so wunderlichen we und we das im alle dise wite welt ze enge wirt.

223. Luther's annotations, "Luther Randbemerkungen zu Taulers Predigten," can be found in the *Weimarer Ausgabe* 9:95–104. Particularly interesting are the comments on V 3, 37, and 41. See Steven Ozment, "An Aid to Luther's Marginal Comments on Johannes Tauler's Sermons," *Harvard Theological Review* 63 (1970): 305–11.

224. On this sermon and its relation to Ruusbroec, see Léonce Reypens, "Der 'Goldene Pfennig' bei Tauler und Ruusbroec," in *Altdeutsche und Altniederlandische Mystik,* 353–62.

225. V 37 (143.18–23): Aber das ist minne, do man hat ein burnen in darbende und in berovbunge, in einem verlossende, das da stande ein stetes unbeweglich quelen und man dabi bestat in rechter gelossenheit, und in der quale ein versmelzen und ein verdorren in dem brande dis darbens und do in glicher gelossenheit: das ist minne und nút als ir wenent. Dis ist die entzúndunge dieser lucernen.

226. For other passages dealing with mystical affliction, see V 21 (85.20–86.19), V 23 (93.17–94.6), V 26 (108.1–109.15), V 28 (115.32–116.2), V 38 (151.26–152.36), V 40 (168.24–169.25), V 41 (171.23–173.26), V 47 (217.3–30), V 50 (226.28–227.29), V 63 (345.9–20), and V 74 (402.1–11).

227. V 47 (211.25–212.2): Kinder, dis ist gar ein behender, naher, vinster, unbekant, ellent weg. . . . Nu diser weg der ist gar vinster, wan alles do wir vor abgesprochen han, das ist in enphallen, der ensmakt in nút, und war si súllent, das ist in unbekant und stont al hie in grossem getrenge, und ist in diser weg wol unbevangen mit vinsternisse, sprach S. Gregorius uf dis wort das der mensche stot in eime unbekentnisse. . . . The passage from Gregory is in *Moralia* 5.7.12 (CC 143:226).

228. V 67 (371.15–18): Und do er fúr alle menschen der verlossenste was, do was er sime vatter aller gevellichest, do er rief 'Got, Got, min Got, wie hast du mich verlossen!' wan er was me verlossen und bitterlicher wan ie heilig verlossen wart. For other passages that single out Christ as the model of dereliction, see V 13 (61.35–62.6), V 14 (67.5–10), V 50 (229.19–230.10), and V 51 (233.20–30).

229. See, e.g., V 7 (32.29–33.5), V 9 (45.29–34), V 26 (108.15–17), V 46 (205.13–31), and V 67 (368.4–12). We can also connect the state of *getrenge* with *mors mystica,* mystical death in Christ, as we see from such passages as V 20 (84.8–11) and V 38 (151.26–152.3).

230. V 39 (162.4–13): In disem so fuert recht der herre den menschen usse im selber in sich. Und do ergetzet er in alles sines ellendes, und werdent alle sine wunden heil, und in dem so zúhet Got den menschen us menschlicher wise in ein goetliche wise, usse alle jomerkeit in ein goetlich sicherheit, und wirt do der mensche als vergottet das alles das der mensche ist und wúrket, das wúrket und ist Got in ime, und wirt als verre uf erhaben úber sin natúrlich wise das er recht wirt von gnaden das Got weslichen ist von naturen. Hie inne voelt und bevint sich der mensche selber verloren haben und enweis noch enbevint noch engevoellet sich niergen; er enweis nút denne ein einvaltig wesen. Other important passages on losing all sense of self and distinction in deep union include V 26 (109.20–30), V 28 (117.30–36), V 56 (263.14–18), and V 62 (340.20–28).

231. Although the supreme level of union is the work of grace, this does not exclude a natural insight into the ground that Tauler admitted was open to all, including pagans such as Plato and Proclus, and even the Free Spirit heretics; see the discussion of V 64 (347.9–24) above, and V 55 (257.37–258.6). Tauler condemned the false, or naturalistic, mysticism of the Free Spirits, but his position on the mystical insight into the ground of the pagan philosophers is more ambiguous, especially because in one sermon (V 13: 64.11–16) he seems to suggest that some pagans at least had received grace. On Tauler's opposition to naturalistic mysticism, see Haas, *Nim din selbes war,* 82.

232. For Tauler's view of final union, see Gandlau, *Trinität und Kreuz,* 321–53; Zekorn, *Gelassenheit und Einkehr,* 173–83; Gnädinger, *Johannes Tauler,* 256–70; Ruh, *Geschichte,* 3:507–12; and especially Wrede, *Unio mystica,* Teil III, 203–81.

233. V 7 (33.25–28): . . . also wurt der geist versunken in Got in goetlicher einikeit, daz er do verlúst alle underscheit, und als daz in dar het braht, daz verlúret do sinnen nammen, also demuetikeit und meinunge und sich selber, und ist ein luter stille heimliche einekeit sunder alle underscheit.

234. See, e.g., V 10 (47.18–21), V 15 (69.11–14), and V 61 (334.18–20).

235. There is a helpful list and references in Gandlau, *Trinität und Kreuz,* 343. For the use of *úberformen,* see especially V 55 (257.13–258.2), V 61 (332.9–15), and V 66 (363.11–15). The

verb suggests the Latin *transformare*, used in 2 Cor. 3:18, one of the premier scriptural texts on mystical transformation in Christ. Tauler quotes the text in V 31 (316.9–14) and V 63 (345.4–6), translating *transformare* by *überformen*.

236. V 56 (263.14–17): Und wer moechte denne gescheiden dise goetliche verre übernatúrliche einunge, do der geist ist in genomen und in gezogen in das abgrúnde sines begines? Wissent: wer es múgelich das man den geist in dem geiste gesehen moechte, man sehe in ane allen zwifel an fúr Got.

237. V 32 (121.26–30): Dis nemment tumbe affehte lúte fleischlichen und sprechent, sú súllent gewandelt werden in goettliche nature, und das ist zuomole boese valsche ketzerige. Von der allerhoehster innigster nehster einunge mit Gotte so ist noch goettliche nature und sin wesen hoch und hoch über alle hoehi, daz get in ein goettliche abgrunde das nimmer keine creature und ouch kein enwurt. Later in the same sermon (122.14–16) Tauler again insists that the divine abyss lies beyond all things. For another attack on heretical views of union, see V 55 (258.4–6).

238. V 37 (146.21–22): In disem wirt die sele alzemole gotvar, gotlich, gottig. Si wirt alles das von gnaden das Got ist von naturen. . . . The same formula can also be found, e.g., in V 6 (25.22–24), V 10 (47.18–21), V 26 (109.23–25), V 29 (300.24–25), and V 39 (162.8–11). Among the sources where Tauler could have found this is William of St. Thierry's *Epistola aurea*, n.263: . . . fieri meretur homo Dei, non Deus, sed tamen quod est Deus: homo ex gratia quod Deus ex natura. See J.-M. Déchanet, ed., *Guillaume de Saint-Thierry: Lettre aux Frères du Mont-Dieu (Lettre d'or)*, SC 301, 182.

239. It is in this sense that Tauler touches, though rarely, on a key theme of Christian mysticism, that is, the notion of *epektasis*, or endless sinking into God; see V 32 (122.14–16) and V 13 (61.19–23).

240. On the coexistence of identity and distance in mystical union, see Wrede, *Unio Mystica*, 214, 233–34.

241. Tauler was also conscious of what we might call a reverse prejudice, as we can see from his comment that when lukewarm religious are criticized, they respond to their critics, *er ist ein beghart* (138.3), that is, a hypocritical heretic.

242. See also V 15 (69.18–30), where he corrects those who misunderstood Eckhart; V 24 (99.3), a brief comment on false freedom; and V 81 (432.18–30), where he discusses the correct way of understanding what it means to go beyond the virtues.

243. For Tauler's view on this opposition, see his comments on the difference between *unrechte friheit* (99.3, 167.22–23, 431.21–22), or *valschen friheit* (218.18, 219.1–2), on the one hand, and what he calls *goetteliche friheit* (24.14), *weseliche friden* (258.24), and *friheit des geistes* (239.19–20), on the other.

244. Gregory the Great, *Moralia* 5.36.66 (CC 143:265–66).

245. V 50 (226.15–228.34); see also V 55 (257.25–26), V 54 (251.15–19), and V 74 (401.20–30).

246. V 50 (228.5–11): Der herre kam als ein blik: der blik was über alle die mosse, die was ze mole so swinde das Elyas stuont in der túrin der húlin und tet den mantel fúr di ovgen. . . . Und das er den mantel fúr die ovgen tet, das was das gesicht. Wie kurtz und wie klein das ist, so ist des ein blik aller naturen ze überswenkig und von blosser nature unlidlich und unbegriffenlich.

247. On divinization, see, e.g., V 7 (33.20–28), V 31 (316.7–17), V 39 (162.5–11), and V 63 (345.4–6).

248. The frequent uses of these terms can be explored through use of the "Wortverzeichnis" in Vetter. Particularly rich uses of *entwerden* can be found in V 30 and 31.

249. V 41 (176.4): . . . und al do versinkt das geschaffen nút in das ungeschaffen nút. . . . For similar formulations, see V 45 (201.6–7), and V 63 (345.27–29). The degree of nothingness is directly proportional to the depth of union, as V 31 puts it: Und so ie das niht so grundeloser ist, so die vereinunge do ie wesenlicher und gewehrlicher wurt; . . . also vil entwerdendes, also vil gewerdendes (314.16–21). For Tauler's teaching on *nicht,* see Minoru

Nambara, "Die Idee des absoluten Nichts in der deutschen Mystik und ihre Entsprechungen im Buddhismus," *Archiv für Begriffsgeschichte* 6 (1960): 209–18. To what extent the human subject remains in the process of annihilation for Tauler is a question that will not be taken up here. Contrary to Wrede (*Unio Mystica*, 253–54, 270–72, and 280), I believe that Tauler thinks that the merely *phenomenal* subject is annihilated in the deepest level of union, though not the ontological root of the subject in our created ground.

250. The need for unknowing appears in many sermons; e.g., V 8 (39.27 and 32), V 25 (307.7–10), V 26 (109.20–25), V 46 (204.20–21), V 47 (212.2), V 54 (252.16–19), V 60 (278.13–17), V 69 (378.33–35), and V 76 (411.15 and 22–23).

251. On *durchbruch* in Tauler, see Bernward Dietsche, "Über den Durchbruch bei Tauler," in *Johannes Tauler. Ein deutsche Mystiker*, 301–20, who takes the term in a broad sense of all movement into the ground, even when the term *durchbruch* itself is not used. It seems to me, however, that Tauler deliberately distances himself from Eckhart and Suso by his rare use of the term.

252. See, e.g., V 43 (183.13–17, 189.23–24), V 47 (214.7–11), V 48 (217.11–14, 217.35–218.1), V 52 (238.17–18), V 55 (257.27–29), and V 74 (402.8–11). In his sermon on the angels (V 68), Tauler ascribes the light and flash to the action of the cherubim (376.7–10).

253. The theme of the inner kingdom of God is the subject of one of Eckhart's most challenging sermons, Jostes no. 82, on which see McGinn, *The Mystical Thought of Meister Eckhart*, 144–47, and chapter 4 above, pp. 179–81.

254. For Luke 17:21, see, e.g., V 29 (301.1–5), V 34 (317.16–19), V 37 (144.1–7), V 62 (337.28–31), etc. On the kingdom of God within in Tauler, see Enders, "Selbsterfahrung als Gotteserfahrung," 661–63. This use of the *regnum Dei* was controversial, because the letter that John Dubheim, bishop of Strassburg, wrote against the Free Spirit heretics in 1317 mentioned as one of their errors a claim to have the kingdom of God within them. See Éric Mangin, "La *Lettre du 13 Août 1317* écrite par l'évêque de Strasbourg contre les disciples du libre esprit," in *700e anniversaire de la naissance de Jean Tauler*, 533.

255. V 66 (358–64) includes a short commentary on the Lord's Prayer and its petition "Thy Kingdom come" (361–62).

256. Christ's three births is the theme of V 1 (7–12), a sermon now generally agreed to be by Eckhart (see Gnädinger, *Johannes Tauler*, 140 n. 44). Other sermons that mention the divine birth include V 7, 11, 15, 28, 29, 31, 33, 40, 41, 49, 51, 52, 54, 56, 63, 67, 69, 73, and 74. For a study, see Jean Reaidy, "Trinité et naissance mystique chez Eckhart et Tauler," in *700e anniversaire de la naissance de Jean Tauler*, 444–55.

257. V 29 (301.18–29): Dis gezúg vindet man in dem grunde unbiltlichen; sicherliche in diseme grunde gebirt der himmelsche vatter sinen eingebornen sun hundert tusent werbe sneller denne ein ougenblik. . . . Denne kummet die vetterliche kraft und ruoffet den menschen in sich durch sinen eingebornen sun, und also der sun wurt geborn uz dem vatter und widerflússet in den vatter, also wurt dis mensche in dem sune von dem vatter geborn und flússet wider in den vatter mit deme sune und wurt eine mit ime. For similar texts on the birth of the Son within the ground of the soul, see, e.g., V 15 (68.34–69.1), V 54 (249.3–9), and V 49 (220.1–30, concerning the eternal birth in Mary).

258. Among the more general appeals to being born or reborn in God, see, e.g., V 31 (315.25–28), V 33 (129.10–13), V 41 (172.15–22 and 173.4–5), V 40 (166–68), V 51 (230–34, on how the cross and the crucified Christ must be born in us), V 52 (239.30–35), V 67 (369.23–28), and V 73 (398.1–11), and V 74 (401.20–24). One text on such birthing quotes Eckhart (V 56 [263.1–13]).

259. Sermons on prayer include V 23, 24, 57, and 78. On interior prayer, see Mieth, *Die Einheit von Vita activa und Vita contemplativa*, 283–90; and Gnädinger, *Johannes Tauler*, 261–72.

260. V 39 (156.16–22): Das gehoert wol zuo einem rechten wesenden ingenomenen verklerten menschen, das wúrken und gebruchen ein werdent und eines von dem andern ungehindert blibe, also es in Gotte ist. Do ist das aller oberste wúrken und das aller luterste gebruchen ein einig ein ane hinderen und ein ieklichs in dem aller hoechsten, und das ein

ieklichs ane des anderen hinderen. Das wúrken ist in den personen, das gebruchen git man dem einvaltigen wesende.

261. V 39 (158.6–8): Dis ist ein engegenwúrtig inwendig ansehent meinen; mit der inwendikeit hat er ein gebruchen; und usser dem selben so kert er sich ze note oder ze nutze us ze wúrkende us dem selben in das selbe.

262. V 55 (255.5–9): Der mensche, als er alle dinge gelies und sich selber in allen dingen, so sol er Gotte [often used of Christ in MHG] volgen úber alle ding mit dem usseren menschen, mit aller uebunge der tugende und mit der gemeinen minne, und mit dem inwendigen menschen in rechter gelossenheit sin selbs in allen wisen, wie die vallent und wie es Got uf in wirffet von innen und von ussen. Many other passages echo this; see, e.g., V 37 (143.25–144.9), V 39 (156.11–22), V 67 (370.19–28), and V 74 (400.8–20).

263. Wrede (*Unio Mystica*, 215–18, 236–40) also studies the differences between Eckhart and Tauler on union.

Chapter 7

1. The VL was begun by Wolfgang Stammler and Karl Langosch. The second edition was primarily edited by Kurt Ruh and several associated editors. Ten volumes were published by Walter de Gruyter of Berlin between 1978 and 1999. Currently under way are two further volumes: Vol. 11: *Nachträge und Corrigenda*, and Vol. 12: *Register*.

2. Some idea of the variety of late medieval German mysticism can be gleaned from the old article of Wolfgang Stammler, "Studien zur Geschichte der Mystik in Norddeutschland," first published in 1922 and reprinted in *Altdeutsche und Altniederländische Mystik*, ed. Kurt Ruh (Darmstadt: Wissenschaftliche Buchgesellschaft, 1964), 386–436.

3. See Werner Williams-Krapp, "Literary Genre and Degrees of Holiness: The Perception of Holiness in Writings by and about Female Mystics," in *The Invention of Saintliness*, ed. Anneke B. Mulder-Bakker (London: Routledge, 2002), 210–11 and 216.

4. Georg Steer, "Der Laie als Anreger und Adressat deutscher Prosaliteratur im 14. Jahrhundert," in *Zur deutschen Literatur und Sprache des 14. Jahrhunderts: Dubliner Colloquium 1981*, ed. Walter Haug, Timothy R. Jackson, and Johannes Janota (Heidelberg: Carl Winter, 1983), 361.

5. Werner Williams-Krapp, "The Erosion of a Religious Monopoly: German Religious Literature in the Fifteenth Century," in *The Vernacular Spirit: Essays on Medieval Religious Literature*, ed. Renate Blumenfeld-Kosinski, Duncan Robertson, and Nancy Bradley Warren (New York: Palgrave, 2002), 241–42, 251–55.

6. For an introduction, see Bernard McGinn, "On Mysticism & Art," *Daedalus* (Spring 2003): 131–34. See also Robert Sukale, "Mystik und Kunst," in *Theologische Realenzyklopädie* (Berlin: Walter de Gruyter, 1977), 23:600–608.

7. Michael Camille, *Gothic Art: Glorious Visions* (New York: Abrams, 1996), 12.

8. Ibid., 23.

9. See especially Jeffrey F. Hamburger, "The Visual and the Visionary: The Image in Late Medieval Monastic Devotion," in *The Visual and the Visionary: Art and Female Spirituality in Late Medieval Germany* (New York: Zone, 1998), 111–48. Also useful are Sixten Ringbom, "Devotional Images and Imaginative Devotions: Notes on the Place of Art in Late Medieval Private Piety," *Gazette des Beaux-Arts*, 6th Ser. 73 (1969): 159–70; and James H. Marrow, "Symbol and Meaning in Northern European Art of the Late Middle Ages and the Early Renaissance," *Simiolus* 16 (1986): 150–72.

10. For a brief overview, see David Freedburg, *The Power of Images: Studies in the History and Theory of Response* (Chicago: University of Chicago Press, 1989), chapter 8, "*Visibilia per invisibilia*: Meditation and the Uses of Theory" (pp. 161–91).

11. Jeffrey F. Hamburger, "Speculations on Speculation: Vision and Perception in the Theory and Practice of Mystical Devotion," in *Deutsche Mystik im abendländische Zusammen-*

hang: Neu erschlossene Texte, neue methodische Ansätze, neue theoretische Konzepte, ed. Walter Haug and Wolfram Schneider-Lastin (Tübingen: Niemeyer, 2000), 353–408, quotation at 359.

12. Richard of St. Victor, *Benjamin Minor* 14 (PL 196:10): . . . quia dulce est ei saltem imaginando eorum memoriam retinere, quorum intelligentiam nondum valet ratiocinando apprehendere. . . . Hanc esse primam viam omni ingrediente ad invisibilium contemplationem nemo ignoret. . . .

13. Bernard of Clairvaux, *Sermones super Cantica* 20.6 (*Sancti Bernardi Opera* 1:118).

14. Thomas of Celano, *Vita Prima* XXX.84–86 (*Fontes Franciscani* [Assisi: Edizioni Porziuncola, 1995], 360–62): Volo enim illius pueri memoriam agere, qui in Bethlehem natus est, et infantilium necessitatum eius incommode, . . . utcumque corporeis oculis pervidere. The vision given to John is described as *a quodam viro virtutis mirabilis visio cernitur.*

15. Bernard McGinn, *The Flowering of Mysticism: Men and Women in the New Mysticism (1200–1350)*, vol. 3 of *The Presence of God: A History of Western Christian Mysticism* (New York: Crossroad, 1998), 270–82.

16. From Gertrude's *Legatus divinae pietatis* 2.5.2, as found in *Gertrude d'Helfta: Oeuvres spirituelles, Tome II, Le Héraut* (SC 139; Paris: Editions du Cerf, 1968): Igitur cum post suscepta vivifica sacramenta, ad locum orationis reversa fuissem, videbatur mihi quasi de dextro latere crucifixi depicti in folio, scilicet de vulnere lateris, prodiret tamquam radius solis, in modum sagittae acutis, qui per ostentum extensus contrahebatur, deinde extendebatur, et sic per moram durans, affectum meum blande allexit.

17. *Le Héraut* 4.12.3 (*Oeuvres spirituelles, Tome IV*, SC 255, 134): Et ideo a nullo debet vilipendi quidquid per imaginationes rerum corporalium demonstratur, sed studere debet quilibet ut per corporalium rerum similitudinem spiritualium delectationum suaves intellectus degustare mereatur. See the discussion in Hamburger, "Visual and the Visionary," 147 (whose translation is used here).

18. Reiner Hausherr, "Über die Christus-Johannes-Gruppen. Zum Problem 'Andachtsbilder' und deutsche Mystik," in *Beiträge zur Kunst des Mittelalters: Festschrift für Hans Wentzel zum 60. Geburtstag*, ed. Rüdiger Beckemann, Ulf-Dietrich Korn, Johannes Zahlten (Berlin: Mann, 1975), 103: "Die Ausformung neuer Bildtypen in der Zeit um 1300 geht sicher auf die gleichen frömmigkeits- und theologiegeschichtlichen Voraussetzungen zurück wie die deutsche Mystik."

19. Erwin Panofsky, "'Imago Pietatis': Ein Beitrag zur Typengeschichte des 'Schmerzensmanns' und der 'Maria Mediatrix,'" in *Festschrift für Max J. Friedländer zum 60. Geburtstag* (Leipzig: E. A. Seemann, 1927), 264–66. The past decades have seen considerable debate over the nature of the *Andachtsbild* that cannot be detailed here. An important caution against the usual understanding of such images has been voiced by Jeffrey F. Hamburger, *Nuns as Artists: The Visual Culture of a Medieval Convent* (Berkeley: University of California Press, 1997), 214: "The ongoing argument over the characteristics of the *Andachtsbild* that sets text against image, private against public, original against imitation, or lay against monastic depends on terminology that would not have been meaningful to those for whom the imagery was made."

20. Marrow, "Symbol and Meaning," 157.

21. On late medieval scenes of the passion iconography, see James H. Marrow, *Passion Iconography in Northern European Art of the Late Middle Ages and Early Renaissance* (Kortrijk: Van Ghemmert, 1979).

22. According to Cousins, in the mysticism of the historical event, "one recalls a significant event in the past, enters into its drama and draws from it spiritual energy, eventually moving beyond the event to union with God." See "Francis of Assisi: Christian Mysticism at the Crossroads," in *Mysticism and Religious Traditions*, ed. Steven Katz (Oxford: Oxford University Press, 1983), 166–67.

23. See Jeffrey F. Hamburger, *St. John the Divine: The Deified Evangelist in Medieval Art and Theology* (Berkeley: University of California Press, 2002).

24. For a survey of some examples, see Bernard McGinn, "Theologians as Trinitarian

Iconographers," in *The Mind's Eye: Art and Theological Argument in the Medieval West*, ed. Jeffrey F. Hamburger and Anne-Marie Bouché (Princeton: Princeton University Press, 2005), 186–207.

25. Jeffrey F. Hamburger, *The Rothschild Canticles: Art and Mysticism in Flanders and the Rhineland circa 1300* (New Haven: Yale University Press, 1990).

26. The 105 current folios of the manuscript (New Haven, Yale University, Rare Book and Manuscript Library, MS 404) contain 46 surviving full page miniatures (of perhaps an original 50), as well as 160 small miniatures, 23 tinted drawings of saints, and 41 historiated initials (Hamburger, *Rothschild Canticles*, 8). These groups are not labeled, or even arranged in order in the present state of the manuscript. Hamburger's reconstruction begins by identifying what he terms prefatory images (chapter 3), and then studies the six types in chapters 4–9: paradisiacal miniatures; Song of Songs miniatures; Marian miniatures; mystical union miniatures; trinitarian miniatures; and miniatures illustrating the *Vitae Patrum*.

27. For the history of illustrations of the Song of Songs, see Otto Gillen, "Braut-Bräutigam," and "Brautmystik," in *Reallexikon zur deutschen Kunstgeschichte*, ed. O. Schmidt (Stuttgart and Munich: Metzler, 1937) 2:1110–24 and 1130–34. The first flowering was in the twelfth century, on which see Isabelle Maliase, "L'Iconographie biblique du *Cantique des Cantiques* au XIIe siècle," *Scriptorium* 46 (1992): 67–73.

28. On this shift, see Bernard McGinn, "The Language of Inner Experience in Christian Mysticism," *Spiritus* 1 (2001): 156–71; and especially Gordon Rudy, *Mystical Language of Sensation in the Later Middle Ages* (New York and London: Routledge, 2002).

29. The Rothschild Canticles illustrate the Song of Songs in two places (ff. 17v–26v and ff. 65v–73r). Hamburger considers the two cycles in chapters 5 and 7 of *The Rothschild Canticles*. In both sets the images are based on the biblical book, though the accompanying texts are anthologies of diverse texts, biblical, liturgical, and ecclesiastical.

30. Hamburger, *Rothschild Canticles*, 71.

31. Rudy, *Mystical Language of Sensation*, chapter 1.

32. On this text from David's *De exterioris et interioris hominis compositione*, and David's teaching in general, see *Flowering of Mysticism*, 113–16.

33. The illustration of Rev. 3:20 (Sto ad ostium et pulso; si quis apperuerit michi introibo et cenabo cum illo et ille mecum) shows the freedom of the creator of the Rothschild Canticles. In Revelation the text is put in Christ's mouth, but here it seems to be expressed by the bride, who has grasped Christ's arm as he moves back into the building.

34. The *Vitis mystica*, a sermon on John 15:1, was probably preached by Bonaventure during a trip to Germany (see *S. Bonaventurae Opera Omnia* 8:158–89). A longer interpolated version of the text circulated under the name of St. Bernard and can be found in PL 184:635–740. This text is found at 643A: . . . per vulnus visibile vulnus amoris invisibilis videamus. The concept goes back to Bernard, *Sermones super Cantica* 61.4 (*Sancti Bernardi Opera* 2:150–51).

35. On this aspect of Bernard's teaching, see Bernard McGinn, *The Growth of Mysticism*, volume 2 of *The Presence of God: A History of Western Christian Mysticism* (New York: Crossroad, 1994), 185–86.

36. The text on f. 65v reads: Deus a lybano uenit et sanctus de monte ombroso et condenso" (Hos. 3:3 in the *Vetus Latina* version). The text was used by Bernard in reference to the incarnation in *Sermones super Cantica* 6.3 (*Sancti Bernardi Opera* 1:27). On this image, see Hamburger, *Rothschild Canticles*, 108.

37. The passage, based on Augustine, *Confessiones* 13.1, reads: Inuoco te Deus meus in animam meam, quam preparas ad capiendum te ex desiderio quo ei inspiras.

38. For studies of the trinitarian images, see Hamburger, *Rothschild Canticles*, chapter 8; and "Revelations and Concealment: Apophatic Imagery in the Trinitarian Miniatures of the *Rothschild Canticles*," *The Yale University Library Gazette,* volume 66, supplement (1991). *Beinecke Studies in Early Manuscripts*, 134–58.

39. François Boespflug, "Apophatisme théologique et abstinence figurative: Sur l'irreprésentabilité de Dieu (le Père)," *Revue des sciences religieuses* 72 (1998): 446–68.

40. On the Old Testament Trinity icon (also known as the "Hospitality of Abraham"), as well as the early theological debates on picturing the Trinity, see Bernard McGinn, "'Trinity Higher Than Any Being!': Imaging the Invisible Trinity," in *Ästhetik des Unsichtbaren: Bildtheorie und Bildgebrauch in der Vormoderne*, ed. David Ganz and Thomas Lentes (Berlin: Reimer, 2004), 76–93, and the literature cited there.

41. The first three trinitarian images are found at the openings from f. 39v to f. 44r. The second series of sixteen begins on f. 74v and concludes on f. 106r. On f. 86v there is a text that does not have a facing picture on 87r, indicating that there were meant to be twenty scenes in all.

42. For an introduction to the variety of forms of trinitarian iconography, see Wolfgang Braunfels, *Die heilige Dreifaltigkeit* (Düsseldorf: Schwann, 1954).

43. Hamburger, "Revelation and Concealment," 134.

44. All twenty text pages contain squares with figures of seers gesturing with awe and attention; sixteen of the nineteen Trinity images contain figures in the corners, most often of two angels above and two humans below. As Hamburger puts it, "The seers enact the response of the viewer, whom they encourage to react to the miniatures as if they were visions" ("Concealment and Revelation," 141).

45. Augustine's *De Trinitate* is cited twelve times, though not at all in the final seven miniatures. Particularly important for the compiler was *De Trin.* 8.4.7, a passage on the necessity but fallibility of imagination. Two long quotations (ff. 39v and 85v) give virtually all of this section of Augustine.

46. F. 103v: Centrum meum ubique locorum; circumferentia autem nusquam. The placing of this Hermetic axiom in God's own mouth is unique. On the axiom and its use by Eckhart, Marguerite Porete, and others, see chapter 1 above, pp. 43–44. An image of the divine nature as the circle whose center is everywhere and whose circumference is nowhere is also found in the Latin commentary on Eckhart's sequence, the "Granum Sinapis."

47. For comments on this image, see Hamburger, *Rothschild Canticles*, 129–30, who connects the circular forms to medieval cosmographic representations; see also "Revelation and Concealment," 147–48.

48. F. 105v: Domine, duc me in desertum tue deitatis et tenebrositatem tui luminis et duc me ubi tu non es. This prayer is glossed by an antiphon from the Feast of St. Lawrence: Mea nox obscurum non habet, sed lux glorie mee omnia inlucessit (cf. Ps. 138:12).

49. F. 105v: Bernardus orauit: domine, duc me ubi es. dixit ei: barnarde [sic], non facio, quoniam si ducerem te ubi sum, annichilareris michi et tibi.

50. See especially Hamburger, *Nuns as Artists*.

51. Romuald Banz, *Christus und die Minnende Seele: Zwei spätmittelhochdeutsche mystische Gedichte* (Breslau: Marcus, 1908; reprint, Hildesheim: G. Olms, 1977). The poem contains 2112 lines divided into twenty-one sections. It is illustrated by twenty images in the two main manuscripts: Einsiedeln, codex 710 [322], and Karlsruhe, codex 106. On the illustrations, see especially Werner Williams-Krapp, "Bilderbogen-Mystik: Zu 'Christus und die minnende Seele': Mit Edition der Mainzer Überlieferung," in *Überlieferungsgeschichtliche Editionen und Studien zur deutschen Literatur des Mittelalters. Kurt Ruh zum 75. Geburtstag*, ed. Konrad Kunze et al. (Tübingen: Niemeyer, 1989), 350–64.

52. Hildegard Elisabeth Keller, *My Secret is Mine: Studies in Religion and Eros in the German Middle Ages* (Leuven: Peeters, 2000), chapters 4–5 (quotation at 191).

53. The text for this illustration is as follows: Hie wile er kestgen iren lib, / Das sy dest minder in der welt belib. / Cristus sprach: Ich müss dir din flaisch beren, / Dass ich mich mug dar inn erneren. / Sy spricht: Du schlechst mich also ser, / Ich mage es nit liden mer (lines 459–64; Banz 281).

54. This experience of being abandoned by God can be found in chapter 8 of her *Memoriale*, in *Il Libro della Beata Angela da Foligno*, ed. Ludger Their and Abela Calufetti (Grottaferrata: Collegio S. Bonaventurae, 1985), 338. See the discussion in McGinn, *Flowering of Mysticism*, 147.

55. "Christus und die minnende sele," lines 1194–95 (Banz, 319): O herr, geflúh dich niemer mer,/ Dess setz ich dir lib und sel.

56. "Christus und die minnende sele," lines 1840–44 (Banz, 351): So wölt ich mich an dich smuken / Und dich an min hertz frúntlich truken / Und fügen in die sele min. / Da müstist ewechlich inne sin.

57. On the formula "du bist mein, ich bin dein," see Friedrich Ohly, "Du Bist Mein, Ich Bin Dein, Du in Mir, Ich in Dir, Ich Du, Du Ich," in *Kritische Bewahrung: Beiträge zur deutschen Philologie. Festschrift für Werner Schröder* (Berlin: Erich Schmidt, 1974), 371–415.

58. *The Hours of Catherine of Cleves: Introduction and Commentaries* by John Plummer (New York: George Braziller, 1966). The manuscript contains nine cycles of "Little Hours." The Hours of the Trinity are recited on Sundays.

59. For a brief history, see Braunfels, *Die heilige Dreifaltigkeit*, xxxv-xliii.

60. On the image of the Man of Sorrows, see Bernhard Ridderbos, "The Man of Sorrows: Pictorial Images and Metaphorical Statements," in *The Broken Body: Passion Devotion in Late-Medieval Culture*, ed. A. A. MacDonald, H. N. B. Ridderbos, and R. M. Schlusemann (Groningen: E. Forsten, 1998), 145–81.

61. The prayer and image appear on f. 183v of a manuscript from Emilia now in the Biblioteca Medicea, Larenziana, and appears as plate 2 in Ribberbos, "Man of Sorrows," 147.

62. Georg Troescher, "Die 'pitié-de-nostre-seigneur' oder die 'Not-Gottes,'" *Wallraf-Richartz Jahrbuch* 9 (1936): 148–68. See also Michael Camille, "Mimetic Identification and Passion Devotion in the Later Middle Ages: A Double-sided Panel by Meister Francke," in *Broken Body*, 192–93.

63. See Herbert Beck and Maraike Bückling, *Hans Multscher: Das Frankfurter Trinitätsrelief. Ein Zeugnis spekulativer Künstlerindividualität* (Frankfurt: Fischer, 1988).

64. Braunfels's general comment on the Throne of Grace in *Die heilige Dreifaltigkeit*, xlii: "Es sind Gebilde von undeutbar sakraler Macht."

65. Hamburger, *Nuns as Artists*, chapter 2.

66. On the background and development of the metaphor of the house as heart, see Gerhard Bauer, *Claustrum Animae: Untersuchungen zur Geschichte der Metapher vom Herzen als Kloster*. Band 1, *Enstehungsgeschichte* (Munich: Wilhelm Fink, 1972).

67. Hamburger, *Nuns as Artists*, chapter 4, especially pp. 144–51, 170–71, and 219.

68. For late medieval passion iconography in northern Europe, see Marrow, *Passion Iconography in Northern European Art*. For the background to medieval passion images, see Hans Belting, *Das Bild und sein Publikum im Mittelalter: Form und Funktion früher Bildtafeln der Passion* (Berlin: G. Mann, 1981).

69. For an introduction to the role of Christ's blood in the history of spirituality, see Réginald Grégoire, "Sang," DS 14:319–33. On the use of blood among late medieval female authors, Caroline Walker Bynum, *Holy Feast and Holy Fast: The Religious Significance of Food to Medieval Women* (Berkeley: University of California Press, 1987), especially 55–56, 64–65, 161–80, and 270–76.

70. On this picture, see Hamburger, *Nuns as Artists*, 1–3.

71. On the infantilization and feminization of the image, see Michael Camille, "Seductions of the Flesh: Meister Francke's Female 'Man' of Sorrow," in *Frömmigkeit im Mittelalter: Politisch-soziale Kontext, visuelle Praxis, körperliche Ausdrucksformen*, ed. Klaus Schreiner and Marc Müntz (Munich: Wilhelm Fink, 2002), 243–69. Camille summarizes: "The devotion of the late Middle Ages was perverse, not, I would suggest, by making Christ into a sexual object but in making him weak, childlike and helpless. Manufacturing a more empathetic God, one more open to projection than the closed, self-contained and triumphal and homo-erotic masculinism produced by the 'other' (Italian) Renaissance" (p. 259).

72. Camille, "Mimetic Identification and Passion Devotion," 190. On the origins of the medieval notion of compassion, see Rachel Fulton, *From Judgment to Passion: Devotion to Christ and the Virgin Mary, 800–1200* (New York: Columbia University Press, 2002).

73. Camille, "Mimetic Identification and Passion Devotion," 204–6.

74. Wilhelm Preger, *Geschichte der deutschen Mystik im Mittelalter*, 3 vols. (Leipzig: Dörffling and Francke, 1874–93). For a recent sketch of the historiography on medieval mysticism, see Otto Langer, *Christliche Mystik im Mittelalter: Mystik und Rationalisierung—Stationen eines Konflikts* (Darmstadt: Wissenschaftliche Buchgesellschaft, 2004), 37–40.

75. The third volume of Ruh's *Geschichte der abendländische Mystik* (Munich: Beck, 1985) deals with Dominican mysticism in late medieval Germany.

76. A classic work is Henri Bremond's *Prayer and Poetry: A Contribution to the Study of Poetical Theory* (London: Burnes Oates & Washbourne, 1927, first published in French in 1926), on which see Clément Moison, *Henri Bremond et la poésie pure* (Paris: Lettres modernes, 1967). See also E. I. Watkin, *Poets and Mystics* (London and New York: Sheed and Ward, 1953); and the papers collected and translated by Paule Plouvier, *Poesia e mistica* (Vatican City: Libreria Editrice Vaticana, 2002). Particularly important are a number of studies by Alois M. Haas, especially "Mechthild von Magdeburg," in *Sermo mysticus: Studien zur Theologie und Sprache in der deutschen Mystik* (Freiburg, Schweiz: Universitätsverlag, 1979), 67–135; and "Dichtung in christlicher Mystik und Zen-Buddhismus," *Zen Buddhism Today* 9 (1992): 86–116.

77. The poem of 4,312 lines was edited by Karl Weinhold, *Lamprecht von Regensburg: Sanct Francisken Leben und Tochter Syon* (Paderborn: Schöningh, 1880). For introductions, see Joachim Heinzle, "Lamprecht von Regensburg," VL 5:522–24; and Margot Schmidt, "Lambert de Ratisbonne," DS 9:142–43. Lamprecht explicitly excludes himself from the enjoyment of mystical graces, which may be why Schmidt characterizes the poem as allegorical rather than mystical.

78. See Keller, *My Secret Is Mine*, 112–15 for an introduction, and 158 and chapter 5 for the role of the passion.

79. The "Tochter Syon" ends with a lengthy description of the wedding of the lovers in the castle of the heart, featuring an analysis of the kiss (lines 4004–4104) and a description of their final union (lines 4188–95), using the phrase "sie ist in im und er in ir" ("She is in him and he is in her" [line 4191]). For a discussion, see Keller, *My Secret Is Mine*, 157–58. Such passages make it difficult to deny that at least some aspects of the poem are deeply mystical.

80. Kurt Ruh ("Mystische Spekulation in Reimversen des 14. Jahrhunderts," in *Kleine Schriften: Band 2, Scholastik und Mystik im Spätmittelalter*, ed. Volker Mertens [Berlin: Walter de Gruyter, 1984], 183–211) lists twenty-six poems as "mystisch-spekulativ." Ruth Meyer ("'Maister Eghart sprichet von wesen bloss': Beobachtungen zur Lyrik der deutschen Mystik," *Zeitschrift für deutsche Philologie: Sonderheft Mystik* 113 [1994]: 66–69) lists fifty-one mystical poems divided into two classes: "mystisch-aszetisch"; and "mystisch-spekulativ."

81. The critical edition of the poem is that of Kurt Ruh, "Textkritik zum Mystikerlied 'Granum Sinapis,'" in *Kleine Schriften* 2:77–93. For an introduction, see Ruh ("Granum sinapis," VL 3:220–24), who justly claims, "Die deutsche Sequenz ist von ungewöhnlicher theologischer Substanz und sprachlich-poetischer Qualität" (p. 221). Ruh also studies the poem in chapter 4, "Dionysische Mystik: 'Granum sinapis,'" in *Meister Eckhart: Theologe. Prediger. Mystiker* (Munich: Beck, 1985), 47–59. Other studies include Maria Bindschedler, "Griechische Gedanke in einem mittelalterlichen mystischen Gedicht," *Theologische Zeitschrift* 4 (1948): 192–212; and Alois M. Haas, "Granum sinapis—An den Grenzen der Sprache," in *Sermo mysticus*, 301–29. The Latin commentary, which is certainly not by Eckhart, has been edited by Maria Bindschedler, *Der lateinische Kommentar zum Granum Sinapis* (Basel: Schwabe, 1949).

82. Walter Haug, "Meister Eckhart und das 'Granum sinapis,'" in *Forschungen zur deutschen Literatur des Spätmittelalters: Festschrift für Johannes Janota*, ed. Horst Brunner and Werner Williams-Krapp (Tübingen: Niemeyer, 2003), 73–92.

83. In dem begin/hô uber si/ist ië daz wort./ô rîcher hort,/da ië begin begin gebâr (Haas, "Granum Sinapis," 304). Notice the characteristic Eckhartian transposition of the past tense of John 1:1 (In principio *erat* Verbum) into the present tense *ist*.

84. Des puntez berk/stîg âne werk,/vorstentlichkeit!/der wek dich treit/in eine wûste wun-derlîch,/dî breit, dî wît,/unmêzik lît./dî wûste hat/noch zît noch stat,/ir wîse dî ist sunderlîch (Haas, ibid.).

85. Wirt als ein kint,/wirt toup, wirt blint!/dîn selbes icht,/mûz werden nicht,/al icht, al nicht trîb uber hôr! (Haas, ibid.).

86. Ō sêle mîn,/genk ûz, got în!/sink al mîn icht/in gotis nicht,/sink in dî grundelôze vlût!/vlî ich von dir,/du kumst zu mir./vorlîs ich mich,/sō vind ich dich:/ô uberweselîches gût (Haas, ibid.). Haug ("Meister Eckhart und das 'Granum sinapis,'" 90–92) argues that the return to the language of positive prayer and personal relation to God at the end of the poem shows that it is not by Eckhart, however much it may use his language and themes.

87. This is suggested by Haug, "Meister Eckhart und das 'Granum sinapis,'" 84–85, and is investigated in greater detail by Charlotte Radler, "The 'Granum Sinapis' Poem and Com-mentary in the Light of Medieval Neoplatonism" (diss., University of Chicago, 2004). There is also a later vernacular comment on the poem that will not be considered here.

88. For uses of Proclus, especially citing the *Liber de Causis* and *Institutio theologica* together (a procedure that may be based on Thomas Aquinas), see the edition of Bindschedler, 50, 70, 78, 112, and 118.

89. Eriugena is cited through the glosses from the *Periphyseon* found in the Paris *corpus Dionysiacum*; see Bindschedler, 32, 80, 94, 120, 126, 146, and 148.

90. For citations of Gallus (twice by name), see Bindschedler, 68, 94–96, 126, 128, 130–32, 144, 150, and 158 (several of these references are not noted by Bindschedler).

91. For a list of sources, see Bindschedler, 17.

92. The defense of Eckhart is a guarded one. In several places in the commentary the author seems to draw back from the more challenging aspects of Eckhart's teaching. Thus, the comment on the verse *hîr ist ein tûfe sunder grunt* has nothing on Eckhart's teaching about the fused ground (ed., 74), and the explanation of the ascent of intellect to the divine moun-tain does not dwell on the nature of *vorstentlichkeit/intellectus* at all (ed., 86–88).

93. On the *desertum mysticum*, see Bindschedler, 86–98, and 136.

94. Bindschedler, *Der lateinische Kommentar*, 146.11–16: "Sink al mîn icht." Hic optat totam quidditatem suam in deum transformari, quod solum in futura vita possibile est, tanta enim excellentia divinae virtutis in futura vita omnibus, qui contemplatione ipsius digni sunt, mani-festabitur, ut nil aliud praeter eam, sive in corporibus, sive in intellectibus, eis eluceat, ut ex libro De quadrifaria divisione naturae plenius habetur. The reference to Eriugena's *Periphy-seon* 1.9 introduces two long quotations drawn from Maximus the Confessor's *Ambigua* as cited by Eriugena (PL 122:449C–450B). It should be noted that neither Eriugena nor Max-imus restricts these divinizing theophanies to the future life.

95. The poem and commentary were first edited by Franz Pfeiffer in his 1857 book on Eckhart. The critical edition and study are in Kurt Ruh, "Seuse Vita c. 52 und das Gedicht und die Glosse 'Vom Überschall,'" in *Kleine Schriften* 2:145–68. See also Alain de Libera, "L'Un ou la Trinité?" *Revue des sciences religieuses* 70 (1996): 40–41. The poem consists of six-teen stanzas of four lines and a final stanza of five, but about five lines are missing.

96. Chapter 52 of Suso's *Life* can be found in the edition of Karl Bihlmeyer, *Seuse: Deutsche Schriften*, 184–90. The word *überschal* is found in chapter 36 (112.4).

97. Stanza V: Der rivier ist ursprunclich da einikeit in weset, / daz einic ein ist durftelos, in im selben ez swebet / in einre dunstren stilheit: ez kan nieman verstan, / wanne in sins selbesheit daz ist ez offenbar (Ruh, "Seuse Vita," 148).

98. Stanza VIII: O gruntlos tiefe abgrunt, in diner tiefe ho, / in diner hoheit nider, wie mac daz sin also? / daz ist uns verborgen in diner tiefe grunt, / doch seit uns sanctus Paulus, ez sül uns werden kunt (Ruh, "Seuse Vita," 148). The reference to Paul is probably to Eph. 3:18–19.

99. Stanzas XV: Daz mens, daz ich meine daz ist wortelos, / ein und ein vereinet, da liuhet bloz gein bloz / in deme unbegrifen der hohen einikeit, / diu alle dinc vernihtet an ir selbesheit. Stanza XVI: Da die zwei abgrunde in einer gelicheit sweben, / gegeistet und ent-

geistet: daz ist ein hohes leben. / da sich got entgeistet da ist dunsterheit/in einer unbekanter bekanter einikeit (Ruh, "Seuse Vita", 149).

100. While there is no full modern history of medieval German preaching, there is a good recent introduction by Hans-Jochen Schiewer, "German Sermons in the Middle Ages," in *The Sermon,* general editor Beverly Mayne Kienzle, Typologie des sources du Moyen Age Occidental, fasc. 81–83 (Turnhout: Brepols, 2000), 861–961.

101. Schiewer, "German Sermons," 862–64.

102. Aside from the bibliography in Schiewer, see the helpful, if now somewhat outdated, lists in Karin Morvay and Dagmar Grube, *Bibliographie der deutschen Predigt des Mittelalters: Veröffentliche Predigten* (Munich: C. H. Beck, 1974). Other important treatments of medieval German preaching include Kurt Ruh, "Deutsche Predigtbücher des Mittelalters," in *Kleine Schriften* 2:296–317; and Georg Steer, "VI. Geistlicher Prosa. 2. Predigt," in *Geschichte der deutschen Literatur,* Band III/2, *Die deutschen Literatur im späten Mittelalter 1250–1370,* ed. Ingeborg Glier (Munich: C. H. Beck, 1987), 318–39; and the papers in *Die deutsche Predigt im Mittelalter,* ed. Volker Mertens and Hans-Jochen Schiewer (Tübingen: Max Niemeyer, 1992). It has been customary to distinguish between the *homilia,* a direct exegesis of a biblical text and its application to life, and *sermo,* a scholastically organized consideration of a theme based on a scriptural text but following a logical development. In practice, since the two ideal types intermingle (though most mystical sermons are closer to the *homilia* ideal), I will use the terms sermon and homily interchangeably. It is also useful to note the obvious: all the MHG sermons that survive are literary works (*Lesepredigt*) whose relation to the actual preached sermon (*Kanzelpredigt*) is not easy to determine.

103. See Schiewer's treatments of mystical sermons in "German Sermons," 874–85, 905–11, 919–21.

104. Schiewer, "German Sermons," 862, 933. See also Williams-Krapp, "Erosion of a Monopoly," in *Vernacular Spirit,* 239–58.

105. Kurt Ruh, "Dominikanische Prediger der Eckhart-Zeit," *Geschichte,* 3:389–414.

106. The Dominican preachers summarized in Ruh's chapter include Giseler von Slatheim, Johannes Franke, Hermann von Loveia, Florentius von Utrecht, Helwic von Germar, Albrecht von Treffurt, Arnold der Rote, Heinrich von Ekkewint, and Johannes von Sterngassen.

107. The text was edited by Philipp Strauch, *Paradisus anime intelligentis (Paradis der fornunftigen sele): Aus der Oxforder Handschrift Cod. Laud. Misc. 479 nach E. Sievers' Abschrift* (Berlin: Weidmann, 1919). This edition has been reissued with a postface by Niklaus Largier and Gilbert Fournier (Hildesheim: Weidmann, 1998).

108. Kurt Ruh provides information about the collection in "'Paradisus anime intelligentis' ('Paradis der fornunftigen sele')," VL 7:298–303, as well as in "Deutsche Predigerbücher des Mittelalters," 312–17; and *Meister Eckhart,* 60–71. Also helpful are Lauri Seppänen, *Studien zur Terminologie des Paradisus anime intelligentis: Beiträge zur Erforschung der Sprache der mittelhochdeutschen Mystik und Scholastik,* Mémoires de la Societé Néophilologique de Helsinki 27 (Helsinki: Societé Néophilologique de Helsinki, 1964); Burkhard Hasebrink, "Studies on the Redaction and Use of the *Paradisus anime intelligentis,*" in *De l'homélie au sermon: Histoire de la prédication médiévale,* ed. Jacqueline Hamesse and Xavier Hermand (Louvain-la-Neuve: Université Catholique, 1993), 143–58; Freimut Löser, "Nachlese: Unbekannte Texte Meister Eckharts in bekannten Handschriften," in *Die deutsche Predigt im Mittelalter,* 125–49; Ria van den Brandt, "Die Eckhart-Predigten der Sammlung *Paradisus anime intelligentis* näher betrachtet," in *Albertus Magnus und der Albertismus: Deutsche philosophische Kultur des Mittelalters,* ed. Maarten J. F. M. Hoenen and Alain de Libera (Leiden: Brill, 1995), 173–87; Schiewer, "German Sermons," 878–80; Alessandra Saccon, "Predicazione e filosofia: il caso del 'Paradisus anime intelligentis,'" in *Filosofia in Volgare nel Medioevo,* ed. Nadia Bray and Loris Sturlese (Louvain-la-Neuve: Féderation Internationale des Instituts d'Études Médiévales, 2003), 81–105; and Niklaus Largier, "Interpreting Eckhart's Incarnation Theology: The Sermon Collection *Paradisus anime intelligentis,*" *Eckhart Review* 13 (Spring 2004): 25–36.

Notes to Pages 321–323

109. The sermons by "meister Hane der calmellita" are nos. 3, 30, and 54. No. 62 (Strauch, 131–33; all subsequent references will be to this edition) is described in the introductory Tabula as from *ein barfuzzin lesemeister.*

110. On paradise of the soul/heart (Gen. 2:8) as a literary and mystical theme, see Friedrich Wilhelm Wodtke, "Die Allegorie des 'Inneren Paradieses' bei Bernhard von Clairvaux, Honorius Augustodunensis, Gottfried von Strassburg und in der deutschen Mystik," in *Festschrift Josef Quint anlässlich seines 65. Geburtstages überreicht,* ed. Hugo Moser, Rudolf Schützeichel, and Karl Stackmann (Bonn: Semmel, 1964), 277–90.

111. Tabula (5.2–5): in disir predigade brudir Gisiler von Slatheim, der lesimeister was zu Kolne und zu Erforte, widir di barfuzin und bewiset daz diz werc der fornunft edilir ist dan daz werc dez willen in deme ewigin lebine, und brichit di bant der barfuzin id est argumenta meisterliche. No. 41 is found in Strauch 90–93.

112. Ruh, "'Paradisus anime,'" VL 7:300.

113. Van den Brandt ("Die Eckhart-Predigten," 176–79) helpfully distinguishes three types of Eckhart sermons on intellect in the *Paradisus anime intelligentis:* (1) Nos. 19, 22, 28, in which intellect is a power of the soul, and therefore not capable of attaining beatitude; (2) nos. 21, 22 (in part), 24, 42, 4, 60, and 33, in which there is a double view of intellect, with the upper intellect identified with the ground, while the lower intellect relates to the created world; and (3) nos. 33 (mostly), 59, and 60 (mostly), in which *forstentnisse* is identified with God.

114. Hasebrink (*"Paradisus anime intelligentis,"* 151) summarizes: "The redactor misunderstands the inner differentiation of Eckhart's sermons and harmonises in favour of an early Eckhart."

115. Hasebrink (*"Paradisus anime intelligentis,"* 152–58) shows how the redactor deliberately edited out linguistic aspects of the sermon genre ("subjectivisms, metaphorical language or apellatives are almost entirely absent," 155), thus crossing the dividing line between sermon and treatise. Steer ("Predigt," 331–32) also emphasizes the pedagogic purpose of the collection. Saccon ("Predicazione e filosofia," 89–99) has a useful discussion of the redactional perspective of the collection.

116. Niklaus Largier, "'Intellectus in deum ascensus': Intellekttheoretische Auseinandersetzungen in Texten der deutschen Mystik," *Deutsche Vierteljahrsschrift für Literaturwissenschaft und Geistesgeschichte* 69 (1995): 423–71, especially 427–28, 459–62; and "Von Hadewijch, Mechthild und Dietrich zu Eckhart und Seuse? Zur Historiographie der 'deutschen Mystik' und der 'deutschen Dominikanerschule,'" in *Deutsche Mystik im abendländische Zusammenhang,* 93–117.

117. On the role of intellect in the *Paradise* collection, see Largier, "'Intellectus in deum ascensus,'" 448–50; Hasebrink, "Studies on the Redaction and Use," 146–52; and Saccon, "Predicazione e filosofia," 99–105.

118. Largier ("Interpreting Eckhart's Incarnation Theology," especially 26–30, 34–35). Largier summarizes: "A common element in all the sermons of the *Paradisus* is their interest in the incarnation not as an historical event but as the birth of God in the soul. . . . The line of interpretation chosen by the author of the *Paradisus* seems primarily to suggest that Eckhart's writings can be read in the context of a more orthodox, namely Dionysian, teaching" (pp. 34–35).

119. No. 17 (42.16–20): . . . und daz die redelichkeit gesamenet hot, da blickit daz forstentnisse in mit einer einveldikeit, und heisit daz der meister di blumen des forstentnisses, wan alse bloume foregeit der frucht, und ist ein gelobin des warin bekentnisses Godes, daz dar noch volgit. Ie mê ein, ie mê gûit; ie mê geteilet und ie gebrechlicher, ie minnir gûit. Ruh (*Geschichte,* 3:399), following Seppänen, refers this teaching on fruit and flower to Aquinas, STh IaIIae, q. 70, a. 1, a connection that seems evident. However, the technical term "flower of the intellect" belongs to the Proclian tradition (*anthos tou nou/flos intellectus*) and demonstrates the importance of the *Proclus Latinus* for the German Dominicans. What Hermann is saying is that the knowledge of God attained here below by the flower of the intellect will

bear fruit in the beatific vision in heaven. The term *flos intellectus* as the equivalent of the *unum anime* is to be found in several of the Latin translations of Proclus (e.g., *Comm. In Parm.* 6 at 1047 and 1071; *De Prov.* 32). On the importance of the term and its influence in German mysticism, see Werner Beierwaltes, "Der Begriff des 'Unum in Nobis' bei Proklos," in *Die Metaphysik im Mittelalter: Ihr Ursprung und ihre Bedeutung*, ed. Paul Wilpert (Berlin: Walter de Gruyter, 1963), 255–66; and Loris Sturlese, "'Homo divinus': Der Prokloskommentar Bertholds von Moosburg und die Probleme der nacheckhartischen Zeit," in *Abendländische Mystik im Mittelalter*, ed. Kurt Ruh (Stuttgart: Metzler, 1986), 149–51, 153–54.

120. No. 17 (43.32–35): nu habe wir, daz Got nicht bekant werdin in dirre vierleige wis, wan alliz daz wir begrifin oder bekennen mugin, daz inist Got nicht . . . daz nicht ist daz hohiste bekentnisse daz wir hi fon Gode gehabin mugin.

121. No. 17 (44.3–8): ez ist zveigirlege bekentnisse da mide man Got irkennit. Ein ist ein roubinde bekentnisse, in deme man beroubit Got allir der dinge di wir hi um zulegin mugin. Daz andere heizet ein richinde oder ein zuleginde bekentnisse. Da lege wir Gode zu alle di edilkeit di wir mugin vindin in allin dingin, und ist dit ein unvollincumen bekentnisse. Ruh, *Geschichte*, 3:400, notes that this terminology seems to be Hermann's creation.

122. No. 17 (44.14–18): sal Got bekant werdin, daz muiz geschehin in zveigirlêge lîchte. Daz eine heizit ein naturlich licht, nicht daz naturliche licht der sele, sundir daz Got ist. Daz andir ist ein ubernaturlich licht und daz ist daz licht der clarheit, und ob wir sprechin daz ez zweigerlêge sî, so ist ez doch einlich. . . .

123. No. 17 (44.27–29): aber etlcihe dinc di hat Got behaldin bi ume selbir: daz sint di dri personen, daz ist di forborgenheit di Got den sinen gelobit hat. 'uch ist gegebin etc.'

124. On Johannes Franke, see Ruh, *Geschichte*, 3:394–98. The *Ego sum via, veritas, et vita* treatise was edited by Franz Pfeiffer, "Predigten und Sprüche deutscher Mystiker," *Zeitschrift für deutsches Alterthum* 8 (1851): 243–51. It was also translated into Dutch.

125. Sermon no. 35 (80.32–35): alleine si in der stedikeit alle zit nicht gestein inmac, doch fon zit zu zit, alse Got in si flizin sal, so muz si ruwin, wan sin inflizin wil ruwe habin, und di sele muz ruwin di sinem influz sal inphahin, wan he me mildekeit hait uz zuflizine wan di sele mugilicheit habe zu inphahine.

126. On Helwic, see Ruh, *Geschichte*, 3:403–5. His sermon no. 43 in the *Paradisus anime intelligentis* is also discussed by Largier, "'Intellectus in deum ascensus,'" 448–50; and Steer, "Predigt," 333. Helwic has been identified as the author of a treatise on friendship, the *De dilectione dei et proximi*, sometimes ascribed to Thomas Aquinas, but this is not sure.

127. No. 52 (115.16–18): 'Praedica verbum'. Sente Paulus sprichit: 'brenge fore daz wort'. He auch sprichit: 'ich beswere uch bi deme der orteiln sal di dodin und di lebinden, daz ir gewinnit ein kint'. The second quotation, an adaptation of 2 Tim. 4:1 with the addition of the reference to birthing, is typical of the free handling of scripture found in Eckhart and his contemporaries. On *praedica* as first "saying within" and then "bringing forth," see Eckhart, In Eccli. n. 69 (LW 2:299.2–3), and Pr. 30 (DW 2:93–94 and 97–98).

128. No. 52 (115.21–22): mochtis di sele inphangin habin, he hette ur di selbe glicheit gegebin, daz si alle dinc hette in der selbin edelkeit.

129. No. 52 (115.29–33): di sele hait eine craft di sundir materien und sundir zit und stat wirkit. Alse di sele in der hohistin craft steit alleine, so sprichit der vadir ein wort in di craft und gebirit sinen son in di craft und inphehit sich selbin in sich selber in dise craft. Also wirt daz ewige wort inphangin in der sele. Dit ist daz kint und daz wort daz wir sullin fore brengin.

130. No. 52 (116.3–6): eia edele sele, haist du daz wort in dir, sprichis herfure! Wanne wirt dit wort forbracht? Alse ein licht der worheit luchtit ez in dem geist und durch den geist in den creftin der sele und in den werkin und sidin und wanelungin.

131. On John of Sterngassen, see Volker Honemann in VL 4:760–62; and Ruh, *Geschichte*, 3:410–14. The most complete account, along with an edition of John's commentary on the Sentences and his surviving MHG works, is Walter Senner, *Johannes von Sterngassen OP und sein Sentenzkommentar*, 2 vols. (Berlin: Akademie Verlag, 1994–95).

132. See, for example, the longest surviving sermon "Surge illuminare Ierusalem" (Isa. 60:1), edited in Senner 2:350–57, which devotes several sections to *luterkeit* (351.7–15, 355.14–357.12). In the longer section John praises emptiness above love and knowledge in a way similar how detachment surpasses love, humility, and mercy in the Ps.-Eckhartian VAbe (DW 5:402–10). In dialogue form, "der maister" says: "Da ist di luterkeit dez herczen an etlicher weyse edler denne minne oder bekenntnisse" (355.21–22). According to John, it is *luterkeit* not *bekenntnisse* or *minne* that unites us with God (357.28–37). See also the praise of *lûterkeit* and *abescheidenheit* in Senner's Predigt 1 (2:347).

133. Pr. "Maria Magdalena sas zuo den fuessen" in Senner 2:361–63.

134. "Maria Magdalena sas" (2:363): Alle creature muossen in der gotheit swîgen. Diu drivaltikeit muos in mir selber swigen. In dem ewigen worte ist nicht der vater sprechende. In dem ewigen worte ist nicht sprechende wac blos wesen. Were gottes persone ab geslagen, noch denne bestuonde er us blossem wesende. Dz ist min selikeit dz ich got mit gotte schouwe. Got, du solt sprechen und ich sol hoeren. Du solt bilden in dem ewigen worte, und ich sol schouwen.

135. Ruh, *Geschichte,* 3:411–13.

136. This sermon, beginning "In allen dingen," does not appear in Senner's edition, but is accepted by Ruh and edited by Wilhelm Wackernagel, *Altdeutsche Predigten und Gebete aus Handschriften* (Basel: H. Richter, 1876), 166–68. The passage quoted is found on 167.16–20: Min sele ist got formelich an irem wesende. Da von ist si al vermügende vnd ir werk ist ewig. Alles das got würken mag das mag si liden. . . . Alle ünser meister künnet nit vinden weder gottes kraft grosser si oder der sele vermügen.

137. This sermon is in Senner 2:358–60. See the comments on this text by Léonce Reypens, "Dieu (connaissance mystique)," DS 3:901–02.

138. "Alle creaturen fragent" (358.16–30 and 359.37–47): und war in mir ein dyapsalma, dz ist ein stilleswigen aller uswendigen dinge, und ein ruowe aller inwendigen dinge, und kant in mir ein himelruorendes suifzenund. min verstentnisse wart entbildet min geist wart entmittelet und min andacht wart entmantelet und persone mines gemuotes wart vernederet. Ich vand in mir ein aller dinge vergessen und ein mines selbes vermissen und ein dich got alleine wissen. . . . Do kam in mich ein mich in dir vergessen unde min vernunft wart in dich gegeistet, unde von dem heiligen geiste wart ich gefueret in den grunt, da der sun inne gebildet ist, unde da erkande ich got in gotte unde des vaters nature in dem sune unde des sunes persone in dem vater unde des heiligen geistes persone in dem vater unde in dem sune.

139. "Alle creaturen fragent: (359.48–61): Es kam in mich ein uiberschouwen und ein uberbegeren und ein uberverstan. Ich vand in mir ein aller dinge vergessen und ein min selbes vergessen und dich got alleine wissen. Do kam in mich ein schowen diner ewikeit und ein bevinden diner selikeit. Ich vand mich allein an dir verstarret. Do kam ich von mir ich mich an dir und dich in mir. Ich vand mich ein wesen mit dir.

140. Kurt Ruh, *Bonaventura deutsch: Ein Beitrag zur deutschen Franziskaner-Mystik und -scholastik* (Bern: Francke, 1956).

141. For Hartwig of Erfurt, see Volker Mertens, "Hartwig (Hartung) von Erfurt," VL 3:532–35; and "Theologie der Mönche—Frömmigkeit der Laien? Beobachtungen zur Textgeschichte von Predigten der Hartwig von Erfurt. Mit einem Textanhang," in *Literatur und Laienbildung im Spätmittelalter und in der Reformationszeit,* ed. Ludger Grenzmann and Karl Stackmann (Stuttgart: J. B. Metz, 1981), 661–85. See also the edition and discussion of an Advent sermon on the birth of the Word in the Soul in Schiewer, "German Sermons in the Middle Ages," 908–11, 953–55.

142. On Jordan, see Adolar Zumkeller, "Jordan von Quedlinburg (Jordanus de Saxonia)," VL 4:853–61, and the same author's article, "Jourdain de Saxe ou de Quedlinburg," DS 8:1423–30. Zumkeller provides an overview of the German Augustinian contribution to mystical literature in "Die Lehrer des geistlichen Lebens unter den deutschen Augustinern vom dreizehnten Jahrhundert bis zum Konzil von Trient," in *Sanctus Augustinus Vitae Spiritualis Magister* (Rome: Analecta Augustiniana, 1956), 239–337 (261–67 on Jordan).

143. An edition of Jordan's *Opera omnia* is planned for the CCCM. On Jordan's democratic and transformational view of sanctity, see E. L. Saak, "*Quilibet Christianus*: Saints in Society in the Sermons of Jordan of Quedlinburg, OESA," in *Models of Holiness in Medieval Sermons*, ed. Beverly Mayne Kienzle (Louvain-la-Neuve: Fédération Internationale des Instituts d'Études Médiévales, 1996), 317–38.

144. For an overall view of Marquard's works, see Nigel F. Palmer, "Marquard von Lindau OFM," VL 6:81–126. Also important are the various studies of Rüdiger Blumrich, especially "Einleitung," in Blumrich, *Marquard von Lindau: Deutsche Predigten. Untersuchungen und Edition* (Tübingen: Niemeyer, 1994), 1*–80*; "Feuer der Liebe. Franziskanische Theologie in den deutschen Predigten Marquards von Lindau," *Wissenschaft und Weisheit* 54 (1991): 44–55; and "Die deutschen Predigten Marquards von Lindau: Ein franziskanischer Beitrag zur *Theologia mystica*," in *Albertus Magnus und der Albertismus: Deutsche philosophische Kultur des Mittelalters*, 155–72.

145. On this treatise, see Palmer, "Marquard von Lindau," VL 6:104.

146. On the mixture of languages in Marquard's oeuvre, see Nigel F. Palmer, "Latein, Volkssprache, Mischsprache: Zum Spruchproblem bei Marquard von Lindau, mit einem Handschriftenverzeichnis der 'Dekalogerklärung' und des 'Auszugs der Kinder Israel,'" in *Spätmittelalterliche geistliche Literatur in der Nationalsprache,* Analecta Carthusiana 106, Band 1. (Salzburg: Universität Salzburg, Institut für Anglistik und Amerikanistik, 1983), 71–110.

147. The John commentary (*Expositio Evangelii "In principio"*) survives in two Latin manuscripts and in five MHG. For an account, see Palmer, "Marquard von Lindau," VL 6:117–18. Loris Sturlese has edited the section of the text attacking Eckhart's view of an eternal creation in his article, "Über Marquard von Lindau und Meister Eckhart," in *Glauben. Wissen. Handeln: Beiträge aus Theologie, Philosophie und Naturwissenschaften zu Grundfragen christlicher Existenz. Festschrift für Philipp Kaiser,* ed. Albert Franz (Würzburg: Echter Verlag, 1994), 277–89 (see especially 283–84). There is also a partial edition of the MHG version by Kurt Ruh, *Franziskanisches Schrifttum im deutschen Mittelalter,* Band 2, *Texte* (Munich: Artemis, 1985), 199–210, where the attack on Eckhart can be found on p. 203.

148. For example, the treatise known as the *Auszug der Kinder Israel,* an allegory of the patriarchs, is based on Richard of St. Victor's *Benjamin minor* (Palmer, "Marquard von Lindau," VL 6:91–92), while the Latin *De arca Noe* is dependent on the two ark treatises of Hugh of St. Victor (Palmer, "Marquard von Lindau," VL 6:109–10).

149. There is a modern edition by Hermann-Josef May, *Marquard von Lindau OFM—De reparatione hominis: Einführung und Textedition* (Frankfurt: Peter Lang, 1977).

150. *De reparatione hominis,* art. 1 (ed., 3–12). Although Marquard makes considerable use of Eckhart in his exegesis of Gen. 2:20–24, he parts company with the Dominican and sides with Augustine in insisting that the image of the Trinity is found in the powers of the soul, not its essence: Haec autem imago non in essentia animae, ut aliqui autumant, sed in potentiis animae, in portione superiori consistit, ut aperte beatus Augustinus libro De civitate dei inquit (9.25–28).

151. Palmer, "Marquard von Lindau," VL 6:89. The *Dekalogerklärung* appears in many forms, often in company with two versions of the *Auszug der Kinder Israels*. There is no modern edition, but a study and reprint of the edition printed at Strassburg in 1516 and 1520 has been made available by Jacobus Willem Van Maren, *Marquard von Lindau: Die Zehe Gebot (Strassburg 1516 und 1520): Ein katechetischer Traktat* (Amsterdam: Ridopi, 1980). In an excursus to his treatment of the tenth commandment, Marquard discusses mystical union, largely on the basis of John Ruusbroec's *Gheestelike Brulocht (Spiritual Espousals)*; see 1516 ed. LIX-LX (modern ed. 112–14).

152. Marquard's sermons, known in seven manuscripts, have been edited by Blumrich, *Marquard von Lindau: Deutsche Predigten*. According to Georg Steer ("Geistliche Prosa," in *Die deutsche Literatur im späten Mittelalter 1250–1370*, 338): "Mit Marquard von Lindau . . . ersteigt die deutsche Predigt des 14. Jahrhunderts einen letzten Gipfel."

153. Along with the studies of Marquard's sources found in the edition and articles of

Blumrich, on the Franciscan's use of Eckhart see Freimut Löser, "Rezeption als Revision: Marquard von Lindau und Meister Eckhart," *Beiträge zur Geschichte der deutschen Sprache und Literatur* 119 (1997): 425–58.

154. See the summary in Löser, "Rezeption als Revision," 455–58.

155. Marquard, Sermon 41 (312.84): Vnd in dem liecht sah er nit, wan er sah got. Marquard's treatment (312.77–313.93) is dependent on Eckhart's Prr. 70 and 71 (DW 3:189, and 227–28).

156. Sermon 19 (131.57–132.63): Die sechsten die nemend die hailgen geschrift vnd ziehend si uff wisen, die ueber vernunft vnd ob bilden vnd ob allem liecht sind, vnd wisend den menschen vsser im selber in ain gancz nit wissen aller ding, als sant Dyonisius in dem buoch 'De mistica theologya' [the reference that follows is actually to DN 1.1 (PG 3:588A)], . . . In dem nit wissen der mensch mit blintheit gesihet vnd mit vnbekantnuest bekennet. The same theme is repeated in Sermon 30 in the treatment of the School of the Holy Spirit: Vnd in diser schuol lernet man gesehen mit blinthait vnd bekennen mit vnbekantnuest (205.106–7).

157. Sermon 16 (120.31–33): . . . daz man in wesenlichen lon schouwet daz grundlos mer der gothait in siner istikait vnd blovsshait, als es bildlos vnd formlovs ist (cf. Sermon 36: 257.158). In Sermon 40 Mary Magdalene in the desert is described as: . . . vnd sich gesenket in daz grundlovs wislovs wesen, daz mavss nit enhavt noch nieman kan begriffen. Sermon 25 (169.72) uses the expression *abgruend der gothait.*

158. Sermon 2 (14.75–76): . . . wan der ist gottez nam, als er genomen wirt in siner blovsser abgeschaidener istigen natur.

159. Sermon 32 (221–30).

160. Marquard's view of the role of philosophy is positive, though limited, as can be seen in Sermon 30 (204.57–69), where pagan wisdom constitutes the third of the six schools that lead to God.

161. Sermon 32 (227.119–223): Ze dem sechsten so lueht die hailig driualtikait in dem bild der vernuenftigen selen, wan da sind dry kreft, in die gott sin bild gedrucket havt so gar adellich, daz sant Augustinus sprichet, waer diss bild sehe, im waer als offenbavr die hailig driualtikait, als daz die sunn gesihteklich an dem himel lovffet. The reference to Augustine is *De Trin.* 15.20.39.

162. Sermon 32 (229.269–70): . . . so hett er doch vnmaessig minn erzoeget, wan er havt doch ain edel bild in die sel gedrucket, davr vmb daz er sinen aingebornen sun in si geber. Blumrich notes the proximity of this to a Pseudo-Eckhart sermon, Pfeiffer XXVI (ed., 100.18–19): Dar umbe hât got dise sêle geschaffen, daz er sînen eingebornen sun in sî gebêre. For other uses of this passage in Marquard, see Löser, "Rezeption als Revision," 432–33, 450–51.

163. Sermon 32 (229.278–230.294). The passage from Eckhart is In Ioh. n.23 (LW 3:19.5–12). Marquard skips Eckhart's third characteristic.

164. Sermon 32 (230.292–94): Ze dem vierden so sol das bild alle zit in gott sin vnd gott in dem bild, als Cristus, der ain bild was des vatters, sprach: 'Der vatter ist in mir, vnd ich in dem vatter'. Here Marquard is actually citing Eckhart's fifth characteristic of the image in In Ioh. n.24 (LW 3:19.13–16).

165. Sermon 32 (230.307–10). On the importance of Marquard's difference from Eckhart on this point, see Blumrich, "Einleitung," *Marquard von Lindau: Deutsche Predigten,* 73*–77*; Löser, "Rezeption als Revision," 437; and Loris Sturlese, "Meister Eckharts Weiterwerken," in *Eckardus Theutonicus, Homo doctus et Sanctus: Nachweise und Berichte zum Prozess gegen Meister Eckhart,* ed. Heinrich Stirnimann and Ruedi Imbach (Freiburg, Switzerland: Universitätsverlag, 1992), 172–73.

166. See, e.g., Sermon 25 (168.30–41); and Sermon 30 (202.14–22).

167. Sermon 31 (217.180–84): . . . vnd haissend es die lerer synderesim. . . . Es ist ain bild goetlicher natur, es ist got navch sipp. Es ist ain liht, daz sunder mittel alle zit entzuendet wirt

von dem hailgen gaist. Blumrich notes the dependence of this passage on Eckhart's Pr. 20a (DW 1:332.3–334.5).

168. Sermon 25 (168.39–41): . . . wav die sehend niderwert in daz guldin brett ires gemuetes, so schovwend vnd sehend si got vnd die gebenedicten driualtikait luchten in dem grund ires gemuetes.

169. Sermon 23 (151.13–15): Ze erst mit usser tugentlicher vebung. Ze dem andern mit inwendigem keren vnd hailger betrahtung in bildlicher wis. Ze dem dritten bildloselich in luterm varainigen vnd schovwen.

170. On love as the form of the virtues, see Sermon 31 (212.14–213.33). For some other treatments of the necessary role of love, see Sermon 2 (20.249–60), Sermon 16 (121.83–86), Sermon 31 (217.161–74), and Sermon 41 (311.39–53).

171. Sermon 39 (292–300). See especially 292.13–293.29 on the law of love; 294.63–295.103 on how the fire of love conforms us to Christ; 295.117–299.242, a section giving six ways in which divine love enkindles the mind; and finally 299.243–300.291, the concluding section on six coals, or motives, for loving God.

172. For remarks on humility, see, e.g., Sermon 5 (41.20–42.31), Sermon 30 (209.234–39), and Sermon 41 (313.129–25).

173. On Marquard's notion of *armut* and its relation to Eckhart, especially the Meister's Pr. 52, see Georg Steer, "Der Armutsgedanke der deutscher Mystiker bei Marquard von Lindau," *Franziskanische Studien* 60 (1978): 289–300. Among the sermons, see especially Sermons 6–7 (48–67).

174. Sermon 2 (12–21).

175. Sermon 2 (14.62–63): . . . daz sich in im die ainvaltig form gottes widerschlueg als in ainem lutern spiegel. . . . Marquard frequently uses mirror images.

176. Sermon 39 (299.239–41): Als vil sich der mensch gelichet Cristo, als vil het er rehter goettlicher minn, wan Cristus leben ist die reht regel goettlicher min. . . .

177. For the use of *ledig* and *blovss* and the relation of these terms to the *Book of Spiritual Poverty*, see Blumrich, "Feuer der Liebe," 46–49.

178. Sermon 5 (41–47).

179. For another treatment of releasement, see Sermon 41, especially 311.54–312.76, and 313.100–314.156.

180. Sermon 1 (8.151–161): . . . wa gottes sun sol kumen in dez menschen hertz vnd gemuet, da muoss ovch ruow sin aller sinnlicher invaell vnd stillhait aller bildlichen creaturen in dez menschen vernunft. Vnd wenn denn der mensch stuond in saemlicher stilli, so waer er kumen in ain nit wissen vnd vergessen sin selbs vnd aller creaturen, vnd wurd denn daz ewig wort gesprochen in die sel. . . . Hier vmb wenn sich creatur nit gebirt in der sel, so kumet den daz ewig wort von den kuengklichen stuelen, vnd sprichet got vatter in die sel sin ewig wort mit allem lust vnd salikait. Blumrich ("Einleitung," 69*) and Löser ("Rezeption als Revision," 449–50) discuss the connections with Eckhart's Prr. 101 and 102.

181. For other treatments of silence in Marquard, see, e.g., Sermon 31 (219.218–26), and Sermon 40 (304.130–305.140). The birth of the Son in the soul is found in many places in the Franciscan; e.g., Sermon 2 (19.233–36), Sermon 8 (77.316–24), and Sermon 16 (119.20–23, and 120.37–39). Sermon 25 (174.234–46) discusses birth into the uncreated world in general fashion.

182. Sermon 30 (206.122–28): Wan vernunft vnd all kreft sind dav berovbet irs werkes vnd aller stilli aines vnwissends vmb sich vnd vmb aellú ding, als sant Dyonisius sprichet [cf. MT 5] mer allain der spicz der minnenden kraft suochet ainikait mit got. Vnd in dem spicz der minnenden kraft wirt got gelobt veber wesenlich mit der veber wallenden minn, die da besoesset wúrken aller ander kreft vnd blovsslich in got gekeret ist, als Vercellensis der abt sprichet. The reference to Gallus is probably to the *Extractio*, the paraphrasing commentary on the Dionysian corpus completed about 1238; see, e.g., the passage on DN 7.1 (*Dionysiaca* 1:696, section 385): Habet praeterea mens unitionem (quam intelligimus summum affectionis apicem quem proprie perfecit dilectio Dei). . . . For more on this passage and the connection

with Gallus, see Blumrich, "Einleitung," 62*–68*; and "Feuer der Liebe," 49–53. The *spicz der minnenden kraft* is also mentioned in Sermon 37 (279.506).

183. On the fire of love, see, e.g., Sermon 2 (20.239–260), Sermon 16 (121.83–86), Sermon 31 (217.161–74), Sermon 39 (294.63–294.103, and 298.215–299.237), and Sermon 40 (302.44–303.67).

184. Sermon 36 (260.267–72): So kommend denn die brinnenden serafin vnd enzúndent daz inre gemuet so inbruenstelich, daz alle vngelichait da verbrinnet vnd daz gemút in dem sússen fúr zerschmilcet vnd mit gott veraint wirt. Vnd denn so ist der mensch ain engelscher mensch worden vnd in so gar grovssen adel geseczet, daz daz nieman gewortigen kan. On the process of "angelization" (i.e., the internalization of the angelic hierarchies as necessary to the ascent to God), introduced by the Victorines and brought to its height by Gallus, see McGinn, *Flowering of Mysticism*, 83–85. Bonaventure's characterization of St. Francis as a *vir hierarchicus* and *vir angelicus* (see *Flowering*, 94) is the likely source for Marquard.

185. Sermon 16 (120.54–121.59): Die minnend kraft oder der will der het aller maist saelikait, wan sider der mensch nit mit vernunft, mer mit der minn dez willen lon verdienet, so sol ovch der kraft aller maist gelonet werden. Ovch vernunft die enphavhet dar an saelikait, daz si got in ir schovwet. Aber der will enpfavhet davr an saelikait, daz er sich in got vindet, vnd daz ist vil edler. For more on the relation of intellect and love, see Sermon 30 (202.13–22), and Sermon 37 (279.499–512).

186. See Sermon 8 (75.240–45)

187. See the text from the "Granum Sinapis" commentary cited above in note 94.

188. For a discussion of union in Marquard, see Blumrich, "Feuer der Liebe," 53–55.

189. Sermon 25 (169.63–83).

190. Sermon 37 (265.79–80): Saemlich edel erhebt menschen stavnd als blovss, als si vff geflossen sind von gott, vnd stavnd als ledig, als do si niht enwavrend. . . . For parallels in Eckhart, see, e.g., Pr. 2 (DW 1:24.8–25.2) and Pr. 52 (DW 3:491.8–9, and 499.2–3).

191. Marquard insists that all union can only take place through inward turning; see Sermon 23 (152.54–59, 153.64–75, and 154.106–08). On vision and union happening only in the realm above all intellect, see, e.g., Sermon 37 (279.492–99).

192. For more on Paul's rapture, see Sermon 31 (218.210–15).

193. Sermon 40 (301–9). In this sermon Marquard makes considerable use of a Pseudo-Origen sermon on the Magdalene that was also used by Eckhart and other late medieval mystics. This homily on the text "Maria stabat ad monumentum foris plorans" (John 20:11), appears to have been produced in the twelfth century, possibly by a Cisterican, and was very popular in the late Middle Ages, in both Latin and vernacular versions. It was printed in the 1535 Basel edition of Origen. For a study, see Freimut Löser, "Jan Milič in europäischer Tradition: Die Magdalen-Predigt des Pseudo-Origenes," in *Deutscher Literatur des Mittelalters in Böhmen und über Böhmen*, ed. Dominique Flieger and Václav Bok (Vienna: Edition Praesens, 2001), 225–45; and the same author's "Pseudo-Origenes," VL 11:1090–95.

194. Marquard's use of the standard arguments for the superiority of the contemplative life (*schovwend leben*) over the active life (304.106–16) needs to be balanced by his adherence to the traditional view that contemplation must yield to active love of neighbor in certain circumstances (see Sermon 23 [155.132–43], and Sermon 40 [309.291–98]). On the relation of action and contemplation Marquard does not break with tradition, as did Eckhart and Tauler.

195. Sermon 40 (303.66–67): . . . davr vmb daz ir gemút alle zit uff gekeret waere gegen iren geminten vnd mit dem allain verainbaert wurde sunder mittel. See 302.33–36 for similar language.

196. Sermon 40 (305.151–53): Die vierd wise ist, so gott sin selbs suessikait der sel inguesset, daz si der kúnstigen froeden enpfinden vnd so gar úbergossen wirt, daz si es inwendig nit mag geliden, es muoss uss brechen mit wunderlichen wisen. The passage goes on to quote Sg. 1:3 as an example of mystical inebriation.

197. Sermon 40 (306.166–69): . . . denn ain luter ainung zwúschen im vnd der sele sunder mittel, vnd nit in formen noch in bilden, mer in luter blovsser ainung sin ewig wort sprichet

in der sele. . . . Further descriptions of Mary's rapture and union are found in 307.208–15 and 229–31.

198. Sermon 40 (307.235–309.298) for the attack on the Free Spirits. See also Sermon 37 (271.256–272.310) for another confrontation, as well as Sermon 23 (154.115–16) for its dismissal of *vngeordnoter frihait.*

199. For an introduction to Geiler's life and writings, see Herbert Kraume, "Geiler, Johannes, von Kaysersberg," VL 2:1141–52. In English there is a study of Geiler's theology by E. Jane Dempsey Douglass, *Justification in Late Medieval Preaching: A Study of John Geiler of Keisersberg,* 2nd ed. (Leiden: Brill, 1989).

200. The most complete study of Geiler's mysticism, both in the *Berg des Schouwens* and in other treatises and sermons, is the unpublished dissertation of Georges J. Herzog, "Mystical Theology in Late Medieval Preaching: John Geiler of Kaysersberg (1445–1510)" (Ph.D. diss., Boston University, 1985), though I cannot agree with the author's claims for Geiler's originality and importance as a mystic. See also Gerhard Bauer, "'Auch einer': Leiden, Weisheit, Mystik und Mystiker bei Johannes Geiler von Kaysersberg," in *Leiden und Weisheit in der Mystik,* ed. Bernd Jaspert (Paderborn: Bonifatius Druck, 1992), 207–33.

201. Wilhelm Oehl's still useful collection of translations, *Deutsche Mystikerbriefe des Mittelalters 1100–1550* (Munich: Georg Müller, 1931), includes five twelfth-century figures.

202. The *Great Book of Letters (Das grosse Briefbuch)* contains twenty-eight letters and seems to have been put together by Suso's spiritual daughter, Elsbeth Stagel. For an edition, see Bihlmeyer, *Heinrich Seuse: Deutsche Schriften,* 405–94. The *Little Book of Letters (Briefbüchlein)* is the fourth part of Suso's own edition of his works, the *Exemplar.* It has eleven letters and is edited in Bihlmeyer, 360–93.

203. Manfred Weitlauff, "Heinrich von Nördlingen," VL 3:845–52, with quotation at 848. See also Weitlauff, "'dein got redender munt machet mich redenlosz . . .' Margareta Ebner und Heinrich von Nördlingen," in *Religiöse Frauenbewegung und mystische Frömmigkeit im Mittelalter,* ed. Peter Dinzelbacher and Dieter R. Bauer (Cologne/Vienna: Böhlau, 1988), 303–52. In English, see Debra L. Stoudt, "The Vernacular Letters of Heinrich von Nördlingen," *Mystics Quarterly* 12 (1986): 19–25; and Margot Schmidt, "An Example of Spiritual Friendship: The Correspondence Between Heinrich of Nördlingen and Margaretha Ebner," in *Maps of Flesh and Light: The Religious Experience of Medieval Women Mystics,* ed. Ulrike Wiethaus (Syracuse: Syracuse University Press, 1993), 74–92.

204. For an edition, see Philipp Strauch, *Margaretha Ebner und Heinrich von Nördlingen: Ein Beitrag zur Geschichte der deutschen Mystik* (Freiburg-im-Breisgau/Tübingen: J. C. B. Mohr, 1882). On the role of letters among the German Dominican nuns and the scribal practices that led to their preservation, see Debra L. Stoudt, "The Production and Preservation of Letters by Fourteenth-Century Dominican Nuns," *Mediaeval Studies* 53 (1991): 309–26. For more on these letters in relation to the Friends of God, see chapter 9, pp. 413–15.

205. Letter XVI, dated to March 25–April 2, 1335 (Strauch, 196.71–73): do wart es in got vergotet, in dem ainigem ain verainet, mit minen gebunden, mit liecht umbfangen, mit frid durchgossen, mit lust durchschosszen. . . .

206. On Christine Ebner, see the *Flowering of Mysticism,* 314–15. Her letters are discussed in Stoudt, "Production and Preservation of Letters," 321–22.

207. The letters of Adelheid Langmann and the Cistercian Ulrich have significant mystical aspects, on which see *Flowering of Mysticism,* 315–17; and the treatment in Stoudt, "Production and Preservation of Letters," 322–24.

208. Many interesting letters remain unedited; e.g., the letters discussed by Kurt Ruh in VL 8:1070–74.

209. The text survives in one fifteenth-century manuscript from Eichstätt, though it more likely dates to the fourteenth century. It was edited by Karl Bihlmeyer, "Kleine Beiträge zur Geschichte der deutschen Mystik," in *Beiträge zur Geschichte der Renaissance und Reformation: Festgabe für Josef Schlecht,* ed. L. Fischer (F. P. Detteren, 1917), 57–58. There is a translation into modern German in Oehl, *Deutsche Mystikerbriefe,* 634–35. See Bernard McGinn, "Vom

verborgenen Gott zum blossen Gott," VL 11:1616–17; and Dorothee Soelle, *The Silent Cry: Mysticism and Resistance* (Minneapolis: Fortress Press, 2001), 83–84.

210. Bihlmeyer 57: Lern Got laszen durch Got, den verporgen Got durch den ploszen Got. . . .

211. Ibid.: . . . pisz billig einen pfeinig verlieszen, das du einen gulden findest, verschutt das wasser, das wein mugst schoppfen! . . . Wiltu fahen fysch, so lern das wasser watten, wiltu lernen Jhesum sehen an dem gestat, so lern yn dem mer vor versincken.

212. Bihlmeyer 57–58: Hor, sich, leyd und sweig, lasz dich yn dem liecht. . . . Mein kint, pisz gedultig und lasz dich, [die] die weill man dir Got ausz deinem grunt deines hertzen nit grebt.

213. Bihlmeyer, 58: O tyeffer schatz, wie wirstu ergraben? O hocher adel, wer mag dich erreichen? O quellenter prun, wer mag dich erschoppfen? O leichter glast, ausz tringende kraft, einfeltiger zuger, blosze verborgenheit, verporgne sicherheit, sichere zwversicht, ein einigs still yn allen dingen, mannigveltigs guttyn einer styl, du styles geschrey, dich mag nymant finden, der dich nit kan lon!

214. See the edition in Preger, *Geschichte der deutschen Mystik im Mittelalter,* 3:417–18. There is a translation into modern German in Oehl, *Deutsche Mystikerbriefe,* 636–37.

215. Preger, 417: Ich beger uech mit dem brinnenden ernst in gnaden warheit, den alle gottesfruent ie gehebt hant, dz due botschaft des ewigen vatters, die er in dir minne sines ewigen geistes uns gesant hât bi sinen ewigen sun . . . . in uech vahe und uech in sich ziehe, also dz uewer usser mentsch in der mentschheit unsers herren jhesu christi und der inner mentsch in dem ewigen wort widerluechtent und antwurtent die liebsten willen des vatters.

216. Preger, 418: . . . durchgânt ze mir alle, die begerent mich, und von minen geburten werden erfuellet. The Vg version is: Transite ad me omnes qui concupiscitis me et a generationibus meis implemini.

217. Ibid.: . . . dz ist uffgerichter mit gantzen begirde ze hoerent den fuergang gottes, doch mit verdachtem antluezt, dz ist mit bekantniss sin selbes unwirdikeit, due in billich schamrot und blug machet in der claren inluechtenden glorie gottes. For Elijah at the cave as a type of mystical consciousness, see Gregory the Great, *Homiliae in Ezechielhem* II.1.17 (*Growth of Mysticism,* 66).

218. Werner Williams-Krapp, "'Dise ding sint dennoch nit ware zeichen der heiligkeit'. Zur Bewertung mystischer Erfahrung im 15. Jahrhundert," in *Frömmigkeitsstile im Mittelalter,* ed. Wolfgang Haubrichs (Göttingen: Vandenhoeck & Ruprecht, 1991), 61–71. See also Werner-Krapp, "Eberhard, Mardach," VL 5:1237–39.

219. On the Dominican reform movement of fifteenth-century Germany and its spirituality, see Michael D. Bailey, "Religious Poverty, Mendicancy, and Reform in the Late Middle Ages," *Church History* 72 (2003): 457–83.

220. This summary of Mardach's unedited letter is based on Williams-Krapp, "Zur Bewertung mystische Erfahrung," 63–66.

221. See Williams-Krapp, "Zur Bewertung," 66–71. On John Nider, the author of the famous *Formicarius,* a collection of exempla on moral and spiritual questions, see Michael D. Bailey, *Battling Demons: Witchcraft, Heresy, and Reform in the Late Middle Ages* (University Park, PA: Pennsylvania State University Press, 2003).

222. On five stories about Eckhart, see Kurt Ruh, "'Eckhart-Legenden,'" VL 2:350–53. The most important of these is "Meister Eckhart's Household" ("Meister Eckharts Wirtschaft") a polylogue between Eckhart, a poor man, and a young virgin over the nature of true poverty. It was first edited by Pfeiffer, *Meister Eckhart,* 625–27. There is an edition of a MHG and Latin version in F. Von der Leyen, "Über einige bisher unbekannte lateinische Fassungen von Predigten des Meisters Eckhehart," *Zeitschrift für deutsche Philologie* 38 (1906): 348–54. Marquard of Lindau, among others, used this text.

223. For an introduction, see Franz-Josef Schweitzer, "'Schwester Katrei,'" VL 8:947–50.

224. The Eckhart connection reflects one of the *Eckhart-Legenden* known as "Meister

Eckharts Tochter," a dialogue between Eckhart and young woman edited by Pfeiffer, *Meister Eckhart*, 625.

225. Franz-Josef Schweitzer, *Der Freiheitsbegriff der deutschen Mystik: Seine Beziehung zur Ketzerei der "Brüder und Schwestern vom freien Geist," mit besonderer Rücksicht auf den pseudo-eckhartischen Traktat "Schwester Katrei" (Edition)* (Frankfurt: Peter Lang, 1981). The edition is found on pp. 322–70 and will be cited by page and line in this account. There is an English translation by Elvira Borgstädt, "The 'Sister Catherine' Treatise," in *Meister Eckhart: Teacher and Preacher*, ed. Bernard McGinn (New York: Paulist Press, 1986), 349–87 (I will use this version with a few modifications). There is a French translation of the Pfeiffer text in *Maître Eckhart: Les Dialogues de Maître Eckhart avec soeur Catherine de Strasbourg* (Mesnil-sur-l'Estrée: Arfuyen, 2004).

226. Many students of medieval heresy have singled out the text as a classic expression of the Free Spirit; e.g., Norman Cohn, *The Pursuit of the Millennium*, rev. and expanded ed. (New York: Oxford, 1970), 175, 179; Gordon Leff, *Heresy in the Later Middle Ages*, 2 vols. (New York: Barnes & Noble, 1967), 1:401–4. Robert Lerner, *The Heresy of the Free Spirit in the Later Middle Ages* (Berkeley: University of California Press, 1972), 215–21, is more cautious, though he admits that the work stretches the boundaries of orthodoxy in places. F.-J. Schweitzer continues to argue that *Sister Katherine* is a Free Spirit product.

227. Schweitzer, *Der Freiheitsbegriff*, 114–15, 266–80. On these heretics, see the discussion in chapter 2, pp. 64–65.

228. Schweitzer 345.25–28: Möchtestu alle creaturen niessen, das söltestu billich tuon, wan wele creatur du nüssest, die treistu vff jn ir vrsprung.

229. This attack (348.31–349.7) comes at the end of a long passage (347.22–349.21) showing the errors of those who have been led into unfaith by following "parables" that lead them to think that they can do all their deeds in one likeness (*das si wellen alle werck in einer gelicheit wircken*: 347.23–24). I take this phrase to mean that works of virtue or sin are all the same if done from the same attitude.

230. Schweitzer 334.37–335.1: Ja, ich bin bewert jn miner ewigen selikeit. Ich han erkrieget jn gnaden, das Christus ist von natur. See also 348.6–8, which again appeals to this axiom.

231. The brief section 1 (322.2–19) begins with the daughter requesting the "shortest way" to perfection. The friar tells her to rid herself of sin first. Section 2 (322.20–323.20) features the friar's advice about the higher stages of love of God. The long section 3 (323.21–328.24) begins with a digression on the nature of hell, but moves on to a dialogue on the fastest way to eternal salvation, highlighting such mystical issues as the nature of true poverty, suffering as an imitation of Christ, and desire for the birth of Christ in the soul (328.2–4). Section 4 (328.25–331.14) includes a discussion of the virtues and the need to leave the self.

232. The sermon "Vom dem edeln menschen" is found in DW 5:106–36.

233. Schweitzer 333.18–20: . . . vnd seczet sich jn ein blosheit. Da züchet si got jn ein goetlich liecht, das si wenet ein mitt got sin, als lange als das wert.

234. Schweitzer 333.34–334.8: Wissest, dis ist allen menschen frömde, vnd wär ich nitt ein sölich pfaffe, das ich es selbe gelesen hett von götlicher kunst, so wer es mir och frömde. Si sprach: Des gan ich üch übel! Ich wolt, das irs mitt leben befunden hetten. Er sprach: . . . Wissest das ich es nitt mitt leben bessessen han, das ist mir aber leit!

235. Schweitzer 335.14–18: Glopt vnd geert sÿ der nam ünsers herren Ihesu Christi, das er mir geoffenbart hett, daz ich got jn im kennen vnd minnen mag, vnd das er min bilder ist gewesen zuo miner ewigen selikeit.

236. Schweitzer 337.35–338.7: Ich bin da, da ich was, ee ich geschaffen wurde; das ist blos got vnd got. Do ist weder engel noch heilig, noch kor, noch himmel, noch dis noch das. . . . . Ir sönd wissen, daz jn gott nütt ist den got. Ir sönd och wissen, daz kein sel jn gott komen mag, si werde e got, als si got was, e si geschaffen würde. Jn die blossen gotheit mag nieman komen, denn wer als blos ist, als er vss got flos.

237. Schweitzer 338.31–36. In a note to this passage (674, n. 22), Schweitzer adduces a similar idea found in Eckhart's RdU (DW 5:205.5 ff.).

238. Schweitzer 339.16–20: Es ist die sele blos vnd nackent aller namhaftiger ding. So staut si ein in ein, also daz si ein fürwert gan hat jn der blossen gotheit, alse das ölei vff dem tuoch: daz flusset alles fürbas.

239. Schweitzer 364.29–38: Do jn aller der vsser trost abgieng, do richte sich die sele vff jnwendig mitt allen irn kreften jn den schöpffer. Do flos der heilge geist dur die krefte jn die sele von dem vatter vnd vom dem sun. . . . Sÿ sachen vnd bekanten den vatter jn dem sun vnd den sun jn dem vatter, vnd bekanten den heilgen geist, der von den zwein personen flos jn ir sele.

240. Schweitzer 369.29–33: Die tochter seit jm also vil von der grössen gottes vnd von den vermügenheit gottes vnd von der fürsichtikeit gottes, das er von allen sinen vssern sinnen kam, vnd das man ime in ein heimliche zelle helfen mueste, vnd lag darinne ein lange wile, e er wider in sich selben kam.

241. These include two women treated in *Flowering of Mysticism*, Margaret the Cripple of mid-thirteenth century Magdeburg (pp. 194–98), and Christina of Hane, a Premonstratensian who died in 1292 (pp. 283–85).

242. In recent decades a rich literature has been devoted to these collections. See especially Siegfried Ringler, *Viten- und Offenbarungsliteratur in Frauenklöstern des Mittelalters: Quellen und Studien* (Munich: Artemis, 1980); and "Gnadenviten aus süddeutschen Frauenklöstern des 14. Jahrhunderts—Vitenschreibung als mystische Lehre," in *"Minnilichui gotes erkennusse": Studien zur frühen abendländischen Mystiktradition. Heidelberger Mystiksymposium vom 16. Januar 1989*, ed. Dietrich Schmidtke (Stuttgart-Bad Canstatt: frommann-holzboog, 1990), 89–104. For a brief overview, see Alois M. Haas, "Nonnenleben und Offenbarungsliteratur," in *Geschichte der deutschen Literatur: Die deutsche Literatur im späten Mittelalter 1250–1370*, ed. Ingeborg Glier (Munich: Beck, 1987), 291–99. Recent literature includes Susanne Bürkle, *Literatur im Kloster: Historische Funktion und rhetorische Legitimation frauenmystischer Texte des 14. Jahrhunderts* (Tübingen and Basel: Francke, 1999); and Béatrice Aklin Zimmermann, "Die Nonnenviten als Modell einer narrativen Theologie," in *Deutsche Mystik im abendländischen Zusammenhang*, 563–80.

243. McGinn, *Flowering of Mysticism*, 298–308, and the literature cited there.

244. On Agnes Blannbekin, whose *Vita et Revelationes* were compiled by her Franciscan confessor about 1318, see McGinn, *Flowering of Mysticism*, 180–83. There is now a translation of the text into English, Ulrike Wiethaus, *Agnes Blannbekin, Viennese Beguine: Life and Revelations* (Cambridge: D.S. Brewer, 2002).

245. Friedrich Sunder's life, *Das Gnaden-Leben des Friedrich Sunder, Klosterkaplan zu Engelthal*, has been edited by S. Ringler, *Viten- und Offenbarungsliteratur*, 391–444 (text) and 144–331 (comment). The text is briefly discussed in McGinn, *Flowering of Mysticism*, 315.

246. Among the early uses of the term, see Richard Kieckhefer, *Unquiet Souls: Fourteenth-Century Saints in Their Religious Milieu* (Chicago: University of Chicago Press, 1984), 6–8. For an overview, see Kate Greenspan, "Autohagiography and Medieval Womens' Spiritual Autobiography," in *Gender and Text in the Later Middle Ages*, ed. Jane Chance (Gainesville: University of Florida, 1996), 216–36, who defines autohagiography broadly as "an account of a holy person's life written or told by the subject" (p. 218).

247. Greenspan, "Autohagiography," 220, 232.

248. For these women, especially Margaret Ebner, see McGinn, *Flowering of Mysticism*, 308–17.

249. Werner Williams-Krapp, "Literary genre and degrees of saintliness. The Perception of holiness in writings by and about female mystics," in *The Invention of Saintliness*, ed. Anneke B. Mulder Bakker (London and New York: Routledge, 2002), 206–16; and "Erosion of a Monopoly," 249–51. The most popular vernacular hagiographical collection, entitled *Der Heiligen Leben*, produced at Nuremberg around 1400, is found in 197 manuscripts, 33 German printings and 8 Dutch printings, according to Williams-Krapp, *Die deutschen und niederländ-*

ischen Legendare des Mittelalters: Studien zu ihrer Überlieferungs-, Text- und Wirkungsgeschichte, (Tübingen: Niemeyer, 1986), 188.

250. See Williams-Krapp, "The invention of saintliness," 207–12, who also notes that only three canonized female mystics, Gertrude of Helfta, Birgitta of Sweden, and Catherine of Siena, were incorporated into the popular collections of saints' lives.

251. André Vauchez, *Sainthood in the Later Middle Ages* (Cambridge: Cambridge University Press, 1997; French ed. 1988), 376–86, 407–12, and 439–43. Of course, the number of mystical women actually canonized was small. Vauchez also notes that although the number of canonizations of lay saints increased, their sanctity was controlled by clerics and that "this springtime of lay sanctity had no tomorrow" (p. 386).

252. See Werner Williams-Krapp, "Raimond von Capua," VL 7:982–86.

253. On the Dominican reform, see Eugen Hillenbrand, "Die Observantenbewegung in der deutschen Ordensprovinz der Dominikaner," in *Reformbemühungen und Observantenbestrebungen im spätmittelalterlichen Ordenswesen,* ed. Kaspar Elm (Berlin: Duncker & Humboldt, 1989), 219–71.

254. On the fourteenth- and fifteenth-century Franciscan reforms, see Duncan B. Nimmo, "The Franciscan Regular Observance," in *Reformbemühungen und Observantenbestrebungen,* 189–205. On the relation of reform to spiritual literature, especially female mysticism, see Werner Williams-Krapp, "Frauenmystik und Ordensreform im 15. Jahrhundert," in *Literarische Interessenbildung im Mittelalter: DFG-Symposion 1991,* ed. Joachim Heinzle (Stuttgart: Metzler, 1993), 301–13; and "Observanzbewegungen, monastische Spiritualität und geistlicher Literatur im 15. Jahrhundert," *Internationales Archiv für Sozialgeschichte der deutschen Literatur* 20 (1995): 1–15.

255. Williams-Krapp, "Frauenmystik und Ordensreform," 312.

256. On the growing concern for discernment of spirits, see chapter 2, pp. 73–78.

257. On John Meyer (1422–1485), see Werner Fechter, "Meyer, Johannes, OP," VL 6:474–89; and Williams-Krapp, "Frauenmystik und Ordensreform," 303–4. Meyer's account of Margaret of Kenzingen is found in his *Buch der Reformacio Predigerordens,* bk. 5, chaps. 11–14. See also the version of the life edited by Heinrich Denifle, "Das Leben der Margaretha von Kentzingen: Ein Beitrag zur Geschichte des Gottesfreundes im Oberland," *Zeitschrift für deutsches Alterthum* 19 (1876): 478–91, and also found in Latin in Bernard Pez, *Bibliotheca Ascetica Antiquo-Nova* (Ratisbon, 1724–25; reprint, 1967), 8:400–412. Meyer showed his interest in female sanctity by producing a second and expanded edition of the lives of the Dominican nuns found in the "St. Katharinentaler Schwesternbuch." See the edition of Ruth Meyer, *Das 'St. Katharinentaler Schwesternbuch': Untersuchung. Edition. Kommentar* (Tübingen: Niemeyer, 1995), 140–81.

258. For introductions to Magdalena, see Peter Dinzelbacher and Kurt Ruh, "Magdalena von Freiburg," VL 5:1117–21; and Peter Dinzelbacher, *Christliche Mystik im Abendland: Ihre Geschichte von den Anfängen bis zum Ende des Mittelalters* (Paderborn: Schöningh, 1994), 396–98. For Magdalena's life and an edition of one of her writings, see Karen Greenspan, "Erklaerung des Vaterunsers: A critical edition of a 15th century mystical treatise by Magdalena Beutler of Freiburg" (diss., University of Massachusetts, 1984). Modern German translations of some of Beutler's letters can be found in Oehl, *Mystikerbriefe,* 519–30, and there is an English translation by Karen Greenspan of part of the life her convent had composed about her in *Medieval Women's Visionary Literature,* ed. Elizabeth Alvida Petroff (New York and Oxford: Oxford University Press, 1986), 350–55.

259. For a treatment of Magdalena in the context of late medieval debates on the issue of fraud investigations, see Dyan Elliott, *Proving Woman: Female Spirituality and Inquisitional Culture in the Later Middle Ages* (Princeton: Princeton University Press, 2004), 197–200.

260. Johannes Nider, *Formicarius,* ed. G. Colvener (Douai, 1602), Liber III, cap. viii, contains his account of Margaret and other, in his view, deluded women. On this section of the *Formicarius,* see Michael D. Bailey, *Battling Demons,* 111–17. The second memorable event in

Magdalena's failed career as mystic and prophetess happened in 1429 when she claimed to have been taken up bodily into heaven for three days and then sent back with a heavenly letter supporting the reform of her house. Forms of such heavenly letters (*Himmelsbriefe*) have been of frequent occurrence in the history of Christianity. The classic example concerns Sunday observance. In the late Middle Ages, some mystics (e.g., Christina Ebner) claimed to have received personal heavenly letters. See Bernhard Schnell, "Himmelsbrief," VL 4:28–33; and Nigel F. Palmer, "Himmelsbrief," *Theologische Realenzyklopädie* (Berlin: Walter de Gruyter, 1977-), 15:344–46. There is a modern translation of Magdalena's heavenly letter in Oehl, *Deutsche Mystikerbriefe*, 525. In the life of Magdalena commissioned by her convent she is credited with the usual horrific ascetical exercises, mystical raptures, and (naturally for a Franciscan woman) the reception of the stigmata.

261. From the partial translation by Karen Greenspan of the still unedited life as found in *Medieval Women's Visionary Literature*, 354.

262. Siegfried Ringler, "Haider, Ursula," VL 3:399–404; and Williams-Krapp, "Frauenmystik und Ordensreform," 310–12.

263. See Siegfried Ringler, "Kügelin, Konrad," VL 5:426–29; Williams-Krapp, "Frauenmystik und Ordensreform," 308–9; and Clément Schmitt, "Élisabeth (Elsbeth) de Reute," DS 4:583–84. I have not seen the edition of Konrad's life of Ursula edited by Karl Bihlmeyer, "Die schwäbische Mystikerin Elsbeth Achler von Reute (d. 1429) und die Überlieferung ihrer Vita," in *Festschrift Philipp Strauch*, ed. G. Baesecke and F. J. Schneider (Halle, 1932), 88–109. Kügelin wrote the life first in Latin at the command of the local bishop, so an attempt at a formal canonization seems to have been intended.

264. For the wider context of sanctity in marriage, see Martina Wehrli-Johns, "Frauenfrömmigkeit ausserhalb des Klosters: Vom Jungfrauenideal zur Heiligung in der Ehe," *Jahrbuch für deutsche Kirchengeschichte* 24 (2000): 17–37.

265. An exceptional example of a male lay holy man from this era is Nicholas of Flüe (1417–87), Swiss farmer and hermit. For a collection of the materials relating to him, see *Bruder Klaus von Flüe: Rat aus der Tiefe*, ed. Anselm Keel (Zurich: Benziger, 1999). For a modern German translation of letters dictated by the illiterate Nicholas, as well as some letters to him, see Oehl, *Deutsche Mystikerbriefe*, 613–31. See also Walter Muschg, *Die Mystik in der Schweiz* (Frauenfeld and Leipzig: Huber, 1935), 383–99.

266. The most complete account of Dorothy and the sources about her is that of Petra Hörner, *Dorothea von Montau: Überlieferung—Interpretation. Dorothea und die osteuropäisches Mystik* (Frankfurt: Peter Lang, 1993). For an overview, see Dinzelbacher, *Christliche Mystik im Abendland*, 349–55.

267. See Anneliese Triller, "Marienwerder, Johannes," VL 6:56–61. John was a trained theologian who taught at the University of Prague until 1386, when the German masters were expelled. Returning to his native Marienwerder, he served in the cathedral there, where he first met Dorothy about 1390. After her death he undertook a decade-long writing campaign to further her cause for canonization, composing four lives, two collections of revelations, and other materials for the canonization process. This is a list of the texts and editions:

- The short *Vita prima* of 1395 in AA.SS.Oct.XIII:493–99.
- The so-called *Vita Lindana* (named after the editor) of 1396 in AA.SS.Oct.XIII:499–560.
- The *Liber de festis (Appariciones venerabilis Domine Dorotheae)*, dating from 1397, a collection of Dorothy's visions in 130 chapters organized according to the liturgical year. It has been edited by Anneliese Triller and Ernst Borchert, *Liber de Festis Magistri Johannis Marienwerder: Offenbarungen der Dorothea von Montau* (Cologne and Vienna: Böhlau, 1992).
- The *Vita Latina* (here abbreviated VL) of 1398, edited by Hans Westphal, *Vita Dorotheae Mantoviensis Magistri Johannis Marienwerder* (Cologne and Graz: Böhlau, 1964).
- The *Septililium venerabilis dominae Dorotheae* (abbreviated Sept.), completed about 1400. This consists of seven treatises detailing Dorothy's spiritual gifts and practices under the headings: (I) Charity; (II) The Mission of the Holy Spirit; (III) The Eucharist; (IV) Con-

temptation; (V) Rapture; (VI) Perfection of the Christian Life; and (VII) Confession. The edition is by Franz Hipler in the *Analecta Bollandiana* 2 (1883): 381–472; 3 (1884): 113–40, 408–48; and 4 (1885): 207–51. This work was widely diffused.

• The MHG life, *Leben der zeligen vrouwen Dorothea* (abbreviated DL), completed between 1400 and 1404 using material from the earlier works, was designed to appeal to a lay audience in detailing Dorothy's sanctity. Four manuscripts survive. On this text, see Hörner, *Dorothea von Montau*, 44–48. The edition is by Max Toeppen in the *Scriptores rerum prussicarum* (Frankfurt: Minerva, 1965; reprint of 1863 edition of Leipzig), 2:179–350. I will use the English translation of Ute Stargardt, *The Life of Dorothea von Montau, a Fourteenth-Century Recluse* (Lewiston: Edwin Mellen, 1997).

For the other MHG sources relating to Dorothy, including a second vernacular life by Nikolaus Humilis, see Hörner, *Dorothea von Montau*, 41–100. Given the repetitious nature of John's writings, I will make use for the most part of the DL.

268. Birgitta's body had passed through Danzig on its way back to Sweden, so Dorothy would have had knowledge of the holy woman and her revelations. She appears as a model in several places, e.g., DL II.22 (ed., 257; trans., 113).

269. DL I.21 (ed., 218; trans., 57): Is komen nicht alleine dy juncvrouwen, und di sust kusch lebin, zcu dem riche der hymle, sundir ouch eliche menschin, di mit rechtim gloubin und gutin werkin gotis holde dirwerbin.

270. Dorothy's life as a married woman who aspired to sanctity has been studied by Elisabeth Schraut, "Dorothea von Montau: Wahrnehmungsweisen von Kindheit und Eheleben einer spätmittelalterlichen Heiligen," in *Religiöse Frauenbewegung und mystische Frömmigkeit im Mittelalter*, ed. Peter Dinzelbacher and Dieter R. Bauer (Cologne and Vienna: Böhlau, 1988), 373–94.

271. DL I.24 (ed., 221; trans., 60).

272. For the canonization materials, see *Die Akten des Kanonisationsprozess Dorotheas von Montau von 1394 bis 1521*, ed. Richard Stachnik (Cologne and Vienna: Böhlau, 1978). For suspicions that Dorothy was a heretic, see the testimony of Metza Hugische on pp. 108–9, as well as the notices on pp. 84 and 473–74.

273. DL II.27 (ed., 269; trans., 126): Czu hant do her nu czu dem irsten meyne beychte hatte gehört, gewan ich gröser lybe czu im, wen czu yrkeynem menschen ich y gewan alzo rysch. Wen ich hatte en czu hant also herczlich lip also meynen bruder, und getrawite im so wol, das ich im dy heymlikeyt meines herczin entplöst hette also vil, als in mir wer gewest, hette mich der herre gelart und mir geholfen enzuhant alczmole aussagin. See the parallel passage in the VL cap. 27e (ed., 149). In DL II.28 (ed., 272; trans., 128), Christ says to Dorothy, "I have united you as two people are bound to one another in marriage, and for this reason each of you shall take on the burdens of the other and one help the other so that you shall come to eternal life; you shall know that no other person has been nor ever will be commended as highly to B [i.e., *Beichtvater*, or confessor] as you have been."

274. On Christina and Peter, see McGinn, *Flowering of Mysticism*, 175–80.

275. DL II.28 (ed., 271–72; trans., 128): . . . du salt öbirgeben gancz deynen willen; was her dir gebewt, das thu, und was her dir vorbewt, das los! For more on Dorothy's obedience to her confessor, see DL III.3 (ed., 287; trans., 151).

276. The failure to get Dorothy of Montau canonized in the fifteenth century had much to do with the complications of the Great Schism, as well as local political issues involving the Teutonic Knights and their rivals for political and ecclesiastical power in the Baltic region. See Ute Stargardt, "The Political and Social Backgrounds of the Canonization of Dorothea von Montau," *Mystics Quarterly* 11 (1985): 107–22. When the Teutonic Order joined the Reformation in the early sixteenth century, her cause experienced a four-century hibernation until it was revived by Catholic refugees from Eastern European Communism in the second half of the twentieth century.

277. Dyan Elliott, "Authorizing a Life: The Collaboration of Dorothea of Montau and John Marienwerder," in *Gendered Voices: Medieval Saints and Their Interpreters*, ed. Catherine M.

Mooney (Philadelphia: University of Pennsylvania Press, 1999), 168–91, especially 168–69, 173, 190–91.

278. See, e.g., VL I.7 (ed., 49–52), Vita Lindana, cap. 4 (AA.SS.Oct.XIII:538), and the discussion in Elliott, "Authorizing a Life," 180–85. See also Dyan Elliott, "*Dominae* or *Dominatae?* Female Mysticism and the Trauma of Textuality," in *Women, Marriage, and Family in Medieval Christendom: Essays in Memory of Michael M. Sheehan, C.S.B.*, ed. Constance M. Rousseau and Joel T. Rosenthal (Kalamazoo: Medieval Institute Publications, 1998), 57–61.

279. We do possess one letter that Dorothy dictated for her daughter in 1394, edited by Richard Stachnik, "Die Geistliche Lehre der Frau Dorothea von Montau an ihre Tochter im Frauenkloster zu Kulm," *Zeitschrift für Ostforschung* 3 (1954): 589–96; see the discussion in Hörner, *Dorothea von Montau,* 41–42, 320–21. In addition, Hörner argues (*Dorothea von Montau,* 42–43, 322–86, 508–9) that the hitherto neglected German concluding chapters to Treatise VII, "De confessione," of the Sept., dictated to John by Dorothy, provides the most direct access to her own mystical views. These concluding chapters (nos. 7–28) were edited by Franz Hipler but unfortunately were not included in his *Analecta Bollandiana* edition. I have not had access to the edition contained in the *Zeitschrift für Geschichte und Alterthumskunde Ermlands* 6 (1877): 81–183.

280. DL I.1 (ed., 201; trans., 36): . . . als in eynen wunsamen anger, noch syner enphenlichkeit mit der hulfe gots zcu lesen di blumen der tugunden, der sie so vol und fruchtbar was, das sie nicht alleyne ire personen, sundir allen libhabern der tugunden zcur salde mogen komen.

281. Kieckhefer, *Unquiet Souls,* 22–33.

282. As might be expected, John often portrays Dorothy's sufferings, both self-inflicted and natural, as examples of imitating Christ's passion; see, e.g., DL I.17; II.17 and 34; and VL II.5 (ed., 68–71).

283. John's Latin works show knowledge of standard authorities, such as Augustine, Gregory, Bernard, and Richard of St. Victor. He also cites Cassian and Pseudo-Dionysius, whom he read along with the commentary of Robert Grosseteste.

284. See Raymond of Capua, *Legenda major S. Caterinae Senensis* II.6, nn. 179–80 (AA.SS.Apr.III:898DF). Raymond cites a different scripture text to support the miracle, Ps. 50:12.

285. DL II.1 (ed., 232; trans., 77–78, slightly altered): . . . do quam unsir herre Jhesus, ir liephabir gros, und rockte ir alds hercze zu, und stys ir vor daz ein nuwe hitzig hertze yn; das fulte wol di selige Dorothea, das man ir ire hercze usczog, und das man ir in des hertzen stat stis eyn hitzeig stucke fleischis, das was zcumol gar heys. In der enphaunge des fleischis adir des nuwen herczen hatte sy so grose lost und freude, daz sy di nymand mochte gancz ussayn. For other accounts of the heart extraction, see VL III.1–2 (ed., 112–16); and Vita Lindana 3 (AA.SS.Oct.XIII:517–18). DL II.29 discusses the three letters, one black, one red, one gold, inscribed on the new heart. In the third list of *Articuli in negotio Canonizationis beate Dorothee vidue dati* of 1403 the exchange of hearts even appears as art. 21 of the investigative procedure for Dorothy's case (*Die Akten,* 23).

286. One of the key themes of the DL is the emphasis on the gradual growth of Dorothy's sanctity; see, e.g., III.25 and 34.

287. DL II.2 (ed., 234; trans., 81): . . . Cristo Jhesu, irme libhabir, der do tegelich vorwunte ere sele und hercze, itzcunt mit den phylin der libe, itzunt mit den stralen und mit den spern der libe; und in der vorwundunge der geschoz fulte sy itzunt smertzen, itzunt suzikeit, itzunt libe und senunge. . . .

288. The self-transparency mentioned here (DL II.2) also appears elsewhere (e.g., III.27) and is reminiscent of the vision of Henry Suso, who sees his soul within him as if gazing through a crystal; see *Life* 5 (Bihlmeyer, 20) and the discussion in chapter 5, p. 228.

289. The 36/37 forms of love appear often in John's writings. Thirty-seven forms are described in DL IV.1 (ed., 332–37; trans., 213–22), while thirty-six are discussed in detail in the first treatise of the Sept. (I.1–35 in *Analecta Bollandiana* 2:400–72). This more theological

treatment in the Sept. includes appropriate citations from scripture and various authorities to help explain the varieties. See also Sept. Pream. and Prol. 2, as well as Vita Lindana 5 (AA.SS.Oct. XIII:547–33). The two lists also are found as separate treatises in MHD; see Hörner, *Dorothea von Montau*, 50–54.

290. Hörner (*Dorothea von Montau*) compares the different lists (pp. 198–207) and also relates these different names of love to Mechthild of Magdeburg's love vocabulary (pp. 494–504).

291. Sept. Prol. 2 (*Analecta Bollandiana* 2:394–98).

292. John's concern to show how Dorothy conforms to the traditional superiority of the contemplative over the active life is more evident in his Latin works than in the DL. See, e.g., Sept. IV.1–7 (*Analecta Bollandiana* 4:207–15).

293. Sept. IV.3 (*Analecta Bollandiana* 4:210): . . . ipsum habere oportet caritatem inebriantem et caritatem violentem, per quam anima ejus supra se elevetur et rapiatur, ut coelestia perspiciat.

294. DL II.36 (ed., 280–81; trans., 139–40). For other passages on the wounds of love in the DL, see, e.g., II.15, III.4 and 38, IV.1 and 2.2. Similar accounts are found in VL II.24, IV.13–16, and VI.24–25. The strange physical wounds that appeared on Dorothy's body from her youth, probably due to a medical condition, are interpreted by John as signs of the saint's interior woundings (DL I.17). Compare with Teresa of Avila's account of her transverberation (*Life*, Chap. 29).

295. DL III.41 (ed., 326–27; trans., 206): Ich fule grose smerczin, wen der herre hat meyn hertcze und alle meyne glid gantcz sere vorwunt mit den strolen und pfeylen seyner libe, dy her gröslichen in das hertcze, in dy armen, in den rocken, in dy schuldirn und anderswo ken dem hertczen in mich geschossin. Ich geen als ein fraw, dy itczunt geberen wil, unde habe keyne rue noch kein frede. . . . Dy czeyt ist nu komen, dovon ich dir czuvor gesagit habe, in der ich gebern sal meyne sele czum ewigin lebin. Dorothy's woundings are often described as inducing a form of pregnancy; see, e.g., DL III.38 and IV.3.4 (ed., 323 and 345; trans., 201 and 238). In Sept. I.9 and 17 such spiritual pregnancy is specifically compared to that of Birgitta of Sweden, with Christ assuring Dorothy that her pregnancies surpass those of the Swedish seer (*Analecta Bollandiana* 2:420–21, 437). For Birgitta's spiritual pregnancy, see *Sancta Birgitta: Revelaciones Book VI*, ed. Birgir Bergh (Stockholm: Almqvist & Wiksell, 1991), cap. LXXXVIII (247–48). There is a treatment of nine ways of spiritually giving birth in Sept. I.27–31 (*Analecta Bollandiana* 2:456–64).

296. For the two forms of spiritual drunkenness, see DL IV.1 (ed., 335–36; trans., 219); as well as Sept. I.18 (*Analecta Bollandiana* 2:438–39). The longest discussion of the grace of inebriation is in Sept. I.17–23 (2:435–50), but there are numerous references in all John's writings; in DL, see also II.16, 17, and 27; III.18, 27, and 29; and IV.3.4.

297. Descriptions of rapture and alienation from the senses are found throughout the DL and John's other texts on Dorothy. See, e.g., DL II.11, 14, 15, and 24; and DL III.32. The most detailed account of Dorothy's raptures is found in Tractatus V of the Sept. (*Analecta Bollandiana* 4:216–22), a mini-treatise using Augustine and Aquinas that analyzes: (1) Quid sit raptus; (2) De his quae sponsae raptum praecedebant; (3) Con comitantia rapti; and (4) Sequentia rapti.

298. For some parallels in John's other accounts, see, e.g., Sept. III.7 (*Analecta Bollandiana* 3:418–20); Vita Lindana 5. nn.119–25 (AA.SS.Oct. XIII:554–57); VL VI.12–19 (ed., 305–16).

299. DL III.28 (ed., 313; trans., 187): Ich wil dir me vorbas früntlicher komen, wen vor. . . . Wyr wellin und miteinander smeltczin in eynen klos, das wir werden miteinander voreynigeth unde seyn alleyne. Do dis der herre sprach, do was dy zele Dorothea von dem fewer der götlichen libe henflissende gleychsam eyne geschmeltczte glockspeyse, und flos mit dem hern in eynen klos. Das fulte dy zele Dorothee gar wol, wy sy eyns wart mit gote unde tiff in en gesencket. This is one of the strongest expressions of mystical union in the DL. For other important passages on union, see II.6 and 25; III.4 and 16; IV.3.3, 3.4, and 3.8. DL III.21 says that these experiences of union sometimes lasted three hours. Here and in the

analysis of union found in the Sept. III.7 (*Analecta Bollandiana* 3:418–20) we do not find any language of unity of indistinction, but rather a rich range of the language of loving oneness of spirit (*unitas spiritus*) rooted in the Song of Songs and 1 Cor. 6:17. The closest that John comes to using some of the more powerful forms of union language comes in Sept. III.27 (3:446).

300. DL III.31 (ed., 317; trans., 192, slightly adapted): Den wen ich wil ein heymelich dinge offenbaren deyner zelin, das ich wil gar heymelich habin, so mache ich deyne sele trunckin, e denne ich dir offenbare meine heymelikeit, so mag sy denne das, das ich mit ir rawme, nicht behaldin noch aussagin. Czu stunden horeth sy das rawmen, und vornimet is nicht irkentlich.

301. DL IV.2.3 (ed., 339; trans., 225–27). The whole second treatise of Sept. is devoted to "De Spiritus sancti missione"; see especially II.5–12 (*Analecta Bollandiana* 3:121–34) which counts the forms of daily sendings of the Spirit.

302. See, e.g., DL II.6 (ed., 237; trans., 85), and the more complete account in Sept. III.7 (*Analecta Bollandiana* 3:419–20).

303. DL III.23 (ed., 308; trans., 178–79): . . . dy worn eyne lautir irleüchtunge irer vorstendikeyt und eyne hitczige entczundung irer libe unde begerunge czu gote. For more on the gifts of illumination and inflammation, see VL VI.8 (ed., 299–300).

304. Sept. VII.1–6 (*Analecta Bollandiana* 4:243–51). For some texts on Dorothy's confessional practice in the German life, see DL I.7, II.2 and 22.

305. André Vauchez compares the role of the Eucharist in Catherine of Siena and Dorothy in his article, "Dévotion eucharistique et union mystique chez les saints de la fin du Moyen Age," in *Atti del Simposio Internazionale Caterininano-Bernardiniano. Siena 1980*, ed. Domenico Maffeir and Paolo Nardi (Siena: Accademia Senese degli Intronati, 1982), 295–300. See also Bynum, *Holy Feast and Holy Fast*, 136–37.

306. DL III.41 (ed., 327; trans., 207): Ich weis nicht, wy ich mag gebeytin! Gleich ap sy spreche: Das beitin ist mir unmögelich, adder alczu bittir addir czu swere.

307. DL II.38 (ed., 281–82; trans., 141–42) is entitled "Das sy eine grosze mertelerinne was und ist."

308. The text has been edited by Ulla Williams and Werner Williams-Krapp, *Die 'Offenbarungen' der Katharina Tucher* (Tübingen: Niemeyer, 1998). A number of the revelations can be precisely dated because of the way Katharina mentions both the feast day and the day of the week on which it fell. See also Karin Schneider, "Tucher, Katharina OP," VL 9:1132–34.

309. An analysis of what is known of Katharina's library is found in the "Einleitung" to *Die 'Offenbarungen,'* 13–23. Katharina's library included a number of biblical texts in translation and commentaries, but concentrated on mystical literature, including William of St. Thierry's *Epistola aurea*, Suso's *Büchlein der ewigen Weisheit*, Marquard of Lindau's *Dekalogtraktat*, Rulman Merswin's *Neunfelsenbuch*, the *Legende* of Catherine of Siena, as well as excerpts from Bernard of Clairvaux and Birgitta's revelations. Birgitta is mentioned by name in revelation no. 5.

310. For remarks on the form of the revelations, see *Die 'Offenbarungen'*, 5–13.

311. The following revelations contain a bridal element: nos. 4, 8, 20, 25, 27, 44, 70, 77, 80, and 86.

312. On the role of the passion, see nos. 2, 6, 9, 12, 13, 14, 15, 21, 22, 31, 32, 41, 51, 54, 73, and 82.

313. In no. 1, Katharina is commanded to go to confession.

314. No. 14 (ed., 36): 'Sich mich an, speiz die sell mit dem leib, wen dv wilt avz meim hertzzen trincken. Daz ist warm vnd niht kalt. Gib mir ein trvnck avf dem krevtz, als man mich magelt mit den henden.' 'Lieber her, wie schol ich dich trencken?' 'Mit eim warn gelaszen gemvt vnd mit eim vnder gang in gehorsam, da mit trenckst dv mich. So wil ich dich trencken avsz meim hertzzen, daz ein avfsprvnck nimt in daz ewig leben.' Katharina uses little of the vocabulary associated with the mysticism of the ground, through the phrase "gelaszen gemvt" also appears in no. 22 (ed., 42.2), and "gelassenhait" in no. 73 (ed., 62.10).

315. In no. 21 (ed., 40–41), we also find a long account of the passion in the form of an address by Mary.

316. No. 8 (ed., 34): Die red mit der sell: 'Mein tavb, mein gemahel, mein vnfermailligtew, kvm, ich wil mich mit dir verainen. . . . So verpirgt er sich vnd ich svch in. Daz siht er wol, vnd ich sih in niht. Wen ich wieder fint, so wirt ich fro vnd sprich: 'O mein schons liep, pelieb pei mir! Schaid dich niht wan mir!' . . . Dez spils, dez kossen, dez lieplichen redens in frevntlicher gegenbvrtigkait, daz vber trift alle irdische lieb, frevd diesser werlt!

317. In no. 9 (ed., 34.29–31) the Blessed Virgin is united with Christ in the "throne of the Holy Trinity." Katharina herself is promised union with Christ and God in a number of texts; see, e.g., nos. 20, 31, 34, 42 (ed., 39.21–24, 46.24–27, 47.8–9, 49.26).

318. For the text of the "Von der seligen Schererin," see Hans-Jochen Schiewer, "Auditionen und Visionen einer Begine: Die 'Selige Schererin', Johannes Mulberg und der Basler Beginenstreit. Mit einem Textabdruck," in *Die Vermittlung geistlicher Inhalte im deutschen Mittelalter: Internationales Symposium, Roscrea 1994,* ed. Timothy R. Jackson, Nigel F. Palmer, and Almut Suerbaum (Tübingen: Niemeyer, 1996), 289–317.

319. On the attack of the Basel Dominicans against the beguines and tertiaries, see Alexander Patschovsky, "Beginen, Begarden und Terziaren im 14. und 15. Jahrhundert: Das Beispiel des Basler Beginenstreits (1400/1404–1411)," in *Festschrift für Eduard Hlawitschka zum 65. Geburtstag,* ed. Karl Rudolf Schnith and Roland Pauler (Munich, 1993), 403–18; and Michael D. Bailey, "Religious Poverty, Mendicancy, and Reform in the Late Middle Ages," *Church History* 72 (2003): 457–83.

320. Schiewer, "Auditionen und Visionen einer Begine," 305.

321. "Von der seligen Schererin" (306.5–14): Do kam ein stimme in einem grossen lieht zuo ir sprechende: "Daz dir got din sel kleide mit sinem liden, so kummet sú erlich vnd ritterlich vnd wol gekleidet fúr in." . . . Do kam die stimme in dem lieht wider vmb zuo ir vnd sprach: "Du bist gesichert ewiges lebens durch daz verdienen vnsers herren."

322. On the role of drinking blood in late medieval mystical women, see Bynum, *Holy Feast and Holy Fast,* especially 55–56, 64–65, 161–80, 270–76 on drinking from Christ's side.

323. On the role of the Eucharist and spiritual communion in the text, see Schiewer, "Auditionen und Visionen," 295–301.

324. "Von der seligen Schererin" (309.120–28): Sú betratete daz wúrdig liden vnsers lieben herren und sú wart verzogen vnd sas ir sel an dem crútze by dem herren vnder sinem hertzen. Vnd unserm herren brach sin hertze vnd daz wúrdige bluot flos vs sinem hertzen in iren munt. Vnd do sú do noch wider zuo ir selber kam, do gedohte sú: "Dir sind grosse ding beschehen. Du hest getruncken vs dem hertzen vnsers herren. Dir ist beschehen also sante Johannes. . . . Waz hestu getruncken? Ich habe getruncken den willen gottes. Ich sencke mich zuo grunde in sinen willen. The passage ends with the visionary quoting Mary's words from Luke 1:46.

325. "Von der seligen Schererin" (317.410–13): Vnd by dem kússen, also sú vnser herre gekússet het vnd die wort zuo ir geret hette, do by merckte sú, daz sú daz sacrament nit solte lossen vnd daz vnser herre ein suon vnd ein vereinung wolte haben mit ir selen.

Chapter 8

1. On this treatise, see Bernard McGinn, *The Flowering of Mysticism: Men and Women in the New Mysticism (1200–1350),* vol. 3 of *The Presence of God: A History of Western Christian Mysticism* (New York: Crossroad, 1998), 113–15. Over four hundred manuscripts survive.

2. On Bonaventure's mystical treatises, see McGinn, *Flowering of Mysticism,* 101–12. The critical edition of Bonaventure's works lists 138 manuscripts for the *Itinerarium mentis in Deum* and no fewer than 299 for the *De triplici via.* The weight of Bonaventure's authority meant that not only were a number of his works translated into various vernaculars, including

MHG, but also many other spiritual and mystical writings came to be ascribed to him. For a survey, see C. Fischer, "Bonaventure (Apocryphes attribuées à saint)," DS 1:1843–56. The most widespread of the works often attributed to him (over two hundred manuscripts) was the *Meditationes vitae Christi* of ca. 1350, on which see McGinn, *Flowering of Mysticism,* 119–20. There is a recent critical edition, *Iohannis de Caulibus Meditaciones Vite Christi olim S. Bonauenturae attributae,* ed. M. Stallings-Taney (CCCM 153; Turnhout: Brepols, 1997).

3. On Rudolph of Biberach, see McGinn, *Flowering of Mysticism,* 117.

4. Hugh of Balma's *Viae Sion Lugent* was to be influential in the mid-fifteenth century debates over the relation of love and knowledge in the mystical ascent and therefore will be treated in more detail in chapter 10, p. 450.

5. A relatively complete list could be assembled from the many entries in the VL. A number of the treatises that have possible Dominican connections have been studied in Kurt Ruh, *Geschichte,* 3:355–88. These include: (1) *Von abegescheidenheit,* once ascribed to Eckhart, but now generally accepted as pseudo-Eckhart; (2) *Vorsmak des êwigen lebennes;* (3) *Traktat von der Minne;* (4) *Die Blume der Schauung;* and (5) the writings ascribed to "Der Meister des Lehrgesprächs," which include the *'Gratia dei' Dialog,* the *'Audi filia' Dialog,* and the *'In principio' Dialog.* Treatises (3) and (5) have more recently been assigned to the Augustinian John Hiltalingen of Basel (ca. 1332–1392); see Karl Heinz Witte, *'In-principio-Dialog': Ein deutschsprachiger Theologe der Augustinerschule des 14. Jahrhunderts aus dem Kreise deutsche Mystik und Scholastik* (Munich: Artemis, 1989); and "Der 'Traktat von der Minne', der Meister des Lehrgesprächs und Johannes Hiltalingen von Basel: Ein Beitrag zur Geschichte der Meister-Eckhart-Rezeption in der Augustinerschule des 14. Jahrhunderts," *Zeitschrift für deutsches Altertum und deutsche Literatur* 131 (2002): 454–87.

6. Franz Pfeiffer, *Meister Eckhart* (Leipzig: C. G. Röder, 1857; reprint, Göttingen: Vandenhoeck & Ruprecht, 1924). These "Tractates" are found on pp. 371–593. The authentic treatises are No. V, "Daz buoch der götlichen troestunge" (pp. 419–48), and No. XVII, "Die rede der underscheidunge" (pp. 543–93). Pfeiffer No. IX, "Von abegescheidenheit," considered authentic by J. Quint and edited in DW 5:400–34, is today generally thought not to be by Eckhart. This mass of pseudo-Eckhartian works alone gives an idea of how many mystical treatises survive from this period.

7. The Franciscans made many important contributions to late medieval German mysticism, as shown by the treatment of Marquard of Lindau in the last chapter. Franciscan spiritual and mystical writings were mostly translations, hagiographical texts, and sermons, as is evident from the two-volume collection edited by Kurt Ruh, *Franziskanisches Schrifttum im deutschen Mittelalter* (Munich: Beck, 1965, 1985). There are a few mystical treatises of Franciscan origin, such as the anonymous *Von der göttlichen Liebe,* edited by Ruh in *Franziskanisches Schrifttum,* 2:232–47.

8. There are several sketches of Augustinian spirituality. In English, see Adolar Zumkeller, "The Spirituality of the Augustinians," in *Christian Spirituality: High Middle Ages and Reformation,* ed. Jill Raitt et al. (New York: Crossroad, 1987), 63–74. More detailed studies include David Gutiérrez, "Eremites de Saint-Augustin," DS 4:983–1018; and for Germany, Adolar Zumkeller, "Die Lehrer des geistlichen Lebens unter den deutschen Augustinern vom dreizehnten Jahrhundert bis zum Konzil von Trient," in *Sanctus Augustinus Vitae Spiritualis Magister* (Rome: Analecta Augustiniana, 1956), 2:239–338. An English version of this essay appears as chapter 3 of Zumkeller's *Theology and History of the Augustinian School in the Middle Ages* (n.p.: Augustinian Heritage Institute, 1996).

9. The most detailed work on Henry of Friemar is Clemens Stroick, *Heinrich von Friemar: Leben, Werke, philosophisch-theologische Stellung in der Scholastik* (Freiburg-im-Breisgau: Herder, 1954). More up-to-date introductions can be found in Adolar Zumkeller, "Henri de Friemar," DS 7:191–97; and Robert G. Warnock, "Heinrich von Friemar der Ältere," VL 3:730–37. I have also profited from the forthcoming paper of Jeremiah Hackett, "The Reception of Meister Eckhart: Mysticism, Philosophy and Theology in Jordanus of Quedlinburg and Henry of Friemar (The Older)."

10. Jordan was briefly noted in chapter 7. For more on Jordan and his extensive, but still mostly unedited writings, see Adolar Zumkeller, "Jordan von Quedlinburg (Jordanus de Saxonia)," VL 4:853–61; and the same author's "Jourdain de Saxe ou de Quedlinburg," DS 8:1423–30.

11. See chapter 2, pp. 76–77.

12. All three works were edited by Adolar Zumkeller, O.S.A., *Henrici de Frimaria, O.S.A. Tractatus ascetico-mystici. Tomus I* (Rome: Augustinianum, 1975).

13. The *Tractatus de adventu Domini* (ed., 66–100) is based on Song of Songs 5:1 ("Veniat dilectus meus in hortum suum"). Henry interprets this verse as expressing the threefold act of the *anima contemplativa*, which structures the three parts of the treatise. Part 1 concerns the *ardentissima affectio* of the soul for the Bridegroom's presence. The long part 2 with three chapters treats the *perfectissima dispositio* of the soul if she is to enjoy the Lord's coming. The key theme here is the proper preparation for and cultivation of the *semen spirituale*, that is, "the influx of divine light" given to the soul who has stripped herself of earthly things (76–77). This reception restores the trinitarian image of God in the soul and leads on to ecstatic states and union with God (82–91). Finally, part 3 deals with the *suavissima refectio*, the spiritual banquet enjoyed by the soul. Here Henry investigates various traditional aspects of mystical consciousness under three headings: what the spiritual banquet is; where and when it is celebrated; and how and in what way it is completed. The rigorous organization is evident. This treatise must date to after 1311, since one passage refers to the first of the errors condemned at the Council of Vienne in that year (86.24–28).

14. *De adventu Verbi*, proem. (3.18–20): . . . quia Verbi aeterni mentalis conceptio videtur esse maxima et suprema gratia omnium donorum, quae in hac vita secundum legem communem animae devotae per gratiam conferuntur.

15. This phrase comes from Bernard McGinn, *The Mystical Thought of Meister Eckhart* (New York: Crossroad, 2002), chapter 4, "The Preacher in Action: Eckhart on the Eternal Birth," 54. This chapter is an extended analysis of these sermons which are now available in DW 4:279–610.

16. Burkhard Hasebrink, *Formen inzitatizer Rede bei Meister Eckhart: Untersuchungen zur literarischen Konzeption der deutschen Predigt* (Tübingen: Niemeyer, 1992), 260–63.

17. The scholastic nature of the work is also seen in the *dubitationes*, or disputed questions, that Henry inserts into the text from time to time (see 12, 35, 36–37, and 42–44).

18. The structure of the work, which survives in five manuscripts, is as follows:

> *Pars I. Dispositio ad conceptionem Verbi per gratiam* (5–33). This preparation stage is based on an exegesis of Luke 1:26–27, the beginning of the Annunciation narrative.
>
> > Four *conditiones gratiosae* are presented: (1) *inspiratio gratiosa* (5–14); (2) *sublimatio virtuosa* (14–41); (3) *aemulatio vigorosa* (21–27); and (4) *illustratio radiosa* (27–33).
>
> *Pars II. Quomodo Verbum in mente per gratiam concipiatur* (34–61). This part deals with the modes of the Word's conception (34–55) and the effects thereof (55–61). It is tied to an exegesis of the Canticle of Simeon ("Nunc dimittis" [Luke 2:29–32]), but also uses Luke 1:28 and 1:42.
>
> > *Primum Principale* (34–48).Three processes by which the Word is conceived in the mind, the centerpiece of the treatise. The processes are: (1) *per modum dulcoris*; (2) *per modum luminis*; and (3) *per modum fulgoris beatificantis*.
> >
> > *Secundum Principale* (48–55). The maternal fecundity by which the Word is conceived.
> >
> > *Tertium Principale* (55–61). The Spiritual Fruits of the Conception. This concerns the effects of contact with God.

Although the Gospel of Luke provides the structural core for Henry's development, the tract uses the Song of Songs more than any other book of the Bible (thirty-eight citations).

19. Among these motifs are (1) the three stages of the spiritual life; (2) action and contemplation; (3) the forms of love; (4) detachment; (5) filiation; (6) contemplation; (7) the experience

of internal sweetness; (8) rapture and ecstasy; (9) union with God; and (10) transformation into the *imago trinitatis.*

20. The word *gratia* appears about seventy times in the treatise.

21. *De adventu Verbi* (9.78–82): Nam per foramen intelligitur consensus liberi arbitrii; quia nullum donum nobis divinitus confertur, nisi per hoc foramen nuntiatur. Unde huius manus per foramen immissio est divinae gratiae per liberum consensum voluntatis vivifica inspiratio.

22. The passage discussed here is found in *De adventu Verbi* (13.199–14.222). The passage from Proclus, found in the *Elementatio theologica,* propositions 30–31, is an expression of the fundamental Neoplatonic paradigm of *monē* (remaining within)—*proodos* (emanating out)—*epistrophē* (returning).

23. *De adventu Verbi* (17.71–74): Secundo sublimatio virtuosa perficitur in suae mentis ab omnibus speciebus creatis omnimoda abstractione, quae convenienter innuitur in nomine "Galilaeae", quae interpretatur transmigratio et signat mentem abstractam et ab omni specie creata evacuatam. . . . Oportet mentem esse virgineam et nulla specie creata ingravidatam, quae debet esse aeterni Verbi virginei conceptiva. In this discussion (17.71–18.93) Henry cites the authority of Dionysius (MT 1.1) and Boethius for the need for such withdrawal. He also says that he has discussed *abstractio* in more detail elsewhere. This seems to be a reference to some lost work, because the other discussions in this work add little to what he says here (see 29.57–59, 30.94–99, 32.155–57, 38.108–12, and 56.24–27). Henry also treats abstraction in the *De adventu Domini* (76.165–177), where he speaks of it as a form of *denudatio,* citing one of Eckhart's favorite scriptural passages (Hos. 2:14) for the meeting between the naked detached soul and the divine One. Henry cites Hosea 2:14 in a similar context discussing the mind's withdrawal from created forms in *De adventu Verbi* 32.148–62.

24. See Bernard McGinn, *The Growth of Mysticism,* volume 2 of *The Presence of God: A History of Western Christian Mysticism* (New York: Crossroad, 1994), 241–45.

25. *De adventu Verbi* (20.154–56): Propter tertium est sciendum, quod sponsus aeternus quiescit tribus modis in isto lectulo conscientiae, prout per suam praesentiam inhabitat tres vires ad rationalem imaginem pertinentes. Henry cites passages from Augustine's *Confessiones* 10.25, 7.10, and 12.16 to illustrate the three modes of presence in the *imago dei.*

26. *De adventu Verbi* (32.159–61): . . . ista verba arcana, quae menti devotae in lumine theorico revelantur, adeo sunt ineffabilia, quod nulla lingua nec aliquo verbo sensibili poterunt declarari.

27. *De adventu Verbi* (38.126–29): Ad istam conceptionem Verbi aeterni mens devota debet summo desiderio aspirare, quia per istam Verbi aeterni praesentiam mens quodam divino amore accenditur. Qui appropriate dici poterit consumptivus eo, quod suo fervore absumat in anima omnem affectum et inclinationem . . . .

28. *De adventu Verbi* (39.155–57): Nam Pater secundum istam [i.e., cognitio notionalis] se personaliter cognoscit et per actum generationis actionem personalem elicit et personam ab eo formaliter distinctam producit . . . . Here Henry cites Augustine, *In Johannis Evangelium* 14.7.42–47.

29. *De adventu Verbi* (40.182–85): Quae quidem nobis debetur duplici iure: primo iure filiationis, qua nos in Dei filios per gratiam adoptavit; secundo iure fraternae participationis, qua Verbum aeternum nostram naturam assumens caro nostra et frater noster esse voluit. The third reason for the appropriateness of the birth of the Word (41.200–208) involves the Son as the influx of divine light.

30. *De adventu Verbi* (41.212–42.219): Nam certum est, quod, cuicumque communicatur realiter et inexistenter praesentia divinae bonitatis, oportet, quod ei ex consequenti communicetur omnis thesaurus gratiae, qui natus est effluere a divina bonitate, sicut etiam, cuicumque communicaretur essentialiter praesentia solis, illi communicaretur effectus lucis et claritatis et omnis alius effectus, qui natus est effluere ab ipso sole. Sed constat, quod per spiritualem conceptionem Verbi ipsum Verbum inexistenter et praesentialiter communicaretur ipsi menti.

31. The citation of 1 Corinthians 6:17, the key biblical proof text for loving union of spirits, is important. Henry also uses it in one of his discussions of union in the *Tractatus de*

adventu Domini (88.92–98). Even though in this passage he uses the language of the divine abyss (*anima rapitur in abyssum divinae vitae*) and cites John 17:20, one of Eckhart's proof texts for indistinct union, Henry's understanding of mystical union is essentially the same as that of the monastic mystics of the twelfth century.

32. *De adventu Verbi* (42.224–28): Quae quidem unitas non intellegitur secundum identitatem realis existentiae, ut quidam erronee posuerunt, sed secundum quandam conformitatis et transformationis similitudinem iuxta illud primae Joannis 3: "Sciamus quod, cum apparuerit, similes ei erimus, quia videbimus eum, sicuti est." The reference given by the editor here, and in another passage in the treatise *De incarnatione Verbi* (130.127–131.147), to Eckhart's Pr. 6 (DW 1:110.8–111.7) is scarcely relevant. Henry may well have had Eckhart in mind, but he summarizes a position, rather than referencing a text.

33. Henry may have been influenced by Richard of St. Victor, *De arca mystica* 5.9–19, who uses biblical figures to illustrate the various kinds of ecstatic experience. Henry refers to the treatise in the *Tractatus de adventu Domini* (91.186–89, citing *De arca mystica* 5.1). The same *Tractatus* (93.33–48) contains another exposition of different forms of the presence of the divine light in the soul illustrated by biblical types. Pharaoh and Nebuchadnezzer illustrate purely intellectual illumination; the Queen of Sheba a purely affective one, while the bride of the Song of Songs experiences God *per intellectum et per affectum*.

34. *De adventu Domini* (83.209–13): Ex qua contingit ipsam ferventer rapi et in sui ipsius exstasim et defectum perduci, quae quidem exstasis annihilatio dicitur, quia mens, quae est in exstasi posita, sibi et omnibus creaturis funditus moritur, in quantum se ipsum nesciens sui et omnium aliorum obliviscitur. On the following page (85.227–47) Henry says that the ecstasy or liquefaction comes about through the contemplation, insofar as this is possible in this life, of the emanations of the persons in the Trinity and the way in which all things preexist indistinctly in God and flow out from him.

35. Heinrich Seuse Denifle, *Das Buch von geistlicher Armuth bisher bekannt als Johann Taulers Nachfolgung des armen Lebens Christi* (Munich: Max Huttler, 1877). For treatments of the text, see A. Chiquot, "Buch von geistlicher Armuth (Das)," DS 1:1976–78; Johannes Auer, "'Das Buch von geistlicher Armut,'" VL 1:1082–85; and especially Ruh, *Geschichte*, 3:517–25, which contains a fairly detailed exposition. I have not seen the 1989 reprint of the Denifle text with modern German translation and study by Niklaus Largier. In English, there is a version by C. F. Kelley, *The Book of the Poor in Spirit by a Friend of God (Fourteenth Century): A Guide to Rhineland Mysticism* (New York: Harper & Brothers, 1954). Kelley's introduction, the only extended treatment in English, is helpful but somewhat antiquated. His translation is a kind of mixed version, based on Denifle and compared with several other forms of the text. I have preferred to make my own version from the MHG in most cases.

36. Laurent Sauer, who Latinized his name as Laurentius Surius (1523–1578), was a key figure in the transmission of German mystical literature to the wider Catholic world of early modern Europe through his translations of real and pseudonymous works of Tauler, Suso, Ruusbroec, and others, between 1540 and 1555. See Augustin Devaux, "Surius (Sauer; Laurent)," DS 14:1325–29.

37. On Daniel Sudermann's role in the transmission of mystical texts, see Monica Pieper, "Sudermann (Daniel)," DS 7:1290–92.

38. A point made by Denifle in his introduction to the edition; *Das Buch*, XII-XIII, and XVI-XX.

39. Kelley ("Introduction," *The Book of the Poor in Spirit*, 3) calls it "the text book of the Rhineland School."

40. E.g., *Das Buch* (44.35–36): . . . der geist uz gat sin selbs nach geschaffenheit, und sich wurffet in ein luter niht. Und daz niht, daz ist daz goetlich bilde daz in den geist getrucket ist.

41. E.g., *Das Buch* (4.34–35): . . . der do wonet in ewikeit und sich einiget in daz einige ein. See also 158.10, and 164.14.

42. *Das Buch* (182.16–30). This passage cites Hosea 2:14, Eckhart's proof text for the desert motif. One Eckhartian theme that does not make an appearance in the book is the notion of

breaking-through into God, though the soul is described as needing to break through, or overcome, all created things (e.g., 138.18 and 193.12 and 15).

43. There are also differences from Tauler. Denifle, in his desire to show that Tauler was not the author of the work, may have overstressed these. For a summary of the differences, see Chiquot, "Buch von geistlicher Armuth," 1977–78.

44. Robert E. Lerner, *The Heresy of the Free Spirit in the Later Middle Ages* (Berkeley: University of California Press, 1972), 223–25. Lerner notes that the book includes in its audience "die in sammenungen sint" (11.37) and that the word *sammenungen* was used in Strassburg to indicate communities of beguines and beghards. Luise Abramowski, "Bemerkungen zur 'Theologia deutsch' und zum 'Buch von geistlicher Armut,'" *Zeitschrift für Kirchengeschichte* 97 (1986): 92–104, argues that beguines and beghards were a part, but scarcely the whole, of the intended audience.

45. On the clerical authorship, see Abramowski, "Bemerkungen," 94–98.

46. The two parts in Denifle's edition comprise pp. 3–90 and 93–193 of his edition. Denifle does not provide chapter numbers, but the manuscript captions he records are the basis for the analysis given here. Kelley (*Book of the Poor in Spirit*) chooses a different arrangement of four parts with more numerous chapter headings and internal divisions to facilitate following an often complex text.

47. *Das Buch* (20.20–23) provides a division of forms of working or activity: . . . Wurcken ist nit anders danne usser niht iht machen, oder usser einem ein anders machen oder eins besser machen danne es vor waz, oder eins, daz do ist, zuo niht machen. . . . This shows the author's scholastic training.

48. On Henry of Friemar's teaching on the discernment of spirits, see chapter 2, pp. 76–77.

49. *Das Buch* (82.32–40): Und daz louffen ist nit nach creaturlichen wise, und da von ist es nit zuo schetzende fur ein bewegunge, mer: es ist nach einer goetlichen wise, und da von ist es unbewegelich, wan der wille in keine wise sich beweget usser got, mer: alle zit in got blibet. Und daz innebliben daz ist sin louffen, und daz louffen ist sin innebliben; und so er aller meist inne verblibet, so er aller meist in got louffet, und so er aller meist in got louffet, so er aller stillest ist und aller unbewegenlichest.

50. *Das Buch* (176.8–11): . . . daz ist ein flissige huote alles des, daz in dem menschen gevallen mag, es sy geistlich oder liplich, daz daz also enpfangen werde, daz es den geist nit enmittele.

51. *Das Buch* (194.2–4): . . . er sol got minnen umb got, und sol sich alles lustes verzihen, und sol got alleine an hangen ane alles warumb.

52. *Das Buch* (3.9–13): 'Waz ist armuot?' Armuot ist ein glicheit gottes. 'Waz ist got?' Got ist ein abgescheiden wesen von allen creaturen. 'Waz ist abgescheiden?' Daz an niht haftet; armuot haftet an niht, und niht an armuot.

53. *Das Buch* (3.21–24): Etliche sprechent daz daz sy die hoeheste armuot und die nehste abgescheidenheit, daz der mensche also sy, als er waz, do er nit enwaz; do verstunt er niht, do enwolt er niht, do waz er got mit got. This is almost a direct quotation from Eckhart's Pr. 52 (DW 2:488.4–6, and 492.3–4).

54. *Das Buch* (4.13–15): . . . so sol er lassen allen underscheit und sol sich in tragen mit ein in ein sunder allen underscheit. . . . The word *underscheit* can mean discernment and/or distinction; both senses seem to work here.

55. On Porete's view of "leaving the virtues behind," see McGinn, *Flowering of Mysticism*, 245, 254.

56. *Das Buch* (8.8–10 and 16–19): . . . got ist ein fri vermugen, also ist armuot ein fri vermugen unbetrungen von nieman, wan sin edel ist friheit. . . . Friheit ist gewar luterkeit und abgescheidenheit, die da sachet ewikeit. Friheit ist ein abgescheiden wesen, daz da got ist oder zuo male got anhangende ist.

57. *Das Buch* (11.18–22): . . . ist ouch nit ein ledig arm mensche gebunden zuo allen den

gesetzden der heiligen cristenheit nach usserliche wise zuo nemende, als ein ander mensche, der sin selbs nit ledig ist worden, wan waz die heilige cristenheit wurket nach usserliche wise, daz wurcket der arme mensche innerlichen in wesen. . . . See the discussion of this passage in Abramowski, "Bemerkungen," 98–99.

58. Some practical advice about a daily schedule is given here (15.26–35). Mornings and evenings, whenever possible, should be set aside for God, while afternoons are the best time for external works and acts of charity.

59. *Das Buch* (19.4–6 and 19–20): . . . und in dem innebliben so entspringet ein naturlich lieht in ime, und daz zoeuget ime underscheit naturlicher warheit, und der underscheit gebirt ime grossen lust. . . . Und dar uz entspringet ein ungeordente friheit, daz er versmahet die gesetzde der heiligen cristenheit.

60. *Das Buch* (113.25–29): . . . so butet ir got sin antlitz und kusset sie. Und kussen ist nit anders wan vereinunge liebes mit liebe, und da gaffet eins daz ander an, und eins ist also gar vergleffet uf daz ander, daz eins ane daz ander nit enmag, also gar sint sie mit minnen zuosamen gebunden.

61. *Das Buch* (118.10–13): Und da verluret der geist sinen namen, daz er me got heisset wan geist, nit daz er got sy, mer: er ist goetlich, und da von wirt er me genammet nach got, wan nach geist.

62. *Das Buch* (118.29–22, and 118.40–119.2): Und so man des ledig ist und alle mittel abe sint, so het man got gegenwurtecliche, und in der gegenwertikeit so schovwet man in an, wan got ist in allen dingen gegenwurtecliche. . . . Wer die werk wurckter eins armen mensch, der ist ein arm mensche, und der ist ouch ein schovwender mensche.

63. *Das Buch* (60.19–24): Und als got der vatter gebirt sunen sun in ime selber und in alle ding, mit der selben geburt fueret got den menschen durch sin liden und durch alle tugent in in. Und als got ewig ist an siner geburt, also ist ouch daz infueren ewig, do mit der mensche durch sin liden wurt gefueret.

64. *Das Buch* (63.20–23): Und die heiden suochent daz blosse wesen der sele, und die kundent nit dar in komen ane cristum. Und dar umb mohtent sie nit got erkennen noch selig gesin, und begertent doch selig zuo sinde.

65. For other passages on *die heiden* that are equally negative, see *Das Buch*, 72.17–23 and 125.15–20. The long discussion found at 161.16–162.2 is more ambiguous, admitting that externally there may be no difference between the good pagan and the poor person and that the internal difference tied to adherence to Christ may be hard to discern.

66. *Das Buch* (64.2–6): Und also hat er ein ewig ingan in got, und er wurt also gar umbegrifen mit got, daz er sich selber verluret, und enweis nit anders danne umb got. Und also ertrincket er in dem grundelosen mer der gotheit, und swimmet in got als ein fisch in dem mere. . . . This is close to Tauler's V 41 (176.10–11): . . . und do hat sich der geist verlorn in Gotz geiste; in dem grundelosen mere ist er ertrunken.

67. *Das Buch* (64.12–18): Daz auge daz ist die intringende minne die sie hat in got, und mit der minne betwinget sie got, daz got muos tuon waz sie wil. . . . Der boge den sie spannet daz ist ir hertze; daz spannet sie und schusset mit einer hitzigen begirde in got und triffet daz rehte zil.

68. Among the other passages in *Das Buch* that emphasize the central role of fixing the mind on the passion, see, e.g., 93–97, 106, and 121–30.

69. *Das Buch* (ed., 97.35–98.23). The treatise does not expend much time on sacramental piety, but it clearly considers it important for the truly poor person.

70. Other important passages on birthing include *Das Buch*, 66.17–28, 68.33–69.21, 118.19–23, 137.25–138.27, 185.17–25, and especially 168.6–169.35.

71. *Das Buch* (101.9–11): Und nach der wise alse der creatur uz geflossen ist von got, nach der selben wise sol sie wieder in fliessen.

72. *Das Buch* (102.30–32): . . . daz ist so der himelsche vatter gebirt sinen sun in der selen. Und die geburt erhebet den geist ueber alle geschaffene ding an got. . . .

73. The need for removing all images to attain to God occurs elsewhere in *Das Buch*; see, e.g., 25.29–26.17; 38.4–9; 44.1–24 (where we find the quotation: *der mensche sol entbildet sin von allen bilden* [44.14], possibly citing Eckhart); 167.24–36; and 177.22–33.

74. *Das Buch* (103.13–20): Und daz nachlouffen daz die vernunft tuot nach dem goetlichen werck, daz ist daz sie sich entbloesset von allen geschaffenen bilden, und mit einem ungeschaffenen lieht in tringet in daz dunsternisse der verborgenen gotheit, und da wurt sie von bekennen kennelos, und von minnen minnelos, daz ist, daz sie nit me bekennet nach creaturlicher wise, mer: nach goetlicher wise, und nit minnen mit irem minnen, mer: nach gottes minnen.

75. For some treatments of the *grunt der sele*, see 55.36, 67.5–7, 68.12–38, 73.1, 100.35, 111.14–19, 136.8, 138.5–6, and 191.9–15.

76. *Das Buch* (192.1–2): . . . wan daz lieht ist einvaltig: hier umb so wil es ouch einen einvaltigen grunt haben. . . .

77. *Das Buch* (192.22–26): . . . nu ist got ungesihtlich und uber alle bilde: und da von so werdent sie betrogen die sich gesihte an nement, wan waz sich in einem einvaltigen lutern grunde gebirt, daz ist also so subtil und also einvaltig, daz ez nieman mit bilden begriffen kan, und da von kan nieman da von gesprechen. . . .

78. *Das Buch* (193.34–37): Und daz sachet der einvaltiger luter grunt uz dem die einvaltige goetliche minne entspringet, und da ist aller groeste lust inne den man in der zit haben mag (here I use Kelley's version, 269).

79. There are a number of helpful introductions to the work: Wolfgang von Hinten, "'Der Franckforter' ('Theologia Deutsch')," VL 2:802–08; Ute Mennecke-Haustein, "'Theologia Deutsch,'" DS 15:459–63; and Christian Peters, "Theologia deutsch," *Theologische Realenzyklopädie* (Berlin: Walter de Gruyter, 1977-) 23:258–62. In English, there are appreciative though outdated accounts by Anna Groh Seesholtz, *Friends of God: Practical Mystics of the Fourteenth Century* (New York: Columbia University Press, 1934), 155–63; and Rufus M. Jones, *The Flowering of Mysticism: The Friends of God in the Fourteenth Century* (New York: Macmillan, 1939), 176–84.

80. Alois M. Haas, Review of Wolfgang von Hinten, *'Der Franckforter' ('Theologia Deutsch'): Kritische Textausgabe* (Munich and Zurich: Artemis, 1982), in *Beiträge zur Geschichte der deutschen Sprache und Literatur* 108 (1986): 297.

81. Steven E. Ozment, *Mysticism and Dissent: Religious Ideology and Social Protest in the Sixteenth Century* (New Haven: Yale University Press, 1973), 17–25, on Luther's use of the text (the quotations from Luther's prefaces are cited from this work). Ozment's chapter 2, "A Common Mystical Writing: The *Theologia Deutsch*," is a good summary of early Protestant use of the treatise. A more extensive survey of Protestant use down to the twentieth century can be found in Bengt Hoffman, "Introduction," *The Theologia Germanica of Martin Luther* (New York: Paulist Press, 1980), 24–34. This volume contains the most recent translation of Luther's 1518 edition of the book.

82. On Castellio and Weigel and the *Theologia Deutsch*, consult Ozment, *Mysticism and Dissent*, 39–60. For more on Weigel and his use of German mysticism, see Andrew Weeks, *Valentin Weigel: Selected Spiritual Writings* (New York: Paulist Press, 2003).

83. For a listing of the editions, see Georg Baring, *Bibliographie der Ausgaben der "Theologia Deutsch" (1516–1961): Ein Beitrag zur Lutherbibliographie. Mit Faksimiledruck der Erstausgabe und 32 Abbildungen* (Baden-Baden: Heitz, 1963).

84. The edition by Wolfgang von Hinten *'Der Franckforter' ('Theologia Deutsch'): Kritische Ausgabe* (Munich: Artemis, 1982), is based on the eight known manuscripts and Luther's two editions, which are independent witnesses. There is a modern German version with introduction by Alois M. Haas, *'Der Franckforter':Theologia Deutsch* (Einsiedeln: Johannes Verlag, 1993). In English there is a recent translation by David Blamires, *The Book of the Perfect Life: Theologia Deutsch—Theologia Germanica* (Walnut Creek, Calif.: AltaMira Press, 2003). I will use this translation unless otherwise noted.

85. Recent studies include Alois M. Haas, "Die 'Theologia Deutsch'. Konstitution eines

mystologisches Texts," in *Das "Einig Ein": Studien zu Theorie und Sprache der deutschen Mystik*, ed. Alois M. Haas and Heinrich Stirnimann (Freiburg, Switzerland: Universitätsverlag, 1980), 369–415; Luise Abramowski, "Bemerkungen zur 'Theologia Deutsch' und zum 'Buch der geistlicher Armut,'" *Zeitschrift für Kirchengeschichte* 97 (1986): 85–105; and Volker Leppin, "Mystische Frömmigkeit und sakramentale Heilsvermittlung im späten Mittelalter," *Zeitschrift für Kirchengeschichte* 112 (2001): 189–204.

86. TD, Prolog (67.1–7): Diss buechelein hat der almechtige, ewige got auss gesprochen durch eynen weissen, vorstanden, worhafftigen, gerechten menschen, synen frunt, der do vor czeitenn gewest ist eyn deutschir herre, eyn prister vnd eyn custos yn der deutschen herren hauss zu franckfurt, vnnd leret manchen liplichen vnderscheit gotlicher warheit vnd besundern, wie vnd wo methe man irkennen moge die warhafftigen, gerechten gotis frundt vnnd auch die vngerechten, falschen, freyen geiste, dy der heiligen kirchen gar schedelich synt (trans. Blamires, 31).

87. Abramowski, "Bemerkungen," 86–88.

88. For example, it does not seem to have been noticed that the argument for the necessity of the incarnation in TD 3 (74.11–14) is based on Anselm.

89. Haas ("Die 'Theologia Deutsch,'" 370–76) provides an analysis of the style of the book.

90. Many Eckhartian themes are integral to the treatise and will be considered below. Others appear only infrequently; e.g., the necessity for removing created images (see 79.7–10 and 87.1–88.4, a citation from Tauler). The term *grunde* appears only once in TD 23 (101.9): . . . vnd diss alczumal yn eyme swigende ynbliben yn syme grunde seyner sele. . . . There is also only a single reference to the birth of the Word in the soul, and it occurs in the final chapter that appears to have been added by the redactor (TD 53 [150.13–15]).

91. Haas ("Die 'Theologia Deutsch,'" 370) summarizes the message as follows: ". . . die gnadenhafter Vergottung des Menschen im Lichte der vermittelnden Vorbildlichkeit des Lebens Christi."

92. The use of oppositions throughout the text is noted by Blamires, "Introduction," *The Book of the Perfect Life*, 26.

93. TD 19 (96.8–11). Since there was no standard German translation of the Bible at that time, the author, like Eckhart, creates his own versions, often paraphrasing for effect. The work contains sixteen citations from Matthew, twelve from John, but only three from Luke and two from Mark. Again, it is unusual to have Matthew's gospel more cited than John's in a mystical text.

94. Haas ("Die 'Theologia Deutsch,'" 412) has an insightful analysis of what he calls "Das fundamentale 'Ich will'" of the treatise.

95. Among the difficult and obscure places, see, for example, 98.6–8, 111.3–14, 122.12–30, and 140.3–11.

96. TD 9 (81.15–18): Ess ist gut ader gut geworden, vnd doch wider diss gut noch das, das man genennen, bekennen ader geczeigen kan, sunder alle vnd vbir alle. Auch darff das nicht yn die sele kommen, wann es bereite dar jnne ist. Ess ist aber vnbekant (trans., 38). For other passages where God is identified with the supreme Good, see TD 32, 43, 44, and 53 (115.1–116.11, 134.1–135.24, 138.12–15, 149.1–4, and 151.70–152.88). Divine unknowability appears in many places, e.g., TD 21 and 42 (98.1–2, and 133.37–42).

97. TD 1 (71.3–5): Das volkommende ist eyn wesen, das yn ym vnnd yn seynem wessen alles begriffen vnd beslossen, vnnd an das vnd usswendig dem keine wares wessen ist, vnnd yn dem alle dingk yr wessen han, wanne es ist aller dinck wessen . . . (trans., 31). The identification of God as *essentia omnium* is a hallmark of Dionysian theology.

98. TD 36 (121.6–7): . . . wan got ist aller wesende wessen vnd aller lebendigenn leben vnd aller wissen wissheit, wan alle ding haben yr wessen werlicher yn got den yn en selber . . . (trans., 67).

99. TD 31 (115.24–25): . . . vnd ist yn ym selber an creatur orspruncklich vnd wessenlich, ader nicht formelich ader wircklich . . . (my trans.).

100. TD 32 (116.27–31): . . . vnnd ess mag keines nymmer gewircket vnd gevbet werden an creatur, wan ess ist yn got an creatur nicht anders dann eyn wessen vnd eyn vrsprung vnd nicht werck. Aber wo diss eyne, das doch disse alle ist, eyn creatur an sich nympt vnd yr geweldig ist vnde ym da czu fuget vnd duncket, das ess sich synes eigens da bekennen mag . . . (trans., 63).

101. TD 51 (144.36–38): Vnd diss magk an creatur nicht gescheen. Dar vmmb sal creatur seyn vnd got wil sie haben, das disser wille seyn eygen werck dar ynne habe vnd wircke, der yn got an werck ist vnd seyn muss (trans., 90).

102. TD 15 (89.1–4): Alles, das yn Adam vnder ging vnd starb, das stunt yn Cristo wider auff vnnd wart lebendig. Alles, das yn Adam auff stunt vnd lebendig wart, das ging yn Cristo vnder vnd starp. Was was vnd ist aber dass? Ich sprech: war gehorsam vnd vngehorsam (trans., 43).

103. On spiritual poverty, see, e.g., chapters 10, 26, and 35 (83.22–25, 105.1–8, and 120.12–27).

104. The language of letting go or releasing, almost always in verb form, is found throughout the TD. Some major appearances are in chapters 19, 23, 27, 35, and 51.

105. The TD uses the words detaching and detachment, though more rarely than the related terms; see, e.g., chapter 8 (79.7–8): . . . sso muss sie [die sele] luter vnnd bloss seyn von allen bilden vnnd ab gescheiden von allen creaturen. . . .

106. A strong expression of the need to get rid of everything belonging to the self already comes in chapter 1 (72.24–26): Wan yn welcher creatur diss volkomen bekant sal werden, da muss creaturlicheit, geschafenheit, ichtheit, selbheit, vorloren werden vnd zu nichte. For similar formulas, see, e.g., 132.14–15 and 135.22–24.

107. TD 43 (137.94–97): . . . wan vnd wo man spricht von Adam vnd vngehorsam vnd von eynem alden menschen, icheit vnnd eigen willen vnd eigenwillikeit, selbwillikeit, ich, meyn, natur, falscheit, tufel, sunde, das ist alles glich vnd eyn. Diss ist alles wider got vnd an got (trans., 83).

108. TD 44 (138.17–18): . . . das alle die willen an gotis willen, das ist aller eygen wille, ist sunde, vnd was uss dem eigen wille geschiet (trans., 84).

109. TD 51 (147.131–34): Aber wer ym volgen sal, der muss alle lassen, wan yn ym was alles gelassen also gar, als ess yn creaturen gelassen wart ader gescheen magk. Auch wer ym volgen wil, der sal das creucze an sich nemen, vnd das creucze is anders nicht den Christus leben . . . (trans., 94). In this context the TD quotes two key Gospel texts about following Christ, Mark 1:20, and Matt. 10:38.

110. See TD 22 (100.30–37). This preparation is described in terms of desire, accepting guidance, and actually setting to work and practicing. Practicing what is not clear.

111. The role of passivity, or suffering God's action, is stressed in many texts; see, e.g., chapters 2, 5, and 23 (74.23–29, 76.20–29, and 101.1–14).

112. V. Leppin in his article "Mystische Frömmigkeit und sakramentale Heilsvermittlung," uses the TD as an example of how the interiorization of sacramental devotion in late medieval mysticism leads to an intensification and enhancement of the value of sacramental practice rather than its diminution.

113. TD 15 (89.19–24): Czu dem waren gehorsam was vnd ist der mensch geschaffen vnd ist den got schuldig. Vnde der gehorsam ist yn Adam vnder gegangen vnd gestorben vnnd ist yn Cristo auff gestanden vnd lebendig worden. . . . Ja die menscheit Cristi was vnd stunt also gar an sich selber vnd an all also ye kein creatur, vnd waz nicht anders dan eyn huss ader eyn wonung gotis (trans., 43).

114. TD 37 (121–22). This chapter notes that the lamentation and misery over sin that characterize the divinized person are based on the suffering that accompanied Christ throughout his life. This is followed by a curious comment that such a person must suffer this "secret suffering" (*hemelich leiden*) until death, and that if a person were to live until Judgment Day, it would still continue (122.21–30). This text, and an echoing reference in the following

chapter (TD 38: 123.6–10), is reminiscent of a similar obscure passage about suffering until the Last Judgment in Mechthild of Magdeburg's *Das fliessende Licht der Gotheit* (6.26)

115. TD 26 (109.88–90): . . . das wil vnd wircket vnd begert anders nicht den gut als gut vnd vmmb gut, vnd da ist anders keyn war vmmb (my trans.). The same point is made in the following chapter (111.8–14).

116. On Tauler's view of mystical dereliction, see chapter 6, pp. 286–89. For a broader study, see Bernard McGinn, "*Vere tu es Deus absconditus:* The Hidden God in Luther and Some Mystics," in *Silence and the Word: Negative Theology and Incarnation,* ed. Oliver Davies and Denys Turner (Cambridge: Cambridge University Press, 2002), 94–114.

117. TD 11 (85.34–36): Disse helle vnd diss hymmelrich seyn czwen gut, sicher wege dem menschen yn der czite, vnd wol ym, der sie recht vnd wol findet, wanne disse helle vorgehet, das hymmelrich bestet (trans., 41).

118. For example, TD 3 (74.20), 16 (93.72–75), 24 (102.10–103.14), and 31 (115.22). The most important discussion is found in chapter 16, which raises the question whether or not it is possible to become by grace what Christ is by nature. The author notes that people deny this because no one can be without sin (92.38–44), but he then goes on to argue that even though no one can be as obedient as Christ, "nu ist doch moglich eynem menschen, also nahe dar czu vnd bey czu kommen, das er gotlich vnd vergotet heisset vnnd ist" (93.71–73).

119. TD 32 (117.49–51): Sich, diss sal seyn vnd ist yn der warheit yn eyme gotlichen ader yn eyme waren, vorgotten menschen, dan er wer anders nicht gotlich ader vorgottet (my trans.).

120. TD 41 (130. 1–4): Man mochte fragen, welchs ader was ist eyn vorgotter ader eyn gotlich mensche. Die antwort: Der durchluchtet vnd durchglantzet ist mit dem ewigen ader gotlichen lichte vnd enbrant mit ewiger vnd gotlicher libe, der ist eyn gotlicher ader vorgotter mensch (my trans.).

121. TD 41 (131.40–46): Das ein mensch vil bekennet von got vnd was gotis eigen ist, vnd er wenet, er wisse vnd bekenne joch, was got ist, hat er nicht libe, sso wirt er nicht gotlich ader vorgott. Ist aber ware libe da mit, so muss sich der mensch an got halden vnd lassen alles, das nicht got ist ader got nicht czu gehoret. . . . Vnd disse liebe voreyniget den menschen mit got, das er nymmer mere do von gescheiden wirt (my trans.). Love as the force that unites us to God is also stressed in chap. 42 (134.65–74).

122. TD 24 (102.1–5): Wo vnd wanne got vnd mensch voreyniget wurden synt, also das man yn der warheit spricht vnd sine die warheit vorgehet, das eyns ist ware, volkommen got vnd ware, volkommen mensch vnd doch mensch got als gar entwichet, das got aldo selber ist der mensche . . . (trans., 52).

123. TD 24 (102.10–103.14): Vnd synt den got alda der selbe mensche ist, sso ist er auch besobelich, befintlich libes vnd leides vnd des gleich. . . . Also ist ess auch, do got vnd mensch eins ist vnd doch got der mensch ist (trans., 53). On the view of union in this and the following chapters 27–28, see Haas, "Die 'Theologia Deutsch,'" 395–96.

124. On the hand metaphor, see TD 10 and 53 (82.9–11, and 152.89–90).

125. For other appearances of the need for annihilation of created reality, especially the will, see 72.23–26, 90.5, 110.7–12, 144.29–30, and 151.42–51.

126. TD 27 (110.7–12): Nichts anders, den das man luterlichen vnd einfeldiclichen vnd gentzlichen yn der warheit eynfeldig sey mit einfeldigen, ewigen willen gotis ader joch czumal an willen sy vnd der geschaffen wille geflossen sey yn den ewigen willen vnd dar jnne vorsmelczet sey vnd czu nichte worden, also das der ewige wille allein do selbist welle thun vnd lasse (trans., 58).

127. TD 20 (97.11–12): Wanne die clymmet also hoch yn yrem eygen lichte vnd yn yr selber, das sie selber wenet, das sie das ewige, ware licht sey . . . (trans., 49).

128. On the devil sowing his seed in the proud rational soul, see chapters 25, 40, and 43 (103.1–104.12, 128.83–129.101, and 136.69–137.97).

129. TD 40 (127.44–50): . . . das ess also hoch stiget vnd klymmet, das ess wenet, ess sey

vber natur vnd ess sey natur ader creatur vnmuglich, also hoch czu kommen. Dar vmmb wenet ess, ess sey got, vnd do von nympt ess sich alles des an, das got czu gehoret, vnd besunder als got ist yn ewikeit vnd nicht als er mensch ist (trans., 73).

130. TD 40 (130.123–26): Aber da das falsch licht ist, do wirt man vnachtsam Cristus leben vnd aller togent, sunder was der natur beqwem vnd lustig ist, das wirt da gesucht vnnd gemeynet. Da von kumpt den falsch, vngeordent freyheit . . . (trans., 76).

131. For an introduction to Gerson as a spiritual writer, see Palémon Glorieux, "Gerson (Jean)," DS 6:314–31; and Brian Patrick McGuire, *Jean Gerson: Early Works* (New York: Paulist Press, 1998).

132. For an introduction to the spiritual and mystical writings of Denys the Carthusian (called *Dionysius exstaticus*), see Anselme Stoelen, "Denys le Chartreux," DS 3:430–49.

133. For an overview of Herp, see Etta Gullick and Optat de Veghel, "Herp (Henri de; Harphius)," DS 7:346–66.

134. For an overview, see Josef Sudbrack, "Johannes von Kastl," VL 4:652–58.

135. P. Josef Sudbrack, S.J., *Die geistliche Theologie des Johannes von Kastl: Studien zur Frömmigkeitsgeschichte des Spätmittelalters*, 2 vols. (Münster: Aschendorff, 1967).

136. On the manuscripts, see the list in Sudbrack, *Die geistliche Theologie*, 2:196–202. For an edition, see *Dell'Unione con Dio di Giovanni di Castel O.S.B.*, ed. Giacomo Huijben (Badia Praglia: Scritti Monastici N. 5, 1926).

137. McGinn, *Growth of Mysticism*, 353–62.

138. On Jacob of Paradise, see Dieter Mertens, "Jakob von Paradies (1381–1465) über die mystische Theologie," *Kartäusermystik und –Mystiker: Dritter internationaler Kongress über die Kartäusergeschichte und –Spiritualität*, Band 5 (Salzburg: Institut für Anglistik und Amerikanistik, 1982), 31–46.

139. For an introduction, see Dennis D. Martin, "Kempf, Nikolaus, von Strassburg," VL 4:1117–24. A full account of Nicholas's life and works may be found in Dennis D. Martin, *Fifteenth-Century Carthusian Reform: The World of Nicholas Kempf* (Leiden: Brill, 1992), especially chapter 5, on mysticism. An edition of Kempf's large treatise (574 pages) can be found in *Nikolaus Kempf: Tractatus de mystica theologia*, ed. Karl Jellouschek, O.S.B., with an introduction by Jeanne Barbet and Francis Ruello, 2 vols. (Salzburg: Institut für Anglistik und Amerikanistik, 1973).

Chapter 9

1. See, for example, the writings of Auguste Jundt in the late nineteenth century, such as his *Histoire du pantheisme populaire au moyen age et au sezième siècle* (Paris, 1875; reprint, Frankfurt: Minerva, 1964); *Les amis de Dieu au 14e siècle* (Paris: Sandoz and Fischbacher, 1879); and *Rulman Merswin et l'Ami de Dieu de l'Oberland: Un problème de psychologie religieuse* (Paris: Fischbacher, 1890). See also Karl Rieder, *Der Gottesfreund vom Oberland: Eine Erfindung des Strassburger Johanniterbruders Nikolaus von Löwen* (Innsbruck: Wagner, 1905).

2. The most complete recent account is that of Bernard Gorceix, *Amis de Dieu en Allemagne au siècle de Maître Eckhart* (Paris: Albin Michel, 1984). There is also an overview by Alois M. Haas, "Gottesfreunde," in *Geschichte der deutschen Literatur: Die deutsche Literatur im späten Mittelalter 1250–1370. Zweiter Teil*, ed. Ingeborg Glier (Munich: C. H. Beck, 1987), 299–303. For an older account, see A. Chiquot, "Amis de Dieu," DS 1:493–500. In English there are four fairly full, but older and in some cases outdated presentations: Anna Groh Seesholtz, *Friends of God: Practical Mystics of the Fourteenth Century* (New York: Columbia University Press, 1934); Rufus M. Jones, *The Flowering of Mysticism: The Friends of God in the Fourteenth Century* (New York: Macmillan, 1939); James M. Clark, *The Great German Mystics* (Oxford: Basil Blackwell, 1949), chapter 5; and Thomas S. Kepler, *Mystical Writings of Rulman Merswin* (Philadelphia: Westminster, 1960). Clark's presentation is generally negative, especially about Rulman

Merswin, whom he describes as a man of "mediocre ability" (p. 81) and as "a garrulous old windbag" (p. 87).

3. For helpful surveys with rich bibliographical references, see Erik Peterson, "Die Gottes-freundschaft: Beiträge zur Geschichte eines religiösen Terminus," *Zeitschrift für Kirchen-geschichte* 42 (1923): 161–202; and Alois M. Haas, "Gottesfreundschaft," in *Mystik im Kontext* (Munich: Wilhelm Fink, 2004), 195–202.

4. Brian Patrick McGuire, *Friendship and Community: The Monastic Experience 350–1250* (Kalamazoo: Cistercian Publications, 1988).

5. See Bernard McGinn, *The Growth of Mysticism*, volume 2 of *The Presence of God: A History of Western Christian Mysticism* (New York: Crossroad, 1994), 312–23. Friendship also plays a role in the mysticism of Bernard of Clairvaux.

6. Thomas Aquinas, STh IIaIIae, q.23, a.5, argues that *caritas . . . est quaedam amicitia hominis ad deum.* For a detailed study, see Richard Egenter, *Gottesfreundschaft: Die Lehre von der Gottesfreundschaft in der Scholastik und Mystik des 12. und 13. Jahrhunderts* (Augsburg: Benno Filser, 1928). A more recent and broader study can be found in Paul J. Wadell, *Friendship and the Moral Life* (Notre Dame: University of Notre Dame Press, 1989).

7. On David of Augsburg and his use of *amicus dei*, see Bernard McGinn, *The Flowering of Mysticism: Men and Women in the New Mysticism (1200–1350)*, vol. 3 of *The Presence of God: A History of Western Christian Mysticism* (New York: Crossroad, 1998), 114; for the more frequent uses by Mechthild, see McGinn, *Flowering of Mysticism*, 223 and 227.

8. For an introduction to fourteenth-century uses, see Richard Egenter, "Die Idee der Gottesfreundschaft im 14. Jahrhundert," in *Aus der Geisteswelt des Mittelalters: Festschrift Martin Grabmann* (Münster: Aschendorff, 1935), 1021–36.

9. RdU 15 (DW 5:241.5–8). The language of Friends of God is found also in BgT (DW 5:54.1–17) and the VeM (DW 5:109.20).

10. Pr. 27 (DW 2:52.8–11): Jâ, in der selben geburt, dâ der vater gebirt sînen eingebornen sun und im gibet die wurzel und alle sîne gotheit und alle sîne saelicheit und im selben niht enbeheltet, in der selben geburt sprichet er uns sîne vriunde (see also 46.7–47.1 in the same sermon).

11. Pr. 86 (DW 3:482.6–8, and 488.7). On Eckhart's use of the friend motif, see Gorceix, *Amis de Dieu*, 68–70.

12. On Pr. 86, see chapter 4, pp. 189–93. Georg Steer, "Die Stellung des 'Laien' im Schrifttum des Strassburger Gottesfreundes Rulman Merswin und der deutschen Domini-kanermystiker des 14. Jahrhunderts," in *Literatur und Laienbildung im Spätmittelalter und in der Reformationzeit: Symposion Wolfenbüttel 1981*, ed. Ludger Grenzmann and Karl Stackmann (Stuttgart: J. B. Metzler, 1984), 650–53, studies Eckhart's importance for the movement, stressing the role of Pr. 86.

13. For the appearances of *gotesvriunt* in the *Schwester Katrei*, see the edition in Franz-Josef Schweitzer, *Der Freiheitsbegriff der deutschen Mystik*, 323.28, 329.7, 340.23 and 32–33, 343.2, 357.28, 359.5–6, and especially 352.26 and 356.32–33. The only appearance of *die fründe gottes* is at 340.23.

14. The index in K. Bihlmeyer, *Heinrich Seuse: Deutsche Schriften*, 581, reveals that Suso uses *gotesfrúnd* once in the *Little Book of Wisdom*, six times in his letters, and twenty-one times in the *Life of the Servant* (twice in the form of *frúnd* without the qualifier).

15. *Leben* 22 (ed. 63:13–14): Daz zoegte got einest eim userwelten gotesfrúnd, und hiess Anna und was och sin gaischlichú tohter. For other references to distinct people under this title, see Bihlmeyer, 59.4, 64.14, 70.1, 142.5, 144.1, and 146.21.

16. The texts for this image are edited in Bihlmeyer, 48*: Diz nagende erbermklich bilde zeoget den strengen vndergang eticher vserwelter gotes fránden.

17. See Louise Gnädinger, *Johannes Tauler: Lebenswelt und mystische Lehre* (Munich: C. H. Beck, 1993), 34–43, and 96–103, for Tauler's exile in Basel (ca. 1338–43) and his contacts with the Friends of God both there and in his home cloister of Strassburg.

18. Tauler mentions the *gotzfründe* more than thirty times in his sermons (Gnädinger,

Johannes Tauler, 96). For a summary of his views, see Marie-Anne Vannier, "Tauler et les Amis de Dieu," in *700e Anniversaire de la naissance de Jean Tauler: Revue des sciences religieuses* 75 (2001): 456–64. See also Gorceix, *Amis de Dieu,* 72–78.

19. Dietmar Mieth, *Die Einheit von Vita activa und Vita contemplativa in den deutschen Predigten und Traktaten Meister Eckharts und bei Johannes Tauler* (Regensburg: Pustet, 1969). Teil III of this work argues that Tauler overcame the bifurcated model of action and contemplation in three ways: (1) by uniting inner and outer prayer; (2) by uniting inner and outer work; and (3) by uniting love of God and love of neighbor in a new way.

20. On Tauler's teaching on mystical union, see above chapter 6, pp. 280–95.

21. See Tauler's sermon for the Fourteenth Sunday after Trinity as found in Ferdinand Vetter, *Die Predigten Taulers,* where this is sermon 47. Hereafter Tauler's sermons will be referred to with V and page and line number. For this passage, see V 47 (213.4–10).

22. V 32 (120.5–7): . . . wanne wiltu fliss haben, so mahtu Got erkriegen und das edel luter guot in allen wisen und wesende do du inner bist. See the whole discussion found in 119.34–120.11.

23. See, for example, Tauler's defense of the role of prelates in V 2 (15.3–12).

24. V 10 (48.36–49.4): Hie scheidet sich die woren frúnt Gottes und die valschen: die valschen kerent alle ding uf sich selber und nement sich der goben an und tragent sú nút Gotte luterliche wider uf mit minne und mit dangberkeit in eime verloeickende sin selbes und gantz gon in Gotte luterliche. Wer dis allermeist hat, der ist der allergantzeste frúnt Gottes. . . .

25. V 49 (223.25–27): Die menschen solten einen gelebten Gotz frúnt úber hundert mile suochen die den rechten weg bekanten und si richte.

26. For other uses of the term *frúnt Gottes,* see V 8 (36.26), V 9 (41.28, 46.12), V 13 (62.37), V 16 (72.3), V 23 (91.12, 93.24), V 33 (130.33), V 36 (158.21), V 39 (157.32), V 41 (174.4), V 44 (193.21), V 52 (239.14), V 55 (253.30), V 71 (385.9), V 73 (395.6), V 76 (407.27, 412.23), V 77 (417.23), as well as six mentions in Sermon C LXXI (Helander ed., 351–61).

27. V 41 (176.12–17): Her nach so wirt der mensche also weselich und als gemein und tugentlich, guetlich und von minsamer wandelunge mit allen menschen gemein und gesellig, doch das man iemer enkeinen gebresten von ime enkan gesehen noch vinden. Und dise menschen sint allen menschen geloebig und barmherzig; si ensint nút strenge noch hertmuotig, denn vil gnedig. Und das enist nút ze glovbende das dise lúte iemer von Gotte múgen gescheiden werden. For similar descriptions under different names, see V 68 (376.18–27) and V 56 (264.23–265.32).

28. V 5 (24.3–5): Ach dis sint minnencliche menschen, sú tragent alle die welt und sint edele súlen der welte; der in disem rehte stunde, daz were ein selig wunnenclich ding.

29. On the notion of mystical saints as pillars, or poles (Arabic: *Qutb*), of the world, see Annemarie Schimmel, *Mystical Dimensions of Islam* (Chapel Hill: University of North Carolina Press, 1975), 57, 200–203, and 369.

30. In the Prologue to *Das fliessende Licht der Gotheit,* Mechthild of Magdeburg had spoken of the crisis of her time as involving "the pillars falling" (*wand wenne die súle vallent;* ed. Neumann Vol. I:4.4). Presumably, this refers to the New Testament understanding of apostles and their episcopal successors as pillars.

31. The *Offenbarungen (Revelations)* of Margaret, along with the correspondence of Henry and Margaret (only one letter of hers survives), were edited by Philipp Strauch, *Margaretha Ebner und Heinrich von Nördlingen: Ein Beitrag zur Geschichte der deutschen Mystik* (Freiburg-im-Breisgau: Herder, 1882; reprint 1966). The MHG text of the letters with an Italian translation and study has been reissued by Lucia Corsini, *Heinrich von Nördlingen e Margaretha Ebner: Le lettere (1332–1350)* (Pisa: Edizioni ETS, 2001). Margaret's *Revelations,* also important for references to the Friends of God, have been translated by Leonard Hinsley, O.P., *Margaret Ebner: Major Works* (New York: Paulist Press, 1993); see especially the "Introduction," 27–41. For an overview of Henry's life and writings, see Manfred Weitlauff, "Heinrich von Nördlingen," VL 3:845–52.

32. Henry mentions Rulman Merswin in Letter LI (ed., 263.81–82) and Letter LIII (ed., 268.31–33).

33. A reference to Suso in Letter XXXI of early 1339 (ed., 216.21–22) is positive, but a later reference in Letter LI of early 1348 (ed., 263.86–87) is more hesitant, perhaps reflecting the accusations of unchastity leveled against the Dominican.

34. Margaret Ebner, *Offenbarungen* (ed., 83–27–84.1): Item ich wart gebeten von dem warhaften friund gotez, den er mir ze grossem trost geben hatt allem minem leben, daz ich ime scribe, waz mir got gebe.

35. Letter XLV, written in 1346 or 1347 (ed., 249–50), mentions a number of Henry's pious friends, including knights and nobles.

36. Letter XLVII (ed., 255.67–72): . . . das min frau die Frickin ze Basel kumen ist mit grossem fröuden ires hertzen, und ir gefelt als wol die ler und die fründ gotz, und das sie mit kristenlicher gehorsame gehaben mag die haillgen sacrament, das sie willen hat ein weil ze beleiben bei gar haillger erber gaistlicher geselschaft, der vil in Basel ist. . . . On Eufemia Frickin, see Strauch, *Margaretha Ebner und Heinrich von Nördlingen*, 322–23; and Corsini, *Le lettere*, 315–16.

37. Letter XXXII of Lent, 1339 (ed., 176.69–73): es begert auch unszer lieber vatter der Tauler und ander gotzfrüind, das du uns in der gemein etwas schribest, was dir dein lieb Jhesus geb und sunderlichen von dem weszen der cristenhait und seiner fruind, die dar under vil lident. See also Letter LI (ed., 263.82–86).

38. See Letter LIII, written in 1349 (ed., 267–68), which tells of the apocalyptic fears of the Friends of God at the time of the Black Death.

39. See, for example, Letter XIII (ed., 189.50–54), Letter XXXIII (ed., 221.62–66), and Letter XLVIII (ed., 257.44–52).

40. On Mechthild and her *Flowing Light*, see McGinn, *Flowering of Mysticism*, 222–44, and the literature cited there.

41. Letter XLIII (ed., 246.117–247.141).

42. Letter XLVI (ed., 252.60–61): hier innen und des glich tunt vor uns usz die groszen gotzfrund des innern menschen geistlich himelfart. Eia! mein und dein got spricht in in. This letter (see 251.36–252.60), as well as Letter XLII (ed., 242.30–33) and Letter XLVIII (ed., 256–59), has quotations, sometimes extensive, from the *Flowing Light*.

43. Letter XXV (ed., 228.82–229.87).

44. On the three stages of Merswin's religious career, see Gorceix, *Amis de Dieu*, 90–98.

45. The MHG edition is by Philipp Strauch, *Merswins Vier anfangenden Jahre: Des Gottesfreundes Fünffmannenbuch (Die sogenannten Autographa)* (Halle: Max Niemeyer, 1927). There is an English version in Thomas S. Kepler, *Mystical Writings of Rulman Merswin*, 39–52, which is helpful, but not always accurate.

46. *Von den vier anfangenden Jahren* (ed., 4.31–5.8): . . . do beschach es, das ein gar geswindes gehes clores lieht kam vnd vmbe fing mich, vnd wart genvomen vnd wart gefvoret [den garten] obbe der erden swebbende ettewie digke den garten vmbe vnd vmbe; vnd was mir ovch in dieseme selben vmbe fürende, wie neiswas gar vsser mosen svose wort zvo mir sprechende were; abber was das lieht vnd das vmbe fvordes was vnd der svosen worte, das weis ich nút, got der weis es wol, wanne es veber alle mine sinneliche vir nvmft was. Abber do diese frelliche kvorze stvonde vs was vnd ich widder zvo mir selber golosen wart, do fant ich mich alleine in dem garten stonde. . . .

47. *Von den vier . . . Jahren* (ed., 22.2–8): do gab got einem menschen in obber landen zvo vir stonde, also das er abbe zvo mir kvomen solte. Nvo do der kam, do gap mir got, das ich mit dem von allen sachns wol redden mvothe; vnd der selbe mensche der war der welte gar alzvomole vnbekant; er wart abbe min heimellicher frúnt . . . (trans. Kepler, 49). The title *Gottesfreund vom Oberland* is generally thought to indicate a geographical origin from the Alpine region, but Alois Haas ("Gottesfreunde," 301) notes that the *Oberland* could just as well be heaven.

48. This may be a reference to to the *Book of the Two Fifteen-Year-Old Boys*, to be discussed below.

49. See especially Heinrich Denifle, "Der Gottesfruend im Oberlande und Nicolaus von Basel," *Historische und politische Blätter* 75 (1875): 17–38, 93–122, 245–66, and 340–54; "Taulers Bekehrung," *Historische und politische Blätter* 84 (1879): 797–815, 877–97; and his book, *Taulers Bekehrung: Kritisch untersucht* (Strassburg: K. J. Trübner, 1879).

50. For a survey of the historiography, see see Gorceix, *Amis de Dieu*, 104–13.

51. Georg Steer, "Die Stellung des 'Laien,'" 645–46.

52. For a list of such texts, see Steer, "Die Stellung des 'Laien,'" 644.

53. The Hospitalar house survived well into the fifteenth century, but Merswin's experiment in a mixed community did not. On the history of the Green Isle, see Gorceix, "De l'Ile Verte au Haut Pays," *Amis de Dieu*, 88–113.

54. This text is cited by Gorceix, *Amis de Dieu*, 94–95.

55. The lay and aristocratic character of the house has been emphasized by Gorceix, *Amis de Dieu*, 144–49, 152–54, and 258–59.

56. The Green Isle house, like the independent circles of Friends of God, was interested in mystical literature and compiled a library of such texts. The earliest surviving manuscript of Suso's *Exemplar* (Strassburg, UB, Ms. 2929) was written for the community.

57. These texts have been studied, edited, and argued about for a century and a half. The most recent survey is by Georg Steer, "Merswin, Rulman," VL 6:420–42. See also the lists and discussion in Gorceix, *Amis de Dieu*, 287–91, and Haas, "Gottesfreunde," 300–301. In English, there are useful, if somewhat dated, discussions in Jones, *Flowering of Mysticism*, chapters 6–7; and Seesholtz, *The Friends of God*, chapters 6–7.

58. The letters were edited by Carl Schmidt, *Nikolaus von Basel: Leben und ausgewählte Schriften* (Vienna: W. Braumüller, 1866), 278–343. The letters are important for the life of the fictional Friend of God. There is a modern German version of six of the letters in Wilhelm Oehl, *Deutsche Mystikerbriefe*, 397–424.

59. Not all of these writings will be discussed here, but the following list will give a sense of this mass of materials.

I. Works ascribed to Merswin: (1) *Book of the First Four Years of His Beginning Life (Büchlein von den Vier Jahren seines anfangenden Lebens)*; (2) *Banner Book (Bannerbüchlein)*; (3) *Book of the Nine Rocks (Neunfelsenbuch)*; (4) *Book of the Three Breakthroughs (Buoch von den dreien durchbrüchen)*; (5) *Seven Works of Mercy (Sieben Werke der Barmherzigkeit)*; and (7) extracts from books 1 and 2 of Ruusbroec's *Spiritual Espousals.*

II. Works ascribed to the Friend of God: (1) *Book of the Two Men (Zweimannenbuch)*; (2) *Book of the Five Men (Fünfmannenbuch)*; (3) *Book of the Two Fifteen-Year-Old Boys (Buch von den fünfzehnjährigen Knaben)*; (4) *Book of the Imprisoned Knight (Buoch von dem gevangen ritter)*; (5) *About the Two Recluses Ursula and Adelheid (Von den beiden Klausnerinnen Ursula und Adelheid)*; (6) *About Two Bavarian Nuns, Margaret and Katherine (Von zwei bayerischen Klosterfrauen, Margarete und Katharina)*; (7) *Book of the Spiritual Stairway (Buch von der geistlichen Stiege)*; (8) *Book of the Spiritual Ladder (Buch von der geistlichen Leiter)*; (9) *Book of the Spark in the Soul (Buch von dem fünkelin in der selen)*; (10) *Lesson to a Young Brother of the Order (Eine letze an einen jungen Ordensbruder)*; (11) *Book of the Self-Willed Worldly Wise (Buoch von eime eigentwilligen weltwisen)*; (12) *Book of a Revelation (Buoch von einre offenbarunge)*; (13) *History of a Young Child of the World (Materie von eime jungen weltlichen manne)*; (14) *The Table (Die tovele)*; (15) *Dialogue of a Brother with a Young Priest named Walter (Dialog eines Klosterbruders mit einem jungen Priester namens Walther)*; (16) *Letters (Briefe)*; and (17) *Masterbook (Meisterbuch).*

60. Steer, "Merswin, Rulman," 438.

61. Nicholas Watson, *Richard Rolle and the Invention of Authority* (Cambridge: Cambridge University Press, 1991).

62. Haas, "Gottesfreunde," 300: . . . und damit die Mystik zur Mystifikation zu werden drohte."

63. The *Buch von den fünfzehnjährigen Knaben* was edited by Carl Schmidt, *Nikolaus von*

Basel: Leben und ausgewählte Schriften, 79–101. There is a summary in Jones, *Flowering of Mysticism*, 124–27.

64. The *Fünfmannenbuch* was edited by Strauch in 1927 in the same volume that contains Merswin's *Vier anfangende Jahre* discussed above.

65. This version has been edited by Carl Schmidt, who mistakenly ascribed it to Nicholas of Basel; see *Nikolaus von Basel: Bericht von der Bekehrung Taulers* (Strassburg, 1875; reprint, Frankfurt: Minerva, 1981). This description cited can be found on p. 61.

66. The version of the text naming Tauler was later reprinted as an introduction to editions of Tauler's sermons in 1521 and 1522. This version, which differs in chapter numbering and other particulars from the text edited by Schmidt, was translated into English by Susanna Winkworth, *The History and Life of the Reverend Doctor John Tauler of Strasbourg; with Twenty-Five of His Sermons* (London: H. R. Allenson, 1905).

67. The connections between Tauler's sermons and the *Meisterbuch* have been studied by Gnädinger, *Johannes Tauler*, 91–96. These include: (1) the superiority of a *lebmeister* over a *lesmeister*, (2) the notion that true conversion takes place between the ages of forty and fifty; (3) devotion to the five wounds of Christ; and (4) emphasis on a holy layman. To these can be added the use of the term "pharisee" to describe unconverted religious.

68. Michel de Certeau, *The Mystic Fable* (Chicago: University of Chicago Press, 1992), 234–37.

69. As Gorceix (*Amis de Dieu*, 170–72) notes, the contrast between the *lebmeister* and *lesmeister*, present in Tauler, is heightened in the Green Isle dossier.

70. *Meisterbuch*, chap. 5 (ed., 26–27): Nuo dar herre der meister, alse es nuo umb úch stot so ist nuo nút me zuo tuonde das ich in lerender wise me zuo úch redende bin; ich sol nuo groesliche begeren von úch geleret zuo werdende, und ich wil ouch nuo hie bliben untze an die zit das ich uwerre bredigen vil gehoere. . . .

71. See Gorceix, *Amis de Dieu*, 176–81, for other texts from the Green Isles that express opposition to Eckhartian-style speculation.

72. A favorite phrase is *zuo grunde gotte in gar grosser demuetikeit* (e.g., chap. 2, p. 11, and chap. 4, p. 25).

73. The sermon is found in chap. 6 (ed., 29–33). The same text was also the basis for Ruusbroec's *Spiritual Espousals*, a text known in Germany.

74. *Meisterbuch*, chap. 6 (ed., 32): Wol uf mir froeiden, es ist zit men sol zuo kirchen gon; und nimet den brútegoum und die brut und fueret sú zuo kirchen, vertruwet sú do suo sammene; und verbindet sú do in alse gar grosser mehelicher minne zuo sammene, . . . das sú weder in zit und in ewikeit niemer me gescheiden werdent. . . . schenket die brut alse gar vuol úberflússiger grosser minnen, also das die brut wurt úberfliessende von minnen und gar und gantz alzuomole in den brúteguom zerflússet, also das die brut alse gar von ir selber kummet und alse gar von minnen trunken wurt, und das sú ir selbes vergisset und aller creaturen beide in zit und in ewikeit mit ir.

75. The edition used is that of Philipp Strauch, *Merswins Neun-Felsen-Buch (Das sogenannte Autograph)* (Halle: Max Niemeyer, 1929). There is an English translation in Kepler, *Mystical Writings of Rulman Merswin*, 55–143. On the *Neunfelsenbuch*, see Steer, "Merswin," 427–29; and Gorceix, *Amis de Dieu*, 204–11. For English summaries, see Seesholtz, *Friends of God*, 151–54; and Jones, *Flowering of Mysticism*, 184–89. It is quite possible that the text as we have it owes something to the editorial work of Nicholas of Louvain.

76. The four discourses are outlined in the prologue (ed., 1.26–2.8). The structure and presentation of the text have led to diverse evaluations. Jones (*Flowering of Mysticism*, 188–89) says it "is one of the most revealing documents that has come to us from 'the Friends of God'"; but Clark (*Great German Mystics*, 79–80) says of the book, "As an allegory it is feeble; as literature it is puerile."

77. For an insightful analysis of the allegorical character of the work, emphasizing how the *Neunfelsenbuch* functions as a parable that reinforces the sense of election in its intended community audience and hides its meaning from the general mass of sinners, see S. L. Clark and

Julian N. Wasserman, "The Soul as Salmon: Merswin's *Neunfelsenbuch* and the Idea of Parable," *Colloquia Germanica* 13 (1980): 47–56. There is also a discussion of Merswin's use of allegorical images in Gorceix, *Amis de Dieu*, 192–211. The *Neunfelsenbuch* contains several treatments of the need for teaching by way of *gelichnisse* (see 16.5–27, 132.10–16, and 166.8–27).

78. In enhancing the authority of the work traditional arguments and topoi abound: (1) God can infuse wisdom on the unschooled (6.17–23); (2) the book's truth is guaranteed by God and written on the heart of Christendom (7.23–33; compare with Mechthild of Magdeburg); and (3) God can write through *sinnen fründen* just as well today as a thousand years ago (7.1–10).

79. *Neunfelsenbuch* (62.4–8): ich wil dir sagen, got der het ein deil heiden und ein deil gudden in diesen citen fil lieber denne fil menschen die cristonnammen hant und doch widder alle cristenliche ordenunge lebbent (trans. Kepler, 90).

80. Clark and Wasserman, "The Soul as Salmon," 53. See also Susan L. Clark and Julian S. Wasserman, "*Purity* and *Das Neunfelsenbuch:* The Presentation of God's Judgment in Two Fourteenth-Century Works," *Arcadia* 18 (1983): 179–84.

81. *Neunfelsenbuch* (93.16–17): . . . das si iren eigin willen wellent ufgebben und wellent eime gottesfründe, demme der weg wol bekant ist, gehorsam sin. . . . The importance of the *gottesfründe*, as might be expected, is found throughout the text. See, e.g., 8.1–10, 48.32, 69.2, 94.31–95.12, 112.10–11, 136.6–7, 140.18, 143.18, 166.26, and especially 160.26–162.34 where the term is used eleven times.

82. *Neunfelsenbuch* (107.20–23): . . . wer uffe diesen fünften fels kuomet und ovch stette duffe blibet, der ist erst kuomen uffe den rehten annefanc der rehten strosen die do ufget zuo demme ursprunge.

83. *Neunfelsenbuch* (112.9–13): . . . daz sint die menschen die sich gotte hant gelosen und hant [sich] den gottes fründen iren eigen willen ufgeben an gottes stat und hant einen ganzen festen willen daz si gehorsam und stette wellent bliben unze in iren tot.

84. *Neunfelsenbuch* (120.36–121.3): . . . diesen menschen wrt zuo etthelichen cithen ein fil wnder kleinnes blickelin usser demme ursprunge und das selbe kuonent si zuo keinnen bilden bringen noch mit keinnen worthen usgesprochen.

85. *Neunfelsenbuch* (127.31–35): . . . wie lúccel dirre menschen sint, so lot doch got die cristenheit uffe diesen menschen geston; du solt ovch wissen, werent diese lúcceln menschen usser der cit, das got die cristenheit an stette liese undergon . . . (trans. Kepler, 122).

86. *Neunfelsenbuch* (141.8–12): In diesem selben worthen do dirre mensche sinnen willen also gar zuo gruonde gotte ufgap, in demme selben ovgenbligke wart diesen menschen die phorthe des ursprunges ufgethon, und wart dirre mensche gelosen in den ursprunc sehhen.

87. *Neunfelsenbuch* (156.32–157.7): Die entwrte sprach: das wil ich dir sagen, du solt wissen das diese menschen iren namen fúrloren hant und sint nammelos worden und sint got worden. . . . [W]elre mensche hie in der cit derzuo kuomet das er umb got úrwirbet das er wrt gelosen in den ursprunc sehhen, der mensche wrt got von gnoden das got ist von nattuoren. For another mention of union, see 153.4–5.

88. The *Bannerbüchlein* was edited by A. Jundt, *Les Amis de Dieu*, 393–402; an excerpt appears in Jundt's *Panthéisme populaire*, 211–14. For studies, see Jones, *Flowering of Mysticism*, 122–24; Gorceix, *Amis de Dieu*, 126–28; and Steer, "Merswin," 426–27.

89. *Panthéisme populaire*, 213: Ich weis in disen ziten nút sichers, wenne alleine zuo fliehende zuo dem gekrútzigeten Cristo: wer nuo mit gantzen trúwen flúhet zuo Cristo, der sol ouch ein gantz getrúwen zuo ime han, das er in nút lasse.

90. The *Buch von dem fünkelin in der selen* was edited by Philipp Strauch in *Sieben bisher unveröffentlichte Traktate und Lektionen* (Halle: Max Niemeyer, 1927), 21–35. For studies, see Gorceix, *Amis de Dieu*, 200–204; Seesholtz, *Friends of God*, 143–45; and Jones, *Flowering of Mysticism*, 131–32.

91. The *Von den drien durchbrúchen* was edited by Auguste Jundt, *Panthéisme populaire*, 215–30. The part of the work that uses the *Von den drin fragen* is found on 215–20 and 227–30.

On the pseudo-Eckhartian work, see Kurt Ruh, "'Von den drîn fragen'" VL 2:234–35. For treatments of the *Book of the Three Breakthroughs*, see Gorceix, *Amis de Dieu*, 176–78; and Seesholtz, *Friends of God*, 163–65.

92. *Von den drien durchbrúchen* (ed., 215): Die erste froge ist: weles der behendeste durchbruch si, den der mensche getun mag, der do gerne zuo dem hoehesten vollekommenesteme lebende keme. Die ander froge ist: weles der sicherste grot si, do der mensche in der zit uffe geston moege noch diseme ersten durchbruche. Die drite froge ist: weles die neheste vereinigunge si, alse sich der mensche in zit mit gotte vereinigen moege.

93. *Von den drien durchbrúchen* (ed., 217): Eine gewore gelossene gelossenheit in dem geiste und in der naturen, . . . also das sich der mensche in allen sinen natúlichen kreften kunde gotte alzuomole zu grunde gelossen. . . . Eine gelossenheit obe aller gelossenheit ist gelossen in in gelossenheit; der mensche solte in solicher gelossenheit und einikeit mit gotte ston also das er ussewendig sin selbes nút befúnde das in verdrússe. . . .

94. *Von den drien durchbrúchen* (ed., 218): Hie von sprach der liebe sancte Paulus: Wer an gotte haftet, der wurt ein geist mit gotte, und in diesem selben entwerdende ist ouch der geist entworden, und ist ein einigesten eine in dem einen worden.

95. *Von den drien durchbrúchen* (ed., 221): Nuo dar, lieber meister Eckhart, ir sagent offentliche an úwerer bredigen von gar grossen vernúnftigen úberschwenckigen dingen, das gar wenig iemand verstot oder nutze ist, und gar ouch wenig frúhte bringet.

96. *Von den dreien durchbrúchen* (ed., 230): Nuo ist eine verborgene aptgrunde in der selen; die aptgrunde die ruffet one underlas und mit einre wilden aptgrúntlichen unbegriffenlicher stimme dem goettlichen aptgrunde alles noch. . . . Aber das hoeheste und das edelste und das nutzeste das ir hie in der zit werden mag, das ist das sú alle wortalle begirde alle gedencke und ouch alle goettliche minne in die sele ziehe, das sú sich alzuomole versencke und ertrencke in den hohen aptgrundelosen grunde der gotheit.

97. For other treatises dealing with stages of ascent, see, e. g., the *Buch von der geistlichen Stiege*, and the *Buch von der geistlichen Leiter*. In the *Buch von den zwei Mannen*, Merswin's fictional account of a conversation between an older and unnamed Friend of God and the young Friend of God from the Land Above, there is a description of seven stages by which one progresses to the status of true Friend of God. See Friedrich Lauchert, *Des Gottesfreundes im Oberland [=Rulman Merswin's] Buch von den zwei Mannen* (Bonn: Hanstein, 1896), 55.14–60.6.

98. *Buch von den fúnkelin* (ed. Strauch, 21.20–22.4): . . . ich wil dir sagen, liber sun, vor fúnftzig joren, do ich noch ein knabe was und under der welte wonende was, in den selben ziten do was ein sprichwort also das die lúte sprechende worent: die katze die ehsse gerne die vische, aber sú wil nút dar noch in das wasser watten.

99. The stages are summarized by Jones, *Flowering of Mysticism*, 131–32; and Gorceix, *Amis de Dieu*, 201–202.

100. *Buch von dem fúnkelin* (ed., 30.31–37): . . . er kumme zuo eime solichen menschen mit voller maht in einer fúrigen flammenden hitzigen foul der minnen und umbeschinet und umbevohet einen alsolichen menschen und zúhet in an sich und in sich und verbirget in in das verwunderte hertze unsers herren Jhesu Christi.

101. On Otto of Passau, see André Schnyder, "Otto von Passua OFM" VL 7:229–34; and Gorceix, *Amis de Dieu*, 108–9.

102. Steer ("Die Stellung," 649) speaks of Merswin as "nur ein unorigineller Rezipient der deutschen Mystik."

Chapter 10

1. The literature on Cusa includes a number of helpful treatments of the role mysticism plays in his thought. Note especially Jasper Hopkins, *Nicholas of Cusa's Dialectical Mysticism: Text, Translation, and Interpretive Study of "De Visione Dei"* (Minneapolis: Arthur J. Banning

Press, 1985); Hans Gerhard Senger, "Mystik als Theorie bei Nikolaus von Kues," in *Gnosis und Mystik in der Geschichte der Philosophie*, ed. Peter Koslowski (Munich: Artemis, 1988), 111–34; Alois Maria Haas, *DEUM MISTICE VIDERE . . . IN CALIGINE COINCIDENCIE: Zum Verhältnis Nikolaus' von Kues zur Mystik*, Vorträge der Aeneas-Sylvius-Stiftung an der Universität Basel 24 (Basel and Frankfurt: Helbing & Lichtenhahn, 1989); Donald F. Duclow, "Mystical Theology and Intellect in Nicholas of Cusa," *American Catholic Philosophical Quarterly* 64 (1990): 111–29; Werner Beierwaltes, "Mystische Elemente im Denken des Cusanus," *Deutsche Mystik im abendländische Zusammenhang: Neu erschlossene Texte, neue methodische Ansätze, neue theoretische Konzepte*, ed. Walter Haug and Wolfram Schneider-Lastin (Tübingen: Niemeyer, 2000), 425–48; and William J. Hoye, *Die mystische Theologie des Nicolaus Cusanus* (Freiburg: Herder, 2004).

2. For a brief life of Cusa, see Donald F. Duclow, "Life and Works," in *Introducing Nicholas of Cusa: A Guide to a Renaissance Man*, ed. Christopher M. Bellitto, Thomas M. Izbicki, and Gerald Christianson (New York: Paulist Press, 2004), 25–56. A classic older account is Edmond Vansteenberghe, *Le Cardinal Nicolaus de Cues (1401–1464): L'action—la pensée* (Paris: Champion, 1920; reprint 1974).

3. Nicholas of Cusa's extensive writings will be cited according to the critical edition of the Heidelberg Academy, *Nicolai de Cusa Opera omnia iussu et auctoritate Academiae Litterarum Heidelbergensis* (Hamburg: Felix Meiner, 1932-). The standard abbreviation for this collection is h. Citations will note the title of the work with book (where needed), chapter, and section number, followed by parentheses including volume number, page, and where necessary line numbers. The *De concordantia catholica* is found in h. XIV. Many translations of Cusa's works are to be found in English. A particularly useful collection for Cusa's mysticism is *Nicholas of Cusa: Selected Spiritual Writings*, translated and introduced by H. Lawrence Bond (New York: Paulist Press, 1997). All translations are my own unless otherwise noted.

4. On Cusa as reformer, see Brian A. Pavlec, "Chap. 3. Reform," in *Nicholas of Cusa: A Guide to a Renaissance Man*, 59–112.

5. DDI, Epistola auctoris n.263 (h. I:163.6–11): Accipe nunc, pater metuende, quae iam dudum attingere variis doctrinarum viis concupivi, sed prius non potui, quousque in mari me ex Graecia redeunte, credo superno dono a patre luminum a quo omne datum optimum, ad hoc ductus sum, ut incomprehensibilia incomprehensibiliter amplecterer in docta ignorantia per transcensum veritatum incorruptibilium humaniter scibilium.

6. Marjorie O'Rourke Boyle, "Cusanus at Sea: The Topicality of Illuminative Discourse," *Journal of Religion* 71 (1991): 180–201.

7. *De coniecturis* 2.14.143 (h. III:143.7–144.15): Homo enim deus est, sed non absolute, quoniam homo; humanus est igitur deus. Homo etiam mundus est, sed non contracte omnia, quoniam homo. Est igitur homo microcosmos aut humanus quidem mundus. . . . Intra enim humanitatis potentiam omnia suo existunt modo.

8. Although Cusa wrote no treatises between late 1453 and 1458, 167 of his sermons come from this five-year period, particularly christological homilies. See Walter Euler, "Proclamation of Christ in Selected Sermons from Cusanus's Brixen Period," in *Nicholas of Cusa and His Age: Intellect and Spirituality*, ed. Thomas M. Izbicki and Christopher M. Bellitto (Leiden: Brill, 2002), 89–103.

9. Cited from *Memoirs of a Renaissance Pope: The Commentaries of Pius II. An Abridgment*, trans. Florence A. Gragg; ed. Leona C. Gabel (New York: Putnam, 1959), 228.

10. On these two works, see F. Edward Cranz, "The *De aequalitate* and *De principio* of Nicholas of Cusa," collected in his volume of studies, *Nicholas of Cusa and the Renaissance*, ed. Thomas M. Izbicki and Gerald Christianson (Aldershot: Ashgate-Variorum, 2000), 61–70. Some 293 of Cusa's sermons survive and they are an important resource for his mystical theology. As of the time of this writing, 167 sermons have appeared in h. XVI–XIX. Cusa preached for the most part in German, but his surviving sermons are the Latin notes and outlines he used, with the exception of Sermon XXIV, a German sermon on the Our Father. For introductions, see Lawrence F. Hundersmarck, "Preaching," in *Nicholas of Cusa: A Guide to a*

Renaissance Man, 232–69; and Walter Euler, "Die Predigten des Nikolaus von Kues," *Trierer theologische Zeitschrift* 110 (2001): 280–93.

11. For an introduction to these treatises, see F. Edward Cranz, "The Late Works on Nicholas of Cusa," in *Nicholas of Cusa and the Renaissance*, 43–60. There is a considerable literature on these works that cannot be discussed here. The treatises certainly develop aspects of Cusa's mysticism in important ways, though not, I believe, beyond the main lines laid down in the DVD.

12. On the role of the *De li non aliud* in Cusa's mystical thought, see Hoye, "Kapitel III: Das Nichtandere," in *Die mystische Theologie Nicolaus von Kues*, 77–90.

13. On the mysticism of the *De apice theoriae*, see Hoye, "Kapitel IV: Der Gipfel der Betrachtung," in *Die mystische Theologie des Nicolaus Cusanus*, 91–123; and H. Lawrence Bond, "Introduction," in *Nicholas of Cusa: Selected Spiritual Writings*, 56–70. Bond argues that this work constitutes a shift in Cusa's thought toward a more positive name of God and more direct form of vision centered on the name *posse ipsum* ("can itself," or "the possible itself"). Hoye (*Die mystische Theologie*, 148–52) argues, correctly I believe, that no divine name is ever final for Cusa.

14. Cusa possessed and studied Eckhart's Latin writings. There is a considerable literature on the influence of the German Dominican on the Renaissance cardinal. Two classic treatments are Herbert Wackerzapp, *Der Einfluss Meister Eckharts auf die ersten philosophischen Schriften des Nikolaus von Kues (1440–1450)* (Münster: Aschendorff, 1962); and Rudolf Haubst, "Nikolaus von Kues als Interpret und Verteidiger Meister Eckhart," in *Freiheit und Gelassenheit: Meister Eckhart heute*, ed. Udo Kern (Grünwald: Kaiser, 1980), 75–96. For some treatments in English, see Donald F. Duclow, "Nicholas of Cusa in the Margins of Meister Eckhart: Codex Cusanus 21," *Nicholas of Cusa in Search of God and Wisdom*, ed. Gerald Christianson and Thomas M. Izbicki (Leiden: Brill, 1991), 57–69; and Elizabeth Brient, "Meister Eckhart and Nicholas of Cusa on the 'Where' of God," in *Nicholas of Cusa and His Age*, 127–50.

15. Cusa's role in relation to modern thought has been the subject of noted contributions. In 1927 Ernst Cassirer hailed Cusa as "the first modern thinker" in his *Individuum und Kosmos in der Philosophie der Renaissance* (English translation, *The Individual and the Cosmos in Renaissance Philosophy* [New York: Harper and Row, 1963]). In 1953 Alexandre Koyré gave Cusa an important role in the development of the modern view of the universe and man's role in it in his book *From the Closed World to the Infinite Universe*. Hans Blumenberg's *The Legitimacy of the Modern Age* (Cambridge, Mass.: MIT Press, 1983; German original, 1966), Part 4, also stresses the significance of Cusa for the origins of modernity, despite his argument that Cusa attempted to save the Middle Ages. For an extended critique of Blumenberg's view, see Jasper Hopkins, *Nicholas of Cusa's Dialectical Mysticism*, 50–93. Louis Dupré (*Passage to Modernity: An Essay in the Hermeneutics of Nature and Culture* [New Haven: Yale University Press, 1993]), has argued that Cusa is a crucial figure at the transition to the first stage of modernity— "probably the last thinker to unite the theocentric and anthropocentric forces that had begun to pull the medieval synthesis apart" (p. 186).

16. A prominent proponent of the view that Cusa is essentially a philosopher is Kurt Flasch, *Nikolaus von Kues—Geschichte einer Entwicklung: Vorlesungen zur Einführung in seine Philosophie* (Frankfurt am Main: Klostermann, 1998). See the critique of Flasch in Hoye, *Die mystische Theologie des Nicolaus Cusanus*, 58–65, 74–78, 82–84, 93–95, 152, and 162–65.

17. *De filiatione* 5.83 (h. IV:59–60): . . . unum est, quod omnes theologizantes aut philosophantes in varietate modorum exprimere conantur. . . . Ita quidem omnes possibiles dicendi modi sub ipsa sunt theologia id ipsum ineffabile qualitercumque exprimere conantes.

18. The relation between reason and faith and the related issue of the respective roles of philosophy and theology in Cusa have been the subject of considerable literature. On the former question, see Jasper Hopkins, *Glaube und Vernunft im Denken des Nikolaus von Kues: Prolegomena zu einem Umriss seiner Auffassung*, Trierer Cusanus Lecture 3 (Trier: Cusanus-Institut, 1996); on the latter, see Werner Beierwaltes, "Das Verhältnis von Philosophie und Theologie

bei Nicolaus Cusanus," *Nikolaus von Kues 1401–2001,* Mitteilungen und Forschungsbeiträge der Cusanus-Gesellschaft [hereafter MFCG] 28 (Trier: Paulinus, 2003), 65–102. Other treatments of these questions include: Rudolf Haubst, "Die leitende Gedanken und Motive der cusanischen Theologie," *Das Cusanus-Jubiläum,* ed. Rudolf Haubst (MFCG 4; Mainz: Matthias-Grünewald, 1964), 257–77; Louis Dupré, "Nature and Grace in Cusa's Mystical Philosophy," *American Catholic Philosophical Quarterly* 64 (1990): 153–70; and Klaus Kremer, *Nicholas of Cusa (1401–1464)* (Trier: Paulinus, 2002), 45–51. A recent major contribution to the study of the relation of philosophy and theology in Cusa is Martin Thurner, *Gott als das offenbare Geheimnis nach Nikolaus von Kues* (Berlin: Akademie Verlag, 2001).

19. *De venatione sapientiae* 8.22 (h. XII:23.12–16): Sed divini nostri theologi revelatione superna didicerunt primam causam, cum omnium assertione sit tricausalis, scilicet efficiens, formalis et finalis, quae per Platonem unum et bonum, per Aristotelem intellectus et ens entium nominatur, esse sic unam quod trina et ita trinam quod una. For more on the partial knowledge of the Trinity among pagan thinkers, see, e.g., *De beryllo* 33–42 (h.XI:36–49).

20. *De venatione sapientiae* 13.38 (h. XII:37.1–2): Patet quomodo philosophi, qui hunc campum non intraverunt, de delectabilissimis venationibus non degustarunt.

21. See, e.g., *De venatione sapientiae* 13.38, 14.41, 21.62–63, 22.67, and 26.73.

22. See Hoye, *Die mystische Theologie des Nicolaus Cusanus,* "Der Vorrang der Theologie vor der Philosophie" (pp. 152–65).

23. Sermo CCXXVI, n. 19 (h. XIX:149): Sunt deinde ut reginae honoratae adhuc in contractiori numero tamquam perfectae in studio philosophiae. Sed una est columba, quae est ut vera theologia.

24. There is a good study of Cusa's exegesis in Klaus Reinhardt, "Nikolaus von Kues in der Geschichte der mittelalterlichen Bibelexegese," MFCG 27 (Trier: Paulinus, 2001), 31–63.

25. William J. Hoye has argued for a nominalistic reading of Cusa, even to the extent of declaring his stance as one of "fideistic positivism." See "The Meaning of Neoplatonism in the Thought of Nicholas of Cusa," *Downside Review* 104 (1986): 10–18; and more mutedly in *Die mystische Theologie des Nicolaus Cusanus,* 141–43, 165–69, 182–83.

26. DDI 3.11.245 (h. I:151.26–27, and 152.1–5): Maiores nostri omnes concordantur asserunt fidem initium esse intellectus. . . . Omnem enim ascendere volentem ad doctrinam credere necesse est his, sine quibus ascendere nequit. Ait enim Ysaias: "Nisi credideritis, non intelligetis." Fides igitur est in se complicans omne intelligibile. Intellectus autem est fidei explicatio. Dirigitur igitur intellectus per fidem, et fides per intellectum extenditur. There are many other passages in which Cusa illustrates how faith seeks understanding; e.g., *De genesi* 175 (h. IV:124).

27. I adopt the term "self-realization" from Beierwaltes, "Das Verhältnis von Philosophie und Theologie," 70, who describes Cusa's position as ". . . eine Einsicht suchende *Selbstvergewisserung des Glaubens,* in der dieser sich seiner reflexiven Voraussetzungen und Entfaltungsmomente bewusst wird."

28. The term *docta ignorantia,* of course, did not originate with Cusa, though it has become primarily associated with him. Augustine appears to have been the first to use it (see, e.g., Ep. 130.15.28 [PL 33:595]), but it was also employed by other authors known to Cusa (e.g., Bonaventure, *Breviloquium* V.6 [*S. Bonaventurae Opera Omnia* V:260a]).

29. Like many medieval thinkers, Cusa distinguished between *ratio,* or discursive thinking, and the higher form of knowing he called *intellectus,* a direct and intuitive grasp of truth. For example, in DVD he uses the three forms of seeing (*visio sensibilis/visio rationalis/visio intellectualis*) as an essential theme—e.g., Praef. 1; 23.97–100, and 24.109–12. However, I agree with Jasper Hopkins that in terms of the relation of faith and human knowing—"Die Unterscheidung zwischen Verstand und Vernunft spielt bei dem Problem des Glaubens keine Rolle" ("Glaube und Vernunft," 26).

30. In DC 1.4.15 (h. III:20) Cusa distinguishes between four levels of existence: All things are in God as *veritas;* in the intellect truly (*vere*); in the soul as a likeness to the truth (*verisimiliter*); and in the body as having lost the likeness with the divine. In this context I can-

not enter into the many investigations of Cusa's epistemology. Among major treatments, see, e.g., *Nikolaus von Kues in der Geschichte des Erkenntnisproblems*, ed. Rudolf Haubst, MFCG 11 (Mainz: Matthias-Grünewald, 1975); and Theo Van Velthoven, *Gottesschau und menschliche Kreativität: Studien zur Erkenntnislehre des Nikolaus von Kues* (Leiden: Brill, 1977).

31. This is clear, for example, from *De venatione sapientiae* 12.31 (h. XII:31.11–13): Hinc, sicut 'quia est' dei est causa scientiae omnium, quia sunt, ita, quia deus quid sit, uti scibilis est, ignoratur, quiditas etiam omnium, uti scibilis est, ignoratur.

32. The theme is found throughout his writings. A forceful summary can be found in Sermo XXI, nn.1–2 (h. XVI:318–19).

33. The importance of this treatise for Cusa's Christology has been emphasized by Harald Schwaetzer, *Aequalitas: Erkenntnistheoretische und soziale Implikationen eines christologischen Begriffs Nikolaus von Kues. Eine Studie zu seiner Schrift* De aequalitate (Hildesheim/Zurich/New York: Georg Olms, 2000).

34. *De aequalitate* 22 (h. X:29.13–30.15): Verbum igitur illud est, sine quo nec pater nec filius nec spiritus sanctus nec angeli nec animae nec omnes intellectuales naturae quicquam intelligere possunt. The theme is present in many other texts; e.g., *De possest* 75 (h. XI.2:87).

35. For a clear statement of the christological center in Cusa, see H. Lawrence Bond, "Nicholas of Cusa and the Reconstruction of Theology: The Centrality of Christology and the Coincidence of Opposites," in *Contemporary Reflections on the Medieval Christian Tradition: Essays in Honor of Ray C. Petry*, ed. George H. Shriver (Durham: Duke University Press, 1974), 81–94.

36. *De apice theoriae* 28 (h. XII:136.1–7): [D]eus trinus et unus, . . . Cuius perfectissima apparitio, qua nulla potest esse perfectior, Christus est nos ad claram contemplationem ipsius posse verbo et exemplo perducens. Et haec est felicitas, quae solum satiat supremum mentis desiderium.

37. E.g., DDI 1.1.3, and 3.9 (h I:6 and 8).

38. DDI 3.11.245 (h. I:153.4–7): Et haec est illa docta ignorantia, per quam ipse beatissimus Paulus ascendens vidit se Christum, quem aliquando solum scivit, tunc ignorare, quando ad ipsum altius elevebatur. For some other references to Paul's ascent in 2 Cor. 12:2, see DDI 3.4.203; Sermo XXXII, nn.1–3 (h. XVII:52–54); and *De apice theoriae* 2 (h. XII:118).

39. DDI 3.11.246 (h.I:153.8–14, and 20; trans. Bond, 197–98): Ducimur igitur nos Christifideles in docta ignorantia ad montem, qui Christus est, quem tangere cum natura animalitatis nostrae prohibiti sumus; et oculo intellectuali dum inspicere ipsum conamur, in caliginem incidimus, scientes intra ipsam caliginem montem esse, in quo solum beneplacitum est habitare omnibus intellectu vigentibus. Quem si cum maiori fidei constantia accesserimus, rapiemur ab oculis sensualiter ambulantium. . . . [C]larius ipsum quasi per nubem rariorem intuemur. On the role of the mountain as a motif for mystical knowing, see Boyle, "Cusanus at Sea," 194–96.

40. Sermo IV, n. 23 (h. XVI:65): Comparatur speculo comprehendens quaecumque magna, quia divina maiestas per fidem attingitur . . . et oculo dextro; sinister oculus est ratio, quae solum de naturalibus iudicat. This entire sermon on "Fides autem catholica," preached on Trinity Sunday of 1431, is an early, but full, treatment of Cusa's notion of faith.

41. Beierwaltes ("Das Verhältnis von Philosophie und Theologie," 74–75) suggests that this Cusan term aptly describes the dialectical relation of faith and reason. On the cooperation between faith and reason in Cusa's thought, see also Jasper Hopkins, "Glaube und Vernunft," 23–29; and Hoye, *Die mystische Theologie des Nicolaus Cusanus*, 180–82.

42. *De venatione sapientiae* 30.89 (h. XII:85.3–5): . . . Dionysius, ille cunctis acutior, deum quaerens repperit in ipso contraria coniuncte verificari privationemque excellentiam esse. . . . On the relation between Dionysius and Cusa, see especially Werner Beierwaltes, "Der verborgene Gott: Cusanus und Dionysius," in *Platonismus im Christentum* (Frankfurt am Main: Klostermann, 1998), 130–71; and chapter 1, "Die Frage nach der mystischen Theologie bei Nikolaus von Kues," in Hoye, *Die mystische Theologie des Nicolaus Cusanus*, 23–48. Treatments on Cusa's use of Dionysius within the context of Renaissance thought include: two papers of

F. Edward Cranz found in his volume *Nicholas of Cusa and the Renaissance*, 109–48; David Luscombe, "Denis the Areopagite in the Writings of Nicholas of Cusa, Marsilio Ficino and Pico della Mirandola," in *Néoplatonisme et philosophie médiévale*, ed. Lino G. Benakis (Turnhout: Brepols, 1997), 93–107; and Hans Gerhard Senger, *Ludus Sapientiae: Studien zum Werk und zur Wirkungsgeschichte des Nikolaus von Kues* (Leiden: Brill, 2002), 228–54. A list of Cusa's extensive citations from Dionysius can be found in Ludwig Baur, *Nicolaus Cusanus und Pseudo-Dionysius im Lichte der Zitate und Randbemerkungen des Cusanus,* Sitzungsberichte der Heidelberger Akademie der Wissenschafter/Phil.-hist. Klasse, 32 Jahrgang 1940/41. 4 Abh. Cusanus-Texte 3. Marginalien 1 (Heidelberg: Carl Winter, 1943), chapter 2, pp. 20–32.

43. Senger, "Mystik als Theorie bei Nikolaus von Kues," 114.

44. Sermo CCLVIII has not yet appeared in h. XIX. For this text, see Hoye, *Die mystische Theologie des Nicolaus Cusanus*, 146.

45. Sermo I, n. 3 (h. XVI:4): Hinc hic Deus tam immensus ab omnibus creaturis innominabilis, inexpressibilis et ad plenum incognoscibilis manet.

46. On Sermones XIX-XXI (h. XVI: 291–331), see H. Lawrence Bond, "Nicholas of Cusa from Constantinople to 'Learned Ignorance': The Historical Matrix for the Formation of *De Docta Ignorantia*," in *Nicholas of Cusa on Christ and the Church*, ed. Gerald Christianson and Thomas M. Izbicki (Leiden: Brill, 1996), 135–63, especially 159–63; and Peter J. Casarella, "*His Name is Jesus*: Negative Theology and Christology in Two Writings of Nicholas of Cusa from 1440," in *Nicholas of Cusa on Christ and the Church*, 281–307, with a translation of Sermo XX on 298–307.

47. Sermo XX, n. 5 (h. XVI: 303): . . . tertio per remotionem, ut defectum, quem reperimus in causato, ab eminentia causae removeamus. These famous three modes of predication are found in DN 7.3.

48. DDI 1.4.12 (h. I:10.27–11.6, and 11.9–11; trans. Bond, 92): Quia igitur maximum absolute est omnia absolute actu quae possunt taliter absque quacumque oppositione, ut in maximo minimum coincidat, tunc super omnem affirmationem est pariter et negationem. Et omne id quod concipitur esse non magis est quam non est. Sed ita est hoc quod est omnia et ita omnia quod est nullum. . . . Aliter enim non esset maximitas absoluta omnia possibilia actu, si non foret infinita et terminus omnium et nullum omnium terminabilis. . . . On the relation between *maximum* and *infinitas*, see Hoye, *Die mystische Theologie des Nicolaus von Kues*, 170–78.

49. A good treatment can be found in Josef Stallmach, *Ineinsfall der Gegensätze und Weisheit der Nichtwissens: Grundzüge der Philosophie des Nikolaus von Kues* (Münster: Aschendorff, 1989). In English, see Jasper Hopkins, *Nicholas of Cusa On Learned Ignorance: A Translation and an Appraisal of De Docta Ignorantia* (Minneapolis: Arthur J. Banning Press, 1981); and Clyde Lee Miller, *Reading Cusanus: Metaphor and Dialectic in a Conjectural Universe* (Washington, D.C.: Catholic University of America Press, 2003), chapter 1.

50. DDI 1.16.43 (h. I:30.21–23; trans., Bond, 107): . . . ita quod penitus omnem oppositionem per infinitum supergreditur. Ex quo principio possent de ipso tot negativae veritates elici, quot scribi aut legi possent.

51. Ibid. Among the texts cited from the Dionysian corpus are MT 1.3, DN 5.8, MT 1.1, and Ep 1. Cusa, of course, was not the first to see God's surpassing of all opposites and therefore of both negation and affirmation as a key to the proper approach to God. Eriugena, another of Cusa's sources, argues the same case in *Periphyseon* 1 (PL 122:458D–460B). On the relation of Cusa and Eriugena, see Werner Beierwaltes, "Cusanus and Eriugena," *Dionysius* 13 (1989): 115–52; and Donald F. Duclow, "Pseudo-Dionysius, John Scotus Eriugena, Nicholas of Cusa: An Approach to the Hermeneutic of the Divine Names," *International Philosophical Quarterly* 12 (1972): 260–78.

52. The notion of *praecisio veritatis* is one of the key Cusan themes that cannot be taken up here. Essentially, God's truth in its *praecisio* goes beyond all that we can know of both God (the *maximum absolutum*) and the world (the *maximum contractum*). See DDI 1.3.

53. The *De Ignota Litteratura* (hereafter DIL) was first edited by Edmond Vansteenberghe,

Le *"De ignota litteratura" de Jean Wenck de Herrenberg contre Nicolas de Cuse* (Münster: Aschendorff, 1910). A superior edition with a translation can be found in Jasper Hopkins, *Nicholas of Cusa's Debate with John Wenck: A Translation and Appraisal of De Ignota Litteratura and Apologia Doctae Ignorantiae* (Minneapolis: Arthur J. Banning Press, 1981). Hopkins keeps the page and line number of the Vansteenberghe edition. This text is from DIL 31.1–2: Rogo quomodo ignorantia docet, cum docere sit actus doctrinae positivus?

54. *Apologia doctae ignorantiae* (herafter *Apologia*; h. II:6.7–10): Unde, cum nunc Aristotelica secta praevalet, quae heresim putat esse oppositorum coincidentiam, in cuius admissione est initium ascensus in mysticam theologiam, in ea secta nutritis haec via penitus insipida. . . .

55. *Apologia* (h. II:7.26–28): Nam mystica theologia ducit ad vacationem et silentium, ubi est visio, quae nobis conceditur, invisibilis Dei. . . . For a further defense of Dionysius's mystical theology and its commentators, including Maximus and Eriugena, see II:19–21.

56. *De filiatione* 6.84 (h. IV: 60): . . . cum sciat deum super omnem affirmationem et negationem ineffabilem, quidquid quisque dicat. . . .

57. *Idiota de sapientia* 2.32 (h V:65.14–17): Est deinde consideratio de deo uti sibi nec positio nec ablatio convenit, sed prout est supra omnem positionem et ablationem. Et tunc responsio est negans affirmationem et negationem et copulationem.

58. The term *theologia coincidentialis* does not appear in Cusa, but *theologia coniunctiva* does. The closest he comes to *theologia coincidentiae* or *coincidentialis* seems to come in Sermo LVII of 1446, which contains a treatment of the coincidences found in the New Testament, especially those of loving and being loved and knowing and being known. He says: Hinc haec est theologia Christiana, quod "fides formata caritate" est cognitio, cui coincidit cognosci. Et haec theologia aliam nobis subinfert, scilicet coincidentiam appropriatorum in Deo . . . (nn. 17–18; h. XVII:283).

59. Edmond Vansteenberghe, *Autour de la docte ignorance: Une controverse sur la théologie mystique au XVe siècle* (Münster: Aschendorff, 1915), "Correspondence de Nicolas de Cuse avec Aindorffer et de Waging," No. 5 (114–15): . . . sed in hoc libello ubi theologiam misticam et secretam vult manifestare possibili modo, saltat supra disuinctionem usque in copulacionem et coicidenciam, seu unionem simplicissimam que non est lateralis sed directe supra omnem ablacionem et posicionem, ubi ablacio coincidit cum posicione, et negacio cum affirmacione; et illa est secretissima theologia, ad quam nullus phylosophorum accessit, neque accedere potest stante principio communi tocius phylosophie, scilicet quod duo contradictoria non coincidunt. Unde necesse est mistice theologizantem supra omnem racionem et intelligenciam, eciam se ipsum linquendo, se in caliginem iniciere. . . .

60. Two studies of the *De possest* are Jasper Hopkins, *A Concise Introduction to the Philosophy of Nicholas of Cusa* (Minneapolis: University of Minnesota Press, 1978); and Peter Casarella, "Nicholas of Cusa on the Power of the Possible," *American Catholic Philosophical Quarterly* 64 (1990): 7–34.

61. *De possest* 15 (h. XI:19.1–20.14): Ducit ergo hoc nomen speculantem super omnem sensum, rationem et intellectum in mysticam visionem, ubi est finis ascensus omnis cognitivae virtutis et revelationis incogniti dei initium. Quando enim supra se ipsum omnibus relictis ascenderit veritatis inquisitor et reperit se amplius non habere accessum ad invisibilem deum, qui sibi manet invisibilis. . . . [P]uta quando ipsum mundum creaturam intelligimus et mundum transcendentes creatorem ipsius inquirimus, se manifestare ipsum ut creatorem suum summa formata fide quaerentibus.

62. On John Wenck, see Rudolf Haubst, *Studien zu Niklaus von Kues und Johannes Wenck: Aus Handschriften der Vatikanischen Bibliothek* (Münster: Aschendorff, 1955). Wenck was not only a conciliarist, but also a determined opponent of the heretical beghards. His own interest in catechetical instruction of the laity is evident in his MHG treatise on the soul edited by Georg Steer, *Johannes Wenck von Herrenberg: Das Büchlein der Seele* (Munich: Fink, 1967).

63. Hopkins, *Nicholas of Cusa's Dialectical Mysticism*, 16.

64. The debate between Wenck and Cusa has sometimes been framed as one about pantheism, but this term has meant so many things in different historical contexts that I avoid it

here. What Cusa and Wenck did disagree about was the meaning of seeing God as the *forma omnis formae* (e.g., *Apologia* 8.12–9.10, and 26.6–7), and whether or not Cusa had claimed that all things coincided with God. On the debate, see Rudolf Haubst, *Studien zu Nikolaus von Kues und Johannes Wenck* (Münster: Aschendorff, 1955); Jasper Hopkins, *Nicholas of Cusa's Debate with John Wenck*, Introduction, 3–18; and Donald F. Duclow, "Mystical Theology and Intellect in Nicholas of Cusa," *American Catholic Philosophical Quarterly* 64 (1990): 115–18. On the role of Eckhart in the debate, see Ingeborg Dengelhardt, *Studien zum Wandel des Eckhartsbildes* (Leiden: Brill, 1967), 50–63.

65. To cite just one example of Wenck's polemic: O quantum spargitur hic venenum erroris et perfidiae, correlario isto destuente omnem processum scientificum ac omnem consequentiam, pariter et tollente omnem oppositionem, pariter et legem contradictionis, et per consequens totam doctrinam Aristotelis, destructo semine omnis doctrinae. . . (DIL 29.15–19).

66. On Cusa's critique of Aristotelianism, see Hans Gerhard Senger, "Aristotelismus vs. Platonismus. Zur Konkurrenze von zwei Archetypen der Philosophie im Spätmittelalter," in *Aristotelisches Erbe im Arabisch-Lateinischen Mittelalter*, ed. Albert Zimmermann (Berlin: Walter de Gruyter, 1986), 53–80. The dialectic of *complicatio-explicatio* (enfolding-unfolding) that Cusa used throughout his thought is another topic that has attracted a large literature. For its background in the Neoplatonic tradition stretching back to Plotinus and Boethius, see Thomas P. McTighe, "A Neglected Feature of Neoplatonic Metaphysics," *Christian Spirituality and the Culture of Modernity: The Thought of Louis Dupré*, ed. Peter Casarella (Grand Rapids: Eerdmans, 1998), 27–49.

67. DIL 19.20–21: . . . veluti fidei nostrae dissona, piarum mentium offensiva, necnon ab obsequio divino vaniter abductiva.

68. DIL 21.1–3: Nam ex quo spiritu haec docta procedat ignorantia, dudum iam Waldensica, Eckhardica, atque Wiclefica praemonstraverunt doctrinationes. On the role of the discernment of spirits in late medieval mysticism, see chapter 2, pp. 76–78.

69. DIL 25.19–21: . . . dicentes Deum esse formaliter omne quod est et se esse Deum per naturam sine distinctione. See the whole treatment found in DIL 24.26–25.14. The beghard condemnation is also mentioned at 29.31–35.

70. DIL 31.22–24: Ex quibus liquet quantum venenositatem scientiae et morum induxerit abstractissima illa intelligentia, nuncupata docta ignorantia, vulgariter "abgescheiden leben."
. . .

71. DIL 41.2–3: . . . ipseque se fatetur penitus ignorans uniones rerum distinctas. . . . Wenck discusses Cusa's misunderstanding of the forms of union at 39.16–23 and 40.25–31.

72. DIL 41.7–10: Nescio an diebus meis unicum scribam sicut hunc umquam viderim tam perniciosum, in materia divinitatis et trinitatis personarum, in materia universitatis rerum, in materia Incarnationis Christi, in materia virtutum theologicalium, in materia ecclesiae.

73. *Apologia* 25.7–12: Aiebat tamen praeceptor se numquam legisse ipsum sensisse creaturam esse creatorem, laudans ingenium et studium ipsius; sed optavit, quod libri sui amoverentur de locis publicis, quia vulgus non est aptus ad ea, quae praeter consuetudinem aliorum doctorum ipse saepe intermiscet, licet per intelligentes multa subtilia et utilia in ipsis reperiantur (this last phrase is an echo of Eckhart's own defense). In *Apologia* 31.13–15, Cusa denies Wenck's attempt to equate his *docta ignorantia* with the Eckhartian *abgeschaiden leben*, which Cusa puts into Latin as *abstracta vita*. This is probably not so much a critique of Eckhart as an attack aimed at Wenck's mistranslation and misunderstanding. On the relation between Eckhart's view of detachment and Cusa, see Reiner Manstetten, "Abgeschiedenheit: Von der negativen Theologie zur negativen Anthropologie: Nikolaus von Kues und Meister Eckhart," *Theologisches Quartalschrift* 181 (2001): 112–31.

74. Cusa is insistent, for example, that the coincidence of opposites cannot be attained by reason, but only by the higher power of *intellectus*; e.g., *Apologia* 14.12–15.16, and 28.15–17.

75. *Apologia* 1.13–15: . . . quod experiantur hanc rem tantum ab aliis viis differre quantum visus ab auditu. . . . On the importance of seeing, consult 10.11–20, 12.19–24, 13.23, 15.16, 17.14–18, 18.17–20, 19.27–20.15, 24.20, 28.23, 29.17, 31.25, 32.3, 34.18, 35.4–8, and 35.13.

76. *Apologia* 9.6 and 15.14–15.

77. For an overview, see Bernard McGinn, "Love, Knowledge and Unio Mystica in the Western Christian Tradition," in *Mystical Union in Judaism, Christianity, and Islam: An Ecumenical Dialogue*, ed. Moshe Idel and Bernard McGinn (New York: Continuum, 1996), 59–86.

78. For a brief analysis of the thought of Gallus, see Bernard McGinn, *The Flowering of Mysticism: Men and Women in the New Mysticism (1200–1350)*, vol. 3 of *The Presence of God: A History of Western Christian Mysticism* (New York: Crossroad, 1998), 78–87, and the literature cited there. The quotation is from Gallus's second commentary on the Song of Songs and is cited in a fuller form in *Flowering*, 79.

79. For these texts and a treatment of Albert's view of Dionysius, see chapter 1, pp. 17–27.

80. Cusa had studied Albert's commentaries on the Dionysian corpus, and he mentions Thomas of Vercelli in *Apologia* 21.2.

81. On the background of the *Cloud*, see J. P. H. Clark, "Sources and Theology in 'The Cloud of Unknowing,'" *Downside Review* 98 (1980): 83–109.

82. The critical edition of this work can be found in *Hugues de Balma: Théologie Mystique*, vols. 1-2, ed. Francis Ruello and Jeanne Barbet, SC 408–9 (Paris: Les Éditions du Cerf, 1995–96). An English translation and study are in Dennis D. Martin, *Carthusian Spirituality: The Writings of Hugh of Balma and Guigo de Ponte* (New York: Paulist Press, 1997).

83. The *quaestio difficilis* can be found in *Hugues de Balma,* 2:182–233; for a translation, see Martin, *Carthusian Spirituality,* 155–70.

84. *Quaestio difficilis* n. 37 (ed. 2:218): . . . nam illud solum de divinis quod sentit adfectus, verissime apprehendit intellectus. It is significant that Hugh defends this view by going on to cite Dionysius's MT 1, but in Thomas Gallus's paraphrase, the *Extractio*: Per unitionem dilectionis, quae est effectiva verae cognitionis, unitur Deo intellectualiter ignoto cognitione multo nobiliori quam sit aliqua intellectualis cognitio.

85. *Quaestio difficilis* n.49 (ed. 2:232): Patet ergo evidenter quod anima vere amans potest consurgere in Deum per adfectum accensum amoris desiderio, sine aliqua cogitatione praevia.

86. Martin, "Introduction," *Carthusian Spirituality,* 19–47, especially 27–34.

87. The critical edition of Gerson's two-part treatise is by André Combes, *Ioannis Carlerii de Gerson De Mystica Theologia* (Lugano: Thesaurus Mundi, 1958). A study and partial translation are in Brian Patrick McGuire, *Jean Gerson: Early Works* (New York: Paulist Press, 1998), 262–333. See also Steven E. Ozment, *Jean Gerson. Selections from* A Deo exivit, Contra curiositatem studentium, *and* De mystica theologia speculativa (Leiden: Brill, 1966).

88. *De mystica theologia* I.8.n.43 (ed. 117): . . . mistica theologia est cognitio experimentalis habita de Deo per coniunctionem affectus spiritualis cum eodem, dum scilicet impletur illud apostoli: "Qui adheret Deo, unus spiritus est"; que nimirum adhesio fit per extaticum amorem, teste beato Dyonisio [actually cited from Hugh of Balma]. Rursus hec eadem mistica theologia dicitur sapientia, prout inter dona reponitur . . . ; vocatur preterea a divino Dyonisio irrationalis et amens sapientia, eo quod superat rationem et mentem, transiliens in affectum, non qualemcumque sed purum ipsique mentali intelligentie correspondentem, quo affectu videtur Deus a mundis corde.

89. *De mystica theologia* II.8. (ed. 172–73): Habet hanc proprietatem mistica theologia quod in affectu reponitur, aliis omnibus scientiis repositis in intellectu. . . .

90. The fundamental work on this controversy remains the study and edition of many of the texts published by Edmond Vansteenberghe, *Autour de la docte ignorance.* Other treatments include Margot Schmidt, "Nikolaus von Kues im Gespräch mit den Tegernseer Mönche über Wesen und Sinn der Mystik," in *Das Sehen Gottes nach Nikolaus von Kues: Akten des Symposions in Trier vom 25. bis 27. September 1986)*, ed. Rudolf Haubst, MFCG 18 (Trier: Paulinus, 1989), 25–49; Haas, *DEUM MISTICE VIDERE . . .* , 11–31; and Hoye, *Die mystische Theologie des Nicolaus Cusanus,* chapter 1.

91. For a sketch of Tegernsee's history and some bibliography, see Morimichi Watanabe, "Monks of Tegernsee," *American Cusanus Society Newsletter* 15 (1998): 20–22.

92. On John Keck, see Heribert Rossmann, "Der Tegernseer Benediktiner Johannes Keck

über die mystische Theologie," in *Das Menschenbild des Nikolaus von Kues und der christliche Humanismus*, ed. Martin Bodeweg, Josef Schmitz, and Reinhold Weier, MFCG 13 (Mainz: Matthias-Grünewald, 1978), 330–52. Keck praised the writings of Bonaventure, Gallus, and Hugh of Balma as the main authorities on mystical theology; nevertheless, he believed that the ecstatic love of mystical theology involved both preparatory cognition, as well as its own form of knowing—Numquam amor exstaticus est sine cognitione affectiva, quae est ipsemet (Rossmann, 352 n. 105).

93. On Bernard of Waging, see Martin Grabmann, "Bayerische Benediktinermystik am Ausgang des Mittelalters," *Benediktinische Monatschrift zur Pflege religiösen und geistigen Lebens* 2(1920):196–202; and Werner Höver, "Bernhard von Waging," VL 1:779–89. The *Laudatorium doctae ignorantiae* is edited in *Autour de la docte ignorance*, 163–68. Bernard had read not only the DDI, but also the *Apologia*, so he was well acquainted with Cusa's developing ideas. Three points are worth noting about this treatise: (1) Bernard, like Cusa, equates *docta ignorantia* with *mystica theologia/theosophia*; (2) like Cusa, he also taught that the vision of God is beyond the coincidence of opposites (see pp. 164, 168); and (3) Bernard insisted that both *cognicio* and *affecio* are needed in the ascent to mystical theology (pp. 164–65).

94. Cusa, Letter of Feb. 12, 1454 (Correspondence no. 9; Vansteenberghe, 122).

95. Letter of Kaspar Ayndorffer to Cusa (Correspondence no. 3; Vansteenberghe, 110): Est autem hec questio, utrum anima devota sine intellectus cognicione, vel etiam sine cogitacione previa vel concomitante, solo affectu seu per mentis apicem quam vocant synderesim Deum attingere possit, et in ipsum immediate moveri aut ferri. Ayndorffer goes on to note that the writings of Hugh of Balma and Gerson, useful as they are, are not sufficient to solve the questions under discussion.

96. See Dennis D. Martin, "Vinzenz von Aggsbach OCart," VL 10:359–65; Augustin Devaux, "Vincent d'Aggsbach," DS 16:804–06; and especially Heribert Rossmann, "Die Stellungnahme der Karthäusers Vinzenz von Aggsbach zur mystischen Theologie des Johannes Gerson," *Karthäusermystik und-Mystiker: Dritter Internationaler Kongress über die Kartäusergeschichte und-Spiritualität*, Analecta Carthusiana 55 (Salzburg: Universität Salzburg, 1982), 5–30.

97. F. J. Worstbrock, "Schlitpacher, Johannes," VL 8:727–48.

98. Heribert Rossmann ("Sprenger, Marquard," VL 9:157–62) gives an introduction; for a more detailed study, see Rossmann, "Der Magister Marquard Sprenger in München und seine Kontroverseschriften zum Konzil von Basel und zur mystischen Theologie," in *Mysterium der Gnade: Festschrift für J. Auer*, ed. Heribert Rossmann and Joseph Ratzinger (Regensburg, 1975), 350–411. Sprenger's most important contribution, the treatise *Elucidatorium mysticae theologiae* of 1453, is not yet edited.

99. Letter to Kaspar Ayndorffer (Correspondence no. 4; Vansteenberghe, 112–13): Inest igitur in omni dilecione qua quis vehitur in Deum, cognicio, licet quid sit id quod diligit ignoret. Est igitur coincidencia sciencie et ignorancie, seu docta ignorancia. . . . [S]ed in raptu multi decipiuntur, qui imaginibus inherent, et visionem fantasticam putant veram. Veritas autem obiectum est intellectus et non nisi invisibiliter videtur, de quo grandis sermo restat pro nunc, neque forte unquam satis explicabilis. The letter ends with Cusa's confession that he himself has not yet tasted how sweet is the Lord (see Ps. 33:9).

100. This text can be found in *Autour de la docte ignorance*, "Ecrits de Vincent d'Aggsbach," no. 1 (Vansteenberghe, 189–201), with the covering letter to Schlitpacher as no. 2 on 201–3.

101. No. 1 (Vansteenberghe, 190): Ecce quomodo principalis conscriptor huius artis nude et plane asserit volentem consurgere etc. . . . ignote vel inscium consurgere oportet, id est sine cogitacione concomitante. Vincent did admit that the unknowing surge into God produced knowledge consequent to the experience, a knowledge he called *supermentalis cognicio*; see no. 3 (Vansteenberghe, 209–10).

102. No. 1 (Vansteenberghe, 195): Theologia mistica est quaedam species vel actus devocionis, vel modus singularis cuiusdam extensionis mentalis in Deum. . . .

103. For Vincent, Hugh of Balma's teaching is like good wine, while Gerson's is *acqua tepida et turbida* (Vansteenberghe, 196).

104. No. 1 (Vansteenberghe, 199): Contemplacio enim a contemplando seu videndo dicitur, mistica vero theologia ab occultacione denominatur; et certe magna differencia est inter visionem et occultacionem.

105. No. 1 (Vansteenberghe, 200): . . . mistice vero theologiae exercitium consistit sollummodo in affectu. Hence, Vincent insists that there can be no content at all, not even a christological or trinitarian one, to mystical theology, but only total ignorance. This position appears to be the reason why, in a later treatise, the *Alterum scriptum de mistica theologia contra Gersonem*, Vincent seems to identify mystical theology with the reception of rapture from God. This text has been edited by Palemon Glorieux, *Jean Gerson: Oeuvres Complètes*, 10 vols. (Paris: Desclée, 1960–73), 10:567–76. See 576: Potest enim misticus discipulus quociescumque voluerit, id est cencies vel amplius, die ac nocte, talem excessum facere, si fuerit rite dispositus. In this treatise Vincent repeats the major points of the earlier work, though with more dependence on Bonaventure.

106. For the attack on "Gerchumar," see the letter to John Schlitpacher of December 19, 1454, which is no. 3 in Vansteenberghe's edition (pp. 205–7). A short attack on Sprenger of uncertain date puts it this way: Magnum chaos positum est inter Vercellinco [i.e., Gallus and Grosseteste] et Gerchumar, et inter contemplacionem et misticam theologiam (ed., 217). Rossmann, "Die Stellungnahme," 21, provides a list of Vincent's contributions to the debate.

107. No. 3 (Vansteenberghe, 205–06): Intitulavit [Cusa] libellum quem fecit occasione illius ymaginis *De visione Dei*, iustius autem intitulasset ipsum "de docta ignorancia" vel "de ignota doctrina." This hints that Vincent may have known Wenck's work. Vincent references other works of Cusa on pp. 207–8.

108. Correspondence no. 5 (Vansteenberghe, 114): . . . Dionysius non aliud intendebat quam aperire Thymoteo quomodo speculatio illa que versatur circa ascensum rationalis nostri spiritus usque ad unionem Dei et visionem illam que est sine velamine non complebitur quamdiu id quod Deus iudicatur intelligitur.

109. No. 5 (Vansteenberghe, 115–16): Et michi visum fuit quod tota ista mistica theologia sit intrare ipsam infinitatem absolutam, dicit enim infinitas contradictoriorum coincidenciam, scilicet finem sine fine; et nemo potest Deum mistice videre nisi in caligine coincidencie, que est infinitas.

110. Correspondence no. 8 (Vansteenberghe, 120): Sed qualis est finis, scilicet Deum videre, eique fruitivo amore inherere feliciter! Sed o visio, o fruitio quanto plus tanto minus, quo propinquius eo longius, quo presentius eo absentius, quanto clarius tanto obscurius!

111. Correspondence no. 9 (Vansteenberghe, 122): . . . perfecta igitur caritas est super coincidenciam contradictoriorum continentis et contenti. Quapropter divina venacio est in altitudine, super hanc oppositorum coincidenciam, ad quam alias homo pertingere nequit, de qua pauca quedam scripsi ut meipsum supra meipsum elevarem.

112. Correspondence no. 15 (Vansteenberghe, 132). Bernard of Waging continued to explore the issues down to the 1460s. Among his most important later contributions is the treatise *De cognoscendo Deum* of 1459, book 9 of which is an interpretation of chapter 7 of Bonaventure's *Itinerarium mentis in Deum* designed to show that the Franciscan includes both love and knowledge at the height of the mystical path. This has been edited by Martin Grabmann, "Die Erklärung des Bernhard von Waging O.S.B. zum Schlusskapitel von Bonaventuras Itinerarium mentis in Deum," *Franziskanische Studien* 8 (1925): 125–35. Bernard's final contribution was a long treatise *De spiritualibus sentimentis et perfectione spirituale* written 1463–64. It is available in a noncritical edition in Bernard Pez, *Bibliotheca Ascetica Antiquo-Nova*, 8 vols. (Ratisbon: J. Peezii, 1724–25; photographic reprint, 1967), V:13–408. The work consists of two parts in Pez's version: ten chapters on the enjoyment of internal sweetness, beginning with a chapter on four kinds of *visio mystica*; and thirty chapters on the fourfold spiritual poverty, largely a translation of the *Book of Spiritual Poverty* (see chapter 8, pp. 377–92). The work deserves further study.

113. Correpondence no. 16 (Vansteenberghe, 135): Christus igitur, qui aperuit felicitatem esse in visone dei, aperuit nobis quod sicut omnia que ad nos aliquo sensu perveniunt videre cupimus, quasi videre sit ultima perfectio sensuum senciencium, sic eciam videre Deum com-

plicat in se, quia ultima perfectio, omnem modum attingendi Deum; ac si videre foret forma et perfectio talium.

114. This section makes use of material from my essay "Seeing and Not Seeing: Nicholas of Cusa's Place in the Mystical Tradition," to appear in *Nicholas of Cusa: Sixth Centenary Studies*, ed. Peter J. Casarella (Washington, D.C.: Catholic University of America Press, 2005).

115. On seeing God in the Hebrew Bible and early Jewish texts, see Friedrich Nötscher, *"Das Angesicht Gottes schauen" nach biblischer und babylonischer Auffassung* (Darmstadt: Wissenschaftlicher Buchgesellschaft, 1969); and Elliot R. Wolfson, *Through a Speculum that Shines: Vision and Imagination in Medieval Jewish Mysticism* (Princeton: Princeton University Press, 1994), chapter 1.

116. For an introduction to both Platonic and Christian *theôria/contemplatio*, see the lengthy multi-author article "Contemplation" in DS 2:1643–2193 (cols. 1716–62 by René Arnou deal with contemplation in ancient philosophy).

117. *Iustini Martyris: Dialogus cum Tryphone*, ed. Miroslav Marcovich (Berlin: Walter de Gruyter, 1997), chapter 2.6 (p. 73).

118. *Dialogus* 4.1 (pp. 76–77). Edward Baert ("Le thème de la vision de Dieu chez S. Justin, Clement d'Alexandrie et S. Grégoire de Nysse," *Freiburger Zeitschrift für Philosophie und Theologie* 12 [1965]: 439–97) provides an introduction to the role of vision in Justin and Clement, discussing this passage on pp. 440–55. On Justin's place in the history of Christian mysticism, see Bernard McGinn, *The Foundations of Mysticism: Origins to the Fifth Century*, volume 1 of *The Presence of God: A History of Western Christian Mysticism* (New York: Crossroad, 1991), 98–100.

119. K. E. Kirk, *The Vision of God: The Christian Doctrine of the "Summum Bonum"* (London: Longmans & Green, 1932); and Vladimir Lossky, *The Vision of God* (London: Faith Press, 1963).

120. Christian Trottmann, *La vision béatifique: Des disputes scolastiques à sa définition par Benoît XII* (Rome: École française de Rome, 1995).

121. In the Sept. 14, 1453, letter (Vansteenberghe, 116), Cusa says that the DVD was originally intended to be a chapter in his *Complementum theologicum*.

122. Among the more interesting treatises explicitly concerned with seeing God in this life was the *De theoria sancta* of the Syriac monk Gregory of Cyprus (ca. 600).

123. The critical edition of the DVD is found in h. VI. Also helpful are the edition and discussion by Jasper Hopkins, *Nicholas of Cusa's Dialectical Mysticism*. There is a good translation in Bond, *Nicholas of Cusa: Selected Spiritual Writings*, 235–89, but here I will make use of my own translations, unless otherwise noted.

124. Cusa's interest in seeing God, both here and hereafter, may have been spurred in part by the discussions between Latins and Greeks about their differing views of *visio dei* at the Council of Ferrara-Florence. The Spanish Dominican Juan Lei produced a treatise reflecting these debates in 1439; see *Tractatus Ioannis Lei O.P. "De visione beata,"* ed. Emmanuel Candal, S.J. (Vatican City: Biblioteca Apostolica Vaticana, 1963).

125. For an introduction to Clement's mysticism, see McGinn, *Foundations of Mysticism*, 101–8.

126. For a consideration of *theôria* in Clement, see Baert, "La thème de la vision," 460–80; and P. T. Camelot, *FOI ET GNOSE: Introduction a l'étude de la connaissance mystique chez Clément d'Alexandrie* (Paris: Vrin, 1945), chapter 4.

127. Clement of Alexandria, *Stromateis* 7.3.13. Clement cites Matt. 5:8 eighteen times—far more than any second-century Christian author before him (e.g., Justin does not use the text at all, and Irenaeus cites it only three times). See *Biblia Patristica: Index des citations et allusions bibliques dans la littérature patristique*, vol. 1, *Des origines à Clément d'Alexandrie et Tertullien* (Paris: CNRS, 1975), 232–33. Clement also quotes 1 Cor. 13:12 fourteen times.

128. See, e.g., *Strom.* 2.10.46, and 7.16.102.

129. Clement, *Protrepticus* 1.8.

130. Werner Beierwaltes, *Visio facialis—sehen ins Angesicht: Zur Coincidenz des endlichen und*

unendlichen Blicks bei Cusanus, Bayerische Akademie der Wissenschaften. Phil.-hist. Klasse. Sitzungsberichte Jahrgang 1988, Heft 1 (Munich: Bayerische Akademie der Wissenschaften, 1988), 34–38, 40–43.

131. *Enneads* V.5.7–10, as found in *Plotinus,* with an English translation by A. H. Armstrong, 7 vols., Loeb Classical Library (Cambridge, Mass.: Harvard University Press, 1966–88), 5:174–87.

132. *Enneads* VI.7.35 (Armstrong 7:194–95).

133. Augustine's discussions of how to understand the various appearances of the Persons of the Trinity described in scripture can be found in the *Enarrationes in Psalmos* 138.8 (PL 37:1788–90), *In Iohannis evangelium* III,17 (PL 35:1403), and especially *De Trinitate* II-IV (PL 42:845–912).

134. Among Augustine's many discussions about seeing God, consult, *Confessiones* VII, IX, and XIII; *De Trinitate* IX-XIV; *De genesi ad litteram* XII; and Epp. 147–148. In addition, a number of places in the *Enarrationes in Psalmos* treat *visio Dei* (e.g., *Ennar.* 97.3, 121.8, 125.9, and 149.4).

135. On the relation between Augustine and Cusa, see Edward F. Cranz, "St. Augustine and Nicholas of Cusa in the Tradition of Western Christian Thought," in *Nicholas of Cusa and the Renaissance,* 73–94.

136. On this aspect of the relation of Dionysius and Cusa, see Beierwaltes, "Der Verborgene Gott: Cusanus und Dionysius"; and William J. Hoye, "Die Vereinigung mit dem gänzlich Unerkannten nach Bonaventura, Nikolaus von Kues und Thomas von Aquin," in *Die Dionysius-Rezeption im Mittelalter,* ed. Tzotcho Boiadjiev, Georgi Kapriev and Andreas Speer (Turnhout: Brepols, 2000), 477–504.

137. For other texts on this higher seeing, which Dionysius often buttresses by quoting 1 Tim. 6:16, consult Ep. 5 (1073A); CH 4.3 (180C); and DN 4.11 (708D).

138. See Beierwaltes, "Cusanus and Eriugena,"115–52, especially 126–30 on *visio absoluta.*

139. Iohannes Scottus Eriugena, *Periphyseon* 3 (PL 122:704B): Visio dei totius uniuersitatis est conditio. Non enim aliud est ei uidere et aliud facere, sed uisio illius uoluntas eius est et uoluntas operatio. For other texts on the *visio dei,* see, e.g., *Peri.* 3 (676C–77A).

140. *Commentarius in Evangelium Iohannis* I.25, in *Jean Scot: Commentaire sur l'Évangile de Jean,* ed. Édouard Jeauneau, SC 180 (Paris: Éditions du Cerf, 1972), 114–26. See also the Irishman's discussion of CH 4.3 in his *Expositiones in Ierarchiam Coelestem* IV.3, ed. Jeanne Barbet, CCCM 31 (Turnhout: Brepols, 1975), 74–82. In *Peri.* V John says that in the final *reditus* the saved never pass beyond the seeing of *theophaniae theophaniarum* (e.g., 998B–1001A). On the contrast between Eriugena, who denies a vision of the divine essence, even in heaven, and standard medieval theology on this issue, see Dominic J. O'Meara, "Eriugena and Aquinas on the Beatific Vision," in *Eriugena Redivivus: Zur Wirkungsgeschichte seines Denkens im Mittelalter und im Übergang zur Neuzeit,* ed. Werner Beierwaltes (Heidelberg: Carl Winter, 1987), 214–36.

141. *Jean Scot: Commentaire sur l'Évangile de Jean,* I.25.95–99 (124–26): Hinc est quod Dionysius ait: "Et si quis eum—deum uidelicet—uidisse dixerit, non eum uidit, sed aliquid ab eo factum." Ipse enim est omnino inuisibilis est, "qui melius nesciendo scitur," et "cuius ignorantia uera est sapientia." The first and third quotations are from Dionysius, Ep 1 (1065A); the central quote is from Augustine, *De ordine* II.16.44 (PL 32:1015).

142. On Eckhart's mysticism of birth out of the ground, see chapter 4 above, pp. 171–77.

143. Dietmar Mieth ("Gottesschau und Gottesgeburt: Zwei Typen christlicher Gotteserfahrung in der Tradition," *Freiburger Zeitschrift für Philosophie und Theologie* 27 [1980]: 204–23) distinguishes two ideal types of mysticism, vision of God and divine birth. Whatever the validity of this broad distinction, it seems that both forms are combined in Cusa. See Niklaus Largier, "The Space of the Word: Birth and Vision in Eckhart and Cusanus" (unpublished).

144. Eckhart, Pr. 5A (DW 1:77.10–13).This passage was condemned as heretical in art. 11 of the Bull "In agro dominico."

145. In the Latin works, see, for example, the treatment of Gen. 32:28 in In Gen. I nn. 296–97, and the discussion of Exod. 20:21 and 33:13–23 in In Ex. nn. 235–38 and nn. 271–81. Isa. 45:15 was a favorite Eckhart scriptural text, which he cites eight times. Also important is the treatment of John 1:18 (In Ioh. nn. 187–98, in LW 3:156–67) and Eckhart's exegesis of John 14:8 (In Ioh. nn. 546–76, in LW 3:477–506). Eckhart often discusses seeing God in his vernacular sermons, e.g., Prr. 3, 9, 15, 23, 32, 36, 45, 57, 59, 73, and 83. Perhaps the most important sermons on seeing God is the group Prr. 69–72 (DW 3:159–254), commenting on scriptural texts on vision (John 16:16, Acts. 9:8, and Matt. 5:1).

146. Pr. 71 (DW 3:211–31).

147. Pr. 12 (DW 1:201.5–8). See also Pr. 76 (DW 3:310–12), as well as Pr. 86 on face-to-face vision (DW 3:487–88). The same teaching is also found in the Latin works; see, e.g., In Gen. II n. 219 (LW 1:697–98), a discussion of Israel's face-to-face vision of God; and In Ioh. n. 107 (LW 3:91–93). Eckhart's teaching often uses the example of the union of the eye and its object in physical seeing (e.g., Pr. 48 [DW 2:416–17]).

148. On William of St.-Thierry's view of face-to-face vision, especially as found in his *Meditativae Orationes* 3, 8, and 10, see McGinn, *Growth of Mysticism*, 247, 261–64. For William as a possible source for Cusa, see Donald F. Duclow, "Mystical Theology and Intellect in Nicholas of Cusa," *American Catholic Philosophical Quarterly* 64 (1990): 121.

149. For studies of the DVD, see *Das Sehen Gottes nach Nikolaus von Kues*, especially the papers of Werner Beierwaltes,"'*Visio facialis*'—Sehen ins Angesicht: Zur Coinzidenz des endlichen und unendlichen Blicks bei Cusanus"; and Wilhelm Dupré, "Das Bild und die Wahrheit" (*Das Sehen*, 91–124 and 125–66). Other useful studies include Beierwaltes, "Mystische Elemente im Denken des Cusanus"; Haas, *DEUM MISTICE VIDERE*; Hoye, *Die mystische Theologie des Nicolaus von Kues*, chapter 2; Louis Dupré, "The Mystical Theology of Nicholas of Cusa's *De visione dei*," and Clyde Lee Miller, "God's Presence: Some Cusan Proposals," both in *Nicholas of Cusa on Christ and the Church*, ed. Gerald Christianson and Thomas M. Izbicki (Leiden: Brill, 1996), 205–20, and 241–49. Also to be noted is the penetrating analysis of Michel de Certeau, "The Gaze of Nicholas of Cusa," in *Diacritics: A Review of Contemporary Criticism* 3 (1987): 2–38; most recently, H. Lawrence Bond, "The 'Icon' and the 'Iconic Text' in Nicholas of Cusa's *De Visione Dei*," in *Nicholas of Cusa and His Age*, 177–97; and Clyde Lee Miller, "The Dialectic of Seeing Being Seen Seeing: *De visione Dei* (1453)," chapter 4 in *Reading Cusanus*.

150. DVD 17.79 (h. VI:63.9–14): Conatus sum me subicere raptui, confisus de infinita bonitate tua, ut viderem te invisibilem et visionem revelatam irrevelabilem. Quo autem perveni, tu scis, ego autem nescio, et sufficit mihi gratia tua, qua me certum reddis te incomprehensibilem esse, et erigis in spem firmam, quod ad fruitionem tui te duce perveniam.

151. For comments on the possible identity of the *icona*, see Bond, "The 'Icon' and the 'Iconic Text,'" 180–83. See also Alex Stock, "Die Rolle der 'Icona Dei' in der Spekulation 'De visione dei,'" in *Das Sehen Gottes nach Nicolaus von Kues*, 50–68.

152. De Certeau, "The Gaze of Nicholas of Cusa," especially 11–21.

153. De Certeau ("The Gaze," 14) speaks of Cusa's exercise as a "mathematical liturgy," but the processional aspect indicates that it is no less monastic. The question of the relation between Cusa's new liturgy with its accompanying *lectio divina* and *meditatio/oratio* and the ordinary practice of the Benedictine life is complicated and deserves further work. For one analysis, see Mark Führer, "The Consolation of Contemplation in Nicholas of Cusa's *De visione dei*," in *Nicholas of Cusa on Christ and the Church*, 221–40, who argues for a close relation of the text to traditional monastic practice and claims that Cusa sought "a revitalization of mental prayer" (p. 224). The relation between the DVD and meditative and contemplative practices is also taken up in Bond, "The 'Icon' and the 'Iconic Text.'"

154. See de Certeau, "The Gaze," 14–23, on the stages of the exercise, especially 20 on the dialogue, "You too?" "Yes."

155. DVD, Pref. 3 (h. VI:6.22–23): . . . credet ei; et nisi crederet, non caperet hoc possibile. This reminiscence of Isa. 7:14 contains a typically Cusan twist.

156. On this point, see Miller, "Dialectic of Seeing Being Seen Seeing," 153–54. Cusa had already advanced this point with regard to our knowing in his treatise *De quaerendo deum* 2.36, where he says: . . . et in luminis ipsius [God] est omnis cognitio nostra, ut nos non simus illi, qui cognoscimus, sed potius ipse in nobis (h. IV:26.7–9).

157. DVD 10.38 (h.VI:35.6–7): Et occurrit mihi, domine, quod visus tuus loquatur; nam non est aliud loqui tuum quam videre tuum. . . .

158. For subsequent references to the visual exercise of the *eicona*, see DVD 1.5, 4.9, 5.13, 6.17 and 19, 9.32 and 35, 10.38, 15.61 and 64, and 22.94.

159. DVD 4.9 (h. VI:13.5–8): . . . et quia visus eiconae te aeque undique respicit et non deserit, quocumque pergas, in te excitabitur speculatio provocaberisque et dices. . . . It is important to note that the term *speculatio*, i.e., true seeing, has the opposite meaning from current use of "speculation" (see Hoye, *Die mystische Theologie des Nicolaus Cusanus*, 105–6).

160. Bond, "The 'Icon' and the 'Iconic Text,'" 184.

161. See, e.g., DVD 6.21 and 7.25 (h. VI:23 and 26–27). On silence in the DVD, see Günter Stachel, "Schweigen vor Gott: Bemerkungen zur mystischen Theologie der Schrift *De visione Dei*," in MFCG 14:167–81.

162. On this form of "reverse dialectic" of the divine presence-in-absence, see Miller, "God's Presence: Some Cusan Proposals," 244–45; and Beierwaltes, "*Visio Facialis*," 18–19.

163. Bond, "The 'Icon' and the 'Iconic Text,'" 192.

164. Many of these essential themes of the DVD are echoed in the *De filiatione* 1.52–54 and 3.62–71, as we shall see below.

165. Bond ("The 'Icon' and the 'Iconic Text,'" 190) notes how each chapter can be considered as a separate meditation.

166. DVD 16.70 (h. VI:57.1–3): Video te, domine deus meus, in raptu quodam mentali, quoniam si visus non satiatur visu nec auris auditu, tunc minus intellectus intellectu.

167. Bernard Lonergan, *Insight: A Study in Human Understanding* (New York: Longmans, 1957).

168. DVD 5.13 (h. VI:17.12–14): Videndo me das te a me videri, qui es deus absconditus. . . . Nec est aliud te videre quam quod tu videas videntem te. There are many other such expressions of fused seeing in the treatise; e.g., 10.40 (h. VI:36.12): Esse creaturae est videre tuum pariter et videri.

169. The *De li non aliud* contains some powerful passages applying Cusa's notion of fused vision to the name "not-other" (e.g., 7.25, 22.103, and 23.104). The passage referred to is at 23.104 (h. XIII:54.15–17): Se igitur et omnia unico et inerrabili contuitu sapientes Deum videre aiunt, quia est visionum visio. On these texts, consult Hoye, *Die mystische Theologie des Nicolaus Cusanus*, 121–22.

170. DVD 7.25–26 (h. VI:26.12–27.2): Et cum sic in silentio contemplationis quiesco, tu, domine, intra praecordia mea respondes dicens: Sis tu tuus et ego ero tuus. . . . Per me igitur stat, non per te, domine. . . . On this famous text, see Klaus Kremer, "Gottes Vorsehung und die menschlicher Freiheit ('Sis tu tuus, et Ego ero tuus')," in *Das Sehen Gottes nach Nicolaus von Kues*, 227–63.

171. DVD 7.26 (h. VI:27.3–4): Quomodo autem ero mei ipsius, nisi tu, domine, docueris me?

172. DVD 16.70 (h. VI:57.6–57.8): Intelligibile enim, quod cognoscit, non satiat nec intelligibile satiat, quod penitus non cognoscit, sed intelligibile, quod cognoscit adeo intelligibile, quod numquam possit intelligi. . . .

173. DVD 16.70 (h. VI:58.11–14): . . . sed solum ille cibus, qui ad eum pervenit et, licet continue deglutiatur, tamen numquam ad plenum potest deglutiari, quoniam talis est, quod deglutiendo non imminuitur, quia infinitus. The passage from Eckhart is from In Eccli. nn. 42–43 (LW 2:271–72). See Donald F. Duclow, "The Hungers of Hadewijch and Eckhart," *Journal of Religion* 80 (2000): 421–41.

174. See Bond, "Introduction," in *Nicholas of Cusa: Selected Spiritual Writings*, 26–36. Bond characterizes coincident theology as follows: "Because we start with God as absolute maxi-

mum in whom maximum and minimum coincide, and because we know God through God's coincident work in Christ, Cusa says, we can, in consequence, see God as the enfolder and unfolder of all reality, and we can see the world in its unity and particularity operating 'coincidentally'" (p. 36).

175. On the difference between the two, see Haas, "DEUM MISTICE VIDERE," 13–15; and Dupré, "Mystical Theology of Nicholas of Cusa's *De visione dei*," 205.

176. These three premises are: (1) whatever can be affirmed of the omnivoyant gaze of the *eicona dei* is eminently true of the absolute uncontracted gaze of God (chap. 2); (2) God's *visus absolutus* embraces all modes of seeing as the *contractio contractionum* (chap. 3); and (3) as the *absoluta ratio*, God enfolds the *rationes* of all things and therefore in God there is no real distinction of his attributes.

177. Miller ("God's Presence: Some Cusan Proposals," 243–47) rightly notes the shift from the investigation of the mutuality of the gaze to the mutuality of the face beginning in chapter 6.

178. On Cusa's image of the *murus paradisi*, or *murus coincidentiae*, see Rudolf Haubst, "Die erkenntnis-theoretische und mystische Bedeutung der 'Mauer der Koincidenz," in *Das Sehen Gottes nach Nikolaus von Kues*, 167–95; Walter Haug, "Die Maurer des Paradieses: Zur mystica theologia des Nicholas Cusanus in 'De visione Dei,'" *Theologische Zeitschrift* 45 (1989): 216–30; Peter Casarella, "Neues zu den Quellen der cusanischen Mauer-Symbolik," MFCG 19: 273–86; and Miller, "Dialectic of Seeing Being Seen Seeing," 161–66.

179. DVD 9.37 (h. VI:35.8–11; trans. Bond, 252): Et iste est murus paradisi, in quo habitas, cuius portam custodit spiritus altissimus rationis, qui nisi vincatur, non patebit ingressus. Ultra coincidentiam contradictoriorum videri poteris et nequaquam citra.

180. Werner Beierwaltes, "Deus Oppositio Oppositorum [Nicolaus Cusanus, *De visione dei* XIII]," *Salzburger Zeitschrift für Philosophie* 8 (1964): 179–81.

181. DVD 10.42 (h. VI:38.18–19): Tu vero, deus meus, ultra nunc et tunc exsistis et loqueris, qui es aeternitas absoluta.

182. DVD 12.50 (h. VI:43.4–6): Sed absolutam cum te video infinitatem, cui nec nomen creatoris creantis nec creatoris creabilis competit, tunc revelate te inspicere incipio et intrare hortum deliciarum. . . . Cusa had considered the paradoxes involved in a "creatable Creator" and a world that is both eternal and temporal in several earlier texts; see, e.g., DDI 2.2.101, and the *De dato patris luminum* 2.97, and 3.104–6.

183. While Cusa does transpose biblical texts about the eschatological vision into this life, he makes it clear that the perfection of *visio facialis* only comes in heaven. See, e.g., *De apice theoriae* 11 (h. XII:125.17–19): . . . quia posse ipsum est solum potens, cum apparuerit in gloria maiestatis, satiare mentis desiderium. Est enim illud quid, quod quaeritur. On the eschatological character of *visio dei*, see Hoye, *Die mystische Theologie des Nicolaus Cusanus*, 57, 102–4, 157, and 162.

184. *De possest* 15 (h. XI:191–4): Ducit ergo hoc nomen speculantem super omnem sensum, rationem et intellectum in mysticam visionem, ubi est finis ascensus omnis cognitivae virtutis et revelationis incogniti dei initium.

185. See Beierwaltes, "*Visio Facialis*," 23–28; and "Mystische Elemente," 429–33, 438; and Miller, "Dialectic of Seeing Being Seen Seeing," 166–72. On the importance of chapter 13 as a key to the book, see also Bond, "The 'Icon' and the 'Iconic Text,'" 190–92.

186. In Cusa the notion of *infinitas* functions much like the term *indistinctum* in Eckhart; see especially In Sap. nn. 144–57 (LW 2:481–94), as discussed in chapter 4 above, pp. 138–40.

187. See Beierwaltes, "Deus Oppositio Oppositorum," 179–82, on the two related meanings of *oppositio oppositorum*: (1) "Nichts von Allem" as found in DVD 13, and the *De non-aliud*; and (2) "Allem in Allem" as taught in the *Compendium* 13 et al.

188. DVD 15.63 (h. VI:53.10–11; trans. Bond, 264): . . . quia id, quod videt in illo aeternitatis speculo, non est figura, sed veritas, cuius ipse videns est figura (trans. Bond). For earlier discussions of the *speculum* motif, see 4.12, 8.30–31, and 12.48. The mirror also played a part in the *De filiatione*, as will be discussed below.

189. DVD 15.65 (h. VI:54.12–14): O inexplicabilis pietas, offers te intuenti te, quasi recipias ab eo esse, et conformes te ei, ut eo plus te diligat, quo appares magis similes ei.

190. On the importance of the last chapters of the DVD, see Dupré, "Mystical Theology of Cusanus' *De visione dei,*" 217–20; Duclow, "Mystical Theology and Intellect in Nicholas of Cusa," 118–29; and Miller, "Dialectic of Seeing Being Seen Seeing," 172–79.

191. Among accounts of Cusa's doctrine of the Trinity, see Rudolf Haubst, *Das Bild des Einen und Dreieinen Gottes in der Welt nach Nikolaus von Kues* (Trier: Paulinus, 1952); Alexandre Ganoczy, *Der dreieinige Schöpfer: Trinitätstheologie und Synergie* (Darmstadt: Wissenschaftliche Buchgesellschaft, 2001); and Jasper Hopkins, "Verständnis und Bedeutung des dreieinen Gottes bei Nikolaus von Kues," in *Nikolaus von Kues 1401–2001: Akten des Symposions in Bernkastel-Kues vom 23. bis 26. Mai 2001,* ed. Klaus Kremer and Klaus Reinhardt, MFCG 28 (Trier: Paulinus, 2003), 135–64. In what follows I will make use of some materials drawn from my article "*Unitrinum seu Triunum*: Nicholas of Cusa's Trinitarian Mysticism," in *Mystics: Presence and Aporia,* ed. Michael Kessler and Christian Sheppard (Chicago: University of Chicago Press, 2003), 90–117.

192. *Apologia* (h. II:23.25–24.4): Scilicet in coincidentia summae simplicitatis et indivisibilitatis atque unitatis et trinitatis. . . . Cum enim dicitur Patrem esse personam et Filium alteram et Spiritum sanctum tertiam, non potest alteritas significatum suum tenere, cum sit haec dictio imposita, ut significet alteritatem ab unitate divisam et distinctam.

193. DDI 1.19.58 (h. I:39.19–21): Coniunge igitur ista, quae videntur opposita, antecedenter, ut praedixi, et non habebis unum et tria vel e converso, sed unitrinum seu trinunum. Et ista est veritas absoluta.

194. Augustine, *De Trinitate* 8.8.12. Several other analogies are presented from 8.10.14 to 9.2.2.

195. Augustine, *De doctrina christiana* 1.5.12 (CSEL 80:10–11): Eadem est tribus aeternitas, eadem incommutabilitas, eadem maiestas, eadem potestas. In patre unitas, in filio aequalitas, in spiritu sancto unitatis aequalitatisque concordia. Et tria haec unum propter patrem, aequalia omnia propter filium, conexa omnia propter spiritum sanctum.

196. For a sketch of the history of this analogy and further literature, see Bernard McGinn, "Does the Trinity Add Up? Transcendental Mathematics and Trinitarian Speculation," in *Praise No Less Than Charity: Studies in Honor of M. Chrysogonus Waddell, Monk of Gethsemani Abbey,* ed. E. Rozanne Elder (Kalamazoo: Cistercian Publications, 2002), 235–64.

197. *Apologia* (h. II:24.6–7): Vir facile omnium, quos legerim, ingenio clarissimus. Cusa did not know Thierry was the author of the *Lectiones in Boethii Librum de Trinitate.*

198. McGinn ("Nicholas of Cusa's Trinitarian Mysticism," 105–9) provides a chart of the trinitarian passages in Cusa's treatises. A similar list can be found in Hopkins, "Verständnis und Bedeutung," 140–43.

199. Sermo XIX, n.6 (h. XVI:296.13–19): Hodie tamen habentes per fidem Trinitatem esse, non esset post fidem rationes Trinitatis difficile invenire, ut dicit Richardus de Sancto Victore in principio De Trinitate, sicut et ipse ibi inquirit, et sicut etiam Anselmus, Augustinus, Damascenus et alii inquisiverunt rationes. . . .

200. DDI 1.7.21 (h. I:16.19–23): Sed quia unitas aeterna est, aequalitas aeterna est, similiter et conexio: hinc unitas, aequalitas et conexio sunt unum. Et haec est illa trina unitas, quam Pythagoras, omnium philosophorum primus, Italiae et Graeciae decus, docuit adorandum. The reference to Pythagoras seems to come from the twelfth-century text *De septem septennis,* which uses the Augustinian formula in the context of a discussion of Pythagoras (see PL 199:961C).

201. For some recent discussions of this work, see Wilhelm Dupré, "Absolute Truth and Conjectural Insight," in *Nicholas of Cusa on Christ and the Church,* 323–38; and Clyde Lee Miller, *Reading Cusanus,* chapter 2.

202. *De coniecturis* 1.1.5 (h. III:8.17–18): Ad cuius assimilationem tanto propinquius erigimur, quanto magis mentem nostram profundaverimus, cuius ipsa unicum vitale centrum existit.

203. DC 1.1.6 (h. III:10.11–13): Quapropter unitas mentis in se omnem complicat multitudinem eiusque aequalitas omnem magnitudinem, sicut et conexio compositionem. Mens igitur unitrinum principium. . . . For later discussions of the triad in this treatise, see 1.2.9 and especially 2.14.145.

204. DC 2.17.171 (h. III:173.9–10): Humanitatem vero individualiter in alteritate contrahibilem alteritatem absolutioris esse unitatis. . . .

205. DC 2.17.182 (h. III:181.1–182.8): Ex te ipso igitur electiones deiformes intueri valebis. Nam conspicis deum, qui est infinita conexio, non ut contractum amabile aliquod diligendum, sed ut absolutissimum infinitum amorem. In eo igitur amore, quo deus diligitur, esse debet simplicissima unitas infinitaque iustitia. . . . Cognoscis etiam hoc esse deum amare quod est amari a deo, cum deus sit caritas. Quanto igitur quid deum plus amaverit, tanto plus divinitatem participat.

206. Cusa uses the following trinitarian triads in the DVD: (1) *amor amans-amor amabilis-utriusque nexus* (17.71–78, 18.80, and 19.83–84); (2) *unitas uniens-unitas unibilis-utriusque unio* (17.71); (3) *intellectus intelligens-intellectus intelligibilis-utriusque nexus* (18.81); and (4) the scriptural *pater-filius-spiritus sanctus* (18.81, and 20.87).

207. Although the most extensive treatments of the love analogy are found in books 8 and 9 of Augustine's *De Trinitate* (e.g., 8.10.14 and 9.2.2), Cusa's analogy of *amor amans-amor amabilis-utriusque nexus* seems closer to a passage in *De Trin.* 15.6.10 (PL 42:1064): Sed ubi ventum est ad charitatem, quae in sancta Scriptura Deus dicta est, eluxit paululum Trinitas, id est, amans, et quod amatur, et amor.

208. DVD 17.73 (h. VI:59.1–2): Illa igitur, quae occurrunt mihi tria esse, scilicet amans, amabilis et nexus, sunt ipsa simplicissima essentia absoluta.

209. DVD 17.75 (h. VI:60.5–61.11): . . . sed video distinctionem amantis et amabilis intra murum coincidentiae unitatis et alteritatis esse. Unde distinctio illa, quae est intra murum coincidentiae, ubi distinctum et indistinctum coincidunt, praevenit omnem alteritatem et diversitatem, quae intelligi potest. Claudit enim murus potentiam omnis intellectus, licet oculus ultra in paradisum respiciat, id autem, quod videt, nec dicere nec intelligere potest.

210. DVD 17.76 (h. VI:61.3–9): Tu enim sic das, domine, quod in me video amorem, quia video me amantem. Et quia video me amare me ipsum, video me amabilem, et naturalissimum nexum me esse video utriusque. Ego sum amans, ego sum amabilis, ego sum nexus. Haubst (*Das Bild des Einen und Dreieinen Gottes*, 79–81) notes the influence of Ramon Llull here.

211. Although he does not use the expression, I think Cusa would have agreed with the formula found among the Cistercian and Victorine mystics—*amor ipse intellectus est.* This is suggested by DVD 24.113 (h. VI:86.5–13), where he says that Christ as Savior teaches us two things: the faith by which the intellect *approaches* God, and the love that actually *unites* us with God. Where Cusa is original is in conceiving of this loving knowledge in terms of his distinctive dialectical view of *docta ignorantia* as the seeing that is not seeing.

212. DVD 18.82 (h. VI:65.1–3): Et sic video humanam rationalem naturam tuae divinae naturae intelligibili et amabili tantum unibilem et quod homo te deum receptibilem capiens transit in nexum, qui ob sui strictitudinem filiationis nomen sortiri potest. . . . The fusion of knowing and loving in face-to-face vision, of course, means that it is in the act of understanding ourselves as capable of always desiring to understand more of God that we see God as Absolute Intellect, and it is in experiencing ourselves as lovers who always desire to love God the more that we come to see that God is Pure Love. This *posse videre* was to be further developed by Cusa in the *De apice theoriae* 11–12 (h. XII:124–26).

213. There are three important discussions of the Trinity in the *De aequalitate*, the third of which is a reformulation of the Augustinian analogy of *memoria-intelligentia-voluntas.* See McGinn, "Nicholas of Cusa's Trinitarian Mysticism," 101–2.

214. Cusa's emphasis on love as *filiatio* does not mean a total exclusion of the language of bridal union of the soul with God (not specifically Christ), which is mentioned in DVD 18.80 (h. VI:64), but this is not a significant theme for the cardinal.

215. A classsic study of Cusa's Christology is Rudolf Haubst, *Die Christologie Nikolaus von Kues* (Freiburg-im-Breisgau: Herder, 1956). In addition, I have found the following articles helpful: H. Lawrence Bond, "Nicholas of Cusa and the Reconstruction of Theology: the Centrality of Christology in the Coincidence of Opposites"; Christoph Schönborn, "'De docta ignorantia' als christozentricher Entwurf," in *Nikolaus von Kues: Einführung in sein philosophisches Denken*, ed. Klaus Jacobi (Freiburg-Munich: Karl Alber, 1979), 138–56; Peter J. Casarella, *"His Name Is Jesus:* Negative Theology and Christology in Two Writings of Nicholas of Cusa from 1440," in *Nicholas of Cusa on Christ and the Church*; Klaus Reinhardt, "Christus, die 'Absolute Mitte' als der Mittler zur Gotteskindschaft," in *Das Sehen Gottes nach Nikolaus von Kues,* 196–226; and "Christus 'Wort und Weisheit' Gottes," in *Weisheit und Wissenschaft: Cusanus im Blick die Gegenwart,* ed. Rudolf Haubst and Klaus Kremer, MFCG 20 (Trier: Paulinus, 1992), 68–97. For a critical survey of recent work on Cusa's Christology, see Hans Gerhard Senger, "Cusanus-Literatur der Jahre 1986–2001: Ein Forschungsbericht," *Recherches de théologie ancienne et médiévale* 69 (2002): 386–94.

216. Part of what follows may be found in more detail in Bernard McGinn, *"Maximum Contractum et Absolutum:* The Motive for the Incarnation in Nicholas of Cusa and his Predecessors," in *Nicholas of Cusa and His Age: Intellect and Spirituality,* 151–75.

217. Augustine, Ep. 174.2 (PL 38:940).

218. A good introduction to the medieval debates can be found in Rudolf Haubst, *Von Sinn der Menschwerdung: "Cur Deus homo"* (Munich: Max Heuber, 1969).

219. Scottus's view can be found in his two comments on book 3, dist. 7, of Peter Lombard's *Sentences,* the *Ordinatio (Opus Oxoniense)* and the *Reportata Parisiensia.*

220. For the logic of the christological presentation of book 3.1–3, see especially Schönborn, "'De docta ignorantia' als christozentrischer Entwurf," 143–56. For the reintegration of faith and reason here, see Louis Dupré, "Nature and Grace in Cusa's Mystical Philosophy," *American Catholic Philosophical Quarterly* 64 (1990): 166–70.

221. DDI 3.3.197 (h. I:126.21–24): Quapropter natura media, quae est medium conexionis inferioris et superioris, est solum illa, quae ad maximum convenienter elevabilis est potentia maximi infiniti dei.

222. DDI 3.3.199 (h. I:127.17–21): . . . per quem cuncta initium contractionis atque finem reciperent, ut per ipsum, qui est maximum contractum, a maximo absoluto omnia in esse contractionis prodirent et in absolutum per medium eiusdem redirent, tamquam per principium emanationis et per finem reductionis. See also 3.3.202.

223. As Schönborn summarizes ("'De docta ignorantia' als christozentricher Entwurf," 148): "Indem Christus als die 'ipsa contractio' bezeichnet wird, ist gesagt, dass an ihm aufscheint, was 'contractio' als Seinsweise des Endlichen ist: in Christus gelangt erst Endlichkeit zu ihrer vollen Bestimmung."

224. In Sermo XLV preached in Mainz in 1444 Cusa explicitly refers to the divergent theological views about the motive of the incarnation and says that his view seeks to conciliate the two positions (see h. XVII:188).

225. See Reinhold Weier, "Christus als 'Haupt' und 'Fundament' der Kirche," in *Nikolaus von Kues, Kirche und Respublica Christiana: Konkordanz, Repräsentanz und Konsens,* ed. Klaus Kremer and Klaus Reinhardt, MFCG 21 (Trier: Paulinus, 1994), 163–82.

226. On the Christology of the last part of the DVD, see especially Reinhardt, "Christus, die 'Absolute Mitte' als der Mittler zur Gotteskindschaft."

227. DVD 23.106 (h. VI:82.8–13): Tu, deus, qui es ipsa bonitas, non potuisti satisfacere infinitae clementiae tuae et largitati tuae, nisi te nobis donares. Nec hoc convenientius et nobis recipientibus possibilius fieri potuit, quam quod nostram assumeres naturam, qui tuam accedere non potuimus. Ita venisti ad nos et nominaris Ihesus salvator semper benedictus.

228. DVD 19.85 (h. VI:67.2–5): Et video Ihesum benedictum hominis filium filio tuo unitum altissime et quod filius hominis non potuit tibi deo patri uniri, nisi mediante filio tuo mediatore absoluto.

229. DVD 19.86 (h. VI:68.3–7): Filiatio igitur humana, quia tu filius hominis, filiationi

divinae in te, Ihesu, altissime unita est, ut merito dicaris filius dei et hominis, quoniam in te nihil mediat inter filium hominis et filium dei. In filiatione absoluta, quae est filius dei, omnis complicat filiatio, cui filiatio humana tua, Ihesu, est supreme unita.

230. Cusa had already begun to explore the issue of filiation in sermons preached prior to the composition of the treatises; see Rudolf Haubst, *Streifzüge in die Cusanische Theologie* (Münster: Aschendorff, 1991), 89–96. In a later sermon preached at Brixen on the Feast of the Annunciation in 1456, he describes filiation in terms of the Eckhartian theme of the birth of the Word in the soul; see Sermo CCXXVI nn. 27–28 (h. XIX:152).

231. See the unpublished paper of David C. Albertson, "Nicholas of Cusa's Ascension Christology in Two Treatises from 1445." My thanks to the author for allowing me to use and quote this paper.

232. On the christological descent into the universe, see especially *De dato patris luminum* 4.111 and 5.122 (h. IV:81–82, and 87).

233. Albertson, "Ascension Christology," 38.

234. For the Eckhartian background of Cusa's view of filiation, see Harald Schwaetzer, "La place d'Eckhart dans la genèse du concept cuséain de 'filiatio dei,'" to appear in *La naissance de Dieu dans l'âme chez Eckhart et Nicolas de Cues*, ed. M.-A. Vannier (Paris: Éditions du Cerf, 2005).

235. DF 3.68 (h. IV:50.9–11): . . . nihil aliud filiationem esse quam translationem illam de umbrosis vestigiis simulacrorum ad unionem cum ipsa infinita ratione. . . .

236. DF 3.70 (h. IV:51.1–3): Filiatio igitur est ablatio omnis alteritatis et diversitatis et resolutio omnium in unum, quae est et transfusio unius in omnia. Et haec theosis ipsa. The *ablatio* that Cusa speaks of here is not to be thought of as a simple removal or negation, but is rather a dialectical recognition of the need for removing or abstracting from created distinction without forgetting its ongoing importance for all conjectural approach to God.

237. DF 6.86 (h. IV:62.5–10): Intellectus autem cum sit intellectualis viva dei similitudo, omnia in se uno cognoscit, dum se cognoscit. Tunc autem se cognoscit, quando se in ipso deo uti est intuetur. Hoc autem tunc est, quando deus in ipso ipse. Nihil igitur aliud est omnia cognoscere quam se similitudinem dei videre, quae est filiatio. Una igitur simplici intuitione cognitiva omnia intuetur.

238. For example, in DVD 20.87 (h. VI:69.14–15) he speaks of union as taking place by "attractio naturae humanae ad divinam in altissimo gradu"; and in 20.88 (h. VI:70.11–12) he says, "sic video naturam tuam humanam in divina natura subsistentem." In only one passage (23.102) does he use a more Chalcedonian language of union in hypostasis or suppositum: Sed video te, domine Ihesu, super omnem intellectum unum suppositum, quia unus Christus es . . . (h. VI: 79.5–7). For the "Nestorian" tone of these chapters, see Dupré, "The Mystical Theology," 218–19; and Jasper Hopkins, "Interpretive Study," in *Nicholas of Cusa's Dialectical Mysticism*, 31–35.

239. John Scottus Eriugena, *Periphyseon* 5 (PL 122 978C–83A).

240. DVD 21.93 (h. VI: 74.17–20): Videt omnis spiritus felix invisibilem deum, et unitur in te, Ihesu, inaccessibili et immortali deo. Et sic finitum in te unitur infinito et inunibili et capitur incomprehensibilis fruitione aeterna, quae est felicitas gaudiossima numquam consumptibilis.

241. See DDI 3.4.204–07 (h. I:130–32).

242. DVD 23.102. In this chapter Cusa goes on to discuss an issue also of intererest to scholastic theology, that is, how in Jesus's death both his body and soul still remained united to divinity.

243. DVD 24.114 (h. VI:86.4–5): Non persuades nisi credere, et non praecipis nisi amare.

244. DVD 25.117 (h. VI:88.7–9): Revelant sibi mutuo secreta sua amoris pleni spiritus et augetur ex hoc cognitio amati et desiderium ad ipsum et gaudii dulcedo inardescit.

245. Cusa continued to insist on the need for both love and knowledge to attain union with Jesus. Especially interesting here is the letter treatise he sent to Nicholas Albergati in 1463, a kind of last will and testament. See the discussion of love and knowledge in nn.

12–13, as well as the reflections on union with Christ in nn. 34–35, as found in Gerda von Bredow, *Das Vermächtnis des Nikolaus von Kues: Der Brief an Nikolaus Albergati nebst der Predigt in Monteoliveto (1463), Cusanus-Texte IV: Briefwechsel des Nikolaus von Kues* (Heidelberg: Carl Winter, 1953), 30, 40. In this work Cusa daringly compares our transformation into Christ with the conversion of the Eucharist elements into the body of Christ (nn. 56–57 on p. 50)—the same kind of comparison that had been condemned as heretical in the case of Meister Eckhart ("In agro dominico," art. 10).

Bibliography

The following bibliography is restricted to secondary studies and does not list the editions of primary sources referred to in the notes to the chapters.

Abramowski, Luise. "Bemerkungen zur 'Theologia deutsch' und zum 'Buch von geistlicher Armut.'" *Zeitschrift für Kirchengeschichte* 97 (1986): 92–104.

Aertsen, Jan A. "Ontology and Henology in Medieval Philosophy (Thomas Aquinas, Meister Eckhart and Berthold of Moosburg)." In *On Proclus and His Influence in Medieval Philosophy*, edited by E. P. Bos and P. A. Meijer, 120–40. Leiden: Brill, 1992.

———. "Der 'Systematiker' Eckhart" (forthcoming).

Albert, Karl. "Meister Eckhart über das Schweigen." In *Festschrift für Lauri Seppänen zum 60. Geburtstag*, 301–9. Tampere: Universität Tampere, 1984.

———. *Meister Eckharts These vom Sein.* Saarbrücken: Universitäts- und Schulbuchverlag, 1976.

———. "Die philosophische Grundegedanke Meister Eckharts." *Tijdschrift voor Philosophie* 27 (1965): 320–39.

Alexis, Raymond. "Die Bibelzitate in Werken des Strassburger Prediger Johannes Tauler: Ein Beitrag zum Problem der vorlutherischen Bibelverdeutschung." *Revue des langues vivants* 20 (1954): 397–411.

Almond, Ian. "How *Not* to Deconstruct a Dominican: Derrida on God and 'Hypertruth.'" *Journal of the American Academy of Religion* 68 (2000): 329–45.

Altrock, Stephanie, and Hans-Joachim Ziegeler. "Vom *diener der ewigen weisheit* zum Autor Heinrich Seuse: Autorschaft und Medienwandel in den illustrierten Handschriften und Drucken von Heinrich Seuse 'Exemplar.'" In *Text und Kultur: Mittelalterliche Literatur 1150–1450*, edited by Ursula Peters, 150–88. Stuttgart: Metzler, 2001.

Ancelet-Hustache, Jeanne. *Master Eckhart and the Rhineland Mystics.* New York: Harper, 1957.

671

Anderson, Wendy Love. "Free Spirits, Presumptuous Women, and False Prophets. Discernment of Spirits in the Late Middle Ages." Ph.D. dissertation, University of Chicago, 2002.

Anzulewicz, Henryk. "Neuere Forschung zu Albertus Magnus: Bestandsaufnahme und Problemstellungen." *Recherches de théologie ancienne et médiévale* 66 (1999): 163–206.

———. "Die platonische Tradition bei Albertus Magnus. Eine Hinführung." In *The Platonic Tradition in the Middle Ages: A Doxographical Approach,* edited by Stephen Gersh and Maarten J. F. M. Hoenen, 207–77. Berlin: Walter de Gruyter, 2002.

———. "Pseudo-Dionysius und das Strukturprinzip des Denkens von Albert des Grossen." In *Die Dionysius-Rezeption im Mittelalter: Internationales Kolloquium in Sofia vom 8. bis 11 April 1999,* edited by T. Boiadjiev, G. Kapriev, and A. Steer, 252–95. Turnhout: Brepols, 2000.

Appel, Heinrich. "Die Syntheresis in der mittelalterlichen Mystik." *Zeitschrift für Kirchengeschichte* 13 (1892): 535-44.

Arbman, Ernst. *Ecstasy or Religious Trance.* 2 vols. Uppsala: Svenska Bokförlaget, 1963.

Aston, Margaret. "Huizinga's Harvest: England and the Waning of the Middle Ages." *Mediaevalia et Humanistica* n.s. 9 (1979): 1–24.

Auer, Johannes. "'Das Buch von geistlicher Armut.'" VL 1:1082–85.

Auerbach, Erich. *Literary Language & Its Public in Late Latin Antiquity and the Middle Ages.* Princeton: Princeton University Press, 1965.

Bach, Josef. *Meister Eckhart: Der Vater der deutschen Speculation.* Vienna: Braumüller, 1864.

Baert, Edward. "Le thème de la vision de Dieu chez S. Justin, Clément d'Alexandrie et S. Grégoire de Nysse." *Freiburger Zeitschrift für Philosophie und Theologie* 12 (1965): 439–97.

Baeumker, Clemens. "Das pseudo-hermetische 'Buch der vierundzwanzig Meister' (Liber XXIV philosophorum)." In *Studien und Charakteristiken zur Geschichte der Philosophie insbesonder des Mittelalters,* 94–214. Münster: Aschendorff, 1927.

Bailey, Michael D. *Battling Demons: Witchcraft, Heresy, and Reform in the Late Middle Ages.* University Park, Pa.: Pennsylvania State University Press, 2003.

———. "Religious Poverty, Mendicancy, and Reform in the Late Middle Ages." *Church History* 72 (2003): 457–83.

Baring, Georg. *Bibliographie der Ausgaben der "Theologia Deutsch" (1516–1961): Ein Beitrag zur Lutherbibliographie. Mit Faksimiledruck der Erstausgabe und 32 Abbildungen.* Baden-Baden: Heitz, 1963.

Bauer, Gerhard. "'Auch einer': Leiden, Weisheit, Mystik und Mystiker bei Johannes Geiler von Kaysersberg." In *Leiden und Weisheit in der Mystik,* edited by Bernd Jaspert, 207–33. Paderborn: Bonifatius, 1992.

———. *Claustrum Animae: Untersuchungen zur Geschichte der Metapher vom Herzen als Kloster.* Band I, *Enstehungsgeschichte.* Munich: Fink, 1972.

Baur, Ludwig. *Nicolaus Cusanus und Pseudo-Dionysius im Lichte der Zitate und Randbemerkungen des Cusanus.* Sitzungsberichte der Heidelberger Akademie der Wissenschaften/Phil.-hist. Klasse, 32 Jahrgang 1940/41. 4 Abh. Cusanus-Texte 3. Marginalien 1. Heidelberg: Carl Winter, 1943.

Beccarisi, Alessandra. "Philosophische Neologismen zwischen Latein und Volkssprache: 'istic' und 'isticheit' bei Meister Eckhart." *Recherches de théologie et philosophie médiévale* 70 (2003): 329–58.

Beck, Herbert, and Maraike Bückling. *Hans Multscher: Das Frankfurter Trinitätsrelief. Ein Zeugnis spekulativer Künstlerindividualität.* Frankfurt: Fischer, 1988.

Beierwaltes, Werner. "Der Begriff des 'Unum in Nobis' bei Proklos." In *Die Metaphysik im Mittelalter: Ihr Ursprung und ihr Bedeutung,* edited by Paul Wilpert, 255–66. Berlin: Walter de Gruyter, 1963.

———. "Cusanus and Eriugena." *Dionysius* 13 (1989): 115–52.

———. "Deus Oppositio Oppositorum [Nicolaus Cusanus, *De visione dei* XIII]." *Salzburger Zeitschrift für Philosophie* 8 (1964): 175–85.

———. "Mystische Elemente im Denken des Cusanus." In *Deutsche Mystik im abendländische Zusammenhang: Neu erschlossene Texte, neue methodische Ansätze, neue theoretische Konzepte,* edited by Walter Haug and Wolfram Schneider-Lastin, 425–48. Tübingen: Niemeyer, 2000.

———. *Platonismus und Idealismus.* Frankfurt: Klostermann, 1972.

———. "Primum est dives per se: Meister Eckhart und der 'Liber de causis.'" In *On Proclus and His Influence in Medieval Philosophy,* edited by E. P. Bos and P. A. Meijer, 141–69. Leiden: Brill, 1992.

———. *Proklus: Grundzüge seiner Metaphysik.* Frankfurt: Klostermann, 1965.

———. "Unity and Trinity East and West." In *Eriugena East and West,* edited by Bernard McGinn and Willemien Otten, 209–31. Notre Dame: University of Notre Dame Press, 1995.

———. "Der verborgene Gott: Cusanus und Dionysius." In Werner Beierwaltes, *Platonismus im Christentum,* 130–71. Frankfurt: Klostermann, 1998.

———. "Das Verhältnis von Philosophie und Theologie bei Nicolaus Cusanus." In *Nikolaus von Kues 1401–2001,* 65–102. *Mitteilungen und Forschungsbeiträge der Cusanus-Gesellschaft* 28. Trier: Paulinus, 2003.

———. *Visio facialis–sehen ins Angesicht: Zur Coincidenz des endlichen und unendlichen Blicks bei Cusanus.* Bayerische Akademie der Wissenschaften. Phil.-hist. Klasse. Sitzungsberichte Jahrgang 1988, Heft 1. Munich: Bayerische Akademie der Wissenschaften, 1988.

Belting, Hans. *Das Bild und sein Publikum im Mittelalter: Form und Funktion früher Bildtafeln der Passion.* Berlin: Mann, 1981.

Benko, Stephen. *Pagan Rome and the Early Christians.* Bloomington, Ind.: Indiana University Press, 1986.

Berger, Kurt. *Die Ausdrücke der Unio mystica im Mittelhochdeutschen.* Berlin: Ebering, 1935.

Bernhart, Joseph. *Die philosophische Mystik des Mittelalters von ihren antiken Ursprüngen bis zur Renaissance.* Munich: Reinhard, 1922.

Biffi, Inos. *Teologia, Storia e Contemplazione in Tommaso d'Aquino.* Milan: Jaca Book, 1995.

Bihlmeyer, Karl. "Einleitung." In *Seuse: Deutsche Schriften,* 3*–163*. Stuttgart: Kohl-hammer, 1907.

———. "Griechische Gedanke in einem mittelalterlichen mystischen Gedicht." *Theologische Zeitschrift* 4 (1948): 192–212.

———."Die schwäbische Mystikerin Elsbeth Achler von Reute (d. 1429) und die Überlieferung ihrer Vita." In *Festschrift Philipp Strauch,* edited by G. Baesecke and F. J. Schneider, 88–109. Halle, 1932.

Bizet, J.-A. "Henri Suso." DS 7:234–57.

———. "Le Mysticisme de Henri Suso: Texte inédit de Jean Baruzi." *Revue d'Histoire de la Spiritualité* 51 (1975): 209–66.

Blamires, David. "Introduction." In *The Book of the Perfect Life,* 1–28. Walnut Creek: AltaMira Press, 2003.

Blank, Walter. "Heinrich Seuses 'Vita': Literarisches Gestaltung und pastorale Funktion des Schriftens." *Zeitschrift für deutsches Altertum und deutsche Literatur* 122 (1993): 285–311.

Blumenberg, Hans. "Ausblick auf eine Theorie der Unbegrifflichkeit." In *Theorie der Metapher,* edited by Anselm Haverkamp, 438–54. Darmstadt: Wissenschaftliche Buchgesellschaft, 1983.

———. "Beobachtungen an Metaphern." *Archiv für Begriffsgeschichte* 15 (1971): 161–214.

———. "Paradigmen zu einer Metaphorologie." *Archiv für Begriffsgeschichte* 6 (1960): 7–142.

Blumrich, Rüdiger. "Die deutschen Predigten Marquards von Lindau: Ein franzis-kanischer Beitrag zur *Theologia mystica.*" In *Albertus Magnus und der Albertismus: Deutsche philosophische Kultur des Mittelalters,* edited by Maarten J. F. M. Hoenen and Alain de Libera, 155–72. Leiden: Brill, 1995.

———. "Feuer der Liebe: Franziskanische Theologie in den deutschen Predigten Marquards von Lindau." *Wissenschaft und Weisheit* 54 (1991): 44–55.

———, and Philipp Kaiser, editors. *Heinrich Seuses Philosophia spiritualis: Quellen, Konzept, Formen und Rezeption.* Wiesbaden: Reichert, 1994.

Boespflug, François. "Apophatisme théologique et abstinence figurative: Sur l'irre-présentabilité de Dieu (le Père)." *Revue des sciences religieuses* 72 (1998): 446–68.

Bond, H. Lawrence. "The 'Icon' and the 'Iconic Text' in Nicholas of Cusa's *De Visione Dei.*" In *Nicholas of Cusa and His Age: Intellect and Spirituality,* edited by Thomas M. Izbicki and Christopher M. Bellitto, 177–97. Leiden: Brill, 2002.

———. "Introduction." In *Nicholas of Cusa: Selected Spiritual Writings,* 3–84. New York: Paulist Press, 1997.

———. "Nicholas of Cusa and the Reconstruction of Theology: The Centrality of Christology and the Coincidence of Opposites." In *Contemporary Reflections on the Medieval Christian Tradition: Essays in Honor of Ray C. Petry,* edited by George H. Shriver, 81–94. Durham: Duke University Press, 1974.

———. "Nicholas of Cusa from Constantinople to 'Learned Ignorance': The His-torical Matrix for the Formation of *De Docta Ignorantia.*" In *Nicholas of Cusa on*

Christ and the Church, edited by Gerald Christianson and Thomas M. Izbicki, 135–63. Leiden: Brill, 1996.

Booth, Edward. *Aristotelian Aporetic Ontology in Islamic and Christian Thinkers.* Cambridge: Cambridge University Press, 1983.

Boss, G., and G. Seel, editors. *Proclus et son influence: Actes du Colloque de Neuchâtel.* Zurich: Éditions du Grand Midi, 1987.

Boyle, Marjorie O'Rourke. "Cusanus at Sea: The Topicality of Illuminative Discourse." *Journal of Religion* 71 (1991): 180–201.

Brady, Thomas A., Jr., Heiko A. Oberman, and James D. Tracy, editors. *Handbook of European History, 1400–1600: Late Middle Ages, Renaissance, and Reformation.* 2 vols. Grand Rapids: Eerdmans, 1996.

Braunfels, Wolfgang. *Die heilige Dreifaltigkeit.* Düsseldorf: Schwann, 1954.

Bremond, Henri. *Prayer and Poetry: A Contribution to the Study of Poetical Theory.* London: Burnes, Oates & Washbourne, 1927.

Brient, Elizabeth. "Meister Eckhart and Nicholas of Cusa on the 'Where' of God." In *Nicholas of Cusa and His Age*, edited by Thomas M. Izbicki and Christopher M. Bellitto, 127–50. Leiden: Brill, 2002.

Bruhl, Adrien. *Liber Pater, origine et expansion du culte dionysiaque à Rome et dans le monde romain.* Paris: de Boccard, 1953.

Brunner, Fernand. "L'analogie chez Maître Eckhart." *Freiburger Zeitschrift für Philosophie und Theologie* 16 (1969): 333–49.

Buning, Marius. "Negativity Then and Now: An Exploration of Meister Eckhart, Angelus Silesius and Jacques Derrida." *The Eckhart Review* (Spring 1995): 19–35.

Bürkle, Susanne. *Literatur im Kloster: Historische Funktion und rhetorische Legitimation frauenmystischer Texte des 14. Jahrhunderts.* Tübingen and Basel: Francke, 1999.

Burr, David. *The Spiritual Franciscans: From Protest to Persecution in the Century after Saint Francis.* Philadelphia: University of Pennsylvania, 2001.

Burrell, David B. *Aquinas. God and Action.* Notre Dame: University of Notre Dame Press, 1979.

———. "Aquinas on Naming God." *Theological Studies* 24 (1963): 183–212.

Bynum, Caroline Walker. *Holy Feast and Holy Fast: The Religious Significance of Food to Medieval Women.* Berkeley: University of California, 1987.

Caciola, Nancy. *Discerning Spirits: Divine and Demonic Possession in the Middle Ages.* Ithaca: Cornell University Press, 2003.

Camelot, P. T. *Foi et Gnose: Introduction à l'étude de la connaissance mystique chez Clément d'Alexandrie.* Paris: Vrin, 1945.

Camille, Michael. *Gothic Art: Glorious Visions.* New York: Abrams, 1996.

———. "Mimetic Identification and Passion Devotion in the Later Middle Ages: A Double-sided Panel by Meister Francke." In *The Broken Body: Passion Devotion in Late-Medieval Culture*, edited by A. A. MacDonald, H. N. B. Ridderbos, and R. M. Schlusemann, 183–210. Groningen: Forsten, 1998.

———. "Seductions of the Flesh: Meister Francke's Female 'Man' of Sorrow." In *Frömmigkeit im Mittelalter: Politisch-soziale Kontext, visuelle Praxis, körperliche*

Ausdrucksformen, edited Klaus Schreiner and Marc Müntz, 243–69. Munich: Fink, 2002.

Caner, Daniel. *Wandering, Begging Monks: Spiritual Authority and the Promotion of Monasticism in Late Antiquity.* Berkeley and Los Angeles: University of California Press, 2002.

Caputo, John D. "Fundamental Themes of Eckhart's Mysticism." *The Thomist* 42 (1978): 197–225.

———. *The Mystical Element in Heidegger's Thought.* Athens, Oh.: Ohio University Press, 1978.

———. "Mysticism and Transgression: Derrida and Meister Eckhart." In *Derrida and Deconstruction*, edited by Hugh J. Silverman, 24–39. London: Routledge, 1989.

———. "The Nothingness of the Intellect in Meister Eckhart's 'Parisian Questions.'" *The Thomist* 39 (1975): 85–115.

Casarella, Peter. "*His Name is Jesus*: Negative Theology and Christology in Two Writings of Nicholas of Cusa from 1440." In *Nicholas of Cusa on Christ and the Church*, edited by Gerald Christianson and Thomas M. Izbicki, 281–307. Leiden: Brill, 1996.

———. "Neues zu den Quellen der cusanischen Mauer-Symbolik." In *Mitteilungen und Forschungsbeiträge der Cusanus-Gesellschaft* 19 (1990): 273–86.

———. "Nicholas of Cusa on the Power of the Possible." *American Catholic Philosophical Quarterly* 64 (1990): 7–34.

Cassirer, Ernst. *The Individual and the Cosmos in Renaissance Philosophy.* New York: Harper and Row, 1963.

Cavicchioli, Curzio. "Meister Eckhart e la morte dello spirito: Un sermone apocrifo." *Rivista di Ascetica e Mistica* 21 (1996): 181–206.

Champollion, Claire. "La place des termes 'gemuete' und 'grunt' dans le vocabulaire de Tauler." In *La mystique rhénane*, 179–92. Paris: Presses Universitaires de France, 1963.

Charles-Saget, Annick. "Non-être et Néant chez Maître Eckhart." In *Voici Maître Eckhart*, edited by Emilie Zum Brunn, 301–18. Grenoble: Jérôme Millon, 1994.

Chiquot, A. "Amis de Dieu." DS 1:493–500.

———. "Buch von geistlicher Armuth (Das)." DS 1:1976–78.

Clark, James M. *The Great German Mystics: Eckhart, Tauler and Suso.* Oxford: Blackwell, 1949.

Clark, J. P. H. "Sources and Theology in 'The Cloud of Unknowing'." *Downside Review* 98 (1980): 83–109.

Clark, Susan L., and Julian S. Wasserman. "*Purity* and *Das Neunfelsenbuch:* The Presentation of God's Judgment in Two Fourteenth-Century Works." *Arcadia* 18 (1983): 179–84.

———. "The Soul as Salmon: Merswin's *Neunfelsenbuch* and the Idea of Parable." *Colloquia Germanica* 13 (1980): 47–56.

Cognet, Louis. *Introduction aux mystiques rhéno-flamands.* Paris: Desclée, 1968.

Cohn, Norman. *The Pursuit of the Millennium.* New York: Oxford, 1970.

Colledge, Edmund. "Introductory Interpretive Essay." In *The Mirror of Simple Souls*, xxv–lxxxvii. Notre Dame: University of Notre Dame Press, 1999.

———, and J. C. Marler. "'Mystical' Pictures in the Suso 'Exemplar' *Ms Strasbourg 2929*." *Archivum Fratrum Praedicatorum* 54 (1984): 293–354.

———, and J. C. Marler. "'Poverty of Will': Ruusbroec, Eckhart and the Mirror of Simple Souls." In *Jan van Ruusbroec: The sources, content, and sequels of his mysticism*, edited Paul Mommaers and N. de Paepe, 14–47. Leuven: Leuven University Press, 1984.

Constable, Giles. *Three Studies in Medieval Religious and Social Thought.* Cambridge: Cambridge University Press, 1995.

"Contemplation." DS 2:1643–2193 (multiauthor).

Cousins, Ewert. "Francis of Assisi: Christian Mysticism at the Crossroads." In *Mysticism and Religious Traditions*, edited by Steven Katz, 163–90. Oxford: Oxford University Press, 1983.

———. "The Humanity and Passion of Christ." In *Christian Spirituality: High Middle Ages and Reformation*, edited by Jill Raitt et al., 375–91. New York: Crossroad, 1987.

Cranz, F. Edward. "The *De aequalitate* and *De principio* of Nicholas of Cusa." In *F. Edward Cranz: Nicholas of Cusa and the Renaissance*, edited by Thomas M. Izbicki and Gerald Christianson, 61–70. Aldershot: Ashgate-Variorum, 2000.

———. "The Late Works of Nicholas of Cusa." In *Nicholas of Cusa and the Renaissance*, 43–60.

———. "St. Augustine and Nicholas of Cusa in the Tradition of Western Christian Thought." In *Nicholas of Cusa and the Renaissance*, 73–94.

Cunningham, Francis L. B. *The Indwelling of the Trinity: A Historico-Doctrinal Study of the Theory of St. Thomas Aquinas.* Dubuque: Priory Press, 1955.

Cupitt, Don. *Mysticism and Modernity.* Oxford: Blackwell, 1998.

d'Alverny, Marie-Thérèse. "Un témoin muet des lottes doctrinales du XIIIe siècle." *Archives d'histoire doctrinale et littéraire du moyen âge* 24 (1949): 223–48.

D'Ancona Costa, Cristina. "Sources et Structure du *Liber de causis*." In C. D'Ancona Costa, *Recherches sur le Liber de causis*, 23–52. Paris: Vrin, 1995.

———. "La doctrine de la création 'mediante intelligentia' dans le *Liber de causis* et dans ses sources." In *Recherches sur Le Liber de causis*, 73–95.

Dannenfeldt, K. H., et al. "Hermetica Philosophica." In *Catalogus Translationum et Commentariorum: Medieval and Renaissance Latin Translations and Commentaries*, edited by P. O. Kristeller et al., 1:137–56. Washington, D.C.: Catholic University of America Press, 1960.

Davies, Oliver. *God Within: The Mystical Tradition of Northern Europe.* London: Darton, Longman, and Todd, 1988.

———. *Meister Eckhart: Mystical Theologian.* London: SPCK, 1991.

———. *Meister Eckhart: Selected Writings.* London: Penguin, 1994.

———. "Why Were Eckhart's Propositions Condemned?" *New Blackfriars* 71 (1990): 433–45.

de Andia, Ysabel. "*'pathôn ta theia*." In *Platonism in Late Antiquity*, edited by Stephen

Gersh and Charles Kannengiesser, 239–58. Notre Dame: University of Notre Dame Press, 1992.

de Certeau, Michel. "The Gaze of Nicholas of Cusa." *Diacritics: A Review of Contemporary Criticism* 3 (1987): 2–38.

———. *The Mystic Fable*. Chicago: University of Chicago Press, 1992.

de Gandillac, Maurice. *Valeur du temps dans la pédagogie spirituelle de Jean Tauler*. Paris/Montréal: Vrin, 1956.

———. "La 'dialectique' du Maître Eckhart." In *Le mystique rhénane*, 59–94. Paris: Presses Universitaires de France, 1963.

de Guibert, Joseph. *Documenta ecclesiastica christianae perfectionis studium spectantia*. Rome: Gregorian University Press, 1931.

Delacroix, Henry. *Essai sur le mysticisme spéculatif en Allemagne au XIVe siècle*. Paris: Alcan, 1900.

de Libera, Alain. *Albert le Grand et la philosophie*. Paris: Vrin, 1990.

———. "À propos de quelques théories logiques de Maître Eckhart: Existe-t-il une tradition médiévale de la logique néo-platonicienne?" *Revue de théologie et de philosophie* 113 (1981): 1–24.

———. *La mystique rhénane d'Albert le Grand à Maître Eckhart*. Paris: Éditions du Seuil, 1994.

———. "On Some Philosophical Aspects of Meister Eckhart's Teaching." *Freiburger Zeitschrift für Philosophie und Theologie* 45 (1998): 151–68.

———. *Le problème de l'être chez Maître Eckhart: Logique et métaphysique de l'analogie*. Geneva: Cahiers de la Revue de théologie et de philosophie, 1980.

———. "L'Un ou la Trinité." *Revue des sciences religieuses* 70 (1996): 31–47.

Dengelhardt, Ingeborg. *Studien zum Wandel des Eckhartsbildes*. Leiden: Brill, 1967.

Denifle, Heinrich Seuse. "Einleitung." In *Das Buch von geistlicher Armuth bisher bekannt als Johann Taulers Nachfolgung des armen Lebens Christi*. Munich: Huttler, 1877.

———. "Der Gottesfruend im Oberlande und Nicolaus von Basel." *Historische und politische Blätter* 75 (1875): 17–38, 93–122, 245–66, and 340–54.

———. "Das Leben der Margaretha von Kentzingen: Ein Beitrag zur Geschichte des Gottesfreundes im Oberland." *Zeitschrift für deutsches Alterthum* 19 (1876): 478–91.

———. "Meister Eckeharts lateinische Schriften und die Grundanschauungen seiner Lehre." *Archiv für Literatur- und Kirchengeschichte des Mittelalters* 2 (1886): 417–615.

———. "Taulers Bekehrung." *Historische und politische Blätter* 84 (1879): 797–815, 877–97.

———. *Taulers Bekehrung: Kritisch untersucht*. Strassburg: Trübner, 1879.

Devaux, Augustin. "Surius (Sauer; Laurent)." DS 14:1325–29.

———. "Vincent d'Aggsbach." DS 16:804–6.

Dietsche, Bernward. "Der Seelengrund nach den deutschen und lateinischen Predigten." In *Meister Eckhart der Prediger: Festschrift zum Eckhart-Gedenkjahr*, edited by Udo M. Nix and Raphael Öchslin, 200–58. Freiburg: Herder, 1960.

Dimier, M.-A. "Pour la fiche *spiritus libertatis*." *Revue du moyen âge latin* 3 (1947): 56–60.

Dinzelbacher, Peter. *Christliche Mystik im Abendland. Ihre Geschichte von den Anfängen bis zum Ende des Mittelalters.* Paderborn: Schöningh, 1994.

———. *Vision und Visionsliteratur im Mittelalter.* Stuttgart: Hiersemann, 1981.

Dinzelbacher, Peter, and Kurt Ruh. "Magdalena von Freiburg." VL 5:1117–21.

Dobie, Robert. "Meister Eckhart's Metaphysics of Detachment." *The Modern Schoolman* 80 (2002): 35–54.

———. "Reason and Revelation in the Thought of Meister Eckhart." *The Thomist* 67 (2003): 409–38.

Dondaine, H. F. *Le Corpus Dionysien de l'université de Paris au XIIIe siècle.* Rome: Edizioni de Storia e Letteratura, 1953.

D'Onofrio, Giulio. *Storia della teologia nel Medioevo.* Vol. 2, *La grande fioritura.* Casale Monferrato: Piemme, 1996.

Douglass, E. Jane Dempsey. *Justification in Late Medieval Preaching: A Study of John Geiler of Keisersberg*, 2nd ed. Leiden: Brill, 1989.

Duclow, Donald F. "Hermeneutics and Meister Eckhart." *Philosophy Today* 28 (1984): 36–43.

———. "The Hungers of Hadewijch and Eckhart." *Journal of Religion* 80 (2000): 421–41.

———. "Life and Works." In *Introducing Nicholas of Cusa: A Guide to a Renaissance Man*, edited by Christopher M. Bellitto, Thomas M. Izbicki, and Gerald Christianson, 25–56. New York: Paulist Press, 2004.

———. "Meister Eckhart on the Book of Wisdom: Commentary and Sermons." *Traditio* 43 (1987): 215–35.

———. "Mystical Theology and Intellect in Nicholas of Cusa." *American Catholic Philosophical Quarterly* 64 (1990): 111–29.

———. "'My Suffering Is God': Meister Eckhart's *Book of Divine Consolation*." *Theological Studies* 44 (1983): 570–86.

———. "Nicholas of Cusa in the Margins of Meister Eckhart: Codex Cusanus 21." In *Nicholas of Cusa in Search of God and Wisdom*, edited by Gerald Christianson and Thomas M. Izbicki, 57–69. Leiden: Brill, 1991.

———. "Pseudo-Dionysius, John Scotus Eriugena, Nicholas of Cusa: An Approach to the Hermeneutic of the Divine Names." *International Philosophical Quarterly* 12 (1972): 260–78.

———. "'Whose Image Is This?' in Eckhart's *Sermones*." *Mystics Quarterly* 15 (1989): 29–40.

Dupré, Louis. "The Mystical Theology of Nicholas of Cusa's *De visione dei*." In *Nicholas of Cusa on Christ and the Church*, edited by Gerald Christianson and Thomas M. Izbicki, 205–20. Leiden: Brill, 1996.

———. "Nature and Grace in Cusa's Mystical Philosophy." *American Catholic Philosophical Quarterly* 64 (1990): 153–70.

———. *Passage to Modernity: An Essay in the Hermeneutics of Nature and Culture.* New Haven: Yale University Press, 1993.

Dupré, Wilhelm. "Absolute Truth and Conjectual Insight." In *Nicholas of Cusa on Christ and the Church*, edited by Gerald Christianson and Thomas M. Izbieki, 323–38. Leiden: Brill, 1996.

———. "Das Bild und die Wahrheit." In *Das Sehen Gottes nach Nikolaus von Kues*, edited by Rudolf Haubst, 125–66. *Mitteilungen und Forschungsbeiträge der Cusanus-Gesellschaft* 18. Trier: Paulinus Verlag, 1989.

Egenter, Richard. *Gottesfreundschaft: Die Lehre von der Gottesfreundschaft in der Scholastik und Mystik des 12. und 13. Jahrhunderts*. Augsburg: Filser, 1928.

Egerding, Michael. "Johannes Taulers Auffassung vom Menschen." *Freiburger Zeitschrift für Philosophie und Theologie* 39 (1992): 105–29.

———. *Die Metaphorik der spätmittelalterlichen Mystik*. 2 vols. Paderborn: Schöningh, 1997.

Elliott, Dyan. "Authorizing a Life: The Collaboration of Dorothea of Montau and John Marienwerder." In *Gendered Voices: Medieval Saints and Their Interpreters*, edited by Catherine M. Mooney, 168–91. Philadelphia: University of Pennsylvania Press, 1999.

———. "*Dominae* or *Dominatae*? Female Mysticism and the Trauma of Textuality." In *Women, Marriage, and Family in Medieval Christendom: Essays in Memory of Michael M. Sheehan, C.S.B.*, edited by Constance M. Rousseau and Joel T. Rosenthal, 57–61. Kalamazoo: Medieval Institute Publications, 1998.

———. *Proving Women: Female Spirituality and Inquisitorial Culture in the Later Middle Ages*. Princeton: Princeton University Press, 2004.

Enders, Markus. *Das mystische Wissen bei Heinrich Seuse*. Paderborn: Schöningh, 1993.

———. "Selbsterfahrung als Gotteserfahrung: Zum Individualitätsbewusstsein bei Johannes Tauler." In *Individuum und Individualität im Mittelalter*, edited by Jan A. Aertsen and Andreas Speer, 642–64. Berlin: Walter de Gruyter, 1996.

Euler, Walter. "Die Predigten des Nikolaus von Kues." *Trierer theologische Zeitschrift* 110 (2001): 280–93.

———. "Proclamation of Christ in Selected Sermons from Cusanus's Brixen Period." In *Nicholas of Cusa and His Age: Intellect and Spirituality*, edited by Thomas M. Izbicki and Christopher M. Bellitto, 89–103. Leiden: Brill, 2002.

Fechter, Werner. "Meyer, Johannes, OP." VL 6:474–89.

Festugière, A.-J. *La révélation d'Hermes Trismégiste*. 4 vols. Paris: Gabalda, 1950–54.

Fidora, Alexander, and Andreas Niederberger. *Von Bagdad nach Toledo: Das "Buch der Ursachen" und seine Rezeption im Mittelalter*. Mainz: Dieterich'sche Verlagsbuchhandlung, 2001.

———. *Vom Einen zum Vielen: Der neue Aufbruch der Metaphysik im 12. Jahrhundert*. Frankfurt: Klostermann, 2002.

Filthaut, Ephrem M., editor. *Heinrich Seuse: Studien zum 600 Todestag, 1366–1966*. Cologne, 1966.

———, editor. *Johannes Tauler: Ein deutsche Mystiker. Gedenkschrift zum 600. Todestag*. Essen: Driewer, 1961.

Fischer, C. "Bonaventure (Apocryphes attribuées à saint)." DS 1:1843–56.

Fischer, Heribert. "Fond de l'Âme: I, Chez Maître Eckhart." DS 5:650–61.

———. "Grundgedanken der deutschen Predigten." In *Meister Eckhart der Prediger*, edited by Udo M. Nix and Raphael Öchslin, 55–59. Freiburg: Herder, 1960.

———. "Zur Frage nach der Mystik in den Werken Meister Eckharts." In *La mystique rhénane*, 109–32. Paris: Presses Universitaires de France, 1963.

Flasch, Kurt. "Die Intention Meister Eckharts." In *Sprache und Begriff: Festschrift für Bruno Liebrucks*, edited by Heinz Röttges, 292–318. Meisenheim am Glan: Hain, 1974.

———. "Meister Eckhart: Versuch ihn aus dem mystischen Strom zu retten." In *Gnosis und Mystik in der Geschichte der Philosophie*, edited by Peter Koslowski, 94–110. Darmstadt: Wissenschaftliche Buchgesellschaft, 1988.

———. *Nikolaus von Kues–Geschichte einer Entwicklung: Vorlesungen zur Einführung in seine Philosophie*. Frankfurt: Klostermann, 1998.

———. "Procedere ut imago: Das Hervorgehen des Intellekts aus seinem göttlichen Grund bei Meister Dietrich, Meister Eckhart und Berthold von Moosburg." In *Abendländische Mystik im Mittelalter*, edited by Kurt Ruh, 125–34. Stuttgart: Metzler, 1986.

Forman, Robert. *Meister Eckhart: Mystic as Theologian*. Rockport: Element Books, 1991.

Fowden, Garth. *The Egyptian Hermes: A Historical Approach to the Late Pagan Mind*. Cambridge: Cambridge University Press, 1986.

Fraioli, Deborah A. *Joan of Arc: The Early Debate*. Woodbridge: Boydell Press, 2000.

Freedburg, David. *The Power of Images: Studies in the History and Theory of Response*. Chicago: University of Chicago Press, 1989.

Führer, Mark L. "Albertus Magnus Theory of Divine Illumination." In *Albertus Magnus: Zum Gedenken nach 800 Jahren: Neue Zugänge, Aspekte und Perspektive*, edited by Walter Senner et al., 141–55. Berlin: Akademie Verlag, 2001.

———. "The Consolation of Contemplation in Nicholas of Cusa's *De visione dei*." In *Nicholas of Cusa on Christ and the Church*, edited by Gerald Christianson and Thomas M. Izbicki, 221–40. Leiden: Brill, 1996.

Fulton, Rachel. *From Judgment to Passion: Devotion to Christ and the Virgin Mary, 800–1200*. New York: Columbia University Press, 2002.

Gadamer, Hans Georg. "Hegel and the Dialectic of the Ancient Philosophers." In *Hegel's Dialectic: Five Hermeneutical Studies*, 5–34. New Haven: Yale University Press, 1976.

Gandlau, Thomas. *Trinität und Kreuz: Die Nachfolge Christi in der Mystagogie Johannes Taulers*. Freiburg: Herder, 1993.

Ganoczy, Alexandre. *Der dreieinige Schöpfer: Trinitätstheologie und Synergie*. Darmstadt: Wissenschaftliche Buchgesellschaft, 2001.

Gersh, Stephen E. "Berthold of Moosburg and the Content and Method of Platonic Theology." In *Nach der Verurteilung von 1277: Philosophie und Theologie an der Universität von Paris im letzten Viertel des 13. Jahrhunderts. Studien und Texte*, edited by Jan A. Aertsen, Kent Emery, Jr., and Andreas Speer, 493–503. Berlin: Walter de Gruyter, 2001.

———. *From Iamblichus to Eriugena: An Investigation of the Prehistory and Evolution of the Pseudo-Dionysian Tradition.* Leiden: Brill, 1978.

Geyer, Bernhard. "Albertus Magnus und Meister Eckhart." In *Festschrift Josef Quint anlässlich seines 65. Geburtstages überreicht,* edited by Hugo Moser et al., 121–26. Bonn: Semmel, 1964.

Gnädinger, Louise. "'Der Abgrund ruft dem Abgrund': Taulers Predigt Beati oculi (V 45)." In *Das "einig Ein": Studien zur Theorie und Sprache der deutschen Mystik,* edited by Alois M. Haas and Heinrich Stirnimann, 167–207. Freiburg, Switzerland: Universitätsverlag, 1980.

———. "Die Altväterzitat im Predigtwerk Johannes Taulers." In *Unterwegs zur Einheit: Festschrift für Heinrich Stirnimann,* edited by Johannes Brantschen and Pietro Selvatico, 253–67. Freiburg, Switzerland: Universitätsverlag, 1980.

———. *Johannes Tauler: Lebenswelt und mystische Lehre.* Munich: Beck, 1993.

Gillen, Otto. "Braut-Bräutigam," and "Brautmystik." In *Reallexikon zur deutschen Kunstgeschichte,* edited by O. Schmidt, 2:1110–24, 1130–34. Stuttgart and Munich: Metzler, 1937.

Glorieux, Palémon. "Gerson (Jean)." DS 6:314–31.

Gorceix, Bernard. *Amis de Dieu en Allemagne au siècle de Maître Eckhart.* Paris: Michel, 1984.

Goris, Wouter. *Einheit als Prinzip und Ziel: Versuch über die Einheitsmetaphysik des "Opus tripartitum" Meister Eckharts.* Leiden: Brill, 1997.

Grabmann, Martin. "Bayerische Benediktinermystik am Ausgang des Mittelalters." *Benediktinische Monatschrift zur Pflege religiösen und geistigen Lebens* 2 (1920): 196–202.

———. "Der Einfluss Alberts der Grossen auf das mittelalterliches Geistesleben: Das deutsche Element in den mittelalterlichen Scholastik und Mystik." In Martin Grabmann, *Mittelalterliches Geistesleben,* 2:325–412. Munich: Heuber, 1936.

———. "Die Erklärung des Bernhard von Waging O.S.B. zum Schlusskapitel von Bonaventuras Itinerarium mentis in Deum." *Franziskanische Studien* 8 (1925): 125–35.

———. "Die Lehre des hl. Thomas von Aquin von der *scintilla animae* in ihre Bedeutung für die deutsche Mystik des Predigerordens." *Jahrbuch für Philosophie und spekulativen Theologie* 14 (1900): 413–27.

Grant, Robert M. "Gnostic Spirituality." In *Christian Spirituality: Origins to the Twelfth Century,* edited by Bernard McGinn, John Meyendorff, and Jean Leclercq, 44–60. Encyclopedia of World Spirituality. New York: Crossroad, 1986.

Greenspan, Karen (Kate). "Autohagiography and Medieval Womens' Spiritual Autobiography." In *Gender and Text in the Later Middle Ages,* edited by Jane Chance, 216–36. Gainesville: University of Florida Press, 1996.

———. "Erklaerung des Vaterunsers: A critical edition of a 15th century mystical treatise by Magdalena Beutler of Freiburg." Dissertation, University of Massachusetts, 1984.

Grégoire, Réginald. "Sang." DS 14:319–33.

Greith, Carl. *Die deutsche Mystik im Prediger-Orden (von 1250–1350).* Freiburg-im-Breisgau: Herder, 1861.

Grundmann, Herbert. "Ketzerverhöre des Spätmittelalters als quellenkritisches Problem." *Deutsches Archiv für Erforschung des Mittelalters* 21 (1965): 519–75.

———. *Religious Movements in the Middle Ages.* Notre Dame: University of Notre Dame Press, 1995.

Guagliardo, Vincent A. "Introduction." In *Thomas Aquinas: Commentary on the Book of Causes,* translated by Vincent A. Guagliardo, Charles R. Hess, and Richard C. Taylor, ix–xxxvii. Washington, D.C.: Catholic University of America Press, 1996.

Guarnieri, Romana."Frères du Libre Esprit." DS 5:1241–68.

———. "Gesuati." In *Dizionario degli Istituti di Perfezione,* edited by Guerrino Pelliccia and Giancarlo Rocca. 11 vols., 4:1116–30. Rome: Edizioni Paoline, 1973–2003.

———. "Il Movimento dello Libero Spirito dalle Origini al Secolo XVI." *Archivio Italiano per la Storia della Pietà* 4 (1965): 353–708.

Guillaumont, Antoine. "Messaliens." DS 10:1074–83.

Gullick, Etta, and Optat de Veghel. "Herp (Henri de; Harphius)." DS 7:346–66.

Gutiérrez, David. "Eremites de Saint-Augustin." DS 4:983–1018.

Haas, Alois Maria. "Aktualität und Normativität Meister Eckharts." In *Eckhardus Theutonicus, homo doctus et sanctus: Nachweise und Berichte zum Prozess gegen Meister Eckhart,* edited by Heinrich Stirnimann and Reudi Imbach, 203–68. Freiburg, Switzerland: Universitätsverlag, 1992.

———. "Die Aktualität Meister Eckhart: Ein Klassiker der Mystik (ca. 1260–1328)." In *Gottes Nähe: Religiöse Erfahrung in Mystik und Offenbarung. Festschrift zum 65. Geburtstag von Josef Sudbruck,* edited by Paul Imhoff, 79–94. Würzburg: Echter, 1990.

———. "'Die Arbeit der Nacht': Mystische Leiderfahrung nach Johannes Tauler." In *Die dunkle Nacht der Sinne: Leiderfahrung und christliche Mystik,* edited by Gotthard Fuchs et al., 9–40. Düsseldorf: Patmos, 1989.

———. "Die Beurteilung der Vita contemplativa und vita activa in der Dominikanermystik des 14. Jahrhunderts." In Alois M. Haas, *Gottleiden–Gottlieben: Zur volksprachlichen Mystik im Mittelalter,* 97–108. Frankfurt: Insel, 1989.

———. *DEUM MISTICE VIDERE . . . IN CALIGINE COINCIDENCIE: Zum Verhältnis Nikolaus' von Kues zur Mystik.* Basel and Frankfurt: Helbing & Lichtenhahn, 1989.

———. "Deutsche Mystik." In *Geschichte der deutschen Literatur III/2: Die deutsche Literatur im späten Mittelalter 1250–1370,* edited by Ingeborg Glier, 234–305. Munich: Beck, 1987.

———. "Dichtung in christlicher Mystik und Zen-Buddhismus." *Zen Buddhism Today* 9 (1992): 86–116.

———. "Gottesfreundschaft." In Alois M. Haas, *Mystik im Kontext,* 195–202. Munich: Fink, 2004.

———. "Granum sinapis–An den Grenzen der Sprache." In Alois M. Haas, *Sermo mysticus. Studien zu Theologie und Sprache der deutschen Mystik*, 301–29. Freiburg, Switzerland: Universitätsverlag, 1979.

———. "Jesus Christus–Inbegriff des Heils und verwirklichte Transzendenz im Geist der deutschen Mystik." In Alois M. Haas, *Geistliches Mittelalter*, 291–314. Freiburg, Switzerland: Universitätsverlag, 1984

———. "Johannes Tauler." In *Sermo mysticus*, 255–95.

———. *Kunst rechter Gelassenheit: Themen und Schwerpunkte von Heinrich Seuses Mystik.* Bern: Lang, 1995.

———. "Mechthild von Magdeburg." In *Sermo mysticus*, 67–135.

———. *Meister Eckhart als normative Gestalt geistlichen Lebens.* 2nd ed. Freiburg: Johannes, 1995.

———. "Meister Eckharts geistliches Predigtprogramm." In *Geistliches Mittelalter*, 317–38.

———. "Meister Eckhart. Mystische Bildlehre." In *Sermo mysticus*, 209–37.

———. "Meister Eckharts Auffassung von Zeit und Ewigkeit." In *Geistliches Mittelalter*, 339–55.

———. "Meister Eckhart und die deutsche Sprache." In *Geistliches Mittelalter*, 215–38.

———. "MORS MYSTICA: Ein mystologisches Motiv." In *Sermo mysticus*, 392–480.

———. "Mystische Erfahrung und Sprache." In *Sermo mysticus*, 19–36.

———. "Das mystische Paradox." In *Das Paradox: Eine Herausforderung des abendländische Denkens*, edited by Paul Geyer and Roland Hagenbüchle, 273–89. Tübingen: Stauffenberg, 1992.

———. *NIM DIN SELBES WAR: Studien zur Lehre von der Selbsterkenntnis bei Meister Eckhart, Johannes Tauler und Heinrich Seuse.* Freiburg, Switzerland: Universitätsverlag, 1971.

———. "The Nothingness of God and its Explosive Metaphors." *The Eckhart Review* 8 (1999): 6–17.

———. ". . . 'Das Persönliche und eigene verleugnen": Mystische vernichtigkeit und verworffenheit sein selbs in Geiste Meister Eckharts." In *Individualität: Poetik und Hermeneutik XIII*, edited Manfred Frank and Anselm Haverkamp, 106–22. Munich: Fink, 1988.

———. "Seinsspekulation und Geschöpflichkeit in der Mystik Meister Eckharts." In *Sein und Nichts in der abendländischen Mystik*, edited by Walter Strolz, 33–58. Freiburg: Herder, 1984.

———. "Schools of Late Medieval Mysticism." In *Christian Spirituality: High Middle Ages and Reformation*, edited by Jill Raitt et al., 140–75. Encyclopedia of World Spirituality. New York: Crossroad, 1987.

———. "Sprache und mystische Erfahrung nach Tauler und Seuse." In *Geistliches Mittelalter*, 239–47.

———. "Die 'Theologia Deutsch': Konstitution eines mystologisches Texts." In *Das "einig Ein": Studien zu Theorie und Sprache der deutschen Mystik*, edited by Alois M.

Haas and Heinrich Stirnimann, 369–415. Freiburg, Switzerland: Universitätsverlag, 1980.

———. "'Trage Leiden geduldiglich': Die Einstellung der deutschen Mystik zum Leiden." *Zeitwende* 57, no. 3 (1986): 154–75.

Haas, Alois Maria, and Kurt Ruh. "Seuse, Heinrich OP." VL 8:1109–29.

Hackett, Jeremiah. "The Reception of Meister Eckhart: Mysticism, Philosophy and Theology in Jordanus of Quedlinburg and Henry of Friemar (The Older)." Forthcoming.

Hadot, Pierre. *Philosophy as a Way of Life: Spiritual Exercises from Socrates to Foucault*, edited with an introduction by Arnold I. Davidson. Oxford: Blackwell, 1995.

Hamburger, Jeffrey F. "Medieval Self-Fashioning: Authorship, Authority and Autobiography in Seuse's *Exemplar*." In *Christ among the Medieval Dominicans*, edited by Kent Emery, Jr., and Joseph P. Wawrykow, 430–61. Notre Dame: University of Notre Dame Press, 1998.

———. *Nuns as Artists: The Visual Culture of a Medieval Convent.* Berkeley: University of California, 1997.

———. "Revelation and Concealment: Apophatic Imagery in the Trinitarian Miniatures of the Rothschild Canticles." Beinecke Studies in Early Manuscripts. *The Yale University Library Gazette* 66, Supplement (1991): 134–58.

———. *The Rothschild Canticles: Art and Mysticism in Flanders and the Rhineland circa 1300.* New Haven: Yale University Press, 1990.

———. *St. John the Divine: The Deified Evangelist in Medieval Art and Theology.* Berkeley: University of California Press, 2002.

———. "Speculations on Speculation: Vision and Perception in the Theory and Practice of Mystical Devotion." In *Deutsche Mystik im abendländische Zusammenhang*, edited by Walter Haug and Wolfram Schneider-Lastin, 353–408. Tübingen: Niemeyer, 2000.

———. "The Use of Images in the Pastoral Care of Nuns: The Case of Heinrich Suso and the Dominicans." *The Art Bulletin* 71 (1988): 20–46.

———. "The Visual and the Visionary: The Image in Late Medieval Monastic Devotion." In Jeffrey F. Hamburger, *The Visual and the Visionary: Art and Female Spirituality in Late Medieval Germany*, 111–48. New York: Zone, 1998.

Hasebrink, Burkhard. "*EIN EINIC EIN:* Zur Darstellung der Liebeseinheit in mittelhochdeutscher Literatur." *Beiträge zur Geschichte der deutschen Literatur und Sprache* 124 (2002): 442–65.

———. *Formen inzitativer Rede bei Meister Eckhart: Untersuchungen zur literarische Konzeption der deutschen Predigt.* Tübingen: Niemeyer, 1992.

———. "GRENZVERSCHIEBUNG: Zu Kongruenz und Differenz von Latein und Deutsch bei Meister Eckhart." *Zeitschrift für deutsches Altertum und deutsche Literatur* 121 (1992): 369–98.

———. "Studies on the Redaction and Use of the *Paradisus anime intelligentis*." In *De l'homélie au sermon: Histoire de la prédication médiévale*, edited by Jacqueline Hamesse and Xavier Hermand, 143–58. Louvain-la-Neuve: Université Catholique, 1993.

Haubst, Rudolf. *Das Bild des Einen und Dreieinen Gottes in der Welt nach Nikolaus von Kues.* Trier: Paulinus, 1952.

———. *Die Christologie Nikolaus von Kues.* Freiburg-im-Breisgau: Herder, 1956.

———. "Die erkenntnis-theoretische und mystische Bedeutung der 'Maurer der Koincidenz.'" In *Das Sehen Gottes nach Nikolaus von Kues,* edited by Rudolf Haubst, 167–95. Mitteilungen und Forschungsbeiträge der Cusanus-Gesellschaft 18. Trier: Paulinus, 1989.

———. "Die leitende Gedanken und Motive der cusanischen Theologie." In *Das Cusanus-Jubiläum,* edited by Rudolf Haubst, 257–77. *Mitteilungen und Forschungsbeiträge der Cusanus-Gesellschaft* 4. Mainz: Matthias-Grünewald, 1964.

———. "Nikolaus von Kues als Interpret und Verteidiger Meister Eckhart." In *Freiheit und Gelassenheit: Meister Eckhart heute,* edited by Udo Kern, 75–96. Grünwald: Kaiser, 1980.

———. *Streifzüge in die Cusanische Theologie.* Münster: Aschendorff, 1991.

———. *Studien zu Niklaus von Kues und Johannes Wenck: Aus Handscriften der Vatikanischen Bibliothek.* Münster: Aschendorff, 1955.

———. *Von Sinn der Menschwerdung: "Cur Deus homo."* Munich: Heuber, 1969.

———, editor. *Nikolaus von Kues in der Geschichte des Erkenntnisproblems. Mitteilungen und Forschungsbeiträge der Cusanus-Gesellschaft* 11. Mainz: Matthias-Grünewald, 1975.

Haucke, Rainer. *Trinität und Denken: Die Unterscheidung der Einheit von Gott und Mensch bei Eckhart.* Frankfurt: Lang, 1986

Haug, Walter. "Johannes Taulers Via negationis." In *Die Passion Christi in Literatur und Kunst des Spätmittelalters,* edited by Walter Haug and Burghart Wachinger, 76–93. Tübingen: Niemeyer, 1993.

———. "Die Maurer des Paradieses: Zur mystica theologia des Nicholas Cusanus in 'De visione Dei.'" *Theologische Zeitschrift* 45 (1989): 216–30.

———. "Meister Eckhart und das 'Granum sinapis.'" In *Forschungen zur deutschen Literatur des Spätmittelalters: Festschrift für Johannes Janota,* edited by Horst Brunner and Werner Williams-Krapp, 73–92. Tübingen: Niemeyer, 2003.

———. "Das Wort und die Sprache bei Meister Eckhart." In *Zur deutschen Literatur und Sprache des 14. Jahrhunderts: Dubliner Colloquium 1981,* edited by Walter Haug, Timothy R. Jackson, Johannes Janota, 25–44. Heidelberg: Winter, 1983.

Hausherr, Irenée. "L'erreur fondamentale et la logique du messalianisme." *Orientalia Christiana Periodica* 1 (1935): 328–60.

Hausherr, Reiner. "Über die Christus-Johannes-Gruppen: Zum Problem 'Andachtsbilder' und deutsche Mystik." In *Beiträge zur Kunst des Mittelalters: Festschrift für Hans Wentzel zum 60. Geburtstag,* edited Rüdiger Beckemann, Ulf-Dietrich Korn, Johannes Zahlten, 79–103. Berlin: Mann, 1975.

Heffner, Blake R. "Meister Eckhart and a Millennium with Mary and Martha." In *Biblical Hermeneutics in Historical Perspective,* edited by Mark S. Burrows and Paul Rorem, 117–30. Grand Rapids: Eerdmans, 1991.

Heinzle, Joachim. "Lamprecht von Regensburg." VL 5:522–24.

Henle, R. J. *Saint Thomas and Platonism.* The Hague: Nijhoff, 1956.

Herlihy, David. *The Black Death and the Transformation of the West,* edited with an introduction by Samuel K. Cohn, Jr. Cambridge, Mass.: Harvard University Press, 1997.

Herzog, George J. "Mystical Theology in Late Medieval Preaching: John Geiler of Kaysersberg (1445–1510)." Ph.D. dissertation, Boston University, 1985.

Hillenbrand, Eugen. "Die Observantenbewegung in der deutschen Ordensprovinz der Dominikaner." In *Reformbemühungen und Observantenbestrebungen im spätmittelalterlichen Ordenswesen,* edited by Kaspar Elm, 219–71. Berlin: Duncker & Humboldt, 1989.

Hlaváček, Ivan. "The Luxemburgs and Rupert of the Palatinate, 1347–1410." In *The New Cambridge Medieval History.* Vol. 6, *c. 1300–1415,* edited by Michael Jones, 551–69. Cambridge: Cambridge University Press, 2000.

Hoenen, Maarten, J.F.M. "Johannes Tauler (d. 1361) in den Niederlanden: Grundzüge eines philosophie- und rezeptionsgeschichtlichen Forschungsprogramms." *Freiburger Zeitschrift für Philosophie und Theologie* 41 (1994): 389–444.

Hof, Hans. *Scintilla Animae: Eine Studie zu einem Grundbegriff in Meister Eckharts Philosophie.* Lund: Gleerup; Bonn: Hanstein, 1952.

Hoffman, Bengt. "Introduction." In *The Theologia Germanica of Martin Luther,* 1–50. New York: Paulist Press, 1980.

Hollywood, Amy. *The Soul as Virgin Wife: Mechthild of Magdeburg, Marguerite Porete, and Meister Eckhart.* Notre Dame: University of Notre Dame Press, 1995.

Honemann, Volker. "Johannes von Sterngassen." VL 4:760–62.

———. "Der Laie als Leser." In *Laienfrömmigkeit im späten Mittelalter: Formen, Funktionen, politisch-soziale Zusammenhänge,* edited by Klaus Schreiner, 241–51. Munich: Oldenbourg, 1992 .

———. "Sprüche der zwölf Meister zu Paris." VL 9:201–5.

Hopkins, Jasper. *A Concise Introduction to the Philosophy of Nicholas of Cusa.* Minneapolis: University of Minnesota Press, 1978.

———. *Glaube und Vernunft im Denken des Nikolaus von Kues: Prolegomena zu einem Umriss seiner Auffassung.* Trierer Cusanus Lecture 3. Trier: Cusanus-Institut, 1996.

———. *Nicholas of Cusa On Learned Ignorance: A Translation and an Appraisal of De Docta Ignorantia.* Minneapolis: Arthur J. Banning, 1981.

———. *Nicholas of Cusa's Debate with John Wenck: A Translation and Appraisal of De Ignota Litteratura and Apologia Doctae Ignorantiae.* Minneapolis: Arthur J. Banning, 1981.

———. *Nicholas of Cusa's Dialectical Mysticism: Text, Translation, and Interpretive Study of De visione dei.* Minneapolis: Arthur J. Banning, 1985.

———. "Verständnis und Bedeutung des dreieinen Gottes bei Nikolaus von Kues." In *Nikolaus von Kues 1401–2001,* edited by Klaus Kremer and Klaus Reinhardt, 135–64. *Mitteilungen und Forschungsbeiträge der Cusanus-Gesellschaft* 28. Trier: Paulinus, 2003.

Hörner, Petra. *Dorothea von Montau: Überlieferung–Interpretation. Dorothea und die osteuropäisches Mystik.* Frankfurt: Lang, 1993.

Höver, Werner. "Bernhard von Waging." VL 1:779–89.

Howells, Edward. *John of the Cross and Teresa of Avila: Mystical Knowing and Selfhood.* New York: Crossroad, 2002.

Hoye, William J. "Gotteserkenntnis per essentiam im 13. Jahrhundert." In *Die Auseinandersetzungen an der Pariser Universität im XIII. Jahrhundert,* edited by Albert Zimmermann, 269–84. Berlin: Walter de Gruyter, 1976.

———. "The Meaning of Neoplatonism in the Thought of Nicholas of Cusa." *Downside Review* 104 (1986): 10–18.

———. *Die mystische Theologie des Nicolaus Cusanus.* Freiburg: Herder, 2004.

———. "Mystische Theologie nach Albert dem Grossen." In *Albertus Magnus: Zum Gedenken nach 800 Jahren,* edited by Walter Senner et al., 587–603. Berlin: Akademie, 2001.

———. "Die Vereinigung mit dem gänzlich Unerkannten nach Bonaventura, Nikolaus von Kues und Thomas von Aquin." In *Die Dionysius-Rezeption im Mittelalter,* edited by Tzotcho Boiadjiev, Georgi Kapriev, and Andreas Speer, 477–504. Turnhout: Brepols, 2000.

Huizinga, Johan. *The Autumn of the Middle Ages.* Translated by Rodney J. Payton and Ulrich Mammitzsch. Chicago: University of Chicago Press, 1996.

Hundersmarck, Lawrence F. "Preaching." In *Introducing Nicholas of Cusa: A Guide to a Renaissance Man,* edited by Christopher M. Bellitto,Thomas M. Izbicki, and Gerald Christianson, 232–69. New York: Paulist Press, 2004.

Imbach, Ruedi. *DEUS EST INTELLIGERE: Das Verhältnis von Sein und Denken in seiner Bedeutung für das Gottesverständnis bei Thomas von Aquin und in den Pariser Quaestionen Meister Eckharts.* Freiburg, Switzerland: Universitätsverlag, 1976.

———. "Le (Néo-)Platonism médiévale, Proclus latin et l'école dominicaine allemande." *Revue de théologie et philosophie* 110 (1978): 427–48.

Iohn, Friedrich. *Die Predigt Meister Eckharts.* Heidelberg: Winter, 1993.

Jones, Rufus M. *The Flowering of Mysticism: The Friends of God in the Fourteenth Century.* New York: Macmillan, 1939.

Jordan, Mark D. "The Names of God and the Being of Names." In *The Existence and Nature of God,* edited by Alfred J. Freddoso, 161–90. Notre Dame: University of Notre Dame Press, 1983.

Jundt, Auguste. *Les amis de Dieu au 14e siècle.* Paris: Sandoz and Fischbacher, 1879.

———. *Histoire du pantheisme populaire au moyen âge et au siezième siècle.* Paris, 1875. Reprint, Frankfurt: Minerva, 1964.

———. *Rulman Merswin et l'Ami de Dieu de l'Oberland: Un problème de psychologie religieuse.* Paris: Fischbacher, 1890.

Kampmann, Irmgard. *"Ihr sollt der Sohn selber sein": Eine fundamentaltheologische Studie zur Soteriologie Meister Eckharts.* Frankfurt: Lang, 1996.

Keel, Anselm, editor. *Bruder Klaus von Flüe: Rat aus der Tiefe.* Zurich: Benziger, 1999.

Keller, Hildegard Elisabeth. "Kolophon im Herzen: Von beschrifteten Mönchen an den Rändern der Paläographie." *Das Mittelalter* 7 (2002): 157–82.

———. *My Secret Is Mine: Studies in Religion and Eros in the German Middle Ages.* Leuven: Peeters, 2000.

Kelley, C. F. *The Book of the Poor in Spirit by a Friend of God (Fourteenth Century): A Guide to Rhineland Mysticism.* New York: Harper, 1954.

———. *Meister Eckhart on Divine Knowledge.* New Haven: Yale University Press, 1977.

Kelly, H. Ansgar. "Inquisition and the Persecution of Heresy: Misconceptions and Abuses." *Church History* 58 (1989): 439–51.

Kepler, Thomas S. *Mystical Writings of Rulman Merswin.* Philadelphia: Westminster, 1960.

Kieckhefer, Richard. "Meister Eckhart's Conception of Union with God." *Harvard Theological Review* 71 (1978): 203–25.

———. "The Notion of Passivity in the Sermons of Tauler." *Recherches de théologie ancienne et médiévale* 48 (1981): 198–211.

———. *Repression of Heresy in Medieval Germany.* Philadelphia: University of Pennsylvania Press, 1979.

———. "The Role of Christ in Tauler's Spirituality." *The Downside Review* 96 (1978): 176–91.

———. *Unquiet Souls: Fourteenth-Century Saints in Their Religious Milieu.* Chicago: University of Chicago Press, 1984.

Kirk, K. E. *The Vision of God: The Christian Doctrine of the "Summum Bonum."* London: Longmans & Green, 1932.

Kirmsee, Kurt. *Die Terminologie des Mystikers Johannes Tauler.* Leipzig: Vogel, 1930.

Klibansky, Raymond. *The Continuity of the Platonic Tradition during the Middle Ages.* London: Warburg Institute, 1939.

Köbele, Susanne. *Bilder der unbegriffenen Wahrheit: Zur Struktur mystischer Rede im Spannungsfeld von Latein und Volkssprache.* Tübingen and Basel: Francke, 1993.

———. *"BÎWORT SÎN:* 'Absolute' Grammatik bei Meister Eckhart." *Zeitschrift für deutsche Philologie* 113 (1994): 190–206.

———. "Meister Eckhart und die 'Hunde des Herrn': Vom Umgang der Kirche mit ihrem Ketzern." *Beiträge zur Geschichte der deutschen Sprache und Literatur* 124 (2002): 48–73.

———. *"PRIMO ASPECTU MONSTRUOSA:* Schriftauslegung bei Meister Eckhart." *Zeitschrift für deutsches Altertum und deutsche Literatur* 122 (1993): 62–81.

Koch, Josef. "Kritische Studien zum Leben Meister Eckharts." *Archivum Fratrum Praedicatorum* 29 (1959): 1–51; 30 (1960): 1–52.

———. "Philosophische und theologische Irrtumslisten von 1270–1329." In Josef Koch, *Kleine Schriften,* 2:423–50. 2 vols. Rome: Edizioni di Storia e Letteratura, 1973.

———. "Zur Analogielehre Meister Eckharts." In *Mélanges offerts à Etienne Gilson,* 327–50. Paris: Vrin, 1959.

Koyré, Alexandre. *From the Closed World to the Infinite Universe.* Baltimore: Johns Hopkins University Press, 1957.

Kraume, Herbert. "Geiler, Johannes, von Kaysersberg." VL 2:1141–52.

Kremer, Klaus. "Gottes Vorsehung und die menschlicher Freiheit ('Sis tu tuus, et Ego ero tuus')." In *Das Sehen Gottes nach Nicolaus von Kues,* edited by Rudolf

Haubst, 227–63. *Mitteilungen und Forschungsbeiträge der Cusanus-Gesellschaft* 18.Trier: Paulinus, 1989.

———. *Nicholas of Cusa (1401–1464).* Trier: Paulinus, 2002.

———. "Das Seelenfunklein bei Meister Eckhart." *Trierer theologische Zeitschrift* 97 (1988): 8–38.

Kristeller, Paul Oskar. "Proclus as a Reader of Plato and Plotinus, and His Influence in the Middle Ages and Renaissance." In *Proclus: Lecteur et interprète des anciens,* 191–211. Paris: CNRS, 1987.

Kunisch, Herman. *Das Wort "Grund" in der Sprache der deutschen Mystik des 14. und 15. Jahrhunderts.* Osnabrück: Pagenkämper, 1929.

Lane, Belden C. *The Solace of Fierce Landscapes: Exploring Desert and Mountain Spirituality.* New York and Oxford: Oxford University Press, 1998.

Langer, Otto. *Christliche Mystik im Mittelalter: Mystik und Rationalisierung–Stationen eines Konflikts.* Darmstadt: Wissenschaftliche Buchgesellschaft, 2004.

———. "Meister Eckharts Lehre vom Seelengrund." In *Grundfragen christliche Mystik,* edited by Margot Schmidt and Dieter R. Bauer, 173–91. Stuttgart-Bad Cannstatt: frommann-holzboog, 1987.

———. *Mystische Erfahrung und spirituelle Theologie: Zu Meister Eckharts Auseinandersetzung mit der Frauenfrömmigkeit seiner Zeit.* Munich and Zurich: Artemis, 1987.

Lanzetta, Beverly. "Three Categories of Nothingness in Meister Eckhart." *Journal of Religion* 72 (1992): 248–68.

Largier, Niklaus. *Bibliographie zu Meister Eckhart.* Freiburg, Switzerland: Universitätsverlag, 1989.

———. "*Figurata locutio:* Philosophie und Hermeneutik bei Eckhart von Hochheim und Heinrich Seuse." In *Meister Eckhart: Lebensstationen–Redesituationen,* edited by Klaus Jacobi, 328–32. Berlin: Akademie Verlag, 1997.

———. "'Intellectus in deum ascensus': Intellekttheoretische Auseinandersetzungen in Texten der deutschen Mystik." *Deutsche Vierteljahrsschrift für Literaturwissenschaft und Geistesgeschichte* 69 (1995): 423–71.

———. "Intellekttheorie, Hermeneutik und Allegorie: Subjekt und Subjektivität bei Meister Eckhart." In *Geschichte und Vorgeschichte der modernen Subjektivität,* edited by Reto Luzius Fetz, Roland Hagenbüchle, and Peter Schulz, 460–86. Berlin and New York: Walter de Gruyter, 1998.

———. "Interpreting Eckhart's Incarnation Theology: The Sermon Collection *Paradisus anime intelligentis.*" *Eckhart Review* 13 (Spring 2004): 25–36.

———. "Der Körper der Schrift: Bild und Text am Beispiel einer Seuse-Handschrift des 15. Jahrhunderts." In *Mittelalter: Neue wege durch einen alten Kontinent,* edited by Jan-Dirk Müller and Horst Wenzel, 241–71. Stuttgart and Leipzig: Hirzel, 1999.

———. "Meister Eckhart: Perspektiven der Forschung, 1980–1993." *Zeitschrift für deutsche Philologie* 114 (1995): 29–98.

———. "Penser la finitude: Création, détachement et les limites de la philosophie dans la pensée de maître Eckhart." *Revue des sciences religieuses* 71 (1997): 458–73.

———. "Recent Work on Meister Eckhart: Positions, Problems, New Perspectives, 1990–1997." *Recherches de théologie et philosophie médiévales* 65 (1998):147–67.

———. "Repräsentation und Negativität: Meister Eckharts Kritik als Dekonstruktion." In *Contemplata aliis tradere: Studien zum Verhältnis von Literatur und Spiritualität*, edited Claudia Brinker et al., 371–90. Frankfurt: Lang, 1995.

———. "Sermo XXV: 'Gratia dei sum id quod sum.'" In *Lectura Eckhardi II*, edited by Georg Steer and Loris Sturlese, 177–203. Stuttgart: Kohlhammer, 2003.

———. "Von Hadewijch, Mechthild und Dietrich zu Eckhart und Seuse? Zur Historiographie der 'deutschen Mystik' und der 'deutschen Dominikanerschule.'" In *Deutsche Mystik im abendländische Zusammenhang*, edited by Walter Haug and Wolfram Schneider-Lastin, 93–117. Tübingen: Niemeyer, 2000.

———. *ZEIT, ZEITLICHKEIT, EWIGKEIT: Ein Aufriss des Zeitproblems bei Dietrich von Freiburg and Meister Eckhart.* Frankfurt: Lang, 1989.

Laurent, M.-H. "Autour de procès de Maître Eckhart." *Divus Thomas* ser. III, 13 (1936): 331–48, and 430–47.

Leclercq, Jean. *Études sur le vocabulaire monastique du moyen âge.* Rome: Herder, 1961.

Leff, Gordon. *The Dissolution of the Medieval Outlook: An Essay on Intellectual and Spiritual Change in the Fourteenth Century.* New York: Harper & Row, 1976.

———. *Heresy in the Later Middle Ages.* 2 vols. New York: Barnes and Noble, 1967.

Leppin, Volker. "Mystische Frömmigkeit und sakramentale Heilsvermittlung im späten Mittelalter." *Zeitschrift für Kirchengeschichte* 112 (2001): 189–204.

Lerner, Robert E. *The Heresy of the Free Spirit in the Later Middle Ages.* Berkeley and Los Angeles: University of California Press, 1972.

———. "New Evidence for the Condemnation of Meister Eckhart." *Speculum* 72 (1997): 347–66.

Lienhard, Joseph T. "On 'Discernment of Spirits' in the Early Church." *Theological Studies* 41 (1980): 505–29.

Lonergan, Bernard J. F. *Grace and Freedom: Operative Grace in the Thought of St. Thomas Aquinas.* New York: Herder & Herder, 1971.

———. *Insight. A Study in Human Understanding.* New York: Longmans, 1957.

Löser, Freimut. "Jan Milič in europäischer Tradition: Die Magdalen-Predigt des Pseudo-Origenes." In *Deutscher Literatur des Mittelalters in Böhmen und über Böhmen*, edited by Dominique Flieger and Václav Bok, 225–45. Vienna: Edition Praesens, 2001.

———. "Nachlese: Unbekannte Texte Meister Eckharts in bekannten Handschriften." In *Die deutsche Predigt im Mittelalter*, edited by Volker Mertens and Hans-Jochen Schiewer, 125–49. Tübingen: Niemeyer, 1992.

———. "*Oratio est cum deo confabulatio:* Meister Eckharts Auffassung vom Beten und seine Gebetspraxis." In *Deutsche Mystik im abendländischen Zusammenhang*, edited by Walter Haug and Wolfram Schneider-Lastin, 283–316. Tübingen: Niemeyer, 2000.

———. "Pseudo-Origenes." VL 11:1090–95.

———. "Rezeption als Revision: Marquard von Lindau und Meister Eckhart." *Beiträge zur Geschichte der deutschen Sprache und Literatur* 119 (1997): 425–58.

Lossky, Vladimir. *Théologie négative et connaissance de Dieu chez Maître Eckhart.* Paris: Vrin, 1960.

———. *The Vision of God.* London: Faith Press, 1963.

Louth, Andrew. *The Wilderness of God.* Nashville: Abingdon, 1991.

Lüers, Grete. *Die Sprache der deutschen Mystik des Mittelalters im Werke der Mechthild von Magdeburg.* Munich: Reinhardt, 1926.

Luscombe, David. "Denis the Areopagite in the Writings of Nicholas of Cusa, Marsilio Ficino and Pico della Mirandola." In *Néoplatonisme et philosophie médiévale,* edited by Lino G. Benakis, 93–107. Turnhout: Brepols, 1997.

Mahnke, Dietrich. *Unendliche Sphäre und Allmittelpunkt: Beiträge zur Genealogie der mathematischen Mystik.* Halle: Niemeyer, 1937.

Maître Eckhart à Paris: Une critique médiévale de l'ontothéologie. Les questions parisiennes no. 1 et no. 2. Paris: Presses Universitaires de France, 1984.

Maliase, Isabelle. "L'Iconographie biblique du *Cantique des Cantiques* au XIIe siècle." *Scriptorium* 46 (1992): 67–73.

Mangin, Éric. "Le *Lettre du 13 Août 1317* écrite par l'Évêque de Strasbourg contre les disciples du Libre Esprit." *Revue des sciences religieuses* 75 (2001): 522–38.

Manstetten, Reiner. "Abgescheidenheit: Von der negativen Theologie zur negativen Anthropologie: Nikolaus von Kues und Meister Eckhart." *Theologisches Quartalschrift* 181 (2001): 112–31.

———. *Esse est Deus: Meister Eckharts christologische Versöhnung von Philosophie und Religion und ihre Ursprünge in der Tradition des Abendlandes.* Munich: Alber, 1993.

Maréchal, Joseph. *Études sur la psychologie des mystiques.* 2 vols. Paris: Alcan/Desclée, 1924–37.

———. "Note d'enseignement théologique: La notion d'extase, d'après l'enseignement traditionnel des mystiques et des théologiens." *Nouvelle revue théologique* 63 (1937): 986–98.

Marrow, James H. *Passion Iconography in Northern European Art of the Late Middle Ages and Early Renaissance.* Kortrijk: Van Ghemmert, 1979.

———. "Symbol and Meaning in Northern European Art of the Late Middle Ages and the Early Renaissance." *Simiolus* 16 (1986): 150–72.

Martin, Dennis D. *Carthusian Spirituality: The Writings of Hugh of Balma and Guigo de Ponte.* New York: Paulist Press, 1997.

———. *Fifteenth-Century Carthusian Reform: The World of Nicholas Kempf.* Leiden: Brill, 1992.

———. "Kempf, Nikolaus, von Strassburg." VL 4:1117–24.

———. "Vinzenz von Aggsbach OCart." VL 10:359–65.

Maurer, Armand. *Master Eckhart: Parisian Questions and Prologues.* Toronto: Pontifical Institute of Medieval Studies, 1974.

McDonnell, Ernest W. *The Beguines and Beghards in Medieval Culture with Special Emphasis on the Belgian Scene.* New Brunswick: Rutgers University Press, 1954.

McEvoy, James. *The Philosophy of Robert Grosseteste.* Oxford: Clarendon Press, 1982.

McGinn, Bernard. "The Abyss of Love." In *The Joy of Learning and the Love of God: Studies in Honor of Jean Leclercq,* edited by E. Rozanne Elder, 95–120. Kalamazoo: Cistercian Publications, 1995.

———. "Asceticism and Mysticism in Late Antiquity and the Middle Ages." In *Asceticism*, edited by Vincent L. Wimbush and Richard Valantasis, 58–74. New York: Oxford University Press, 1995.

———. "Do Christian Platonists Really Believe in Creation?" In *God and Creation: An Ecumenical Symposium*, edited by David B. Burrell and Bernard McGinn, 197–223. Notre Dame: University of Notre Dame Press, 1990.

———. "Does the Trinity Add Up? Transcendental Mathematics and Trinitarian Speculation in the Twelfth and Thirteenth Centuries." In *Praise No Less Than Charity: Studies in Honor of M. Chrysogonus Waddell*, 235–64. Kalamazoo: Cistercian Publications, 2002.

———. "Eckhart's Condemnation Reconsidered." *The Thomist* 44 (1980): 390–414.

———. "'Evil-sounding, Rash, and Suspect of Heresy': Tensions between Mysticism and Magisterium in the History of the Church." *Catholic Historical Review* 90 (2004): 193–212.

———. *The Flowering of Mysticism*. See *The Presence of God*

———. "Foreword." In Gershom Scholem, *On the Kabbalah and Its Symbolism*, vii–xviii. Reprint. New York: Schocken, 1996.

———. *The Foundations of Mysticism*. See *The Presence of God*

———. "God as Eros: Metaphysical Foundations of Christian Mysticism." In *New Perspectives on Historical Theology: Essays in Memory of John Meyendorff*, edited by Bradley Nassif, 189–209. Grand Rapids: Eerdmans, 1996.

———. "The God beyond God: Theology and Mysticism in the Thought of Meister Eckhart." *Journal of Religion* 61 (1981): 1–19.

———. *The Growth of Mysticism*. See *The Presence of God*

———. "The Human Person as Image of God: II, Western Christianity." In *Christian Spirituality Origins to the Fifth Century*, edited by Jean Leclercq, Bernard McGinn, John Meyendorff, 312–30. Encyclopedia of World Spirituality. New York: Crossroad, 1985.

———. "The Language of Inner Experience in Christian Mysticism." *Spiritus* 1 (2001): 156–71.

———. "The Language of Love in Jewish and Christian Mysticism." In *Mysticism and Language*, edited by Steven T. Katz, 202–35. New York: Oxford University Press, 1992.

———. "Love, Knowledge and *Unio mystica* in the Western Christian Tradition." In *Mystical Union in Judaism, Christianity, and Islam: An Ecumenical Dialogue*, edited by Moshe Idel and Bernard McGinn, 59–86. New York: Continuum, 1996.

———. "*Maximum Contractum et Absolutum*: The Motive for the Incarnation in Nicholas of Cusa and Some of His Predecessors." In *Nicholas of Cusa and His Age: Intellect and Spirituality*, edited by Thomas M. Izbicki and Christopher M. Bellitto, 149–75. Leiden: Brill, 2002.

———. "Meister Eckhart on God as Absolute Unity." In *Neoplatonism and Christian Thought*, edited by Dominic O'Meara, 128–39. Albany: SUNY Press, 1982.

———. *The Mystical Thought of Meister Eckhart: The Man from Whom God Hid Nothing*. New York: Crossroad, 2001.

———. "Mystical Union in Judaism, Christianity, and Islam." In *The Encyclopedia of Religion*, 2nd ed. (forthcoming).

————. "On Mysticism & Art." *Daedalus* (Spring 2003): 131–34.

————. "Ocean and Desert as Symbols of Mystical Absorption in the Christian Tradition." *Journal of Religion* 74 (1994):155–81.

————. "The Originality of Eriugena's Spiritual Exegesis." In *Iohannes Scottus Eriugena: The Bible and Hermeneutics*, edited by Gerd Van Riel, Carlos Steel, and James McEvoy, 55–80. Leuven: Leuven University Press, 1996.

————. *The Presence of God: A History of Western Christian Mysticism.* Vol. 1, *The Foundations of Mysticism: Origins to the Fifth Century;* Vol. 2, *The Growth of Mysticism: Gregory the Great through the Twelfth Century;* Vol. 3, *The Flowering of Mysticism: Men and Women in the New Mysticism–1200–1350.* New York: Crossroad, 1991, 1994, 1998.

————. "A Prolegomomenon to the Role of the Trinity in Meister Eckhart's Mysticism." *Eckhart Review* (Spring 1997): 51–61.

————. "*Quo vadis?* Reflections on the Current Study of Mysticism." *Christian Spirituality Bulletin* (Spring 1998): 13–21.

————. "St. Bernard and Meister Eckhart." *Citeaux* 31 (1980): 373–86.

————. "*SAPIENTIA JUDAEORUM*: The Role of Jewish Philosophers in Some Scholastic Thinkers." In *Continuity and Change: The Harvest of Late Medieval and Reformation History. Essays Presented to Heiko A. Oberman on his 70th Birthday*, edited by Robert J. Bast and Andrew C. Gow, 206–28. Leiden: Brill, 2000.

————. "Seeing and Not Seeing: Nicholas of Cusa's Place in the Mystical Tradition." In *Nicholas of Cusa: Sixth Centenary Studies*, edited by Peter J. Casarella. Washington, D.C.: Catholic University of America Press, 2005 (forthcoming).

————. "Sermo IV. 'Ex ipso, per ipsum et in ipso sunt omnia.'" In *Lectura Eckhardi I: Predigten Meister Eckharts von Fachgelehrten gelesen und gedeutet*, edited by Georg Steer and Loris Sturlese, 289–316. Stuttgart: Kohlhammer, 1998.

————. "Sermo XXIX. 'Deus unus est.'": In *Lectura Eckhardi II: Predigten Meister Eckharts von Fachgelehrten gelesen und gedeutet*, edited by Georg Steer and Loris Sturlese, 205–32. Stuttgart: Kohlhammer, 2003.

————. "Sermo XLIX. 'Cuius est imago haec et superscriptio?'" In *Lectura Eckhardi III*, edited by Georg Steer and Loris Sturlese. Stuttgart: Kohlhammer, 2005 (forthcoming).

————. "Theologians as Trinitarian Iconographers." In *The Mind's Eye: Art and Theological Argument in the Medieval West*, edited by Jeffrey F. Hamburger and Anne-Marie Bouché, 186–207. Princeton: Princeton University Press, 2005.

————. "'Trinity Higher Than Any Being!' Imaging the Invisible Trinity." In *Ästhetik des Unsichtbaren: Bildtheorie und Bildgebrauch in der Vormoderne*, edited by David Ganz and Thomas Lentes, 76–93. Berlin: Reimer, 2004.

————. "*Unitrinum seu Triunum*: Nicholas of Cusa's Trinitarian Mysticism." In *Mystics: Presence and Aporia*, edited by Michael Kessler and Christian Sheppard, 90–117. Chicago: University of Chicago Press, 2003.

————. "*Vere tu es Deus absconditus*: The Hidden God in Luther and Some Mystics." In *Silence and the Word: Negative Theology and Incarnation*, edited by Oliver

Davies and Denys Turner, 94–114. Cambridge: Cambridge University Press, 2002.

———. "Visions and Critiques of Visions in Late Medieval Mysticism." In *Rending the Veil: Concealment and Secrecy in the History of Religions*, edited by Elliot R. Wolfson, 87–112. New York: Seven Bridges, 1999.

———. "Vom verborgenen Gott zum blossen Gott." VL 11:1616–17.

———, editor. *Meister Eckhart and the Beguine Mystics: Hadewijch of Brabant, Mechthild of Madgeburg, and Marguerite Porete.* New York: Continuum, 1994.

McGuire, Brian Patrick. *Friendship and Community: The Monastic Experience 350–1250.* Kalamazoo: Cistercian Publications, 1988.

———. *Jean Gerson: Early Works.* New York: Paulist Press, 1998.

McIntosh, Mark A. *Discernment and Truth: The Spirituality and Theology of Knowledge.* New York: Crossroad, 2004.

McLaughlin, Eleanor. "The Heresy of the Free Spirit and Late Medieval Mysticism." *Mediaevalia et Humanistica* n.s. 4 (1973): 37–54.

McTighe, Thomas P. "A Neglected Feature of Neoplatonic Metaphysics." In *Christian Spirituality and the Culture of Modernity: The Thought of Louis Dupré*, edited by Peter Casarella, 27–49. Grand Rapids: Eerdmans, 1998.

Meersseman, Giles. "La contemplation mystique d'après le Bx. Albert est-elle immédiate?" *Revue Thomiste* 36 (1931): 408–21.

Mennecke-Haustein, Ute. "'Theologia Deutsch.'" DS 15:459–63.

Merle, Hélène. "*DEITAS*: quelques aspects de la signification de ce mot d'Augustin à Maître Eckhart." In *Von Meister Dietrich zu Meister Eckhart*, edited by Kurt Flasch, 12–21. Hamburg: Meiner, 1984.

Mertens, Dieter. "Jakob von Paradies (1381–1465) über die mystische Theologie." In *Kartäusermystik und -Mystiker: Dritter internationaler Kongress über die Kartäusergeschichte und -Spiritualität*, Band 5, 31–46. Salzburg: Institut für Anglistik und Amerikanistik, 1982.

Mertens, Volker, and Hans-Jochen Schiewer, editors. *Die deutsche Predigt im Mittelalter.* Tübingen: Niemeyer, 1992.

———. "Hartwig (Hartung) von Erfurt." VL 3: 532–35.

———. "Theologie der Mönche–Frömmigkeit der Laien? Beobachtungen zur Textgeschichte von Predigten der Hartwig von Erfurt: Mit einem Textanhang." In *Literatur und Laienbildung im Spätmittelalter und in der Reformationszeit*, edited by Ludger Grenzmann and Karl Stackmann, 661–85. Stuttgart: Metzler, 1981.

Meyendorff, John. "Messalianism or Anti-Messalianism? A Fresh Look at the 'Macarian' Problem." In *KYRIAKON: Festschrift Johannes Quasten*, edited by Patrick Granfield and Joseph Jungmann, 2:585–90. 2 vols. Munster: Aschendorff, 1970.

Meyer, Ruth. "'Maister Eghart sprichet von wesen bloss': Beobachtungen zur Lyrik der deutschen Mystik." *Zeitschrift für deutsche Philologie. Sonderheft Mystik* 113 (1994): 63–82.

———. *Das 'St. Katharinentaler Schwesternbuch': Untersuchung. Edition. Kommentar.* Tübingen: Niemeyer, 1995.

Michel, Paul. *'Formosa deformitas': Bewältigungsformen des Hässlichen in mittelalterlichen Literatur.* Bonn: Bouvier, 1976.

———. "Heinrich Seuse als Diener des göttlichen Wortes: Persuasive Strategien bei der Verwendung von Bibelzitaten im Dienste seiner pastoralen Aufgaben." In *Das "einig Ein,"* edited by Alois M. Haas and Heinrich Stirnimann, 281–367. Freiburg, Switzerland: Universitätsverlag, 1980.

Mieth, Dietmar. *Christus–Das Soziale im Menschen.* Düsseldorf: Patmos, 1972.

———. *Die Einheit von Vita Activa und Vita Passiva in den deutschen Predigten und Traktaten Meister Eckharts und bei Johannes Tauler.* Regensburg: Pustet, 1969.

———. "Gottesschau und Gottesgeburt: Zwei Typen Christlicher Gotteserfahrung in der Tradition." *Freiburger Zeitschrift für Theologie und Philosophie* 27 (1980): 204–23.

———. "Die theologische transposition der Tugendethik bei Meister Eckhart." In *Abendländische Mystik im Mittelalter,* edited by Kurt Ruh, 63–79. Stuttgart: Metzler, 1986.

Miethke, Jürgen. "Der Prozess gegen Meister Eckhart im Rahmen der spätmittelalter Lehrzuchtverfahren gegen Dominikanertheologen." In *Meister Eckhart: Lebensstationen–Redesituationen,* edited by Klaus Jacobi, 353–75. Berlin: Akademie Verlag, 1997.

Milem, Bruce. *The Unspoken Word: Negative Theology in Meister Eckhart's German Sermons.* Washington, D.C.: Catholic University of America Press, 2002.

Miller, Clyde Lee. "God's Presence: Some Cusan Proposals." In *Nicholas of Cusa on Christ and the Church,* edited by Gerald Christianson and Thomas M. Izbicki, 241–49. Leiden: Brill, 1996.

———. *Reading Cusanus: Metaphor and Dialectic in a Conjectural Universe.* Washington, D.C.: Catholic University of America Press, 2003.

Minio-Paluello, Lorenzo. "Moerbeke, William of." In *Dictionary of Scientific Biography,* 9:334–40. New York: Scribner, 1974.

Miquel, Pierre. "La place et le rôle de l'expérience dans la théologie de saint Thomas." *Recherches de théologie ancienne et médiévale* 39 (1972): 63–70.

Misch, Georg. *Geschichte der Autobiographie,* Vol. IV. 1. Frankfurt: Schulte-Bulmker, 1967.

Moison, Clément. *Henri Bremond et la poésie pure.* Paris: Lettres modernes, 1967.

Mojsisch, Burkhard. "'Causa essentialis' bei Dietrich von Freiburg und Meister Eckhart." In *Von Meister Eckhart zu Meister Dietrich,* edited by Kurt Flasch, 106–14. Hamburg: Meiner, 1984.

———. "'Ce moi': La conception du moi de Maître Eckhart." *Revue des sciences religieuses* 70 (1996): 18–30.

———. "'Dynamik der Vernunft' bei Dietrich von Freiberg und Meister Eckhart." In *Abendländisches Mystik im Mittelalter,* edited by Kurt Ruh, 135–44. Stuttgart: Metzler, 1986.

———. *Meister Eckhart: Analogie, Univozität und Einheit.* Hamburg: Meiner, 1983.

———. "*Nichts* und *Negation:* Meister Eckhart und Nikolaus von Kues." In *Historia philosophiae medii aevi: Studien zur Geschichte der Philosophie des Mittelalters,* edited by Burkhard Mojsisch, 2:675–93. Amsterdam: Grüner, 1991.

————. "Predigt 48: 'alliu glîchu dinc minnent sich.'" In *Lectura Eckhardi I*, edited by Georg Steer and Loris Sturlese, 151–62. Stuttgart: Kohlhammer, 1998.

Molloy, Noel. "The Trinitarian Mysticism of St. Thomas." *Angelicum* 57 (1980): 373–88.

Moran, Dermot. "Pantheism from John Scottus Eriugena to Nicholas of Cusa." *American Catholic Philosophical Quarterly* 64 (1990): 131–52.

Morard, Meinrad. "Ist, istic, istikeit bei Meister Eckhart." *Freiburger Zeitschrift für Philosophie und Theologie* 3 (1956): 169–86.

Morvay, Karin, and Dagmar Grube. *Bibliographie der deutschen Predigt des Mittelalters: Veröffentliche Predigten.* Munich: Beck, 1974.

Müller, Gunther. "Scholastikerzitate bei Tauler." *Deutsche Vierteljahrsschrift für Literaturwissenschaft und Geistesgeschichte* 1 (1923): 400–418.

Murk-Jansen, Saskia. *Brides in the Desert: The Spirituality of the Beguines.* London: Darton, Longman and Todd, 1998.

Murnion, William E. "St. Thomas Aquinas's Theory of the Act of Understanding." *The Thomist* 37 (1973): 88–118.

Muschg, Walter. *Die Mystik in der Schweiz.* Frauenfeld and Leipzig: Huber, 1935.

Nambara, Minoru. "Die Idee des absoluten Nichts in der deutschen Mystik und seine Entsprechungen im Buddhismus." *Archiv für Begriffsgeschichte* 6 (1960): 143–277.

Newman, Barbara. "Henry Suso and Medieval Devotion to Christ the Goddess," *Spiritus* 2 (2002): 1–14.

————. "Possessed by the Spirit: Devout Women, Demoniacs, and the Apostolic Life in the Thirteenth Century." *Speculum* 73 (1998): 733–70.

————. "What Did It Mean to Say 'I Saw'? The Clash between Theory and Practice in Medieval Visionary Culture." *Speculum* 80 (2005): 1–43.

Nimmo, Duncan B. "The Franciscan Regular Observance." In *Reformbemühungen und Oberservantenbestrebungen im spätmittelalterlichen Ordenswesen*, edited by Kaspar Elm, 189–205. Berlin: Duncker & Humblot, 1989.

Nötscher, Friedrich. *"Das Angesicht Gottes schauen" nach biblischer und babylonischer Auffassung.* Darmstadt: Wissenschaftliche Buchgesellschaft, 1969.

Nuchelmans, Gabriel. *Secundum/tertium adiacens: Vicissitudes of a Logical Distinction.* Amsterdam: Koninklijke Nederlandse Akademie, 1992.

Oakley, Francis. *The Western Church in the Later Middle Ages.* Ithaca: Cornell University Press, 1979.

Oberman, Heiko A. *The Dawn of the Reformation: Essays in Late Medieval and Early Reformation Thought.* Edinburgh: T & T Clark, 1986.

————. *The Harvest of Medieval Theology: Gabriel Biel and Late Medieval Nominalism.* Cambridge, Mass.: Harvard University Press, 1963.

Oechslin, R.-L. "Eckhart et la mystique trinitaire." *Lumière et vie* 30 (1956): 99–120.

Oehl, Wilhelm. *Deutsche Mystikerbriefe des Mittelalters 1100–1550.* Munich: Müller, 1931.

Ohly, Friedrich. "Du Bist Mein, Ich Bin Dein, Du in Mir, Ich in Dir, Ich Du, Du

Ich." In *Kritische Bewahrung: Beiträge zur deutschen Philologie. Festschrift für Werner Schröder*, 371–415. Berlin: Schmidt, 1974.

Oliger, Livarius. *De secta Spiritus Libertatis in Umbria saec. XIV: Disquisitio et Documenta.* Rome: Edizioni di Storia e Letteratura, 1943.

O'Meara, Dominic J. "Eriugena and Aquinas on the Beatific Vision." In *ERIUGENA REDIVIVUS: Zur Wirkungsgeschichte seines Denkens im Mittelalter und im Übergang zur Neuzeit*, edited by Werner Beierwaltes, 224–36. Heidelberg: Winter, 1987.

Ozment, Steven. *The Age of Reform 1250–1550: An Intellectual and Religious History of Late Medieval and Reformation Europe.* New Haven: Yale University Press, 1980.

———. "An Aid to Luther's Marginal Comments on Johannes Tauler's Sermons." *Harvard Theological Review* 63 (1970): 305–11.

———. *Homo spiritualis: A Comparative Study of the Anthropology of Johannes Tauler, Jean Gerson and Martin Luther (1509–16) in the Context of their Theological Thought.* Leiden: Brill, 1969.

———. *Mysticism and Dissent: Religious Ideology and Social Protest in the Sixteenth Century.* New Haven: Yale University Press, 1973.

Pagnoni-Sturlese, Maria-Rita. "A propos du néoplatonisme d'Albert le Grand." *Archives de philosophie* 43 (1980): 635–54.

Palmer, Nigel F. "Himmelsbrief." *Theologische Realenzyklopädie*, 15:344–46. Berlin: Walter de Gruyter, 1977–.

———. "Latein, Volkssprache, Mischsprache: Zum Spruchproblem bei Marquard von Lindau, mit einem Handschriftenverzeichnis der 'Dekalogerklärung' und des 'Auszugs der Kinder Israel.'" In *Spätmittelalterliche geistliche Literatur in der Nationalsprache.* Analecta Carthusiana 106, Band 1, 70–110. Salzburg: Universität Salzburg, Institut für Anglistik und Amerikanistik, 1983

———. "Marquard von Lindau OFM." VL 6:81–126.

Panofsky, Erwin. "'Imago Pietatis': Ein Beitrag zur Typengeschichte des 'Schmerzensmanns' und der 'Maria Mediatrix.'" In *Festschrift für Max J. Friedländer zum 60. Geburtstag*, 261–308. Leipzig: Seemann, 1927.

Patschovsky, Alexander. "Beginen, Begarden und Terziaren im 14. und 15. Jahrhundert: Das Beispiel des Basler Beginenstreits (1400/4–1411)." In *Festschrift für Eduard Hlawitschka zum 65. Geburtstag*, edited by Karl Rudolf Schnith and Roland Pauler, 403–18. Munich, 1993.

———. "Strassburger Beginenverfolgerung im 14. Jahrhundert." *Deutsches Archiv für Erforschung des Mittelalters* 30 (1974): 56–198.

———. "Was Sind Ketzer? Über den geschichtlichen Ort der Häresien im Mittelalter." In *Eine finstere und fast unglaubliche Geschichte? Mediävistische Notizen zu Umberto Ecos Monchsroman 'Der Name der Rose,'* edited by Max Kerner, 169–90. Darmstadt: Wissenschaftliche Buchgesellschaft, 1988.

Pavlec, Brian A. "Reform." In *Introducing Nicholas of Cusa*, edited by Christopher M. Bellitto, Thomas M. Izbicki, and Gerald Christianson, 59–112. New York: Paulist Press, 2004.

Pelster, Franz. "Eine Gutachten aus dem Eckehart-Prozess in Avignon." In *Aus der*

Geisteswelt des Mittelalters: Festgabe Martin Grabmann, 1099–1124. Münster: Aschendorff, 1935.

Pepin, Jean. "'Stilla aquae modica multo infusa vino, ferrum ignitum, luce perfusus aer': L'origine de trois comparisons familières à la théologie mystique médiévale." *Divinitas 11 (Miscellanea André Combes):* 331–75

Peters, Christian. "Theologia deutsch." In *Theologische Realenzyklopädie,* 23:258–62. Berlin: Walter de Gruyter, 1977– .

Peters, Edward. *Inquisition.* New York: Free Press, 1988.

———, and Walter P. Simons, "The New Huizinga and the Old Middle Ages." *Speculum* 74 (1999): 587–620.

Peterson, Erik. "Die Gottesfreundschaft: Beiträge zur Geschichte eines religiösen Terminus." *Zeitschrift für Kirchengeschichte* 42 (1923): 161–202.

Phillips, Dayton. *Beguines in Medieval Strassburg: A Study of the Social Aspect of Beguine Life.* Stanford: Stanford University Press, 1941.

Pieper, Monica. "Sudermann (Daniel)." DS 7:1290–92.

Pleuser, Christine. *Die Benennungen und der Begriff des Leides bei J. Tauler.* Berlin: Schmidt, 1967.

Plouvier, Paule. *Poesia e mistica.* Vatican City: Libreria Editrice Vaticana, 2002.

Plummer, John. *The Hours of Catherine of Cleves: Introduction and Commentaries.* New York: Braziller, 1966.

Preger, Wilhelm. *Geschichte der deutschen Mystik im Mittelalter.* 3 vols. Leipzig: Dörffling & Franke, 1874–93.

Quint, Josef. "Mystik und Sprache, Ihr Verhältnis zueinander, insbesondere in der spekulativen Mystik Meister Eckeharts." In *Altdeutsche und altniederländische Mystik,* edited by Kurt Ruh, 113–51. Wege der Forschung 23. Darmstadt: Wissenschaftliche Buchgesellschaft, 1964.

Radler, Charlotte. "The '*Granum Sinapis*' Poem and Commentary in the Light of Medieval Neoplatonism." Dissertation, University of Chicago, 2004.

Rahner, Hugo. "Die Gottesgeburt: Die Lehre der Kirchenväter von der Geburt Christi aus den Herzen der Kirche und der Gläubigen." In Hugo Rahner, *Symbole der Kirche: Die Ekklesiologie der Väter,* 7–41. Salzburg: Müller, 1964.

Rapp, Francis. "Le couvent des dominicains de Strasbourg à l'époque de Tauler." In *Cheminer avec Jean Tauler: Pour le 7e centenaire de sa naissance (La vie spirituelle)* 155 (2001): 59–74.

Reinhardt, Klaus. "Christus, die 'Absolute Mitte' als der Mittler zur Gotteskindschaft." In *Das Sehen Gottes nach Nikolaus von Kues,* edited by Rudolf Haubst, 196–226. *Mitteilungen und Forschungsbeiträge der Cusanus-Gesellschaft* 18. Trier: Paulinus, 1989.

———. "Christus 'Wort und Weisheit' Gottes." In *Weisheit und Wissenschaft: Cusanus im Blick die Gegenwart,* edited by Rudolf Haubst and Klaus Kremer, 68–97. *Mitteilungen und Forschungsbeiträge der Cusanus-Gesellschaft* 20. Trier: Paulinus, 1992.

———. "Nikolaus von Kues in der Geschichte der mittelalterlichen Bibelexegese." In *Mitteilungen und Forschungsbeiträge der Cusanus-Gesellschaft* 27, 31–63. Trier: Paulinus, 2001.

Renna, Thomas. "Angels and Spirituality: The Augustinian Tradition to Eckhardt." *Augustinian Studies* 16 (1985): 29–37.

Reynolds, Lyndon P. "*Bullitio* and the God beyond God: Meister Eckhart's Trinitarian Theology." *New Blackfriars* 70 (1989): 169–81, 235–44.

Reypens, Léonce. "Âme (son fond, ses puissances et sa structure d'après les mystiques)." DS 1:433–69.

———. "Dieu (connaissance mystique)." DS 3:883–929.

———. "Der 'Goldene Pfennig' bei Tauler und Ruusbroec." In *Altdeutsche und Altniederlandische Mystik*, edited by Kurt Ruh, 353–62. Darmstadt: Wissenschaftliche Buchgesellschaft, 1964.

Ricoeur, Paul. *The Symbolism of Evil.* New York: Harper, 1967.

Ridderbos, Bernhard. "The Man of Sorrows: Pictorial Images and Metaphorical Statements." In *The Broken Body: Passion Devotion in Late-Medieval Culture*, edited by A. A. MacDonald, H. N. B. Ridderbos, and R. M. Schlusemann, 145–81. Groningen: Forsten, 1998.

Rieder, Karl. *Der Gottesfreund vom Oberland: Eine Erfindung des Strassburger Johanniterbruders Nikolaus von Löwen.* Innsbruck: Wagner, 1905.

Ringbom, Sixten. "Devotional Images and Imaginative Devotions: Notes on the Place of Art in Late Medieval Private Piety." *Gazette des Beaux-Arts*, 6th Ser. 73 (1969): 159–70.

Ringler, Siegfried. "Gnadenviten aus süddeutschen Frauenklöstern des 14. Jahrhunderts–Vitenschreibung als mystische Lehre." In *"Minnilichui gotes erkennusse": Studien zur frühen abendländischen Mystiktradition*, edited Dietrich Schmidtke, 89–104. Stuttgart-Bad Canstatt: frommann-holzboog, 1990.

———. "Haider, Ursula." VL 3: 399–404.

———. "Kügelin, Konrad." VL 5:426–29.

———. *Viten- und Offenbarungsliteratur in Frauenklöstern des Mittelalters: Quellen und Studien.* Munich: Artemis, 1980.

Rorem, Paul. *Pseudo-Dionysius: A Commentary on the Texts and an Introduction to Their Influence.* New York: Oxford University Press, 1993.

Rossmann, Heribert. "Der Magister Marquard Sprenger in München und seine Kontroverseschriften zum Konzil von Basel und zur mystischen Theologie." In *Mysterium der Gnade: Festschrift für J. Auer*, edited by Heribert Rossmann and Joseph Ratzinger, 350–411. Regensburg: Pustet, 1975.

———. "Sprenger, Marquard." VL 9:157–62.

———. "Die Stellungnahme der Karthäusers Vinzenz von Aggsbach zur mystischen Theologie des Johannes Gerson." In *Karthäusermystik und -Mystiker: Dritter Internationaler Kongress über die Kartäusergeschichte und-Spiritualität*, 5–30. Analecta Carthusiana 55. Salzburg: Universität Salzburg, 1982.

———. "Der Tegernseer Benediktiner Johannes Keck über die mystische Theologie." In *Das Menschenbild des Nikolaus von Kues und der christliche Humanismus*, edited by Martin Bodeweg, Josef Schmitz and Reinhold Weier, 330–52. *Mitteilungen und Forschungsbeiträge der Cusanus-Gesellschaft* 13. Mainz: Matthias-Grünewald, 1978.

Roy, Lucien. *Lumière et Sagesse: La grace mystique dans la Théologie de saint Thomas d'Aquin.* Montréal: Studia Collegii Maximi Immaculatae Conceptionis, 1948.

Rudy, Gordon. *Mystical Language of Sensation in the Later Middle Ages.* New York and London: Routledge, 2002.

Ruello, Francis. *Les "Noms divins" et leur "Raisons" selon Albert le Grand commentateur du "De Divinis Nominibus."* Paris: Vrin, 1963.

Ruh, Kurt. *Bonaventura deutsch: Ein Beitrag zur deutschen Franziskaner-Mystik und -Scholastik.* Bern: Francke, 1956.

———. "Dionysius Areopagita im deutschen Predigtwerk Meister Eckharts, Perspektiven der Philosophie." *Neues Jahrbuch* 13 (1987): 207–23.

———. "'Eckhart-Legenden.'" VL 2:350–53.

———. *Franziskanisches Schrifttum im deutschen Mittelalter.* 2 vols. Munich: Beck, 1965, 1985.

———. *Geschichte der abendländische Mystik.* Band III, *Die Mystik des deutschen Predigerordens und ihre Grundlegung durch die Hochscholastik.* Munich: Beck, 1996.

———. "Granum sinapis." VL 3:220–24.

———. *Kleine Schriften.* Band II, *Scholastik und Mystik im Spätmittelalter,* edited by Volker Mertens. Berlin: Walter de Gruyter, 1984.

———. *Meister Eckhart: Theologe. Prediger. Mystiker.* Munich: Beck, 1985.

———. "Das mystische Schweigen und die mystische Rede." In *Festschrift für Ingo Reiffenstein zum 60. Geburtstag,* 463–72. Göppingen: Kümmerle, 1988.

———. "Neuplatonische Quellen Meister Eckharts." In *Contemplata aliis tradere: Studien zum Verhältnis von Literatur und Spiritualität,* edited by Claudia Brinker et al., 317–52. Frankfurt: Lang, 1995.

———. "'Paradisus anime intelligentis' ('Paradis der fornunftigen sele')." VL 7:298–303.

———. "Sendbrief." VL 8:1070–73.

Saak, E. L. "*Quilibet Christianus*: Saints in Society in the Sermons of Jordan of Quedlinburg, OESA." In *Models of Holiness in Medieval Sermons,* edited by Beverly Mayne Kienzle, 317–38. Louvain-la-Neuve: Fédération Internationale des Instituts d'Études Médiévales, 1996.

Saccon, Alessandra. "Predicazione e filosofia: Il caso del 'Paradisus anime intelligentis.'" In *Filosofia in Volgare nel Medioevo,* edited by Nadia Bray and Loris Sturlese, 81–105. Louvain-la-Neuve: Féderation Internationale des Instituts d'Études Médiévales, 2003.

Scheeben, Heribert Christian. "Der Konvent der Predigerbrüder in Strassburg–Die religiöse Heimat Taulers." In *Johannes Tauler: Ein deutscher Mystiker. Gedenkschrift zum 600. Todestag,* edited by Ephrem Filtaut, 37–74. Essen: Driewer, 1961.

Schiewer, Hans-Jochen. "Auditionen und Visionen einer Begine: Die 'Selige Schererin,' Johannes Mulberg und der Basler Beginenstreit. Mit einem Textabdruck." In *Die Vermittlung geistlicher Inhalte im deutschen Mittelalter: Internationales Symposium, Roscrea 1994,* edited by Timothy R. Jackson, Nigel F. Palmer, and Almut Suerbaum, 289–317. Tübingen: Niemeyer, 1996.

———. "German Sermons in the Middle Ages." In *The Sermon,* general editor Beverly Mayne Kienzle, 861–961. Typologie des sources du Moyen Âge Occidental, fasc. 81–83. Turnhout: Brepols, 2000.

Schimmel, Annemarie. *Mystical Dimensions of Islam*. Chapel Hill: University of North Carolina Press, 1975.

Schleusener-Eichholz, Gudrun. *Das Auge im Mittelalter*. 2 vols. Munich: Fink, 1985.

Schmidt, Carl. *Nicolaus von Basel: Bericht von der Bekehrung Taulers*. Strassburg, 1875; photomechanical reprint, Frankfurt: Minerva, 1981.

Schmidt, Carl, editor. *Nikolaus von Basel: Leben und ausgewählte Schriften*. Vienna: Braumüller, 1866.

Schmidt, Margot. "An Example of Spiritual Friendship: The Correspondence Between Heinrich of Nördlingen and Margaretha Ebner." In *Maps of Flesh and Light: The Religious Experience of Medieval Women Mystics*, edited by Ulrike Wiethaus, 74–92. Syracuse: Syracuse University, 1993.

———. "Lambert de Ratisbonne" DS 9:142–43.

———. "Miroir." DS 10:1290–1303.

———. "Nikolaus von Kues im Gespräch mit den Tegernseer Mönche über Wesen und Sinn der Mystik." In *Das Sehen Gottes nach Nikolaus von Kues*, edited by Rudolf Haubst, 25–49. *Mitteilungen und Forschungsbeiträge der Cusanus-Gesellschaft* 18. Trier: Paulinus, 1989.

Schmitt, Clément. "Élisabeth (Elsbeth) de Reute." DS 4:583–84.

Schmoldt, Benno. *Die deutsche Begriffssprache Meister Eckharts: Studien zur philosophischen terminologie des Mittelhochdeutschen*. Heidelberg: Quelle & Meyer, 1954.

Schneider, Karin. "Tucher, Katharina OP." VL 9:1132–34.

Schneider, Richard. "The Functional Christology of Meister Eckhart." *Recherches de théologie ancienne et médiévale* 35 (1968): 291–332.

Schnell, Bernhard. "Himmelsbrief." VL 4:28–33.

Schnyder, André. "Otto von Passua OFM." VL 7:229–34.

Scholem, Gershom. "Mysticism and Society." *Diogenes* 58 (1967): 1–24.

———. "Religious Authority and Mysticism." In Gershom Scholem, *On the Kabbalah and Its Symbolism*, 5–31. New York: Schocken, 1965.

Schönborn, Christoph. "'De docta ignorantia' als christozentricher Entwurf." In *Nikolaus von Kues: Einführung in sein philosophisches Denken*, edited by Klaus Jacobi, 138–56. Freiburg-Munich: Alber, 1979.

Schönfeld, Andreas. *Meister Eckhart: Geistliche Übungen. Meditationspraxis nach den "Reden der Unterweisung."* Mainz: Matthias-Grünewald, 2002.

Schraut, Elisabeth. "Dorothea von Montau: Wahrnehmungsweisen von Kindheit und Eheleben einer spätmittelalterlichen Heiligen." In *Religiöse Frauenbewegung und mystische Frömmigkeit im Mittelalter*, edited by Peter Dinzelbacher and Dieter R. Bauer, 373–94. Cologne and Vienna: Böhlau, 1988.

Schreiner, Klaus. "Laienfrömmigkeit–Frömmigkeit von Eliten oder Frömmigkeit des Volkes? Zur sozialen Verfasstheit laikaler Frömmigkeitspraxis im späten Mittelalter." In *Laienfrömmigkeit im späten Mittelalter: Formen, Funktionen, politisch-soziale Zusammenhänge*, edited by Klaus Schreiner, 1–78. Munich: Oldenbourg, 1992.

Schultheiss, Peter, and Ruedi Imbach, *Die Philosophie im Mittelalter: Ein Handbuch mit einem bio-bibliographischen Repertorium.* Düsseldorf: Artemis & Winkler, 2000.

Schürmann, Reiner. *Meister Eckhart: Mystic and Philosopher.* Bloomington: Indiana University, 1978.

Schwaetzer, Harald. *Aequalitas: Erkenntnistheoretische und soziale Implikationen eines christologischen Begriffs Nikolaus von Kues. Eine Studie zu seiner Schrift* De aequalitate. Hildesheim, Zurich, and New York: Olms, 2000.

———. "La place d'Eckhart dans la genèse du concept cuséain de 'filiatio dei.'" In *La naissance de Dieu dans l'âme chez Eckhart et Nicolaus de Cues,* edited by M.-A. Vannier. Paris: Éditions du Cerf, 2005 (forthcoming).

Schwartz, Yossef. "'*Ecce est locus apud me':* Maimonides und Eckharts Raumvorstellung als Begriff des Göttlichen." In *Raum und Raumvorstellungen im Mittelalter,* edited by Jan A. Aertsen and Andreas Speer, 348–64. Berlin: Walter de Gruyter, 1998.

———. "Metaphysiche oder theologische Hermeneutik? Meister Eckhart in Spuren des Maimonides und Thomas von Aquin" (forthcoming).

Schweitzer, Franz-Josef. *Der Freiheitsbegriff der deutschen Mystik: Seine Beziehung zur Ketzerei der "Brüder und Schwestern vom freien Geist," mit besonderer Rücksicht auf den pseudoeckhartischen Traktat "Schwester Katrei" (Edition).* Frankfurt: Lang, 1981.

———. "'Schwester Katrei.'" VL 8:947–50.

Schwietering, Julius. "Zur Autorschaft von Seuses Vita." In Julius Schwietering, *Mystik und höfische Dichtung im Hochmittelalter,* 107–22. Tübingen: Niemeyer, 1960.

Seesholtz, Anna Groh. *Friends of God: Practical Mystics of the Fourteenth Century.* New York: Columbia University Press, 1934.

Sells, Michael A. *Mystical Languages of Unsaying.* Chicago and London: University of Chicago Press, 1994.

Senger, Hans Gerhard. "Aristotelismus vs. Platonismus: Zur Konkurrenze von zwei Archetypen der Philosophie im Spätmittelalter." In *Aristotelisches Erbe im Arabisch-Lateinischen Mittelalter,* edited by Albert Zimmermann, 53–80. Berlin: Walter de Gruyter, 1986.

———. "Cusanus-Literatur der Jahre 1986–2001: Ein Forschungsbericht." *Recherches de théologie ancienne et médiévale* 69 (2002): 386–94.

———. *Ludus Sapientiae: Studien zum Werk und zur Wirkungsgeschichte des Nikolaus von Kues.* Leiden: Brill, 2002.

———. "Mystik als Theorie bei Nikolaus von Kues." In *Gnosis und Mystik in der Geschichte der Philosophie,* edited by Peter Koslowski, 11–34. Munich: Artemis, 1988.

Senner, Walter, editor. "Heinrich Seuse und der Dominikanerorden." In *Heinrich Seuses Philosophia spiritualis: Quellen, Konzepte, Formen und Rezeption,* edited by Rüdiger Blumrich and Philipp Kaiser, 3–31. Wiesbaden: Reichert, 1994.

———. *Johannes von Sterngassen OP und sein Sentenzkommentar.* 2 vols. Berlin: Akademie Verlag, 1994–95.

———. "Meister Eckhart in Köln." In *Meister Eckhart: Lebensstationen–Redesituationen*, edited by Klaus Jacobi, 207–37. Berlin: Akademie Verlag, 1997.

———. "Rhineland Dominicans, Meister Eckhart, and the Sect of the Free Spirit." In *The Vocation of Service to God and Neighbour*, edited by Joan Greatrex, 121–33. Turnhout: Brepols, 1998.

Senner, Walter, editor. *Albertus Magnus: Zum Gedenken nach 800 Jahren. Neue Zugänge, Aspekte und Perspektiven*. Berlin: Akademie Verlag, 2001.

Seppänen, Lauri. *Studien zur Terminologie des Paradisus anime intelligentis: Beiträge zur Erforschung der Sprache der mittelhochdeutschen Mystik und Scholastik*. Mémoires de la Societé Néophilologique de Helsinki 27, Helsinki: Societé Néophilologique de Helsinki, 1964.

Simons, Walter. *Cities of Ladies: Beguine Communities in the Medieval Low Countries, 1200–1565*. Philadelphia: University of Pennsylvania, 2001.

Soelle, Dorothee. *The Silent Cry: Mysticism and Resistance*. Minneapolis: Fortress, 2001.

Solignac, Aimé. "NOUS et MENS." DS 11:459–69.

———. "Synderesis." DS 14:407–12.

Speer, Andreas, and Wouter Goris. "Das Meister-Eckhart-Archiv am Thomas-Institut der Universität zu Köln: Die Kontinuität der Forschungsaufgaben." *Bulletin de philosophie médiévale* 37 (1995): 149–74.

Spoerri, Bettina. "Schrift des Herzens: Zum vierten Kapitel der 'Vita' Heinrich Seuses." In *Homo Medietas: Aufsätze zu Religiosität, Literatur und Denkformen des Menschen vom Mittelalter bis in die Neuzeit. Festschrift für Alois Maria Haas zum 65. Geburtstag*, edited by Claudia Brinker-von der Heyde and Niklaus Largier, 299–315. Bern: Lang, 1999.

Stachel, Günter. "Schweigen vor Gott: Bemerkungen zur mystischen Theologie der Schrift *De visione Dei*." In *Mitteilungen und Forschungsbeiträge der Cusanus-Gesellschaft* 14, 167–81. Trier: Paulinus, 1980.

Stallmach, Josef. *Ineinsfall der Gegensätze und Weisheit der Nichtwissens: Grundzüge der Philosophie des Nikolaus von Kues*. Münster: Aschendorff, 1989.

Stammler, Wolfgang. "Studien zur Geschichte der Mystik in Norddeutschland." In *Altdeutsche und Altniederländische Mystik*, edited by Kurt Ruh, 386–436. Darmstadt: Wissenschaftliche Buchgesellschaft, 1964.

Stargardt, Ute. *The Life of Dorothea von Montau, a Fourteenth-Century Recluse*. Lewiston: Mellen, 1997.

———. "The Political and Social Backgrounds of the Canonization of Dorothea von Montau." *Mystics Quarterly* 11 (1985): 107–22.

Steer, Georg. "Der Armutsgedanke der deutschen Mystiker bei Marquard von Lindau." *Franziskanische Studien* 60 (1978): 289–300.

———. "Bernhard von Clairvaux als theologische Authorität für Meister Eckhart, Johannes Tauler und Heinrich Seuse." In *Bernhard von Clairvaux: Rezeption und Wirkung im Mittelalter und in der Neuzeit*, edited by Kaspar Elm, 249–59. Wiesbaden: Harrassowitz, 1994.

———. "Geistlicher Prosa: 2, Predigt." In *Geschichte der deutschen Literatur*. Band

III/2, *Die deutschen Literatur im späten Mittelalter 1250–1370*, edited by Ingeborg Glier, 318–39. Munich: Beck, 1987.

———. *Johannes Wenck von Herrenberg: Das Büchlein der Seele*. Munich: Fink, 1967.

———. "Der Laie als Anreger und Adressat deutscher Prosaliteratur im 14. Jahrhundert." In *Zur deutschen Literatur und Sprache des 14. Jahrhunderts*, edited by Walter Haug, Timothy R. Jackson, and Johannes Janota, 354–67. Heidelberg: Winter, 1983.

———. "Meister Eckharts Predigtzyklus *von der êwigen geburt:* Mutmassungen über die Zeit seiner Entstehung." In *Deutsche Mystik im abendländische Zusammenhang*, edited by Walter Haug and Wolfram Schneider-Lastin, 253–81. Tübingen: Niemeyer, 2000.

———. "Merswin, Rulman." VL 6:420–42.

———. "Predigt 101: 'Dum medium silentium tenerent omnia.'" In *Lectura Eckhardi I*, edited by Georg Steer and Loris Sturlese, 247–88. Stuttgart: Kohlhammer, 1998.

———. "Die Stellung des 'Laien' im Schrifttum des Strassburger Gottesfreundes Rulman Merswin und der deutschen Dominikanermystiker des 14. Jahrhunderts." In *Literatur und Laienbildung im Spätmittelalter und in der Reformationzeit*, edited by Ludger Grenzmann and Karl Stackmann, 643–60. Stuttgart: Metzler, 1984.

Stewart, Columba. *'Working the Earth of the Heart': The Messalian Controversy in History, Texts, and Language to AD 431*. Oxford: Clarendon Press, 1991.

Stirnimann, Heinrich, and Ruedi Imbach, editors. *Eckardus Theutonicus, homo doctus et sanctus: Nachweise und Berichte zum Prozess gegen Meister Eckhart*. Freiburg, Switzerland: Universitätsverlag, 1992.

———. "Mystik und Metaphorik: Zu Seuses Dialog." In *Das "einig Ein,"* edited by Alois M. Haas and Heinrich Stirnimann, 230–43. Freiburg, Switzerland: Universitätsverlag, 1980.

———. "Seuses Morgengruss." In *Homo Medietas*, edited by Claudia Brinker-von der Heyde and Niklaus Largier, 317–21. Bern: Lang, 1999.

Stock, Alex. "Die Rolle der 'Icona Dei' in der Spekulation 'De visione dei.'" In *Das Sehen Gottes nach Nicolaus von Kues*, edited by Rudolf Haubst, 50–68. *Mitteilungen und Forschungsbeiträge der Cusanus-Gesellschaft* 18. Trier: Paulinus, 1989.

Stoelen, Anselme. "Denys le Chartreux." DS 3:430–49.

Stoudt, Debra L. "The Production and Preservation of Letters by Fourteenth-Century Dominican Nuns." *Mediaeval Studies* 53 (1991): 309–26.

———. "The Vernacular Letters of Heinrich von Nördlingen." *Mystics Quarterly* 12 (1986): 19–25.

Strauss, Gerhard. "Ideas of *Reformatio* and *Renovatio* from the Middle Ages to the Reformation." In *Handbook of European History 1400–1600*. Vol. 2, *Visions, Programs, Outcomes*, edited by Thomas A. Brady, Heiko A. Oberman, and James D. Tracy, 1–30. Grand Rapids: Eerdmans, 1996.

Stroick, Clemens. *Heinrich von Friemar: Leben, Werke, philosophisch-theologische Stellung in der Scholastik*. Freiburg-im-Breisgau: Herder, 1954.

Sturlese, Loris. "Albert der Grosse und die deutsche philosophische Kultur des Mittelalters." *Freiburger Zeitschrift für Philosophie und Theologie* 28 (1981): 133–47.

———. "Alle origini della mistica tedesca: Antichi testi su Teodorico di Freiburg." *Medioevo* 3 (1977): 36–44.

———. *Die deutsche Philosophie im Mittelalter: Von Bonifatius bis zu Albert dem Grossen 748–1280.* Munich: Beck, 1993.

———. "Il dibattito sul Proclo latino nel medioevo fra l'università di Parigi e lo Studium di Colonia." In *Proclus et son influence*, edited by G. Boss and G. Seel, 261–85. Zurich: Éditions du Grand Midi, 1985.

———. "Dietrich von Freiburg." VL 2:127–38.

———. "'Homo divinus': Der Prokloskommentar Bertholds von Moosburg und die Probleme der nacheckhartischen Zeit." In *Abendländische Mystik im Mittelalter*, edited by Kurt Ruh, 145–61. Stuttgart: Metzler, 1986.

———. "Die Kölner Eckhartisten: Das Studium generale der deutschen Domini-kaner und die Verurteilung der Thesen Meister Eckharts." In *Die Kölner Univer-sität im Mittelalter*, edited by Albert Zimmermann, 192–211. Berlin: Walter de Gruyter, 1989.

———. *Meister Eckhart: Ein Porträt (Eichstätter Hochschulreden 90).* Regensburg: Pustet, 1993.

———. "Meister Eckhart in der Bibliotheca Amploniana: Neues zur Datierung des 'Opus tripartitum.'" In *Der Bibliotheca Amploniana: ihre Bedeutung im Spannungs-feld von Aristotelismus, Nominalismus und Humanismus*, edited by Andreas Speer, 434–46. Berlin and New York: Walter de Gruyter, 1995.

———. "Mysticism and Theology in Meister Eckhart's Theory of the Image." *Eck-hart Review* (March 1993): 18–31.

———. "Un nuovo manoscritto delle opere latine di Eckhart e il suo significato per la ricostruzione del testo e della storia del Opus tripartitum." *Freiburger Zeitschrift für Philosophie und Theologie* 32 (1985): 145–54.

———. "A Portrait of Meister Eckhart." *Eckhart Review* (Spring 1996): 7–12.

———. "Proclo ed Ermete in Germania da Alberto Magno a Bertoldo di Moos-burg: Per una prospettiva di ricerca sulla cultura filosofica tedesca nel secolo delle sue origini (1250–1350)." In *Von Meister Dietrich zu Meister Eckhart*, edited by Kurt Flasch, 22–33. Hamburg: Meiner, 1984.

———. "Saints et magiciens: Albert le Grand en face d'Hermès Trismégiste." *Archives de Philosophie* 43 (1980): 615–34.

———. "Tauler im Kontext: Die philosophischen Voraussetzungen des "Seelen-grundes" in der Lehre des deutschen Neoplatonikers Berthold von Moosburg." *Beiträge zur Geschichte der deutschen Sprache und Literatur* 109 (1987): 390–426.

Sudbrack, P. Josef. *Die geistliche Theologie des Johannes von Kastl: Studien zur Fröm-migkeitsgeschichte des Spätmittelalters*, 2 vols. Münster: Aschendorff, 1967.

———. "Johannes von Kastl." VL 4:652–58.

Sukale, Robert. "Mystik und Kunst." *Theologische Realenzyklopädie,* 23:600–608. Berlin: Walter de Gruyter, 1977–.

Sweeney, Leo. "Doctrine of Creation in the *Liber de causis*." In *An Etienne Gilson*

Tribute, edited by Charles J. O'Neil, 274–89. Milwaukee: Marquette University Press, 1959.

Tarrant, Jacqueline. "The Clementine Decrees on the Beguines: Conciliar and Papal Versions." *Archivum Historiae Pontificiae* 12 (1974): 300–307.

Taylor, Richard C. "A Critical Analysis of the Structure of the *Kalīm fī mahd al-khair (Liber de causis).*" In *Neoplatonism and Islamic Thought,* edited by Parvis Morewedge, 11–40. Albany: SUNY Press, 1992.

———. "The *Kalīm fī mahd al-khair (Liber de causis)* in the Islamic Philosophic Milieu." In *Pseudo-Aristotle in the Middle Ages: The "Theology" and Other Texts,* edited by Jill Kraye, W. F. Ryan, and C. B. Schmitt, 37–52. London: Warburg Institute, 1986.

Theisen, Joachim. *Predigt und Gottesdienst: Liturgische Strukturen in den Predigten Meister Eckharts.* Frankfurt: Lang, 1990.

———. "Tauler und die Liturgie." In *Deutsche Mystik im abendländischen Zusammenhang,* edited by Walter Haug and Wolfram Schneider-Lastin, 409–23. Tübingen, Niemeyer, 2000.

Thijssen, J. M. M. H. *Censure and Heresy at the University of Paris 1200–1400.* Philadelphia: University of Pennsylvania Press, 1998.

Thurner, Martin. *Gott als das offenbare Geheimnis nach Nikolaus von Kues.* Berlin: Akademie Verlag, 2001.

Tierney, Brian. *Foundations of the Conciliar Theory: The Contributions of the Medieval Canonists from Gratian to the Great Schism.* Cambridge: At the University Press, 1955.

Tobin, Frank. "Creativity and Interpreting Scripture: Meister Eckhart in Practice." *Monatshefte* 74 (1982): 410–18.

———. "Eckhart's Mystical Use of Language: The Contexts of *eigenschaft.*" *Seminar* 8 (1972): 160–68.

———. "Henry Suso and Elsbeth Stagel: Was the *Vita* a Cooperative Effort?" In *Gendered Voices: Medieval Saints and Their Interpreters,* edited by Catherine M. Mooney, 118–35. Philadelphia: University of Pennsylvania Press, 1999.

———. "Introduction." In *Henry Suso: The Exemplar, with Two German Sermons,* 19–26. New York: Paulist Press, 1989.

———. "Mechthild of Magdeburg and Meister Eckhart: Points of Comparison." In *Meister Eckhart and the Beguine Mystics,* edited by Bernard McGinn, 44–61. New York: Continuum, 1994.

———. *Meister Eckhart: Thought and Language.* Philadelphia: University of Pennsylvania Press, 1986.

———. "Meister Eckhart and the Angels." In *In hôhem prîse: A Festschrift in Honor of Ernst S. Dick,* edited by Winder McConnell, 379–93. Göppingen: Kümmerle, 1989.

Torrell, Jean-Pierre. *Saint Thomas Aquinas.* Vol. 1, *The Person and the Work;* Vol. 2, *Spiritual Master.* Washington, D.C.: Catholic University of America Press, 1996, 2003.

Triller, Anneliese. "Marienwerder, Johannes." VL 6:56–61.

Troescher, Georg. "Die 'pitié-de-nostre-seigneur' oder die 'Not-Gottes.'" *Wallraf-Richartz Jahrbuch* 9 (1936): 148–68.

Trottmann, Christian. *La vision béatifique: Des disputes scolastiques à sa définition par Benoît XII.* Rome: École Française de Rome, 1995.

Trusen, Winfried. *Der Prozess gegen Meister Eckhart: Vorgeschichte, Verlauf und Folgen.* Paderborn: Pustet, 1988.

———. "Meister Eckhart vor seinen Richtern und Zensoren." in *Meister Eckhart: Lebensstationen–Redesituationen,* edited by Klaus Jacobi, 335–52. Berlin: Akademie Verlag, 1997.

Tugwell, Simon. "Albert: Introduction." In *Albert and Thomas: Selected Writings,* 3–129. New York: Paulist Press, 1988.

———. "The Spirituality of the Dominicans." In *Christian Spirituality: High Middle Ages and Reformation,* edited by Jill Raitt et al., 15–31. Encyclopedia of World Spirituality. New York: Crossroad, 1987.

Turner, Denys. *The Darkness of God: Negativity in Christian Mysticism.* Cambridge: Cambridge University Press, 1995.

Ueda, Shizuteru. *Die Gottesgeburt in der Seele und der Durchbruch zur Gott: Die mystische Anthropologie Meister Eckharts und ihre Konfrontation mit der Mystik der Zen Buddhismus.* Gütersloh: Mohn, 1965.

Ulrich, Peter. *Imitatio et configuratio: Die philosophia spiritualis Heinrich Seuses als Theologie der Nachfolge des Christus passus.* Regensburg: Pustet, 1995.

van den Brandt, Ria. "Die Eckhart-Predigten der Sammlung *Paradisus anime intelligentis* näher betrachtet." In *Albertus Magnus und der Albertismus: Deutsche philosophische Kultur des Mittelalters,* edited by Maarten J. F. M. Hoenen and Alain de Libera, 173–87. Leiden: Brill, 1995.

van den Broek, Roelof, and Cis van Heertum, editors. *From Poimandres to Jacob Böhme: Gnosis, Hermetism and the Christian Tradition.* Amsterdam: In de Pelikaan, 2000.

Van Engen, John. "The Church in the Fifteenth Century." In *Handbook of European History 1400–1600.* Vol. 1, *Structures and Assertions,* edited by Thomas A. Brady, Jr., Heiko A. Oberman, and James D. Tracy, 305–30. Grand Rapids: Eerdmans, 1995.

Vannier, Marie-Anne, editor. *Cheminer avec Jean Tauler: Pour le 7e centenaire de sa naissance. La vie spirituelle* 155 (March 2001).

———. "Déconstruction de l'individualité ou assomption de la personne chez Eckhart?" In *Individuum und Individualität im Mittelalter,* edited by Jan. A. Aertsen and Andreas Speer, 622–41. Berlin: Walter de Gruyter, 1996.

———. "Eckhart à Strasbourg (1313–1323/24)." In *Dominicains et Dominicaines en Alsace XIIIe–XXe S.,* edited by Jean-Luc Eichenlaub, 197–208. Colmar: Éditions d'Alsace, 1996.

———. "L'homme noble, figure de l'ouevre d'Eckhart à Strasbourg." *Revue des sciences religieuses* 70 (1996): 73–89.

———. "Tauler et les Amis de Dieu." In *700e Anniversaire de la naissance de Jean Tauler. Revue des sciences religieuses* 75 (2001): 456–64.

Vannini, Marco. "*Praedica Verbum:* La *generazione* della parola dal silenzio in Meister Eckhart." In *Il Silenzio e La Parola da Eckhart à Jabès*, edited by Massimo Baldini and Silvano Zucal, 17–31. Trent: Morcelliana, 1987.

Vansteenberghe, Edmond. *Autour de la docte ignorance: Une controverse sur la théologie mystique au XVe siècle.* Münster: Aschendorff, 1915.

———. *Le Cardinal Nicolaus de Cues (1401–1464): L'action–la pensée.* Paris: Champion, 1920. Reprint, 1974.

———. *Le "De ignota litteratura" de Jean Wenck de Herrenberg contre Nicolas de Cuse.* Münster: Aschendorff, 1910.

Van Steenberghen, Fernand. *Aristotle in the West: The Origins of Latin Aristotelianism.* Louvain: Nauwelaerts, 1955.

Van Velthoven, Theo. *Gottesschau und menschliche Kreativität: Studien zur Erkenntnislehre des Nikolaus von Kues.* Leiden: Brill, 1977.

Vauchez, André. "Dévotion eucharistique et union mystique chez les saints de la fin du Moyen Âge." In *Atti del Simposio Internazionale Cateriniano-Bernardiniano: Siena 1980*, edited by Domenico Maffeir and Paolo Nardi, 295–300. Siena: Accademia Senese degli Intronati, 1982.

———. *Sainthood in the Later Middle Ages.* Cambridge: Cambridge University Press, 1997.

Verdeyen, Paul. "Le procès d'Inquisition contre Marguerite Porete et Guiard de Cressonessart (1309–1310)." *Revue d'histoire ecclésiastique* 81 (1986): 48–94.

Villegas, Diana L. "Discernment in Catherine of Siena." *Theological Studies* 58 (1997): 19–38.

Völker, Ludwig. "'Gelassenheit': Zur Entstehung des Wortes in der Sprache Meister Eckharts und seiner Überlieferung in der nacheckhartschen Mystik bis Jacob Böhme." In *'Getempert und Gemischet' für Wolfgang Mohr zum 65. Geburtstag*, edited by Franz Hundsnurscher and Ulrich Müller, 281–312. Göppingen: Kümmerle, 1972.

Völker, Walther. "Abschluss: Die Auslegung von Cap. 1 der 'Mystischen Theologie' in den Kommentataren des Mittelalters und der neueren Zeit als Beispiel für das Fortwirken und die Umformung der Areopagitischen Gedanken." In Walther Völker, *Kontemplation und Ekstase bei Pseudo-Dionysius Areopagita*, 218–63. Wiesbaden: Steiner, 1958.

Vollmann, Benedikt K. "Stil und Anspruch des 'Horologium Sapientiae.'" In *Heinrich Seuses Philosophia spiritualis*, edited by Rüdiger Blumrich and Philipp Kaiser, 83–93. Wiesbaden: Reichert, 1994.

von Balthasar, Hans Urs. *The Glory of the Lord: A Theological Aesthetics.* Vol. 5, *The Realm of Metaphysics in the Modern Age.* San Francisco: Ignatius, 1991.

———. "The Gospel as Norm and Test of All Spirituality in the Church." In Hans Urs von Balthasar, *Spirituality in Church and World*, 7–23. New York: Paulist Press, 1965.

———. *Thomas und die Charismatik: Kommentar zu Thomas von Aquin Summa Theologica Quaestiones II II 171–182. Besondere Gnadengaben und die zwei menschlichen Lebens.* Freiburg: Johannes, 1996.

von der Leyen, F. "Über einige bisher unbekannte lateinische Fassungen von Predigten des Meisters Eckhehart." *Zeitschrift für deutsche Philologie* 38 (1906): 348–54.

von Hinten, Wolfgang. "'Der Franckfurter' ('Theologia Deutsch')." VL 2:802–8.

von Hügel, Friedrich. *The Mystical Element of Religion as Studied in Catherine of Genoa and Her Friends.* 2 vols. Reprint, London: James Clarke & J. M. Dent, 1961.

von Ivanka, Endré. "Apex mentis: Wanderung und Wandlung eines stoischen Terminus." *Zeitschrift für katholischen Theologie* 72 (1950): 129–76.

von Siegroth-Nellessen, Gabriele. *Versuch einer exakten Stiluntersuchung für Meister Eckhart, Johannes Tauler und Heinrich Seuse.* Munich: Fink, 1979.

Wackernagel, Wolfgang. "Maître Eckhart et le discernement mystique: A propos de la rencontre de Suso avec 'la (chose) sauvage sans nom.'" *Revue de Théologie et de Philosophie* 129 (1997): 113–26.

———. "Some Legendary Aspects of Meister Eckhart: The Aphorisms of the Twelve Masters." *Eckhart Review* (Spring 1998): 30–41.

———. *YMAGINE DENUDARI: Éthique de l'image et métaphysique de l'abstraction chez Maître Eckhart.* Paris: Vrin, 1991.

Wackerzapp, Herbert. *Der Einfluss Meister Eckharts auf die ersten philosophischen Schriften des Nikolaus von Kues (1440–1450).* Münster: Aschendorff, 1962.

Wadell, Paul J. *Friendship and the Moral Life.* Notre Dame: University of Notre Dame Press, 1989.

Waldschütz, Erwin. *Denken und Erfahren des Grundes: Zur philosophischen Deutung Meister Eckharts.* Vienna-Freiburg-Basel: Herder, 1989.

———. "Probleme philosophische Mystik am Beispiel Meister Eckharts." In *Probleme philosophischer Mystik: Festschrift für Karl Albert zum siebigsten Geburtstag,* edited Elenor Jain and Reinhard Margreiter, 71–92. Sankt Augustin: Academia, 1991.

Walz, A. "'Grund' und 'Gemüt' bei Tauler." *Angelicum* 40 (1963): 328–698.

Warnock, Robert G. "Heinrich von Friemar der Ältere." VL 3:730–37.

Watanabe, Morimichi. "Monks of Tegernsee." *American Cusanus Society Newsletter* XV (1998): 20–22.

Watkin, E. I. *Poets and Mystics.* London and New York: Sheed and Ward, 1953.

Watson, Nicholas. *Richard Rolle and the Invention of Authority.* Cambridge: Cambridge University Press, 1991.

Wéber, Eduoard. "Eckhart et l'ontothéologisme: Histoire et conditions d'une rupture." In *Maître Eckhart à Paris,* 13–83. Paris: Presses Universitaires de France, 1984.

———. "L'interprétation par Albert le Grand de la Théologie Mystique de Denys le Ps.-Aréopagite." In *Albertus Magnus: Doctor Universalis 1280/1980,* edited by Gerbert Meyer, Martina Wehrli-Johns, and Albert Zimmermann, 409–39. Mainz: Matthias Grünewald, 1980.

———. "La théologie de la grâce chez Maître Eckhart." *Revue des sciences religieuses* 70 (1996): 48–72.

Wehrli-Johns, Martina. "Frauenfrömmigkeit ausserhalb des Klosters: Vom Jungfrauenideal zur Heiligung in der Ehe." *Jahrbuch für deutsche Kirchengeschichte* 24 (2000): 17–37.

———. "Mystik und Inquisition: Die Dominikaner und die sogenannte Häresie des Freien Geistes," In *Deutsche Mystik im abendländischen Zusammenhang*, edited by Walter Haug and Wolfram Schneider-Lastin, 223–52. Tübingen: Niemeyer, 2000.

Weier, Reinhold. "Christus als 'Haupt' und 'Fundament' der Kirche." In *Nikolaus von Kues, Kirche und Respublica Christiana: Konkordanz, Repräsentanz und Konsens*, edited by Klaus Kremer and Klaus Reinhardt, 163–82. *Mitteilungen und Forschungsbeiträge der Cusanus-Gesellschaft* 21. Trier: Paulinus, 1994.

Weilner, Ignaz. *Johannes Taulers Bekehrungsweg: Die Erfahrungsgrundlagen seiner Mystik.* Regensburg: Pustet, 1961.

Weintraub, Karl Joachim. *The Value of the Individual: Self and Circumstance in Autobiography.* Chicago: University of Chicago Press, 1978.

Weisheipl, James A. "Mystic on Campus: Friar Thomas." In *An Introduction to the Medieval Mystics of Europe*, edited by Paul Szarmach, 135–59. Albany: SUNY Press, 1984.

Weiss, Bardo. *Die Heilsgeschichte bei Meister Eckhart.* Mainz: Matthias Grünewald, 1965.

Weitlauff, Manfred. "'dein got redender munt machet mich redenlosz . . .': Margareta Ebner und Heinrich von Nördlingen." In *Religiöse Frauenbewegung und mystische Frömmigkeit im Mittelalter*, edited Peter Dinzelbacher and Dieter R. Bauer, 303–52. Cologne/Vienna: Böhlau, 1988.

———. "Heinrich von Nördlingen." VL 3:845–52.

Welte, Bernhard. *Meister Eckhart: Gedanken zu seinem Gedanken.* Freiburg: Herder, 1979.

Wilde, Mauritius. *Das neue Bild vom Gottesbild: Bild und Theologie bei Meister Eckhart.* Freiburg, Switzerland: Universitätsverlag, 2000.

Williams-Krapp, Werner. "Bilderbogen-Mystik: Zu 'Christus und die minennde Seele'. Mit Edition der Mainzer Überlieferung." In *Überlieferungsgeschichtliche Editionen und Studien zur deutschen Literatur des Mittelalters: Kurt Ruh zum 75. Geburtstag*, edited by Konrad Kunze et al., 350–64. Tübingen: Niemeyer, 1989.

———. "'Dise ding sint dennoch nit ware zeichen der heiligkeit': Zur Bewertung mystischer Erfahrung im 15. Jahrhundert." In *Frömmigkeitsstile im Mittelalter*, edited by Wolfgang Haubrichs, 61–71. Göttingen: Vandenhoeck & Ruprecht, 1991.

———. "Eberhard, Mardach." VL 5:1237–39.

———. "The Erosion of a Religious Monopoly: German Religious Literature in the Fifteenth Century." In *The Vernacular Spirit: Essays on Medieval Religious Literature*, edited by Renate Blumenfeld-Kosinski, Duncan Robertson, and Nancy Bradley Warren, 239–59. New York: Palgrave, 2002.

———. "Frauenmystik und Ordensreform im 15. Jahrhundert." In *Literarische Interessenbildung im Mittelalter. DFG-Symposion 1991*, edited by Joachim Heinzle, 301–13. Stuttgart: Metzler, 1993.

———. "Henry Suso's *Vita* between Mystagogy and Hagiography." In *Seeing and Knowing: Women and Learning in Medieval Europe 1200–1500*, edited by Anneke B. Mulder-Baker, 35–47. Turnhout: Brepols, 2004.

———. "Literary Genre and Degrees of Holiness: The Perception of Holiness in Writings by and about Female Mystics." In *The Invention of Saintliness*, edited by Anneke B. Mulder-Bakker, 206–18. London: Routledge, 2002.

———. "'*Nucleus totius perfectionis*': Die Altväterspiritualität in der *Vita* Heinrich Seuses." In *Festschrift für Walter Haug und Burghart Wachinger*, 1:405–21. 2 vols. Tübingen: Niemeyer, 1992.

———. "Observanzbewegungen, monastische Spiritualität und geistlicher Literatur im 15. Jahrhundert." *Internationales Archiv für Sozialgeschichte der deutschen Literatur* 20 (1995): 1–15.

———. "Raimond von Capua." VL 7:982–86.

Wilms, Hieronymus. "Das Seelenfünklein in der deutschen Mystik." *Zeitschrift für Aszese und Mystik* 12 (1937): 157–66.

Wippel, John F. "The Condemnations of 1270 and 1277 at Paris." *Journal of Medieval and Renaissance Studies* 7 (1977): 169–201.

Witte, Karl Heinz. "Der 'Traktat von der Minne,' der Meister des Lehrgesprächs und Johannes Hiltalingen von Basel: Ein Beitrag zur Geschichte der Meister-Eckhart-Rezeption in der Augustinerschule des 14. Jahrhunderts." *Zeitschrift für deutsches Altertum und deutsche Literatur* 131 (2002): 454–87.

———. '*In-principio-Dialog*': Ein deutschsprachiger Theologe der Augustinerschule des 14. Jahrhunderts aus dem Kreise deutsche Mystik und Scholastik. Munich: Artemis, 1989.

Wodtke, Friedrich Wilhelm. "Die Allegorie des 'Inneren Paradieses' bei Bernhard von Clairvaux, Honorius Augustodunensis, Gottfried von Strassburg und in der deutschen Mystik." In *Festschrift Josef Quint anlässlich seines 65. Geburtstages überreicht*, edited by Hugo Moser, Rudolf Schützeichel, and Karl Stackmann, 277–90. Bonn: Semmel, 1964.

Wolfson, Elliot R. *Through a Speculum that Shines: Vision and Imagination in Medieval Jewish Mysticism.* Princeton: Princeton University Press, 1994.

Woods, Richard. *Mysticism and Prophecy: The Dominican Tradition.* London: Darton, Longman and Todd, 1998.

Worstbrock, F. J. "Schlitpacher, Johannes." VL 8:727–48.

Wrede, Gösta. *Unio Mystica: Probleme der Erfahrung bei Johannes Tauler.* Uppsala: Almqvist & Wiksell, 1974.

Wyser, Paul. "Taulers Terminologie vom Seelengrund." In *Altdeutsche und Altniederlandische Mystik*, edited by Kurt Ruh, 324–52. Darmstadt: Wissenschaftliche Buchgesellschaft, 1964.

Yates, Frances A. *Giordano Bruno and the Hermetic Tradition.* Chicago: University of Chicago Press, 1964.

Zekorn, Stefan. *Gelassenheit und Einkehr: Zu Grundlage und Gestalt geistlichen Lebens bei Johannes Tauler.* Würzburg: Echter, 1993.

Zimmermann, Béatrice Aklin. "Die Nonnenviten als Modell einer narrativen Theologie." In *Deutsche Mystik im abendländischen Zusammenhang*, edited by Walter Haug and Wolfram Schneider-Lastin, 563–80. Tübingen: Niemeyer, 2000.

Zorzi, M. Benedetta. "*Melos* e *Iubilus* nelle *Enarrationes in Psalmos* di Agostino: Una questione di mistica agostiniana." *Augustinianum* 42 (2002): 383–413.

Zum Brunn, Émilie. "Dieu n'est pas être." In *Maître Eckhart à Paris: Une critique médiévale de l'ontothéologie: Les Questions parisiennes no. 1 et no. 2*, 84–108. Paris: Presses Universitaries de France, 1984.

——, and Alain de Libera. *Métaphysique du Verbe et théologie négative*. Paris: Beauchesne, 1984.

Zumkeller, Adolar. "Henri de Friemar." DS 7:191–97.

——. "Jourdain de Saxe ou de Quedlinburg." DS 8:1423–30.

——. "Jordan von Quedlinburg (Jordanus de Saxonia)." VL 4: 853–61.

——. "Die Lehrer des geistlichen Lebens unter den deutschen Augustinern vom dreizehnten Jahrhundert bis zum Konzil von Trient." In *Sanctus Augustinus Vitae Spiritualis Magister*, 239–338. Rome: Analecta Augustiniana, 1956.

——. "The Spirituality of the Augustinians." In *Christian Spirituality: High Middle Ages and Reformation*, edited by Jill Raitt et al., 63–74. New York: Crossroad, 1987.

——. *Theology and History of the Augustinian School in the Middle Ages*. n.p.: Augustinian Heritage Institute, 1996.

Index of Subjects

Index of Names

Abelard, 506
Abramowski, Luise, 394, 636, 637, 639
Adalbert, 354
Adelheid (the *reclusa*), 66, 510
Adelheid Langmann, 351, 621
Aelred of Rievaulx, 408
Aeneas Sylvius Piccolomini. *See* Pius II (pope)
Aertsen, Jan. A., 536, 545
Agnes Blannbekin, 350
Agnes of Hungary (queen), 102
Alan of Lille, 40, 43, 317, 502
Albergati, Nicholas, 668
Alberigo, 487, 506, 508, 509
Albert, Karl, 540, 544
Albert of Brünn, 510
Albert of Lauingen. *See* Albert the Great
Albert the Great, 3, 11–47, 58, 59, 65, 89, 92, 95, 96, 126, 143, 245, 246, 247, 255, 317, 322, 336, 405, 449, 487– 495, 498, 503, 507, 509, 521, 528, 588, 657
Albertson, David C., 479, 668
Albrecht of Treffurt, 321
Alexis, Raymond, 587
Alfarabi, 18, 20, 491
al-Ghazzali, 584
al-Hallaj, 584
Allmand, Christopher, 486
Almond, Ian, 555–57
Altrock, Stephanie, 570
Alverny, Marie-Thérèse d', 502
Amaury of Bene, 507

Ambrose, 45, 49, 332
Ambrose Traversari, 455
Amphilochius of Iconium, 54
Anastasius, 488
Ancelet-Hustache, Jeanne, 515
Anderson, Wendy Love, 513, 514, 515
Andia, Ysabel de, 498
André Vauchez, 351
Angela of Foligno, 60, 262, 286, 305, 310, 355, 508, 572
Anselm of Canterbury, 151, 332, 440, 471, 492, 639
Antonio Correr (cardinal), 72
Antonio Zeno, 71
Anzulewicz, Hendryk, 487, 488, 489
Appel, Heinrich, 592
Arbman, Ernst, 580
Aristotle, 12, 13, 14, 18, 20, 24, 25, 28, 31, 36, 40, 95, 108, 232, 246, 255, 269, 332, 379, 437, 446, 487, 489, 491, 494, 495, 497, 545, 548, 555, 564, 588, 656
Arndt, John, 393
Arnou, Rene, 660
Arsenius, 205, 221, 573
Aston, Margaret, 1, 485
Athanasius, 551
Athenagoras, 54
Auer, Johannes, 635
Auerbach, Erich, 531
Augustine, 14, 37, 39, 45, 49, 53, 88, 102, 111, 113, 128, 134, 144, 146, 152, 161, 181, 190, 202, 207, 212, 223, 233, 244, 245,

Kaspar Ayndorffer, 452, 453, 455, 456, 658
Katharina Tucher, 361–62, 363, 365, 630, 631
Keats, John, 1
Keck, John. *See* John Keck
Keller, Hildegard Elisabeth, 309, 315, 574, 577, 590, 609, 611
Kelley, C. F., 527, 537, 635, 636, 638
Kelly, H. Ansgar, 506
Kempf, Nicholas. *See* Nicholas Kempf
Kepler, Thomas S., 642, 645, 647
Kerlinger, Walter, 511
Kertz, Karl G., 551
Kieckhefer, Richard, 63, 202, 270, 274, 291, 356, 506, 509, 563, 565, 572, 597, 598, 624, 628
Kihm, M. Engratis, 600
Kirk, K. E., 458, 660
Kirmsee, Kurt, 518, 591, 595
Klibansky, Raymond, 503
Köbele, Susanne, 86, 114, 117, 121, 516, 517, 522, 526, 528, 529, 530, 531, 532, 534, 535, 549
Koch, Josef, 506, 521, 528, 542
Konrad Kügelin, 353, 626
Konrad of Füssen, 341
Kraume, Herbert, 621
Kremer, Klaus, 550, 652, 663
Kristeller, Paul Oskar, 45, 503
Kügelin, Konrad. *See* Konrad Kügelin
Kunisch, Herman, 86, 517
Künzle, Pius, 198, 570, 571, 572, 580

Lachance, Paul, 572
Lambert, 511
Lambert of Burn, 69
Lamprecht of Regensburg, 315
Lane, Belden C., 562
Langer, Otto, 118, 517, 524, 533, 611
Langmann, Adelheid. *See* Adelheid Langmann
Langosch, Karl, 606
Lanzetta, Beverly, 547
Largier, Niklaus, 102, 110, 122, 192, 209, 322, 323, 519, 520, 521, 522, 525, 527, 528, 529, 530, 535, 536, 538, 540, 549, 552, 554, 556, 557, 558,

561, 566, 568, 570, 571, 572, 574, 613, 614, 615, 635, 661
Lauchert, Friedrich, 649
Laurent, M.-H., 526, 527
Laurentius Surius, 378, 586, 635
Layton, Bentley, 504
Leclercq, Jean, 31, 497, 573
Leff, Gordon, 66, 485, 606, 507, 510, 511, 512, 513, 623
Leppin, Volker, 639, 640
Lerner, Robert E., 106, 379, 505, 506, 507, 508, 509, 510, 511, 513, 526, 527, 584, 623, 636
Lewis of Bavaria, 5, 103, 199, 241–42, 408, 413–14, 571
Leyen, F. Von der, 622
Libera, Alain de, 14, 15, 179, 487, 489, 490, 491, 503, 504, 515, 519, 528, 537, 538, 540, 541, 542, 545, 548, 550, 563, 566, 612
Lichtmann, Maria, 534
Lienhard, Joseph T., 513
Livy, 505
Llull, Ramon, 666
Lohr, Charles, 500
Lombard, Peter, 501
Lonergan, Bernard, J. 464, 497, 498, 554, 663
Lorenzo Giustiniani, 72
Löser, Freimut, 555, 556, 613, 618, 620
Lossky, Vladimir, 137, 458, 536, 542, 543, 544, 545, 554, 660
Louth, Andrew, 562
Loveia, Hermann von, 613
Lucentini, Paolo, 43, 501, 502
Lüers, Grete, 518
Luscombe, David, 654
Luther, Martin, 3, 275, 287, 392, 393, 398, 520, 598, 602, 638

Macarius the Great, 55, 418
Macrobius, 45, 502
Magdalena Beutler (Beutlerin). *See* Magdalena of Freiburg
Magdalena of Freiburg, 352, 625–26
Mahnke, Dietrich, 502
Maimonides, 110, 113, 185, 441, 442–43, 495, 523, 529, 538, 546, 566

Index of Passages

Genesis

1:1	127, 128, 538
1:26	129, 146, 548
2:8	481, 614
2:20–24	617
3:1	548
3:24	467
18	307
29–30	190
32:28	662
32:30	24, 456

Exodus

3:14	125, 140, 170, 309
5:3	178
6:4	249
20:21	662
24:10	456
24:18	173
33:11	24, 408
33:13–23	662
33:20	324, 456

Numbers

12:8	456

Judges

8:22	408

3 Kings

19:11–13	292, 342
19:12–13	284

Job

3:23	288, 602
4:12	171, 559
4:13	286
4:15	602
7:1	573
17:2	602
17:16	602
33:14	133
33:15–16	540

Psalms

26:8	280
30:1	226
30:23	226
33:9	658
41	264, 281
41:8	250, 262, 263, 319, 582, 594
44:11	217
46:2	601
67:28	226
80:2	601
81:6	388
84:9	133
138:12	609
138:17 (Vg)	408
148:7–12	327

Proverbs

31:26	545

Ecclesiastes

1:7	127, 372
23:11	325
24:11	327

Song of Songs

1:1	361
1:2	387
1:6	306
1:15	372
2:4	306, 358
2:5	306, 392
2:6	305
2:7	306
3:1–4	530
3:6	178
4:9	389
5:1	633
5:4	371
6:7–9	438
7:11	372
8:14	306

Isaiah

6:5	456
7:9	438
7:14	662
11:2	278
45:15	249, 456, 465, 662
55:9	309